ALL·IN·ONE

CompTIA A+™

Certification

EXAM GUIDE

Eleventh Edition (Exams 220-1101 & 220-1102)

ABOUT THE SERIES EDITOR

Michael Meyers is the industry's leading authority on CompTIA A+ and CompTIA Network+ certifications. He was the president and co-founder of Total Seminars, LLC, a major provider of computer and network repair curriculum and seminars for thousands of organizations throughout the world, and a member of CompTIA. Today, Mike works as Vice President of marketing for National Cyber Group (www.nationalcyber.com).

Mike has written numerous popular textbooks, including the best-selling *Mike Meyers' CompTIA A+ Guide to Managing and Troubleshooting PCs*, *Mike Meyers' CompTIA Network+ Guide to Managing and Troubleshooting Networks*, and *Mike Meyers' CompTIA Security+ Certification Guide*, plus many more.

About the Authors

Travis A. Everett is a software developer, writer, and editor who writes open-source software in his spare time (and occasionally blogs about it). In addition to holding an MFA in creative writing from Old Dominion University, Travis owns exactly one-third of an original copy of *Wolfenstein 3D* on floppy disk and rewatches *The Matrix* regularly. Travis is CompTIA A+ certified.

Andrew Hutz may be the newest guy on the Total Seminars writing staff, but he brings ten years of writing experience in both IT and the music industry. When not working for Total Seminars, Andrew deals with risk management in the cybersecurity arena, where he blogs at https://tgasec.wordpress.com. Andrew holds the CompTIA A+ and CompTIA Security+ certifications and is working toward his bachelor's degree in software development and security.

About the Editor in Chief

Melissa Layne, EdD, has dedicated over 25 years in the field of education in various capacities. Roles include serving as a clinical professor teaching and developing several pre-service teacher courses at Sam Houston State University, a director of research, AVP for research and innovation, editor in chief for four academic journals, and founding editor for two of those journals. She has authored over 50 peer-reviewed academic articles and book chapters on virtual environments and online learning. Dr. Layne has also led internships for graduate students in scholarly communications, editorial processes, peer review, and publishing. She loves to mess around in her flower garden and spend time with her four children and three grandchildren.

About the Technical Editor

Mark Edward Soper has worked with computers and related technologies for over 30 years and specializes in technology education through training, writing, and public speaking. He has authored and co-authored 40 books on technology topics ranging from CompTIA A+ certification to Microsoft Windows, networking, and troubleshooting. Mark has also taught these and other topics across the United States.

Mark has CompTIA A+ and Microsoft MOS – Microsoft Excel 2013 certifications, and currently teaches Microsoft Office classes for University of Southern Indiana and Ivy Tech Community College. Mark blogs at https://markesoper.com.

Special Mention: Michael Smyer

Our resident super-nerd **Michael Smyer** really stepped up to the plate in supporting the book production and helping get Melissa Layne up to speed in record time. Many thanks Michael—your ongoing magic with graphics combined with your jumping into the editor slot kept the book going when we needed it most.

ALL · IN · ONE

CompTIA A+™ Certification

EXAM GUIDE

Eleventh Edition (Exams 220-1101 & 220-1102)

Mike Meyers, Series Editor
Travis A. Everett
Andrew Hutz

New York   Chicago   San Francisco
Athens   London   Madrid   Mexico City
Milan   New Delhi   Singapore   Sydney   Toronto

1 2 3 4 5 6 7 8 9   DSS   27 26 25 24 23

Library of Congress Control Number: 2022944277

ISBN   978-1-264-60990-1
MHID   1-264-60990-6

Sponsoring Editor Tim Green	**Technical Editor** Mark Edward Soper	**Production Supervisor** Thomas Somers
Editorial Supervisor Janet Walden	**Copy Editor** William McManus	**Composition** KnowledgeWorks Global Ltd.
Project Editor Rachel Fogelberg	**Proofreader** Rick Camp	**Illustration** KnowledgeWorks Global Ltd.
Acquisitions Coordinator Caitlin Cromley-Linn	**Indexer** Ted Laux	**Art Director, Cover** Jeff Weeks

To Amanda Lee Simpson

~SuperMuse

She walks in beauty, like the night
Of cloudless climes and starry skies;
And all that's best of dark and bright
Meet in her aspect and her eyes;
Thus mellowed to that tender light
Which heaven to gaudy day denies.

~Lord Byron

CONTENTS AT A GLANCE

CONTENTS

ACKNOWLEDGMENTS

As the author of the first edition, way back in 1998, through the tenth edition of *CompTIA A+ Certification All-in-One Exam Guide*, I am now switching hats to the series editor role. One thing remains the same: the hard-working, dedicated, and talented people who also proudly wear their own hats, but wear several of them at a time to make sure this book eventually lands in your hands. So, on that note, I'd like to acknowledge the many people who contributed their talents to make this book possible:

To my in-house editor in chief, Melissa Layne: Way to dive into the deep end, eh? You did a great job and I'm glad to have you on board.

To my executive editor, Timothy Green: What are you gonna do with me now working as a series editor? I know, the same as we always do. Let's do it again, eh?

To Mark Edward Soper, technical editor: Fantastic job, Mark! Very much a pleasure to work with you. The book is much better because of your input and insight.

To Rachel Fogelberg, project editor for McGraw Hill: Thank you for your patience, persistence, and perfectionism.

To Caitlin Cromley-Linn, editorial coordinator at McGraw Hill: Every complex project needs someone keeping the wheels on the bus and everyone organized. You did a great job, thanks.

To Bill McManus, copy editor: Bill, words can't express what an awesome editing job you did on this edition. Your skill continues to amaze me. Thank you!

To Janet Walden, editorial supervisor at McGraw Hill: It was a joy to work with you again. I couldn't have asked for a better team. In fact, I asked for the best team and got exactly what I wanted!

To Rick Camp, proofreader: Awesome work!

INTRODUCTION

The field of computing has changed dramatically over the decades since the introduction of the IBM Personal Computer (PC) in 1981, and so has the job of the people who build, maintain, and troubleshoot computers. A *PC tech* for many years serviced IBM-compatible desktop systems running a Microsoft operating system (OS), such as DOS or, later, Windows. All a tech needed to service an early Windows machine was a Phillips-head screwdriver and knowledge of the hardware and OS.

An IBM-compatible PC, circa 1989

The personal computing landscape today includes a zillion devices in all shapes, sizes, and purposes. How many computing devices do you interact with every day? Seriously, count them.

Here's my typical contact in a day. My smartphone alarm clock awakens me in the morning. I use either a Windows or macOS desktop to check the morning news and my e-mail by connecting to other computers over the Internet. At the gym, my smart watch keeps track of my exercises and my heart rate. The computer in my car handles navigation and traffic reports for my daily commute. At the office I'm literally surrounded by dozens of computing devices, because everyone has a desktop or laptop computer, a tablet, a smartphone, plus any number of wearable devices. Behind the scenes, these devices constantly interact with and offload work to a wide array of online services.

We're all PCs!

Someone needs to set up, secure, manage, maintain, and troubleshoot all of these devices. Because you're reading this book, I'm guessing that *you* are that someone. You're going to need a lot of knowledge about many systems to be a modern personal computer technician. A modern PC tech, therefore, works with many devices running many different systems. Almost everything uses networking to interconnect, and a PC tech makes those connections happen.

 NOTE This book uses the term "personal computer" and the initials "PC" generically to refer to any kind of personal computing device. PCs here mean things that techs interact with, can set up, and repair.

This book teaches you everything you need to know to become a great tech. It might seem like a lot of information at first, but I'll show you how each system functions and interacts, so you learn the patterns they all follow. At some point in the process of reading this book and working on computers, it will all click into place. You've got this!

Along the way, you'll pick up credentials that prove your skill to employers and clients. The rest of this chapter explains those credentials and the steps you need to take to gain them.

CompTIA A+ Certification

Nearly every profession has some criteria that you must meet to show your competence and ability to perform at a certain level. Although the way this works varies widely from one profession to another, all of them will at some point make you take an exam or series of exams. Passing these exams proves that you have the necessary skills to work at a certain level in your profession, whether you're an aspiring plumber, teacher, barber, lawyer, or PC tech.

If you successfully pass these exams, the organization that administers them grants you certification. You receive some piece of paper or pin or membership card that you can show to potential clients or employers. This certification gives those potential clients or employers a level of confidence that you can do what you say you can do. Without this certification, either you will not find suitable work in that profession or no one will trust you to do the work.

Modern PC techs attain the CompTIA A+ certification, the essential credential that shows competence in the modern field of information technology (IT), a fancy way of saying *computing technology plus all the other stuff needed to connect and support computers.* CompTIA A+ is an industry-wide, vendor-neutral certification program developed and sponsored by the Computing Technology Industry Association (CompTIA). You achieve this certification by taking two computer-based exams consisting of multiple-choice and performance-based questions. The exams cover what technicians should know after 12 months of hands-on work on personal computing devices, experience obtained either from a job or as a student in the lab. CompTIA A+ certification enjoys wide recognition throughout the computer industry. To date, more than 1,000,000 technicians have become CompTIA A+ certified, making it the most popular of all IT certifications.

Who Is CompTIA?

CompTIA is a nonprofit industry trade association based in Downers Grove, Illinois. It consists of over 20,000 members in 102 countries. You'll find CompTIA offices in such diverse locales as Amsterdam, Dubai, Johannesburg, Tokyo, and São Paulo.

CompTIA provides a forum for people in these industries to network (as in meeting people), represents the interests of its members to the government, and provides certifications for many aspects of the computer industry. CompTIA sponsors CompTIA A+, CompTIA Network+, CompTIA Security+, and other certifications. CompTIA works hard to watch the IT industry and constantly looks to provide new certifications to meet the ongoing demand from its membership. Check out the CompTIA Web site at https://www.comptia.org for details on the other certifications you can obtain from CompTIA.

CompTIA began offering CompTIA A+ certification back in 1993. When it debuted, the IT industry largely ignored CompTIA A+ certification. Since that initial stutter, however, the CompTIA A+ certification has grown to become the de facto requirement for entrance into the PC industry. Many companies require CompTIA A+ certification for all of their PC support technicians, and the CompTIA A+ certification is widely recognized both in the United States and internationally.

The Path to Other Certifications

Most IT companies—big and small—see CompTIA A+ certification as the entry point to IT. Where you go next depends on a lot of things, such as your interests and the needs of your organization. Let's look at other CompTIA certifications first and then explore vendor-specific options from Microsoft and Cisco.

CompTIA Core Series

CompTIA A+ is part of the CompTIA *Core Series* of certifications. Many techs flow from CompTIA A+ to other certifications in the Core Series before specializing. The Core Series consists of four certifications:

- CompTIA IT Fundamentals (ITF+)
- CompTIA A+ (1101 is called *Core 1*; 1102 is called *Core 2*)
- CompTIA Network+
- CompTIA Security+

(For the record, I have no idea why A+ gets "sub" names and the other three exams don't. Just go with it.)

CompTIA ITF+ covers essentials of computer literacy, such as everything any modern worker needs to know about computing just to function. That includes information about computing device types, what you can do with computers, how networks work, and basic security. If you already have the requisite experience to pursue the CompTIA A+ certification, you don't need to backtrack to ITF+. Recommending CompTIA ITF+ to newbies is a good idea, though, as ITF+ will fill in a lot of gaps for people.

CompTIA Network+ continues the good work you started in the CompTIA A+ networking sections. We live in an interconnected world. Techs need to know networking inside and out to handle jobs at bigger organizations. Getting Network+ certified proves your skills as a network tech, including your understanding of network hardware, infrastructure, installation, and troubleshooting. Network+ is the next logical step after the A+ certification. CompTIA A+ is not a prerequisite to take your Network+ exam, but it is highly recommended.

Similarly, *CompTIA Security+* picks up from the network security sections in both CompTIA A+ and Network+, taking you much deeper into how to secure networks against attacks and best practices for every security-conscious organization. I recommend taking Security+ after Network+; this rounds out your essential skill set all the way up to enterprise tech, if this is the career route you wish to take.

CompTIA Specialty Series

CompTIA offers several tracks to pursue post–Core Series. These offer either specialization in an IT subfield or building on the skills you've already acquired. Let me explain the Infrastructure Pathway, Cybersecurity Pathway, Data and Analytics Pathway, and Professional Skills tracks.

NOTE For more information about the CompTIA certification pathways and all its certifications, go here:
https://www.comptia.org/certifications/which-certification

Moving to the *Infrastructure Pathway* means turning to the machines and operating systems that beat at the heart of enterprise organizations. There are three certifications in this series:

- CompTIA Linux+
- CompTIA Server+
- CompTIA Cloud+

Many organizations rely on Linux-powered servers to accomplish much of the dedicated hardware tasks. The servers and server infrastructure require specialized knowledge. Also, much of the industry is moving to cloud-based computing, so understanding how to take an organization there successfully is increasingly important for IT professionals.

The *Cybersecurity Pathway* goes deep into the Dark Arts of network security—how to protect *against* bad people, not how to be a successful criminal mastermind—with three certifications:

- CompTIA Cybersecurity Analyst (CySA+)
- CompTIA PenTest+
- CompTIA Advanced Security Practitioner (CASP+)

These certifications show that you know your skills at analyzing a network of any size, can test for vulnerabilities, and can harden the network dramatically. You can leverage all the information learned in the Core Series, using it as the foundation for becoming a security guru.

The *Data and Analytics Pathway* covers the toolkit you'll use to take raw data and transform it into the kinds of statistics, visualizations, and reports that support data-driven business decisions. This pathway only has two certifications as of the time of publication, but CompTIA has announced plans to add more certifications in the future:

- CompTIA Data+
- CompTIA Data Systems

CompTIA Data+ shows that you know how to mine data for patterns and trends, analyze the results, and communicate the insights you find. CompTIA Data Systems covers skills required to work with databases.

The *Professional Skills* series offers three exams, but they're geared to unique skillsets used every day in IT:

- CompTIA Project+
- CompTIA Cloud Essentials+
- CompTIA Certified Technical Trainer (CTT+)

Project management is wildly important in managing big IT projects. Project managers use the Project+ certification to show their credentials. Cloud Essentials+ is all about what you—not the IT hero, but the business manager—need to know about cloud computing. CTT+ is for people like me, a certification that shows you know how to teach IT skills to adults.

None of the Professional Skills certifications seem obvious or logical to pursue after the Core Series certifications, but they're situational. If, for example, you find yourself in a position where getting project management credentials will greatly benefit you and your organization, Project+ makes a lot of sense.

Microsoft Technical Certifications

Microsoft operating systems control a huge portion of all installed networks, and those networks need qualified support people to make them run. Pursuing Microsoft's series of certifications for networking professionals is a natural next step after completing the CompTIA certifications. Microsoft offers a whole slew of certifications paths such as Data Science, Dev Ops Engineer, AI Engineer, and more. You can find additional details on the Microsoft Docs Web site:

https://docs.microsoft.com/certifications

Cisco Certification

Cisco routers pretty much run the Internet and most intranets in the world. A *router* is a networking device that controls and directs the flow of information over networks, such as e-mail messages, Web browsing, and so on. Cisco provides multiple levels of IT certification for folks who want to show their skills at handling Cisco products, such as the Cisco Certified Network Associate (CCNA), plus numerous specialty certifications. See the Cisco Certifications Web site here for more details:

https://www.cisco.com/c/en/us/training-events/training-certifications/certifications.html

CompTIA A+ Objectives

CompTIA splits A+ certification into two exams: CompTIA A+ Core 1 (220-1101) *and* CompTIA A+ Core 2 (220-1102). It's common to refer to these two exams as the "2022" exams to differentiate them from older CompTIA exams.

Although you may take either of the two exams first, I recommend taking 220-1101 followed by 220-1102. The 220-1101 exam concentrates on understanding a wide range of terminology and technology, how to do fundamental tasks such as upgrading RAM, basic network and mobile device support, and fundamental concepts of virtualization and cloud computing. The 220-1102 exam builds on the first exam, concentrating on operating system support, security and software, troubleshooting scenarios, and operational procedures.

Both of the exams are extremely practical, with little or no interest in theory, aside from troubleshooting. They include 60–90 multiple-choice questions (single and multiple response) and 3–8 performance-based questions (PBQs). PBQs are problems that are skills-based and configured as labs, virtual environments, or simulations that you must solve.

The number of multiple-choice questions depends on how many PBQs you get. You can get partial credit for the PBQs, so even if you can't complete them, do as much as you can in case you qualify for partial credit. The following is an example of the type of multiple-choice questions you will see on the exams:

Your laser printer is printing blank pages. Which item should you check first?

A. Printer drivers

B. Toner cartridge

C. Printer settings

D. Paper feed

The correct answer is B, the toner cartridge. You can make an argument for any of the others, but common sense (and skill as a PC technician) tells you to check the simplest possibility first. For an excellent example of a PBQ, visit this link: https://demosim .comptia.io/

Be aware that CompTIA may add new questions to the exams at any time to keep the content fresh. The subject matter covered by the exams won't change, but new questions may be added periodically at random intervals. Be sure and check the CompTIA Web site before final preparation for the exams. This policy puts strong emphasis on understanding concepts and having solid PC-tech knowledge rather than on trying to memorize specific questions and answers that may have been on the exams in the past. No book or Web resource will have all the "right answers" because those answers change constantly. Luckily for you, however, this book not only teaches you what steps to follow in a particular case, but also explains how to be a knowledgeable tech who understands *why* you're doing those steps. That way, when you encounter a new problem (or exam question), you can work out the answer. This will help you pass the exams and function as a master tech.

Windows-Centric

The CompTIA A+ exams cover six different operating systems and many versions within each OS. When you review the exam objectives a little later in this section, though, you'll see that the majority of content focuses on the Microsoft Windows operating systems you would expect to find on a PC at a workstation or in a home. The operating systems are primarily the focus of the CompTIA A+ 1102 exam and cover a specific and limited scope of questions on macOS, Linux, Chrome OS, iOS, and Android.

Objectives in the exams cover the following operating systems:

- Windows 10 Home, Windows 10 Pro, Windows 10 Enterprise
- Windows 11
- macOS
- Linux
- Chrome OS
- iOS
- Android

Try This!

Recommending an OS

Imagine this scenario. One of your first clients wants to upgrade her computing gear and doesn't know which way to go. It's up to you to make a recommendation. This is a great way to assess your knowledge at the start of your journey into CompTIA A+ certification, so try this!

Open a Web browser on a computer or smartphone and browse to my favorite tech store, Newegg (https://www.newegg.com). Scan through their computer systems. What operating systems seem to be most common? What can you get from reading reviews of, say, Chrome OS versus Windows 11? Does Newegg sell any Apple products?

Don't get too wrapped up in this exercise. It's just a way to ease you into the standard research we techs do all the time to stay current. We'll revisit this exercise in later chapters so you can gauge your comfort and knowledge level over time.

Exam 220–1101

The questions on the CompTIA A+ 220-1101 exam fit into one of five domains. The number of questions for each domain is based on the percentages shown in the following table.

Domain (Exam 220-1101)	Percentage
1.0 Mobile Devices	15%
2.0 Networking	20%
3.0 Hardware	25%
4.0 Virtualization and Cloud Computing	11%
5.0 Hardware and Network Troubleshooting	29%

The 220-1101 exam tests your knowledge of computer components, expecting you to be able to identify just about every common device on PCs, including variations within device types. Here's a list:

- Hard drives
- Solid-state drives (SSDs)
- Removable storage (flash drives, memory cards, and optical drives)
- Motherboards
- Power supplies
- CPUs
- RAM

- Monitors
- Input devices, such as keyboards and touchscreens
- Video and multimedia cards
- Network and modem cards
- Cables and connectors
- Heat sinks, fans, and liquid cooling systems
- Laptops and mobile devices
- Printers and multifunction devices
- Network switches, cabling, and wireless adapters
- Biometric devices

The 220-1101 exam tests you on mobile devices (including laptops). While the smartphone and tablet market covers an impossibly wide array of hardware and software, the 220-1101 exam focuses on Apple iOS and Google Android devices. You'll need to know how to interact with the hardware and software.

The 220-1101 exam tests extensively on networking. You need to know how to set up a typical local area network (LAN), for example, understanding cabling standards, network protocols, and Windows configuration.

The 220-1101 exam tests your ability to install, configure, and maintain all the hardware technology involved in a personal computer. You need to be able to install and set up a hard drive, for example, and configure devices in Windows.

The 220-1101 exam will quiz you on cloud computing and virtualization technologies. You'll need to know about available cloud services such as online storage and applications only available via the Internet. You'll get asked about the purpose of virtual machines in a network environment and their resource and security requirements.

The 220-1101 exam requires you to know a lot about hardware and network troubleshooting. You'll get questions, for example, on how to fix a network failure.

Exam 220-1102

The CompTIA A+ 220-1102 exam covers four domains. This table lists the domains and the percentage of questions dedicated to each domain.

Domain (Exam 220-1102)	Percentage
1.0 Operating Systems	31%
2.0 Security	25%
3.0 Software Troubleshooting	22%
4.0 Operational Procedures	22%

The 220-1102 exam covers the configuration, repair, and troubleshooting of operating systems—primarily Microsoft Windows, but you'll also get questions on Apple macOS and some very basic questions on Linux distributions. You have to know your way around Windows and understand the tasks involved in updating, upgrading, and installing Windows as well. You need to know the standard diagnostic tools available in Windows so that you can fix problems and work with higher-level techs. Make sure you know Windows; probably a quarter of the questions are going to challenge you on this.

So what versions of Windows are covered on the CompTIA A+ 220-1102 exam? Let's refer directly to the CompTIA A+ Certification Exam Core 2 Objectives to find out:

NOTE ON WINDOWS 11

Versions of Microsoft® Windows® that are not end of Mainstream Support (as determined by Microsoft), up to and including Windows 11, are intended content areas of the certification. As such, objectives in which a specific version of Microsoft Windows is not indicated in the main objective title can include content related to Windows 10 and Windows 11, as it relates to the job role.

You need to know your way around the macOS interface. Plus, the 220-1102 exam tests you on accessing and properly using various tech tools for running maintenance, backup, and so forth. The exam goes into lots of detail on iOS and Android configuration, such as setting up e-mail and securing the devices.

In general, security is a big topic on the 220-1102 exam. You need to know quite a bit about computer security, from physical security (door locks to retinal scanners), to knowledge of security threats (malware and viruses), to the ways in which to secure an individual computer. This also includes coverage of how to recycle and dispose of computer gear properly.

You'll also be tested on methods for securing networks. You'll need to know how to access a small office/home office (SOHO) router or wireless access point and configure that device to protect your network.

Much as the 220-1101 exam requires you to know a lot about hardware and network troubleshooting, the 220-1102 exam covers software troubleshooting (including some security problems) in great detail. You'll get questions, for example, on how to troubleshoot instability in Windows, on why a mobile device won't auto-rotate, and even on what procedure you should use to remove malware.

Finally, this exam puts a lot of emphasis on operational procedures, such as safety and environmental issues, communication, and professionalism. You need to understand how to avoid hazardous situations. The exam tests your ability to communicate effectively with customers and coworkers. You need to understand professional behavior and demonstrate that you have tact, discretion, and respect for others and their property.

The Path to Certification

You become CompTIA A+ certified, in the simplest sense, by taking and passing two computer-based exams. There are no prerequisites for taking the CompTIA A+ certification exams (although there's an assumption of computer literacy, whether or not you have one of the computer literacy certifications). There is no required training course and no training materials to buy. You *do* have to pay a testing fee for each of the two exams.

You pay your testing fees, go to a local testing center to take the test or take it online. You immediately know if you have passed or failed, whether you take it in person or online. By passing both exams, you become CompTIA A+ certified.

To stay certified, every three years you'll need to do one of the following: (1) retake the exams; (2) perform sufficient continuing education as specified by CompTIA; or (3) pass a higher-level certification.

Retaking the exams isn't that hard to understand, but the continuing education requirement is a bit more complex. Instead of trying to explain it all here, please review CompTIA's documentation:

https://www.comptia.org/continuing-education

Most importantly, if you pursue the continuing education path, you'll need to earn 20 Continuing Education Units (CEUs) each three-year period to renew your CompTIA A+ certification. How do you earn these CEUs? You can participate in industry events and seminars, complete a presentation, participate in IT training, or teach a course. The number of CEUs that you earn by completing each of these requirements varies, and each requires that you submit documentation to CompTIA for review.

Finally, you can keep your CompTIA A+ certification current by passing a higher-level certification. For example, if you pass and get your CompTIA Network+ certification, that extends your A+ certification for another three years. Likewise, getting your CompTIA Security+ certification extends your A+ and Network+ certifications for three years. This is the path I recommend. It keeps you growing professionally and adding to your skills while keeping your certifications current.

How Do I Take the Exams?

To take the CompTIA A+ exams, you may go to an authorized testing center or take your exams over the Internet. Pearson VUE administers the CompTIA A+ exams. You'll find thousands of Pearson VUE testing centers scattered across the United States and Canada, as well as in over 186 other countries around the world. You may take the exam at any testing center. To locate a testing center and schedule an exam, call Pearson VUE at 877-551-7587 or visit their Web site at https://home.pearsonvue.com. To schedule an Internet-based exam through OnVUE, go to https://www.onvue.com. You'll need a solid Internet connection and a webcam, such as one built into most portable computers. Pearson VUE will accommodate any special needs, although this may limit your selection of testing locations.

Exam Costs

The cost of the CompTIA A+ exams depends on whether you work for a CompTIA member or not. At the time of this writing, the cost for non-CompTIA members is $239 (U.S.) for each exam. International prices vary, but you can check the CompTIA Web site for international pricing. Of course, the prices are subject to change without notice, so always check the CompTIA Web site for current pricing.

Very few people pay full price for the exam. Virtually every organization that provides CompTIA A+ training and testing also offers discount *vouchers*. You buy a discount voucher and then use the voucher number instead of a credit card when you schedule the exam. Vouchers are sold per exam, so you'll need two vouchers to take the two CompTIA A+ exams. Total Seminars is one place to get discount vouchers. You can call Total Seminars at 800-446-6004 or 281-922-4166, or get vouchers via the Web site: https://www.totalsem.com. No one should ever pay full price for CompTIA A+ exams.

How to Pass the CompTIA A+ Exams

CompTIA designed the A+ exams to test the knowledge of a technician with only 12 months of experience, so keep it simple! The exams aren't interested in your ability to overclock DDR4 CAS latency in system setup or whether you can explain the differences between Intel and AMD chipsets. Think in terms of practical knowledge and standards. Read this book, do whatever works for you to memorize the key concepts and procedures, take the practice exams on the media accompanying this book, review any topics you miss, and you should pass with no problem.

 NOTE Those of you who just want more knowledge in managing and troubleshooting PCs can follow the same strategy as certification-seekers. Think in practical terms and work with the PC as you go through each chapter.

Some of you may be in or just out of school, so studying for exams is nothing novel. But if you haven't had to study for and take an exam in a while, or if you think maybe you could use some tips, you may find the next section valuable. It lays out a proven strategy for preparing to take and pass the CompTIA A+ exams. Try it. It works.

Obligate Yourself

The very first step you should take is to schedule yourself for the exams. Have you ever heard the old adage "Heat and pressure make diamonds?" Well, if you don't give yourself a little "heat," you'll end up procrastinating and delay taking the exams, possibly forever. Do yourself a favor. Using the following information, determine how much time you'll need to study for the exams, and then call Pearson VUE or visit their Web site and schedule the exams accordingly. Knowing the exams are coming up makes it much easier to put down the game controller and crack open the book. You can schedule an exam as little as a few weeks in advance, but if you schedule an exam and can't take it at the scheduled time, you must reschedule at least a day in advance or you'll lose your money.

Set Aside the Right Amount of Study Time

After helping thousands of techs get their CompTIA A+ certification, we at Total Seminars have developed a pretty good feel for the amount of study time needed to pass the CompTIA A+ certification exams. The following table provides an estimate to help you plan how much study time you must commit to the CompTIA A+ certification exams. Keep in mind that these are averages. If you're not a great student or if you're a little on the nervous side, add 10 percent; if you're a fast learner or have a good bit of computer experience, you may want to reduce the figures.

To use the table, just circle the values that are most accurate for you and add them up to get your estimated total hours of study time.

Tech Task	None	Once or Twice	Every Now and Then	Quite a Bit
		Amount of Experience		
Installing an adapter card	6	4	2	1
Installing and configuring hard drives and SSDs	10	8	6	2
Connecting a computer to the Internet	8	6	4	2
Installing printers and multifunction devices	16	8	4	2
Installing RAM	8	6	4	2
Installing CPUs	8	7	5	3
Repairing printers	6	5	4	3
Repairing boot problems	8	7	7	5
Repairing portable computers	8	6	4	2
Configuring mobile devices	4	3	2	1
Building complete systems	12	10	8	6
Using the command line	8	8	6	4
Installing and optimizing Windows	10	8	6	4
Using Windows 10	8	6	4	2
Using Windows 11	8	6	4	2
Using Linux	8	6	6	3
Using macOS	8	4	4	2
Configuring NTFS, Users, and Groups	6	4	3	2
Configuring a wireless network	6	5	3	2
Configuring a software firewall	6	4	2	1
Using cloud services	3	2	2	1
Removing malware	4	3	2	0
Using OS diagnostic tools	8	8	6	4
Installing and configuring virtual machines	6	4	2	1

To that value, add hours based on the number of months of direct, professional experience you have had supporting PCs, as shown in the following table:

Months of Direct, Professional Experience	Hours to Add to Your Study Time
0	50
Up to 6	30
6 to 12	10
Over 12	0

A total neophyte often needs roughly 240 hours of study time. An experienced tech shouldn't need more than 60 hours.

Total hours for you to study: _____.

A Strategy for Study

Now that you have a feel for how long it's going to take to prepare for the exams, you're ready to develop a study strategy. I suggest a strategy that has worked for others who've come before you, whether they were experienced techs or total newbies.

This book accommodates the different study agendas of these two groups of students. The first group is experienced techs who already have strong PC experience but need to be sure they're ready to be tested on the specific subjects covered by the CompTIA A+ exams. The second group is those with little or no background in the computer field. These techs can benefit from a more detailed understanding of the history and concepts that underlie modern PC technology, to help them remember the specific subject matter information they must know for the exams. I'll use the shorthand terms Old Techs and New Techs for these two groups. If you're not sure which group you fall into, pick a few chapters and go through some end-of-chapter questions. If you score less than 70 percent, go the New Tech route.

I have broken most of the chapters into four distinct parts:

- **Historical/Conceptual** Topics that are not on the CompTIA A+ exams but will help you understand more clearly what is on the CompTIA A+ exams
- **1101** Topics that clearly fit under the CompTIA A+ 220-1101 exam domains
- **1102** Topics that clearly fit under the CompTIA A+ 220-1102 exam domains
- **Beyond A+** More advanced issues that probably will not be on the CompTIA A+ exams—yet

The beginning of each of these parts is clearly marked with a large banner that looks like this:

Historical/Conceptual

Those of you who fall into the Old Tech group may want to skip everything except the 1101 and 1102 parts in each chapter. After reading the sections in those parts, jump immediately to the questions at the end of the chapter. The end-of-chapter questions concentrate on information in the 1101 and 1102 sections. If you run into problems, review the Historical/Conceptual sections in that chapter. Note that you may need to skip back to previous chapters to get the Historical/Conceptual information you need for later chapters.

After going through every chapter as described, Old Techs can move directly to testing their knowledge by using the free practice exams on the media that accompanies the book. Once you start scoring above 90 percent, you're ready to take the exams. If you're a New Tech—or if you're an Old Tech who wants the full learning experience this book can offer—start by reading the book, *the whole book*, as though you were reading a novel, from page 1 to the end without skipping around. Because so many computer terms and concepts build on each other, skipping around greatly increases the odds that you will become confused and end up closing the book and firing up your favorite game. Not that I have anything against games, but unfortunately that skill is *not* useful for the CompTIA A+ exams!

Your goal on this first read is to understand concepts, the *whys* behind the *hows*. Having a PC nearby as you read is helpful so you can stop and inspect the PC to see a piece of hardware or how a particular concept manifests in the real world. As you read about hard drives, for example, inspect the cables. Do they look like the ones in the book? Is there a variation? Why? It is imperative that you understand why you are doing something, not just how to do it on one particular system under one specific set of conditions. Neither the exams nor real life as a PC tech will work that way.

If you're reading this book as part of a managing and troubleshooting PCs class rather than a certification-prep course, I highly recommend going the New Tech route, even if you have a decent amount of experience. The book contains a lot of details that can trip you up if you focus only on the test-specific sections of the chapters. Plus, your program might stress historical and conceptual knowledge as well as practical, hands-on skills.

The CompTIA A+ certification exams assume that you have basic user skills. The exams really try to trick you with questions on processes that you may do every day and not think much about. Here's a classic: "To move a file from the C:\DATA folder to the D:\ drive using File Explorer, what key must you hold down while dragging the file?" If you can answer that without going to your keyboard and trying a few likely keys, you're better than most techs! In the real world, you can try a few wrong answers before you hit on the right one, but for the exams, you have to *know* it. Whether Old Tech or New Tech, make sure you are proficient at user-level Windows skills, including the following:

- Recognizing all the components of the standard Windows desktop (Start menu, notification area, etc.)
- Manipulating windows—resizing, moving, and so on
- Creating, deleting, renaming, moving, and copying files and folders within Windows
- Understanding file extensions and their relationship with program associations
- Using common keyboard shortcuts/hotkeys
- Installing, running, and closing a Windows application

When you do your initial read-through, you may be tempted to skip the Historical/Conceptual sections—don't! Understanding the history and technological developments behind today's personal computing devices helps you understand why they work—or don't work—the way they do. Basically, I'm passing on to you the kind of knowledge you might get by apprenticing yourself to an older, experienced PC tech.

After you've completed the first read-through, go through the book again, this time in textbook mode. If you're an Old Tech, start your studying here. Try to cover one chapter at a sitting. Concentrate on the 1101 and 1102 sections. Get a highlighter and mark the phrases and sentences that bring out major points. Be sure you understand how the pictures and illustrations relate to the concepts being discussed.

Once you feel you have a good grasp of the material in the book, you can check your knowledge by using the practice exams included on the media accompanying this book. You can take these in Practice mode or Exam mode. In Practice mode, you can use the Assistance window to get a helpful hint for the current questions, use the Reference feature to find the chapter that covers the question, check your answer for the question, and see an explanation of the correct answer. In Exam mode, you answer all the questions and receive an exam score at the end, just like the real thing. You can also adjust the number of questions in Practice or Exam mode by using the Customize option.

Both modes show you an overall grade, expressed as a percentage, as well as a breakdown of how well you did on each exam domain. The Review Questions feature lets you see which questions you missed and what the correct answers are. Use these results to guide further studying. Continue reviewing the topics you miss and taking additional exams until you are consistently scoring in the 90 percent range. When you get there, you are ready to pass the CompTIA A+ certification exams.

Study Tactics

Perhaps it's been a while since you had to study for a test. Or perhaps it hasn't, but you've done your best since then to block the whole experience from your mind. Either way, savvy test-takers know that certain techniques make studying for tests more efficient and effective.

Here's a trick used by students in law and medical schools who have to memorize reams of information: write it down. The act of writing something down (not typing, *writing*) in and of itself helps you to remember it, even if you never look at what you wrote again. Try taking separate notes on the material and re-creating diagrams by hand to help solidify the information in your mind.

Another oldie but goodie: make yourself flash cards with questions and answers on topics you find difficult. A third trick: take your notes to bed and read them just before you go to sleep. Many people find they really do learn while they sleep!

Contact

If you have any problems, any questions, or if you just want to argue about something, feel free to send an e-mail to the authors (total@totalsem.com).

For any other information you might need, contact CompTIA directly at their Web site: https://www.comptia.org.

Safety and Professionalism

In this chapter, you will learn how to
- Present yourself with a proper appearance and professional manner
- Talk to customers in a professional, productive manner
- Discuss the tools of the trade and preparations necessary to deal with problems proactively
- Use common safety procedures
- Apply the best practice methodology to resolve problems

I am a "nerd" and I consider the term a compliment. Nerds are smart and like to work with technology—these are the good aspects of nerd-dom. On the other hand, many people think of the term nerd as an insult. Nerds are rarely portrayed in a positive manner in the media, and I think I know why. Nerds generally suffer from some pretty serious social weaknesses. These weaknesses are classics: bad clothing, shyness, and poor communication skills. If you've ever seen an episode of the TV show *The Big Bang Theory*, you know what I'm talking about.

This chapter covers some basic life skills to enable you to enjoy your nerdiness and yet function out in the real world. You'll learn how to act as a professional and how to communicate effectively. After you're well on your way to the beginnings of social graces, we'll discuss some of the hazards (such as static electricity) you may run into in your job and the tools you can use to prevent problems. After all, nerds who cannot stay organized—or who break equipment or themselves—need to learn some tricks to keep everything organized and safe. The chapter finishes with a discussion about troubleshooting. You'll learn the CompTIA A+ troubleshooting methodology, an excellent tool that will serve you well in your studies and career as a tech.

1102

The Professional Tech

A professional tech displays professionalism, which might seem a little trite if it weren't absolutely true. The tech presents a professional appearance and follows a proper ethical code. I call the latter the Traits of a Tech. Let's look at these two areas in more detail.

Professional Appearance and Attire

Americans live in a casual society. The problem with casual is that perhaps our society is becoming *too* casual. Customers often equate casual clothing with a casual attitude. You might think you're just fixing somebody's computer, but you're doing much more than that. You are saving precious family photos. You are keeping a small business in operation. This is serious stuff, and nobody wants an unclean, slovenly person doing these important jobs. Look at Figure 1-1. This is our resident illustrator (among other job descriptions), Ford Pierson, casually dressed to hang with his buddies.

Figure 1-1
Casual Ford

I have a question for you. If you ran a small business and your primary file server died, leaving 15 employees with nothing to do, how would you feel about Ford as a tech coming into your office looking like this? I hope your answer would be "not too confident." Every company has some form of dress code for techs. Figure 1-2 shows Ford dressed in fairly typical *business casual* attire, with a company polo shirt, khaki pants, and dark shoes (trust me on that score). Please also note that both his shirt and his pants are wrinkle free. All techs either know how to iron or know the location of the nearest cleaners.

Business casual is standard for techs, but you also need to *match the required attire of the given environment.* If you get invited to a fancy dinner at a conference, for example, don't show up in a polo shirt and khakis, but wear appropriate *formal* clothes, like a nice dress, elegant pants and blouse, coat and tie and slacks, and so forth.

While we are looking at this model of a man, do you appreciate that his hair is combed and his face is cleanly shaven? It's too bad I can't use scratch-and-sniffs, but if I could, you'd also notice that Professional Ford took a shower, used some deodorant, and brushed his teeth.

Figure 1-2
Professional Ford

I hope that most of the people who read this smile quietly to themselves and say, "Well, of course." The sad truth tells me otherwise. Next time you look at a tech, ask yourself how many of these simple appearance and hygiene issues were missed. Then make a point not to be one of the unkempt techs.

The Traits of a Tech

When I was a Boy Scout in the United States, we learned something called the Boy Scout Law, a list of traits that define the ethics of a Boy Scout. Even though I haven't been active in Boy Scouts for a long time, I still have the Scout Law memorized: "A Scout is trustworthy, loyal, helpful, friendly, courteous, kind, obedient, cheerful, thrifty, brave, clean, and reverent."

My goal here isn't a sales pitch for scouting in any form, but rather to give you an idea of what we are trying to achieve: a list of ethics that will help you be a better technician. The list you are about to see is my own creation, but it does a great job of covering the CompTIA A+ objectives. Let's dive into the traits of a tech: honesty/integrity, dependability/responsibility, and sensitivity.

Honesty/Integrity

Honesty and integrity are not the same thing, but for a tech, they are so closely related that it is best to think of them as one big ethic. *Honesty* means to tell the truth, and *integrity* means doing the right thing.

It's simple to say you have to be honest, but be warned that our industry often makes it difficult. IT technicians get a lot of leeway compared to most starting jobs, making dishonesty tempting. One of the biggest temptations is lying to your boss. A new tech driving around in a van all day may find it convenient to stretch the truth on how long he took for lunch or how far along he is on the next job. Being up front and honest with your boss is pretty obvious and easy to understand.

Being honest with your customers is a lot harder. Don't sell people goods and services they don't need, even if you get a cut of what you sell. Don't lie to your customers about a problem. If you can't explain the problem to them in plain English, don't create techno-babble (see note) and don't be afraid to say, "I don't know." Too many techs seem to think that not knowing exactly what a problem might be reflects poor skill. A skilled tech can say, "I don't know, but I know how to figure it out, and I will get you the right answer."

NOTE   *Techno-babble* is the use of (often nonsensical) jargon and technical terms to intimidate and silence a challenge to a technical issue.

A computer tech must bring integrity to the job, just like any other service professional. You should treat anything said to you and anything you see as a personal confidence, not to be repeated to customers, coworkers, or bosses. Here's Mike's Rule of Confidentiality: "Unless it's a felony or an imminent physical danger, you didn't see nothin'." You'll learn more about dealing with prohibited content in Chapter 27.

There is an exception to this rule. Sometimes you need to separate paying customers from in-house users. A paying customer is someone who doesn't work for your company and is paying for your services. An in-house user is someone who works for the same company you work for and is not directly paying for your services. It's often your job (but not always) to police in-house IT policies. Here's a great example. If you are at a customer's site and you see a sticky note with a *password* on a user's monitor, you say nothing. If you are in-house and you see the same thing, you probably need to speak to the user about the dangers of exposing passwords.

You have a lot of power when you sit in front of someone's computer. You can readily read private e-mail, discover Web sites surfed, and more. With a click of the Start button, you can know the last five programs the user ran, including Word and Solitaire, and the last few documents the user worked on. Don't do this; you really don't want to know. Plus, if you are caught violating a customer's privacy, you not only will lose credibility and respect, but you could also lose your job. *You need to deal appropriately with customers' confidential and private materials.* This includes files on the computer, items on a physical desktop, and even pages sitting in a printer tray.

Every user's password represents a potential danger spot for techs. We're constantly rebooting computers, accessing protected data, and performing other jobs that require passwords. The rule here is to *avoid learning other folks' passwords at all costs* (see Figure 1-3). If you know a password to access a mission-critical machine and that machine ends up compromised or with data missing, who might be blamed? You, that's who, so avoid learning passwords! If you only need a password once, let the user type it in for you. If you anticipate accessing something multiple times (the more usual situation), ask the user to change the password temporarily.

It's funny, but people assume ownership of things they use at work. John in account-ing doesn't call the computer he uses anything but "my PC." The phone on Susie's desk

Figure 1-3
Don't do this!

isn't the company phone, it's "Susie's phone." Regardless of the logic or illogic involved with this sense of ownership, a tech needs to respect that feeling. You'll never go wrong if you follow the *Ethic of Reciprocity*, also known as the *Golden Rule:* "Do unto others as you would have them do unto you." In a tech's life, this can translate as "Treat people's things as you would have other people treat yours." Don't use or touch anything—keyboard, printer, laptop, monitor, mouse, phone, pen, paper, or cube toy—without first asking permission. Follow this rule at all times, even when the customer isn't looking.

Dependability/Responsibility

Dependability and responsibility are another pair of traits that, while they don't mean the same thing, often go together. A dependable person performs agreed-upon actions. A responsible person is answerable for her actions. Again, the freedom of the typical IT person's job makes dependability and responsibility utterly critical.

Dependable techs show up for job appointments and show up on time. Failure to show up for an appointment not only inconveniences the customer but also can cost your customer a lot of money in lost time and productivity. So, *be on time.*

If you or your company makes an appointment for you, show up. Be there. Don't let simple problems (such as bad traffic) prevent you from showing up on time. Take some time to prepare. Figure out traffic times. Figure out if preceding appointments will cause a problem, and check for traffic. There is a popular old saying in the United States, "Five minutes early is on time, and on time is late." Sometimes events take place that prevent you from being on time. *If late, contact the customer immediately* and give him or her your best estimate of when you will arrive. A simple apology wouldn't hurt, either.

Responsibility is a tricky subject for IT folks. Certainly, you should be responsible for your actions, but the stakes are high when critical data and expensive equipment are at risk. Before you work on a computer, always ask the customer if there are up-to-date backups of the data. If there aren't, offer to make backups for the customer, even if this incurs an extra charge for the customer. If the customer chooses not to make a backup, make sure he or she understands, very clearly, the risk to the data on the system you are about to repair.

NOTE Most computer repair companies require a signed Authorization of Work or Work Authorization form to document the company name, billing information, date, scope of work, and that sort of thing. Even if you do your own repairs, these forms can save you from angst and from litigation. You can create your own or do an Internet search for examples.

Sensitivity

Sensitivity is the ability to appreciate another's feeling and emotions. Sensitivity requires observing others closely, taking time to appreciate their feelings, and acting in such a way that makes them feel comfortable. I've rarely felt that technicians I've met were good at sensitivity. The vast majority of nerds I know, including myself, tend to be self-centered and unaware of what's going on around them. Let me give you a few tips I've learned along the way.

Understand that the customer is paying for your time and skills. Also understand that your presence invariably means something is wrong or broken, and few things make users more upset than broken computers. When you are "on the clock," you need to show possibly very upset customers that you are giving their problem your full attention. To do this, you need to avoid distractions. If you get a personal call, let it roll over to voicemail. If you get a work-related call, politely excuse yourself, walk away for privacy, and keep the call brief. Never speak badly of a customer; you never know where you'll run into them next.

Last, *be culturally sensitive*. We live in a diverse world of races, religions, etiquettes, and traditions. If a customer's religious holiday conflicts with your work schedule, the customer wins. If the customer wants you to take off your shoes, take them off. If the customer wants you to wear a hat, wear one. *Use appropriate professional titles, when applicable.* If a customer's title is "Doctor," for example, use the title even if you don't recognize the field of medicine. When in doubt, always ask the customer for guidance.

Effective Communication

When you deal with users, managers, and owners who are frustrated and upset because a computer or network is down and they can't work, your job requires you to take on the roles of detective and psychologist. Talking with frazzled and confused people and getting answers to questions about how the personal computing device got into the state it's in takes skill. Communicating clearly and effectively is important.

This section explores techniques for *effective communication*. It starts with assertive communication and then looks at issues involving respect. We'll examine methods for eliciting useful answers in a timely fashion. The section finishes with a discussion about managing expectations and professional follow-up actions.

Assertive Communication

In many cases, a computer problem results from user error or neglect. As a technician, you must show users the error of their ways without creating anger or conflict. You do this by using assertive communication. Assertive communication isn't pushy or bossy, but it's also not the language of a pushover. *Assertive communication* first requires you to show the other person that you understand and appreciate the importance of his feelings. Use statements such as "I know how frustrating it feels to lose data," or "I understand how infuriating it is when the network goes down and you can't get your job done." Statements like these cool off the situation and let customers know you are on their side. Avoid using the word "you," as it can sound accusatory.

The second part of assertive communication is making sure you state the problem clearly without accusing the user directly. Here's an example: "Help me understand how the network cable keeps getting unplugged during your lunch hour." Last, tell the user what you need to prevent this error in the future. "Please call me whenever you hear that buzzing sound," or "Please check the company's approved software list before installing anything." Always use "I" and "me," and never make judgments. "I can't promise the keyboard will work well if it's always getting dirty" is much better than "Stop eating cookies over the keyboard, you slob!"

Respectful Communication

Generally, IT folks support the people doing a company's main business. You are there to serve their needs and, all things being equal, to do so at their convenience, not yours.

You don't do the user's job, but you should *respect* that job and person as an essential cog in the organization. Communicate with users the way you would like them to communicate with you, were the roles reversed. Again, this follows the Ethic of Reciprocity.

Don't assume the world stops the moment you walk in the door and that you may immediately interrupt a customer's work to do yours. Although most customers are thrilled and motivated to help you the moment you arrive, this may not always be the case. Ask the magic question, "May I start working on the problem now?" Give customers a chance to wrap up, shut down, or do anything else necessary to finish their business and make it safe for you to do yours.

Engage the user with the standard rules of civil conversation. *Actively listen. Avoid interrupting the customer* as he or she describes a problem; *just listen and take notes.* You might hear something that leads to resolving the problem. Rephrase and repeat the problem back to the customer to verify you understand the issue ("So the computer is locking up three times a day?"). Use an even, nonaccusatory tone, and although it's okay to try to explain a problem if the user asks, *never condescend* and *do not argue with a customer.*

Maintain a positive attitude in the face of adversity. Don't get defensive if you can't figure something out quickly and the user starts hassling you. Remember that an angry customer isn't really angry with you—he's just frustrated—so don't take his anger personally. Instead, take it in stride; smile, *project confidence*, and assure him that computer troubleshooting sometimes takes a while.

Avoid distractions that take your focus away from the user and his or her computer problem. Things that break your concentration slow down the troubleshooting process immensely. Plus, customers will feel insulted if you start texting or talking to coworkers while interacting with the customer. You're not being paid to socialize, so turn those cell phones to vibrate. That's why the technogods created voicemail. Avoid personal interruptions or personal calls. Never take any call except one that is potentially urgent. If a call is potentially urgent, explain the urgency to the customer, step away, and deal with the call as quickly as possible.

Also, avoid texting and accessing social media sites while on the job. Checking Facebook or tweeting while your customer waits for his computer to get fixed is rude. And definitely never disclose experiences with customers via social media outlets.

Try This!

Apply the Ethic of Reciprocity

The Ethic of Reciprocity appears in almost every religion on the planet, with versions attributed to Confucius, Jesus, Moses, and Mohammed, among others. Just for practice, try the Ethic of Reciprocity out in nontechnical situations, such as when buying something from the corner store or grocery. Consciously analyze how the clerk behind the counter would want a customer to interact with him or her. Now put yourself in the clerk's shoes. How would you want a customer to communicate with you? Act accordingly!

If you discover that the user caused the problem, either through ignorance or by accident, don't dismiss the customer's problem, but avoid being judgmental or insulting about the cause. We all screw up sometimes, and these kinds of mistakes are your job security. *You get paid because people make mistakes and machines break.* Chances are you'll be back at that workstation six months or a year later, fixing something else. By becoming the user's advocate and go-to person, you create a better work environment. If a mistaken action caused the problem, explain in a positive and supportive way how to do the task correctly, and then have the user go through the process while you are there to reinforce what you said.

Getting Answers

Your job as a tech is to get the computer fixed, and the best way to start that process is to determine what the computer is doing or not doing. You must start by talking to the customer. Allow the customer to explain the problem fully while you record the information.

Although each person is different, most users with a malfunctioning computer or peripheral will be distraught and perhaps defensive about the problem. There are methods for dealing with difficult customers or situations. You need to ask the right questions *and* listen to the customer's answers. Then ask the proper follow-up questions with the goal of *getting answers* that will help you troubleshoot the problem.

Always avoid accusatory questions because they won't help you in the least (see Figure 1-4). "What did you do?" generally gets a confused or defensive "Nothing" in reply, which doesn't get you closer to solving the problem. First, ask questions that help clarify customer statements. Repeat what you think is the problem after you've listened all the way through the user's story.

Figure 1-4
Never accuse!

Follow up with fact-seeking questions. "When did it last work?" "Has it ever worked in this way?" "Has any software changed recently?" "Has any new hardware been added?" Ask *open-ended questions* to narrow the scope of the problem ("Which applications are running when the computer locks up?").

By keeping your questions friendly and factual, you show users that you won't accuse them or judge their actions (see Figure 1-5). You also show them that you're there to help them. After the initial tension drops away, you'll often get more information: for instance, a recitation of something the user might have tried or changed. These clues can help lead to a quick resolution of the problem.

Figure 1-5
Keeping it
friendly

Remember that you may know all about computer technology, but the user probably does not. This means a user will often use vague and/or incorrect terms to describe a particular computer component or function. That's just the way it works, so don't bother to correct the user. Wherever possible, use proper language and avoid jargon, acronyms, and slang when applicable. They simply confuse the already upset user and can make you sound like you're talking down to the user. Just ask direct, factual questions in a friendly tone, using simple, non-jargon language to zero in on what the user was trying to accomplish and what happened when things went wrong. Use visual aids when possible. Point at the machine or go to a working computer to have the user show what went wrong or what she did or tried to do.

People do usually want to get a handle on what you are doing—in a simplified way. You don't want to overwhelm them, but don't be afraid to use simple analogies or concepts to give them an idea of what is happening. If you have the time (and the skills), use drawings, equipment, and other visual aids to make technical concepts clearer. If a customer is a closet tech and is really digging for answers—to the point that it's affecting your ability to do your job—compliment her initiative, and then direct her to outside training opportunities. Better yet, tell her where she can get a copy of this book!

Beyond basic manners, never assume just because you are comfortable with friendly or casual behavior that the customer will be too. Even a casual user will expect you to behave with professional decorum. On the flip side, don't allow a user to put you in an awkward or even potentially dangerous or illegal situation. Never do work outside the scope of your assigned duties without the prior approval of your supervisor (when possible, in such cases, try to direct users to someone who *can* help them). You are not a babysitter. Never volunteer to "watch the kids" while the customer leaves the job site or tolerate a potentially unsafe situation if a customer isn't properly supervising a child. Concentrate on doing your job safely and efficiently, and maintain professional integrity.

Expectations and Follow-Up

Users are terrified when their computers and networks go down so hard that they need to call in a professional. Odds are good that they've left critical, or at least important, data on the computer. Odds are equally good they need this computer to work to do their job. When they're ready to lay down money for a professional, they're expecting you to make their system exactly the way it was before it broke. Hopefully you can do exactly that for them, but you also must deal with their expectations and let them know what to expect.

Equally, you should give your customers some follow-up after the job is finished. We've already covered data backups and Authorization of Work forms (and those are very important), but you need to keep the customers' needs in mind. You also want to keep the customer satisfied, should they need more help in the future. Here are a few items you should consider.

Timeline

If you can give the customer a best guess as to how long the repair will take, you'll be a hero. Don't be afraid to hold off on your time frame prediction until you've diagnosed the machine. If you truly don't have a feel for the time involved, tell the customer that and then tell him or her what you'll need to know before you can make the prediction.

Set and meet expectations, establish the timeline, and communicate status with the customer. Stick to the timeline. If you finish more quickly, great! People love a job that goes faster than predicted. If you're moving past the predicted time frame, contact the customer and tell him or her as soon as possible. Let him or her know what's happened, explain why you need more time, and give the customer a new time frame. The biggest secret here is to keep in communication with the customer on any change in status. People understand delays—they take place in our lives daily. People resent not knowing why a delay is occurring, especially when a precious computer is at stake.

Options

Many times with a computer issue, you can fix the problem and avoid a similar problem in the future in several ways. These options boil down to money. Offer repair/replacement options, as needed, and let the customer decide which route to take.

Route A might replace a faulty component with an upgraded component and a backup in case the new component fails in the future. Route B might replace the faulty device with an upgraded device. Route C might do an even device swap. Provide options and let the customer decide.

Documentation

At the completion of work, provide proper documentation of the services provided. Describe the problem, including the time and day you started work, the solution (again including the time and day the work ended), the number of hours you worked, and a list of all parts you replaced. If the customer owns the replaced parts, offer them to the customer (this is especially true if you replace any storage media). This documentation may or may not include your charges.

Follow-Up

Follow up with the customer/user at a later date to verify satisfaction. This can be simple follow-up, usually just a phone call, to confirm that the customer is happy with your work. This gives the customer a chance to detail any special issues that may have arisen, and it also adds that final extra touch that ensures he or she will call you again when encountering a technical problem.

Be Prepared!

Effective communication with your customer enables you to *start* the troubleshooting process, getting details about the problem and clues about things that happened around the same time. To continue troubleshooting, though, you need to be adept at handling computing devices. That starts with knowing how to handle computer components safely and how to use the tools of a tech. You also need a very clear troubleshooting methodology to guide your efforts. Let's look at these issues.

Electrostatic Discharge (ESD)

All computing devices use electricity. As long as the electricity runs properly through the circuits and wires as designed, all is good. There are times when electricity improperly jumps from one place to another in ways that cause damage, an *electromagnetic pulse (EMP)*. An EMP shows up in many ways. Lightning is a form of EMP. Lightning hitting your electrical equipment certainly makes for a bad day! Nuclear detonations also create a massive EMP burst (yikes!), but the EMP of most concern to techs is *electrostatic discharge (ESD)*.

ESD simply means the passage of a static electrical charge from one item to another. Have you ever rubbed a balloon against your shirt, making the balloon stick to you? That's a classic example of static electricity. When that static charge discharges, you may not notice it happening—although on a cool, dry day, I've been shocked so hard by touching a doorknob that I could see a big, blue spark! I've never heard of a human being getting anything worse than a rather nasty shock from ESD, but I can't say the same thing about computers. ESD will destroy the sensitive parts of any computing device, so it is essential that you take steps to avoid ESD when working on a PC or other computing device.

NOTE All computing devices are well protected against ESD on the outside. Unless you take a screwdriver or pry tool and open up a PC or other computing device, you don't need to concern yourself with ESD.

Antistatic Tools

ESD only takes place when two objects that store different amounts (the hip electrical term to use is *potential*) of static electricity come in contact. The secret to avoiding ESD is to keep you and the parts of the computer you touch at the same electrical potential, otherwise known as grounding yourself to the computing device. You can accomplish this by connecting yourself to the computer via a handy little device called an *electrostatic discharge (ESD) strap*. This simple device consists of a wire that connects on one end to an alligator clip and on the other end to a small metal plate that secures to your wrist with an elastic strap. You snap the alligator clip onto any handy metal part of the computer and place the ESD strap on either wrist. Figure 1-6 shows a typical electrostatic discharge (ESD) strap in use.

Figure 1-6
Electrostatic
discharge (ESD)
strap in use

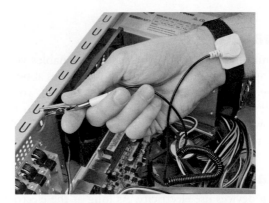

EXAM TIP Static electricity, and therefore the risk of ESD, is much more prevalent in dry, cool environments.

NOTE Make sure the metal plate on the ESD strap touches the skin of your wrist. Don't put it on over the sleeve of a long-sleeved shirt.

Electrostatic discharge (ESD) straps are standard equipment for anyone working on a computing device, but other tools might also come in handy. One of the big issues when working with a computer occurs if you find yourself pulling out parts from the computer and setting them aside. The moment you take a piece out of the computer, it no longer has contact with the systems and may pick up static from other sources. Techs use antistatic mats to eliminate this risk. An *electrostatic discharge mat*—or *ESD mat*—acts as a point of common potential; it's typical to purchase a combination ESD strap and mat that all connect to keep you, the computer, and any loose components at the same electrical *potential* (see Figure 1-7).

Figure 1-7
Electrostatic discharge (ESD) strap and mat combination

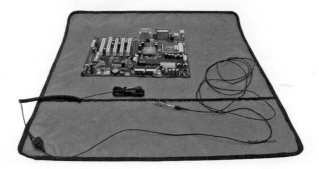

 EXAM TIP Always put components in an antistatic bag, not on the bag.

ESD straps and mats use tiny *resistors*—devices that stop or *resist* the flow of electricity—to prevent a static charge from racing through the device. These resistors can fail over time, so it's always a good idea to read the documentation that comes with your antistatic tools to see how to test those small resistors properly.

Any electrical component not in a computer case needs to be stored in an *antistatic bag*, a specially designed bag that sheds whatever static electricity you have when you touch it, thus preventing any damage to components stored within (see Figure 1-8). Almost all components come in an antistatic bag when purchased. Experienced techs never throw these bags away, as you never know when you'll want to pull a part out and place it on a shelf for a while.

Although having an ESD strap with you at all times would be ideal, the reality is that from time to time you'll find yourself in a situation where you lack the proper antistatic tools. This shouldn't keep you from working on the computer—if you're careful! Before working on a computer in such a situation, take a moment to touch the power supply—I'll show you where it is in Chapter 2—to make sure you are at the same

Figure 1-8
Antistatic bag

electrical potential as the computer. Repeat every once in a while as you work. Although this isn't as good as a wrist strap, this *equipment grounding* is better than nothing at all.

Use these tools for proper component handling and storage: ESD straps, ESD mats, antistatic bags, and equipment grounding.

Try This!

Antistatic Protection Devices

In some circumstances, an antistatic protection device such as an ESD strap could get in the way. Manufacturers have developed some alternatives to the wrist strap, so try this:

1. Take a field trip to a local computer or electronics store.

2. Check out their selection of antistatic devices. Can you find anything other than wrist straps or mats?

3. Do a Web search for "static control products." Can you find anything other than wrist straps or mats?

4. Report what options you can find for protecting your equipment from ESD. Weigh the pros and cons and decide what you would use in various situations.

The last issue regarding ESD is that never-ending question—should you work with the computing device plugged in or unplugged? The answer is simple: Do you really want to be physically connected to a computer that is plugged into an electrical outlet? Granted, the chances of electrocution are slim, but why take the risk?

EXAM TIP Always disconnect power before repairing a personal computing device.

Removing the power applies also when working on portable computers. Disconnect both the battery and the power cord from the wall outlet and remove the battery. With mobile devices such as tablets and smartphones, this creates an issue because the battery is inside the case. Chapter 25 covers the special skills needed for working on mobile devices.

Electromagnetic Interference (EMI)

A magnetic field interfering with electronics is *electromagnetic interference (EMI)*. EMI isn't nearly as dangerous as ESD, but it can cause permanent damage to some components and erase data on some storage devices. You can prevent EMI by keeping magnets away from computer equipment. Certain components are particularly susceptible to EMI, especially storage devices like hard drives.

The biggest problem with EMI is that we often use magnets without even knowing we are doing so. Any device with an electrical motor has a magnet. Many telephones have magnets. Power bricks for laptops and speakers also have magnets. Even a lowly screwdriver might have a magnet. Keep them away!

Radio Frequency Interference (RFI)

Do you ever hear strange noises on your speakers even though you aren't playing any sounds? Do you ever get strange noises on your cell phone? If so, you've probably run into *radio frequency interference (RFI)*. Many devices emit radio waves:

- Cell phones
- Wireless network cards/access points
- Cordless phones
- Baby monitors
- Microwave ovens

In general, the radio waves that these devices emit are very weak, and almost all electronic devices are shielded to prevent RFI. A few devices, speakers in particular, are susceptible to RFI. RFI will never cause any damage, but it can be incredibly irritating. The best way to prevent RFI is to keep radio-emitting devices as far away as possible from other electronics.

RFI becomes a big problem when two devices share the same frequencies. Baby monitors, Internet of things (IoT) devices (like wireless surveillance cameras), and many wireless networks share the same range of frequencies. They sometimes interfere with each other, causing poor signals or even blocking signals completely. These devices need to be tuned to avoid stomping on each other's frequencies. In Chapter 20 you'll see how to tune a wireless network to prevent RFI.

NOTE Computer gear manufacturers package their products in a variety of ways to shield against accidental damage, whether that's physical damage, ESD, EMI, or RFI. The typical pink translucent computer bag is coated with a film that prevents the bag from producing static electricity and mildly protects the contents against physical contact (and thus damage). Two types of metal bags offer shielding against EMI and RFI as well as ESD. These are the silvery bags (such as shown previously in Figure 1-8) you'll see hard drives packed in, for example, and the black-and-silver woven bags you'll sometimes see. These bags are easy to purchase online and are a cheap insurance policy to protect your expensive components.

Physical Tools

The basic *tech toolkit* consists of a *Phillips-head screwdriver* and not much else—seriously—but a half-dozen tools round out a fully functional toolkit. Most kits have a star-headed Torx wrench, a nut driver or two, a pair of plastic tweezers, a little grabber tool (the technical term is *parts retriever*), a hemostat, and both Phillips-head and flat-head screwdrivers (see Figure 1-9).

Figure 1-9
Typical
technician toolkit

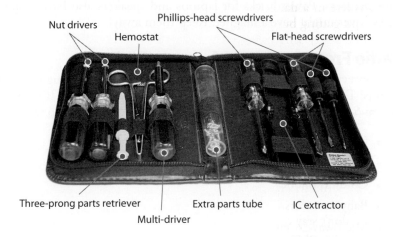

Nut drivers
Hemostat
Phillips-head screwdrivers
Flat-head screwdrivers
Three-prong parts retriever
Multi-driver
Extra parts tube
IC extractor

I'll add a few more tools to this toolkit as the book progresses that you'll want for a not-so-basic toolkit. Those more advanced tools will be introduced as your knowledge grows.

You already own another great tool, the camera in your smartphone or tablet. It's amazing how handy it is to photograph screw locations, cable connections, or other conditions so that you can later retrieve those images when you reinstall something.

A lot of techs throw in an extension magnet to grab hard-to-reach bits that drop into cases (an exception to the "no magnets" rule). Many also add a magnifying glass and a flashlight for those hard-to-read numbers and text on the printed circuit boards (PCBs) that make up a large percentage of devices inside the system unit. Contrary to what you might think, techs rarely need a hammer.

Mobile devices such as tablets and smartphones require more complex kits that include specialized tools, such as prying tools (called *spudgers*—isn't that a great word?). There are many excellent toolkits available for purchase; I recommend the toolkits sold by iFixit (https://www.ifixit.com) and use one myself (Figure 1-10). These kits are inexpensive and reliable, plus iFixit has hundreds of free videos that walk you through many scenarios using the kits.

Figure 1-10
Author's go-to iFixit toolkit (several of the implements on the right side are types of spudger)

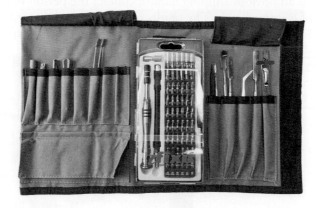

Personal Safety

IT techs live in a dangerous world. We're in constant danger of tripping, hurting our backs, and getting burned by hot components. You also need to keep in mind what you wear (in a safety sense). Let's take a moment to discuss these *personal safety* issues and what to do about them.

CAUTION When thinking about safety, maintain *compliance with government regulations.* You may be required to wear certain protective gear or take extra precautions while in the workplace. Make sure you also follow any environmental rules for the disposal of old parts, especially with things like batteries and toner cartridges, which may contain hazardous or toxic materials. Check with your employer or your local government's Web site for more information.

If you don't stay organized, hardware technology will take over your life. Figure 1-11 shows a corner of my office, a painful example of cable "kludge."

Figure 1-11
Mike's cable kludge

Cable messes such as these are dangerous tripping hazards. While I may allow a mess like this in my home office, all cables in a business environment are carefully tucked away behind computer cases, run into walls, or placed under cable runners. If you see a cable that is an obvious tripping hazard, contact the person in charge of the building to take care of it immediately. The results of ignoring such hazards can be catastrophic (see Figure 1-12). Use proper cable management to avoid these dangers.

Figure 1-12
What a strange,
bad trip it's been.

Another personal safety issue is heavy boxes. Computers, printers, monitors—everything we use—all seem to come to us in heavy boxes. Use proper lifting techniques. Remember never to lift with your back; lift with your legs, and always use a hand truck if available. Pay attention to weight limitations on the devices you use to move anything heavy. You are never paid enough to risk your own health.

You also need to watch out for hot components. It's hard to burn yourself unless you open up a computer, printer, or monitor. First, watch for anything with a cooling fan like the one shown in Figure 1-13. If you see a cooling fan, odds are good that something is hot enough to burn you—such as the metal *cooling fins* below the fan. Also look for labels or stickers warning about hot components. Last, when in doubt, move your hand over components as if you were checking the heat on a stove.

 NOTE A non-contact thermometer is another useful tool to have on hand. Not only is it more precise than your hand, it can read the temperature of components deep in hard-to-reach corners of a device.

Disconnect a computer from its electrical source before you work on it, if possible. In the rare event where you need to work on a live system, take caution. Provide *electrical fire safety* equipment in rooms or locations that have a fire risk, such as server rooms. All those

Figure 1-13
Checking for hot
cooling fins

electronics and all that juice make a dangerous combination in those rare circumstances in which bad things happen. Keep properly rated (Class C) fire extinguishers handy.

EXAM TIP When you build out a computer space, such as a server closet (the room that has a lot of important computers in it), use standard carpentry safety techniques. Wear an *air filter mask*, when cutting drywall, for example. Wear *safety goggles* when using power tools.

Finally, remove any jewelry or loose-hanging clothing before working on a computer. If you have long hair, you might consider tying it back in a ponytail. You don't want anything getting caught in a fan or stuck on a component. This can save you and your components a lot of pain.

1101

Troubleshooting Methodology

An effective *troubleshooting methodology* follows a set of steps to diagnose and fix a computer. Troubleshooting methodology includes talking to users to determine how and when the problem took place, determining a cause, testing, verification, and documentation. Techs use a number of good troubleshooting methodologies. Luckily for those taking the CompTIA A+ 220-1101 certification exam, CompTIA clearly defines their vision of troubleshooting methodology:

5.1 Given a scenario, apply the best practice methodology to resolve problems.

1. *Identify the problem*
   - Gather information from the user, identify user changes, and, if applicable, perform backups before making changes
   - Inquire regarding environmental or infrastructure changes

2. *Establish a theory of probable cause* (question the obvious)

- If necessary, conduct external or internal research based on symptoms

3. *Test the theory* to determine the cause

- Once the theory is confirmed, determine the next steps to resolve the problem

- If the theory is not confirmed, re-establish a new theory or *escalate*

4. *Establish a plan of action* to resolve the problem and implement the solution

- Refer to the vendor's instruction for guidance

5. *Verify* full system functionality and, if applicable, implement preventive measures

6. *Document* the findings, actions, and outcomes

Identify the Problem

There's a reason you're standing in front of a computer to repair it: something happened that the user of the computer has identified as "not good." First, you need to *identify the problem* by talking to the user. Get the user to show you what's not good. Is it an error code? Is something not accessible? Is a device not responding?

Then ask the user that classic tech question (remember your communication skills here!): "Has anything recently changed on the computer that might have made this problem appear?" What you're really saying is: "Have you messed with the computer? Did you install some evil program? Did you shove a USB drive in so hard that you broke the connection?" Of course, you never say these things; simply ask nicely without accusing so the user can help you troubleshoot the problem (see Figure 1-14).

Figure 1-14
Tech asking
nicely

Ask also if any changes have happened in the environment around the workstation. Check for any infrastructure changes that might cause problems.

In most troubleshooting situations, it's important to back up critical files before making changes to a system. To some extent, this is a matter of proper ongoing maintenance, but if some important bit of data disappears and you don't have a backup, you know who the user will blame, don't you? (We cover backup options in detail in Chapter 14.)

EXAM TIP   The CompTIA A+ certification exams assume that all techs should back up systems *every time* before working on them, even though that's not how it works in the real world.

Establish a Theory of Probable Cause (Question the Obvious)

Now it's time to analyze the issue and come up with a theory as to what is wrong, a *theory of probable cause*. Personally, I prefer the word "guess" at this point because very few errors are so obvious that you'll know what to do. Fall back on your knowledge of the *computing process* to localize the issue based on the symptoms. Keep your guesses…err…theories…simple. One of the great problems for techs is their desire to overlook the obvious problems in their desire to dig into the system (see Figure 1-15).

Figure 1-15
Ford the Tech misses the obvious.

NOTE   Chapter 2 walks you through the computing process in some detail, showing how all the parts interact to "make the magic happen." The combination of a solid troubleshooting methodology and a fundamental understanding of the computing process is the core knowledge for techs for fixing things.

Research   In many situations, you'll need to access other resources to root out the most probable cause of the problem. Therefore, if necessary, you should conduct external or internal research based on the symptoms.

Use the Internet for external research. With the Internet quite literally at the fingertips of anyone with access to a smartphone or tablet, a short search online can result in swift answers to tech problems. If the customer's computer displays an error message, for example, put the whole error message into a search engine.

Internal research means asking other techs on-site for help. It means checking company records regarding a particular machine (for example, checking a problem-tracking database where previous issues have been recorded). This kind of search will reveal any known problems with the machine or with the user's actions.

Outside the Case   Take a moment to look for clues before you open up the case. Most importantly, use all your senses in the process.

What do you see? Is a connector mangled or a plastic part clearly damaged? Even if that connector or part works fine, the physical abuse could provide extra information. If the user can't connect to a network, check the cable. Did something roll over it to break the thin internal wires? Is that a jelly smear near the jammed optical drive door? (No pun intended, really!) A visual examination of the external computer is important.

When you put your hand on the system unit (that's the case that houses all the computer parts), does it feel hot? Can you feel or hear the vibrations of the fans? If not, that would be a clue to an overheating or overheated computer. Modern computers can run when overly hot, but generally run very sluggishly.

If you spend a moment listening to the computer, you might get some clues to problem sources. A properly running computer doesn't make a lot of sound, just a regular hum from the spinning fans. If you hear clicking or grinding sounds, that's a very bad sign and a very important clue! We'll cover data storage devices—a classic cause of clicking and grinding sounds—in detail in Chapters 8 and 9.

Finally, don't forget your nose. If you smell the unmistakable odor of ozone, you know that's the smell electronic components give off when they cook or are simply running much too hot.

Test the Theory to Determine the Cause

Okay, so you've decided on a theory that makes sense. It's time to *test the theory* to see if it fixes the problem. A challenge to fixing a computer is that the theory and the fix pretty much prove themselves at the same time. In many cases, testing your theory does nothing more than verify that something is broken. If that's the case, then replace the broken part.

If your theory doesn't pan out, you should come up with a new theory and test it. (In CompTIA speak, if the theory is not confirmed, you need to re-establish a new theory.) If you verify and the fix lies within your skill set, excellent.

At this point, you need to check in with management to make certain you have permission to make necessary changes. Always consider corporate policies, procedures, and impacts before implementing changes. Having the boss walk in frowning while you're elbows-deep in a machine with the question "Who gave you permission?" can make for a bad day!

If you don't have the skills—or the permissions—to fix the issue, you need to *escalate* the problem.

Escalation is the process your company (or sometimes just you) goes through when you—the person assigned to repair a problem—are not able to get the job done. It's okay to escalate a problem because no one can fix every problem. All companies should have some form of escalation policy. It might mean calling your boss. It might mean filling out and sending some in-house form to another department. Escalation is sometimes a more casual process. You might want to start researching the problem online; you might want to refer to in-house documentation to see if this problem has appeared in the past. (See "Document Findings, Actions, and Outcomes" later in this chapter.) You may want to call a coworker to come check it out (see Figure 1-16).

Figure 1-16
Ford the Tech asks for help from Scott.

Establish a Plan of Action to Resolve the Problem

At this point, you should have a good sense of the problem, including the scope and necessary permissions to do the job. You need to *establish a plan of action* to resolve the problem and implement the solution. Sometimes the plan requires a few steps before you can implement the solution. You might need additional resources such as known-good replacement parts. A backup of user data should be part of establishing a plan of action.

When working on vendor-specific equipment, refer to the vendor's instructions for guidance on how to troubleshoot. Often the vendor knows the quirks or possible failure points in their gear because many of their customers have broken things in the same place or same fashion.

Verify and Prevent

Fantastic! Through either your careful work or escalation, you've solved the problem, or so you think. Remember two items here. First, even though *you* think the problem is fixed, you need to *verify* with the customer/user that it's fixed. Second, try to do something to prevent the problem from happening again in the future, if possible.

Verify Full System Functionality   You need to verify full system functionality to make sure the user is happy. Let's say a user can't print. You determine that the Print Spooler service is stalled due to a locked-up laser printer. You reset the printer and all of the jobs start printing. Job done, right?

The best way to verify full system functionality is to have the user do whatever she needs to do on the repaired system for a few minutes while you watch. Any minor errors will quickly become apparent, and you might learn some interesting aspects of how the user does her job. Knowing what your users do is critical for good techs to help them do their jobs better (see Figure 1-17).

Figure 1-17
Ford the Tech
sticks around and
watches.

If Applicable, Implement Preventive Measures   A very smart tech once told me, "A truly good support tech's work goal should be to never have to get out of his chair." That's a pretty tall order, but it makes sense to me. Do whatever you can to prevent this problem from repeating. For some problems, there are obvious actions to take, such as making sure anti-malware is installed so a computer doesn't get infected again. Sometimes there's no action to take at all: nothing can prevent a hard drive that decides to die. But you can take one more critical action in almost every case: education. Take advantage of the time with the user to informally train him about the problem. Show him the dangers of malware or tell him that sometimes hard drives just die. The more your users know, the less time you'll spend out of your chair.

Document Findings, Actions, and Outcomes

Based on his famous quote, "Those who cannot remember the past are condemned to repeat it," I think the philosopher George Santayana would have made a great technician. As a tech, the last step of every troubleshooting job should be to *document* your findings, actions, and outcomes. This documentation might be highly formalized in some organizations, or it might just be a few notes you jot down for your own use, but you must document! What was the problem? What did you do to fix it? What worked? What didn't? The best guide to use for documentation is: "What would I have liked to have known about this problem before I walked up to it?" Good documentation is the strongest sign of a good tech (see Figure 1-18).

Figure 1-18
Ford documents
a successful fix.

Documenting problems helps you track the troubleshooting history of a computing device over time, enabling you to make longer-term determinations about retiring it or changing out more parts. If you and fellow techs fix a specific problem with Mary's laptop several times, for example, you might decide to swap out her whole system rather than fix it a fourth time.

Documenting helps fellow techs if they have to follow up on a task you didn't finish or troubleshoot a machine you've worked on previously. The reverse is also true. If you get a call about Frank's computer, for example, and check the records to find other service calls on his computer, you might find that the fix for a particular problem is already documented. This is especially true for user-generated problems. Having documentation of what you did also means you don't have to rely on your memory when your coworker asks what you did to fix the weird problem with Jane's computer a year ago!

Documenting also comes into play when you or a user has an accident on-site. If your colleague Joe drops a monitor on his foot and breaks both the monitor and his foot, for example, you need to fill out an *incident report*, just as you would with any kind of accident: electrical, chemical, or physical. An incident report should detail what happened and where it happened. This helps your supervisors take the appropriate actions quickly and efficiently.

Chapter Review

Questions

1. Which of the following would be most appropriate for the workplace? (Select two.)

   A. Clean, pressed khaki trousers

   B. Clean, wrinkle-free T-shirt

   C. Clean, wrinkle-free polo shirt

   D. Clean, pressed jeans

2. While manning the help desk, you get a call from a distraught user who says she has a blank screen. What would be a useful follow-up question? (Select two.)

   A. Is the computer turned on?

   B. Is the monitor turned on?

   C. Did you reboot?

   D. What did you do?

3. At the very least, what tool should be in every technician's toolkit?

   A. Pliers

   B. Hammer

   C. Straight-slot screwdriver

   D. Phillips-head screwdriver

4. When is it appropriate to yell at a user?

   A. When he screws up the second time.

   B. When he interrupts your troubleshooting.

   C. When he screws up the fifth time.

   D. Never.

5. When troubleshooting a software problem on Phoebe's computer and listening to her describe the problem, you get a text from your boss. Which of the following is the most appropriate action for you to take?

   A. Excuse yourself, walk out of the cubicle, and text your boss.

   B. Pick up Phoebe's phone and dial your boss's number.

   C. Wait until Phoebe finishes her description and then ask to use her phone to call your boss.

   D. Wait until Phoebe finishes her description, run through any simple fixes, and then explain that you need to call your boss on your cell phone.

6. You are at a customer's workstation to install several software and hardware updates, a process that will take a while and require several reboots of the computer. What should you do about the password to the user's account?

    A. Require the customer to sit with you throughout the process so she can type in her password each time.

    B. Ask the user to write down her password for you to use.

    C. Ask the user to change her password temporarily for you to use.

    D. Call your supervisor.

7. Which of the following is a good practice after completing a troubleshooting call at someone's office?

    A. Follow up with a call within a couple of days to make sure everything is going well with the fixed computer.

    B. Make copies of any passwords you used at the site for future reference.

    C. Document any particularly important people you met for future reference.

    D. Do nothing. Your work is finished there.

8. Which tool helps you avoid accidental static discharge by keeping you at the same electrical potential as the computer on which you're working?

    A. Antistatic spray

    B. Antistatic bag

    C. ESD wrist strap

    D. Phillips-head screwdriver

9. Once you have ascertained the computer's problem and backed up the critical data, what should you do?

    A. Establish a theory of probable cause.

    B. Start fixing the machine.

    C. Question users more to find out how they caused the problem.

    D. Document.

10. What should you do after successfully repairing a machine?

    A. Do nothing; your job is done.

    B. Admonish the user for causing so much work for the IT department.

    C. Document your findings.

    D. Lock it down so the user can't cause the same problem again.

Answers

1. **A, C.** Khaki trousers and a polo shirt trump jeans and a T-shirt every time.

2. **A, B.** Go for the simple answer first. When faced with a blank screen, check to see if the computer and the monitor are turned on.

3. **D.** Every tech's toolkit should have a Phillips-head screwdriver, at the very least.

4. **D.** Don't get angry or yell at clients.

5. **D.** Focus on the customer and don't use her things.

6. **C.** In this circumstance, asking for a temporary password is the right answer. Make sure the user changes her password back before you leave the site.

7. **A.** A simple follow-up builds goodwill and trust. This is a very important step to take after completing a job.

8. **C.** An ESD wrist strap keeps you at the same electrical potential as the computer.

9. **A.** You should establish a theory of probable cause once you have ascertained the problem and backed up data.

10. **C.** At the end of a repair you should always document your findings.

The Visible Computer

In this chapter, you will learn how to

- Describe how computing devices work
- Identify common connectors and devices on typical computer systems
- Discuss features common to operating system software

Charles Babbage didn't set out to change the world. He just wanted to perform mathematical calculations without worrying about human error, something all too common in his day. Babbage was a mathematician in the nineteenth century, a time well before anyone thought to create electronic calculators or computers (see Figure 2-1). When he worked on complex math, the best "computers" were people who computed by hand. They solved equations using pen or pencil and paper.

Figure 2-1
Charles Babbage, father of the computer

Babbage dreamed of machines that would calculate mechanically, making sure the results were always right. Although his ideas were ahead of his time, inventors in the mid-twentieth century picked up the concepts and created huge calculating machines that they called *computers*.

This chapter explores how computing devices work. We'll look first at the computing process, then turn to hardware components common to all devices. The chapter finishes with a discussion about software, exploring commonality among all operating systems and specific functions of application programming.

Historical/Conceptual

The Computing Process

In modern terms, a *computer* is an electronic device that can perform calculations. The most common types use special programming languages that people, known as *computer programmers*, have written and compiled to accomplish specific tasks.

When most people hear the word "computer," they picture *general* computing devices, machines that can do all sorts of things. The typical *personal computer (PC)* running Microsoft Windows is used for various tasks (see Figure 2-2). You can use it to manage your money and play games, for example, without doing anything special to it, such as adding new hardware.

Figure 2-2
A typical
desktop PC

Here are some other general-purpose computing devices:

- Apple Mac
- Apple iPad
- Smartphone
- Laptop (see Figure 2-3)

Figure 2-3
A laptop

Plenty of other devices do *specific* computing jobs, focusing on a single task or set of similar tasks. You probably encounter them all the time. Here's a list of common specific-purpose computers:

- Internet of Things (IoT) thermostat
- Digital watch
- Router
- Wi-Fi picture frame
- Xbox Series X
- Roku
- Point of sale (POS) system (see Figure 2-4)

Figure 2-4
A point of sale computer in a gasoline pump

This list isn't even close to complete! Plus, there are computers *inside* a zillion other devices. Here are some:

- Modern refrigerators
- Every automobile built since the mid-1990s
- Airplanes
- Boats
- Mall lighting systems
- Zambonis
- Home security alarms

You get the idea. Computers help the modern world function.

Modern computer techs need to know how different types of computing devices work so they can support the many devices used by their clients. This diversity is also reflected in the CompTIA A+ exams.

If the list of devices to support seems overwhelming, relax. The secret savior for modern techs is that computing devices function similarly to each other. Once you know what a device should enable a user to do, you'll be able to configure and troubleshoot successfully.

The Computing Parts

A modern computer consists of three major components:

- Hardware
- Operating system
- Applications

The *hardware* is the physical stuff that you can touch or hold in your hand. With a smartphone, for example, you hold the phone. On a typical personal computer, you touch the keyboard or view images on the monitor.

The *operating system (OS)* controls the hardware and enables you to tell the computer what to do. The operating system often appears as a collection of windows and little icons you can click or touch (see Figure 2-5). Collectively these are called the *user interface (UI),* which means the software parts with which you can interact. The UI that offers images or icons to select (as opposed to making you type commands) is called a *graphical user interface (GUI).*

Applications (or programs) enable you to do specialized tasks on a computer, such as

- Type a letter
- Send a message from your computer in Houston to your friend's computer in Paris
- Wander through imaginary worlds with people all over Earth

Very simple computing devices might have an operating system with only a few features that give you choices. A digital camera, for example, has a menu system that enables you to control things like the quality of the picture taken (see Figure 2-6).

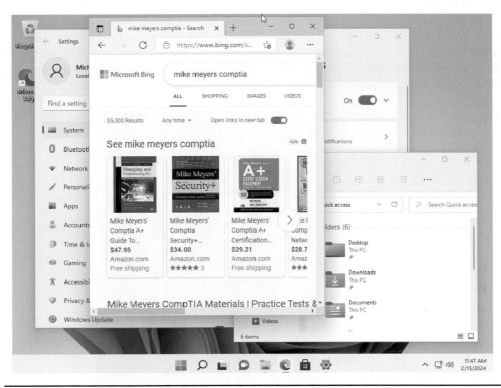

Figure 2-5 The Microsoft Windows 11 operating system

Figure 2-6
Changing
settings on a
digital camera

More complicated devices offer more choices. A Samsung Galaxy Z Fold phone, for example, does some cool things right out of the box, way more than just phone calls! But all smartphones also have access to an online store with massive selections of applications. Just download the applications (known as *apps*) to do all sorts of things that Samsung didn't include (see Figure 2-7).

Figure 2-7
Google Play store

Finally, multipurpose computers like the typical Windows PC or macOS computer offer applications to help you do everything from write a book on CompTIA A+ certification to talk with someone on the other side of the world, with full audio and video (see Figure 2-8).

Figure 2-8
Video call with
Apple's FaceTime

Stages

At the most basic level, computers work through three stages, what's called the *computing process:*

- Input
- Processing
- Output

You start the action by doing something—clicking the mouse, typing on the keyboard, or touching the touch screen. This is *input.* The parts inside the device or case take over at that point as the operating system tells the hardware to do what you've requested. This is *processing.*

In fact, at the heart of every computing device is a *central processing unit (CPU),* usually a single, thin wafer of silicon and tiny transistors (see Figure 2-9). The CPU handles the majority of the processing tasks and is, in a way, the "brain" of the computer.

Figure 2-9
An AMD Ryzen
CPU installed on
a motherboard

 NOTE Chapter 3 gives a lot more information on CPUs and other processing components.

Once the computer has processed your request, it shows you the result by changing what you see on the display or playing a sound through the speakers. This is *output.* A computer wouldn't be worth much if it couldn't demonstrate that it fulfilled your commands! Figure 2-10 shows the computing process.

Figure 2-10
The computing
process

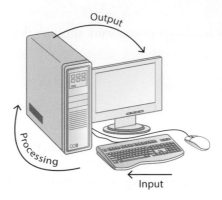

Modern computing devices almost always have two other stages:

- Data storage
- Network connection

Data storage means saving a permanent copy of your work so that you can come back to it later. It works like this. First, you tell the computer to save something. Second, the CPU processes that command and stores the data. Third, the computer shows you something, such as a message saying that the data is stored. Any work that you *don't* save is lost when you turn the computer off or exit the application.

Most computing devices connect to other devices to access other resources. A *network connection* often describes how one computer connects to one or more other computers. And it doesn't just apply to a couple of office computers. Every smartphone, for example, can connect to the Internet and play a video from YouTube (assuming you have a signal from a cell tower and a data plan).

At this point, students often ask me a fundamental question: "Why should I care about the computing process?" The answer to this question defines what makes a good computer technician. Here's my response.

Why the Process Matters to Techs

Because the computing process applies to *every* computing device, it provides the basis for how every tech builds, upgrades, and repairs such devices. By understanding both the components involved and how they talk to each other, you can work with *any* computing device. It might take a couple minutes to figure out how to communicate with the device via input, for example, but you'll quickly master it because you know how all computing devices work.

Breaking It Down

The whole computer process from start to finish has a lot of steps and pieces that interact. The more you understand about this interaction and these pieces, the better you can troubleshoot when something goes wrong. *This is the core rule to being a great tech.*

We'll turn to our knowledge of these "steps and pieces" as we tackle troubleshooting scenarios throughout the book, remembering the essential question a tech should ask when facing a problem: What can it be? Or, in slightly longer fashion: What could cause the problem that stopped this device from functioning properly?

1101

Computing Hardware

Later chapters examine specific computing hardware, such as CPUs and mass storage devices. CompTIA expects competent techs to know what to call every connector, socket, and slot in a variety of computing devices. Rather than describe all of those briefly here, I decided to create a photo walkthrough naming points of interest and the chapters that discuss them.

 EXAM TIP Memorize the names of the components, connectors, and terms discussed and displayed in this section. You'll see them in future chapters, in the real world, and on the CompTIA A+ 1101 exam.

This section serves as a visual introduction to the components and connections. Plus, it should work great as a set of study sheets for memorizing names just before taking the CompTIA A+ 1101 exam. The images that follow indicate the chapters where you'll find information about a component or connection standard.

Figure 2-11 shows a typical desktop PC. The input and output devices should be familiar to most.

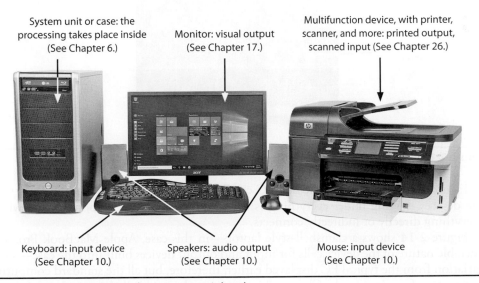

Figure 2-11   Desktop PC with common peripherals

Figure 2-12 shows the back of a PC's system unit, where you'll find the many connection points called *ports*. Some ports connect to output devices such as monitors. Other ports are exclusively used for input devices. Most (such as the universal serial bus, or USB) handle both input and output.

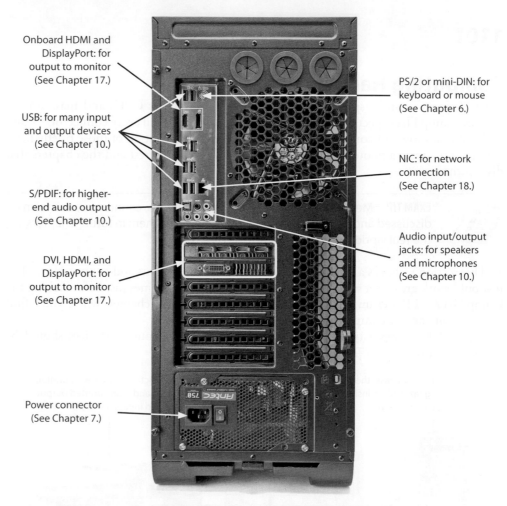

Figure 2-12 The business end of a desktop PC

Figure 2-13 reveals the inside of a PC case, where you'll find the processing and storage devices. Hiding under everything is the motherboard, the component into which everything directly or indirectly connects.

Figure 2-14 shows a clamshell-style laptop—in this case, Apple MacBook Pro. The portable nature of the device calls for input and output devices built into the case—some variation from the typical PC displayed earlier, therefore, but all the standard computing component functions apply. Chapter 23 goes into a lot of detail about each component displayed here.

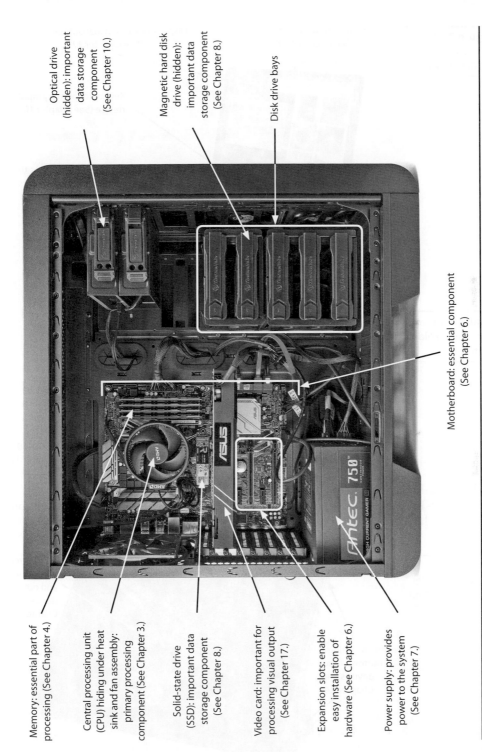

Optical drive (hidden): important data storage component (See Chapter 10.)

Magnetic hard disk drive (hidden): important data storage component (See Chapter 8.)

Disk drive bays

Motherboard: essential component (See Chapter 6.)

Memory: essential part of processing (See Chapter 4.)

Central processing unit (CPU) hiding under heat sink and fan assembly: primary processing component (See Chapter 3.)

Solid-state drive (SSD): important data storage component (See Chapter 8.)

Video card: important for processing visual output (See Chapter 17.)

Expansion slots: enable easy installation of hardware (See Chapter 6.)

Power supply: provides power to the system (See Chapter 7.)

Figure 2-13 Inside the system unit

Figure 2-14
Laptop
(a MacBook Pro)

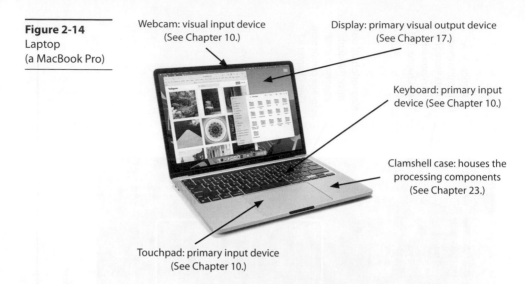

Webcam: visual input device
(See Chapter 10.)

Display: primary visual output device
(See Chapter 17.)

Keyboard: primary input
device (See Chapter 10.)

Clamshell case: houses the
processing components
(See Chapter 23.)

Touchpad: primary input device
(See Chapter 10.)

Figure 2-15
Ports on an older
laptop

USB port: for many input and output devices
(See Chapter 10.)

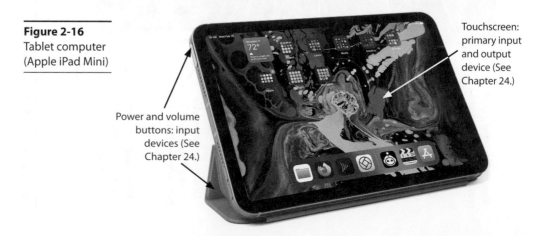

Secure Digital (SD) card slot: removable
data storage port (See Chapter 10.)

Thunderbolt 2 port: general-purpose
input/output connection (See Chapter 10.)

Figure 2-15 shows the side of a laptop with three different connection types.

Figure 2-16 shows a tablet computer, an Apple iPad. Note that the screen has a touch interface, which makes it both an input and output device.

Figure 2-16
Tablet computer
(Apple iPad Mini)

Touchscreen:
primary input
and output
device (See
Chapter 24.)

Power and volume
buttons: input
devices (See
Chapter 24.)

We could continue with any number of computing devices in the same picture show, but at this point the uniformity of computing component functions should be clear. They all work similarly, and, as a competent tech, you should be able to support just about any customer device. Let's turn now to a feast of software.

 SIM Check out the excellent Chapter 2 Challenge! sim on motherboard matching at https://www.totalsem.com/110X. It's a cool sim that helps names stick in your head.

1102

Computing Software

Any premade set of binary instructions that a CPU can read and react to is software. All applications are software. Operating systems such as Microsoft Windows or Apple's iOS running on your iPhone are also software. Care and feeding of your computer's software is important work. Reflecting that importance, the CompTIA A+ 1102 exam covers a lot of software, mostly operating system tools. You'll need to know how to install and support applications, of course, as that's an essential role for a CompTIA A+ tech.

The exam explores four workstation operating systems, Microsoft Windows (versions 10 and 11 only), Apple macOS, Linux, and Google Chrome OS. Note that the exam covers common Linux features, but not distribution-specific features. The book follows this pattern as well.

 EXAM TIP Linux comes in a dizzying variety of versions, called distributions or *distros*. The CompTIA A+ 1102 exam focuses on features common to all distros.

In addition to the workstation operating systems, the CompTIA A+ 1102 exam covers three smartphone/tablet operating systems: Google Android, Apple iOS, and Apple iPadOS.

Common Operating System Functions

All OSs are not created equal, but every OS provides certain functions. Here's a list:

- The OS communicates, or provides a method for other programs to communicate, with the hardware of the PC or device. Operating systems run on specific hardware. For example, if you have a 32-bit CPU, you need to install a 32-bit version of an operating system. With a 64-bit CPU, you need a 64-bit OS (Chapter 3 explains 32- vs. 64-bit processors).

- The OS creates a *user interface (UI)*—a visual representation of the computer on the monitor that makes sense to the people using the computer.
- The OS enables users to determine the available installed programs and run, use, and shut down the programs of their choice.
- The OS enables users to add, move, and delete the installed programs and data.
- The OS provides a method to secure a system from all sorts of threats, such as data loss or improper access.

All operating systems enable you to use programs, but the formats vary so widely that you can't just install any program on any OS. Programmers do extra work to build separate versions of a program that can run on more than one OS. This is one example of what the CompTIA A+ 1102 exam calls *compatibility concerns between OSs*. The software your users need can restrict the list of acceptable OS choices, and the OS choice limits available software. This can also affect how well users on multiple operating systems can collaborate!

Another common compatibility concern is whether a specific OS can communicate with a given piece of hardware. A device that works well with one OS may work poorly or not at all with another! One OS may need no extra software to work with a device, while another OS might need a special program installed to control it. Likewise, brand-new hardware may not work well on any OS until the OS receives updates to support the new hardware.

Almost every chapter in this book explores the interaction of OS and hardware. Chapter 11 examines adding and removing programs. Many security features show up in multiple chapters, such as Chapter 13 and Chapter 27. The rest of this chapter focuses on the user interface and the file structures.

User Interfaces

This section tours the various operating system *desktop styles/user interfaces*. Like the hardware tours earlier, this section serves a double purpose. First, you need to know the proper names for the various UI features and understand their functions. Second, it serves as a handy quick review section before you take the CompTIA A+ 1102 exam.

 NOTE Chapter 24 details the operating systems for mobile devices—iOS, iPadOS, and Android.

Windows

Figure 2-17 shows the standard interface for Windows 11, a traditional multipurpose computer. Windows uses a graphical user interface primarily, so you engage with the mouse or other pointing device and click on elements. The background is called the *Desktop*. The open apps are File Explorer—the file browser in Windows 11—and the Microsoft Store for purchasing apps, games, movies, and so on.

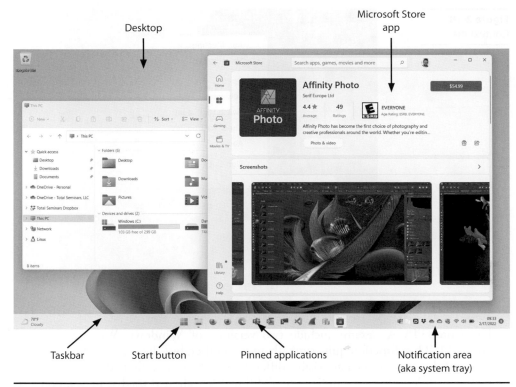

Figure 2-17 Windows 11 with apps open

Other visible items are as follows:

- Click the *Start button* to get access to applications, tools, files, and folders.
- The *pinned applications* enable you to launch a program with a single left-click.
- The *taskbar* shows running programs.
- The *notification area* shows programs running in the background. Many techs also call it the *system tray*.

Interacting with the Windows interface involves using a mouse or touchpad to move the cursor and either left-clicking or right-clicking the icons to achieve different goals. Left-clicking selects an item; double left-clicking opens an item. Right-clicking opens a *context menu* from which you can select various options. Figure 2-18 shows the context menu for the Zoom app (for video conferencing) that's running in the background. (Most people refer to a left-click simply as a *click*. This section makes the left/right distinction clear, so you learn how to access tools properly.)

NOTE The context menu offers options specific to the icon you right-click. Right-clicking a file, for example, gives you a context menu that differs greatly from when you right-click an application.

Figure 2-18
Context menu

The CompTIA A+ exams include two versions of Windows: Windows 10 and Windows 11. They function quite similarly to each other, but the user interface is different. One of the most immediate visible differences is the center-aligned Start menu and pinned apps in Windows 11, unlike the traditional left-aligned taskbar in Windows 10 (see Figure 2-19). Note that these are just the defaults. In Windows 10, you can move the taskbar to any screen edge you want. In Windows 11, you are stuck with the taskbar on the bottom of the screen, but you can left align the Start menu and pinned apps if you prefer the classic Windows look.

The Start menu—the go-to place for launching applications in Windows—differs a lot between Windows 11 and Windows 10. In Windows 11, clicking the Start button or pressing the Windows logo key on the keyboard brings up a menu that has a "Type here to search" box, pinned apps, and recommended files (see Figure 2-20). The last of those are simply the six most recent files you opened so the entries change frequently.

 EXAM TIP   The CompTIA A+ 1102 exam objectives specifically call out Windows 10 features, tools, and Control Panel utilities for the look and feel and location of these various tech tools. This book will make explicit references to Windows 10 where appropriate, so you won't miss questions on the exam.

Figure 2-19 Windows 10 desktop showing left-aligned taskbar and open Start menu

Figure 2-20
Results of
clicking the Start
menu or pressing
the Windows
logo key in
Windows 11

The Start menu has one more trick up its sleeve for us techs. Pressing WINDOWS LOGO KEY + X on the keyboard or right-clicking the Start menu brings up the *Quick Link* menu (see Figure 2-21). This extremely handy menu gives us quick access to most of the utilities and apps we need to keep Windows running smoothly.

Figure 2-21
Accessing the
Quick Link menu
by right-clicking
the Start menu

Fortunately, most of the time we are not fixing Windows, but using it to get work done. One feature Windows has to help us stay productive takes advantage of widescreen monitors with the *side-by-side apps* feature. Select an open application and press WINDOWS LOGO KEY + LEFT ARROW and the application will pin to the left half of the monitor. Any other open applications will appear as smallish icons on the right so you can quickly pin your choice to the right half of the monitor (Figure 2-22). Do the reverse with another application, and it'll pin to the right half of the monitor. With apps like Microsoft Word, where each document opens in a unique window, side-by-side apps make it easy to compare two documents.

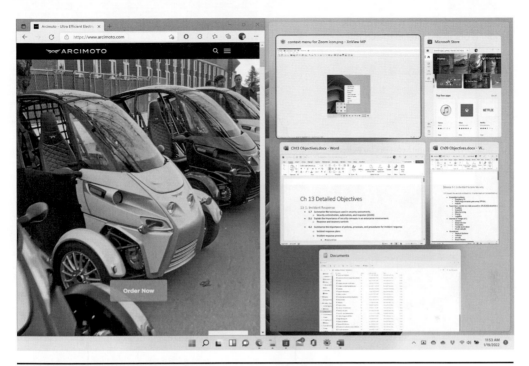

Figure 2-22 Edge browser pinned left; other running apps ready to be pinned right

 NOTE The Microsoft Store enables you to acquire and download Windows apps directly from Microsoft. Microsoft has updated the Microsoft Store many times, tying it together with its Xbox gaming system, for example. The Microsoft Store is the place to get touch-first apps, meaning programs designed specifically with touchscreen interfaces in mind.

macOS

The macOS operating system interface offers similar functions to those found on Windows. The background of the main screen is called the *Desktop*, and running along the bottom of the desktop is the *Dock*, which holds your running and pinned applications (very similar to the Windows taskbar). Along the top of the screen is probably the most distinctive feature of macOS, the *menu bar*. The menu bar is divided into a few sections, with the Apple and app menus taking up the left side, and the status menus (similar to the Windows notification area) taking up the right. Figure 2-23 shows the typical macOS interface.

Menu bar for essential access to tools
(Finder is discussed later in the chapter.)

Open application
windows

Desktop

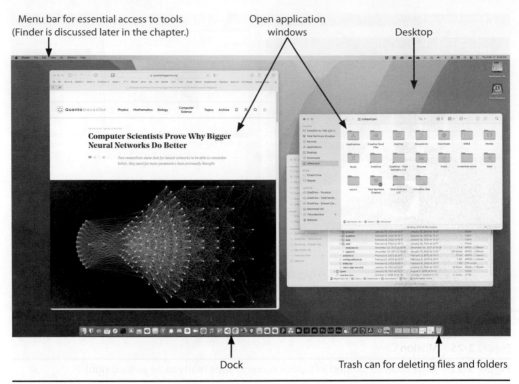

Dock

Trash can for deleting files and folders

Figure 2-23   macOS

Pressing the Mission Control button on an Apple keyboard (see Figure 2-24) brings up a feature, called *Mission Control,* that lets you see all your open apps at a glance and quickly switch between them, as shown in Figure 2-25. You can also access Mission Control by pressing and holding the CONTROL/CTRL key and then pressing the UP ARROW key.

The macOS interface supports *Spaces*—essentially *multiple Desktops*—that can have different backgrounds and apps but keep the same Dock. You can optimize your workflow, for example, by putting your primary program full screen on Desktop 1 and putting your e-mail client on Desktop 2 (see Figure 2-26). New messages won't disturb you when working, but you can access the second Desktop easily when you want with Mission Control. Press and hold the CONTROL key and press the RIGHT ARROW and LEFT ARROW keys to scroll through Spaces.

Figure 2-24
Mission Control
button on
keyboard

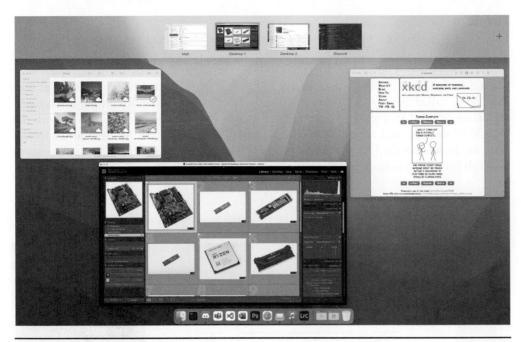

Figure 2-25   Mission Control showing three open apps and four Desktops

Figure 2-26   Switching between multiple Desktops

Linux

Linux is a popular, free, open source operating system that's been around since the mid-1990s. Over the years, there have been hundreds of different versions or *distributions (distros)* of Linux. The reason for all the distro versions depends on what a distro is needed to do. Unlike Windows or macOS, different Linux distros offer a variety of user interfaces, called *desktop environments (DEs)*. They offer similar functions to those in Windows or macOS. Figure 2-27 shows a popular Linux distro, Ubuntu Linux, with the GNOME desktop and notes the various features. Frequently used utilities and applications are locked on the Dock on the left side of the screen. Most distros give you options for Web browsing, e-mail, accessing files and folders, and so on.

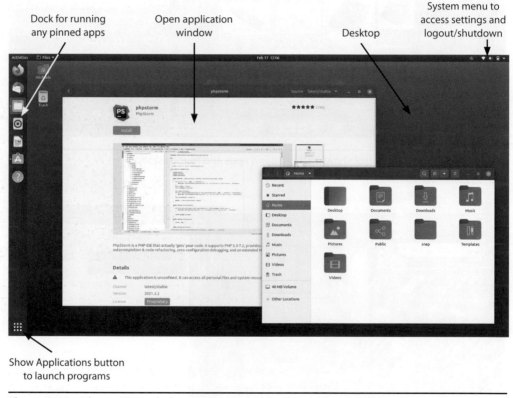

Figure 2-27   Ubuntu Linux desktop environment

Command-Line Interface

Long before there were pretty GUIs with their mice pointers and icons, operating systems used a *command-line interface (CLI)*. Although the CLI is an old concept, every operating system still has at least one, and for good reason: the CLI works when the GUI just can't do the job. The CLI is a tech's best friend, and you must learn to be comfortable working in the CLI. Chapter 15 is devoted to the command line, but let's look at one example of what the command line can do—in this case, using Windows.

On Windows, the default CLI is called PowerShell. To access it, open the Quick Links menu (right-click the Start button) and select Windows Powershell (or Windows Terminal in Windows 11). A new window will open with a prompt patiently waiting for you to conjure some command-line magic (see Figure 2-28).

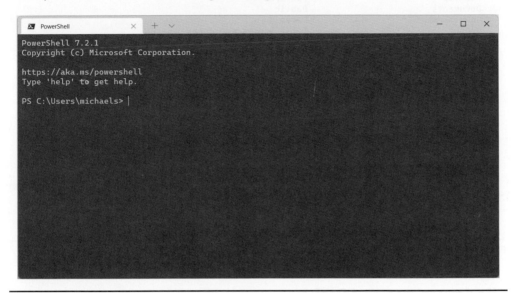

Figure 2-28   A PowerShell prompt in Windows 11

 NOTE   Microsoft provides two PowerShell choices: one that says PowerShell and another that says PowerShell (Admin). PowerShell (Admin) is more powerful but requires you to have administrative rights. For now, choose either.

At the command prompt, type **dir** and press ENTER. The dir *command-line utility* displays all the files and folders in a specific directory—probably your user folder for this exercise—and displays folder and file names as well as other information. (A *directory* is the same thing as a folder.) The dir command is just one of many command-line tools. You'll learn much more about dir in Chapter 15.

macOS has a superb CLI called Terminal. The Terminal CLI looks like the Windows CLI but the commands are different. On a Mac, the dir command doesn't work. You need to type **ls** to see the contents of a folder in Terminal (see Figure 2-29).

Linux is even more dependent on the CLI. You can be a pretty good tech with Windows or a macOS and not know much about the CLI. Not so in Linux. The command line in Linux (also called Terminal) is an essential tool. You can get there in most distros by pressing CTRL-ALT-T. (See Chapter 15 for a lot of details about essential Linux commands.)

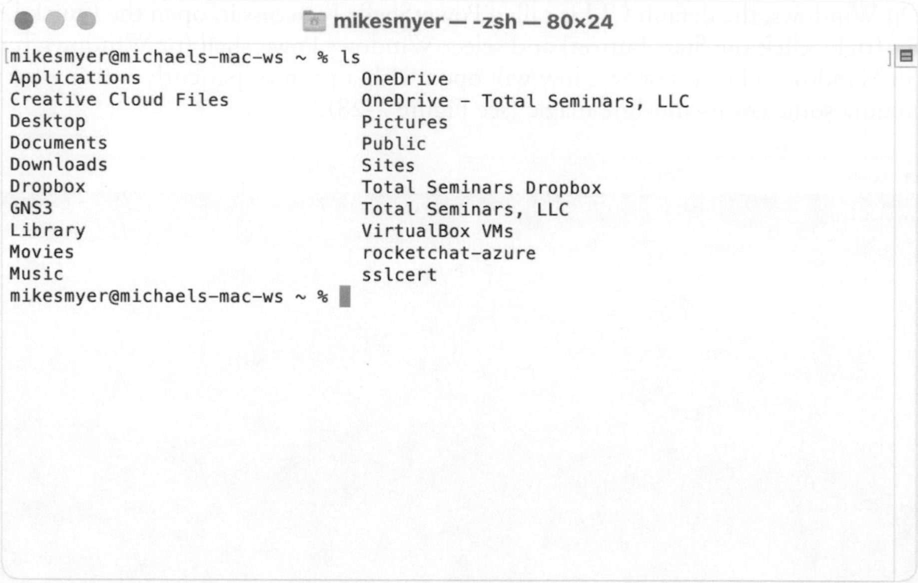

```
● ● ●                          🏠 mikesmyer — -zsh — 80×24
[mikesmyer@michaels-mac-ws ~ % ls
Applications                    OneDrive
Creative Cloud Files            OneDrive - Total Seminars, LLC
Desktop                         Pictures
Documents                       Public
Downloads                       Sites
Dropbox                         Total Seminars Dropbox
GNS3                            Total Seminars, LLC
Library                         VirtualBox VMs
Movies                          rocketchat-azure
Music                           sslcert
mikesmyer@michaels-mac-ws ~ % ▊
```

Figure 2-29   Running the ls command in Terminal

File Structures and Paths

Knowing where to find specific content—files and the folders in which they reside—helps techs help users do their day-to-day tasks more efficiently. Almost every operating system stores files in folders in a tree pattern. The root of the tree is the drive or disk, followed by a folder, subfolder, sub-subfolder, and so on, until you get to the desired file. The drive or disk gets some designation, most usually a *drive letter* nomenclature that looks like "C:". Chapter 9 goes into gory detail on how modern operating systems implement systems for storing data.

Windows

Windows has important folders that help organize programs and documents. They sit in the *root directory*—where the operating system is installed—and vary depending on the version of Windows. The following sections walk through the locations of important folders.

Windows *File Explorer* enables you to browse and select files and folders stored on all the storage locations available to the computer. Figure 2-30 shows File Explorer displaying the contents of the Documents folder in Windows 10. Note the title of the window is *Documents*. The tool, regardless of the title, is File Explorer.

The default file and folder view in Windows has a couple of notable features that you can see in Figure 2-30. Note the "July 15" file? That X icon says Windows recognizes the file as a Microsoft Excel spreadsheet, which means almost certainly the actual filename is July 15.xlsx. The .xlsx is the *file extension*, hidden by default, that tells the OS which application to use with the file. This pairing of application with file extension is called *file association*.

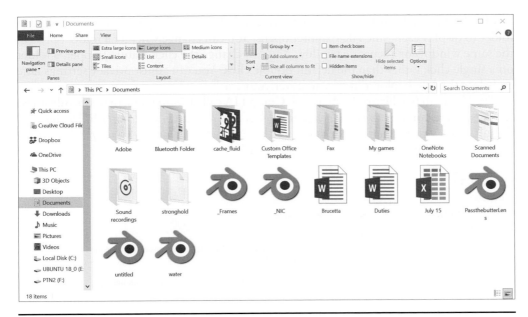

Figure 2-30   File Explorer

Note also that Figure 2-30 has the View tab displayed—that's the ribbon at the top of the window. To change the default view, make changes here. Accessing the *File Explorer Options*—CompTIA's term for Folder Options in File Explorer—enables you to make changes in default behavior with the tool. To get to Folder Options in Windows 11, in the toolbar, click the three horizontal dots next to the View menu option and select Options. In Windows 10, select the View tab and click Options. Both paths open a similar dialog box (see Figure 2-31).

Figure 2-31
Windows 11
Folder Options,
General tab

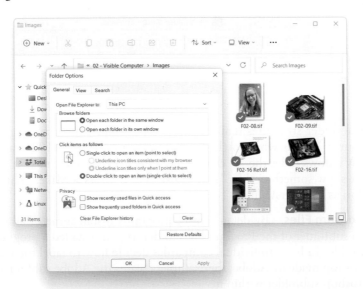

On the General tab (*General options* in CompTIA speak), you can set the default folder to display each time File Explorer opens. You can change whether a folder opens in the same window or a separate window. You can change the click feature to open a folder on a single click rather than the default double click. You can adjust privacy settings here and clear the File Explorer history to cover your tracks.

The View tab (see Figure 2-32), which CompTIA calls *View options*, presents Advanced settings where you can *Show hidden files, folders, and drives*. (File Explorer hides them by default.) You can toggle file extensions on here (deselect *Hide extensions for known file types*.) You have many options here. Experiment!

Figure 2-32
Windows 11
Folder Options,
View tab

The folder structures that follow here use standard formatting for describing folder structures. This is what you'll see on the CompTIA A+ 1102 exam and in almost any OS. Windows hides the "\" characters at the beginning to make it prettier. File Explorer might show something like "Local Disk (C:) > Users > Mike." This translates in proper fashion as C:\Users\Mike.

C:\Program Files By default, most programs install some or all of their essential files into a subfolder of the Program Files folder. If you installed a program, it should have its own folder in here. Individual companies decide how to label their subfolders. Installing Photoshop made by Adobe, for example, creates the Adobe subfolder and then an Adobe Photoshop subfolder within it.

C:\Program Files (x86)   The 64-bit editions of Windows create two directory structures for program files. The 64-bit applications go into the C:\Program Files folder, whereas the 32-bit applications go into the C:\Program Files (x86) folder. The separation makes it easy to find the proper version of whatever application you seek.

Personal Documents   Windows uses subfolders in the C:\Users folder to organize files for each user on a PC. Figure 2-33 shows the default folders for a user named Mike. Let's quickly survey the ones you most likely need to know for the CompTIA A+ exams:

- **C:\Users\Mike\Desktop**   This folder stores the files on the user's Desktop. If you delete this folder, you delete all the files placed on the Desktop.
- **C:\Users\Mike\Documents**   This is the Documents or My Documents folder for that user. (Only Windows 7 uses My Documents. The others use Documents.)
- **C:\Users\Mike\Downloads**   Microsoft's preferred download folder for applications to use. Most applications use this folder, but some do not.
- **C:\Users\Mike\Music**   This is the default location for music you download. My guess is that more people have music in iTunes, but that's just me.
- **C:\Users\Mike\Pictures**   Pictures is the default location for images imported into the PC, although the Pictures library can (and does) draw from many folder locations.
- **C:\Users\Mike\Videos**   Videos is the default location for movies and homebrewed videos imported into a PC.

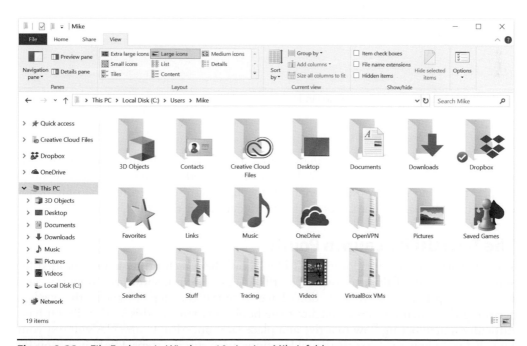

Figure 2-33   File Explorer in Windows 10 viewing Mike's folders

macOS

Finder holds the keys to files and folders in macOS. Figure 2-34 shows Finder open to display Mike's Users folder. Note that, although its style differs from the Windows screen shown in Figure 2-33, it has functionally similar folders. These are the default locations for files on the Desktop, in Documents, Downloads, Music, Pictures, and so on. Each user account on the Mac will have a unique Users folder that is inaccessible by other users on that computer.

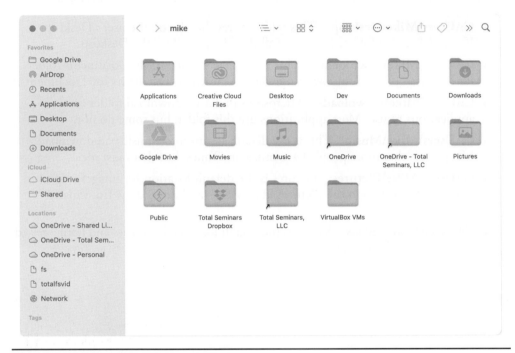

Figure 2-34   Mike's Users directory in Finder

Linux

Ready to be shocked? Not surprisingly, Linux uses pretty much the same structure for user organization (see Figure 2-35). I guess once something seems logical to enough people, there's no reason to add confusion by changing the structure. The only major difference is the name: Linux uses the Home folder, rather than the Users folder.

The Tech Utility Launch Points

Every OS has two or three locations (I like to call them tech utility launch points) for some, most, or all of their tech-specific utilities. This section shows you how to access those areas, primarily so that we don't have to repeat the steps to get to them when accessing them many times throughout the book. Just refer to this section if you have difficulty remembering how to arrive at a place later on. Also, CompTIA will test your knowledge on how to access these tool locations, with specific steps. Use this section for the last-minute cram before taking the exams.

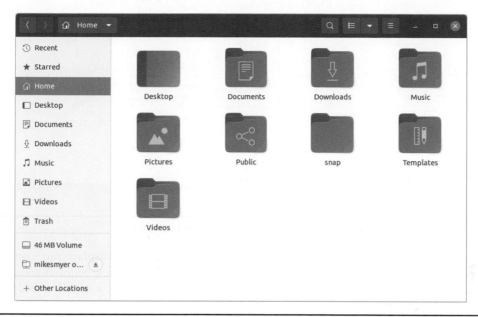

Figure 2-35 Mike's Home directory in File Manager

Windows

Microsoft has refined and changed Windows with every version. For example, Windows 10 and Windows 11 modifications included aspects to tech tools such as their *location* and *level of importance*. These changes often trigger strong opinions among techs of all ages on such details. Despite these opinions, Microsoft does a fine job innovating and advancing their technology and will continue to do so. Techs will simply need to keep up with new updates and tools so they keep their knowledge and skills current with each new version.

Windows offers many tech tool areas, including Settings, Control Panel, and Administrative Tools. A lot of tools appear to be standalone tools, but they're specialized manifestations of a toolset called the Microsoft Management Console. Let's look at all these now.

NOTE Most of these tools may be accessed in both Windows 10 or 11 via the Quick Link menu by right-clicking the Start button.

Settings Settings provides a central location and a consistent interface for most of the important tech tools in Windows (see Figure 2-36). Introduced way back with Windows 8, Settings is slowly taking over many utilities from the venerable Control Panel.

Control Panel The *Control Panel*, an ancient but still used launch point, handles many of the maintenance, upgrade, and configuration aspects of Windows.

Figure 2-36   Settings app in Windows 10 (left) and Windows 11 (right)

The Control Panel opens in Category view by default, which displays the icons in groups like Hardware and Sound, as shown in Figure 2-37. This view requires an additional click (and sometimes a guess about which category includes what you need), so many techs use Classic view.

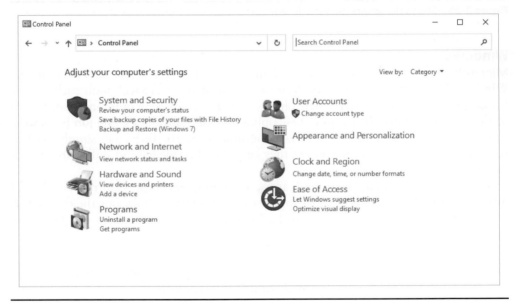

Figure 2-37   Windows 10 Control Panel Category view

Administrative Tools (renamed *Windows Tools* in Windows 11) is one example of the many powerful utilities found in the Control Panel. The Administrative Tools utility enables you to set up hard drives, manage devices, test system performance, and much more (see Figure 2-38).

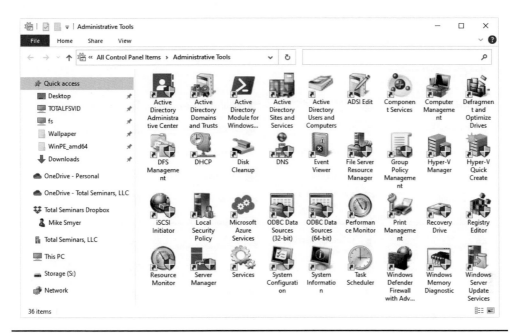

Figure 2-38   Administrative Tools open showing many utilities

NOTE   *Device Manager* enables you to examine the state of all the hardware and drivers in a Windows computer. As you might suspect from that description, techs spend a lot of time with this tool. You'll see Device Manager referenced many more times both in this book and during your career as a PC tech.

The CompTIA A+ 1102 exam specifically assumes Classic view with large icons, so you should do what every tech does: switch from Category view to Classic view. In Control Panel, select either Large icons or Small icons from the View by drop-down list for a similar effect. Figure 2-39 shows the Windows 11 Control Panel in Large icons view.

Many programs, called *applets*, populate the Control Panel. The names and selection of applets vary depending on the version of Windows and whether any installed programs have added applets. But all versions of Windows have applets that enable you to control specific aspects of Windows, such as the appearance, installed applications, and system settings. You will get details on each applet as we put them into use over the course of this book.

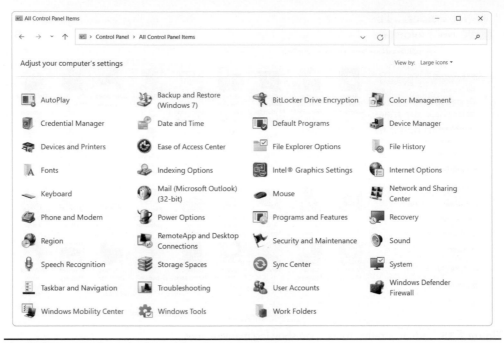

Figure 2-39 Windows 11 Control Panel Large icons view

macOS

macOS has two key launch points for techs: the System Preferences app and the Utilities folder. You can access both quickly.

System Preferences

To access *System Preferences,* click the Apple icon (top-left corner of screen) and select System Preferences from the Apple menu to open the app (see Figure 2-40). From System Preferences you have access to almost all settings you will need to administer a macOS system.

Figure 2-40
Accessing System
Preferences

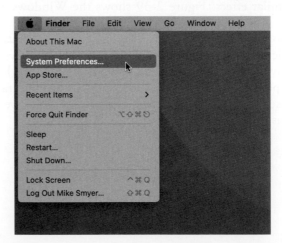

Utilities Folder   The second launch point is the *Utilities* folder, located neatly in the Applications folder. Because of its importance, Apple provides a quick shortcut to access it. With the Finder in focus, click Go on the menu bar and select Utilities (see Figure 2-41). Alternatively, use the hot-key combination: COMMAND-SHIFT-U. The Utilities folder gives you access to the tools you need to perform services on a Mac beyond what's included in System Preferences, including Activity Monitor and Terminal. The latter is the command-line interface for macOS that we already touched on, a very powerful tool for techs that we explore in detail in Chapter 15.

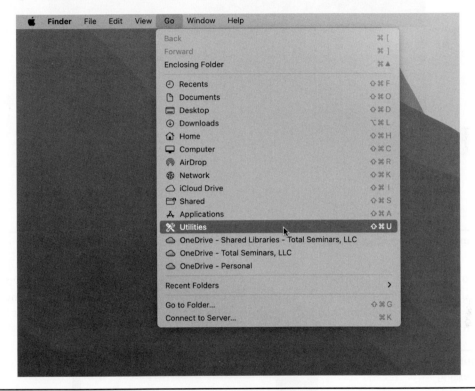

Figure 2-41   Accessing the Utilities folder

Linux

Linux lacks the handy, one-stop launch points available in Windows and macOS. Instead, the various desktop environments have their own launch points. Here are the locations of the launch points for common desktop environments KDE Plasma Desktop and Gnome 3.

KDE Plasma Desktop   The most common launch point in KDE Plasma Desktop is the System *Settings app*. To access System Settings, open the Application Launcher by clicking the button in the lower left of the screen. From the launcher, either search for **System Settings** or click Applications then the Settings category. From here, open the System Setting application (see Figure 2-42).

Figure 2-42   Accessing KDE's System Settings

Gnome 3   The main utility launch point in Gnome 3 is the System menu, shown in Figure 2-43, which you access by clicking the downward-pointing triangle on the menu bar. From here, you can access the Settings app and log out or shut down/restart the computer.

Figure 2-43
Accessing
Gnome 3's
System menu

Smartphone OSs

Your smartphone's OS also has utility launch points, just not as many as a traditional desktop like Windows or macOS. For instance, Figure 2-44 shows the iOS Settings app—the first place to go to configure anything on your iOS phone. Android phones also use a launch point called Settings.

Figure 2-44
Apple iOS
Settings app

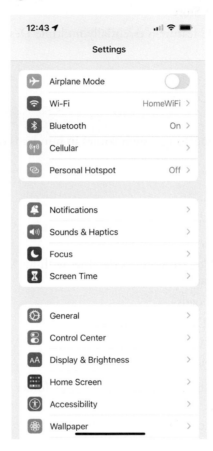

Chapter Review

Questions

1. What is the oldest version of Windows covered on the CompTIA A+ 220-1102 exam?

    A. Windows Server 2016

    B. Windows 8 Enterprise

    C. Windows 10

    D. Windows 11

2. Which of the following is the utility used to download apps in Windows?

   A. Play Store

   B. Apple Spaces

   C. Microsoft Store

   D. Windows Store

3. What macOS feature is essentially multiple Desktops?

   A. Charms

   B. Desktop

   C. Mission Control

   D. Spaces

4. The Linux operating system comes in hundreds of different versions, known as _____.

   A. Desktops

   B. Distros

   C. Dispersions

   D. Domiciles

5. The user, Mike, has downloaded files with his Web browser. Where will they be stored by default?

   A. C:\Downloads

   B. C:\Mike\Desktop\Downloads

   C. C:\Users\Mike\Downloads

   D. C:\Users\Mike\Desktop\Downloads

6. 32-bit programs are installed into which folder by default in a 64-bit edition of Windows?

   A. C:\Program Files

   B. C:\Program Files (x32)

   C. C:\Program Files\Wins\Old

   D. C:\Program Files (x86)

7. Which macOS feature is functionally equivalent to Windows File Explorer?

   A. Finder

   B. Dock

   C. Quartz

   D. File Manager

8. Which of the following Windows utilities is slowly replacing the ancient Windows Control Panel?

   A. Device Manager

   B. Settings

   C. Administrative Tools

   D. Terminal

9. What feature of macOS is the equivalent of the command-line interface in Windows?

   A. Dock

   B. Spaces

   C. Terminal

   D. Unity

10. Both Apple and Android smartphones have a utility called _____.

    A. Settings

    B. Control

    C. Command Center

    D. Control Center

Answers

1. **C.** Windows 10 is the oldest version of Windows covered on the CompTIA A+ 220-1102 exam.

2. **C.** Microsoft Store is used to download apps in Windows.

3. **D.** *Spaces* is the term Apple uses for multiple Desktops in macOS.

4. **B.** Different versions of Linux are known as distros, short for distributions.

5. **C.** The default download location in Windows is C:\Users\<user name>\Downloads.

6. **D.** By default, 32-bit applications install into the C:\Program Files (x86) folder.

7. **A.** Finder is the equivalent of File Explorer.

8. **B.** Settings is slowly taking over many utilities from the Control Panel.

9. **C.** Terminal is the equivalent of the Windows command-line interface.

10. **A.** Both Apple and Android smartphones have a utility called Settings.

8. Which utility or identification, Windows utility is slowly replacing the ancient Windows Control Panel?

A. Device Manager

B. Settings

C. Administrative Tools

D. regedit

9. What feature of macOS is the equivalent of the command-line interface in Windows?

A. Dock

B. Spaces

C. Terminal

D. Chute

10. Both Apple and Android smartphones have a utility called _____.

A. Settings

B. Control

C. Command Center

D. Control Center

Answers

1. C. Windows 10 is the oldest version of Windows covered on the CompTIA A+ 220-1102 exam.

2. C. Microsoft Store is used to download apps in Windows.

3. D. Spaces is the term Apple uses for its multiple Desktops feature.

4. B. Different versions of Linux are known as distros, short for distributions.

5. C. The default download location if Windows is C:\Users\ Dept user named O owloads.

6. D. By default, 32-bit applications install into the c:\Program Files (x86) folder.

7. A. Finder is the equivalent of File Explorer.

8. B. Settings is slowly taking over many utilities from the Control Panel.

9. C. Terminal is the equivalent of the Windows Command-line interface.

10. A. Both Apple and Android smartphones have a utility called Settings.

CPUs

3

In this chapter, you will learn how to
- Identify the core components of a CPU
- Describe the relationship of CPUs with memory
- Explain the varieties of modern CPUs
- Select and install a CPU
- Troubleshoot CPUs

The *central processing unit (CPU)*, also called the *microprocessor*, is a single silicon-based electronic chip that makes your computer...well, a computer. Desktop computers, laptops, smartphones, even tiny computers in a smartwatch or a washing machine have a CPU. A CPU invariably hides on the motherboard below a heat sink and often a fan assembly as well. CPU makers name their microprocessors in a fashion similar to the automobile industry: CPUs get a make and a model, such as Intel Core i9, Qualcomm Snapdragon 8 Gen 1, or AMD Ryzen 7. But what's happening inside the CPU to make it able to do the amazing things asked of it every time you step up to the keyboard?

This chapter delves into microprocessors in detail. We'll first discuss how processors work and the components that enable them to interact with the rest of the computer. The second section describes how CPUs work with memory. The third section takes you on a tour of modern CPUs. The fourth section gets into practical work, selecting and installing CPUs. The final section covers troubleshooting CPUs in detail.

 EXAM TIP CompTIA only uses the term *CPU*, not *microprocessor*. Expect to see CPU on the 1101 exam.

Historical/Conceptual

CPU Core Components

Although the computer might seem to act quite intelligently, comparing the CPU to a human brain hugely overstates its capabilities. A CPU functions more like a very powerful calculator than like a brain—but, oh, what a calculator! Today's CPUs add, subtract, multiply, divide, and move billions of numbers per second. Processing that much information so quickly makes any CPU look intelligent. It's simply the speed of the CPU, rather than actual intelligence, that enables computers to perform feats such as accessing the Internet, playing visually stunning games, or editing photos.

A good technician needs to understand some basic CPU functions to support computing devices, so let's start with an analysis of how the CPU works. If you wanted to teach someone how an automobile engine works, you would use a relatively simple example engine, right? The same principle applies here. Let's begin our study of the CPU with the granddaddy of all PC CPUs: the Intel 8088, invented in the late 1970s. This CPU defined the idea of the modern microprocessor and contains the same basic parts used in the most advanced CPUs today.

The Man in the Box

Begin by visualizing the CPU as a man in a box (see Figure 3-1). This is one clever guy. He can perform virtually any mathematical function, manipulate data, and give answers *very quickly*.

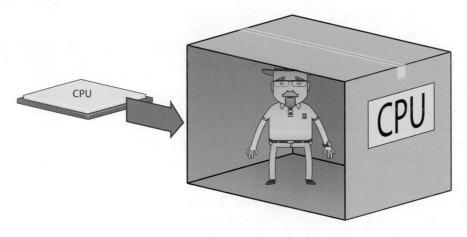

Figure 3-1   Imagine the CPU as a man in a box.

This guy is potentially very useful to us, but there's a catch—he lives in a tiny, closed box. Before he can work with us, we must come up with a way to exchange information with him (see Figure 3-2).

Imagine that we install a set of 16 light bulbs, 8 inside his box and 8 outside his box. Each of the 8 light bulbs inside the box connects to one of the 8 bulbs outside the box to form a pair. Each pair of light bulbs is always either on or off. You can control the 8 pairs of bulbs by using a set of 8 switches outside the box, and the Man in the Box can also control them by using an identical set of 8 switches inside the box. This light-bulb communication device is called the external data bus (EDB).

Figure 3-2   How do we talk with the Man in the Box?

Figure 3-3 shows a cutaway view of the external data bus. When either you or the Man in the Box flips a switch on, *both* light bulbs go on, and the switch on the other side is also flipped to the on position. If you or the Man in the Box turns a switch off, the light bulbs on both sides are turned off, along with the other switch for that pair.

Figure 3-3   Cutaway of the external data bus—note that one light bulb pair is on.

Can you see how this works? By creating on/off patterns with the light bulbs that represent different pieces of data or commands, you can send that information to the Man in the Box, and he can send information back in the same way—*assuming that you agree ahead of time on what the different patterns of lights mean.* To accomplish this, you need some sort of codebook that assigns meanings to the many patterns of lights that the EDB might display. Keep this thought in mind while we push the analogy a bit more.

Before going any further, make sure you're clear on the fact that this is an analogy, not reality. There really is an EDB, but you won't see any light bulbs or switches on the CPU. You can, however, see little wires sticking out of many CPUs (see Figure 3-4). If you apply voltage to one of these wires, you in essence flip the switch. Get the idea? So, if that wire had voltage and if a tiny light bulb were attached to the wire, that light bulb would glow, would it not? By the same token, if the wire had no power, the light bulb would not glow. That is why the switch-and-light-bulb analogy may help you picture these little wires constantly flashing on and off.

Figure 3-4
Close-up of
the underside
of a CPU

Now that the EDB enables you to communicate with the Man in the Box, you need to see how it works by placing voltages on the wires. This brings up a naming problem. It's a hassle to say something like "on-off-on-off-on-on-off-off" when talking about which wires have voltage. Rather than saying that one of the EDB wires is on or off, use the number 1 to represent on and the number 0 to represent off (see Figure 3-5). That way, instead of describing the state of the lights as "on-off-on-off-on-on-off-off," I can instead describe them by writing "10101100."

In computers, wires repeatedly turn on and off. As a result, we can use this "1 and 0," or binary, system to describe the state of these wires at any given moment. (See, and you just thought computer geeks spoke in binary to confuse normal people. Ha!) There's much more to binary numbering in computing, but this is a great place to start.

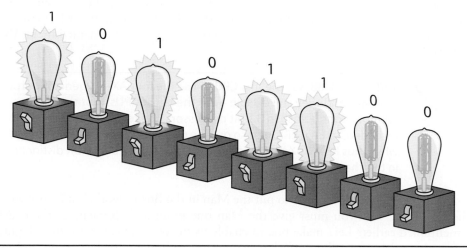

Figure 3-5   Here "1" means on, "0" means off.

Registers

The Man in the Box provides good insight into the workspace inside a CPU. The EDB gives you a way to communicate with the Man in the Box so you can give him work to do. But to do this work, he needs a worktable; in fact, he needs at least four worktables. Each of these four worktables has 16 light bulbs. These light bulbs are not in pairs; they're just 16 light bulbs lined up straight across the table. Each light bulb is controlled by a single switch, operated only by the Man in the Box. By creating on/off patterns like the ones on the EDB, the Man in the Box can use these four sets of light bulbs to work math problems. In a real computer, these worktables are called registers (see Figure 3-6) and store internal commands and data.

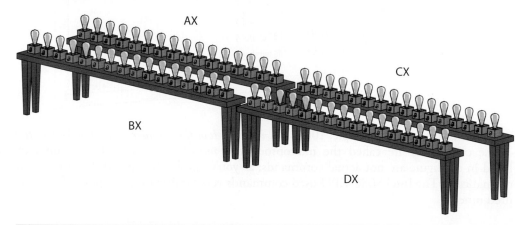

Figure 3-6   The four general-purpose registers

Registers provide the Man in the Box with a workplace for the problems you give him. All CPUs contain a large number of registers, but for the moment let's concentrate on the four most common ones: the *general-purpose registers*. Intel named them AX, BX, CX, and DX.

NOTE The 8088 was the first CPU to use the four AX–DX general-purpose registers, and they still exist in even the latest CPUs. (But they have a lot more light bulbs!) In 32-bit processors, the registers added an E for extended, so EAX, EBX, and so on. The 64-bit registers get an R (I don't know why), thus RAX, RBX, and so on. We'll get to the 32-bit/64-bit distinction later in the chapter.

Great! We're just about ready to put the Man in the Box to work, but before you close the lid on the box, you must give the Man one more tool. Remember the codebook I mentioned earlier? Let's make one to enable us to communicate with him. Figure 3-7 shows the codebook we'll use. We'll give one copy to him and make a second for us.

Figure 3-7
CPU codebook

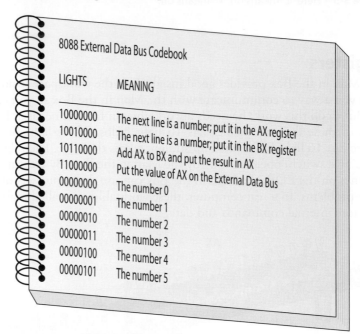

In this codebook, for example, 10000111 means *Move the number 7 into the AX register*. These commands are called the microprocessor's *machine language*. The commands listed in the figure are not actual commands; as you've probably guessed, I've simplified dramatically. The Intel 8088 CPU used commands very similar to these, plus a few hundred others.

Here are some examples of machine language for the Intel 8088:

10111010	The next line of code is a number. Put that number into the DX register.
01000001	Add 1 to the number already in the CX register.
00111100	Compare the value in the AX register with the next line of code.

By placing machine language commands—called *lines of code*—onto the EDB one at a time, you can instruct the Man in the Box to do specific tasks. All of the machine language commands that the CPU understands make up the CPU's *instruction set.*

So here is the CPU so far: the Man in the Box can communicate with the outside world via the EDB; he has four registers he can use to work on the problems you give him; and he has a codebook—the instruction set—so he can understand the different patterns (machine language commands) on the EDB (see Figure 3-8).

Figure 3-8 The CPU so far

Clock

Okay, so you're ready to put the Man in the Box to work. You can send the first command by lighting up wires on the EDB. How does he know when you've finished setting up the wires and it's time to act?

Imagine there's a bell inside the box activated by a button on the outside of the box. Each time you press the button to sound the bell, the Man in the Box reads the next set of lights on the EDB. Of course, a real computer doesn't use a bell. The bell on a real CPU is a special wire called the *clock wire* (most diagrams label the clock wire CLK).

A charge on the CLK wire tells the CPU that another piece of information is waiting to be processed (see Figure 3-9).

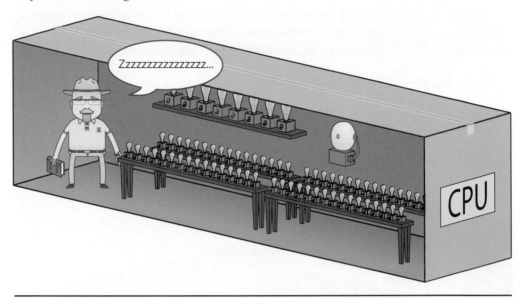

Figure 3-9   The CPU does nothing until activated by the clock.

For the CPU to process a command placed on the EDB, a certain minimum voltage must be applied to the CLK wire. A single charge to the CLK wire is called a *clock cycle*. The CPU requires at least two clock cycles to act on a command, and usually more. A CPU may require hundreds of clock cycles to process some commands (see Figure 3-10).

Figure 3-10   The CPU often needs more than one clock cycle to get a result.

The maximum number of clock cycles that a CPU can handle in a given period of time is referred to as its *clock speed*. The clock speed is the fastest speed at which a CPU can operate, determined by the CPU manufacturer. The Intel 8088 processor had a clock speed of 4.77 MHz (4.77 million cycles per second), extremely slow by modern standards, but still a pretty big number compared to using a pencil and paper. High-end CPUs today run at speeds in excess of 5 GHz (5 billion cycles per second). You'll see these "hertz" terms a lot in this chapter, so here's what they mean:

1 hertz (1 Hz) = 1 cycle per second

1 megahertz (1 MHz) = 1 million cycles per second

1 gigahertz (1 GHz) = 1 billion cycles per second

A CPU's clock speed is its *maximum* speed, not the speed at which it *must* run. A CPU can run at any speed, as long as that speed does not exceed its clock speed. Many CPU models have the clock speed printed clearly (see Figure 3-11). Other models might have a cryptic code.

Figure 3-11
Clock speed
printed on CPU
(3.30 GHz)

The *system crystal* determines the speed at which a CPU and the rest of the PC operate. The system crystal is usually a quartz oscillator, very similar to the one in a wristwatch, soldered to the motherboard (see Figure 3-12).

The quartz oscillator sends out an electric pulse at a certain speed, many millions of times per second. This signal goes first to a clock chip that adjusts the pulse, usually increasing the pulse sent by the crystal by some large multiple. (The folks who make motherboards could connect the crystal directly to the CPU's clock wire, but then if you wanted to replace your CPU with a CPU with a different clock speed, you'd need to replace the crystal too.) As long as the computer is turned on, the quartz oscillator, through the clock chip, fires a charge on the CLK wire, in essence pushing the system along.

Figure 3-12
One of many
types of system
crystals

Visualize the system crystal as a metronome for the CPU. The quartz oscillator repeatedly fires a charge on the CLK wire, setting the beat, if you will, for the CPU's activities. If the system crystal sets a beat slower than the CPU's clock speed, the CPU will work just fine, though at the slower speed of the system crystal. If the system crystal forces the CPU to run faster than its clock speed, it can overheat and stop working. Before you install a CPU into a system, you must make sure that the crystal and clock chip send out the correct clock pulse for that particular CPU. In the old days, this required very careful adjustments. With today's systems, the motherboard talks to the CPU. The CPU tells the motherboard the clock speed it needs, and the clock chip automatically adjusts for the CPU, making this process now invisible.

 NOTE Aggressive users sometimes intentionally overclock CPUs by telling the clock chip to multiply the pulse faster than the CPU's designed speed. They do this to make slower (cheaper) CPUs run faster and to get more performance in demanding programs. See the "Overclocking" section later in this chapter.

Back to the External Data Bus

One more reality check. We've been talking about tables with racks of light bulbs, but of course real CPU registers don't use light bulbs to represent on/1 and off/0. Registers are tiny storage areas on the CPU made up of microscopic semiconductor circuits that hold charges. It's just easier to imagine a light bulb lit up to represent a circuit holding a charge; when the light bulb is off, there is no charge.

Figure 3-13 is a diagram of an 8088 CPU, showing the wires that comprise the external data bus and the single clock wire. Because the registers are inside the CPU, you can't see them in this figure.

Figure 3-13
Diagram of
an Intel 8088
showing the
external data bus
and clock wires

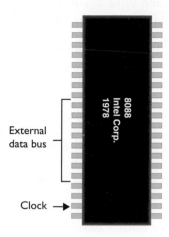

External
data bus

8088
Intel Corp.
1978

Clock

Now that you have learned what components are involved in the process, try the following simple exercise to see how the process works. In this example, you tell the CPU to add 2 + 3. To do this, you must send a series of commands to the CPU; the CPU will act on each command, eventually giving you an answer. Refer to the codebook in Figure 3-7 to translate the instructions you're giving the Man in the Box into binary commands.

Did you try it? Here's how it works:

1. Place 10000000 on the external data bus (EDB).

2. Place 00000010 on the EDB.

3. Place 10010000 on the EDB.

4. Place 00000011 on the EDB.

5. Place 10110000 on the EDB.

6. Place 11000000 on the EDB.

When you finish step 6, the value on the EDB will be 00000101, the decimal number 5 written in binary.

Congrats! You just added 2 + 3 by using individual commands from the codebook. This set of commands is known as a program, which is a series of commands sent to a CPU in a specific order for the CPU to perform work. Each discrete setting of the EDB is a line of code. This program, therefore, has six lines of code.

Memory

Now that you've seen how the CPU executes program code, let's work backward in the process for a moment and think about how the program code gets to the external data bus. The program itself is stored on the hard drive. In theory, you could build a computer that sends data from the hard drive directly to the CPU, but there's a problem—the hard drive is too slow. Even the ancient 8088, with its clock speed of 4.77 MHz, could conceivably process several million lines of code every second. Modern CPUs crank out billions of lines every second. Hard drives simply can't give the data to the CPU at a fast enough speed.

Computers need some other device that takes copies of programs from the hard drive and then sends them, one line at a time, to the CPU quickly enough to keep up with its demands. Because each line of code is nothing more than a pattern of eight ones and zeros, any device that can store ones and zeros eight-across will do. Devices that in any way hold ones and zeros that the CPU accesses are known generically as *memory*.

Many types of devices store ones and zeros perfectly well—technically even a piece of paper counts as memory—but computers need memory that does more than just store groups of eight ones and zeros. Consider this pretend program:

1. Put 2 in the AX register.
2. Put 5 in the BX register.
3. If AX is greater than BX, run line 4; otherwise, go to line 6.
4. Add 1 to the value in AX.
5. Go back to line 1.
6. Put the value of AX on the EDB.

This program has an IF statement, also called a *branch* by CPU makers. The CPU needs a way to address each line of this memory—a way for the CPU to say to the memory, "Give me the next line of code" or "Give me line 6." Addressing memory takes care of another problem: the memory must store not only programs but also the result of the programs. If the CPU adds 2 + 3 and gets 5, the memory needs to store that 5 in such a way that other programs may later read that 5, or possibly even store that 5 on a hard drive. By addressing each line of memory, other programs will know where to find the data.

Memory and RAM

Memory must store not only programs, but also data. The CPU needs to be able to read and write to this storage medium. Additionally, this system must enable the CPU to jump to *any* line of stored code as easily as to any other line of code. All of this must be done at or at least near the clock speed of the CPU. Fortunately, this magical device has existed for many years: *random-access memory (RAM)*. Chapter 4 develops the concept in detail, so for now let's look at RAM as an electronic spreadsheet, like one you can generate in Microsoft Excel (see Figure 3-14). Each cell in this spreadsheet can store only a one

Figure 3-14
RAM as a
spreadsheet

1	0	0	0	0	0	1	1
0	1	0	0	0	0	0	0
0	0	0	0	1	1	0	1
0	1	0	1	0	0	0	0
0	0	0	0	0	0	0	1
0	1	0	1	1	0	1	0
0	0	1	1	1	1	0	0
0	0	0	0	1	0	0	1
1	1	1	0	0	0	0	0
0	0	1	0	1	1	1	0
1	0	0	0	0	0	0	0
1	0	1	0	1	0	1	0

or a zero. Each cell is called a bit. Each row in the spreadsheet is 8 bits across to match the EDB of the 8088. Each row of 8 bits is called a *byte*. In PCs, RAM transfers and stores data to and from the CPU in byte-sized chunks. RAM is therefore arranged in byte-sized rows. Here are the terms used to talk about quantities of bits:

- Any individual 1 or 0 = a bit
- 4 bits = a nibble
- 8 bits = a byte
- 16 bits = a word
- 32 bits = a double word
- 64 bits = a paragraph or quad word

The number of bytes of RAM varies from PC to PC. In earlier PCs, from around 1980 to 1990, the typical system would have only a few hundred thousand bytes of RAM. Today's systems often have billions of bytes of RAM.

Let's stop here for a quick reality check. Electronically, RAM looks like a spreadsheet, but real RAM is made of groups of semiconductor chips soldered onto small cards that snap into your computer (see Figure 3-15). In Chapter 4, you'll see how these groups of chips actually make themselves look like a spreadsheet. For now, don't worry about real RAM and just stick with the spreadsheet idea.

Figure 3-15
Typical RAM

The CPU accesses any one row of RAM as easily and as fast as any other row, which explains the "random access" part of RAM. Not only is RAM randomly accessible, it's also fast. By storing programs on RAM, the CPU can access and run them very quickly. RAM also stores any data that the CPU actively uses.

Computers use *dynamic RAM (DRAM)* for the main system memory. DRAM needs both a constant electrical charge and a periodic refresh of the circuits; otherwise, it loses data—that's what makes it dynamic rather than static in content. The refresh can cause some delays, because the CPU has to wait for the refresh to happen, but modern CPU manufacturers have clever ways to get by this issue, as you'll see when you read about modern processor technology later in this chapter.

Don't confuse RAM with mass storage devices such as hard drives and flash drives. You use hard drives and flash drives to store programs and data permanently. Chapters 8 through 10 discuss permanent storage in intimate detail.

Address Bus

So far, the entire PC consists of only a CPU and RAM. But the CPU and the RAM need some connection so they can talk to each other. To do so, extend the external data bus from the CPU so it can talk to the RAM (see Figure 3-16).

Figure 3-16
Extending the
EDB

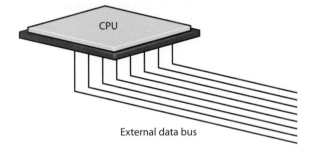

Wait a minute. This is not a matter of just plugging the RAM into the EDB wires! RAM is a spreadsheet with thousands and thousands of discrete rows, and you need to look at the contents of only one row of the spreadsheet at a time, right? So how do you connect the RAM to the EDB in such a way that the CPU can see any one given row but still give the CPU the capability to look at *any* row in RAM?

We need some type of chip between the RAM and the CPU to make the connection. The CPU needs to be able to say which row of RAM it wants, and the chip should handle the mechanics of retrieving that row of data from the RAM and putting it on the EDB. This chip comes with many names, but for right now just call it the *memory controller chip (MCC)*.

The MCC contains special circuitry so it can grab the contents of any line of RAM and place that data or command on the EDB. This in turn enables the CPU to act on that code (see Figure 3-17).

Once the MCC is in place to grab any discrete byte of RAM, the CPU needs to be able to tell the MCC which line of code it needs. The CPU therefore gains a second set

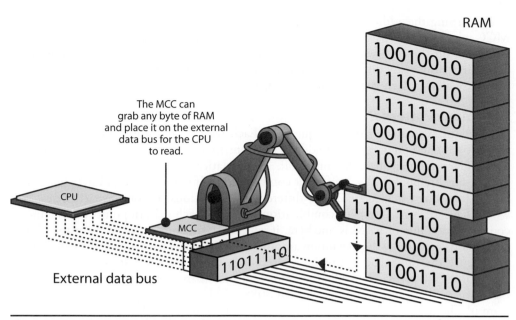

Figure 3-17 The MCC grabs a byte of RAM.

of wires, called the *address bus*, with which it can communicate with the MCC. Different CPUs have different numbers of wires (which, you will soon see, is very significant). The 8088 had 20 wires in its address bus (see Figure 3-18).

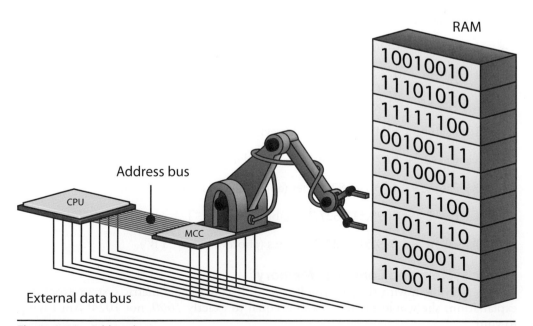

Figure 3-18 Address bus

By turning the address bus wires on and off in different patterns, the CPU tells the MCC which line of RAM it wants at any given moment. Every different pattern of ones and zeros on these 20 wires points to one byte of RAM. There are two big questions here. First, how many different patterns of on-and-off wires can exist with 20 wires? And second, which pattern goes to which row of RAM?

How Many Patterns?

Mathematics can answer the first question. Each wire in the address bus exists in only one of two states: on or off. If the address bus consisted of only one wire, that wire would at any given moment be either on or off. Mathematically, that gives you (pull out your old pre-algebra books) $2^1 = 2$ different combinations. If you have two address bus wires, the address bus wires create $2^2 = 4$ different combinations. If you have 20 wires, you would have 2^{20} (or 1,048,576) combinations. Because each pattern points to one line of code and each line of RAM is one byte, if you know the number of wires in the CPU's address bus, you know the maximum amount of RAM that a particular CPU can handle.

Because the 8088 had a 20-wire address bus, the most RAM it could handle was $2^{20} = 1,048,576$ bytes. The 8088, therefore, had an *address space* of 1,048,576 bytes. This is not to say that every computer with an 8088 CPU had 1,048,576 bytes of RAM. Far from it! The original IBM PC only had a measly 65,536 bytes—but that was considered plenty back in the Dark Ages of Computing in the early 1980s.

Okay, so you know that the 8088 had 20 address wires and a total address space of 1,048,576 bytes. Although this is accurate, no one uses such an exact term to discuss the address space of the 8088. Instead, you say that the 8088 had one *megabyte* (1 MB) of address space.

What's a "mega"? Well, let's get some terminology down. Dealing with computers means constantly dealing with the number of patterns a set of wires can handle. Certain powers of 2 have names used a lot in computing. The following list explains.

1 kilo = 2^{10} = 1024 (abbreviated as "K")

1 kilobyte = 1024 bytes (abbreviated as "KB")

1 mega = 2^{20} = 1,048,576 (abbreviated as "M")

1 megabyte = 1,048,576 bytes (abbreviated as "MB")

1 giga = 2^{30} = 1,073,741,824 (abbreviated as "G")

1 gigabyte = 1,073,741,824 bytes (abbreviated as "GB")

1 tera = 2^{40} = 1,099,511,627,776 (abbreviated as "T")

1 terabyte = 1,099,511,627,776 bytes (abbreviated as "TB")

Metric System and Computer Memory

There's a problem with that list you just read. If you asked a metric system expert for explanation, she would say that a *kilo* is equal to exactly *1000*, not 1024! Am I lying to you?

Well, yes, I am, but not out of malice. I'm just the messenger of yet another weird aspect to computing. Here's what happened, a long time ago.

In the early days of computing there arose a need to talk about large values, but the words hadn't been invented. In one case, the memory address folks were trying to describe permutations. They used values based on powers of 2 as just described. No one had ever invented terms for 1024 or 1,048,576, so they used kilo and mega, as 1000 was close enough to 1024 and 1,000,000 was close enough to 1,048,576.

In the meantime, computer people measuring quantities such as CPU speeds and hard drive capacities didn't count with powers of 2. They just needed regular 1000 for kilo and 1,000,000 for mega.

From the early 1980s until around 1990, nobody cared about this weird thing where one word could mean two values. Everything was fine until the math nerds and the attorneys started making trouble. To fix this, in 1998 the International Electrotechnical Committee (IEC) invented special prefixes for binary values I call the *ibis* (pronounced *eee-bees*).

1 kibi = 2^{10} = 1024 (abbreviated as "Ki")

1 mebi = 2^{20} = 1,048,576 (abbreviated as "Mi")

1 gibi = 2^{30} = 1,073,741,824 (abbreviated as "Gi")

1 tebi = 2^{40} = 1,099,511,627,776 (abbreviated as "Ti")

To follow this revised naming convention, you should say, "the 8088 processor could address one mebibyte (MiB) of memory." The problem is that *no one* but math nerds uses these ibis. If you buy RAM, the manufacturers use the term gigabyte even though technically they should use gibibyte. Welcome to the weird world of counting in IT. Let's get back to memory.

 NOTE The jury is still out on correct pronunciation of the ibis. You will find ardent supporters of "keebeebyte" and equally passionate supporters of "kehbeebyte." It doesn't really matter, because the rest of us just say "kilobyte."

Which Pattern Goes to Which Row?

The second question is a little harder: "Which pattern goes to which row of RAM?" To understand this, let's take a moment to discuss binary counting. In binary, only two numbers exist, 0 and 1, which makes binary a handy way to work with wires that turn on and off. Let's try to count in binary: 0, 1…what's next? It's not 2—you can only use zeros and ones. The next number after 1 is 10! Now let's count in binary to 1000: 0, 1, 10, 11, 100, 101, 110, 111, 1000. Try counting to 10000. Don't worry; it hardly takes any time at all.

Super; you now count in binary as well as any math professor. Let's add to the concept. Stop thinking about binary for just a moment and think about good old base 10 (regular numbers). If you have the number 365, can you put zeros in front of the 365, like this:

000365? Sure you can—it doesn't change the value at all. The same thing is true in binary. Putting zeros in front of a value doesn't change a thing! Let's count again to 1000 in binary. In this case, add enough zeros to make 20 places:

00000000000000000000

00000000000000000001

00000000000000000010

00000000000000000011

00000000000000000100

00000000000000000101

00000000000000000110

00000000000000000111

00000000000000001000

Hey, wouldn't this be a great way to represent each line of RAM on the address bus? The CPU identifies the first byte of RAM on the address bus with 00000000000000000000. The CPU identifies the last RAM row with 11111111111111111111. When the CPU turns off all the address bus wires, it wants the first line of RAM; when it turns on all the wires, it wants the 1,048,576th line of RAM. Obviously, the address bus also addresses all the rows of RAM in between. So, by lighting up different patterns of ones and zeros on the address bus, the CPU can access any row of RAM it needs.

 NOTE   Bits and bytes are abbreviated differently. Bits get a lowercase b, whereas bytes get a capital B. So for example, 4 Kb is 4 kilobits, but 4 KB is 4 kilobytes. The big-B little-b standard applies all the way up the food chain, so 2 Mb = 2 megabits; 2 MB = 2 megabytes; 4 Gb = 4 gigabits; 4 GB = 4 gigabytes; and so on.

1101

Modern CPUs

CPU manufacturers have achieved stunning progress with microprocessors since the days of the Intel 8088, and the rate of change doesn't show any signs of slowing. At the core, though, today's CPUs function similarly to the processors of its predecessors. The *arithmetic logic unit (ALU)*—that's the Man in the Box—still crunches numbers many millions of times per second. CPUs rely on memory to feed them lines of programming as quickly as possible.

This section brings the CPU into the present. We'll first look at models you can buy today, and then we'll turn to essential improvements in technology you should understand.

Developers

In a basic sense, to produce a CPU requires three processes. First, a developer creates the *industry standard architecture (ISA)* for the CPU. That's the *instruction set,* essentially how the CPU will handle code and interact with other components, like you read about earlier in this chapter. You'll see the ISA described as the CPU platform. Second, a developer designs the chip floorplan, how all the transistors and other physical parts of the CPU interconnect. Third, a *fabrication* company puts all the designs into action and creates the physical CPU according to all the architecture and design specifications.

 NOTE CPUs fit into a CPU socket on a motherboard. There are many socket types, and a CPU only fits into a specific socket. We'll explore CPU sockets in the section "Selecting and Installing CPUs" later in this chapter.

Three companies create the vast majority of CPUs today and all three approach the three processes differently. *Intel* Corporation makes x86-64 architecture processors and, for the most part, designs the chip and handles the fabrication as well. *Advanced Micro Devices, Inc. (AMD)* also makes x86-64 architecture processors and designs the chips. AMD is (these days) a *fabless semiconductor* company, meaning it relies on another company to produce the physical processors. Finally, *Arm Ltd.* makes *Advanced RISC Machine (ARM)* architecture processors. Arm licenses its processors to many other companies, such as Apple, Samsung, and Qualcomm, who design the chips. These companies in turn use fabrication companies to make the physical processors.

 EXAM TIP The CompTIA A+ 1101 exam objectives spell out the original (now unused) acronym for ARM, *Advanced RISC Machine (ARM)*.

Microsoft Windows, many versions of Linux, and some versions of Apple macOS run on the *x86-64 architecture,* meaning their developers wrote the operating systems to use the x86-64 instruction set. Some versions of Google Chrome OS also run on the x86-64 architecture.

 EXAM TIP The CompTIA A+ 1101 exam objectives reverse the numbers for x86-64, so you'll see them as *x64/x86*. Or perhaps that's meant to be shorthand for x64 vs. x86. You know the distinctions, so you won't miss anything on the exam.

Current versions of Windows, macOS, Linux, and Chrome OS and *every* version of modern mobile devices—Apple iOS and iPadOS and Google Android—run on ARM, which makes the *ARM* instruction set indisputably the most used CPU platform in the world by far.

Every computer requires hardware designed around a specific CPU platform. An Intel-based system, for example, requires a motherboard designed for a specific set of Intel processors. An AMD-based system likewise requires an AMD-based motherboard. ARM systems differ somewhat because most of them have the ARM processor integrated into the motherboard along with other components, what's called a *system on a chip (SoC)*. We'll revisit SoCs later in the book after we've covered a lot more hardware components.

Model Names

CPU makers differentiate product lines by using different product names, and these names have changed over the years. For a long time, Intel used *Pentium* for its flagship model, just adding model numbers to show successive generations—Pentium, Pentium II, Pentium III, and so on. AMD used the *Athlon* brand in a similar fashion. Intel uses the Core brand name for the most part these days; AMD goes with Ryzen (see Figure 3-19).

Figure 3-19
AMD Ryzen 7
glamour shot

 NOTE　Arm Ltd. processors do not have model names or code names because they license their processors to other companies such as Apple, Samsung, and Qualcomm.

Most discussions on PC CPUs focus on four end-product lines: desktop PC, budget PC, portable/mobile PC, and server computers. Table 3-1 displays many of the current product lines and names.

Microarchitecture

CPU makers continually develop faster, smarter, and generally more capable CPUs. In general, each company comes up with a major new design, called a *microarchitecture*, every few years. They try to minimize the number of model names in use, however, most

Market	Intel	AMD
Enthusiast	Core i7/i9	Ryzen 9, Threadripper
Mainstream desktop	Core i7/i5/i3	Ryzen 5, Ryzen 7
Budget desktop	Pentium, Celeron	Ryzen 5
Portable/mobile	Core i7/i5/i3 (mobile), Mobile Celeron	Ryzen 9/7/5/3
Server	Xeon	EPYC
Workstation	Xeon	Ryzen PRO, Ryzen Threadripper

Table 3-1   Current Intel and AMD Product Lines and Names

likely for marketing purposes. This means that they release CPUs labeled as the same model, but the CPUs inside can be very different from earlier versions of that model. CPU companies use code names to keep track of different variations within models (see Figure 3-20). As a tech, you need to know both the models and code names to be able to make proper recommendations for your clients. One example illustrates the need: the Intel Core i7.

Figure 3-20
Same branding, but different capabilities

NOTE   The processor number helps a lot when comparing processors once you decode the meanings. We need to cover more about modern processors before introducing processor numbers. Look for more information in the upcoming section "Deciphering Processor Numbers."

Intel released the first Core i7 in the summer of 2008. By spring of 2012, the original microarchitecture—code named Nehalem—had gone through five variations, none of which worked on motherboards designed for one of the other variations. Plus, in 2011, Intel introduced the Sandy Bridge version of the Core i7 that eventually had two desktop versions and a mobile version, all of which used still other sockets. Just about every year since then has seen a new Core i7 based on improved architectures with different code names such as Ivy Bridge, Haswell, Broadwell, and so on. As we go to print, Intel has released the 12th-generation Core i7 processors, codenamed Golden Cove + Gracemont. By the time you read this book, another generation and variations within those generations will be common. And they're all called "Core i7."

At this point, a lot of new techs throw their hands in the air. How do you keep up? How do you know which CPU will give your customer the best value for his or her money and provide the right computing firepower for his or her needs? Simply put, you need to research efficiently.

Your first stop should be the manufacturers' Web sites. Both companies put out a lot of information on their products.

- https://www.intel.com
- https://www.amd.com

You can also find many high-quality tech Web sites devoted to reporting on the latest CPUs. When a client needs an upgrade, surf the Web for recent articles and make comparisons. Because you'll understand the underlying technology from your CompTIA A+ studies, you'll be able to follow the conversations with confidence. Here's a list of some of the sites I use:

- https://arstechnica.com
- https://www.anandtech.com
- https://www.tomshardware.com
- https://www.extremetech.com

Finally, you can find great, exhaustive articles on all things tech at Wikipedia:

- https://www.wikipedia.org

NOTE Wikipedia is a user-generated, self-regulated resource. I've found it to be accurate on technical issues the majority of the time, but you should always check other references as well. Nicely, most article authors on the site provide their sources through footnotes. You can often use the Wikipedia articles as jumping-off points for deeper searches.

Desktop Versus Mobile

Mobile devices, such as portable computers, have needs that differ from those of *desktop* computers, notably the need to consume as little electricity as possible. This helps in two ways: extending battery charge and creating less heat.

Both Intel and AMD have engineers devoted to making excellent mobile versions of their CPUs that sport advanced energy-saving features (see Figure 3-21). These mobile CPUs consume much less power than their desktop counterparts. They also run in very low power mode and scale up automatically if the user demands more power from the CPU. If you're surfing the Web at an airport terminal, the CPU doesn't draw too much power. If you switch to playing an action game, the CPU kicks into gear. Saving energy by making the CPU run more slowly when demand is light is generically called *throttling*.

Figure 3-21
Desktop vs.
mobile, fight!

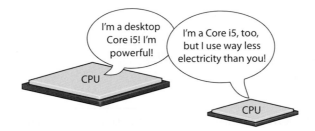

Unfortunately, this picture gets more complicated when you throw in heat. Because most portable and mobile computing devices are very compact, they can't dissipate heat as quickly as a well-cooled desktop system. Mobile CPUs can scale up to handle demanding tasks, but they'll start accumulating heat quickly. As this heat nears levels that could damage the CPU, it will engage in *thermal throttling* to protect itself. A system trying to do demanding work with only a fraction of its full power available may grind to a halt!

NOTE   The industry describes how much heat a busy CPU generates with a figure (measured in watts) called its *thermal design power (TDP)*. The TDP can give you a rough idea of how much energy a CPU draws and what kind of cooling it will need. It can also help you select more efficient CPUs.

TDP has been trending down over time (especially in recent years), but it may help to have a sense of what these values look like in the real world. The CPUs in a smartphone or tablet typically have a TDP from 2 to 15 watts, laptop CPUs range from 7 to 65 watts, and desktop CPUs tend to range from 50 to 140 watts.

Many of the technologies developed for mobile processors migrate back into their more power-hungry desktop siblings. That's a bonus for the planet (and maybe your power bill).

ARM processors took the opposite road from Intel and AMD, blossoming as mobile-only CPUs for many years and then gradually making the transition to desktop and server systems. With their incredibly efficient energy, processing power, and heat ratios, ARM is rapidly cutting into the desktop and server landscape.

Technology

Although microprocessors today still serve the same function as the venerable 8088—crunching numbers—they do so far more efficiently. Engineers have altered, enhanced, and improved CPUs in a number of ways. This section looks at eight features:

- Clock multipliers
- 64-bit processing
- Virtualization support
- Parallel execution

- Multicore processing
- Integrated memory controller (IMC)
- Graphics processing unit (GPU)
- Security

 NOTE CompTIA A+ looks at CPU technologies in a fairly simplistic way, in terms of speed, raw processing capabilities, and power consumption. Most of this chapter discusses CPUs the same way. The "Beyond A+" section at the end of the chapter introduces several important differentiating concepts and technologies that matter a lot once you move beyond a simple desktop computer. Plus, Chapter 23 and Chapter 24 explore important variations and innovations in CPUs designed for the mobile market.

Clock Multipliers

All modern CPUs run at some multiple of the system clock speed. The system bus on my Ryzen 7 machine, for example, runs at 100 MHz. The clock multiplier goes up to ×32 at full load to support the 3.2 GHz maximum speed. Originally, CPUs ran at the speed of the bus, but engineers early on realized the CPU was the only thing doing any work much of the time. If the engineers could speed up just the internal operations of the CPU and not anything else, they could speed up the whole computing process. Figure 3-22 shows a nifty program called CPU-Z displaying my CPU details. Note that all I'm doing is typing at the moment, so the CPU has dropped the clock multiplier down to ×15.5 and the CPU core speed is only 1546 MHz.

Figure 3-22
CPU-Z showing the clock speed, multiplier, and bus speed of a Ryzen 7 processor hardly breaking a sweat

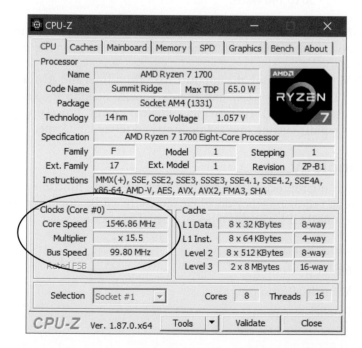

Try This!

CPU-Z

Imagine a scenario where you're dumped into an office full of unfamiliar PCs. There's no documentation about the systems at all, so your boss tells you to get cracking and find out as much as possible about each PC ASAP. Try this! Download a copy of the very popular and free CPU-Z utility from https://www.cpuid .com. CPU-Z gives you every piece of information you'll ever want to know about a CPU. Copy it to a thumb drive, then insert it into a bunch of different computers. (Ask permission, of course!) What kinds of processors do you find in your neighbors' computers? What can you tell about the different capabilities?

Today's CPUs report to the motherboard through a function called CPUID (CPU identifier). The motherboard sets the speed and multiplier automatically. You can manually override this automatic setup on many motherboards. See "Overclocking," later in this chapter, for details.

64-Bit Processing

Over successive generations of microprocessors, engineers have upgraded many physical features of CPUs. The EDB gradually increased in size, from 8 to 16 to 32 to 64 bits wide. The address bus similarly jumped, going from 20 to 24 to 32 bits wide (where it stayed for a decade).

The technological features changed as well. Engineers added new and improved registers, for example, that used fancy names like multimedia extensions (MMX) and Streaming SIMD Extensions (SSE). A mighty shift started several years ago and continues to evolve: the move to 64-bit computing.

Most new CPUs support 64-bit processing, meaning they can run a compatible 64-bit operating system, such as Windows 10 or Windows 11, and 64-bit applications. They also support 32-bit processing for 32-bit operating systems, such as some Linux distributions, and 32-bit applications. The general-purpose registers also make the move up to 64-bit. The primary benefit to moving to 64-bit computing is that modern systems can support much more than the 4 GB of memory supported with 32-bit processing.

With a 64-bit address bus, CPUs can address 2^{64} bytes of memory, or more precisely, 18,446,744,073,709,551,616 bytes of memory—that's a lot of RAM! This number is so big that gigabytes and terabytes are no longer convenient, so we now go to an exabyte (2^{60}), abbreviated *EB*. A 64-bit address bus can address 16 EB of RAM.

In practical terms, 64-bit computing greatly enhances the performance of programs that work with large files, such as video editing applications. You'll see a profound improvement moving from 4 GB to 8 GB or 16 GB of RAM with such programs.

 EXAM TIP The primary benefit of 64-bit computing is to support more than 4 GB of memory, the limit with 32-bit processing.

x86   CPUs from the early days can be lumped together as *x*86 CPUs, because they used an instruction set that built upon the earliest Intel CPU architecture. The Intel Core 2 Duo, for example, could run a program written for an ancient 80386 processor that was in fashion in the early 1990s.

x64   When the 64-bit CPUs went mainstream, marketing folks needed some way to mark applications, operating systems, and so on such that consumers could quickly tell the difference between something compatible with their system or something not compatible. Since you generally cannot return software after you open it, this is a big deal. The marketing folks went with *x*64, and that created a mess.

x86-64   The earlier 32-bit stuff had been marketed as *x*86, not *x*32, so now we have *x*86 (old, 32-bit stuff) versus *x*64 (current, 64-bit stuff). It's not pretty, but do you get the difference? To make matters even worse, however, *x*64 processors quite happily handle *x*86 code and are, by definition, *x*86 processors too! It's common to marry the two terms and describe current 64-bit CPUs as *x*86-64 processors.

Virtualization Support

Intel and AMD have built in support for running more than one operating system at a time, a process called virtualization support. Virtualization support is very cool and gets its own chapter later in the book (Chapter 22), so I'll skip the details here. The key issue from a CPU standpoint is that virtualization used to work entirely through software. Programmers had to write a ton of code to enable a CPU—which was designed to run one OS at a time—to run more than one OS at the same time. Think about the issues involved. How does the memory get allocated, for example, or how does the CPU know which OS to update when you type something or click an icon? With hardware-based virtualization support, CPUs took a lot of the burden off the programmers and made virtualization a whole lot easier.

Parallel Execution

Modern CPUs can process multiple commands and parts of commands in parallel, known as *parallel execution.* Early processors had to do everything in a strict, linear fashion. The CPUs accomplish this parallelism through multiple pipelines, dedicated cache, and the capability to work with multiple threads or programs at one time. To understand the mighty leap in efficiency gained from parallel execution, you need insight into the processing stages.

Pipelining   To get a command from the data bus, do the calculation, and then send the answer back out onto the data bus, a CPU takes at least four steps (each of these steps is called a *stage*):

1. **Fetch**   Get the data from the EDB.
2. **Decode**   Figure out what type of command needs to be executed.
3. **Execute**   Perform the calculation.
4. **Write**   Send the data back onto the EDB.

Smart, discrete circuits inside the CPU handle each of these stages. In early CPUs, when a command was placed on the data bus, each stage did its job and the CPU handed back the answer before starting the next command, requiring at least four clock cycles to process a command. In every clock cycle, three of the four circuits sat idle. Today, the circuits are organized in a conveyer-belt fashion called a *pipeline*. With pipelining, each stage does its job with each clock-cycle pulse, creating a much more efficient process. The CPU has multiple circuits doing multiple jobs, so let's add pipelining to the Man in the Box analogy. Now, it's *Men* in the Box (see Figure 3-23)!

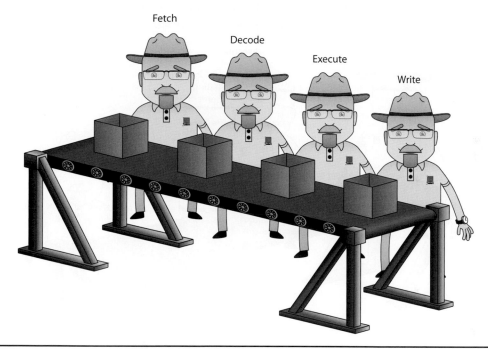

Figure 3-23   Simple pipeline

Pipelines keep every stage of the processor busy on every click of the clock, making a CPU run more efficiently without increasing the clock speed. Note that at this point, the CPU has four stages: fetch, decode, execute, and write—a four-stage pipeline. No CPU ever made has fewer than four stages, but advancements in caching (see "Cache," next) have increased the number of stages over the years. Current CPU pipelines contain many more stages, up to 20 in some cases.

Pipelining isn't perfect. Sometimes a stage hits a complex command that requires more than one clock cycle, forcing the pipeline to stop. Your CPU tries to avoid these stops, or *pipeline stalls*. The decode stage tends to cause the most pipeline stalls; certain commands are complex and therefore harder to decode than other commands. Current processors use multiple decode stages to reduce the chance of pipeline stalls due to complex decoding.

The inside of the CPU is composed of multiple chunks of circuitry to handle the many types of calculations your PC needs to do. For example, one part, the *arithmetic logic unit (ALU)* (or *integer unit*), handles integer math: basic math for numbers with no decimal point. A perfect example of integer math is 2 + 3 = 5. The typical CPU spends most of its work doing integer math. CPUs also have special circuitry to handle complex numbers, called the *floating point unit (FPU)*. With a single pipeline, only the ALU or the FPU worked at any execution stage. Worse yet, floating point calculation often took many, many clock cycles to execute, forcing the CPU to stall the pipeline until the FPU finished executing the complex command (see Figure 3-24). Current CPUs offer multiple pipelines to keep the processing going (see Figure 3-25).

Figure 3-24 Bored integer unit

Cache When you send a program to the CPU, you run lots of little programs all at the same time. Okay, let's be fair here: *you* didn't run all these little programs—you just started your Web browser or some other program. The moment you double-clicked that icon, Windows started sending many programs to the CPU. Each of these programs breaks down into some number of little pieces, called *threads*, and data. Each thread is a series of instructions designed to do a particular job with the data.

Modern CPUs don't execute instructions sequentially—first doing step 1, then step 2, and so on—but rather process all kinds of instructions. Most applications have certain instructions and data that get reused, sometimes many times.

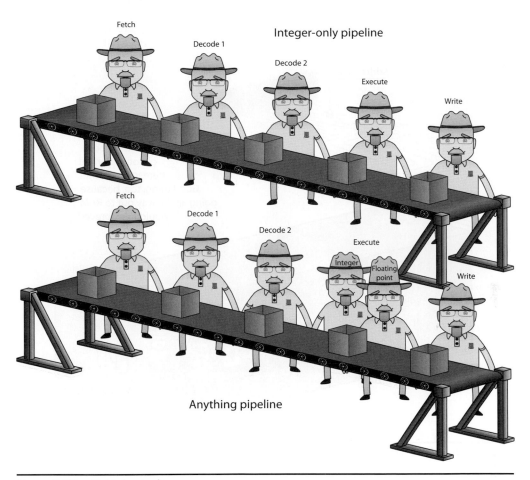

Figure 3-25 Multiple pipelines

Pipelining CPUs work fantastically well as long as the pipelines stay filled with instructions. Because the CPU runs faster than the RAM can supply it with code, you'll always get pipeline stalls—called *wait states*—because the RAM can't keep up with the CPU. To reduce wait states, CPUs come with built-in, very high-speed RAM called *static RAM (SRAM)*. This SRAM preloads as many instructions as possible and keeps copies of already run instructions and data in case the CPU needs to work on them again (see Figure 3-26). SRAM used in this fashion is called a *cache*.

The SRAM cache inside the early CPUs was tiny, only about 16 KB, but it improved performance tremendously. In fact, it helped so much that many motherboard makers began adding a cache directly to the motherboards. These caches were much larger, usually around 128 to 512 KB. When the CPU looked for a line of code, it first went to the built-in cache; if the code wasn't there, the CPU went to the cache on the motherboard. The cache on the CPU was called the *L1 cache* because it was the one the CPU first tried

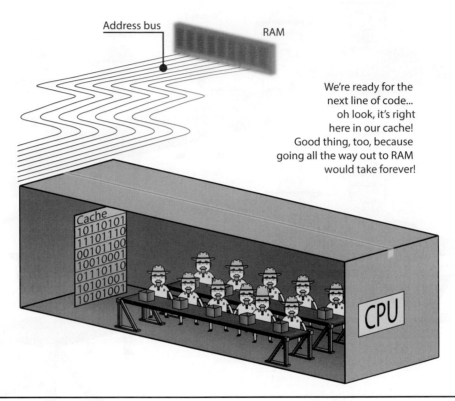

Figure 3-26   SRAM cache

to use. The cache on the motherboard was called the *L2 cache*, not because it was on the motherboard, but because it was the second cache the CPU checked.

Eventually, engineers took this cache concept even further and added the L2 cache onto the CPU package, then eventually right onto the CPU chip. Many modern CPUs include three caches (see Figure 3-27): an L1, an L2, and an *L3 cache* (Intel calls it Smart Cache).

The L2 cache on the early CPUs that had L2 cache included on the CPU package ran at a slower clock speed than the L1 cache. The L1 cache was in the CPU and thus ran at the speed of the CPU. The L2 cache connected to the CPU via a tiny set of wires on the CPU package. The first L2 caches ran at half the speed of the CPU.

The inclusion of the L2 cache on the chip gave rise to some new terms to describe the connections between the CPU, MCC, RAM, and L2 cache. The address bus and external data bus (connecting the CPU, MCC, and RAM) were lumped into a single term called the frontside bus, and the connection between the CPU and the L2 cache became known

Figure 3-27
CPU-Z displaying the cache information for a Ryzen 7 processor

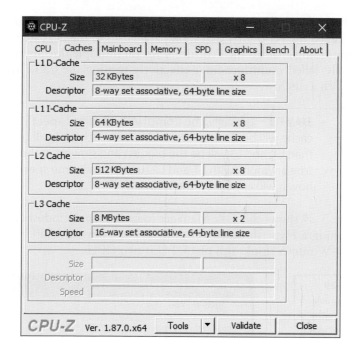

as the backside bus (see Figure 3-28). (These terms don't apply well to current computers, so they have fallen out of use. See the "Integrated Memory Controller" section later in this chapter.)

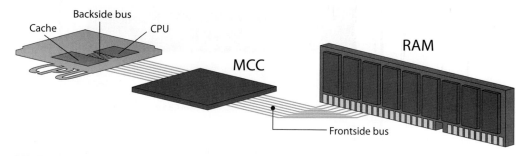

Figure 3-28   Frontside and backside buses

NOTE   To keep up with faster processors, motherboard manufacturers began to double and even quadruple the throughput of the frontside bus. Techs sometimes refer to these as *double-pumped* and *quad-pumped* frontside buses.

Multithreading   At the peak of the single-CPU 32-bit computing days, Intel released a CPU called the Pentium 4 that took parallelism to the next step with Hyperthreading. Hyperthreading enabled the Pentium 4 to run multiple threads at the same time, what's generically called multithreading, effectively turning the CPU into two CPUs on one chip—with a catch.

EXAM TIP   Typically, the CompTIA A+ exams expect you to know that L1 cache will be the smallest and fastest cache; L2 will be bigger and slower than L1; and L3 will be the biggest and slowest cache. (This is not completely true anymore, with L1 and L2 running the same speed in many CPUs, but it is how it will appear on the exams.)

Figure 3-29 shows the Task Manager in an ancient Windows XP computer on a system running a Hyperthreaded Pentium 4. Note how the CPU box is broken into two groups—Windows thinks this one CPU is two CPUs.

Figure 3-29
Windows Task Manager with the Performance tab displayed for a system running a Hyperthreaded Pentium 4

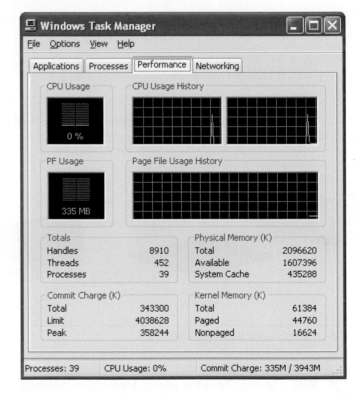

Multithreading enhances a CPU's efficiency but with a couple of limitations. First, the operating system and the application must be designed to take advantage of the feature. Second, although the CPU simulates the actions of a second processor, it doesn't double the processing power because the main execution resources are not duplicated.

Multicore Processing

Microarchitecture hit a plateau back in 2002 when CPU clock speeds hit a practical limit of roughly 4 GHz, motivating the CPU makers to find new ways to get more processing power for CPUs. Although Intel and AMD had different opinions about 64-bit CPUs, both decided at virtually the same time to move beyond the *single-core* CPU (one CPU) and combine two CPUs (or *cores*) into a single chip, creating a *dual-core* architecture. A dual-core CPU has two execution units—two sets of pipelines—but the two sets of pipelines share caches and RAM. A single-core CPU has only one set of everything.

Today, multicore CPUs—with four, six, or eight cores—are common. Higher-end CPUs have up to 32 cores! With each generation of multicore CPU, both Intel and AMD have tinkered with the mixture of how to allocate the cache among the cores. Figure 3-30 shows another screenshot of CPU-Z, this time displaying the cache breakdown of an Ice Lake–based Core i7.

Figure 3-30
CPU-Z showing the cache details of an Ice Lake Core i7

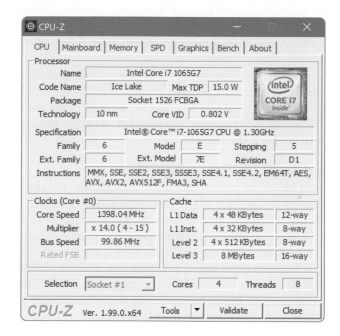

Figure 3-30 reveals specific details about how this Intel CPU works with cache. This Core i7 has L1, L2, and L3 caches of 320 KB, 2 MB, and 8 MB, respectively. (The L1 cache divides into 48-KB chunks to handle data—the *D-Cache*—and another 32-KB chunk for instructions—the *I-Cache*.) Each core has dedicated L1 and L2 caches. All four cores share the giant L3 cache. That pool of memory enables the cores to communicate and work together without having to access the radically slower main system RAM as much.

CPU manufacturers engineered the cores in multicore CPUs to divide up work independently of the OS, known as multicore processing. This differs from Hyperthreading, where the OS and applications must be written specifically to handle the multiple threads. Note that even with multicore processors, applications must be modified or optimized for this parallelism to have a huge impact on performance.

Because one great technology advancement isn't enough, both Intel and AMD make multicore CPUs that incorporate Hyperthreading as well. The Intel Core i9-12900K, for example, sports 16 cores, Hyperthreading, 16 MB of L2 cache and 30 MB of L3 cache, and Turbo Boost to crank the clock speed over 5 GHz when the system needs it.

SIM   This is a great time to head over to the Chapter 3 Show! and Click! sims to see how to download and use the CPU-Z utility. Check out "What is CPU-Z?" here: https://www.totalsem.com/110X.

Integrated Memory Controller

All current microprocessors have an *integrated memory controller (IMC),* moved from the motherboard chip into the CPU to optimize the flow of information into and out from the CPU. An IMC enables faster control over things like the large L3 cache shared among multiple cores.

Just like in so many other areas of computing, manufacturers implement a variety of IMCs in their CPUs. In practice, this means that different CPUs handle different types and capacities of RAM. I'll save the details on those RAM variations for Chapter 4. For now, add "different RAM support" to your list of things to look at when making a CPU recommendation for a client.

Integrated Graphics Processing Unit

As you'll read about in much more detail in Chapter 17, the video processing portion of the computer—made up of the parts that put a changing image on the monitor—traditionally has a discrete microprocessor that differs in both function and architecture from the CPUs designed for general-purpose computing. The generic term for the video processor is a *graphics processing unit (GPU).* I'll spare you the details until we get to video in Chapter 17, but it turns out that graphics processors can handle certain tasks much more efficiently than the standard CPU. Integrating a GPU into the CPU enhances the overall performance of the computer while at the same time reducing energy use, size, and cost. With the proliferation of mobile devices and portable computers today, all these benefits have obvious merit.

Security

All modern processors employ the *NX bit* technology that enables the CPU to protect certain sections of memory. This feature, coupled with implementation by the operating system, stops malicious attacks from getting to essential operating system files. Microsoft calls the feature Data Execution Prevention (DEP), turned on by default in every OS (see Figure 3-31).

Figure 3-31
DEP in
Windows 10

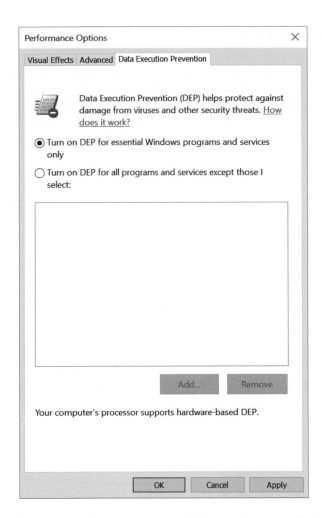

Everybody calls the NX bit technology something different (but you don't need to memorize any of this for the exams):

- **Intel**   XD bit (eXecute Disable)
- **AMD**   Enhanced Virus Protection
- **ARM**   XN (eXecute Never)

Selecting and Installing CPUs

Now that you know how CPUs work, it's time to get practical. This last section discusses selecting the proper CPU, installing several types of processors, and troubleshooting the few problems techs face with CPUs.

Selecting a CPU

When selecting a CPU, you need to make certain you get one that the motherboard can accommodate. Or, if you're buying a motherboard along with the CPU, then get the right CPU for the intended purpose. Chapter 11 discusses computer roles and helps you select the proper components for each role. You need to have a lot more knowledge of all the pieces around the CPU to get the full picture, so we'll wait until then to discuss the "why" of specific processors. Instead, this section assumes you're placing a new CPU in an already-acquired motherboard. You need to address two key points in selecting a CPU that will work. First, does the motherboard support Intel CPUs or AMD CPUs? Second, what CPU socket does the motherboard have?

NOTE As mentioned previously, ARM processors come in a complete package with the motherboard and other components. You'll never "install" an ARM processor.

To find answers to both those questions, you have two sources: the motherboard book or manual and the manufacturer's Web site. Figure 3-32 shows a page from the manual for an ASUS motherboard listing the supported processors and the socket type.

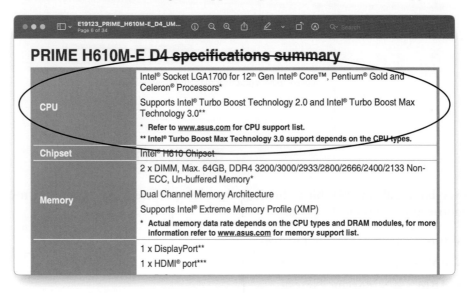

Figure 3-32 Supported processors and socket type

Just as Intel and AMD make many types of CPUs, motherboards are manufactured with various different types of sockets. There have been hundreds of sockets developed over the years. Table 3-2 charts a few of the more popular ones in production today.

Socket	Platform	CPU
LGA 2066	Intel	Core i3/i5/i7, Xeon (Skylake, Kaby Lake, Cascade Lake)
LGA 1200	Intel	Core i5/i7/i9, Xeon (Comet Lake, Rocket Lake)
LGA 1700	Intel	Core i5/i7/i9, Xeon (Alder Lake)
AM4	AMD	Ryzen
TR4	AMD	Ryzen Threadripper
AM5	AMD	AMD Zen 4

Table 3-2 Common Sockets

 EXAM TIP   The CompTIA A+ 1101 exam objectives do not list any specific CPU sockets, but previous versions frequently included questions about them. Hopefully you won't run into one of these questions, but it's not a bad idea to know the sockets just in case. Beyond the exam, just make sure that you understand that every CPU has a specific socket into which it fits and make sure a client's motherboard has the socket that works with a suggested CPU.

Deciphering Processor Numbers

Intel and AMD use different processor numbering schemes that help you compare multiple CPUs with similar names, such as Core i5. AMD and Intel both have fairly similar numbering schemes. Here's the scoop on both.

Intel processor numbers follow a very clear pattern. An Intel Core i7 7500 U processor, for example, maps out like this:

- Intel Core = brand
- i7 = brand modifier
- 7 = generation
- 500 = SKU numbers
- U = alpha suffix (U indicates that it's a desktop processor using ultra-low power)

Contrast the previous processor with an Intel Core i7 12700K, where the numbers map like this:

- Intel Core = brand
- i7 = brand modifier
- 12 = generation
- 700 = SKU numbers
- K = alpha suffix (K indicates that the processor is unlocked and therefore overclockable)

AMD processor nomenclature is similar. Here's the breakdown for an AMD Ryzen 7 5800X:

- AMD Ryzen = brand
- 7 = market segment/power (higher number is more powerful)
- 5 = generation
- 8 = performance level
- 00 = model number
- X = power suffix (X indicates high-performance)

Try This!

Processor Research

Both Intel and AMD maintain accessible Web sites with exhaustive information about their recent CPUs. All three Web sites listed here provide details you can use for client support and for recommendations when dealing with specific sockets for upgrades. Try this! Put one or more of the following links into a Web browser and explore the CPUs. Then tuck the URLs into your tech toolkit for later reference when needed.

- https://ark.intel.com
- https://www.amd.com/en/products/processors-desktop
- https://www.amd.com/en/products/processors-laptop

Installation Issues

When installing a CPU, you need to use caution not to bend any of the tiny pins on the CPU or the socket. Plus, you must make certain that the power supply can supply enough electricity for the processor to function along with all the other components on the computer. Third, you must provide adequate cooling. Finally, you can decide whether to leave the CPU at stock settings or overclock it.

CPU Socket Types

The location of the pins differs between Intel and AMD CPUs. With Intel-based motherboards, the sockets have hundreds of tiny pins that line up with contacts on the bottom of the CPU (see Figure 3-33). Intel CPUs use a *land grid array (LGA)* package for socketed CPUs, where the underside of the CPU has hundreds of contact points that line up with the socket pins.

Figure 3-33
Intel-based
socket with pins

AMD CPUs have the pins; the sockets have holes (see Figure 3-34). The pins on the AMD *pin grid array (PGA)* CPUs align with the holes in the sockets.

All CPUs and sockets are keyed so you can't (easily) insert them incorrectly. Look at the underside of the CPU on the left side of Figure 3-35. Note that the pins do not make a perfect square, because a few are missing. Now look at the top of the CPU on the right in Figure 3-35. See the little mark at the corner? The socket also has tiny markings so you can line the CPU up properly with the socket.

Figure 3-34
AMD-based
socket without
pins

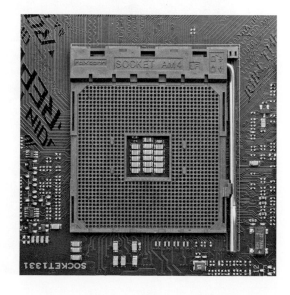

Figure 3-35
Underside and
top of a CPU

In both socket styles, you release the retaining mechanism by pushing the little lever down slightly and then away from the socket (see Figure 3-36). You next raise the arm fully, and then move the retaining bracket (see Figure 3-37).

Align the processor with the socket and gently drop the processor into place. If it doesn't go in easily, check the orientation and try again. These sockets are generically called *zero insertion force (ZIF) sockets,* which means you never have to use any force at all.

Figure 3-36
Moving the
release arm

Figure 3-37
Fully opened
socket

Cooling

CPUs work very hard and thus require power to function. In electrical terms, CPUs consume *wattage* or *watts*, a unit of electrical power, just like a 100-watt light bulb consumes power whenever it's on. (See Chapter 7 for more details about electricity.) Have you ever touched a light bulb after it's been on for a while? Ouch! CPUs heat up, too.

To increase the capability of the CPUs to handle complex code, CPU manufacturers have added a lot of microscopic transistors over the years. The more transistors the CPU has, the more power they need and thus the hotter they get. CPUs don't tolerate heat well, and modern processors need active cooling solutions just to function at all. Almost every CPU uses a combination of a heat sink and fan assembly to wick heat away from the CPU. A *heat sink* is a copper or other metal device designed to dissipate heat from whatever it touches. Figure 3-38 shows the standard Intel heat sink and fan. Here are some cooling options:

EXAM TIP A heat sink by itself (no fan) on a chip provides *passive cooling*. A heat sink and fan combination provides *active cooling*. You'll sometimes hear the latter described as an *active heat sink*.

- **OEM CPU coolers** Original equipment manufacturer (OEM) heat-sink and fan assemblies are included with most Intel and AMD retail-boxed CPUs. OEM in this case means that Intel makes the heat-sink/fan assemblies. Rather confusingly, you'll see the term "OEM CPUs" used to mean CPUs you buy in bulk or not in the retail packaging. These are still made by Intel or AMD and are

Figure 3-38
Intel stock heat-sink and fan assembly

functionally identical to the retail versions. They don't come bundled with CPU coolers. Crazy, isn't it? OEM CPU coolers have one big advantage: you know absolutely they will work with your CPU.

- **Specialized CPU coolers** Many companies sell third-party heat-sink and fan assemblies for a variety of CPUs. These usually exceed the OEM heat sinks in the amount of heat they dissipate. These CPU coolers invariably come with eye-catching designs to look really cool inside your system (see Figure 3-39)—some are even lighted.

Figure 3-39
Cool retail heat sink

The last choice is the most impressive of all: liquid cooling! *Liquid cooling* works by running some liquid—usually water—through a metal block that sits on top of your CPU, absorbing heat. The liquid gets heated by the block, runs out of the block and into something that cools the liquid, and is then pumped through the block again. Any liquid-cooling system consists of three main parts:

- A hollow metal block that sits on the CPU
- A pump to move the liquid around
- Some device to cool the liquid

And of course, you need plenty of hosing to hook them all together. Figure 3-40 shows a typical liquid-cooled CPU.

Figure 3-40
Liquid-cooled
CPU

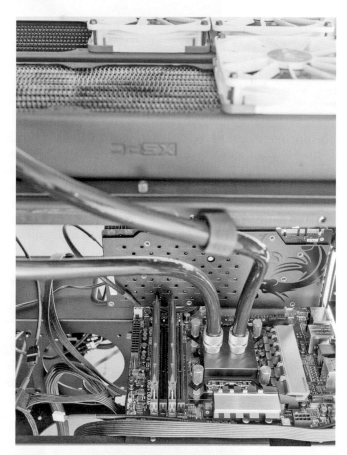

Several companies sell liquid-based cooling systems. Although they look impressive and certainly cool your CPU, unless you're overclocking or want a silent system, a good fan will more than suffice.

Once you have a heat-sink and fan assembly sorted out, you need to connect it to the motherboard. To determine the orientation of the heat-sink and fan assembly, check the power cable from the fan. Make sure it can easily reach the three- or four-wire standout on the motherboard (see Figure 3-41). If it can't, rotate the heat sink until it can. (Check the motherboard manual if you have trouble locating the CPU fan power standout.)

Figure 3-41
CPU fan power
standout on
motherboard

Next, before inserting the heat sink, you need to add a small amount of *thermal paste* (also called *thermal compound, heat dope,* or *nasty silver goo*). Many heat sinks come with some thermal paste already on them in the form or a thermal pad; the thermal pad on these pre-doped heat sinks is covered by a small square of tape—take the tape off before you snap it to the CPU. If you need to put thermal paste on from a tube, know that you need to use only a tiny amount of this compound (see Figure 3-42). Spread it on as thinly, completely, and evenly as you can. Unlike so many other things in life, you *can* have too much thermal paste!

Figure 3-42
Applying thermal
paste

You can secure heat sinks in various ways, depending on the manufacturer. Stock Intel heat sinks have four plungers that you simply push until they click into place in corresponding holes in the motherboard. AMD stock heat sinks generally have a bracket that you secure to two points on the outside of the CPU socket and a latch that you swivel to lock it down (see Figure 3-43).

Figure 3-43
AMD stock
heat-sink and fan
assembly

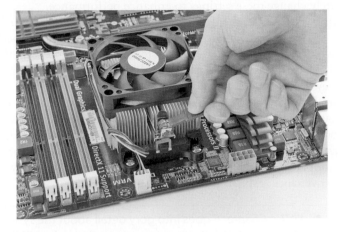

Finally, you can secure many aftermarket heat-sink and fan assemblies by screwing them down from the underside of the motherboard (see Figure 3-44). You have to remove the motherboard from the case or install the heat sink before you put the motherboard in the case.

Figure 3-44
Heat-sink and
fan assembly
mounted to
motherboard
with screws

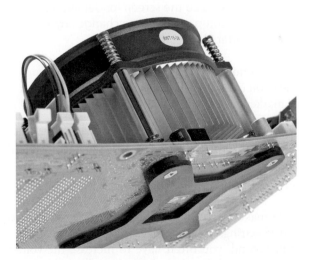

For the final step, plug the fan power connector into the motherboard standout. It won't work if you don't!

Overclocking

For the CPU to work, the motherboard speed, multiplier, and voltage must be set properly. In most modern systems, the motherboard uses the CPUID functions to set these options automatically. Some motherboards enable you to adjust these settings manually by moving a jumper, changing a CMOS setting, or using software; many enthusiasts deliberately change these settings to enhance performance.

Starting way back in the days of the Intel 80486 CPU, people intentionally ran their systems at clock speeds higher than the CPU was rated, a process called *overclocking*, and it worked. Well, *sometimes* the systems worked, and sometimes they didn't. Intel and AMD have a reason for marking a CPU at a specific clock speed—that's the highest speed they guarantee will work.

Before I say anything else, I must warn you that intentional overclocking of a CPU immediately voids most warranties. Overclocking has been known to destroy CPUs. Overclocking might make your system unstable and prone to *system lockups*, *reboots*, and *unexpected shutdowns*. I neither applaud nor decry the practice of overclocking. My goal here is simply to inform you of the practice. You make your own decisions. If a client wants to overclock, explain the potential consequences.

 NOTE Chapter 5 goes into gory detail about the system setup utility and the area in which it stores important data (called *CMOS*), but invariably students want to experiment at this point, so I'll give you some information now. You can access the system setup utility by pressing some key as the computer starts up. This is during the text phase, well before it ever says anything about starting Windows. Most systems require you to press the DELETE key, but read the screen for details. Just be careful once you get into the system setup utility not to change anything you don't understand. And read Chapter 5!

CPU makers do not encourage overclocking. Why would you pay more for a faster processor when you can take a cheaper, slower CPU and just make it run faster? Bowing to enthusiast market pressure, however, both Intel and AMD make utilities that help you overclock their respective CPUs:

- **Intel Extreme Tuning Utility (Intel XTU)** Don't skip the additional Performance Tuning Protection Plan if you go this route.
- **AMD Overdrive Utility** No extra warranty is provided here; you're on your own.

Most people make a couple of adjustments to overclock successfully. First, through jumpers, CMOS settings, or software configuration, you would increase the bus speed for the system. Second, you often have to increase the voltage going into the CPU by just a little to provide stability. You do that by changing a jumper or CMOS setting (see Figure 3-45).

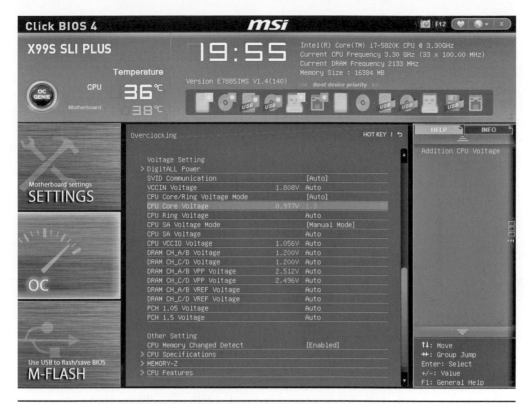

Figure 3-45 Manually overriding CPU settings in the system setup utility

Overriding the defaults can completely lock up your system, to the point where even removing and reinstalling the CPU doesn't bring the motherboard back to life. (There's also a slight risk of toasting the processor, although all modern processors have circuitry that shuts them down quickly before they overheat.) Most motherboards have a jumper setting or a button called *CMOS clear* or *CLRTC* (see Figure 3-46) that makes the CMOS go back to default settings. Before you try overclocking on a modern system, find the CMOS-clear jumper or button and make sure you know how to use it! Hint: Look in the motherboard manual.

Figure 3-46
CMOS-clear
jumper

CMOS-clear jumper

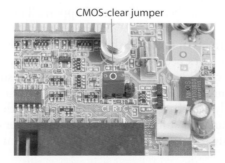

To clear the CMOS, turn off the PC. Then locate one of those tiny little plastic pieces (officially called a *shunt*) and place it over the two jumper wires for a moment. Next, restart the PC and immediately go into CMOS and restore the settings you need.

Troubleshooting CPUs

Troubleshooting CPU issues falls into two categories: overheating and catastrophic failures, with overheating being far more common than the latter. Once a CPU is installed properly and functioning, it rarely causes problems. The only exception is when you ask a CPU to do too much too quickly. Then you'll get a sluggish PC. The Intel Atom processor in my vintage netbook, for example, does a great job if I'm surfing the Web, working on e-mail, or writing stellar chapters of your favorite textbook. But if I try to play a game more advanced than *Half-Life* (the original, circa 1998), the machine stutters and complains and refuses to play nice.

The vast majority of problems with CPUs come from faulty installation or environmental issues that cause overheating. Very rarely will you get a catastrophic failure, but we'll look at the signs of that, too.

Symptoms of Overheating

Failure to install a CPU properly results in either nothing—that is, you push the power button and nothing at all happens—or a system lock-up in a short period of time. Because of the nature of ZIF sockets, you're almost guaranteed that the issue isn't the CPU itself, but rather the installation of the heat-sink and fan assembly. Here's a checklist of possible problems that you need to address when faced with a CPU installation problem:

1. Too much thermal paste can impede the flow of heat from the CPU to the heat sink and cause the CPU to heat up rapidly. All modern CPUs have built-in fail-safes that tell them to shut down before getting damaged by heat.

2. Not enough thermal paste or thermal paste spread unevenly can cause the CPU to heat up and consequently shut itself down.

3. Failure to connect the fan power to the motherboard can cause the CPU to heat up and shut itself down.

The fan and heat-sink installation failures can be tricky the first few times you encounter them. You might see the text from the system setup. You might even get into an installation of Windows before the crash happens. The key is that as soon as you put the CPU under load—that is, make it work for a living—it heats up beyond where the faulty heat-sink connection can dissipate the heat and then shuts down.

With a system that's been running fine for a while, environmental factors can cause problems. An air conditioning failure in my office last summer, deep in the heart of very hot Texas, for example, caused machines throughout the office to run poorly. Some even shut down entirely. (At that point it was time to close the doors and send the staff to the beach, but that's another story.) A client called the other day to complain about his computer continuously rebooting and running slowly. When I arrived on the scene, I found a house with seven cats. Opening his computer case revealed the hairy truth: the CPU fan was so clogged with cat hair that it barely spun at all! A quick cleaning with a computer vacuum and a can of compressed air and he was a happily computing client.

The CPU needs adequate ventilation. The CPU fan is essential, of course, but the inside of the case also needs to get hot air out through one or more exhaust fans and cool air in through the front vent. If the intake vent is clogged or the exhaust fans stop working or are blocked somehow, the inside of the case can heat up and overwhelm the CPU cooling devices. This will result in *sluggish performance* (the CPU slows down to minimize heat), *intermittent shutdowns* (when the CPU hits a certain thermal level), or spontaneously rebooting.

Catastrophic Failure

You'll know when a catastrophic error occurs. The PC will suddenly get a blue screen of death (BSoD), what's technically called a Windows Stop error (see Figure 3-47). On macOS, by comparison, you might get a spinning pinwheel that doesn't stop or a kernel panic (i.e., automatic restart). (CompTIA calls the BSoD and pinwheel *proprietary crash screens.*)

Figure 3-47
Blue Screen
of Death

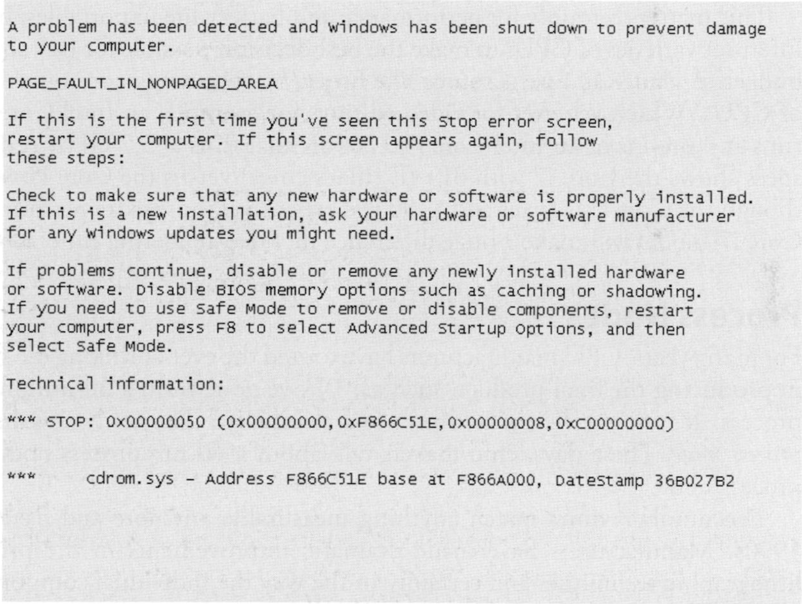

```
A problem has been detected and windows has been shut down to prevent damage
to your computer.

PAGE_FAULT_IN_NONPAGED_AREA

If this is the first time you've seen this Stop error screen,
restart your computer. If this screen appears again, follow
these steps:

Check to make sure that any new hardware or software is properly installed.
If this is a new installation, ask your hardware or software manufacturer
for any windows updates you might need.

If problems continue, disable or remove any newly installed hardware
or software. Disable BIOS memory options such as caching or shadowing.
If you need to use Safe Mode to remove or disable components, restart
your computer, press F8 to select Advanced Startup Options, and then
select Safe Mode.

Technical information:

*** STOP: 0x00000050 (0x00000000,0xF866C51E,0x00000008,0xC00000000)

***      cdrom.sys - Address F866C51E base at F866A000, DateStamp 36B027B2
```

Or the entire computer will simply stop and the screen will go black, perhaps accompanied by a loud pop. The acrid smell of burnt electronics or ozone will grace your nasal passages. You might even see trails of smoke coming out of the case. You might not know immediately that the CPU has smoked, but follow your nose. Seriously. Sniff the inside of the case until you find the strongest smell. If it's the CPU, that's bad news. Whatever electrical short hit it probably caused damage to the motherboard too, and you're looking at a long day of replacement and rebuilding.

Beyond A+

Knowing certain aspects of CPUs that fall outside the scope of the CompTIA A+ 1101 exam helps techs make informed choices for clients when recommending CPUs. This section explores hybrid core CPU architecture and process node variations.

Hybrid Cores

CPU developers have models that combine high-power/high-wattage cores—*performance cores*—with low-power/high-*efficiency cores* to create multicore CPUs with tremendous versatility. ARM introduced the concept more than a decade ago (branding it as *big .LITTLE*) to create CPUs that could work fast and hard when necessary, but ran using only the high-efficiency cores for tasks that didn't need a lot of horse power, thus maximize battery life in mobile devices.

This model has come to x86-64 as well. Intel's Alder Lake CPUs, for example, have 16 cores, 8 for performance and 8 for efficiency. One example for how the performance cores are more powerful is they're multithreaded, with each core able to run two threads while the efficiency cores are limited to one thread.

This matters certainly for performance and battery life in portables, but also in how to interpret varieties of CPUs to make the best decision possible for task solving at a specific budget. A glance at a parts source like https://www.newegg.com quickly shows varieties of CPUs. Which is better for video editing, for example, an Intel Core i7-12700K that runs at 3.6 GHz or an Intel Core i5-12600K that runs at 3.7 GHz? A deeper look at the specs shows the Core i7 with 8P+4E (that's cores) versus the Core i5 with 6P+4E. Even though the Core i5 is faster and $100 less expensive, those extra performance cores in the Core i7 model will make a huge difference in video-rendering time. Know your cores!

Process Nodes

For many years, CPU manufacturers have touted the ever-shrinking die size and efficiency in producing the final product, such as, "We've gone from a 60-nm process to a 45-nm process. It's more efficient and uses less electricity." The term now has morphed into *process node*. These days, chip makers talk about a 10-nm process node or even a 3-nm process node.

The numbers don't match anything measurable anymore and haven't since the late 1990s. Manufacturers have made dramatic improvements in the printing process or lithographic techniques and certainly in the way the individual components of the CPU work. When a manufacturer comes up with a new improvement, it markets the improvement as a "shrinking of the process node." The tinier number matters from a marketing standpoint and will point you to changes that can end up making a big difference in processing capabilities when you're rolling out a new data center or some other high-end set of systems.

Chapter Review

Questions

1. What do registers provide for the CPU?

   A. Registers determine the clock speed.

   B. The CPU uses registers for temporary storage of internal commands and data.

   C. Registers enable the CPU to address RAM.

   D. Registers enable the CPU to control the address bus.

2. What function does the external data bus have in the PC?

   A. The external data bus determines the clock speed for the CPU.

   B. The CPU uses the external data bus to address RAM.

   C. The external data bus provides a channel for the flow of data and commands between the CPU and RAM.

   D. The CPU uses the external data bus to access registers.

3. What is the function of the address bus in the PC?

   A. The address bus enables the CPU to communicate with the memory controller chip.

   B. The address bus enables the memory controller chip to communicate with the RAM.

   C. The address bus provides a channel for the flow of data and commands between the CPU and RAM.

   D. The address bus enables the CPU to access registers.

4. Which of the following terms are measures of CPU speed?

   A. Megahertz and gigahertz

   B. Megabytes and gigabytes

   C. Megahertz and gigabytes

   D. Frontside bus, backside bus

5. Which CPU feature enables the microprocessor to support running multiple operating systems at the same time?

   A. Clock multiplying

   B. Caching

   C. Pipelining

   D. Virtualization support

6. Into which socket could you place an Intel Core i5 (Alder Lake)?

   A. Socket LGA 1700

   B. Socket LGA 2066

   C. Socket C

   D. Socket AM4

7. Which feature enables a single-core CPU to function like two CPUs?

   A. Hyperthreading

   B. SpeedStep

   C. Virtualization

   D. *x*64

8. What steps do you need to take to install a Core i7 CPU into an AM4 motherboard?

   A. Lift the ZIF socket arm; place the CPU according to the orientation markings; snap on the heat-sink and fan assembly.

   B. Lift the ZIF socket arm; place the CPU according to the orientation markings; add a dash of thermal paste; snap on the heat-sink and fan assembly.

   C. Lift the ZIF socket arm; place the CPU according to the orientation markings; snap on the heat-sink and fan assembly; plug in the fan.

   D. Take all of the steps you want to take because it's not going to work.

9. A client calls to complain that his computer starts up, but crashes when Windows starts to load. After a brief set of questions, you find out that his nephew upgraded his RAM for him over the weekend and couldn't get the computer to work right afterward. What could be the problem?

   A. Thermal paste degradation

   B. Disconnected CPU fan

   C. Bad CPU cache

   D. There's nothing wrong. It usually takes a couple of days for RAM to acclimate to the new system.

10. Darren has installed a new CPU in a client's computer, but nothing happens when he pushes the power button on the case. The LED on the motherboard is lit up, so he knows the system has power. What could the problem be?

    A. He forgot to disconnect the CPU fan.

    B. He forgot to apply thermal paste between the CPU and the heat-sink and fan assembly.

    C. He used an AMD CPU in an Intel motherboard.

    D. He used an Intel CPU in an AMD motherboard.

Answers

1. **B.** The CPU uses registers for temporary storage of internal commands and data.

2. **C.** The external data bus provides a channel for the flow of data and commands between the CPU and RAM.

3. **A.** The address bus enables the CPU to communicate with the memory controller chip.

4. **A.** The terms megahertz (MHz) and gigahertz (GHz) describe how many million or billion (respectively) cycles per second a CPU can run.

5. **D.** Intel and AMD CPUs come with virtualization support, enabling more efficient implementation of virtual machines.

6. **A.** You'll find Core i5 processors in several socket types, but the Alder Lake varieties fit LGA 1700.

7. **A.** Intel loves its Hyperthreading, where a single-core CPU can function like a dual-core CPU as long as it has operating system support.

8. **D.** Intel and AMD processors are not compatible at all.

9. **B.** Most likely, the nephew disconnected the CPU fan to get at the RAM slots and simply forgot to plug it back in.

10. **B.** The best answer here is that he forgot the thermal paste, though you can also make an argument for a disconnected fan.

RAM

In this chapter, you will learn how to
- Identify the different types of DRAM packaging
- Explain the varieties of RAM
- Select and install RAM
- Perform basic RAM troubleshooting

Whenever people come up to me and start professing their computer savvy, I ask them a few questions to see how much they really know. In case you and I ever meet and you decide you want to "talk tech" with me, I'll tell you my first two questions now so you'll be ready. Both involve *random-access memory (RAM)*, the working memory for the CPU.

1. "How much RAM is in your computer?"
2. "What is RAM and why is it so important that every PC has enough?"

Can you answer either of these questions? Don't fret if you can't—you'll know how to answer both before you finish this chapter. Let's start by reviewing what you know about RAM thus far.

When not in use, programs and data are held in a mass storage device such as a solid-state drive (SSD), USB thumb drive, optical drive, or some other device that can hold data while the computer is off. When you load a program in Windows, your PC copies the program from the mass storage device to RAM and then runs it (see Figure 4-1).

You saw in Chapter 3 that the CPU uses *dynamic random-access memory (DRAM)* as RAM for all PCs. Just like CPUs, DRAM has gone through evolutionary changes over the years, resulting in improved DRAM technologies such as SDRAM, RDRAM, and DDR RAM. This chapter starts by explaining how DRAM works, and then discusses the types of DRAM used over the past several years and how they improve on the original DRAM. The third section, "Working with RAM," goes into the details of finding and installing RAM. The chapter finishes with troubleshooting RAM problems.

Historical/Conceptual

Understanding DRAM

As discussed in Chapter 3, DRAM functions like an electronic spreadsheet, with numbered rows containing cells and each cell holding a one or a zero. Now let's look at what's physically happening. Each spreadsheet cell is a special type of semiconductor that can hold a single bit—one or zero—by using microscopic capacitors and transistors. DRAM makers put these semiconductors into chips that can hold a certain number of bits. The bits inside the chips are organized in a rectangular fashion, using rows and columns.

Each chip has a limit on the number of lines of code it can contain. Think of each line of code as one of the rows on the electronic spreadsheet; one chip might be able to store a million rows of code while another chip might be able to store over a billion lines. Each chip also has a limit on the width of the lines of code it can handle. One chip might handle 8-bit-wide data while another might handle 16-bit-wide data. Techs describe chips by bits rather than bytes, so they refer to ×8 and ×16, respectively. Just as you could describe a spreadsheet by the number of rows and columns—John's accounting spreadsheet is huge, 48 rows × 12 columns—memory makers describe RAM chips the same way. An individual DRAM chip that holds 1,048,576 rows and 8 columns, for example, would be a *1M × 8* chip, with "M" as shorthand for "mega," just like in megabytes (2^{20} bytes). It is difficult if not impossible to tell the size of a DRAM chip just by looking at it—only the DRAM makers know the meaning of the tiny numbers on the chips (see Figure 4-2), although sometimes you can make a good guess.

Figure 4-2
What do these
numbers mean?

NOTE Serious RAM enthusiasts can enjoy chip specifics available at memory maker Web sites. Check out the charts at Micron, for example: https://www.micron.com/products/dram/ddr4-sdram/part-catalog.

Organizing DRAM

Because of its low cost, high speed, and ability to contain a lot of data in a relatively small package, DRAM has been the standard RAM used in all computers—not just PCs—since the mid-1970s. DRAM can be found in just about everything, from automobiles to automatic bread makers.

The PC has very specific requirements for DRAM. The original 8088 processor had an 8-bit frontside bus. Commands given to an 8088 processor were in discrete 8-bit chunks. You needed RAM that could store data in 8-bit (1-byte) chunks, so that each time the CPU asked for a line of code, the *memory controller chip (MCC)* could put an 8-bit chunk on the data bus. This optimized the flow of data into (and out from) the CPU. Although today's DRAM chips may have widths greater than 1 bit, all DRAM chips back then were 1 bit wide, meaning only sizes such as 64 K × 1 or 256 K × 1 existed—always 1 bit wide. So how was 1-bit-wide DRAM turned into 8-bit-wide memory? The solution was quite simple: just take eight 1-bit-wide chips and use the MCC to organize them electronically to be eight wide (see Figure 4-3).

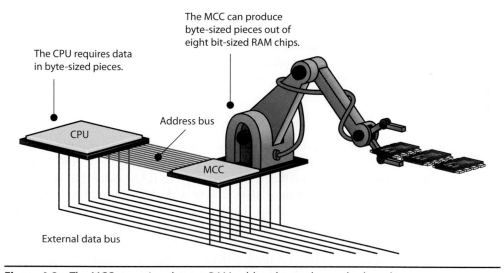

Figure 4-3 The MCC accessing data on RAM soldered onto the motherboard

Practical DRAM

Okay, before you learn more about DRAM, I need to clarify a critical point. When you first saw the 8088's machine language in Chapter 3, all the examples in the "codebook" were exactly 1-byte commands. Figure 4-4 shows the codebook again—see how all the commands are 1 byte?

Figure 4-4
Codebook again

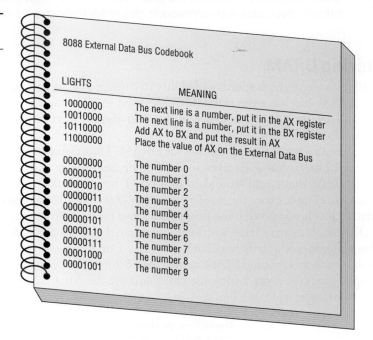

8088 External Data Bus Codebook

LIGHTS	MEANING
10000000	The next line is a number, put it in the AX register
10010000	The next line is a number, put it in the BX register
10110000	Add AX to BX and put the result in AX
11000000	Place the value of AX on the External Data Bus
00000000	The number 0
00000001	The number 1
00000010	The number 2
00000011	The number 3
00000100	The number 4
00000101	The number 5
00000110	The number 6
00000111	The number 7
00001000	The number 8
00001001	The number 9

Well, the reality is slightly different. Most of the 8088 machine language commands are 1 byte, but more-complex commands need 2 bytes. For example, the following command tells the CPU to move 163 bytes "up the RAM spreadsheet" and run whatever command is there. Cool, eh?

```
1110100110100011
```

The problem here is that the command is 2 bytes wide, not 1 byte. So how did the 8088 handle this? Simple—it just took the command 1 byte at a time. It took twice as long to handle the command because the MCC had to go to RAM twice, but it worked.

So, if some of the commands are more than 1 byte wide, why didn't Intel make the 8088 with a 16-bit frontside bus? Wouldn't that have been better? Well, Intel did. Intel invented a CPU called the 8086. The 8086 predates the 8088 and was absolutely identical to the 8088 except for one small detail: it had a 16-bit frontside bus. IBM could have used the 8086 instead of the 8088 and used 2-byte-wide RAM instead of 1-byte-wide RAM. Of course, they would have needed to invent an MCC that could handle that kind of RAM (see Figure 4-5).

Why did Intel sell the 8088 to IBM instead of the 8086? There were two reasons. Nobody had invented an affordable MCC or RAM that handled 2 bytes at a time. Sure, chips had been invented, but they were *expensive*, and IBM didn't think anyone would want to pay $12,000 for a personal computer. So IBM bought the Intel 8088, not the Intel 8086, and all our RAM came in bytes. But as you might imagine, it didn't stay that way for long.

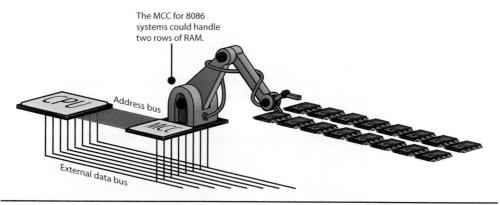

The MCC for 8086 systems could handle two rows of RAM.

Figure 4-5   Pumped-up 8086 MCC at work

DRAM Sticks

As CPU data bus sizes increased, so too did the need for RAM wide enough to fill the bus. The Intel 80386 CPU, for example, had a 32-bit data bus and thus the need for 32-bit-wide DRAM. Imagine having to line up 32 one-bit-wide DRAM chips on a motherboard. Talk about a waste of space! Figure 4-6 shows motherboard RAM run amuck.

Figure 4-6   That's a lot of real estate used by RAM chips!

DRAM manufacturers responded by creating wider DRAM chips, such as ×4, ×8, and ×16, and putting multiples of them on a small circuit board called a *stick* or *module*. Figure 4-7 shows an early stick, called a *single inline memory module (SIMM)*, with eight DRAM chips. To add RAM to a modern machine, you need to get the right stick or sticks for the particular motherboard. Your motherboard manual tells you precisely what sort of module you need and how much RAM you can install.

Figure 4-7
A 72-pin SIMM

Modern CPUs are a lot smarter than the old Intel 8088. Their machine languages have some commands that are up to 64 bits (8 bytes) wide. They also have at least a 64-bit frontside bus that can handle more than just 8 bits. They don't want RAM to give them a puny 8 bits at a time! To optimize the flow of data into and out of the CPU, the modern MCC provides at least 64 bits of data every time the CPU requests information from RAM.

Modern DRAM sticks come in 32-bit- and 64-bit-wide data form factors with a varying number of chips. Many techs describe these memory modules by their width, so we call them ×*32* and ×*64*. Note that this number does *not* describe the width of the individual DRAM chips on the module. When you read or hear about *by whatever* memory, you need to know whether that person is talking about the DRAM width or the module width. When the CPU needs certain bytes of data, it requests those bytes via the address bus. The CPU does not know the physical location of the RAM that stores that data, nor the physical makeup of the RAM—such as how many DRAM chips work together to provide the 64-bit-wide memory rows. The MCC keeps track of this and just gives the CPU whichever bytes it requests (see Figure 4-8).

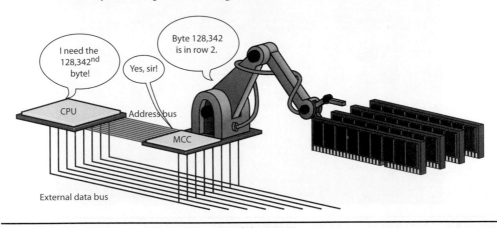

Figure 4-8 The MCC knows the real location of the DRAM.

Try This!

Dealing with Old RAM

Often in the PC world, old technology and ways of doing things are reimplemented with some newer technology. A tech who knows these ancient ways will have extra opportunities. Many thousands of companies—including hospitals, auto repair places, and more—use very old proprietary applications that keep track of medical records, inventory, and so on. If you're called to work on one of these ancient systems, you need to know how to work with old parts, so try this.

Obtain an old computer. Ask your uncle, cousin, or Great Aunt Edna if they have a PC collecting dust in a closet that you can use. Failing that, go to a secondhand store or market and buy one for a few dollars.

Open up the system and check out the RAM. Remove the RAM from the motherboard and then replace it to familiarize yourself with the internals. You never know when some critical system will go down and need repair immediately—and you're the one to do it!

Consumer RAM

If modern DRAM modules come in sizes much wider than a byte, why do people still use the word "byte" to describe how much DRAM they have? Convention. Habit. Rather than using a label that describes the electronic structure of RAM, common usage describes the *total capacity of RAM on a stick in bytes*. John has a single 8-GB stick of RAM on his motherboard, for example, and Sally has two 4-GB sticks. Both systems have a total of 8 GB of system RAM. That's what your clients care about. Having enough RAM makes their systems snappy and stable; not enough RAM means their systems run poorly. As a tech, you need to know more, of course, to pick the right RAM for many different types of computers.

Types of RAM

Development of newer, wider, and faster CPUs and MCCs motivates DRAM manufacturers to invent new DRAM technologies that deliver enough data at a single pop to optimize the flow of data into and out of the CPU.

SDRAM

Most modern systems use some form of *synchronous DRAM (SDRAM)*. SDRAM is still DRAM, but it is *synchronous*—tied to the system clock, just like the CPU and MCC, so the MCC knows when data is ready to be grabbed from SDRAM. This results in little wasted time.

SDRAM made its debut in 1996 on a stick called a *dual inline memory module (DIMM)*. The early SDRAM DIMMs came in a wide variety of pin sizes. The most common pin sizes found on desktops were the 168-pin variety. Laptop DIMMs came in 68-pin, 144-pin (see Figure 4-9), or 172-pin *micro-DIMM* packages, as well as the 72-pin, 144-pin, or 200-pin *small-outline DIMM (SO-DIMM)* form factors (see Figure 4-10). With the exception of the 32-bit 72-pin SO-DIMM, all these DIMM varieties delivered 64-bit-wide data to match the 64-bit data bus of every CPU since the original Pentium.

Figure 4-9
144-pin micro-DIMM (photo courtesy of Micron Technology, Inc.)

Figure 4-10
A (168-pin) DIMM above a (144-pin) SO-DIMM

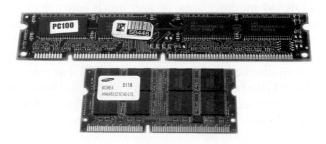

 EXAM TIP Some manufacturers (and CompTIA) drop the hyphen: *SODIMM*. You might see the RAM package spelled as SO-DIMM, SODIMM, or even SoDIMM.

To take advantage of SDRAM, you needed a PC designed to use SDRAM. If you had a system with slots for 168-pin DIMMs, for example, your system used SDRAM. A DIMM in any one of the DIMM slots could fill the 64-bit bus, so each slot was called a *bank*. You could install one, two, or more sticks and the system would work. Note that on laptops that used the 72-pin SO-DIMM, you needed to install two sticks of RAM to make a full bank, because each stick only provided half the bus width.

SDRAM was tied to the system clock, so its clock speed matched the frontside bus. Five clock speeds were commonly used on the early SDRAM systems: 66, 75, 83, 100, and 133 MHz. The RAM speed had to match or exceed the system speed, or the computer would be unstable or wouldn't work at all. These speeds were prefixed with a "PC" in the front, based on a standard forwarded by Intel, so SDRAM speeds were PC66 through PC133. For a Pentium III computer with a 100-MHz frontside bus, you needed to buy SDRAM DIMMs rated to handle it, such as PC100 or PC133.

DDR SDRAM

AMD and many major system and memory makers threw their support behind a new RAM technology, *double data rate SDRAM (DDR SDRAM)*. DDR SDRAM basically copied a proprietary memory solution developed by Rambus, doubling the throughput of SDRAM by making two processes for every clock cycle. This synchronized (pardon the pun) nicely with the Athlon and later AMD processors' double-pumped frontside bus. DDR SDRAM could not run as fast as RDRAM (DDR SDRAM's more expensive and less popular predecessor)—although relatively low frontside bus speeds made that a moot point—but cost only slightly more than regular SDRAM.

 NOTE   RDRAM, short for *Rambus DRAM* (named for the company that developed it, Rambus, Inc.), was initially introduced as a replacement for regular SDRAM. While faster than SDRAM, RDRAM was ultimately rejected by the industry due to delays in development and high prices compared to its predecessor.

DDR SDRAM for desktops come in 184-pin DIMMs. These DIMMs match 168-pin DIMMs in physical size but not in pin compatibility (see Figure 4-11). The slots for the two types of RAM appear similar as well but have different guide notches, so you can't insert either type of RAM into the other's slot. DDR SDRAM for laptops come in either 200-pin SO-DIMMs or 172-pin micro-DIMMs (see Figure 4-12).

 NOTE   Most techs drop some or all of the SDRAM part of DDR SDRAM when engaged in normal geekspeak. You'll hear the memory referred to as DDR, DDR RAM, and the weird hybrid, DDRAM.

Following the lead of AMD and other manufacturers, the PC industry adopted DDR SDRAM as the standard system RAM. In the summer of 2003, Intel relented and stopped producing motherboards and memory controllers that required RDRAM.

Figure 4-11
DDR SDRAM

Figure 4-12
172-pin DDR
SDRAM micro-
DIMM (photo
courtesy of
Kingston/Joint
Harvest)

One thing is sure about PC technologies: any good idea that can be copied will be copied. One of Rambus' best concepts was the *dual-channel architecture*—using two sticks of RDRAM together to increase throughput. Manufacturers released motherboards with MCCs that support dual-channel architecture using DDR SDRAM. Dual-channel DDR motherboards use regular DDR sticks, although manufacturers often sell RAM in matched pairs, branding them as dual-channel RAM.

Dual-channel DDR requires two identical sticks of DDR and they must snap into two paired slots. Many motherboards offer four slots (see Figure 4-13).

Figure 4-13
A motherboard
showing four
RAM slots. By
populating the
same-colored
slots with
identical RAM,
you can run in
dual-channel
mode.

SIM I've got a great Chapter 4 Challenge! sim on calculating RAM speeds at https//www.totalsem.com/110X. Check it out right now!

NOTE DDR SDRAM was improved in the form of DDR2. DDR2 was faster and more power efficient than the original DDR and found widespread adoption in the industry before eventually being replaced by DDR3, DDR4, and now DDR5. While no longer used in PCs, DDR2 modules can still sometimes be found in use as memory for some older devices such as printers.

1101

Current motherboards use one of three speeds of RAM, DDR3, DDR4, and DDR5. Let's start with DDR3.

DDR3

DDR3 boasts higher speeds, more efficient architecture, and around 30 percent lower power consumption than DDR2 RAM. Just like its predecessor, DDR3 uses a 240-pin DIMM, albeit one that is slotted differently to make it difficult for users to install the wrong RAM in their system without using a hammer (see Figure 4-14). DDR3 SO-DIMMs for portable computers have 204 pins. Neither fits into a DDR2 socket.

Figure 4-14
DDR2 DIMM on top of a DDR3 DIMM

DDR2
DDR3

 EXAM TIP The CompTIA 220-1101 exam loves to test you on pin counts with RAM! It will challenge your knowledge of the various RAM types including DDR3, DDR4, and DDR5. Make sure you know their individual characteristics and differences. DDR3 DIMMs have 240 pins, for example, and DDR3 SO-DIMMs have 204 pins.

In addition to having an impressive 8-bit buffer for bandwidth, some DDR3 (and later) modules also include a feature called *XMP*, or *Extreme Memory Profile*, that enables power users to overclock their RAM easily, boosting their already fast memory. DDR3 modules also use higher-density memory chips, up to 16-GB DDR3 modules. AMD's version of XMP is called *AMP*, for *AMD Memory Profile*.

 NOTE Do not confuse DDR*x* with GDDR*x*; the latter is a type of memory used solely in video cards (e.g., GDDR5). See Chapter 17 for the scoop on video-specific types of memory.

Some motherboards that support DDR3 also support features called *triple-channel memory architecture* or *quad-channel memory architecture*, which work a lot like dual-channel, but with three or four sticks of RAM instead of two. More recently, Intel and AMD systems have switched back to dual-channel, although there's plenty of systems out there using triple- or quad-channel architectures.

EXAM TIP Be sure you are familiar with single-, dual-, triple-, and quad-channel memory architectures.

Table 4-1 shows common DDR3 speeds. Note that DDR3 I/O speeds are quadruple the clock speeds, whereas DDR2 I/O speeds are only double the clock. This speed increase is due to the increased buffer size, which enables DDR3 to grab twice as much data every clock cycle as DDR2 can.

Core RAM Clock Speed	DDR I/O Speed	DDR3 Speed Rating	PC Speed Rating
100 MHz	400 MHz	DDR3-800	PC3-6400
133 MHz	533 MHz	DDR3-1066	PC3-8500
166 MHz	667 MHz	DDR3-1333	PC3-10667
200 MHz	800 MHz	DDR3-1600	PC3-12800
233 MHz	933 MHz	DDR3-1866	PC3-14900
266 MHz	1066 MHz	DDR3-2133	PC3-17000
300 MHz	1200 MHz	DDR3-2400	PC3-19200

Table 4-1 DDR3 Speeds

DDR4

DDR4 arrived on the scene in late 2014 with much fanfare and slow adoption, although it's the mainstream channel memory architecture now. DDR4 offers higher density and lower voltages than DDR3, and can handle faster data transfer rates. In theory, manufacturers could create DDR4 DIMMs up to 512 GB. DIMMS running DDR4 top out at 64 GB, compared to the 16 GB max of DDR3, but run at only 1.2 V. (There's a performance version that runs at 1.35 V and a low-voltage version at 1.05 V too.)

NOTE While DDR4 DIMMs generally won't exceed 64 GB, some manufacturers have pushed the envelope, creating individual DIMMs with up to a whopping 256 GB. These high-capacity DIMMs are almost exclusively intended for enterprise-level use.

DDR4 uses a 288-pin DIMM, so DDR4 DIMMs are not backward compatible with DDR3 slots. DDR4 SO-DIMMs have 260 pins that are not compatible with DDR3 204-pin SO-DIMM slots. Some motherboard manufacturers have released boards that offer support for both DDR3 and DDR4, by providing both slot types.

With DDR4, most techs have switched from bit rate to megatransfers per second (MT/s), a way to describe the number of data transfer operations happening at any given second. For DDR4, the number is pretty huge. To determine DDR4 bandwidth, multiply the clock speed in MHz by 8. The result is not only the bandwidth in MT/s, but also the DDR4 speed rating. To determine the PC speed rating, multiply the DDR4 speed rating by 8 again. Table 4-2 shows *some* DDR4 speeds and labels.

Clock Speed	Bandwidth	DDR4 Speed Rating	PC Speed Rating
200 MHz	1600 MT/s	DDR4-1600	PC4-12800
266 MHz	2133 MT/s	DDR4-2133	PC4-17000
300 MHz	2400 MT/s	DDR4-2400	PC4-19200
400 MHz	3200 MT/s	DDR4-3200	PC4-25600
[… *Skipping a whole bunch here in the middle …*]			
563 MHz	4500 MT/s	DDR4-4500	PC4-36000
575 MHz	4600 MT/s	DDR4-4600	PC4-36800
588 MHz	4700 MT/s	DDR4-4700	PC4-37600

Table 4-2   Standard DDR4 Varieties

DDR5

In 2017, channel memory architecture manufacturers began working on a successor to DDR4, and in 2020, they launched the first commercially available DDR5 DRAM chip. Much like previous upgrades to DDR, *DDR5* boasts the potential for doubled bandwidth, decreased power consumption, and quadrupled DIMM capacity. The highest currently available bandwidth at the time of writing is 7200 MT/s. Power consumption is more efficient as well, with the voltage per DIMM decreasing to 1.1 V from 1.2 V. Power management is handled by an onboard circuit known as a *power management integrated circuit*, or *PMIC*, as opposed to DDR4 that was managed by the motherboard. The range of available DIMM sizes has gone from a maximum of 64 GB all the way up to a whopping 256 GB. As with previous improvements in DDR technology, DDR5 is not backward compatible with DDR4. DDR5 DIMMs have 288 pins, like DDR4 (see Figure 4-15), while SO-DIMMs slightly increase the pin count from 260 to 262.

Figure 4-15
DDR5 (top) vs.
DDR4 (bottom)
pin comparison

To determine the bandwidth of DDR5 RAM, take the channel memory architecture clock speed in MHz and multiply by 8. This number is both the bandwidth in MT/s and the DDR5 speed rating. To find the PC speed rating, multiply the DDR5 speed rating by 8 again. Table 4-3 shows the bandwidth and speed ratings for some varieties of DDR5 RAM.

Clock Speed	Bandwidth	DDR5 Speed Rating	PC Speed Rating
300 MHz	4800 MT/s	DDR5-4800	PC5-38400
325 MHz	5200 MT/s	DDR5-5200	PC5-41600
350 MHz	5600 MT/s	DDR5-5600	PC5-44800
375 MHz	6000 MT/s	DDR5-6000	PC5-48000
400 MHz	6400 MT/s	DDR5-6400	PC5-51200
425 MHz	6800 MT/s	DDR5-6800	PC5-54400
450 MHz	7200 MT/s	DDR5-7200	PC5-57600

Table 4-3   Standard DDR5 Varieties

While DDR5 hasn't quite achieved a high enough bandwidth to double that of the fastest DDR4 DIMMs yet, it's important to remember DDR4 also took time to reach its maximum potential after its initial release. Channel memory architecture manufacturers announce new DDR5 breakthroughs fairly regularly, and although DDR5 has yet to be widely adopted, there is no reason to think that it won't eventually find the same success as its DDR forebears.

RAM Variations

Within each class of RAM, you'll find variations in packaging, speed, quality, and the capability to handle data with more or fewer errors. Higher-end systems often need higher-end RAM, so knowing these variations is of crucial importance to techs.

Double-Sided DIMMs

Every type of RAM stick comes in one of two types: *single-sided RAM* and *double-sided RAM*. As their name implies, single-sided sticks have chips on only one side of the stick. Double-sided sticks have chips on both sides (see Figure 4-16). Double-sided sticks are basically two sticks of RAM soldered onto one board. There's nothing wrong with double-sided RAM sticks other than the fact that some motherboards either can't use them or can only use them in certain ways—for example, only if you use a single stick and it goes into a certain slot.

Latency

Different types of RAM respond to electrical signals at varying rates. When the memory controller starts to grab a line of memory, for example, a slight delay occurs; think of it as the RAM getting off the couch. After the RAM sends out the requested line of memory, there's another slight delay before the memory controller can ask for another line—the RAM sat back down. The delay in RAM's response time is called its *latency*.

If two types of RAM have the same speed rating, RAM with a lower latency (such as CL17) is slightly faster than RAM with a higher latency (such as CL19) because it responds more quickly. The CL refers to clock cycle delays. The 17 means that the memory delays 17 clock cycles before delivering the requested data; the 19 means a 19-cycle delay. Because it's measured in clock cycles, CL is relative to the clock speed of

Figure 4-16
Double-sided
DDR SDRAM

the RAM—a 19-cycle delay takes up more real-world time at a lower clock speed than it will at a higher clock speed.

Back when DDR2 and DDR3 were the latest and greatest, these latency numbers were a big deal. Gamers and other PC enthusiasts paid a handsome premium for lower-latency RAM. (See Figure 4-17.) When DDR4 debuted, its relatively high CL numbers made enthusiasts question the memory companies, afraid it would be too slow. In real-world tests, DDR4's higher clock speeds result in latencies in line with the older DDR3. It's still worth looking at latency when you go memory shopping, but it's a lot less important than it used to be.

Figure 4-17
Ancient RAM
stick

NOTE Latency numbers reflect how many clicks of the system clock it takes before the RAM responds. If you speed up the system clock—say, from 200 MHz to 266 MHz—the same stick of RAM might take an extra click before it can respond. When you take RAM out of an older system and put it into a newer one, you might get a seemingly dead PC, even though the RAM fits in the DIMM slot. Many motherboards enable you to adjust the RAM timings manually. If yours does so, try raising the latency to give the slower RAM time to respond. See Chapter 5 to learn how to make these adjustments (and how to recover if you make a mistake).

From a tech's standpoint, you need to get the proper RAM for the system you're working on. If you put a high-latency stick in a motherboard set up for a low-latency stick, you'll get an unstable or completely dead PC. Check the motherboard manual or RAM manufacturer's Web site and get the quickest RAM the motherboard can handle, and you should be fine.

Today's PCs that need to watch for RAM errors use a special type of RAM called *error correction code RAM (ECC RAM)*. ECC is a major advance in error checking on DRAM. ECC detects and corrects any time a single bit is flipped, on-the-fly. It can detect but *not correct* a double-bit error. The checking and fixing come at a price, however, as ECC RAM is always slower than non-ECC RAM.

ECC DRAM comes in every DIMM package type and can lead to some odd-sounding numbers. You can find DDR3 (see Figure 4-18) or DDR4 RAM sticks, for example, that come in 240-pin, 72-bit versions. Similarly, you'll see 200-pin, 72-bit SO-DIMM format. The extra 8 bits beyond the 64-bit data stream are for the ECC. All DDR5 DIMMs have a variant of ECC built right into the chip itself, which protects against bit-flips in the chip. This differs from classic ECC, which protects against bit-flips in transit. DDR5 DIMMs are also available with or without classic ECC functionality.

Figure 4-18
Stick of ECC
DDR3 with nine
memory chips

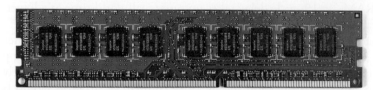

You might be tempted to say, "Gee, maybe I want to try this ECC RAM." Well, don't! To take advantage of ECC RAM, you need a motherboard designed to support ECC. Only expensive motherboards for high-end systems use ECC. The special-use-only nature of ECC makes it fairly rare in desktop systems. Plenty of techs with years of experience have never even seen ECC RAM.

 NOTE Some memory manufacturers call the technology *error checking and correction (ECC)*. Don't be thrown off if you see the phrase—it's the same thing, just a different marketing slant for error correction code.

Registered and Buffered Memory

When shopping for memory, especially for ECC memory, you are bound to come across the terms *registered RAM* or *buffered RAM*. Either term refers to a small register installed on some memory modules to act as a buffer between the DIMM and the memory controller. This little extra bit of circuitry helps compensate for electrical problems that crop up in systems with lots of memory modules, such as servers and big professional workstations.

The key thing to remember is that a motherboard will use either buffered or *unbuffered RAM* (that's typical consumer RAM), not both. If you insert the wrong module in a system you are upgrading, the worst that will happen is a blank screen and a lot of head scratching.

EXAM TIP   The CompTIA A+ 1101 exam covers DDR3, DDR4, and DDR5. You won't find DDR or DDR2 on the exam.

Working with RAM

Whenever people ask me what single hardware upgrade they can do to improve their system performance, I always tell them the same thing—add more RAM. Adding more RAM can improve overall system performance, processing speed, and stability—if you get it right. Botching the job can cause dramatic system instability, such as frequent, random crashes and reboots. Every tech needs to know how to install and upgrade system RAM of all types.

To get the desired results from a RAM upgrade, you must first determine if insufficient RAM is the cause of system problems. Second, you need to pick the proper RAM for the system. Finally, you must use good installation practices. Always store RAM sticks in antistatic packaging whenever they're not in use, and use strict ESD handling procedures. Like many other pieces of the PC, RAM is *very* sensitive to ESD and other technician abuse (see Figure 4-19).

Figure 4-19
Don't do this! Grabbing the contacts is a bad idea!

Do You Need More RAM?

Two symptoms point to the need for more RAM in a PC: general system sluggishness and excessive hard drive accessing. If programs take forever to load and running programs seem to stall and move more slowly than you would like, the problem could stem from insufficient RAM.

A friend with an older Windows system complained that her PC seemed snappy when she first got it but now takes a long time to do the things she wants to do with it, such as photograph retouching in Adobe Photoshop. Over the years, new applications and updates to her existing operating system and applications piled up until her system, with only 4 GB of RAM, was woefully insufficient for her tasks—she kept maxing out the RAM and thus the system slowed to a crawl. I replaced her single 4-GB stick with a pair of 8-GB sticks and suddenly she had the speedy workstation she desired.

Another common example of RAM-related sluggishness, and one that most of us have encountered at some point in time, is related to Web browser tabs. Over the years, Web browsers have become more complex, incorporating new features, plug-ins, and additional security measures, among other additions. As a result, they have become more resource intensive, and Web browsing habits that had no effect on your system's performance five years ago will bring that same system to its knees today. As with the previous example, adding more RAM will almost certainly fix the problem.

Excessive hard drive activity when you move between programs points to a need for more RAM. Every computer has the capability to make a portion of your hard drive look like RAM in case you run out of real RAM.

Virtual Memory

Computers use a portion of the hard drive (or solid-state drive) as an extension of system RAM called *virtual memory*. The operating system uses part of the available drive space to save a *page file* or *swap file*. When a computer starts running out of real RAM because you've loaded too many programs, the system swaps less-used programs from RAM to the page file, opening more space for programs currently active. All versions of Windows, macOS, and Linux use virtual memory. Let's use a typical Windows PC as an example of how paging works.

 EXAM TIP   While virtual memory is generally the terminology you'll hear out in the wild, you may see it referred to as *"virtual RAM"* on the exam. (See Chapter 22 for an entirely different type of virtual RAM.)

Let's assume you have a PC with 8 GB of RAM. Figure 4-20 shows the system RAM as a thermometer with gradients from 0 to 8 GB. As programs load, they take up RAM, and as more and more programs are loaded (labeled A, B, and C in the figure), more RAM is used.

Figure 4-20
A RAM thermometer showing that more programs take more RAM

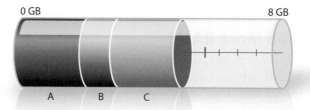

At a certain point, you won't have enough RAM to run any more programs (see Figure 4-21). Sure, you could close one or more programs to make room for yet another one, but you can't keep all of the programs running simultaneously. This is where virtual memory comes into play.

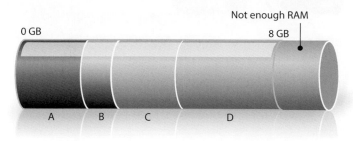

Figure 4-21   Not enough RAM to load program D

Windows' virtual memory starts by creating a page file that resides somewhere on your hard drive. The page file works like a temporary storage box. Windows removes running programs temporarily from RAM into the page file so other programs can load and run. If you have enough RAM to run all your programs, Windows does not need to use the page file—Windows brings the page file into play only when insufficient RAM is available to run all open programs.

 NOTE   Virtual memory is a fully automated process and does not require any user intervention. This is true of virtual memory in Windows, macOS, and Linux.

To load, Program D needs a certain amount of free RAM. Clearly, this requires unloading some other program (or programs) from RAM without actually closing any programs. Windows looks at all running programs—in this case A, B, and C—and decides which program is the least used. That program is then cut out of or swapped from RAM and copied into the page file. In this case, Windows has chosen Program B (see Figure 4-22). Unloading Program B from RAM provides enough RAM to load Program D (see Figure 4-23).

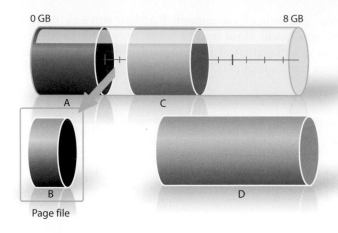

Figure 4-22 Program B being unloaded from channel memory architecture

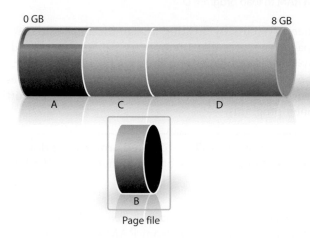

Figure 4-23 Program B stored in the page file, making room for Program D

It is important to understand that none of this activity is visible on the screen. Program B's window is still visible, along with those of all the other running programs. Nothing tells the user that Program B is no longer in RAM (see Figure 4-24).

So what happens if you click on Program B's window to bring it to the front? The program can't actually run from the page file; it must be loaded back into RAM. First, Windows decides which program must be removed from RAM, and this time Windows chooses Program C (see Figure 4-25). Then it loads Program B into RAM (see Figure 4-26).

Swapping programs to and from the page file and RAM takes time. Although no visual clues suggest that a swap is taking place, the machine slows down quite noticeably as Windows performs the swaps. Page files are a crucial aspect of Windows operation.

Figure 4-24
You can't tell whether a program is swapped or not.

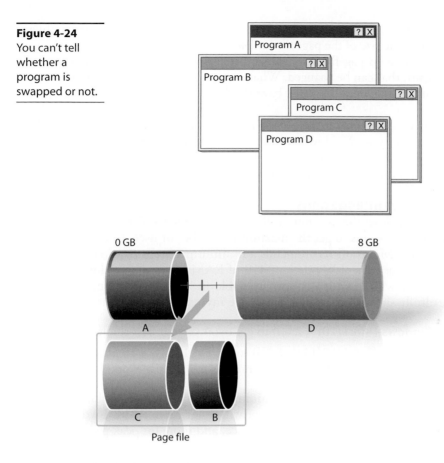

Figure 4-25 Program C is swapped to the page file.

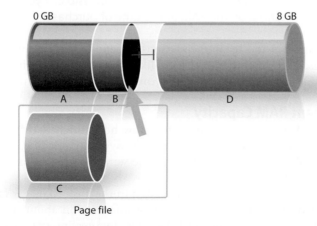

Figure 4-26 Program B is swapped back into RAM.

Windows handles page files automatically, but occasionally you'll run into problems and need to change the size of the page file or delete it and let Windows re-create it automatically. The page file is pagefile.sys. You can often find it in the root directory of the C: drive, but again, that can be changed. Wherever it is, the page file is a hidden system file, which means in practice that you'll have to play with your folder-viewing options to see it.

If Windows needs to access the page file too frequently, you will notice the hard drive access LED going crazy as Windows rushes to move programs between RAM and the page file in a process called *disk thrashing*. Windows uses the page file all the time, but excessive disk thrashing suggests that you need more RAM.

System RAM Recommendations

Microsoft sets very low the minimum RAM requirements listed for the various Windows operating systems to get the maximum number of users to upgrade or convert, and that's fine. Microsoft recommends a minimum system requirement of 1 GB of RAM for 32-bit versions of Windows, 2 GB of RAM for 64-bit versions, and 4 GB of RAM for Windows 11, which is only available in a 64-bit version. I think that results in dreadfully sluggish computers. Here are my recommendations:

- **32-bit Windows (8/8.1/10)** 2 GB to get by; 4 GB for best results
- **64-bit Windows (8/8.1/10/11)** 8 GB to get by; 16 GB for a solid machine; 32+ GB for any machine doing serious, processor-intensive work

The latest versions of macOS require a minimum of 4 GB of RAM. Like Windows, however, the 64-bit-only OS does much better with a lot more RAM. I would go with 8 GB at a minimum, 16 GB for good performance, and more for peak performance.

 NOTE Beware sealed systems! Almost all smartphones and tablets are sealed. Today many desktop and laptop systems—in the past easily upgraded by a good tech—are sealed, making upgrades impossible. If you get a sealed system, don't scrimp on the RAM at the time of purchase!

Linux RAM requirements and recommendations depend entirely on which distribution (distro) is being used. The mainstream distros, like Ubuntu, have requirements similar to Windows and macOS, but many distros get by on very minimal system requirements.

Determining Current RAM Capacity

Before you go get RAM, you obviously need to know how much RAM you currently have in your PC. Windows displays this amount in the System Control Panel applet (see Figure 4-27). You can also access the screen with the WINDOWS-PAUSE/BREAK keystroke combination on standard keyboards.

Windows also includes the handy Performance tab in the Task Manager (as shown in Figure 4-28). The Performance tab includes a lot of information about the amount of RAM being used by your PC. Access the Task Manager by pressing CTRL-SHIFT-ESC and selecting the Performance tab.

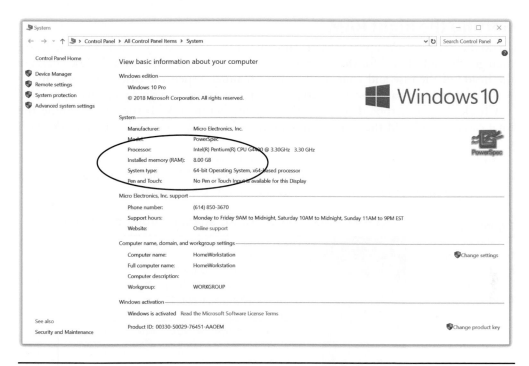

Figure 4-27 Mike's Windows 10 system only has 8 GB of RAM.

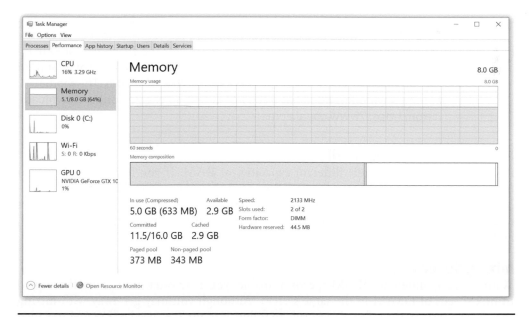

Figure 4-28 Performance tab in Windows 10 Task Manager

Getting the Right RAM

To do the perfect RAM upgrade, determine the optimum capacity of RAM to install and then get the right RAM for the motherboard. Your first two stops toward these goals are the inside of the case and your motherboard manual. Open the case to see how many sticks of RAM you have installed currently and how many free slots you have open.

Check the motherboard book or RAM manufacturer's Web site to determine the total capacity of RAM the system can handle and what specific technology works with your system.

You can't put DDR4 into a system that can only handle DDR3 SDRAM, after all, and it won't do you much good to install a pair of 8-GB DIMMs when your system tops out at 8 GB. Figure 4-29 shows the RAM limits for an ASUS-brand motherboard.

Figure 4-29
The motherboard book shows how much RAM the motherboard will handle.

ROG RAMPAGE VI EXTREME specifications summary

CPU	Intel® Socket 2066 for Intel® Core™ X-Series Processor 79xx, 78xx Series Supports 14nm CPU Supports Intel® Virtual RAID on CPU (VROC)* Supports Intel® Turbo Boost Max Technology 3.0* * **Support of these features depends on the CPU types.**
Chipset	Intel® X299 Chipset
Memory	8 x DIMM, max. 128GB, DDR4 4200+(O.C.)* / 4000(O.C.)* / 3866(O.C.)* / 3600(O.C.)* / 3333(O.C.)* / 3300(O.C.)* / 3200(O.C.)* / 3000(O.C.)* / 2800(O.C.)* / 2666(O.C.)* / 2400(O.C.)* / 2133 MHz, non-ECC, un- buffered memory Quad channel memory architecture

NOTE The freeware CPU-Z program tells you the total number of slots on your motherboard, the number of slots used, and the exact type of RAM in each slot—very handy. CPU-Z not only determines the latency of your RAM but also lists the latency at a variety of motherboard speeds. The media accompanying this book has a copy of CPU-Z, so check it out or download it from https://www.cpuid.com.

Mix and Match at Your Peril

All motherboards can handle different capacities of RAM. If you have three slots, you may put a 4-GB stick in one and an 8-GB stick in the other with a high chance of success. To ensure maximum stability in a system, however, shoot for as close as you can get to uniformity of RAM. Choose RAM sticks that match in technology, capacity, speed, and latency (CL).

Mixing Speeds

With so many different DRAM speeds available, you may often find yourself tempted to mix speeds of DRAM in the same system. Although you may get away with mixing speeds on a system, the safest, easiest rule to follow is to use the speed of DRAM specified in the motherboard book, and make sure that every piece of DRAM runs at that speed.

In a worst-case scenario, mixing DRAM speeds can cause the system to lock up every few seconds or every few minutes. You might also get some data corruption. Mixing speeds sometimes works fine, but don't do your tax return on a machine with mixed DRAM speeds until the system has proven to be stable for a few days. The important thing to note here is that you won't break anything, other than possibly data, by experimenting.

Okay, I have mentioned enough disclaimers. Modern motherboards provide some flexibility regarding DRAM speeds and mixing. First, you can use DRAM that is faster than the motherboard specifies. For example, if the system needs PC-19200 DDR4, you may put in PC-25600 DDR4 and it should work fine. Faster DRAM is not going to make the system run any faster, however, so don't look for any system improvement.

Second, you can sometimes get away with putting one speed of DRAM in one bank and another speed in another bank, as long as all the speeds are as fast as or faster than the speed specified by the motherboard. Don't bother trying to put different-speed DRAM sticks in the same bank with a motherboard that uses dual-channel DDR.

Installing DIMMs

Installing DRAM is so easy that it's one of the very few jobs I recommend to non-techie folks. First, attach an antistatic wrist strap or touch some bare metal on the power supply to ground yourself and avoid ESD. Then swing the side tabs on the RAM slots down from the upright position. Pick up a stick of RAM—don't touch those contacts—and line up the notch or notches with the raised portion(s) of the DIMM socket (see Figure 4-30). A good hard push down is usually all you need to ensure a solid connection. Make sure that the DIMM snaps into position to show it is completely seated. Also, notice that the one or two side tabs move in to reflect a tight connection.

Figure 4-30
Inserting a DIMM

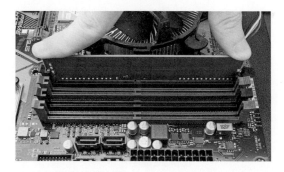

Your motherboard should detect and automatically set up any DIMM you install, assuming you have the right RAM for the system, using a technology called *serial presence detect (SPD)*. RAM makers add a handy chip to modern sticks called the SPD chip (see Figure 4-31). The SPD chip stores all the information about your DRAM, including size, speed, ECC or non-ECC, registered or unregistered, and other more technical bits of information.

Figure 4-31
SPD chip on
a stick

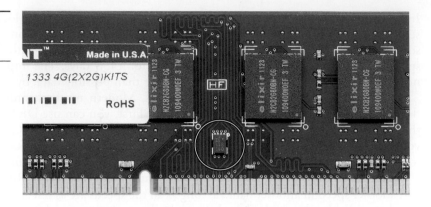

When a PC boots, it queries the SPD chip so that the MCC knows how much RAM is on the stick, how fast it runs, and other information. Any program can query the SPD chip. Take a look at Figure 4-32 with the results of the popular CPU-Z program showing RAM information from the SPD chip.

Figure 4-32
CPU-Z showing
RAM information

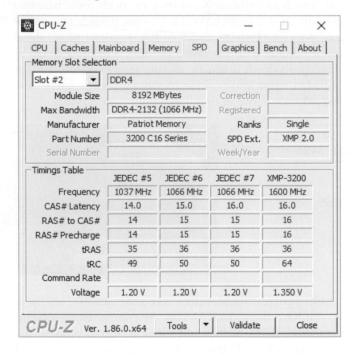

All new systems count on SPD to set the RAM timings properly for your system when it boots. If you add a RAM stick with a bad SPD chip, you'll get a POST error message and the system will not boot. You can't fix a broken SPD chip; you just buy a new stick of RAM.

Installing SO-DIMMs in Laptops

It wasn't that long ago that adding RAM to a laptop was either impossible or required you to send the system back to the manufacturer. Long ago, laptop makers used expensive, proprietary, custom-made RAM packages that were hard to handle. Wide acceptance of SO-DIMMs solved these problems for a time—until ultra-thin laptops started turning up with soldered-on RAM. Most larger laptops still provide relatively convenient access to their SO-DIMMs, making it easy to add or replace RAM.

Access to RAM usually requires removing a panel or lifting up the keyboard—the procedure varies among laptop manufacturers. Figure 4-33 shows a typical laptop RAM access panel. You can slide the panel off to reveal the SO-DIMMs. Slide the pins into position and snap the SO-DIMM down into the retaining clips (see Figure 4-34).

Figure 4-33
A RAM access panel on a laptop

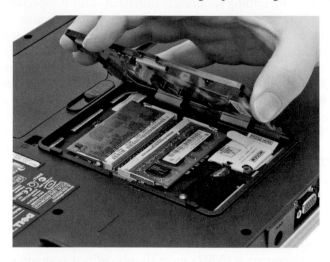

Figure 4-34
Snapping in a SO-DIMM

Before doing any work on a laptop, turn the system off, disconnect it from the AC wall socket, and remove all batteries. If you are working on a laptop with a built-in battery, consult the service manual and look for a *service mode*, or similarly named, procedure. Enabling this mode will cut off power from the installed battery, making the laptop safe to work on. Finally, as always, use an antistatic wrist strap to keep ESD from damaging the system.

Troubleshooting RAM

"Memory" errors show up in a variety of ways on modern systems, including system lockups, page faults, and other error screens. These errors can indicate bad RAM but often point to something completely unrelated. This is especially true with intermittent problems. Techs need to recognize these errors and determine which part of the system caused the memory error. Then they need to follow up with various testing methods.

System lockups and page faults (they often go hand in hand) in Windows can indicate a problem with RAM. A system lockup is when the computer stops functioning. A *page fault* is a milder error that can be caused by memory issues but not necessarily system RAM problems. Certainly page faults *look* like RAM issues because Windows generates frightening error messages filled with long strings of hexadecimal digits, such as "KRNL386 caused a page fault at 03F2:25A003BC." Just because the error message contains a memory address, however, does not mean that you have a problem with your RAM. Write down the address. If it repeats in later error messages, you probably have a bad RAM stick. If Windows displays different memory locations, you need to look elsewhere for the culprit.

Every once in a while, something potentially catastrophic happens within the PC, some little electron hits the big red panic button, and the operating system has to shut down certain functions before it can save data. This panic button inside the PC is called a *non-maskable interrupt (NMI),* more simply defined as an interruption the CPU cannot ignore. An NMI manifests as a *proprietary crash screen*. In Windows 10, for example, the crash screen is what techs call the *blue screen of death (BSoD)*—a bright blue screen with a scary-sounding error message on it (see Figure 4-35).

Windows 10/11 display a blue screen with a sad face and the words to the effect of Windows has a problem. Restart the machine. A macOS machine might display a spinning rainbow wheel sometimes called the *spinning pinwheel of death (SPoD)* or, more likely, will simply restart.

Bad RAM sometimes triggers an NMI, although often the culprit lies with buggy programming or clashing code. The BSoD/SPoD varies across Windows and macOS versions and operating systems, and it would require a much lengthier tome than this one to cover all the variations. Suffice it to say that RAM *could* be the problem when that delightful blue screen or pinwheel appears.

Figure 4-35
Blue screen
of death

Finally, intermittent memory errors can come from a variety of sources, including a dying power supply, electrical interference, buggy applications, buggy hardware, and so on. These errors show up as lockups, general protection faults, and page faults, but they never have the same address or happen with the same applications. I always check the power supply first.

Once you discover that you may have a RAM problem, you have a couple of options. First, several companies manufacture hardware RAM-testing devices. Second, you can use the method I use—*replace and pray*. Open the system case and replace each stick, one at a time, with a known-good replacement stick. (You have one of those lying around, don't you?) This method, although potentially time-consuming, certainly works. With PC prices as low as they are now, you could simply replace the whole system for less than the price of a dedicated RAM tester.

Third, you could run a software-based tester on the RAM. Because you have to load a software tester into the memory it's about to scan, there's always a small chance that simply starting the software RAM tester might cause an error. Still, you can find some pretty good free ones out there. Windows 7 and later include the *Windows Memory Diagnostic* tool, which can automatically scan your computer's RAM when you encounter a problem. If you're using another OS, my favorite tool is the open source Memtest86+ (https://www.memtest.org). The Memtest86+ software exhaustively checks your RAM and reports bad RAM when it finds it (see Figure 4-36).

 NOTE A *general protection fault (GPF)* is an error that can cause an application to crash. Often GPFs are caused by programs stepping on each other's toes. Chapter 16 goes into more detail on GPFs and other Windows errors.

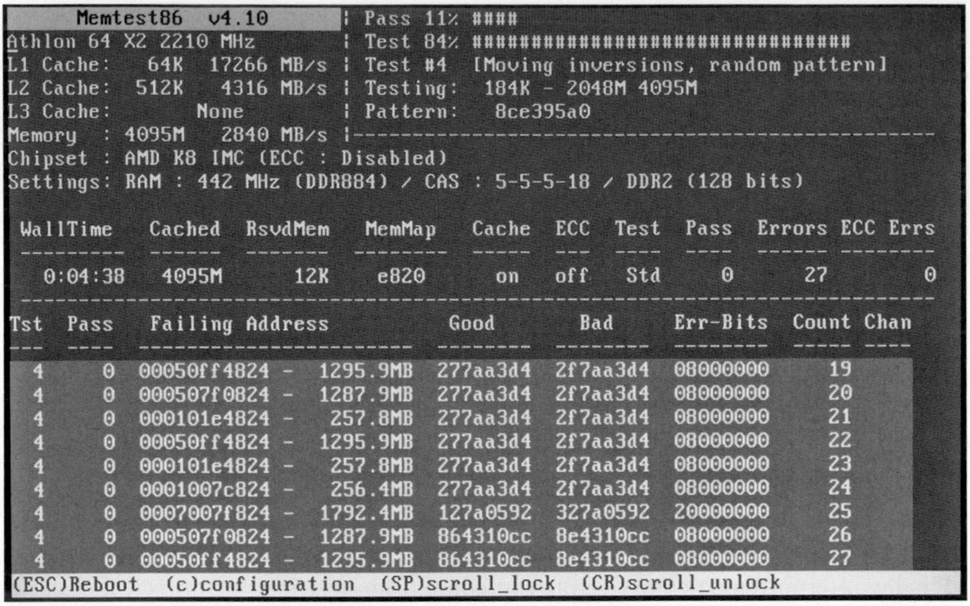

```
     Memtest86   v4.10    ┊ Pass 11% ####
Athlon 64 X2 2210 MHz     ┊ Test 84% ###################################
L1 Cache:     64K  17266 MB/s ┊ Test #4  [Moving inversions, random pattern]
L2 Cache:  512K   4316 MB/s ┊ Testing:  184K - 2048M 4095M
L3 Cache:        None     ┊ Pattern:    8ce395a0
Memory  : 4095M   2840 MB/s ┊--------------------------------------------
Chipset : AMD K8 IMC (ECC : Disabled)
Settings: RAM : 442 MHz (DDR884) / CAS : 5-5-5-18 / DDR2 (128 bits)

 WallTime   Cached  RsvdMem   MemMap   Cache  ECC  Test  Pass  Errors ECC Errs
 --------   ------  -------   ------   -----  ---  ----  ----  ------ -------
   0:04:38   4095M     12K     e820     on   off  Std    0     27        0

Tst  Pass   Failing Address        Good        Bad    Err-Bits  Count Chan
---  ----   ---------------        ----        ---    --------  ----- ----
 4    0    00050ff4824 -  1295.9MB  277aa3d4  2f7aa3d4  08000000   19
 4    0    000507f0824 -  1287.9MB  277aa3d4  2f7aa3d4  08000000   20
 4    0    000101e4824 -   257.8MB  277aa3d4  2f7aa3d4  08000000   21
 4    0    00050ff4824 -  1295.9MB  277aa3d4  2f7aa3d4  08000000   22
 4    0    000101e4824 -   257.8MB  277aa3d4  2f7aa3d4  08000000   23
 4    0    0001007c824 -   256.4MB  277aa3d4  2f7aa3d4  08000000   24
 4    0    0007007f824 -  1792.4MB  127a0592  327a0592  20000000   25
 4    0    000507f0824 -  1287.9MB  864310cc  8e4310cc  08000000   26
 4    0    00050ff4824 -  1295.9MB  864310cc  8e4310cc  08000000   27
(ESC)Reboot   (c)configuration   (SP)scroll_lock   (CR)scroll_unlock
```

Figure 4-36   Memtest86+ detecting failing RAM

Chapter Review

Questions

1. Steve adds a second 8-GB 288-pin DIMM to his PC, which should bring the total RAM in the system up to 16 GB. The PC has an Intel Core i7 4-GHz processor and four 288-pin DIMM slots on the motherboard. When he turns on the PC, however, only 8 GB of RAM shows up in Windows Settings app. Which of the following is most likely to be the problem?

   A. Steve failed to seat the RAM properly.

   B. Steve put DDR4 in a DDR3 slot.

   C. The CPU cannot handle 16 GB of RAM.

   D. The motherboard can use only one RAM slot at a time.

2. Scott wants to add 8 GB of PC3-12800 DDR3 to an aging but still useful desktop system. The system has a 200-MHz motherboard and currently has 4 GB of non-ECC DDR3 RAM in the system. What else does he need to know before installing?

   A. What speed of RAM he needs

   B. What type of RAM he needs

   C. How many pins the RAM has

   D. If the system can handle that much RAM

3. What is the primary reason that DDR4 RAM is faster than DDR3 RAM?

   A. The core speed of the DDR4 RAM chips is faster.

   B. The input/output speed of the DDR4 RAM is faster.

   C. DDR3 RAM is dual-channel and DDR4 RAM is quad-channel.

   D. DDR3 RAM uses 240-pin DIMMs and DDR4 uses 288-pin DIMMs.

4. What is the term for the delay in the RAM's response to a request from the MCC?

   A. Variance

   B. MCC gap

   C. Latency

   D. Fetch interval

5. How does an NMI manifest on a macOS system?

   A. Blue screen of death.

   B. Spinning pinwheel of death.

   C. Interrupt of death.

   D. NMIs only happen on Windows systems.

6. Silas has an AMD-based motherboard with two sticks of DDR3 RAM installed in two of the three RAM slots, for a total of 8 GB of system memory. When he runs CPU-Z to test the system, he notices that the software claims he's running single-channel memory. What could be the problem? (Select the best answer.)

   A. His motherboard only supports single-channel memory.

   B. His motherboard only supports dual-channel memory with DDR2 RAM, not DDR3.

   C. He needs to install a third RAM stick to enable dual-channel memory.

   D. He needs to move one of the installed sticks to a different slot to activate dual-channel memory.

7. Which of the following Control Panel applets will display the amount of RAM in your PC?

   A. System

   B. Devices and Printers

   C. Device Manager

   D. Action Center

8. What is the best way to determine the total capacity and specific type of RAM your system can handle?

   A. Check the motherboard book.

   B. Open the case and inspect the RAM.

   C. Check the Device Manager.

   D. Check the System utility in the Control Panel.

9. Gregor installed a third stick of known-good RAM into his Core i7 system, bringing the total amount of RAM up to 12 GB. Within a few days, though, he started having random lockups and reboots, especially when doing memory-intensive tasks such as gaming. What is most likely the problem?

   A. Gregor installed DDR2 RAM into a DDR3 system.

   B. Gregor installed DDR3 RAM into a DDR4 system.

   C. Gregor installed RAM that didn't match the speed or quality of the RAM in the system.

   D. Gregor installed RAM that exceeded the speed of the RAM in the system.

10. Cindy installed a second stick of DDR4 RAM into her Core i5 system, bringing the total system up to 16 GB. Within a short period of time, though, she begin experiencing blue screens of death. What could the problem be?

    A. She installed faulty RAM.

    B. The motherboard could only handle 12 GB of RAM.

    C. The motherboard needed dual-channel RAM.

    D. There is no problem. Windows always does this initially but gets better after crashing a few times.

Answers

1. **A.** Steve failed to seat the RAM properly.

2. **D.** Scott needs to know if the system can handle that much RAM.

3. **B.** The input/output speed of DDR4 RAM is faster than that of DDR3 RAM (although the latency is higher).

4. **C.** Latency is the term for the delay in the RAM's response to a request from the MCC.

5. **B.** A non-maskable interrupt on a macOS system often results in the spinning pinwheel of death.

6. **D.** Motherboards can be tricky and require you to install RAM in the proper slots to enable dual-channel memory access. In this case, Silas should move one of the installed sticks to a different slot to activate dual-channel memory architecture. (And he should check the motherboard manual for the proper slots.)

7. **A.** You can use the System applet to see how much RAM is currently in your PC.

8. **A.** The best way to determine the total capacity and specific type of RAM your system can handle is to check the motherboard book.

9. **C.** Most likely, Gregor installed RAM that didn't match the speed or quality of the RAM in the system.

10. **A.** If you have no problems with a system and then experience problems after installing something new, chances are the something new is at fault.

Firmware

In this chapter, you will learn how to
- Define and explain the function of firmware, UEFI, BIOS, CMOS, ROM
- Distinguish among various system setup utility options
- Troubleshoot using the power-on self-test (POST)
- Maintain BIOS/UEFI settings

In Chapter 3 you saw how the address bus and data bus connect RAM to the CPU via the memory controller to run programs and transfer data. Assuming you apply power in the right places, you don't need anything else to make a simple computer. The only problem with such a simple computer is that it would bore you to death—there's no way to do anything with it! A PC needs devices such as keyboards and mice to provide input, and output devices such as monitors and speakers to communicate the current state of the running programs to you. A computer also needs permanent storage devices, such as solid-state drives, to store programs and data when you turn off the computer.

This chapter discusses in detail the software that controls a PC at its core. We'll start with a couple of sections on why and how it all works, and then we'll look at hardware and self-testing circuits. The chapter finishes with the finer points of maintaining this essential programming and hardware.

1101

We Need to Talk

For a keyboard or a monitor or a hard drive to work with a CPU, they must communicate via some kind of physical connection. More than that, these peripherals (usually) can't connect directly to the CPU. This communication requires a *controller*, a chip that connects the device to the CPU (see Figure 5-1).

Figure 5-1
A controller
chip acts as
an interface.

Getting the CPU to communicate with a controller starts with a physical interconnection—a communication bus (that means *wires*) that enables the CPU to send commands to and from devices. To make this connection, let's extend the data bus and the address bus throughout the motherboard, connecting all of the computer's controllers to the CPU (see Figure 5-2).

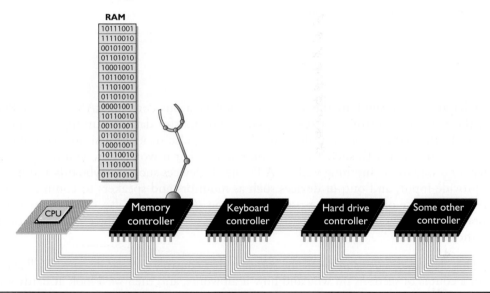

Figure 5-2 Data bus and address bus extended

Early motherboards were covered in controller chips. Figure 5-3 shows a very early motherboard, absolutely packed with controller chips (as well as many other chips).

Starting around 1990, chip manufacturers began to combine multiple controller chips into specifically designed *chipsets* to reduce chip count and to standardize communication between the CPU and devices. Early chipsets such as the Intel 430VX shown in Figure 5-4 consisted of two paired chips called the *northbridge* and *southbridge*.

Chipsets were in pairs for many years, roughly from 1990 to around 2010. Today's CPUs have controllers built into the CPU itself, such as the memory and display controllers. With so many chipset functions now built into the CPU, almost all chipsets are now a single chip—Intel's name for this chip is *Platform Controller Hub (PCH)*.

Figure 5-3
Early motherboard, loaded with controller chips

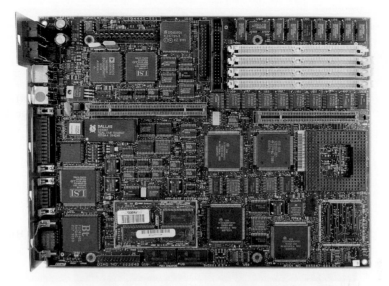

Figure 5-4
Ancient 430VX chipset showing northbridge and southbridge

Figure 5-5 shows where the CPU and PCH are located on an Intel motherboard. AMD (and most of the tech industry) still refers to the single chip as the chipset, even though it's no longer a "set" of chips.

NOTE Even though chipsets are often single-chip solutions, it's common tech speak to say "chipset" (even though "set" implies more than one chip).

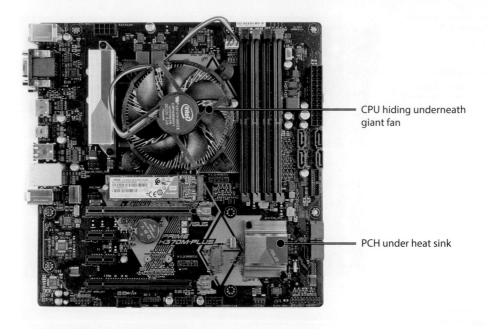

CPU hiding underneath giant fan

PCH under heat sink

Figure 5-5 Intel CPU and PCH

The chipset extends the data bus to every device on the PC. The CPU uses the data bus to move data to and from all the devices of the PC. Data constantly flows on the data bus among the CPU, chipset, RAM, and other devices on the PC (see Figure 5-6).

The concept that the CPU uses the address bus to talk to the devices isn't difficult to fathom, but how does the CPU know what to say to them? How does it know, for example,

Figure 5-6
Everything
connecting

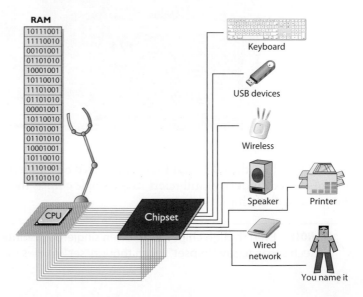

all the patterns of ones and zeros to place on the address bus to tell the hard drive it needs to send a file? Let's look at the interaction between the keyboard and CPU for insight into this process.

Talking to the Keyboard

Let's step back a moment and consider a world without chipsets, where every device had its own controller. The keyboard provides a great example of how the buses and support programming help the CPU get the job done. In early computers, the keyboard connected to the data bus via a special chip known as the *keyboard controller*. Don't bother looking for this chip on your motherboard—chipsets long ago replaced keyboard controller chips.

Even though dedicated keyboard controller chips no longer exist, the way the keyboard controller functions with the CPU has changed only a small amount in the past decades, making it a perfect tool to illustrate how the CPU talks to a device.

NOTE Techs commonly talk about various functions of the chipset as if those functions were still handled by discrete chips. You'll hear about memory controllers, keyboard controllers, drive controllers, USB controllers, and so on, even though all these controllers are now combined into the CPU or chipset.

The keyboard controller was one of the last single-function chips to be absorbed into the chipset. Figure 5-7 shows a typical keyboard controller from those days. Electronically, it looked like Figure 5-8.

Figure 5-7
A dedicated keyboard chip on a pre-1990 motherboard

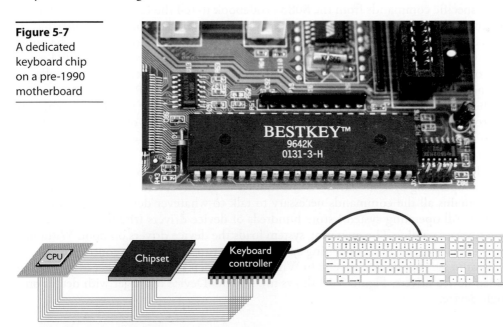

Figure 5-8 Electronic view of the keyboard controller

Every time you press a key on your keyboard, a scanning chip in the keyboard notices which key you pressed. Then the scanner sends a coded pattern of ones and zeros—called the *scan code*—to the keyboard controller. Every key on your keyboard has a unique scan code. The keyboard controller stores the scan code in its own register. Does it surprise you that the lowly keyboard controller has a register similar to a CPU? Lots of chips have registers—not just CPUs (see Figure 5-9).

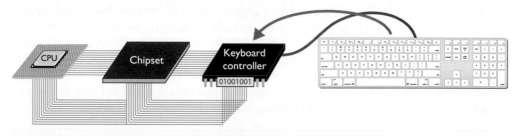

Figure 5-9   Scan code stored in keyboard controller's register

How does the CPU get the scan code out of the keyboard controller? While we're at it, how does the CPU tell the keyboard to type capital letters if CAPS LOCK is on or to turn the NUM LOCK LED (light-emitting diode) on and off, to mention just a few other jobs the keyboard needs to do for the system? The point is that the keyboard controller must be able to respond to multiple commands, not just one.

The keyboard controller accepts commands exactly as you saw the CPU accept commands in Chapter 3. Remember when you added 2 to 3 with the 8088? You had to use specific commands from the 8088's codebook to tell the CPU to do the addition and then place the answer on the external data bus. The keyboard controller has its own codebook—much simpler than any CPU's codebook, but conceptually the same. If the CPU wants to know what key was last pressed on the keyboard, the CPU needs to know the command (or series of commands) that orders the keyboard controller to put the scan code of the letter on the external data bus so the CPU can read it.

The CPU doesn't magically or otherwise automatically know how to talk with any controller; it needs some sort of programming—a codebook of commands, ready to go in memory, to speak to that particular controller. We call this codebook a *device driver*.

A device driver is code, sitting on the PC's mass storage, that's loaded into memory as your operating system starts. As mentioned above, a device driver is a codebook that contains all the commands necessary to talk to whatever device it was written to support. All operating systems store hundreds of device drivers (the number of device drivers varies wildly). The operating system loads the device drivers on boot. Without a correct device driver, your operating system cannot run that specific controller.

Want to see your device drivers? In Windows you open Device Manager to see all your loaded device drivers. Figure 5-10 shows my system's Device Manager with details on a single device.

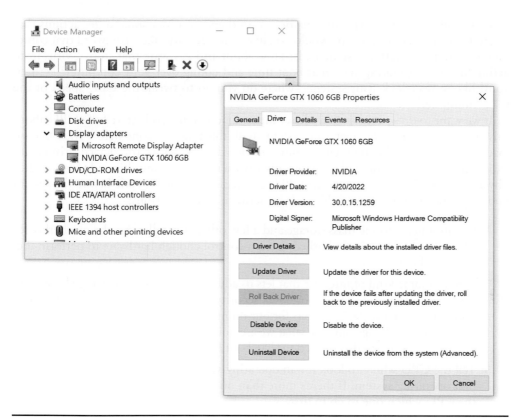

Figure 5-10   Windows device drivers seen from the Device Manager utility

Whoa. Wait! We got a HUGE problem here! How can your operating system boot up and load device drivers if the system doesn't even know how to talk to the mass storage where the operating system and device drivers are stored (see Figure 5-11)? Even if the operating system could somehow magically not need a device driver, how do you tell the system where the operating system is located to load it? What if you like to install multiple operating systems—how does the system know which operating system to start?

Figure 5-11
How do you
talk to a device
without a device
driver?

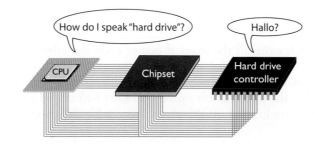

Forget all about the device drivers for a second and consider some other actions that might be really nice at boot-up. Would you like some security, like a password that comes even before the operating system loads? How about anti-malware that stops a virus from acting like your operating system at boot time and taking over your computer? Perhaps you'd like to overclock your system—where do you go to tweak the CPU speed or the CPU multiplier?

If we want to do actions such as these, then we need some code to tell the CPU about this. This code isn't in the operating system, as all this must be done before the OS even loads! We need to add some code, some "device drivers before the device drivers," to make all these actions take place. Not only do we need to create this code, we need to physically place it somewhere so the CPU can access and run the code before the system boots up. To sum up, we need this code to perform three functions:

1. Communicate to the mass storage and a few other controllers on the motherboard. Once that function is established, we can control enough hardware to perform the next two items.

2. Develop some kind of interface that lets us add to, configure, and change boot-time features of our systems, like boot order, security, and much more. We'll need some more of those basic device drivers for our monitor, keyboard, and maybe mouse to input those changes and see what we are doing. We might even need network drivers if we want to do cool actions like boot from another host on a network.

3. Tell the CPU where to look for an operating system so the system can boot into that operating system. If there's more than one bootable device, we need to tell the CPU which one to go to first.

(There are a lot more functions than just those three, but these will get us started on our learning path.)

Luckily for us, the code to do these functions exists on every computer—and has been since the first PCs back in the early 1980s. The code exists on your motherboard on a chip. OK, but what chip technology should the motherboard use? RAM won't work, because all the data is erased every time we turn off the computer. We cannot use a hard drive, as that requires a driver. We need some type of permanent program storage device that does not depend on other peripherals to work. It must plug directly into the address/system bus so the CPU can talk to it. And we need that storage device to sit on the motherboard. What we need is called ROM.

ROM

Motherboards store all the magical bits of code described in the previous section on a special type of device called a *read-only memory (ROM)* chip. A ROM chip stores code exactly like RAM, but with two important differences. First, ROM chips are *nonvolatile*, meaning that the information stored on ROM isn't erased when the computer is turned off. Second, traditional ROM chips are read-only, meaning that once you store a program on one, you can't change it unless you go through a specific reprogramming process. There are many types of ROM, but for the past 20 years or so, all motherboards use a type of ROM called *flash ROM*. Figure 5-12 shows a typical flash ROM chip on a motherboard.

Figure 5-12
Typical flash ROM

 EXAM TIP   Programs stored on ROM chips—flash or any other kind of ROM chip—are known collectively as *firmware*, as opposed to programs stored on dynamic media, which are collectively called *software*.

Great! We now have a flash ROM chip sitting on every motherboard. Now we need to load it with firmware to solve the three functions described in the previous section. Enter something amazing called UEFI!

UEFI

Modern systems use firmware programming called the *Unified Extensible Firmware Interface (UEFI)*. UEFI is a programming standard that defines how we configure utilities that every system needs: device drivers, boot support, and system setup—all on the motherboard's flash ROM chip. UEFI essentially provides the programming that enables the CPU to communicate with other hardware. You've seen UEFI in action during a system's boot, although it's easily missed if you're not paying attention (see Figure 5-13).

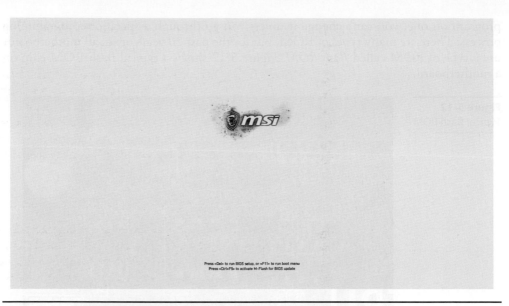

Press <Del> to run BIOS setup, or <F11> to run boot menu
Press <Ctrl+F5> to activate M-Flash for BIOS update

Figure 5-13 UEFI data appearing during the boot-up of a desktop system.

The correct term for UEFI "device drivers" is *services*. UEFI provides services to support most of the hardware on your system. These services don't support as many features as true device drivers, but they are good enough to support configuring and booting a system.

NOTE There's no standardization on how to pronounce UEFI, by the way. Microsoft initializes it: "U-E-F-I." Others say "you-fee" or "you-fie." For a job interview, stick with initializing it. You can't go wrong that way.

BIOS

All current systems use UEFI and have since around 2010. However, before UEFI was invented these functions were known as BIOS (basic input/output system). BIOS was very ancient, originally designed to be run on the Intel 8088 CPU back in 1981. System makers are very conservative, so BIOS hung on long after everything else on a typical PC was upgraded and improved. UEFI has completely replaced BIOS but the term BIOS is still out there and very commonly used. For example, most techs continue to call the system's UEFI the BIOS. Maybe PC techs are also conservative? Bottom line? Be ready to use either word interchangeably.

EXAM TIP The CompTIA A+ 1101 objectives list the term BIOS/UEFI, so if you see a question that says BIOS, just think UEFI.

CMOS and the System Setup Utility

Flash ROM is *read-only*, but there's a problem: every UEFI needs a tiny bit of writable memory. UEFI knows you have RAM, but how much RAM does UEFI need? You want to add a boot-up password, so where do you tell UEFI to store that password? This writable memory is a tiny bit of specialized RAM hooked up to a small battery to keep it working when the PC is off and unplugged. We call this memory *complementary metal-oxide semiconductor (CMOS)*. Today the CMOS is built into the chipset, but back in the old days CMOS was a dedicated chip (see Figure 5-14).

Figure 5-14
Old-style CMOS chip

If the data stored in CMOS about a piece of hardware (or about its fancier features) is different from the specs of the actual hardware, the computer cannot access that piece of hardware (or use its fancier features). It is crucial that this information be correct. If you change any of the previously mentioned hardware, you must update CMOS to reflect those changes. You need to know, therefore, how to change the data in CMOS.

Every UEFI comes with a *system setup utility* that enables you to access and modify CMOS data. On a completely new system, with no operating system installed, you'll see something like the system setup utility shown in Figure 5-15. After the OS is installed, these screens effectively disappear. I'll show you how to access them in a little bit.

NOTE The terms *CMOS setup program/utility*, *CMOS*, system setup, and *system setup utility* are functionally interchangeable today. You'll even hear the program referred to as the BIOS/UEFI setup utility, BIOS/UEFI settings, or UEFI firmware settings.

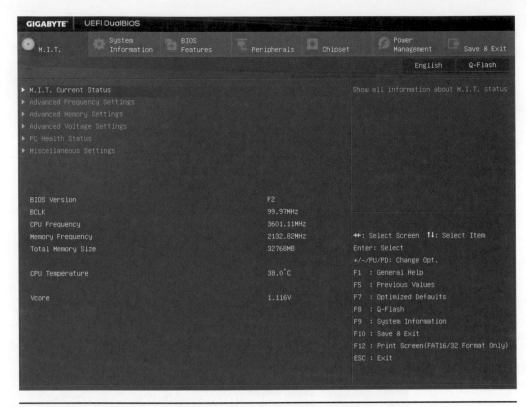

Figure 5-15 Gigabyte system setup utility

Touring the System Setup Utility

Every BIOS/UEFI maker's system setup utility looks a little different. Some are graphical like the one shown in Figure 5-15 and some are more textual, but don't let that confuse you. They all contain basically the same settings; you just have to be comfortable poking around the different interfaces. To avoid doing something foolish, *do not save anything* unless you are sure you have it set correctly.

Accessing System Setup

You access the system setup utility by pressing one or more utility-specific keys when the system is booting. Turn off your system and then turn it on again. Watch the screen closely! On some systems you'll read text on the screen telling you what key(s) to press, as shown in Figure 5-16. Many boot screens do not show up like that figure!

Figure 5-16
Boot screen with
system setup
instructions

There's no standard key to press here, but the two most common keys are DELETE and F2. When in doubt just do a Web search for the right keys for your system. Figure 5-17 shows the instructions to access the system setup on a Microsoft Surface (from the Microsoft Web site).

The UEFI settings can be adjusted only during system startup. To load the UEFI firmware settings menu:

1. Shut down your Surface.

2. Press and hold the volume-up button on your Surface and at the same time, press and release the power button.

3. When you see the Surface logo, release the volume-up button.
   The UEFI menu will display within a few seconds.

Figure 5-17   Microsoft.com instructions for how to access system setup on a Surface device

Don't be afraid to experiment. There's no danger in trying combinations until something works! If you press a key and the system boots to an operating system, then you're either too slow or pressing the wrong key. No worries—just reboot the system and try again.

NOTE   Every system setup utility has its own look and feel. Don't let these differences bother you, and remember they all do roughly the same thing, so poke around and explore! As long as you don't save your changes you won't hurt anything.

Let's start by touring a graphical system setup. Figure 5-18 shows a typical, simple graphical setup screen. This particular system setup utility has two modes: EZ and Advanced (not all system setups offer this EZ/Advanced option, thing but it's nice when they do).

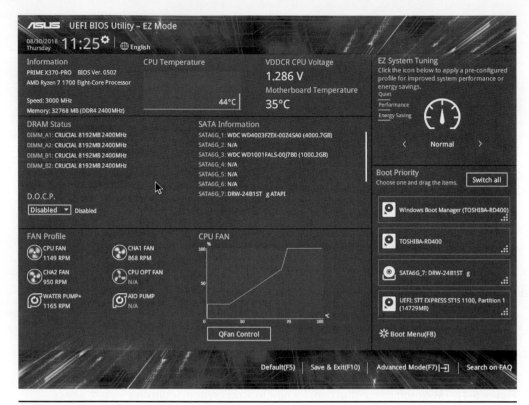

Figure 5-18   ASUS UEFI system setup utility

Click the option to go into Advanced Mode and you'll get a much more versatile utility (see Figure 5-19) for changing the interface configurations. The Main tab offers some *BIOS component information*, such as the amount of RAM and speed of CPU, plus a couple of options to modify the language and date and time.

The Main tab (not all system setups have a Main tab option, but many do) enables you to configure passwords by setting an administrator or user password. (The default for the pictured UEFI BIOS is Access Level: Administrator. Click the Security option to change access information. UEFI setup screens differ somewhat, but you'll find similar options in all of them.)

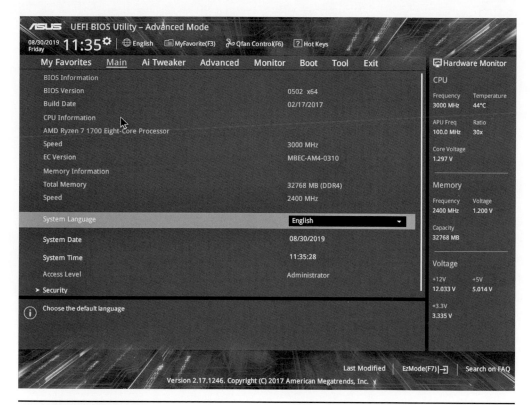

Figure 5-19 Main tab

An *administrator password* locks or unlocks access to the system setup utility. A *user password* locks or unlocks the computer booting to an operating system. Set a *BIOS/UEFI password* when you encounter a scenario like installing computer kiosks at a convention or installing systems in a public library. A *BIOS/UEFI password* is required to login into a computer's BIOS/UEFI to stop casual miscreants from messing with your accessible systems.

Things get far more interesting in the other tabs. Selecting the Ai Tweaker tab, for example, enables you to delve into the Dark Arts of overclocking both the CPU and RAM (see Figure 5-20). You can change the clock multiplier, clock speeds, voltages, and more here. This is a great place to go to fry a new CPU!

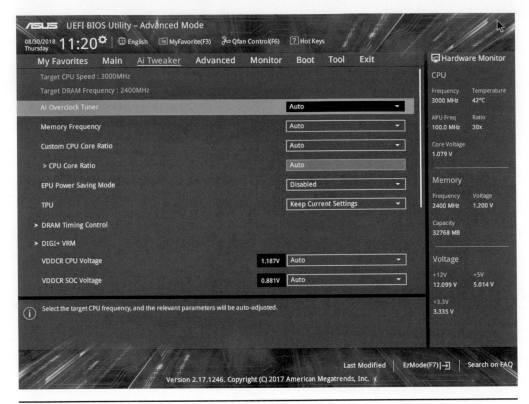

Figure 5-20 Ai Tweaker tab

The Advanced tab (see Figure 5-21) gives component information about CPUs, hard drives and optical drives, and all the built-in components, such as USB ports. In this tab, as you drill down to each subcategory, you can configure drive settings, enable and disable devices, and more.

The Boot tab (see Figure 5-22) enables you to adjust boot settings. You can select devices to boot by priority, setting the *boot sequence* used by the motherboard. (See "The Boot Process" later in this chapter for more information.) You can determine how the system will react/inform if booting fails, and more.

The Tool tab (see Figure 5-23) has a couple of very important features. The ASUS EZ Flash 3 Utility enables you to update the motherboard firmware. See the "Flashing

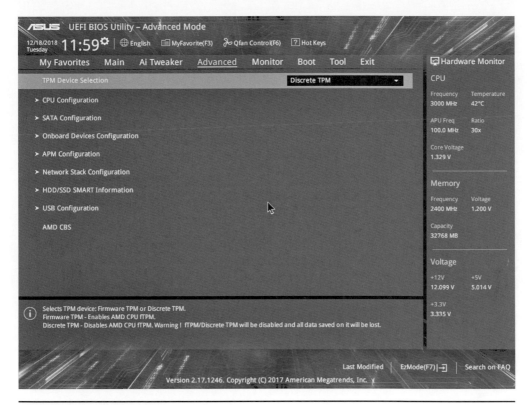

Figure 5-21 Advanced tab

the ROM" section later in this chapter for more details. The Tool tab also shows RAM information. That's the SPD option (for *serial presence detect*) you should recognize from Chapter 4.

So you don't start thinking that all system setups look the same, let's switch to a UEFI motherboard on an Intel-based portable computer with a more text-based interface. This isn't nearly as pretty as the first system setup but it still does the job. As we go through the screens, pay attention to the options listed on the screen. I'll call out features that the graphical AMD-based UEFI didn't have.

The Information tab (see Figure 5-24) offers straightforward information about the CPU and RAM amount, and cryptic information about the hard drive. Other tabs do more.

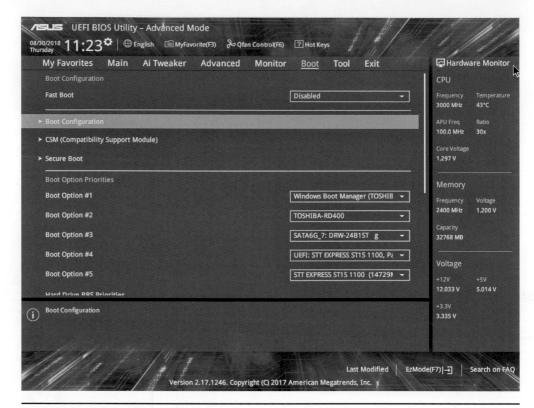

Figure 5-22 Boot tab

The Configuration tab (see Figure 5-25) shows a number of built-in devices that you configure or enable/disable here. Because this is a laptop, it has an option to turn on/off wireless networking capabilities.

There are two interesting options here that are covered in detail in other chapters but warrant a brief discussion now. The Intel Virtual Technology option enables or disables virtualization support for virtual machines. A virtual machine is a powerful type of program that enables you to run a second (or third or fourth), software-based machine inside your physical PC. It re-creates the motherboard, hard drives, RAM, network adapters, and more, and is just as powerful as a real PC. To run these virtual machines, however, you'll need a very powerful PC—you are trying to run multiple PCs at the same time, after all.

To support this, CPU manufacturers have added *hardware-assisted virtualization*. Intel calls its version Intel Virtualization Technology (Intel VT for short), and AMD calls its version AMD Virtualization (AMD-V) technology. This technology helps the virtual machines use your hardware more efficiently and is controlled by the BIOS. This feature is disabled by default in BIOS, so if your virtual machine requires hardware-assisted virtualization, you'll need to enable it here.

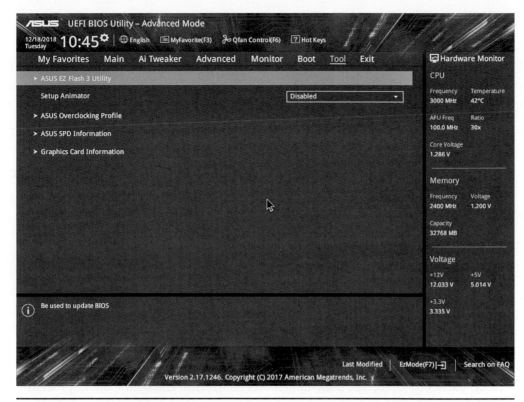

Figure 5-23 Tool tab

Figure 5-24
Information tab

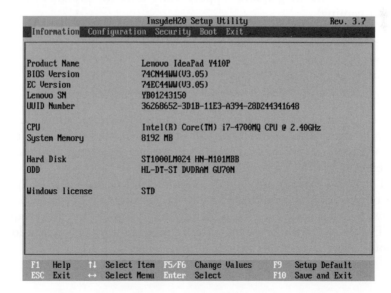

Figure 5-25
Configuration
tab

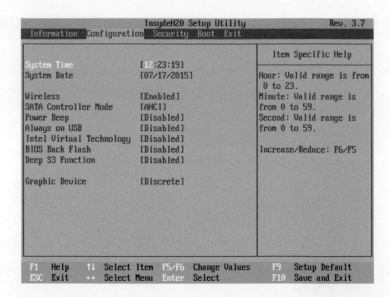

```
                                InsydeH20 Setup Utility              Rev. 3.7
       Information  Configuration  Security  Boot  Exit

                                                    Item Specific Help

       System Time            [12:23:19]
       System Date            [07/17/2015]       Hour: Valid range is from
                                                   0 to 23.
       Wireless               [Enabled]          Minute: Valid range is
       SATA Controller Mode   [AHCI]             from 0 to 59.
       Power Beep             [Disabled]         Second: Valid range is
       Always on USB          [Disabled]         from 0 to 59.
       Intel Virtual Technology [Disabled]
       BIOS Back Flash        [Disabled]         Increase/Reduce: F6/F5
       Deep S3 Function       [Disabled]

       Graphic Device         [Discrete]




       F1   Help      ↑↓  Select Item  F5/F6  Change Values   F9   Setup Default
       ESC  Exit      ↔   Select Menu  Enter  Select          F10  Save and Exit
```

NOTE Chapter 22 covers virtual machines in gory detail. Stay tuned!

This particular laptop has built-in graphics courtesy of the Intel Core i7 processor, plus it has a dedicated add-on video card for gaming. The Graphic Device option, set here to Discrete, means to use the dedicated video card when possible. This uses more electricity than the graphics support using only the processor, but it makes for way better gaming!

NOTE Chapter 17 goes into video options (and gaming) in modern systems.

The Security tab (see Figure 5-26) offers a lot more options for configuring BIOS security than found on the Main tab of the AMD-based system. You see the Administrator Password and User Password options, but there's also an option to set a couple of different hard drive passwords.

The *Secure Boot* feature you can see on the Security tab is a UEFI protocol that secures the boot process by requiring properly signed software. This includes boot software and software that supports specific, essential components. Secure Boot requires an Intel CPU, a UEFI BIOS, and an operating system designed for it, such as Windows. See the "Secure Boot" section later in this chapter for more details.

Figure 5-26
Security tab

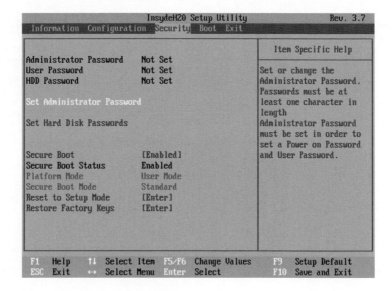

```
                        InsydeH2O Setup Utility          Rev. 3.7
     Information  Configuration  Security  Boot  Exit

                                              ┌─────────────────────────┐
                                              │   Item Specific Help    │
    Administrator Password   Not Set          │                         │
    User Password            Not Set          │ Set or change the       │
    HDD Password             Not Set          │ Administrator Password.  │
                                              │ Passwords must be at     │
    Set Administrator Password                │ least one character in   │
                                              │ length                   │
    Set Hard Disk Passwords                   │ Administrator Password   │
                                              │ must be set in order to  │
                                              │ set a Power on Password  │
    Secure Boot              [Enabled]        │ and User Password.       │
    Secure Boot Status       Enabled          │                         │
    Platform Mode            User Mode        │                         │
    Secure Boot Mode         Standard         │                         │
    Reset to Setup Mode      [Enter]          │                         │
    Restore Factory Keys     [Enter]          │                         │
                                              └─────────────────────────┘

    F1   Help    ↑↓  Select Item  F5/F6  Change Values   F9   Setup Default
    ESC  Exit    ↔   Select Menu  Enter  Select          F10  Save and Exit
```

NOTE Secure Boot is an example of a tool that uses *drive encryption*. Various types of encryption—essentially scrambling the information to make it inaccessible to bad guys—secure all sorts of processes and data in modern computing. We'll hit the subject in several places later in the book. Chapter 11 discusses drive encryption specifically in more detail.

Noteworthy BIOS/UEFI Security Settings

Motherboard manufacturers, BIOS/UEFI writers, and programmers have implemented all kinds of security features over the years. This section mentions a couple you might run into on various motherboards (or on a certain exam in your near future).

Boot Options

Imagine a desktop computer with two hard drives. How does your computer know which drive to access to boot the system? Imagine you're a tech and in order to work on a system with malware, you need to boot the system from a special thumb drive loaded with anti-malware. You need a way to select what device you wish to boot from, and the system setup enables you to do exactly that!

On this particular system setup there's a Boot tab (see Figure 5-27) that enables you to set *boot options* to determine which bootable device gets priority. This tab is where you provide support for booting to a USB device as well. It looks a little different from the graphical example presented earlier. See "The Boot Process" later in this chapter for more explanation.

USB Permissions

Allowing your system to boot to a USB drive is a bit of a problem. What if a bad guy managed to insert a bootable USB drive into your unattended computer? Well, the bad guy could then copy the drive, maybe join your network and copy other drives, add

Figure 5-27
Boot tab

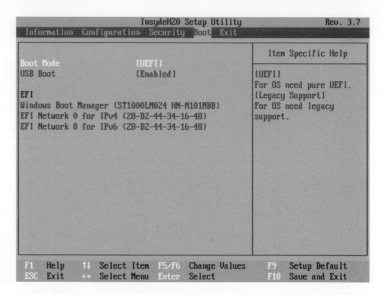

malware, and so forth. Therefore, it's important to consider the risk of leaving all your USB ports enabled. In high-security environments such as law enforcement, turning off USB ports is common practice (see Figure 5-28).

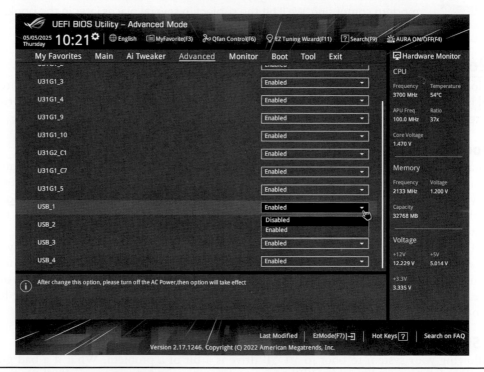

Figure 5-28   Turning off a USB port

Fan Considerations

Today's computers, especially desktop systems, have substantial cooling needs, and that means fans, lots of fans! Fans are wonderful tools for keeping your systems cool but they come with challenges. First, fans get louder the faster they spin, so it's nice to make sure your fans spin as slowly as possible. Second, if a fan dies, your system will overheat, causing rebooting and in some cases permanent damage.

Every desktop system setup (and many laptop setups as well) come with fan settings to deal with exactly these issues. Figure 5-29 shows an example of fan settings in a system setup utility.

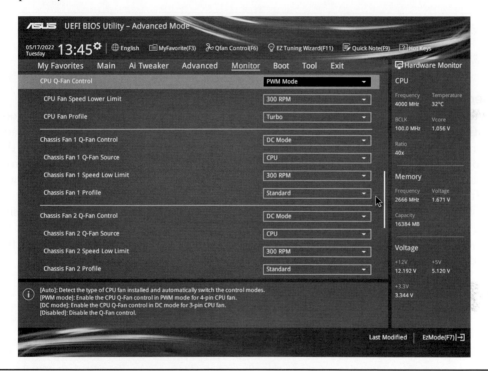

Figure 5-29   Fan temp and speed settings

 NOTE   System setup fan settings vary wildly on a system-by-system basis.

Trusted Platform Module

The *Trusted Platform Module (TPM)* acts as a secure cryptoprocessor, which is to say that it is a hardware platform for the acceleration of cryptographic functions and the secure storage of associated information. Just think of the TPM as a storage place for very secure keys used by all kinds of software on your system. The specification for the TPM is published by the Trusted Computing Group, an organization whose corporate members include Intel, Microsoft, AMD, IBM, Lenovo, Dell, Hewlett Packard Enterprise, and many others.

The TPM can be a small circuit board plugged into the motherboard (a hardware security module), or it can be built directly into the chipset. The system setup utility usually contains settings that can turn the TPM on or off and enable or disable it.

TPMs can be used in a wide array of cryptographic operations, but one of the most common uses of TPMs is hard disk encryption. For example, the BitLocker Drive Encryption feature of Microsoft Windows requires TPM if you want to encrypt entire disk drives or SSDs (which will be discussed in further detail in Chapter 11). Other possible uses of TPMs include digital rights management (DRM), network access control, application execution control, and password protection.

 EXAM TIP BIOS security-related options can include TPM, passwords, Secure Boot, and drive encryption. You'll hear more about these topics in other chapters.

Secure Boot

We live in a world where malware can exist just about everywhere. There are pretty good anti-malware solutions—once the operating systems has started—but your system traditionally has no anti-malware support *during* the boot process. The PC industry saw this problem and developed a security standard called Secure Boot to respond to the security of the boot-up area. Secure Boot's goal is to make sure that a device only loads firmware/software trusted by the Original Equipment Manufacturer (OEM).

The secret to getting your system to trust a piece of firmware or software is to first sign the code using a digital signature. We'll cover digital signatures in later chapters, but for now imagine the firmware/software storing a note that says, "I am trustworthy—feel free to check my special code that proves it" (see Figure 5-30).

Windows boot loader (bootmgr.efi)

```
00006cc0:  4d69 6372 6f73 6f66 7420 436f 7270 6f72   Microsoft Corpor
00006cd0:  6174 696f 6e31 3630 3406 0355 0403 0c2d   ation1604..U...-
00006ce0:  4d69 6372 6f73 6f66 7420 5769 6e64 6f77   Microsoft Windows
00006cf0:  7320 5365 6375 7265 2042 6f6f 7420 5661   s Secure Boot Va
00006d00:  7269 6162 6c65 2053 6967 6e65 7230 8201   riable Signer0..
00006d10:  2230 0d06 092a 8648 86f7 0d01 0101 0500   "0...*.H........
00006d20:  0382 010f 0030 8201 0a02 8201 0100 c494   .....0..........
00006d30:  929c 5737 7b6f 2a1a c9c5 abe4 8e3f c0f7   ..W7{o*......?..
00006d40:  3033 f6c2 0317 95a1 3b53 19b1 9c60 5e9a   03......;S...`^.
0000  50:  6323 3215 7709 4990 fb30 67e7 7384 833e   c#2.w.I..0g.s..>
      50  cdc6 89c7 71e1 da19 c43a 3e44 4cf0   2P....q....:>DL.
      6  6a20 8bfa e7e3 b4a1 11be b880 95e4   5.j ............
      3cf2 f141 3267 67a9 8395 9481 c0d8   .3<..A2gg.......
      0286 8ac7 c716 458e df81 43d4 e05e   w.......E...C..^
      4ae9 fe13 3d31 568b a19a 8d6e d9c0   7.J...=1V....n..
      5320 37a4 13c7 7574 c59e fbe1 2b8e   .6S 7...ut....+.
```

Digital signature

Figure 5-30 Code must be signed to be trustworthy.

When your system runs a signature check of each piece of boot software and the UEFI drivers, it also checks the core operating system files as well. If the signatures are valid, the PC passes control to the operating system and the system boots.

Exiting and Saving BIOS/UEFI Settings

Of course, all system setup utilities provide some method to Save Changes, Discard Changes, Exit Saving Changes, or Exit Discarding Changes (see Figure 5-31). Use these options as needed for your situation. Exit Discarding Changes is particularly nice for those folks who want to poke around the CMOS setup utility but don't want to mess anything up. Use it!

NOTE People serious about tweaking UEFI settings for maximum performance (overclocking) or minimum energy use (underclocking) can use a feature in some system setup utilities to save customized settings. Various utilities call them presets or profiles—essentially, it's a "save these settings as" option. If something isn't quite right with the changes, go back into setup, make some changes, and try again. If you're done fiddling for the day and want to play with a stable machine, pick the profile you created that is the stable machine. See "Care and Feeding of BIOS/UEFI" later in this chapter for the ultimate undo features.

Figure 5-31
Exit options

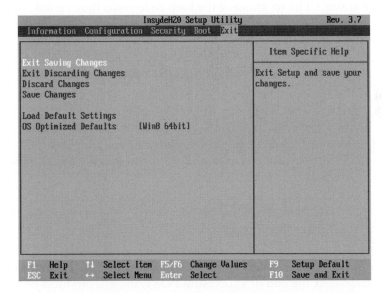

The CMOS setup utility would meet all the needs of a modern system for BIOS if manufacturers would just stop creating new devices. That's not going to happen, of course, so let's turn now to devices that need to have BIOS loaded from elsewhere.

Power-On Self-Test (POST)

BIOS isn't the only program on *system ROM*. When the computer is turned on or reset, it initiates a special program called the *power-on self-test (POST)*. The POST program checks out the system every time the computer boots. To perform this check, the POST sends out a command that says to all of the devices, "Check yourselves out!" All of the standard devices in the computer then run their own built-in diagnostic—the POST doesn't specify what they must check. The quality of the diagnostic is up to the people who made that particular device.

Let's consider the POST for a moment. Suppose some device—let's say it's the keyboard controller chip—runs its diagnostic and determines that it is not working properly. What can the POST do about it? Only one thing really: tell the human in front of the PC! So how does the computer tell the human? PCs convey POST information to you in two ways: beep codes and text messages.

Before and During the Video Test: The Beep Codes

The computer tests the most basic parts of the computer first, up to and including the video card. In early PCs, you'd hear a series of beeps—called *beep codes* or POST beeps—if anything went wrong. By using beeps before and during the video test, the computer could communicate with you. (If a POST error occurs before the video is available, obviously the error must manifest itself as beeps, because nothing can display on the screen.) The meaning of the beep code you'd hear varied among different BIOS manufacturers. You could find the beep codes for a specific motherboard in its motherboard manual.

 NOTE CompTIA refers to beep codes as *POST beeps*.

Most modern PCs have only two beep codes: one for bad or missing video (one long beep followed by two or three short beeps), and one for bad or missing RAM (a single beep that repeats indefinitely).

 CAUTION You'll find lots of online documentation about beep codes, but it's usually badly outdated.

You'll hear three other beep sequences on most PCs (although they're not officially beep codes). At the end of a successful POST, the PC produces one or two short beeps, simply to inform you that all is well. Most systems make a rather strange noise when the RAM is missing or very seriously damaged. Unlike traditional beep codes, this code repeats until you shut off the system. Finally, your speaker might make beeps for reasons that aren't POST or boot related. One of the more common is a series of short beeps after the system's been running for a while. That's a CPU alarm telling you the CPU is approaching its high heat limit.

Text Errors

After the video has tested okay, any POST errors display on the screen as text errors. If you get a text error, the problem is usually, but not always, self-explanatory (see Figure 5-32). Text errors are far more useful than beep codes, because you can simply read the screen to determine the bad device.

Figure 5-32
POST text error messages

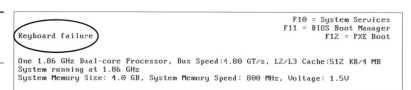

```
                                                          F10 = System Services
                                                          F11 = BIOS Boot Manager
 (Keyboard failure)                                             F12 = PXE Boot

 One 1.86 GHz Dual-core Processor, Bus Speed:4.80 GT/s, L2/L3 Cache:512 KB/4 MB
 System running at 1.86 GHz
 System Memory Size: 4.0 GB, System Memory Speed: 800 MHz, Voltage: 1.5V
```

POST Cards

Beep codes, numeric codes, and text error codes, although helpful, can sometimes be misleading. Worse than that, an inoperative device can sometimes disrupt the POST, forcing the machine into an endless loop. This causes the PC to act dead—no beeps and nothing on the screen. In this case, you need a device, called a *POST card*, to monitor the POST and identify which piece of hardware is causing the trouble.

POST cards are simple cards that snap into expansion slots on your system. A small, two-character LED readout on the card indicates which device the POST is currently testing (see Figure 5-33).

Figure 5-33
POST card in action

POST cards used to be essential tools for techs, but today I use them only when I have a "dead" PC to determine at which level it's dead. If the POST card shows no reading, I know the problem is before the POST and must be related to the power, the CPU, the RAM, or the motherboard. If the board posts, then I know to look at more issues, such as the drives and so on.

The Boot Process

All PCs need a process to begin their operations. Once you feed power to the PC, the tight interrelation of hardware, firmware, and software enables the PC to start itself, to "pull itself up by the bootstraps" or boot itself.

When you first power on the PC, the power supply circuitry tests for proper voltage and then sends a signal down a special wire called the *power good* wire to awaken the CPU. The moment the power good wire wakes it up, every Intel and clone CPU immediately sends a built-in memory address via its address bus. This special address is the same on every Intel and clone CPU, from the oldest 8086 to the most recent microprocessor. This address is the first line of the POST program on the system ROM! That's how the system starts the POST. After the POST has finished, there must be a way for the computer to find the programs on the hard drive to start the operating system. What happens next differs between the old BIOS way and the UEFI way.

In the older BIOS environment, the POST passes control to the last BIOS function: the bootstrap loader. The *bootstrap loader* is little more than a few dozen lines of BIOS code tacked to the end of the POST program. Its job is to find the operating system. The bootstrap loader reads CMOS information to tell it where to look first for an operating system. Your PC's system setup utility has an option that you configure to tell the bootstrap loader which devices to check for an operating system and in which order—that's the *boot sequence* (see Figure 5-34).

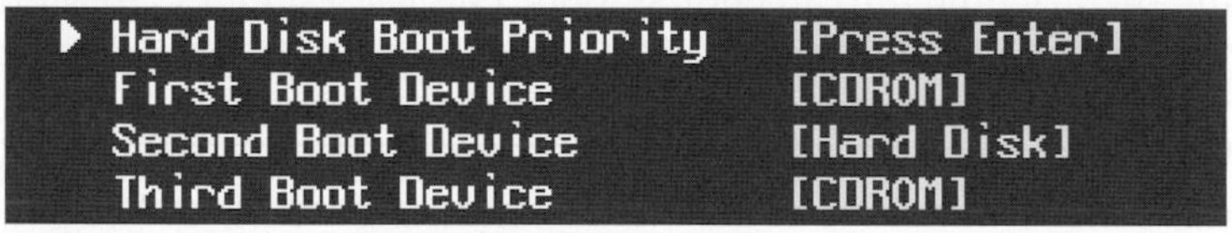

Figure 5-34
System Setup
boot sequence

> Hard Disk Boot Priority   [Press Enter]
> First Boot Device   [CDROM]
> Second Boot Device   [Hard Disk]
> Third Boot Device   [CDROM]

Almost all storage devices—hard disk drives, solid-state drives, optical drives, and USB thumb drives—can be configured to boot an operating system by setting aside a specific location called the *boot sector*. If the device is bootable, its boot sector contains special programming designed to tell the system where to locate the operating system. Any device with a functional operating system is called a *bootable disk* or a *system disk*. If the bootstrap loader locates a good boot sector, it passes control to the operating system and removes itself from memory. If it doesn't, it goes to the next device in the boot sequence you set in the CMOS setup utility. The boot sequence is an important tool for techs because you can set it to load in special bootable devices so you can run utilities to maintain PCs without using the primary operating system.

In UEFI systems, the POST hands control of the boot process to the Boot Manager, which checks the boot configuration, and then loads the operating system boot loader directly (see Figure 5-35). There's no need for scanning for a boot sector or any of that. UEFI firmware stores the Boot Manager and boot configuration.

Some BIOS include a feature that enables a PC to use a *preboot execution environment (PXE)*. A PXE enables you to boot a PC without any local storage by retrieving an OS from a server over a network. You'll see more on PXE when we talk about installing Windows in Chapter 11.

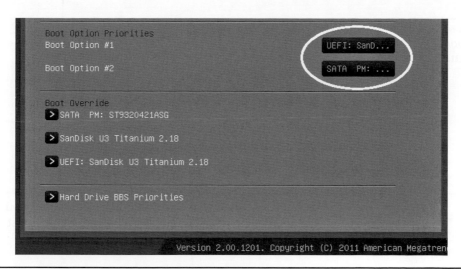

```
Boot Option Priorities
Boot Option #1                              UEFI: SanD...

Boot Option #2                              SATA PM: ...


Boot Override
 > SATA PM: ST9320421ASG

 > SanDisk U3 Titanium 2.18

 > UEFI: SanDisk U3 Titanium 2.18


 > Hard Drive BBS Priorities



           Version 2.00.1201. Copyright (C) 2011 American Megatren
```

Figure 5-35   UEFI boot mode with Boot Manager options displayed

Care and Feeding of BIOS/UEFI

BIOS/UEFI and system setup are areas in your PC that you don't go to very often. BIOS/UEFI itself is invisible. The only real clue you have that it even exists is the POST. The system setup utility, on the other hand, is very visible if you start it. While system setup utilities today work acceptably well without ever being touched, you're an aspiring tech, and all self-respecting techs start up the system setup utility and make changes. That's when most system setup utility problems take place.

This section shows you how to navigate a system setup utility and change settings. Keep in mind that you should make only as many changes at one time as you can remember. Document the original settings and the changes on a piece of paper or take a photo so that you can restore the original settings if necessary. Don't make changes unless you know what they mean! It's easy to screw up a computer fairly seriously by playing with CMOS settings you don't understand.

Default/Optimized Settings

Every system setup utility has a couple of reset options, commonly called Load Default Settings and OS Optimized Defaults (see Figure 5-36). These options keep you from having to memorize all of those weird settings you'll never touch. Default or Fail-Safe sets everything to very simple settings—you might occasionally use this setting when very low-level problems such as freeze-ups occur and you've checked more obvious areas first. Optimized sets the system to the best possible speed/stability for the system. You would use this option after you've tampered with the system setup too much and need to put it back like it was!

Figure 5-36
Options for
resetting CMOS

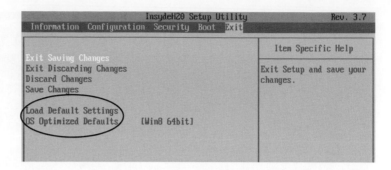

NOTE Remember that if you don't save your changes, you can't hurt your system setup. Don't be afraid to poke around in your system setup—just don't save anything!

Clearing CMOS

You read about the process for clearing system settings back in Chapter 3, but the process is worth repeating here. When you mess up a setting (by overclocking too much or disabling something that should have remained enabled—or vice versa) that renders the computer dead, you can reset the CMOS back to factory defaults and start over.

Almost every motherboard has a dedicated set of wires called *CLRTC* or something similar (see Figure 5-37).

Figure 5-37
CMOS RTC clear
wires

NOTE Many techs use older language to describe the reset CMOS RTC RAM, simply *CMOS clear*, describing both the process and the motherboard option.

Turn off and unplug the computer, then open the case to access the motherboard. Find the CMOS RTC clear wires. Move the shunt (the little plastic and metal jumper thing) from wires 1 and 2 to wires 2 and 3 (see Figure 5-38). Wait for 10 seconds and then move the shunt back to the default position. Plug in and boot the system.

Figure 5-38
Changing shunt
location to clear
CMOS RAM

 NOTE Manufacturers of enthusiast boards designed for easy overclocking experimentation know you're going to screw up during the overclocking process. You'll often find a dedicated clear CMOS button hardwired to the motherboard. Now that's service!

If that doesn't work or if you get one of the truly odd motherboards without CLRTC jumpers, power down the system and unplug. Pry out the little coin battery (described next) and wait for several seconds. Reinstall and reboot.

Losing CMOS RTC Settings

As mentioned before, your CMOS RAM needs a continuous trickle charge to keep the internal clock running and remember its settings. Motherboards use some type of battery, usually a 3-volt Lithium-Ion coin battery, to give the CMOS RAM the charge it needs when the computer is turned off (see Figure 5-39). This is called the *CMOS battery*. Typical systems use a *CR2032* battery. (What does your system use?)

Figure 5-39
A CMOS battery

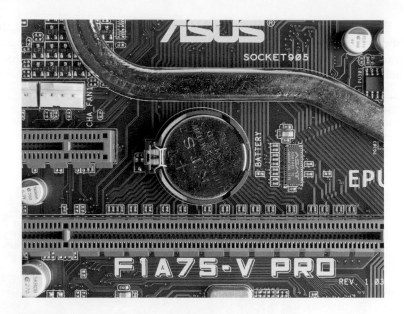

If some mishap suddenly erases the information on the CMOS RAM, the computer might not boot or you'll get nasty-looking errors at boot. Any PC will boot to factory defaults if the CMOS clears, so the chances of not booting are slim—but you'll still get errors at boot. Here are a few examples of errors that point to a lost CMOS information scenario:

- CMOS configuration mismatch
- CMOS date/time not set
- BIOS time and settings reset
- No boot device available
- CMOS battery state low

Here are some of the more common reasons for losing CMOS data:

- Pulling and inserting cards
- Touching the motherboard
- Dropping something on the motherboard
- Dirt on the motherboard
- Faulty power supplies
- Electrical surges

If you run into any of these scenarios, or if the clock in Windows resets itself to January 1st every time you reboot the system, the battery on the motherboard is losing its charge and needs to be replaced. To replace the battery, use a screwdriver to pry the battery's catch gently back. The battery should pop up for easy removal. Before you install the new battery, double-check that it has the same voltage and amperage as the old battery. To retain your CMOS settings while replacing the battery, simply leave your PC plugged into an AC outlet. The 5-volt soft power on all modern motherboards provides enough electricity to keep the CMOS charged and the data secure. Of course, I know you're going to be *extremely* careful about ESD while prying up the battery from a live system!

Flashing the ROM

Flash ROM chips can be reprogrammed to update their contents. With flash ROM, when you need to update your system BIOS to add support for a new technology, you can simply run a small command-line program, combined with an update file, and voilà, you have a new, updated BIOS! This is called a *firmware update*. Different BIOS makers use slightly different processes for *flashing the BIOS*, but, in general, you insert a removable disk of some sort (usually a USB thumb drive) containing an updated BIOS file and use the updating utility in system setup.

 CAUTION A failed BIOS/UEFI update—where something goes wrong during the process—can *brick* a computer or device. The failure turns a computing device into a brick, useless for anything but a paperweight.

Some motherboard makers provide Windows-based flash ROM update utilities that check the Internet for updates and download them for you to install. Most of these utilities also enable you to back up your current BIOS so you can return to it if the updated version causes trouble. Without a good backup, you could end up throwing away your motherboard if a flash BIOS update goes wrong, so you should always make one.

Finally, a lot of motherboards these days have system setup utilities that can connect directly to the Internet and access updates that way. Figure 5-40 shows one such update utility.

Just a word of caution to complete the BIOS update section. Don't update your BIOS unless you have some compelling reason to do so. Some common reasons are supporting larger drive capacities, supporting faster RAM speeds, and security enhancements. As the old saying goes, "If it ain't broke, don't fix it!"

 NOTE While techs usually talk about "flashing the BIOS," CompTIA refers to this process also as "firmware updates."

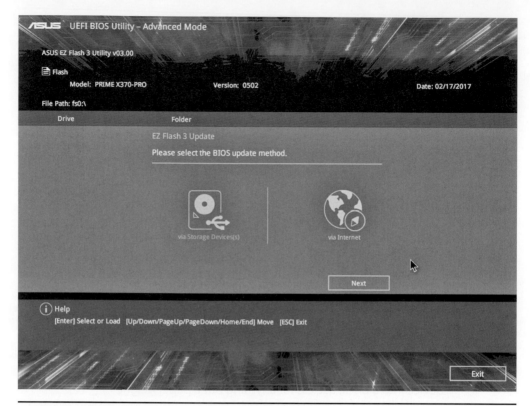

Figure 5-40 ROM-updating program for an ASUS motherboard

Chapter Review

Questions

1. What does BIOS/UEFI provide for the computer? (Choose the best answer.)

   A. The physical interface for various devices such as USB and Thunderbolt ports

   B. The programming that enables the CPU to communicate with other hardware

   C. Memory space for applications to load into from the hard drive

   D. Memory space for applications to load into from the main system RAM

2. What does nonvolatile mean when discussing memory?

   A. The memory erases itself every time the system is rebooted.

   B. The memory saves the code to mass storage during reboot.

   C. The stored information isn't erased when the computer is turned off.

   D. The stored information is not backed up to mass storage.

3. What is the predominant form of ROM used in systems today called?

   A. PROM

   B. EPROM

   C. EEPROM

   D. Flash ROM

4. Henry wants to change the boot order on his system. Which BIOS/UEFI feature must Henry use to do this?

   A. Power-on self-test

   B. Flash ROM

   C. System setup utility

   D. Disk Management

5. Which of the following keystrokes will most likely enable access to the system setup utility?

   A. SHIFT-PRINT SCREEN

   B. CTRL-ALT-DEL

   C. F10

   D. DELETE

6. While poking around his system setup, Troy notices a setting for PXE. What is a PXE used for?

   A. A PXE enables you to boot your system from removable media.

   B. A PXE enables your system to boot into a UEFI shell.

   C. A PXE enables your system to boot from a disk drive.

   D. A PXE enables your system to boot from a networked system.

7. Davos finds that a disgruntled former employee decided to sabotage her computer when she left by putting a password in CMOS that stops the computer from booting. What can Davos do to solve this problem?

   A. Davos should boot the computer while holding the left SHIFT key. This will clear the CMOS information.

   B. Davos should try various combinations of the former employee's name. The vast majority of people use their name or initials for CMOS passwords.

   C. Davos should find the CLRTC jumper on the motherboard. Then she can boot the computer with a shunt on the jumper to clear the CMOS information.

   D. Davos should find a replacement motherboard. Unless she knows the CMOS password, there's nothing she can do.

8. Richard over in the sales department went wild in CMOS and made a bunch of changes that he thought would optimize his PC. Now most of his PC doesn't work. The computer powers up, but he can only get to CMOS, not into Windows. Which of the following tech call answers would most likely get him up and running again?

   A. Reboot the computer about three times. That'll clear the CMOS and get you up and running.

   B. Open up the computer and find the CLRTC jumper. Remove a shunt from somewhere on the motherboard and put it on the CLRTC jumper. Reboot and then put the shunt back where you got it. Reboot, and you should be up and running in no time.

   C. Boot into the CMOS setup program and then find the option to load a plug-and-play operating system. Make sure it's set to On. Save and exit CMOS; boot normally into Windows. You should be up and running in no time.

   D. Boot into the CMOS setup program and then find the option to load OS Optimized Defaults. Save and exit CMOS; boot normally into Windows. You should be up and running in no time.

9. Every time Jill boots her system, it goes through POST, beeps once, and then loads Windows normally. What is this beep code telling her?

   A. Everything is OK.

   B. Bad CPU.

   C. Bad RAM.

   D. Missing keyboard.

10. Amanda's old system uses DDR5 RAM but doesn't support the latest speeds. Which of the following should she consider as a course of action?

   A. Update the motherboard flash ROM.

   B. Replace the flash ROM.

   C. Reset the flash ROM.

   D. Replace the motherboard.

Answers

1. **B.** BIOS/UEFI provides the programming that enables the CPU to communicate with other hardware.

2. **C.** Nonvolatile memory means the stored information isn't erased when the computer is turned off.

3. **D.** The predominant form of ROM used in system's today is called flash ROM

4. **C.** Henry needs to use the system setup utility.

5. **A.** Which keystroke used to access the system setup utility varies depending on the UEFI system, but the most common from the choices offered is the DELETE key.

6. **D.** A preboot execution environment (PXE) enables your system to boot from a networked system.

7. **C.** Davos should find the CLRTC jumper on the motherboard and then boot the computer with a shunt on the jumper to clear the CMOS information.

8. **D.** Please don't hand Richard a screwdriver! Having him load Optimized Default settings will most likely do the trick.

9. **A.** On almost all systems, a single beep indicates everything is OK.

10. **A.** It's fairly common to update your flash ROM for reasons such as achieving faster RAM speeds.

Motherboards

In this chapter, you will learn how to
- Explain how motherboards work
- Recognize modern expansion buses
- Upgrade and install motherboards
- Troubleshoot motherboard problems

The *motherboard* provides the foundation for the personal computer. Every piece of hardware, from the CPU to the lowliest expansion card, directly or indirectly plugs into the motherboard. The motherboard contains the wires—called *traces*—that make up the buses of the system. It holds the vast majority of the ports used by the peripherals, and it distributes the power from the power supply (see Figure 6-1). Without the motherboard, you literally have no PC.

Figure 6-1
Traces visible beneath the CPU socket on a motherboard

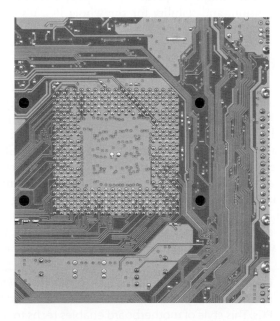

This chapter starts with an explanation of how motherboards work, identifying various types or form factors of motherboards, including distinguishing features. The second section examines expansion capabilities on motherboards, specifically the types of expansion slots you'll run into in the wild, and how to install expansion cards. The third section goes through the pragmatic steps of upgrading and installing motherboards. The chapter finishes with techniques for troubleshooting motherboard problems.

Historical/Conceptual

How Motherboards Work

Three variable and interrelated characteristics define modern motherboards: form factor, chipset, and components. The *form factor* determines the physical size of the motherboard as well as the general location of components and ports. The *chipset* defines the type of processor and RAM the motherboard requires and determines to a degree the built-in devices the motherboard supports, including the expansion slots. Finally, the built-in components determine the core functionality of the system.

Almost all chipsets used in desktops and laptops are made by either Intel or AMD. It's fitting that the two biggest CPU manufacturers for Windows-, macOS-, and Linux-based computers would also produce the essential supporting chipsets.

Any good tech should be able to make a recommendation to a client about a particular motherboard simply by perusing the specs. Because the motherboard determines function, expansion, and stability for the whole PC, it's essential that you know your motherboards!

Layers of the PCB

Modern motherboards are layered *printed circuit boards (PCBs),* copper etched onto a nonconductive material and then coated with some sort of epoxy for strength. The layers mask some of their complexity. You can see some of the traces on the board, but every motherboard is four or more layers thick. The layers contain a veritable highway of wires, carrying data and commands back and forth between the CPU, RAM, and peripherals.

The layered structure enables multiple wires to send data without their signals interfering with each other. The layered approach allows the manufacturer to add complexity and additional components to the board without extending the overall length and width of the board. Shorter traces also allow signals to travel faster than they would if the wires were longer, as would be necessary if motherboards did not use layers. The multiple layers also add strength to the board itself, so it doesn't bend easily.

 EXAM TIP   CompTIA A+ 1101 exam objective 3.4 focuses specifically on motherboards you find in classical Windows and Linux-based desktop PCs. This style of motherboard enables techs to do things such as update components. Thus, this chapter uses the term "PC" pretty much throughout.

Form Factors

Motherboard form factors are industry-standardized shapes and layouts that enable motherboards to work with cases and power supplies. A single form factor applies to all three components. All motherboards come in a basic rectangular or square shape but vary in overall size and in the layout of built-in components (see Figure 6-2). You need to install a motherboard in a case designed to fit it, so the ports and slot openings on the back fit correctly.

Figure 6-2
Typical
motherboard

The power supply and the motherboard need matching connectors, and different form factors define different connections. Given that the term "form factor" applies to the case, motherboard, and power supply—the three parts of the PC most responsible for moving air around inside the PC—the form factor also defines how the air moves around in the case.

To perform motherboard upgrades and provide knowledgeable recommendations to clients, techs need to know their form factors. The PC industry has adopted—and dropped—a number of form factors over the years with such names as AT, ATX, and ITX. Let's start with the granddaddy of all PC form factors, AT.

NOTE In case your curiosity has run rampant, yes, the form factor initials stand for words. AT was Advanced Technology; ATX stands for Advanced Technology Extended; and ITX stands for Information Technology Extended. No one used or uses the full terms. Stick with the initials.

AT Form Factor

The AT form factor (see Figure 6-3), invented by IBM in the early 1980s, was the predominant form factor for motherboards through the mid-1990s. AT is now obsolete.

Figure 6-3
AT-style
motherboard

The AT motherboard had a few size variations (see Figure 6-4), ranging from large to very large. The original AT motherboard was huge, around 12 inches wide by 13 inches deep. PC technology was new and needed lots of space for the various chips necessary to run the components of the PC.

Figure 6-4
AT motherboard
(bottom)
and Baby AT
motherboard
(top)

The single greatest problem with AT motherboards was the lack of external ports. When PCs were first invented, the only devices plugged into the average PC were a monitor and a keyboard. That's what the AT was designed to handle—the only dedicated connector on an AT motherboard was the keyboard port (see Figure 6-5).

Figure 6-5
Keyboard
connector on
the back of an AT
motherboard

Over the years, the number of devices plugged into the back of the PC has grown tremendously. Your average PC today has a keyboard, a mouse, a printer, some speakers, a monitor, and—if your system's like mine—four to six USB devices connected to it at any given time. These added components created a demand for a new type of form factor, one with more dedicated connectors for more devices. Many attempts were made to create a new standard form factor. Invariably, these new form factors integrated dedicated connectors for at least the mouse and printer, and many even added connectors for video, sound, and phone lines.

1101

ATX Form Factor

There continued to be a tremendous demand for a new form factor, one that had more standard connectors and also was flexible enough for possible changes in technology. This demand led to the creation of the ATX form factor in 1995 (see Figure 6-6). ATX got off to a slow start, but by around 1998, ATX overtook AT to become the most common form factor, a distinction it holds over 20 years later.

ATX is distinct from AT in the lack of an AT keyboard port, replaced with a rear panel that has all necessary ports built in. Note the mini-DIN (PS/2) keyboard and mouse ports at the left of Figure 6-7, standard features on some ATX boards. You recall those from Chapter 2, right?

The ATX form factor includes many improvements over AT. The position of the power supply creates better air movement. The CPU and RAM are placed to provide easier access, and the rearrangement of components prevents long expansion cards from colliding with the CPU or northbridge. Other improvements, such as placing the RAM closer to the northbridge and CPU than on AT boards, offer users enhanced performance as well. The shorter the wires, the easier to shield them and make them capable of handling double or quadruple the clock speed of the motherboard. Figure 6-8 shows AT and ATX motherboards—note the radical differences in placement of internal connections.

ATX motherboards come in three variations to accommodate different types of cases. So far, you've seen the full-sized ATX form factor, which is 12 by 9.6 inches.

The microATX motherboard (see Figure 6-9) floats in at a svelte 9.6 by 9.6 inches (usually), or about 30 percent smaller than standard ATX, yet uses the standard ATX connections.

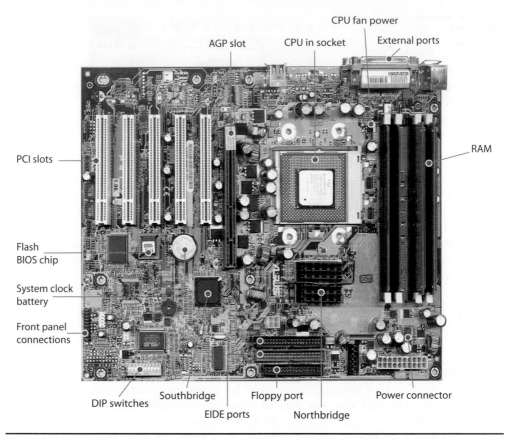

CPU fan power

AGP slot   CPU in socket   External ports

PCI slots

RAM

Flash
BIOS chip

System clock
battery

Front panel
connections

DIP switches   Southbridge   Floppy port   Power connector

EIDE ports   Northbridge

Figure 6-6   Early ATX motherboard

Figure 6-7
ATX ports

Figure 6-8
AT (left) and
ATX (right)
motherboards
for quick visual
comparison

Figure 6-9
A microATX
motherboard

A microATX motherboard fits into a standard ATX case or in the much smaller microATX cases. Note that not all microATX motherboards have the same physical size. You'll sometimes see microATX motherboards referred to with the Greek symbol for micro, as in µATX.

ITX

VIA Technologies started the process to create a small form factor (SFF) motherboard, the Information Technology eXtended, or *ITX*. The ITX itself wasn't a success, but VIA in turn created smaller form factors that today populate the SFF market, specifically Mini-ITX.

Mini-ITX (see Figure 6-10) is a miniscule 6.7 by 6.7 inches and competes head to head with the virtually identical microATX.

One of the great benefits of these SFF motherboards is the tiny amount of power needed to support them. ITX power supplies are quite small compared to a typical power supply. Lower power usage produces less heat, thus enabling passive cooling on many SFF systems. The lack of fan noise makes them ideal for media center PCs.

 NOTE   CompTIA lists ITX as a motherboard form factor. Straight ITX doesn't exist in the real world, but Mini-ITX is quite common.

Figure 6-10
A Mini-ITX
motherboard

Proprietary Form Factors

Several major PC makers make motherboards that work only with their cases. These *proprietary* motherboards enable these companies to create systems that stand out from the generic ones and, not coincidently, push you to get service and upgrades from their authorized dealers. Some of the features you'll see in proprietary systems are *riser cards* (also known as daughter boards)—part of a motherboard separate from the main one but connected by a cable of some sort—and unique power connections.

Try This!

Motherboard Varieties

Motherboards come in a wide variety of form factors. Go to your local computer store and check out what is on display. Note the different features offered by ATX, microATX, and Mini-ITX motherboards. ATX is common, but does the store stock Mini-ITX or proprietary motherboards? Did the clerk use tech slang and call the motherboards "mobos"? (It's what most of us call them outside of formal textbooks, after all!)

Chipset

You learned in the previous chapter that every motherboard has a chipset, one or more discrete integrated circuit chips that support the CPU's interfacing to all the other devices on the motherboard. The chipset determines the type of processor the motherboard accepts, the type and capacity of RAM, and the sort of internal and external devices that the motherboard supports. Chipsets vary in features, performance, and stability, so they factor hugely in the purchase or recommendation of a particular motherboard. Good techs know their chipsets!

Because the chipset facilitates communication between the CPU and other devices in the system, its component chips are relatively centrally located on the motherboard (see Figure 6-11). As you'll recall from Chapter 5, chipsets were originally composed of two primary chips: the northbridge and the southbridge.

Figure 6-11
Chipset hidden under cooling fins on modern motherboards

The northbridge chip handled RAM, while the southbridge handled some expansion devices and mass storage drives, such as hard drives. Some motherboard manufacturers added (or still add) a third chip called the *Super I/O chip* to handle these chores, especially in dealing with legacy devices. Figure 6-12 shows a typical Super I/O chip.

Today, other chips have absorbed many of the functions of the classic chipset. The CPU handles the memory controller features the northbridge used to do. The primary expansion bus communication (see "Expansion Bus" later in this chapter) goes through the CPU as well, something the southbridge handled back in the day. Most techs refer to the remaining support chips on the motherboard as the chipset, although the terms northbridge and southbridge are dead.

Figure 6-12
Super I/O
chip on ASUS
motherboard

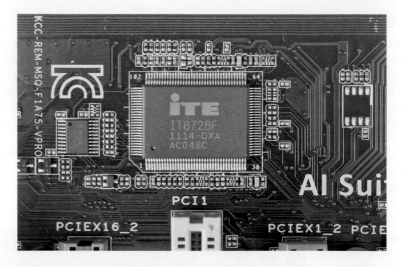

The system ROM chip provides part of the BIOS for the chipset, but only at a bare-bones, generic level. The chipset still needs support for the rest of the things it can do. So how do expansion devices get BIOS? From software drivers, of course, and the same holds true for modern chipsets. You have to load the proper drivers for the specific OS to support all of the features of today's chipsets. Without software drivers, you'll never create a stable, fully functional PC. Most motherboards ship with an optical disc with drivers, support programs, and extra-special goodies such as antivirus software (see Figure 6-13).

Figure 6-13
Driver disc
for ASUS
motherboard

Different chipsets offer support for a lot of different hardware options, including type of memory slot (DDR4 or DDR5), number and version of USB ports, various mass storage devices, integrated network connections, video support, and so on. Figure 6-14 shows a schematic with typical chipset chores for an Intel Z690 chipset.

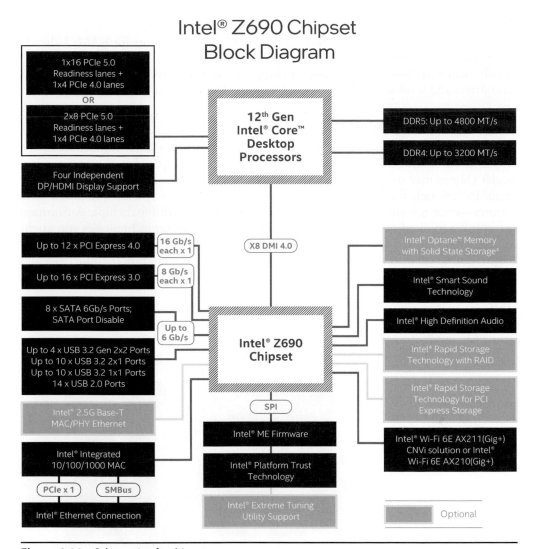

Figure 6-14 Schematic of a chipset

Good techs need to know the hot chipsets in detail. The chipset defines almost every motherboard feature short of the CPU itself. Techs love to discuss chipsets and expect a fellow tech to know the differences between one chipset and another. You also need to be able to recommend a motherboard that suits a client's needs. Chapter 11 covers choosing components and building PCs for specific purposes, such as video editing and gaming. One of the most important choices you'll make in building a custom rig is selecting a chipset.

Standard Components

Every motherboard provides a socket (or two) for a CPU and slots for RAM. I already covered the variety of both sockets (in Chapter 3) and slot types (in Chapter 4), so I won't rehash them here. You'll also find ports to support standard mass storage devices, such as hard drives and solid-state drives (covered in more detail in Chapter 8).

Additional Components

The connections and capabilities of a motherboard sometimes differ from those of the chipset the motherboard uses. This disparity happens for a couple of reasons. First, a particular chipset may support eight USB ports, but to keep costs down, the manufacturer might include only four ports. Second, a motherboard maker may choose to install extra features—ones not supported by the chipset—by adding additional chips. A common example is a motherboard that supports an old serial port. Other technologies you might find are built-in sound, hard drive RAID controllers, network cards, and more. Some motherboards have added convenience features, such as case fan power connectors and running lights so you can see what you're working on.

USB

All chipsets support USB, but it seems no two motherboards offer the same port arrangement. My motherboard supports eight USB ports, for example, but if you look on the back of the motherboard, you'll only see four USB ports (see Figure 6-15).

Figure 6-15
USB connectors showing on back of PC

Most motherboards have *headers—internal connectors*—to plug in header cables for additional external ports. These headers are standardized, so many cases have built-in front USB ports that have header cables attached (see Figure 6-16). This is very handy for USB devices you might want to plug and unplug frequently, such as thumb drives or digital cameras.

Figure 6-16
Front USB
connections

Sound

Most motherboards come with onboard sound support. As with USB, a lot of motherboards have a port for connecting to audio jacks on the front of the case, another example (like USB) of *front panel connectors*. These enable you to plug headphones or microphones into the front rather than the rear of the case, a very convenient feature. These connectors are identical to the ones used on sound cards, so we'll save more discussion for Chapter 10.

Networking

Most desktop motherboards come with at least one RJ-45 jack for attaching a network cable. The networking support is built into the chipset or comes as an additional chip soldered to the motherboard. Chapter 18 covers the physical aspects of networking in detail.

Video

Many motherboards sport one or more video ports for attaching a display. These vary a lot, from the venerable VGA to the HDMI and DisplayPort that are common today. Chapter 17 discusses video in depth, so we'll save further discussion until then.

RAID

RAID stands for *redundant array of independent* (or *inexpensive*) *disks* and is very common on motherboards. There are many types of RAID, such as *mirroring* (the process of using two drives to hold the same data, which is good for safety, because if one drive dies, the other still has all of the data) or *striping* (making two drives act as one drive by spreading data across them, which is good for speed). RAID is a very cool but complex topic that's discussed in detail in Chapter 8.

Case Fan Support

Every motherboard has a CPU fan power connector, as you'll recall from Chapter 3, usually a four-wire connector that supports three-wire fans too. Some motherboards offer one or more fan power connectors for case fans. These are almost always only three-wire connectors. The case fans plugged into the motherboard can be monitored and controlled in Windows, unlike case fans connected only to the power supply, so they add a nice feature.

Expansion Bus

Expansion slots have been part of the PC from the very beginning. Way back then, IBM created the PC with an eye to the future; the original IBM PC had slots built into the motherboard—called *expansion slots*—for adding expansion cards and thus new functions to the PC. (Specific expansion cards such as video, sound, capture, and NIC are discussed later in Chapter 17.) The slots and accompanying wires and support chips on the first PC and on the latest and greatest PC are called the *expansion bus*.

Structure and Function of the Expansion Bus

As you've learned, every device in the computer—whether soldered to the motherboard or snapped into a socket—connects to the external data bus and the address bus. The expansion slots are no exception. They connect to the rest of the PC through the chipset. Exactly *where* on the chipset varies depending on the system. On newer systems, the expansion slots connect to the CPU (see Figure 6-17) because modern CPUs contain a lot of controller features that used to be in the chipset. In older systems, the expansion slots connected directly to the chipset (see Figure 6-18). Finally, many systems have more than one type of expansion bus, with slots of one type connecting to the CPU and slots of another type connecting to the chipset (see Figure 6-19).

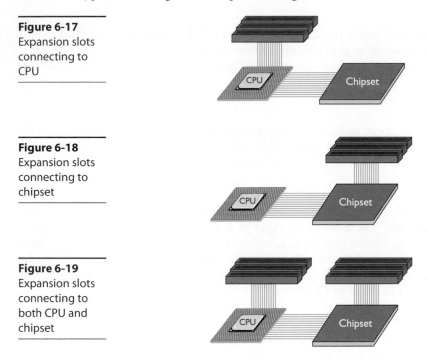

Figure 6-17
Expansion slots connecting to CPU

Figure 6-18
Expansion slots connecting to chipset

Figure 6-19
Expansion slots connecting to both CPU and chipset

The chipset provides an extension of the address bus and data bus to the expansion slots, and thus to any expansion cards in those slots. If you plug a hard drive controller card into an expansion slot, it functions just as if it were built into the motherboard, albeit with one big difference: speed. As you'll recall from Chapter 3, the system crystal—the clock—pushes the CPU. The system crystal provides a critical function for the entire PC, acting like a drill sergeant calling a cadence, setting the pace of activity in the computer. Every device soldered to the motherboard is designed to run at the speed of the system crystal. A 200-MHz motherboard, for example, has its chipset chips all timed by a 200-MHz crystal (see Figure 6-20).

Figure 6-20
The system
crystal sets the
speed.

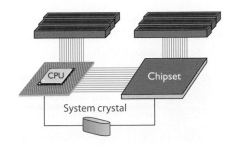

Clock crystals aren't just for CPUs and chipsets. Pretty much every chip in your computer has a CLK wire and needs to be pushed by a clock chip, including the chips on your expansion cards. Suppose you buy a device that did not come with your computer—say, a graphics card. The chips on the graphics card need to be pushed by a CLK signal from a crystal. If PCs were designed to use the system crystal to push that graphics card, graphics card manufacturers would need to make graphics cards for every possible motherboard speed. You would have to buy a 100-MHz graphics card for a 100-MHz system or a 200-MHz graphics card for a 200-MHz system.

That would be ridiculous, and IBM knew it when they designed the PC. They had to make an extension to the external data bus that *ran at its own standardized speed*. You would use this part of the external data bus to snap new devices into the PC. IBM achieved this goal by adding a different crystal, called the *expansion bus crystal*, which controlled the part of the external data bus connected to the expansion slots (see Figure 6-21).

Figure 6-21
Function of
system and
expansion bus
crystals

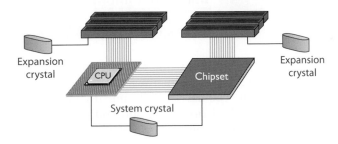

The expansion slots run at a much slower speed than the frontside bus. The chipset acts as the divider between the two buses, compensating for the speed difference with wait states and special buffering (storage) areas. No matter how fast the motherboard runs, the expansion slots run at a standard speed. In the original IBM PC, that speed was about 14.318 MHz ÷ 2, or about 7.16 MHz. Luckily, modern expansion buses run much faster! Let's start with the oldest of the modern expansion slots, PCI.

PCI

Intel introduced the *Peripheral Component Interconnect (PCI)* bus architecture (see Figure 6-22) in the early 1990s, and the PC expansion bus was never again the same. Intel made many smart moves with PCI, not the least of which was releasing PCI to the public domain to make PCI very attractive to manufacturers. PCI provided a wider, faster, more flexible alternative than any previous expansion bus. The exceptional technology of the new bus, combined with the lack of a price tag, made manufacturers quickly drop older buses and adopt PCI.

Figure 6-22
PCI expansion bus slots

PCI really shook up the PC world with its capabilities. The original PCI bus was 32 bits wide and ran at 33 MHz, which was superb, but these features were expected and not earth-shattering. The coolness of PCI came from its capability to coexist with other expansion buses. When PCI first came out, you could buy a motherboard with both PCI and older slots. This was important because users could keep their old expansion cards and slowly migrate to PCI. Equally impressive was that PCI devices were (and still are) self-configuring, a feature that led to the industry standard that became known as plug and play (PnP). Finally, PCI had a powerful burst-mode feature that enabled very efficient data transfers.

PCI Express

PCI Express (PCIe) is still PCI, but it uses a point-to-point *serial* connection instead of PCI's shared *parallel* communication. Consider a single 32-bit chunk of data moving from a device to the CPU. In PCI parallel communication, 32 wires each carry one bit of that chunk of data. In serial communication, only 1 wire carries those 32 bits. You'd think that 32 wires are better than 1, correct?

First of all, PCIe doesn't share the bus. A PCIe device has its own direct connection (a point-to-point connection) to the CPU, so it does not wait for other devices.

Plus, when you start going really fast (think gigabits per second), getting all 32 bits of data to go from one device to another at the same time is difficult, because some bits get there slightly faster than others. That means you need some serious, high-speed checking of the data when it arrives to verify that it's all there and in good shape. Serial data doesn't have this problem, as all of the bits arrive one after the other in a single stream. When data is really going fast, a single point-to-point serial connection is faster than a shared 32-wire parallel connection.

And boy howdy, is PCIe ever fast! A PCIe connection uses one wire for sending and one for receiving. Each of these pairs of wires between a PCIe controller and a device is called a *lane*. Each direction of a lane runs at 2.5 gigatransfers per second (GTps) with PCIe 1.*x*, 5 GTps with PCIe 2.*x*, 8 GTps with PCIe 3.*x*, and a whopping 16 GTps with PCIe 4.0! Better yet, each point-to-point connection can use 1, 2, 4, 8, 12, or 16 lanes to achieve a maximum theoretical bandwidth of up to 256 GTps. The *transfer rate* describes the number of operations happening per second. With serial communication, you almost get a one-to-one correlation between transfer rate and binary data rate. The effective data rate drops a little bit because of the *encoding scheme*—the way the data is broken down and reassembled—but full-duplex data throughput can go up to a whopping 32 GBps on a ×16 connection.

 EXAM TIP You need to know the various motherboard expansion slots for the CompTIA 220-1101 exam, especially PCI and PCIe.

The most common PCIe slot is the 16-lane (×16) version most often used for video cards, as shown in Figure 6-23. The first versions of PCIe motherboards used a combination of a single PCIe ×16 slot and a number of standard PCI slots. (Remember, PCI is designed to work with other expansion slots, even other types of PCI.)

Figure 6-23
PCIe ×16 slot (center) with PCI slots (top and bottom)

The bandwidth provided by a ×16 slot is far more than anything other than a video card would need, so most PCIe motherboards also contain slots with fewer lanes. Currently ×1 is the most common general-purpose PCIe slot (see Figure 6-24). You'll also see ×4 slots on some motherboards.

Figure 6-24
PCIe ×1 slot (top)

Unfortunately for us techs, you can't always know how fast a PCIe slot is just by its size. Here are a few of the most-common factors that can affect how these slots perform:

- The slot may be wired for fewer lanes than its size suggests. You will most often see this where a ×16 slot is wired up to only 4 or 8 lanes. If you put a video card that expects 16 lanes in a slot like this, it will work at a fraction of its capacity.

- Some motherboards don't have enough lanes for each slot to use its maximum at the same time. In this case, adding expansion cards to a system might slow down already-connected devices.

- Lower PCIe versions have less bandwidth available—and some motherboards support different PCIe versions on different slots. The CPU you select can also dictate the effective PCIe version.

- PCIe lanes can be used for some other things on the board as well, and their speed/functionality can be affected by the number of slots/lanes in use (and vice versa). Some examples include network interfaces, newer generations of USB and Thunderbolt, and M.2 (a slot used for high-performance SSDs—we'll take a closer look at M.2 in Chapter 8).

There's no great way to just know exactly how each slot will perform. Make sure to check your motherboard manual to understand how many lanes each slot actually supports under different conditions. Don't go by physical size alone! When you talk about the lanes, such as ×1 or ×16, use "by" rather than "ex" for the multiplication mark. So "by 1" and "by 16" are the correct pronunciations.

Try This!

Shopping Trip

So, what's the latest PCIe motherboard out there? Get online or go to your local computer store and research higher-end motherboards. What combinations of PCIe slots can you find on a single motherboard? Which motherboard has the most PCIe lanes? Why? Jot them down and compare specifications.

Installing Expansion Cards

Installing an expansion card successfully—another one of those bread-and-butter tasks for the PC tech—requires at least four steps. First, you need to know that the card works with your system and your operating system. Second, you have to insert the card in an expansion slot properly and without damaging the card or the motherboard. Third, you need to provide drivers for the operating system—*proper* drivers for the *specific* OS. Fourth, you should always verify that the card functions properly before you walk away from the PC.

 EXAM TIP The four steps involved in installing expansion cards apply to all types of expansion cards. The CompTIA A+ exams will ask you about cards ranging from common—sound, video, and networking—to other specific cards for USB, Thunderbolt, and modem connections. They'll ask about wireless and cellular networking cards, storage cards, video capture cards, and more, all of which we'll cover in their proper chapters in this book. You install any of them using the same four steps: knowledge, physical installation, device drivers, and verification.

Step 1: Knowledge

Learn about the device you plan to install—preferably before you purchase it! Does the device work with your system and operating system? Does it have drivers for your operating system? If you use a recent version of Windows, the answer to these questions is almost always "yes." If you're attempting to install an old device or if you're trying to install a very unique device in a less-common operating system such as Linux, these questions become important. A lot of older hardware simply won't work with newer versions of Windows, especially Windows 10/11. Check the device's documentation and check the device manufacturer's Web site to verify that you have the correct drivers. While you're checking, make sure you have the latest version of the driver; most devices get driver updates more often than the weather changes in Texas.

Step 2: Physical Installation

To install an expansion card successfully, you need to take steps to avoid damaging the card, the motherboard, or both. This means knowing how to handle a card and avoiding electrostatic discharge (ESD) or any other electrical issue. You also need to place the card firmly and completely into an available expansion slot.

Optimally, a card should always be in one of two places: in a computer or in an antistatic bag. When inserting or removing a card, be careful to hold the card only by its edges. Do not hold the card by the slot connectors or touch any components on the board (see Figure 6-25).

Figure 6-25
Where to handle
a card

If possible, use an antistatic wrist strap properly attached to the PC, as noted in Chapter 1. If you don't have a wrist strap, you can use the tech way of avoiding ESD by touching the power supply after you remove the expansion card from its antistatic bag. This puts you, the card, and the PC at the same electrical potential and thus minimizes the risk of ESD.

Modern systems have a trickle of voltage on the motherboard at all times when the computer is plugged into a power outlet. Chapter 7 covers power for the PC and how to deal with it in detail, but here's the short version: *Always unplug the PC before inserting an expansion card!* Failure to do so can destroy the card, the motherboard, or both. It's not worth the risk.

Never insert or remove a card at an extreme angle. This may damage the card. A slight angle is acceptable and even necessary when removing a card. Always secure the card to the case with a connection screw or other retaining mechanism. This keeps the card from slipping out and potentially shorting against other cards. Also, many cards use the screw connection to ground the card to the case (see Figure 6-26).

Many technicians have been told to clean the slot connectors if a particular card is not working. This is almost never necessary after a card is installed and, if done improperly, can cause damage. You should clean slot connectors only if you have a card that's been on the shelf for a while and the contacts are obviously dull.

Figure 6-26
Always secure all
cards properly.

Never use a pencil eraser for this purpose. Pencil erasers can leave behind bits of residue that wedge between the card and slot, preventing contact and causing the card to fail. Grab a can of electronic contact cleaning solution and use it instead. Electronic contact cleaning solution is designed for exactly this purpose, cleans contacts nicely, and doesn't leave any residue. You can find electronic contact cleaning solution at any electronics store or online.

A fully inserted expansion card sits flush against the back of the PC case—assuming the motherboard is mounted properly, of course—with no gap between the mounting bracket on the card and the screw hole on the case. If the card is properly seated, no contacts are exposed above the slot. Figure 6-27 shows a properly seated (meaning fitted snugly in the slot) expansion card.

Step 3: Device Drivers

You know from Chapter 5 that all devices, whether built into the motherboard or added along the way, require BIOS. For almost all expansion cards, that BIOS comes in the form of *device drivers*—software support programs—loaded automatically by the operating system or manually from a USB drive or from an optical disc provided by the card manufacturer.

Figure 6-27
Properly seated
expansion card;
note the tight
fit between case
and mounting
bracket and the
evenness of the
card in the slot.

Installing device drivers is fairly straightforward. You should use the correct drivers—kind of obvious, but you'd be surprised how many techs mess this up—and, if you're upgrading, you might have to unload current drivers before loading new drivers. Finally, if you have a problem, you may need to uninstall the drivers you just loaded or roll back to earlier, more stable drivers.

Getting the Correct Drivers   To be sure you have the best possible driver you can get for your device, you should always check the manufacturer's Web site. The drivers that come with a device may work well, but odds are good that you'll find a newer and better driver on the Web site. How do you know that the drivers on the Web site are newer? First, take the easy route: look on the disc. Often the version is printed right on the optical media. If it's not printed there, you're going to have to load the disc in your optical drive (if you have one) and poke around. Many driver discs have an AutoRun screen that advertises the version. If nothing is on the pop-up screen, look for a Readme file (see Figure 6-28).

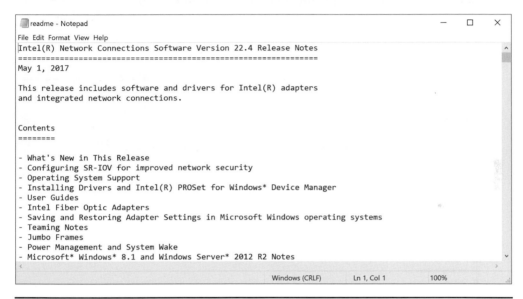

Figure 6-28   Part of a Readme file showing the driver version

If you don't have optical media or an optical drive to install a driver, the easiest way to identify a driver is to do it manually by following the steps below.

For Windows 10 and 11:

1. Open *Device Manage* by right-clicking the Windows *Start* menu. Select *Device Manager*.

2. Click *Yes* if prompted for permission from User Account Control.

3. Expand the branch for the device driver version you want to check.

4. Right-click on the device and select *Properties*.

5. Navigate to the *Driver* tab and note the *Driver Version* presented.

Driver or Device?   In almost all cases, you should install the device driver after you install the device. Without the device installed, the driver installation will not see the device and will give an error screen. The only exceptions to this rule are USB devices—with these you should always install the driver first. (The other excellent external connection,

Thunderbolt, works great however you install drivers when you're in macOS. With Windows? It totally depends on the hardware manufacturer. Read the documentation.)

Removing the Old Drivers   Some cards—and this is especially true with video cards—require you to remove old drivers of the same type before you install the new device. To do this, you must first locate the driver in Device Manager. Right-click the device driver you want to uninstall and select Uninstall device (see Figure 6-29).

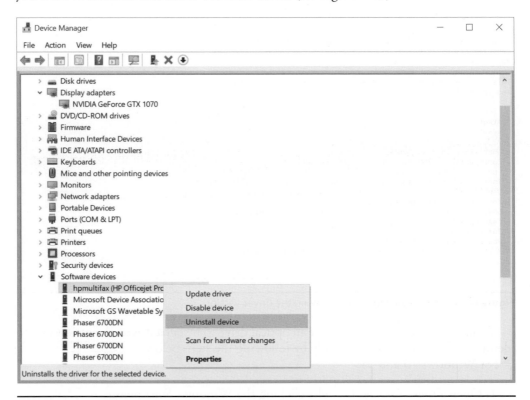

Figure 6-29   Uninstalling a device

Unsigned Drivers   Microsoft truly wants your computer to work, so they provide an excellent and rigorous testing program for hardware manufacturers called the *Windows Hardware Compatibility Program*. The drivers get a digital signature that says Microsoft tested them and found all was well.

Some older versions of Windows had support for *unsigned drivers* automatically enabled. These are drivers that have not gone through the Windows Hardware Compatibility Program, so their software does not have a digital signature from Microsoft. Modern versions of Windows (10 and 11) can support unsigned drivers, but this is disabled by default.

Installing the New Driver You have two ways to install a new driver in Windows. The first option is to let Windows detect the new hardware and find the proper device driver. The second method is to install the drivers manually by downloading them from the manufacturer or using the installation disc. Most installation media give clear options so you can choose what you want to install (see Figure 6-30).

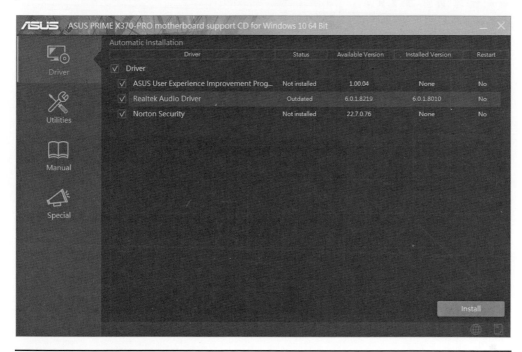

Figure 6-30 Installation menu

 NOTE To install drivers in a Windows computer, you need to have the proper permission. I'm not talking about asking somebody if you're allowed to install the device. Permissions are granted in Windows to enable people to do certain things, such as add a printer to a local computer or install software, or to stop people from being able to do such tasks. Specifically, you need administrative permissions to install drivers. See Chapter 13 for more on permissions.

Driver Rollback All versions of Windows offer the nifty feature of rolling back to previous drivers after an installation or driver upgrade. If you decide to live on the edge and install beta drivers for your video card, for example, and your system becomes fright-fully unstable, you can revert to the drivers that worked before. (Not that I've ever had to use that feature, of course.) To access the rollback feature, simply open Device Manager and access the properties for the device you want to adjust. On the Driver tab (see Figure 6-31), you'll find the Roll Back Driver button.

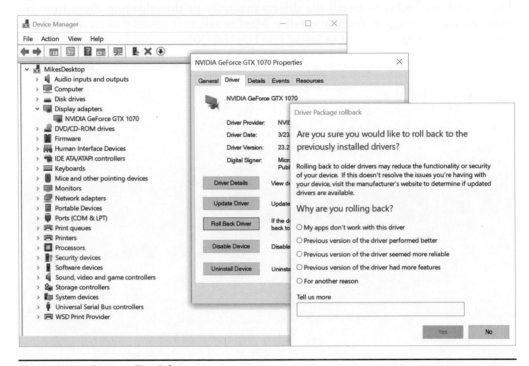

Figure 6-31   Driver rollback feature

Step 4: Verification

As a last step in the installation process, inspect the results of the installation and verify that the device works properly. Immediately after installing, you should open Device Manager and verify that Windows sees the device (see Figure 6-32). Assuming that Device Manager shows the device working properly, your next check is to put the device to work by making it do whatever it is supposed to do. If you installed a printer, print something; if you installed a scanner, scan something. If it works, you're finished!

Beta Drivers

Many PC enthusiasts try to squeeze every bit of performance out of their PC components, much as auto enthusiasts tinker with engine tunings to get a little extra horsepower out of their engines. Expansion card manufacturers love enthusiasts, who often act as free testers for their unpolished drivers, known as beta drivers. Beta drivers are fine for the most part, but they can sometimes cause amazing system instability—never a good thing! If you use beta drivers, make sure you know how to uninstall or roll back to previous drivers.

Figure 6-32
Device Manager
shows the device
working properly.

Troubleshooting Expansion Cards
===============================

A properly installed expansion card rarely makes trouble; it's the botched installations that produce headaches. Chances are high that you'll have to troubleshoot an expansion card installation at some point, usually from an installation you botched personally.

The first sign of an improperly installed card usually shows up the moment you first try to get that card to do whatever it's supposed to do, and it doesn't do it. When this happens, your primary troubleshooting process is a reinstallation—after checking in with Device Manager.

Other chapters in this book cover specific hardware troubleshooting. For example, troubleshooting video cards is covered in Chapter 17. Use this section to help you decide what to look for and how to deal with the problem.

Device Manager provides the first diagnostic and troubleshooting tool in Windows. After you install a new device, Device Manager gives you many clues if something has gone wrong.

Occasionally, Device Manager may not even show the new device. If that happens, verify that you inserted the device properly and, if needed, that the device has power. Run the Add Hardware Wizard and see if Windows recognizes the device (see Figure 6-33). In Windows, you run the program by clicking Start and typing the name of the executable in the Search bar: **hdwwiz.exe**.

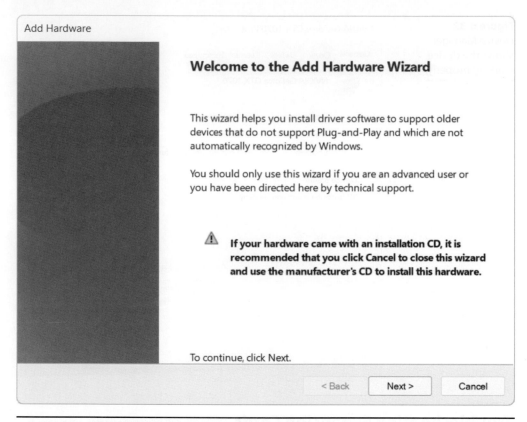

Figure 6-33   Running Add Hardware Wizard in Windows 11

If Device Manager doesn't recognize the device at this point, you have one of two problems: either the device is physically damaged and you must replace it, or the device is an onboard device, not a card, and is turned off in CMOS.

Device Manager rarely completely fails to see a device. More commonly, device problems manifest themselves in Device Manager via error icons:

- A black "!" on a triangle indicates that a device is missing (see Figure 6-34), that Windows does not recognize a device, or that there's a device driver problem. A device may still work even while producing this error.

- A black downward-pointing arrow on a white field indicates a disabled device. This usually points to a device that's been manually turned off, or a damaged device. A device producing this error will not work.

The "!" symbol is the most common error symbol and usually the easiest to fix. First, double-check the device's connections. Second, try reinstalling the driver with the Update Driver button. To get to the Update Driver button, right-click the desired device in Device Manager and select *Update driver* to open the updating wizard (see Figure 6-35).

Figure 6-34
An "!" in Device
Manager,
indicating a
problem with the
selected device

Figure 6-35
Updating the
driver

If you get a downward-pointing arrow, first check that the device isn't disabled. Right-click the device and select Enable. If that doesn't work (it often does not), try rolling back the driver (if you updated the driver) or uninstalling (if it's a new install). Shut the system down and make triple-sure you have the card physically installed.

Then redo the entire driver installation procedure, making sure you have the most current driver for that device. If none of these procedures works, return the card—it's almost certainly bad.

Upgrading and Installing Motherboards

To most techs, the concept of adding or replacing a motherboard can be extremely intimidating. It really shouldn't be; motherboard installation is a common and necessary part of PC repair. It is inexpensive and easy, although it can sometimes be a little tedious and messy because of the large number of parts involved. This section covers the process of installation and replacement and shows you some of the tricks that make this necessary process easy to handle.

Choosing the Motherboard and Case

Choosing a motherboard and case can prove quite a challenge for any tech, whether newly minted or a seasoned veteran. You first have to figure out the type of motherboard you want, such as AMD- or Intel-based. Then you need to think about the form factor, which of course influences the type of case you'll need. Third, how rich in features is the motherboard and how tough is it to configure? You have to read the motherboard manual to find out. Finally, you need to select the case that matches your space needs, budget, and form factor. Now look at each step in a little more detail.

 EXAM TIP Being able to select and install a motherboard appropriate for a client or customer is something every CompTIA A+ technician should know.

First, determine what motherboard you need. What CPU are you using? Will the motherboard work with that CPU? Because most of us buy the CPU and the motherboard at the same time, make the seller guarantee that the CPU will work with the motherboard. How much RAM do you intend to install? Are extra RAM sockets available for future upgrades? Chapter 11 covers items needed for specialized PCs.

Try This!

Building a Recommendation

Family, friends, and potential clients often solicit the advice of a tech when they're thinking about upgrading their PC. This solicitation puts you on the spot to make not just any old recommendation, but one that works with the needs and budget of the potential upgrader. To handle this scenario successfully, you need to manage expectations and ask the right questions like these:

What does the upgrader want to do that compels him or her to upgrade? Write it down! Some of the common motivations for upgrading are to play that hot new game or to take advantage of new technology. What's the minimum system needed to run tomorrow's action games? What do you need to make multimedia sing? Does the motherboard need to have SuperSpeed USB 3.0 or SuperSpeed USB 10 Gbps (USB 3.2 Gen 2) built in to accommodate digital video or some other special purpose?

How much of the current system does the upgrader want to save? Upgrading a motherboard can very quickly turn into a complete system rebuild. What form factor is the old case? If it's a microATX case, that constrains the motherboards you can use with it to microATX. If the desired motherboard is a full-sized ATX board, you'll need to get a new case. Does the new motherboard possess the same type of CPU socket as the old motherboard? If not, that's a sure sign you'll need to upgrade the CPU as well.

What about RAM? If the old motherboard was using DDR3 SDRAM, and the new motherboard requires DDR4, you'll need to replace the RAM. If you need to upgrade the memory, it is best to know how many channels the new RAM interface supports, because performance is best when all channels are populated.

Once you've gathered information on motivation and assessed the current PC of the upgrader, it's time to get down to business: field trip time! This is a great excuse to either physically go to the computer store and check out the latest motherboards and gadgets or simply visit their website. Don't forget to jot down notes and prices. By the end of your in-person or virtual field trip, you should have the information to give the upgrader an honest assessment of what an upgrade will entail, at least in monetary terms. Be honest—in other words, don't just tell upgraders what you think they want to hear—and you won't get in trouble.

A number of excellent motherboard manufacturers currently exist. Some of the more popular brands are ASUS, AsRock, GIGABYTE, and MSI. Your supplier may also have some lesser-known but perfectly acceptable brands of motherboards. As long as the supplier has an easy return policy, it's fine to try one of these.

Second, make sure you're getting a form factor that works with your case. Don't try to put a regular ATX motherboard into a microATX case!

Third, all motherboards come with a technical manual, better known as the *motherboard book* (see Figure 6-36). You must have this book! This book is your primary source for all of the critical information about the motherboard. If you set up CPU or RAM timings incorrectly in CMOS, for example, and you have a dead PC, where would you find the CMOS-clear jumper? Where do you plug in the speaker? Even if you let someone else install the motherboard, insist on the motherboard book; you will need it.

Figure 6-36
Motherboard box
and book

NOTE If you have a motherboard with no manual, you can usually find a copy of the manual in Adobe Acrobat (.PDF) format online at the manufacturer's Web site. Make sure you match the revision number of the motherboard as well as the model number. It's a good idea to grab and print a copy to keep with the motherboard. I often tape a copy of the manual (either hard copy, burned onto a disc, or copied to a USB drive) in the case where I installed the motherboard. A good spot is in an unused drive bay. Just don't cover any vents!

Fourth, pick your case carefully. Cases come in many sizes: slimline, desktop, mini-tower, mid-tower, tower, and cube. You can also get specialized cases, such as tiny cases for entertainment systems or ones that fit the same format as a stereo receiver or DVD player. The latter case is called a home theater PC (HTPC), an example of which is shown in Figure 6-37.

Figure 6-37
An HTPC

Slimline and desktop models generally sit on the desk, beneath the monitor. The various tower cases usually occupy a bit of floor space next to the desk. The mini-tower and mid-tower cases are the most popular choices. Make sure you get a case that fits your motherboard—most microATX cases are too small for a regular ATX motherboard. Cube cases generally require a specific motherboard, so be prepared to buy both pieces at the same time. A quick test-fit before you buy saves a lot of return trips to the supplier.

Better cases offer tool-free component installation, so you don't have to screw down cards or drives. They just snap into place. You'll still need a trusty screwdriver to secure the motherboard, though. No installation is completely tool-free yet.

Power supplies sometimes come with the case. Watch out for "really good deal" cases because that invariably points to a cheap or missing power supply. You also need to verify that the power supply has sufficient wattage. This issue is handled in Chapter 7.

Installing the Motherboard

If you're replacing a motherboard, first remove the old motherboard. Begin by removing all of the cards. Also remove anything else that might impede removal or installation of the motherboard, such as a hard drive. Keep track of your screws—the best idea is to return the screws to their mounting holes temporarily, at least until you can reinstall the parts. Sometimes you even have to remove the power supply temporarily to enable access to the motherboard.

 EXAM TIP   The CompTIA A+ exams may test you on the basics of installing a motherboard, so you need to know this section.

Unscrew the motherboard. *It will not simply lift out.* The motherboard mounts to the case via small connectors called *standoffs* that screw into the bottom of the case (see Figure 6-38). Screws then go into the standoffs to hold the motherboard in place. Be sure to place the standoffs properly before installing the new motherboard.

 CAUTION   Watch out for ESD here! Remember that it's very easy to damage or destroy a CPU and RAM with a little electrostatic discharge. It's also fairly easy to damage the motherboard with ESD. Always wear your antistatic wrist strap.

When you insert the new motherboard, do not assume that you will put the screws and standoffs in the same place as they were in your old motherboard. When it comes to the placement of screws and standoffs, only one rule applies: anywhere it fits. Do not be afraid to be a little tough here! Installing motherboards can be a wiggling, twisting, knuckle-scraping process.

 CAUTION   Pay attention to the location of the standoffs if you're swapping a motherboard. If you leave a screw-type standoff beneath a spot on the motherboard where you can't add a screw and then apply power to the motherboard, you run the risk of frying the motherboard.

Figure 6-38
Standoff in a
case, ready for
the motherboard

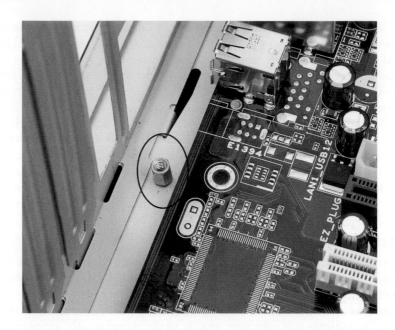

The next part of motherboard installation is connecting the LEDs, buttons, and front-mounted ports on the front of the box. This is sometimes easier to do before you install the motherboard fully in the case. You can trace the wire leads from the front of the case to the appropriate standoffs on the motherboard. These usually include the following:

- Soft power button
- Reset button
- Speaker
- Hard drive activity light
- Power light
- USB
- Sound
- Thunderbolt

These wires have specific pin connections to the motherboard. Although you can refer to the motherboard book for their location, usually a quick inspection of the motherboard will suffice for an experienced tech (see Figure 6-39).

You need to follow a few rules when installing these wires. First, the lights are LEDs, not light bulbs; they have a positive side and a negative side. If they don't work one way, turn the connector around and try the other. Second, when in doubt, guess. Incorrect installation only results in the device not working; it won't damage the computer. Refer to the motherboard book for the correct installation. The third and last rule is that, with the exception of the soft power switch on an ATX system, you do not need any of these wires for the computer to run.

Figure 6-39
Motherboard
wire connections
labeled on the
motherboard

NOTE A lot of techs install the CPU, CPU fan, and RAM into the motherboard before installing the motherboard into the case. This helps in several ways, especially with a new system. First, you want to make certain that the CPU and RAM work well with the motherboard and with each other—without that, you have no hope of setting up a stable system. Second, installing these components first prevents the phenomenon of *flexing* the motherboard. Some cases don't provide quite enough support for the motherboard, and pushing in RAM can make the board bend. Third, attaching a CPU fan can be a bear of a task, one that's considerably easier to do on a table top than within the confines of a case. A lot of third-party CPU fan and heat-sink assemblies mount on brackets on the bottom of the motherboard, requiring installation before placement in the case.

No hard-and-fast rule exists for determining the function of each wire. Often the function of each wire is printed on the connector (see Figure 6-40). If not, track each wire to the LED or switch to determine its function.

Finally, install the motherboard into the case fully and secure it with the appropriate screws. Once you get the motherboard mounted in the case, with the CPU and RAM properly installed, it's time to insert the power connections and test it. A POST card can be helpful with the system test because you won't have to add the speaker, a video card, monitor, and keyboard to verify that the system is booting. If you have a POST card, start the system, and watch to see if the POST takes place—you should see a number of POST codes before the POST stops. If you don't have a POST card, install a keyboard, speaker, video card, and monitor. Boot the system and see if the BIOS information shows up on the screen. If it does, you're probably okay. If it doesn't, it's time to refer to the motherboard book to see where you made a mistake.

Figure 6-40
Sample of case
wires

If you get no power at all, check to make sure you plugged in all the necessary power connectors. If you get power to fans but get nothing on the screen, you could have several problems. The CPU, RAM, or video card might not be connected to the motherboard properly. The only way to determine the problems is to test. Check the easy connections first (RAM and video) before removing and reseating the CPU. Also, see Chapter 7 for more on power issues.

Troubleshooting Motherboards

Motherboards fail. Not often, but motherboards and motherboard components can die from many causes: time, dust, cat hair, or simply slight manufacturing defects made worse by the millions of amps of current sluicing through the motherboard traces. Installing cards, electrostatic discharge, flexing the motherboard one time too many when swapping out RAM or drives—any of these factors can cause a motherboard to fail. The motherboard is a hard-working, often abused component of the PC. Unfortunately for the common tech, troubleshooting a motherboard problem can be difficult and time-consuming. Let's wrap up this chapter with a look at symptoms of a failing motherboard, techniques for troubleshooting, and the options you have when you discover a motherboard problem.

Symptoms

Motherboard failures commonly fall into three types: catastrophic, component, and ethereal. With a *catastrophic failure,* the computer just won't boot. It might have been working just fine; you hear a pop—a *loud noise*—followed by the acrid smell of ozone, and then you have a dead computer. Use your nose to lead you to a popped capacitor or other motherboard component. Check the power and hard drive activity *indicator lights* on the front of the PC. Assuming they worked before, having them completely flat points to power supply failure or motherboard failure.

 SIM   Check out the Chapter 6 Challenge! sim, "Label Motherboard," over at https://www.totalsem.com/110x. It'll help you remember all the motherboard components in case you get a performance-based challenge on the CompTIA A+ 1101 exam.

This sort of problem happens to brand-new systems because of manufacturing defects—often called a *burn-in failure*—and to any system that gets a shock of ESD. Burn-in failure is uncommon and usually happens in the first 30 days of use. Swap out the motherboard for a replacement and you should be fine. If you accidentally zap your motherboard when inserting a card or moving wires around, be chagrined. Change your daring ways and wear an antistatic wrist strap!

Component failure happens rarely and appears as flaky connections between a device and motherboard, or as intermittent problems. A hard drive plugged into a faulty controller on the motherboard, for example, might show up in CMOS autodetect but be inaccessible in Windows. Another example is a USB port that worked fine for months until a big storm took out the external modem hooked to it, and now it doesn't work, even with a replacement modem.

The most difficult of the three types of symptoms to diagnose are those I call *ethereal* symptoms. Stuff just doesn't work all of the time. The PC reboots itself. You get a blue screen of death (BSoD) in the midst of heavy computing, such as right before you smack the villain and rescue the damsel. What can cause such symptoms? If you answered any of the following, you win the prize:

- Faulty component
- Buggy device driver
- Buggy application software
- Slight corruption of the operating system
- Power supply problems

Err…you get the picture.

What a nightmare scenario to troubleshoot! The Way of the Tech knows paths through such perils, though, so let's turn to troubleshooting techniques now.

Techniques

Troubleshooting a potential motherboard failure requires time, patience, and organization. Some problems will certainly be quicker to solve than others. If the hard drive doesn't work as expected, as in the previous example, check the settings on the drive.

Try a different drive. Try the same drive with a different motherboard to verify that it's a good drive. Like every other troubleshooting technique, what you're trying to do with motherboard testing is to isolate the problem by eliminating potential causes.

Use a modern POST card with a good diagnostic screen. You'll find cards that plug into both PCI and PCIe slots, for example, and even USB-based POST cards that enable quick diagnostic tests on portable computers. See Figure 6-41.

Figure 6-41 USB POST card (left) and PCI POST card (right)

This three-part system—check, replace, verify good component—works for both simple and more complicated motherboard problems. You can even apply the same technique to ethereal-type problems that might be anything, but you should add one more verb: *document*. Take notes on the individual components you test so you don't repeat efforts or waste time. Plus, taking notes can lead to the establishment of patterns. Being able to re-create a system crash by performing certain actions in a specific order can often lead you to the root of the problem. Document your actions. Motherboard testing is time-consuming enough without adding inefficiency.

Options

Once you determine that the motherboard has problems, you have several options for fixing the three types of failures. If you have a catastrophic failure, you must replace the motherboard. Even if it works somewhat, don't mess around. The motherboard should provide bedrock stability for the system. If it's even remotely buggy or problematic, get rid of it!

CAUTION If you've lost components because of ESD or a power surge, you would most likely be better off replacing the motherboard. The damage you can't see can definitely sneak up to bite you and create system instability.

If you have a component failure, you can often replace the component with an add-on card that will be as good as or better than the failed device. One example of this is a card that can replace the built-in SATA ports on the motherboard (see Figure 6-42).

Figure 6-42
PCIe SATA card

If your component failure is more a technology issue than physical damage, you can try upgrading the BIOS on the motherboard. As you'll recall from Chapter 5, every motherboard comes with a small set of code that enables the CPU to communicate properly with the devices built into the motherboard. You can quite readily upgrade this programming by *flashing the BIOS*: running a small command-line program to write a new BIOS in the flash ROM chip. Refer to Chapter 5 for the details on flashing.

 NOTE Flashing the BIOS for a motherboard can fix a lot of system stability problems and provide better implementation of built-in technology. What it cannot do for your system is improve the hardware. If AMD comes out with a new, improved, lower-voltage A-Series CPU, for example, and your motherboard cannot scale down the voltage properly, you cannot use that CPU—even if it fits in your motherboard's Socket AM4. No amount of BIOS flashing can change the hardware built into your motherboard.

Finally, if you have an ethereal, ghost-in-the-machine type of problem that you have finally determined to be motherboard related, you have only a couple of options for fixing the problem. You can flash the BIOS in a desperate attempt to correct whatever it is, which sometimes does work and is less expensive than the other option, which is replacing the motherboard.

Chapter Review

Questions

1. Which of the following statements about the expansion bus is true?

    A. The expansion bus runs at the speed of the system clock.

    B. The expansion bus crystal sets the speed for the expansion bus.

    C. The CPU communicates with RAM via the expansion bus.

    D. The frontside bus is another name for the expansion bus.

2. What does a black down arrow next to a device in Device Manager indicate?

    A. A compatible driver has been installed that may not provide all of the functions for the device.

    B. The device is missing, or Windows cannot recognize it.

    C. The system resources have been assigned manually.

    D. The device has been disabled.

3. Which of the following is a serial expansion bus?

    A. PCI-X

    B. PCI

    C. PCIe

    D. AGP

4. Which of the following form factors dominates the PC industry?

    A. AT

    B. ATX

    C. ITX

    D. BTX

5. Amanda bought a new system that, right in the middle of an important presentation, gave her a blue screen of death. Now her system won't boot at all, not even to CMOS. After extensive troubleshooting, she determined that the motherboard was at fault and replaced it. Now the system runs fine. What was the most likely cause of the problem?

    A. Burn-in failure

    B. Electrostatic discharge

    C. Component failure

    D. Power supply failure

6. Martin bought a new motherboard to replace his older ATX motherboard. As he left the shop, the tech on duty called after him, "Check your standoffs!" What could the tech have meant?

    A. Standoffs are the connectors on the motherboard for the front panel buttons, such as the on/off switch and reset button.

    B. Standoffs are the metal edges on some cases that aren't rolled.

    C. Standoffs are the metal connectors that attach the motherboard to the case.

    D. Standoffs are the headers that enable a motherboard to support more than four USB ports.

7. Solon has a very buggy computer that keeps locking up at odd moments and rebooting spontaneously. He suspects the motherboard. How should he test it?

    A. Check settings and verify good components.

    B. Verify good components and document all testing.

    C. Replace the motherboard first to see if the problems disappear.

    D. Check settings, verify good components, replace components, and document all testing.

8. When Jane proudly displayed her new motherboard, the senior tech scratched his beard and asked, "What kind of northbridge does it have?" What could he possibly be asking about?

    A. The PCI slot

    B. The PCIe slot

    C. The chipset

    D. The USB controller

9. What companies dominate the chipset market? (Select two.)

    A. AMD

    B. Intel

    C. NVIDIA

    D. SiS

10. If Windows recognizes a device, where will it appear?

    A. Device Manager

    B. C:\Windows\System32\Devices

    C. Desktop

    D. Downloads

Answers

1. **B.** A separate expansion bus crystal enables the expansion bus to run at a different speed than the frontside bus.

2. **D.** The device has been disabled.

3. **C.** PCIe is a serial expansion bus, while the older PCI, PCI-X, and AGP are all parallel expansion busses.

4. **B.** Almost all modern motherboards follow the ATX form factor.

5. **A.** Although all of the answers are plausible, the best answer here is that her system suffered burn-in failure.

6. **C.** Standoffs are the metal connectors that attach the motherboard to the case.

7. **D.** Solon needs to check settings, verify good components, replace components, and document all testing.

8. **C.** The tech is using older terminology to refer to the chips—the chipset—that help the CPU communicate with devices.

9. **A, B.** AMD and Intel produce the vast majority of the chipsets used in personal computers.

10. **A.** Windows displays recognized devices in Device Manager.

CHAPTER 7

Power Supplies

In this chapter, you will learn how to

- Explain the basics of electricity
- Describe the details of powering the PC
- Install and maintain power supplies
- Explain power supply troubleshooting and fire safety

Computers need electricity to run. Where this electricity comes from depends on the device. Mobile devices use batteries (covered in detail in Chapter 23). Desktop computers need a special box—the *power supply unit (PSU)*—that takes electricity from the wall socket and transforms it into electricity your computer can use. Figure 7-1 shows a typical power supply.

Figure 7-1
Power supply
about to be
mounted inside a
system unit

As simple as this appears on the surface, power supply issues are of critical importance for techs. Problems with power create system instability, crashes, and data loss—all things most computer users would rather avoid! Good techs know an awful lot about powering the PC, from understanding the basic principles of electricity to knowing the many variations of PC power supplies. Plus, you need to know how to recognize power problems and implement the proper solutions. Too many techs fall into the "just plug it in" camp and never learn how to deal with power, much to their clients' unhappiness.

 EXAM TIP Some questions on the CompTIA A+ 220-1101 exam might refer to a power supply as a *PSU*, for *power supply unit*. A power supply also falls into the category of field replaceable unit (FRU), which refers to the typical parts a tech should carry, such as RAM and a hard drive.

Historical/Conceptual

Understanding Electricity

Electricity is a flow of negatively charged particles, called electrons, through matter. All matter enables the flow of electrons to some extent. This flow of electrons is very similar to the flow of water through pipes; so similar that the best way to learn about electricity is by comparing it to how water flows through pipes. Let's talk about water for a moment.

Water comes from the ground, through wells, aquifers, rivers, and so forth. In a typical city, water comes to you through pipes from the water supply company that took it from the ground. What do you pay for when you pay your water bill each month? You pay for the water you use, certainly, but built into the price of the water you use is the surety that when you turn the spigot, water will flow at a (more or less) constant rate. The water sits in the pipes under pressure from the water company, waiting for you to turn the spigot.

Electricity works essentially the same way as water. Electric companies gather or generate electricity and then push it to your house under pressure through wires. Just like water, the electricity sits in the wires, waiting for you to plug something into the wall socket, at which time it'll flow at a (again, more or less) constant rate. You plug a lamp into an electrical outlet and flip the switch, electricity flows, and you have light. You pay for the quantity of reliable, constant-voltage electricity your home or business uses.

The pressure of the electrons in the wire is called *voltage* and is measured in units called *volts (V)*. See Figure 7-2.

Figure 7-2
Electrical voltage
as water pressure

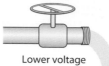

Lower voltage   Higher voltage

The number of electrons moving past a certain point on a wire is called the *current* (or *amperage*), which is measured in units called *amperes (amps or A)*. See Figure 7-3.

Figure 7-3
Electrical
amperage as
amount of water
flowing

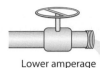
Lower amperage

Higher amperage

The amps and volts needed so that a particular device will function is expressed as how much *wattage (watts or W)* that device needs. The correlation between the three is remarkably simple math: V × A = W. Let's see how this formula helps PC techs.

Wires of all sorts—whether copper, tin, gold, or platinum—have a slight *resistance* to the flow of electrons, just as water pipes have a slight amount of friction that resists the flow of water. Resistance to the flow of electrons is measured in *ohms (Ω)*.

- Pressure = voltage (V)
- Volume flowing = amperes (A)
- Power = wattage (W)
- Resistance = ohms (Ω)

NOTE   Types of matter that allow electrons to move easily are known as *conductors*. Types of matter that inhibit electron movement are called *insulators*.

A particular thickness of wire only holds so much current at a time. If you push too much through, the wire will overheat and break, much as an overloaded water pipe will burst. To make sure you use the right wire for the right job, all electrical wires have an amperage rating, such as 20 amps. If you try to push 30 amps through a 20-amp wire, the wire will break, and electrons will seek a way to return into the ground. Not a good thing, especially if the path back to ground is through you!

Circuit breakers and ground wires provide the basic protection from accidental overflow. A circuit breaker is a heat-sensitive or electromagnetically operated electrical switch rated for a specified amperage. If you push too much amperage through the circuit breaker, the wiring inside detects the increase in heat or current and automatically opens, stopping the flow of electricity before the wiring overheats and breaks. You reset the circuit breaker to reestablish the circuit, and electricity flows once more through the wires. A ground wire provides a path of least resistance for electrons to flow back to ground in case of an accidental overflow.

Many years ago, home and building electrical supplies used fuses instead of circuit breakers. Fuses are small devices with a tiny filament designed to break if subjected to too much current. Unfortunately, fuses had to be replaced every time they blew, making circuit breakers much more convenient. Even though you no longer see fuses in a building's electrical circuits, many electrical devices—such as a PC's power supply—often still use fuses for their own internal protection. Once blown, these fuses are not replaceable by users or technicians without special training and tools.

 TIP An electrical outlet must have a ground wire to be suitable for PC use.

Electricity comes in two flavors: *direct current (DC),* in which the electrons flow in one direction around a continuous circuit, and *alternating current (AC),* in which the flow of electrons alternates direction back and forth in a circuit (see Figure 7-4). Most electronic devices use DC power, but all power companies supply AC power because AC travels long distances much more efficiently than DC.

Figure 7-4
Diagrams
showing DC and
AC flow

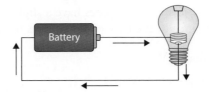

Direct current (DC)
• Constant power in one direction
• Best for electronics

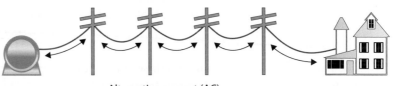

Alternating current (AC)
• Power alternates back and forth
• Best for long distance

1101

Powering the PC

Your PC uses DC voltage, so some conversion process must take place before the PC can use AC power from the power company. The power supply in a computer converts high-voltage AC power from the wall socket to low-voltage DC. The first step in powering the PC, therefore, is to get and maintain a good supply of AC power. Second, you need a power supply to convert AC to the proper voltage and amperage of DC power for the motherboard and peripherals. Finally, you need to control the by-product of electricity use—namely, heat. Let's look at the specifics of powering the PC.

Supplying AC

Every PC power supply must have standard AC power from the power company. The power supply gets that power with a power cord that plugs into an electrical outlet on one end and to the power supply via a standard *IEC-320* connector on the other. In the United States, standard AC comes in somewhere between input 110 and 120 V, often written as ~115 VAC (volts of alternating current). Most of the rest of the world uses 230 VAC, so modern power supplies are designed to support both voltages, aka *dual voltage*. Not only are they dual voltage, but they're also autosensing. Just plug in the power supply and it automatically adjusts to whatever voltage is offered.

Older power supplies were also dual voltage but not autosensing. These power supplies came with a voltage-selection switch and are referred to as fixed-input. Figure 7-5 shows the back of a power supply. Note the three components, from top to bottom: the hard on/off switch, the 115/230 switch, and the IEC-320 connector.

Figure 7-5
Back of fixed-input power supply, showing typical switches and power connection

 CAUTION Be careful with fixed-input power supplies! Flipping the voltage selection switch on the back of a power supply will wreak havoc on a PC. Moving the switch to 230V in the United States makes for a great practical joke (as long as the PC is off when you do it)—the PC might try to boot up but probably won't get far. You don't risk damaging anything by running at half the AC that the power supply is expecting. In countries that run 230V standard, on the other hand, firing up the PC with this switch set to ~115 can cause the power supply to die a horrid, smoking death. Watch that switch!

Testing Your Power Source

Before you plug any critical components into an AC outlet, take a moment to test the outlet first by using a multimeter or a device designed exclusively to test outlets. Failure to test AC outlets properly can result in inoperable or destroyed equipment, as well as possible electrocution. The IEC-320 plug has three holes, called hot, neutral, and ground. These names describe the function of the wires that connect to them behind the wall plate. The hot wire carries electrical voltage, much like a pipe that delivers water. The neutral wire carries no voltage, but instead acts like a water drain, completing the circuit by returning electricity to the local source, normally a breaker panel. The ground wire makes it possible for excess electricity to return safely to the ground, such as in a short-circuit condition.

When testing AC power, you want to check for three things: that the hot outputs approximately 115 V (or whatever the proper voltage is for your part of the world), that the neutral connects to ground (0 V output), and that the ground connects to ground (again, 0 V). Figure 7-6 shows the voltages at an outlet. You can use a *multimeter*—often also referred to as a *volt-ohm meter (VOM)* or *digital multimeter (DMM)*—to measure several aspects of electrical current. A multimeter consists of two probes, an analog or digital meter, and a dial to set the type of test you want to perform. Refer to Figure 7-7 to become familiar with the components of the multimeter.

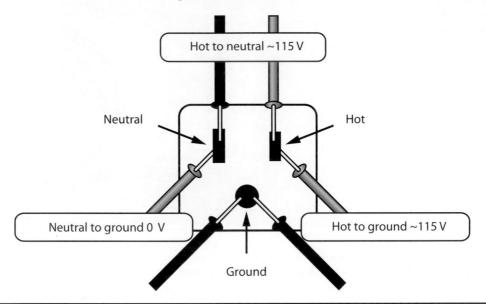

Figure 7-6   Outlet voltages

Note that some multimeters use symbols rather than letters to describe AC and DC settings. For example, the *V* with the solid line above a dashed line in Figure 7-8 refers to direct current. The *V~* stands for alternating current.

AC Adapters

Many computing devices use an AC adapter rather than an internal power supply. AC adapters tend to look the same, a black box with two cables. One cable goes to a wall power outlet, and the other cable plugs into your device (see Figure 7-9).

Figure 7-7
Author's ancient
but reliable Radio
Shack digital
multimeter

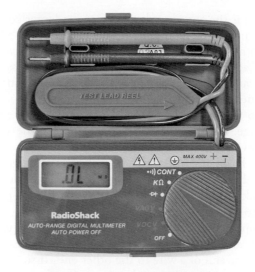

Figure 7-8
Multimeter
featuring DC and
AC symbols

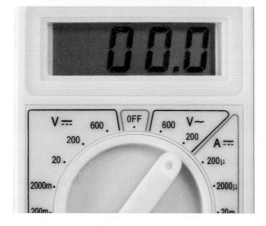

Figure 7-9
Typical
AC adapter

Even though it sits outside a device, an AC adapter converts AC current to DC, just like a power supply. Unlike internal power supplies, AC adapters are rarely interchangeable. Although manufacturers of different devices often use the same kind of plug on the end of the AC adapter cable, these adapters are not necessarily interchangeable. In other words, just because you can plug an AC adapter from your friend's laptop into your laptop does not mean it's going to work.

You need to make sure that three things match before you plug an AC adapter into a device: voltage, amperage, and polarity. If either the voltage or amperage output is too low, the device won't run. If the polarity is reversed, it won't work, just like putting a battery in a flashlight backward. If either the voltage or amperage—especially the former—is too high, on the other hand, you can very quickly toast your device. Don't do it! Always check the voltage, amperage, and polarity of a replacement AC adapter before you plug it into a device.

Most multimeters offer at least four types of electrical tests: continuity, resistance, AC voltage (VAC), and DC voltage (VDC). Continuity tests determine whether electrons can flow from one end of a wire to the other end. If so, you have continuity; if not, you don't. You can use this setting to determine if a fuse is good or to check for breaks in wires. If your multimeter doesn't have a continuity tester (many cheaper multimeters do not), you can use the resistance tester. A broken wire or fuse will show infinite resistance, while a good wire or fuse will show no resistance. Testing AC and DC voltages is a matter of making sure the measured voltage is what it should be.

Try This!

Using a Multimeter to Test AC Outlets

Every competent technician knows how to use a multimeter, so if you haven't used one in the past, get hold of one and work through this scenario. Your boss tasks you with checking the existing electrical outlets in a new satellite location for the company. Caution: During this exercise, do *not* physically touch any of the metal parts of the probes or sockets!

First you need to set up the meter for measuring AC. Follow these steps:

1. Move the selector switch to the AC V (usually red). If multiple settings are available, put it into the first scale higher than 120 V (usually 200 V). *Auto-range* meters set their own range; they don't need any selection except AC V.

2. Place the black lead in the common (–) hole. If the black lead is permanently attached, ignore this step.

3. Place the red lead in the V-Ohm-A (+) hole. If the red lead is permanently attached, ignore this step.

Once you have the meter set up for AC, go through the process of testing the various wires on an AC socket. Just don't put your fingers on the metal parts of the leads when you stick them into the socket! Follow these steps:

1. Put either lead in hot, the other in neutral. You should read 110 to 120 VAC.

2. Put either lead in hot, the other in ground. You should read 110 to 120 VAC.

3. Put either lead in neutral, the other in ground. You should read 0 VAC.

If any of these readings is different from what is described here, it's time to call an electrician.

Using Special Equipment to Test AC Voltage

A number of good AC-only testing devices are available. With these devices, you can test all voltages for an AC outlet by simply inserting them into the outlet. Be sure to test all of the outlets the computer system uses: power supply, external devices, and monitor. Although convenient, these devices aren't as accurate as a multimeter. My favorite tester is a seemingly simple tool available from a number of manufacturers. This handy circuit tester (see Figure 7-10) provides three light-emitting diodes (LEDs) that describe everything that can go wrong with a plug.

Figure 7-10
Circuit tester

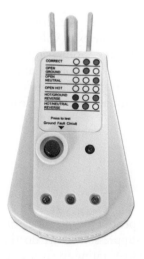

1102

Equipment Grounding

Computer equipment safety starts with proper grounding. The ground wire functions as an emergency outlet for excess current in case of any short or malfunction of a device. Don't assume that a convenient three-prong outlet has proper grounding, especially in older buildings. Use a multimeter to check that ground wire.

Protecting the PC from Spikes and Sags in AC Power

If all power companies could supply electricity in smooth, continuous flows with no dips or spikes in pressure, the next two sections of this chapter would be irrelevant. Unfortunately, no matter how clean the AC supply appears to a multimeter, the truth is that voltage from the power company tends to drop well below (sag) and shoot far above (*power surge* or spike) the standard 115 V (in the United States). These sags and spikes usually don't affect lamps and refrigerators in such scenarios, but they can keep your PC from running or can even destroy a PC or peripheral device. Two essential devices handle spikes and sags in the supply of AC: surge suppressors and uninterruptible power supplies.

 EXAM TIP Large sags in electricity are also known as *brownouts*. When the power cuts out completely, it's called a *blackout*.

Surge Suppressors   Surges or spikes are far more dangerous than sags. Even a strong sag only shuts off or reboots your PC; any surge can harm your computer, and a strong surge destroys components. Given the seriousness of surges, every PC should use a *surge suppressor* device that absorbs the extra voltage from a surge to protect the PC. The power supply does a good job of surge suppression and handles smaller surges without a problem. But the power supply takes a lot of damage from larger surges and will eventually fail. To protect your power supply, a dedicated surge suppressor works between the power supply and the outlet to protect the system from power surges (see Figure 7-11).

Figure 7-11
Surge suppressor

Most people tend to spend a lot of money on their PC and for some reason suddenly get cheap on the surge suppressor. Don't do that! Make sure your surge suppressor has the UL LCC 1449 for 330-V rating to ensure substantial protection for your system. UL (https://www.ul.com) is a U.S.-based, not-for-profit, widely recognized industry testing laboratory whose testing standards are very important to the consumer electronics industry.

Additionally, check the joules rating before buying a new surge suppressor. A *joule* is a unit of electrical energy. How much energy a surge suppressor can handle before it fails is described in joules. Most authorities agree that your surge suppressor should rate at a minimum of 2000 joules—and the more joules, the better the protection. My surge suppressor rates at 3500 joules.

While you're protecting your system, don't forget that surges also come from telephone and cable connections. If you use anything with copper cables—cable modems, or even an old DSL modem—make sure to get a surge suppressor that includes support for these types of connections. Many manufacturers make surge suppressors with telephone line protection (see Figure 7-12).

Figure 7-12
Surge suppressor with cable and telephone line protection

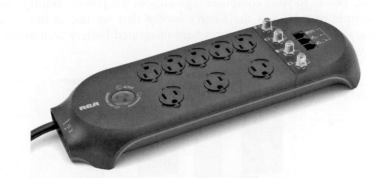

No surge suppressor works forever. Make sure your surge suppressor has a test/reset button so you'll know when the device has—as we say in the business—turned into an extension cord. If your system takes a hit and you have a surge suppressor, call the company! Many companies provide cash guarantees against system failure due to surges, but only if you follow their guidelines.

 CAUTION No surge suppressor in the world can handle the ultimate surge, the electrical discharge of a lightning strike. If your electrical system takes such a hit, you can kiss your PC and any other electronic devices goodbye if they were plugged in at the time. Always unplug electronics during electrical storms!

 NOTE Surge suppression isn't just about joules. Surge suppressors are also rated in clamping voltage, in which an overvoltage condition is "clamped" to a more manageable voltage for a certain amount of time. Good consumer suppressors can clamp 600 volts down to 180 volts or less for at least 50 microseconds and can do so on either the hot line or neutral line.

If you want really great surge suppression, you need to move up to *power conditioning*. Your power lines take in all kinds of strange signals that have no business being in there, such as electromagnetic interference (EMI) and radio frequency interference (RFI). Most of the time, this line noise is so minimal it's not worth addressing, but occasionally events (such as lightning) generate enough line noise to cause weird things to happen to your PC (keyboard lockups, messed-up data). All better surge suppressors add power conditioning to filter out EMI and RFI.

Uninterruptable Power Supply   An uninterruptable power supply (UPS) protects your computer (and, more importantly, your data) in the event of a power sag or power outage. Figure 7-13 shows a typical UPS. It essentially contains a big battery that provides AC power to your computer regardless of the power coming from the AC outlet. An example of a UPS is the *battery backup* that we use in our personal computers, laptops, and tablets. These devices have integrated battery technology that charges the device with DC power.

Figure 7-13
UPS

All UPSs are measured in both watts (the true amount of power they supply in the event of a power outage) and in *volt-amps (VA)*. Volt-amps is the amount of power the UPS could provide if the devices took power from the UPS in a perfect way. Your UPS provides perfect AC power, moving current smoothly back and forth 60 times a second (or 50 in other parts of the world). Power supplies, monitors, and other devices, however, may not take all of the power the UPS has to offer at every point as the AC power moves back and forth, resulting in inefficiencies. If your devices took all of the power the UPS offered at every point as the power moved back and forth, VA would equal watts.

EXAM TIP   You'll want to be familiar with the technology and use of surge suppressors and battery backup systems for the CompTIA A+ 220-1102 exam.

If the UPS makers knew ahead of time exactly what devices you planned to plug into their UPS, they could tell you the exact watts, but different devices have different efficiencies, forcing the UPS makers to go by what they can offer (VAs), not what your devices will take (watts). The watts value they give is a guess, and it's never as high as the VAs. The VA rating is always higher than the wattage rating.

Because you have no way to calculate the exact efficiency of every device you'll plug into the UPS, go with the wattage rating. You add up the total wattage of every component in your PC and buy a UPS with a higher wattage. You'll spend a lot of time and mental energy figuring precisely how much wattage your computer, monitor, drives, and so on require to get the proper UPS for your system. But you're still not finished! Remember that the UPS is a battery with a limited amount of power, so you then need to figure out how long you want the UPS to run when you lose power.

NOTE   There are two main types of UPS: online, where devices are constantly powered through the UPS's battery, and standby, where devices connected to the UPS receive battery power only when the AC sags below ~80–90 V. Another type of UPS is called line-interactive, which is similar to a standby UPS but has special circuitry to handle moderate AC sags and surges without the need to switch to battery power.

The quicker and far better method to use for determining the UPS you need is to go to any of the major surge suppressor/UPS makers' Web sites and use their handy power calculators. My personal favorite is on the APC by Schneider Electric Web site: https://www.apc.com (type **UPS selector** in the search field). APC makes great surge suppressors and UPSs, and the company's online calculator will show you the true wattage you need—and teach you about whatever new thing is happening in power at the same time.

Every UPS also has surge suppression and power conditioning, so look for the joule and UL 1449 ratings. Also look for replacement battery costs—some UPS replacement batteries are very expensive. Last, look for a UPS with a USB or Ethernet (RJ-45) connection. These handy UPSs come with monitoring and maintenance software (see Figure 7-14) that tells you the status of your system and the amount of battery power available, logs power events, and provides other handy options.

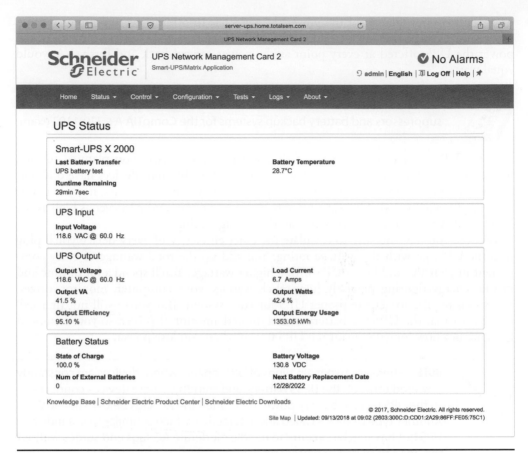

Figure 7-14   UPS management application

Table 7-1 gives you a quick look at the low end and the higher end of UPS products.

Brand	Model	Outlets Protected	Backup Time	Price	Type
APC	BE425M	3 @ 120 V	3 min @ 200 W, 10 min @ 100 W	$49.99	Standby
APC	Pro BR 1000MS	4 @ 120 V	4 min @ 600 W, 64 min @ 100 W	$184.99	Standby
CyberPower	CPS1500AVR	6 @ 120 V	18 min @ 950 W, 6 min @ 475 W	$497.00	Line-interactive

Table 7-1   Typical UPS Devices

1101

Supplying DC

After you've ensured the supply of good AC electricity for the PC, the power supply unit takes over, converting public utility voltage AC (115/120 V in the United States, 230 V in many other countries) into several DC voltages (notably, 3.3 V, 5 V, and 12 V) usable by the delicate interior components. Power supplies come in a large number of shapes and sizes, but the most common size by far is the standard 150 mm × 140 mm × 86 mm desktop PSU shown in Figure 7-15.

Figure 7-15
Desktop PSU

The PC uses the 12-V current to power motors on devices such as hard drives and optical drives, and it uses the 3.3- and 5-V current for support of onboard electronics. Manufacturers may use these voltages any way they wish, however, and may deviate from these assumptions. Power supplies also come with standard connectors for the motherboard and interior devices.

Power to the Motherboard

Modern motherboards use a 20- or 24-pin *P1 power connector*. Some motherboards may require special 4-, 6-, or 8-pin connectors to supply extra power (see Figure 7-16). We'll talk about each of these connectors in the form factor standards discussion later in this chapter.

Figure 7-16
Motherboard
power
connectors

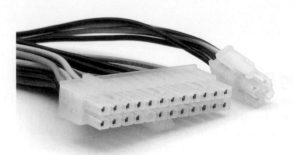

Power to Peripherals: Molex, Mini, and SATA

Many devices inside the PC require power. These include hard drives, solid-state drives, optical drives, and fans. The typical PC power supply has at least three types of connectors that plug into peripherals: Molex, mini, and SATA. (Higher-end video cards get their own connector(s) as well, covered a little later in this chapter.)

Molex Connectors   Now over 50 years old, the Molex connector supplies 5-V and 12-V current for fans and older drives (see Figure 7-17). It has notches, called *chamfers*, that guide its installation. The tricky part is that Molex connectors require a firm push to plug in properly, and a strong person can defeat the chamfers, plugging a Molex in upside down. Not a good thing. *Always* check for proper orientation before you push it in!

Figure 7-17
Molex connector

Mini Connectors   A few power supplies still support the *mini connector* or *Berg connector* (see Figure 7-18). The mini supplies 5 V and 12 V to peripherals. Originally adopted as the standard connector on 3.5-inch floppy disk drives, you'll still see the occasional device needing this connector.

Figure 7-18
Mini connector

Try This!

Testing DC

A common practice for techs troubleshooting a system is to test the DC voltages coming out of the power supply. Even with good AC, a bad power supply can fail to transform AC to DC at voltages needed by the motherboard and peripherals. The best way to learn how to perform this common technique is to try it yourself, so grab your trusty multimeter and walk through the following steps on a powered-up PC with the side cover removed. Note that you must have P1 connected to the motherboard and the system must be running (you don't have to be in Windows or Linux, of course).

1. Switch your multimeter to DC, somewhere around 20 V DC if you need to make that choice. Make sure your leads are plugged into the multimeter properly: red to hot, black to ground. The key to testing DC is that which lead you touch to which wire matters. Red goes to hot wires of all colors; black *always* goes to ground. If your wires are all the same color, look up a pin-out diagram for the connector. For a Molex connector, pin 1 will be 12 V and pin 4 will be 5 V; a quick way to tell is with the chamfers up, pin 1 is on the left.

2. Plug the red lead into the red wire socket (pin 4) of a free Molex connector and plug the black lead into one of the two black wire sockets (pins 2 or 3). You should get a reading of ~5 V. What do you have?

3. Now move the red lead to the yellow socket (pin 1). What voltage do you get?

4. Testing the P1 connector is a little more complicated. You push the red and black leads into the top of P1, sliding in alongside the wires until you bottom out. Leave the black lead in one of the black wire ground sockets. Move the red lead through all of the colored wire sockets. What voltages do you find?

 CAUTION As with any power connector, plugging a mini connector into a device the wrong way will almost certainly destroy the device. Check twice before you plug one in!

SATA Power Connectors Serial ATA (SATA) drives need a 15-pin *SATA power connector* (see Figure 7-19). The larger pin count supports the SATA hot-swappable feature and 3.3-, 5-, and 12-V devices. The 3.3-V pins are not used in any current iteration of SATA drives and are reserved for possible future use. All three generations of SATA use the same power connectors. SATA power connectors are L shaped, making it almost impossible to insert one incorrectly into a SATA drive. No other device on a computer uses the SATA power connector. For more information about SATA drives, see Chapter 8.

Figure 7-19
SATA power
connector

Splitters and Adapters   You may occasionally find yourself without enough connectors to power all of the devices inside your PC. In this case, you can purchase splitters to create more connections (see Figure 7-20). You might also run into the phenomenon of needing a SATA connector but having only a spare Molex. Because the voltages on the wires are the same, a simple adapter will take care of the problem nicely.

Figure 7-20
Molex splitter

ATX

The original ATX power supplies had two distinguishing physical features: the motherboard power connector and soft power. Motherboard power came from a single cable with a 20-pin P1 motherboard power connector. ATX power supplies also had at least two other cables, each populated with two or more Molex or mini connectors for peripheral power.

When plugged in, ATX systems have 5 V running to the motherboard. They're always "on," even when powered down. The power switch you press to power up the PC isn't a true power switch like the light switch on the wall in your bedroom. The power switch on an ATX system simply tells the computer whether it has been pressed. The BIOS or operating system takes over from there and handles the chore of turning the PC on or off. This is called soft power.

Using soft power instead of a physical switch has several important benefits. Soft power prevents a user from turning off a system before the operating system has been shut down. It enables the PC to use power-saving modes that put the system to sleep and then wake it up when you press a key, move a mouse, or receive an e-mail (or other network traffic). (See Chapter 23 for more details on sleep mode.)

All of the most important settings for ATX soft power reside in CMOS setup. Boot into CMOS and look for a Power Management section. Take a look at the Power Button Function option in Figure 7-21. This determines the function of the on/off switch. You may set this switch to turn off the computer, or you may set it to the more common *4-second delay*.

Figure 7-21
Soft power
setting in CMOS

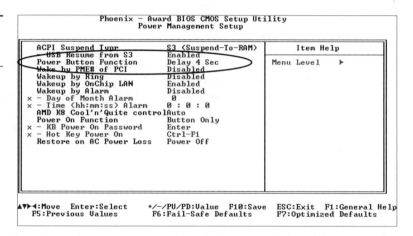

ATX did a great job supplying power for more than a decade, but over time more powerful CPUs, multiple CPUs, video cards, and other components began to need more current than the original ATX provided. This motivated the industry to introduce several updates to the ATX power standards: ATX12V 1.3, EPS12V, multiple rails, ATX12V 2.0, other form factors, and active PFC.

ATX12V 1.3   The first widespread update to the ATX standard, ATX12V 1.3, came out in 2003. This introduced a 4-pin motherboard power connector, unofficially but commonly called the *P4 power connector*, that provides more 12-V power to assist the 20/24-pin P1 motherboard power connector. Any power supply that provides a P4 connector is called an ATX12V power supply. The term "ATX" was dropped from the ATX power standard, so if you want to get really nerdy you can say—accurately— that there's no such thing as an ATX power supply. All power supplies—assuming they have a P4 connector—are ATX12V or one of the later standards.

TIP SATA also supports a slimline connector that has a 6-pin power segment and a micro connector that has a 9-pin power segment.

The ATX12V 1.3 standard also introduced a 6-pin auxiliary connector—commonly called an *AUX* connector—to supply increased 3.3- and 5-V current to the motherboard (see Figure 7-22). This connector was based on the motherboard power connector from the precursor of ATX, called *AT*.

Figure 7-22
Auxiliary power
connector

The introduction of these two extra power connectors caused the industry some teething problems. In particular, motherboards using AMD CPUs tended to need the AUX connector, while motherboards using Intel CPUs needed only the P4. As a result, many power supplies came with only a P4 or only an AUX connector to save money. The biggest problem with the ATX12V standard was the lack of enforcement—it made a lot of recommendations but few requirements, giving PSU makers too much choice (such as choosing or not choosing to add AUX and P4 connectors) that weren't fixed until later versions.

EPS12V Server motherboards are thirsty for power, and sometimes ATX12V 1.3 just didn't cut it. An industry group called the Server System Infrastructure (SSI) developed a non-ATX standard motherboard and power supply called EPS12V. An EPS12V power supply came with a 24-pin main motherboard power connector that resembled a 20-pin ATX connector, but it offered more current and thus more stability for motherboards. It also came with an AUX connector, an ATX12V P4 connector, and a unique 8-pin connector. That's a lot of connectors! EPS12V power supplies were not interchangeable with ATX12V power supplies.

EPS12V may not have seen much life beyond servers, but it introduced a number of power features, some of which eventually became part of the ATX12V standard. The most important issue was something called *rails*.

Rails Generally, the PC's power comes from a single transformer that takes the AC current from a wall socket and converts it into DC current that is split into three primary DC voltage rails: 12 V, 5 V, and 3.3 V. Groups of wires run from each of these voltage rails to the various connectors.

Each rail has a maximum amount of power it can supply. Normal computer use rarely approaches this ceiling, but powerful computers with advanced processors and graphics cards require more power than some rails can provide. In the past, 12-V rails only supplied about 18 amps, which wasn't enough to power all that high-end equipment.

The most popular solution was to include multiple 12-V rails in the power supply. This worked fine, but you needed to make sure that you weren't drawing all the power from the same 12-V rail. The key circuitry that monitors the amount of amperage going through each rail, called the over-current protection (OCP), will shut down the power supply if the current goes beyond its cap. In a *single-rail* system, a single OCP circuit monitors all the pathways. In a *multi-rail* system, each pathway gets its own OCP circuit.

When first implemented, multi-rail power supplies didn't do a great job balancing the circuitry, so enthusiasts still ran into problems with systems shutting down under heavy load. This has been fixed since 2008 or so, so any multi-rail PSU you buy today can handle whatever you throw at it.

Today's power supply manufacturers produce single- and multi-rail high-amperage PSUs. You can find power supplies now with 12-V rails pushing 70 amps or more!

ATX12V 2.0 The ATX12V 2.0 standard incorporated many of the good ideas of EPS12V, starting with the 24-pin connector. This 24-pin motherboard power connector is backward compatible with the older 20-pin connector, so users don't have to buy a new motherboard if they use an ATX12V 2.0 power supply. ATX12V 2.0 requires two 12-V rails for any power supply rated higher than 230 W. ATX12V 2.0 dropped the AUX connector and requires SATA hard drive connectors.

Many ATX12V 2.0 power supplies have a convertible *20-to-24-pin motherboard adapter*. These are handy if you want to make a nice "clean" connection, because many 20-pin connectors have interfaces that prevent plugging in a 24-pin connector. You'll also see many 24-pin connectors constructed in such a way that you can slide off the extra four pins. Figure 7-23 shows 20-pin and 24-pin connectors; Figure 7-24 shows a convertible adapter. Although they look similar, those extra four pins won't replace the P4 connector. They are incompatible!

Figure 7-23
20- and 24-pin
connectors

Figure 7-24
Convertible
motherboard
power connector

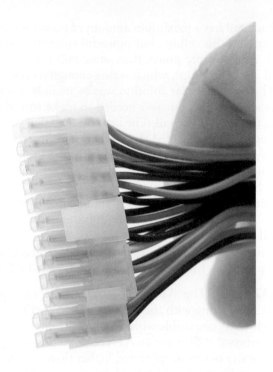

Many modern ATX motherboards feature an 8-pin CPU power connector like the one found in the EPS12V standard to help support high-end CPUs that demand a lot of power. This connector is referred to by several names, including EPS12V, EATX12V, and ATX12V 2x4. One half of this connector will be pin compatible with the P4 power connector, and the other half may be under a protective cap. Be sure to check the motherboard installation manuals for recommendations on when to use the full 8 pins. For backward compatibility, some power supplies provide an 8-pin power connector that can split into two 4-pin sets, one of which is the P4 connector.

Another notable connector is the auxiliary PCI Express (PCIe) power connector. Figure 7-25 shows the 6-pin PCIe power connector. Some motherboards add a Molex socket for PCIe, and some cards come with a Molex socket as well. Higher-end video cards have one or two sockets that require specific PCIe *6/8-pin power connectors*. The 8-pin PCIe connector should not be confused with the EPS12V connector, as they are not compatible. Some PCIe devices with the 8-pin connector will accept a 6-pin PCIe power connection instead, but this may put limits on their performance. Often, you'll find that 8-pin PCIe power cables have two pins at the end that you can detach for easy compatibility with 6-pin devices.

Figure 7-25
PCI Express 6-pin
power connector

 SIM Check out the Chapter 7 Challenge! sim, "ID PSU Connector," over at https://www.totalsem.com/110X. It'll help you identify and memorize the standard power supply connectors.

Niche-Market Power Supply Form Factors The demand for smaller and quieter PCs led to the development of niche-market power supply form factors. All use standard ATX connectors but differ in size and shape from standard ATX power supplies.

Here are some of the more common specialty power supply types:

- **Mini-ITX** and **microATX** Smaller power supply form factors designed specifically for mini-ITX and microATX cases, respectively
- **TFX12V** A small power supply form factor optimized for low-profile ATX systems
- **SFX12V** A small power supply form factor optimized for systems using FlexATX motherboards (see Figure 7-26)

Figure 7-26
SFX power
supply

 NOTE You'll commonly find niche-market power supplies bundled with computer cases (and often motherboards as well). These form factors are rarely sold alone.

Active PFC   Visualize the AC current coming from the power company as water in a pipe, smoothly moving back and forth, 50 or 60 times each second. A PC's power supply, simply due to the process of changing this AC current into DC current, is like a person sucking on a straw on the end of this pipe. It takes gulps only when the current is fully pushing or pulling at the top and bottom of each cycle and creating an electrical phenomena—similar to the back pressure sometimes seen in water pipes—that's called *harmonics* in the power industry. These harmonics create the humming sound you hear from electrical components. Over time, harmonics damage electrical equipment, causing serious problems with the power supply and other electrical devices on the circuit. Once you put a few thousand PCs with power supplies in the same local area, harmonics can even damage the electrical power supplier's equipment!

Good PC power supplies come with *active power factor correction (active PFC)*, extra circuitry that smooths out power coming from the wall before passing it to the main power supply circuits. This smoothing process eliminates any harmonics (see Figure 7-27). Never buy a power supply that does not have active PFC—all power supplies with active PFC will announce it on the box.

Figure 7-27
Power supply
advertising
active PFC

[ENGLISH] Model: Neo HE 550

- ATX12V v2.2 and EPS12V compliant.
- Dual CPU and dual core ready.
- Advanced cable management system improves internal airflow and reduces system clutter by allowing you to use only the cables that you need.
- Universal Input automatically accepts line voltages from 100V to 240V AC.
- Active PFC (Power Factor Correction) delivers environmentally-friendlier power.
- Up to 85% efficiency reduces heat generation and saves power and money.
- Dedicated voltage outputs to deliver more stable power.
- Voltage feedback and tight ±3% regulation for improved system stability.
- Three +12V output circuits provide maximum stable power for the CPU independently and for other peripherals.
- Dual PCI Express graphics card power connectors.
- Low-speed 80mm fan delivers whisper-quiet cooling and ensures quiet operation by varying fan speed in response to load and conditions.

Wattage Requirements

Every device in a PC requires a certain wattage to function. A typical hard drive draws about 15 W of power when accessed, for example, whereas an AMD Ryzen 9 5900X draws a whopping 105 W at peak usage. The total wattage of all devices combined is the minimum you need the power supply to provide.

When selecting a power supply for a system, in other words, make sure the power supply provides enough wattage to run the number of devices in the system. Also, the power supply needs to be able to support all the *types* of devices to be powered in the system. This is where knowing the *wattage rating* of your system is important. The wattage rating represents the amount of energy that's converted from the power outlet to your computer's internal power components. For example, a computer with a 75 percent power supply would consume approximately 400W if it generated 300W of power internally. I updated the video card in a system the other day, for example, from a card that required a single 6-wire power cable to one that required two 8-wire power cables (see Figure 7-28). The power supply clearly had to have the latter capability.

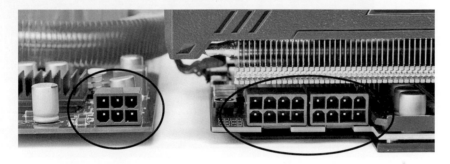

Figure 7-28   Big jump in power requirements!

If the power supply cannot produce the wattage a system needs, that PC won't work properly or at all. Because most devices in the PC require maximum wattage when first starting, the most common result of insufficient wattage is a paperweight that looks like a PC. This can lead to some embarrassing moments. You might plug in a new hard drive for a client, push the power button on the case, and nothing happens—a dead PC! Eek! You can quickly determine if insufficient wattage is the problem. Unplug the drive and power up the system. If the system boots up, the power supply is a likely suspect. The only fix for this problem is to replace the power supply with one that provides more wattage (or leave the new drive out—a less-than-ideal solution).

NOTE   An undersized power supply may not necessarily result in a complete paperweight. Some graphics cards that are dependent on additional rail power from a PSU may continue to operate but will do so at reduced frame rates. That means your games won't play well, but the computer will function in other capacities. See Chapter 17 for the scoop on power-hungry video cards.

No power supply can convert 100 percent of the AC power coming from the power company into DC current, so all power supplies provide less power to the system than the wattage that they draw from the wall. The difference is lost in heat generation. The amount of this differential is advertised on the box. ATX12V 2.0 standards require a power supply to be at least 70 percent efficient, but many power supplies operate with better than 80 percent efficiency. Figure 7-29 shows a power supply clearly displaying its rating.

Figure 7-29
PSU efficiency
rating

Power supplies are typically graded for their efficiency under a voluntary standards program called *80 Plus*. Under 80 Plus, power supplies are rated from 80 percent to 94 percent efficiency for a given load and badged with "metal labels" such as Bronze (80 percent), Gold (90 percent), or Titanium (94 percent) levels. These levels are achieved within a narrow range of watts provided, while lower levels of efficiency are achieved at higher and lower power draw. Power and efficiency curves are usually provided in the power supply documentation. More efficiency can tell you how many watts the system draws to supply sufficient power to the PC in actual use. The added efficiency means the power supply wastes less power, saving you money.

 EXAM TIP The CompTIA A+ 1101 exam does not require you to figure precise wattage needs for a particular system. When building a PC for a client, however, you do need to know this stuff!

One common argument these days is that people buy power supplies that provide far more wattage than a system needs and therefore waste power. This is untrue. A power supply provides only the amount of power your system needs. If you put a 1500-W power supply into a system that needs only 250 W, that big power supply will put out only 250 W to the system. So buying an efficient, higher-wattage power supply gives you two benefits. First, running a power supply at less than 100 percent load helps it live longer. Second, you'll have plenty of extra power when adding new components.

Don't cut the specifications too tightly for power supplies. All power supplies produce less wattage over time, simply because of wear and tear on the internal components. If you build a system that runs with only a few watts of extra power available from the power supply initially, that system will most likely start causing problems within a year or less. Do yourself or your clients a favor and get a power supply that has more wattage than you need.

As a general recommendation for a new system, use at least a 550-W power supply. This is a common wattage and gives you plenty of extra power for booting as well as for whatever other components you might add to the system in the future.

Try This!

Calculating Power Needs

The Internet has some great tools to help you determine power needs for specific computer systems. As noted earlier in the chapter, I recently upgraded from a decent video card to a high-end gaming card (and added another solid-state drive for more storage), after which I used an online tool to determine whether I needed to upgrade the power supply for a stable system. You will find yourself in similar situations as a tech, so try this!

Open a Web browser and check out the OuterVision Power Supply Calculator at https://outervision.com/power-supply-calculator. Enter the details on your desired systems and let this amazing tool do the math for you. Note the calculator compares efficiency information and even makes a recommended purchase for you (and not from OuterVision). It's a very slick, very convenient tool. Bookmark it!

Installing and Maintaining Power Supplies

Although installing and maintaining power supplies takes a little less math than selecting the proper power supply for a system, they remain essential skills for any tech. Installing takes but a moment and maintaining is almost as simple. Let's take a look.

Installing

The typical power supply connects to the PC with four standard computer screws, mounted in the back of the case (see Figure 7-30). Unscrew the four screws and the power supply lifts out easily (see Figure 7-31). Insert a new power supply that fits the case and attach it by using the same four screws.

Figure 7-30
Mounting screws
for power supply

Figure 7-31
Removing power
supply from
system unit

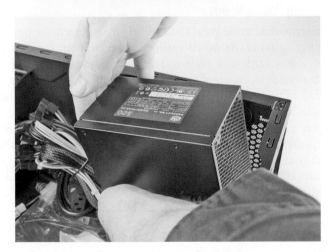

Handling ATX power supplies requires special consideration. Understand that an ATX power supply *never turns off*. As long as that power supply stays connected to a power outlet, the power supply will continue to supply 5 V to the motherboard. Always unplug an ATX system before you do any work! For years, techs bickered about the merits of leaving a PC plugged in or unplugged when servicing it. ATX settled this issue forever. Roughly half of all ATX power supplies provide a real on/off switch on the back of the PSU (see Figure 7-32). If you really need the system to be shut down with no power to the motherboard, use this switch.

Figure 7-32
On/off switch for
an ATX system

When working on an ATX system, you may find that using the power button is inconvenient. Perhaps you're not using a case, or you haven't bothered to plug the power button's leads into the motherboard. That means there is no power button. One trick when in that situation is to use a metal key or a screwdriver to contact the two wires to start and stop the system (see Figure 7-33).

Figure 7-33
Shorting the soft
on/off jumpers

Your first task after acquiring a new power supply is simply to make sure that it works. Insert the motherboard power connectors before starting the system. If you have video cards with power connectors, plug them in too. You can wait to plug in other connectors such as hard drives until you have one successful boot—or if you're feeling lucky, just plug everything in!

Cooling

Heat and computers are not the best of friends. Cooling is therefore a vital consideration when building a computer. Electricity equals heat. Computers, being electrical devices, generate heat as they operate, and too much heat can seriously damage a computer's internal components.

The *power supply fan* provides the basic cooling for the PC (see Figure 7-34). It not only cools the voltage regulator circuits *within* the power supply but also provides a constant flow of outside air throughout the interior of the computer case. A dead power supply fan can rapidly cause tremendous problems, even equipment failure. If you ever turn on a computer and it boots just fine but you notice that it seems unusually quiet, check to see if the power supply fan has died. If it has, quickly turn off the PC and replace the power supply.

Figure 7-34
Power supply fan

Some power supplies come with a built-in sensor to help regulate the airflow. If the system gets too hot, the power supply fan spins faster (see Figure 7-35).

Figure 7-35
3-wire fan sensor connector

Case fans are large, square fans that snap into special brackets on the case or screw directly to the case, providing extra cooling for key components (see Figure 7-36). Most cases come with a case fan, and no modern computer should really be without one or two.

Figure 7-36
Case fan

The single biggest issue related to case fans is where to plug them in. Case fans may come with standard Molex connectors, which are easy to plug in, or they may come with three-pronged power connectors that connect to the motherboard. You can get adapters to plug three-pronged connectors into Molex connectors or vice versa. But if your fans support it, I recommend plugging into the motherboard so the system can monitor the fan speed.

Maintaining Airflow

A computer is an enclosed system, and computer cases help the fans keep things cool: everything is inside a box. Although many tech types like to run their systems with the side panel of the case open for easy access to the components, in the end they are cheating themselves. Why? A closed case enables the fans to create airflow. This airflow substantially cools off interior components. When the side of the case is open, you ruin the airflow of the system, and you lose a lot of cooling efficiency.

An important point to remember when implementing good airflow inside your computer case is that hot air rises. Warm air always rises above cold air, and you can use this principle to your advantage in keeping your computer cool.

In the typical layout of case fans for a computer case, an intake fan is located near the bottom of the front bezel of the case. This fan draws cool air in from outside the case and blows it over the components inside the case. Near the top and rear of the case (usually near the power supply), you'll usually find an exhaust fan. This fan works the opposite of the intake fan: it takes the warm air from inside the case and sends it to the outside.

Another important part of maintaining proper airflow inside the case is ensuring that slot covers are covering all empty expansion bays (see Figure 7-37). To maintain good airflow inside your case, you shouldn't provide too many opportunities for air to escape. Slot covers not only assist in maintaining a steady airflow; they also help keep dust and smoke out of your case.

Figure 7-37
Slot covers

 TIP   Missing slot covers can cause the PC to overheat!

Reducing Fan Noise

Fans generate noise. In an effort to ensure proper cooling, many techs put several high-speed fans into a case, making the PC sound like a jet engine. You can reduce fan noise by using manually adjustable fans, larger fans, or specialty "quiet" fans. Many motherboards enable you to control fans through software.

Manually adjustable fans have a little knob you can turn to speed up or slow down the fan (see Figure 7-38). This kind of fan can reduce some of the noise, but you run the risk of slowing down the fan too much and thus letting the interior of the case heat up. A better solution is to get quieter fans.

Figure 7-38
Manual fan
adjustment
device

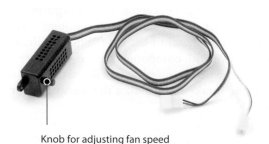

Knob for adjusting fan speed

Larger fans that spin more slowly are another way to reduce noise while maintaining good airflow. Fans sizes are measured in millimeters (mm) or centimeters (cm). Traditionally, the industry used 80-mm power supply and cooling fans, but today you'll find 92-mm, 120-mm, 140-mm, and even larger fans in power supplies and cases.

Because the temperature inside a PC changes depending on the load put on the PC, the best solution for noise reduction combines a good set of fans with temperature sensors to speed up or slow down the fans automatically. A PC at rest uses less than half of the power of a PC running a video-intensive computer game and therefore makes a lot less heat. Virtually all modern systems support three fans through three 3-pin fan connectors on the motherboard. The CPU fan uses one of these connectors, and the other two are for system fans or the power supply fan.

Assuming your fans are installed with 3-wire connections, you can monitor and control your fans. Before you start messing with fans, keep in mind that on most system you never have to touch anything in terms of fans because the system and the OS work together to turn them on and off as needed.

Most system setup utilities provide some amount of control over fans plugged into the motherboard. Figure 7-39 shows typical system settings for the fans in system setup.

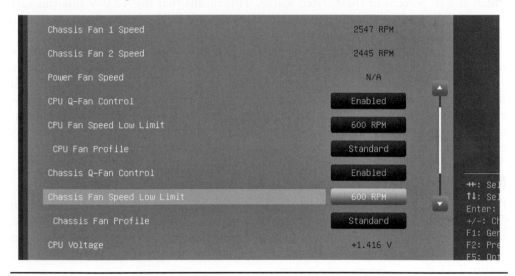

Figure 7-39   System setup

Troubleshooting Power Supplies

Power supplies fail in two ways: sudden death and slowly over time. When they die suddenly, the computer will not start and the fan in the power supply will not turn. In this case, verify that electricity is getting to the power supply before you do anything. Avoid the embarrassment of trying to repair a power supply when the only problem is a bad outlet or an extension cord that is not plugged in. If the system has electricity, the best way to verify that a power supply is working or not working is to use a multimeter to check the voltages coming out of the power supply (see Figure 7-40).

Figure 7-40
Testing one
of the 5-V DC
connections

Do not panic if your power supply puts out slightly more or less voltage than its nominal value. The voltages supplied by most PC power supplies can safely vary by as much as ±10 percent of their stated values. This means that the 12.0-V line can vary from roughly 10.8 to 13.2 V without exceeding the tolerance of the various systems in the PC. The 5.0- and 3.3-V lines offer similar tolerances.

Be sure to test every connection on the power supply—that means every connection on your main power as well as every Molex and mini. Because all voltages are between −20 and +20 VDC, simply set the multimeter to the 20-V DC setting for everything. If the power supply fails to provide power, throw it out the window and get a new one— even if you're a component expert and a whiz with a soldering iron. Don't waste your time or your company's time; the price of new power supplies, and the danger of a nasty or even deadly shock, makes replacement the obvious way to go.

No Motherboard

Power supplies will not start unless they're connected to a motherboard, so what do you do if you don't have a motherboard you trust to test? First, try an ATX tester. Many companies make these devices. Look for one that supports both 20- and 24-pin motherboard connectors as well as all of the other connectors on your power supply. Figure 7-41 shows a power supply tester.

NOTE Many CMOS utilities and software programs monitor voltage, saving you the hassle of using a multimeter. Of course, you have to have enough functionality to get into the CMOS utilities!

EXAM TIP Be sure you are familiar with power-testing tools such as multimeters and power supply testers.

Figure 7-41
ATX power
supply tester

When Power Supplies Die Slowly

If all power supplies died suddenly, this would be a much shorter chapter. Unfortunately, the majority of PC problems occur when power supplies die slowly over time. This means that one of the internal electronics of the power supply has begun to fail. The failures are *always* intermittent and tend to cause some of the most difficult to diagnose problems in PC repair. The secret to discovering that a power supply is dying lies in one word: intermittent. Whenever you experience intermittent problems, your first guess should be that the power supply is bad. Here are some other clues you may hear from users:

- "Whenever I start my computer in the morning, it starts to boot, and then locks up. If I press CTRL-ALT-DEL two or three times, it will boot up fine."

- "Sometimes when I start my PC, I get an error code. If I reboot, it goes away. Sometimes I get different errors."

- "My computer will run fine for an hour or so. Then it locks up, sometimes once or twice an hour."

- "It takes a couple of tries—plugging and unplugging—with a new USB device before my system recognizes it."

Sometimes something bad happens and sometimes it does not. That's the clue for replacing the power supply. And don't bother with the multimeter; the voltages will show up within tolerances, but only *once in a while* they will spike and sag (far more quickly than your multimeter can measure) and cause these intermittent errors. When in doubt, change the power supply. Power supplies break in computers more often than any other part of the PC except components with moving parts. You might choose to keep extra power supplies on hand for swapping and testing.

Fuses and Fire

Inside every power supply resides a simple fuse. If your power supply simply pops and stops working, you might be tempted to go inside the power supply and check the fuse. This is not a good idea. First off, the capacitors in most power supplies carry high-voltage charges that can hurt a lot if you touch them. Second, fuses blow for a reason. If a power supply is malfunctioning inside, you want that fuse to blow because the alternative is much less desirable.

Failure to respect the power of electricity will eventually result in the most catastrophic of all situations: an electrical fire. Don't think it can't happen to you! Keep a fire extinguisher handy. Every computer workbench needs a fire extinguisher, but make sure you have the right one. The fire prevention industry has divided fire extinguishers into five fire classes:

- **Class A** Ordinary free-burning combustible, such as wood or paper
- **Class B** Flammable liquids, such as gasoline, solvents, or paint
- **Class C** Live electrical equipment
- **Class D** Combustible metals such as titanium or magnesium
- **Class K** Cooking oils, trans-fats, or fats

As you might expect, you should use only a Class C fire extinguisher on a burning computing device. All fire extinguishers are required to have their type labeled prominently on them. Many fire extinguishers are multiclass in that they can handle more than one type of fire. The most common fire extinguisher is type ABC—it works on all common types of fires, though it can leave residue on computing equipment.

 TIP If your power supply is smoking or you smell something burning inside of it, stop using it now. Unplug and replace it with a new power supply.

Redundant Power Supplies

Two is always better than one! You will never have to worry about power failure when you have a *redundant power supply (RPS),* which is where two identical RPS power supplies are used in a server (see Figure 7-42). When both power supplies are in use by the host computer and the electrical load is between them, this is known as load balancing. So, for example, if the computer needs 500 watts, both power supplies will provide 250 watts, but if one fails, the other can then jump up to giving the whole 500 watts.

Modular Power Supplies

It's getting more and more popular to make PCs look good on both the inside and the outside. Unused power cables dangling around inside PCs creates a not-so-pretty picture and can impede airflow. To help stylish people, manufacturers created modular power supplies. (see Figure 7-43).

Figure 7-42
Redundant
power supply

Figure 7-43
Modular power
supply

Modular cables are cool! You add only the lines you need for your system. On the other hand, some techs claim that modular cables hurt efficiency because the modular connectors add resistance to the lines. You make the choice: Is a slight reduction in efficiency worth a clean look?

Chapter Review

Questions

1. What is the proper voltage for a U.S. electrical outlet?

   A. 120 V

   B. 60 V

   C. 0 V

   D. −120 V

2. What voltages does an ATX12V P1 connector provide for the motherboard?

   A. 3.3 V, 5 V

   B. 3.3 V, 12 V

   C. 5 V, 12 V

   D. 3.3 V, 5 V, 12 V

3. What sort of power connector do better video cards require?

   A. Molex

   B. Mini

   C. PCIe

   D. SATA

4. Joachim ordered a new power supply but was surprised when it arrived because it had an extra 4-wire connector. What is that connector?

   A. P2 connector for plugging in auxiliary components

   B. P3 connector for plugging in case fans

   C. P4 connector for plugging into modern motherboards

   D. Aux connector for plugging into a secondary power supply

5. What should you keep in mind when testing DC connectors?

   A. DC has polarity. The red lead should always touch the hot wire; the black lead should touch a ground wire.

   B. DC has polarity. The red lead should always touch the ground wire; the black lead should always touch the hot wire.

   C. DC has no polarity, so you can touch the red lead to either hot or ground.

   D. DC has no polarity, so you can touch the black lead to either hot or neutral but not ground.

6. What voltages should the two traditionally colored hot wires on a Molex connector read?

   A. Red = 3.3 V; Yellow = 5 V

   B. Red = 5 V; Yellow = 12 V

   C. Red = 12 V; Yellow = 5 V

   D. Red = 5 V; Yellow = 3.3 V

7. Why is it a good idea to ensure that all the slots in your computer case are covered with slot covers?

   A. To maintain good airflow inside your case.

   B. To help keep dust and smoke out of your case.

   C. Both A and B are correct reasons.

   D. Trick question! Leaving a slot uncovered doesn't hurt anything.

8. A PC's power supply provides DC power in what standard configuration?

   A. Two primary voltage rails, 12 volts and 5 volts, and an auxiliary 3.3-volt connector

   B. Three primary voltage rails, one each for 12-volt, 5-volt, and 3.3-volt connectors

   C. One primary DC voltage rail for 12-volt, 5-volt, and 3.3-volt connectors

   D. One voltage rail with a 12-volt connector for the motherboard, a second voltage rail with a 12-volt connector for the CPU, and a third voltage rail for the 5-volt and 3.3-volt connectors

9. What feature of ATX systems prevents a user from turning off a system before the operating system has been shut down?

   A. Motherboard power connector

   B. CMOS setup

   C. Sleep mode

   D. Soft power

10. How many pins does a SATA power connector have?

   A. 6

   B. 9

   C. 12

   D. 15

Answers

1. **A.** U.S. outlets run at 120 V.

2. **D.** An ATX12V power supply P1 connector provides 3.3, 5, and 12 volts to the motherboard.

3. **C.** Better video cards require one or two 6- or 8-pin PCIe connectors.

4. **C.** The P4 connector goes into the motherboard to support more power-hungry chips.

5. **A.** DC has polarity. The red lead should always touch the hot wire; the black lead should touch a ground wire.

6. **B.** A Molex connector's red wires should be at 5 volts; the yellow wire should be at 12 volts.

7. **C.** Both A and B are correct reasons. Keeping the slots covered helps keep a good airflow in your case and keeps the dust and smoke away from all those sensitive internal components.

8. **B.** The standard PC power supply configuration has three primary voltage rails, one each for 12-volt, 5-volt, and 3.3-volt connectors.

9. **D.** The soft power feature of ATX systems prevents a user from turning off a system before the operating system has been shut down.

10. **D.** SATA power connectors have 15 pins.

Mass Storage Technologies

In this chapter, you will learn how to

- Explain how hard drives work
- Identify mass storage interface connections
- Describe how to protect data with RAID
- Describe hard drive installation

Of all the hardware on a PC, none gets more attention—or gives more anguish—than mass storage drives. There's a good reason for this: if a drive breaks, you lose data. As you probably know, when data goes, you have to redo work, restore from a backup, or worse, just kiss the data goodbye. It's good to worry about data, because that data runs the office, maintains the payrolls, and stores the e-mail.

This chapter focuses on how drives work, beginning with the internal layout and organization of drives. You'll look at the different types of drives used today and how they interface with the PC. The chapter covers how more than one drive may work with other drives to provide data safety and improve speed through a feature called RAID. The chapter wraps up with an extensive discussion on how to install drives properly into a system. Let's get started.

 NOTE Chapter 9 continues the hard drive discussion by adding in the operating systems, showing you how to prepare drives to receive data, and teaching you how to maintain and upgrade drives in modern operating systems.

Historical/Conceptual

How Hard Drives Work

Hard drives come in two major types. First are hard disk drives (HDDs) that store data on spinning platters, with moving read/write heads. Second are the more recent solid-state drives (SSDs), which are faster, contain no moving parts, and have become the predominant form of mass storage for most systems. Let's look at both types of hard drives.

Hard Drives

A traditional *hard disk drive (HDD)* is composed of individual disks, or *platters*, with read/write heads on actuator arms controlled by a servo motor—all contained in a sealed case that prevents contamination by outside air (see Figure 8-1).

Figure 8-1
An enclosed HDD (top) and an opened HDD (bottom)

The aluminum platters are coated with a magnetic medium. Two tiny read/write heads service each platter, one to read/write on top of the platter and the other to read/write on the bottom of the platter (see Figure 8-2). Each head has a bit-sized *transducer* to read or write to each spot on the drive. Many folks refer to traditional HDDs as *magnetic hard drives, spinning drives, spindles, mechanical drives,* or sometimes *spinning rust*.

Figure 8-2
Read/write heads on actuator arms

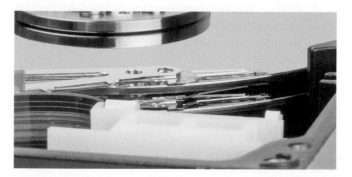

1101

Spindle (or Rotational) Speed

Hard drives rotate at a set *spindle speed,* with the spinning platters measured in *revolutions per minute (RPM)*. The faster the spindle speed, the faster the drive stores and retrieves data. By far the two most common speeds are 5400 RPM and 7200 RPM. Higher performance drives (which are also far less common) run at 10,000 and 15,000 RPM.

Faster drives generally equate to better performance, but they also generate more noise and heat. Excess heat cuts the life of hard drives dramatically. A rise of 5 degrees (Celsius) may reduce the life expectancy of a hard drive by as much as two years. Airflow through a system's case makes or breaks your system stability, especially when you add new drives that increase the ambient temperature. Hot systems get flaky and lock up at odd moments. Many things can impede the airflow—jumbled-up ribbon cables (used by older storage systems, USB headers, and other attachments), drives squished together in a tiny case, fans clogged by dust or animal hair, and so on. Fewer and fewer systems these days even have any traditional hard drives, so many modern cases tuck the drive bays away at the bottom-front (see Figure 8-3), sometimes under a PSU shroud that keeps the drives and power supply out of sight. This prevents the drives from obstructing airflow to more heat-sensitive components. An optional intake fan at the bottom-front of the case can help cool the drives themselves.

Figure 8-3
Hard drive bays in a modern case layout

Technicians need to consider airflow when adding a new hard drive to an older system. Get into the habit of tying off non-aerodynamic cables, adding front fans to cases when systems lock up intermittently, and making sure any fans run well. Finally, if a client wants a new drive for a system in a tiny minitower with only the power supply fan to cool it off, be gentle, but definitely steer the client to one of the lower RPM or SATA SSD drives discussed later in this chapter.

Form Factors

Hard disk drives are manufactured in two standardized form factors, 2.5-inch and 3.5-inch (see Figure 8-4). You'll see both form factors in desktops and servers; most laptops use the 2.5-inch form factor.

Figure 8-4
2.5-inch drive stacked on top of a 3.5-inch drive

The form factor only defines size. The connections and the storage technology inside these drives can vary.

Solid-State Drives

Booting up a computer takes time in part because a traditional hard drive needs to spin up before the read/write heads can retrieve data off the drive and load it into RAM. All of the moving metal parts of a platter-based hard drive use a lot of power, create a lot of heat, take up space, wear down over time, and take a lot of nanoseconds to get things done. A *solid-state drive (SSD)* addresses these issues nicely.

In technical terms, solid-state technology and devices are based on the combination of semiconductors and transistors used to create electrical components with no moving parts. That's a mouthful! In simple terms, SSDs use flash memory chips to store data instead of all those pesky metal spinning parts used in platter-based hard drives (see Figure 8-5).

Figure 8-5
A solid-state
drive

Solid-state drives are everywhere today. Desktops and laptops use SSDs, and smart-phones, USB thumb drives, and other handheld devices all use SSD in some form for mass storage.

SSDs for personal computers come in one of three form factors: the 2.5-inch form factor previously mentioned and two flat form factors called *mSATA* and *M.2* (see Figure 8-6). mSATA and M.2 drives connect to specific mSATA or M.2 slots on motherboards (see Figure 8-7). Many current motherboards offer two or more M.2 slots.

Figure 8-6
M.2 SSD

Figure 8-7
M.2 SSD installed
in motherboard

TIP Although you can still buy mSATA cards as we go to print, the technology is on its way out for both laptop and desktop computers, replaced by M.2. The latter standard is half the physical size and offers substantially better performance.

M.2 slots come in a variety of configurations, keyed for different sorts of mass storage uses. The keys have a letter associated. M.2 slots that use Key B, Key M, or Keys B+M support mass storage devices, for example, like in Figure 8-7. Other slots like Key A and Key E are used in wireless networking devices. The specifics of the keys are beyond the current CompTIA A+ exam, but M.2 looks like it's here to stay, so you need to be aware of the variations.

M.2 SSDs come in a few different sizes to allow them to be used in a variety of systems and circumstances. They are designated with a four-digit (or occasionally five-digit) number. The first two digits indicate the width in millimeters, and the remaining digits represent the length. An M.2 SATA drive or NVMe drive (introduced later in the chapter) with the designation 2280 would therefore be 22 mm wide by 80 mm long. The most common dimensions for M.2 SSDs are 2242, 2260, 2280, and 22110 (see Figure 8-8 for a size comparison). Longer drives are able to accommodate more flash memory chips and, therefore, have greater potential storage capacity.

SSDs use nonvolatile flash memory such as *NAND* that retains data when power is turned off or disconnected. (See Chapter 10 for the scoop on flash memory technology.)

Figure 8-8
M.2 SSD size comparison in relation to a standard ATX motherboard

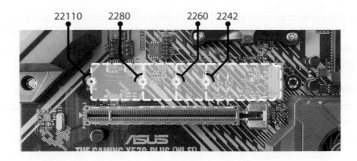

Cost

SSDs cost more than HDDs. Less expensive SSDs typically implement less reliable *multi-level cell (MLC)* memory technology in place of the more efficient *single-level cell (SLC)* technology to cut costs. The most popular type of memory technology in SSDs is *3D NAND*, a form of MLC that stacks cells vertically, providing increased density and capacity.

NOTE Sometimes, an SSD will be less expensive than SATA and NVMe drives because it doesn't use a DRAM cache. Watch out for this, as these SSDs can be significantly slower than an SSD that uses a DRAM cache in some instances.

Solid-state drives operate internally by writing data in a scattershot fashion to high-speed flash memory cells in accordance with the rules contained in the internal SSD controller. That process is hidden from the operating system by presenting an electronic façade to the OS that makes the SSD appear to be a traditional magnetic hard drive.

Performance Variables

There are three big performance metrics to weigh when you buy an SSD: how fast it can read or write long sequences of data stored in the same part of the drive, how fast it can read or write small chunks of data scattered randomly around the drive, and how quickly it responds to a single request. The value of each metric varies depending on what kind of work the drive will do. Before we dive into how you should weigh each metric, let's look at how the storage industry measures the sequential read/write performance, random read/write performance, and latency of individual SSDs.

Sequential Read/Write Performance A common measure of a storage device's top speed is its *throughput*, or the rates at which it can read and write long sequences of data. We usually express a device's *sequential read* and *sequential write* throughput in megabytes per second (MBps). Most drives read a little faster than they write.

For context, traditional hard drives generally have sequential read/write speeds that top out at 200 MBps; SATA SSDs can hit 600 MBps; and NVMe SSDs roll at 2500 MBps or faster. These numbers are useful if you know your drives will frequently read and write huge files, but very few real-world systems do.

Random Read/Write Performance   Because real-world drives rarely get to read and write huge files all day, we also look at a drive's *random read*, *random write*, and *mixed random* performance. Basically, we measure how many times per second a device can read or write small, fixed-size chunks of data at random locations on the drive.

The labels for these measurements often reflect the size of the data chunk (usually 4 KB), so you may see them called *4K Read*, *4K Random Write*, *4K Mixed*, and so on. These measurements are all typically expressed as a number of *input/output operations per second* (IOPS), but you may also see them expressed in MBps. For context, traditional hard drives typically clock in at fewer than 150 IOPS, whereas the latest NVMe SSDs boast *hundreds of thousands* of IOPS.

Latency   It's also useful to look at a drive's *response time*, *access time*, or *latency*, which measures how quickly it responds to a single request. Latency is usually expressed in milliseconds (ms) or microseconds (µs). Low-latency storage is critical for high-performance file and database servers, but the latency of most modern drives is fine for general use. For context, traditional hard drives often have latencies under 20 ms, whereas SSDs commonly clock in well under 1 ms.

A lot of factors determine which combination of performance and price makes sense for a specific situation. A typical machine, for example, doesn't put a huge demand on the SSD. Users boot up the computer and then open an application or two and work. The quality of the SSD matters for boot-up time and application load, but the machine will rarely break a sweat after that. A workstation for high-end video editing, on the other hand, may read and write massive files for hours on end. A large file server may need to read and write thousands of tiny files a minute.

In practical terms, you can get by with a cheaper, lower performing SSD in a general-use computer, but need to spend more for a higher performing SSD in demanding circumstances. When it comes to picking exactly which high-performance SSD, the throughput, IOPs, and latency metrics help you avoid overpaying for performance characteristics that don't matter for your use.

Connecting Mass Storage

Setting up communication between a CPU and a mass storage drive requires two main items. First, there must be standardized physical connections between the CPU, the drive controller, and the physical drive. These connections must send data between these devices as quickly as possible while still retaining good security (see Figure 8-9).

Figure 8-9
Standardized physical connections are essential.

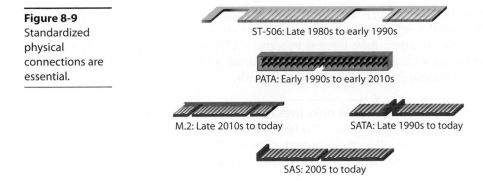

ST-506: Late 1980s to early 1990s

PATA: Early 1990s to early 2010s

M.2: Late 2010s to today   SATA: Late 1990s to today

SAS: 2005 to today

Second, the CPU needs to use a standardized protocol, sort of like a special language, so it knows how to speak to the mass storage device to read and write data to the device (see Figure 8-10).

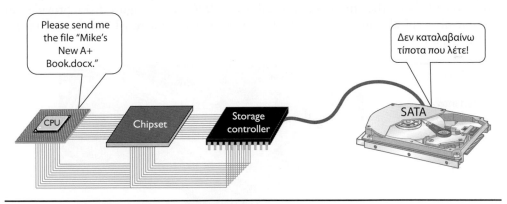

Please send me the file "Mike's New A+ Book.docx."

Δεν καταλαβαίνω τίποτα που λέτε!

CPU   Chipset   Storage controller   SATA

Figure 8-10   We need a common language!

In most cases, the standards bodies that define both the physical connections and the language used for communications are the same organization. For the last 25+ years, the Storage Networking Industry Association's Small Form Factor (SFF) committee has defined mass storage standards, the most important to CompTIA A+ techs being *ATA/ATAPI*.

NOTE   Check out the Storage Networking Industry Association's Web site (https://www.snia.org) for a good source for mass storage standards.

The *Advanced Technology Attachment (ATA)* standards started with version 1 way back in 1990, going through ATA/ATAPI version 7. Let's make it even easier, because only two versions of this standard have interest to techs: PATA and SATA. *Parallel ATA (PATA)* was introduced with ATA/ATAPI version 1. *Serial ATA (SATA)* was introduced with ATA/ATAPI version 7. Let's look at both standards.

NOTE The CompTIA objectives refer to PATA drives as *Integrated Drive Electronics (IDE)* drives. The term *IDE* refers to any hard drive with a built-in controller. All hard drives are technically IDE drives, although we only use the term IDE when discussing PATA drives.

PATA

PATA drives are easily recognized by their data and power connections. PATA drives used unique 40-pin ribbon cables. These ribbon cables usually plugged directly into a system's motherboard. Note that the exam will call these *IDE cables*. Figure 8-11 provides an example of a typical connection. All PATA drives used a standard Molex power connector (see Figure 8-12).

Figure 8-11
PATA cable plugged into a motherboard

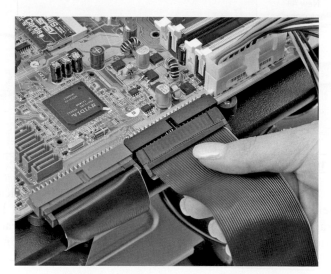

Figure 8-12
Molex connector

EXAM TIP CompTIA may still ask you about IDE cables and Molex power connectors, so be sure to familiarize yourself with them when preparing for the exam.

As a technology standard, ATA went through seven major revisions, each adding power, speed, and/or capacity to storage system capabilities. I could add 15 pages discussing the changes, but they're not particularly relevant for modern techs. There is one feature added back then that we still use today, though, called *S.M.A.R.T.*

ATA/ATAPI version 3 introduced *Self-Monitoring, Analysis, and Reporting Technology (S.M.A.R.T.),* an internal drive program that tracks errors and error conditions within the drive. This information is stored in nonvolatile memory on the drive and can be examined externally with S.M.A.R.T. reader software. There are generic S.M.A.R.T. reading programs, and every drive manufacturer has software to get at the vendor-specific information being tracked. Regular usage of S.M.A.R.T. software will help you create a baseline of hard drive functionality to predict potential drive failures.

SATA

For all its longevity as the mass storage interface of choice for the PC, parallel ATA had problems. First, the flat ribbon cables impeded airflow and could be a pain to insert properly. Second, the cables had a limited length, only 18 inches. Third, you couldn't hot-swap PATA drives. You had to shut the computer down completely before installing or replacing a drive. Finally, the technology had simply reached the limits of what it could do in terms of throughput. It was time to revamp both the connection and the language for ATA/ATAPI drives.

Serial ATA addressed these issues. SATA creates a point-to-point connection between the SATA device—magnetic hard drives, solid-state drives, optical media drives—and the SATA controller, the *host bus adapter (HBA)*. SATA drives at first glance look identical to PATA devices, but take a closer look at the cable and power connectors, and you'll see significant differences (see Figure 8-13).

Figure 8-13
SATA hard disk
power (left)
and data (right)
cables

Because SATA devices send data serially instead of in parallel, the SATA interface needs far fewer physical wires—only 7 connectors instead of the 40 typical of PATA—resulting in much thinner cabling. Thinner cabling means better cable control and better airflow through the PC case, resulting in better cooling.

Further, the maximum SATA-device cable length is more than twice that of a PATA cable—about 40 inches (1 meter) instead of 18 inches. This facilitates drive installation in larger cases.

 EXAM TIP The CompTIA A+ 1101 exam objectives refer to the 40-pin PATA ribbon cable as an *IDE cable*. They're the same thing, so don't miss this one on the exam!

SATA did away with the two drives per cable of PATA. Each drive connects to one port. Further, there's no maximum number of drives—many motherboards today support up to eight SATA drives (see Figure 8-14). Want more? Snap in a SATA HBA into an expansion slot and load 'em up with even more drives.

Figure 8-14
SATA cable plugged into typical motherboard (note the other available socket)

The biggest news about SATA is in data throughput. As the name implies, SATA devices transfer data in serial bursts instead of parallel, as PATA devices do. Typically, you might not think of serial devices as being faster than parallel, but in this case, a SATA device's single stream of data moves much faster than the multiple streams of data coming from a parallel ATA device—theoretically, up to 30 times faster. SATA drives come in three common SATA-specific varieties: *1.5 Gbps*, *3 Gbps*, and *6 Gbps*, which have a maximum throughput of 150 MBps, 300 MBps, and 600 MBps, respectively. It should be noted that if a system has an (external) eSATA port (discussed next), it will operate at the same revision and speed as the internal SATA ports.

NOTE Number-savvy readers might have noticed a discrepancy between the names and throughput of SATA drives. After all, SATA 1.0's 1.5-Gbps throughput translates to 192 MBps, a lot higher than the advertised speed of a "mere" 150 MBps. The encoding scheme used on SATA drives takes about 20 percent of the transferred bytes as overhead, leaving 80 percent for pure bandwidth.

Traditionally you do not connect or disconnect mass storage devices to a running system. Connecting a mass storage device to a fully functioning and powered-up computer may result in less than optimal results. The result may be as simple as the component not being recognized or as dire as a destroyed component or computer.

Enter the era of the hot-swappable device. Hot-swapping entails two elements, the first being the capacity to plug a device into the computer without harming either. The second is that once the device is safely attached, it will be automatically recognized and become a fully functional component of the system. SATA was the first popular mass storage technology to support hot swapping.

SATA Express (SATAe) ties capable drives directly into the PCI Express bus on motherboards. SATAe drops both the SATA link and transport layers, embracing the full performance of PCIe. The lack of overhead greatly enhances the speed of SATA throughput, with each lane of PCIe 3.0 capable of handling up to 8 Gbps of data throughput. A drive grabbing two lanes, therefore, could move a whopping 16 Gbps through the bus. Without the overhead of earlier SATA versions, this translates as 2000 MBps!

NOTE Each SATA variety is named for the revision to the SATA specification that introduced it, with the exception of SATAe:
SATA 1.0: 1.5 Gbps/150 MBps
SATA 2.0: 3 Gbps/300 MBps
SATA 3.0: 6 Gbps/600 MBps
SATA 3.2: up to 16 Gbps/2000 MBps

SATAe (also known as SATA 3.2) has unique connectors (see Figure 8-15) but provides full backward compatibility with earlier versions of SATA. Note that the center and left portions of the port look just like regular SATA ports. They function that way too, so you can plug two regular SATA drives into a SATAe socket. Feel free to upgrade your motherboard! Oh yeah, did I forget to mention that? You'll need a motherboard with SATAe support to take advantage of these superfast versions of SATA drives.

Figure 8-15
SATAe connector

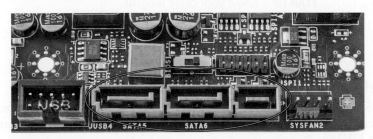

eSATA and Other External Drives

External SATA (eSATA) extended the SATA bus to external devices, as the name would imply. The eSATA drives used connectors that looked similar to internal SATA connectors, but were keyed differently so you couldn't mistake one for the other. Figure 8-16 shows an eSATA connector on the back of a motherboard.

Figure 8-16
eSATA connector

External SATA used shielded cable in lengths up to 2 meters outside the PC and was hot-swappable. eSATA extended the SATA bus at full speed, mildly faster than the fastest USB connection when it was introduced.

 EXAM TIP eSATA withered when USB 3.0 hit the market and quickly disappeared. You'll only find it today on very old systems and drive enclosures, and on the CompTIA A+ exam.

Current *external enclosures* (the name used to describe the casing of external HDDs and SSDs) use the USB (3.0, 3.1, 3.2, or C-type) ports or Thunderbolt ports for connecting external hard drives. Chapter 10 goes into the differences among these types of ports in detail. The drives inside the enclosures are standard SATA HDDs or SSDs.

 EXAM TIP Know your cable lengths:
PATA (IDE): 18 inches
SATA: 1 meter
eSATA: 2 meters

Refining Mass Storage Communication

The original ATA standard defined a very specific series of commands for the CPU to communicate with the drive controller. The current drive command sets are AHCI and NVMe.

AHCI

Current versions of Windows support the *Advanced Host Controller Interface (AHCI)*, an efficient way to work with SATA HBAs. Using AHCI unlocks some of the advanced features of SATA, such as native command queuing and hot-swapping.

Native command queuing (NCQ) is a disk-optimization feature for SATA drives. It takes advantage of the SATA interface to achieve faster read and write speeds that are simply impossible with the old PATA drives. Also, while SATA supports hot-swapping ability, the motherboard and the operating system must also support this.

AHCI mode is enabled at the CMOS level (see "BIOS Support: Configuring CMOS and Installing Drivers" later in this chapter) and generally needs to be enabled before you install the operating system. Enabling it after installation will cause Windows to Blue Screen. How nice.

When you plug a SATA drive into a running Windows computer that does not have AHCI enabled, the drive doesn't appear automatically. With AHCI mode enabled, the drive should appear in Computer immediately, just what you'd expect from a hot-swappable device.

Successfully Switching SATA Modes Without Reinstalling

You can attempt to switch to AHCI mode in Windows without reinstalling. This scenario might occur if a client has accidentally installed Windows in Legacy/IDE mode, for example, and finds that the new SSD he purchased requires AHCI mode to perform well.

First, back up everything before attempting the switch. Second, you need to run through some steps in Windows before you change the BIOS/UEFI settings. Windows 10 and 11 use an elevated command prompt exercise with the bcdedit command. (The command line is covered in Chapter 15.)

A quick Google search for "switch from ide to ahci windows" will reveal several excellent walkthroughs of the process for Windows 10 and 11. Back everything up first!

NVMe

AHCI was designed for spinning SATA drives to optimize read performance as well as to effect hot-swappability. As a configuration setting, AHCI works for many SSDs as well, but it's not optimal. That's because for an SSD to work with the operating system, the SSD has to include some circuitry that the OS can see that makes the SSD appear to be a traditional spinning drive. Once a read or write operation is commenced, the virtual drive circuits pass the operation through a translator in the SSD that maps the true inner guts of the SSD.

The *Non-Volatile Memory Express (NVMe)* specification supports a communication connection between the operating system and the SSD directly through a PCIe bus lane, reducing latency and taking full advantage of the wicked-fast speeds of high-end SSDs (see Figure 8-17). NVMe SSDs come in a few formats, such as an add-on expansion card using a PCIe slot on the motherboard, a 2.5-inch drive that works with a SATAe connector, and the most common style, M.2 format. NVMe drives are more expensive than other SSDs but offer much higher speeds.

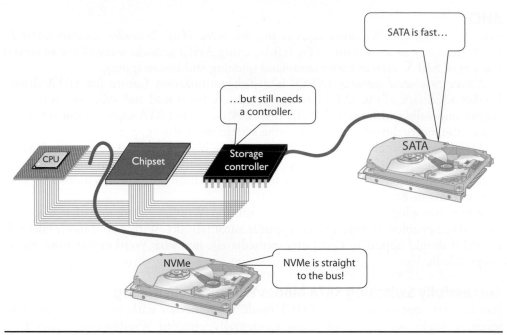

Figure 8-17 NVMe enables direct-to-the-bus communication.

Protecting Data with RAID

Ask experienced techs "What is the most expensive part of a PC?" and they'll all answer in the same way: "It's the data." You can replace any single part of your PC for a few hundred dollars at most, but if you lose critical data—well, let's just say I know of two small companies that went out of business just because they lost a hard drive full of data.

SCSI

SATA-connected HDDs and SSDs dominate the personal computer market, but another drive technology, called the *small computer system interface (SCSI),* rules the roost in the server market. SCSI has been around since the earliest days of HDDs and has evolved over the years from a parallel to a wider parallel to—and this should be obvious by now—a couple of super-fast serial interfaces. SCSI devices—parallel and serial—use a standard SCSI command set, meaning you can have systems with both old and new devices connected and they can communicate with no problem. SCSI drives used a variety of ribbon cables, depending on the version.

Serial Attached SCSI (SAS) hard drives provide fast and robust storage for servers and storage arrays today. The latest SAS interface, SAS-4, provides speeds of up to 22.5 Gbps. SAS controllers also support SATA drives, which is cool and offers a lot of flexibility for techs, especially in smaller server situations. SAS implementations offer more than a dozen different connector types. Most look like slightly chunkier versions of a SATA connector.

Data is king; data is your PC's *raison d'être*. Losing data is a bad thing, so you need some method to prevent data loss. Of course, you can do backups, but if a hard drive dies, you have to shut down the computer, reinstall a new hard drive, reinstall the operating system, and then restore the backup. There's nothing wrong with this as long as you can afford the time and cost of shutting down the system.

A better solution, though, would save your data if a hard drive died and enable you to continue working throughout the process. This is possible if you stop relying on a single hard drive and instead use two or more drives to store your data. Sounds good, but how do you do this? Well, you could install some fancy hard drive controller that reads and writes data to two hard drives simultaneously (see Figure 8-18). The data on each drive would always be identical. One drive would be the primary drive and the other drive, called the *mirror* drive, would not be used unless the primary drive failed. This process of reading and writing data at the same time to two drives is called *disk mirroring*.

Figure 8-18
Mirrored drives

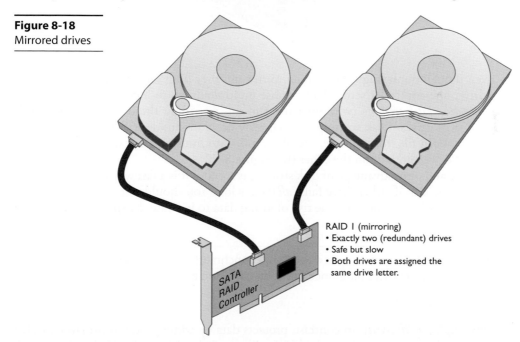

If you really want to make data safe, you can use a separate controller for each drive. With two drives, each on a separate controller, the system will continue to operate even if the primary drive's controller stops working. This super-drive mirroring technique is called *disk duplexing* (see Figure 8-19). Disk duplexing is also marginally faster than disk mirroring because one controller does not write each piece of data twice.

Figure 8-19
Duplexing drives

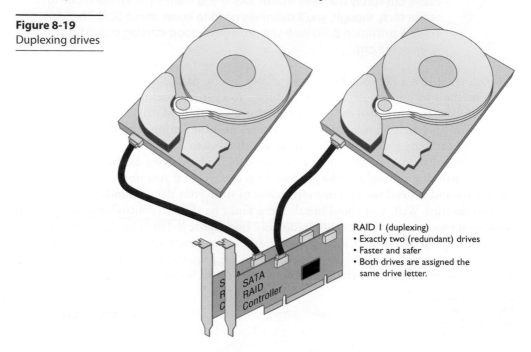

RAID 1 (duplexing)
• Exactly two (redundant) drives
• Faster and safer
• Both drives are assigned the same drive letter.

Even though duplexing is faster than mirroring, they both are slower than the classic one-drive, one-controller setup. You can use multiple drives to increase your hard drive access speed. *Disk striping* (without parity) means spreading the data among multiple (at least two) drives. Disk striping by itself provides no redundancy. If you save a small Microsoft Word file, for example, the file is split into multiple pieces; half of the pieces go on one drive and half on the other (see Figure 8-20).

The one and only advantage of disk striping is speed—it is a fast way to read and write to hard drives. But if either drive fails, *all* data is lost. You should not do disk striping—unless you're willing to increase the risk of losing data to increase the speed at which your hard drives store and retrieve data.

 NOTE In practice (as opposed to benchmarking) you won't experience any performance difference between mirroring and striping.

Disk striping with parity, in contrast, protects data by adding extra information, called *parity data*, that can be used to rebuild data if one of the drives fails. Disk striping with parity requires at least three drives, but it is common to use more than three. Disk striping with parity combines the best of disk mirroring and plain disk striping. It protects data and is quite fast. The majority of network servers use a type of disk striping with parity.

Figure 8-20
Disk striping

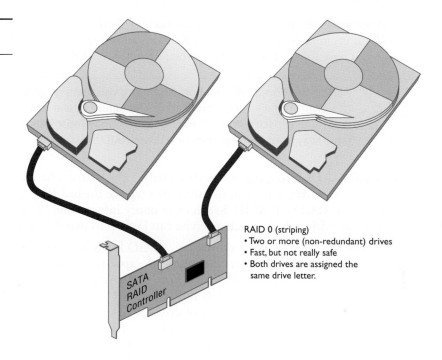

RAID 0 (striping)
• Two or more (non-redundant) drives
• Fast, but not really safe
• Both drives are assigned the
  same drive letter.

SATA
RAID
Controller

NOTE There is actually a term for a storage system composed of multiple independent disks of various sizes, *JBOD*, which stands for *just a bunch of disks* (or *drives*). Many drive controllers support JBOD.

RAID

A couple of sharp guys in Berkeley back in the 1980s organized many of the techniques for using multiple drives for data protection and increasing speeds as the *redundant array of independent* (or *inexpensive*) *disks (RAID)*. An *array* describes two or more drives working as a unit. They outlined several forms or "levels" of RAID that have since been numbered 0 through 6 (plus a couple of special implementations). Only a few of these RAID types are in use today: 0, 1, 5, 6, 10, and 0+1.

- **RAID 0—Disk striping** Disk striping requires at least two drives. It does not provide redundancy to data. If any one drive fails, all data is lost. I've heard this called *scary RAID* for that very reason.

- **RAID 1—Disk mirroring/duplexing** RAID 1 arrays require at least two hard drives, although they also work with any even number of drives. RAID 1 is the ultimate in safety, but you lose storage space because the data is duplicated; you need two 2-TB drives to store 2 TB of data.

- **RAID 5—Disk striping with distributed parity** Instead of dedicated data and parity drives, RAID 5 distributes data and parity information evenly across all drives. This is the fastest way to provide data redundancy. RAID 5 requires at least three drives. RAID 5 arrays effectively use one drive's worth of space for parity. If, for example, you have three 2-TB drives, your total storage capacity is 4 TB. If you have four 2-TB drives, your total capacity is 6 TB.

NOTE RAID 5 sounds great on paper and will seem great on your CompTIA A+ exam, but it's out of favor today. The failure rate of drives combined with the huge capacity (and rebuilding times) mean most RAID implementations shy away from the "lose only one drive" RAID 5.

- **RAID 6—Disk striping with extra parity** If you lose a hard drive in a RAID 5 array, your data is at great risk until you replace the bad hard drive and rebuild the array. RAID 6 is RAID 5 with extra parity information. RAID 6 needs at least four drives, but in exchange you can lose up to two drives at the same time.

- **RAID 10—Nested, striped mirrors** RAID levels have been combined to achieve multiple benefits, including speed, capacity, and reliability, but these benefits must be purchased at a cost, and that cost is efficiency. Take for instance RAID 10, also called RAID 1+0 and sometimes a "stripe of mirrors." Requiring a minimum of four drives, a pair of drives is configured as a mirror, and then the same is done to another pair to achieve a pair of RAID 1 arrays. The arrays look like single drives to the operating system or RAID controller. So now, with two drives, we can block stripe across the two mirrored pairs (RAID 0). Cool, huh? We get the speed of striping and the reliability of mirroring at the cost of installing two bytes of storage for every byte of data saved. Need more space? Add another mirrored pair to the striped arrays!

- **RAID 0+1—Nested, mirrored stripes** Like RAID 10, RAID 0+1 (or a "mirror of stripes") is a nested set of arrays that works in opposite configuration from RAID 10. It takes a minimum of four drives to implement RAID 0+1. Start with two RAID 0 striped arrays, then mirror the two arrays to each other. Which is better: the RAID 10 or the RAID 0+1? Why not do a bit of research and decide for yourself?

EXAM TIP Make sure that you are familiar with RAID levels 0, 1, 5, and 10. Know the minimum number of drives in a given level array, and how many failures a given array can withstand and remain functional.

RAID Level	Minimum Drives	Number of Functional Failures
RAID 0	2	0
RAID 1	2	1
RAID 5	3	1
RAID 6	4	2
RAID 10	4	Up to 2

Implementing RAID

RAID levels describe different methods of providing data redundancy or enhancing the speed of data throughput to and from groups of hard drives. They do not say *how* to implement these methods. Literally thousands of methods can be used to set up RAID. The method you use depends largely on the level of RAID you desire, the operating system you use, and the thickness of your wallet.

The obvious starting place for RAID is to connect at least two hard drives in some fashion to create a RAID array. Specialized RAID controller cards support RAID arrays of up to 15 drives—plenty to support even the most complex RAID needs. Dedicated storage boxes with built-in RAID make implementing a RAID solution simple for external storage and backups.

Once you have hard drives, the next question is whether to use hardware or software to control the array. Let's look at both options.

Software Versus Hardware

All RAID implementations break down into either software or hardware methods. Software is often used when price takes priority over performance. Hardware is used when you need speed along with data redundancy. Software RAID does not require special controllers; you can use the regular SATA controllers to make a software RAID array. But you do need "smart" software. The most common software implementation of RAID is the built-in RAID software that comes with Windows. The Disk Management program in Windows Server versions can configure drives for RAID 0, 1, or 5, and it works with PATA or SATA (see Figure 8-21). The Storage Spaces feature in Windows 10 and 11 can do RAID 0 and 1.

NOTE   Chapter 9 discusses RAID solutions implemented in Windows.

Windows Disk Management is not the only software RAID game in town. A number of third-party software programs work with Windows or other operating systems.

Software RAID means the operating system is in charge of all RAID functions. It works for small RAID solutions but tends to overwork your operating system easily, creating slowdowns. When you *really* need to keep going, when you need RAID that doesn't even let the users know a problem has occurred, hardware RAID is the answer.

NOTE   See Chapter 9 for a thorough discussion of *Storage Spaces*, a software RAID implementation available in Windows.

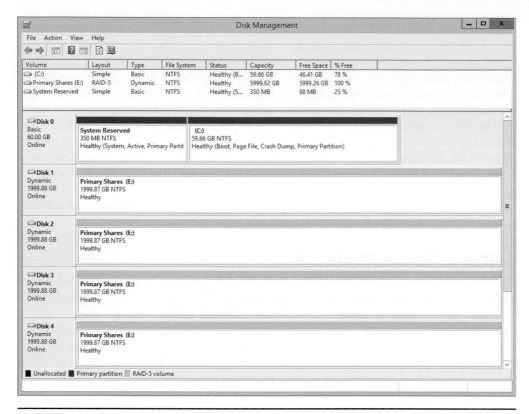

Figure 8-21 Disk Management tool of Computer Management in Windows Server

Hardware RAID centers on an *intelligent* controller that handles all of the RAID functions (see Figure 8-22). Unlike regular PATA/SATA controllers, these controllers have chips with their own processor and memory. This allows the card or dedicated box, instead of the operating system, to handle all the work of implementing RAID.

Figure 8-22
Serial ATA RAID
controller

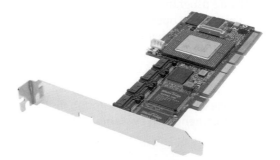

Most traditional RAID setups in the real world are hardware-based. Almost all of the many hardware RAID solutions provide *hot-swapping*—the ability to replace a bad drive without disturbing the operating system. Hot-swapping is common in hardware RAID.

Hardware-based RAID is invisible to the operating system and is configured in several ways, depending on the specific chips involved. Most RAID systems have a special configuration utility in flash ROM that you access after CMOS but before the OS loads. Figure 8-23 shows a typical firmware program used to configure a hardware RAID solution.

Figure 8-23
RAID
configuration
utility

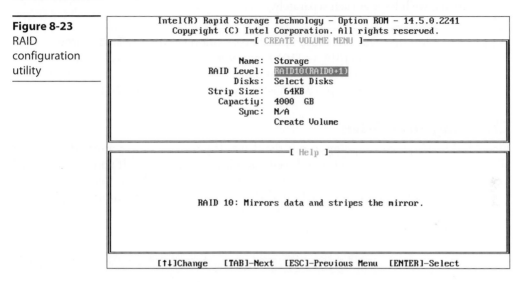

```
        Intel(R) Rapid Storage Technology - Option ROM - 14.5.0.2241
            Copyright (C) Intel Corporation. All rights reserved.
============================[ CREATE VOLUME MENU ]============================

                       Name:  Storage
                 RAID Level:  RAID10(RAID0+1)
                      Disks:  Select Disks
                 Strip Size:     64KB
                   Capactiy:  4000  GB
                       Sync:  N/A
                              Create Volume


==================================[ Help ]==================================




            RAID 10: Mirrors data and stripes the mirror.




=============================================================================
       [↑↓]Change    [TAB]-Next   [ESC]-Previous Menu   [ENTER]-Select
```

SIM   Check out the Chapter 8 Challenge! sim, "Storage Solution," to examine best RAID practices at https://www.totalsem.com/100x.

Dedicated RAID Boxes

Many people add a dedicated RAID box to add both more storage and a place to back up files. These devices take two or more drives and connect via one of the ports on a computer, such as USB or Thunderbolt (on modern systems) or FireWire or eSATA (on older systems). (See Chapter 10 for details on USB and FireWire.) Figure 8-24 shows an external RAID box (also called an *enclosure*). This model is typical, offering three options for the two drives inside: no RAID, RAID 0, or RAID 1.

Figure 8-24
Western Digital
RAID enclosure

Installing Drives

Installing a drive is a fairly simple process if you take the time to make sure you have the right drive for your system, configure the drive and system setup properly, and do a few quick tests to see if it's running properly. Since PATA and SATA have different cabling requirements, we'll look at each separately.

EXAM TIP Don't let the length of explanation about installation throw you during CompTIA A+ 1101 exam prep. PATA installation is much more complicated than SATA installation, so we've devoted more ink to the process here. SATA is what you will most likely see in the field and on the exam.

Choosing Your Drive

First, decide where you're going to put the drive. If you have a new motherboard, just slip the drive into the M.2 socket and secure it with the tiny screw. If you plan to install a 3.5-inch HDD or 2.5-inch SSD, then you need to go old school. Look for an open SATA connection. Is it part of a dedicated RAID controller? Many motherboards with built-in RAID controllers have a CMOS setting that enables you to turn the RAID controller on or off (see Figure 8-25).

Figure 8-25
Settings for RAID in CMOS

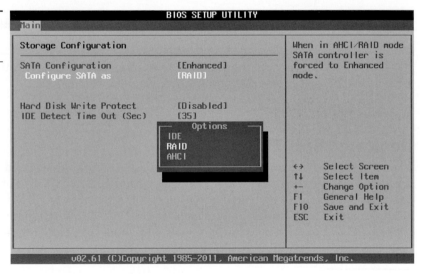

Second, make sure you have room for the drive in the case. Where will you place it? Do you have a spare power connector? Will the data and power cables reach the drive? A quick test fit is always a good idea.

Try This!

Managing Heat with Multiple Drives

Adding three or more fast magnetic hard drives into a cramped PC case can be a recipe for disaster to the unwary tech. While the heat generated may not threaten the fabric of the time-space continuum, heat reduces the life expectancy of drives and computers. You have to manage the heat inside a RAID-enabled system because such systems usually have more than the typical quantity of drives found in desktop computers. The easiest way to do this is to add fans.

Open up the PC case and look for built-in places to mount fans. How many case fans do you have installed now? What size are they? What sizes can you use? (Most cases have 120-mm and larger fans.) Jot down the fan locations of the case and take a trip to the local PC store or online retailer to check out the fans.

Before you get all fan-happy and grab the biggest and baddest fans to throw in your case, don't forget to think about the added noise level. Try to achieve a compromise between keeping your case cool enough and avoiding early deafness.

Cabling SATA Drives

Installing SATA hard disk drives is relatively easy and straightforward process because there are no jumper settings to worry about at all, as SATA supports only a single device per controller channel. Simply connect the power and plug in the controller cable as shown in Figure 8-26—the OS automatically detects the drive and it's ready to go. The keying on SATA controller and power cables makes it impossible to install either incorrectly.

 NOTE Some older SATA drives have jumpers, but they are used to configure SATA version/speed (1.5, 3.0) or power management. The rule of one drive for one controller applies to these drives, just like more typical jumperless SATA drives.

Every modern motherboard has two or more SATA ports (or *SATA connectors*) built in, as shown in Chapter 6. The ports are labeled (SATA 1, SATA 2, and so forth up to however many are included). Typically, you install the primary drive into SATA 1, the next into SATA 2, and so on. With nonbooting SATA drives, such as in M.2 motherboards, it doesn't matter which port you connect the drive to.

Figure 8-26   Properly connected SATA cable

Connecting Solid-State Drives

SATA SSDs possess the same connectors as magnetic SATA drives, so you install an SSD as you would any SATA drive. SATA SSDs usually come in 2.5-inch laptop sizes. Just as with earlier hard drive types, you either connect SSDs correctly and they work, or you forget to plug in the power cable and they don't.

M.2 and mSATA drives slip into their slot on the motherboard or add-on card, then either clip in place or secure with a tiny screw (see Figure 8-27). Both standards are keyed, so you can't install them incorrectly.

Keep in mind the following considerations before implementing a HDD/SDD migration:

- Do you have the appropriate drivers and firmware for the SSD? Newer Windows versions will load the most currently implemented SSD drivers. As always, check the manufacturer's specifications as well.

- Do you have everything important backed up? Good!

Figure 8-27
mSATA SSD
secured on
motherboard

BIOS Support: Configuring CMOS and Installing Drivers

Every device in your PC needs BIOS support, whether it's traditional BIOS or UEFI. Hard drive controllers are no exception. Motherboards provide support for the SATA hard drive controllers via the system BIOS, but they require configuration in CMOS for the specific hard drives attached.

In the old days, you had to fire up CMOS and manually enter hard drive information whenever you installed a new drive. Today, this process is automated.

Configuring Controllers

As a first step in configuring controllers, make certain they're enabled. Most controllers remain active, ready to automatically detect new drives, but you can disable them. Scan through your CMOS settings to locate the controller on/off options (see Figure 8-28 for typical settings). This is also the time to check whether the onboard RAID controllers work in both RAID and non-RAID settings.

Autodetection

If the controllers are enabled and the drive is properly connected, the drive should appear in system setup through a process called *autodetection*. Autodetection is a powerful and handy feature that takes almost all the work out of configuring hard drives. Motherboards use a numbering system to determine how drives are listed—and every motherboard uses its own numbering system! Though not described in the figure, one common numbering method uses the term *channels* for each controller. The first boot device is channel 1, the second is channel 2, and so on. So instead of names of drives, you see numbers. Look at Figure 8-29.

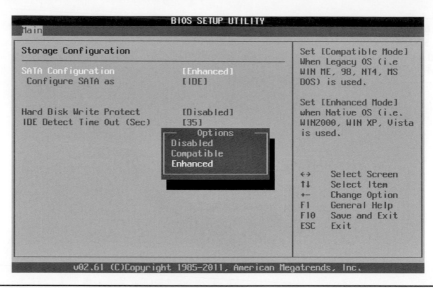

Figure 8-28 Typical controller settings in CMOS

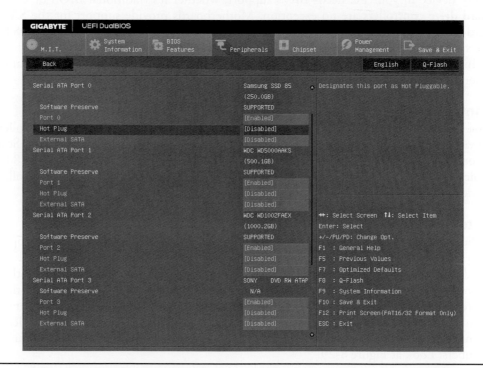

Figure 8-29 Standard system setup features

Whew! Lots of hard drives! This motherboard supports six SATA connections. Each connection has a number, with an M.2 SSD on SATA 0, hard drives on SATA 1 and SATA 2, and the optical drive on SATA 3. Each was autodetected and configured by the BIOS without any input from me. Oh, to live in the future!

Boot Order

If you want your computer to run, it's going to need an operating system to boot. You assign *boot order* priority to drives and devices in CMOS.

Figure 8-30 shows a typical boot-order screen, with a first, second, and third boot option. Many users like to boot first from the optical drive and then from a hard drive. This enables them to put in a bootable optical disc if they're having problems with the system. Of course, you can set it to boot first from your hard drive and then go into CMOS and change it when you need to—it's your choice.

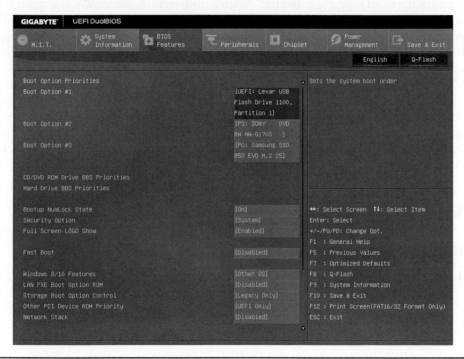

Figure 8-30   Boot order

Most modern CMOS setup utilities include a second screen for determining the boot order of your hard drives. You might want to set up a boot order that starts with the optical drive, followed by the hard drive, and then the USB thumb drive, but what if you have more than one hard drive? This screen enables you to set which hard drive goes first. If you have a different operating system on each hard drive, this can be very helpful.

Enabling AHCI

On motherboards that support AHCI, you implement it in CMOS. You'll generally have up to three options/modes/HBA configurations: IDE/SATA or compatibility mode, AHCI, or RAID. Don't install modern operating systems in compatibility mode; it's included with some motherboards to support ancient (Windows XP) or odd (some Linux distros, perhaps?) operating systems. AHCI works best for current HDDs and SSDs, so make sure the HBA configuration is set to AHCI.

Troubleshooting Hard Drive Installation

The best friend a tech has when it comes to troubleshooting hard drive installation is the autodetection feature of the CMOS setup utility. When a drive doesn't work, the most obvious question, especially during installation, is "Did I plug it in correctly? Or did I plug both data and power in correctly?" With autodetection, the answer is simple: If the system doesn't see the drive, something is wrong with the hardware configuration. Either a device has physically failed or, more likely, you didn't give the hard drive power, plugged a cable in improperly, or messed up some other connectivity issue. To troubleshoot hard drives, simply work your way through each step to figure out what went wrong.

Make sure the BIOS recognizes the hard drive. Use the CMOS setup program to check. Check the physical connections, then run through these issues in CMOS. Is the controller enabled? Similarly, can the motherboard support the type of drive you're installing? If not, you have a couple of options. You may be able to flash the BIOS with an upgraded BIOS from the manufacturer or get a hard drive controller that goes into an expansion slot.

Chapter Review

Questions

1. Which of the following is a common spindle speed for an HDD?

   A. 5200

   B. 7200

   C. 9200

   D. Not applicable. HDDs have no moving parts.

2. Which form factor connects directly to a dedicated motherboard socket?

   A. 2.5-inch SSD

   B. 3.5-inch SSD

   C. M.2 SSD

   D. eSATA SSD

3. Which of the following is an advantage of an NVMe SSD?

   A. Lower cost

   B. Higher potential storage capacity

   C. The ability to hot-swap the drive

   D. Faster read/write speeds

4. Which of the following is not an SSD form factor?

   A. M.2

   B. 3.5 inch

   C. 2.5 inch

   D. mSATA

5. How do SSDs avoid the need to use moving mechanical parts?

   A. By using magnetic platters

   B. By being placed in an external enclosure

   C. By using flash memory

   D. By using SATA connectors

6. What is the maximum cable length of an internal SATA device?

   A. 2 meters

   B. 12 inches

   C. 18 inches

   D. 1 meter

7. What is the maximum number of SATA drives you can have on a system?

   A. One

   B. Two

   C. Eight

   D. There is no maximum other than the limitations of your motherboard/host card.

8. Which SATA version offers the least overhead (and thus best performance)?

   A. AHCI

   B. SATA 2.0

   C. PATA 3.0

   D. SATAe

9. Which standard supports magnetic SATA drives most efficiently?

   A. AHCI

   B. CMOS

   C. SATA-IO

   D. SATA 3.2

10. Which RAID standard requires at least four drives?

    A. RAID 1

    B. RAID 4

    C. RAID 5

    D. RAID 10

Answers

1. **B.** Common spindle speeds on magnetic hard drives are 5400, 7200, 10,000, and 15,000 RPM.

2. **C.** The M.2 (and mSATA) SSD has a dedicated motherboard socket.

3. **D.** NVMe SSDs offer significantly faster read/write speeds than mechanical hard drives or SATA SSDs.

4. **B.** 3.5 inch is a form factor for mechanical hard drives, not SSDs.

5. **C.** SSDs use flash memory such as NAND in place of the less reliable spinning disks used by mechanical HDDs.

6. **D.** The maximum cable length of an internal SATA device is 1 meter.

7. **D.** There is no maximum number of SATA drives you can have on a system beyond the limits imposed by the number of ports on your motherboard/host card.

8. **D.** SATA Express (SATAe) uses the PCIe bus and has none of the traditional SATA overhead.

9. **A.** The AHCI standard supports magnetic SATA drives efficiently.

10. **D.** RAID 10 requires at least four drives.

Implementing Mass Storage

In this chapter, you will learn how to
- Explain the partitions available in Windows
- Discuss hard drive formatting options
- Partition and format hard drives
- Maintain and troubleshoot hard drives

From the standpoint of your PC, a freshly installed hard drive is nothing more than a huge pile of unorganized storage space. Sure, CMOS recognizes it as a drive—always a step in the right direction—but your operating system is clueless without more information. Your operating system must organize that storage so you can use the drive to store data. This chapter covers that process.

Historical/Conceptual

After you've successfully installed a hard drive, you must perform two more steps to translate a drive's raw media into something the system can use: partitioning and formatting. Partitioning is the process of electronically subdividing a physical drive into one or more units called partitions. After partitioning, you must format the drive. Formatting installs a file system onto the drive that organizes each partition in such a way that the operating system can store files and folders on the drive. Several types of file systems are used by Windows. This chapter will go through them after covering partitioning.

NOTE This chapter uses the term "hard drive" as a generic term that covers all the drive types you learned about in Chapter 8. Once you get into Windows, the operating system doesn't particularly care if the drive is a magnetic hard disk drive (HDD) or a solid-state drive (SSD). The tools and steps for preparing the drives for data are the same.

The process of partitioning and formatting a drive is one of the few areas remaining on the software side of PC assembly that requires you to perform a series of fairly complex manual steps. The CompTIA A+ 220-1102 exam tests your knowledge of *what* these processes do to make the drive work, as well as the steps needed to partition and format hard drives in Windows.

This chapter continues the exploration of hard drive installation by explaining the concepts of partitioning and formatting, and then going through the process of partitioning and formatting hard drives. The chapter wraps with a discussion on hard drive maintenance and troubleshooting issues, the scope of which includes all the operating systems covered on the current exams.

Hard Drive Partitions

Before a magnetic disk drive leaves the factory, it is magnetically preset with millions (hundreds of millions on really big drives) of storage areas known as sectors. Older hard drives had 512-byte sectors; modern drives use 4096-byte Advanced Format (AF) sectors. Figure 9-1 shows a close-up of several sectors on a typical HDD.

Figure 9-1
Sectors on
an HDD

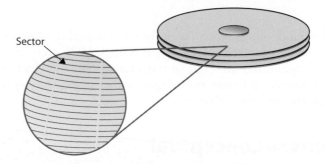

Solid-state drives come from the factory with each NAND chip storing millions (hundreds of millions on really big drives) of 4096-byte storage areas known as *pages*. A group of pages are combined into a *block*. The size of a block varies, but 128 pages per block isn't uncommon. Figure 9-2 shows a simplified concept of how this looks.

The CPU and operating system never talk to these internal structures. Instead, the controller on the HDD or SSD uses *logical block addressing (LBA)* to present all these storage chunks as nothing more than a number that starts at LBA0 and goes until every sector or page has an LBA number (see Figure 9-3). These LBA chunks are also called *blocks*.

LBA makes addressing any form of mass storage easy, and that's how the operating system interacts with the mass storage, via blocks. The operating system presents to the user files and folders, not LBA addresses. We must organize mass storage in a way that enables us to store and retrieve files, create folders, and so on. The first step to doing this is partitioning.

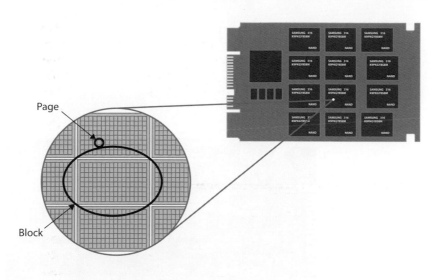

Figure 9-2 SSD pages and blocks

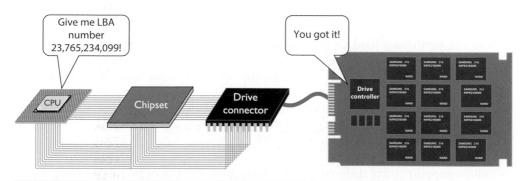

Figure 9-3 LBA in action

If you think of a hard drive as an empty building filled with many rooms (the blocks), partitioning is what organizes the rooms into something bigger (like suites or companies) and gives each bigger entity a name (see Figure 9-4). Partitioning takes a single physical drive and electronically organizes it into one or more . . . partitions. With that analogy, think of partitions as collections of rooms in the building. Partitions provide tremendous flexibility in hard drive organization. With partitions, you can organize a drive to suit your personal taste.

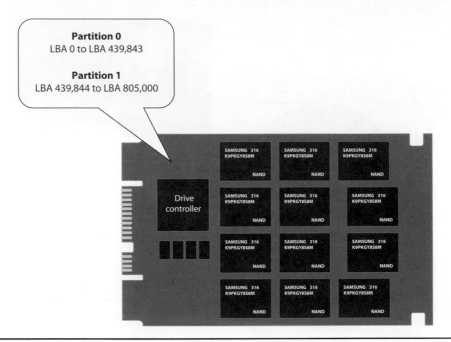

Figure 9-4 Partitions on an SSD

You can partition a hard drive to store more than one operating system: store one OS in one partition and create additional partitions for another OS. Granted, most people use only one OS, but if you want the option to boot to either Windows or Linux, partitions are the key.

1102

Windows supports three different partitioning methods: the older master boot record (MBR) partitioning scheme, Windows' proprietary dynamic storage partitioning scheme, and the GUID partition table (GPT). (I'll cover all three of these in their respective sections, following this introduction.) Microsoft calls a hard drive that uses either the MBR partitioning scheme or the GPT partitioning scheme a *basic disk* and calls a drive that uses the dynamic storage partitioning scheme a *dynamic disk*.

A single Windows system with three hard drives may have one of the drives partitioned with MBR, another with GPT, and the third set up as a dynamic disk, and the system will run perfectly well. The bottom line? You get to learn about three totally different types of partitioning. I'll also cover a few other partition types, such as hidden partitions, and tell you when you can and should make your partitions.

Master Boot Record

The first sector of an MBR hard drive contains the *master boot record (MBR),* code that informs the system about installed operating systems. To clarify, hard drives that use the MBR partitioning scheme have a tiny bit of data that is also called the "master boot record." While your computer boots up, BIOS looks at the first sector of your hard drive for instructions. At this point, it doesn't matter which OS you use or how many partitions you have. Without this bit of code, your OS will never load.

 NOTE Techs often refer to MBR-partitioned drives as "MBR drives." The same holds true for GPT-partitioned drives, which many techs refer to as "GPT drives."

The master boot record also contains the *partition table,* which describes the number and size of partitions on the disk (see Figure 9-5). MBR partition tables support up to four partitions—the partition table is large enough to store entries for only four partitions. The instructions in the MBR use this table to determine which partition contains the active operating system.

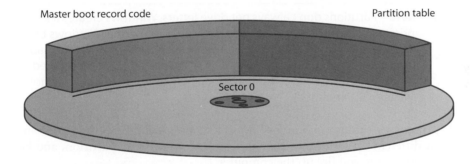

1. The master boot record looks for a partition with an operating system.

2. The partition table tells the master boot record where to look.

Master boot record code

Partition table

Sector 0

Figure 9-5 The master boot record

After the MBR locates the appropriate partition, the *partition boot sector* loads the OS on that partition. The partition boot sector stores information important to its partition, such as the location of the OS boot files (see Figure 9-6).

 EXAM TIP Only one master boot record and one partition table within that master boot record exist per MBR disk. Each partition has a partition boot sector.

Figure 9-6
Using the master
boot record to
boot an OS

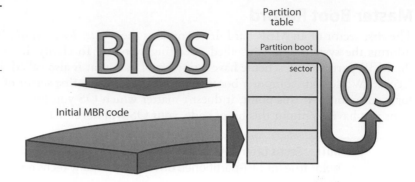

Initial MBR code

MBR partition tables support two types of partitions: primary partitions and extended partitions. *Primary partitions* are designed to support bootable operating systems. *Extended partitions* are not bootable. A single MBR disk may have up to four primary partitions or up to three primary partitions and one extended partition.

Primary Partitions and Multiple Operating Systems

Primary partitions are usually assigned drive letters and appear in Windows Explorer/File Explorer (once you format them). The first lettered primary partition in Windows is always C:. After that, you can label the partitions D: through Z:.

 NOTE Partitions don't always get drive letters. Windows creates a small primary partition named "System Reserved" for essential Windows boot files. See also the section "Mounting Partitions as Folders," later in this chapter, for details. In a related topic, the first primary Windows partition is called "C:" because early PCs had one or two floppy drives installed and they got the "A:" and "B:" labels.

Only primary partitions can boot operating systems. On an MBR disk, you can easily install four different operating systems, each on its own primary partition, and boot to your choice each time you fire up the computer.

Every primary partition on a single drive has a special setting stored in the partition table called *active* that determines the *active partition*. During boot-up, the BIOS/POST reads the MBR to find the active partition and boots the operating system on that partition. Only one partition can be active at a time because you can run only one OS at a time (see Figure 9-7).

To control multiboot setups, many people use a free Linux-based boot manager called Grand Unified Bootloader (GRUB), shown in Figure 9-8. When the computer boots, the boot manager software yanks control from the MBR and asks which OS you want to boot. Once a partition is set as active, the partition boot sector loads the operating system.

Partition table
Partition 1
C:
Windows 11
Active
Partition 2
D:
Partition 3
E:
Partition 4
F:

Figure 9-7 The active partition containing Windows

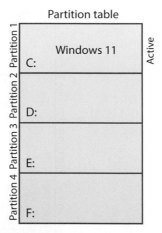

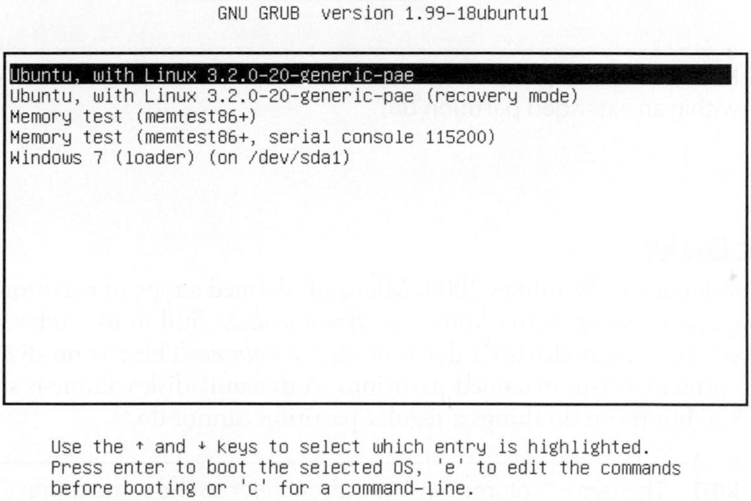

GNU GRUB version 1.99-18ubuntu1
Ubuntu, with Linux 3.2.0-20-generic-pae
Ubuntu, with Linux 3.2.0-20-generic-pae (recovery mode)
Memory test (memtest86+)
Memory test (memtest86+, serial console 115200)
Windows 7 (loader) (on /dev/sda1)
Use the ↑ and ↓ keys to select which entry is highlighted.
Press enter to boot the selected OS, 'e' to edit the commands
before booting or 'c' for a command-line.

Figure 9-8 GRUB in action

Extended Partitions

With a four-partition limit, an MBR disk would be limited to only four drive letters if using only primary partitions. Extended partitions were invented to get around this limit. An extended partition may contain multiple *logical drives,* each of which can get a drive letter (see Figure 9-9).

Figure 9-9
An extended
partition
containing
multiple logical
drives

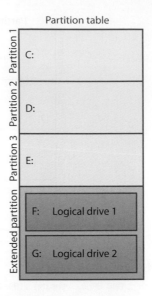

Partition table

NOTE Extended partitions do not receive drive letters, but the logical drives within an extended partition do.

Dynamic Disks

With the introduction of Windows 2000, Microsoft defined a type of partitioning called *dynamic storage partitioning*, better known as *dynamic disks*. Still in use today, Microsoft calls a drive structure created with a dynamic disk a *volume*. There is no dynamic disk equivalent to primary versus extended partitions. A dynamic disk volume is still technically a partition, but it can do things a regular partition cannot do.

NOTE The terms "volume" and "partition" refer to the same thing: a defined chunk of a hard drive.

First off, when you turn a hard drive into a dynamic disk, you can create as many volumes on it as you want. You're not limited to four partitions.

Second, you can create—in software—new drive structures that you can't do with MBR drives. Specifically, you can implement RAID, span volumes over multiple drives, and extend volumes on one or more drives. Table 9-1 shows you which volume types Windows 10/11 and Windows Server supports, and here are the explanations of the volumes:

- *Simple volumes* work a lot like primary partitions. If you have a hard drive and you want to make half of it E: and the other half F:, for example, you create two volumes on a dynamic disk. That's it.

Table 9-1
Dynamic Disk
Compatibility

Volume	Windows 10/11	Windows Server
Simple	X	X
Spanned	X	X
Striped	X	X
Mirrored	X	X
RAID 5		X

- *Spanned volumes* use unallocated space on multiple drives to create a single volume. Spanned volumes are a bit risky: if any of the spanned drives fails, the entire volume is lost.

- *Striped volumes* are RAID 0 volumes. You may take any two unallocated spaces on two separate hard drives and stripe them. But again, if either drive fails, you lose all of your data.

- *Mirrored volumes* are RAID 1 volumes. You may take any two unallocated spaces on two separate hard drives and mirror them. If one of the two mirrored drives fails, the other keeps running.

- *RAID 5 volumes,* as the name implies, are for RAID 5 arrays. A RAID 5 volume requires three or more dynamic disks with equal-sized unallocated spaces.

NOTE Windows 10 and 11 can use a software RAID system called Storage Spaces that's distinct from dynamic disks. See the appropriately named section of this chapter for the scoop.

GUID Partition Table

MBR partitioning came out a long time ago, in an age where 32-MB hard drives were thought to be larger than you would ever need. While it's lasted a long time as the partitioning standard for bootable drives, back around 2010 a new kid appeared in town with the power to outshine the aging partitioning scheme and assume all the functions of the older partition style.

The *GUID partition table (GPT)* partitioning scheme shares a lot with the MBR partitioning scheme, overcoming many of the MBR scheme's limitations. Here are the big improvements:

- While MBR drives were limited to four partitions, a GPT drive can have an almost unlimited number of primary partitions. Microsoft has limited Windows to 128 partitions.

- MBR partitions were no larger than 2.2 TB, but GPT partitions have no such restrictions. Well, there is a maximum size limit, but it's so large, we measure it in zettabytes. A zettabyte, by the way, is roughly a billion terabytes.

On paper, a GPT drive looks a lot like an MBR drive, except it's arranged by LBA instead of sectors (see Figure 9-10). LBA 0, for instance, is the *protective MBR*. This is a re-creation of the master boot record from MBR drives so that disk utilities know it is a GPT drive and don't mistakenly overwrite any partition data.

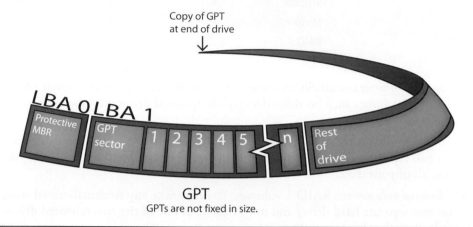

Figure 9-10   GUID partition table

Instead of the old master boot record and partition table, GPT drives use a GPT header and partition entry array. Both are located at the beginning and end of the drive so there is a protected backup copy. The partitions on a GPT drive go between the primary and backup headers and arrays, as shown in Figure 9-10.

You can configure Windows 10 and 11 to boot from GPT only if you use a UEFI motherboard. In other words, if you're trying to install a current version of Windows on an ancient motherboard, you're stuck with MBR. The same is true of macOS. Most Linux distributions can boot from GPT partitions with older BIOS or UEFI firmware.

NOTE   Okay, if GPT stands for GUID partition table, I guess we had better see what GUID stands for, eh? A *globally unique identifier (GUID)* provides a reference number for an object or process that has an almost impossibly small chance of duplication. The number is, therefore, *unique* to a specific object or process.

Other Partition Types

The partition types supported by Windows are not the only partition types you may encounter; other types exist. One of the most common is called the *hidden partition*. A hidden partition is really just a primary partition that is hidden from your operating system. Only special BIOS tools may access a hidden partition. Hidden partitions are used by some PC makers to hide a backup copy of an installed OS that you can use to restore your system if you accidentally trash it—by, for example, learning about partitions and using a partitioning program incorrectly.

A *swap partition* is another special type of partition, but swap partitions are found only on Linux and UNIX systems. A swap partition's only job is to act like RAM when your system needs more RAM than you have installed. Windows has a similar function with a *page file* that uses a special file instead of a partition, as you'll recall from Chapter 4.

When to Partition

Partitioning is not a common task for an already-setup system. The two most common situations likely to require partitioning are when you install an OS on a new system, and when you add an additional drive to an existing system. When you install a new OS, the installation program asks you how you would like to partition the drive. When you add a new hard drive to an existing system, every OS has a built-in tool to help you partition it.

Each version of Windows offers a different tool for partitioning hard drives. For more than 20 years, through the days of DOS and early Windows (up to Windows Me), we used a command-line program called FDISK to partition drives. Modern versions of Windows use a graphical partitioning program called *Disk Management,* shown in Figure 9-11. You'll find it in the Quick Links menu or Computer Management in Administrative Tools. (Windows has an advanced command-line disk management tool as well, called *diskpart,* discussed in detail in Chapter 16.)

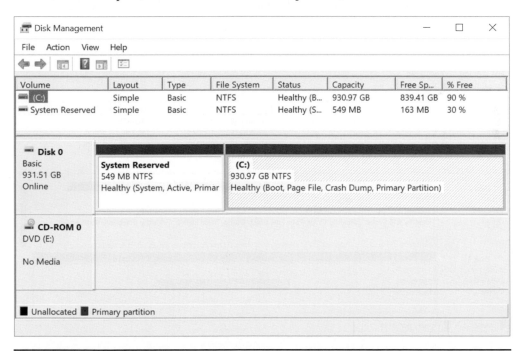

Figure 9-11 Windows 10 Disk Management tool in Computer Management

Linux uses several tools for partitioning. The oldest is called *fdisk*—yes, the same name as the DOS/Windows tool (though case-sensitive). That's where the similarities end, however, as Linux fdisk has a totally different command set. Even though every copy of Linux comes with the Linux fdisk, it's rarely used because so many better partitioning tools are available. One of the GUI Linux partitioning tools is called GParted and is even conveniently provided by Ubuntu's live CD.

In the early days of PCs, you couldn't change a partition's size or type (other than by erasing it) once you'd made it with any Microsoft tools. A few third-party tools, led by PartitionMagic, gave techs the tools to resize partitions without losing the data the partitions held. Current Microsoft Windows tools allow you to resize free space. Windows enables you to resize partitions nondestructively by shrinking or expanding existing partitions with available free space.

 SIM Check out the excellent Chapter 9 Show! and Click! simulations, both titled "Resizing a Partition," at the Total Seminars Training Hub: https://www.totalsem.com/110X. These give you a quick shot at addressing probable simulation questions on the 1102 exam.

Partition Naming Problems

So far, you've learned that MBR and GPT disks use partitions and that dynamic disks use volumes. Unfortunately, when you create a new partition or volume in current versions of Windows (10 and 11), the tool (Disk Management) only shows that you're about to create a volume. See Figure 9-12.

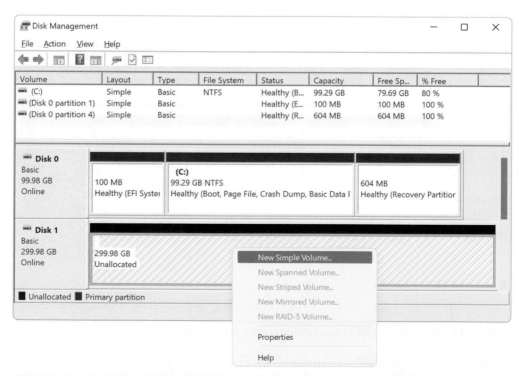

Figure 9-12 Note that the context menu only mentions volumes, not partitions.

When working with older MBR disks, and even though the context menu says "New Simple Volume," you create partitions on basic disks. Figure 9-13 shows Disk Management in Windows 11 with a basic disk with four partitions. The first three (from left to right) are primary partitions. The fourth and fifth structures on the right are a logical drive and some blank, unpartitioned "Free space" in an extended partition.

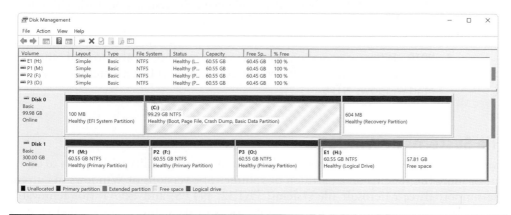

Figure 9-13 Drive with four partitions displayed in Disk Management

Hard Drive Formatting

Once you've partitioned a hard drive, that partition is nothing more than a large number of blocks. Your operating system needs to store files, files with names like VacationMemories .mp4 or chrome.exe. We need to organize those blocks (see Figure 9-14).

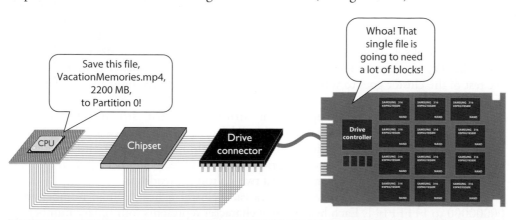

Figure 9-14 Big files require many blocks.

Formatting, the process of making a partition into something that stores files, does two things. First, it creates a *file system*—an organization of all the blocks contained in that partition, enabling file storage and retrieval. Second, formatting creates a root directory in the file system to enable the partition to store folders. You must format every partition/volume so they can hold and retrieve data.

Every operating system has its own file systems. For the Apple folks, macOS uses APFS. Linux users have lots to choose from; most use ext4, but you will see others with names like BTRFS, XFS, ZFS, and so on. Windows has file systems with names like NTFS, FAT32, and exFAT. Let's first understand what a file system does (using Windows as an example), and then we will discuss the differences.

 NOTE Different operating systems may or may not be able to read other operating systems' file systems. For example, most Linux systems easily read Windows' NTFS.

File Systems in Windows

Every version of Windows comes with a built-in formatting utility with which to create one or more file systems on a partition or volume. The versions of Windows in current use support three Microsoft file systems: FAT32, NTFS, and exFAT (for removable media). All Windows file systems organize blocks of data into groups called *clusters.* The size of each cluster varies according to the file system and the size of the partition. Windows uses clusters to overcome some of the limitations in addressing inherent to each file system. (I'll add charts with each file system to show how the clusters scale.)

FAT32

The base storage area for hard drives is a block; each block stores up to 4096 bytes of data. In a small partition, each cluster is made up of one block. If a file is larger than 4096 bytes, it will use as many clusters as needed to store the file. The OS needs a method to fill one cluster, find another that's unused, and fill it, continuing to fill clusters until the file is completely stored. Once the OS stores a file, it must remember which cluster holds the file, so it can be retrieved later. If an OS stores a file smaller than 4096 bytes, the rest of the cluster goes to waste. We accept this waste because most files are far larger than 4096 bytes.

MS-DOS version 2.1 first supported hard drives using a data structure and indexing system to keep track of stored data on the hard drive, and Microsoft called this structure the *file allocation table (FAT).* Think of the FAT as nothing more than a card catalog that keeps track of which clusters store the various parts of a file. The official jargon term for a FAT is *data structure,* but it is more like a two-column spreadsheet.

The left column (see Figure 9-15) gives each cluster a hexadecimal number from 00000000 to FFFFFFFF. Each hexadecimal character represents four binary numbers or 4 bits. Eight hex characters, therefore, represent 32 bits. If you do the math (2^{32}), you'll find that there are over four billion clusters that can be tracked or indexed.

Figure 9-15
32-bit FAT

LBA number	Status
00000000	
00000001	
00000002	
00000003	
00000004	
00000005	

FFFFFFFA	
FFFFFFFB	
FFFFFFFC	
FFFFFFFD	
FFFFFFFE	
FFFFFFFF	

NOTE Hexadecimal characters cover the decimal numbers 0–15, numbering from 0–9 and then A–F; each character reflects the state of four binary characters. You add them up to make the number. So, 0000 in binary shows zero numbers and the hex number is 0. When you go up numerically in binary to 0001, this represents the number 1 in decimal and also in hex. The key to hex is when you reach the number 10. In binary, this looks like this: 1010. But because hex sticks with a single digit, it's represented as A. B translates as 11 in decimal or 1011 in binary, and so on.

We call this type of FAT a *32-bit FAT* or *FAT32*. And it's not just hard drives and SSDs that have FATs. Many USB flash drives use FAT32.

The right column of the FAT contains information on the status of clusters. All hard drives, even brand-new drives fresh from the factory, contain faulty blocks that cannot store data because of imperfections in the construction of the drives. The OS must locate these bad blocks, mark them as unusable, and then prevent any files from being written to them. This mapping of bad blocks is one of the functions of *high-level formatting*. After the format program creates the FAT, it marches through every block of the entire partition, writing and attempting to read from each block sequentially. If it finds a bad block, it places a special status code (0000FFF7) in the block's FAT location, indicating that the cluster is unavailable for use. Formatting also marks the good blocks with code 00000000 (see Figure 9-16).

NOTE *High-level formatting*, as noted, creates the FAT and then creates a blank root directory. This process is known in Microsoft speak as a quick format. At your option, you can cause the format utility to test every sector to mark out the unusable ones in the FAT. This is called a full format.

Figure 9-16
Bad blocks
marked

LBA number	Status	
00000000	00000000	
00000001	00000000	
00000002	00000000	
00000003	00000000	
00000004	0000FFF7	Bad block
00000005	00000000	

FFFFFFFA		
FFFFFFFB	00000000	
FFFFFFFC	0000FFF7	Bad block
FFFFFFFD	00000000	
FFFFFFFE	00000000	
FFFFFFFF	00000000	

FAT32 in Action

Suppose you have a system with a drive using FAT32. When an application such as Microsoft Word tells the OS to save a file, Windows starts at the beginning of the FAT, looking for the first space marked "open for use" (00000000), and begins to write to that cluster. If the entire file fits within that one cluster, Windows places the code *0000FFFF* (last cluster) into the cluster's status area in the FAT. That's called the *end-of-file marker*. Windows then goes to the folder storing the file and adds the filename and the cluster's number to the folder list. If the file requires more than one cluster, Windows searches for the next open cluster and places the number of the next cluster in the status area, filling and adding clusters until the entire file is saved. The last cluster then receives the end-of-file marker (0000FFFF).

Let's run through an example of this process, starting by selecting an arbitrary part of the FAT: from 03213ABB to 03213AC7. Assume you want to save a file called mom.txt. Before saving the file, the FAT looks like Figure 9-17.

Windows finds the first open cluster, 03213ABB, and fills it. But the entire mom.txt file won't fit into that cluster. Needing more space, the OS goes through the FAT to find the next open cluster. It finds cluster 03213ABC. Before filling 03213ABC, the value *03213ABC* is placed in 03213ABB's status. Even after filling two clusters, more of the mom.txt file remains, so Windows must find one more cluster. The 03213ABD cluster has been marked 0000FFF7 (bad block), so Windows skips over 03213ABD, finding 03213ABE.

Before filling 03213ABE, Windows enters the value *03213ABE* in 03213ABC's status. Windows does not completely fill 03213ABE, signifying that the entire mom.txt file has been stored. Windows enters the value *0000FFFF* in 03213ABE's status, indicating the end of file (see Figure 9-18).

Figure 9-17
The initial FAT

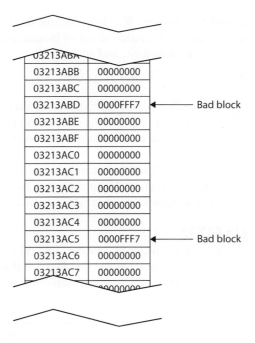

Figure 9-18
End of file
reached

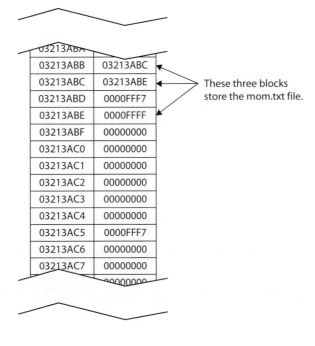

After saving all of the clusters, Windows locates the file's folder (yes, folders also are stored on blocks, but they get a different set of blocks, somewhere else on the disk) and records the filename, size, date/time, and starting cluster, like this:

```
mom.txt      13234 05-19-23 2:04p 03213ABB
```

If a program requests that file, the process is reversed. Windows locates the folder containing the file to determine the starting cluster and then pulls a piece of the file from each cluster until it sees the end-of-file cluster. Windows then hands the reassembled file to the requesting application.

Clearly, without the FAT, Windows cannot locate files. FAT32 automatically makes two copies of the FAT. One FAT backs up the other to provide special utilities a way to recover a FAT that gets corrupted—a painfully common occurrence.

Cluster Sizes in FAT32

Cluster sizes scale according to the file system. FAT32 offers 4-KB cluster sizes up to a partition size of 2 GB, which matches the size of a 4-KB block. Larger partitions require clusters with more blocks, thus reducing somewhat the efficiency of that drive. Table 9-2 shows the scaling effect in FAT32.

Table 9-2 FAT32 Cluster Sizes	Drive Size	Cluster Size
	512 MB to 1023 MB	4 KB
	1024 MB to 2 GB	4 KB
	2 GB to 8 GB	4 KB
	8 GB to 16 GB	8 KB
	16 GB to 32 GB	16 KB
	>32 GB	32 KB

FAT32 is still very much commonly used today, though not for operating system partitions. Rather, you'll see it on smaller (< 32-GB) flash-media USB drives.

Fragmentation

Continuing with the example, let's use Microsoft Word to save two more files: a letter called Important Document 31.docx and a letter named System Storage.docx. The Important Document 31.docx file takes the next three clusters—03213ABF, 03213AC0, and 03213AC1—and System Storage.docx takes two clusters—03213AC2 and 03213AC3 (see Figure 9-19).

Assuming these files are all in the same folder, the file information looks like this:

```
mom.txt                    13234   05-19-23 2:04p 03213ABB
Important Document 31.docx   9276   05-19-23 2:07p 03213ABF
System Storage.docx          5434   05-19-23 2:10p 03213AC2
```

Figure 9-19
Three files saved

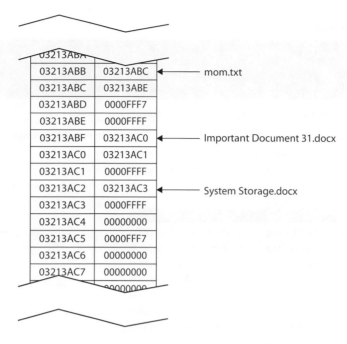

03213ABA	
03213ABB	03213ABC	← mom.txt
03213ABC	03213ABE
03213ABD	0000FFF7
03213ABE	0000FFFF
03213ABF	03213AC0	← Important Document 31.docx
03213AC0	03213AC1
03213AC1	0000FFFF
03213AC2	03213AC3	← System Storage.docx
03213AC3	0000FFFF
03213AC4	00000000
03213AC5	0000FFF7
03213AC6	00000000
03213AC7	00000000

Now suppose you erase mom.txt. Windows does not delete the block entries in the FAT for mom.txt when it erases the file. Windows only alters the information in the folder, simply changing the first letter of mom.txt to the lowercase Greek letter σ (sigma), as shown next. This causes the file to "disappear" as far as the OS knows. It won't show up, for example, in Windows Explorer, even though the data still resides on the hard drive for the moment.

```
σom.txt                13234   05-19-23 2:04p 03213ABB
```

Note that under normal circumstances, Windows does not actually delete files when you press the DELETE key. Instead, Windows moves the file listing (but not the actual blocks) to a special hidden directory that you can access via the Recycle Bin. The files themselves are not actually deleted until you empty the Recycle Bin.

Because the data for mom.txt is intact, you could use some program to change the σ back into another letter and thus get the document back. A number of third-party undelete tools are available. Figure 9-20 shows one such program at work. Just remember that if you want to use an undelete tool, you must use it quickly. The space allocated to your deleted file may soon be overwritten by a new file.

EXAM TIP CompTIA may ask you how to recover a deleted file. If the file is still in the Recycle Bin, simply browse to the Recycle Bin, right-click the deleted file, and select Restore. If the file was deleted and bypassed the Recycle Bin or for any other reason is no longer there, Windows does not have a built-in file restore utility. You must install Microsoft's utility, or a third-party utility, to attempt recovery.

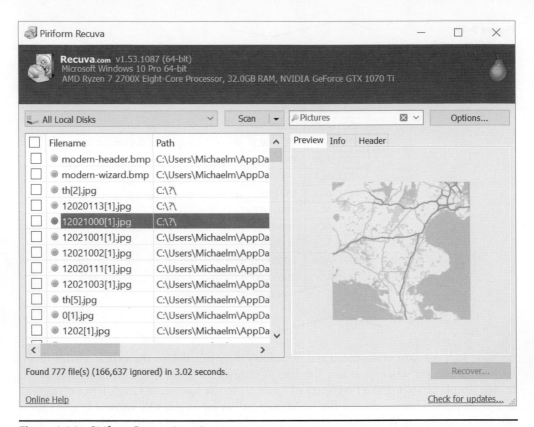

Figure 9-20 Piriform Recuva in action

Let's say you just emptied your Recycle Bin. You now save one more file, Taxrec.xls, a big spreadsheet that will take six clusters, into the same folder that once held mom.txt. As Windows writes the file to the drive, it overwrites the space that mom.txt used, but it needs three more clusters. The next three available clusters are 03213AC4, 03213AC6 (skipping cluster 03213AC5, which is marked bad), and 03213AC7 (see Figure 9-21).

Notice that Taxrec.xls is in two pieces, thus *fragmented*. *Fragmentation* takes place all of the time on FAT32 systems. Although the system easily negotiates a tiny fragmented file split into only two parts, excess fragmentation slows down the system during hard drive reads and writes. This example is fragmented into two pieces; in the real world, a file might fragment into hundreds of pieces, forcing the read/write heads to travel all over the hard drive to retrieve a single file. You can dramatically improve the speed at which the hard drive reads and writes files by eliminating this fragmentation.

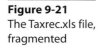

Figure 9-21

The Taxrec.xls file, fragmented

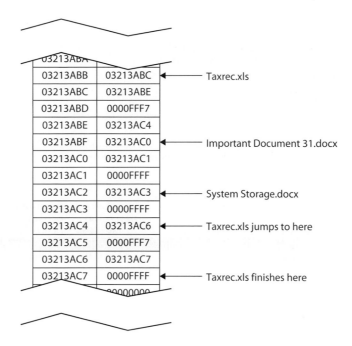

Windows 10 and 11 come with an app called Optimize Drives (known in older versions of Windows as Disk Defragmenter) that can rearrange the files into neat contiguous chunks (see Figure 9-22). Windows does this automatically by default. Defragmentation is crucial for ensuring the top performance of a mechanical hard drive. The "Maintaining and Troubleshooting Hard Drives" section of this chapter gives the details on working with Optimize Drives in Windows.

SSDs also have fragmentation of a sort, but the nature of an SSD means almost any page is as easily accessed as any other. In the first-generation SSDs, once data was written into a memory cell, it stayed there until the drive was full. Even if the cell contained file contents from a "deleted" file, the cell was not immediately erased or overwritten, because the SSD controller had no way to know the cell's contents were deleted as far as the OS was concerned.

Because SSD memory cells have a finite number of times that they can be written to before wearing out, the first generation of SSDs waited until all the cells of an SSD were filled before erasing and reusing a previously written cell.

SSDs have a feature called *trim* that enables the OS to issue commands to clean up and reuse deleted areas. Windows runs trim automatically, so there's rarely any reason at all to defragment any SSD—but we will develop this more when we discuss troubleshooting later in this chapter.

NTFS

The Windows format of choice these days is the *New Technology File System (NTFS)*. NTFS came out a long time ago with the first version of Windows NT, thus the name. Over the years, NTFS has undergone several improvements. NTFS uses clusters of blocks and file allocation tables, but in a much more complex and powerful way compared to FAT32.

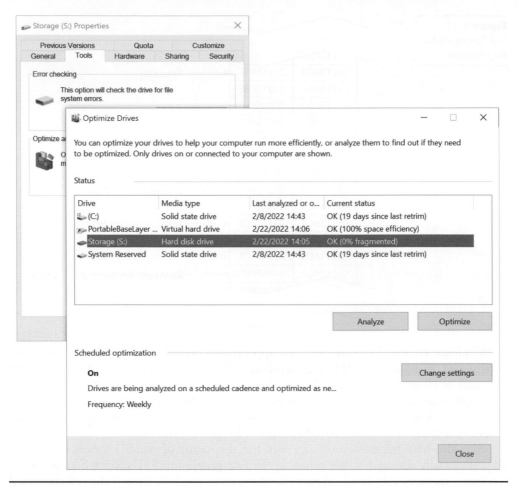

Figure 9-22   Windows 10 Optimize Drives

NTFS offers six major improvements and refinements: redundancy, security, compression, encryption, disk quotas, and cluster sizing.

TIP   If you have a geeky interest in what version of NTFS you are running, open a Command Prompt as an administrator and type this command: **fsutil fsinfo ntfsinfo c:**. Then press ENTER.

NTFS Structure

NTFS utilizes an enhanced file allocation table called the *master file table (MFT)*. An NTFS partition keeps a backup copy of the most critical parts of the MFT in the middle of the disk, reducing the chance that a serious drive error can wipe out both the MFT and the MFT copy. Whenever you defragment an NTFS partition, you'll see a small, immovable chunk somewhere on the drive, often near the front; that's the MFT (see Figure 9-23).

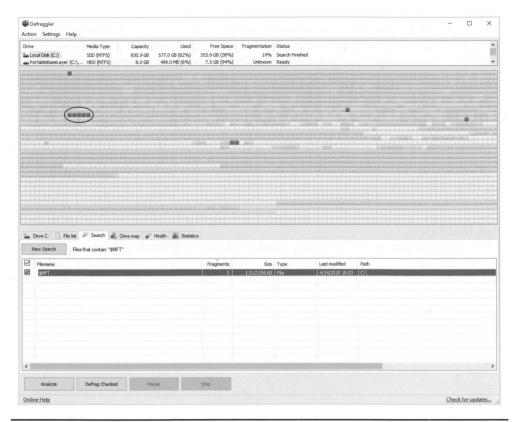

Figure 9-23 The NTFS MFT appears in a defragmenter program as the highlighted blocks.

Security

NTFS views individual files and folders as objects and provides security for those objects through a feature called the *access control list (ACL)*. Future chapters go into this in much more detail.

NOTE Microsoft has never released the exact workings of NTFS to the public.

Compression

NTFS enables you to compress individual files and folders to save space on a hard drive. Compression makes access time to the data slower because the OS must uncompress files every time you use them, but in a space-limited environment, sometimes that's what you have to do. Windows Explorer/File Explorer displays filenames for compressed files in blue.

NOTE Sometimes compression makes access faster. In cases where the CPU can decompress faster than the storage system can give it bytes, compressing the files means that the disk will have fewer bytes to send and the CPU can just rip right through them, expanding them into memory.

Encryption

One of the big draws with NTFS is file encryption, making files unreadable to anybody who doesn't have the right key. You can encrypt a single file, a folder, or a folder full of files. Microsoft calls the encryption utility in NTFS the *encrypting file system (EFS)*, but it's simply an aspect of NTFS, not a standalone file system. You'll learn more about encryption when you read Chapter 13.

Disk Quotas

NTFS supports *disk quotas,* enabling administrators to set limits on drive space usage for users. To set quotas, you must log on as an Administrator, right-click the hard drive name, and select Properties. In the Drive Properties dialog box, select the Quota tab and make changes. Figure 9-24 shows configured quotas for a hard drive. Although rarely used on single-user systems, setting disk quotas on multiuser systems prevents any individual user from monopolizing your hard disk space.

Figure 9-24
Hard drive
quotas in
Windows 10

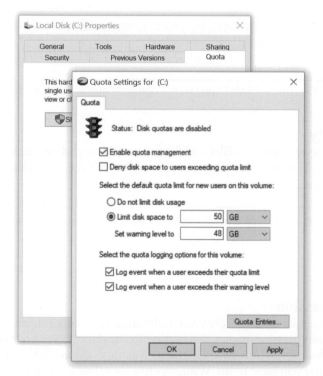

Cluster Sizes

NTFS uses clusters, much like FAT32. The numbers equate to block size until you get to very large partitions. Table 9-3 shows the default cluster sizes for NTFS.

Table 9-3	Drive Size	Cluster Size
NTFS Cluster Sizes	7 MB to 16 TB	4 KB
	16 to 32 TB	8 KB
	32 to 64 TB	32 KB
	64 to 128 TB	64 KB
	128 to 256 TB	128 KB

By default, NTFS supports partitions up to ~16 TB on a dynamic disk (though only up to 2 TB on a basic disk). By tweaking the cluster sizes, you can get NTFS to support partitions up to 16 exabytes, or 18,446,744,073,709,551,616 bytes! That might support any and all upcoming hard drive capacities for the next 100 years or so.

 EXAM TIP NTFS supports partitions from 16 TB by default, but that goes up to 8 petabytes.

With so many file systems, how do you know which one to use? In the case of internal hard drives, you should use the most feature-rich system your OS supports. For all modern versions of Windows, use NTFS. External hard drives and flash drives still often use FAT32 because NTFS features such as the ACL and encryption can make access difficult when you move the drive between systems, but with that exception, NTFS is your best choice on a Windows-based system.

exFAT

Everyone loves USB flash drives. Their ease of use and convenience make them indispensable for those of us who enjoy sharing a program, some photos, or a playlist. But people today want to share more than just a few small files, and they can do so with larger flash drives. As flash drives grow bigger in capacity, however, the file system becomes a problem.

The file system we have used for years on flash drives, FAT32, does not work on drives larger than 2 TB. Worse, FAT32 limits *file* size to 4 GB. Because there is frequent need to physically transport many files that are often larger than 4 GB, Microsoft developed a replacement for FAT32.

 EXAM TIP FAT32 only supports drives up to 2 TB and files up to 4 GB.

The newer file system, called *exFAT*, breaks the 4-GB file-size barrier, supporting files up to 16 exabytes (EB) and a theoretical partition limit of 64 zettabytes (ZB). Microsoft recommends a partition size of up to 512 TB on today's larger USB flash drives, which should be enough for a while. The exFAT file system extends FAT32 from 32-bit cluster entries to 64-bit cluster entries in the file table. Like FAT32, on the other hand, exFAT still lacks all of NTFS's extra features such as permissions, compression, and encryption.

NOTE An exabyte is 2^{60} bytes; a zettabyte is 2^{70} bytes. For comparison, a terabyte is 2^{40} bytes. Remember from your binary practice that each superscript number doubles the overall number, so $2^{41} = 2$ TB, $2^{42} = 4$ TB, and so on. That means a zettabyte is really, really big!

File Systems in macOS

From 1998 to 2017, MacOS used *Hierarchical File System Plus (HFS+)*. Since 2017, however, all new Macs (and existing systems upgrading macOS) use the *Apple File System (APFS)* by default. Unlike HFS+, APFS is optimized for SSDs, allows for full disk encryption, and enables snapshots, among other improvements. Like Windows and Linux, macOS can read and write to several different file systems, such as FAT32 and exFAT, though only read NTFS.

File Systems in Linux

Most Linux distributions use a file system known as the *Fourth Extended File System (ext4)* by default. Some older distros use one of its predecessors, such as *ext2* or *ext3*. The ext4 file system supports volumes up to 1 exabyte (EB) with file sizes up to 16 TB and is backward compatible with ext2 and ext3. In other words, you can mount an ext3 volume as an ext4 volume with no problems. You don't need to know the details of ext3 or ext4, just that they are Linux file systems and that ext4 supports volumes up to 1 EB with file sizes up to 16 TB.

NOTE Linux file system capabilities exceed those of both macOS and Windows, being able to read and write to NTFS, FAT32, exFAT, HFS+, APFS (with a little bit of command-line elbow grease), and ext4. Sweet!

Many Linux distributions, especially at the enterprise level (big data centers), use ZFS file system or its newer cousin, BTRFS (pronounced "butter eff ess"). Both offer powerful copy and disk management features that go well beyond the scope of CompTIA A+. For more information on ZFS and most likely the file system wave of the future, even in Windows, start with the Wikipedia article about ZFS and follow the links to the sources.

The Partitioning, Formatting, and Pooling Process

Now that you understand the concepts of partitioning and formatting, let's go through the process of setting up an installed hard drive by using different partitioning and formatting tools. At the end of the section, we'll look at the process of creating a storage pool by creating a virtual disk. If you have access to a system, try following along with these descriptions. Don't make any changes to a drive you want to keep, because both partitioning and formatting are destructive processes. The pooling process is also destructive. You cannot follow the procedure in that discussion unless you have a few drives to erase.

Bootable Media

Imagine you've built a brand-new PC. The hard drive has no OS, so you need to boot up something to set up that hard drive. Any software that can boot up a system is by definition an operating system. You need an optical disc or USB flash drive with a bootable OS installed. Any removable media that has a bootable OS is generically called a boot device or boot disc. Your system boots off of the boot device, which then loads some kind of OS that enables you to partition, format, and install an OS on your new hard drive. Boot devices come from many sources. All Windows OS installation media are boot devices (see Figure 9-25), as are Linux installation media.

Figure 9-25 Windows 10 bootable media

Boot devices may also be a medium that has an image of an installation disc. These images are usually stored as a file with a name that has an extension of ".iso." Image files may be on a traditional boot device, such as a disc or flash drive, but they can come from anyplace, such as on a network drive.

Every boot device has partitioning tools and a way to format a new partition. A hard drive must have a partition and has to be formatted to support an OS installation.

Partitioning and Formatting with the Installation Media

When you boot up Windows installation media and the installation program detects a hard drive that is not yet partitioned, it prompts you through a sequence of steps to partition and format the hard drive. Chapter 11 covers the entire installation process, but we'll jump ahead and dive into the partitioning part of the installation here to see how this is done.

The process of partitioning and formatting when installing Windows is straightforward. You'll go through a couple of installation screens (see Figure 9-26) where you select things such as language and get prompted for a product key and acceptance of the license agreement. Eventually you'll get to the *Where do you want to install Windows?* dialog box (see Figure 9-27).

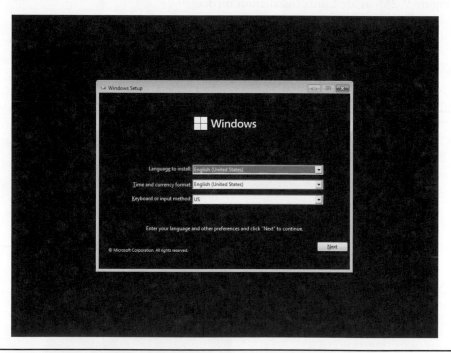

Figure 9-26 Starting the Windows installation

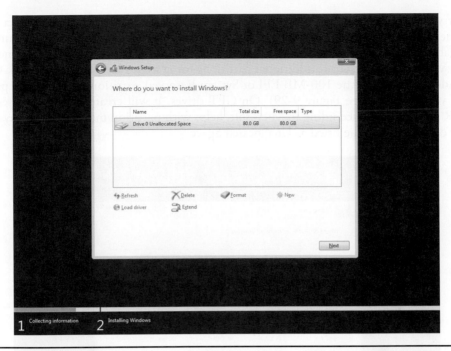

Figure 9-27   Where do you want to install Windows?

Click Next to do the most common partitioning and formatting action: creating a single C: partition, making it active, and formatting it as NTFS. Note that Windows creates three partitions: an EFI or System Reserved partition, the C: partition, and a Recovery partition. This is normal, the way the system was designed to work. Figure 9-28 shows a typical Windows installation in Disk Management.

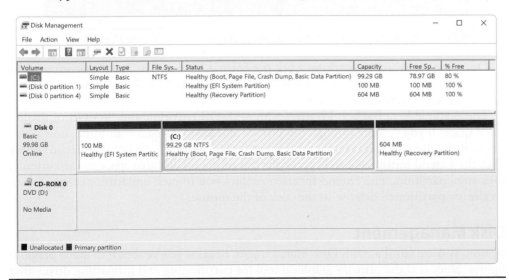

Figure 9-28   Disk Management showing Windows 11's default partitions

If you want to do any custom partitioning or delete existing partitions, select one of the options. To create a new partition, click the New button. Type in an amount in megabytes that you want to use for a new partition, then click Apply. You will get a notice that Windows might create additional partitions for system files. When you click OK, Windows will create the 100-MB EFI or System Reserved partition as well as the partition you specified (see Figure 9-29). On GPT drives, it will create a 16-MB Reserved MSR partition that, according to Microsoft, helps with partition management. Any leftover drive space will be listed as Unallocated Space.

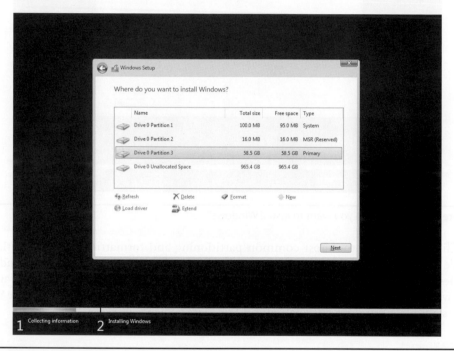

Figure 9-29   New partition with System Reserved partition and Unallocated Space

Once you create a new partition, click the Format button. The installer won't ask you what file system to use. Newer Windows versions can read FAT32 drives, but they won't install to such a partition by default.

The example here has a 1-TB drive with a 58-GB partition and 965 GB of unallocated space. If you've gone through this process and have changed your mind, now wanting to make the partition use the full terabyte, what do you have to do? You can simply click the Extend button and then apply the rest of the unallocated space to the currently formatted partition. The Extend function enables you to tack unpartitioned space onto an already partitioned drive with the click of the mouse.

Disk Management

By now, you are familiar with Disk Management, because you've seen it in many previous figures. Since it is the primary graphical tool for partitioning and formatting drives after installation, I want to go into more depth on some of its features. The Run Command for Disk Management, dskmgmt.msc, allows you to do just about everything you need to do to a hard drive or solid-state drive in one handy tool, including initialization, creating volumes, change drive letters, using dynamic disks, extending drives, and more. You can find Disk Management in the Quick Links menu, under Administrative Tools, or can just type **disk management** in the Start menu and open it directly (see Figure 9-30).

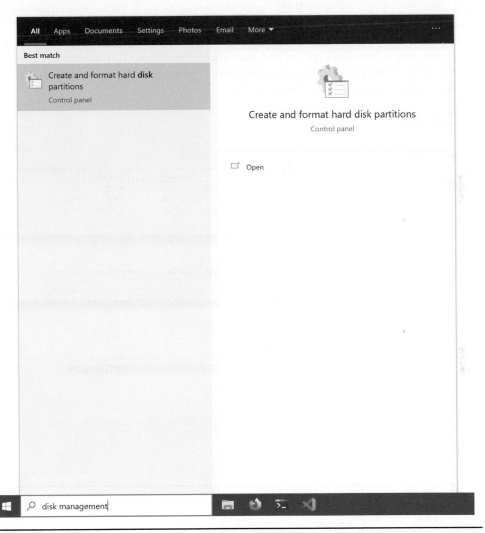

Figure 9-30   Opening Disk Management directly (shown as Create and format hard disk partitions)

   NOTE   Windows offers a command-line tool for managing mass storage: *diskpart,* the successor to FDISK. It's incredibly powerful and useful (and dangerous without adequate knowledge). Chapter 16 discusses diskpart in more detail.

Disk Initialization

Every hard drive in a Windows system has special information placed onto the drive through a process called *disk initialization*. (CompTIA refers to this as *initializing* a disk.) This initialization information includes identifiers that say "this drive belongs in this system" and other information that defines what this hard drive does in the system. If the hard drive is part of a software RAID array, for example, its RAID information is stored in the initialization. If it's part of a spanned volume, this is also stored there.

All new drives must be initialized before you can use them. When you install an extra hard drive into a Windows system and start Disk Management, it notices the new drive and starts the Hard Drive Initialization Wizard. If you don't let the wizard run, the drive will be listed as unknown (see Figure 9-31).

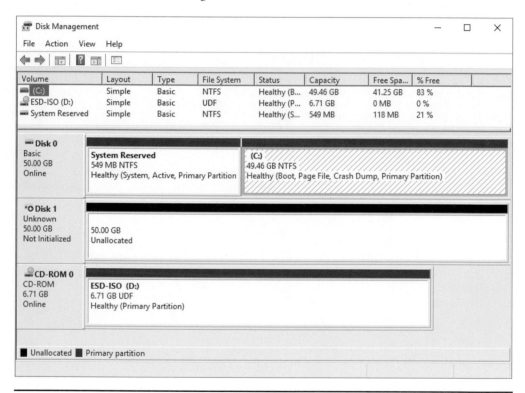

Figure 9-31   Unknown drive in Disk Management

To initialize a disk, right-click the disk icon and select Initialize. You will get the option to select MBR or GPT as a partition style (see Figure 9-32). Once a disk is initialized, you can see the status of the drive—a handy tool for troubleshooting.

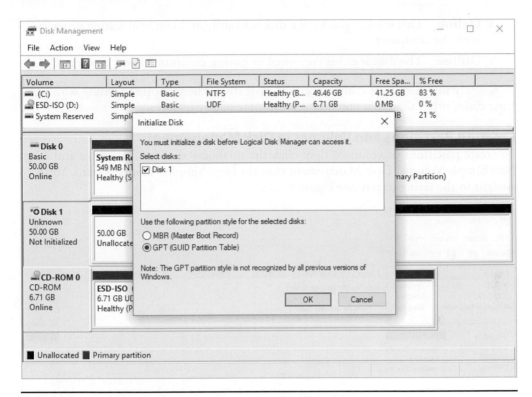

Figure 9-32 Initializing a drive

Disk Management enables you to view the *drive status* of every mass storage device in your system. Hopefully, you'll mostly see each drive listed as Healthy, meaning that nothing is happening to it and things are going along swimmingly. You're also already familiar with the Unallocated and Active statuses, but here are a few more to be familiar with for the CompTIA A+ exams and real life as a tech:

- **Foreign drive** You see this when you move a dynamic disk from one computer to another.

- **Formatting** As you might have guessed, you see this when you're formatting a drive.

- **Failed** Pray you never see this status, because it means that the disk is damaged or corrupt and you've probably lost some data.

- **Online** This is what you see if a disk is healthy and communicating properly with the computer.
- **Offline** The disk is either corrupted or having communication problems.

A newly installed drive is always set as a basic disk. There's nothing wrong with using basic disks, other than that you miss out on some handy features.

Creating Partitions and Volumes in Disk Management

To create partitions or volumes, right-click the unallocated part of the drive and select New Simple Volume. Disk Management runs the New Simple Volume Wizard. You'll go straight to the sizing screen (see Figure 9-33).

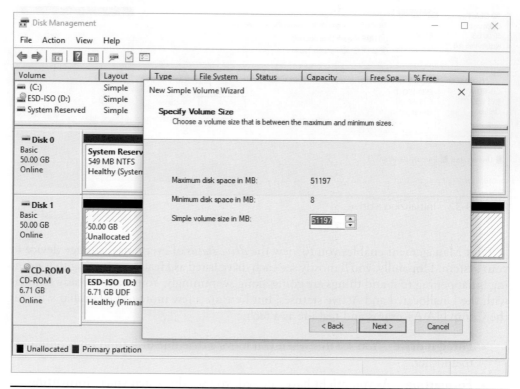

Figure 9-33 Specifying the simple volume size in the New Simple Volume Wizard

Specify a volume size and click Next. The wizard will ask if you want to assign a drive letter to the volume, mount it as a folder to an existing volume, or do neither (see Figure 9-34). In almost all cases, you'll want to give simple volumes a drive letter.

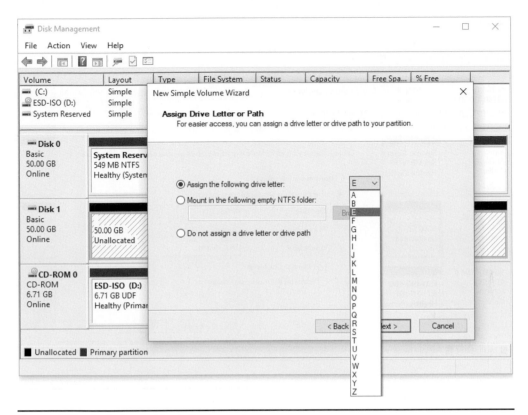

Figure 9-34 Assigning a drive letter to a volume

 NOTE Disk Management does *not* enable you to specify whether you want a primary or extended partition when you create a volume on MBR drives. The first three volumes you create will be primary partitions. Every volume thereafter will be a logical drive in an extended partition. The command-line tool, diskpart, offers options not available in Disk Management. Check out Chapter 16 for more details.

The last screen of the New Simple Volume Wizard asks for the type of format you want to use for this partition (see Figure 9-35). If your partition is 32 GB or less, you can make the drive FAT32 or NTFS. Windows requires NTFS on any partition greater than 32 GB. Although FAT32 supports partitions up to 2 TB, Microsoft wants you to use NTFS on larger partitions and creates this limit. With today's multi-terabyte drives, there's no good reason to use anything other than NTFS in Windows.

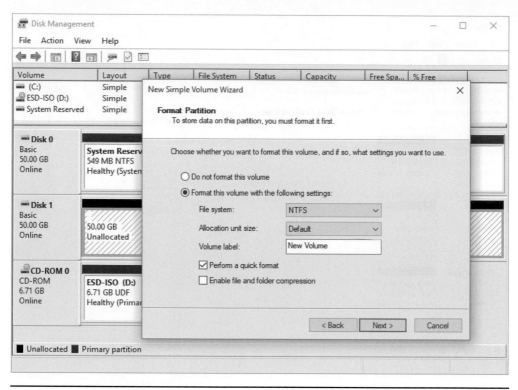

Figure 9-35   Choosing a file system type

In addition to the file system selection, you are offered a checkbox to perform a quick format or a full format. A quick format does not test the blocks as part of the format process, while the full format option does. (See "Formatting a Partition" later in this chapter for more details.)

You have a few more tasks to complete at this screen. You can add a volume label if you want. You can also choose the size of your clusters (Allocation unit size). You can sure speed up the format if you select the Perform a quick format checkbox. This will format your drive without checking every block. It's fast and a bit risky, but new hard drives almost always come from the factory in perfect shape—so you must decide whether to use it or not.

Last, if you chose NTFS, you may enable file and folder compression. If you select this option, you'll be able to right-click on any file or folder on this partition and compress it. To compress a file or folder, choose the one you want to compress, right-click, and select Properties. Then click the Advanced button and turn compression on (see Figure 9-36). Compression is handy for opening up space on a hard drive that's filling up.

Figure 9-36
Turning on
compression

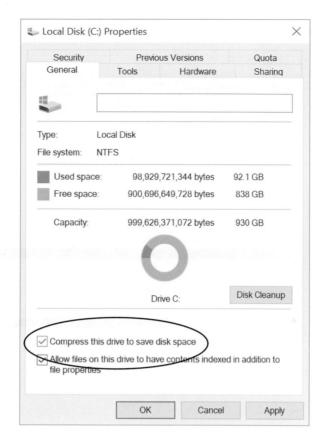

Dynamic Disks

You create dynamic disks from basic disks in Disk Management. Once you convert a drive from a basic disk to a dynamic disk, primary and extended partitions no longer exist; dynamic disks are divided into volumes instead of partitions. Because current versions of Windows call partitions *volumes*, the change to dynamic disk isn't obvious at all.

 TIP When you move a dynamic disk from one computer to another, it shows up in Disk Management as a foreign drive. You can import a foreign drive into the new system by right-clicking the disk icon and selecting Import Foreign Disks.

To convert a basic disk to dynamic, just right-click the drive icon and select Convert to Dynamic Disk (see Figure 9-37). The process is very quick and safe, although the reverse is not true. The conversion from dynamic disk to basic disk first requires you to delete all volumes off the hard drive.

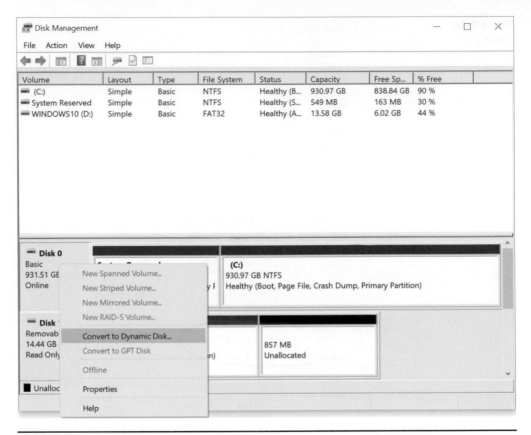

Figure 9-37 Converting to a dynamic disk

Once you've converted the disk, you can make one of the five types of volumes on a dynamic disk: simple, spanned, striped, mirrored, or RAID 5. You'll next learn how to implement the three most common volume types. The final step involves assigning a drive letter or mounting the volume as a folder.

Simple Volumes   A simple volume acts just like a primary partition. If you have only one dynamic disk in a system, it can have only a simple volume. It's important to note here that a simple volume may act like a traditional primary partition, but it is very different because you cannot install an operating system on it.

In Disk Management, right-click on any unallocated space on the dynamic disk and choose New Simple Volume to run the New Simple Volume Wizard (see Figure 9-38). You'll see a series of screens that prompt you on size and file system, and then you're finished. Figure 9-39 shows Disk Management with three simple volumes.

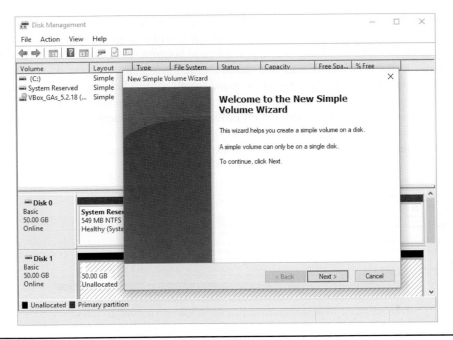

Figure 9-38   Starting the New Simple Volume Wizard

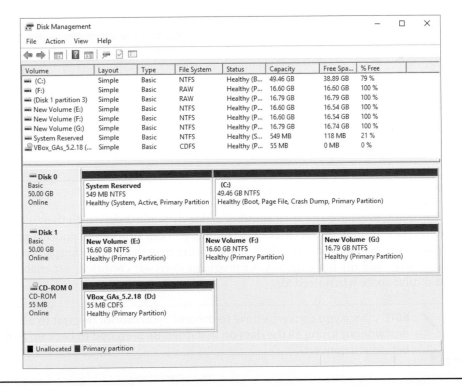

Figure 9-39   Simple volumes

Spanning Volumes You can extend the size of a simple volume to any unallocated space on a dynamic disk. You can also extend the volume to grab extra space on completely different dynamic disks, creating a spanned volume. This capability is very helpful if you manage an older system that needs a little more space but you don't have time or inclination to upgrade. To extend or span, simply right-click the volume you want to make bigger, and choose Extend Volume from the options (see Figure 9-40). This opens the Extend Volume Wizard, which prompts you for the location of free space on a dynamic disk and the increased volume size you want to assign (see Figure 9-41). If you have multiple drives, you can span the volume just as easily to one of those drives.

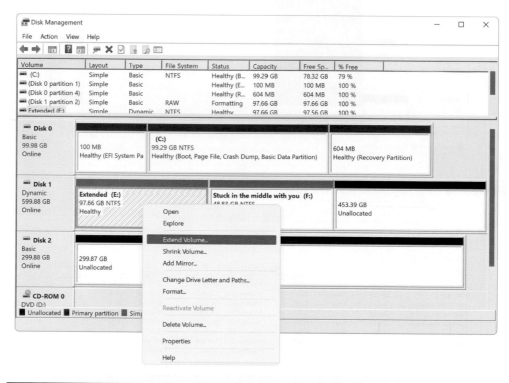

Figure 9-40   Selecting the Extend Volume option

The capability to extend and span volumes makes dynamic disks worth their weight in gold. If you start running out of space on a volume, you can simply add another physical hard drive to the system and span the volume to the new drive. This keeps your drive letters consistent and unchanging so your programs don't get confused, yet enables you to expand drive space when needed.

 NOTE   Once you convert a drive to dynamic, you cannot revert it to a basic disk without losing all the data on that drive. Be prepared to back up all data before you convert.

Figure 9-41
The Extend
Volume Wizard

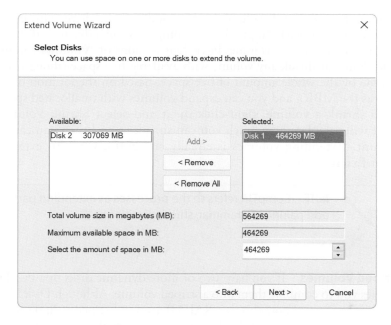

You can extend or span any simple volume on a dynamic disk, not just the "one on the end" in the Disk Management console. You simply select the volume to expand and the total volume increase you want. Figure 9-42 shows a simple 97.66-GB volume named Extended that has been enlarged an extra 453.39 GB in a portion of the hard drive,

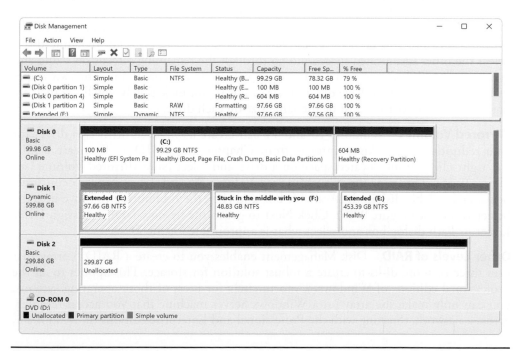

Figure 9-42   Extended volume

skipping the 48.83-GB volume in the middle of the drive. This created a 551.05-GB volume. Windows has no problem skipping areas on a dynamic disk.

You can also shrink volumes in current versions of Windows without using dynamic disks. You can shrink any volume with available free space (though you can't shrink the volume by the whole amount of free space, based on the location of unmovable sectors such as the MBR), and you can expand volumes with unallocated space on the drive.

To shrink a volume, right-click on it and select Shrink Volume. Disk Management will calculate how much you can shrink it, and then you can choose up to that amount. Extending volumes is equally straightforward. To extend, right-click and select Extend Volume.

 NOTE CompTIA refers to the processes as extending partitions and, in an odd pairing of grammar, shrink partitions.

Striped Volumes   If you have two or more dynamic disks in a PC, Disk Management enables you to combine them into a striped volume. Although Disk Management doesn't use the term, you know this as a RAID 0 array. A striped volume spreads out blocks of each file across multiple disks. Using two or more drives in a group called a *stripe set*, striping writes data first to a certain number of clusters on one drive, then to a certain number of clusters on the next drive, and so on. It speeds up data throughput because the system has to wait a much shorter time for a drive to read or write data. The drawback of striping is that if any single drive in the stripe set fails, all the data in the stripe set is lost.

To create a striped volume, right-click on any unused space on a drive, choose New Volume, and then choose Striped. The wizard asks for the other drives you want to add to the stripe, and you need to select two unallocated spaces on other dynamic disks. Select the other unallocated spaces and go through the remaining screens on sizing and formatting until you've created a new striped volume (see Figure 9-43). The two stripes in Figure 9-43 appear to have different sizes, but if you look closely you'll see they are both 300 GB. All stripes must be the same size on each drive.

Mirrored Volumes   Windows 10 and 11 can create a *mirror set* with two drives for data redundancy. You know mirrors from Chapter 8 as RAID 1. To create a mirror, right-click on unallocated space on a drive and select New Mirrored Volume (see Figure 9-44). This runs the New Mirrored Volume Wizard. Click Next to continue. Select an available disk in the Available box and click the Add button to move it to the Selected box (see Figure 9-45). Click Next to get to the by-now-familiar Assign Drive Letter or Path dialog box and select what is appropriate for the PC.

Other Levels of RAID   Disk Management enables you to create a RAID 5 array that uses three or more disks to create a robust solution for storage. This applies to all the Professional editions of Windows. Unfortunately for users of those operating systems, you can only make the array on a Windows Server machine that you access remotely across a network. (Starting with the Professional and Enterprise editions of Windows 8,

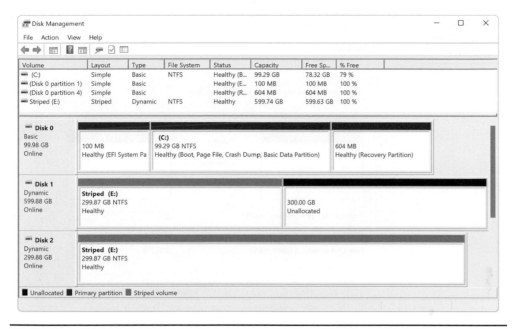

Figure 9-43 Two striped drives

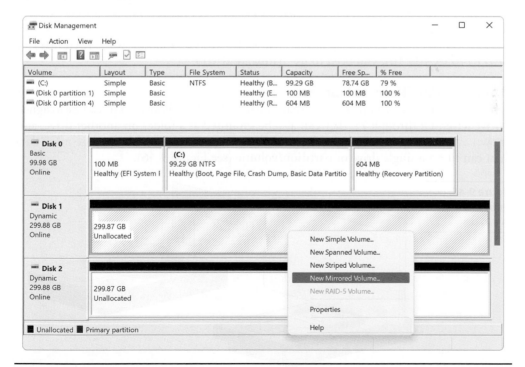

Figure 9-44 Selecting a new mirror

Figure 9-45
Selecting drives
for the array

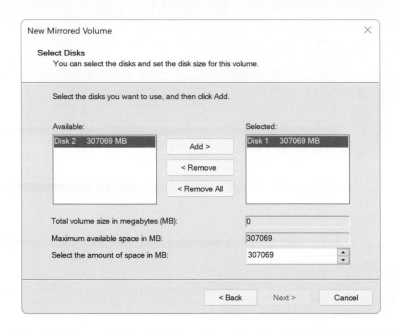

Microsoft includes Storage Spaces, an alternative way to do software pseudo-RAID in the form of pooling; one option closely resembles RAID 5. See the "Storage Spaces" section later in the chapter for more details.)

Disk Management cannot do any nested RAID arrays. So if you want RAID 0+1 or RAID 1+0 (RAID 10), you need to use hardware RAID.

Mounting Partitions as Folders

While partitions and volumes, other than the one Windows boots from, can be assigned a drive letter, D: through Z:, they can also be mounted as a folder on another drive, also known as a *mount point*. This enables you to use your existing folders to store more data than can fit on a single drive or partition/volume (see Figure 9-46).

Figure 9-46
Mounting a drive
as a folder

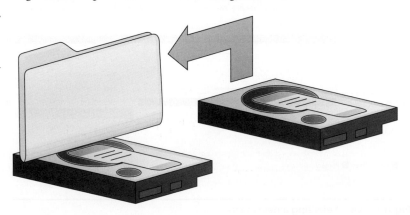

Imagine you use your Documents folder on a Windows machine to store your digital photos. As your collection grows, you realize your current 500-GB SSD is running out of space. You're willing to buy another drive, but you have a great organizational structure in your existing Documents folder and you don't want to lose that. You don't have to move everything to the new hard drive, either.

After you install the new hard drive, you can *mount* the primary partition (or logical drive) as a folder within the existing Documents folder on your C: drive (for example, C:\Users\Mike\Documents\My Photos). At this point the drive doesn't have a letter (though you could add one later, if you wanted). To use the new drive, just drop your files into the My Photos folder. They'll be stored on the second drive, not the original 500-GB drive (see Figure 9-47). Amazing!

Figure 9-47
Adding photos to the mounted folder stores them on the second hard drive.

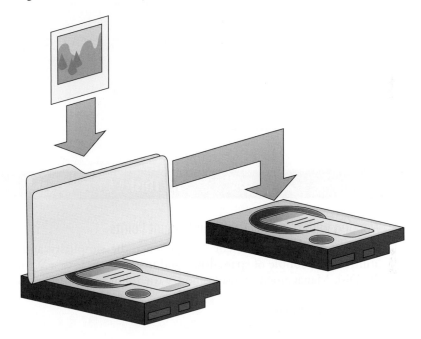

To create a mount point, right-click on an unallocated section of a drive and choose New Simple Volume. This opens the appropriately named wizard. In the second screen, you can select a mount point rather than a drive letter (see Figure 9-48). Browse to a blank folder on an NTFS-formatted drive or create a new folder and you're in business.

NOTE To be clear, you never actually split a partition. If you want to turn one partition into two, you need to remove the existing partition and create two new ones, or shrink the existing partition and add a new one to the unallocated space. If you see the term on the exam, know that this is what CompTIA means.

Figure 9-48
Choosing to
create a mounted
volume

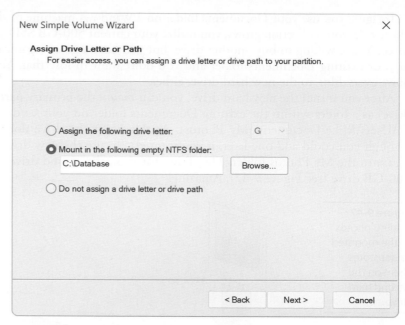

New Simple Volume Wizard   ✕

Assign Drive Letter or Path
For easier access, you can assign a drive letter or drive path to your partition.

○ Assign the following drive letter: G ⌄

● Mount in the following empty NTFS folder:
C:\Database   Browse...

○ Do not assign a drive letter or drive path

    < Back   Next >   Cancel

Try This!

Working with Dynamic Drives and Mount Points

Play with Disk Management to experience the simplicity and elegance of the utility. Get a couple of spare drives and install them into a Windows PC. Open the Disk Management console and try the following setup options:

1. Make a mirror set.

2. Make a stripe set.

3. Make them into a single volume spanned between both drives.

4. Make a single volume that takes up a portion of one drive, and then extend that volume onto another portion of that drive. Finally, span that volume to the other hard drive as well.

5. Create a volume of some sort—you decide—and then mount that volume to a folder on the C: drive.

You'll need to format the volumes after you create them so you can see how they manifest in Windows Explorer/File Explorer. Also, you'll need to delete volumes to create a new setup. To delete a volume, right-click on the volume and choose Delete Volume. It's almost too easy.

Assigning/Changing Drive Letters and Paths

Disk Management enables you to modify the drive letter, path, or mount point on currently installed mass storage devices. Right-click a drive and select Change Drive Letter and Paths. You can assign a desired drive letter to an optical drive—say, from D: to Z:, for example. Or, you can change a hard drive from D: to a non-letter-named mount point so it shows up in Windows Explorer/File Explorer as a subfolder. You have a ton of flexibility with Disk Management.

 EXAM TIP Disk Management is the go-to tool in Windows when adding drives or adding arrays to a system.

Formatting a Partition

You can format any Windows partition/volume in Windows Explorer/File Explorer. Just right-click on the drive name and choose Format. You'll see a dialog box that asks for the type of file system you want to use, the cluster size, and a volume label (see Figure 9-49). You can also do a quick format or compress the volume. The Quick Format option tells Windows not to test the blocks and is a handy option when you're in a hurry—and feeling lucky.

Figure 9-49
Format New
Volume
dialog box

Disk Management is today's preferred formatting tool for Windows. When you create a new partition or volume, the wizard also asks you what type of format you want to use. Always use NTFS unless you're that rare and strange person who wants to dual-boot some ancient version of Windows.

All OS installation media partition and format as part of the OS installation. Windows simply prompts you to partition and then format the drive. Read the screens and you'll do great.

Storage Spaces

With Windows 10 and 11, you can group one or more physical drives of any size into a single *storage pool*. These drives can be internal HDD or SSD or external storage connected via USB. It's pretty sweet. *Storage Spaces* functions like a RAID management tool, except it goes well beyond the typical tool. Here's the scoop.

First off, to run the tool, get to the Start screen and type **storage spaces**. Storage Spaces will show up in the Search. Click on it to run the program. The opening screen gives you pretty much a single option, to *Create a new pool and storage space* (see Figure 9-50). Click that option.

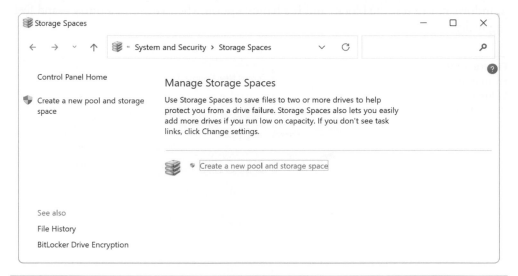

Figure 9-50   Storage Spaces waiting to create the first pool

Storage Spaces will show you the available installed physical drives (see Figure 9-51). Select the drives you want to include in the pool and click the Create pool button.

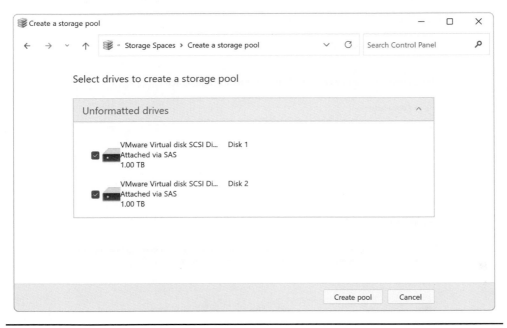

Figure 9-51   Drives available to use in a storage pool

Once you've created a pool, you need to select what Microsoft calls the *resiliency mechanism*, which essentially means providing one or more layers of redundancy so you can lose a hard drive or two and not lose any data. Sounds a lot like RAID, doesn't it? Figure 9-52 shows the Create a storage space window with a *Two-way mirror* storage layout. Here's where Storage Spaces gets pretty much cooler than any RAID management tool.

Storage Spaces offers three different types of storage spaces:

- *Simple spaces* are just pooled storage, like JBOD, that has multiple drives of whatever capacity added together to form a single virtual drive. Simple spaces provide no resiliency, so if a drive fails, the data goes away. These are good for temporary storage, scratch files, and the like.

- *Mirror spaces* keep more than one copy of the data, like in a RAID mirror array, so you can lose one or more drives and still save your data. The number of drives in the array determines which mirror options you have. A two-way mirror requires at least two drives; a three-way mirror requires five or more. Mirror spaces work like RAID 1 or RAID 10, providing excellent redundancy and resiliency, and robust performance.

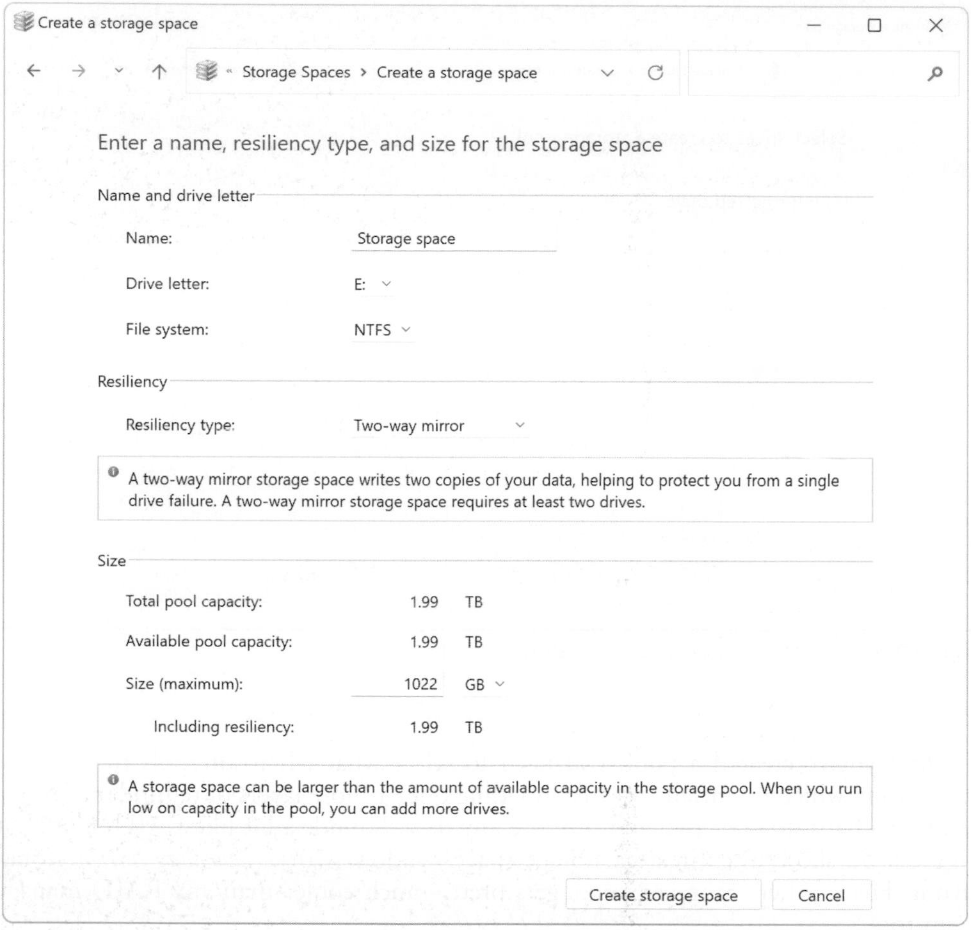

Figure 9-52 Ready to create the storage space

- *Parity spaces* add another layer of resiliency to the array, similar to how a RAID 5 or RAID 6 provides redundancy. The added resiliency comes with both an upside and a downside. The good thing about parity spaces is that they are more space efficient than two-way mirroring. In two-way mirroring, for every 10 GB of data to be stored, 20 GB of storage must be installed. With parity spaces, for every 10 GB of stored data, only 15 GB of storage needs to be installed. The downside is that the performance overhead to manage parity spaces can have a significant impact on overall performance. Microsoft recommends using parity spaces for big files that don't change a lot, like your movie collection. You can lose one drive and recover in a three-drive parity space. It takes a seven-drive parity space (at minimum) to enable you to recover from a two-drive loss.

When a disk fails in a space, Storage Spaces sends a warning through the standard Windows Action Center messaging. You can open Storage Spaces to reveal the failed drive and replace the drive readily.

 EXAM TIP   A storage pool is a collection of physical drives that enables you to flexibly add and expand capacity. Storage spaces are virtual drives that are created from storage pool free space. Storage spaces have resiliency and fixed provisioning.

Storage Spaces enables you to do one more very cool action: future-proof your storage needs. The thin provisioning feature means you can create a space with more capacity than your current physical drives provide. You might have a storage pool composed of two 2-TB drives and one 3-TB drive, laid out as a two-way mirror. Rather than limit your new space to a 3-TB capacity, you can assign whatever capacity you want, such as 12 TB, because you know your movie collection will grow. When you start to reach the capacity of the physical drives in the pool, Storage Spaces will tell you and enable you to add more physical capacity at that time. Thin provisioning means you don't have to redo an array or space when you reach the limits of current hardware.

 NOTE   SSDs work great with some space types and not others. With a simple two-way or three-way mirror, go for it. You'll add some speed and lots of resiliency. With parity spaces, on the other hand, the nature of how SSDs function inside might cause premature failure. It's best to use HDDs with parity spaces.

Maintaining and Troubleshooting Hard Drives

Hard drives are complex mechanical and electrical devices. With platters spinning at thousands of rotations per minute, they also generate heat and vibration. All of these factors make hard drives susceptible to failure. In this section, you will learn some basic maintenance tasks that will keep your hard drives healthy, and for those inevitable instances when a hard drive fails, you will also learn what you can do to repair them.

 NOTE   The "Maintaining and Troubleshooting Hard Drives" section applies primarily to HDDs, not SSDs. The few parts that apply to the latter have been salted into the discussion.

Pay attention to the terminology used both on the CompTIA A+ exam and in the field. Current storage for drives focuses on blocks and logical block addressing. A block is one step above the physical layout of the drive, which gives a lot of flexibility in the media. Microsoft continues to use the term cluster to refer to locations in their file allocation tables. With NTFS, a cluster and a block are pretty much the same thing, a 4-KB chunk of a drive (until you get partitions larger than 16 TB).

The official term for a cluster is an allocation unit. You'll see all three terms used interchangeably in the field.

Maintenance

Hard drive maintenance can be broken down into two distinct functions: checking the disk occasionally for failed blocks, and keeping data organized on the drive so it can be accessed quickly.

Error Checking

Individual blocks on hard drives sometimes go bad. There's nothing you can do to prevent this from happening, so it's important that you check occasionally for bad blocks on drives. The tools used to perform this checking are generically called error-checking utilities, although the term for an older Microsoft tool—*chkdsk* (pronounced "checkdisk")—is often used. Chkdsk is a command-line utility. Microsoft has a graphical version of this tool, which is called *Error checking* in Windows 10 and 11. macOS uses the *Disk Utility*. Linux offers a command-line tool called *fsck*. Whatever the name of the utility, each does the same job: when the tool finds bad blocks, it puts the electronic equivalent of orange cones (placing 0000FFF7 in the FAT/MFT) around them so the system won't try to place data in those bad blocks.

 EXAM TIP The CompTIA A+ exam objectives mention chkdsk specifically, but not Error checking. Even without the shout-out in the objectives, expect a question on disk maintenance that refers to Error checking.

Most error-checking tools do far more than just check for bad blocks. They go through all the drive's filenames, looking for invalid names and attempting to fix them. They look for blocks that have no filenames associated with them (we call these *lost chains*) and erase them or save them as files for your review. From time to time, the underlying links between parent and child folders are lost, so a good error-checking tool checks every parent and child folder. With a folder such as C:\Test\Data, for example, the tool makes sure that the Data folder is properly associated with its parent folder, C:\Test, and that C:\Test is properly associated with its child folder, C:\Test\Data.

To access Error checking on a Windows system, open Windows Explorer/File Explorer, right-click on the drive you want to check, and choose Properties to open the drive's Properties dialog box (see Figure 9-53). Select the Tools tab and click the Check or Check now button.

In macOS, you'll find Disk Utility in the Utilities folder. When open, you'll get one option to try and fix any problems with your disk, First Aid (see Figure 9-54). First Aid checks for errors and will attempt to repair them if it can. You can run First Aid on a disk while macOS is booted, but sometimes Disk Utility won't be able to work its magic on your disk because it's in use and can't be unmounted. If this happens, you need to reboot the system and press COMMAND-R until the Recovery partition loads. You can then load Disk Utility from here and run First Aid on the ailing disk again.

Figure 9-53
The Tools tab in the Properties dialog box

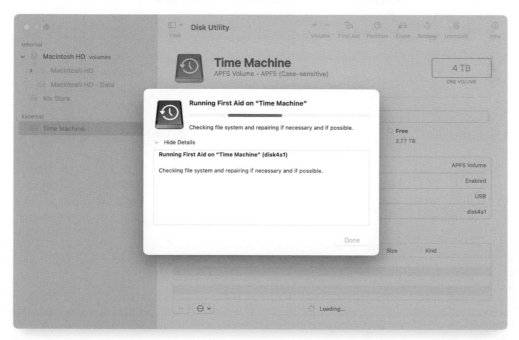

Figure 9-54 Disk Utility options

Defragmentation

You read about fragmentation earlier in this chapter. Fragmentation of blocks increases your hard disk drive access times dramatically. It's a good idea to *defragment*—or *defrag*—your traditional spinning drives as part of monthly maintenance. You access the defrag tool Optimize Drives the same way you access Error checking—right-click a drive in Windows Explorer/File Explorer and choose Properties—except you click the Optimize or Defragment now button on the Tools tab to open Optimize Drives.

Defragmentation is not interesting to watch but Windows today makes it a non-event by automatically defragging HDDs once a week by default (see Figure 9-55). While this takes care of dealing with spinning hard drives, what about the SSDs that most of our systems use today? In that case, Windows still needs to optimize the drive, but it will perform a retrim, which is jargon for letting the SSD know what sectors are not being used by the file system. This lets the SSD controller erase them so they can be used again in the future. Like the classic defragmentation on an HDD we discussed earlier, this is important for keeping your SSD performance at its peak.

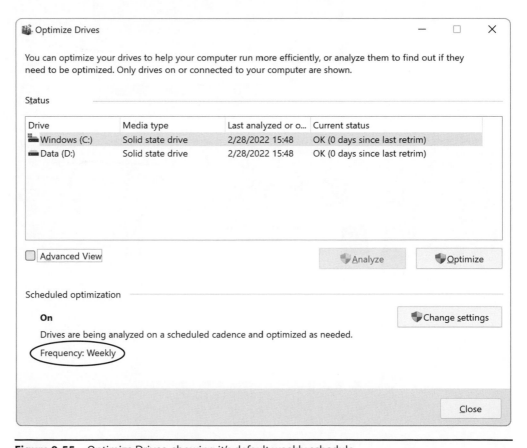

Figure 9-55   Optimize Drives, showing it's default weekly schedule

Disk Cleanup

Did you know that the average hard drive is full of trash? Not the junk you intention-ally put in your hard drive such as the terabytes of video of your cat Sparkles sitting in every box she can fit into. This kind of trash is all the files that you never see that Windows keeps for you. Here are a few examples:

- **Files in the Recycle Bin**   When you delete a file, it isn't really deleted. It's placed in the Recycle Bin in case you decide you need the file later. I just checked my Recycle Bin and found around 3 GB worth of files (see Figure 9-56). That's a lot of trash!

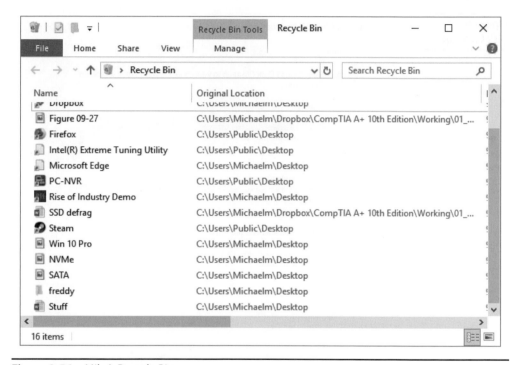

Figure 9-56   Mike's Recycle Bin

- **Temporary Internet files**   When you go to a Web site, your browser keeps copies of the graphics and other items so the page will load more quickly the next time you access it.

- **Downloaded program files**   This is for the legacy Web technologies of ActiveX and Java applets, so this should always be 0, but if you're dealing with an older corporate PC, you might run across some items in here. You can see these in the Internet Options applet by clicking the Settings button under the Browsing history label. Click the View objects button on the Temporary Internet Files and History Settings dialog box. You'll generally find only a few tiny files here.

- **Temporary files**   Many applications create temporary files, and for one reason or another, these temporary files sometimes aren't deleted. The location of these files varies with the version of Windows, but they always reside in a folder called "Temp."

Every hard drive eventually becomes filled with lots of unnecessary trash. All versions of Windows tend to act erratically when the drives run out of unused space. Fortunately, all versions of Windows have a powerful tool called Disk Cleanup (see Figure 9-57). You can access Disk Cleanup in Windows by clicking the Start button and typing **disk cleanup**. Click its icon to run the program.

Figure 9-57
Disk Cleanup

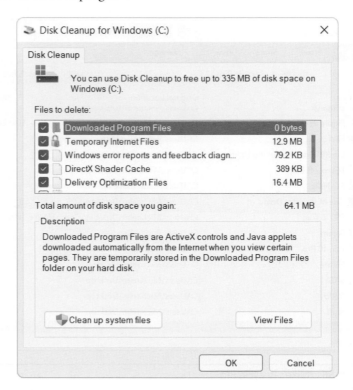

Disk Cleanup gets rid of the four types of files just described (and a number of others). Run Disk Cleanup once a month or so to keep plenty of space available on your hard drive.

 NOTE   Starting in Windows 10, Disk Cleanup's functionality called Storage Sense is built into the Storage section of the Settings app. You can still run classic Disk Cleanup, but Storage Sense will run automatically by default. There are also other options here (every OS has third-party disk cleanup utilities), and on macOS you can use the built in Storage Management app.

1101

Troubleshooting Hard Drive Implementation

There's no scarier computer problem than an error that points to trouble with a hard drive. This section looks at some of the more common problems that occur with hard drives and how to fix them. These issues fall into four broad categories: installation errors, data corruption, dying hard drives, and RAID issues.

Installation Errors

Installing a drive and getting to the point where it can hold data requires four distinct steps: connectivity, system setup, partitioning, and formatting. If you make a mistake at any point on any of these steps, the drive won't work. The beauty of this is that if you make an error, you can walk back through each step and check for problems. The "Troubleshooting Hard Drive Installation" section in Chapter 8 covered physical connections and CMOS system setup, so this section concentrates on the latter two issues.

Partitioning   Partitioning errors generally fall into two groups: failing to partition at all, and making the wrong size or type of partition. You'll recognize the former type of error the first time you open Windows Explorer/File Explorer after installing a drive. If you forgot to partition it, the drive won't even show up in Windows Explorer/File Explorer, only in Disk Management. If you made the partition too small, that'll become painfully obvious when you start filling it up with files.

The fix for partitioning errors is simply to open Disk Management and do the partitioning correctly. Just right-click and select Extend Volume to correct the mistake. Remember that deleting any volume will permanently delete any data on that drive.

Formatting   Failing to format a drive makes the drive unable to hold data. Accessing the drive in Windows results in a drive "is not accessible" error, and from a C:\> prompt, you'll get an "Invalid media type" error. Format the drive unless you're certain that the drive has a format already. Corrupted files can create the invalid media error. Check the upcoming "Data Corruption" section for the fix.

Most of the time, formatting is a slow, boring process. But sometimes the drive makes "bad sounds" and you start seeing errors like the one shown in Figure 9-58 at the top of the screen. Remember, an *allocation unit* is another term for a block or cluster.

The drive has run across a bad cluster and is trying to fix it. For years, I've told techs that seeing this error a few times doesn't mean anything; every drive comes with a few bad spots. This is no longer true. Modern drives hide a significant number of extra blocks that they use to replace bad blocks automatically. If a new drive gets a lot of "Trying to recover lost allocation unit" errors, you can bet that the drive is dying and needs to be replaced. Get the hard drive maker's diagnostic tool to be sure. Bad clusters are reported by S.M.A.R.T. (introduced in Chapter 8), one of several S.M.A.R.T. errors possible.

Figure 9-58
The "Trying
to recover
lost allocation
unit" error

```
A:\>format C:/s

WARNING:  ALL DATA ON NON-REMOVABLE DISK
DRIVE C:  WILL BE LOST!
Proceed with Format  (Y/N)?y

Formatting  30709.65M

Trying to recover lost allocation unit 37,925
```

Mental Reinstallation   Focus on the fact that all of these errors share a common thread—you just installed a drive! Installation errors don't show up on a system that has been running correctly for three weeks; they show up the moment you try to do something with the drive you just installed. If a newly installed drive fails to work, do a "mental reinstallation." Does the drive show up in the UEFI or traditional BIOS setup screens? No? Then recheck the data and power cables. If it does show up, did you remember to partition and format the drive? Did it need to be set to active? These are commonsense questions that come to mind as you march through your mental reinstallation. Even if you've installed thousands of drives over the years, you'll be amazed at how often you do things such as forget to plug in power to a drive. Do the mental reinstallation—it really works!

Data Corruption

All hard drives occasionally get corrupted data in individual blocks. Power surges, accidental shutdowns, corrupted installation media, and viruses, along with hundreds of other problems, can cause this *data loss/corruption*. In most cases, this type of error shows up while Windows is running. Figure 9-59 shows a classic example.

You may also see Windows error messages saying one of the following:

- "The following file is missing or corrupt"
- "The download location information is damaged"
- "Unable to load file"
- "… is not a valid Win32 application"
- "Bootmgr is missing…Press CTRL+ALT+DEL to restart"
- "Your PC ran into a problem…This problem caused your PC to restart"
- "This app can't run on your PC"

Figure 9-59   A corrupted data error

If core boot files become corrupted, you may see text errors at boot, such as the following:

- "Error loading operating system"
- "An error occurred while attempting to read the boot configuration data"

The first fix for any of these problems is to run the Error checking utility. Error checking will go through and mark bad blocks and, hopefully, move your data to a good block. If the same errors continue to appear after you run the Error checking utility, there's a chance that the drive has too many bad blocks and may need to be recycled.

Almost all drives today take advantage of built-in *error correction code (ECC)* that constantly checks the drive for bad blocks. If the ECC detects a bad block, it marks the block as bad in the drive's internal error map. Don't confuse this error map with a FAT. The partitioning program creates the FAT. The drive's internal error map was created at the factory on reserved drive heads and is invisible to the system. If the ECC finds a bad block, you will get a corrupted data error as the computer attempts to read the bad block. Disk-checking utilities fix this problem most of the time.

Dying Hard Drive

Physical problems are rare, thankfully, but they are devastating when they happen. If a hard drive is truly damaged physically, there is nothing that you or any service technician can do to fix it. Fortunately, hard drives are designed to take a phenomenal amount of punishment without failing. Physical problems manifest themselves in several ways. One common problem you start getting are *extended read/write times*, which is caused by a connection to a file being interrupted or terminated and could result in data corruption. Other signs that the hard drive might be dying is that the drive works properly but makes a lot of noise, or the drive seems to disappear. You might get a failure to boot after experiencing any of these events.

Windows will give you error messages with read/write failures. Good hard drives don't fail to read or write. Only dying ones have these problems.

All mechanical hard drives make noise—the hum as the platters spin and the occasional slight scratching noise as the read/write heads access sectors are normal. However, if your drive begins to make any of the following sounds, it is about to die:

- Continuous high-pitched squeal
- Loud *clicking sounds*, a short pause, and then another series of clicking sounds
- Continuous *grinding noises* or rumbling

Another way you can tell if your hard drive is having issues is by looking at the computer's *light-emitting diode (LED)*, which is located on the front of the computer case. There are LEDs that provide information on the health of the computer. The activity LED (green) and the status LED (bicolor, green/amber) can help you diagnose a hard drive problem such as if a drive has failed (or if there is a predicted failure reported by the drive), the slot is empty, the drive is rebuilding, etc.

If all else fails, back up your critical data and replace the drive. Windows comes a with a decent backup utility, but don't be afraid to research third-party options if it doesn't meet your needs. The cloud backup services are particularly nice options because they provide off-site protection in addition to backing up your data.

 NOTE   Most hard drives have a three-year warranty. Before you throw away a dead drive, check the hard drive maker's Web site or call them to see if the drive is still under warranty. Ask for a return material authorization (RMA). You'll be amazed how many times you get a newer, and sometimes larger, hard drive for free. It never hurts to check!

You'll know when a drive simply dies. If it's the drive that contains your operating system, the system will lock up. When you try to restart the computer, you'll see this error message or something similar to it:

```
Bootable Device Not Found
```

If it's a second drive, it will simply stop showing up in Windows Explorer/File Explorer. The first thing to do in either case is to access the system setup program and see if autodetect sees the drive. If it does, you do not have a physical problem with the drive.

If autodetect fails, shut off the system and remove the data cable, but leave the power cable attached. Restart the system and listen to the drive. If the drive spins up, you know it is getting good power. This is usually a clue that the drive is probably good. In that case, you need to look for more mundane problems such as an unplugged data cord or jumpers incorrectly set (PATA only). If the drive doesn't spin up, try another power connector. If it still doesn't spin up and you've triple-checked the jumpers and data cable, you have a problem with the onboard electronics and the drive is dead.

If the drive is an SSD, the troubleshooting process is similar: either the power or motherboard controller is bad, a power or data cable has failed, or the drive electronics are dead. Start with the power cable, changing it for a known-good one. Then try a known-good data cable using the original motherboard connection. Next, try a different motherboard connector. Still haven't got it? It's likely a bad drive, but you should confirm so by testing it in another known-good computer to see if it is detected by UEFI/BIOS and then by Windows Disk Management.

NOTE If you ever lose a hard drive that contains absolutely critical information, you can turn to a company that specializes in hard drive data recovery. The job will be expensive—prices usually start around $1000 (USD)—but when you have to have the data, such companies are your only hope. Do a search for "data recovery" for companies in this line of business.

Troubleshooting RAID

For the most part, drive problems in a RAID array are identical to those seen on individual drives. There are a couple of errors unique to RAID, however, that need their own separate discussion.

Drive Not Recognized   If you're using hardware RAID and the configuration firmware doesn't recognize one of the drives, first check to make sure the drives are powered and that they are connected to the proper connections. This is especially true of motherboards with onboard RAID that require you to use only certain special RAID connectors.

RAID Stops Working   When one of the drives in a RAID array fails, several things can happen depending on the type of array and the RAID controller. With RAID 0, the effect is dramatic. Many enthusiasts use RAID 0 for their OS drive to make it snappier. If you're running such a rig that then loses a drive, you'll most likely get a critical stop error that manifests as some sort of *proprietary crash screen*. Windows will show a Blue Screen of Death (BSoD), for example. On reboot, the computer will fail to boot or you'll get a message such as *Missing Drive in OS* or *Bootable device not found*. You lose all your data because there's no redundancy on a stripe set. You may see error messages before the crash related to read/write failures. On macOS machines, a failing drive or array may result in the Spinning Pinwheel of Death (SPoD). If there are no other systemic problems such as low RAM or low disk space, it's time to break out RAID- or disk-diagnostic tools such as S.M.A.R.T. reader software.

All the other levels of RAID tend to do nothing extraordinary when one drive in the array fails. When you reboot the system, that's when the RAID controller (if hardware) or Windows (if you've used the built-in tools) will squeal and tell you that a drive has failed.

Often, the failure of a drive will cause access to the contents of the drive to slow to a crawl, and that *slow performance* is your clue to check Device Manager or the RAID controller firmware. Some drive failures will cause the computer to crash. Others will show no effects until you get the error messages at reboot.

Regardless of the reason a RAID stops working or the effects, the fix is simple. Replace the failed drive and let the RAID rebuild itself. Life is good. If you need to know the reason for the failure, trying running S.M.A.R.T. reader software on the failed drive. If the drive electronics have some functionality, you may get results.

RAID Not Found

The CompTIA A+ 220-1101 exam objectives use the term "RAID not found," which doesn't really exist as an error but instead implies a series of errors where an existing RAID array suddenly fails to appear. The problem with these errors is that they vary greatly depending on the make and model of hardware RAID or (heaven forbid) if you used software RAID.

A properly functioning hardware RAID array will always show up in the configuration utility. If an existing array stops working and you enter the configuration utility only to find the array is gone, you have big trouble. This points to either dead drives or faulty controllers. In either case they must be replaced.

If the array is gone but you can still see the drives, then the controller may have broken the array on its own. This is a rare action that some controllers take to try to save data. You should at least try to rebuild the array using whatever tools the controllers provide.

Chapter Review

Questions

1. Which is the most complete list of file systems Windows can use?

    A. FAT32, NTFS

    B. FAT32, exFAT, NTFS

    C. FAT32

    D. NTFS

2. Which of the following correctly identifies the four possible entries in a file allocation table?

    A. Filename, date, time, size

    B. Number of the starting cluster, number of the ending cluster, number of used clusters, number of available clusters

    C. An end-of-file marker, a bad-block marker, code indicating the cluster is available, the number of the cluster where the next part of the file is stored

    D. Filename, folder location, starting cluster number, ending cluster number

3. What program does Microsoft include with Windows to partition and format a drive?

   A. Format

   B. Disk Management console

   C. Disk Administrator console

   D. System Commander

4. What does NTFS use to provide security for individual files and folders?

   A. Dynamic disks

   B. ECC

   C. Access control list

   D. MFT

5. Jaime wishes to check her hard drive for errors. What tool should she use in Windows 11?

   A. FDISK

   B. Format

   C. Disk Management

   D. Error checking

6. To make your files unreadable by others, what should you use?

   A. Clustering

   B. Compression

   C. Disk quotas

   D. Encryption

7. How can you effectively expand the capacity of an NTFS drive?

   A. Create an extended partition to extend the capacity.

   B. Install a second drive and mount it to a folder on the original smaller NTFS drive.

   C. Convert the drive to a dynamic disk and create a mirrored set.

   D. Format the drive with the Quick Format option.

8. Which configuration requires three same-sized volumes?

   A. RAID 5

   B. Mirrored set

   C. Spanned volume

   D. Striped volume

9. Which of the following partitioning schemes enable the creation of more than four partitions or volumes on a single hard drive? (Select two.)

   A. MBR

   B. GPT

   C. Dynamic disk

   D. MFT

10. Which storage option in Windows 10 or 11 offers the best mix of resiliency and performance with two drives?

    A. Simple space

    B. Two-way mirror space

    C. Three-way mirror space

    D. Parity space

Answers

1. **B.** Modern versions of Windows can use FAT32 and NTFS for hard drives, and exFAT for removable flash-media drives.

2. **C.** The four possible entries in a file allocation table are an end-of-file marker, a bad-block marker, code indicating the cluster is available, and the number of the cluster where the next part of the file is stored.

3. **B.** Windows uses the Disk Management console to partition and format a drive.

4. **C.** Because NTFS views individual files and folders as objects, it can provide security for those objects through an Access control list.

5. **D.** Error checking is used to check a drive for errors.

6. **D.** To make your files unreadable by others, use encryption.

7. **B.** You can effectively expand the capacity of an NTFS drive by installing a second drive and mounting it to a folder on the original smaller NTFS drive.

8. **A.** RAID 5 requires three same-sized volumes.

9. **B, C.** Both GPT and dynamic disk partitioning schemes enable the creation of more than four partitions or volumes on a single hard drive.

10. **B.** A two-way mirror space efficiently and effectively uses two drives for resilience and performance. A simple space offers no resiliency; the other options require three or more drives.

Essential Peripherals

In this chapter, you will learn how to
- Explain how to support multipurpose connectors
- Identify and install standard peripherals on a computer
- Identify and install common removable storage devices and their media

Modern computing devices sport a variety of peripherals—stuff you plug into the system unit—that extend and enhance their capabilities. This chapter looks at common ports first, then turns to a laundry list of standard peripherals. The chapter finishes with a discussion of various mass storage devices, such as flash drives and the fading but not yet gone optical disc technologies.

 NOTE This chapter does *not* cover ports or devices used for standalone monitors, such as the typical computer desktop display. That's such a big and important topic that it gets its own chapter! Chapter 17 covers monitors and their ports in detail.

1101

Supporting Common Ports

Whenever you're dealing with a device that isn't playing nice, you need to remember that you're never dealing with just a device. You're dealing with a device *and* the port to which it is connected. Before you start troubleshooting the device, you need to look at the issues and technologies of some of the more common input/output (I/O) ports and see what needs to be done to keep them running well.

Serial Ports

Techs at times have to support or service older gear, such as installed point-of-sale systems or networking components soldiering on in the background. Many of these old devices connect to computers using *serial connections*, which use the Recommended Standard

232 (RS232), introduced way back in 1960. A *serial port* manifests as a 9-pin, D-shell male socket, called a *DB9* or an *RS232*. You won't find serial ports on anything made in the last decade, but CompTIA thinks they're important enough to include in the CompTIA A+ 1101 objectives. Figure 10-1 shows a serial connector on a cable and a DB9 port.

Figure 10-1
DB9 connector and port

 EXAM TIP You don't need to know how serial ports work to get through the CompTIA A+ 1101 exam. Just remember the names of the ports and connectors, DB9 and RS232.

USB Ports

Universal serial bus (USB) connects almost every type of peripheral one might consider today. Most folks have used USB ports and USB devices, but let's go beyond the user level and approach USB as techs.

Understanding USB

The core of USB is the *USB host controller*, an integrated circuit normally built into the chipset. The host controller acts as the interface between the system and every USB device that connects to it. Connected to the host controller is a *USB root hub*, the part of the host controller that makes the physical connection to the USB ports. Every USB root hub is a bus, similar in many ways to an expansion bus. Figure 10-2 shows one possible diagram of the relationship between the host controller, root hub, and USB ports.

Figure 10-2
Host controller, root hub, and USB ports in a typical system

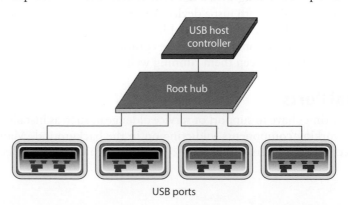

USB host controller

Root hub

USB ports

A single host controller supports up to 127 USB devices, though real-life circumstances create sharper limits. Even if a host controller supports a certain number of USB ports, there's no guarantee that the motherboard maker will supply that many ports. To give a common example, the AMD X370 chipset supports 16 USB ports, but only a few motherboard makers supply that many USB ports.

A USB host controller is the boss (primary) of any device (secondary) that plugs into that host controller. The host controller sends commands and provides power to USB devices. The host controller is *upstream*, controlling devices connected *downstream* to it (see Figure 10-3). The host controller is shared by every device plugged into it, so speed and power are reduced with each new device.

Figure 10-3
Host controller
and USB mouse
showing
upstream/
downstream

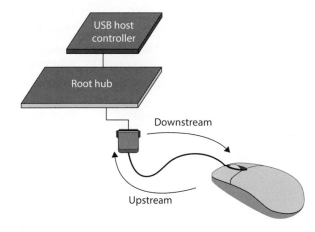

USB Standards and Compatibility

When advancing compliance programs, the Universal Serial Bus Implementers Forum (USB-IF), authorizes the use of their USB-IF Platform Interoperability test lab for vendors to test specific USB Technology. Products that are early to implement new USB standards are encouraged to attend the USB-IF Platform Interoperability Lab for certification and compliance testing.

Once certified, USB-IF also emphasizes to vendors the importance and value of consistent messaging on USB product packaging, marketing materials, and advertising as the USB standard has gone through many revisions in the past including:

- USB 1.1 was the first widely adopted standard and defined two speeds: Low-Speed USB, running at a maximum of 1.5 Mbps (plenty for keyboards and mice), and Full-Speed USB, running at up to 12 Mbps.

- The *USB 2.0* standard introduced Hi-Speed USB running at 480 Mbps.

- *USB 3.0* is capable of speeds of up to 5 Gbps—ten times faster than USB 2.0. USB 3.0 is marketed as SuperSpeed USB. It's also referred to as *USB 3.1 Gen 1*, though *not* on the CompTIA A+ exams.

- USB 3.1 can handle speeds up to 10 Gbps. It's marketed as SuperSpeed USB 10 Gbps or *USB 3.1 Gen 2.*

- USB 3.2 supports speeds up to 20 Gbps using a pair of 10-Gbps lanes. This version is labeled "2×2" to represent 2nd generation, 2 lanes.

If you think all of those names and numbers are confusing, you're right. Table 10-1 provides a quick reference to help you sort it all out.

Name	Standard	Maximum Speed	Common Usage
Low-Speed USB	USB 1.1	1.5 Mbps	Keyboards, mice
Full-Speed USB	USB 1.1	12 Mbps	Headphones, Bluetooth devices
Hi-Speed USB	USB 2.0	480 Mbps	Webcams, card scanners, older wireless adapters, older flash-media drives
SuperSpeed USB	USB 3.0	5 Gbps	Flash-media drives, external storage, cameras, current wireless adapters
SuperSpeed USB 10 Gbps	USB 3.1 (Now USB 3.2 Gen 1 and USB 3.2 Gen 2)	10 Gbps	Flash-media drives, external storage, networking
SuperSpeed USB 20 Gbps	USB 3.2 2×2	20 Gbps	Very high-speed external storage, networking, and video

Table 10-1   USB Standards

USB 2.0 is fully backward compatible with USB 1.1 devices, while USB 3.0/3.1 is backward compatible with USB 2.0 devices. Older devices won't run any faster than they used to, however. To take advantage of the fastest USB speeds, you must connect a USB device to a USB port at least as fast as the device. Backward compatibility may enable you to use a faster USB device with a slower port, but a quick bit of math tells you how much time you're sacrificing when you're transferring a 2-GB file at 480 Mbps instead of 10 Gbps!

NOTE   Each standard defines more than just the speed. Because they were incorporated into the newer standard, many Low-Speed and Full-Speed USB devices are also USB 2.0 devices. SuperSpeed Plus, Enhanced SuperSpeed and SuperSpeed+ are defined in the USB specifications. However these terms are not intended to be used in product names, messaging, packaging, or any other consumer-facing content.

Most people want to take advantage of these amazing speeds, but what do you do if your motherboard doesn't have built-in SuperSpeed USB ports? One option is to add an adapter card like the one shown in Figure 10-4.

Figure 10-4
USB expansion
card

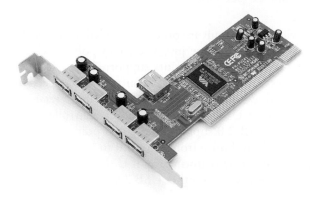

Motherboards capable of both USB 1.1 and USB 2.0 usually share the available USB ports (see Figure 10-5). For every USB port on your computer, a Low-Speed or Full-Speed device uses the USB 1.1 host controller, whereas a Hi-Speed device uses the USB 2.0 host controller.

Figure 10-5
Shared USB ports
for 1.1 and 2

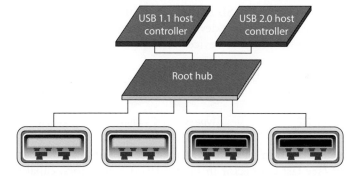

USB 3.0 and 3.1, on the other hand, are different enough from USB 2.0 that they typically use separate host controllers. You can plug older USB devices into a USB 3.0 or 3.1 port, as noted, but they will run at the slower speeds. The only ports that work at 10 Gbps are the USB 3.1 ports (see Figure 10-6).

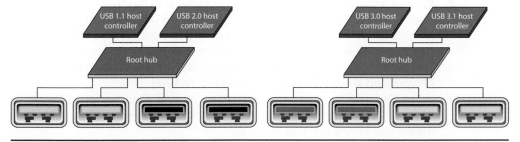

Figure 10-6   Shared USB ports for all speeds of USB

NOTE The USB ports tend to follow a color scheme. USB 2.0 ports are usually black; 3.0 ports are dark blue; 3.1/3.2 ports are teal; and USB 3.2 2×2 ports are red (see Table 10-2).

USB devices have built-in processes, called *end points*, that use USB controller resources. Some devices have just a few end points, while others have many. Unfortunately, the number of end points supported by a USB controller is limited. When enough devices are connected to a controller to exceed the limit, devices may not work and Windows will generate a *USB controller resource warning*. Fortunately, the fix is simple: move USB devices to another controller. While USB 3.*x* is faster than USB 2.0 ports, USB 2.0 supports more end points. Moving low-performance devices such as keyboards and mice from USB 3.0 to USB 2.0 ports can free up USB 3.0 end points without affecting performance. If USB resources are low across USB 3.0 devices, move some of the devices to other USB 3.0 controllers.

USB Cables and Connectors

When USB 1.1 was introduced, the standard defined two types of connectors: USB A and USB B. USB A connectors plug upstream toward the host controller (which is why you see them on the PC) and USB B connectors plug downstream into USB devices.

The A and B plugs come in sizes: "standard" USB A/USB B, miniUSB A/miniUSB B, and microUSB A/microUSB B (see Figure 10-7). The mini and microUSB A connectors were basically ignored; most devices come hard wired. The miniUSB B and microUSB B connectors connect smaller devices such as cameras and smartphones.

Figure 10-7
USB type A and B
connectors

Type-A   Type-B   Mini-B   Micro-B   Micro-B 3.0

The introduction of USB 3.0 required an upgraded USB A connector and new Micro-B (see last connector in Figure 10-7) connectors, capable of handling the much greater speeds. USB 1.1 and 2.0 cables used four-pin connectors, while USB 3.0/3.1 A and B ports and connectors use nine pins. The USB 3 A connector looks exactly like the older USB A connectors, sneaking the new pins into the same old USB A connector.

 NOTE The naming conventions for the various USB plugs and ports have changed over time. The most recent specification calls the original full-sized A and B connectors *Standard-A* and *Standard-B*. Most people in the industry call them *Type-A* and *Type-B* (refer to Figure 10-7). You'll also most commonly see the mini and micro versions of the connectors as *Mini-A*, *Mini-B*, *Micro-A*, *Micro-B*, and *Micro-B 3.0* (also shown in Figure 10-7).

The CompTIA A+ 1101 exam objectives get even muddier, using the nonstandard terms *miniUSB* and *microUSB*. I can only assume CompTIA means USB Mini-B and USB Micro-B.

The USB industry introduced color schemes to identify the different port types (see Figure 10-8). Table 10-2 lists the colors and the standards.

Figure 10-8
Blue USB 3.0 ports (left) and teal USB 3.1 ports (center)

Table 10-2
USB Connector Colors

USB Standard	Port Color
USB 1.1	White
USB 2.0	Black
USB 3.0	Blue
USB 3.1/USB 3.2	Teal
USB 3.2 2×2	Red

 NOTE It's not uncommon to see laptops with red, orange, or yellow USB A ports. These are "always on" ports to charge other devices even if the laptop is turned off. There is no standard to these colors.

The keyed USB Standard-A connector has proven remarkably difficult to insert. The long-running joke on it, for example, is that it takes three tries to insert a plug: up position, down position, and then, finally, the superposition (which is the up position when you try it again).

The USB-IF standards body released the universal *USB Type-C* plug and port to address the problem with A and to unify the connector types. USB Type-C replaces both A and B plugs of all sizes.

 EXAM TIP The naming conventions for USB Type-C connectors are all over the place, just like with A and B connectors. A lot of industry folks shorten and hyphenate the connector to *USB-C*. That's also how you'll see it on the CompTIA A+ 1101 exam.

USB Type-C uses 24 pins, can be inserted in either orientation, fully supports USB 3.1, and even supports other busses such as Thunderbolt (see "Thunderbolt Ports" later in this chapter). USB Type-C is quickly replacing microUSB as the dominant USB connection for devices (see Figure 10-9).

Figure 10-9
USB Type-C
connector

 NOTE In general, your connection will operate at the speed of the slowest device involved. If you have a USB 2.0 device connected to a USB 3.x port on your PC, it will operate at USB 2.0 speeds.

Cable length is an important limitation to keep in mind with USB. USB 1.1 and USB 2.0 specifications allow for a maximum cable length of 5 meters. Although most USB devices never get near this maximum, some devices, such as digital cameras, can come with cables at or near the maximum 5-meter cable length. The USB 3.x standards don't define a maximum cable length. Because USB is a two-way (bidirectional) connection, as the cable grows longer, even a standard, well-shielded, 20-gauge, twisted-pair USB cable begins to suffer from electrical interference. To avoid these problems, I stick to cables that are no more than about 2 meters long, except in special circumstances. My staff photographer, for example, has a 4.5-meter cable between his camera (at the photo station) and his Mac. It works just fine in the studio.

 EXAM TIP Numerous manufacturers make USB A to B adapters of various sorts. These enable you to use an all A cable, for example, to connect a printer to a PC.

USB Hubs

Each USB host controller supports up to 127 USB devices, but as mentioned earlier, most motherboard makers provide only six to eight real USB ports. So what do you do when you need to add more USB devices than the motherboard provides ports? You can add more host controllers (in the form of internal cards), or you can use a USB hub. A *USB hub* is a device that extends a single USB connection to two or more USB ports, almost always directly from one of the USB ports connected to the root hub. Figure 10-10 shows a typical USB hub. USB hubs are often embedded into peripherals. The monitor shown in Figure 10-11 comes with a built-in USB hub—very handy!

Figure 10-10
USB hub

Figure 10-11
Monitor with
built-in USB hub

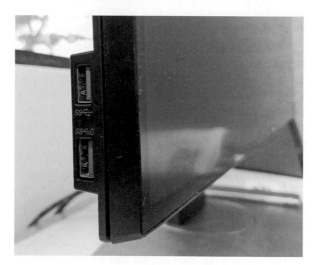

Hubs also come in powered and bus-powered versions. If you choose to use a general-purpose USB hub like the one shown in Figure 10-10, and you have power-hungry devices like external bus-powered hard drives, use a powered hub. A single USB port only provides 500 milliamps of power, which must be split among all the devices connected to an unpowered hub. This means a single power-hungry device connected to the hub can take all the power for itself, starving the other ports of power.

Troubleshooting USB Issues

The biggest troubleshooting challenge you encounter with USB is a direct result of its widespread adoption and ease of use. Pretty much every modern PC comes with multiple USB ports, and anyone can easily pick up a cool new USB device at the local computer store. The problems arise when all of this USB installation activity gets out of control, with too many devices using the wrong types of ports or pulling too much power. Happily, by following a few easy steps, you can avoid or eliminate these issues.

Windows, Linux, Chrome, and macOS include many built-in drivers for USB devices. You can count on the OSs to recognize keyboards, mice, and other basic devices with their built-in drivers. Just be aware that if your new mouse or keyboard has some extra buttons, the default USB drivers might not support them. To be sure I'm not missing any added functionality, I always install the driver that comes with the device or an updated one downloaded from the manufacturer's Web site.

Another tough issue is power. A mismatch between available and required power for USB devices results in scary error codes and can result in nonfunctioning or malfunctioning USB devices. If you're pulling too much power, you must disconnect devices off that root hub until the error goes away. Install an add-in USB expansion card if you need to use more devices than your current USB hub supports.

One of the options available to us in Windows is to control USB power when the computer is off. Turning off USB power when the computer is shut down is a good way to conserve battery power, because otherwise the computer is providing power to devices that are not needed when the computer is off. This control is called *USB selective suspend*. It is controlled through the Control Panel under Power Options in the Advanced settings menu. USB selective suspend can be set differently, depending on whether the computer is plugged in or running on battery. When enabled, USB ports are placed in a low power state when the computer is off and restored to full power function when the computer operates. With USB selective suspend enabled, great power savings are available for portable computers that are connected to power-hungry devices such as USB hard drives.

There's one more problem with USB power: sometimes USB devices go to sleep and won't wake up. Actually, the system is telling them to sleep to save power. You should suspect this problem if you try to access a USB device that was working earlier but that suddenly no longer appears in Device Manager. To fix this, head to Device Manager to inspect the hub's Properties, then open the Power Management tab and uncheck the *Allow the computer to turn off this device to save power* checkbox, as shown in Figure 10-12.

 SIM Check out the Chapter 10 Challenge! sim, "USB Speeds," to prepare for questions on the CompTIA A+ 1101 exam. You'll find it here: https://www .totalsem.com/1100X.

"My USB port still doesn't work!" There's a couple of reasons, besides circuit failure, that can affect all of the USB ports in a computer and that fall under a category that CompTIA calls *USB permissions*. That's a highfalutin term that means USB settings in the UEFI/ BIOS. Many BIOS setup programs include several settings that impact USB port operations. One setting enables or disables all onboard USB ports. This can be necessary if the USB controller chip on the motherboard fails but the rest of the board still functions. You can add USB ports with an add-on card that has USB ports. The BIOS settings won't impact USB ports on an add-on card.

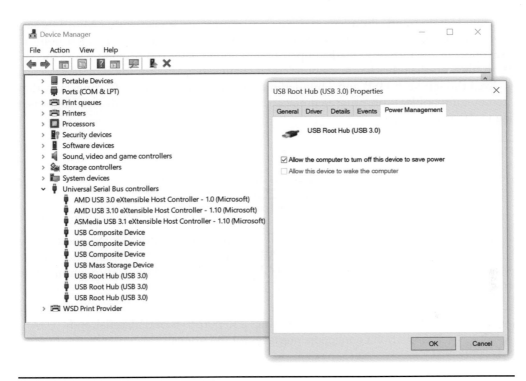

Figure 10-12   Power Management tab

Another setting is backward compatibility. We're used to having USB ports that support older versions of USB. That is typically a default USB configuration that is set in the UEFI/BIOS setup program. But it doesn't have to be. In some BIOS setup programs, backward compatibility can be disabled. This would prevent USB 2.0 devices from working when plugged into USB 3 ports. If you plug a mouse or keyboard into a USB 3 port and it doesn't work, troubleshoot by trying it in a USB 2.0 port and by checking the USB settings in the BIOS setup program.

Thunderbolt Ports

Intel and Apple developed *Thunderbolt* ports as a high-speed alternative to existing technologies such as USB, tapping the PCI Express bus for up to six external peripherals (Thunderbolt functions alongside USB these days.) PC developers have adopted the technology and you will find it standard on many laptop and desktop systems these days. If you have a custom-built PC, assuming your motherboard is Thunderbolt-ready, you can readily upgrade by purchasing PCIe *Thunderbolt cards*. Thunderbolt supports video (up to a single 4K video monitor—see Chapter 17) and audio signals. It handles data storage devices just fine, too.

Thunderbolt 1 and Thunderbolt 2 connect computing devices with a Mini Display-Port (mDP) connector. Thunderbolt 3 uses a USB Type-C connector. Thunderbolt can use copper or fiber cabling. With copper, Thunderbolt chains can extend up to 3 meters. With fiber, on the other hand, a Thunderbolt chain can extend up to 60 meters.

Even though both USB and Thunderbolt use the same USB Type-C connector, they are not compatible, prompting manufacturers to mark their ports with clear logos (see Figure 10-13).

Figure 10-13
Thunderbolt and
USB logos

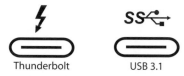

And did I mention that Thunderbolt offers amazing bandwidth? Thunderbolt 1 runs full duplex at 10 Gbps, so it compares to USB 3.1. Thunderbolt 2 combines internal data channels, enabling throughput at up to 20 Gbps. Thunderbolt 3 offers throughput up to 40 Gbps at half the power consumption of Thunderbolt 2. Nice!

 EXAM TIP Know the characteristics and purposes of USB, serial, and Thunderbolt connection interfaces for the exams.

General Port Issues

No matter what type of port you use, if it's not working, you should always check out a few issues. First of all, make sure you can tell a port problem from a device problem. Your best bet here is to try a second known-good device in the same port to see if that device works. If it does *not*, you can assume the port is the problem. It's not a bad idea to reverse this and plug the device into a known-good port.

If you're pretty sure the port's not working, you can check a few things: make sure the port is turned on. Almost any I/O port on a motherboard can be turned off in system setup. Reboot the system and find the device and see if the port's been turned off. You can also use Windows Device Manager to enable or disable most ports. Figure 10-14 shows a disabled USB controller in Device Manager; you'll see a small down-pointing arrow in Windows. To enable the port, right-click the device's icon and choose Enable.

Ports need drivers just as devices need drivers. All operating systems have excellent built-in drivers for all common ports, so if you fail to see an active port (and you know the port is enabled in system setup), you can bet the port itself has a physical problem.

Figure 10-14
Disabled USB
controller in
Device Manager
in Windows 10
and 11

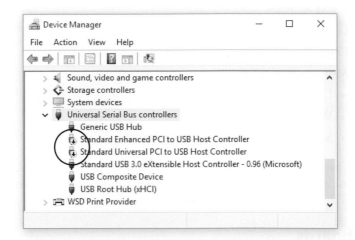

Try This!

Expansion Opportunities

Manufacturers constantly update and produce expansion cards and peripherals to give consumers the latest technology, so try this! Check your system for USB or Thunderbolt ports. What does it have? Then go to an online retailer such as https://www.newegg.com and search for upgrades. Can you get a PCIe USB 3.1 card with Type-C ports? What about an add-on Thunderbolt card? As a related search, check the availability of powered and unpowered USB hubs. What variations can you get?

Common Peripherals

Peripherals enhance the capabilities of computing devices. Common peripherals include keyboards and mice, but there are many more. The CompTIA A+ 220-1101 exam explores a lot of peripherals. Here's a list for this chapter:

- Keyboards
- Pointing devices (mouse and touchpad)
- Biometric devices
- Smart card readers
- Barcode scanners/QR scanners
- Touch screens

- KVM switches
- Game controllers and joysticks
- Digitizers
- Multimedia devices
  - Digital cameras
  - Webcams
  - Sound processors, speakers, and microphones

You probably don't use all of these "common" devices every day, so I'll cover each of them in detail. (Later chapters explore other common peripherals, such as video capture cards, TV tuners, printers, and scanners.)

Keyboards

The *keyboard* is both the oldest and still the primary way you input data into a PC. All modern operating systems come with perfectly good drivers for any keyboard, although some fancier keyboards may come with specialized features (screens, lights, programmable keys) that require special drivers to operate properly.

Modern keyboards connect via USB port, whether wired or wireless. In the last few years there's been a resurgence of the ancient but fast PS/2 port. Figure 10-15 shows a combination mouse/keyboard PS/2 port on a modern motherboard.

Figure 10-15
Combination mouse/keyboard PS/2 (circular connector, top left)

 NOTE Wireless keyboards remove the cable between you and the PC. Make sure to keep a complete set of spare batteries around.

There's not much to do to configure a standard keyboard. The only configuration tool you might need in Windows is the Keyboard Control Panel applet. This tool enables you to change the repeat delay (the amount of time you must hold down a key before the keyboard starts repeating the character), the repeat rate (how quickly the character is repeated after the repeat delay), and the default cursor blink rate. Figure 10-16 shows the default Windows Keyboard Properties dialog box. Some keyboard makers provide drivers that add extra tabs.

Figure 10-16
Keyboard Control
Panel applet

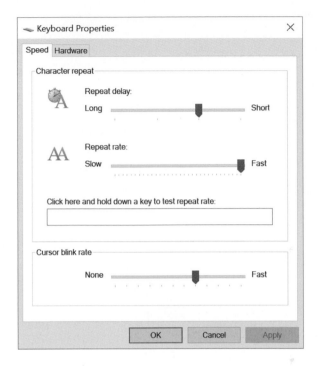

Windows and Linux share the same standard QWERTY keyboards, including the CTRL and ALT *modifier keys* that enable you to do certain keyboard shortcuts. (Press CTRL-Z to undo an action, for example.) Windows-specific keyboards also come with the WINDOWS LOGO modifier key. Apple keyboards have three modifier keys: CONTROL, OPTION, and COMMAND. The first two correspond to CTRL and ALT; the COMMAND key is the macOS special modifier key. You can use Windows keyboards with macOS, but you need to go into the Keyboard preferences in System Preferences to map the modifier keys properly (see Figure 10-17).

Keyboards might be easy to install, but they do fail occasionally. Given their location—right in front of you—the three issues that cause the most keyboard problems stem from spills, physical damage, and dirt.

Spilling a soda onto your keyboard can make for a really bad day. If you're quick and unplug the keyboard from the PC before the liquid hits the electrical components, you might be able to save the keyboard. It'll take some cleaning, though. More often than not, you'll get a sticky, ill-performing keyboard that is not worth the hassle—just replace it!

Other common physical damage comes from dropping objects onto the keyboard, such as a heavy book (like the one in your hands). This can have bad results! Most keyboards are pretty resilient, though, and can bounce back from the hit.

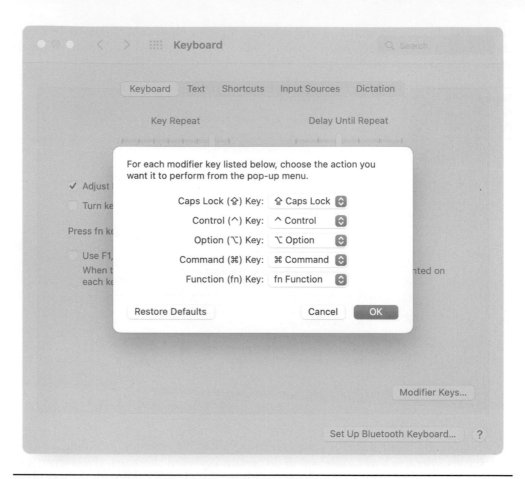

Figure 10-17   Keyboard options in macOS System Preferences

Clean grime off the keys by using a cloth dampened with a little water, or if the water alone doesn't do the job, use a bit of isopropyl alcohol on a cloth (see Figure 10-18).

Figure 10-18
Cleaning keys

Dirty keys might be unsightly, but dirt under the keys might cause the keyboard to stop working completely. When your keys start to stick, grab a bottle of compressed air and shoot some air under the keys. Do this outside or over a trash can—you'll be amazed how much junk gets caught under the keys!

The bottom line when it comes to stuck keys is that the keyboard's probably useless with the stuck key, so you might as well try to clean it. Worse comes to worst, you can always buy another keyboard.

Pointing Devices

Have you ever tried to use Windows, Chrome, or macOS without a mouse or other device to move the cursor? It's not fun, but it can be done. All techs eventually learn the navigation hot keys for those times when mice fail, but all in all we do love our mice. There are two common pointing devices, mice and touchpads. A mouse moves the cursor as you move the mouse; a touchpad moves the cursor as you move your fingers over its surface.

Now you can get the best of both by using what's called a multi-touch gesture. A gesture is a combination of using a mouse, touchpad, or finger movements and mouse clicks to perform a function. With two fingers together, for example, you can scroll up and down on a page by moving your fingers up and down on the touchpad. Have a bunch of Windows open and want see the all at once? With three fingers swipe up on the touchpad. See something interesting on a Web page or PDF? Pinch in with two fingers to zoom in; then spread your fingers to zoom out just like on your phone.

Apple's Magic Trackpad and Microsoft's Precision Touchpad have both upped the ante in the area of multi-touch gestures. Many of the gestures come directly from multi-touch phones and tablets and will be the same on macOS, Chrome, and Windows. But each OS does have a few unique gestures, so make sure to head over to the respective Web sites of Apple and Microsoft for an up-to-date list.

In Windows, you can adjust your mouse or touchpad settings through the Mouse Control Panel applet or Settings app. Figure 10-19 shows the Windows 10 Settings app and Control Panel applet. macOS has both Mouse and Trackpad applets in System Preferences.

Modern pointing devices require little maintenance and almost never need cleaning, as the optics that make them work are never in contact with the grimy outside world. On the rare occasion where an *optical mouse* begins to act erratically, try using a cloth or damp cotton swab to clean out any bits of dirt that may be blocking the optics (see Figure 10-20).

Biometric Devices

Biometric devices scan and remember unique aspects of various body parts, such as your iris, face, head image, or fingerprint, using some form of sensing device. This information is used as a key to prevent unauthorized people from accessing whatever the biometric device is securing. Chrome, macOS, and Windows 10 and 11 have built-in

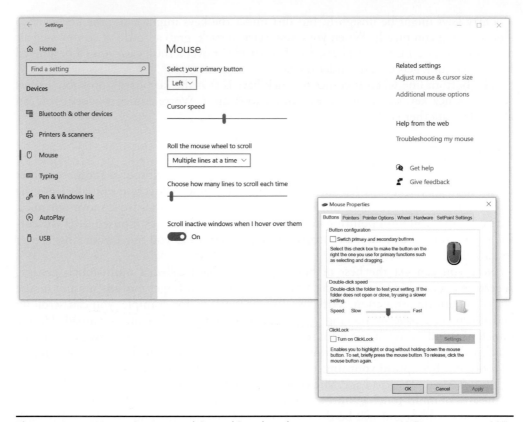

Figure 10-19   Mouse Settings and Control Panel applet

Figure 10-20
Cleaning an
optical mouse

support for using biometrics like fingerprint scanners (see Figure 10-21) and facial recognition to secure user accounts. Windows uses Windows Hello to manage biometric authentication; in Figure 10-22, I'm training my system to recognize my face using a Windows Hello–compatible infrared camera.

Figure 10-21
Laptop with built-in fingerprint scanner

Figure 10-22
Training Windows Hello facial recognition

Biometric security is very common with smartphones. Both Apple and Android vendors support fingerprint scanners for phones that have that feature. This replaces password/pin security. Figure 10-23 shows the Android fingerprint scanner learning a new fingerprint. When asked by Android or an application, you simply press your finger against the fingerprint scanner. It confirms your identity (assuming your fingerprint matches), and then special software that comes with the scanner supplies your credentials.

Figure 10-23
Fingerprint
scanner on an
Android phone

Biometric devices are also used for recognition. Recognition is different from security in that the biometric device doesn't care who you are; it just wants to know what you're doing. The best example of this is voice recognition. Voice recognition programs convert human voice input into commands or text. Apple, Microsoft, and Google use voice recognition in many forms, including Siri in iOS and Cortana in Windows 10 and 11 (both can respond to input for searching and other functions). Google uses voice recognition in its flagship office productivity app, Google Docs, so students can speak in addition to type.

No matter what biometric device you use, you use the same steps to make it work:

1. Install the device.

2. Register your identity with the device by following the setup routine to register your unique fingerprints, retina, face, etc.

3. Configure software to tell the device what to do when it recognizes your scanned identity.

Barcode Scanner/QR Scanner

Barcode scanners read standard *Universal Product Code (UPC)* barcodes or *Quick Response (QR)* codes (see Figure 10-24), primarily to track inventory. Scanners enable easy updating of inventory databases stored on computing devices.

Figure 10-24
UPC code (left)
and QR code
(right)

Two types of barcode scanners are commonly found with personal computers: pen scanners and hand scanners. Pen scanners look like an ink pen and must be swiped across the barcode (see Figure 10-25). Hand scanners are held in front of the UPC code while a button is pressed to scan. All barcode scanners emit a tone to let you know the scan was successful.

Figure 10-25
Barcode hand
scanner

Barcode scanners use USB ports or go wireless. No configuration is usually necessary, other than making sure that the barcode scanner works with whatever database or point-of-sale software you use.

Touch Screens

A *touch screen* is a monitor with some type of sensing device across its face that detects the location and duration of contact, usually by a finger or stylus. All touch screens then supply this contact information to the PC as though it were a click event from a mouse. Touch screens are used in situations for which conventional mouse/keyboard input is either impossible or impractical:

- Smartphones
- Smart watches
- Fitness monitors
- Information kiosks
- Point-of-sale systems
- Tablets
- E-readers

Touch screens can be separated into two groups: built-in screens like the ones in smartphones, and standalone touch screen monitors like those in many point-of-sale systems. From a technician's standpoint, you can think of a standalone touch screen as a monitor with a built-in mouse. These touch screens have a separate USB port for the "mouse" part of the device, along with drivers you install just as you would for any USB mouse.

Windows includes a Control Panel applet for configuring the touch screens on tablet PCs, such as the Microsoft Surface. Windows also has a Tablet applet in Settings that has Tablet Mode options for standard touchscreen-enabled computers, such as many laptops (see Figure 10-26). You can use these applets to adjust how you interact with the touch screen just as you would with the Mouse or Keyboard applets. The applets enable you to configure what happens when you tap, double-tap, use gestures called "flicks," and more.

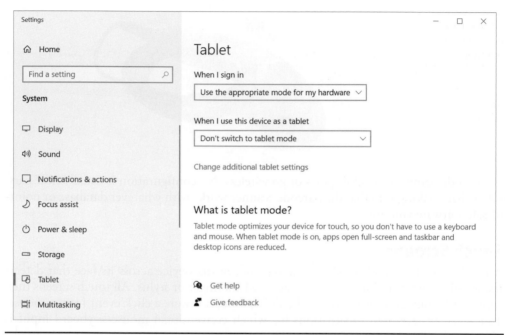

Figure 10-26 Tablet Mode in Windows 10 and 11 Settings

KVM Switches

A *keyboard, video, mouse (KVM) switch* is a hardware device that most commonly enables multiple computers to be viewed and controlled by a single mouse, keyboard, and screen. Some KVM switches reverse that capability, enabling a single computer to be controlled by multiple keyboards, mice, or other devices. KVM switches are especially useful in data centers where multiple servers are rack mounted, space is limited, and power is a concern. An administrator can use a single KVM switch to control multiple server systems from a single keyboard, mouse, and monitor.

There are many brands and types of KVM switches. Some enable you to connect to only two systems, and some support hundreds. Some even come with audio output jacks to support speakers. Typical KVM switches come with two or more sets of wires that are used for input devices such as PS/2 or USB mice and video output (see Figure 10-27).

Figure 10-27
A typical KVM
switch

To use a KVM switch, you simply connect a keyboard, mouse, and monitor to the KVM switch and then connect the KVM switch to the desired computers. Once connected and properly configured, assigned keyboard hotkeys—a combination of keys typically assigned by the KVM switch manufacturer—enable you to toggle between the computers connected to the KVM switch. In most cases, you simply tap the SCROLL LOCK key twice to switch between sessions.

Installing a KVM switch is not difficult; the most important point to remember is to connect the individual sets of cables between the KVM ports and each computer one at a time, keeping track of which keyboard, mouse, and video cable go to which computers. (I highly recommend labeling and using twist or zip ties.)

If you get the connections wrong, the KVM switch won't function as desired. If you connect a mouse and keyboard wires to the correct KVM port, for example, but attach the same computer's video cable to a different port on the KVM switch, you won't get the correct video when you try to switch to that computer. The same holds true for the mouse and keyboard cables. Don't cross the cables!

Game Controllers and Joysticks

Whether you're racing through tight turns at top speeds or flying a state-of-the-art jet fighter, having the right controller for the job is important for an enjoyable gaming experience. Two peripherals are commonly used for controlling PC games, game controllers and joysticks.

Some PC games, especially those that were designed to be played on consoles like the Microsoft Xbox or Sony PlayStation, are best enjoyed when using a game controller. A game controller has an array of buttons and triggers to affect movement and actions on the screen (see Figure 10-28).

Over the past decade, flight simulator programs have declined in popularity, and so have *joysticks* (see Figure 10-29). Once a required component of a gamer's arsenal, you only need joysticks now if you are a *serious* flight simulator fan. Most modern games are controlled by game controller or mouse and keyboard.

Figure 10-28
Xbox wireless
game controllers

Figure 10-29
A joystick

Game controllers and joysticks have used plenty of connectors over the years, including the eponymous joystick connector. These days, they all connect to computers via USB or wireless connections. Depending on the complexity of the controller, you may need to install drivers to get a game controller or joystick working.

You'll need to configure a game controller or joystick to make sure all the buttons and controls work properly. In Windows, go to the Devices and Printers applet. Depending on your game controller or joystick, you'll be able to configure the buttons, sticks, triggers, and more (see Figure 10-30). You can calibrate the analog sticks so they accurately register your movements. You can even adjust the amount of vibration used by the controller's force feedback (if available). Force feedback adds vibration or resistance to the controller to mirror what's happening in the game.

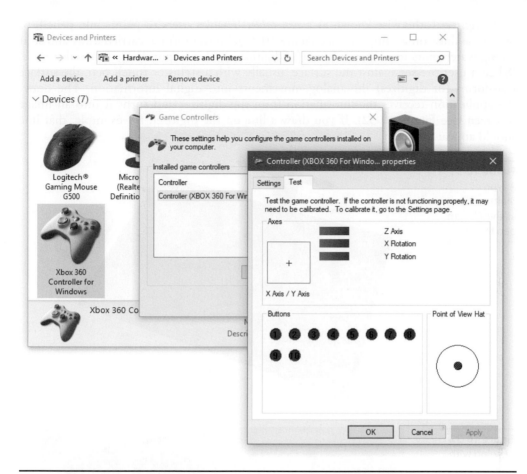

Figure 10-30   Game controller properties

   NOTE   You might also need to configure your controller from within the game you want to play. Most games are set to use keyboard and mouse controls by default. You'll need to play around with the settings to enable your game controller.

Once you've set up your controller, you should be ready to take to the skies, or the streets, or wherever else you go to game.

Digitizers

PCs and Macs have quickly become the most powerful and flexible tools available for visual artists. Given the number of applications dedicated to producing various visual styles—including painting, sketching, animation, and more—digital art stands toe-to-toe with its more traditional counterpart. It's only reasonable that a category of hardware would appear to help users take advantage of these tools.

A *digitizer* (otherwise known as a *pen tablet*) enables users to paint, ink, pencil, or otherwise draw on a computer (see Figure 10-31). Now, don't get carried away and start taking watercolors to your monitor. The digitizer receives input using a special surface. When a user presses against the surface, usually with a stylus or touch pen, the surface transforms (or digitizes) the analog movements into digital information. The drawing application receives the information from the digitizer and turns it into an image onscreen (see Figure 10-32). If you draw a line on the digitizer, for example, that line should appear onscreen.

Figure 10-31
A type of digitizer known as the Wacom pen tablet

Figure 10-32
Drawing with a digitizer

NOTE Not all digitizers are designed for digital art. Some are used for handwriting, technical drawings, writing complex characters, or even as a replacement pointing device.

Most digitizers connect via a USB or wireless connection. You'll need to install drivers before you connect the device, although they should be included in the box. The digitizer should also include a configuration utility. Here you can adjust the pressure sensitivity of the stylus, configure buttons on the tablet, and set the portion of the screen to which the tablet can draw.

People interact with simple digitizer technology a lot in the form of *signature pads*, devices that enable you to sign your name and have that signature converted to digital. Every time you sign a credit card pad, for example, you use a signature pad.

Multimedia Devices and Formats

Multimedia devices like digital cameras and webcams enable sharing of photographs and video chats with friends and family around the world. Almost all mobile devices come with some capability to produce and record multimedia.

Digital Cameras

Digital cameras capture every moment of life today and are essential tools for everything from note-taking to capturing your child's first steps. Because digital cameras seem to be integrated with every new gadget, I need to clarify that this section will be talking about dedicated cameras. Because these digital cameras interface with computers, CompTIA A+ certified techs need to know the basics.

Storage Media   Digital cameras save pictures and videos onto some type of *removable storage media*. The most common removable storage media used in modern digital cameras is the *Secure Digital (SD)* card (see Figure 10-33). Consumer digital cameras are fading because we all have one built into our smartphones. The days of the SD card have become numbered in favor of smaller, faster, and higher capacity digital cards. There are others you might run across as you get into professional cameras. (For details about removable storage media, see the discussion in the "Storage Devices" section later in this chapter.)

Figure 10-33
Secure Digital
card

Connection   Digital cameras either plug directly into a USB port (see Figure 10-34) or connect to a Wi-Fi network. Another common option is to connect the camera's storage media to the computer, using one of the many digital media readers available.

Figure 10-34
Camera
connecting
to USB port

You can find readers designed specifically for SD cards, as well as other types. Plenty of readers can handle multiple media formats. Many computers come with a decent built-in SD card reader (see Figure 10-35).

Figure 10-35
Digital media
reader built into
computer

Webcams

Cameras in or on computer monitors, often called *webcams* because their most common use is for Internet video communication, enable people to interact over networks with both voice and video. Webcams range greatly in quality and price.

Webcams vary in both image and sound capture quality. Because webcams are mostly used for video chat, they tend to be marketed similar to other video cameras using terms like 720p, HD, and 4K. The most common dedicated webcams today provide a 1080p experience.

NOTE   Unfamiliar with terms such as 1080p? Pixels? All is covered in Chapter 17.

Figure 10-36 shows two of my editors chatting via webcam using Microsoft Teams.

Figure 10-36
Video chatting
by webcam
with Teams

Most people who use online video also want a *microphone*. Many webcams come with microphones, or you can use a standalone device. Those who do a lot of video chatting may prefer to get a good-quality headset with which to speak and listen.

Sound Components

Virtually every computing device today comes with four critical components for capturing and outputting sound: a sound device built into the motherboard or a dedicated sound card, speakers, microphone, and recording/playback software. This section explores each component. But let's start with how *digital* devices (computers) deal with *analog* input/output (sound waves).

Analog to Digital (and Vice Versa) Sound   Computers capture (record) sound waves in electronic format through a process called *sampling*. In its simplest sense, sampling means capturing the state or quality of a particular sound wave a set number of times each second. The sampling rate is measured in units of thousands of cycles per second, or kilohertz (KHz). The more often a sound is sampled, the better the reproduction of that sound. Most sounds in computing are recorded with a sampling rate ranging from 11 KHz (very low quality, like an ancient telephone) to 192 KHz (ultra-high quality, better than the human ear).

NOTE   Every modern motherboard comes with sound-processing capabilities built in. Techs refer to built-in sound as built-in sound, even when there's no expansion card for sound. People use dedicated *Sound card* expansion cards for specific tasks, such as turning a computer into a recording studio device. For typical use, the built-in sound suffices for most users.

Sounds vary according to their loudness (*amplitude*), how high or low their tone (*frequency*), and the qualities that differentiate the same note played on different instruments (*timbre*). All the characteristics of a particular sound wave—amplitude, frequency, timbre—need to be recorded and translated into ones and zeros to reproduce that sound accurately within the computer and out to your speakers.

The number of characteristics of a particular sound captured during sampling is measured by the *bit depth* of the sample. The greater the bit depth used to capture a sample, the more characteristics of that sound can be stored and thus re-created. An 8-bit sample of a Slash guitar solo, for example, captures 2^8 (256) characteristics of that sound per sample. It would sound like a cheap recording of a recording, perhaps a little flat and thin. A 16-bit sample, in contrast, captures 2^{16} (65,536) different characteristics of his solo and reproduces all the fuzzy overtones and feedback that gives Slash his unique sound.

The last aspect of sound capture is the number of tracks of sound you capture. Most commonly, you can capture either a single track (*monaural*) or two tracks (*stereo*). More advanced captures record many more sound tracks, but that's a topic for a more advanced sound capture discussion.

The combination of sampling frequency and bit depth determines how faithfully a digital version of a sound captures what your ear would hear. A sound capture is considered *CD quality* when recorded at 44.1 KHz, with 16-bit depth and in stereo. Most recording programs let you set these values before you begin recording. Figure 10-37 shows the configuration settings for Audacity, a free and powerful sound recording and editing tool.

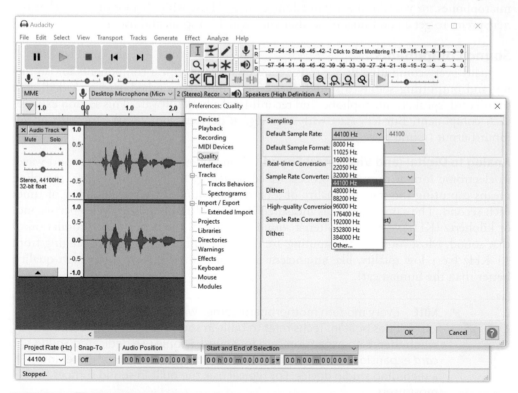

Figure 10-37   Audacity's quality settings

Recorded Sound Formats Audio files have numerous file formats, both uncompressed and compressed. The granddaddy of all sound formats is *pulse code modulation (PCM)*. PCM was developed in the 1960s to carry telephone calls over the first digital lines. With just a few minor changes to allow for use in PCs, the PCM format is still alive and well, although it's better known as the WAV format in the PC world. WAV files are great for storing faithfully recorded sounds and music, but they do so at a price. WAV files can be large, especially when sampled at high frequency and depth. A 4-minute song at 44.1 KHz and 16-bit stereo, for example, weighs in at a whopping 40-plus MB.

What's interesting about sound quality is that the human ear cannot perceive anywhere near the subtle variations of sound recorded at 44.1 KHz and 16-bit stereo. Clever programmers have written algorithms to store full-quality WAV files as compressed files, discarding unnecessary audio qualities of that file. These algorithms—really nothing more than a series of instructions in code—are called compressor/decompressor programs or, more simply, *codecs*. You've most likely encountered the Fraunhoffer MPEG-1 Layer 3 codec, more often called by its file extension, *MP3*. Today there are many common formats, one of the most popular one being *Advanced Audio Encoding (AAC),* the format used for Apple iPhone and iPad, YouTube Music, and more.

Streaming media is a data file that is downloaded and played on your computer and immediately discarded. Streaming media is incredibly popular and has spawned an entire industry of Internet radio stations and music services.

Speaker Support You'd be hard pressed to find a motherboard without built-in sound (see Figure 10-38). Every motherboard at the very least supports two speakers or a pair of headphones, but most motherboards support five or more speakers in discrete channels. These multiple speakers provide surround sound—popular not only for games but also for those who enjoy watching movies on their personal computers. The motherboard shown in Figure 10-38, for example, has outputs for many speakers.

Figure 10-38
A motherboard with multiple speaker connections

Another popular speaker addition is a *subwoofer*. A subwoofer provides the amazing low-frequency sounds that give an extra dimension to your movies, music, and games. Almost all modern systems support both surround sound and a subwoofer and advertise this with a nomenclature such as Dolby Digital or DTS. The nomenclature for multiple speakers follows a simple format, the number of speakers plus the subwoofer. A *2.1* system, for example, has two satellite speakers and a sub (see Figure 10-39). A *5.1* system has five satellites and a sub.

Figure 10-39
A 2.1 speaker set

Jacks　Virtually every system comes with at least three connections, called *jacks* when used with sound: one for a stereo speaker system, one for a microphone, and one for a secondary input called line in. If you look at the back of a motherboard with built-in sound, you'll invariably see at least these three connections. On most systems, the main stereo speaker jack is green, the line in jack is blue, and the microphone jack is pink. You'll often find plenty of other connectors as well. Refer back to Figure 10-39.

Here's a list of some of the standard audio jacks:

- **Main speaker out**　Just what it sounds like, the main speaker output is where you plug in the standard speaker connector.

- **Line out**　Some systems will have a separate line out jack that is often used to connect to an external device such as a DVD or MP3 player. This enables you to output sounds from your computer.

- **Line in**　The line in port connects to an external device such as a DVD or MP3 player to enable you to import sounds into your computer.

- **Rear out**　The rear out jack connects to the rear speakers for surround sound audio output.

- **Analog/digital out**　The multifunction analog/digital out jack acts as a special digital connection to external digital devices or digital speaker systems, and it also acts as the analog connection to center and subwoofer channels.

- **Microphone**　The microphone port connects to an external microphone for voice input.

Many sound processors also come with a special *Sony/Philips Digital Interface (S/PDIF* or *SPDIF)* connector that enables you to connect your sound card directly to a 5.1 speaker system or receiver (see Figure 10-40). Using a single S/PDIF instead of a tangle of separate wires for each speaker greatly simplifies your sound setup. S/PDIF connections come in two types, optical and coaxial. The optical variety looks like a square with a small door (at right in Figure 10-40). The coaxial is a standard

RCA connector (at left), the same type used to connect a DVD player to your stereo. It doesn't matter which one you use; just make sure you have an open spot on your receiver or speakers.

Figure 10-40
S/PDIF
connectors

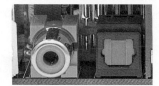

Configure speakers and speaker settings with the Sound applet/preferences. (Go to the Control Panel in Windows; System Preferences in macOS.)

NOTE Both HDMI and DisplayPort are capable of carrying audio to, say, a TV or stereo receiver. This is very handy as you only need one cable for audio and video, making everything nice and tidy. If you have a video card that can send audio over HDMI/DisplayPort, its ports will be listed as playback devices along with your traditional speaker and S/PDIF ports in the Windows Settings/Sound dialog (Windows 10 and 11) and Sound applet (all versions) in the Control Panel.

Microphones Speakers are great for listening to music, but what if you're a musician looking to record your own music? Or, more likely, an office worker needing to jump on a Zoom call? In either of these cases, you'll need a microphone of some sort to get audio into your computer. Assuming your computer doesn't already have a microphone built in, you'll need to connect an external one via USB (see Figure 10-41), built-in audio interface, or sound card. A *microphone* records sound by turning vibrations into an electronic signal. Microphones are mainly used for recording voices, though you can easily record any other sounds.

Figure 10-41
A large-
diaphragm USB
microphone

Headsets   If you want to listen to music without disturbing others or if you want to chat with your friends over Discord while gaming (see Figure 10-42), you'll probably want a headset. Headsets come with or without a microphone and use the same connectors as speakers and microphones. Headsets without microphones more commonly use 1/8-inch RCA jacks, while headsets with microphones more commonly use USB, although there are many exceptions to that rule.

Figure 10-42
Headsets are great for gaming.

Many systems have moved to dedicated USB audio boxes for recording or listening. Figure 10-43 shows a USB audio interface, the Focusrite Scarlett 2i2 (left), and a Schiit *digital-to-analog converter (DAC)* for listening to music.

Figure 10-43
Scarlett audio interface and Schiit DAC

Video Formats

Video files can be massive, so let's take a moment to see how video files are stored. With an audio file, as discussed earlier, this is a simple process. You pick a format such as AAC and save the file. Video is far more complicated.

A video is two or more separate tracks—moving picture and audio—that each go through a compression algorithm (codec). Otherwise, the resulting files would be huge, even for short videos. The compressed tracks then get wrapped up into a *container file*, what's often called a *wrapper*. When you receive a file saved in a standard wrapper, such as .MOV for a QuickTime Movie file, you have no way to know for certain which codecs were used to compress the video or audio tracks inside that container file (see Figure 10-44).

Figure 10-44
A standard container file holds multiple tracks, each encoded separately.

Codecs   Video files use standard audio codecs for the audio tracks, such as WAV or MP3, but vary wildly in the type of video codecs used. Just as with audio codecs, video codecs take a video stream and compress it by using various algorithms. Here are some of the standard video codecs:

- MPEG-2 Part 2, used for DVDs, broadcast TV.
- H.264, used for everything from smartphone video and streaming video to Blu-ray movies.
- H.265, half the size of H.264 at the same quality. Used to support 4K video.
- VP9, Google's competitor to H.265, used in places like Android devices.
- AV1, another competitor to H.265, designed by a group of companies including Amazon, Intel, Microsoft, and Google. YouTube is one its main users.

Wrappers   When both the video and audio streams of your video file are compressed, the file is placed into some sort of container file or wrapper. The key thing to note here is that the wrapper file doesn't necessarily specify how the video or audio tracks were encoded. You can look at two seemingly identical movie files—for example, both saved with the .MP4 file extension—and find that one will play audio and video just fine in Windows Media Player, but the other one might play only the audio and not the video because Media Player lacks the specific codec needed to decode the video stream. Here are some of the more common video wrappers you might run across:

- AVI (note this ends in the letter "I", not numeral 1), a container file for Windows (not used much these days)
- MOV, the standard format for Apple QuickTime
- MP4, probably the most common format these days, used for H.264 and H.265 video
- MKV, the Matroska Multimedia Container, a free and open container format with native support in Windows 10 and 11

Removable Storage Devices

Removable media refers to any type of mass storage device that you may use in one system and then easily remove from that system and use in another. Today's highly networked computers have reduced the need for removable media as a method of sharing programs and data, but removable media has so many other uses that it's still going strong. Removable media is the perfect tool for software distribution, data archiving, and system backup.

This section covers the most common types of removable media used today. For the sake of organization, the removable media types are broken down into these groups:

- **Flash memory**   From USB thumb drives to flash memory cards
- **Optical discs**   Any shiny disc technology, such as DVDs and Blu-ray Discs

We can add external drives to this mix, meaning any hard drive, SSD, or optical drive that connects to a PC via an external cable. These drives manifest just like an internal drive, as you studied in Chapter 8 and Chapter 9, so there's nothing special to discuss here.

Flash Memory

Flash memory, the same flash memory that replaced ROM chips for system BIOS, found another home in personal computing devices in the form of removable mass storage devices. Flash memory comes in two families: USB thumb drives and memory cards. *USB thumb drives* are flash devices that have a standard USB connector. *Memory card* is a generic term for a number of tiny cards used in cameras, smartphones, and other devices. Both of these families can manifest themselves as drives in modern OSs, but they usually perform different jobs. USB thumb drives have replaced virtually all other rewritable removable media as the way people transfer files or keep copies of important programs. My thumb drives (yes, I have two on me at all times) keep backups of my current work, important photos, and a stack of utilities I need to fix computers. Memory cards are very small and make a great way to store data on cameras and smartphones and then transfer that data to your computer.

Flash Drives

Moving data between computers has historically been a pain, but *USB flash memory drives,* also known as thumb drives, jump drives, and flash drives, make the process much easier (see Figure 10-45). For a low price, you can get a 128-GB *USB flash memory* drive that holds a ton of data.

The smallest thumb drives are slightly larger than an adult thumbnail; others are larger and more rounded. The drives are hot-swappable in all modern operating systems. You simply plug one into any USB port and it appears in File Explorer or on the Desktop as a removable storage device. After you plug the drive into a USB port, you can copy or move data to or from the drive and then unplug the unit and take it with you. You can read, write, and delete files directly from the drive. Because these are USB devices, they don't need an external power source. The nonvolatile flash memory is solid-state, so it's shock resistant and is supposed to retain data safely for a decade.

Figure 10-45
Thumb drives

Figure 10-45
Thumb drives

Current systems enable you to boot from a thumb drive, replacing the traditional CDs and DVDs with fast flash drives. Most of the classic bootable-utility-CD makers have created USB versions that seek out your thumb drive and add an operating system with the utilities you wish to use.

NOTE   Change the boot order in system setup when you want to boot from a USB flash drive. If you use the wrong boot order, the BIOS will ignore the thumb drive and go straight to the SSD or hard disk.

Memory Cards

Memory cards are the way people store data on small appliances. Memory cards come in several formats, so let's start by making sure you know the more common ones.

CompactFlash   *CompactFlash (CF)* is the oldest removable flash media card standard (see Figure 10-46). CF cards come in two sizes: CF I (3.3 mm thick) and CF II (5 mm thick). CF II cards are too thick to fit into CF I slots.

Figure 10-46
CF card

Secure Digital   *Secure Digital (SD)* cards, as mentioned earlier, are common but becoming less so. About the size of a postage stamp, you'll see SD cards in just about any type of device that uses flash media.

In addition to full-size SD cards, there are two smaller forms called *mini Secure Digital (miniSD)* cards and *micro Secure Digital (microSD)* cards. Today the miniSD format has fallen out of use, but full-size SD is still popular in cameras and microSD is often found in other small devices where its small size is an advantage. Figure 10-47 shows the full-size and micro forms of SD cards.

Figure 10-47
SD and microSD cards

SD cards come in three storage capacities. *Standard SD* cards store from 4 MB to 4 GB, *Secure Digital High Capacity (SDHC)* cards store 4 GB to 32 GB, and *Secure Digital Extended Capacity (SDXC)* cards have a storage capacity of 32 GB to 2 TB. Early SD card readers and devices cannot read the SDHC or SDXC cards, though the latter standards provide backward compatibility.

When it comes to figuring out how fast a given SD card is, things start to get complicated. Card speeds matter when it comes to intensive uses like high-quality video and high-resolution or high-speed photography.

To try and make it easy for users to pick a card that will be fast enough for their use, the people behind the SD cards have created a few standards to communicate performance. These standards roughly break down into three different generations. The first-generation cards use the *speed class* (2, 4, 6, and 10) ratings to indicate the card's minimum MB/s write speed; a Class 10 card should write at a minimum of 10 MB/s.

The second generation of speed ratings coincided with the introduction of the new *Ultra High Speed (UHS)* bus. These cards use the *UHS Speed Class* standard; Class U1 cards should both read and write at a minimum of 10 MB/s, while U3 cards should read and write at a minimum of 30 MB/s.

The third generation of performance standards is the *Video Speed Class*. These standards are designed to support the newest video standards such as 4K and even 8K. The slowest class is V6, supporting 6 MB/s, but it goes all the way up to V90, which guaranties 90 MB/s write speed. If this wasn't confusing enough, modern cards often sport indicators for more than one (if not all) of these speed rating systems.

But wait, there's more! The speed classes we've looked at guarantee that a card can continuously write at the indicated rate or higher. Ratings like this are critical for figuring out whether a card can keep up with a device like a video camera. But these days, SD cards are just as likely to be used in a smartphone as they are in a camera. That's where the *Application Performance Class* ratings come in. This standard has two classes, A1 and

A2. They both support a minimum of 10 MB/s sustained write. Where they differ is how many *input/output operations per second (IOPS)* the card can do. The A1 class can sustain 1500 IOPS while reading and 500 IOPS while writing. The A2 class can keep up with at least 4000 IOPS while reading and 2000 IOPS while writing. These performance characteristics don't matter much when a card is writing video, but they make all the difference when multiple smartphone apps are using it.

Beyond these ratings, SD cards often have a maximum read speed (in MB/s) printed on the card or packaging. This practice started years ago with cards oriented toward professionals, but has become relatively common on cards of any quality. If you're wondering why the maximum write speed isn't also on the card, that's a great question; while it isn't printed on any card we've seen yet, product listings for high-performance SD cards typically mention the maximum write speed.

Because there's a wide variety of SD cards available with different qualities, two cards of the same capacity can vary wildly in price and performance. It's important to evaluate each card's properties to avoid wasting money on performance you don't need, or thinking you got a great deal on a massive card only to find it can't keep up with your brand-new professional video camera.

 EXAM TIP Some high-end cameras use a card format called *XQD*, which offers very high-speed transfers and capacities of 2+ TB. This format is *not* on the exam. XQD has been joined at the high end by *CFexpress* (also not on the exam) that uses NVMe.

Card Readers Whichever type of flash memory you use, your computer must have a *card reader* to access the data on the card directly. A number of inexpensive USB card readers are available today (see Figure 10-48), and many computers and home printers come with built-in SD readers—handy to have when you want to pull the photos from your camera for editing or quickly print a photo.

Figure 10-48
USB card reader

Whichever type of flash memory you have, understand that it acts exactly like any other mass storage drive. If you wish, you can format a memory card or copy, paste, and rename files.

Optical Media

Optical disc is the generic term for shiny, 12-centimeter-wide discs. The drives that support them are called *optical drives*. This section examines optical discs, finishing with the details about installing optical drives. Optical drives are dying or dead, replaced by flash media and streaming Internet feeds. You'll see them on legacy computers and the CompTIA A+ exams. Memorize the contents of this section for the exams, then just let optical media go.

CD, DVD, and Blu-ray Disc drives and discs come in a variety of flavors and formats. *Compact disc (CD)* is a medium that was originally designed in the early 1980s as a replacement for vinyl records. The *digital versatile disc (DVD)* first eliminated VHS cassette tapes from the commercial home movie market, and grew into a contender for backups and high-capacity storage. *Blu-ray Disc (BD)* became the only high-definition and 4K, high-capacity optical format.

Going beyond those big three household names, the term "optical disc" refers to technologies such as CD-ROM, CD-R, CD-RW, DVD, DVD+RW, BD-R, BD-RE, and so on. Each of these technologies will be discussed in detail in this chapter—for now, understand that although "optical disc" describes a variety of exciting formats, they all basically boil down to the same physical object: that little shiny disc.

CD-Media

The best way to understand optical disc technologies is to sort out the many varieties available, starting with the first: the compact disc. All you're about to read is relevant and fair game for the CompTIA A+ certification exams.

CDs store data by using microscopic pits burned into a glass master CD with a powerful laser. Expensive machines create plastic copies of the glass master that are then coated with a reflective metallic coating. CDs store data on one side of the disc only. The CD drive reads the pits and the non-pitted areas (lands) and converts the pattern into ones and zeros.

CD Formats The first CDs were designed for playing music and organized the music in a special format called *CD-Digital Audio (CDDA)*, which we usually just call CD-audio. CD-audio divides the CD's data into variable-length tracks; on music CDs, each song gets one track. CD-audio is an excellent way to store music, but it lacks advanced error checking, file support, or directory structure, making it a terrible way to store data. For this reason, The Powers That Be created a special method for storing data on a CD, called—are you ready—*CD-ROM*. The CD-ROM format divides the CD into fixed sectors, each holding 2353 bytes.

At first glance you might think, "Why don't CD-ROMs just use a FAT or an NTFS format like hard drives?" Well, first of all, they could. There's no law of physics that prevented the CD-ROM world from adopting any file system. The problem is that the CD makers did not want CD-ROM to be tied to Microsoft's or Apple's or anyone else's file format. In addition, they wanted non-PC devices to read CDs, so they invented their own file system just for CD-ROMs called *ISO-9660*. This format is sometimes referred to by the more generic term *CD File System (CDFS)*. The vast majority of data CD-ROMs today use this format.

CD-ROM Speeds   The first CD-ROM drives processed data at roughly 150,000 bytes per second (150 KBps), copying the speed from the original CD-audio format. Although this speed is excellent for listening to music, the CD-ROM industry quickly recognized that installing programs or transferring files from a CD-ROM at 150 KBps was the electronic equivalent of watching paint dry. Since the day the first CD-ROM drives for PCs hit the market, there has been a desire to speed them up to increase their data throughput. Each increase in speed is measured in multiples of the original 150-KBps drives and given an × to show speed relative to the first (1×) drives. Here's a list of the common CD-ROM speeds, including most of the early speeds that are no longer produced:

1× 150 KBps	24× 3600 KBps
2× 300 KBps	36× 5400 KBps
4× 600 KBps	48× 7200 KBps
16× 2400 KBps	72× 10800 KBps

CD-R   Making CD-ROMs requires specialized, expensive equipment and substantial expertise, so a relatively small number of CD-ROM production companies do it. Yet, since the day the first CD-ROMs came to market, demand was high for a way that ordinary PC users could make their own CDs. The CD industry made a number of attempts to create a technology that would let users record, or *burn*, their own CDs.

In the mid-1990s, the CD industry introduced the CD-recordable (CD-R) standard, which enables affordable CD-R drives, often referred to as *CD burners*, to add data to special CD-R discs. Any CD-ROM drive can then read the data stored on the CD-R, and all CD-R drives can read regular CD-ROMs. CD-R discs come in two varieties: a 74-minute disc that holds approximately 650 MB, and an 80-minute variety that holds approximately 700 MB (see Figure 10-49). A CD-R burner must be specifically designed to support the longer, 80-minute CD-R format, but most drives you'll encounter can do this.

Figure 10-49
A CD-R disc, with its capacity clearly labeled

CD-R discs function similarly to regular CD-ROMs, although the chemicals used to make them produce a brightly colored recording side on almost all CD-R discs. CD-ROM discs, in contrast, have a silver data side. CD-R technology records data by using organic dyes embedded into the disc. CD-R burners have a second burn laser, roughly ten times as powerful as the read laser, that heats the organic dye. This causes a change in the reflectivity of the surface, creating the functional equivalent of a CD-ROM's pits.

CD-R drives have two speeds that matter: the record speed and the read speed, both expressed as multiples of the 150-KBps speed of the original CD-ROM drives. The record speed, which is listed first, is always equal to or slower than the read speed. For example, a CD-R drive with a specification of 8×24× would burn at 8× and read at 24×.

CD-RW   Just as CD-R drives could both burn CD-R discs and read CD-ROMs, a newer type of drive called CD-rewritable (CD-RW) took over the burning market from CD-R drives. Although this drive has its own type of CD-RW discs, it also can burn to CD-R discs, which are much cheaper.

CD-RW technology enables you not only to burn a disc, but to *burn over* existing data on a CD-RW disc. The CD-RW format essentially takes CD-media to the functional equivalent of a 650-MB flash-media drive. Once again, CD-RW discs look exactly like CD-ROM discs with the exception of a colored bottom side. Figure 10-50 shows all three formats.

Figure 10-50
CD-ROM, CD-R, and CD-RW discs

A CD-RW drive works by using a laser to heat an amorphous (noncrystalline) substance that, when cooled, slowly becomes crystalline. The crystalline areas are reflective, whereas the amorphous areas are not. Because both CD-R and CD-RW drives require a powerful laser, making a drive that could burn CD-Rs and CD-RWs was a simple process, and plain CD-R drives disappeared almost overnight. Why buy a CD-R drive when a comparably priced CD-RW drive could burn both CD-R and CD-RW discs?

CD-RW drive specs have three multiplier values. The first shows the CD-R write speed, the second shows the CD-RW rewrite speed, and the third shows the read speed. Write, rewrite, and read speeds vary tremendously among the various brands of CD-RW drives; here are just a few representative samples: 8×4×32×, 12×10×32×, and 48×24×48×.

Windows and CD-Media   Virtually all optical drives use the same interface as your mass storage drives. You just plug in the drive and, assuming you didn't make any physical installation mistakes, the drive appears in Windows (see Figure 10-51).

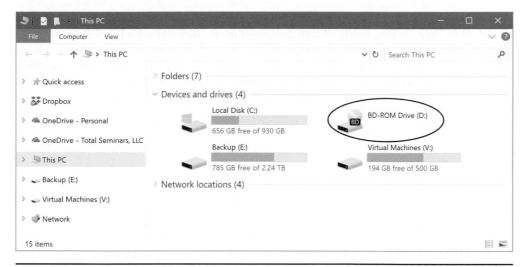

Figure 10-51   Optical drive in Windows

DVD-Media

For years, the video industry tried to create an optical-media replacement for videotape. The DVD was developed by a large consortium of electronics and entertainment firms during the early 1990s and released as digital *video* discs in 1995. The transformation of DVD to a data storage medium required a name change to digital *versatile* discs. You'll still hear both terms used. The industry also uses the term *DVD-video* to distinguish the movie format from the data formats. With the exception of the DVD logo stamped on all commercial DVDs (see Figure 10-52), DVDs look exactly like CD-media discs, but that's pretty much where the similarities end.

Figure 10-52
Typical
DVD-video

The single best word to describe DVD is *capacity*. The lowest capacity DVD holds 4.37 GB of data, or two hours of standard-definition video. The highest capacity DVD versions store roughly 16 GB of data, or more than eight hours of video. DVD uses a number of technologies, but three are most important. First, DVD uses smaller pits than CD-media, and packs them much more densely. Second, DVD comes in both *single-sided (SS)* and *double-sided (DS)* formats. As the name implies, a DS disc holds twice the data of an SS disc, but it also requires you to flip the disc to read the other side. Third, DVDs come in *single-layer (SL)* and *dual-layer (DL)* formats. DL formats use two pitted layers on each side, each with a slightly different reflectivity index. Table 10-3 shows the common DVD capacities.

DVD Version	Capacity
DVD-5 (12 cm, SS/SL)	4.37 GB, more than two hours of video
DVD-9 (12 cm, SS/DL)	7.95 GB, about four hours of video
DVD-10 (12 cm, DS/SL)	8.74 GB, about four and a half hours of video
DVD-18 (12 cm, DS/DL)	15.90 GB, more than eight hours of video

Table 10-3   DVD Versions/Capacities

DVD-ROM   DVD-ROM is the DVD equivalent of the standard CD-ROM data format except that it's capable of storing up to almost 16 GB of data. Almost all DVD-ROM drives also fully support DVD-video, as well as most CD-ROM formats. Most DVD drives sold with PCs are DVD-ROM drives.

Recordable DVD   The IT industry has no fewer than *three* distinct standards of recordable DVD-media: DVD-R, DVD-RW, and DVD-RW DL. DVD-R discs work like CD-Rs. You can write to them but not erase or alter what's written. DVD-RW discs can be written and rewritten, just like CD-RW discs. DVD-RW DL can be written to on two layers, doubling the capacity. Most DVD drives can read all formats.

 EXAM TIP   Apple stopped including optical drives on both desktop and portable systems a long time ago. Because optical media enjoys some popularity, Apple gave macOS machines *Remote Disc*, the capability to read optical media from an optical drive in another system.

Blu-ray Disc Media

Blu-ray Disc is the last generation in optical disc formatting and storage technology (see Figure 10-53). Because of its near-perfect audio and video quality; mass acceptance by industry-leading computer, electronics, game, music, retail, and motion picture companies; and huge storage capacities of up to 25 GB (single-layer disc), 50 GB (dual-layer disc), and 100 GB (BDXL), Blu-ray Disc technology enjoyed wild popularity until flash memory prices dropped in the 2010s to basically kill off all optical media.

Figure 10-53
Standard
Blu-ray Disc

NOTE If you own an Xbox One (except the Series S) or PlayStation 3 or later, you already have a Blu-ray Disc player. That's the optical format the game system uses.

BD-ROM BD-ROM (read only) is the Blu-ray Disc equivalent of the standard DVD-ROM data format except, as noted earlier, it can store much more data and produces superior audio and video results. Almost all BD-ROM drives are fully backward compatible and support DVD-video as well as most CD-ROM formats. If you want to display the best possible movie picture quality on your HDTV, you should get a Blu-ray Disc player and use Blu-ray Discs in place of DVDs. Most new computer systems don't come standard with optical drives installed. You can often custom-order a system with a Blu-ray Disc drive, or you can simply connect one yourself. Figure 10-54 shows a Blu-ray Disc drive.

Figure 10-54
A combination
CD/DVD/Blu-ray
Disc drive

BD-R and BD-RE   Blu-ray Discs come in two writable formats, BD-R (recordable) and BD-RE (rewritable). You can write to a BD-R disc one time. You can write to and erase a BD-RE disc several times. There are also BD-R and BD-RE versions of mini Blu-ray Discs.

Installing Optical Drives

From ten feet away, optical drives of all flavors look absolutely identical. Figure 10-55 shows a CD-RW drive, a DVD drive, and a BD-R drive. Can you tell them apart just by a glance? In case you were wondering, the CD-RW drive is on the bottom, the DVD drive is next, and finally the BD-R drive is on the top. If you look closely at an optical drive, you will normally see its function either stamped on the front of the case or printed on a label somewhere less obvious (see Figure 10-56).

Figure 10-55
CD-RW, DVD, and
BD-R drives

Figure 10-56
Label on optical
drive indicating
its type

Most internal optical drives use SATA. External optical drives often use USB or Thunderbolt connections. Plug them in and go.

Chapter Review

Questions

1. Jason put in a recommendation that his company upgrade the SD cards used in the company smartphones from 32-GB SDHC A1 to 128-GB SDXC A2. What is the advantage of A2 cards over A1 cards?

   A. A2 cards offer much greater capacity than A1 cards.

   B. A2 cards offer much faster sustained write speeds than A1 cards.

   C. A2 cards cost a lot less than A1 cards and offer similar performance.

   D. A2 cards sustain faster IOPS than A1 cards.

2. What happens to bus speed and power usage when you plug multiple devices into a USB hub?

   A. The bus speed stays constant, but power usage increases.

   B. The bus speed increases because each device brings a little burst; power usage increases.

   C. The bus speed decreases because all devices share the same total bandwidth; power usage increases.

   D. The bus speed decreases because all devices share the same total bandwidth; power usage decreases.

3. Which cable is used to transfer information between two devices using a serial communication protocol?

   A. Thunderbolt cable

   B. Video cable

   C. Hard drive cable

   D. Serial cable

4. You take a tech call from a user who complains that she gets an error message, "Hub power exceeded," when she plugs her new thumb drive into her USB keyboard's external USB port. Worse, the device won't work. What's most likely the problem?

   A. Her USB port is defective.

   B. She has a defective thumb drive.

   C. She plugged a Hi-Speed device into a Full-Speed port.

   D. She plugged one too many devices into the USB hub.

5. What is the fastest speed that Hi-Speed USB 2.0 can go?

   A. 12 Mbps

   B. 120 Mbps

   C. 400 Mbps

   D. 480 Mbps

6. What is the maximum cable length for USB 2.0?

   A. 1.2 meters

   B. 1.2 yards

   C. 5 meters

   D. 5 feet

7. How many speakers are in a 5.1 setup?

   A. Five speakers plus a subwoofer

   B. Six speakers plus a subwoofer

   C. Seven speakers plus a subwoofer

   D. Eight speakers plus a subwoofer

8. Which multimedia device is used for Internet video communication, which allows people to interact over networks with both voice and video?

   A. Speaker

   B. Microphone

   C. Webcam

   D. Sound processor

9. Which optical disc type offers the most capacity writing and rewriting data files?

   A. DVD-R

   B. DVD+RW DL

   C. BD-RE

   D. BD-RW

10. Jack downloaded a video shared by a friend, ourfamilyholiday.avi. When he opens it in his media player software, he hears sound but gets no picture. What's the most likely problem and solution?

   A. His media player software doesn't support AVI files. He needs to install a new media player.

   B. His computer is a Mac; he needs to play the file on a Windows system.

   C. His computer lacks the proper video codec. He needs to update the codecs installed on his computer.

   D. The video is corrupt. His friend needs to share it with him again.

Answers

1. **D.** A1 and A2 Application Performance Class ratings refer to the IOPS rating of the card, with A2 cards offering better performance than A1. This matters for smartphones with multiple apps running. SDHC and SDXC refer to the capacity of a card's storage.

2. **C.** The bus speed decreases because all devices share the same total bandwidth; power usage increases.

3. **D.** A serial cable transfer information between two devices using a serial communication protocol.

4. **D.** Just like the error message said, the thumb drive drew too much power for the hub to handle.

5. **D.** Hi-Speed USB 2.0 has a theoretical maximum of 480 Mbps.

6. **C.** USB has a maximum cable length of 5 meters.

7. **A.** A 5.1 setup has five speakers and one subwoofer.

8. **C.** A webcam allows people to interact over networks with both voice and video.

9. **C.** BD-RE offers the highest rewritable capacity of the discs mentioned here.

10. **C.** Most likely, Jack's system lacks the video codec needed for the video portion of the file. He needs to update the codecs on his machine.

Answers

CHAPTER 11

Installing and Upgrading Operating Systems

In this chapter, you will learn how to

- Recognize current Windows editions
- Install and upgrade Windows
- Describe Windows post-installation best practices

This chapter's title is slightly deceptive, as it might be more accurate to call it "Installing and Upgrading Microsoft Windows." With that being said, there are operating systems out there other than Windows. Linux installations use a similar general installation process as Windows and are easily upgraded through the command line. ChromeOS and macOS come preinstalled on devices and are upgraded through regular software updates rather than by the release and installation of entirely new versions like you'd see with Windows (for example, Windows 10 to 11). The odds of you manually installing either of these are next to zero, and that's by design.

There's a good reason to make this chapter mainly about Windows. Microsoft Windows comes in many variations compared to macOS, ChromeOS, or any individual version of Linux (there are many different versions of Linux, known as distributions or "distros," but these are each separate projects). It's also installed on something like 90 percent of all the desktop, laptop, and server computers in the world, so understanding Windows is always a great skill to possess.

This chapter puts together a lot of what you know about hardware from the previous ten chapters and layers on the essential component that makes Windows PCs so excellent: Windows. We'll start by exploring the different Windows versions and editions and then turn to installing and upgrading Windows. The final section covers post-installation tasks.

1102

Windows Versions and Editions

There's an interesting page at Wikipedia.org titled "List of Microsoft Windows versions" that lists every version of Windows from the original Windows 1.0 back in 1985 to Windows 11 today. A quick scan of that page lists over 40 PC versions of Windows over the years! Fortunately, the CompTIA A+ 1102 exam objectives define only one version: Microsoft Windows 10. The Windows 10 operating system is designed to run on classic personal computers, both desktop and laptop systems, which are still the cornerstone for many of us.

Let's take a moment to differentiate between Windows *versions* and Windows *editions*. Windows 10 is a version. Windows 11 is another version. Each version of Windows is in turn broken down into editions that address specific needs. Windows 10 is available in multiple editions, with names such as Windows 10 Home and Windows 10 Enterprise. CompTIA A+ 220-1102 exam objective 1.1 specifies exactly four Windows 10 editions:

- Windows 10 Home
- Windows 10 Pro (not "Professional")
- Windows 10 Pro for Workstations
- Windows 10 Enterprise

What About Windows 11?

Every CompTIA A+ update has always been basically—almost comically—one version behind the latest version of Windows since Windows 7. With the introduction of the CompTIA A+ 220-1101/1102 exams, CompTIA added the following note to the A+ 1102 exam objectives:

NOTE ON WINDOWS 11

Versions of Microsoft® Windows® that are not at the end of Mainstream Support (as determined by Microsoft), up to and including Windows 11, are intended content areas of the certification. As such, objectives in which a specific version of Microsoft Windows is not indicated in the main objective title can include content related to Windows 10 and Windows 11, as it relates to the job role.

There's a little room for interpretation here, but my 30 years of working with CompTIA gives me some insight. I interpret CompTIA's note to mean that, other than very specific questions that point exactly to only Windows 10, Windows 10 and 11 are so similar that if a question says "Windows," then it doesn't matter which edition of

Windows you're thinking in your head, as the question applies to both Windows 10 and 11—so don't worry about the version!

NOTE   Windows 11 has the same editions as Windows 10.

Windows 10 Home

Windows 10 Home is the most basic of the Windows 10 editions listed in CompTIA A+ 220-1102 exam objective 1.1. Designed for home users, Windows 10 Home lacks many features that are offered in the other three editions that we'll review. The important point to remember about Windows 10 Home is that it only supports 128 GB of RAM. That might sound like a lot of RAM to you, but Microsoft doesn't want you to use Windows Home for anything even remotely resembling a server, so it hobbles Home to make sure you don't use it for anything but a basic home system.

Workgroups vs. Domains

Speaking of keeping your Windows Home at home, it also lacks another very important feature: the ability to log on to a Windows domain. Windows domains require a special version of Windows called Windows Server. If you have a home network that lacks a Windows Server system (like almost all home networks), your network devices are members of a workgroup. Let's examine both workgroups and domains, as understanding these concepts is important to help you choose the Windows edition you need.

Workgroups

A workgroup is the most fundamental network organization used in Windows networks. In a workgroup, every computer stores all its own users and passwords (see Figure 11-1). These are known as *local usernames*. A workgroup setup is inexpensive because it doesn't require an expensive server system running expensive Windows Server software, nor does it require any special skills. It just works.

Domains

A Windows domain is a much more complex and powerful setup than a workgroup. First, you need a dedicated server system. This system usually sits in a rack in a closet and does nothing but...serve. This system runs Windows Server, a powerful and expensive (thousands of dollars per copy) version of Windows (see Figure 11-2).

Possibly the most popular feature of Windows Server is the *domain*. In a Windows domain, the individual computers log on to the server itself. This server stores its own set of "domain" usernames and passwords that are completely separate from the local usernames. Using domains instead of workgroups has too many advantages to list here,

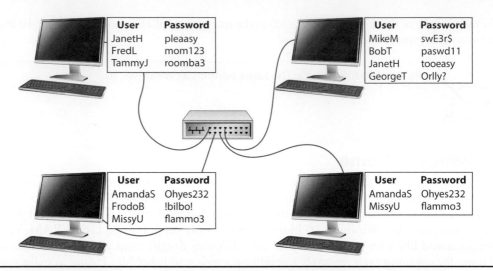

Figure 11-1   In a Windows workgroup every system has its own usernames and passwords.

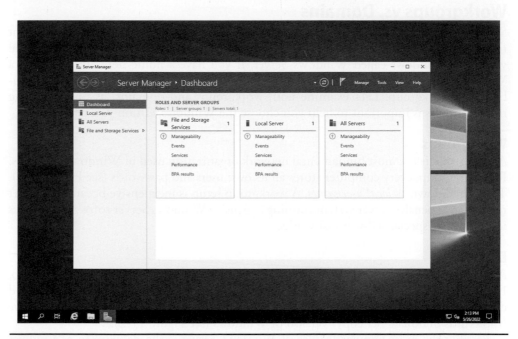

Figure 11-2   Windows Server 2019 with the Server Manager console displayed

but one of them is *single sign-on (SSO)*, which lets you use the same username and password to sign on to any computer in the domain (see Figure 11-3). There are many more advantages to Windows domains that make the added cost worthwhile.

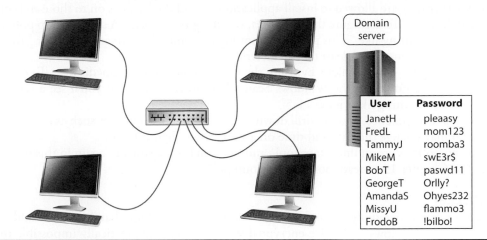

Figure 11-3   Windows domain

Windows domains are fantastic, but purchasing Window Server is beyond the pocketbook of many home users. Windows Home systems cannot become part of a domain, to do that, you'll need something like Windows Pro.

 NOTE   Head over to Chapters 13 and 19 for more details about Windows domains and how your system may join them and use them.

Windows 10 Pro

The limits of Windows Home make it unattractive for anything but the most basic home user. If you want to see what Windows is all about, you need to start with *Windows 10 Pro*. For starters, Windows 10 Pro supports up to 2 TB of RAM and is the most basic edition of Windows that supports joining a Windows domain (see Figure 11-4). Once you step up to Windows Pro and beyond, you gain access to some very powerful features. Here are some of those features and how they work.

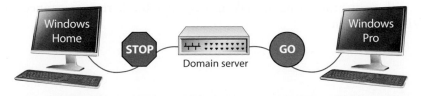

Figure 11-4   Unlike Windows 10 Pro, Windows 10 Home can't use a Windows domain.

Group Policies

Microsoft Windows has some amazing features when it comes to security. You can require users to use complex passwords, you can limit when people log on, you can control whether they are allowed to install applications...and the list goes on to thousands of security features. To configure these features, you use *group policies*. A single group policy might be something like "This person cannot log on remotely to their system" or "Your login password must be at least ten characters."

You configure group policies by using the Group Policy Editor, gpedit.msc. To open it, simply type **gpedit** in the Windows Search bar, press ENTER, and you'll see a screen that looks something like Figure 11-5.

With a little practice, you can drill down and make practical changes such as configuring who may change the date and time on a system (see Figure 11-6).

Group policies are an important topic and one you'll see again and again in this book. Head to Chapter 13 to read more about group policies.

BitLocker

BitLocker is an incredibly powerful drive encryption technology that Microsoft added way back in Windows 7. A drive encrypted with BitLocker is practically impossible to break, and the encryption is completely transparent to the user: when the user logs off, the drive is encrypted, and when the user logs on, the drive is unencrypted.

Be careful! If you want to use BitLocker, make sure you choose any Windows edition other than Windows Home, which lacks BitLocker support.

 NOTE BitLocker can protect more than just your laptop's boot disk. With BitLocker to Go, you can encrypt removable drives, such as an external hard drive, keeping its files safe if it ever falls into the wrong hands.

Remote Desktop Protocol

Remote Desktop Protocol (RDP) is the primary tool for remote connectivity between individual Windows systems. A great example is Windows Server systems. Most servers running Windows Server either sit in a rack system in a closet (for smaller organizations), sit in a data center (for larger organizations), or exist in the cloud (for everything in between). Because you're likely not going to be standing in front of a Windows server, you need to have some kind of remote connection tool to communicate with that server.

RDP allows different tools to make that remote connection. Figure 11-7 shows the most popular tool, Remote Desktop Connection. This tool has been around for decades with very little changes, making easy, graphical, remote connections with other Windows systems.

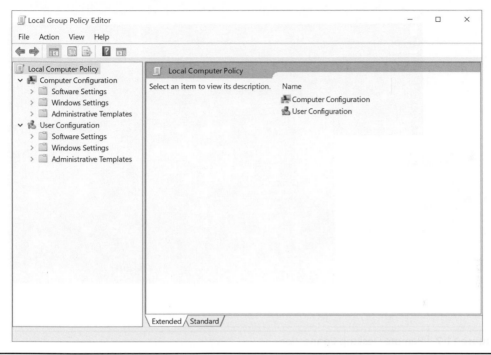

Figure 11-5   Default Local Group Policy Editor window

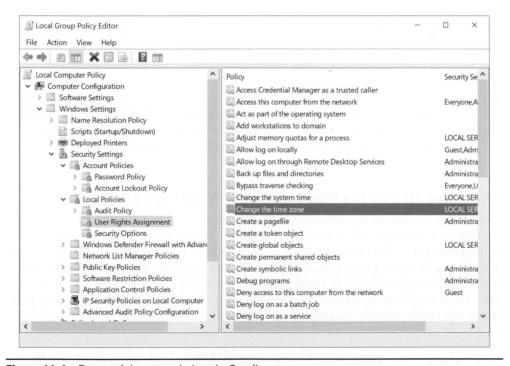

Figure 11-6   Date and time permissions in Gpedit

Figure 11-7   Remote Desktop Connection

According Microsoft's documentation, Windows Home lacks Remote Desktop Protocol support. Although you'll find the Remote Desktop Connection program in Windows Home, it doesn't work! There are weird workarounds to make RDP work on Windows 10 Home…but maybe you should just avoid the Home edition if you want to do remote connections.

TIP   As you see in this section, there are many features available on every edition of Windows except Windows Home. It's for this and many more reasons that your author truly dislikes Windows Home. Don't use it if you can avoid it.

Windows 10 Pro for Workstations/Windows 10 Enterprise

The last two Windows 10 editions you need to know for the CompTIA A+ 1102 exam are *Windows 10 Pro for Workstations* and *Windows 10 Enterprise*. These two editions are so similar that it makes sense to talk about them in one shot. First, both editions support domain membership, group policies, BitLocker, and Remote Desktop Protocol. Second, both editions support up to 6 TB of RAM, far more than most motherboards can support. These are powerful, high-end operating systems designed to support the most powerful workstation systems available.

NOTE A workstation is a powerful computer that someone sits at and does real work. A server serves resources, but no one sits at it and does work.

The only significant difference between Windows 10 Pro for Workstations and Windows 10 Enterprise is a special feature unique to Windows 10 Enterprise called *long-term servicing branch (LTSB)*. LTSB has three major features: it turns off automatic updates, as it assumes your hosts are being administered in house; it removes the Microsoft Store; it skips installing the Edge web browser. If you want real control over your system, get Windows Enterprise.

Well, there's one small problem with Windows 10 Enterprise—it's not available to the retail market. You must purchase Enterprise through a Microsoft sales representative.

What Version of Windows Do I Have?

There are many ways to identify your Windows version and edition, but one of the easiest is to run the System Information Utility (msinfo32.exe) (see Figure 11-8).

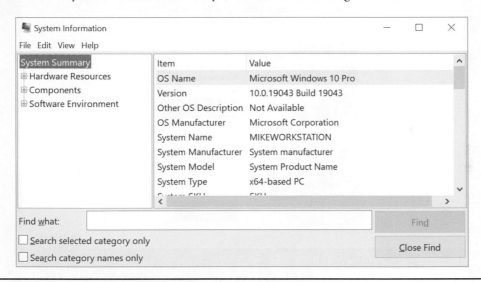

Figure 11-8 Version and edition details in System Information

Use the following table as a quick reference of the pertinent Windows 10 editions:

Edition	RAM	Domain?	RDP?	Group Policy?	BitLocker?	LTSB?
Windows 10 Home	128 GB					
Windows 10 Pro	2 TB	Y	Y	Y	Y	
Windows 10 Pro for Workstations	6 TB	Y	Y	Y	Y	
Windows 10 Enterprise	6 TB	Y	Y	Y	Y	Y

Installing and Upgrading Windows

You're not really a true PC tech until you've installed your first version of Windows, so let's get to installing! This section looks at media selection, types of installation, then the installation and upgrade process. It completes with a discussion on troubleshooting installations.

Media Sources

At its most basic, a Windows installation has two steps. First, boot the system from the OS installation media. Second, answer the installation wizard's initial queries and let it do its thing. At the end of the 20- to 40-minute process, you'll be looking at a Welcome screen (see Figure 11-9) and be ready to begin your love affair with the PC.

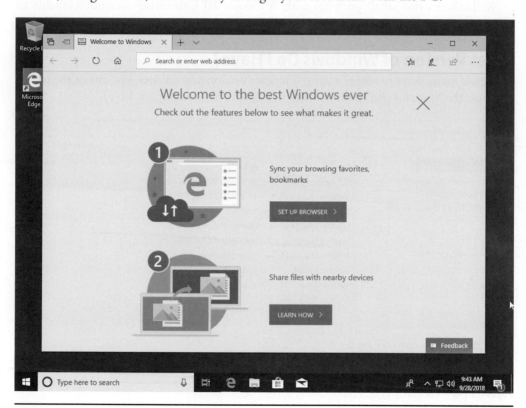

Figure 11-9   Windows 10 Welcome screen

 EXAM TIP   Successful installation results in a properly formatted boot drive with the correct partitions/formats.

Windows offers a surprising number of *boot methods*, giving you many options to get the process started. The most common way to start—historically at least—is to insert a Windows installation DVD, change the boot order in the system setup utility, and power up the system.

Today we usually boot to a drive inserted into a USB port. That includes flash drives or external drives. Any number of *external/hot-swappable drives* will do the job. Microsoft will even sell you a Windows 10 installation thumb drive (see Figure 11-10).

Figure 11-10   Windows flash installation media

 EXAM TIP   Microsoft has shifted with the times. The primary way to install Windows 10 and 11 is to download an ISO image and write that image to some bootable media. With the Windows Media Creation Tool (a quick download from Microsoft), you can easily make that bootable media a DVD or USB flash drive. CompTIA refers to this as the "internet-based boot method."

Don't feel like plugging something into the computer? No problem. You can access Windows installation files over a network. See "Installing Windows over a Network," a little later in this chapter, for details.

Finally, many system builders add a small, hidden partition to the primary hard drive containing an image of the factory-fresh version of Windows. In the event of a corrupted or very messy instance of Windows, you can reboot, access this *recovery partition*, and reinstall Windows. Chapter 16 covers recovery partitions and other forms of restoration in some detail.

 EXAM TIP CompTIA A+ 220-1102 exam objective 1.9 offers "internal hard drive (partition)" as a viable boot method for installing Windows. My best guess is that CompTIA means the hidden recovery partition.

Types of Installation

You can install Windows in several ways. A *clean install* of an OS involves installing it onto an empty hard drive or completely replacing an existing installation. An *upgrade installation* means installing an OS on top of an earlier installed version, thus inheriting all previous hardware and software settings. You can combine versions of Windows by creating a *multiboot installation*. Let's look at all the options.

Clean Install

A clean install means your installation ignores a previous installation of Windows, wiping out the old version as the new version of Windows installs. A clean install is also performed on a new system with a completely blank mass storage drive. The advantage of doing a clean install is that you don't carry problems from the old OS over to the new one. The disadvantage is that you need to back up and then restore all your data, reinstall all your applications, and reconfigure the desktop and each application to the user's preferences. You typically perform a clean install by setting CMOS to boot from the optical drive or USB before the hard drive or SSD. You then boot off a Windows installation disc/drive, and Windows gives you the opportunity to partition and format the hard drive or SSD during the installation process.

Upgrade Installation

For decades, if you wanted to take advantage of a new version of some operating system, you had to grab (usually purchase) the new version and go through a process called an upgrade installation. You might find yourself in a situation where you need to upgrade an older version of Windows to Windows 10 or 11, so let's talk about an upgrade installation.

In an upgrade installation, the new OS installs into the same folders as the old OS, or in tech speak, the new installs *on top of* the old. The new OS replaces the old OS, but retains data and applications and also inherits all of the personal settings (such as font styles, desktop themes, and so on). The best part is that you don't have to reinstall your favorite programs. Figure 11-11 shows the start of the Windows 10 installation, asking if you want an upgrade installation.

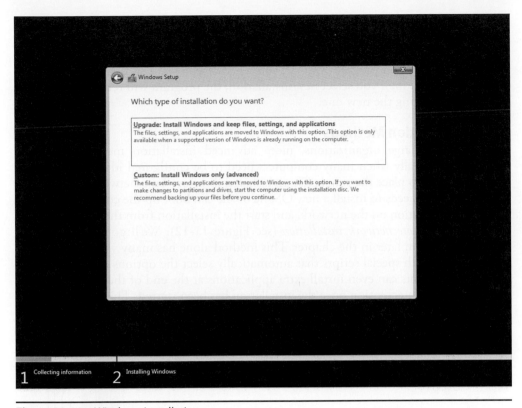

Figure 11-11 Windows installation

 EXAM TIP Microsoft often uses the term *in-place upgrade* to define an upgrade installation, so you might see it on the CompTIA A+ 1102 exam. On the other hand, Microsoft documentation also uses the term for a completely different process, called a *repair installation*, so read whatever questions you get on the exam carefully for context. For repair installations, see Chapter 16.

Before you begin an upgrade of Windows, *always* back up all user data files! You can use the backup tools in Windows or a third-party tool, but don't skip this step. You should also make sure that applications and drivers have support or are backward compatible. Naturally, you should doublecheck to ensure that your hardware is compatible with the Windows version you're installing.

To begin the upgrade of Windows, you should run the appropriate program from the optical disc or USB drive. This usually means inserting a Windows installation disc/disk into your system while your old OS is running, which autostarts the installation program. The installation program will ask you whether you want to perform an upgrade or a new installation; if you select new installation, the program will remove the existing OS before installing the new one.

Other Installation Methods

In medium to large organizations, more advanced installation methods are often employed, especially when many computers need to be configured identically. A common method is to place the source files in a shared directory on a network server. Then, whenever a tech needs to install a new OS, he or she can boot up the computer, connect to the source location on the network, and start the installation from there. This is called generically a *remote network installation* (see Figure 11-12). We'll go deeper into this type of installation later in the chapter. This method alone has many variations and can be automated with special scripts that automatically select the options and components needed. The scripts can even install extra applications at the end of the OS installation, all without user intervention once the installation has been started. This type of installation is called an *unattended installation*.

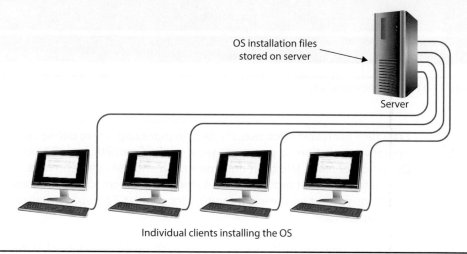

OS installation files
stored on server

Server

Individual clients installing the OS

Figure 11-12   Remote network installation

Another type of installation that is very popular for re-creating standard configurations is an *image deployment* (see Figure 11-13). An image is a complete copy of a hard drive volume on which an operating system and any desired application software programs have been preinstalled. Images can be stored on servers, optical discs, or flash-media drives, in which case the tech runs special software on the computer that copies the image onto the local hard drive or SSD. Images can also be stored on special network servers, in which case the tech connects to the image server by using special software that copies the image from the server to the local HDD or SSD. A leader in this technology for many years was Norton Ghost, which was available from Symantec. That Symantec is no more, but the enterprise-focused Symantec Ghost Solution Suite continues on as a product offered by Broadcom. Other similar programs are Clonezilla and Acronis True Image.

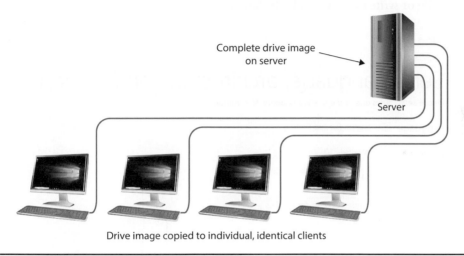

Figure 11-13 Image deployment over a network

The OS Installation Process

At the most basic level, installing any operating system follows a standard set of steps. You turn on the computer, insert an operating system disc/disk into the optical drive or USB port, or access the media some other way, and follow the installation wizard until you have everything completed. Along the way, you'll accept the *end-user license agreement (EULA)*—the terms and conditions for using the OS—and enter the product key that says you're not a pirate. The product key is invariably located on the installation disc's case or USB packaging. Ah, but there is a devil in the details!

First, you need to decide on a clean install, an upgrade install, or a multiboot install. Review the steps covered earlier in this chapter to make your decision. The following is an example of a clean install of Windows.

Second, Windows isn't the only operating system out there. Even though the following example uses Windows, keep in mind that both macOS and all Linux desktop distributions share similar installation steps.

Windows 10 Clean install Process

Start by booting your computer from some sort of Windows 10 installation media, which you can create with the free Media Creation Tool from Microsoft. This tool lets you select the language, edition, and architecture for the Windows install you are performing (see Figure 11-14). With those details out of the way, you can then create either an ISO file or write directly to a USB flash drive.

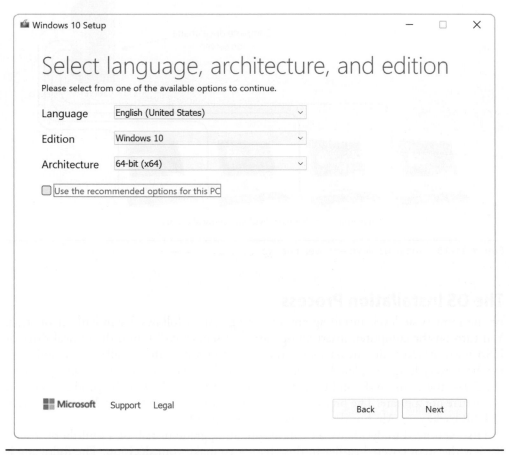

Figure 11-14 Windows Media Creation Tool

Once you're booted into the installer, Windows will ask for language, time and currency, and keyboard settings, as shown in Figure 11-15. These are sometimes called *regional settings.* Click Next to proceed.

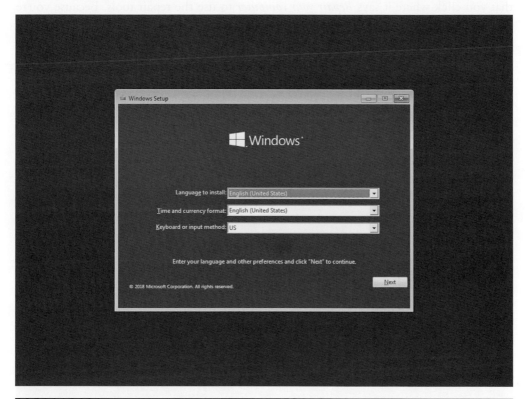

Figure 11-15 Windows regional settings

 EXAM TIP Early in the installation process, if you're installing Windows onto drives connected via a RAID controller, you'll be prompted to press F6 to *load alternative third-party drivers if necessary.* Nothing happens immediately when you respond to this request. You'll be prompted later in the process to insert a driver disc.

The next screen starts the installation process, but note the lower-left corner. This screen also enables techs to start the installation disc's repair tools (see Figure 11-16). You'll learn more about those tools in Chapter 16, but for now all you need to know is that you click where it says *Repair your computer* to use the repair tools. Because you're just installing Windows in this chapter, click Install now.

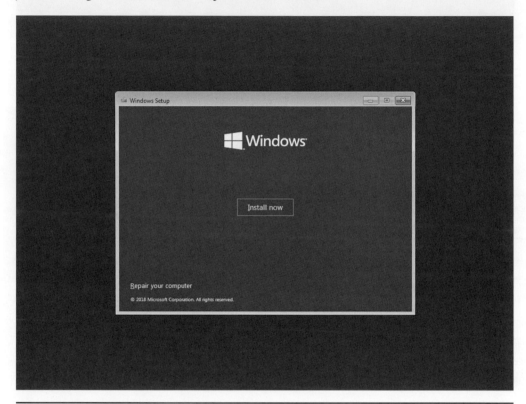

Figure 11-16   The Windows Setup welcome screen

The next screen prompts you to enter your product key before you do anything else, as you can see in Figure 11-17. The product key comes with the installation media. You should never lose it.

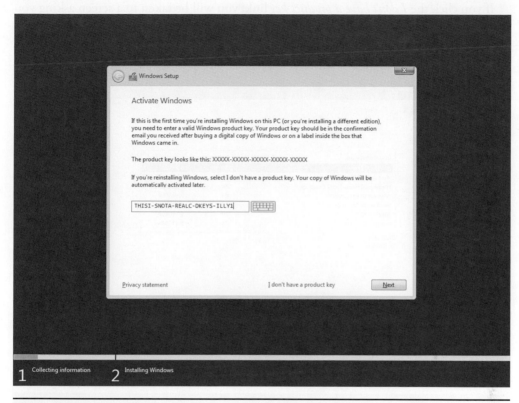

Figure 11-17 The Windows product key screen

Every Windows installation disc/disk contains all of the available editions within a version. The product key not only verifies the legitimacy of your purchase; it also tells the installer which edition you purchased.

If you click the *I don't have a product key* link, you will be taken to a screen asking you which version of Windows you would like to install (see Figure 11-18).

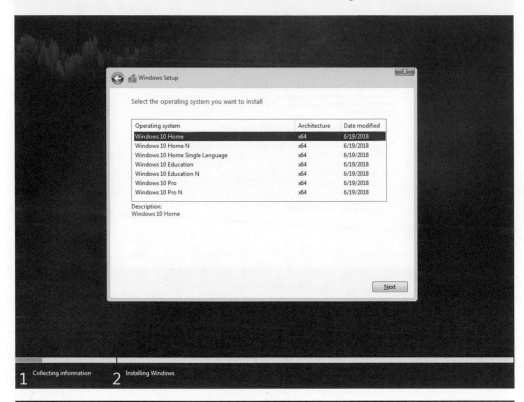

Figure 11-18 Choosing the edition of Windows you want to install

Lest you start to think that you've discovered a way to install Windows without paying for it, you should know that doing this simply installs a 30-day trial of the operating system. After 30 days, you will no longer be able to boot to the desktop without entering a valid product key that matches the edition of Windows you installed.

After you enter the product key and click Next, you'll encounter Microsoft's EULA, shown in Figure 11-19. You must accept the license terms and click Next to proceed.

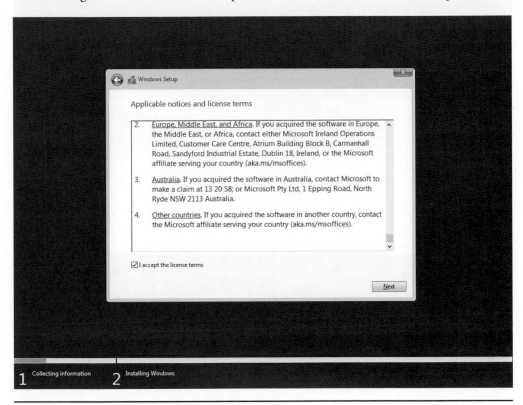

Figure 11-19   The Windows EULA

On the next page, you get to decide whether you'd like to do an upgrade installation or a clean install. Windows calls the clean install a *Custom* installation, as you can see in Figure 11-20. This option enables customization of various items, such as partitions.

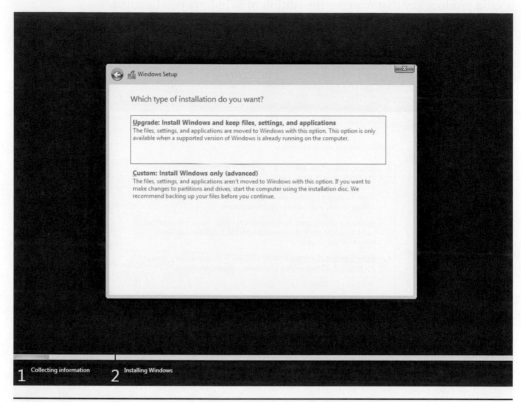

Figure 11-20   Choose your installation type.

Figure 11-21 shows how you can partition hard drives and choose a destination partition for Windows. From this screen, you can click the New link to display a variety of partitioning options.

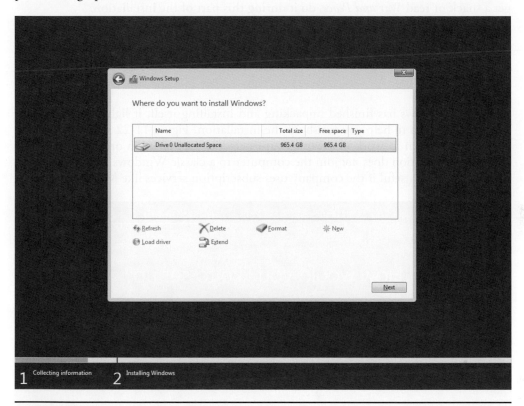

Figure 11-21   The partitioning screen

Once you've partitioned drives and selected a partition into which to install Windows, the installation process takes over, copying files, expanding files, installing features, and just generally doing lots of computerish things. This can take a while, so if you need to get a snack or read *War and Peace*, do it during this part of the installation.

NOTE It doesn't take *that* long to install Windows. Windows 10 is far snappier than its predecessors, especially on an SSD.

When Windows has finished unpacking and installing itself, it lights up the oh-so-irritating Cortana to help you finish up the installation. Figure 11-22 shows where you configure a system to work in a workgroup (personal use) or in an organization. Note that the latter option does *not* join the computer to a classic Windows Active Directory domain, but it is useful if the company uses subscription services like Microsoft 365.

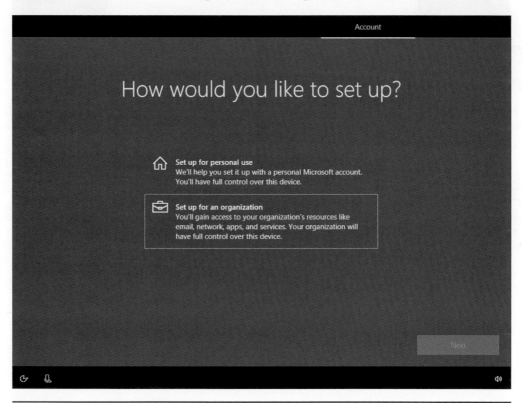

Figure 11-22 Choosing personal or organization

This following screen (see Figure 11-23) asks you to set up a username and password for your main user account. All operating systems require the creation of this account. Cortana asks you to choose a username and tries to get you to open a Microsoft account if you don't already have one. I skip the Microsoft account and simply create a regular local account on the computer. My editors use Microsoft accounts. Choose the option that works best for you.

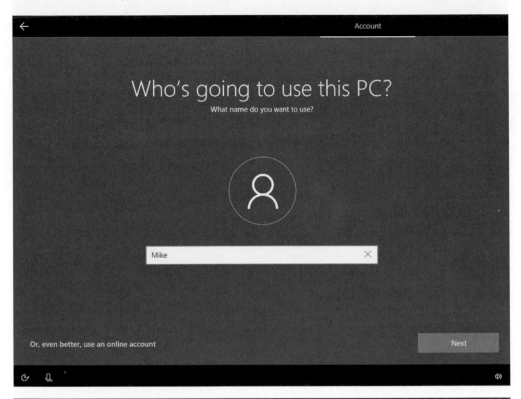

Figure 11-23   Choosing a username

 EXAM TIP   Expect a question on *workgroup vs. domain setup* on the CompTIA A+ 1102 exam. Choosing the *Set up for personal use* option in Figure 11-22 puts you squarely in a workgroup. Installing a computer in a classic Windows Active Directory domain requires a lot of steps on behalf of the domain administrator. The computer needs to be joined to the domain. A user needs a domain account set up. Windows Active Directory domains accentuate security; they require more aggressive setup.

Microsoft and Apple are big on users logging in with accounts tied not to the PC, but to online Microsoft and Apple. These accounts provide some amount of convenience and are acceptable for home users, but any organization larger than the smallest mom-and-pop shops will skip these and use more traditional accounts. Your author recommends you do the same.

Microsoft also adds another installation feature at this point, privacy settings (see Figure 11-24). Turning everything off on this screen still doesn't prevent Microsoft from taking some amount of information.

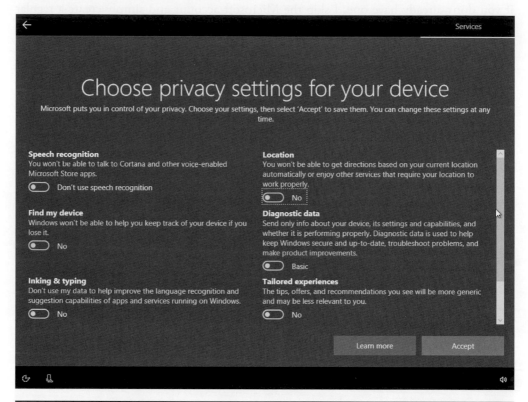

Figure 11-24   Choosing privacy settings for your device

 NOTE   Activation is mandatory, but you can skip this step during installation. You have 30 days in which to activate the product, during which time it works normally. If you don't activate it within that time frame, the OS will be labeled as not genuine and you won't receive updates. Don't worry about forgetting, though, because once it's installed, Windows frequently reminds you to activate it with a balloon message over the tray area of the taskbar. The messages even tell you how many days you have left.

Once you're past the privacy settings screen, Windows gets to work on the installation (see Figure 11-25) and warns you that it may take some time and that you should not turn off your PC. Awfully polite for a piece of software, don't you think?

Figure 11-25
Okay, Windows,
thanks for the
warning!

This might take several minutes

Don't turn off your PC

Installing Windows over a Network

Techs working for big corporations can end up installing Windows a lot. When you have a hundred PCs to take care of and Microsoft launches a new update of Windows, you don't want to have to walk from cubicle to cubicle with an installation disc, running one install after the other. You already know about automated installations, but network installations take this one step further.

Imagine another scenario. You're still a tech for a large company, but your boss has decided that every new PC will use an image with a predetermined set of applications and configurations. You need to put the image on every workstation, but most of them don't have optical drives. Network installation saves the day again!

The phrase "network installation" can involve many different tools depending on which version of Windows you use. Most importantly, the machines that receive the installations (the *clients*) need to be connected to a server. That server might be another copy of regular Windows, or it might be a full-fledged server running Windows Server. The serving PC needs to host an image, which can either be the default installation of Windows or a custom image, often created by the network administrator.

All of the server-side issues should be handled by a network administrator—setting up a server to deploy Windows installations and images goes beyond what the CompTIA A+ exams cover.

On the client side, you'll need to use the *Preboot Execution Environment (PXE)*. PXE uses multiple protocols such as IP, DHCP, and DNS to enable your computer to boot from a network location. That means the PC needs no installation disc or USB drive. Just plug your computer into the network and go! Okay, it's a little more complicated than that.

To enable PXE, you'll need to enter system setup; in CompTIA speak, you need to configure the *BIOS (on-board NIC)* for PXE boot. Find the screen that configures your NIC (see Figure 11-26). If there is a PXE setting there, enable it. You'll also need to change the boot order so that the PC boots from a network location first.

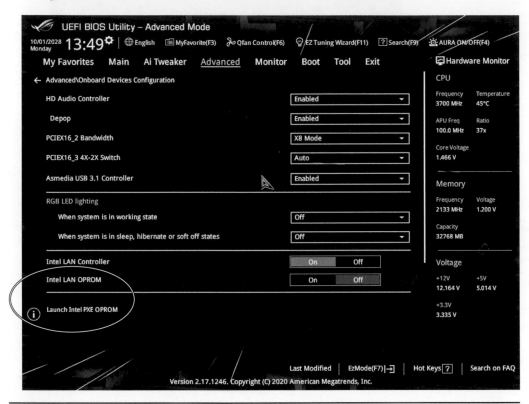

Figure 11-26   Setting up PXE in system setup

 NOTE   Most, but not all, NICs support PXE. To boot from a network location without PXE, you can create boot media that forces your PC to boot from a mapped network location.

When you reboot the PC, you'll see the familiar first screens of the boot process. At some point, you should also see an instruction to "Press F12 for network boot." (It's almost always F12.) The PC will attempt to find a server on the network to which it can connect. When it does, you'll be asked to press F12 again to continue booting from the network, as you can see in Figure 11-27.

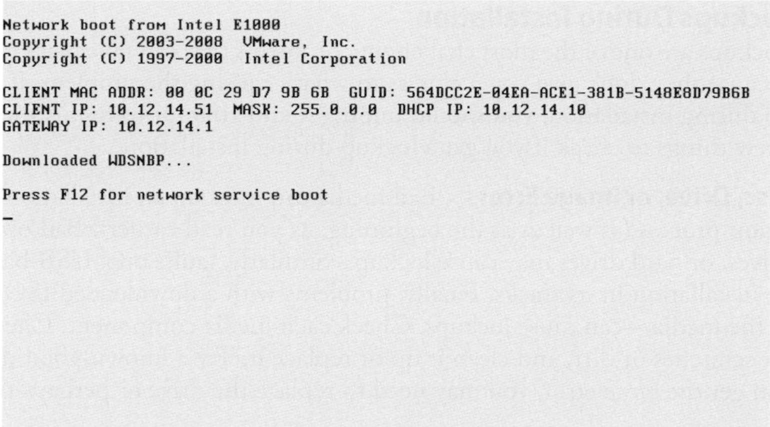

Figure 11-27
Network boot

```
Network boot from Intel E1000
Copyright (C) 2003-2008  VMware, Inc.
Copyright (C) 1997-2000  Intel Corporation

CLIENT MAC ADDR: 00 0C 29 D7 9B 6B   GUID: 564DCC2E-04EA-ACE1-381B-5148E8D79B6B
CLIENT IP: 10.12.14.51   MASK: 255.0.0.0   DHCP IP: 10.12.14.10
GATEWAY IP: 10.12.14.1

Downloaded WDSNBP...

Press F12 for network service boot
_
```

Depending on how many images are prepared on the server, you'll either be taken directly to the Windows installation screen or be asked to pick from multiple images. Pick the option you need, and everything else should proceed as if you were installing Windows from the local optical drive.

Troubleshooting Installation Problems

The term "installation problem" is rather deceptive. The installation process itself almost never fails. Usually, something else fails during the process that is generally interpreted as an "install failure." Let's look at some typical installation problems and how to correct them.

Media Errors

If you're going to have a problem with a Windows installation, have a media error, like a scratched DVD or a corrupted USB drive. It's always better to have the error right off the bat as opposed to when the installation is nearly complete.

No Boot Device Present When Booting Off the Windows Installation Disc

Either the installation media is bad or the system setup is not set to look at that installation media first. Access the system setup utility as discussed in Chapter 5.

Graphical Mode Errors

Once the graphical part of the installation begins, errors can come from a number of sources, such as hardware or driver problems. Failure to detect hardware properly by any version of Windows Setup can be avoided by simply researching compatibility beforehand. Or, if you decided to skip that step, you might be lucky and only have a hardware detection error involving a noncritical hardware device. You can troubleshoot this problem at your leisure. In a sense, you are handing in your homework late, checking out compatibility, and finding a proper driver after Windows is installed.

Lockups During Installation

Lockups are one of the most challenging problems that can take place during installation, because they don't give you a clue as to what's causing the problem. If your system locks up during installation, you should unplug it and attempt to restart the process. Here are a few things to check if you get a lockup during installation.

Disc, Drive, or Image Errors   Bad media can mess up an installation during the installation process (as well as at the beginning, as you read earlier). Bad optical discs, optical drives, or hard drives may cause lockups. Similarly, faults on a USB-based drive can stop an installation in its tracks. Finally, problems with a downloaded ISO image—also part of the media—can cause lockups. Check each media component. Check the optical disc for scratches or dirt, and clean it up or replace it. Try a known-good disc in the drive. If you get the same error, you may need to replace the drive or perhaps the ISO.

Log Files   Windows versions before Windows 10 generate a number of special text files called *log files* that track the progress of certain processes. Windows creates different log files for different purposes. The Windows installation process creates about 20 setup log files, organized by installation phase. Each phase creates a setuperr.log file to track any errors during that phase of the installation. Windows 10 creates a setup.etl file (among others) in the %WINDIR%/Panther folder that you can open with Event Viewer.

Try This!

Locating Windows Setup Log Files

1. If you are using a pre–Windows 10 version, go to the following Microsoft Web site: https://technet.microsoft.com/en-us/library/Hh824819.aspx. For Windows 10 and 11, check out https://docs.microsoft.com/en-us/windows-hardware/manufacture/desktop/windows-setup-log-files-and-event-logs.

2. Identify the specific log file locations and descriptions.

3. Using Windows Explorer or File Explorer on your PC, navigate to the specific log file locations and see if you can find your setup log files.

Who knows, you may be on your way to becoming a Microsoft log file reader!

Windows stores these log files in the Windows directory (the location in which the OS is installed). These operating systems have powerful recovery options, so the chances of ever actually having to read a log file, understand it, and then get something fixed because of that understanding are pretty small. What makes log files handy is when you call Microsoft or a hardware manufacturer. They *love* to read these files, and they actually have people who understand them. Don't worry about trying to understand log files for the CompTIA A+ exams; just make sure you know the names of the log files and their location. Leave the details to the übergeeks.

Post-Installation Tasks

You might think that's enough installation work for one day, but your task list has a few more things. They include updating the OS with patches, upgrading drivers, restoring user data files, and migrating and retiring systems.

Windows Updates

Someone once described an airliner as consisting of millions of parts flying in close formation. I think that's also a good description for an operating system. And we can even carry that analogy further by thinking about all of the maintenance required to keep an airliner safely flying. Like an airliner, the parts (programming code) of your OS were created by different people, and some parts may even have been contracted out. Although each component is tested as much as possible, and the assembled OS is also tested, it's not possible to test for every possible combination of events. Sometimes a piece is simply found to be defective. Generically, the fix for such a problem is a corrective program called a *patch*.

In the past, Microsoft provided patches for individual problems. They also accumulated patches up to some sort of critical mass and then bundled them together as a *service pack*, but Windows 7 was the last version to get one. Today, Windows simply sends individual *updates* to your system via the Internet.

Immediately after installing Windows, Windows will install the latest updates on the computer. The easiest way to accomplish this task it to turn on *Windows Update*. Chapter 14 covers this process more thoroughly.

Upgrading Drivers

During installation, you may decide to go with the default drivers that come with Windows and then upgrade them to the latest drivers after the fact. This is a good strategy because installation is a complicated task that you can simplify by installing old but adequate drivers. Maybe those newest drivers are just a week old—waiting until after the Windows installation to install new drivers gives you a usable driver to go back to if the new driver turns out to be a lemon.

Restoring User Data Files (If Applicable)

Remember when you backed up the user data files before your upgrade installation? You don't? Well, check again, because now is the time to restore that data. Your method of restoring depends on how you backed up the files in the first place. If you used a third-party backup program, you need to install it before you can restore those files, but if you used Backup and Restore, you are in luck, because they are installed by default. If you did something simpler, such as copying to optical discs, USB or other external drive, or a network location, all you have to do is copy the files back to the local hard drive. Good luck!

 NOTE Backup and Restore is called System Restore in Windows 10.

Installing Essential Software

The final step in the post-installation process is to install the software that makes the computer work the way you or your client wants. If you install software that requires a license key, have it ready. Similarly, if you install subscription software such as Microsoft Office 365, make sure you have accurate usernames and passwords available. Don't forget to install Steam and download essential leisure applications!

Migrating and Retiring Systems

Seasons change and so does the state of the art in computing. At a certain point in a computer's life, you'll need to retire an old system. This means you must move the data and users to a new system or at least a new hard drive—a process called *migration*—and then safely dispose of the old system. Microsoft offers a few tools to accomplish this task, and because it's important to know about them for the CompTIA A+ exams (not to mention for your next new computer purchase), I'm going to go over them.

Third-Party Migration Tools

Windows has always been pretty good about providing tools to make migration of single systems fairly straightforward.

User State Migration Tool

If you're the sort of computer user who demands maximum functionality and power from your operating system, you'll probably want to use the *User State Migration Tool (USMT)*. The USMT's primary use is in businesses because it has to be run in a Windows Server Active Directory domain. If you need to migrate many users, the USMT is the tool.

 NOTE USMT is extremely handy for large-scale Windows operating system deployments. Microsoft provides a detailed overview that includes the benefits and limitations of USMT. Take a look here: https://docs.microsoft .com/en-us/windows/deployment/usmt/usmt-overview.

Migration Practices

When talking about migration or retirement in terms of security, you need to answer one question: What do you do with the old system or drive?

All but the most vanilla new installations have sensitive data on them, even if it's simply e-mail messages or notes-to-self that would cause embarrassment if discovered. Most PCs, especially in a work environment, contain a lot of sensitive data. You can't just format C: and hand over the drive.

Follow three principles when migrating or retiring a computer. First, migrate your users and data information in a secure environment. Until you get passwords properly in place and test the security of the new system, you can't consider that system secure. Second, remove data remnants from hard drives that you store or give to charity. Third, recycle the older equipment; don't throw it in the trash. PC recyclers go through a process of deconstructing hardware, breaking system units, keyboards, printers, and even monitors into their basic plastics, metals, and glass for reuse.

The easiest way for someone to compromise or access sensitive data is to simply walk up and take it when you're not looking. This is especially true when you are in the process of copying information to a new, unprotected system. Don't set a copy to run while you go out to lunch, but rather be there to supervise and remove any remnant data that might still reside on any mass storage devices, especially hard drives.

Data Destruction

You might think that, as easy as it seems to be to lose data, you could readily get rid of data if you tried. That's definitely not the case with magnetic media such as hard drives. When you delete something in Windows, or even empty the Recycle Bin, the "deleted" data remains on your storage device until new data overwrites it, or replaces it. (This "deleted" data is also what you see as free space in Windows.) This can be a big security hole when you dispose of a drive.

Cleaning a drive completely is very difficult. You can either physically destroy the hard drive or *sanitize* it using a software utility. Physical destruction isn't complicated—you bust up the drive into tiny little bits or melt it. Methods to accomplish physical destruction include *drilling*, *shredding*, and *degaussing* (reducing or removing the magnetic fields that store data on HDDs). Incineration pretty much clears all data. Keep in mind that, as hard drives advance and pack more data into smaller spaces, you'll need to break the hard drive into smaller pieces to prevent anyone from recovering your data.

 EXAM TIP Professional hard drive disposal services are third-party vendors that will guarantee they have truly, thoroughly destroyed drives by issuing a *certificate of destruction/recycling*. This certificate brings peace of mind, among other things, that precious data won't slip into unwanted hands.

Sanitizing your drive means the hard drive will still function once the data has been destroyed. There are several more or less effective ways to do this. The CompTIA A+ exam wants you to know the difference between a standard format and a *low-level format*. You already learned about standard formatting back in Chapter 9, so how is low-level formatting different? With older drives (pre-1990s), low-level formatting would create the physical marks on the disk surface so that the drive knew where to store data; in process, it erased the data from the drive. This was initially done at the factory, but utilities existed to repeat this operation later. As drives became more complex, hard drive manufacturers disabled the ability to perform low-level formats outside the factory.

Today, the term "low-level formatting" is often used to describe a zero-fill or overwrite operation. This process returns the drive to a state as close to like-new as possible by writing zeros to every location on the drive.

There are a number of *erasing/wiping* utilities to erase any old, deleted data that hasn't been overwritten yet. Simply put, this overwrites the free space on your drive with junk data that makes the original data harder to recover. There are literally hundreds of drive wiping tools you can use in Windows. Figure 11-28 shows a popular utility called CBL Data Shredder.

Figure 11-28
CBL Data
Shredder in
action

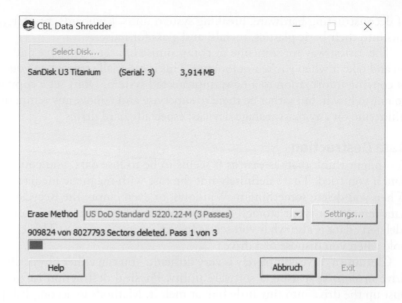

Recycle

An important and relatively easy way to be an environmentally conscious computer user is to follow *recycling or repurposing best practices*. Recycling products such as paper and printer cartridges not only keeps them out of overcrowded landfills but also ensures that the more toxic products are disposed of in the right way. Safely disposing of hardware containing hazardous materials, such as computer monitors, protects both people and the environment.

Anyone who's ever tried to sell a computer more than three or four years old learns a hard lesson: they're not worth much, if anything at all. It's a real temptation to take that old computer and just toss it in the garbage, but never do that!

First of all, many parts of your computer—such as various circuit boards—contain hazardous materials that pollute the environment. Luckily, thousands of companies now specialize in computer recycling and will gladly accept your old computer. If you have enough computers, they might even pick them up. If you can't find a recycler, call your local municipality's waste authority to see where to drop off your system.

An even better alternative for your old computer is donation. Many organizations actively look for old computers to refurbish and to donate to schools and other organizations. Just keep in mind that the computer can be too old—not even a school wants a computer more than five or six years old.

No Installation Is Perfect

Even when the installation seems smooth, issues may slowly surface, especially in the case of upgrades. Be prepared to reinstall applications or deal with new functions that were absent in the previous OS. If things really fall apart, you can go back to the previous OS. Or, if you have an OEM computer (one built by, for example, Dell or HP instead of by you), your computer likely came with a special recovery partition on its hard drive, a recovery disc, or a recovery USB flash drive; you can use any of these to restore your operating system to its factory settings. You usually invoke a system recovery by pressing a certain key during boot-up—usually F10 or F11—and then following a set of prompts.

The procedures I've laid out in this chapter may seem like a lot of work—how bad could it be to grab installation media, fling a copy of Windows onto a system, and, as the saying goes, let the chips fall where they may? Plenty bad, is how bad. Not only is understanding these procedures important for the CompTIA A+ certification exams, but these procedures can also save your, ah, hide once you're a working PC tech and tasked to install the latest version of Windows 10 on the boss's new computer!

Chapter Review

Questions

1. Which of the following is not a way to physically destroy data on a hard drive?

    A. Drilling

    B. Shredding

    C. Low-level formatting

    D. Degaussing

2. Michael's hard drive is causing an installation lockup. What should he check first to view specific installation steps and track errors?

    A. Patch

    B. Log files

    C. Recovery partition

    D. Service pack

3. Cindy's client wants a new workstation. The client's small business has ten current workstations connected in a Windows domain, and the client wants the new workstation to be part of that domain. What edition of Windows 10 should Cindy install on the new computer to accomplish this goal and provide the best value?

    A. Windows 10 Starter Edition

    B. Windows 10 Home

    C. Windows 10 Pro

    D. Windows 10 Enterprise

4. You will need a dedicated server system in order to set up a Windows _____ computer.

    A. 10 Pro

    B. Domain

    C. 10 Enterprise

    D. 10 Home

5. What tool enables installing Windows over a network?

   A. Windows DVD

   B. NetBoot

   C. PXE

   D. Windows can't be installed over a network.

6. When you install an operating system alongside an existing operating system, what do you create?

   A. A clean install

   B. An upgrade installation

   C. A multiboot installation

   D. A network installation

7. If you do not complete the activation process for Windows, what will happen to your computer?

   A. Nothing. Activation is optional.

   B. The computer will work fine for 30 days and then Windows will be disabled.

   C. Microsoft will not know how to contact you to provide upgrade information.

   D. It will work if you check the "I promise to pay for Windows later" box.

8. If Windows locks up during the installation, what should you do?

   A. Press CTRL-ALT-DEL to restart the installation process.

   B. Push the Reset button to restart the installation process.

   C. Press the ESC key to cancel the installation process.

   D. Unplug the computer and restart the installation process.

9. Which term describes the process of getting the latest version of your operating system?

   A. Hot fix

   B. Hot pack

   C. Update

   D. Service release

10. Which tool is handy for large-scale Windows OS deployments that have to be run in a Windows Server Active Directory domain and need to migrate many users?

   A. BitLocker

   B. RDP

   C. PXE

   D. User State Migration Tool

Answers

1. **C.** Low-level formatting does not physically destroy the hard drive, allowing it to be reused.

2. **B.** Because optical drives and hard drives can cause installation lockups, Michael should first check the setup log files to examine specific installation steps and track errors.

3. **C.** Windows 10 Pro offers the best choice here. The Enterprise edition would also work, but it costs more and adds features the client doesn't need.

4. **B.** A Windows domain requires a lot of steps on behalf of the domain administrator and the computer needs to be joined to the domain. A user needs a domain account set up before anything else.

5. **C.** The Preboot Execution Environment, or PXE, enables installation of Windows over a network.

6. **C.** An OS added to an existing OS creates a multiboot system.

7. **B.** If you do not complete the activation process for Windows 7, the computer will work fine for 30 days and then Windows will be disabled.

8. **D.** If Windows locks up during the installation, you should unplug the computer and restart the installation process.

9. **C.** An update is used to get the latest version of your operating system, including fixes for bugs and security flaws.

10. **D.** The UMST is the go-to tool for large-scale Windows operating system deployments (such as large businesses) that have to be run in a Windows Server Active Directory domin and need to migrate many users.

CHAPTER 12

Working with Operating Systems

In this chapter, you will learn how to

- Explore Registry components
- Explore and use Windows tools and settings
- Understand the differences between Windows Administrative Tools and Processes, Applications, and Services
- Identify common features and tools of macOS

Windows is powerful, easy to use, surprisingly idiot proof, backwardly compatible, and robust. A large part of Windows' power is hidden—*under the hood*—in programs and processes that Microsoft doesn't want normal users to see. For the record, I think hiding anything normal users don't need is a smart idea. Technicians, on the other hand, need to not only understand these processes and programs, but also know how to use, configure, and fix them when needed. This chapter doesn't focus solely on Windows though! Here is a look at what this chapter will cover: the Registry, Windows 10 features and tools, using Windows 10 Control Panel utilities and settings, Windows 11 features that differ from Windows 10 features, and identifying common features and tools of macOS. Let's dig in!

1102

Registry

The *Registry* is a critical database, core to every Windows system, that stores everything about a PC, including information on all the hardware, network information, user preferences, file types, passwords, desktop color...virtually everything you might find in Windows. Almost any form of configuration you do to a Windows system involves editing the Registry, and your system will not boot into Windows without a properly configured Registry. Every version of Windows stores the numerous Registry files (called *hives*) in the \%SystemRoot%\ System32\config folder and each user account folder. Although you rarely have to access these files directly, every competent tech should know how to access the Registry, understand its basic components, and know how to manually edit the Registry. So, without further ado, let's explore the Registry!

Accessing the Registry

When you use Windows' Settings or Control Panel (or just about any other utility), you are editing the Registry; however, there are some situations where a tech might need to access the Registry directly.

You can access and open the Registry directly by using the go-to command in the *Registry Editor* (also known by its executable name, *regedit*) on your machine and compare what you see to the examples in this chapter. To open the Registry Editor, enter **regedit** in the Start | Search bar. You can also run regedit from the command line.

Registry Components

The Registry is organized in a tree structure similar to the folders on the file system. Once you open the Registry Editor in Windows, you will see five main subgroups, or *root keys*:

- HKEY_CLASSES_ROOT
- HKEY_CURRENT_USER
- HKEY_LOCAL_MACHINE
- HKEY_USERS
- HKEY_CURRENT_CONFIG

Try opening one of these root keys by clicking the plus sign to its left; note that more subkeys are listed underneath. A subkey also can have other subkeys, or *values*. Values define aspects of the subkey. Figure 12-1 shows an example of a subkey with some values. Notice that the Registry Editor shows only keys—root keys and subkeys—on the left and values on the right. Each of the root keys has a specific function, so let's take a look at them individually.

HKEY_CLASSES_ROOT

Historically, the HKEY_CLASSES_ROOT root key defined the standard class objects used by Windows. A *class object* is a named group of functions that defines what you can do with the object it represents. Pretty much everything that has to do with files on the system is defined by a class object. The Registry, for example, uses two class objects to define the JPG image file. One object is located at HKEY_CLASSES_ROOT\.jpg and the other object is located at HKEY_CURRENT_USER\Software\Classes\.jpg and covers user-specific associations for JPG files.

This root key combines class objects from \Software\Classes under both HKEY_CURRENT_USER and HKEY_LOCAL_MACHINE to provide backward compatibility for older applications.

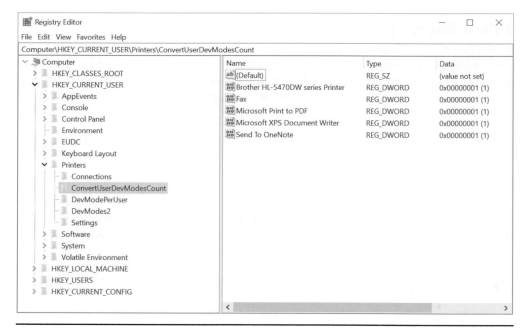

Figure 12-1 Typical Registry root keys, subkeys, and values

HKEY_CURRENT_USER and HKEY_USERS

Windows is designed to support more than one user on the same system, storing personalized information such as desktop colors, screensavers, and the contents of the desktop for every user that has an account on the system. HKEY_CURRENT_USER stores the current user settings, and HKEY_USERS stores all of the personalized information for each user. While you certainly can change items such as the screensaver here, the better way is to right-click on the desktop and select Personalize.

HKEY_LOCAL_MACHINE

The HKEY_LOCAL_MACHINE root key contains all the data for a system's non-user-specific configurations. This encompasses every device and every program in your computer.

HKEY_CURRENT_CONFIG

If the values in HKEY_LOCAL_MACHINE have more than one option, such as two different monitors, this root key defines which one is currently being used. Because most people have only one type of monitor and similar equipment, this area is almost never touched.

SIM Check out the excellent trio of sims on "Registry Files Location" in the Chapter 12 section of the online TotalSims here: https://www.totalsem.com/training-simulations/.The combination of Type!, Show!, and Click! sim will prepare you for any scenario-based question on the Windows Registry.

Talkin' Registry

When describing a Registry setting, we use a simple nomenclature. For example, I once moved my copy of *World of Warcraft* from my C: drive to my D: drive and had problems when the program started. I went online to https://www.blizzard.com (home of Blizzard Entertainment, the folks who make *World of Warcraft*) and contacted the support staff, who gave me instructions to access the Registry and make this change:

> *Go to HKLM\SOFTWARE\Blizzard Entertainment\World of Warcraft and change the GamePath object and the InstallPath object to reflect the new drive letter of your new WoW location.*

To do so, I opened the Registry Editor. Using this nomenclature, I was able to find the location of these Registry settings. Figure 12-2 shows this location. Compare this image to the path described in the instructions from Blizzard. Note that HKEY_LOCAL_MACHINE is abbreviated as HKLM.

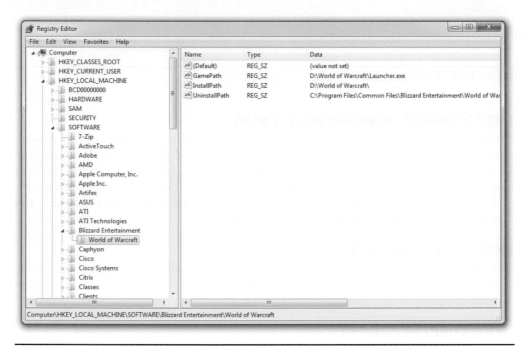

Figure 12-2   Editing the Registry to move *World of Warcraft* to a new drive

To describe the location of a specific Registry value, like where the Blizzard tech told me to go, requires a little bit of repetition. To wit, in the previous example, World of Warcraft is a subkey to Blizzard Entertainment, which is in turn a subkey to the root key HKLM. The World of Warcraft subkey has four values. All keys have the (Default) value, so in this case the World of Warcraft subkey offers three functional values.

Values must have a defined type of data they store:

- **String value** These are the most flexible type of value and are very common. You can put any form of data in these.
- **Binary value** These values store nothing more than long strings of ones and zeros.
- **DWORD value** These values are like Binary values but are limited to exactly 32 bits.
- **QWORD value** These values are like Binary values but are limited to exactly 64 bits.

There are other types of values, but these four are used for most Registry entries.

Manual Registry Edits

The most common scenario where you need to access the Registry directly is when you're directed to do so by a tech support Web site, a vendor's patch, or a tech support technician. Be careful! When you do find yourself using the Registry Editor to access the Registry, you risk breaking things in Windows: applications might not start, utilities might not work, or worst of all, your computer might not boot. To prevent these problems, always make a backup of the Registry before you change anything. Once the backup is in a safe place (I like to use a thumb drive, personally), reboot the system to see if the changes you made had the desired result. If it worked, great. If not, you'll need to restore the old Registry settings using your backup. Let's watch this in action.

One of the more common manual Registry edits is to delete autostarting programs. I want to prevent a program installed by my Logitech GamePanel keyboard and mouse from autostarting. The most common place for making this change is here:

```
HKLM\SOFTWARE\Microsoft\Windows\CurrentVersion\Run
```

Opening the Registry Editor and going to this subkey, you'll see something like what's shown in Figure 12-3.

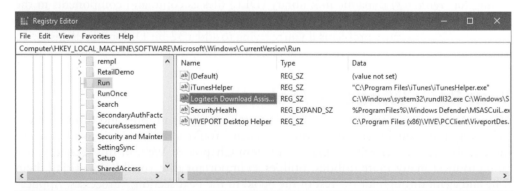

Figure 12-3 Mike's Run subkey

Before I delete these keys, I'm going to save a copy of my Registry. The Registry Editor's Export feature enables you to save either the full Registry or only a single root key or subkey (with all subkeys and values under it). Select Run from the left pane and then click File | Export. Save the subkey as a Registration file with the extension .reg. Be sure to put that file somewhere you'll remember. Should you need to restore that key, use the File | Import command, or just right-click the icon and click Merge as shown in Figure 12-4.

Figure 12-4
Merging keys
from a backup file

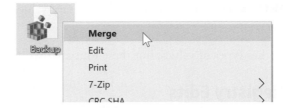

Command-Line Registry Editing Tools

Windows includes a couple of command-line tools to edit the Registry (plus a lot more in PowerShell). The two that you might need on occasion are reg and regsvr32.

NOTE If the command-line interface is new to you, you might want to flag this section and skip it for now, then return to it after reading about the command line and how it works in Chapter 15.

The *reg* command is a full Registry editing tool. You can view Registry keys and values, import and export some or all of a Registry, and even compare two different versions of a Registry. The tool is so powerful that it has multiple levels of help so you can tailor a command to accomplish very tight Registry edits. For example, typing **reg /?** brings up a list of 12 specific operations that you can search for help on, such as reg query /? and reg add /?.

The *regsvr32* command, in contrast with reg, can modify the Registry in only one way, adding (or *registering*) dynamic link library (DLL) files as command components in the Registry. By default, if you run regsvr32 in a 64-bit version of Windows, the 64-bit version runs. This can cause problems if you're trying to add a 32-bit DLL to the Registry. To accomplish the latter, run the regsvr32.exe file in the %SystemRoot%Syswow64 folder.

Your Basic Windows Toolset

Microsoft Windows comes with a dizzying number of built-in tools and utilities to do, well, everything you'll ever want to do to a system. You've already started to see some of these tools—remember Disk Management from Chapter 8? Well, in this section you're going to meet many more utilities, utilities so important that you'll be revisiting them time and again throughout the rest of the book! In the next section, "Processes, Applications, and Service Tools," you'll be introduced to yet another set of tools which are a bit different from the ones we are about to discuss. The difference, you ask? Let's see if you can figure it out after reading about both!

System Configuration

Techs use *System Configuration* (also known by its executable name, *msconfig*) to edit and troubleshoot operating system and program startup processes and services. System Configuration is an old tool but one we turn to again and again!

To start the System Configuration utility, go the Start | Search bar, enter **msconfig**, and click OK or press ENTER. The program runs after you provide the necessary credentials, depending on the User Account Control (UAC) setup.

The System Configuration utility offers a number of handy features, distributed across the following tabs:

- **General** Select the type of startup you would like to use for the next boot (see Figure 12-5). You can perform a normal startup with all device drivers and services launching normally, a diagnostic startup with only basic devices and services, or a selective startup where you choose whether to load system services, load startup items, or use original boot configuration.

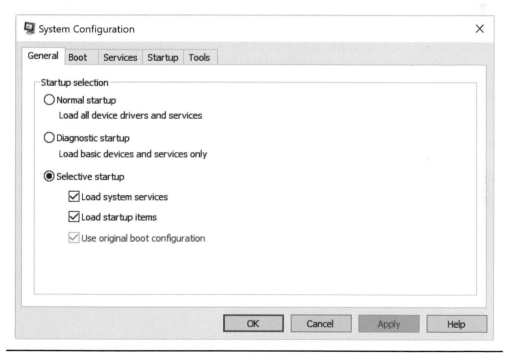

Figure 12-5 Windows 10 System Configuration

- **Boot** This tab contains advanced boot features. Here you can see every copy of Windows you have installed, set a default OS, or delete an OS from the boot menu. You can set up a safe boot, or adjust advanced options like the number of cores or amount of memory to use. Selecting Safe boot, by the way, will force Windows to start in Safe mode on every reboot until you deselect it. *Safe mode* loads minimal, generic, trusted drivers and is used for troubleshooting purposes.

- **Services** This tab is similar to the Services tab in the Task Manager. You can enable or disable any or all services running on your PC.

- **Startup** This tab lets you launch Task Manager to enable you to toggle on or off any startup programs (programs that load when you launch Windows). This is perhaps the most useful tab, especially if Windows is slow to load on your PC.

- **Tools** This tab lists many of the tools and utilities available in Windows, including Event Viewer, Performance Monitor, Command Prompt, and so on. There's nothing here that you can't find elsewhere in Windows, but it's a handy list all the same.

Windows Settings

Settings is the "one-stop-shop" utility for the vast majority of tools you'll use to work on a Windows system (see Figure 12-6). Introduced back in 2012 with Windows 8, Settings is slowly replacing the Control Panel, the traditional place to configure Windows. This creates a bit of a problem for Windows users in that, as you'll see later in this chapter, the Control Panel is still alive and well. In fact, the Control Panel is still critical for access to some utilities. This means that any given utility on your Windows system may only be accessible from Settings, only accessible from the Control Panel, or in some case accessible from both Settings and Control Panel. Sheesh! Let's dive into some of the Settings categories that you are most likely to see on the CompTIA A+ 1102 exam.

Be careful with terminology here. Microsoft calls Settings an application (app) and it uses the term *categories* for the choices inside Settings, such as "System" or "Privacy." Strange terms, but hey, it's Microsoft, so we live with these things.

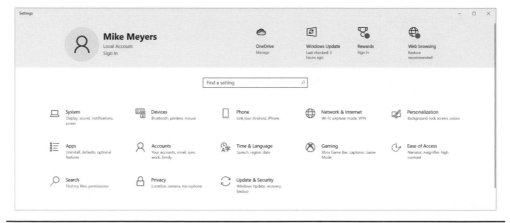

Figure 12-6 Windows Settings

Time & Language

The *Time & Language* category is used to set the time and date, add languages to your PC, and adjust speech settings. Time & Language has four sections on the left: Date & time, Region, Language, and Speech.

Date & Time   In the Date & Time section, you'll see the current date and time displayed at the top of the screen. Next, you'll see *Set time automatically* and *Set time zone automatically* options; if you set both toggles to On, Windows will automatically set the date and time based on your device's current location. If these toggles are set to Off, you can click Change to change the date, time, and time zone manually.

Region   In the Region section, you can choose your country or region from a drop-down menu. Your region determines which apps you can use from the Windows Store (not all apps are available in all regions) and will also help app makers deliver localized content. Your region does not affect your Windows display language.

Language   In the Language section, you can add languages and keyboards. To do this, click Add a language and choose the language you want to add. This will add that language's keyboard to your PC. You can switch between keyboards by clicking the language taskbar button and pick the keyboard you want to use, or you can use the keyboard shortcut WINDOWS KEY-SPACEBAR to toggle between added keyboards.

Speech   The last section in the Time & Language tab is the Speech section. Here, you can tweak some Cortana settings, such as picking what language you use to interact with your device. You can also choose the default voice for apps. This is where you can pick things such as a male or female voice and specific accents that match the country in which the computer is being used.

So that was a lot of detail, but the intent was to walk you through one section of Settings to help you understand what the workflow looks like. In the sections that follow we will talk about what other Settings do, but without the same level of detail. That said, you should open Settings and poke around to make sure you understand how everything works.

Update & Security

We use the Update & Security category for three main jobs. First, the Windows Update and Delivery Optimization sections enable you to configure how and when Windows and Store app updates are delivered. Second, the Windows Security section provides a button to launch the Windows Security app to configure anti-malware, firewalls and other security functions. Third, the Backup section and the Recovery section provide options to make backups and to restore those backups, respectively.

Update & Security also gives you access to Windows Activation, Find my device, For developers (special Windows features that are intended only for developers), and the Windows Insider Program for those who like the most cutting-edge updates (Microsoft calls these *preview builds*). Also extremely handy are the Troubleshooter tools (for a quick diagnosis and automatic fix when things go wrong with Windows) and the Device Encryption tool, specifically Bitlocker, which helps protect your information

Personalization

The *Personalization* category lets you change how Windows looks to suit your preferences. You can change the background on your desktop, colors, folder options, icons, and much more! If you have Windows, take some time to explore all of the items you can personalize. It's all about you!

Apps

Windows is useless without the many applications we use to get work (or play) done. The Apps category lists all the apps installed on your system, enables you to uninstall any of the listed apps, and view and change what apps autostart when your system starts up. Some of the awesome apps offered include Microsoft Edge, Microsoft Office, Dropbox, OneDrive, Skype, and more.

Privacy

Virtually every tech company collects a certain amount of information about their users, such as what you do with their product, where you are using it, and what else you are doing at the time. They claim that they do this to diagnose common problems by bringing together information from thousands, if not millions, of users and that such information can also be used to customize your experience. Well, yes, some of that is accurate, but they also collect a heck of a lot of other data that they don't do anything with but use it to put eerily accurate advertisements in front of you; a process known as monetization of data.

Think about apps that you may have installed on your phone. One of my favorite apps is a combination flashlight and magnifying glass. It's great for reading menus in dark restaurants, but why do the app's creators need to know my location and be able to access my microphone? They don't, but we have grown so accustomed to giving up this type of data that we don't think much about it. However, when we are tasked with creating secure systems, we have to consider potential negative outcomes.

The Privacy category enables you to limit the extent to which you're targeted for advertising. It also has a list of permissions that apps may want (such as access to your camera or microphone), enabling you to control whether *any* app can have the permission or to control which apps do.

System

The System category is, in my opinion, a big pile of settings that Microsoft couldn't find a better home for anywhere else. Lots of different settings are exposed in the System category. You can access Display options (e.g., fonts and layout) here. Moving from the visual to auditory you will find the Sound settings. Here you can select the audio input and output devices you want to use, troubleshoot them, customize volume levels, and access Bluetooth settings and connected devices.

In the Notifications & actions section, you can set the sounds you want to associate with different types of alerts, as well as where on your screen they appear. Notifications can be annoying, but they are important because they alert you to crucial incoming items. The next section of System, Focus assist, enables you to assign priority levels to different types of notifications, so you aren't interrupted every time a spam message comes in. Power & sleep is an important section that is already well covered in Chapter 23. There are plenty of other options under Settings, you have to scroll down to see all of them. Luckily, CompTIA isn't going to quiz you on every feature under System.

Devices

The Devices category enables you to make mundane adjustments to attached devices. From the main Settings window, open Devices and you will see several sections, including Bluetooth & other devices, Printers & scanners, Mouse, Touchpad, and so forth.

(Please note that what you see may vary depending on what devices your administrator wants you to have access to.) To understand what is available, just click through the Devices list. For Bluetooth & other devices, you will see the Bluetooth On/Off toggle and, when set to On, a list of devices that are or may be connected. Printers & scanners lets you see the printers you have access to, add new ones, and print to Desktop, and it provides some troubleshooting services. Mouse lets you choose button and speed settings. A quick review of the other items will inform you of what you can do, but again, these are more mundane options that are provided to let you make quick adjustments or carry out simple tasks related to devices.

Network & Internet

If you need to do anything related to connecting your system to a network or the Internet, the Network & Internet category is the place to go. Here you get quick access to your connection status, adapter settings, network sharing options, as well as dial-up, VPN, and proxy settings. Many of the available options are covered in Chapters 18, 19, 20, and 21, so check out those chapters to see the Network & Internet category in action!

Gaming

If you have ever played a newer game on an older system, or even on a newer system that is underpowered, you know that the system can freeze up or, at the very least, drop frames. Either one of these events can suck all of the joy out of gameplay. The Gaming category is here to help prevent this from happening. Here you will find options specific to Xbox Game Bar, as well as the general Game Mode option. When you select Game Mode and toggle to the On position, your system will be optimized for more stable graphics performance while you're playing a game. In addition, Game Mode prevents Windows Update from restarting Windows to install updates (but just while you're running a game).

Accounts

Whether it's a personal computer or a work computer, there may be more than one person using it, and each of those people may have differing roles and responsibilities. For example, on your personal computer you probably wouldn't want your eight-year-old child to have the same levels of access that you do. In your job, you might share a workstation and not want someone else looking at your data or messing up tasks that you may have been working on for weeks. To meet needs like this, the Accounts category includes a wide range of options for configuring Windows accounts, privileges, and permissions which will be discussed next in Chapter 13.

Control Panel

Before Windows Settings there was the *Control Panel*. Like Windows Settings, the Control Panel is an application from which you can launch a number of different utilities. However, in the Control Panel each of these utilities is called an *applet*. For many years, the Control Panel was the place for users and administrators to configure Windows systems—but the role it plays has been steadily shrinking since the introduction of the Settings app in Windows 8. In fact, the CompTIA A+ 1102 objectives only mention the Control Panel in the context of Windows 10 (though it is still soldiering on in Windows 11, at least for now). Figure 12-7 shows the Control Panel in its default (Category) view.

Figure 12-7   Control Panel default view

The Control Panel offers two ways to find the applets. At the top right of the panel, you will see a View by drop-down menu. Choose Category to view the main categories, which you can drill down into to find applets by function. Choose View by | Large icons or View by | Small icons to view the complete list of applets (Figure 12-8 shows Large icons view).

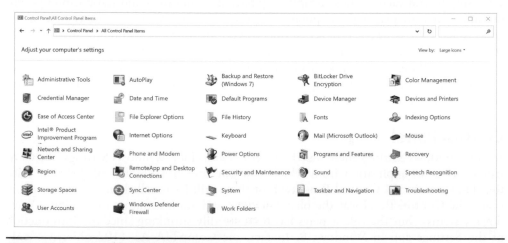

Figure 12-8   Control Panel Large icons view

The CompTIA A+ 1102 exam objectives list 15 specific Control Panel applets you need to know for the exam. All 15 applets are described in this book, but many of them are discussed in other chapters that pertain to their specific usage. This chapter covers six applets that don't fit well anywhere else, so let's take a look at them and explore what they do.

NOTE As you can see in Figure 12-8, the Control Panel includes many more applets than the 15 applets CompTIA lists! If CompTIA doesn't list them, I don't cover them in the book.

System

The System applet opens Windows Settings in the About section of the System category, displaying information about the computer. This includes the version of Windows, processor speed, RAM, if it's 32-bit or 64-bit, if pen or touch is enabled, computer name, workgroup, and if Windows is activated. This is one of the first places you go to view specifics on the system you are working with.

EXAM TIP The CompTIA A+ 1102 objectives ask about scenarios where you'd use the System applet, which *used* to open the System Properties dialog box. From the Control Panel on a Windows 10 computer, right-click System and choose Open to open the traditional System applet. From there, click one of the links in the left navigation pane (other than Device Manager) or click the Change settings link to open the System Properties dialog box. Keep this in mind when you take a closer look at the System Properties dialog box in Chapter 14.

Sound

The Sound applet, as the name implies, has everything to do with sound settings. Here you can choose and configure sound output devices, sound input devices, and default Windows sounds. The Sound applet is one of the tools that exists in both Windows Settings and the Control Panel. Figure 12-9 compares the Sound Control Panel applet (left) to the Sound section of the System category in Windows Settings (right). At first glance they look very different, but if you open both tools and click through their options, you'll see that they do basically the same job. Having said that, never assume that both Windows Settings and the Control Panel always have the same features.

Indexing Options

Indexing describes the way a computer gathers information about files to make it easier to find what you are looking for and stores the file information in a database-type format. This makes the search process much faster. Imagine having to open every folder and look through it to find what you need. Indexing solves this problem by creating a directory that you can reference and access files from. However, not every folder is indexed, as there are many folders that you will seldom, if ever, use. To speed up processing, these folders

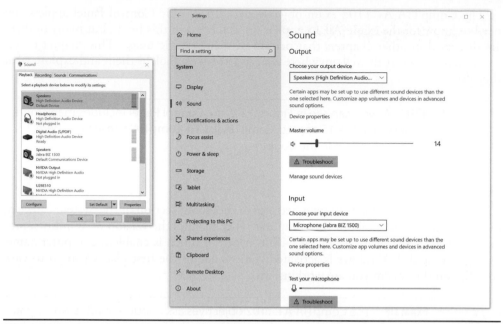

Figure 12-9 Sound Control Panel applet (left) compared to the Sound settings in Windows Settings (right)

are excluded from the initial indexing. However, if there is something you want to index, because you use it frequently, the Indexing Options tool lets you select files and folders that you want indexed.

To index selected files or folders, click Indexing Options in the Control Panel. You will see a list of the folders that are indexed. As just noted, very few folders are actually indexed by default, with Figure 12-10 serving as an example of what you might expect to see.

Ease of Access

Microsoft works hard to make Windows usable by folks with physical limitations, and Ease of Access Center in Control Panel is the place to go to adapt the OS to those needs. For those with sight impairment, you can launch Magnifier to enable them to enlarge part of the screen and launch Narrator to read the screen out loud. For those who need help with keyboard and mouse control, Ease of Access provides features such as On-Screen Keyboard, Sticky Keys (key combinations can be typed one key at a time), and Filter Keys (ignores double taps).

Administrative Tools

Administrative Tools is a special setting of File Explorer that enables you to open a specific set of applets—it's like a super applet launcher! You've already seen some of these applets in earlier chapters—such as Disk Cleanup and Defragment back in Chapter 9. We'll also cover a number of these applets in this and later chapters. For now just know that you can launch many applets from this one super applet (see Figure 12-11)!

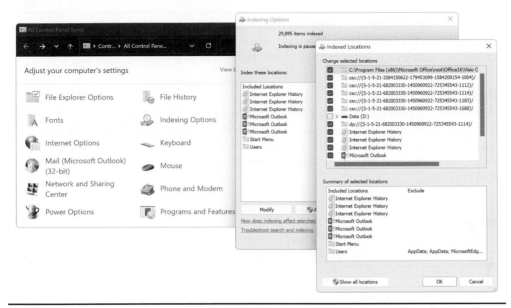

Figure 12-10 Indexing options in the Windows Control Panel

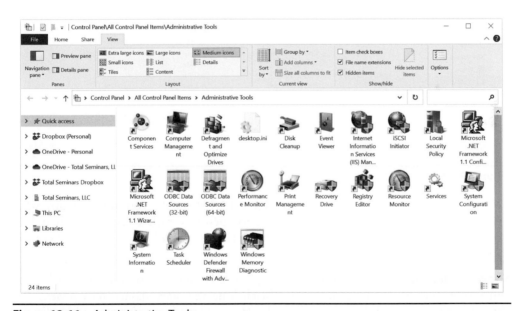

Figure 12-11 Administrative Tools

Don't let the many applets in Administrative Tools intimidate you. Only a select few of these applets are on the exam and we will talk about them in detail as appropriate, including in this chapter. What's important here is that you recognize Administrative Tools and know that it's located in the Control Panel.

TIP Windows 11 renames Administrative Tools to Windows Tools. Still sitting in the Control Panel and with a few different applets, it does roughly the same job—a super applet that starts other applets!

File Explorer Options

File Explorer is your go-to tool for file manipulation in Windows. Here you can delete, copy, and move files. You can create folders and move or copy those folders as well. Equally, you can double-click on any file to launch it or run it. I have File Explorer open 50 percent of the time on my machine. Figure 12-12 shows the contents of the C:\ drive on my system.

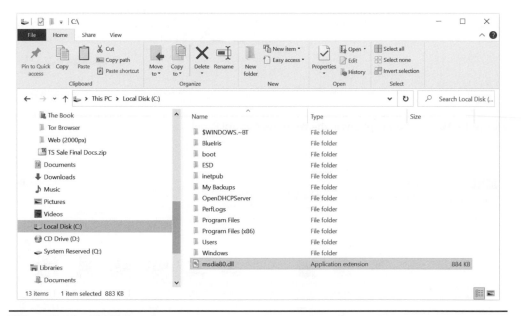

Figure 12-12 File Explorer

The File Explorer Options applet (see Figure 12-13) enables you to personalize what File Explorer shows you. Want File Explorer to open to Quick access rather than This PC? Set that here. Want to see the file extensions for every file? This applet is where you do that.

Show Hidden Files A very popular setting in File Explorer Options is to show hidden and system files. By clicking the View tab, clicking the *Show hidden files, folders, and drives* radio button, and then unchecking the *Hide protected operating system files (Recommended)* checkbox, you'll be able to see all files on your system. Compare Figure 12-14 to Figure 12-12 and you'll see the difference.

Showing hidden files is an important function for File Explorer Options, but the CompTIA A+ 1102 exam objectives explicitly list three others, so let's take a look at them.

Figure 12-13
File Explorer
Options

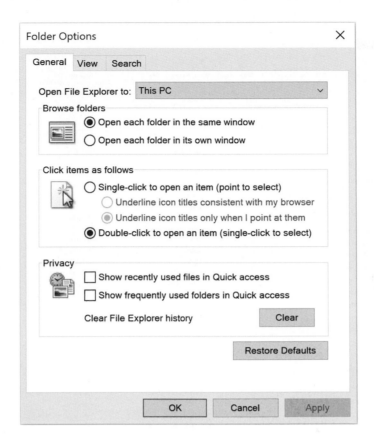

Show or Hide Extensions   Computer filenames have two parts, such as mydog.jpg. The first part of the name is the title that you or someone else gave the file. The second part is the type of file. In the mydog.jpg example, the file is a picture of my dog. We know this because of the descriptive title and because .jpg is a type of format that is used for images. This latter part of the name is known as the *file extension*. For some reason, though, Microsoft doesn't think that users need to know the type of file they are looking at and therefore has hidden all of the extensions by default. If you want to see file extensions in File Explorer, go to the View tab and uncheck the *Hide extensions for known file types* checkbox.

View Options   The previous sections discussed two of the most frequent options you will interact with in the View tab of File Explorer Options. However, as you've seen, there are many other options on the View tab. Take a few minutes to explore them. You will see options such as *Always show icons, never thumbnails, Hide empty drives, Always show availability status,* and so forth. These are all options that administrators commonly tinker with, and ones you will likely learn on the job.

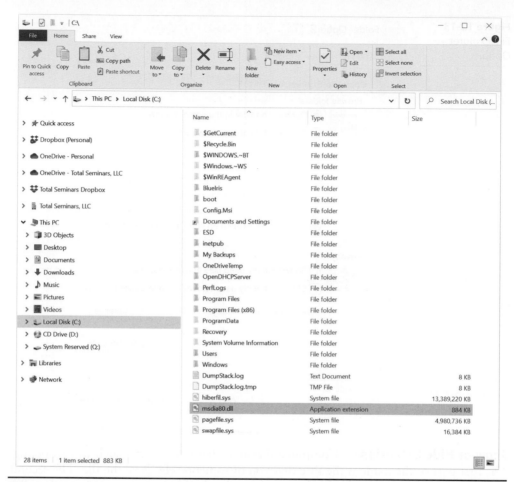

Figure 12-14   File Explorer with hidden and operating system files visible

General Options   File Explorer comes with many default settings. Most folks like the defaults, but for reasons ranging from privacy to personal preference, some users may want to change this interface. In File Explorer Options, click the General tab. The first option you see, Open File Explorer to, enables you to specify if you want to open File Explorer to Quick access or This PC. The Privacy section, at the bottom of the General tab, allows you to specify whether you want to show recently used files and frequently used folders in Quick access. Both options are checked by default, but you can uncheck either or both.

The other two sections in the General tab deal far more with personal preference. The first, *Browse folders*, allows you to specify whether you want folders to open in the same window or a new window. The second, *Click items as follows*, allows you to adjust how click behaviors work: either point at an item to select it and click once to open it, or click once to select an item and click twice to open it.

Processes, Applications, and Services Tools

Recall from Chapter 3 that CPUs run *threads*—bits of programs that are fed into the CPU. Let's take a moment and develop this concept. A program is machine code, manifesting as a file, that the CPU can read from RAM. When the program is sitting on your hard drive, nothing is happening. When you click on the file, a copy of the program is loaded from the hard drive onto RAM. At this point the program is running and is called a process. As the CPU runs the program, it grabs a few lines of code from RAM and processes them.

NOTE   A running program in Windows is called a process.

Dealing with processes in their many forms is a big part of understanding what's happening "under the hood." Windows is a multitasking operating system, running lots of processes simultaneously. Many of these processes appear in a window (or full screen) when you open them and end when you close that window. These processes are called *applications*.

There's an entire class of processes that, due to the nature of their job, don't require a window of any form. These processes run invisibly in the background, providing a large number of necessary support roles. Collectively, these are called services.

A big part of troubleshooting a Windows system is dealing with processes and services. We start them up and turn them off. We need to configure which applications autostart when the computer boots up. We need to make sure that we don't overload our system with too many processes and services. Perhaps we need to schedule a program to run at a certain time. For these scenarios and so many more, Windows comes with many utilities to help us tweak our processes, applications, and services. Let's take a look at these tools now.

Task Manager

Microsoft offers the Windows *Task Manager* as the one-stop-shop for anything you need to do with applications, processes, and services. The Task Manager is an old utility that dates back to some of the earliest versions of Windows, but it has been updated with almost every version of Windows. By default, the Task Manager starts in a simplified mode that makes it easy for new users to kill problem apps, if needed (see Figure 12-15).

The quickest way to open the Task Manager is to press CTRL-SHIFT-ESC. There are many other ways to open the Task Manager, including a few that you might see on the CompTIA A+ 1102 exam: go to Start | Search, type **taskmgr**, and press ENTER; or press CTRL-ALT-DELETE and select Task Manager.

NOTE   The Task Manager is, in my opinion, the most useful and most used of all the utilities on a typical Windows system.

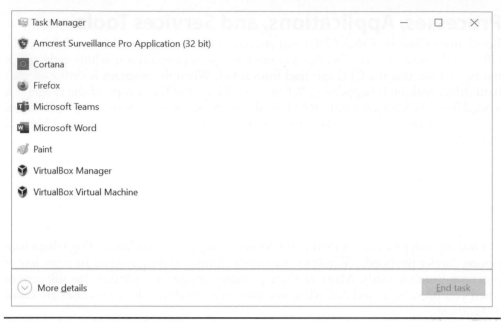

Figure 12-15 Default Task Manager

For some users, the simplified mode is all they'll ever need—but the real power of the Task Manager is in its detailed mode, which you can access by clicking the *More details* button. Once you have switched into detailed mode you can see that the Task Manager has several tabs. Every one of these tabs is incredibly useful and deserves a separate discussion, so let's look at each in turn, starting with the Processes tab.

Processes Tab

If you really want to tap the power of the Task Manager, there's no better place to start than the *Processes tab* (see Figure 12-16). Since everything is a process, and the Processes tab shows you every running process, this is the one place that enables you to see and control every process running on your computer.

Most processes also provide a description to help you understand what the process is doing, although you'll probably need to scroll right to see this information.

 NOTE If you don't see the Processes tab, click the More details button at the bottom of the Task Manager window.

All processes have certain common features that you should recognize:

- A process is named after its executable file, which usually ends in .exe but can also end with other extensions.
- A single process may spawn many instances of the same process, as shown in Figure 12-16.

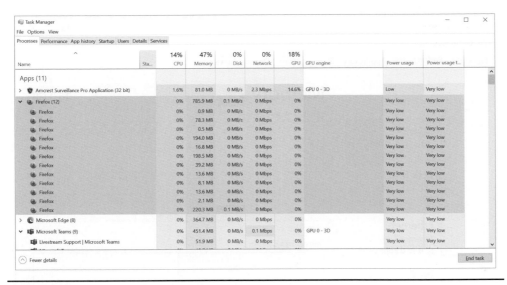

Name	Sta...	14% CPU	47% Memory	0% Disk	0% Network	18% GPU	GPU engine	Power usage	Power usage t...
Apps (11)									
> 🛡 Amcrest Surveillance Pro Application (32 bit)		1.6%	81.0 MB	0 MB/s	2.3 Mbps	14.6%	GPU 0 - 3D	Low	Very low
∨ 🦊 Firefox (12)		0%	785.9 MB	0.1 MB/s	0 Mbps	0%		Very low	Very low
🦊 Firefox		0%	0.9 MB	0 MB/s	0 Mbps	0%		Very low	Very low
🦊 Firefox		0%	78.3 MB	0 MB/s	0 Mbps	0%		Very low	Very low
🦊 Firefox		0%	0.5 MB	0 MB/s	0 Mbps	0%		Very low	Very low
🦊 Firefox		0%	194.0 MB	0 MB/s	0 Mbps	0%		Very low	Very low
🦊 Firefox		0%	16.8 MB	0 MB/s	0 Mbps	0%		Very low	Very low
🦊 Firefox		0%	198.5 MB	0 MB/s	0 Mbps	0%		Very low	Very low
🦊 Firefox		0%	39.2 MB	0 MB/s	0 Mbps	0%		Very low	Very low
🦊 Firefox		0%	13.6 MB	0 MB/s	0 Mbps	0%		Very low	Very low
🦊 Firefox		0%	8.1 MB	0 MB/s	0 Mbps	0%		Very low	Very low
🦊 Firefox		0%	13.6 MB	0 MB/s	0 Mbps	0%		Very low	Very low
🦊 Firefox		0%	2.1 MB	0 MB/s	0 Mbps	0%		Very low	Very low
🦊 Firefox		0%	220.3 MB	0.1 MB/s	0 Mbps	0%		Very low	Very low
> 🌐 Microsoft Edge (8)		0%	364.7 MB	0 MB/s	0 Mbps	0%		Very low	Very low
∨ 📧 Microsoft Teams (9)		0%	451.4 MB	0 MB/s	0.1 Mbps	0%	GPU 0 - 3D	Very low	Very low
📧 Livestream Support	Microsoft Teams		0%	51.9 MB	0 MB/s	0 Mbps	0%		Very low	Very low

Figure 12-16 Lots of Firefox processes!

- All processes have a username to identify who started the process. A process started by Windows has the username System.

- All processes have a process identifier (PID). To identify a process, you use the PID, not the process name. You can see all PIDs in the Details tab.

Try This!

Closing Applications
Launch Notepad and then start up the Task Manager. On the Processes tab in the Task Manager, right-click the Notepad application and select Go to details. It takes you to the process in the Details pane. Right-click and select End task to close the application.

Performance Tab
The *Performance tab* is a great resource to get an overview of resource usage on your system. On this one page you get a graphical view of how much your system is taxing your CPU, RAM (see Figure 12-17), storage, and network connections and even how hard your GPU is working. When you run into scenarios where your system or the Internet seems to run too slowly or stop, this is a great first place to check.

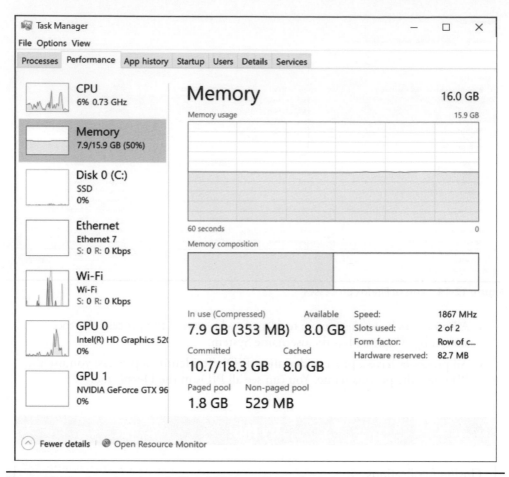

Figure 12-17   I'm using about half my RAM according to the Task Manager.

App History Tab

The App history tab tracks how much CPU time and network bandwidth all your applications have used since the last time you reset tracking. I don't find App history useful, and it seems CompTIA agrees—it isn't listed as a Task Manager tab in A+ 1102 exam objective 1.3.

Startup Tab

Too many programs automatically starting up when you start Windows? The Startup tab shows you all the autostarting programs. You can disable autostarting programs (see Figure 12-18) to see how the system runs without them, but you cannot permanently remove them from autostarting—a bit frustrating, Microsoft!

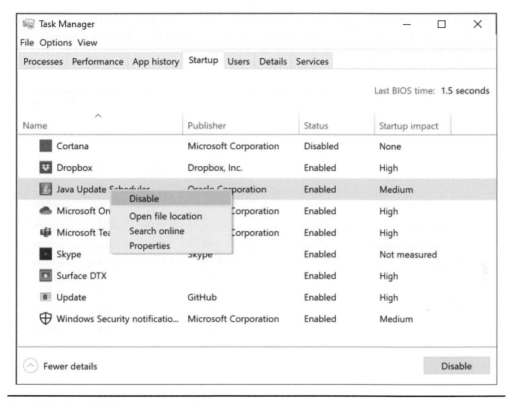

Figure 12-18 Disabling an autostarting program

Microsoft has a weird relationship with autostarting programs. Windows has been around since the 1980s, and over the years Microsoft has come up with many ways to autostart both programs and services. This means there is no single utility to answer the question "What's autostarting on my system?" To find this answer, download Microsoft's free Autoruns utility at https://docs.microsoft.com/en-us/sysinternals/downloads/autoruns.

TIP Microsoft's Sysinternals offers many more great tools in addition to Autoruns. Want to lose six hours of your life filled with nerdy joy? Go to https://docs.microsoft.com/en-us/sysinternals/ and start playing with the hundreds of powerful tools invented by Microsoft's CTO of the Azure product team, Mark Russinovich. Mark's been writing Windows utilities for over 25 years, and all us techs love him.

Users Tab

Windows is designed to support multiple users. Twenty or thirty years ago it was common for a single computer to have, for example, one user from 8 a.m. to 4 p.m. and another user from 4 p.m. to midnight. We tend to forget this as we live in a world where everyone has their own computer(s). Yet with networking and the Internet, it's possible for one person to log on at the computer (locally) while others log on remotely. The Users tab shows the applications running on a per-user basis (see Figure 12-19). You can also right-click on a username and sign them out.

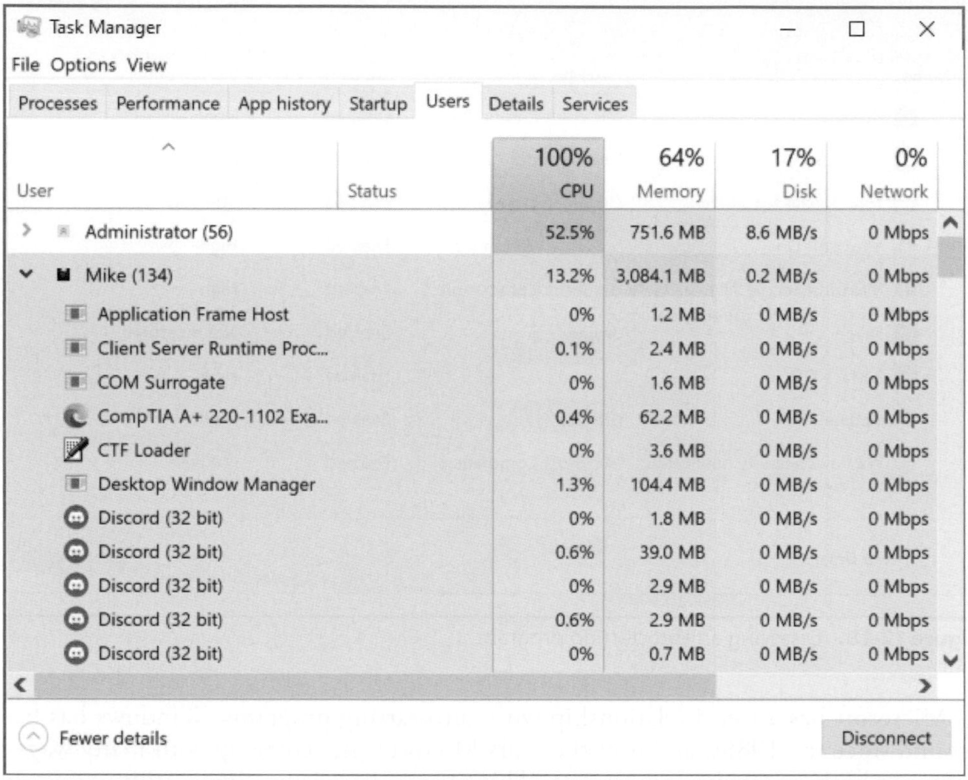

Figure 12-19 Users tab

The Users tab is the place to go if you want to see who's logged in and which programs each logged-in user is running. But, if you want to see a list of everything that's running along with which user is running it, the Details tab is where you want to go.

Details Tab

The main Processes tab is a great overview of your running processes, but to see the PID and User name columns, switch to the *Details tab*, as shown in Figure 12-20. The Details tab also enables you to pull a neat trick for dealing with stubborn, hard-to-kill programs with more than one process; right-click on a process and select *End process tree* to kill the process and child processes it launched.

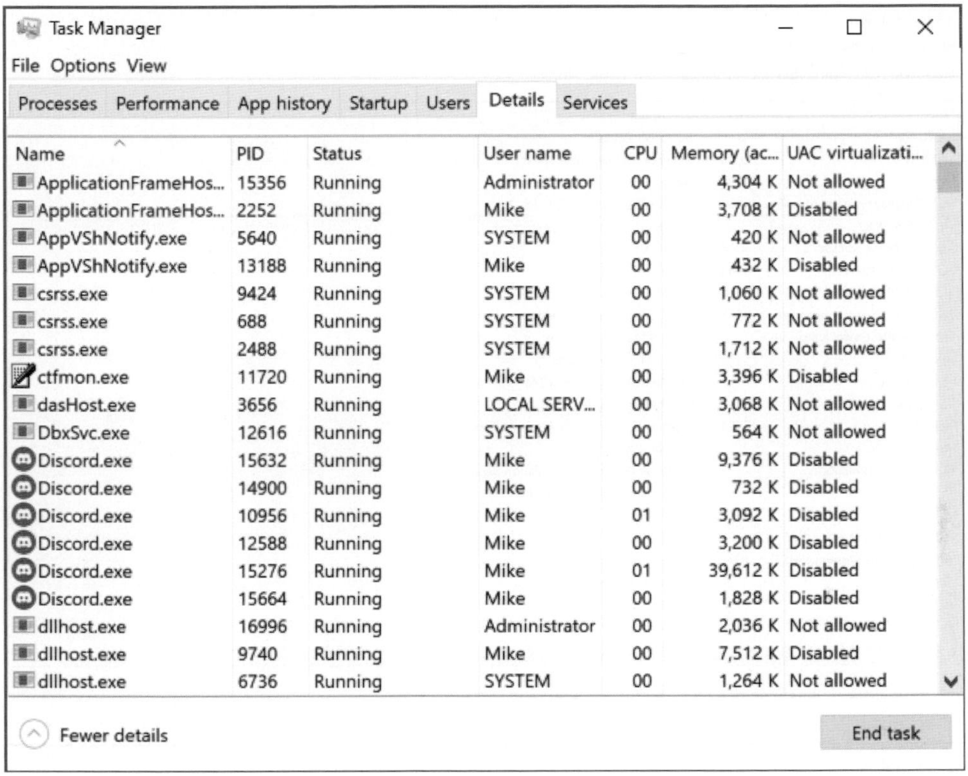

Figure 12-20 Details tab

Shockingly, the Details tab isn't listed along with the other Task Manager tabs in CompTIA A+ 1102 objective 1.3. I think this a huge error on CompTIA's part. The Details tab, even though not on the exam, has many features such as usernames and PIDs. Usernames and PIDs are on the exam, so let's just use the details as a tool to understand the CompTIA A+ objectives even better.

Services Tab

We've spent a lot of time talking about how the Task Manager allows us to manipulate one genre of processes known as applications, so it's easy to forget there's an entire other genre of processes that are not applications: services. Services are the soul of your Windows system. Services don't show up on your screen but they do the hundreds of background tasks critical to making Windows run.

Services need to be started either manually, by another process, or autostarted. You'll run into scenarios where a service becomes erratic and needs to be stopped. Sometimes too many services load up and slow down your system. This is where the Service tab comes into play (see Figure 12-21).

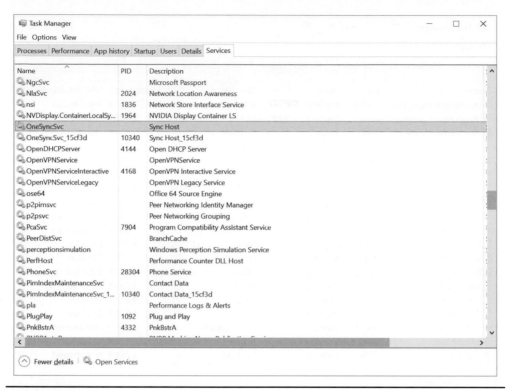

Figure 12-21 Services tab

The *Services tab* allows you to start, stop, or restart any service. You cannot, however, use the Services tab to set up a service to autostart or even just pause a service for a moment. This is a job for a different utility. Take a look at the bottom of the Services tab. See the option called Open Services? Click this to open the ancient but still useful Services utility. At first glance the Services utility looks pretty much like Task Manager's Services tab, but it actually does much more. Check out Figure 12-22 to see some of the settings that you can configure for a service by right-clicking its name in the Services utility and choosing Properties.

EXAM TIP You can open the Services utility from the Start | Search bar by typing **services.msc** and pressing ENTER.

Resource Monitor

The Task Manager should always be your first choice for quick checks on system usage, but there are times where you might need more detail and more control. In these cases, it's time to use Resource Monitor. Think of *Resource Monitor (resmon)* as a super Task Manager with all the same features, plus many more (see Figure 12-23) You can access Resource Monitor from the Performance tab in the Task Manager, from the Control Panel under Administrative Tools, or just by typing **resource monitor** or **resmon** in the Start | Search bar.

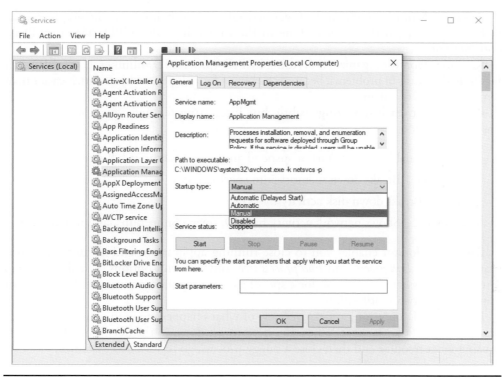

Figure 12-22   Services utility showing properties

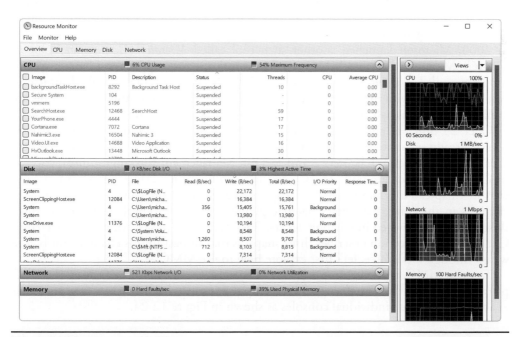

Figure 12-23   Resource Monitor

Resource Monitor starts on the Overview tab. This is handy, and the graphs on the right are pretty, but the work is done in the four other tabs: CPU, Memory, Disk, and Network.

Resource Monitor organizes everything by PID (process ID) number. Using PIDs can facilitate diagnosis of problems, because tracking a four-digit number is much easier than remembering a text string.

Beyond that, each tab brings subtle but interesting features you don't see in the Task Manager:

- **CPU**   Enables you to start or suspend any process without killing it
- **Memory**   Breaks down memory into specific types
- **Disk**   Breaks down disk activity by PID
- **Network**   Shows network activity by PID, open connections, and much more

Resource Monitor enables you to close running applications and all associated programs with the *End process* and *End process tree* context menu options. It makes sense to put the options here, so you can look specifically at programs jamming CPU usage, for example, or network utilization.

In general, if you want a quick overview of what's happening with your system's processes, use the Task Manager. When you need to get down to the details of what process is using what resource and then close a buggy process, go to Resource Monitor.

Microsoft Management Console

Microsoft has always had a challenge with the organization of its many built-in utilities. Tools like the Control Panel and Windows Settings are examples of Microsoft's ongoing desire to organize utilities into what I personally see as "tools to launch tools." Back in 2000, Microsoft launched another such tool called *Microsoft Management Console (MMC)*. Microsoft describes MMC as a framework used to support and launch special programs called *snap-ins*. On your system, MMC is an executable file called mmc.exe. A snap-in is a file with the file extension .msc. Not all Windows Administrative Tools are available as snap-ins, which CompTIA lists as "Additional tools" in 1102 objective 1.3

Over 25 different snap-ins are preinstalled in a typical Windows system. In fact, you've already encountered some snap-ins in previous chapters! Remember Device Manager (devmgmt.msc) in Chapters 2 and 5? Disk Management (diskmgmt.msc), covered in Chapter 8? Those are both MMC snap-ins. Group Policy Editor (gpedit.msc), covered in Chapter 11, is another MMC snap-in. We will see more MMC snap-ins in later chapters in the context of their related topics. For example, Local Users and Groups (lusrmgr.msc) is covered in Chapter 13 and Task Scheduler (taskschd.msc) is covered in Chapter 14. This section describes three snap-ins that fit best in this chapter. But before we go through these three, let's first explore how to use MMC.

To open MMC, type **mmc** into the Start | Search bar and (after confirming the UAC prompt) press ENTER. This brings up an empty console, that is, MMC is a tool that enables you to create individual consoles as shown in Figure 12-24.

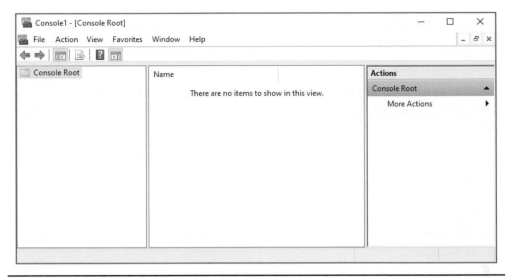

Figure 12-24   Blank MMC

An empty MMC console is useless without loading one or more snap-ins. Choose File | Add/Remove snap-in to see a list of available snap-ins. To add a snap-in, click its name in the Available snap-ins list on the left and click the Add button to add it to the Selected snap-ins list on the right (see Figure 12-25). Keep clicking and adding until you have the snap-ins you want for this console and then click OK to finish.

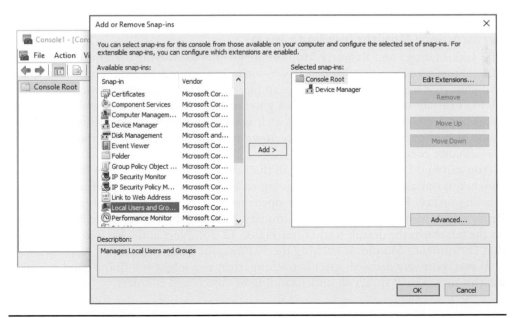

Figure 12-25   Loading snap-ins

TIP Many snap-ins will run either on a local system or on a network computer.

You don't have to run MMC to start a snap-in. If you know the filename of the snap-in you want to run, just type the filename in the Start | Search bar, press ENTER, and that snap-in starts without your needing to first open MMC. Of course, the trick is to know the names of these snap-ins. CompTIA wants you to know the names of eight specific snap-ins. Table 12-1 lists these snap-ins and their corresponding filenames.

Event Viewer	eventvwr.msc
Disk Management	diskmgmt.msc
Task Scheduler	taskschd.msc
Device Manager	devmgmt.msc
Certificate Manager	certmgr.msc
Local Users and Groups	lusrmgr.msc
Performance Monitor	perfmon.msc
Group Policy Editor	gpedit.msc

Table 12-1 MMC snap-ins and filenames

Now that you know how to run MMC and snap-ins, I'll give you a tour of the three snap-ins listed in Table 12-1 that are not covered in other chapters.

Performance Monitor (perfmon.msc)

The Task Manager and Resource Monitor are great at identifying current problems, but what about problems that happen when you're not around to see them? What about problems that happen over time? For example, what if your system is always running at a CPU utilization of 60 percent—is that good or bad? Windows comes with tools to log resource usage so you can track metrics such as CPU and RAM usage over time. In Windows, a good tech turns to *Performance Monitor* as the primary tool for tracking system performance over time.

You can find Performance Monitor in the Administrative Tools applet in the Control Panel. You can also open the tool by going to Start | Search, typing **perfmon.msc**, and pressing ENTER. Performance Monitor opens to a screen that displays some text about Performance Monitor and a System Summary. Clicking the Performance Monitor item on the left shows the default tracker (see Figure 12-26). Note at the bottom of the screen that Performance Monitor is tracking the % Processor Time counter.

If you want very detailed, specific tracking, then you might still find a good reason to use this tool. That requires an understanding of objects and counters.

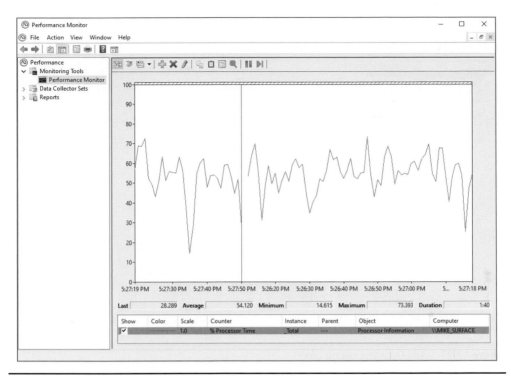

Figure 12-26 Default Performance Monitor

Objects and Counters   Two tool types define the usefulness of Performance Monitor: object and counter. An *object* is a system component that is given a set of characteristics and can be managed by the operating system as a single entity. A *counter* tracks specific information about an object. The processor object counter %Processor Time shown in Figure 12-26, for example, tracks the percentage of elapsed time the processor uses to execute a non-idle thread. Many counters can be associated with an object.

Working with the Tools   Performance Monitor gathers real-time data on objects, such as memory, physical disk, processor, and network, and displays this data as a graph (line graph), histogram (bar graph), or simple report. When you first open it, Performance Monitor shows data in graph form. The data displayed is from the set of counters listed below the chart. If you want to add counters, click the Add button (the one that looks like a plus sign). Select one of the many different objects you can monitor. Once you've chosen an object, the Add Counters dialog box includes a helpful feature: you can select a counter and click the Show description checkbox to learn about the counter, as shown in Figure 12-27.

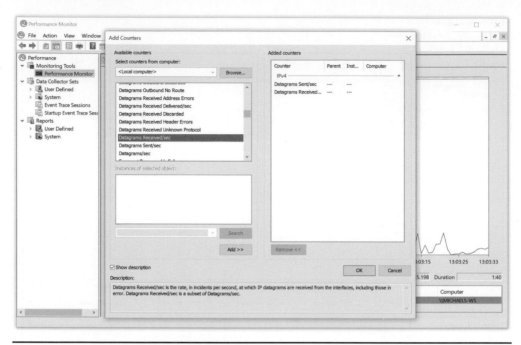

Figure 12-27   Add Counters dialog box

NOTE   You can add counters from your local machine or from other Windows machines on your network

The big question here is "Which counters should I add?" Well, to understand fully which counters to use in which situation takes a lifetime of learning, but you can narrow down your options by considering what you want to look at. For instance, in a scenario where the Internet is running slower than normal, you may want to consider a counter that tracks the network bandwidth. If you're worried you are running low on RAM, use a counter that shows total memory use. In the end, when a CompTIA A+ 1102 exam question asks you which counters to use in a particular scenario, a little common sense is all you need. In the real world where things are more complex, you can always turn to online recommendations or use a premade data collector set that ships with Windows.

Data Collector Sets   *Data Collector Sets* are groups of counters you can use to make reports. You can make your own Data Collector Sets (User Defined), or you can just grab one of the predefined system sets. Once you start a Data Collector Set, you can use the Reports option to see the results (see Figure 12-28). Data Collector Sets not only help you choose counter objects to track, but also enable you to schedule when you want them to run. Pretty cool, right?

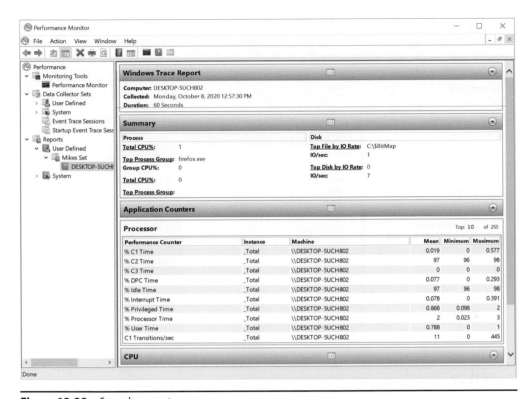

Figure 12-28 Sample report

 EXAM TIP UNIX-based operating systems (like macOS and various Linux distros) use a logging standard called syslog to create information placed in log files. Applications use syslog standards to write about issues happening to or about the application. Syslog is network-friendly, so it's common to have a single syslog server just to collect syslog data from multiple systems. Programs use syslog standards to write logs that other syslog standard applications in turn read. You'll find the log files at /var/log in most Linux distros. There is also third-party support for syslog in Windows, so it's not limited to UNIX-based systems.

Event Viewer (eventvwr.msc)

Event Viewer is Windows' default tattletale program, spilling the beans about thousands of interesting happenings (Windows calls them *events*) that your system monitors and logs. Your system monitors many different logs by default, and you can add more logs or change what they see if you'd like. Event Viewer is the tool you use to read and understand these logs. Be patient with Event Viewer! It is akin to learning chess. You can get the basics of Event Viewer quickly, but it takes a lifetime to master.

You can open Event Viewer from Control Panel | Administrative Tools or by typing **eventvwr.msc**, and pressing ENTER. You can also just start typing **Event Viewer** in the

Start | Search bar and press ENTER when it pops up in the results. The default interface isn't too interesting. Get into the good part of Event Viewer by expanding the Windows Logs option on the left to see something like Figure 12-29.

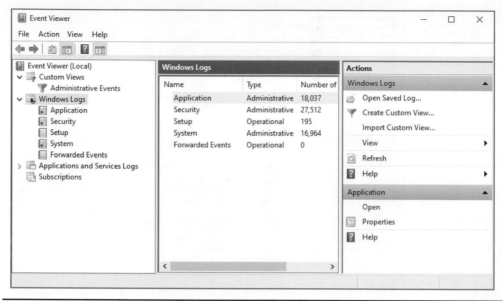

Figure 12-29 Event Viewer showing Windows Logs

 TIP A log file is a record of events. Windows logs are binary files. You must read them through tools like Event Viewer.

Windows Logs   There are four important Windows Logs: Application, Security, Setup, and System. Collectively and by default these four logs are all that most techs need to diagnose what's happening on a system. Make sure you know what type of events each of these four logs stores:

- **Application**   Records anything that has to do with applications or programs outside of the Windows system files themselves
- **Security**   Records security events such as failed logons
- **Setup**   Tracks setup and update events for your Windows system
- **System**   Tracks anything having to do with your Windows operating system

Your system may have more logs than just these four. That's fine. For the exam and for real life, stick with the big four.

Clicking System should list quite a few events. Even the tamest Windows machine generates lots of events, and that's OK. By default, the top (the most recent) event is selected and the bottom of Event Viewer shows details about that event (see Figure 12-30).

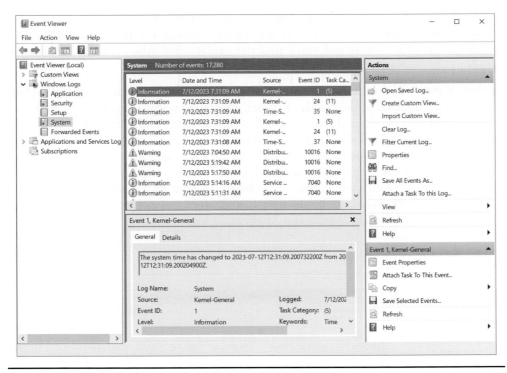

Figure 12-30 Individual event in Event Viewer

Event Levels   Not all events are created equal. Some are extremely serious, requiring some form of action or at least your notification, while others are just letting you know something took place. Windows defines five different event levels:

- **Verbose**   Extra information that is probably only useful when debugging an application.
- **Information**   Something happened that went well, such as a successful backup.
- **Warning**   An event that isn't an error but may warn about one, like low disk space.
- **Error**   Something went wrong, such as a file not loading.
- **Critical**   Something a little more serious happened, like the system unexpectedly powering off instead of shutting down cleanly.

   NOTE   If you're an old-timer like me, you might wonder where the Audit Success and Audit Failure levels went. Once upon a time, Audit Success and Audit Failure were special levels used only for the Security log. Microsoft didn't get rid of this concept completely—but they aren't considered levels anymore. If you take a gander at the Security log, you'll find Audit Success and Audit Failure in the *Keywords* column. They still indicate successful or failed security actions like a successful logon or failed access to a file.

The first time you investigate individual events, you're going to be intimidated. No worries, as most Windows events aren't very easy to understand. In most cases you just search for the error online and you'll find the explanation. Also remember that error details might give you a clue as to the problem.

Custom Views Going through the default logs poses a problem: a single log can include tens or even hundreds of thousands of events. Plus, who wants to go through every log when there is a single, filtered place to see all or at least some of them? That place is Custom Views in the Event Viewer navigation pane.

Event Viewer comes with a premade Custom View called Administrative Events that does a good job of tracking warning and error events across your logs. You can (and probably should) make your own custom views based on your own needs by clicking New View. Figure 12-31 shows the results of a custom view called Critical Only that only shows critical errors for the System and Application log.

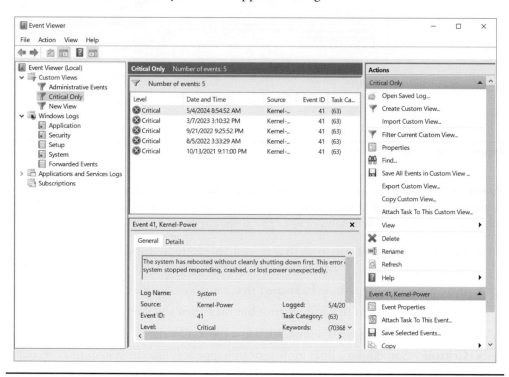

Figure 12-31   Event Viewer showing only Critical events

Certificate Manager (certmgr.msc)

A *certificate* is, in essence, a digital key that enables your programs to encrypt data that may only be read by a corresponding key on the receiver's side. Certificates are the cornerstone of pretty much every encrypted communication done between devices on the Internet. Your system is full of certificates, and the Certificate Manager gives you access to all of them.

Honestly, there's not much reason to go into the Certificate Manager unless you're instructed to. I'll save the big discussion of certificates for Chapter 27, so for now let's just make sure you know how to start Certificates Manager. Like the other snap-ins discussed here, you can access Certificate Manager from Control Panel | Administrative Tools, or by typing either **certmgr.msc** or **Certificate Manager** in the Start | Search bar and pressing ENTER. All will lead you to the default screen, as shown in Figure 12-32.

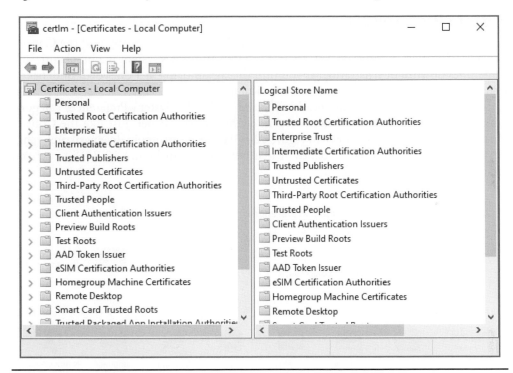

Figure 12-32   Default Certificate Manager screen

So, returning to the question at the beginning of the "Your Basic Windows Toolset" section on the difference between those tools and the ones we just discussed, what *is* the difference? Your Basic Windows Toolset includes a number of Microsoft Management Console snap-ins found in the Windows folder (e.g., Task Scheduler, Event Viewer). Your Processes, Applications, and Services tools either run in the background, execute programs using one or more threads, or are executable by the user when logged in. Now, let's switch gears and tackle a different animal—macOS preferences and features.

macOS Preferences and Features

Where the rubber meets the road, Windows and macOS are both just operating systems. Since users need many of the same things from *any* operating system they use, Windows and macOS are actually pretty similar. They both have places to go to configure the OS, set up file synchronization, search the device, and more. Let's look at a few things you'll need to understand for configuring and working with macOS.

NOTE The CompTIA A+ 1102 exam objectives don't cover macOS in anywhere near as much detail as they cover Windows. I'll stick to what you need to know for the exam here—but be prepared to roll up your sleeves and use macOS for a few months if you need to have a working knowledge of it.

System Preferences

As you may have noticed in the sections on the Windows Settings app and the Control Panel, the location of different settings in a modern Windows system is a bit chaotic and sometimes downright frustrating. If you find this as annoying as I do, you'll understand one small reason why macOS has many dedicated users.

In macOS, most settings are neatly collected under the System Preferences category, which works like a more consistent version of the Control Panel. Just like the Control Panel, System Preferences (shown in Figure 12-33) collects settings in dozens of preference *panes*. It also includes a handy-dandy search box (shown in Figure 12-34) in case you aren't sure where an option lives.

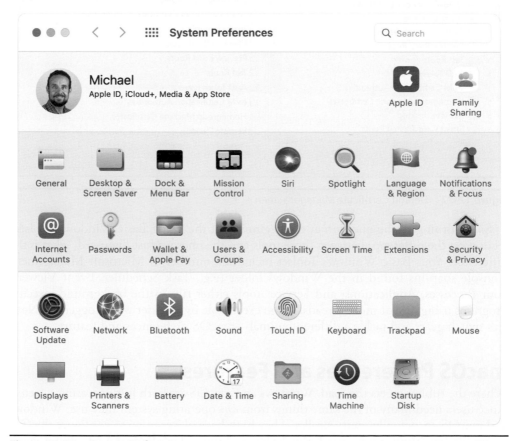

Figure 12-33 System Preferences

Figure 12-34   Finding an option in System Preferences

NOTE   As we were about to go to press, Apple announced that it has redesigned System Preferences for macOS Ventura (and renamed it to System Settings). Make sure to explore the new System Settings app if you have to support devices running macOS Ventura or newer!

You shouldn't need to know all the preference panes for the exam—the CompTIA A+ 1102 exam objectives only call out seven: Displays, Network, Printers, Scanners, Privacy, Accessibility, and Time Machine. Let's take a look at each.

EXAM TIP   In addition to these seven preferences, the CompTIA A+ 1102 exam objectives for macOS also cover a few features and tools that you interact with mainly or entirely through System Preferences. You'll find settings for the Dock and Mission Control (which you saw way back in Chapter 2) as well as for Apple ID, FileVault, and Spotlight (which are introduced a little later in this chapter). You probably won't have to answer questions about configuring them, but I recommend knowing that they're available via System Preferences just in case!

Displays

Much like the display settings in Windows, this is the place to go to configure things like your display's resolution, brightness, and color, and configure how multiple displays are arranged. The settings here differ from device to device based on their capabilities.

For example, the main reason to come here is to arrange multiple displays. Figure 12-35 shows how the Display preference pane puts this option front-and-center when you have a second display connected and otherwise opens to settings for the lone display. The display-specific preferences enable you to configure things like the resolution, color profile, refresh rate, and rotation—but the precise options will depend on the display's features.

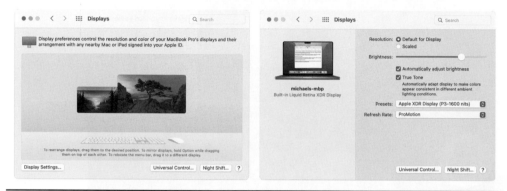

Figure 12-35   Display preferences with multiple displays (left) and a single display (right)

Network

Since we haven't discussed networking in much detail yet (we'll get there in Chapters 18 through 21), I'll keep this pretty light for now. The most common network operation that your average user needs is just to connect to or disconnect from a wireless network or turn Wi-Fi off altogether—and you can accomplish both of these via the Wi-Fi *status menu* on the right side of the menu bar (see Figure 12-36).

The Network preferences pane (see Figure 12-37) is where to look if you need to fiddle with a whole slate of network settings that we haven't had a chance to talk about yet: setting up rare network types, configuring preferred Wi-Fi networks, TCP/IP settings, and DNS settings, and configuring many more advanced options. Don't worry about what these are for now—just remember where to find them and keep an eye out for these topics in the network chapters.

Printers & Scanners

The CompTIA A+ 1102 objectives list separate preference panes called Printers and Scanners—but in reality there is a *single* preference pane called Printers & Scanners (shown in Figure 12-38) for configuring printers, document/photo scanners, and combination all-in-one printer/scanner devices. We'll take a closer look at these devices in Chapter 26, so for now you just need to know that Printers & Scanners is where you'd go to add or remove a printer or scanner, check on supply levels, and check up on a document that seems to be stuck in the print queue.

Figure 12-36
Selecting a
wireless network
in macOS

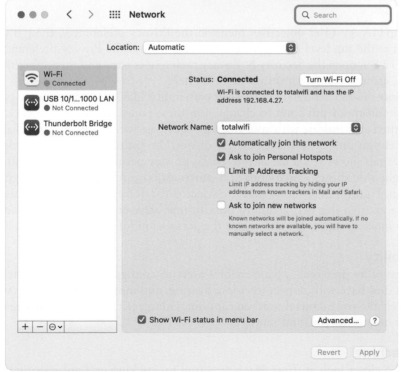

Figure 12-37   Network preference pane

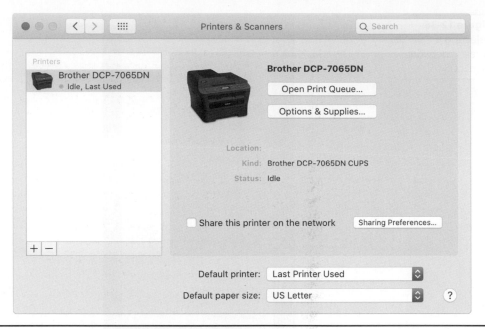

Figure 12-38 Printers & Scanners preference pane

Privacy

The CompTIA A+ 1102 objectives mention the Privacy preferences, though you won't find them at the top level of System Preferences. To find the Privacy preferences shown in Figure 12-39, open the Security & Privacy preferences pane and then select the Privacy tab. There are a few different things to notice here.

First, note the lock icon in the lower-left corner. Just like in Windows, some preferences require administrator privileges to change. On these panes, you'll have to click this lock icon and then authenticate with your fingerprint or password before making changes.

Whether you unlock to make changes or not, the list on the left side of the Privacy preferences tab shows you a list of the special privacy permissions available, and the list on the right side shows which apps and processes have requested or been granted the permission. Figure 12-39 shows that I've selected the Screen Recording permission, and that I have granted this permission to the Chrome browser and Microsoft Teams. If you unlock to make changes, you can toggle the permission for a given process.

Accessibility

The Accessibility preferences pane enables users to configure macOS to better support any needs they have with respect to vision, hearing, and motor control. This is where you can go to enable voice control, turn on captions, enlarge parts of the screen, cause macOS to narrate menus for you, and more.

Time Machine

We'll take a closer look at *Time Machine*, a tool for backing up (and restoring) files and folders on your Mac, in Chapter 14. For now, it's enough to know that the Time Machine

Figure 12-39   Privacy preferences in the Security & Privacy pane

preferences pane enables you to turn on backups, specify where to store them, control which files are backed up, and configure whether Time Machine should take new backups if your device is running on battery power.

EXAM TIP   Speaking of basic tools for your Mac and your Linux systems, you'll notice that there is no "built-in" antivirus program for these operating systems, while Windows has the built-in Windows Defender. Traditionally, issues such as Apple's strong security awareness or Linux's assumption of high technical skill makes these operating systems traditionally less interesting to malware and, in turn, subject to fewer attacks compared to a Windows system.

However, more and more macOS and Linux administrators turn to antivirus/antimalware for these systems. There's plenty of third-party options for Mac and Linux antivirus, both free and for pay, that do a fine job of keeping malware at bay. Check out our complete antivirus/antimalware discussion in Chapter 27 for more details!

Apple ID

An Apple ID is, more or less, Apple's version of a Microsoft account. It's a global account that you register with Apple that enables you to synchronize data and preferences among multiple devices (through Apple's *iCloud* service). The main difference is that you can log in to a Windows system with a Microsoft account, while an Apple ID is just associated with your local account after you log in.

The CompTIA A+ 1102 exam objectives don't focus on Apple ID as part of System Preferences—but the Apple ID preference pane is the place to go to log in, log out, update account data, configure which kinds of data are synchronized via iCloud (shown in Figure 12-40), see which devices are associated with your Apple ID, and locate a device if Find My Mac is enabled.

Figure 12-40   iCloud synchronization options in the Apple ID preferences pane

EXAM TIP The CompTIA A+ 1102 exam objectives mention *corporate restrictions* in the context of Apple ID. My best guess is that CompTIA is referring to something called a *Managed Apple ID*, which organizations can set up through the *Apple Business Manager*. While a personal Apple ID enables all kinds of data synchronization and other cool features, some organizations see these features as a risk to the organization and its data—and therefore implement Managed Apple IDs to restrict which features employees can use when they log in to the organization's network.

AirDrop

Your series editor is a Windows guy, but Apple sure does a great job creating some very nifty utilities that really just don't happen in the Windows world. AirDrop is one example of that kind of nifty. Got a file you want to share with another Apple product nearby? Select the file and choose Share | AirDrop. You will see every AirDrop-enabled device in your nearby space. Just drag the file to the systems you wish—nifty!

Watch for scenarios where AirDrop doesn't work. First, make sure the other device is AirDrop capable. Second, make sure that both your device and the other device are discoverable (Go | AirDrop in Finder) Last, make sure each system's firewall has "Block All Incoming Connections" disabled.

Spotlight

Spotlight has long been the global system search tool on macOS—it can find files, preferences, Web pages, contacts, and events, and can even serve as a calculator. The Spotlight search experience has been so good for so long that Windows (via Start | Search) and most Linux distros all include a similar global search tool these days. To access Spotlight, just press COMMAND-SPACE and then start typing your query.

NOTE The Spotlight preferences pane enables you to control which types of search results show up in Spotlight and to exclude specific folders from the Spotlight index.

Keychain

On macOS, *Keychain* (which you can investigate via the *Keychain Access* app) is responsible for managing sensitive passwords and certificates. We'll talk a little more about certificates in Chapters 21 and 27, so for now let's focus on passwords.

Keychain remembers many kinds of common password (like your aunt's Wi-Fi password) automatically. Keychain will supply the password automatically when you join the network. If you need to see it later, you can pop open Keychain Access, find the password item, toggle Show password, and then provide your own user-account password (or fingerprint scan) to reveal the prerecorded password (as shown in Figure 12-41).

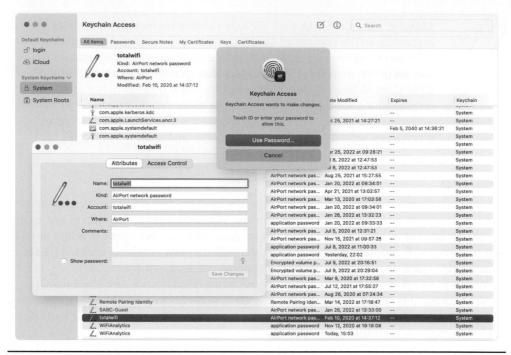

Figure 12-41   Revealing a Wi-Fi password in Keychain Access

NOTE   Keychain has a few more neat tricks. First, it can synchronize through iCloud, so you can have access to all of your passwords on all of your Apple devices. Second, it can also manage *Secure Notes* if you need to keep any notes-to-self under lock and key.

FileVault

In the early 2000s, Apple first introduced its FileVault storage encryption feature. FileVault makes it easy to encrypt a storage device so that some snoop can't plug it in to another system and read your files without having to log in. FileVault has become a little less important in recent years—all of the internal storage devices on modern Macs are encrypted by default—but I still think it's a pretty cool idea.

The main difference between the default encryption and FileVault is that macOS automatically unlocks the default encryption when you turn on the device, while a storage volume encrypted by FileVault is only unlocked once you log in to your account. If you lose or give a device away without FileVault enabled, it will be *much* harder for some snoop to recover your files.

NOTE   To enable FileVault, visit the FileVault tab in the Security & Privacy preferences pane.

Chapter Review

Questions

1. Which of the following does Windows do if you enable Game Mode?

   A. It increases the color quality.

   B. It disables some security protections that often interfere with modern games.

   C. It increases mouse or trackpad sensitivity.

   D. It prevents Windows Update from restarting Windows.

2. What is Audit Success?

   A. A Registry Editor option to ensure a Registry change won't render the system unbootable

   B. A Windows Update utility to visualize what fraction of updates are installed within one week

   C. A keyword used to indicate successful actions in the Security log found within Event Viewer

   D. A high level of login security in the Updates and Security settings that audits even successful login attempts

3. When using Performance Monitor, which settings are defined to track resource usage? (Select two.)

   A. Processes

   B. Objects

   C. Counters

   D. Values

4. Which of the following are organized inside the Registry's root keys? (Select two.)

   A. Subkeys

   B. Subfolders

   C. Values

   D. Objects

5. Which of the following root keys contains the data for a system's non-user-specific configurations?

   A. HKEY_LOCAL_MACHINE

   B. HKEY_USERS

   C. HKEY_CURRENT_USER

   D. HKEY_CLASSES_ROOT

6. Which macOS tool, feature, or preference pane performs a function similar to the Certificate Manager MMC snap-in?

   A. Apple ID

   B. Keychain

   C. FileVault

   D. Network

7. How do you open the Registry Editor from the command prompt?

   A. regedit

   B. reg

   C. regeditor

   D. rgstry

8. Sven calls the Help Desk to complain that a certain program has locked up. In such a scenario, which tool should you use to force the program to quit and how do you open the tool?

   A. Task Manager; press CTRL-SHIFT-ESC to open

   B. Task Manager; press CTRL-T-M to open

   C. Performance Monitor; open in Administrative Tools

   D. Performance Monitor; press CTRL-P-M to open

9. What tool enables you to track resource usage by PID, rather than a text string, for easier problem diagnosis?

   A. Performance Monitor

   B. PID Monitor

   C. Resource Monitor

   D. Task Manager

10. If a user has never used Task Manager before, which tab will be selected when it opens?

    A. Details tab

    B. More Details tab

    C. Processes tab

    D. None of the above

Answers

1. **D.** Game Mode prevents Windows Update from interrupting gameplay by restarting Windows to install updates.

2. **C.** Audit Success (along with Audit Failure) is a keyword unique to the Security log in Event Viewer.

3. B, C. To track resource usage in Performance Monitor, you need to configure objects and counters.

4. A, C. The Registry's root keys are further organized into subkeys and values.

5. A. The system's non-user-specific configurations are stored in the HKEY_LOCAL_ MACHINE root key of the Registry.

6. B. On macOS, Keychain (more specifically, the Keychain Access app) enables users to browse and manage certificates.

7. A. From the command prompt, you use regedit to open the Registry Editor.

8. A. The Task Manager is the tool you need to use to force a program to close in Windows. The easiest way to access the tool is to press CTRL-SHIFT-ESC simultaneously.

9. C. Resource Monitor organizes everything by PID (process ID) number. Using PIDs often can facilitate diagnosis of problems, because tracking a four-digit number is much easier than remembering a text string.

10. D. If a user hasn't previously changed to Task Manager's More details view, it will open in the Fewer details view (which has no tabs).

Users, Groups, and Permissions

In this chapter, you will learn how to

- Create and administer Windows users and groups
- Define and use NTFS permissions for authorization
- Share a Windows computer securely
- Secure PCs with policies and User Account Control

Your computer's mass storage is filled with files that need protection. You might have personal Word documents, spreadsheets, photos, and videos that you do not want others to access. You have critical files, such as the operating system itself, that cannot be accidentally deleted. You have browser histories and download folders full of files that you want and need. So how are these protected from others, even others who may use the same computer from time to time? The answer is user accounts, groups, and permissions.

Through the combination of user accounts and groups and NTFS permissions, Windows provides incredibly powerful file and folder security. This user/group/NTFS combination scales from a single computer up to a network of computers spanning the world.

When learning about users, groups, and NTFS permissions, it's helpful to know how NTFS works on a single PC with multiple users logging on and off during the day. To that end, this chapter focuses on Windows security from the point of view of a single, or *standalone*, machine. Chapter 19 takes over where this chapter stops and will revisit these topics in more detail and show you how the same tools scale up to help you protect a computer in a networked environment.

This chapter begins by examining user accounts, passwords, and groups, then turns to the high level of granular security afforded by NTFS. The third section describes methods for sharing and accessing shared content. The chapter wraps with a look under the hood at security policies and User Account Control.

1102

Authentication with Users and Groups

Security begins with a *standard account*, a unique combination of a username and an associated password, stored in a database on your computer, that grants the user access to the system. Although we normally assign a standard account to a human user, standard accounts are also assigned to everything that runs programs on your computer. For example, every Windows system has a SYSTEM account that Windows uses when it runs programs. Two mechanisms enable standard account security: authentication and authorization.

Authentication is the process of identifying and granting access to some user, usually a person, who is trying to access a system. In Windows, authentication is most commonly handled by a password-protected user account. The process of logging into a system is where the user types in an active username and password.

NOTE Authentication is the process of giving a user access to a system. Authorization determines what an authenticated user can do to a system.

Once a user authenticates, he or she needs *authorization*: the process that defines what resources an authenticated user may access and what they may do with those resources. Authorization for Windows' files and folders is controlled by the NTFS file system, which assigns permissions to users and groups. These permissions define exactly what users may do to a resource on the system. Let's continue our discussion of authentication with an overview of user accounts, passwords, and groups, then look at configuring users and groups in Windows.

NOTE Although this section primarily describes the use of user accounts, passwords, and groups in Windows, understand that all operating systems— without exception—use user accounts, passwords, and groups.

Standard Accounts

Every *standard account* (previously called user account) has a username and a password. A username is a text string that identifies the user account assigned to a system. Three examples of possible usernames are "Mike1" or "john.smith" or "some.person@outlook.com." Associated with every username is a password: a unique key known only by the system and the person using that username.

Every Windows system stores the user accounts as an encrypted database of usernames and passwords. Windows calls each record in this database a *local user account* (see Figure 13-1).

Figure 13-1
Windows logon
screen

Usernames and passwords are
stored here:
C:\Windows\System32\config\SAM

Once upon a time, the story ended here. These days, it's increasingly common to use a *global user account* that you register with your OS developer. On Chrome OS, the *only* way to get the full experience is by logging in with an account you register with Google. The opposite is true on Linux, where local user accounts (tied to a specific computer and user) rule. For its part, macOS still uses local user accounts—but you can *also* link your local account with your Apple ID to enable additional features. Windows combines all three approaches, supporting traditional local user accounts, the ability to link your Microsoft account with a local account to enable synchronization, as well as the ability to directly log in to Windows with your Microsoft account.

NOTE   *Global user account* is my term. Each company has its own name for its global accounts, such as a Microsoft account, Apple ID, or Google Account. Still, you get the idea, right?

Global accounts function like local accounts but add the benefit of synchronizing some of your stuff with the global account settings. My custom desktop picture at home, for example, matches the desktop picture on my laptop computer. I log in to both machines with my Microsoft account.

EXAM TIP   The CompTIA A+ 1102 exam objectives want you to know the difference between using a local account and a global Microsoft account. Logging in with a Microsoft account will automatically enable a number of features on your device such as alternative authentication options (which we'll look at in a moment), full-device encryption, file and setting synchronization, the ability to lock your device if it is lost, and more. It also enables you to reset your password if you forget it. Keep in mind that these features come at the expense of a greater risk that someone halfway around the world can log in to your account and access your data.

Creating a standard account (local or global) not only adds a username to a database, it also generates several folders on a computer. In Windows, for example, each standard account gets unique personal folders, such as Documents, Desktop, Pictures, Music, and more. By default, only a person logged in as a specific user can access the personal folders for that standard account. So, the next step is to secure that local standard account.

NOTE Your organization may also have its own equivalent of a global standard account. We'll take a closer look at single sign-on (SSO) using organizational accounts (via Active Directory) in Chapter 19.

Groups

A *group* is a container that holds user accounts and defines the capabilities of its members. A single account can be a member of multiple groups. Groups are an efficient way of managing multiple users, especially when you are dealing with a whole network of accounts. Standalone computers rely on groups too, though Windows obscures this a little, especially with Home edition users.

Groups make Windows administration much easier in two ways. First, you can assign a certain level of access for a file or folder to a group instead of to just a single standard account. You can make a group called Accounting, for example, and put all standard accounts for the accounting department in that group. If a person quits, you don't need to worry about assigning all the proper access levels when you create a new account for his or her replacement. After you make an account for the new person, just add that account to the appropriate access group! Second, Windows provides numerous built-in groups with various access levels already predetermined.

While all Windows editions come with many of these built-in groups, Windows Home edition handles them very differently than more advanced editions. For starters, make sure you are aware of the following groups for the exam:

- **Administrators** Any account that is a member of the *Administrators group* has complete *administrator privileges*. Administrator privileges grant complete control over a machine. It is common for the primary user of a Windows system to have her account in the Administrators group.

  When you create the Jane user account, in other words, and make Jane an administrator, you place the Jane account in the Administrators group. Because the Administrators group has all power over a system, Jane has all power over the system.

EXAM TIP The default administrator account is named *Administrator*. You should use this default only if no other administrators can log on. Best practice is to make a complex password for Administrator; write it down and put it in a safe for emergency use. *Change the default administrator's user account/password* to reflect one or more of the user accounts added to the Administrators group.

- **Power Users** Members of the *Power Users group* are almost as powerful as members of the Administrators group, but they cannot install new devices or access other users' files or folders unless the files or folders specifically provide them access.

- **Standard Account (Users)**   Members of a *Standard Account group* cannot edit the Registry or access critical system files. They can create groups but can manage only those they create. While *all* users are members of this group, there's a special name for members of *just* this group: *standard account* (or standard users).

  If you change the Jane account from administrator to standard user, you specifically take the Jane account out of the Administrators group (the Jane account is already in the Standard Users group). Nothing happens with her personal files or folders, but what the Jane account can do on the computer changes rather dramatically.

- **Guests group**   The *Guests group* enables someone who does not have an account on the system to log on by using a guest account. You might use this feature at a party, for example, to provide casual Internet access to guests, or at a library terminal. Most often, the guest account remains disabled. *Guest users* (which includes the usually disabled guest account) can't change settings, install anything, or access the personal files of other user accounts.

Standard Account and Elevated Privileges

The typical scenario with Windows machines is to have a single primary standard account—a standard user—and a local administrator account for doing important tasks like installing or uninstalling apps, updating software, and so on. When you're logged in as a standard user and need to do something that requires an administrator account, you have a couple of options. You could log out and log back in as an administrator, but that's clunky. Windows gives you a way to open and run utilities with the context menu of a right-click, called *Run as administrator*, or generically, *using elevated privileges*. The mechanism that will pop when you want to do something beyond your standard account level is called User Account Control (UAC). See the "Beyond Sharing Resources" section at the end of this chapter for the gory details.

Configuring Users and Groups in Windows

Windows comes with many tools to help you create, modify, and delete users. Groups are a different story, though, so let's focus on where you can go configure both users and groups: the *Local Users and Groups (lusrmgr.msc)* MMC snap-in, shown in Figure 13-2. You can access Local Users and Groups several different ways, but I prefer to right-click on Start, select Computer Management, and select Local Users and Groups in the left pane.

NOTE   For reasons that will be described shortly, Windows 10 Home edition does not have Local Users and Groups.

Local Users and Groups has two folders: Users and Groups. By default, the Users folder should already be selected. If not, click the Users folder now. Note the existing user accounts shown in Figure 13-2. Do you see Administrator? Do you see Michaelm?

Do you see Guest? Note the down arrow on the Guest user (and others) to show that they are disabled.

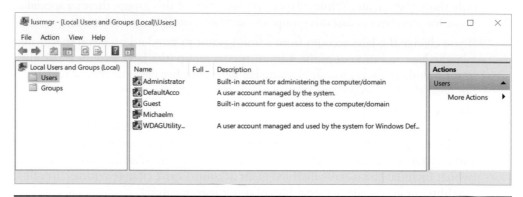

Figure 13-2 Local Users and Groups

Create a standard account (JimT) by right-clicking the whitespace below the existing standard accounts and selecting New User from the context menu. You then add the information to create the new account as shown in Figure 13-3.

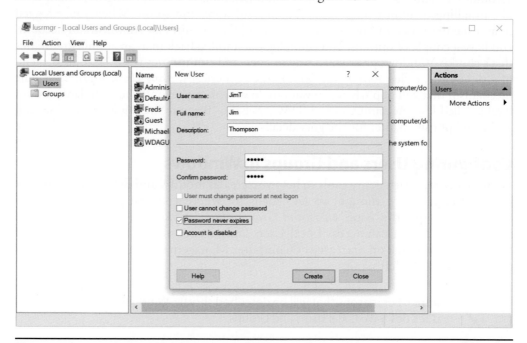

Figure 13-3 Creating a new user account called JimT

By default, all new user accounts are automatically added to the Users group. Click the Groups folder to see the many default groups. Figure 13-4 shows the default groups in Windows 10. Do you see Users, Power Users, Guests, and Administrators?

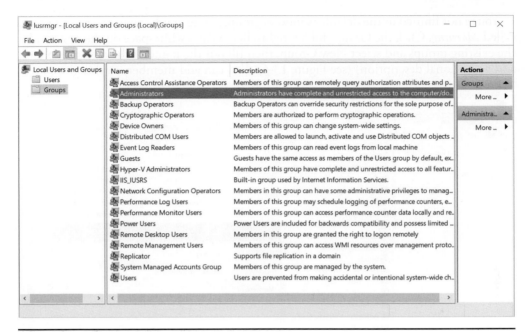

Figure 13-4   Default groups

Let's add the JimT standard account to the Administrators group. Double-click the Administrators group and select Add. Enter JimT into the Select Users dialog box (see Figure 13-5), then click OK.

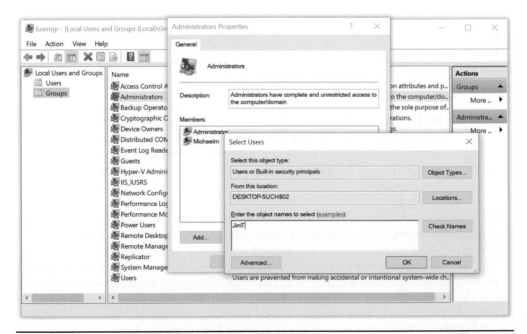

Figure 13-5   Adding JimT to the Administrators group

You're not limited to the default Windows groups. Here are the steps to create a group called *Morning*. Click the Groups folder, right-click on any whitespace on the right under the existing groups and select New Group, then fill out the name of the new group (and add an optional description) (see Figure 13-6). You can add members to this group.

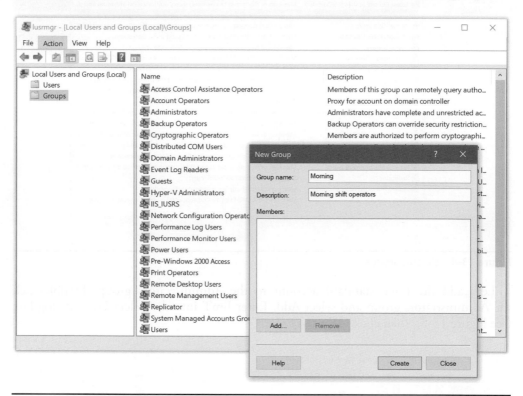

Figure 13-6   Creating the Morning group

 NOTE   To create and manage users, you must run Local Users and Groups as an administrator. The easiest way to do this is to open a command prompt with elevated privileges, type **lusrmgr.msc**, and press ENTER. See Chapter 15 for the scoop on running commands from the command-line interface.

Local Users and Groups is a perfectly fine tool for dealing with local users and groups on a single Windows system. Microsoft offers other tools as well. The newest and most important of these is the Accounts app located in Settings (see Figure 13-7).

The Accounts app is more for configuring your personal account than adding users or moving an account into a group. You can work with other users, however, by moving to the *Family & other users* menu option and clicking *Add someone else to this PC* (see Figure 13-8). Good luck creating a local user account though, because Microsoft hides this ability, pressuring you to use or create a Microsoft account.

Figure 13-7   Accounts app home

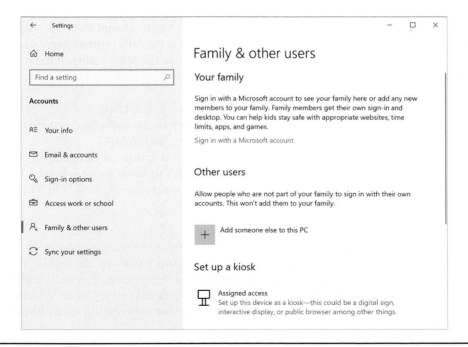

Figure 13-8   Family & other users

The *User Accounts Control (UAC)* utility in Windows 10 (see Figure 13-9) is handy for making more technical changes to your account. Here you can change (but not create) your group memberships and make simple changes to your account and other accounts (like changing the account name of a local non-domain account). You need to be a member of the Administrators group to make these changes. We will be discussing UAC more in-depth in the "User Accounts Control" section coming up.

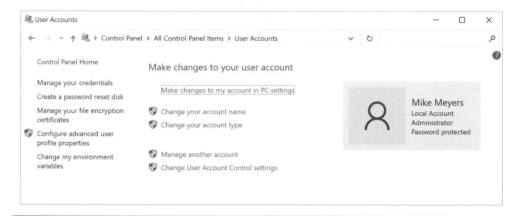

Figure 13-9 User Accounts in Windows 10

 EXAM TIP You can perform most account-management tasks via the Settings app, but CompTIA wants you to also be familiar with the traditional way to do this: the User Accounts applet in Control Panel. Don't be surprised if you get a question where User Accounts is the only right answer—but in the real world most of the actions you take in the applet will just redirect you to the Settings app or some other interface!

If you're not using the Windows 10 Home edition, Local Users and Groups is still the best way to go if you're comfortable with the power of the tools (and don't try to do something dangerous such as deleting the administrator account).

Whew! All this hubbub with local user accounts and groups is designed to do one thing only: get a user logged on to a Windows system. But once a user is logged on, it's time to see what they can do to the data. That's where authorization with NTFS kicks in.

Authentication Options

When it comes to actually authenticating with (or logging in to) a computer, the standard for most computers has long been a username and password. As mobile devices (the focus of Chapters 24 and 25) have revolutionized computing, they've also affected how we authenticate. In particular, there are now several ways to log in to Windows—and a new Account | Sign-in option page in Settings for configuring them (shown in Figure 13-10).

Figure 13-10
Sign-in options
in Windows 11
Settings app

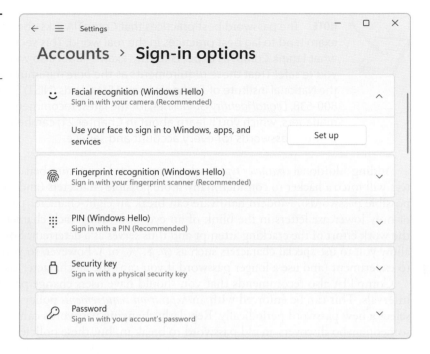

The CompTIA A+ 1102 exam objectives don't expect you to know about *all* of these options (CompTIA refers to them as "login OS options), so I'll just focus on the ones you do need to know about. Since every account still needs to have a good password, I'll start there and discuss some password-related best practices.

Username and Passwords

Usernames and passwords help secure user accounts. For starters, never use a similar name and password. Protect your passwords. Never give out passwords over the phone. If someone learns your username and password, he or she can log on to your computer. Even if the user account has only limited permissions—perhaps it can only read files, not edit them—you still have a security breach.

Make your users choose good passwords. I once attended a security seminar, and the speaker had everyone stand up. She then began to ask questions about our passwords— if we responded yes to the question, we had to sit down. She began to ask questions like these:

"Do you use the name of your spouse as a password?"
"Do you use your pet's name?"

By the time she had asked about 15 questions, only 6 people out of some 300 were still standing. The reality is that most of us choose passwords that are amazingly easy to hack. Make sure users have a *strong password*: at *least* eight characters long, including letters (some uppercase), numbers, and non-alphanumeric symbols. Many organizations have their employees, clients, customers, etc., use these *complexity requirements* to ensure they've chosen a hard-to-guess password.

NOTE The password best practices that CompTIA asks about on the A+ 1102 exam tend to lag best practices in the real world. This section focuses on what I think CompTIA expects for the exam—but I also want to make sure you're safe! Treat these requirements as the *bare* minimum and check out the National Institute of Technology and Standards (NIST) Special Publication 800-63B, *Digital Identity Guidelines*, for the latest recommendations. Password managers, which you'll learn about in Chapter 21, can help you use long, unique passwords for every account and service.

Adding additional *character types* such as uppercase letters, numbers, and special characters will force a hacker to consider many more possible characters (and many, many more possible passwords). Modern hardware can break an eight-character password consisting of only lowercase letters in the blink of an eye—but using each character type increases the work effort of the cracking attempt and thus serves as a deterrent. Some systems won't allow you to use special characters such as @, $, %, or \, however, so you need may need to experiment (and use a longer password if you can't use all character types).

CompTIA also recommends that you should have users change passwords at regular intervals. This can be enforced with an *expiration requirements* policy that forces users to select a new password periodically. Regularly changing passwords can make it harder for someone who discovers an old password to break in, but these policies are hard to maintain in the real world. For starters, users tend to forget passwords when they change too often, leading to an even bigger security problem.

If your organization forces everyone to change passwords often, some people will just adopt a numbering system to help them remember. In a simpler era, I worked at a company that required me to change my password at the beginning of each month. So, I took a root password—let's say it was "m3y3rs5"—and added a number to the end representing the current month. So, when June rolled around, for example, I would change my password to "m3y3rs56." I was pretty proud of this system at the time, but anyone who discovered one of my older passwords could have guessed my new password and broken into my system in a heartbeat!

NOTE Every secure organization sets up various security policies and procedures to ensure that security is maintained. Windows has various mechanisms to implement such things as requiring a strong password, for example. Chapter 27 goes into detail about setting up Local Policies and Group Policy.

Windows requires you to create a password hint or password questions for your local accounts. This clue appears above the reset password option after your first logon attempt fails.

CAUTION Blank passwords or passwords that are easily visible on a sticky note provide no security. Always insist on non-blank passwords, and do not let anyone leave a password sitting out in the open.

Fingerprints and Facial Recognition

Nothing quite makes me feel like I'm both living in the future and in line at the DMV like setting up a computer to authenticate by scanning my fingerprints or recognizing my face (refer back to Chapter 10 for *fingerprint* and *facial recognition*).

NOTE Before you can even set up these (or many other) *biometric* authentication options, your computer will need special equipment—like a fingerprint scanner or a good front-facing camera.

When you decide to set up one of these options for the first time, your device will give you instructions on what it needs you to do with your fingers or face in order for it to collect sufficient information to authenticate you with later. As shown in Figure 13-11, fingerprint setup requires you to place your finger on the scanner repeatedly at slightly different angles, while facial recognition setup instructs you to center your face in the frame and look directly at the camera.

Figure 13-11 Adding fingerprint (left) and facial recognition (right) with Windows Hello

Personal Identification Number

Traditionally, a *personal identification number (PIN)* is usually a 4- or 6-digit numeric code that provides a little extra security—most often in a banking or financial context such as debit card transactions and accessing an ATM. This definition isn't all that much help in understanding the PIN's role in logging in to Windows, though!

The first thing to know is that the PIN is only an option when you log in to Windows with a Microsoft account. Second, it doesn't *have* to be a numeric PIN—you can check the *Include letters and symbols* checkbox (shown in Figure 13-12) to enable the "PIN" to be a strong password. Third, you'll have to set up a PIN to use biometric authentication options—Windows wants you to have a backup option in case you damage your scanner, camera, fingers, or face! Fourth, if the PIN is numbers only, it can't be a number pattern. Finally, the PIN is specific to the device you set it up on—setting up a PIN on one device won't enable you to use it on your other devices.

Figure 13-12
Creating a
Windows
Hello PIN

> **NOTE** *Single sign-on (SSO)* is yet another login OS option where users can
> authenticate through a single domain account that enables access to all
> machines on the domain, thus the term *single sign-on*. Single sign-on is
> further discussed in Chapter 19.

Authorization Through NTFS

User accounts and passwords provide the foundation for securing a Windows computer, enabling users to authenticate to log on to a PC. After you've created a user account, you need to determine what the user can do with the available resources (files, folders, applications, and so on). This *authorization* process uses the NT File System (NTFS) as the primary tool.

NTFS Permissions

Every file and folder on an NTFS partition has a list that contains two sets of data. First, the list details every user and group that has access to that file or folder. Second, the list specifies the *level* of access that each user or group has to that file or folder. The level of access is defined by a set of restrictions called NTFS permissions. *NTFS permissions* are rulesets, connected to every folder and file in your system, that define exactly what any account or group can or cannot do to the file or folder.

NTFS permissions are quite detailed and powerful. You can, for example, set up NTFS permissions to enable a user account to edit a file but not delete it. You could also configure NTFS permissions to enable any member of a user group to create a subfolder for a folder. You can even configure a folder so that one group may be able to read the files but not delete them, modify them, or even see them in File Explorer.

NTFS file and folder permissions are powerful and complicated. Entire books have been written just on NTFS permissions. Fortunately, the CompTIA A+ 220-1102 exam tests your understanding of only the following basic concepts of NTFS permissions:

- **Ownership** When you create a new file or folder on an NTFS partition, you become the *owner of* that file or folder. This is called *ownership*. Owners can do anything they want to the files or folders they own, including changing the permissions to prevent anybody, even administrators, from accessing them.

- **Take Ownership permission** With the Take Ownership permission, anyone with the permission can seize control of a file or folder. Administrator accounts have Take Ownership permission for everything. Note the difference here between owning a file and accessing a file. If you own a file, you can prevent anyone from accessing that file. An administrator whom you have blocked, however, can take that ownership away from you and *then* access that file!

- **Change permission** Another important permission for all NTFS files and folders is the Change permission. An account with this permission can give or take away permissions for other accounts.

- **Folder permissions** *Folder permissions* define what a user may do to a folder. One example might be "List folder contents," which gives the permission to see what's in the folder.

- **File permissions** *File permissions* define what a user may do to an individual file. One example is Read & Execute, which gives a user account the permission to run an executable program.

The primary way to set NTFS permissions is through the Security tab of the Properties of a folder or file (see Figure 13-13). The Security tab contains two main areas. The top area shows the list of accounts that have permissions for that resource. The lower area shows exactly what permissions have been assigned to the selected account.

You add or remove NTFS permissions by first selecting the user or group you wish to change and then clicking Edit to open a Permissions dialog box. To add an NTFS permission, select the Allow checkbox next to the NTFS permission you want to add.

Figure 13-13
The Security tab enables you to set permissions.

You remove an NTFS permission by deselecting the Allow checkbox next to the NTFS permission you want to remove. The Deny checkbox is not used very often and has a very different job—see the next section, "Inheritance."

Here are the standard NTFS permissions for a folder:

- **Full Control**   Enables you to do anything you want to the folder
- **Modify**   Enables you to read, write, and delete both files and subfolders
- **Read & Execute**   Enables you to see the contents of the folder and any subfolders as well as run any executable programs or associations in that folder
- **List Folder Contents**   Enables you to see the contents of the folder and any subfolders
- **Read**   Enables you to view a folder's contents and open any file in the folder
- **Write**   Enables you to write to files and create new files and folders
- **Full Control**   Enables you to do anything you want to the file
- **Modify**   Enables you to read, write, and delete the file

- **Read & Execute** Enables you to open and run the file
- **Read** Enables you to open the file
- **Write** Enables you to open and write to the file

Here are a few important points about NTFS permissions:

- To see the NTFS permissions on a folder or file, access the file's or folder's Properties dialog box and open the Security tab.
- NTFS permissions are assigned both to user accounts and groups, although it's considered a best practice to assign permissions to groups and then add user accounts to groups instead of adding permissions directly to individual user accounts.
- Permissions are cumulative. If you have Full Control on a folder and only Read permission on a file in the folder, you get Full Control permission on the file.
- Whoever creates a folder or a file has complete control over that folder or file. This is ownership.
- If an administrator wants to access a folder or file they do not have permission to access, they may go through the Take Ownership process.

Take some time to think about these permissions. Why would Microsoft create them? Think of scenarios where you might want to give a group Modify permission. Also, you can assign more than one permission. In many situations, administrators give users both the Read and Write permissions to files or folders.

Inheritance

Inheritance determines which NTFS permissions any newly introduced files or subfolders contained in a folder receive. To understand how a new folder (shown in Figure 13-14) gets its permissions, techs need to know how inheritance works.

Figure 13-14
What are the new folder's permissions?

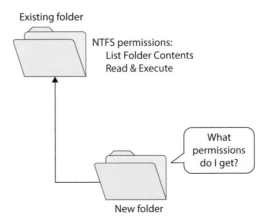

Existing folder

NTFS permissions:
   List Folder Contents
   Read & Execute

What permissions do I get?

New folder

The base rule of Windows inheritance is that any new files or folders placed into a folder automatically get all the NTFS permissions of the parent folder. So if, for example, you have Read & Execute access to a folder and someone else copies a file to that folder, you will automatically get Read & Execute permissions (see Figure 13-15).

Figure 13-15
Here are your permissions.

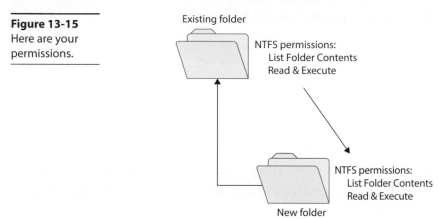

Existing folder

NTFS permissions:
List Folder Contents
Read & Execute

NTFS permissions:
List Folder Contents
Read & Execute

New folder

All versions of Windows have inheritance turned on by default, which most of the time is a good idea. If you access a folder's Properties dialog box, click the Security tab, and then click the Advanced button, you'll see a button that says either *Disable inheritance* or *Enable inheritance*. If you wanted to turn off inheritance, you could click this button. Don't do that. Inheritance is good. Inheritance is expected.

If you look closely at Figure 13-16, you'll see that there are two grayed-out NTFS Allow permissions. That's how Windows tells you that the permissions are inherited. These checkmarks can't be changed, so what do you do if you need to make a change?

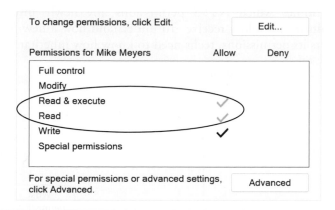

Figure 13-16 Inherited permissions

You can edit the permissions by clicking the Edit button above the permissions list. This opens a new dialog (shown in Figure 13-17) where the checkmarks appear as checkboxes.

Figure 13-17
Editing
permissions

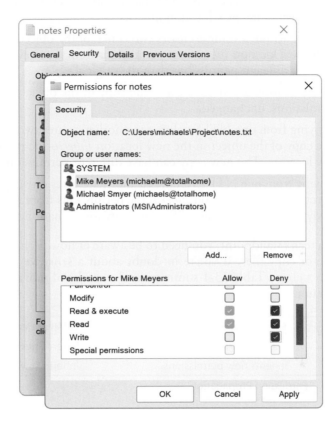

Permission Propagation

Permission propagation determines what NTFS permissions are applied to files that are moved or copied into a new folder. Be careful here! You might be tempted to think, given you've just learned about inheritance, that any new files/folders copied or moved into a folder would just inherit the folder's NTFS permissions, but this is not always true. It depends on two issues: whether the data is being copied or moved, and whether the data is coming from the same volume or a different one. So, we need to consider these situations:

- Copying data within one NTFS-based volume creates two copies of the object. The copy of the object in the new location inherits...

- Moving data within one NTFS-based volume creates one copy of the object. That object retains its permissions, unchanged.

- Copying data between two NTFS-based volumes creates two copies of the object. The copy of the object…

- Moving data between two NTFS-based volumes creates one copy of the object. The object in the new location inherits…

- Copying within a volume creates two copies of the object. The copy of the object in the new location *inherits* the permissions from that new location. The new copy can have different permissions than the original.

- Moving within a volume creates one copy of the object. That object *retains* its permissions, unchanged.

- Copying from one NTFS volume to another creates two copies of the object. The copy of the object in the new location *inherits* the permissions from that new location. The new copy can have different permissions than the original.

- Moving from one NTFS volume to another creates one copy of the object. The object in the new location *inherits* the permissions from that new location. The newly moved file can have different permissions than the original.

From a tech's standpoint, you need to be aware of how permissions can change when you move or copy files. If you're in doubt about a sensitive file, check it before you sign off to a client. Table 13-1 summarizes the results of moving and copying between NTFS volumes.

	Same Volume	Different Volume
Move	Keeps original permissions	Inherits new permissions
Copy	Inherits new permissions	Inherits new permissions

Table 13-1   Permission Propagation

 EXAM TIP   Current versions of Windows refer to sections of an HDD or SSD as *volumes*, as you'll recall from Chapter 9. Earlier versions—and many techs and exams in your near future—refer to such groupings as *partitions*. Be prepared for either term.

Any object that you put on a FAT partition loses any permissions because FAT doesn't support NTFS permissions. This applies in most current scenarios involving FAT32- or exFAT-partitioned mass storage devices, such as the ubiquitous thumb drives that all of us use for quick copying and moving of files from device to device.

Techs and Permissions

You must have local administrative privileges to do almost anything on a Windows machine, such as install updates, change drivers, and install applications; most administrators hate giving out administrative permissions (for obvious reasons). If an administrator does give you administrative permission for a PC and something goes wrong with that system while you're working on it, you immediately become the primary suspect!

If you're working on a Windows system administered by someone else, make sure that administrator understands what you are doing and how long you think it will take. Have the administrator create a new temporary account for you that's a member of the Administrators group. Never ask for the password to a permanent administrator account! That way, you won't be blamed if anything goes wrong on that system: "Well, I told Janet the password when she installed the new hard drive . . . maybe she did it!" When you have fixed the system, *make sure the administrator deletes the account you used.*

Permissions in Linux and macOS

While the CompTIA A+ 1102 exam concentrates hard on Windows users, groups, and permissions, this is a good time to consider that Linux and macOS also have their own concepts pertaining to users, groups, and permissions. Let's take a short jaunt into Linux and macOS users, groups, and permissions. We'll look at the chmod and chown commands because they are listed as objectives for the CompTIA A+ 1102 exam.

 NOTE Understanding this section requires some understanding of the Linux command line. You may need to refer to Chapter 15 to practice some of the commands shown here.

Just as in Windows, every file and folder on a Linux or macOS system has permissions. You can easily see this if you go to a Linux terminal and type this command: ls -l. This shows a detailed list of all the files and folders in a location, like the following example. Chapter 15 discusses the ls command in a lot more detail, but this is enough for our present discussion.

```
drwxrwxr-x 2 mikemeyers mi6      4096 Oct  2 18:35 agent_bios
-rw-rw-r-- 1 mikemeyers mi6     34405 Oct  2 18:39 datafile
-rwxrwxrwx 1 mikemeyers mi6      7624 Oct  2 18:39 honeypot
-rw-rw-r-- 1 mikemeyers users     299 Oct  2 18:36 launch_codes
-rw-rw-r-- 1 mikemeyers mi6       905 Oct  2 18:36 passwords.txt
```

Let's zero in on one line of this output:

```
-rwxrwxrwx 1 mikemeyers mi6      7624 Oct  2 18:39 honeypot
```

First, let's get the nonessential details out of the way: The 1 is about links (admins may need to care about these); mikemeyers is the owner and mi6 is the group. The file size is 7624; the date and time are next. The filename is honeypot.

Now note the string -rwxrwxrwx. Each of those letters represents a permission for this file. Ignore the dash at the beginning. That is used to tell us if this listing is a file, directory, or shortcut. What we have left are three groups of rwx. The three groups, in order, stand for:

- **Owner**   Permissions for the owner of this file or folder
- **Group**   Permissions for members of the group for this file or folder
- **Everyone**   Permissions for anyone for this file or folder

The letters r, w, and x represent the following permissions:

- **r**   Read the contents of a file
- **w**   Write or modify a file or folder
- **x**   Execute a file or list the folder contents

Figure 13-18 shows the relationships.

Figure 13-18
UNIX-style file permissions

Let's look at another example:

```
-rw-rw-r-- 1 mikemeyers users   299 Oct  2 18:36 launch_codes
```

- This file is called launch_codes. The owner of this file is me. This file is in the users group.
- The owner, mikemeyers, has read and write privileges (rw-).
- The group, users, has read and write privileges (rw-).
- No one has execute permissions (x) because this is just a text file, not a script or program.
- Everyone can read the launch_codes file (r--). We should probably fix that.

chown Command

The *chown* command enables you to change the owner and the group with which a file or folder is associated. The chown command uses the following syntax:

```
chown <new owner> filename
```

To change the group, use the following syntax:

```
chown <owner>:<group> filename
```

So, to change the owner of launch_codes to sally, type

```
chown sally launch_codes
```

To change the group to mi6, type

```
chown sally:mi6 launch_codes
```

If you retype the **ls -l** command, you would see the following output:

```
-rw-rw-r-- 1 sally mi6    299 Oct  2 18:36 launch_codes
```

Be aware that the chown command needs superuser privileges (sudo or su). Refer to Chapter 15 for details.

chmod Command

The *chmod* command is used to change permissions. Sadly, it uses a somewhat nonintuitive addition system that works as follows:

```
r: 4
w: 2
x: 1
```

For example, we can interpret the permissions on

```
-rw-rw-r-- 1 mikemeyers mi6      299 Oct  2 18:36 launch_codes
```

as follows:

- Owner's permissions are 6: 4 + 2 (rw-)
- Group's permissions are 6: 4 + 2 (rw-)
- Everyone's permissions are 4: 4 (r--)

The chmod command uses the following syntax to make permission changes:

```
chmod <permissions> <filename>
```

Using this nomenclature, we can make any permission change desired using only three numbers. The current permissions can be represented by 664. To keep the launch codes out of the wrong hands, just change the 4 to a 0: 660. To make the change, use the chmod command as follows:

```
chmod 660 launch_codes
```

To give everyone complete control, give everyone read + write + execute. 4 + 2 + 1 = 7. So, use the command as follows:

```
chmod 777 launch_codes
```

NOTE The *most common* syntax for the chmod command uses three digits, from 0 to 7, but the command technically supports four digits (and even an entirely different *symbolic* syntax). Run the command **man chmod** for more details.

Sharing Resources Securely

By using NTFS, Windows makes private the folders and files in a specific user's personal folders (Documents, Music, Pictures, and so on). In other words, only the user who created those documents can access those documents. Members of the Administrators group can override this behavior, but members of the Users group (standard users) cannot. To make resources available to multiple users on a shared Windows machine requires you to take extra steps and actively share.

Sharing Folders and Files

The primary way to share resources on a single computer is to give users or groups NTFS permissions to specific folders and files. This process requires you to a right-click on a file or folder, select Properties, and click the Security tab. You'll notice the Security tab has two sections. The top section is a list of users and groups that currently have NTFS permissions to that folder, and the bottom section is a list of NTFS permissions for the currently selected users and groups (see Figure 13-19).

Figure 13-19
Folder Security
tab

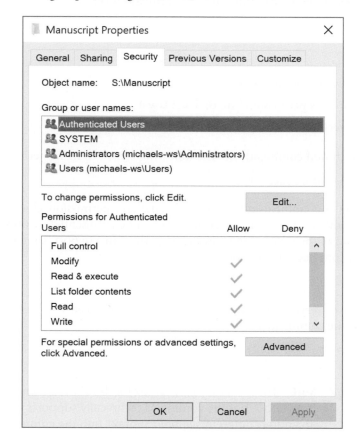

To add a new user or group, click the Edit button. In the Permissions dialog box that opens, you not only can add new users and groups but also can remove them and edit existing NTFS permissions (see Figure 13-20).

 NOTE The Sharing tab in Figure 13-19 accesses the Sharing Wizard, discussed shortly. It's about network shares rather than NTFS sharing.

Figure 13-20
Permissions
dialog box

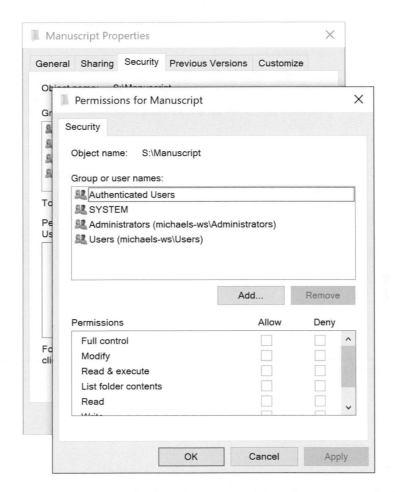

While the method just shown works for all versions of Windows, it's a tad old fashioned. Windows provides the *Sharing Wizard*, which is less powerful but easier to use. To use this method, pick anything you want to share (even a single file) in File Explorer. Then simply right-click on it and choose Give access to | Specific people, which opens the Network access dialog box, shown in Figure 13-21, where you can select specific user accounts from a drop-down list.

Once you select a user account, you can then choose what permission level to give to that user. Note that your account is listed as Owner. You have two choices for permissions to give to others: Read and Read/Write (see Figure 13-22). *Read* simply means the user has read-only permissions. *Read/Write* gives the user read and write permissions and the permission to delete any file the user contributed to the folder.

 NOTE If the computer in question is on a Windows domain, the Network access dialog box lets you search the network for user accounts in the domain. This makes it easy to share throughout the network. See Chapter 19 to learn about Windows domains.

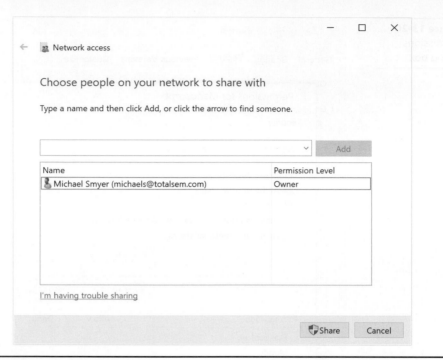

Figure 13-21 Network access dialog box

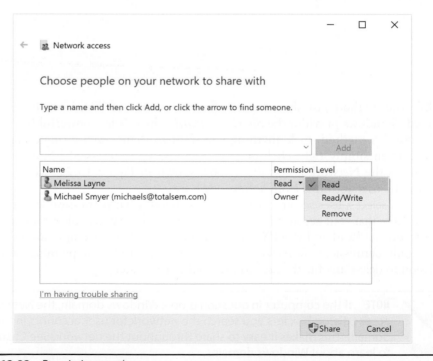

Figure 13-22 Permissions options

Locating Shared Folders

Before you walk away from a computer, you should check for any unnecessary or unknown (to you) shared folders on the hard drives. This enables you to make the computer as secure as possible for the user. When you look in File Explorer, shared folders don't just jump out at you, especially if they're buried deep within the file system. A shared C: drive is obvious, but a shared folder all the way down in D:\temp\backup\Simon\secret_share would not be obvious, especially if none of the parent folders were shared.

Windows comes with a handy tool for locating all the shared folders on a computer, regardless of where they reside on the drives. The Computer Management console in Administrative Tools has a Shared Folders option under System Tools. Under Shared Folders are three options: Shares, Sessions, and Open Files. Select Shares to reveal all the shared folders (see Figure 13-23).

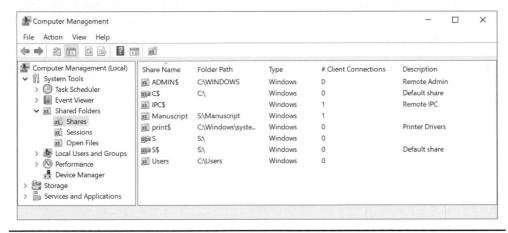

Figure 13-23   Shared Folders tool in Computer Management

You can double-click on any share to open the Properties dialog box for that folder. At that point, you can make changes to the share—such as users and permissions— just as you would from any other sharing dialog box. A close look at the screenshot in Figure 13-23 might have left some of you with raised eyebrows. What kind of share is ADMIN$ or C$?

Every version of Windows since Windows NT way back in the early 1990s comes with several default shares, notably all hard drives—not optical drives or removable devices, such as thumb drives—plus the %systemroot% folder (usually C:\Windows) and a couple of others, depending on the system. These *administrative shares* give local administrators administrative access to these resources, whether they log on locally or remotely. (In contrast, shares added manually are called *local shares*.)

Administrative shares are odd ducks. You cannot change the default permissions on them. You can delete them, but Windows will re-create them automatically every time you reboot. They're hidden, so they don't appear when you browse a machine over the network, though you can map them by name. Keep the administrator password safe, and these default shares won't affect the overall security of the computer.

Protecting Data with Encryption

The scrambling of data through encryption techniques provides the only true way to secure your data from access by any other user. Administrators can use the Take Ownership permission to seize any file or folder on a computer, even those you don't actively share. Thus, you need to implement other security measures for that data that needs to be ultra-secure. Depending on the Windows edition, you have between zero and three encryptions tools: Windows Home edition has basically no security features. Advanced editions of Windows such as Windows Pro, Windows Pro for Workstations, and Windows Enterprise add a system that can encrypt files and folders called Encrypting File System. Finally, the most advanced editions feature drive encryption through *BitLocker*.

Encrypting File System

The professional editions of Windows offer a feature called the *Encrypting File System (EFS)*, an encryption scheme that any user can use to encrypt individual files or folders on a computer.

To encrypt a file or folder takes seconds. Right-click on the file or folder you want to encrypt and select Properties. On the General tab of the Properties dialog box for that object, click the Advanced button (see Figure 13-24) to open the Advanced Attributes dialog box. Check the *Encrypt contents to secure data* checkbox (see Figure 13-25).

Figure 13-24
Click the Advanced button on the General tab.

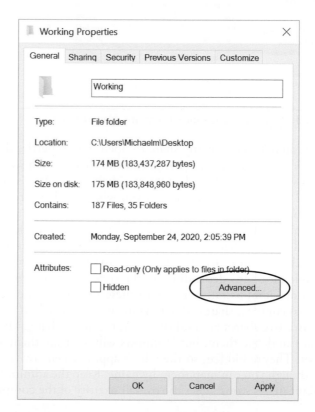

Figure 13-25
Selecting
encryption

Click OK to close the Advanced Attributes dialog box and then click OK again to close the Properties dialog box, and you've locked that file or folder from any user account aside from your own.

As long as you maintain the integrity of your password, any data you encrypt by using EFS is secure from prying. That security comes at a potential price, though, and your password is the key. The Windows security database stores the password (securely, not plain text, so no worries there), but that means access to your encrypted files is based on that specific installation of Windows. If you lose your password or an administrator resets your password, you're locked out of your encrypted files permanently. (There are some very complex ways to try to recover the files, but they're likely to fail—I wouldn't count on them working!) Also, if the computer dies and you try to retrieve your data by installing the hard drive in another system, you're likewise out of luck. Even if you have an identical username on the new system, the security ID that defines that user account will differ from what you had on the old system.

NOTE If you use EFS, you may want to back up your file encryption certificates in case something terrible happens. You can back them up by selecting *Manage your file encryption certificates* in the User Accounts Control Panel applet. One of the steps in the dialog this opens will enable you to save a password-protected backup.

And one last caveat. If you copy an encrypted file to a drive formatted as anything but NTFS, you'll get a prompt saying that the copied file will not be encrypted. If you copy to a drive with NTFS, the encryption stays. The encrypted file—even if on a removable disk—will only be readable on your system with your login.

BitLocker Drive Encryption

Windows Pro and better offer full drive encryption through *BitLocker Drive Encryption*. BitLocker encrypts the whole drive, including every user's files, so it's not dependent on any one account. The beauty of BitLocker is that if your hard drive is stolen, such as in the case of a stolen portable computer, all the data on the hard drive is safe. The thief can't get access, even if you have a user on that system who failed to secure his or her data through EFS.

BitLocker requires a special Trusted Platform Module (TPM) chip on the motherboard to function. The TPM chip (which we looked at in Chapter 5) validates on boot that the computer has not changed—that you still have the same operating system installed, for example, and that the computer wasn't hacked by some malevolent program. The TPM also works in cases where you move the BitLocker drive from one system to another.

NOTE BitLocker can use a USB flash drive to store its recovery key if you don't have a TPM chip. While this is better than nothing, you do sacrifice some of the security that a TPM chip provides.

If you have a legitimate BitLocker failure (rather than a theft) because of tampering or moving the drive to another system, you need to have a properly created and accessible recovery key or recovery password. The key or password is generally created at the time you enable BitLocker and should be kept somewhere secure, such as a printed copy in a safe or a file on a network server accessible only to administrators.

To enable BitLocker, double-click the BitLocker Drive Encryption icon in the Classic Control Panel, or select Security in Control Panel Home view and then click Turn on BitLocker (see Figure 13-26).

BitLocker To Go enables you to apply BitLocker encryption to removable drives, like USB-based flash drives. Although it shares a name, BitLocker To Go applies encryption and password protection, but doesn't require a TPM chip. Still, every little bit counts when it comes to securing data.

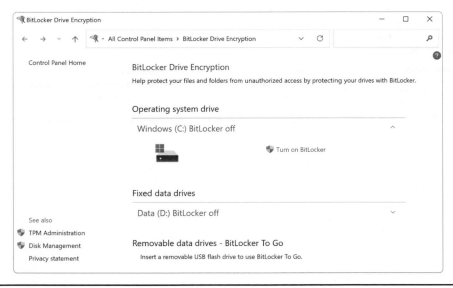

Figure 13-26   Enabling BitLocker Drive Encryption

Beyond Sharing Resources

As you've just seen, users and groups are powerful tools for authenticating users to systems as well as authorizing NTFS permissions, but that's not where their power ends. There are two more areas where we use users and groups to go beyond logging on to a system or sharing folders and files: security policies and User Account Control. Let's discuss security policies first and then cover User Account Control.

Security Policies

Security policies are rules applied to users and groups—and they can do just about everything NTFS permissions can't. Would you like to configure your system so that the Accounting group can log on only between 9 A.M. and 5 P.M.? There's a security policy for that. How about forcing anyone who logs on to your system to use a password that's at least eight characters long? There's a security policy for that as well. Windows provides thousands of preset security policies that you may use simply by turning them on in a utility called *Local Security Policy (secpol.msc)*.

You can access this tool through Control Panel's Administrative Tools, but all of us cool kids just open a command line and run **secpol.msc**. However, if you choose to access this tool, it will look something like Figure 13-27.

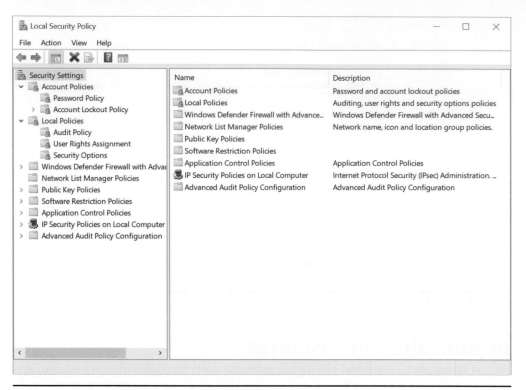

Figure 13-27 Local Security Policy utility

EXAM TIP The Group Policy Editor *(gpedit.msc)* includes the same items as Local Security Policy (in its Security folder)—plus many other policies. Local Security Policy is the most direct way to work with security policies, but CompTIA left it out of the exam objectives this time around. Look for Group Policy Editor (introduced in Chapter 11) if you see a question about editing security policies on the CompTIA A+ 1102 exam—but be flexible if Local Security Policy is the only good answer.

Local Security Policy has a number of containers that help organize the many types of policies on a typical system. Under each container are subcontainers or preset policies. As an example, let's set a local security policy that causes user passwords to expire every 30 days—better known as account password expiration or password age. To do this, open the Account Policies container and then open the Password Policy subcontainer.

Look at the Maximum password age setting. Local user accounts passwords expire after 42 days by default on Windows. On almost all versions of Windows, your local user accounts passwords expire after 42 days. You can easily change this to 30 days just by double-clicking Maximum password age and adjusting the setting in the Properties dialog box, as shown in Figure 13-28. You can also set the value to 0 and the password will never expire.

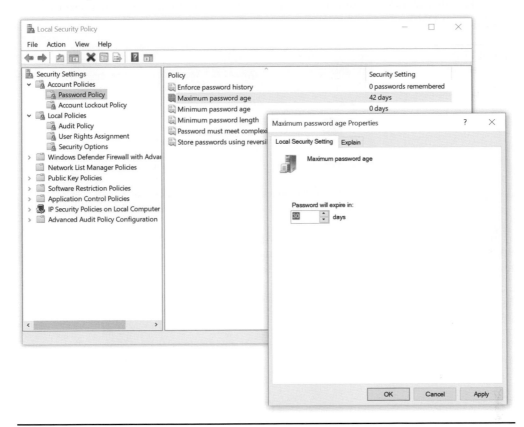

Figure 13-28   Editing Maximum password age in Local Security Policy

 NOTE   Policies are useful for configuring local systems, but they *really* shine when you can apply them to every system in your entire network or apply different policies to systems in different departments. Keep an eye out for *domains* in Chapter 19 to learn more about applying policies to many systems at once.

User Account Control

The *User Account Control (UAC)* starting way back in Vista to stop unauthorized changes to Windows. These potential changes can come from installing applications or malicious software, among other things. You'd think consumers would applaud such a feature, right?

When picking the poster child for the "327 Reasons We Hated Vista" list, I'll bet most folks put Vista's UAC at the very top. Vista's UAC manifested as a pop-up dialog box that seemed to appear every time you tried to do *anything* on a Vista system (see Figure 13-29).

Figure 13-29
UAC in action.
Arrgh!

It's too bad that UAC got such a bad rap. Not only is UAC an important security update for all versions of Windows, both macOS and Linux/UNIX have an equivalent feature. Figure 13-30 shows the equivalent feature on a Mac.

Figure 13-30
UAC equivalent
on a Mac

If every other major operating system uses something like UAC, why was Microsoft slammed so hard when it unveiled UAC in Windows Vista? The reason was simple: Windows users are spoiled rotten, and until UAC came along, the vast majority of users had no idea how risky their computing behavior was.

The problem started years ago when Microsoft created NTFS. NTFS uses robust user accounts and enables fine control over how users access files and folders—but at a cost: NTFS in its pure form is somewhat complicated.

User accounts have always been a bit of a challenge. The only account that can truly do *anything* on a Windows system is the administrator. Sure, you can configure a system with groups and assign NTFS permissions to those groups—and this is commonly done on large networks with a full-time IT staff—but what about small offices and home networks? These users almost never have the skill sets to deal with the complexities of users and groups, which often results in systems where the user accounts are all assigned administrator privileges by default—and that's when it gets dangerous (see Figure 13-31).

Figure 13-31
The danger of administrator privileges in the wrong hands!

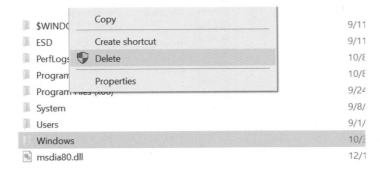

User Account Control enables users to know when they are about to do something that has serious consequences. Here are some examples of common actions that require administrator privileges:

- Installing and uninstalling applications
- Installing a driver for a device (e.g., a video card)
- Installing Windows Updates
- Adjusting Windows Firewall settings
- Changing a user's account type
- Browsing to another user's directory

Before Vista, Microsoft invented the idea of the Power Users group to give users almost all the power of an administrator account (to handle most of the situations just described) without actually giving users the full power of the account. Assigning a user to the Power Users group still required someone who knew how to do this, however, so most folks at the small office/home level simply ignored the Power Users group (see Figure 13-32).

Clearly, Microsoft needed a better method to prevent people from running programs that they should not run. If users have the correct privileges, however—or the ability to "escalate" their privileges to that of an administrator—then they should be able to do what they need to do as simply as possible. Microsoft needed to make the following changes:

- The idea of using an administrator account for daily use needed to go away.
- Any level of account should be able to do anything as easily as possible.

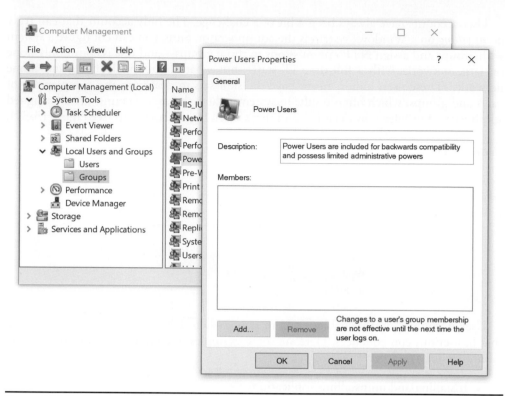

Figure 13-32 Power Users group—almost never used at the small office/home level

- If a regular account wants to do something that requires administrator privileges, the user of the regular account will need to enter the administrator password.

- If a user with administrator privileges wants to run something that requires administrator privileges, the user will not have to reenter his or her password, but the user will have to respond to an "Are you sure?"–type dialog box so he or she appreciates the gravity of the action—thus, the infamous UAC dialog box.

NOTE Both Linux and macOS have a UAC command-line function called *sudo*. Check it out in Chapter 15.

How UAC Works

UAC works for both standard accounts and administrator accounts. If a standard user attempts to do something that requires administrator privileges, he or she sees a UAC dialog box that prompts for the administrator password (see Figure 13-33).

Figure 13-33
Prompting for
an administrator
password in
Windows 10

NOTE The official name for the UAC dialog box is the "UAC consent prompt."

If a user with administrator privileges attempts to do something that requires administrator privileges, a simpler UAC dialog box appears, like the one shown in Figure 13-34.

Figure 13-34
Classic UAC
prompt

UAC uses small shield icons to warn you ahead of time that it will prompt you before certain tasks, as shown in Figure 13-35. Microsoft updated this somewhat redundant feature in subsequent versions of Windows after Vista, as you'll soon see.

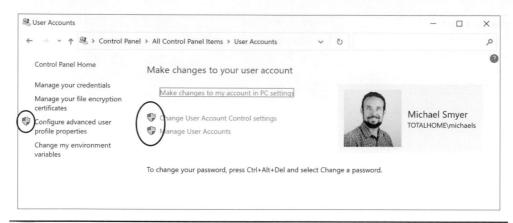

Figure 13-35   Shield icons in User Accounts

UAC gives users running a program an opportunity to consider their actions before they move forward. It's a good thing, but spoiled Windows users aren't accustomed to something that makes them consider their actions. As a result, one of the first things everyone learned how to do when Vista came out was to turn off UAC. While it's all but impossible to truly shut down UAC, reducing the impact of UAC is easy.

UAC in Modern Windows

Microsoft may be a huge company, but it still knows how to react when its customers speak out about features they don't like. Modern Windows versions have a refined, less "in-your-face" UAC that makes the feature much easier to use. Let's break down how it works.

A More Granular UAC

Microsoft did some research on why UAC drove users nuts, concluding that the problem wasn't UAC itself but the "I'm constantly in your face or you can turn me off and you get no help at all" aspect. To make UAC less aggressive, Microsoft introduced four UAC levels. To see these levels, start typing **user account control** in the Search field and select the option to Change User Account Control settings to open the Control Panel app (see Figure 13-36). You can also go to the User Accounts applet in Control Panel and select Change User Account Control settings, as shown in Figure 13-37. This takes you to the same UAC Settings dialog box shown in Figure 13-36.

In Figure 13-36, you can see a slider with four levels. The top level (Always notify) means you want UAC to display the aggressive consent form every time you do anything that typically requires administrator access. The bottom option (Never notify) turns off UAC. The two levels in the middle are very similar. Both do the following:

- Don't notify me when I make changes to Windows settings.
- Notify me only when apps/programs try to make changes to my computer.

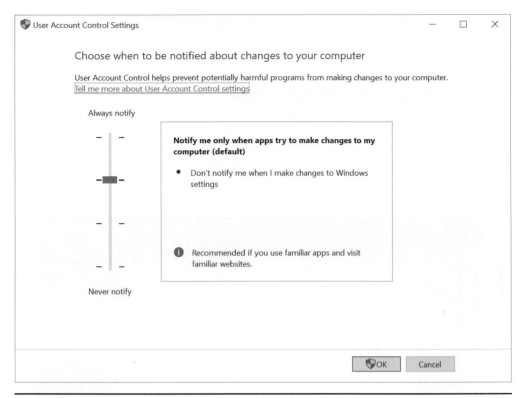

Figure 13-36   Four levels of UAC

Figure 13-37
Change User
Account Control
settings option in
Windows 10

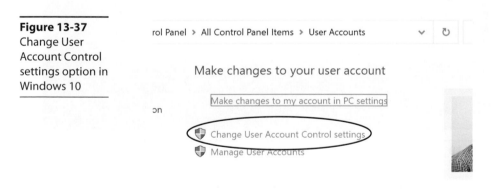

The only difference is that the second-from-top level dims the desktop (blocking all other actions) when it displays the consent form prompted by an app's attempt to make changes, whereas the third-from-top level doesn't dim the desktop (allows all other actions) when it displays the consent form.

EXAM TIP Make sure you know what each of the four UAC levels does.

Program Changes Versus Changes I Make

So, what's the difference between a program making a change and you making a change? Look at Figure 13-38. In this case, Windows is set to the second-from-top option. Because this is a program trying to make changes (and Windows is set to the second-from-top UAC level), the UAC consent form appears and darkens the desktop. If you lower the UAC level to the third-from-top option, you still see a consent form, but now it acts like a typical dialog box.

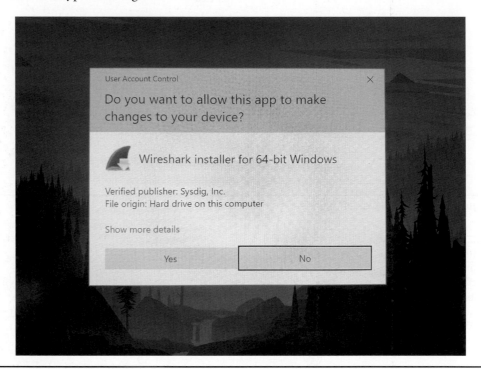

Figure 13-38 Darkened UAC

 EXAM TIP The default behavior for UAC in Windows is the second-from-top option, which results in a screen similar to Figure 13-38.

A program such as the Wireshark installer is very different from a feature *you* want to change. Notice the options with shields shown earlier in Figure 13-35. Each of these options isn't a program—each is merely a feature built into Windows. Those shields tell you that clicking the feature next to a shield will require administrator privileges. If you set UAC to any of the three lower settings, you'd go straight to that feature without *any* form of UAC consent prompt. Of course, this isn't true if you don't have administrator privileges. If you're a standard user, you'll still be prompted for a password.

 EXAM TIP CompTIA A+ 1102 exam objective 1.2 includes a Windows command-line utility—*net user*—that can pull some neat user-related tricks such as adding and deleting users, setting passwords, and enabling or disabling an existing account. It can come in handy when you want to downgrade accounts to keep users from clicking through UAC prompts. Windows won't let you downgrade the last administrator account on a system, but you *can* enable the super-secret hidden administrator account, give it a secure password, and *then* remove administrator privileges from the accounts. Just run **net user administrator SuperSecurePassword /active:yes** to enable the administrator account and set its password.

Overall, the improvements to UAC show that it has a place on everyone's computer. UAC might cause an occasional surprise or irritation, but that one more "Are you sure?" could mean the difference between safe and unsafe computing.

Chapter Review

Questions

1. The process of identifying and giving access to users is known as which of the following?

   A. Authentication

   B. Authorization

   C. Acceptance

   D. Administration

2. Which of the following is a unique combination of a username and an associated password stored in a database on your computer?

   A. Group

   B. Power Users

   C. User account

   D. User information

3. The process that defines what an authenticated user may access and what they can do with the resources is known as which of the following?

    A. Restriction

    B. Authentication

    C. Authorization

    D. Administration

4. Which of the following is the name of a container that holds user accounts and defines the capabilities of its users?

    A. Users

    B. Group

    C. Storage

    D. RAM

5. Which of the following refers to administrative privileges that provide complete control over a machine?

    A. User privileges

    B. Power Users privileges

    C. Administrator privileges

    D. Standard user privileges

6. Almost as powerful as members of the Administrators group, members of which group cannot install new devices or access other users' files or folders unless the files or folders specifically provide them access?

    A. User group

    B. Administrator group

    C. Power Users group

    D. Standard User group

7. Which types of groups cannot edit the Registry or access system files. They can create groups but may only manage those they create.

    A. Administrator group

    B. User group

    C. Power Users group

    D. Standard User group

8. Which of these is not a requirement for using fingerprint authentication in Windows?

    A. Setting up a PIN number

    B. Logging in with a PIN number

    C. Logging in with a Microsoft account

    D. Repeatedly placing your finger on the scanner

9. Which of the following defines exactly what any particular account can or cannot do to a file or folder?

   A. Admin permissions

   B. User permissions

   C. NTFS permissions

   D. Group permissions

10. Which of the following is an NTFS permission that enables an account to seize control of a file or folder?

    A. Take Charge

    B. Take Ownership

    C. Seize and Desist

    D. Take Away

Answers

1. **A.** Every Windows system has an authorization system account that Windows uses when it runs programs.

2. **C.** Security begins with a user account, a unique combination of a username and an associated password, stored in a database on the computer, that grants the user access to the system.

3. **C.** Authorization for Windows files and folders is controlled by the NTFS file system, which assigns permissions to users and groups. These permissions define exactly what users may do to a resource on the system.

4. **B.** A single group account can be a member of multiple groups. Groups are an efficient way of managing multiple users, especially when you are dealing with a whole network of accounts.

5. **C.** Administrator privileges grant complete control over a machine. It is common for the primary user of a Windows system to have their account linked to the Administrators group.

6. **B.** Almost as powerful as members of the Administrators group, members of the Power Users group cannot install new devices or access other users' files or folders unless the files or folders specifically provide them access.

7. **B.** User groups cannot edit the Registry or access system files. They can create groups but may only manage those they create.

8. **B.** Users will have to use a Microsoft account, set up a PIN, and repeatedly place their finger on the scanner in order to use fingerprint authentication.

9. **C.** NTFS permissions are the primary tool for authorization and provide many configuration options for user access and security.

10. **B.** Administrators have Take Ownership permission for everything and can use this to take ownership away from someone and then access their files.

14

Maintaining and Optimizing Operating Systems

In this chapter, you will learn how to
- Perform operating system maintenance tasks
- Optimize operating systems
- Prepare for problems

Every computer running a modern operating system (OS) requires both occasional optimization to keep the system running snappily and ongoing maintenance to make sure nothing goes wrong. The people who develop Windows, macOS, and the many Linux distros use decades of experience with operating systems to find ways to make the tasks of maintaining and optimizing surprisingly easy and automatic, but there's still plenty to know about how to keep things humming along.

This chapter covers maintenance and optimization, so let's make sure you know what these two terms mean. *Maintenance* is work you do from time to time to keep the OS running well, such as running utilities to clean up junk on your mass storage devices. An *optimization* is a change you make to a system to make it better—a good example is adding RAM or installing a useful program. This chapter covers the standard maintenance and optimization activities performed on Windows, macOS, and Linux, and the tools techs use to perform them.

Even the best maintained, most perfectly optimized computer is going to run into trouble. Hard drives crash, careless coworkers delete files, and lightning strikes. The secret isn't to try to avoid trouble, because trouble *will* find you, but rather to make sure you're ready to deal with problems when they arise. This is one area that very few users do well, and it's our job as techs to make recovery from trouble as painless as possible. OS developers give us plenty of tools to prepare for problems—we just need to make sure we use them.

NOTE This chapter covers maintenance and optimization techniques for all the operating systems currently on the CompTIA A+ 1102 exam. But, like the exams and the reality of market share, Windows features a lot more than macOS or Linux.

1102

Maintaining Operating Systems

Operating systems need patching to support the latest hardware and defend against newly discovered security problems. Systems also need regular maintenance to stay in good working order. Today, operating systems handle many of these jobs automatically. This section looks at the most common maintenance jobs that techs need to understand on modern systems and the tools that make it happen.

Patch Management

There's no such thing as a perfect operating system. First, all operating system makers come up with new features and improvements. Second, bad actors discover weaknesses and generate malware to take advantage of those weaknesses. The process of keeping software updated in a safe and timely fashion is known as *patch management* (because it entails installing *patches* to fix one issue or another). Microsoft regularly releases updates to Windows to head off malware attacks, fix code errors, support new hardware, add new features, and so on. Patch management isn't only for Windows. Both macOS and Linux require patch management, and I'll cover those needs as well.

Windows Patch Management

In modern Windows, updates are handled through the appropriately named *Windows Update*. In Windows 11 it has its own top-level category in the Settings app, but it's nestled in the Update & Security category in Windows 10. Since its introduction over two decades ago, Windows Update has gone through many iterations; fortunately, CompTIA cares only that you know how it works on Windows 10 and newer.

 EXAM TIP As you saw in Chapter 12, the Update and Security category in Windows 10 includes a lot of seemingly unrelated settings. When the category was removed in Windows 11, most of these unrelated settings found new homes in the System category and the Privacy & Security category. If you don't remember what these settings are, make a note to go back and review them!

Windows has two types of updates. *Quality updates* are the classic problem-fixing patches that you know and love. *Feature updates* essentially are new versions of Windows released once or twice a year. Here is a rundown of key points you need to know about feature updates:

- They are a reinstall of Windows.
- They used to be named by year and month (such as 1703 and 1809) and have marketing names, like *Creators update* or *November 2019 Update*. Since 2020, the names have indicated which half of the year they came out in (20H2, 21H1, 21H2, and so on) and the marketing names have indicated the month and year of release, like *November 2021 Update*.

- They are controlled by what channel you are on: Insiders, Semi-Annual Channel (Targeted), Semi-Annual Channel, or Long-Term Servicing Branch. The LTSB is only available in the Enterprise license.

Users can't turn off updates, though they can pause them for up to five weeks and set an active-hours window during which the OS won't reboot to install updates. Users cannot prevent Windows updates, although they may uninstall some non-system updates via Control Panel | Programs and Features | View installed updates. (There's also a link to this interface from Settings | Update & Security | Windows Update | View update history in Windows 10 and Settings | Windows Update | Update history in Windows 11.)

 EXAM TIP Since modern operating systems tend to receive regular bug fixes and feature updates, it's more important than it used to be to understand that each released version of an OS will (at the whims of whoever develops it) pass through a few phases that we call its *life cycle*. The vendor's life cycle limitations dictate if the OS will receive feature updates and bug fixes and for how long. They usually receive security updates for longer than feature updates, but even these stop coming when they reach their *end-of-life (EOL)* date. They may also dictate if you can upgrade to the latest version for free (or for a reduced rate).

Patch Management in macOS and Linux

Like Windows, both macOS and Linux take an automated approach to patching and alert you when software needs to be updated. With macOS 12.4, for example, you access updates through the *Software Update* pane in System Preferences (see Figure 14-1). Most desktop-focused Linux distros have a GUI updating tool like the Software Updater in Ubuntu (see Figure 14-2).

Figure 14-1 Software Update advanced options in macOS

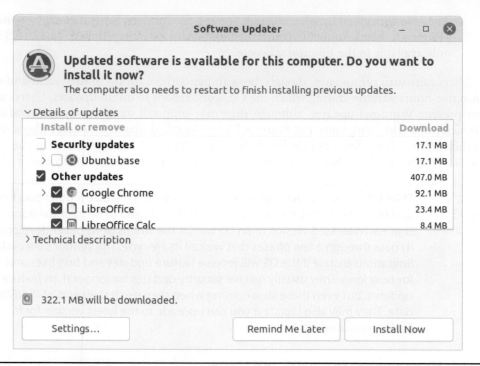

Figure 14-2   Software Updater in Ubuntu Linux

Scheduling Maintenance

Maintenance only works properly when you do it at regular intervals. In the early days of computing, techs and system administrators had a whole arsenal of maintenance tools—some bundled with the operating system and others made by independent vendors—that they used to keep their systems in good order. In that world, it was important to know how to schedule critical maintenance tasks to run regularly.

Over the years, modern operating systems have gotten pretty good at automatically performing essential maintenance on their own internal schedules. I'm much less sure that you'll put this knowledge to use—but I (and CompTIA) want to make sure you know where to start if your organization needs you to schedule an internal script or third-party tool for regular maintenance.

NOTE   You might see scripts or tools used to back up data (which we'll discuss later in the chapter), audit the software installed on a system, and so on. Scheduling can also be important for non-maintenance reasons, like supporting power users doing technical work. You might, for example, need to help a researcher schedule a script that downloads the latest version of a massive data set every night so that it's ready by morning. We'll talk a little more about scripting in Chapter 15.

Scheduling Maintenance in Windows

Modern versions of Windows use a single Administrative Tool (and MMC snap-in), *Task Scheduler* (*taskschd.msc*), to schedule maintenance. You can choose an executable program and define when you want that program to run. The key to running scheduled maintenance is to know the names of the executable programs and any special switches you may need to enter.

Task Scheduler divides tasks into triggers, actions, and conditions. *Triggers* are actions or schedules that start a program. *Actions* are steps that define both the program to run and how it is to run. *Conditions* are extra criteria that must be met for the program to run. (Is the system idle? Is it connected to the Internet?) To create a basic task, all you need to do is name it, set how often it should run, and decide what it should do.

Many Windows utilities include built-in scheduling options. Here's the twist, though: they're still using Task Scheduler (although Windows won't let you directly edit the schedule for many built-in programs in Task Scheduler). You can open up Task Scheduler and see the scheduled task for Disk Defragmenter, for example, but to change it you must use the scheduler built into Optimize Drives, as shown in Figure 14-3.

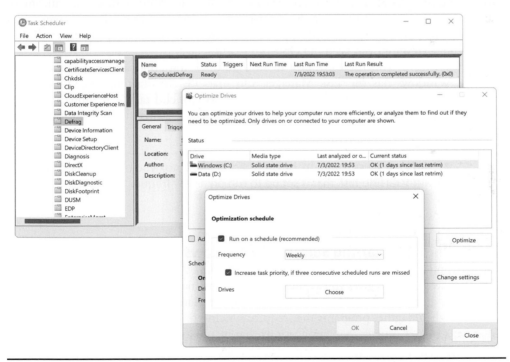

Figure 14-3 Optimize Drives scheduler and corresponding task in Task Scheduler

Scheduling Maintenance in macOS and Linux

Unix-like operating systems—including macOS and Linux—have two main ways to run all sorts of tasks automatically. The first is *cron*, which provides a simple (and fairly universal) mechanism for running a command or program at some fixed interval.

The second option is something called an *init system*, which is basically in charge of all the processes running on a Unix-like OS. The *idea* of the init system is universal, but there are actually quite a few different ones out there. The two you're most likely to encounter are *launchd* on macOS and *systemd* on Linux. There aren't any hard-and-fast rules here, but an init system will give you some way to register a new task, set it to run on a schedule, and configure settings that dictate exactly when, why, and how it should run.

 NOTE You shouldn't see cron or init systems on the exam, but a good tech should know what these are in case they come up in conversation!

Controlling Autostarting Software

A lot of software loads when you boot up any computing device, such as small programs that provide support for the various functions of the operating system. As you add applications and peripherals to a system, some of them also add software that loads automatically at startup. Most of the time these autostarting programs are welcome—you want that latest peripheral to work, right? Sometimes, though, autostarting programs will slow down your system or even keep the OS from loading cleanly.

Every OS gives you the capability to stop autostarting applications, processes, and services. Windows has the Task Manager. On macOS, autostarting programs usually manifest as either account-specific *Login Items* or as launchd tasks. In Linux, you may find them in the Startup Applications folder or as tasks registered with the init system (usually systemd).

 NOTE It's less common, but on macOS and Linux you may also find an autostarting task that is set up to run on a very frequent schedule in cron.

Controlling Autostarting Software in Windows

Startup applications and services have been in the *Task Manager* (press CTRL-SHIFT-ESC) since Windows 8. This gives you a quick way to see the status (enabled or disabled) of each application and a handy guide to the startup impact that program has (see Figure 14-4). As you might imagine, programs that require syncing of a lot of files across the Internet will have a higher impact than applications that just load local files.

 EXAM TIP Before Windows 8, we used the System Configuration (msconfig) utility (introduced in Chapter 12) to control autostarting applications, but now the Startup tab in System Configuration just links to the Startup tab in Task Manager. If you see a question about controlling startup applications on the exam, look for Task Manager first—but be prepared to choose System Configuration if Task Manager isn't a choice. You can also control startup applications from within the Apps category of the Settings app.

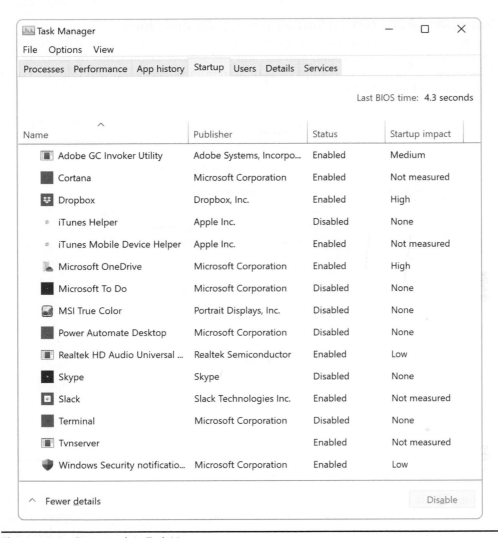

Name	Publisher	Status	Startup impact
Adobe GC Invoker Utility	Adobe Systems, Incorpo...	Enabled	Medium
Cortana	Microsoft Corporation	Enabled	Not measured
Dropbox	Dropbox, Inc.	Enabled	High
iTunes Helper	Apple Inc.	Disabled	None
iTunes Mobile Device Helper	Apple Inc.	Enabled	Not measured
Microsoft OneDrive	Microsoft Corporation	Enabled	High
Microsoft To Do	Microsoft Corporation	Disabled	None
MSI True Color	Portrait Displays, Inc.	Disabled	None
Power Automate Desktop	Microsoft Corporation	Disabled	None
Realtek HD Audio Universal ...	Realtek Semiconductor	Enabled	Low
Skype	Skype	Disabled	None
Slack	Slack Technologies Inc.	Enabled	Not measured
Terminal	Microsoft Corporation	Disabled	None
Tvnserver		Enabled	Not measured
Windows Security notificatio...	Microsoft Corporation	Enabled	Low

Figure 14-4 Startup tab in Task Manager

To enable or disable an application, right-click it and select the corresponding option. When you reboot the system next, the behavior of the application will be changed according to your previous action.

SIM Nervous about using the Task Manager? Check out the excellent Chapter 14 Click! sim, "Manage Tasks with Task Manager," at https://www .totalsem.com/110x. You'll get a very nice walkthrough with no risk to your system.

Controlling Autostarting Software in macOS and Linux

The main user-friendly way to set up autostarting software in macOS is by adding a Login Item to the user's account. You can add and remove Login Items by selecting the desired user in the Users & Groups pane of System Preferences and selecting the Login Items tab (see Figure 14-5).

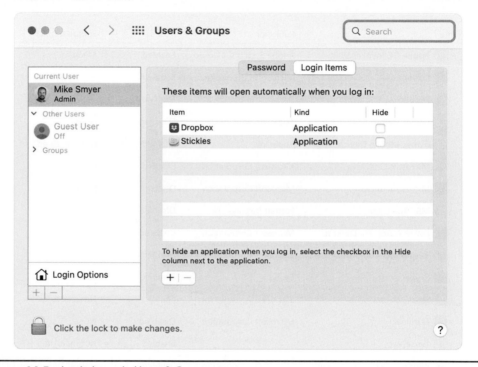

Figure 14-5 Login Items in Users & Groups pane

Some Linux distros, such as Ubuntu, have something very similar. To access the preferences, open the applications menu, type **startup**, and launch Startup Applications. From there, deselect the checkbox next to a program you don't want to start at boot and you're done (see Figure 14-6).

On Unix-like systems (including macOS and Linux), some autostarting software will just register a task with the init system and configure it to run when the system starts. Init systems aren't as easy to control without getting your hands messy—the main way to control them is from the command line. On macOS you'll control launchd with a command called *launchctl*, and on any Linux distro that uses systemd you can control it with a command called *systemctl*.

NOTE The launchctl and systemctl commands are both complex, but you won't see questions about them on the exam.

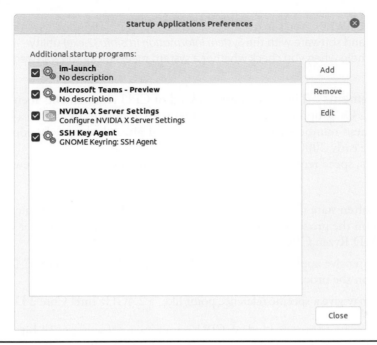

Figure 14-6 Disabling an autostarting program in Startup Applications Preferences

Optimizing Operating Systems

Maintenance means keeping the performance of an OS from degrading with time and use. Of course, you don't just want to keep trouble at bay—you want to make your systems better, stronger, faster! Anything you do that makes Windows better than it was before, such as adding a piece of software or hardware to make something run better, is an *optimization*.

Installing and Removing Software

Installing and removing software is part of the normal life of any computing device. Each time you add or remove software, you make changes and decisions that can affect the system beyond whatever the program does, so it pays to know how to do it right. This section looks at software requirements, how software is distributed, how it can impact an organization and its systems, and how to install and remove it.

Software Requirements

They may not always be stated clearly, but all software has *requirements*—a list of things you need before you can run the software. When application developers state the requirements clearly, they often list the minimum requirements to run it at all, the suggested requirements for it to perform well, or both. Less frequently, the developers may break out requirements for different features (a video app, for example, may have different requirements for low- and high-quality video). The CompTIA A+ 1102 objectives focus on the most common hardware and OS requirements, so I'll break each one down.

EXAM TIP You can get a *very* detailed report on a Windows system's hardware and software with the *System Information (msinfo32.exe)* utility—it can be a big help when you check whether a system meets picky software requirements.

CPU Requirements   The most common kind of CPU requirements focus on the processor's speed. Once upon a time speed requirements almost always stated a specific clock speed, but these numbers have become less useful after clock speeds stopped growing rapidly in the early 2000s.

These days, speed requirements can be surprisingly vague. Here are a few patterns you might see:

- They often state the processor line/family ("Intel Core i5 or equivalent") and may mention the processor generation ("An Intel 7th generation Core or newer CPU, or AMD Ryzen CPU").
- Less-intensive applications may set a low bar like "1 GHz or faster" (or not even mention the processor).
- They may give a specific reference point like "a 2.4GHz Intel Core 2 Duo or faster."

The next most common kind of CPU requirements focus on 32-bit versus 64-bit support. If the software is 64-bit, you'll need a 64-bit CPU. If the software is 32-bit, it'll depend on your OS (Windows still supports 32-bit software, but macOS stopped supporting 32-bit software in 2019).

NOTE You probably won't need to think much about 32-bit versus 64-bit support unless you need to support devices with 32-bit CPUs. 64-bit CPUs and software are the norm these days. In fact, Microsoft stopped offering the 32-bit version of Windows to manufacturers in 2020, and there is no 32-bit version of Windows 11. Don't think this means you can forget about CPU architecture compatibility after the exam! The industry is in the early days of a transition from x86-based CPUs to ARM-based CPUs. Some applications are already ARM-compatible—but there's still a lot of work to do.

From time to time, you'll also run into software with two more kinds of CPU requirement for a certain number of CPU cores, or specific CPU features (such as the multimedia extensions, streaming extensions, and virtualization support we discussed in Chapter 3).

Graphics Requirements   Many graphically demanding applications (video games, graphics and video editors, video players, and so on) state specific graphics requirements. These requirements often take the form of a comparison to a popular graphics card (such as "GeForce GTX 1070 or equivalent"), but the CompTIA A+ 1102 objectives focus on something more specific: dedicated graphics cards versus integrated ones.

NOTE Graphically demanding applications aren't the *only* reason to require a powerful GPU. Some kinds of science and research software take advantage of specialized GPU hardware. Specialized GPU hardware is just plain better at some tasks than the system's CPU and RAM.

Back in Chapter 3 we talked about CPUs that have a built-in graphics processing unit (GPU)—and we'll take a closer look at both *dedicated* and *integrated* GPUs in Chapter 17—so for now we'll just focus on how this difference manifests in software requirements.

The main things to understand here are that integrated GPUs tend to be less powerful (but more efficient) than dedicated ones, and that some software demands a lot from your GPU without really pushing your CPU very hard. When the GPU is integrated with the CPU, applications like this may require a CPU that is *much* newer and more powerful than what they require if the GPU is dedicated.

Figure 14-7 shows part of the requirements for streaming very high-quality video in Netflix's Windows app. Note that they don't even specify a specific CPU if you have dedicated ("discrete") graphics—Netflix assumes *any* CPU will do the job if you have a dedicated GPU!

- **If using an integrated GPU:** An Intel 7th generation Core or newer CPU, or AMD Ryzen CPU.

- **If using a discrete GPU:** A Nvidia Geforce GPU that meets these requirements, or an AMD Radeon RX 400 series or newer GPU.

Figure 14-7 Integrated and discrete GPU requirements for Netflix

For the same reason, the requirements for very demanding software like video games often assume dedicated graphics. You may need to do your own research to figure out whether a system with integrated graphics can keep up. If the requirements say how much system RAM and video RAM (VRAM) the program requires, remember that systems with integrated GPUs generally have to share a single pool of RAM for the system and graphics. Requirements like this may just refer to a specific card (such as "AMD Radeon RX 400 series or newer") or may even spell out the amount of video RAM (as in "Nvidia GeForce GTX 1050 or higher with at least 3 GB of video RAM").

RAM Requirements Since RAM stores working data and code for running applications, software requirements often state how many megabytes or gigabytes of RAM you'll need. For example, Netflix suggests a minimum of 3 GB for HD video streaming. Understanding what kind of applications users will use—and which ones they'll need to run simultaneously—is one key to ensuring their system will be up to the task.

Storage Requirements Every bit of software you install on a system (including the OS) will take up some storage space—so most software will state how much storage space it requires. Much like RAM, this will usually be some number of megabytes or gigabytes. For example, the current version of the Mozilla Firefox Web browser requires at least 200 MB of storage, while a recent game such as *Battlefield 2042* will tie up a massive 100 GB!

NOTE Storage has become fairly cheap over the years, so most general-use workstations won't have too much trouble here. The main exceptions will be systems with older SSDs (especially laptops), users who need to work with media files or large databases, and users who install modern video games.

Application and OS Compatibility Applications need to be developed to fit the way each OS does things, so few applications support *every* OS. Newer versions of the OS may have changes that prevent older software from running. Newer software also tends to take advantage of new OS features that keep it from working on older versions of an OS.

Each developer ends up making its own decisions about how much time and effort it wants to invest in supporting multiple platforms. You can find tons of small apps out in the world made by one person or a small company that *only* support macOS or Windows (or any other OS). An app may also only have resources to ensure it works on the latest version of the supported operating systems. Major software developers are more likely to support the last few versions of an OS, and to support more than one OS.

Mere support isn't always the end of the story. Some software won't perform as well on an older OS, or it may have some features that only work on newer versions. In this case, the developers often specify which version they *recommend*.

NOTE Updating the OS or the software can break compatibility. If every device in your organization auto-installs the latest updates, a bad update could stop work for hours or days. To manage this risk, some organizations try updates out on test machines first so that they can ensure everything works right. They may also update systems in phases so that the *whole* organization isn't affected if testing missed a problem.

External Hardware Tokens One constant over the long history of commercial software is piracy. Users and software publishers have been battling each other at least since Bill Gates wrote his now-famous letter to the Home Brew Computer Club back in the 1970s. This protracted war has led to many anti-piracy technologies over the years, with some being more onerous than others for us techs to deal with.

Many computer users are likely familiar with common practices like "CD" or license keys and monthly subscriptions tied to an account. The CompTIA A+ 1102 objectives mention another anti-piracy technique that you *probably* haven't seen—though it is very common in applications for musicians and artists. These programs often require an *external hardware token*: a USB device containing software licenses that must be plugged into the system for the software to run. A common brand is iLok, whose latest USB-C based token can hold up to 1500 authorizations.

Distribution Methods

The methods for distributing software have morphed over the years. For a long time, most software was distributed on removable media like floppy disks (back when I still had a full head of hair) or optical discs (first CD-ROMs and later DVD-ROMs). These days, we download most application software from the Internet. If it's still distributed on physical media, it'll almost certainly be on a USB flash drive.

Most of the time, the thing you download is an application installer. Less frequently, it may be a standalone executable or an ISO image (which your OS can mount as if it were a disc in an optical drive). In all of these cases, it *can* also be wrapped up in a container file such as .zip or .tar or .gz. If so, you'll need to extract the actual application or its installer from the container file.

 NOTE   Software distribution is a bit more complicated than this in the real world. For example, some organizations store approved software installers and updates on their own internal server. This can help make it clear what's approved and avoid wasting bandwidth on hundreds of systems all downloading the same files. Some organizations also insist on building most of the software they use from scratch to ensure that it hasn't been compromised (in which case you'll almost certainly obtain it from an internal server).

Other Considerations for New Applications

An important part of considering whether to install a new application is coming to grips with how it will impact the devices you install it on, the networks those devices are connected to, the people in your organization, and the organization as a whole. Taken together, these considerations underscore the importance of carefully thinking through how new software might impact all corners of your organization *before* you start installing.

Impact on Devices   Installing a new application on a device unavoidably *changes* it. Not only will the device have less storage and some new capabilities, that new application might add an always-running service that reduces battery life, causes performance problems, or creates security vulnerabilities that could ultimately compromise the device.

Impact on Network   Every application you install on a device *could* also affect any networks the device joins. A new application that uses the network might unexpectedly trigger security rules, making you rethink whether to keep the security rules or ditch the software. Some applications will need new firewall exemptions, and an administrator will have to decide whether or not to add them.

You should also weigh how many systems you expect to run the new application—and how all of them running it at once will go. An app that regularly scans your network for other devices it knows how to interact with may not cause trouble when it's only installed on one computer, but it might slow the network to a crawl when a hundred computers run it. A new video-conferencing app may work fine when you test it with five systems, but then clog the office's Internet connection when everyone tries to join the same remote meeting from their workstation.

Impact to Operation   New applications can affect your organization's operations in a number of different ways. Here are a few potential scenarios:

- Installing a new application may interrupt whatever the users and technicians would otherwise be doing, creating a backlog or affecting deadlines—especially if the installation causes problems.

- A new application may add to your organization's ongoing workload. It might just lead to more support requests, require extra account or configuration management, and add to the list of OS compatibility tests your organization needs to perform.

- If the organization has a limited number of licenses for an application, you may need new processes to keep track of which users have which license key, enable users to request access, and decide what to do if there isn't one available when they need it.

Impact on Business   Assessing how a new application might impact your organization and the business it carries out entails understanding how the new application might impact the organization's devices, networks, and people—and considering whether the risks and benefits are acceptable.

Is it acceptable if machines perform worse after an installation? If a new application will perform poorly on the oldest devices in the office, should they be replaced before rolling out the application? Should you abort the deployment of a video-conferencing application if it causes bandwidth problems in some offices, or plan to upgrade each office's Internet connection instead? If someone needs temporary access to an expensive application that you don't have a spare license for, should you deny the request, purchase a new license, or ask someone already using a license if they can live without it for a few months?

The answers to these questions can save or cost a business money, affect whether important work gets done or not, and potentially compromise the organization's security. In short, all of these concerns bubble up—where applications should support (or at least not undermine) the organization's ability to meet its long-term goals.

Installing Software in Windows

Many moons ago, Windows used a feature called AutoRun to—wait for it—automatically run a program on any removable media you inserted. This was convenient, but it also made inserting a strange optical disc or flash drive really risky! These days, Windows just asks what you'd like to do if you insert removable media that contains an installer (look for the option to *Install or run program from your media*).

 EXAM TIP   The CompTIA A+ 1102 objectives recommend disabling AutoRun for exactly these security reasons. If your system doesn't prompt you, you should be able to manually navigate to and run the installer or right-click on the device in File Explorer and look for the option to *Show more options* or *Install or run program from your media.*

If your application comes as an ISO image, double-clicking it will cause Windows to mount it and show you the contents in File Explorer. From here, you can run the installer (if there are many executables, it may not be clear which one you should run—you can open the "autorun" file in Notepad to see which executable it would have run). If you downloaded the installer directly, just double-click it.

User Account Control (UAC) in Windows complicates the installation process a bit. You will most likely be prompted by UAC when installing an application, giving you time to review what is happening to your system in case you did not intend to install the program. If you are using an administrator account, you can simply click Yes or Continue and finish the installation (see Figure 14-8).

Figure 14-8
Installation UAC

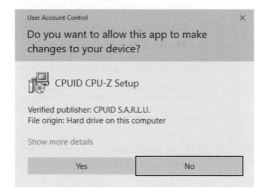

If you are logged in with a less privileged account, you will need to enter a username and password of an account with administrative privileges. Some installers have trouble letting UAC know that they need more privileges and simply fail no matter what account you are logged in with. In those cases, it is best to right-click the installer icon and select Run as administrator to give the installer the access it expects from the start.

Assuming all is well, you typically must accept the terms of a software license before you can install an application. These steps are not optional; the installation simply won't proceed until you accept all terms the software manufacturer requires (see Figure 14-9). You may also be asked to make several decisions during the installation process. For example, you may be asked where you would like to install the program and if you would like certain optional components installed. It is best to accept the suggested settings unless you have a very specific reason for changing the defaults.

Modern versions of Windows also come with the Microsoft Store. Microsoft tests Store applications to ensure they're malware-free and safe for use (see Figure 14-10). The Microsoft Store represents only a small percentage of application installations; most people prefer to use more traditional methods of software installation for Windows systems.

Installing Software in macOS
You have a couple of options for installing software in macOS. One method involves the Mac App Store, which you can get to via the Apple menu. Installing via the App Store is just like installing an app on your phone. You click a button, and the app installs (see Figure 14-11). Alternatively, you can directly download an installer. Let's look at the most common patterns.

Figure 14-9
Accepting
software terms

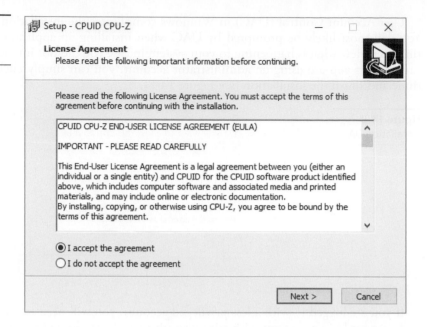

Figure 14-10   Microsoft Store

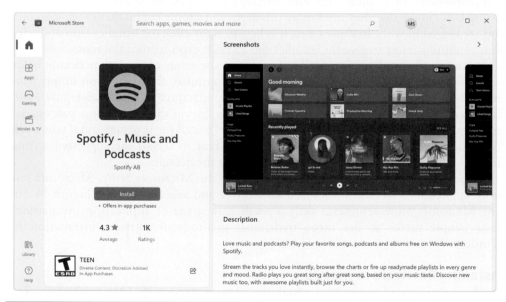

Most of the time, you'll end up with an Apple Disk Image (.dmg) file—a collection of files that macOS can mount as a volume visible within Finder. This volume often contains a macOS application bundle (.app) file containing all of the app's executables, resources, and other files. You can run the application it contains by double-clicking

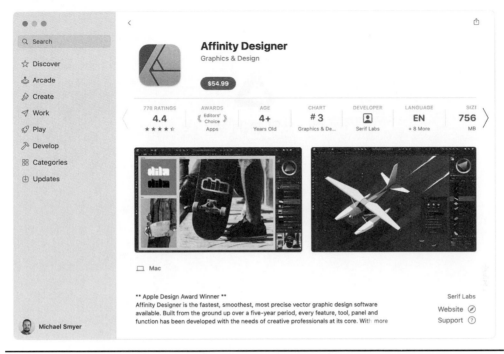

Figure 14-11 Affinity Designer offered on the Mac App Store in macOS

the file, but that won't install it. To install it, you need to drag it to the Applications folder. Disk images that include an .app file often include a shortcut to the Applications folder—and usually some kind of nudge to remind you to drag the .app bundle over, as shown in Figure 14-12.

If the disk image *doesn't* contain an .app file, it'll probably contain an application installer (.pkg) file. Double-clicking this installer will launch an installer program similar to those that are common in Windows.

Installing Software in Linux

Linux distros differ in the process of installing applications (*packages* in Linux parlance). Many distros such as Pop! OS have a "store" similar to the Microsoft Store or the Mac App Store (see Figure 14-13). These stores can differ from distro to distro—some also handle updating and patching your applications, and some do not. Another way to install applications in many distros is to download a package file, double-click it, and select Install from the options.

EXAM TIP Linux (and its different distros) can be a bit of a mess when it comes to updates and patches. There's no one-stop shop for updating both your OS and all of your applications. You may have to go to more than one place (such as the distro app store or its software updater) to get everything updated. Welcome to Linux!

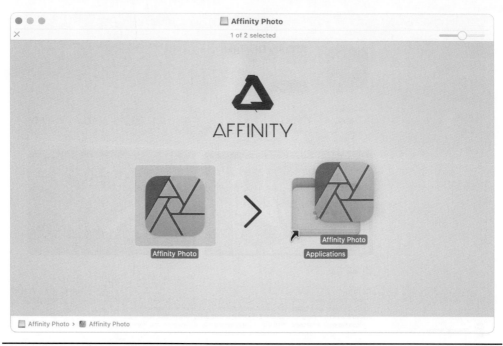

Figure 14-12 Installing a new app by dragging it to the Applications folder

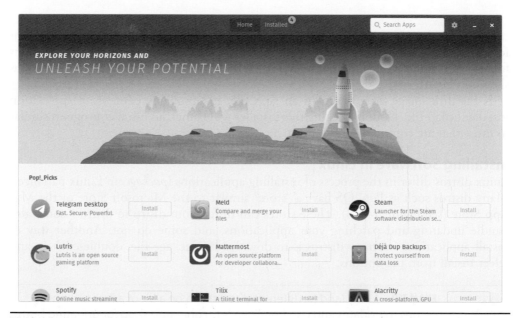

Figure 14-13 Pop!_Shop app store

But the most common way to install new apps is through a built-in package manager like Ubuntu's Advanced Package Tool (APT). You can use it via the apt-get or apt command from the Terminal. (See Chapter 15 for more details on the Terminal interface.) As an interesting side note, Ubuntu's "store" actually uses APT underneath its GUI.

 NOTE You won't find them on the CompTIA A+ 1102 exam, but if you support Linux on user workstations, you may also run into Flatpak and Snap. Both of these are alternative packaging formats that are a little bit more self-contained than the traditional package-manager approach that you'll learn more about in Chapter 15.

Removing Software

Each installed program takes up space on a computer's hard drive, and programs that you no longer need waste space that could be used for other purposes. Removing unnecessary programs is an important piece of optimization.

You remove a program from a Windows PC in much the same manner as you install it. That is, you use the application's own uninstall program, when possible. You normally find the uninstall program listed in the application's folder in the Start menu, as shown in Figure 14-14.

Figure 14-14
Uninstall me!

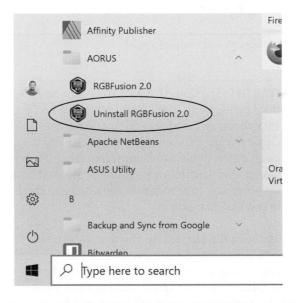

If an uninstall program is not available, use the *Programs and Features* applet in the Control Panel (see Figure 14-15) or *Apps & features* in Settings to remove the software. You select the program you want to remove and click the Uninstall/Change button. Windows displays a message warning you that the program will be permanently removed from your PC. If you're certain you want to continue, click Yes.

NOTE The Uninstall/Change button varies depending on the program. Not all programs can be changed.

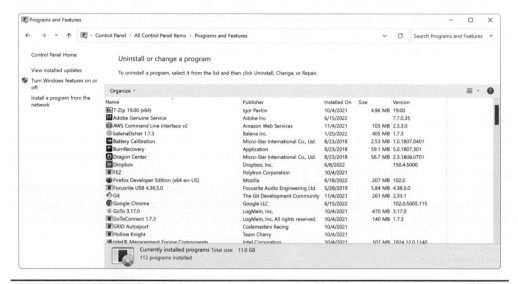

Figure 14-15 Programs and Features applet

EXAM TIP The CompTIA A+ 1102 exam objectives want you to know about the Apps settings in the Settings app. When you enter the Settings app, click the Apps category and *Apps & features* will be the first item listed. Other things you'll find here are the ability to control *default apps* that open different file extensions, change settings for Windows' built-in video player, and another way to control the startup applications on your system (another way to accomplish the tasks you can perform with the Startup tab in the Task Manager).

You may then see a message telling you that a shared file that appears to no longer be in use is about to be deleted, and asking your approval. Generally speaking, it's safe to delete such files. If you do not delete them, they will likely be orphaned and remain unused on your hard disk forever. In some cases, clicking the Uninstall/Change or Change/Remove button starts the application's uninstall program (the one you couldn't find before). This is a function of the program you're attempting to remove. The end result should be the removal of the program and all of its pieces and parts, including files and Registry entries.

Uninstalling applications in macOS varies based on how they were installed. Mac App Store apps are removed very similarly to apps on your phone. First, open the Launchpad app from the Dock or Applications folder (it looks like a rocket ship), then click and

hold on any app icon until all the icons start to wiggle. As shown in Figure 14-16, an ×
in a circle will appear on the upper left of any app that can be removed. Click the × to
remove the app. If you accidentally remove an app you wanted, you can re-download it
from the Mac App Store.

Figure 14-16 Uninstalling App Store–purchased applications using the Launchpad app

For all other macOS apps, removing them comes down to two options. Drag the app
to the Trash or run the uninstaller if the app came with one. Of the two, the first option
of just deleting the app is the most common, with a dedicated uninstaller only being
available for some of the larger (and often cross-platform) apps like Photoshop. Be aware
that deleting an app can leave behind various files on the system, most often a few user
preference files and other customizations in the user's Library folder.

Removing software in mainstream Linux distros is just as easy as installing it. Open
the software manager, find the app, and then click Uninstall (see Figure 14-17). The
underlying package manager, which we'll work with directly in Chapter 15, will handle
all the deleting and cleanup for you.

Adding or Removing Windows Components/Features

When you installed Windows, it included certain features by default. It installed Notepad, network support, and games on your computer. You can remove these Windows
components from your system if you like and add other components as well.

The *old* way to do this is to open the Programs and Features applet in the Control
Panel, and then click the *Turn Windows features on or off* link on the left. Click Yes or
Continue if prompted by UAC and you will be presented with the Windows Features
dialog box. To toggle a feature on or off, simply click its checkbox.

Figure 14-17   Removing an application in Ubuntu Linux

Microsoft's *new* ways, however, never cease to amaze me! In the Settings app, Microsoft has tucked away the option to *Turn Windows features on or off* under Apps | Optional features | More Windows features—and added a whole new alternative. The Optional features page itself lists a lot of optional features that are very similar to—but different from—the list you'll find under *More Windows features* or *Turn Windows features on or off*. Figure 14-18 shows both of these optional-feature interfaces side by side.

 EXAM TIP   Since the objectives cover both the Programs and Features applet of Control Panel and the Apps category of the Settings app, I'm not sure if CompTIA will ask you about optional features in either or both places. Make sure to play around with both and have a sense of what options are in each menu.

Performance Options

One optimization you can perform on Windows is setting Performance Options. *Performance Options* are used to configure CPU, RAM, and virtual memory (page file) settings. To access these options right-click on the Start button and select System (which will open the System | About page in the Settings app), and then scroll down and click the *Advanced system settings* link. This opens the Advanced tab of the System Properties dialog box; click the Settings button in the Performance section.

The Performance Options dialog box has three tabs: Visual Effects, Advanced, and Data Execution Prevention (see Figure 14-19). The Visual Effects tab enables you to adjust visual effects that impact performance, such as animations, thumbnails, and transparencies. Try clicking the top three choices in turn and watch the list of settings. Notice the tiny difference between the first two choices (*Let Windows choose what's best for my computer* and *Adjust for best appearance*). The third choice, *Adjust for best*

Figure 14-18 The Windows Features dialog box (left) and Optional features settings page (right)

performance, turns off all visual effects, and the fourth option is an invitation to make your own adjustments.

If you're on a computer that barely supports Windows, turning off visual effects can make a huge difference in the responsiveness of the computer. For the most part, though, just leave these settings alone.

The Advanced tab, shown in Figure 14-20, has two sections. Under the Processor scheduling section, you can choose to adjust for best performance of either Programs or Background services. The Virtual memory section of this tab enables you to modify the size and location of the page file.

Data Execution Prevention (DEP) works in the background to stop viruses and other malware from taking over programs loaded in system memory. It doesn't prevent viruses from being installed on your computer, but it does make them less effective. By default, DEP is only enabled for critical operating system files in RAM, but the Data Execution Prevention tab enables you to turn on DEP for all running programs. It works, but you might take a performance hit or find that some applications crash with DEP enabled for

Figure 14-19
Windows 10
Performance
Options
dialog box

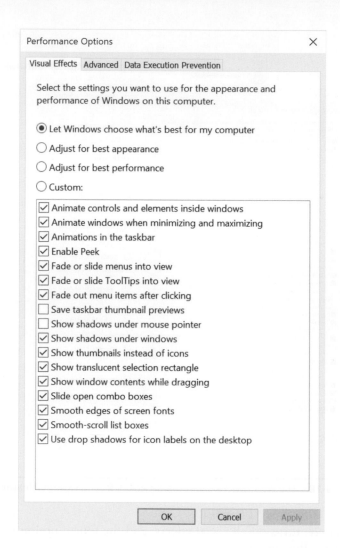

all programs. Like other options in Performance Options, leaving the default DEP settings is the best option most of the time.

EXAM TIP The CompTIA A+ 1102 objectives no longer mention these performance options by name, but they *do* still expect you to recognize scenarios where you might use the System applet in the Control Panel. The problem with this is that opening the System applet in Windows 10 and 11 just redirects to the System | About page in the Settings app. Traditionally, the System applet *was* the System Properties dialog box that we opened in this section. Even though it doesn't square with how Windows works these days, be prepared to recognize the System applet as the place to go for scenarios like tweaking visual effects for low-power systems, changing the size or location of the page file (virtual memory), and changing the DEP settings!

Figure 14-20
Advanced tab
of Performance
Options dialog
box

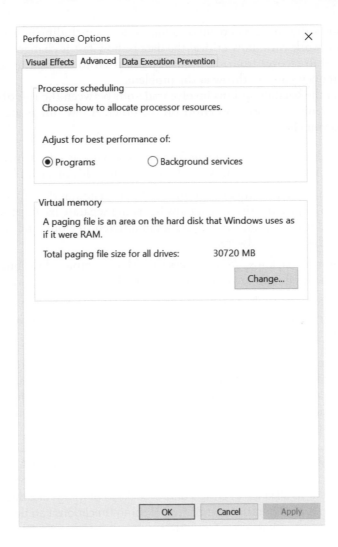

Preparing for Problems
=======================

Techs need to prepare for problems. You must have critical system files and data backed up and tools in place before trouble inevitably strikes. Every modern operating system has options for backing up data and, as you might imagine, they all offer different features. Windows offers System Restore to recover from problems, too. This section focuses first on backups generally—concepts that apply regardless of how big or small your organization is, what kind of data it has, how many different operating systems you support, and so on. From there, we'll look at specific tools.

Backup and Recovery Options

This section focuses on broad questions like what to back up, where to put it, and how long to keep older backups. There aren't perfect answers to these questions for everyone—the answers depend on a ton of factors including how you work, what kind of data you work with, how critical the data is, how fast it changes, what kind of problems you need to recover from, how quickly you need to be back up and running, and how much money you can throw at the problem.

All of the backup options involve trade-offs between the risk of data loss on one hand and convenience, cost, and effort on the other. A few things are true no matter which options you choose:

- Making multiple copies of data ensures that it is safe. However, making multiple copies is more expensive and increases the odds of a data leak.

- Similar to how investors limit risk by diversifying their investment portfolio, you can reduce the risk of data loss by taking separate backups with more than one backup program, keeping copies in different regions, and storing them on a mix of different hardware.

- Storing backups *offsite* reduces the risk of complete loss, but it also increases the time it takes to recover unless you also keep an *onsite* copy.

- Automatic backups take a little more work to set up, but they beat the socks off manual backups once you've got everything ironed out. Manual backups are better than nothing, but people will forget to do them.

Another big question is how much data you can afford to store. Storage is cheap, but the cost of storing many copies of frequent backups still adds up fast. Different backup methods and software use many strategies—such as compression, deduplication, incremental backups that only record changes since the previous backup, and so on—to cut down on the amount of data stored.

NOTE Keep in mind that the scope of the CompTIA A+ 1102 exam is limited to backing up workstations, but the concepts discussed here apply to all kinds of critical data—backups of things like databases, network configurations, and internal communications can be even more important than backups of workstations!

Types of Backup

The CompTIA A+ 1102 objectives want you to know about four specific types of *workstation* backup:

- A *full backup* is a snapshot of a workstation's files at some point in time. It takes a while to copy all the files, but recovering from a complete copy is faster than recovering using more than one type of backup.

- Once you have a full backup, some software can capture an *incremental backup* that only stores what has changed since the last incremental backup. Each incremental backup is faster and wastes less space. The downside is that you'll need the full backup and every incremental backup to restore (and stepping through each slows the restore process down a little). Each incremental backup is faster than normal backups.

- Instead of storing the changes since the previous backup (as an incremental backup does), a *differential backup* includes all changes since the last full backup. Differential backups are a great deal if your data doesn't change rapidly—but each differential backup will be slower than the last if your data does change rapidly.

- A *synthetic backup* (also known as a synthetic *full* backup) is created by merging the previous full backup and all subsequent incremental backups to create a backup that is identical to a new full backup. The goal is being able to restore as quickly as you could from a full backup without taking the time and resources to take a full backup every time.

Backup Media

The CompTIA A+ 1102 objectives have surprisingly little to say about what kind of *media* your backups get saved to, but you should have an idea of what the main options are. Organizations may not choose just the fastest or cheapest media—they may back up to more than one media to increase the odds that critical data won't get lost. You might recall Chapter 10 covers storage.

Hard Drives   Traditional magnetic hard drives and SSDs are often used for backups, though they'll often be mounted in an external enclosure or connected to a storage server of some sort. Don't use a partition on the same drive the data is on—one of the risks you want to protect against is the device failing! It's a little more reasonable (but not ideal) to back up to a secondary internal drive; it will protect against a drive failure, but not against a burst pipe that drowns the whole system. SSDs are very fast, but traditional large hard drives are more cost-efficient.

Magnetic Tapes   Ages ago, using magnetic tapes was the main option for serious data backup. A lot of people think tape is dead, but it's still there, chugging along. It's a rock-solid solution for organizations that archive gobs of data and aren't in a hurry to replace it.

Optical Discs   The waning popularity of optical drives and their media is making these less used—and they generally don't store enough data to play a role in large-scale backup operations. Some optical formats have surprisingly short lives, while others should still be readable in several decades if stored with care. Given this, you might see optical media used for personal backups or to archive important data.

Flash Media   In my experience, flash devices such as USB thumb drives and SD cards can fail unexpectedly, so I wouldn't depend on them alone for backups. They can be a good way to back up data on a device in the field that isn't connected to a network—but I would transfer the backups to a more durable media as soon as possible.

Online (Cloud) Storage   We'll take a closer look at the cloud in Chapter 22, so for now I'll focus on the basics. Cloud storage services entail paying someone else (such as Amazon Web Services) to host near-infinite amounts of data. You put your data in the bucket and pay based on your usage, and the provider deals with the details of managing the massive fleet of storage devices that power the service. Online storage is a simple way to store a copy of your data offsite if you don't have another secure location, but recovering the data can take longer when you have to download it.

For the same reasons, cloud storage can be tedious for very large backups. With a sustained 10-Mbps speed, it would take over a day to upload even a terabyte of data. This may not be a big deal for your parent's photo collection, but it is such a big deal that organizations looking to transfer gobs of data into or out of cloud storage can throw stacks of cash at Amazon to have a few of their finest rumble up to their doorstep in an AWS Snowmobile—a semi-truck hauling a shipping container stuffed to the gills with over 100,000 terabytes of data storage capacity. If they really mean business, Amazon will even throw in a security escort vehicle.

Backup Testing

Expect a question or two on the CompTIA A+ 1102 exam about backup testing or verifying a backup. The rule is simple: always verify your backups. You could easily invest a dozen years of time and money taking daily backups and following best practices like storing encrypted copies in multiple physical locations and cloud accounts, only to discover—when disaster strikes—that you can't successfully recover the data the backups contain. Backup strategies that don't involve verifying your backups are just fanciful. You might as well leave your failed hard drives under your pillow for the tooth fairy.

Unfortunately, verifying backups isn't as simple as it sounds. The gold standard is being able to restore whatever you backed up—whether files or disk images—and end up with exactly what you *expect* to have. Reality is tricky, though. Imagine, as soon as you take a backup, you compare the backup with the files on disk to make sure they're identical. If files on your disk are corrupt, verifying the backup just guarantees that you've meticulously copied the corrupt files.

Backup tools worth your time and money will provide a way to verify that a backup hasn't changed since it was saved, but this is no substitute for periodically verifying that you can restore and actually use backups of any critical system images, applications, files, and data. In practice, this means:

- If your backup software can verify backups, do this every time you back up.
- No matter what your backup software does, regularly test the actual backups. Systems should restore and boot, and all critical applications should run. It's hard to check everything, but critical files should open correctly in appropriate software. Critical applications should be carefully tested to make sure essential settings, configuration, and data are working.

 EXAM TIP The CompTIA A+ 1102 objectives mention backup testing *frequency*. I'm not sure if CompTIA has hard numbers in mind, so let's step back and think about how you'd decide how frequently to test backups. The main factors are how critical systems and data are to your organization as a whole and how relatively important different systems or data are. A business that could fail if it lost critical systems or data—like a bank— might be taking backups hourly or even *continuously* and testing them weekly. Very few workstations will be that critical, so you'll likely back them up nightly or weekly and test recovery monthly or quarterly.

Backup Rotation Schemes

Early in this section I mentioned that all the backup options involve trade-offs between the risk of data loss on one hand and cost, convenience, and effort on the other. After weighing these trade-offs, organizations often settle on a set of practices that they think will help them meet their goals. Since backups tend to take up a lot of storage space, these practices often entail a *backup rotation scheme* (or strategy) that dictates which kind of backups to take, when to take them, what media to store them on, and where to keep those media. The backup rotation scheme choreographs the whole process of taking backups, moving them to safer locations, and eventually *overwriting* the old backups once they aren't needed.

The key to understanding backup rotation schemes is knowing the risk and benefit of overwriting. If you never overwrite any of your old backups, you'll constantly accumulate new storage devices. This would be *great* for your ability to roll back the clock to the day before trouble started, but you'd need a lot of money—and a lot of space for your growing archive of backups. A scheme for how often to overwrite old backups enables you to use a smaller number of storage devices.

Every organization must decide which backup rotation scheme works best for its needs. However, a good place to start is with the *3-2-1 backup rule*: keep at least three copies of your data on at least two different types of media (i.e., hard drives, tapes, optical disks, cloud storage) and store at least one copy offsite. Let's think through how to design a scheme based on this rule.

Why not just buy an SSD and two hard drives, use a different one each day, and keep one offsite? This *would* satisfy the 3-2-1 backup rule on the cheap—but it also means that you'd be overwriting *all* copies of your data every three days. If an important file gets corrupted or deleted and you don't notice before the third backup starts, you won't be able to recover the data!

 NOTE   Cycling through a single set of devices like this is known as a *first in, first out (FIFO)* rotation scheme. If you're curious, there are plenty of other schemes (and variations on them) out there.

There's one specific rotation scheme CompTIA wants you to know for the A+ 1102 exam, so let's look at how it works and consider how it satisfies the 3-2-1 backup rule without falling into this trap.

A basic *grandfather-father-son (GFS)* rotation scheme might use the SSD to back up four days a week, use one of the hard drives on the last day of each week, and use the other hard drive on the last day of each month—and store the monthly copy offsite. A scheme like this gives us at least a week to notice trouble. We can extend the scheme to buy more time by adding storage devices to each backup cycle (like using nine devices to keep three daily backups, three weekly backups, and three monthly backups) and by adding more cycles (like a yearly backup).

Backing Up Personal Data

The most important data on your computer is data: your documents, e-mail messages and contacts, Web favorites, photographs, and other files. To handle backing up personal data, Windows offers several backup utilities. macOS and Linux of course have backup tools as well.

Windows Backup and Restore

Windows includes the automated and simple *Backup and Restore* Control Panel applet. The process begins by asking where you want to save your backup (see Figure 14-21).

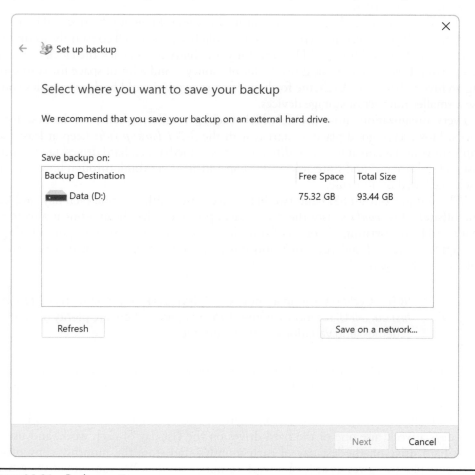

Figure 14-21   Backup options

NOTE If you're wondering why the applet shows up in the Control Panel as "Backup and Restore (Windows 7)," I imagine it's because Microsoft caused an uproar when they removed Backup and Restore in Windows 8/8.1. When they brought it back in Windows 10, I think they wanted to make darned sure everyone knew they listened and restored the tool as it existed in Windows 7.

After you choose the backup location and click Next, Windows asks what you want to back up. As you can see in Figure 14-22, there are two choices: *Let Windows choose (recommended)* and *Let me choose*.

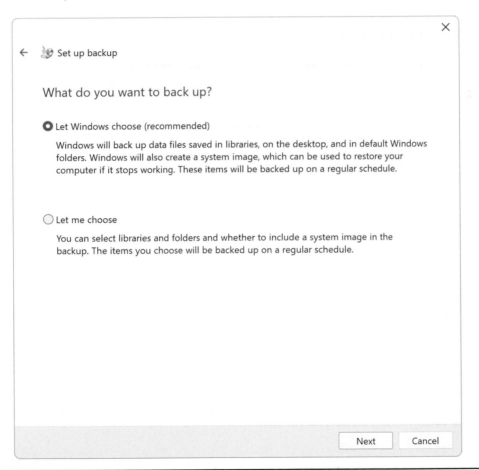

Figure 14-22 What do you want to back up?

If you select *Let Windows choose (recommended)*, you'll back up each user's personal data. Assuming you have enough space in your backup location, Windows will automatically add a system image that includes the entire Windows operating system, every installed program, all device drivers, and even the Registry.

Selecting *Let me choose* is equally interesting. Windows enables you to pick individual users' files to back up (see Figure 14-23). This can be handy when you store important files outside of the folders the *Let Windows choose* option covers.

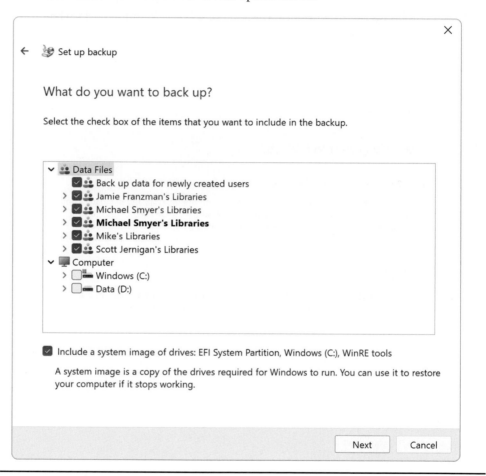

Figure 14-23 Backup showing a list of users

By selecting a user, you can choose libraries or the user's personal folders to back up, as shown in Figure 14-24. Also note the checkbox that gives you the option to make a system image, just as if you selected the *Let Windows choose (recommended)* option.

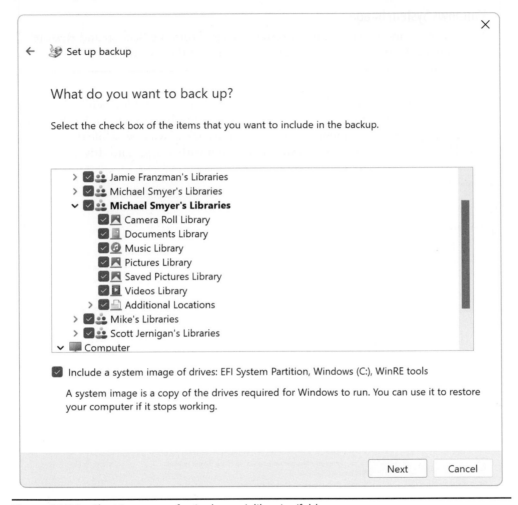

Figure 14-24 Showing some of a single user's libraries/folders

---

Try This!

Windows System Images

You can also choose to create just a system image. From the Backup and Restore applet, select *Create a system image* on the left side of the screen.

Once you complete the wizard, Windows starts backing up your files. While the backup runs, you can monitor its progress with an exciting progress bar (see Figure 14-25). If you can't handle that much excitement, you can close the backup window while the OS backs up files. The process can take many hours on a system with a large hard drive.

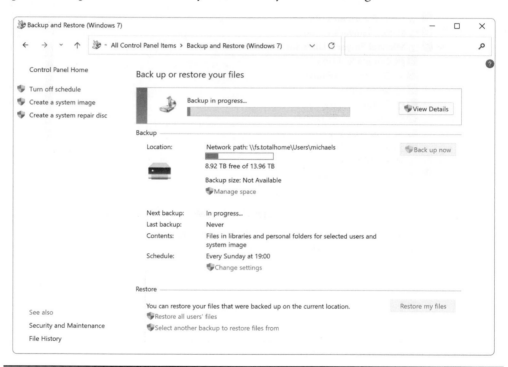

Figure 14-25   Backup in progress . . .

Windows File History

The *File History* Control Panel applet focuses on backing up your personal files and folders (see Figure 14-26) and includes the ability to restore previous versions of individual files. File History requires a second drive and is not enabled by default. You can use any type of HDD or SSD as the second drive, internal or external. (You could choose to back up to a second partition on the same drive, I suppose, but what would be the point?)

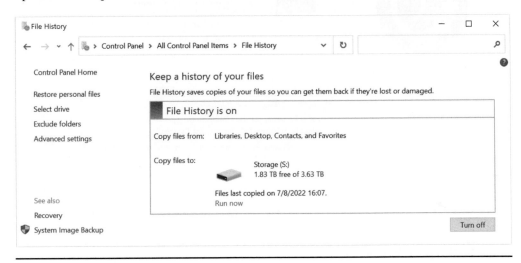

Figure 14-26   Windows File History

Note that File History won't back up all your personal files unless you either add them to the default libraries or create custom libraries. File History does *not* replace full system backups!

Time Machine in macOS

macOS includes *Time Machine* to create full system backups (see Figure 14-27). These backups are called *local snapshots*. Time Machine enables you to recover some or all files in the event of a crash; it also enables you to *restore* deleted files and recover previous versions of files. Time Machine requires an external HDD or SSD, or you can use a shared network drive. Find Time Machine in System Preferences.

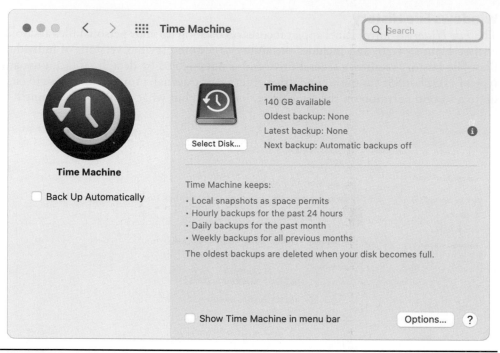

Figure 14-27   Time Machine

Backups in Linux

Different Linux distros offer different tools for backing up files, folders, and drives. Ubuntu Linux uses Déjà Dup, although the name of the app is *Backups* (see Figure 14-28). Déjà Dup will happily back up your files to wherever you tell it, such as an external drive, network share, or even a folder on your main hard drive (not recommended if you care about your files!). Déjà Dup backs up a user's Home folder by default; that's where most users store all personal documents. Déjà Dup will store files and versions of files permanently, as long as the storage location has sufficient space.

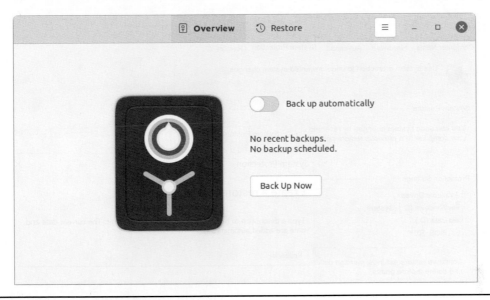

Figure 14-28   Backups app in Ubuntu Linux

System Restore in Windows

Every technician has war stories about the user who likes to add the latest gadget and cool software to his computer. Then the user is amazed when things go very, very wrong: the system locks up, refuses to boot, or simply acts weird. This guy also can't remember what he added or when. All he knows is that you should be able to fix it—fast.

The *System Restore* tool enables you to create a *restore point*, a *snapshot* of a computer's configuration at a specific point in time. If the computer later crashes or has a corrupted OS, you can restore the system to its previous state, specifically *restore system files and settings*.

When System Restore is turned on, it makes a number of restore points automatically. To make your own restore point, right-click the Start button and select System, and then scroll down the About page and click the System protection link. The System Properties dialog box opens with the System Protection tab showing. Click the Create button to open the dialog box shown in Figure 14-29. Name your restore point appropriately and then click Create.

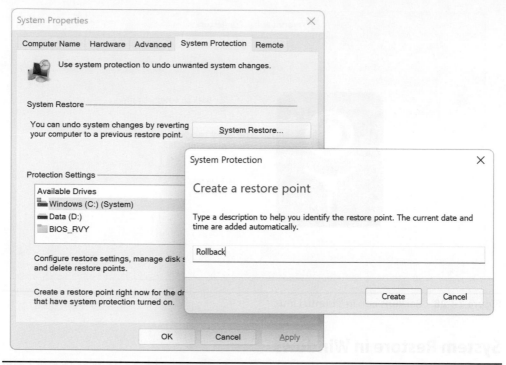

Figure 14-29   Creating a manual restore point in Windows

EXAM TIP   Microsoft started disabling System Restore by default in Windows 10. I've heard rumors about it being unreliable after a few (not most) Windows updates—but CompTIA's malware-removal procedure (which you'll learn in Chapter 27) assumes you'll have it enabled. If you find yourself needing to roll back a Windows machine with no restore points, you may need to look at a much more drastic fix: using Windows' Reset this PC feature, which we will talk about in Chapter 16.

After your new restore point is created, you can locate it by clicking the System Restore button on the System Protection tab to open the System Restore window, which might also show restore points that have already been made for you automatically (see Figure 14-30).

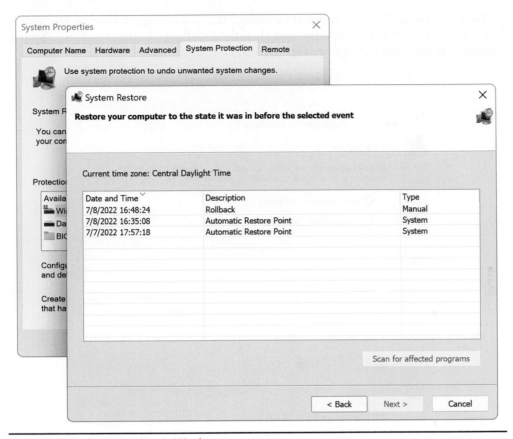

Figure 14-30   Restore points in Windows

The System Restore tool creates some restore points automatically, including every time you install new software. If installing a program causes your computer to malfunction, simply restore the system to a point before you installed it. During the restore process, only settings and programs are changed (it won't touch user files). This feature is absolutely invaluable for overworked techs. A simple restore fixes many user-generated problems. To restore to a previous time point, return to the System Restore window as previously described, select the restore point you want to return to, and click Next.

To turn System Restore on or off or change the space usage, return to the System Protection tab of System Properties and click the Configure button to change System Restore configuration settings (see Figure 14-31).

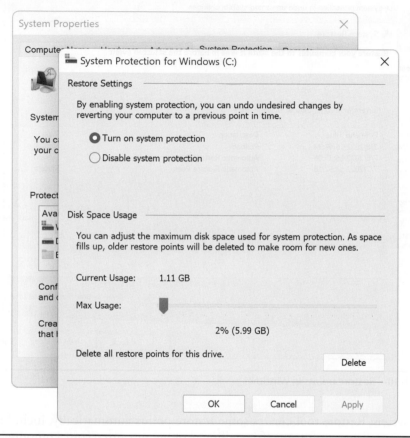

Figure 14-31 System Restore settings and disk space usage options

Beyond A+

Third-Party Backup Tools

The backup tools built into an operating system are often enough for your average single-system user, but many power users and organizations will find themselves using third-party backup tools to meet specific needs. These needs can be simple, like wanting to use a single tool to back up and restore on multiple operating systems. They can also be quite complex, like keeping continuous offsite backups of all of an organization's critical systems.

There are countless backup tools in the world, but they all fall more or less into three main categories: tools, applications, and services.

A backup *tool* is a program (command line or graphical) that can capture some type of backup and save it to a local device or network location. There are tons of backup tools with different features, but in general they give you a lot of control over your backups. This control means you'll usually have to make a lot of decisions beyond just picking out a tool, but it can also help reduce costs and minimize the risk of losing access to your old backups if the vendor goes out of business.

 NOTE   Remember that it's also a good idea to use more than one backup tool. This can really save your skin if there's a bug in an update to your backup tool that causes it to start saving unrestorable backups.

A backup *appliance* is an all-in-one combination of hardware and software from some provider built for the exact purpose of making and storing backups. A backup appliance might live right next to the device(s) it backs up, in a nearby server rack, or in a remote data center—but the key is that backup appliances are a lot less do-it-yourself than a simple backup tool. These appliances store a copy of your data inside the device, and they can often upload one or more copies of the data to offsite locations.

A backup *service* is a little bit like a backup appliance minus the dedicated local hardware. These all-in-one backup services include software for working with backups that is integrated with the provider's online (cloud) backup storage service. These services are usually very simple to set up and get started with, but they do come with an ongoing subscription cost—and could leave your organization at the provider's mercy if it goes out of business or increases rates.

Chapter Review

Questions

1. What tool enables you to select the programs and services that load when Windows starts?
   A. Task Manager
   B. System Configuration
   C. msconfig
   D. Task Scheduler

2. What tool enables you to run a maintenance script based on specific conditions on Windows?
   A. Task Manager
   B. System Configuration
   C. msconfig
   D. Task Scheduler

3. What does System Information do?

   A. Provides you with a report about the hardware resources, components, and software environment in your computer

   B. Enables you to select which programs and services start when Windows boots up

   C. Enables you to schedule hard drive defragmentation, chkdsk scans, and other computer tasks

   D. Enables you to perform automatic custom backups of your files and settings

4. What tool enables you to correct a corrupted Windows operating system by reverting your computer to a previous state?

   A. Windows Restore

   B. Restore State Manager

   C. Time Machine

   D. System Restore

5. What is Data Execution Prevention (DEP)?

   A. A technology that prevents viruses from taking over programs loaded in system memory

   B. A technology that enables you to set permissions for different users on your computer

   C. A technology that prevents programs from being installed on your computer

   D. A technology that prevents files from being written to your hard drive

6. Which of the following is *not* a file extension you'd expect to see in the process of downloading and installing an app on macOS?

   A. .app

   B. .dmg

   C. .msc

   D. .pkg

7. Which of the following enables you to schedule maintenance tasks on macOS and Linux?

   A. systemd

   B. launchd

   C. Task Scheduler

   D. cron

8. Joan is looking for the quickest way to take very frequent backups of an important database. Which of the following media would be best?

   A. Cloud storage

   B. Magnetic tapes

   C. Solid-state drives

   D. Magnetic hard drives

9. What tool is used in macOS to perform full system backups?

   A. Backup and Restore

   B. File History

   C. Time Machine

   D. iCloud

10. What Windows feature enables you to back up your important files and folders regularly?

    A. Time Machine

    B. Backup and Restore

    C. System Snapshot

    D. File History

Answers

1. **A.** The Task Manager enables you to select the programs and services that load when Windows starts. (System Configuration used to do this, but it now redirects you to the Task Manager.)

2. **D.** Task Scheduler enables you to set up a maintenance task that will run when certain triggers occur and specified conditions are met.

3. **A.** System Information gives you a wide variety of information about your system.

4. **D.** Using System Restore, you can restore your computer to a previous restore point.

5. **A.** Data Execution Prevention prevents viruses from taking control of programs loaded into memory.

6. **C.** The .msc extension is associated with Windows MMC snap-ins.

7. **D.** While systemd, launchd, and Task Scheduler can all schedule maintenance tasks, only cron is available on *both* macOS and Linux.

8. **C.** Joan should check out solid-state drives, which offer more speed in exchange for a higher price.

9. **C.** macOS uses Time Machine to perform full system backups.

10. **D.** File History enables you to perform backups of important files and folders regularly.

Working with the Command-Line Interface

In this chapter, you will learn how to

- Explain the operation of the command-line interface
- Describe fundamental commands
- Explain file manipulation
- Describe additional useful Windows commands
- Describe additional helpful macOS and Linux commands
- Explain scripting languages and platforms

Whenever I teach a class of new techs and we get to the section on working with the command line, I'm invariably met with a chorus of moans and a barrage of questions and statements like "Why do we need to learn this old stuff?" and "Is this ritualistic hazing appropriate in an IT class?"

For techs who master the interface, the command line provides a powerful, quick, and flexible tool for working on a computer. Learning that interface and understanding how to make it work is not only useful, but also necessary for all techs who want to go beyond baby-tech status. You simply cannot work on modern computers without knowing the command line! I'm not the only one who thinks this way. The CompTIA A+ 220-1102 certification exam tests you on a variety of command-line commands, both in Windows and Linux, for doing everything from renaming a file to rebuilding a system file.

If you're interested in moving beyond Windows and into Unix-like operating systems such as Linux and macOS, you'll find that pretty much all of the serious work is done at the command line.

The command line is popular for many reasons. Let's consider three for this chapter. First, if you know what you're doing, you can do most jobs more quickly by typing a text command than by clicking through a graphical user interface (GUI). Second, a *command-line interface (CLI)* uses fewer system resources, so it's the natural choice for jobs where you don't want (or couldn't even run) a full-blown GUI. Third, you can combine multiple text commands to automate complex tasks.

This chapter gives you a tour of the Windows, Linux, and macOS command-line interfaces, explaining how they work and what's happening behind the scenes. You'll learn the concepts and master essential commands. You'll work with files and folders and learn about scripting. It's all fun! A good tactic for absorbing the material in this chapter is to try out each command as it's presented.

 NOTE If you're using a Windows system, this is a great opportunity to jump ahead to Chapter 22 and try some virtualization. Consider loading up a virtual machine and installing Linux so you can practice the Linux command line. Check out and install my favorite virtualization tool, Oracle VirtualBox at https://www.virtualbox.org, and then download an ISO file from https://ubuntu.com.

1102

Deciphering the Command-Line Interface

A command-line interface is a little like a voice assistant (such as Amazon's Alexa, Apple's Siri, and Google Assistant), but instead of talking and getting a response, you type and get a response. When you say the magic words to wake up a voice assistant, it'll do *something* (make a noise, light up, change its screen, etc.) to indicate that it heard you and is ready for your request. A CLI tells you it's ready to receive commands by displaying a specific set of characters called a *prompt*. Here's an example of a generic prompt:

```
>: Computer: Want to play a game?
>: _
```

You type a command and press ENTER to send it:

```
>: Computer: Want to play a game?
>: You: What kind of game?
>: _
```

Much like a voice assistant, the computer evaluates what you entered and responds. A computer generally responds by displaying the information you requested, a list of things the command did, a request for more information, or an error message if it couldn't understand or perform your request. When it finishes, it displays a new prompt to show that it is ready for your next instruction:

```
>: Computer: Want to play a game?
>: You: What kind of game?
>: Computer: A very fun game...
>: _
```

Running commands from the command line is equivalent to interacting with buttons, icons, and menus in a GUI. The results are basically the same: you tell the computer to do something and it responds.

Getting the Most out of the CLI

When you're trying to find your sea legs, the big difference between CLIs and GUIs is that everything you can do in a GUI has to take up space on the screen (or be tucked away in menus that take up space). It's much easier to *discover* what you can do with a GUI, but it also means that GUIs for complex tasks are stuffed with deeply nested menus and panels that take time to navigate. The CLI can be faster for many tasks once you are sure-footed, but it is much less *discoverable*: you must learn (and then *know*) which commands exist and what they do.

Start a separate file (or even a notebook) for your own notes about the command line. Keep track of the different shells and commands you encounter, write a short summary of what each one does, and maintain a list of situations where you've found each helpful. Every time you have to go ask a mentor, friend, coworker, or search engine what command to use for some task, make sure to update your notes!

Shells

The command line, like a GUI, is just another way to interface with a computer. The command line interprets input and sends it to the OS in a form the OS understands, and then shows the results. The tool that interprets input is called the *command-line interpreter*, also known as the *shell*.

 EXAM TIP The CompTIA A+ 1102 objectives don't mention PowerShell or any of its key concepts. I'm including some PowerShell basics because I think you should learn how to use it—but the Windows examples in this chapter focus on Command Prompt because that's what you'll see on the exam.

While most operating systems have only one GUI, that's not the case with the shell. Every operating system has the ability to interface with different types of shells. The default in Windows is now PowerShell, but the traditional Command Prompt (we nerds call it cmd) is still there. If you use Linux or macOS, you'll be spoiled with choices. Some of the most common are the GNU Bourne-Again Shell (bash), Z shell (zsh), Fish shell (fish), and C shell (csh). Many (but not all) Linux distributions (aka distros) have long used *bash* as their default shell—and so did macOS until it switched to zsh in late 2019. It's a rite of nerd passage to experiment with different shells.

 NOTE There are *way* more shells than I'm listing here. The most common shells are everywhere because they're as old as the hills—aside from Fish (2005) and PowerShell (2006), the other shells I listed got their start between 1978 and 1993! If you want to take something more modern for a spin, my favorites are Elvish, Nushell, Oil, and Xonsh.

Accessing the Command-Line Interface in Windows

You access the command-line interface in Windows by starting the shell program Command Prompt. We touched on accessing the CLI in Chapter 2, but let's develop this procedure more here.

A common way to access the command-line interface is through the Start menu or the Start screen's Search bar. Type **cmd** from the Start screen. Command Prompt appears as the best match (see Figure 15-1). Press ENTER.

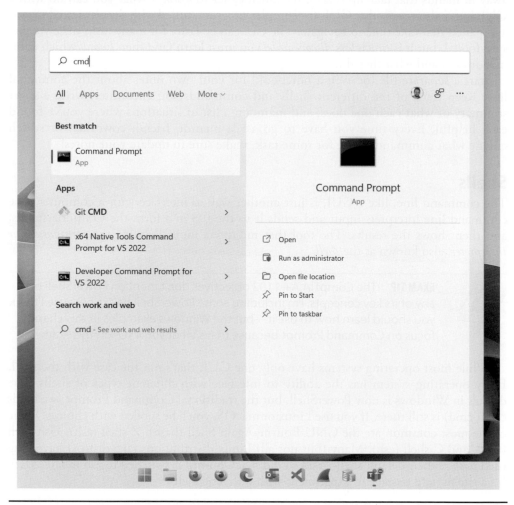

Figure 15-1 Starting Command Prompt in Windows 11

On Windows 11, Command Prompt opens in the brand new Windows Terminal, so it looks a little different than it does in Windows 10 (see Figure 15-2). To close the CLI, you can either click the Close box in the upper-right corner, as on any other window, or simply type **exit** and press ENTER.

Figure 15-2 The command-line interface in Windows 11 (top) and 10 (bottom)

Try This!

Opening Windows GUI Programs from the Command Line

Keep in mind as you go through this chapter that the command line is just another tool for communicating with the system, so try this! At a command line, type **notepad** and press ENTER. What happens? The graphical program Notepad opens up, just as if you'd double-clicked on its icon. Here's another: type **explorer** and press ENTER. Voilà! File Explorer loads.

If you try to run a command that requires elevated or administrative privileges on Windows, you receive a UAC "Windows needs your permission to continue" dialog box. (You learned about UAC in Chapter 13.) You can also manually run a command with elevated privileges by right-clicking on a command-prompt shortcut and then selecting *Run as administrator*. If Windows prompts for the administrator password or credentials, enter whatever is needed.

NOTE You can create a shortcut to a Windows command prompt with elevated privileges by right-clicking on the desktop and selecting New | Shortcut. For the location of the item, type **cmd** and click Next. Type **cmd** to name the shortcut, and click Finish. The shortcut appears on the Desktop. Next, right-click the shortcut and select the Advanced button. In the Advanced Properties dialog box, check the *Run as administrator* box and click OK. You have now created a Windows command-prompt shortcut that will always run with administrative privileges.

Accessing the Command-Line Interface in macOS and Linux

Linux and macOS have very similar command lines. Both come with a default *terminal emulator* (its name comes from the fact that it emulates iconic old-school hardware terminals that were common from the 1960s to the 1990s—but you can just think of it as a GUI application that enables you to use a shell). The default in macOS is named *Terminal*, and different distros of Linux use different emulators, such as Konsole Terminal and GNOME Terminal. To make things easy, we'll use the command-line interface in Ubuntu Linux which is also conveniently named *Terminal*.

NOTE Linux and macOS are so similar because they are both heavily influenced by the old UNIX operating system. It may not be obvious from their GUIs, but the relationship is clear at the command line. Throughout this chapter I'll use "UNIX" or "UNIX-like" or "UNIXes" when Linux and macOS are equivalent and I'll call them out by name when they differ.

To open Terminal in macOS, either launch the Terminal app from the Utilities folder (located in the Applications folder) or activate Spotlight (COMMAND-SPACEBAR), type **terminal**, and press ENTER to bring up the macOS Terminal (see Figure 15-3).

The way to open a terminal emulator in Linux varies depending on the Linux distro you use. Generally, every desktop-focused Linux distro has some form of finder or search function on the desktop that works similarly to the search tools in macOS and Windows. Find this tool and then type **terminal** and press ENTER to start the program. This brings up the terminal window, as shown in Figure 15-4.

Figure 15-3
macOS Terminal

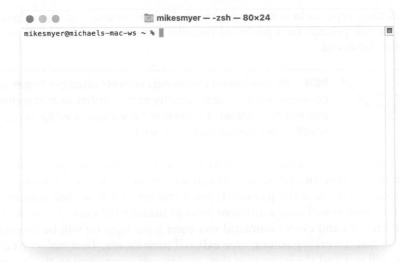

Figure 15-4
Linux Terminal

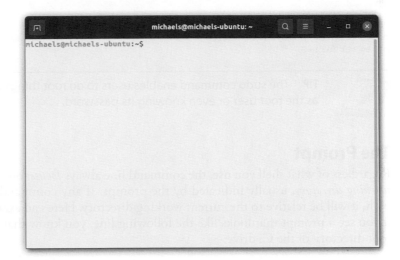

TIP *Spotlight* is a phenomenal search tool in macOS. It indexes your drive(s), not just for filenames, but for content. That means you can search for specific files, of course, plus all sorts of other things, like apps, e-mail messages, music, contacts, and even flight information! Try it!

UNIXes also enable you to run commands with advanced privileges, called *super user* or *root privileges*. Two commands do the trick: *su* and *sudo*. Even though this advanced privileges function is equivalent to the elevated privileges in Windows, UNIXes handle this elevation differently. First, open Terminal. Whenever you need to run a command as root, type **sudo** followed by the desired command and then press ENTER. The system will prompt for a password (usually; it can be configured not to) and then execute the command.

NOTE While running commands with elevated privileges is the most common use of su and sudo, try to remember su as standing for *substitute user identity* instead of *super user*. When you need to run commands as any specific user, you can use su or sudo.

If the system doesn't have sudo, it should have its older cousin *su*. With su, you typically just type **su** and press ENTER; it will prompt you for the root password. Once you successfully enter the password, you'll end up in a new shell session for the root user. This session will have a different prompt (usually the character at the end changes from a $ to a #) and every command you enter from then on will be executed as root. When you finish working as root, type **exit** and press ENTER. Terminal won't close like before—it will just end the inner root shell session and return you to the outer session. You can see how the prompt changes in the following example:

```
mike@server:~$ su
Password:_
root@server:/home/mike# exit
mike@server:~$
```

TIP The sudo command enables users to do root things without logging in as the root user or even knowing its password.

The Prompt

Regardless of what shell you use, the command line always *focuses* on a specific folder, the *working directory*, usually indicated by the prompt. If any commands use a relative file path, it will be relative to the current working directory. Here's an example: in Windows, if you see a prompt that looks like the following line, you know that the focus is on the root directory of the C: drive:

```
C:\>
```

In a UNIX-like OS the prompt is subtly different, but functionally the same. First, these systems don't use the Windows drive lettering concept: all forms of storage are simply mounted as folders. Second, prompts on these systems usually show the logged-on user and system as well as the current directory. Third, paths on these systems use a forward slash (/) instead of a backslash (\). This prompt shows user mike is on the "server" system and is in the home directory:

```
mike@server:/home$
```

In Windows, if you see a prompt that looks like Figure 15-5, you know that the focus is on the \Diploma\APLUS\ folder of the C: drive. If you're working with files from the command line, it's important to focus the prompt on the drive and folder where you want to work.

Figure 15-5
Command prompt indicating focus on the C:\ Diploma\APLUS\ folder

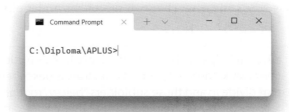

Closing the Terminal

Closing a command prompt is easy and is done the same way in Windows, macOS, and Linux. From the CLI you want to close, just type **exit** and press ENTER. This techni-cally just exits the shell itself, but many terminal emulators will automatically close the window or tab when the shell terminates. If yours doesn't, manually close the tab or window as well.

```
mike@server:/home$ exit
```

Drives and Folders

When working from the command line, you need to be able to focus the prompt at the specific drive and folder that contains the files or programs with which you want to work. This can be a little more complicated than it seems.

Before we get too deep here, let's review what you studied in Chapter 9. Windows assigns drive letters to each hard drive partition and to every recognized form of mass stor-age. HDD/SSD partitions usually start with the letter C:. Thumb drives, external drives, and optical drives get the next available drive letter after the last hard drive partition.

UNIXes do not use drive letters. Instead, the boot partition is defined as the root drive, shown as just a slash: /. All other storage—partitions, optical discs, thumb drives, and so on—must go through a process called *mounting* to enable the OS to treat them as folders. These folders are most often mounted to a single folder off the root drive called /mount or /media in Linux and /Volumes in macOS.

TIP Windows partitions are also mounted (that's what happens when they get a drive letter), although Microsoft rarely uses that term.

Whatever the names of the drives, all operating systems use a hierarchical directory tree to organize the contents of these drives. All files are put into groups called *folders*, although you'll often hear techs use the interchangeable term *directory*. Any file not in a folder *within* the tree—that is, any file in the folder at the root of the directory tree—is said to be in the *root directory*. A folder inside another folder is called a *subfolder*. Any folder can have multiple subfolders. A subfolder may have subfolders. Two or more files with the same name can exist in different folders on a PC, but two files in the same folder cannot have the same name. In the same way, no two subfolders under the same folder can have the same name, but two subfolders under different folders can have the same name.

NOTE It helps to visualize a directory tree as upside down, because in geekspeak, the trunk, or root directory, is described as "above" the folders that divide it, and those subfolders "below" root are spoken of as being "above" the other subfolders inside them. For example, "The file is in the Adobe folder under Program Files."

When describing a drive in Windows, you use its letter and a colon. For example, the hard drive would be represented by C:. To describe the root directory, put a backslash (\) after the C:, as in C:\. To describe a particular directory, add the name of the directory. For example, if a PC has a directory in the root directory called Test, it is C:\Test. Subdirectories in a directory are displayed by adding backslashes and names. If the Test directory has a subdirectory called System, it is shown like this: C:\Test\System. This naming convention provides for a complete description of the location and name of any file. If the C:\Test\System directory includes a file called test2.txt, it is C:\Test\System\test2.txt.

The location of a file is called its *path*. An *absolute path* specifies the file's exact location, while a *relative path* is just enough to find it from a starting point (such as the working directory). Think of this like an address. If a buddy on the other side of the world wanted to send you a gift, you'd need to give them a complete address. But if you're having pizza delivered from a few blocks over, a street and number should be enough for the delivery driver to find your house. The absolute path for the test2.txt file is C:\Test\System\test2.txt, but System\test2.txt would be enough to find it from C:\Test. Here are some examples of possible Windows paths:

```
C:\Program Files
C:\Users\mike\Desktop
F:\FRUSCH3\CLEAR
D:\
```

UNIXes also use paths. Folder names are separated by a forward slash (/), however, instead of the backslash used by Windows. Also, Windows and macOS are not usually case sensitive, while Linux is. For example, in Linux it's perfectly acceptable to have two folders called "Mike" and "mike" inside the same folder. Windows and macOS do not allow this. Here are some examples of UNIX paths:

```
/usr/local/bin
/Applications/Utilities
/home/mike/Desktop
/
```

While it is hard to generalize about prompts on UNIXes—they differ from shell to shell and users often customize them—they usually show your folder location a bit differently than Windows. Generally, your default prompt points at the /home/<username>/ folder. By default, however, the prompt on most UNIXes just shows a tilde (~), as follows:

```
mike@server:~$
```

The ~ is really just a shorthand for your user's *home directory*; in this case it means my working directory is /home/mike. Yes, a little confusing, but welcome to UNIX! There's a handy utility, *pwd*, that tells you the full path of the current working directory if you're unsure:

```
mike@server:~$ pwd
/home/mike
```

Here are key points to remember about folder names and filenames:

- Folders and files may have spaces in their names.
- The only disallowed characters in Windows are the following eleven: * " / \ [ ] : ; | = ,
- In UNIX the only disallowed character is a forward slash: /

Mastering Fundamental Commands

It's time to try using the command line, but before you begin, a note of warning is in order: the command-line interface is picky and unforgiving. It will do what you *say*, not what you *mean*, so it always pays to double-check that those are one and the same before you press ENTER and commit the command. One careless keystroke can result in the loss of crucial data, with no warning and no going back. In this section, you'll explore the structure of commands and then play with basic commands to navigate and manipulate your OS's folder structure.

Structure: Syntax and Switches

All commands in every command-line interface use a similar structure and you run them the same way. You type the name of the command, followed by the target of that command and any modifications of that command that you want to apply, and then press ENTER to execute the command. You specify a modification with its *switch* or *option* (often a special character such as / or - followed by one or more letters, numbers, or words), which usually follows either the command or the target, depending on the command. The proper way to write a command is called its *syntax*.

 NOTE From this point on, I'll just assume you have a terminal open and ready. I'll also use the word *run* when I want you to type a command and then press ENTER. If I just tell you to *type* something, look for more instructions before you press ENTER.

The command generally won't understand if you spell anything incorrectly or use a \ when the syntax calls for a /. Since the CLI doesn't have an easy-to-discover button or menu for every command, *you* have to learn the correct syntax for each. (There's no shame in looking it up each time—there are plenty of commands I can't keep straight—but it will slow you down.) Consider these two common forms (the brackets are just placeholders—you wouldn't type them):

```
[command] [target (if any)] [switches]
```

or

```
[command] [switches] [target (if any)]
```

How do you know what switches are allowed? How do you know whether the switches come before or after the target? Don't just guess, look it up!

Teaching Yourself to Fish

There are thousands of commands out in the world. Some of them do something so simple they don't have any options; others are monsters with hundreds and hundreds of options. How do you know what switches are allowed and what they do? How do you know whether the switches come before or after the target? You look up the command's *documentation*.

If you want to find out the syntax and switches used by a particular command in Windows Command Prompt, run the command itself with the **/?** switch to get help:

```
[command name] /?
```

PowerShell has a dedicated command for this—just run **Get-Help** with the command you're interested in:

```
Get-Help [command name]
```

In UNIX, run **man** (manual) with the name of the command you're interested in:

```
man [command name]
```

Any of these commands searches for a matching manual entry (commonly called a *manual page* or *man page*) and—if it finds an entry—opens it in an interactive reader (which is commonly called a *pager*—we'll talk *more* about these in a minute). You should be able to scroll through the document with your mouse-wheel, trackpad, or arrow keys; press the Q key to quit the interactive reader when you're done.

 EXAM TIP In the real world, there are a bewildering number of ways to get command help (including a few I'm leaving out). The CompTIA 1102 exam objectives, however, only mention the /? switch on Windows, and the man command for Linux.

Command Types

I need to take you down a rabbit hole to learn something that trips up a lot of new CLI users, especially on UNIX: there's more than one type of command, and the command type affects how to look up information about it. The most important types are *builtins* (which are actually part of your shell) and standalone *external* commands.

On a UNIX-like OS, you can run the **type** builtin followed by a command to see what type it is. Here's a command we've already looked at:

```
mike@server:~$ type pwd
pwd is a shell builtin
```

Generally speaking, the manual won't have an entry for a builtin *unless it is also an external command.* Read that again! Yes—it's possible to have more than one version of a command. If you run **type** again with the **-a** (all) switch, it will show if there is more than one version. When you actually run this command, your shell will use the one at the top of the list):

```
mike@server:~$ type -a pwd
pwd is a shell builtin
pwd is /bin/pwd
```

There's no tried and true way to find the right information for builtins; it varies from shell to shell. Bash and Fish, for example, both have a built-in help command (the former displays a summary, the latter opens a Web page)—but Z shell lists them all on the "zshbuiltins" manual page. Take the time to learn how your shell handles this! Sooner or later, it'll save you a lot of confusion.

 NOTE   Some external commands just don't have a manual page (or you might have to do extra work to find, enable, or install its man page). As a last resort, try running the command with the **--help** or **-h** switch.

Getting help in Windows is a little more consistent, but the method does still differ depending on which shell you use. In PowerShell, for example, the Get-Command *cmdlet* is roughly equivalent to the type builtin. The following command shows that, in PowerShell, pwd is an alias (an alternative name) for a cmdlet named Get-Location:

```
PS C:\> Get-command pwd
CommandType     Name                      Version   Source
-----------     ----                      -------   ------
Alias           pwd -> Get-Location(2)Viewing Directory Contents: dir and ls
```

The Windows *dir* command and the UNIX ls command show you the contents of the working directory. If you're like most techs, you'll use dir or ls more often than any other command. When you open a command-line window in Windows, it opens focused on your user folder. You will know this because the prompt looks like C:\Users*User name*>. When you run **dir**, you will see something like:

```
C:\Users>dir
 Volume in drive C has no label.
 Volume Serial Number is 98F4-E484

 Directory of C:\Users

07/16/2023  10:52 AM    <DIR>          .
07/16/2023  10:52 AM    <DIR>          ..
12/20/2022  06:59 PM    <DIR>          DefaultAppPool
08/14/2024  10:42 AM    <DIR>          Mike
07/16/2023  02:07 AM    <DIR>          Public
               0 File(s)              0 bytes
               5 Dir(s)  295,888,113,664 bytes free
C:\Users>
```

The default prompts in Linux don't show the full path, but on my Ubuntu Linux system, running ls shows the following in my home directory:

```
mike@server:~$ ls
Desktop      Downloads   Public      Videos
Documents    photo.jpg   timmy.doc
mike@server:~$
```

If you are following along, remember that different computers contain different folders, files, and programs; you will see something different from these examples. If a lot of text scrolls quickly down the screen in Windows, try running **dir /p** (the /p is for pause). The /p switch is a lifesaver when you need to skim a large directory. Just press SPACEBAR to display the next screen.

NOTE   Some commands give you the same result whether you include spaces or not. Running dir/p and dir /p, for example, produces the same output. Some commands, however, *require* spaces between the command and switches. Get into the habit of putting spaces between your command and switches and you won't run into problems.

In UNIX, you can get the same result as dir /p by running **ls | more**. The | symbol is an "operator" called a *pipe*. You are telling the shell to take the output of ls and, instead of sending it directly to the screen, "pipe" it through the more command (more is a *pager*—a command that enables you to browse through multipage documents). The pipe operator works in all three operating systems and is incredibly powerful. You'll see lots more of the pipe operator later in this chapter.

NOTE   If you try to follow along in PowerShell, be prepared for output and switches to differ. PowerShell has its own take on many classic Command Prompt commands! Its dir command, for example, has no equivalent to the /p switch. Instead, you can run **dir | more** like you would in UNIX.

dir Command

When you run a simple **dir** command, you will see file entries that list the creation date, creation time, file size in bytes, filename, and extension:

```
09/04/2023    05:51 PM              63,664 photo.jpg
```

You'll also see directory entries that list the creation date, creation time, *<DIR>* to tell you it is a folder, and the folder name:

```
12/31/2023  10:18 AM     <DIR>          Windows
```

Next, run **dir /w** and note that it only lists filenames, arranged in columns across your screen. Finally, run **dir /?** to list all the command's switches, as shown in Figure 15-6.

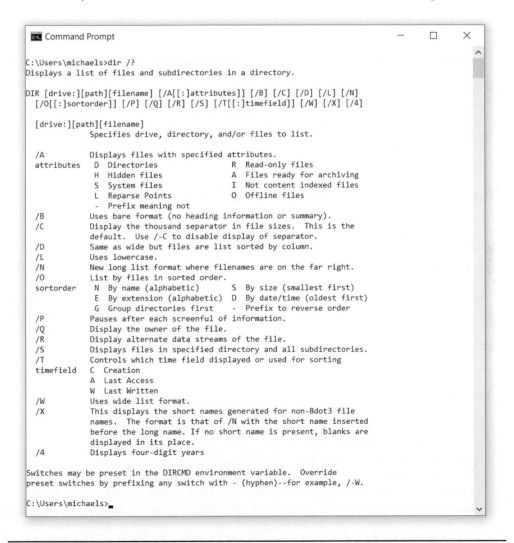

Figure 15-6   Running **dir /?** in Windows lists all possible switches for the dir command.

ls Command

The ls command, which is for listing the contents of directories, has gobs of options that control things like what it lists, in how much detail, and in what order. For now let's just cover one of the more important options: -l.

> **NOTE** As with many fundamental UNIX commands, you can find different variants of ls (with different options) on different systems.

Running **ls** with the **-l** (or long listing) switch outputs detailed information about all the files:

```
$ ls -l
-rw-rw-r-- 0 mike 2313443 Jun 13 15:27 photo.jpg
```

We'll discuss this output in more detail as we continue through the chapter.

> **NOTE** You can often use more than one switch or option to modify a command (though some options conflict with each other). For example, try running **ls -a -l -h** in macOS or Linux. With many commands, you can run multiple switches together. With ls, for example, **ls -alh** works just fine, with all three switches applied.

Changing Directory Focus: The cd Command

The *cd* command, which changes the current working directory, works in every operating system (although there are differences). To use it, run **cd** followed by the directory you want to focus on.

In Windows, for example, run **cd \obiwan** to go to the Obiwan directory inside the root directory. If the system has an Obiwan directory there, the prompt changes focus to that directory and appears as C:\Obiwan>. If no Obiwan directory exists or if you accidentally type something like **obiwam**, you get the error "The system cannot find the path specified." If only I had a dollar for every time I've seen that one! I usually get them because I've typed too fast. If you get this error, check what you typed and try again.

Errors Are Good!

Consider errors in general for a moment—not just command-prompt errors such as "Invalid directory," but any error, including errors in the GUI. Many new computer users freeze in horror when they see an error message. Do not fear error messages. Error messages are good! Love them. Worship them. They will save you.

Seriously, think how confusing it would be if the computer didn't tell you when you messed up. Error messages tell you what you did wrong so you can fix it. You absolutely cannot hurt your PC in any way by typing the dir or cd command incorrectly. Take advantage of this knowledge and experiment. Intentionally make mistakes to familiarize yourself with the error messages. Have fun and learn from errors!

Ok, let's get back to the cd command. Run **cd ** to focus on the root directory. You can use the cd command to point the prompt to any directory. For example, you could run **cd \obiwan\my\hope** from a C:\ prompt, and the prompt would change to C:\Obiwan\my\hope>—assuming, of course, that your system *has* a directory called C:\Obiwan\my\hope. (I can't be the only one, right?)

Once the prompt has changed, run **dir** again. You should see a different list of files and directories. Every directory holds different files and subdirectories, so when you point the prompt to different directories, the dir command shows you different contents.

Changing directory focus in UNIX is similar to doing so in Windows, but you use a / instead of a \. Using the same example just shown for Windows, from the root directory run **cd /obiwan**. To go to the /Obiwan/my/hope directory, run **cd /Obiwan/my/hope**.

 NOTE On UNIXes it is considered bad manners to create files and folders in the root (/) directory. In fact, you need "root" permissions to do such a thing. This is because of Linux's history as a multiuser system. Such restrictions keep users from inconveniencing everyone by breaking the underlying OS.

So far, the examples in this section all start with a slash (indicating the root directory). These *absolute* paths list the entire path from the root directory to the target directory. Absolute paths are great when you know exactly where you're going, but *relative* paths (those without a leading slash) come in handy when you need to browse.

When you run **cd obiwan** without the leading slash, it will look for a subdirectory of the current working directory. For example, you could go to the C:\Obiwan directory from the root directory simply by typing **cd obiwan** at the C:\> prompt. You can then move one level at a time, like this:

```
C:\>cd obiwan
C:\Obiwan>cd my
C:\Obiwan\my>cd hope
```

You can also jump multiple directory levels in one step, like this:

```
C:\>cd obiwan\my\hope
C:\Obiwan\my\hope>
```

These tricks also work for UNIX, but of course you always use a forward slash instead of a backslash as needed:

```
mike@server:~$ cd obiwan
mike@server:~/Obiwan$
```

A final trick: run **cd ..** to move the focus *up* a single directory level (cd ../.. would move it up two levels):

```
C:\Obiwan\my>cd ..
C:\Obiwan>
```

Take some time to experiment moving the prompt focus around the directories of your PC, using the cd and dir commands. Use dir to find a directory, and then use cd to move the focus to that directory. Remember, cd \ (or cd / in any UNIX) always gets you back to the root directory.

Moving Between Drives

Because Windows has drive letters and the UNIXes do not, they have very different techniques for moving between drives. Let's start with Windows and then we'll take a look at the UNIX-likes.

Moving Between Drives in Windows

The cd command is *not* used to move between Windows' drive letters. To focus the prompt on another drive, just type the drive letter and a colon—and then press ENTER just like it is a command. If you need to go find some files on your handy-dandy USB thumb drive (E:), just run **e:** and the prompt will focus on the USB drive:

```
C:\Users\mike>e:
E:\>
```

Run **c:** to return to the C: drive (note that it restored the same focus I had before changing drives):

```
E:\>c:
C:\Users\mike>
```

Just for fun, try typing in a drive letter that you know doesn't exist on your system. For example, I know that my system doesn't have a W: drive. If I type in a nonexistent drive on a Windows system, I get the following error:

```
The system cannot find the drive specified.
```

Try inserting an optical disc or a thumb drive and entering its drive letter to focus on its drive. Run **dir** to see the contents of the removable media and run **cd** to explore any folders it contains. Now return focus to the C: drive.

Using the dir, cd, and drive letter commands, you can access any folder on any storage device on your system. Make sure you are comfortable navigating with them.

Moving Between Drives in macOS and Linux

So if UNIXes don't use drive letters, how do you access your other drive partitions, optical media, thumb drives, and so on? Well, all media is mounted as a folder within a single hierarchy (but the location of those folders varies). In macOS, look in the /Volumes folder. In Ubuntu Linux, look in the /mnt folder for drives and the /media/<user name> folder for removable media. In other Linux distributions, well, you're going to have to explore—good thing you know how to use cd and ls, eh? The following commands show my optical drive and a thumb drive in an Ubuntu Linux system:

```
mike@server:/media/mike$ ls -l
drwx------ 3 mike mike 4096 Dec 31 1969 THUMBDRIVE
dr-xr-xr-x 6 mike mike 2048 May 13 10:15 Age of Empires
mike@server:/media/mike$
```

Making Directories: The md/mkdir Command

Now that you have learned how to navigate in a command-prompt world, it's time to make stuff—starting with a new directory to practice in. Run **cd \Users\<your user-name>** if your prompt isn't already focused on your home directory (or **cd ~** on a UNIX).

To make a directory, use the *md* command in Windows. Alternatively, you can use the *mkdir* command, which works in all operating systems. Run **md practice** to create a practice directory:

```
C:\Users\mike>md practice
```

Windows executes the command but doesn't volunteer any information about what it did. Run **dir** to confirm that you have, in fact, created a new directory:

```
C:\>dir
 Volume in Drive C is
 Volume Serial Number is 1734-3234
Directory of C:\Users\mike
08/21/2024  03:58 PM    <DIR>          .
08/21/2024  03:58 PM    <DIR>          ..
08/21/2023  09:55 AM    <DIR>          Desktop
07/15/2023  08:25 AM    <DIR>          Documents
08/20/2023  09:16 AM    <DIR>          Downloads
07/15/2023  08:25 AM    <DIR>          Favorites
07/15/2023  08:25 AM    <DIR>          Music
07/15/2024  08:25 AM    <DIR>          Pictures
08/21/2022  03:58 PM    <DIR>          practice
07/15/2023  08:25 AM    <DIR>          Videos
               1 File(s)            240 bytes
              10 Dir(s)  216,876,089,344 bytes free
```

Note that that, unlike the other directory names, the name of our practice directory shows up in all lowercase. Windows displays both cases in file and folder names but rarely makes any distinction with commands—which is a nice way to say Windows doesn't support case. Try running **md Practice** to see what happens. This also happens in the Windows GUI—go to your desktop and try to make two folders, one called files and the other called FILES, and see what Windows tells you.

To create a files subdirectory in the practice directory, first run **cd practice** to focus on the practice directory:

```
C:Users\mike>cd practice
```

Then run **md files** to make a files directory:

```
C:Users\mike\practice>md files
```

NOTE Ensure the prompt points to the directory you want to contain the new subdirectory before you execute the md command.

When you're finished, run **dir** to see the new files subdirectory. Just for fun, try the process again and add a games directory under the practice directory. Run **dir** to verify success.

Creating folders in a UNIX-like OS is again identical, but you must use the mkdir command. Here is the same example just given but done on my Ubuntu system:

```
mike@server:~$ mkdir practice
```

You can see the results by running the **ls** command:

```
mike@server:~$ls
practice
```

Don't forget that Linux is case sensitive. It will happily let you make folders for bills, BILLS, BiLLS, and so on.

Removing Directories: The rd/rmdir Command

Removing subdirectories works exactly like making them. First, get to the directory that contains the subdirectory you want to delete, and then execute either the *rmdir* or *rd* command. The rmdir command works equally well in Windows, macOS, and Linux, but the rd command only works in Windows.

 NOTE If you don't mind the extra typing, you can also use absolute paths to work with files without first navigating with cd.

Let's get rid of some folders! This time I'll use Linux as the example while we delete the files subdirectory in our ~/practice directory (remember ~ means your home directory). First, run **cd ~/practice** to navigate to where the files subdirectory is located. Then run **rmdir files**. If you received no response, you probably did it right! Run **ls** to confirm the files subdirectory is gone. Windows works the same, although we tend to use the shorter rd command.

Next, we'll remove the whole practice directory. Run **cd ..** to navigate back to your home directory and then run **rmdir practice** to remove it:

```
mike@server:~$ rmdir practice
rmdir: failed to remove 'practice': Directory not empty
```

There's a big, fat asterisk here—these commands won't just delete a directory that contains files or subdirectories. They'll complain like rmdir did here or ask you for confirmation (as it does in PowerShell). The message may look annoying, but the commands are being helpful! It's easy to delete more than you intended, and there is no Recycle Bin when deleting from the command line, so this speedbump gives you a chance to think twice about what you mean. Always follow the maxim "Check twice and delete once."

To remove a folder *and all of its contents* in Linux, we turn to the very handy rm command. (More on rm a little later in the chapter—see "Deleting Files.") Just run **rm** with the **-r** (recursive) switch as shown:

```
mike@server:~$ rm -r practice
```

Windows folks can use the rd command followed by the /s switch to delete a directory as well as all files and subdirectories:

```
C:\Users\mike>rd practice /s
practice, Are you sure (Y/N)?
```

Pressing the Y key eliminates both C:\Users\mike\practice and C:\Users\mike\practice\games.

 EXAM TIP Make sure you know how to use md, mkdir, rd, rmdir, rm, and cd for the CompTIA A+ 220-1102 exam.

Running a Program in Windows

To run most programs from the Windows command line, simply type the name of the program and then press ENTER. Remember MMC from the previous chapter? To run the mmc.exe program, just run the filename, in this case **mmc** (see Figure 15-7). Note that you do not have to type the .exe extension, although you can. Congratulations! You have just run another application from the command line.

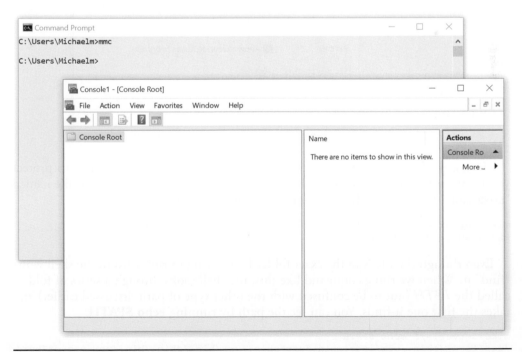

Figure 15-7 Running mmc in Windows

NOTE Windows includes a lot of command-line tools for specific jobs such as starting and stopping services, viewing computers on a network, converting hard drive file systems, and more. This book discusses these task-specific tools in the chapters that reflect their task. Chapter 19 goes into detail on the versatile and powerful net command, for example.

Running a Program in macOS and Linux

As much as I like to tell folks how similar UNIX and Windows command lines are, one place they differ is what counts as a program. For starters, executable programs on UNIXes don't need a special extension such as .exe. You can give the execute permission to any file—whether it's compiled code or a text file—as shown in Figure 15-8.

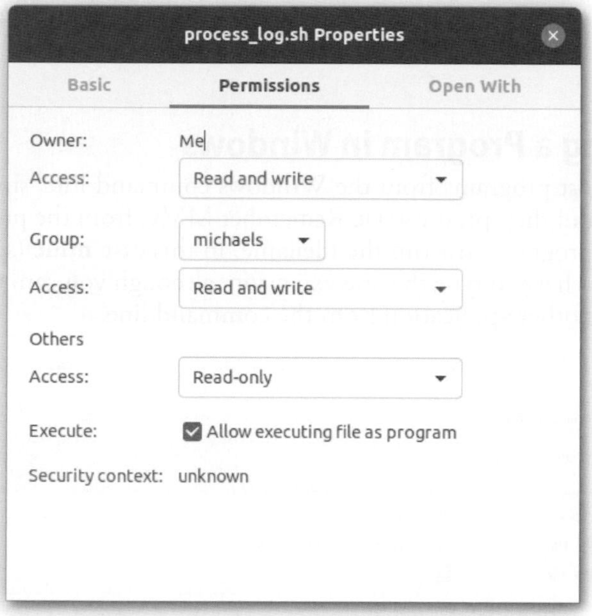

Figure 15-8
Showing file properties in Ubuntu

process_log.sh Properties			✕
Basic	**Permissions**	Open With	

Owner: Me

Access: Read and write ▾

Group: michaels ▾

Access: Read and write ▾

Others

Access: Read-only ▾

Execute: ☑ Allow executing file as program

Security context: unknown

Since *any* file could be an executable, UNIX shells add an extra wrinkle to protect you from running the wrong thing. Here's what happens if I download some file named "executable" to my home directory and try to run **executable**:

```
mike@server:~$ executable
executable: command not found
```

Even though the file is in the exact folder I am trying to run it from, the shell won't "find" it. When we run a command like this, the shell looks through a series of folders called the *PATH* (not to be confused with the other type of path discussed earlier) and takes the first one it finds. You can see the path by running **echo $PATH**:

```
mike@server:~$ echo $PATH
/usr/local/sbin:/usr/local/bin:/usr/sbin:/usr/bin:/sbin:/bin:/usr/games:/usr/
local/games
```

As you can see, my home directory isn't in this list. If I want the shell to run an executable that isn't in one of these directories (*on my PATH*, as we say), I have to be more specific. To run an executable in my working directory, I have to prefix it with "./" (the . is shorthand for the working directory):

```
mike@server:~$ ./executable
-bash: ./executable: Permission denied
```

Oops! This can be a surprise if you don't expect it. Remember: since execute is a file permission, you'll get a permission error if you try to run something that isn't marked executable. Don't get the wrong idea, though—just because you can *mark* anything as executable doesn't mean you can execute *anything*. For example, here's what happens when I mark an image file as executable and then try to run it:

```
mike@server:~$ ./image.png
-bash: ./image.png: cannot execute binary file: Exec format error
```

In reality, this means it's up to you to verify you are even trying to use a program. You cannot just start programs haphazardly in macOS or Linux. You make a point to know your executable before you run it.

Investigating Files

UNIXes also very often include an *incredibly* helpful command when it comes to identifying random, untrusted files: the file command. (And if they don't come with it, you can always install it.) For example, here's what the file command has to say about a PNG image file and the ls command on both macOS and Linux (in that order):

```
./image.png: PNG image data, 64 x 64, 8-bit/color RGBA, non-interlaced
/bin/ls: Mach-O 64-bit executable x86_64
/bin/ls: ELF 64-bit LSB pie executable, x86-64, version 1 (SYSV), dynamically
linked, interpreter /lib64/ld-linux-x86-64.so.2, for GNU/Linux 3.2.0, BuildID
[sha1]=a65f86cd6394e8f583c14d786d13b3bcbe051b87, stripped
```

Even though I marked this image as executable, the file command isn't fooled!

Working with Files

This section deals with basic file manipulation. You will learn how to inspect, copy, move, rename, and delete files. The examples in this section are based on a C: root directory with the following files and directories:

```
C:\>dir
 Volume in drive C has no label.
 Volume Serial Number is 4C62-1572

 Directory of C:\

05/26/2023  11:37 PM                 0 AILog.txt
05/29/2023  05:33 PM             5,776 aoedoppl.txt
05/29/2023  05:33 PM             2,238 aoeWVlog.txt
07/12/2023  10:38 AM    <DIR>          books
```

```
07/15/2023    02:45 PM                    1,708 CtDrvStp.log
06/04/2023    10:22 PM      <DIR>               Impressions Games
09/11/2023    11:32 AM      <DIR>               NVIDIA
01/03/2023    01:12 PM      <DIR>               pers-drv
09/14/2023    11:11 AM      <DIR>               Program Files
09/12/2023    08:32 PM                       21 statusclient.log
07/31/2023    10:40 PM                      153 systemscandata.txt
03/13/2023    09:54 AM                1,111,040 t3h0
04/21/2023    04:19 PM      <DIR>               temp
01/10/2023    07:07 PM      <DIR>               WebCam
12/31/2023    10:18 AM      <DIR>               WINDOWS
01/03/2023    09:06 AM      <DIR>               WUTemp
              6 File(s)        1,120,936 bytes
              9 Dir(s)    94,630,002,688 bytes free
```

Because you probably don't have a PC with these files and directories, follow the examples but use what's on your drive. In other words, create your own folders and copy files to them from various folders currently on your system.

Reading Plaintext Files

Most files on your computer are in file formats that aren't very accessible to humans without special tools. If you want to view or edit a picture, you'll need a program that understands image file formats. But many programs and operating systems (especially the UNIX-like ones) have plaintext files that contain configurable options or documentation. You can open these files in Notepad or another GUI editor, but it's often faster to read them directly from the command line!

The *simple* way to read a file is to run a command that will write the file's contents to your terminal in one go. This doesn't help much with long files, but it's fine for short ones. On any UNIX, you can use the *cat* command to write out the contents of one or more files. No, it isn't named for the furry household predator! It's short for *concatenate*—to join things together. When you run cat with more than one filename, it writes out all the files joined into one long stream.

 EXAM TIP Forgive me for withholding something to avoid confusion. The CompTIA A+ 1102 objectives list just one command for reading files: cat. It's available in UNIX and even PowerShell—but the objectives just list it as a Linux command. I'm leaving out the Windows Command Prompt equivalent. It isn't in the objectives, and it has the same name as a UNIX command we've discussed. Focus on cat for the exam!

Now that I've shown you the *simple* way to read a file, I want to show you the *easy* way: just run **more** followed by the name or path of the file. The *more* command is a simple pager (remember, a pager is an interactive reader) that advances one line when you press ENTER and one page when you press SPACEBAR. To exit, just scroll to the end of the file or press Q. It's usually present in UNIX and Windows in both Command Prompt and PowerShell.

NOTE There's an even better pager than more. The *less* command is an advanced pager that can navigate both forward and backward in the file (with your arrow keys, scroll wheel, trackpad, etc.) and recognizes gobs of keyboard shortcuts for jumping around in a file, searching its contents, and so on. As they say, less is…more!

Using Wildcards to Locate Files

Imagine having 273 files in one directory. A few of these files have the extension .docx, but most do not. You are looking only for files with the .docx extension. Instead of flipping through pages of irrelevant files, you can use wildcards to list just the ones you want.

A *wildcard* is one of two special characters—asterisk (*) and question mark (?)—that you can use in place of all or part of a filename, often so that a command-line command will act on more than one file at a time. Wildcards work with all command-line commands that take filenames.

NOTE I'm glossing over a big, geeky difference between Windows and UNIX here. Windows shells don't *expand* wildcards (convert them into a list of matching files)—they leave it up to each command. UNIX shells generally expand the wildcards (unless quoted) and pass the list of matching files to the command. You can run echo * and echo "*" on both systems to see the difference.

Most (but not all) Windows commands that work with files will support wildcards. Relatively few UNIX commands directly support wildcards—most rely on the shell to do it for them (a well-known exception is the find command, which comes up later in the chapter). Just file this away in the back of your mind and pull it out any time you're confused as heck about how some wildcard is (or isn't) working.

A great example is the dir command. When you execute a plain dir command, it finds and displays all the files and folders in the specified directory; however, you can also narrow its search by adding a filename. For example, if you run **dir ailog.txt** while in your root (C:\) directory, you get the following result:

```
C:\>dir ailog.txt
 Volume in drive C has no label.
 Volume Serial Number is 4C62-1572
 Directory of C:\
05/26/2023  11:37 PM                 0 AILog.txt
               1 File(s)             0 bytes
               0 Dir(s)  94,630,195,200 bytes free
```

But what if you want to see all files with the extension .txt? You can use the * wildcard, which matches any number of characters (the ? wildcard, by contrast, matches any single character). Run **dir *.txt** to see something like this:

```
 Volume in drive C has no label.
 Volume Serial Number is 4C62-1572

 Directory of C:\
```

```
05/26/2023  11:37 PM                     0 AILog.txt
05/29/2023  05:33 PM                 5,776 aoedoppl.txt
05/29/2023  05:33 PM                 2,238 aoeWVlog.txt
07/31/2023  10:40 PM                   153 systemscandata.txt
               4 File(s)          8,167 bytes
               0 Dir(s)  94,630,002,688 bytes free
```

Wildcards also substitute for parts of filenames. This dir command will list files that start with the letter *a*:

```
C:\>dir a*
 Volume in drive C has no label.
 Volume Serial Number is 4C62-1572

 Directory of C:\

05/26/2023  11:37 PM                     0 AILog.txt
05/29/2023  05:33 PM                 5,776 aoedoppl.txt
05/29/2023  05:33 PM                 2,238 aoeWVlog.txt
               3 File(s)          8,014 bytes
               0 Dir(s)  94,629,675,008 bytes free
```

Wildcards in UNIX shells work basically the same as in Windows. Head over to the /usr/sbin directory on a typical UNIX system and try using a wildcard with the ls command. Here's what comes up when I run **ls z* -l** on my Linux system:

```
mike@server:/usr/sbin$ ls z* -l
-rwxr-xr-x 1 root root  63784 Dec 16  2023 /usr/sbin/zic
-rwxr-xr-x 1 root root 117088 Jul 21  2023 /usr/sbin/zramctl
```

We've used wildcards only with the dir and ls commands in the previous examples, but virtually every command that deals with files and folders will take wildcards. Let's examine some more commands and see how they use wildcards.

 SIM   Check out the four "Wildcard" sims in the Chapter 15 section of https://www.totalsem.com/110X. The two Type! sims plus the Show! and the Click! will prepare you for any number of performance-based questions CompTIA throws at you in the 1102 exam.

Deleting Files

To delete files, you use the *del* (or *erase*) command in Windows and the *rm* command in UNIXes. Deleting a file in the GUI gives you the luxury of retrieving accidentally deleted files from the Recycle Bin. The command line, however, shows no mercy to the careless. If you accidentally erase a file, don't expect to get it back without restoring it from a backup. Again, the rule here is to *check twice and delete once*.

To delete one file in Windows, use the del command followed by the filename. For example, to delete the file reportdraft1.docx, run

```
del reportdraft1.docx
```

In UNIX, use **rm** in place of del:

```
rm reportdraft1.docx
```

Nothing appears on the screen, but you can run dir or ls to confirm it's gone.

You can use wildcards with the del and rm commands to delete multiple files at once. For example, to delete all files with the extension .txt in a folder, you can run this in any UNIX:

```
rm *.txt
```

You can place the wildcard anywhere in the name. If you exported reportdraft1 in multiple formats, you could run **del reportdraft1.*** to delete them all.

Copying and Moving Files

Being able to copy and move files from the command line is crucial to all technicians. Because of its finicky nature and many options, the copy command is also rather painful to learn, especially if you're used to dragging icons around a GUI. The following tried-and-true, five-step process makes it easier, but the real secret is to get in front of a prompt and just copy and move files around until you're comfortable. Keep in mind that the only difference between copying and moving is whether the original is left behind (*copy*) or not (*move*). Once you've learned the copy command, you've also learned the move command! In UNIXes, the copy command is *cp* and the move command is *mv*.

Mike's Five-Step copy/move Process

There's about 10,000 different ways to copy and move files. To make learners' lives easier, I've been teaching folks how to copy and move files for years with this handy five-step process. As you grow more confident, don't be afraid to try your own methods in the operating system of your choice to learn the full power of the commands. But first, follow this process step by step:

1. Focus the prompt on the directory containing the file(s) you want to copy or move.

2. Type **copy** or **move** (Windows) or **cp** or **mv** (macOS and Linux) and a space.

3. Type the *name(s)* of the file(s) to be copied/moved (with or without wildcards) and a space.

4. Type the *path* of the new location for the file(s).

5. Press ENTER.

Let's try an example using Windows. The directory Jedi (in my \Users folder) contains the file notes.txt. Copy this file to a USB thumb drive (E:).

1. Type **cd Jedi** to focus the prompt on the Jedi directory.

   ```
   C:\Users\mike>cd Jedi
   ```

2. Type **copy** and a space.

   ```
   C:\Users\mike\Jedi>copy
   ```

3. Type **notes.txt** and a space.

```
C:\Users\mike\Jedi>copy notes.txt
```

4. Type **e:**.

```
C:\Users\mike\Jedi>copy notes.txt e:\
```

5. Press ENTER.

The entire command and response would look like this:

```
C:\Users\mike\Jedi>copy notes.txt e:\
1 file(s) copied
```

You can focus the prompt on the E: drive and run **dir** to confirm the notes.txt file is there. Let's try another example, this time in macOS or Linux. Suppose 100 files are in the ~/Jedi directory, 30 of which have the .odf extension, and suppose you want to move those files to ~/Screenplays/sw2024. Follow these steps:

1. Type **cd Jedi** to focus the prompt on the correct folder.

```
mike@server:~$ cd Jedi
```

2. Type **mv** and a space.

```
mike@server:~/Jedi$ mv
```

3. Type ***.odf** and a space.

```
mike@server:~/Jedi$ mv *.odf
```

4. Type **~/Screenplays/sw2024/**.

```
mike@server:~/Jedi$ mv *.odf ~/Screenplays/sw2024/
```

5. Press ENTER.

```
mike@server:~/Jedi$
```

This won't give you any feedback at all unless you use special switches. You can confirm the move with **ls**.

Pruning and Grafting Folder Trees

There's a number of situations where you find yourself wanting to grab a folder, complete with all of the subfolders and any files that might be anywhere in any of the folders, and copy or move the whole "pile" in one command. We call this process *pruning and grafting* and it's a place where the command line shines in comparison to GUI file manipulation. Done properly, command-line pruning and grafting is faster and gives you much finer control of the process.

In Windows, the standard copy and move commands can work only in one directory at a time, making them a poor choice for copying or moving files in multiple directories. To help with these multi-directory jobs, Microsoft added the *xcopy* command. (Note that there is no xmove, only xcopy.) We'll also look at robocopy, cp, and mv.

xcopy

The *xcopy* command functions similarly to copy, but xcopy has extra switches that give it the power to work with multiple directories. Here's how it does that. Let's say I have a directory called Logs in the root of my C: drive. The Logs directory has three subdirectories: Jan, Feb, and Mar. All of these directories, including the Logs directory, contain about 50 files. If I wanted to copy all of these files to my E: drive in one command, I would use xcopy in the following manner:

```
xcopy c:\Logs e:\Logs /s
```

Because xcopy works on directories, you don't have to use filenames as you would in copy, although xcopy certainly accepts filenames and wildcards. The /s switch tells xcopy to copy all subdirectories that aren't empty. The /e switch tells xcopy to copy empty subdirectories. When you have a lot of copying to do over many directories, xcopy is the tool to use.

robocopy

Microsoft introduced the *robocopy* command—short for Robust File Copy—many years ago as an add-on tool for Windows Server to enable techs to manage files and folders more quickly and efficiently than with xcopy or copy. The robocopy command enables you to, for example, copy the files and folders from one computer to another across a network, fully replicating the structure on the destination system *and* deleting anything on that system that wasn't part of the copy.

The robocopy syntax does not resemble xcopy—don't get them mixed up! Here's the basic syntax:

```
robocopy [source] [destination] [options]
```

Here's an example of the command in action. The following command would copy all files and subfolders from a local machine's D:\testserver\website folder to a shared folder on the remote server \\liveserver\website:

```
robocopy d:\testserver\website \\liveserver\website /mir
```

The /mir (mirror) switch tells robocopy to copy everything from the source and make the destination mirror it. That means robocopy will delete anything in the destination that doesn't match the source folders and files.

That's not even the tip of the robocopy iceberg! It can copy encrypted files. It enables an administrator to copy files even if the administrator account is expressly denied access to those files. It will also resume copying after an interruption at the spot it stopped. For the full syntax, run

```
robocopy /?
```

Their power and utility make the del, copy/move, xcopy, and robocopy commands indispensable for a PC technician, but that same power and utility can cause disaster. Only a trained Jedi, with The Force as his ally . . . well, wrong book, but the principle remains: Beware of the quick and easy keystroke, for it may spell your doom. Think twice and execute the command once. The data you save may be yours!

EXAM TIP Know xcopy and robocopy for the CompTIA A+ 220-1102 exam.

cp and mv (again!)

If you really want to see some powerful commands, let's head over to Linux. Unlike Windows, you can both move and copy folders and their contents, using the same cp and mv commands we saw earlier for regular copying and moving. Let's say I have a folder called /home/mike/Backups. The Backups folder has ten subfolders and hundreds of files. I want to save a copy of these files to a folder called /mnt/storage. To do this I only need to run **cp** with the **-R** (recursive) switch (remember that the ~ in my prompt shows that the working directory is my home folder):

```
mike@server:~$ cp -R Backups /mnt/storage
```

If I want to move all of that to storage instead of copy, I use the mv command. Interestingly, the mv command doesn't even need a special switch—just run it with the folder to move and the destination:

```
mike@server:~$ mv Desktop/Backups /mnt/storage
```

Assorted Windows Commands

As a proficient IT technician in the field, you need to be familiar with a whole slew of command-line tools and other important utilities. The CompTIA A+ 220-1102 exam focuses in on several of them, and although many have been discussed in detail in previous chapters, it is extremely important that you understand and practice with chkdsk, format, hostname, gpupdate, gpresult, sfc, shutdown, and winver.

chkdsk (/f /r)

The *chkdsk* (checkdisk) command scans, detects, and repairs file system issues and errors. You can run the chkdsk utility from a command line with the switches /f and /r. The /f switch attempts to fix file system–related errors, while the /r switch attempts to locate and repair bad sectors. To run successfully, chkdsk needs direct access to a drive. In other words, the drive needs to be "unlocked." For example, if you run **chkdsk /f /r** and chkdsk does not consider your drive unlocked, you will receive a "Cannot lock current drive" message, meaning that another process has the drive locked and is preventing chkdsk from locking the drive itself. After this, chkdsk presents you with the option to run it the next time the system restarts (see Figure 15-9).

format

After the previous chapters, you should have an expert-level knowledge of (or, at the very least, a passing familiarity with) formatting and partitioning hard drives. Formatting, you may remember, is the process of writing a new file system to a volume (or partition,

Figure 15-9
The chkdsk /f
/r utility and
switches on a
locked drive

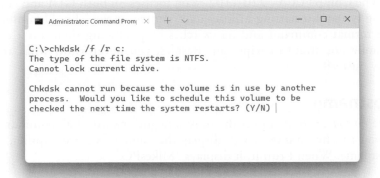

```
C:\>chkdsk /f /r c:
The type of the file system is NTFS.
Cannot lock current drive.

Chkdsk cannot run because the volume is in use by another
process.  Would you like to schedule this volume to be
checked the next time the system restarts? (Y/N)
```

if you're old school) so it can hold an operating system or data. We have already discussed the various built-in Windows utilities available to provide the formatting of drives, and you no doubt know that many third-party formatting tools are out there. In this chapter, you just need to become familiar with the format command and its switches.

The *format* command, you may have guessed, enables you to format volumes from the command line. Figure 15-10 shows an example of the format command in action. Note the complex switches that let me specify which file system to use, which volume, that I want compression, and so on. The very best way to familiarize yourself with the format command and its available switches is to run **format /?** from the command line.

Figure 15-10
The format
command
in action

```
C:\>format e: /FS:exFAT /v:Flash
Insert new disk for drive E:
and press ENTER when ready...
The type of the file system is RAW.
The new file system is EXFAT.
Verifying 3.6 GB
Initializing the File Allocation Table (FAT)...
Creating file system structures.
Format complete.
        3.6 GB total disk space.
        3.6 GB are available.

        32,768 bytes in each allocation unit.
    119,017 allocation units available on disk.

            32 bits in each FAT entry.

Volume Serial Number is A88E-4597

C:\>
```

The CompTIA A+ 220-1102 exam focuses on both GUI and command-line operating system formatting utilities and options, so you should familiarize yourself with the format command and its switches by practicing them on a test system you are literally not afraid to wipe out. Besides, you never know what antiques CompTIA may dust off.

hostname

The *hostname* command is the most straightforward of all command-line commands. If you run **hostname**, it will display the name of your computer, also known as the hostname. When I run it, it displays "MikesPC."

winver

There's one really odd duck in the list of Windows "commands" in the 1102 objectives: winver. I personally disagree that it's even a command! When you run *winver*, it opens a GUI information panel that displays some version information about Windows. I guess you might do this if you're already working in the CLI, but you could also just use the Start menu to search for **winver** and launch it directly.

 EXAM TIP The 1102 objectives might be confusing winver with the older ver command (which is an actual Command Prompt builtin). If you're running Command Prompt, ver will write a Windows version number to your terminal. Keep winver in mind if you see a question about checking the Windows version from the command line.

gpupdate

Group policies define various security settings for Windows systems, such as password complexity, logon attempts, and permissions for users to install software. Group policies can apply to a standalone system or to systems on a domain. It takes time for a group policy change to propagate throughout a domain, but you can force a workstation to update to new policies by running *gpupdate* on the workstation. Here is an example of gpupdate in action:

```
C:\Windows\system32>gpupdate
Updating policy…

Computer Policy update has completed successfully.
User Policy Update has completed successfully.

C:\Windows\32\system32>
```

Check out Chapter 27 to see exactly what gpudate is doing.

gpresult

If you need a quick overview of all security policies applied to a single user or computer, the *gpresult* tool is for you. You can run **gpresult** for any user or computer on your network (assuming you have a valid username and password) and you can ask for detailed or summary information. This command shows the summary results for user michaelm on the local computer:

```
C:\>gpresult /USER michaelm /R

Microsoft (R) Windows (R) Operating System Group Policy Result tool v2.0
c 2018 Microsoft Corporation. All rights reserved.
Created on 8/20/2023 at 1:54:20 PM
RSOP data for TOTALBOGUS\michaelm on MIKEPC : Logging Mode
---------------------------------------------------------
OS Configuration:           Member Workstation
OS Version:                 6.3.9600
Site Name:                  N/A
Roaming Profile:            N/A
Local Profile:              C:\Users\michaelm
Connected over a slow link?: No

USER SETTINGS
--------------
    CN=michaelm,CN=Users,DC=totalbogus
    Last time Group Policy was applied: 8/20/2023 at 1:39:10 PM
    Group Policy was applied from:      dc1.totalbogus
    Group Policy slow link threshold:   500 kbps
    Domain Name:                        TOTALBOGUS
    Domain Type:                        Windows 2008 or later

    Applied Group Policy Objects
    ----------------------------
        Default Domain Policy
    The following GPOs were not applied because they were filtered out
    -----------------------------------------------------------------
        Local Group Policy
         Filtering:  Not Applied (Empty)
    The user is a part of the following security groups
    ---------------------------------------------------
        Domain Users
        Everyone
```

sfc

The Windows *sfc (System File Checker)* command scans, detects, and restores important Windows system files, folders, and paths. Techs often turn to sfc when Windows isn't quite working correctly and use it to find and fix critical Windows system files that have become corrupt. If you run sfc and it finds issues, it attempts to replace corrupted or missing files from cached DLLs (backups of those system files) located in the Windows\System32\Dllcache\ directory. Without getting very deep into the mad science involved, just know that you can use sfc to correct corruption. To start sfc from a command line, run **sfc /scannow**. To familiarize yourself with sfc's switches, run **sfc /?** (see Figure 15-11).

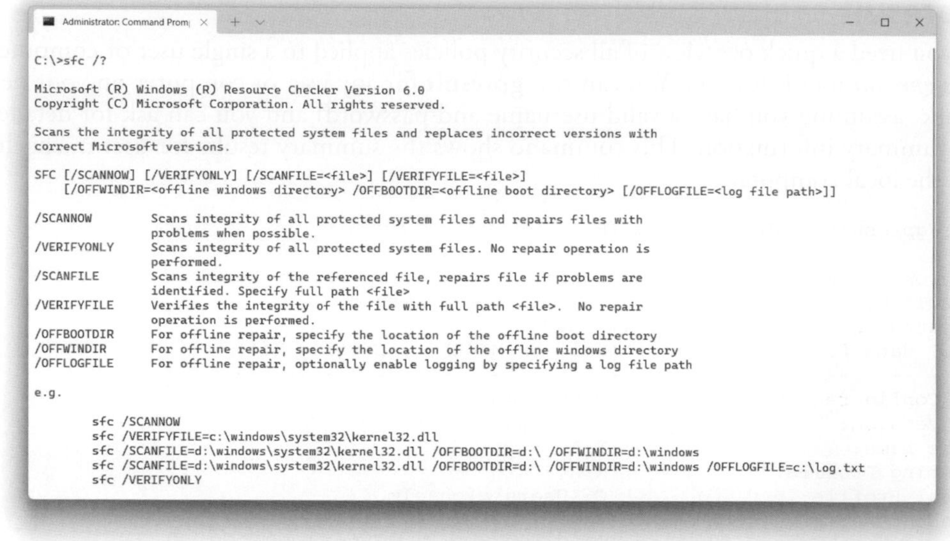

```
C:\>sfc /?

Microsoft (R) Windows (R) Resource Checker Version 6.0
Copyright (C) Microsoft Corporation. All rights reserved.

Scans the integrity of all protected system files and replaces incorrect versions with
correct Microsoft versions.

SFC [/SCANNOW] [/VERIFYONLY] [/SCANFILE=<file>] [/VERIFYFILE=<file>]
    [/OFFWINDIR=<offline windows directory> /OFFBOOTDIR=<offline boot directory> [/OFFLOGFILE=<log file path>]]

/SCANNOW        Scans integrity of all protected system files and repairs files with
                problems when possible.
/VERIFYONLY     Scans integrity of all protected system files. No repair operation is
                performed.
/SCANFILE       Scans integrity of the referenced file, repairs file if problems are
                identified. Specify full path <file>
/VERIFYFILE     Verifies the integrity of the file with full path <file>.  No repair
                operation is performed.
/OFFBOOTDIR     For offline repair, specify the location of the offline boot directory
/OFFWINDIR      For offline repair, specify the location of the offline windows directory
/OFFLOGFILE     For offline repair, optionally enable logging by specifying a log file path

e.g.

    sfc /SCANNOW
    sfc /VERIFYFILE=c:\windows\system32\kernel32.dll
    sfc /SCANFILE=d:\windows\system32\kernel32.dll /OFFBOOTDIR=d:\ /OFFWINDIR=d:\windows
    sfc /SCANFILE=d:\windows\system32\kernel32.dll /OFFBOOTDIR=d:\ /OFFWINDIR=d:\windows /OFFLOGFILE=c:\log.txt
    sfc /VERIFYONLY
```

Figure 15-11   Checking sfc options with sfc /? at a command line

shutdown

The *shutdown* command enables you to do exactly that to a local or remote computer—shut it down (or reboot it). The cool part of the tool is that you can use a number of switches to control and report the shutdown. A network administrator could use this tool to restart a computer remotely, for example, like this:

```
shutdown /r /m \\devserver
```

The /r switch tells shutdown to have the computer reboot rather than just shut down. If you want to see the full syntax for shutdown, run the following:

```
shutdown /?
```

Keyboard Shortcuts

You might find yourself repeatedly typing the same commands, or at least very similar commands, when working with a CLI. Microsoft provides several ways to access previous commands. First, run **dir** from the command line. Next, press F1, and the letter *d* appears. Press F1 again. Now the letter *i* appears after the *d*. Do you see what is happening? The F1 key rebuilds the previous command one letter at a time. Pressing F3 rebuilds the entire command at once. Now try running these three commands:

```
dir /w
hostname
md Skywalker
```

Now press the UP ARROW key. Keep pressing it till you see your original dir command—it's a history of all your old commands. Now use the RIGHT ARROW key to add /w to the end of your dir command. Windows command history is very handy.

UNIX shells come with their own shortcuts, some of which match those in Windows. (Actually, Windows copied many of the handier shortcuts, like the history feature, from the UNIX world.) UNIXes take command history one step further and can (depending on configuration) remember it even if you close the terminal or reboot the machine. For example, you can search your history with the CTRL-R combination. This can pay for itself if you have to figure out a long, complex command one day and need to use it again two weeks later!

Assorted macOS and Linux Commands

macOS and Linux generally come with a big pile of preinstalled command-line utilities—and you can install thousands and thousands more. Even if we're just talking about Linux, the list of preinstalled commands can vary widely from distro to distro. In fact, one of the most interesting challenges to learning the CLI is that for almost any task, there is more than one tool for the job (see the nano and vi commands, later). What you are going to see here are the commands listed by the CompTIA A+ objectives—you could spend the rest of your life learning CLI commands!

See Running Processes: top and ps

The 1102 objectives cover *two* commands you can use to see the processes running on your system, so you'll need to know what each one does, and how they differ. The (very old) *ps* command provides detailed and customizable information about the processes running on your system at the moment you run the command. The *top* command is an interactive, continuously updating monitor of what's running—and by default it focuses on resource-hungry processes. Generally, use top to monitor or investigate system performance, and use ps to look for specific processes.

top

When you just run top by itself, you get the default settings: the screen divided with the top portion showing system and resource information and the lower portion showing running processes. Figure 15-12 shows that the defaults can differ between systems.

Once you start top, you use your keyboard to control it. Different versions of top have different options, so the first thing to try is to press ? for information about all of the interactive options. You can press Q to close this help view, and press Q from the main resource view to close top entirely.

 NOTE You need to know top for the 1102 exam, but there's room for more than one resource monitor in your life! Not only are there *improved* versions of top, such as htop and ytop, but you can also find top-like tools for detailed monitoring of things like storage, graphics, or network performance—and much more. Explore!

```
michaels@michaels-ubuntu: ~

top - 08:58:14 up 19 min,  1 user,  load average: 0.06, 0.12, 0.29
Tasks: 323 total,   2 running, 321 sleeping,   0 stopped,   0 zombie
%Cpu(s):  4.4 us,  1.2 sy,  0.0 ni, 94.5 id,  0.0 wa,  0.0 hi,  0.0 si,  0.0 st
MiB Mem :  15879.4 total,  11896.9 free,   1332.1 used,   2650.4 buff/cache
MiB Swap:   2048.0 total,   2048.0 free,      0.0 used.  14010.5 avail Mem

  PID USER      PR  NI    VIRT    RES    SHR S  %CPU  %MEM     TIME+ COMMAND
15495 root      20   0  268996  82264  45808 R  20.6   0.5   0:31.76 Xorg
34040 michaels  20   0  744652  45056  34032 S  16.6   0.3   0:00.92 gnome-s+
15640 michaels  20   0 4545796 281016 106692 S  13.6   1.7   0:34.32 gnome-s+
  521 root       0 -20       0      0      0 D   1.0   0.0   0:00.74 kworker+
33964 michaels  20   0   20624   4056   3292 R   1.0   0.0   0:00.08 top
   26 root      20   0       0      0      0 S   0.7   0.0   0:01.27 ksoftir+
   75 root      20   0       0      0      0 I   0.7   0.0   0:01.22 kworker+
   13 root      20   0       0      0      0 I   0.3   0.0   0:00.86 rcu_sch+
    1 root      20   0  169016  12888   8136 S   0.0   0.1   0:03.66 systemd
    2 root      20   0       0      0      0 S   0.0   0.0   0:00.00 kthreadd
    3 root       0 -20       0      0      0 I   0.0   0.0   0:00.00 rcu_gp
    4 root       0 -20       0      0      0 I   0.0   0.0   0:00.00 rcu_par+
    6 root       0 -20       0      0      0 I   0.0   0.0   0:00.00 kworker+
    7 root      20   0       0      0      0 I   0.0   0.0   0:00.01 kworker+
    9 root       0 -20       0      0      0 I   0.0   0.0   0:00.00 mm_perc+
   10 root      20   0       0      0      0 S   0.0   0.0   0:00.00 rcu_tas+
   11 root      20   0       0      0      0 S   0.0   0.0   0:00.00 rcu_tas+
```

```
mikesmyer — top ~ — top — 80×24

Processes: 599 total, 2 running, 597 sleeping, 2614 threads          08:58:37
Load Avg: 1.68, 1.81, 2.39  CPU usage: 17.51% user, 9.44% sys, 73.4% idle
SharedLibs: 310M resident, 50M data, 18M linkedit.
MemRegions: 114046 total, 1834M resident, 106M private, 818M shared.
PhysMem: 8139M used (2096M wired), 51M unused.
VM: 20T vsize, 3099M framework vsize, 4625462(0) swapins, 4996483(0) swapouts.
Networks: packets: 1334830/1520M in, 289253/71M out.
Disks: 2917742/56G read, 578449/27G written.

PID   COMMAND      %CPU TIME      #TH   #WQ  #PORT MEM     PURG   CMPRS   PGRP PPID
92    systemstats  27.9 00:10.35  5     4    103-  2644K-  0B     640K    92   1
161   WindowServer 14.1 13:41.63  15    6    2533+ 916M+   5632K+ 82M-    161  1
180   coreaudiod    9.0 04:12.74  15    5    881+  21M+    0B     9628K   180  1
4147  top           7.6 00:01.12  1/1   0    30+   5180K+  0B     0B      4147 3621
1628  Music         5.6 03:58.00  25    5    840   222M    592K   112M-   1628 1
0     kernel_task   4.7 10:50.92  201/4 0    0     293M-   0B     0B      0    0
4152  screencaptur  3.3 00:00.14  6     4    189-  4012K+  620K+  0B      406  406
162   tccd          3.1 00:11.16  3     2    58+   4152K-  24K    1380K-  162  1
164   loginwindow   2.9 00:06.57  5     3    511+  30M-    0B     13M-    164  1
167   trustd        2.1 00:51.24  3     2    112   4436K+  124K   1980K-  167  1
1     launchd       2.1 00:42.33  4     3    2870+ 22M+    0B     10M-    1    0
424   siriactionsd  1.8 00:01.61  4     3    114+  4204K+  0B     2796K-  424  1
150   bluetoothd    1.5 01:39.17  8     4    271-  5212K-  120K   1424K   150  1
349   com.apple.Ap  1.5 00:55.09  3     2    168   760K+   0B     196K    349  1
```

Figure 15-12 top running on Linux (above) and macOS (below)

ps

The *ps* command is so old that it has two totally different types of switch sets! If you just run ps by itself, it won't list much. We would have to get *very* deep in the weeds to understand exactly why—so instead we'll run one of the most common examples of ps: **ps aux**. The "aux" bit here is actually three separate switches (using the older *legacy* switch set): a = processes for all users, u = show process owner, and x = process not attached to a terminal.

```
mike@server:~$ ps aux
USER         PID %CPU %MEM    VSZ   RSS TTY      STAT START   TIME COMMAND
root           1  0.0  0.2  33968  4416 ?        Ss   11:08   0:00 /sbin/init
```

Note that ps aux usually writes out a ton of lines. I'm going to cut most of them out for space, but before we look at any more, let's discuss what these columns actually mean:

- USER: Who is running this process
- PID: The process ID number assigned to the process
- %CPU: What percentage of CPU power this process is using
- %MEM: What percentage of memory this process is using
- VSZ: Total paged memory in kilobytes
- RSS: Total physical memory in kilobytes
- TTY: The terminal that is taking the process's output
- STAT: S = waiting, R = running, l = multithreaded, + = foreground process
- START: When the process was started
- TIME: Length of time process has been running
- COMMAND: Name of the executable that created this process

Now for a few more lines of output:

```
root        2188  0.0  0.0      0     0 ?        S    11:08   0:04 [kworker/0:2]
mike        2218  0.0  1.5 574732 30908 ?        Sl   11:08   0:03 gnome-terminal
mike        2225  0.0  0.0  14828  1916 ?        S    11:09   0:00 gnome-pty-helpe
mike        2226  0.0  0.2  26820  5244 pts/10   Ss   11:09   0:00 bash
mike        2267  0.0  1.0 571544 20856 ?        Sl   11:09   0:00 update-notifier
root        2570  0.0  0.0      0     0 ?        S    14:19   0:00 [kworker/u2:1]
root        2577  0.0  0.0      0     0 ?        S    14:29   0:00 [kworker/u2:0]
root        2578  0.0  0.0      0     0 ?        S    14:34   0:00 [kworker/u2:2]
mike        2579  0.0  0.1  22648  2568 pts/10   R+   14:34   0:00 ps aux
mike@server:~$
```

EXAM TIP For mysterious reasons, the CompTIA 1102 exam objectives ignore both the UNIX *kill* command (used for killing processes) and the Windows equivalent, taskkill. In my experience, the most common reason to run ps is to find the PID of a process I want to kill! Keep ps in mind if a question mentions looking up information about specific processes on Linux or macOS.

A big problem with ps aux is the enormous output I mentioned. There are a number of ways to make dealing with this output easier (including different commands), but the most common is to pipe its output into a pager (like less, or more) for reading, or pipe it into a filter such as grep, which we'll discuss next.

grep

The *grep* command is a *filter*: it enables you to search through text files or command output to find specific information and filter out the rest. For example, finding a specific process is easy if you combine grep with the ps command. Let's say LibreOffice froze while opening a document and I need to kill it. I have no idea what the PID is, but I can use grep with ps to find it. I know the command uses the word "libre," so I type

```
mike@server:~$ ps aux | grep libre
mike      2524   0.0   0.2 145804   5652 ?          Sl    14:12    0:00 /usr/lib/
libreoffice/program/oosplash --writer
mike      2543   0.0   5.5 1140216 114080 ?         Sl    14:12    0:01 /usr/lib/
libreoffice/program/soffice.bin --writer --splash-pipe=5
```

So I see there are two processes from LibreOffice: 2524 and 2543. Cool! The grep command can find any string of text and show you the line it was in. This is only a light overview of one of the most powerful tools in UNIX. If you need to look in anything to find a string of text, grep is a good place to start.

find

Another big workhorse on UNIX is the *find* command, which can plow through all of the files and folders in a directory (and all of its subdirectories) and output a list containing only the ones that match some criteria of your choosing. When I say criteria, the following are some good examples:

- Its file is bigger than, smaller than, or exactly some size.
- It was created or modified before, on, or after some date (or some number of seconds/minutes/hours/days ago).
- It has (or doesn't have) certain permissions.
- Its name does (or doesn't) match a pattern.

If you just run **find** all by itself, find will plow through all of the files in your current working directory without using any criteria at all—it'll list all of them! Give it a try (though it will output a lot if you are in a big directory). If that doesn't output much, run **find /etc/** to get the same effect on a specific directory.

This isn't very useful on its own, so let's try out some criteria. Imagine you are asked to collect and archive all PDF documents in any user's home directory on a Linux laptop, wipe the device, and reinstall the OS. One of the find command's many options is perfect for this job: the -iname option adds a *case-insensitive* name criteria that can use a wildcard pattern. Here's how this search looks on my system (though I'm just including a few matches):

```
mike@server:~$ find /home/ -iname "*.pdf"
/home/mike/Downloads/CompTIA A+ 220-1101 Exam Objectives (4.0).pdf
/home/mike/Downloads/CompTIA A+ 220-1102 Exam Objectives (4.0).pdf
/home/mike/research/the-UNIX-command-language-(1976).pdf
/home/mike/Downloads/receipts/United Airlines - Flight Check In.pdf
. . .
```

This searches each user's home directory within the /home/ directory, and prints out every file that ends with the .pdf extension (regardless of case—including .PDF, .Pdf, and so on). Fair warning: if you don't have permission to read all of the user directories on your system, find will emit a permission error for each one it can't search.

NOTE find is one of the UNIX commands that has built-in support for wildcards. Remember: You need to quote "*.pdf" to keep your shell from expanding the wildcard before it reaches the find command. If you fail to quote it, you'll almost certainly end up with an error message or the wrong results.

Package Managers: apt-get and yum

The CompTIA A+ 1102 objectives don't have much to say about what is, to my mind, one of the most revolutionary concepts to come out of the whole spectrum of UNIX-like operating systems: package managers. The objectives do, however, mention two commands that are at least related to package management—and that's all the invitation I need!

Back in *ye olde days*, installing software on UNIX could be a lot like walking to school in the snow, uphill both ways! If you needed an application, you often had to dig around for the source code and try to compile it on your system. Sometimes this worked on the first try, and other times you'd just discover that it depended on yet more code that you had to find, then manually set up configuration files . . . ugh!

Over the years many improvements have been made to the availability, acquisition, and installation of UNIX software, culminating in tools called *package managers* that empower you to install and update software—including the other software it depends on—with a few commands.

NOTE The commands in the 1102 objectives (apt-get and yum) are associated with the official system package managers for two major branches of the Linux family tree. They aren't the only game in town, though! In fact, package managers are so useful that the concept has even made the leap to Windows. Go ask the Internet about a few of my favorites: Chocolatey, Scoop, and winget (Windows); Homebrew (macOS and Linux); and Nix (macOS and Linux).

apt-get/APT

For Linux distros in the Debian family tree (like Ubuntu and Mint), we use APT, the *advanced packaging tool*. The *apt-get* command enables you to manage (install, uninstall, update, and so on) APT packages—assuming you know the name of the program you wish to install. Many Linux users prefer monitoring systems with something a little flashier than the original top program, such as htop. To download and install the latter program, start by running the following:

```
mike@server:~$ sudo apt-get update
```

Have APT update its *package index*, the list of all the available packages (software). You can technically skip this step, but you might end up installing an old version or, if the package is new enough, not finding it. Once APT's index has been updated, run this next:

```
mike@server:~$ sudo apt-get install htop
```

That's it! Got htop already installed but want the newest version? No problem! Just use **apt-get** again:

```
mike@server:~$ sudo apt-get upgrade htop
```

The only downside to apt-get is that you need to know the name of the package you want to install. While there are command-line tools that help (apt-cache), many people prefer to use the graphical search tool their Linux distro provides, such as the Ubuntu Software Center.

As useful as APT is for fetching and installing single applications, that's not where its real power lies. *System* package managers can manage *all* the software (minus anything you compiled yourself) on the system; they are what you use to keep the whole system up to date, just as Windows Update handles much of the software on Windows. All that it takes to upgrade all the packages on your system is to run

```
mike@server:~$ sudo apt-get update
mike@server:~$ sudo apt-get upgrade
```

If apt-get finds any out-of-date packages, it will let you know which ones and ask you to confirm the upgrade, then away it goes to download and update your system. Keeping your system up to date in this way is critical to close any security vulnerabilities that might be lurking on your system.

yum/RPM

For Red Hat–based systems (such as Fedora and CentOS), we use *Red Hat Package Manager (RPM)*. As with APT, there's a convenient command line you can use to manage RPM packages: the *yum* command. There a lot of little differences between these package managers and the commands for working with them, but the essentials are virtually the same as with apt-get. Here are the commands we used to install htop, but for yum:

```
mike@server:~$ sudo yum update
mike@server:~$ sudo yum install htop
```

> **NOTE** There are multiple ways to use both APT and RPM. I've stuck to apt-get and yum here to avoid confusing you with alternatives before the exam. If you spend much time working with Linux, look into the alternatives later!

nano

You will sometimes need to edit raw text files in UNIX, and it's good to know you can do it from the command line (especially if you don't have access to a full GUI). The family tree of command-line editors is big, with a long history and heated arguments about which one is best.

The previous iteration of the CompTIA A+ exam objectives (220-1002) focused on a fairly ubiquitous editor, *vi*, which you'll find bundled in some form or another with most UNIXes. Figuring out how to edit a file (or even just exit) with vi in some ways is a rite of passage. Only after you have mastered vi's nonintuitive and perhaps even downright weird interface can you truly start to think of yourself as a UNIX Terminal Jedi master.

Luckily for you (unless you already happen to know vi, or have strong opinions about CLI text editors), the current CompTIA A+ 1102 objectives now focus on an easier-to-learn editor: GNU *nano*. You'll still find nano on most UNIXes, but it is a *little* less common than vi—tuck the name vi away in your pocket in case you need to edit a file on a system without nano! Let's get started with nano by creating a new text file called "fred" (the same command will also edit an existing file):

```
mike@server:~$ nano fred
```

You'll now be in the nano text editor, staring at a blank file, as shown in Figure 15-13. The big thing to notice here is at the bottom of the screen, where nano lists a few important keyboard shortcuts (each prefixed with ^ to indicate that you should press CTRL and the indicated key simultaneously). The most important ones are in the bottom-left corner: Get Help, and Exit. Press CTRL + G once to access the help menu, and CTRL + X once to return to the edit view.

To make basic edits in nano, all you need to do is move your cursor around with your keyboard and type or delete as needed. Enter a few lines of text, such as shown in Figure 15-14, press ENTER at the end of each line, and use the BACKSPACE key if you make an error.

To save your new file and quit nano, press CTRL + X. If you exit with unsaved changes (a "modified buffer"), nano will prompt you to save them, discard them, or cancel and return to the editor. Just press Y to save the changes. It's important to know how to use a common editor such as nano or vi, but for day-to-day work most UNIX people usually reach for one of the hundreds of alternatives. Check out other terminal-based editors such as vim, joe, or emacs, and graphical editors such as gedit or gVim.

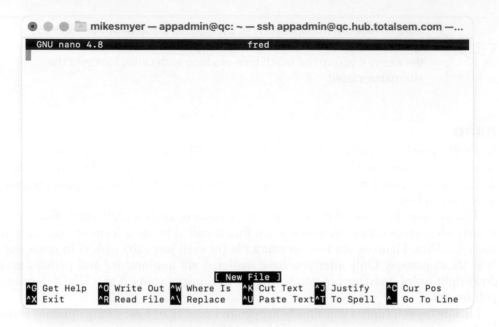

Figure 15-13   nano open

Figure 15-14   nano with text

dd

The *dd* command is primarily used to create an exact, bit-by-bit image of any form of block storage, meaning mass storage devices such as hard drive volumes, thumb drives, and optical media. In its most simple form, the dd command is just

```
$ dd if=<source block device> of=<destination image file location>
```

There's no way to show you all the possible uses for dd, so I'll just show three of the typical places I use it. Let's start with something simple: copying a hard drive.

Be careful here—some people joke that dd stands for "Disk Destroyer" for a reason! This powerful tool will wreak havoc on your data if not used correctly. There are a number of issues that I'm not covering here that could greatly affect the success of running the dd command. While all of the following commands are valid, simply running them on your systems without understanding these subtleties can wipe drives. You have been warned!

Copying a Hard Drive

Let's say you have a hard drive (sda) you want to copy onto another hard drive (sdb). In this case we will say they are exactly the same size. The following command will copy the entire sda drive, partition table, file systems . . . everything to the sdb drive:

```
dd if=/dev/sda of=/dev/sdb
```

Backing Up a Thumb Drive

Let's say you have thumb drive full of important files you really want to back up. Using dd as follows, you can copy the entire USB drive and make an image file (I chose to call it thumbBackup.bak) and place that image file on your Desktop:

```
dd if=/dev/sdc of=/home/mike/Desktop/thumbBackup.bak
```

Wiping a Disk

I have a drive (sdb) that I want to totally wipe. The dd command can take input from anywhere, but in this case I'll use Linux's random number generator, /dev/urandom, to write a stream of random bits completely over the entire drive. It's not a perfect wipe, but it will stop all but the most sophisticated tools.

```
dd if=/dev/urandom of=/dev/sdb
```

df

The *df* (display free disk space) command makes it easy to diagnose the most common storage-space issues on UNIX systems. You can just run **df** by itself, but I always run **df -h** (the -h switch uses human-friendly units):

```
$ df -h
Filesystem      Size  Used Avail Use% Mounted on
devtmpfs        1.6G     0  1.6G   0% /dev
tmpfs            16G  425M   16G   3% /dev/shm
tmpfs           7.9G  6.7M  7.9G   1% /run
tmpfs            16G  504K   16G   1% /run/wrappers
```

```
/dev/nvme0n1p3   250G   195G   43G   83%  /
/dev/nvme0n1p1   500M   140M  361M   28%  /boot
tmpfs            3.2G    92K  3.2G    1%  /run/user/1000
```

One quick command is all I need to know that the primary volume (mounted at the root directory /) is about 83% full.

shutdown

In Windows, you can shut down or restart the system from a terminal using the *shutdown* command. Run the command as follows:

```
shutdown <options> <time>
```

By far the most common time is *now*. To shut down the system immediately, run

```
shutdown now
```

To restart the system, run **shutdown** with the **-r** option:

```
shutdown -r now
```

Scripting

Up until now, we've entered commands into the CLI one by one. Most of the time all you need is one or two commands, but sometimes you will find yourself running the same series of commands to perform a task over and over. When you find yourself in this situation, it might be a good idea to write a *script*—a small program that helps automate a task by collecting a series of commands and giving them a name.

Early in the chapter—when we looked at shells—I pointed out that a shell is the command-line interpreter that interprets the commands you run. It's time to let you in on a secret. Shells can also execute a text file by interpreting each line as if it were a command you typed and ran. We call these text files *shell scripts*. Each command shell has its own *shell scripting language*—and all of the commands I've shown you so far use a little slice of it.

The rest of each shell's *scripting language* is for controlling when and how the shell runs the commands in a script—but you can make a super simple shell script by just copying a few shell commands to a new file and saving it. Imagine you have an application (importantapp.exe) that requires a weekly maintenance restart, where you run the following commands:

```
kill /IM importantapp.exe /P gudpwd1    (shut down the application)
cd \ProgramData\importantapp\Data        (Go to a specific location)
del *.tmp                                (delete the temporary files)
copy config.ini config.bak /Y            (back up config; overwrites
                                           last week's backup)

importantapp.exe                         (start the application)
```

Typing these commands one after the other every week is tedious, and you may mistype or misremember them. Instead, you can put them in a text file (using Notepad, for example), give it a name like weeklyrestart.bat, and just run the script each week. (Look for more on the .bat file extension in the next section.)

The most-productive techs use scripts all the time to automate a zillion tasks. My office is relatively small, but it has a lot of computers to keep up with. My sysad (systems administrator) Michael's morning routine includes checking the status of every one of those computers, looking for errors, proper functioning, and so forth. It would take him all day to visit each machine—even over the network—to check its status. Michael created scripts that automate this task. He sits at his Mac with his morning coffee, opens Terminal, runs a few scripts, and reviews the reports they kick out. Sweet!

Script Types and Languages

Scripting is a kind of *programming*; a scripting language is a type of *programming language* for writing scripts. As with any kind of programming, there are many different scripting languages designed for a variety of purposes. The CompTIA A+ objectives expect you to be able to identify the file types for six different scripting languages.

Table 15-1 lists and describes common scripting languages and their file extensions.

Language	File Extension	Description
Batch File	.bat	Batch files are the shell scripting language for the old-school Command shell on Windows and DOS (yes, that DOS).
PowerShell	.ps1	*PowerShell* is a shell scripting language written from the ground up for automating modern Windows systems. Replaces batch files in most situations.
Bash (or Bourne Again) shell script	.sh	By convention, the first line of a UNIX shell script file specifies which shell should execute the script (and thus, which specific shell scripting language it is written in). These files often have a .sh file extension, but it is not necessary.
Python	.py	Python is a flexible programming language with simple syntax that makes it well suited for writing both simple scripts and large applications.
JavaScript	.js	JavaScript is a browser scripting language developed back in the 1990s to enhance Web pages, but these days you can find it in command-line programs, extensions for many desktop applications, and much more.
Visual Basic Script	.vbs	Visual Basic Script is a legacy scripting language for Windows and other Microsoft applications. Slowly being replaced by other languages like PowerShell.

Table 15-1 Common Languages and Their File Extensions

NOTE The first three scripting languages in Table 15-1 are *shell* scripting languages, but the other three are more general scripting languages. In a shell scripting language, any normal command you would run is a valid part of the language. This is not true in the more general scripting languages (but they have many other useful features).

Ask Not What You Can Do for Scripting

Like I said before, scripts help automate computing tasks. They *do* things. Which things? Unfortunately, you can't automate one of the big tricks to scripting: figuring out exactly which tasks to automate in the first place. The closest you can get is knowing the basic capabilities of scripting, seeing how other people like to automate, and building habits that make it easier to automate when the time comes.

Use Cases for Scripting

I'm not alone, here—CompTIA also thinks it's a great idea for you to know what other people do with scripting. Before we run through the *use cases for scripting* that you should know for the CompTIA A+ 1102 exam, I want to make something clear: automation and scripting are huge topics and the CompTIA A+ objectives just scratch the surface. If you find this stuff interesting, dive beyond the CompTIA A+ objectives and teach yourself some code.

NOTE There is often more than one way to automate something. When it comes to Windows systems, Group Policy (which we'll take a closer look at in Chapter 27) can help with these same use cases.

Basic Automation It's hard to know exactly what CompTIA means by "basic automation," but in my mind basic automation is all about writing *little* scripts for things you do every day or week or month. Maybe that's resetting a browser profile to troubleshoot constant crashing. Maybe that's resetting default applications after users accidentally change them. Maybe that's resetting file permissions that keep getting messed up for some unknown reason.

The point is, it's usually up to you and your colleagues to spot these opportunities, figure out how to automate them, and share what you discover. I'll take a closer look at how to recognize these in the upcoming "Automatic Habits" section.

Restarting Machines For exactly the same reason that "Have you tried turning it off and back on?" is an essential troubleshooting step, it's common for organizations to set up automation for restarting machines. Nightly or weekend reboots are common for workstations that live in a lab or office with predictable hours.

There's more variety when it comes to laptops and servers. Scripts for restarting laptops may give users advanced warning, let the user defer the restart if they are busy, or reschedule it at a specific time. Scripts for restarting servers might cautiously confirm another server with spare capacity is available, stop the flow of new requests, and wait for the server to finish everything in its queue before rebooting.

Remapping Network Drives   In many organizations, users need to work with files that are stored on file servers that they access over the network. One way to do this is by mapping the relevant network shares to a drive letter on the user's system, and it's common for organizations that work this way to have scripts for ensuring the right network shares get set up. This might mean setting up one set of shares for everyone, or setting up department-specific shares depending on which user logs in.

Installation of Applications   Much as with network shares, organizations often need to ensure that their users' computers have certain applications installed and properly configured. Scripts can both set up applications on new systems and help deploy new applications to existing systems—without having to lay hands on each device.

Automated Backups   Backups can help minimize the pain of disasters, hardware failures, and updates gone wrong. We'll take a closer look at backup procedures in Chapter 28, so for now it's enough to know that manual backups are fine in some cases—but critical systems and data should be backed up automatically. Good scripts enable you to back up exactly what you need as often as you need.

Gathering of Information/Data   A big part of good system administration is just gathering information. Sometimes we need to gather a lot of information on a single system—such as a comprehensive report on the hardware and configuration of a system that keeps crashing at odd times, or a forensic audit of a device that might have been hacked or used in a crime. Other times, we need to collect information about a whole lot of systems—maybe their network configuration, list of installed apps, or free storage space. Scripts enable you to collect everything you need in exactly the right way every time.

Initiating Updates   System and software updates are tricky to manage just right. If your organization doesn't update its devices quickly enough, it could end up being the low-hanging fruit that cyber criminals target for extortion. But if its devices take every update as soon as it's available, everyone's work could be disrupted (and data could be lost) if vendors push out a real lemon of an update.

Scripting these updates can enable your organization to avoid being the guinea pig or installing known-bad updates—but also ensure devices do get updated regularly. Scripting can also make it possible to roll out updates in stages and discover incompatibilities before they affect everyone.

Automatic Habits

Here's an all-too-common automation tragedy: I'll go to manually fix something for the umpteenth time only to realize that I've been down this same road before. I'll pop open an editor, sketch out the steps, and start filling in commands. Then, midway through, I'll run into some roadblock. Maybe it requires a complex decision, or I just can't figure out why the script is doing what I wrote instead of what I meant. I'll fight it for a while, end up frustrated that I can't automate the whole task, throw out the script, and do it manually (in a huff!).

Don't do this! When it comes to automating something complex, the best way to set yourself up for success is to develop habits that give you a head start on the automation process and then automate gradually.

The most important habits here are all about notetaking: keep detailed notes, save command-line history and logs alongside them, organize them in a way that makes sense to you, make sure to refer back to them, and update them as you learn more. Do what works for you and your organization. When it's time to automate a task, a good set of notes will answer important questions and save time!

The next key habit is to keep an eye out for signs a script could save you time. This is an art, but one good hint is when you catch yourself flipping back through your command history to find a whole sequence of commands to run them all again. Another is when you have to visit a search engine or check your notes just to remember some steps, what order they belong in, or how to run them.

Once you suspect a task deserves a script, the last habit is to automate it gradually. Start with the easy parts, and then (if you have time) take another bite each time you repeat the task. Automating gradually is all about avoiding two mistakes:

- Putting tons of work into a script you never end up running.
- Letting "perfect" be the enemy of "better." Yes, it is really (*really!*) gratifying to completely automate a complex task, but it's better to start saving time and energy today.

 NOTE One of my favorite scripting tips of the last few years comes from Dan Slimmon, who recommends kicking off your gradual automation with the *opposite* of a script that does things: write the task up as a script that just tells *you* what to do, step by step. Each time you run through it, you'll have a chance to check the instructions for accuracy, refine the process, and automate easy steps.

Here Be Dragons

Before I pat you on the head and send you off into the world armed only with a text editor and a shell, I have to share some hard truths: scripting can be just as dangerous and frustrating as it is powerful. Most of the risks that come with scripting are just the dark side of the command line's incredible power.

One big way scripts cause trouble is that they tend to be *fragile*—a script can be very sensitive to small differences between the system you run it on and the one the author wrote it on, unless the script's author anticipated such differences. Maybe the script assumes a directory will exist but it doesn't, or that some command will be installed and it isn't.

Once one thing goes wrong, the best scripts will try to stop, reverse any changes they've already made, and display a message about what went wrong. Many scripts aren't this good—they'll just keep right on going (with some changes failing, and others succeeding). When this happens, you'll have to manually fix whatever went wrong and clean up after the script.

When it comes to using scripts, here are three specific considerations you should keep in mind for the CompTIA A+ 1102 exam:

- If you can install software on a system from the command line, scripts can also install software. If you (or your users) run scripts that other people wrote without carefully reading the scripts to understand what they'll do, there's a very real chance of *unintentionally introducing malware*.

- If there's a way to change a setting from the command line, it's possible for a script to change it! Not only does this mean that a malicious script could intentionally change system settings to make a system easier to compromise, but it also means that there's a risk of *inadvertently changing system settings* when you (or your users) run a script. This risk increases greatly when a script encounters errors!

- While it isn't exactly common for scripts to cause system or application stability problems, it is still good to be aware that they are basically little programs—it is possible for them cause *browser or system crashes due to mishandling of resources*.

The best way to deal with these risks is to exercise caution and diligence. Train your users not to run untrusted scripts. Read scripts before you run them. Run them on test systems before you run them on systems that work for a living. Back up systems before you try out new scripts on them. Test new scripts on a fraction of your organization's systems before deploying them everywhere.

Beyond A+

Anatomy of a Script

We use programming languages to tell computers to do something to some piece of data. You've solved math problems in school, so you are already halfway to understanding this. In a simple math problem like 3 + 4, you have two numbers, and a symbol that tells you what operation (addition, in this case) to perform.

To do this math problem, you need to know the rules. You learned the rules of arithmetic back in grade school, right? In arithmetic, each of these numbers is a *value*; the rules tell you to add two numbers when you see the + sign.

But what if the equation looked a little different? What would you do if it was 3 + cow? That doesn't make sense! Cow isn't a number, it's a word for a large, grass-eating bovine. You and I know this, but a C and a 3 are both just bytes to the computer. How does it know that it can't add them?

Data Types

To be able to treat numbers and words differently, programming languages need a new concept—data types. A data type is a defined category, like *number* or *word*. In many programming languages, these rules dictate important details, such as *you can't add the number 3 and the word cow because the two values have different data types*.

The number 3 is an *integer* (i.e., a whole number) data type, and cow (i.e., a word) is what programmers call a *string* data type. Here's where it gets a little more complicated, but stick with me and it'll become clearer!

A way to think of a string is as a *sequence of characters*, like c – o – w. Most programming languages require that you identify a string with 'single' or "double" quotes, so 'cow' or "cow" in this example. While only some characters are valid integers, all characters can be valid in a string.

Every programming language dictates the actions the computer can perform on strings (like joining two strings together, breaking one string into pieces, checking how many characters are in a string, and so on). While the rules of arithmetic dictate that you can't add 3 + cow (probably because it would upset the cow), many languages combine two strings when you "add" them. Adding "brown" + "cow" produces "brown cow" (and a happier cow).

NOTE Some languages have additional data types for more specific circumstances (like a special type for dates, or fractional numbers).

Strings also make it possible to keep the computer from interpreting something as an equation to solve. For example, if I tried to write my office phone number like 281-922-4166, a computer wouldn't have any choice but to compute the result of 281 minus 922 minus 4166 (it's -4807, an integer data type). If I write "281-922-4166" instead, a computer will leave the digits intact.

Variables

As soon as the computer thinks it's done with this value (whether it's -4807 or "281-922-4166"), it will forget it. If you need to use the value more than once, you must tell the computer to save it. Most programming languages tell the computer to remember the value by *naming* it; we call these named values *variables*. I could save my office phone number as the variable phone number:

```
phone_number = "281-922-4166"
```

Conditionals and Basic Loops

Once you move beyond the most basic shell scripts—those that are just a list of commands—you often need to control when and how different commands run. Not surprisingly, scripting languages and programming languages give you excellent tools, called *control constructs*, to control what they should do under different conditions.

NOTE I've included some scripting examples in this section. Each one uses the *Python* language. If you try to copy them into a script file for another language, they probably won't work!

The most basic control constructs are *conditionals*. Conditionals enable you to specify code that should run only when some condition is (or is not) met. Most languages have *keywords*, such as an "if" statement. The "if" statement specifies a condition, and what code to run if the condition is met. Here's a simple example:

```
animal = "cow"
if animal == "cat":
    print("meow")
```

Here's what each line means:

1. The *animal* variable holds a string value "cow".

2. The if statement checks to see if the animal variable contains a value of "cat".

3. If it contains "cat", the computer will print the word "meow" to the terminal. If not, nothing will happen.

In this case, the script would never print "meow" because the condition *is not met*. Conditionals are a critical building block for all but the most basic scripts and programs. As described earlier in this chapter, one of the main reasons to write a script in the first place is because you need to do something many times. In programming, a good way to accomplish this is with a loop. Basic *loops* are another kind of conditional that tell the computer to run the code over and over *until the condition is (or is not) met*. Depending on the language, you'll usually see loops indicated with keywords like *for* and *while*. Here's an example:

```
cows = 0
while cows < 4:
    print("moo")
    cows = cows + 1
```

This loop will run until the number of cows *is* 4, so it will print "moo" four times—one for each cow. Because the value in the cows variable is an integer, we can do math with it. Each time the loop runs, it prints "moo" once and adds one to the number of cows.

 NOTE Different languages have different control structures. Most of them have at least a few. Take the time to learn the control structures of languages you deal with—it's much easier to figure out what a script does once you know them.

Comments

Scripting and programming languages usually have a way to insert special text—called a *comment*—that helps anyone reading the script later (including the writer, a few months on!) understand what's going on. The computer ignores this text, as it's only for the humans. Leaving comments is a really good idea even if you don't expect anyone else to ever read your script. Comments are a great way to describe the problem a script exists to solve. You should also use them to describe how, when, and where to use the script.

Each language has its own comment syntax, though *most* languages share two common formats. Three of the languages (PowerShell, Python, and UNIX shell) use a single format, which begins a comment with the # symbol. The comment symbol can start a line or follow statements on the same line. Let's take a look:

```
# This script makes all of the cows moo.
# Be careful with this power.
cows = 0 # start with no cows
while cows < 4: # only 4 cows allowed to moo :(
    print("moo") # moo, cow, moo
    cows = cows + 1 # add one cow
```

The comments in this example describe the goal of the script—make all the cows moo—and caution the user of the script. They note that the script starts with no cows and limits the total number of cows to four, and so on.

The other three languages are all a little different, so they'll be easy to tell apart. JavaScript:

```
// This is a single-line comment in JavaScript
/* This is a multiline comment
in JavaScript */
```

Batch file:

```
REM This is the older way to comment in Batch files
:: But many newer scripts use this format.
```

Visual Basic Script:

```
' Visual Basic Script's comments start with a single quote.
```

Comments are absolutely essential for humans who need to work on scripts and programs. Nothing's worse than trying to remember how many cows will moo a year after you write the script!

Environment Variables

Any system you access has important values stored in variables that make up what we call the *environment* of a running program. Some of these values are set systemwide, but these values can also be set by the user, the script/program, or even the shell it is running in. These values, which we call *environment variables,* tell running programs all sorts of things, like what the current directory or user is, or where to store temporary files. Figure 15-15 shows the default environment variables for programs run under the michaels user account.

We also use environment variables to configure scripts because they make it easy for many different users to customize how the same script will behave on a given system without having to edit the script itself. Here's an example of Windows Command shell environment variables in a batch file (remember that *REM* here means *comment*):

```
@echo off
REM prints the name of the currently logged-in account
echo You are logged in as %username%
REM prints the currently logged-in user's main folder
echo Your home directory is %homepath%
```

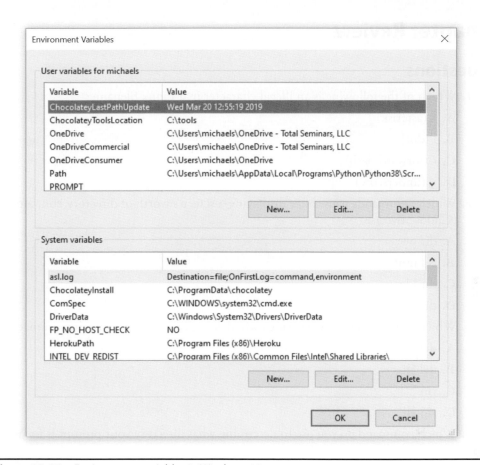

Figure 15-15 Environment variables in Windows 10

The text surrounded by percent signs (for example, %username%) is an environment variable in batch that will change depending on the user running the script. If I run the script, it'll say "Mike" and print the location of my home directory.

UNIXes have a set of environmental variables that are similar to those in Windows, but they look a bit different. Here is the same script as the previous one but written for a UNIX system:

```
#!/bin/bash
# Prints the name of the currently logged-in account
echo You are logged in as $USER
# Prints the currently logged-in user's main folder
echo Your home directory is $HOME
```

Most scripts that are meant for use on multiple different systems will depend on at least a few environment variables. Once you can read and understand the control structures in a script, it's a good idea to learn what the most common environment variables contain and train yourself to mentally substitute them as you read. When you encounter an unfamiliar environment variable, get curious—ask a search engine about it!

Chapter Review

Questions

1. Which of the following is an illegal character in a Linux filename?

   A. * (asterisk)

   B. . (dot)

   C. / (forward slash)

   D. _ (underscore)

2. Which commands pause after displaying a screen's worth of directory contents? (Choose two.)

   A. dir p

   B. ls | more

   C. dir | less

   D. dir /p

3. Which of the following commands will delete all the files in a directory in macOS?

   A. del *

   B. del all

   C. rm *

   D. rm all

4. Which command do you use to determine what directory your prompt is focusing on in Linux?

   A. dir

   B. path

   C. pwd

   D. prompt

5. Which Windows command is functionally equivalent to the Linux ls command?

   A. dir

   B. command

   C. copy

   D. dd

6. What do you type before a macOS command to access help for that command?

   A. Get-Help

   B. ?

   C. man

   D. /?

7. Which of the following UNIX commands will show detailed information about the contents of a folder?

   A. ls -l

   B. ls -e

   C. ls -h

   D. ls -k

8. Which UNIX command enables you to see a continually updating list of active processes?

   A. ps

   B. zsh

   C. top

   D. kill

9. Of the following, which best describes the function of the Windows gpresult command?

   A. Lists all recently updated group policies

   B. Lists the group policies applied to a user

   C. Lists all changes to a user's group policies since the last refresh

   D. Lists any and all conflicting group policies

10. How do you run a command at the Windows command prompt with administrative privileges?

   A. Enter an elevated username and password at the command prompt.

   B. Right-click a command-prompt shortcut and then select Run as PowerUser.

   C. Right-click a command-prompt shortcut and then select Run as administrator.

   D. The cmd command only runs with administrator privileges.

Answers

1. **C.** Any of these characters are acceptable in a Linux filename except the forward slash (/), which is used exclusively as a path separator.

2. **B, D.** The ls | more and dir /p commands in UNIX and Windows, respectively, pause a long listing at the end of the page.

3. **C.** Type **rm** * and press ENTER to delete all files in a directory in macOS.

4. **C.** The pwd command enables you to determine the current folder location in Linux.

5. **A.** The Windows dir command accomplishes a similar function to the Linux ls command.

6. **C.** Access the help for a macOS command by typing **man [command name]**.

7. **A.** Type **ls -l** and press ENTER to see detailed information about a folder in UNIX systems.

8. **A.** ps is the UNIX command that enables you to see a continually updating list of active processes.

9. **B.** The gpresult command in Windows lists group policies applied to a user.

10. **C.** To run a command at the Windows command prompt with administrative privileges, right-click a command-prompt shortcut and then select Run as administrator.

CHAPTER 16

Troubleshooting Operating Systems

In this chapter, you will learn how to
- Perform common Windows OS troubleshooting steps
- Identify symptoms of and troubleshoot common Windows OS problems
- Identify symptoms of and troubleshoot problems related to motherboards, RAM, CPU, and power

As we have discussed in previous chapters, you can perform regular maintenance, keep your system updated, and be vigilant with respect to security, but inevitably something will go wrong. Sometimes the cause is human error, but quite often things simply go wrong with both software and hardware. Knowing what to check and how to address issues will be a very large part of your job.

In this chapter we'll look first at some common Windows troubleshooting procedures that can serve as a good foundation for dealing with all kinds of issues. From there, we'll consider a list of more specific symptoms that you should know about. Finally, we will wrap up with talking about how to identify and troubleshoot hardware-related issues. All of these are major themes on the CompTIA A+ 1101 and 1102 exams, so take time to digest this material.

 NOTE We are going to be doing a lot of troubleshooting in this chapter, so now is a good time to turn back to Chapter 1 and review CompTIA's troubleshooting methodology.

1102

Common Windows Troubleshooting Procedures

Learning how to troubleshoot and fix specific problems efficiently is part of becoming a great troubleshooter, but in my mind it's even more important to know how to hit the ground running when you honestly have *no clue* why a system is acting up. In this section

651

we'll look at several troubleshooting procedures for Windows that you can fall back on to get your systems up and running in a pinch. Buckle up!

> **NOTE** The CompTIA A+ 1102 objectives call these troubleshooting *steps*, but I'm using the word *procedures* because they aren't a well-ordered list of things you should follow sequentially.

Turning Things Off and Back On

For as long as we've had computers, turning them off and back on has been an important troubleshooting procedure. Because software and hardware can both have tiny defects, the longer a system runs without a reboot, the more likely it is to run into trouble. One common cause of this slow descent into chaos is programs that don't properly clean up and release the resources they've been using, preventing the system from allocating those resources to other applications. This is most common with memory—so common, in fact, that we have a special term for it: a *memory leak*.

You can waste a lot of time trying to figure out what's going wrong only for a reboot to instantly clear up the problem. As long as there isn't a good reason *not* to reboot a system, I'd reboot it any time you run into a problem that you don't recognize, just to see if it clears up. You might feel like rebooting is throwing up your hands in defeat, but there will *always* be problems that we have to manage with reboots until some developer or manufacturer releases an update.

Don't think these kinds of problems just apply to programs that you run as a user. Long-running services wear a lot of important hats in modern operating systems. Compared to in-your-face desktop applications, it's easy to forget all about services when they behave themselves. But they *are* still software—and most software has bugs and defects.

No matter which app you are using, when some general feature of your OS stops working—maybe it can't connect to the network, print a document, or find files that you *know* are there—there's a decent chance a misbehaving or crashed service is to blame. In the "Services Not Starting" section later in this chapter, I'll show you how Windows will warn you if a particularly important service fails to start when you boot the system.

One way to troubleshoot cases like this is to try to *restart services* to see if the problem goes away. In *my* opinion, you'll often be able to reboot a system when you run into a problem like this. It is rarely even obvious which service to restart! The main time you'd want to go to the effort of restarting services is when there's a good reason you can't reboot—perhaps the system is acting as a database server or in the middle of processing a massive print job.

CompTIA, however, wants you to know that restarting services is a common troubleshooting procedure (especially if Windows notifies you that a critical service failed to start). It's possible the service failed for a temporary reason and giving it a swift kick may get it going again.

NOTE   Refer to Chapter 12 for the lowdown on how to stop and start services with both the Task Manager and the Services MMC snap-in.

System File Check

Most of the time Windows will either work just fine or collapse in a heap, but if you use it long enough, you'll eventually run into cases where it's acting strange. Whenever problems like this persist even after I reboot, the hair tends to stand up on my arms. As you'll see in Chapter 27, erratic behavior is one of the telltale signs of a malware infestation. But there *are* still some simpler explanations to rule out before you panic.

Back in Chapter 15 I showed you a cool little Windows utility called *sfc (System File Checker)*. It'll search your system files to ensure they're all present and not corrupted—and *try* to replace the files if there's a problem. It isn't the best thing since sliced bread, but running it is a good idea to rule out these kinds of issues if a system's misbehaving.

EXAM TIP   The CompTIA A+ 1102 exam objectives call this troubleshooting procedure *system file check,* but the actual tool is named *System File Checker.* Don't get tripped up by this difference if it pops up on the exam!

Uninstall/Reinstall/Update Applications

From time to time, an application will just break on you. Most of the time it'll be broken from the moment you install it or break right after you update the application or your OS. Once in a blue moon, the application will just break for no obvious reason. It'll work fine one time, and then…not at all.

If a program isn't working quite right, a good first step is to see if it has any updates available and, if so, apply the updates and confirm you still see the problem on the newest version. If the program destabilizes the system, you should uninstall it before doing anything else.

If the program broke after you updated it or the OS, either one might have a bug or might no longer be compatible with the other. Verify that the program and OS are still compatible. If not, you might need to update the OS to a newer version, or even set aside a system to run an older (compatible) version of the OS. It's also possible that the software requirements have changed—make sure to verify them.

Less frequently, a program may just stop working out of the blue even though nothing's changed recently. Many programs read and write data to files on the system as they run, and even the tiniest problem in these data files could crash the program. These incompatibilities can be caused by things like an application crash, the power going out, or restoring older copies of the data files. Uninstalling and reinstalling the program may clear the bad data and get you on your way.

Some programs store data files in locations that aren't deleted when you uninstall the program, so they'll keep right on failing after you reinstall them. In this case, you'll need to research the file locations (they differ from program to program) and manually delete them.

If none of these steps help—especially if you know the software is running fine on similar systems—the failure may actually be an early sign of hardware trouble. The specifics can vary from program to program, but an application that tickles your system just right can easily turn up early signs of failure in almost any component or peripheral plugged into your system!

NOTE Refer back to Chapter 14 if you need to refresh your knowledge of compatibility problems between programs and the OS or review the actual process of updating, uninstalling, or reinstalling applications.

Resource Requirements

When a system or its applications start misbehaving out of nowhere, it's natural to focus on the exact program or feature that isn't working, or recent changes such as updates. That'll *usually* lead you in the right direction, but it can also blind you to the obvious.

Our systems are constantly changing in ways that can affect the resources available to our programs and OS. Every new application we install takes more resources. Every file we create or download takes up a little storage space. Every time the OS or an application automatically updates, it may use more resources, fewer resources, or just a different balance of them.

When we're having unexplained trouble, good techs aren't afraid to ask simple questions like whether the device meets the system requirements for the OS and programs the user is trying to run. If the answer is *no*, the solution is usually to move the user to a newer system or *add resources* (upgrade the RAM, storage, processor, graphics card, and so on) to the existing one.

EXAM TIP The CompTIA A+ 1102 objectives refer to this troubleshooting procedure as *verify requirements*. These are the *system requirements* (CPU, RAM, graphics, storage, and so on) discussed in Chapter 14. Be prepared to see the follow-on procedure—add resources—on the exam as well.

Recovering When Windows Breaks

When things get hairy enough that Windows can't even load or work right, you can usually get the system running again with a special set of tools called the *Windows Recovery Environment*.

EXAM TIP Techs often refer to the Windows Recovery Environment as *WinRE* or *Windows RE*. Because the CompTIA A+ 1102 objectives don't refer directly to WinRE—they just refer to the options you'll find inside it—I'm not sure if you'll see any of these names on the exam. Microsoft also refers to the options themselves as the *System Recovery Options*. To be safe, be ready to recognize all of these names plus the names of the individual options!

WinRE includes an impressive, powerful set of both automated and manual utilities that collectively diagnoses and fixes all but the most serious of Windows boot problems. Although WinRE does all the hard work for you, you still need to know how to access and use it. When faced with a failure-to-boot scenario in modern versions of Windows, WinRE is one of your primary tools.

In Windows, you can access WinRE in a few ways depending on the state of your system. First, if your system boots, you can hold SHIFT while clicking the Restart button on the Start menu or login screen. Alternatively, from the Settings app, open the Update & Security category (System category in Windows 11), click Recovery, and then click Restart now in the Advanced startup section. But if you can't boot Windows, you can boot from the Windows installation media and select Repair your computer (see Figure 16-1).

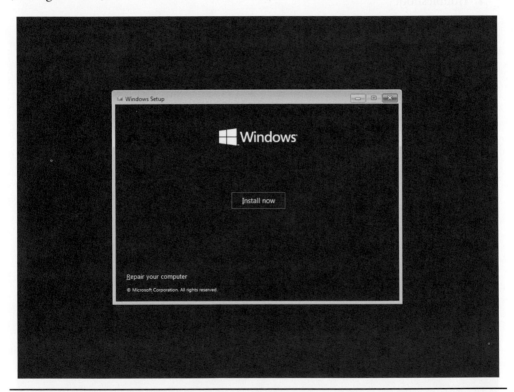

Figure 16-1 Repair your computer option on the Windows 11 installer

You can also create Windows installation media by downloading it directly from Microsoft (https://www.microsoft.com/software-download/) and making a bootable USB drive. If you're already using a Windows machine, select the version of Windows you want to install and download the corresponding *Windows media creation tool*. Insert a USB drive and run the media creation tool to create a bootable USB drive. (If you aren't already using a Windows machine, you'll need to download the ISO file and look up how to create a bootable USB drive on your OS.)

Using the advanced startup options to boot into WinRE usually works, so it's a good place to start. You should access WinRE from the Windows installation media if your system is too messed up to boot WinRE or you think the system may have malware.

WinRE offers few choices initially, so you'll have to click around a bit to find the good stuff. Don't be surprised if you see something different than what's shown in the screenshots in this section—Microsoft likes to fiddle with the options from version to version, and they can also differ from system to system. In Windows 11, the main menu starts (see Figure 16-2) with a few options:

- Continue
- Use a device
- Troubleshoot
- Turn off your PC

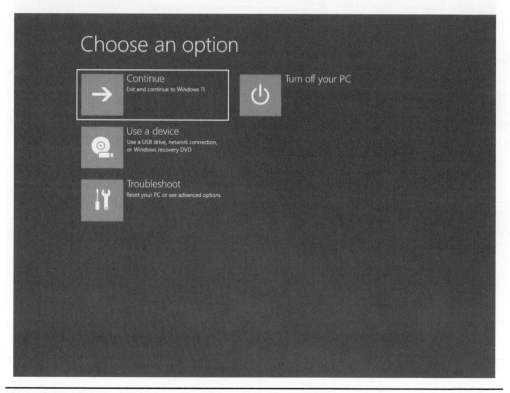

Figure 16-2 Recovery Environment main screen in Windows 11

Click the Troubleshoot option to see a couple more options, as shown in Figure 16-3. (If you boot from the installation media, clicking Troubleshoot will take you directly to the Advanced options screen discussed next.)

- Reset this PC
- Advanced options

Figure 16-3   WinRE Troubleshoot screen

Clicking Advanced options reveals another menu (see Figure 16-4) that shows a lot of options (you may have to click *See more recovery options* to see them all). I want to discuss seven of these (you may see them in a different order):

- System Restore
- Startup Settings
- Uninstall Updates
- System Image Recovery (not shown in Figure 16-4)
- Startup Repair
- Command Prompt
- UEFI Firmware Settings (if your system has UEFI)

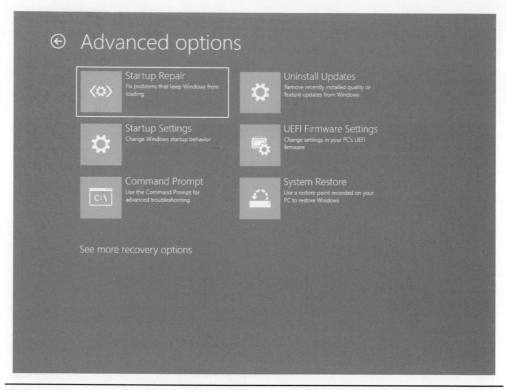

Figure 16-4   WinRE Advanced options screen

Let's look at the details of these options plus *Reset this PC*.

 EXAM TIP   Make sure you know how to access the Windows Recovery Environment and what each of the available tools does.

System Restore

System Restore enables you to go back to a time when your computer worked properly. This option gives those of us who make many *restore points*—snapshots of a system at various points in time—a handy way to return a system to a previous state (see Figure 16-5).

 NOTE   As we discussed back in Chapter 14, System Restore is now disabled by default. So, if you are attempting to fix a Windows machine by rolling back with System Restore, there is a good chance you will find that there are no snapshots available.

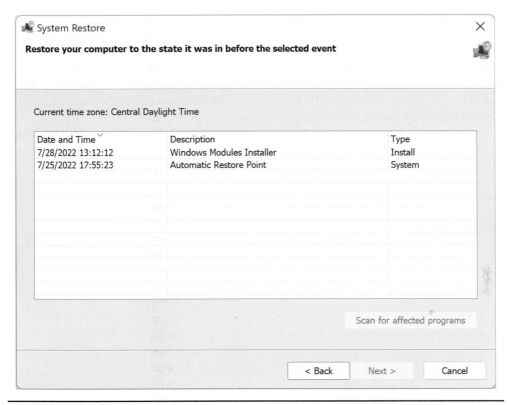

Figure 16-5 System Restore list of restore points

Startup Settings

It isn't in the CompTIA A+ 1102 exam objectives, but the *Startup Settings* option enables you to control some special troubleshooting and developer modes that Windows can start up in. Sooner or later, there's a good chance you'll need to use these settings to access *Safe Mode* (a staple of Windows troubleshooting for decades)!

Uninstall Updates

Use the Uninstall Updates option in the very off chance that Microsoft pushes out an update that breaks things in your system. It's happened in the past, so Microsoft includes this option just in case. You'll likely never need to use it.

System Image Recovery

Use the System Image Recovery tool to restore a system after a catastrophe. This is a great tool if you manage a set of uniform systems, typical in many workplaces. Keep a default image on hand, including OS settings, network settings, and applications, and you can quickly *reimage* a borked computer to get clients up and running. You can keep a simpler image as well, one that reloads the OS for further customization.

If you have the drive containing the system image plugged in when you first run the wizard, it should detect your latest backup and give you the option to restore it. After you select the image you want to restore, the utility presents you with some additional options that affect how it will reimage your system.

After you click Finish on the confirmation screen, which also contains a final warning, the restore process begins. The utility removes the old system data and then copies the backed-up system image to the hard drive(s). Once the process completes, your system reboots and should start up again with all of your data and programs just where you left them when you last backed up.

Startup Repair

The *Startup Repair* utility serves as a one-stop, do-it-all option (see Figure 16-6). When run, it performs a number of repairs, including:

- Repairs a corrupted Registry by accessing the backup copy on your hard drive
- Restores critical boot files
- Restores critical system and driver files
- Rolls back any non-working drivers
- Rolls back updates
- Runs chkdsk
- Runs a memory test to check your RAM

Figure 16-6
Startup Repair's rather bare-bones interface for Windows 11 in action

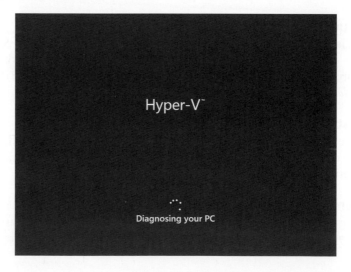

Startup Repair fixes almost any Windows boot problem (Windows can even start it automatically if it detects a boot problem). In fact, if you have a system with one hard drive containing a single partition with Windows installed, you'd have trouble finding something Startup Repair *couldn't* fix. Upon completion, Startup Repair will let you know whether it succeeded and where to find a log file called srttrail.txt that lists exactly what the program found, what it fixed, and what it failed to do. Its content may look cryptic, but you can type anything you find in this file into a search engine and easily find more information.

 EXAM TIP The CompTIA 1102 exam objectives have their own terms for referring to these WinRE procedures. They refer to System Restore as *restore*, Uninstall Updates as *roll back updates*, System Image Repair as *reimage*, and Startup Repair as *repair Windows*. Make sure you recognize these names for the exam!

Command Prompt

The nerdiest option in the WinRE menu is Command Prompt. The WinRE command prompt functions similarly to the regular cmd shell in Windows, covered in Chapter 15. WinRE's command prompt enables you to do some low-level rocket's surgery on your system in order to recover from thorny problems.

The WinRE command prompt contains utilities for repairing or modifying the low-level structure that points to the files your system needs to boot up (bootrec and bcdedit), utilities for working with your system's storage devices and file systems (diskpart, fsinfo, fsutil), and more. Luckily for you, the CompTIA A+ 1102 objectives cover many fewer of these utilities than previous versions of the CompTIA A+ objectives. Know that these tools are here in case you need them someday—but for now I'll focus on the only one you'll see on the exam: diskpart.

 NOTE The Startup Repair tool runs many of these command-prompt utilities automatically. You need to use the WinRE command prompt only for unique situations where the Startup Repair tool fails.

The *diskpart* utility is a fully featured partitioning tool. It lacks many of the safety features built into Disk Management (covered in Chapters 8 and 9), so proceed with caution. You can, for example, delete any partition of any type at any time. Starting diskpart opens a special command prompt as shown here:

```
C:\Windows\system32>diskpart
Microsoft DiskPart version 10.0.17134.345
Copyright (C) Microsoft Corporation.
On computer: MIKESPC
DISKPART>
```

You can list volumes (or partitions on basic disks):

```
DISKPART> list volume
  Volume ###  Ltr  Label      Fs     Type      Size     Status     Info
  ----------  ---  --------   -----  --------   -------  ---------  -------
  Volume 0    D                      DVD-ROM       0  B  No Media
  Volume 1    C    New Volume  NTFS   Partition  1397 GB  Healthy    System

DISKPART>
```

Select a volume to manipulate (you may also select an entire drive):

```
DISKPART> select volume 1
Volume 1 is the selected volume.
DISKPART>
```

You can run commands at the diskpart prompt to add, change, or delete volumes and partitions on drives, mount or dismount volumes, and even manipulate software-level RAID arrays. Use the **format** command to format a newly created volume.

Run the **clean** command at the diskpart prompt to wipe all partition and volume information off the currently selected disk. This tool handles nasty corruptions that simply won't let Windows boot and serves as my last-ditch step before I toss a drive.

UEFI Firmware Settings

Getting into system settings in UEFI-based motherboards can be a challenge. Although pressing the DELETE key repeatedly works sometimes, the opportunity flashes by very quickly. The UEFI Firmware Settings option enables you to access the system setup utility when you restart your computer via the Recovery option in Settings. Use the UEFI Firmware Settings option when you're tweaking things like CPU or RAM timings, or you want to change the boot order for some reason.

 EXAM TIP   CompTIA won't ask about the UEFI Firmware Settings option on the CompTIA A+ 1102 exam—but it *is* a helpful little option when you're already in WinRE.

Reset This PC

When less aggressive options (such as Startup Repair or System Restore) fail to get you back up and running, you may need to bite the bullet and reinstall Windows. Luckily, Microsoft makes this pretty easy—it's exactly what the *Reset this PC* option mentioned earlier in this section does. As a reminder, to access it from the main WinRE menu, click Troubleshoot and you'll find it listed with Advanced options (refer to Figure 16-3). Reset this PC has two suboptions with dramatically different outcomes:

- **Keep my files**   Reinstalls Windows but preserves your files and settings and any applications purchased from the Windows Store. Note well: this option *deletes every other application on your system.*

- **Remove everything**   Nukes your system—all apps, programs, user files, user settings—leaving you with a fresh installation of Windows. Use it as a last resort when troubleshooting a PC. And back up your data first.

EXAM TIP If you're wondering where Reset this PC *gets* this fresh copy of Windows, you're asking a *great* question. Back in Chapter 11 I mentioned that systems often keep a spare copy of the OS on a hidden *recovery partition*. That's exactly what Reset this PC is doing—using the copy hidden in the recovery partition to reinstall Windows. You might also see this referred to as a *repair installation* on the CompTIA A+ 1102 exam.

Rebuild Windows Profiles

Each user account on a Windows machine has an associated *user profile* that records settings such as Desktop preferences (like background and color), shortcuts, and other icons. A corrupt profile can block a user from logging in and getting access to his or her stuff. Corrupt profiles can also manifest as very slow profile load times. Anti-malware software can sometimes corrupt a profile, as can upgrading from one version of Windows to another. You have two options to rebuild a Windows profile: perform several direct Registry edits or create a new user account and copy the old profile settings to the new account.

The Registry edits are a little complex, so here are the steps. The first step is to get into Safe Mode (you'll find this in the WinRE Advanced options | Startup Settings discussed earlier). Once in Safe Mode, access an elevated command prompt. (Type **cmd** in the Search field, right-click the Command Prompt option, and select Run as administrator.) Type **regedit** and press ENTER to open the Registry Editor. Navigate to the following string to get to the screen shown in Figure 16-7:

```
HKEY_LOCAL_MACHINE\SOFTWARE\Microsoft\Windows NT\CurrentVersion\ProfileList
```

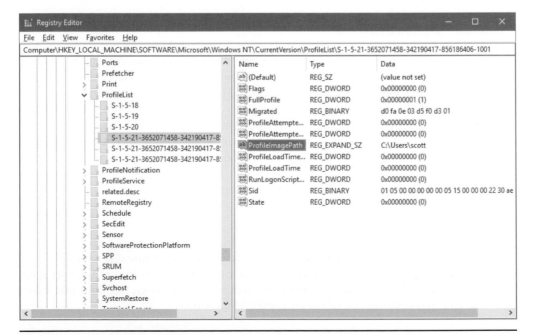

Figure 16-7 ProfileList in Registry

Click the ProfileList arrow on the left to see a set of entries that start with S-1-5. Select the one that matches the messed-up profile. Figure 16-7 shows a user named Scott (which you can barely make out in the ProfileImagePath on the right pane). At the bottom of the right pane, double-click the State entry, set the value to 0 (see Figure 16-8), and click OK.

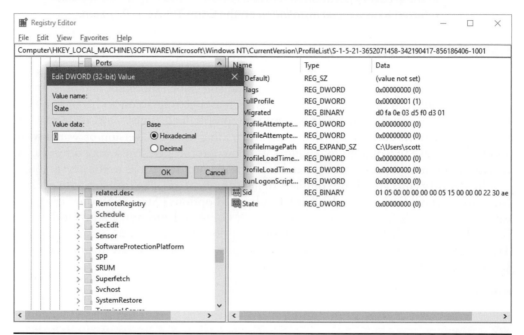

Figure 16-8   Setting the State to 0

Here's the last step. If you have an option for RefCount on the right, double-click it and set the value to 0. If you don't have that entry, create it: Edit | New | DWORD (32-bit) Value. Close the Registry Editor and reboot the computer. That profile should work.

If the profile doesn't work, then the next option is to create a new user account and essentially duplicate the earlier profile. Boot back into Safe Mode and open an elevated command prompt. You need an administrator account to create a new user, so that's what you're about to access. To activate the super-secret-hidden local administrator account, the command to use is *net user*. Type **net user** and press ENTER:

```
net user administrator /active:yes
```

Reboot the computer and log in as the local administrator you just activated. Create a new user account: Settings | Accounts | Other users | Add someone else to this PC (see Figure 16-9). Give the account a unique name. Go to the Users folder of the corrupted account and copy all the contents to the new account's Users folder, but do it one folder at a time to avoid copying any of the corrupted hidden files.

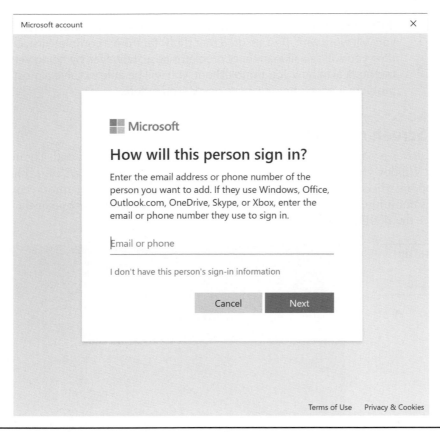

Figure 16-9   Creating a new user account in Windows 10

When you reboot the computer, you should be able to log on to the newly created account and access all the old/corrupt accounts files. Once *verified*, log back on as administrator, delete the corrupted account, and rename the new account to the same as the old account.

Both processes for recovering a corrupted user profile are clunky, but they work. Expect to see a question or two on this topic on the CompTIA A+ 1102 exam.

Troubleshooting Common Windows OS Symptoms

If you have used the same PC for any period of time, you know things will inevitably go wrong. An application might crash, the system drags along incredibly slowly, or it might present you with the dreaded BSoD! This is when most users reach for tech support. But we're not most users, we're techs! In this section, we are going to cover the most common symptoms that crop up when using Windows and how to troubleshoot them.

NOTE Remember that these are just some of the most common issues you will work with. Rest assured that this is far from a complete list. Over time you will see all manner of problems arise; however, by being very methodical in how you troubleshoot, you will be able to solve almost any problem—even ones you have never seen before.

Blue Screen of Death

Device driver problems that stop Windows from loading look pretty sad. Figure 16-10 shows a Windows Stop error, better known as the *Blue Screen of Death (BSoD)*. The BSoD only appears when something causes an error from which Windows cannot recover. The BSoD is not limited to device driver problems, but device drivers are one of the reasons you'll see the BSoD.

Figure 16-10
BSoD in
Windows 10

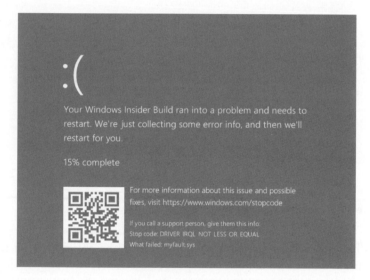

Whenever faced with a scenario where you get a BSoD, read what it says. Windows BSoDs tell you the name of the file that caused the problem and usually suggest a recommended action (aside from the automatic restart). Once in a while these are helpful.

BSoD problems due to device drivers almost always take place immediately after you've installed a new device and rebooted. Take out the device and reboot. If Windows loads properly, head over to the device manufacturer's Web site. A new device producing this type of problem is a serious issue that should have been caught before the device was released. In many cases, the manufacturer will have updated drivers available for download or will recommend a replacement device. If Windows doesn't load properly, try the Startup Repair procedure discussed earlier.

Sluggish Performance

One day you realize that your once blazingly fast computer now runs at snail's pace. What happened? Where did the almost instantaneous startup go? Why are you watching apps load up in minutes rather than in seconds?

Like humans, computers tend to accumulate clutter over time. By the time you notice it, it's usually already started to affect your computer's performance. One source of clutter is programs that start automatically when you boot the device and consume resources that you'd probably rather use for something else. We talked about controlling autostarting software in Chapter 14, and that's exactly the cure for this disease.

To stop these unwanted programs from wasting time and resources, bring up the Task Manger's Startup tab (see Figure 16-11) and review the enabled applications for any you don't need. This tab shows the publisher of the app, whether autostart is enabled or disabled, and even an estimate of how much resource impact the app has at startup. If you aren't sure what a program is, you can right-click it and either select Properties to open its Properties dialog box or select Search online to find more information on the Web. As a bonus, the Startup tab can also be a useful place to look if you suspect your system may have some malware, but we'll save that discussion for a little later.

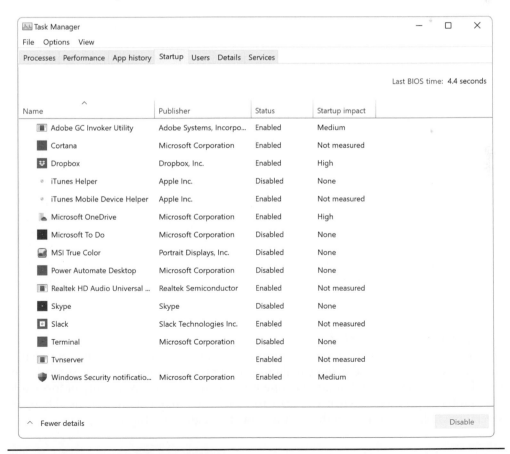

Figure 16-11   Startup tab in Task Manager

Once you've reviewed the list and decided which apps are essential to run at startup, it's time to get your computer back up to "ludicrous speed" where it belongs. It's as simple as right-clicking the app you want to disable and clicking Disable. Don't worry if you decide later that you want to use the app after all; you can always launch it normally from the Start menu or a desktop shortcut.

 NOTE There is always the possibility that a sluggish system is being slowed down by malware. If you can't find an obvious cause for the slowdown, it is a good idea to run a virus scan—just in case.

Boot Problems

Most failed-boot scenarios require you to determine where the fault occurred: with the hardware and configuration, or in Windows. Boot problems are pretty straightforward. Imagine that a user calls and says "My PC won't boot" or "My computer is dead." At this point, your best tools are knowledge of the boot process and asking lots of questions. Here are some I use regularly:

- "What displays on the screen—if anything—after you press the power button on the case?"
- "What do you hear—if anything—after you press the power button on the case?"
- "Is the PC plugged in?"
- "Do you smell anything weird?"

Hardware problems can give you a blank screen on boot-up, so you follow the tried-and-true troubleshooting methodology for hardware. Make sure everything is plugged in and turned on.

If the user says that the screen says "No boot device detected" and the system worked fine before, it *could* mean something as simple as the computer has attempted to boot to an incorrect device, such as to something other than the primary hard drive. This scenario happens all the time. Someone plugs a thumb drive into a USB port and the CMOS is configured to boot to removable media before hard drives—boom! "No boot device detected" error. The first few times it happened to me, I nearly took my machine apart before experiencing that head-slapping moment. I removed the thumb drive and then watched Windows boot normally.

Frequent Shutdowns

If you have used Windows for any amount of time, there is about a 99 percent chance that you have experienced a sudden shutdown. This can be extremely frustrating, not only because of lost time, but also because it poses the very real possibility of lost work. The problem gets worse when you start to experience frequent shutdowns. There are several possible causes, but on the software side there are three biggies.

Fast Startup

Windows has a feature called *fast startup* that, as the name implies, allows your computer to boot up quicker than normal. However, fast is not always better. One example of this has to do with drivers. If your system has a lot of drivers installed, fast startup may not give them all enough time or resources to boot properly and, as a result, they will crash. In turn, this will cause Windows to shut down at some random point thereafter. You can disable fast startup but you have to go through a bit of a maze to get there, so let's walk through it together.

In Windows 10, go to Settings | System | Power & sleep. Once you're in the Power & sleep menu, look for the Related settings section and click Additional power settings. In the Power Options window that opens, click *Choose what the power buttons do* on the left and then click *Change settings that are currently unavailable*. Under Shutdown settings, uncheck the Turn on fast startup (recommended) checkbox (see Figure 16-12) and then click the Save changes button to save your changes. See what I meant when I said it was a bit of a maze? That was a lot of different menus!

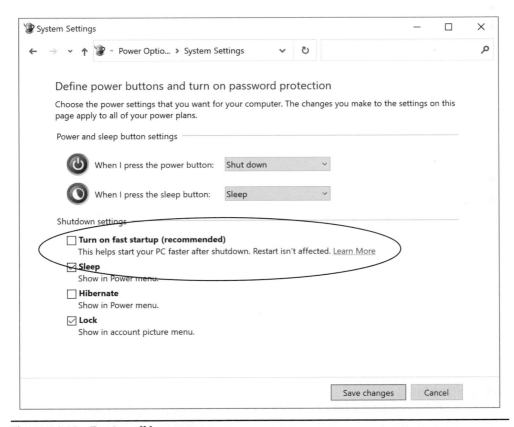

Figure 16-12   Turning off fast startup

Sleep Mode

Sleep mode is intended to save power when you are away from your computer. However, sometimes your computer might shut down instead of going to sleep. So, if you notice that Windows is shutting down while you are away from your computer, this is the likely culprit. When this is the case, you will want to disable sleep mode.

To do this in Windows 11, go to Settings | System | Power & battery. On this screen you will see two drop-down menus under Screen and sleep: *On battery power, PC goes to sleep after* and *When plugged in, PC goes to sleep after*. Set both menus to Never, as shown in Figure 16-13.

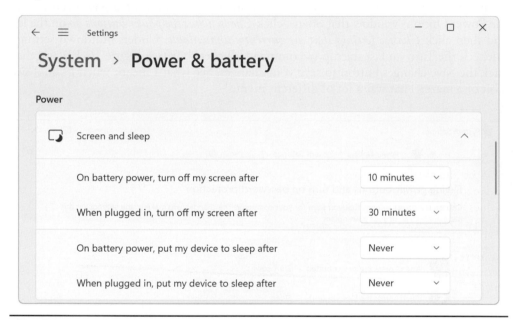

Figure 16-13 Setting sleep mode to Never

 EXAM TIP The CompTIA A+ 1102 exam objectives want you to know about something else you can do with these power options. *Choose what closing the lid does* enables you to configure a laptop to automatically shut down, sleep, hibernate—or even keep on running—when you close the lid. You might want to use different options if you use your laptop on the go rather than stationary on your desk all day.

Driver Problems

If neither of the previous solutions resolves the issue of frequent shutdowns, it is likely that you have an issue with a driver. Specifically, you may have a driver that needs updated or you have a driver that has become corrupted. Follow the same procedure you used for unruly drivers back in the "Blue Screen of Death" section.

Services Not Starting

Windows loads many services as it starts. In a scenario where a critical service fails to start, Windows informs you with an error message. The important word here is *critical*. Windows will not report *all* service failures at this point. If a service that is less than critical to Windows doesn't start, the OS usually waits until you try to use a program that needs that service before it prompts you with an error message (see Figure 16-14).

Figure 16-14
Service error

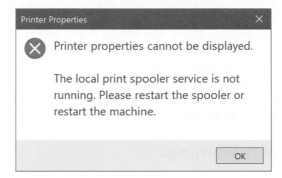

To work with your system's services, go to the Control Panel | Administrative Tools | Services and verify that the service you need is running. If not, restart the service. Also notice that each service has a Startup Type—Automatic, Manual, or Disabled—that defines when it starts. It's very common to find that a service has been set to Manual when it needs to be set to Automatic so that it starts when Windows boots (see Figure 16-15).

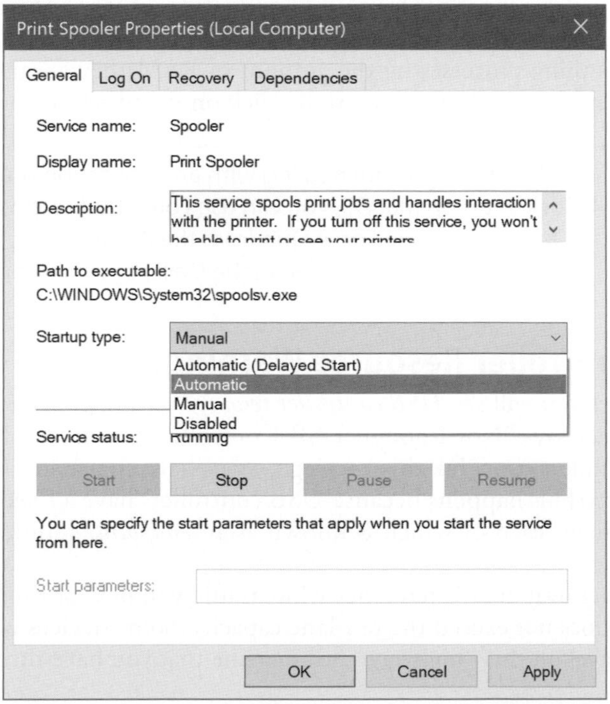

Figure 16-15
Autostarting a
service

Applications Crashing

Occasionally, an application gets released that isn't ready for prime time and bugs in the code cause the application or even the operating system to crash. I've seen this most often with games rushed to market near the winter holidays. The results of this rushed code can be pretty spectacular. You're right in the middle of a thrilling fight with the bad guy and then what happens? A crash to desktop (CTD).

Poorly written or buggy programs and device drivers can have awful effects on you and your clients. Some of the scenarios caused by such programs are the computer locking up or unexpectedly shutting down. The system might spontaneously shut down and restart. That kind of improper shutdown can cause problems—especially if a program was in the middle of editing an important file!

The problem here is that these crashes can also be caused by hardware. You've got to keep in mind all of these things as you approach troubleshooting a crash. Look out for more on hardware causes later in the chapter.

Low Memory Warnings

Imagine you are listening to music, writing a report in Word, and have a few dozen too many browser tabs open for research. All of the sudden you get a *low memory warning*, or more specifically, a message pops up that says "Your computer is low on memory."

Wait. How can that be? Is my RAM going bad? The answer is *usually* that the running programs are using nearly all of your system's available memory. So, what do you do? The easiest thing is to close tabs and applications that you don't need—but if an open program is suffering from a memory leak, you may have to reboot to get a fresh start.

There is also a more precise way of evaluating what is hogging your system's memory. Open the Processes tab in the Task Manager and click the Memory column head to arrange running processes by the amount of RAM they are using. If you locate an app that is using too much memory, right-click on it and select End task.

 EXAM TIP If you are dealing with an application that is hogging memory or locked up on macOS, you can use Force Quit to close it. You can access Force Quit by selecting Force Quit from the Apple menu, by holding the OPTION key and right-clicking the app in the Dock, or via the Activity Monitor app.

USB Controller Resource Warnings

Sometimes you will see *USB controller resource warnings*, or more specifically, a message pop up that says "Not Enough USB Controller Resources." Most of the time there is a very simple reason for this message—you have too many things plugged into your USB ports. This happens because USB controllers have a fixed number of communication channels, each of which is known as an *endpoint*. Think of endpoints as lanes on a highway.

On a highway that is ten lanes wide, traffic will flow normally as long as the amount of traffic does not exceed the ten-lane capacity. Some devices will require more than one lane to travel on this "highway." So, imagine that you have three pieces of hardware that each require four lanes and they are trying to run on the ten-lane highway—at this point you don't have enough USB controller resources.

To fix the problem, you will have to assess what devices you have connected and potentially disconnect some. If your system has a mix of USB versions, it may help to move some USB 3.0 devices to a USB 2.0 port or vice versa. If you have to choose, reserve the higher-version ports for high-bandwidth devices like storage drives or video interfaces.

System Instability

System instability is something of a catch-all term. Even in perfectly configured systems there will be occasional errors, but when those errors start to become more frequent and more diverse, we can say that the system is unstable. These types of errors can be occurring in the OS, apps, or various other places. Plus, the older a system gets, the more likely it is to experience stability issues.

It's easy enough to know if your own system is unstable by just paying careful attention to it. But how do you determine this if it's *not* your system? Fortunately, *Reliability Monitor* in Windows can give you a quick overview of how often the system locks up or crashes. To open it, go to the Control Panel | Security and Maintenance, click the Maintenance drop-down arrow, and click View reliability history. Reliability Monitor generates a report and displays it in the default Days view (see Figure 16-16). This lets you see all the errors that have occurred on each day over the last few weeks.

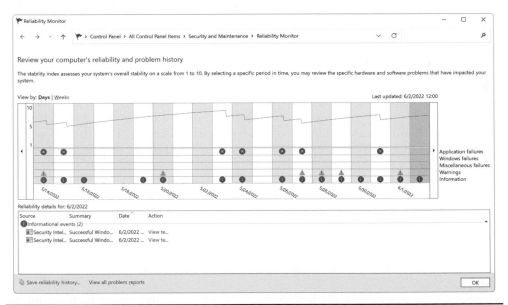

Figure 16-16   Reliability Monitor

As shown on the right side of Figure 16-16, the graph has several categories, including Application failures, Windows failures, Miscellaneous failures, Warnings, and Information. In addition to the types of errors, you will also be able to see when they are occurring and get additional information. In short, blue circle icons with an *i* are informational and not indicative of problems. A red circle icon with an × indicates where something bad went wrong. A yellow triangle icon with an ! denotes where a warning occurred. Therefore, when you see lots of recuring red and yellow icons, it's a clear indication that a system is potentially unstable. Checking Reliability Monitor isn't a perfect way gauge system stability, but it is a good place to keep tabs on the general health of your system and diagnose emerging problems.

No OS Found

The first time you see this error message, it will likely make you panic a little—I sure did! It's pretty unnerving to think that your OS and data might be gone, but the key is to remain calm and work through this systematically. Back in Chapter 14 we discussed the single best way to beat back this sense of dread: regularly back up your data and confirm that you can recover a working system from it. Having rock-solid confidence that you'll be able to recover whatever was on the system makes it way easier to focus on the problem.

Back in Chapter 5, we discussed how the system firmware (aka BIOS) looks for an OS to boot from. If it can't find one, then it displays an "Operating system not found" error. Some causes are relatively simple to resolve, like bad BIOS configurations, while others can be related to a dying or dead hard drive. Here are a few common tactics/steps that you can use to troubleshoot and fix the underlying problem.

First, verify whether you (or someone else) left any new removable media (such as a flash drive or optical disc) in the system. If so, see if the system boots correctly without it connected. If it boots right up, the system is trying to boot from removable media that isn't bootable. If it doesn't, you should reboot and enter the system setup utility to confirm that the hard drive containing your OS comes first in the *boot sequence* (which is also called the boot priority or boot order).

As a quick refresher, accessing the system setup utility varies from manufacturer to manufacturer. It usually requires pressing ESC, DEL, or one of the FN keys during the boot process. A quick search online should identify which key your PC uses. For more details on accessing the system setup utility and changing the boot sequence, refer back to Chapter 5.

 NOTE If your hard drive doesn't even show up in the system setup utility, make sure it's connected correctly. If that doesn't help, try resetting the system setup utility's settings to default. If you still don't see your hard drive, it's probably having hardware issues (which will require an entirely different type of troubleshooting and potentially expert repair).

If the correct drive is already first in the boot sequence, the master boot record we talked about back in Chapter 9 may be corrupt and need to be rebuilt. First, boot to a Windows recovery drive (or installation media) and navigate to the System Recovery Options that you read about earlier in this chapter in the "Recovering When Windows Breaks" section. From here, you have two options: the *easy* way and the *quick* way.

The easy way is to just launch the Startup Repair utility and go do something else while it runs. I recommended the easy way, but if you're feeling impatient, you can do this a little faster if you're willing to roll up your sleeves and learn the bootrec and bcdedit commands. I'm not going to go into detail here because you won't see these commands on the CompTIA A+ 1102 exam.

Slow Profile Load

As I discussed earlier in the "Rebuild Windows Profiles" section, user profiles are a very useful part of Windows, but they can start to load slowly (or not at all) if they get corrupted. This can be a drag on its own, but combine it with some of the causes of sluggish performance we dealt with earlier in the chapter, and it becomes a real nuisance.

Earlier, in the "Frequent Shutdowns" section, we discussed how sometimes Fast startup can cause problems because there are too many processes trying to start at once. That is also a possibility here, so first disable Fast startup if it's enabled and see if this makes any difference in load time.

Another possibility is that there is too much stuff on your desktop. We have all been there—it is easy to create a new file and place the copy on your desktop, swearing that you will put it in the proper folder later. However, later never seems to come and the next thing you know you have a few gigs of data on your desktop. Try temporarily moving these files into a folder that isn't on your desktop to see if it helps.

If none of these did the trick, it's time to turn to the procedure that I laid out in the "Rebuild Windows Profiles" section earlier in the chapter.

Time Drift

A lot of people who haven't looked under the hood take the concept of "time" for granted. If you've ever noticed the time on something like a wall or stove clock drifting slowly out of step with the time your cellphone shows, you've brushed up against a fundamental truth: all clocks drift apart, and the best we can do is resynchronize them occasionally.

The clock inside every computer is subject to *time drift* (also known as clock drift) and slowly diverges from the actual time (and may do so more rapidly when the system works hard). Since many applications are dependent on precise time measurements, time drift can cause applications to not start, crash, or perform poorly. Because security protocols frequently use keys that expire after a certain amount of time, it can also cause security and login problems.

To keep their clocks mostly right, modern operating systems regularly (once a week for Windows) synchronize with time servers that exist just for this purpose. Microsoft has set up its own at time.windows.com. As long as time drift isn't causing trouble, it's usually okay to ignore it between syncs. If you have systems suffering enough time drift to cause problems—or you notice that the gap continues to grow—there are a few things to consider.

If the systems are continuing to drift beyond a week, they may not be configured (or able) to communicate with the time server. The easy way to check this is to open the Time & Language category in the Settings app, ensure that *Set time automatically* is enabled, and click *Sync now* to see if the process completes. If it can't reach the time server, it'll show a spinner for a few minutes and then a "Time synchronization failed" message (as shown in Figure 16-17); this likely indicates that the system is offline or network settings need adjustment (which we'll discuss in detail in Chapters 18 through 21).

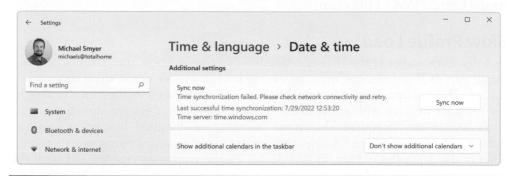

Figure 16-17   A failed time synchronization

If the time synchronizes just fine but the system keeps experiencing time-related problems, it may be a hardware issue (see the upcoming "Inaccurate System Date/Time" section).

   EXAM TIP   I don't think CompTIA will expect you to be able to troubleshoot network-related time synchronization failures on the A+ 1102 exam. *If* they did, the right answers probably involve ensuring the system is using a well-known time server (like time.windows.com) or using the ping command to verify that the time server is reachable. Keep an eye out for ping in Chapters 18–21.

1101

Troubleshooting Problems Related to Motherboard, CPU, RAM, and Power

So far in this chapter, we have discussed problems related to the OS and applications from a software perspective. Unfortunately, trouble with the hardware in your system can cause many of the same symptoms—and to be a good troubleshooter, you need to be able to recognize when you can and can't rule out hardware problems.

In the early chapters of this book, we discussed how computers are built and how each component plays a critical role in maintaining the overall health of the system. We covered CPUs in Chapter 3, RAM in Chapter 4, motherboards in Chapter 6, and power supplies in Chapter 7. Each chapter included a "Troubleshooting" section in which I called out common symptoms and problems related to the component covered in that chapter. For easy review, I want to close out this chapter by taking a moment to sweep up several hardware problems related to motherboards, CPUs, RAM, and power that you'll need to recognize for the 1101 exam.

Power-On Self-Test

As we discussed in Chapter 5, when you start your PC, it runs through the *power-on self-test (POST)* that checks your computer's hardware to make sure everything is working correctly before booting the OS. If the computer passes the POST, you will mostly likely hear a single beep and then Windows will start booting. If a component fails the POST, you will either hear a beep code (a sequence of beeps) or, on some of the more recent motherboards, see the power light or internal LED blinking. Check your motherboard's manual for details on what the beep codes, also known as POST codes, mean for your PC and then start troubleshooting the problem component.

Proprietary Crash Screens

In the first part of this chapter, we discussed the BSoD from a software perspective, with an emphasis on bad drivers or applications. However, a BSoD that occurs during the initial boot sequence could also be caused by bad hardware, with drivers being a leading culprit. As was the case with software, be systematic in testing components, removing only one at a time, starting with any that were recently installed. macOS systems display a spinning pinwheel (also called a beachball) to indicate an issue.

 EXAM TIP The CompTIA A+ 1101 exam objectives list this symptom as *proprietary crash screens (blue screen of death [BSOD]/pinwheel)*. Be prepared to see all three of these terms together, or to know that they're all associated if you see them separately!

Black Screen

Though it is far from the worst thing that could go wrong, a black (or blank) screen can be extremely frustrating because it provides absolutely no information suggesting what the problem might be. So, if your computer is powered on but you are seeing a black screen, where do you start?

 EXAM TIP We'll take a much closer look at all kinds of hardware- and software-related display and graphics troubleshooting issues in Chapter 17. In this section, I'll keep the focus on basic hardware issues pertaining to your motherboard, RAM, CPU, and power.

If the computer was running fine earlier and the screen has suddenly gone black, confirm that the monitor is plugged in, turned on, and properly connected to your computer. These may seem like no-brainer checks, but modern video cables don't have screw mounts like the old ones—a pet or a user with restless legs can easily knock one loose.

If it's not the monitor, see if it comes back on after a reboot. If so, leave it alone until it happens regularly. A one-time occurrence could be the computer's fault, but it can also be caused by something like a power fluctuation. It's annoying, but it's worse to spend tons of time troubleshooting and fiddling with options, think you've fixed it, only to be confused when it happens few months later during a bad storm.

If the cables seem fine and the monitor is powered on, connecting it to a different system is a quick way to sort out whether the display or the computer is to blame. It's also worth trying a different set of known-good cables in case those are the problem. If it's the cables, replace them. If it's the display, stay tuned for more display-specific troubleshooting in Chapter 17.

When it seems like the computer is the problem, a black screen usually indicates that some hardware is misconfigured, misconnected, or not working. If you are hearing or seeing any of the POST codes discussed earlier, follow the procedure for troubleshooting POST codes.

If you *don't* hear or see a POST code but you've been tinkering inside your case lately, ensure any components you touched are properly connected. If you added a component, see if the display comes on without it. Booting a system with the RAM mis-seated (or with no RAM at all), for example, can cause the computer to power on, issue no POST codes, but never boot up.

We'll talk more about the difference between integrated and dedicated graphics in Chapter 17, but one more common issue arises when you're trying to use a video connector on the motherboard but the integrated graphics are disabled in the system setup. In this case, consult your motherboard manual and perform a CMOS reset (this will restore the default settings, which should have the integrated graphics enabled).

No Power

You press the power button and nothing happens. What do you do now? First, make sure that that wall socket is getting electricity, your computer is plugged in, surge suppressors are turned to the on position, and the power cord is properly plugged in to the computer.

Next, open your system and verify that the CPU and motherboard cables are connected. If all of these things are hooked up correctly and nothing happens when you press the power button, look for indicator lights on the motherboard. If you don't see anything, then you likely have a bad power supply.

If you do see indicator lights on the motherboard, things get a little more complicated. However, you should move on to checking that your front-panel button is connected properly. Look inside your case near the front panel for a small bundle of wires that connects to your motherboard to enable the power button, front USB ports, and any number of other ports and features your specific case may have. The connector typically has two rows of pins and is encased in a plastic box. Remove the side panel on your computer and make sure the cable is tightly connected.

If your system starts but fails to boot, refer to the previous section on POST. If nothing happens, you likely have additional hardware issues and may need to take a closer look at the hardware.

Sluggish Performance

In the first part of this chapter, we discussed how preventing apps from running at startup can improve performance. Unfortunately, just about every component in a computer can fail suddenly or fail slowly—and slowly failing components often cause performance or stability problems.

 NOTE   In this section I'm assuming that you've already followed the steps for troubleshooting software-related sluggishness. This includes adding resources such as additional RAM or a newer CPU if the system isn't meeting your needs. In the real world, you'll be simultaneously considering software and hardware causes of sluggishness.

If the sluggishness started after you installed new hardware, disconnect the new device and uninstall the associated driver. If your system speeds up, you have found the cause. The manufacturer's Web site may provide a new driver or another workaround so that you can go on happily using their product.

If you haven't changed anything and the sluggishness is new, you'll want to check up on your existing components. Since overheating can cause sluggish performance, a good place to start is by following the recommendations in the next section, "Overheating." Beyond heat issues, you need to see if individual components are failing.

I like to keep in stock some spare known-good components like RAM modules, CPUs, hard drives, and motherboards for both emergency repairs and troubleshooting unexplained performance problems. I also keep a spare working system to swap the components into. Work one component at a time. I like to start with the RAM because it's easiest—but go with your gut after that.

 TIP   If you want to make an investment in your own future sanity, pick out one or more computer performance benchmark suites, occasionally run them on your systems, and keep a copy of the results. It's a bit of extra work, but having a few snapshots of how the device used to perform can enable you to diagnose a failing component by just rerunning the benchmark suite and comparing the results.

Overheating

If your computer starts freezing up, randomly shutting down or restarting, making strange noises, or displaying strange graphical glitches, and you can feel heat radiating off of it, you are probably dealing with *overheating*. When a computer starts to overheat, ensure it is well ventilated. Check that all the vents are clear and not blocked by pet hair or other obstructions. (May you never see the matted mess that cat hair can make of a computer's vents and heatsinks!)

Make sure you're grounded, as discussed in Chapter 1, and open the computer to give it a good cleaning. Dust and hair building up over the years can form a component-smothering blanket. Use a can of compressed air to give the system a good cleaning, paying particular attention to areas around the vents, fan, and power supply.

Once all the vents and fans are clean and clear and the system has had a good cleaning, ensure that there aren't other sources of heat near the system.

 NOTE Consider using compressed air on a particularly dusty computer only if you are outside or in a well-ventilated area that will be easy to clean up afterward.

If a good dusting doesn't help, check the fans (not just your case fans—but also any on components inside). Over time, fans can begin to run slowly and seize up. An easy way to tell if your fan is bad is to unplug it and spin it with your finger. If it stops suddenly or slows down too quickly, you likely need a new one. Other signs are if the fan makes any strange noise, visibly wobbles, or obviously runs slower than other fans in the case. The good news is that fans are cheap.

If the system is running hot, you should also notice the fans spinning faster as it warms. Listen closely when you're gaming or doing other processing-intensive tasks; can you hear the fans spin up and get louder? If not, make sure the system setup utility is set to ramp up fan speeds when things start to get hot.

Once you've made sure that the PC is clean and the fans are spinning and installed correctly, it's a good idea to keep an eye on the actual temperature of the CPU and GPU (these generate a lot of heat and are most likely to be damaged by overheating). You can usually check the CPU temp in the system setup utility, but you can't really do this while you're playing a game or editing a movie. There are many free utilities you can use to keep an eye on the CPU and GPU temps when performing processing-intensive tasks. One of my favorites is HWiNFO64.

Burning Smell

When overheating reaches a critical stage, you may notice a burning smell. It may remind you of an electrical fire, melting plastic, some combination of the two, or another "hot" smell. Regardless, your nose will tell you when something is on fire. This can be a symptom of both extreme overheating and a sudden electrical failure.

If you're in the room when this happens, disconnect the system from power ASAP and observe it for long enough to know whether opening the case is safe. Don't open it if it's actively smoking (and get your handy-dandy Class C fire extinguisher ready).

 NOTE This is, in my mind, where cases with one or more big windows are worth whatever they cost. It's hard to put a price on being able to quickly confirm whether there's an active fire!

Once you're sure nothing is on fire, open the case to investigate (but be careful—accumulated dust or a critically overheated component could catch fire when exposed to the inflow of oxygen). Move your hand around the components without touching them to identify any hot spots (focus on the CPU, GPU, and anything else with a fan). If nothing feels unusually hot, see if you can sniff out where the offending smell is coming from.

If there was smoke but neither of these steps locates a source, you need to visually inspect any dust for signs of burning, dust the computer out, break it down, and visually inspect every component for scorch marks (often around connectors and capacitors). You do *not* want to try to boot up a computer with electrical damage, so I recommend treating everything in the computer as a loss unless you can locate an obvious cause of the smoke.

Frequent Shutdowns

Earlier in this chapter we looked at several software issues that can cause frequent shutdowns, but hardware issues can cause the same problem. Rule out the easy things first. If a system starts to overheat, it *should* thermal throttle or even shut itself down to avoid damage or fire. These measures might not be enough, so it's still a good idea to check for overheating.

Since most systems will automatically reboot after they encounter a proprietary crash screen such as a BSoD, it's a good idea to investigate whether these crashes are at fault. Shutdowns can also be a side-effect of instability caused by problems in the motherboard firmware. If random or frequent reboots have always been a problem, or they start right after a firmware update, look for a newer version or flash the firmware you were using previously. (For more on this process, refer to "Flashing the ROM" in Chapter 5.)

Just like sluggish performance, frequent shutdowns can also be a sign of slowly failing hardware, so the recommendations in the "Sluggish Performance" section may help identify a troublesome component.

If none of the previously described items are the cause of frequent shutdowns, check all connections to make sure there is not a short or loose connector. Finally, dust and corrosion can wreak havoc long before that. Dust or corrosion in motherboard slots (mainly RAM and PCIe) or on the component pins themselves can also cause flaky connections and occasional shutdowns. This is where careful cleaning comes in. Depending on the contaminant, the cleaning tool of choice might be compressed air and a microfiber cloth, a cotton swap with a dab of isopropyl alcohol on it, or even a pencil eraser (it can help clean the gold-plated contacts, but I always treat this as a last recourse).

Application Crashes

We looked at software issues that can cause application crashes earlier in the chapter, but hardware issues can cause the same problem. Suppose you're playing a graphically intensive game, when the screen and Windows both lock up. As we saw earlier, the program might just be buggy, but it could also be the case that the video card is slowly failing and throws a fit when you push it too hard. It could be that the system accessed a section of RAM that has gone bad.

You've already confirmed that software isn't causing the problem, so you should rule out problems like overheating and loose connectors. If the problem is happening regularly, the best way to figure out which component is causing the problem is to swap them out one by one with a known good component until the problem goes away.

Grinding Noise

You turn on your computer and you hear a grinding noise. Nothing strikes fear in the heart of both car and computer owners like unexpected metallic grinding noises. Luckily, there are only two things in modern computers that make this type of noise: fans and traditional magnetic hard drives.

If you have only solid-state drives, then you immediately know it is a fan—you don't have to worry about a catastrophic loss of data. If you have a traditional magnetic hard drive or more than one fan, you'll need to open the case and listen carefully to identify where the grinding is coming from. It can also help to place a finger on the outside of a hard drive or fan to feel for vibrations.

In both cases, the result is the same: the component is on its way out and you should promptly replace it.

 NOTE If it's the hard drive, you'll also need to consider its data. When was the last backup? What might you lose if you replace the drive now? If there is critical data on the drive that you don't have backed up, shut off the computer until you're ready to back up the drive. (A hard drive making this noise might last for months—or minutes.) If it's a boot drive, I'd attach it to another system to perform the backup. It could fail at any time, and the extra stress of booting the OS from it isn't worth the risk!

Capacitor Swelling

In the world of motherboards, a *capacitor* is a tiny electrical component that helps regulate the voltage going to other components, like video cards and hard drives, to prevent power spikes from damaging them. Age, overcurrent, and design or manufacturing defects can all cause capacitors to bulge (usually at the top)—and the CompTIA A+ 1101 exam objectives refer to this as *capacitor swelling*. Capacitors can even split open and leak some of the chemicals inside.

As part of routine cleaning, you should examine capacitors on the motherboard for bulges. If you see any, it is time to either replace the motherboard or send it off for service. (You can technically replace a capacitor yourself if you're comfortable with a soldering gun—but that's well beyond what you'll need to know for the CompTIA A+ 1101 exam!)

 NOTE Since we usually don't peek inside smaller devices such as laptops and cellphones, it's good to keep an eye out for bumps or bulges in the case of these devices. It might be swollen capacitors—but the lithium batteries contained within our laptops and phones can also swell (and potentially burst into flames). We will go over that specific problem in Chapter 23.

Inaccurate System Date/Time

Small discrepancies between the time your computer and other devices report usually come down to time drift, covered earlier in this chapter, but *large* discrepancies (months or even *years*) tend to have a completely different cause: the CMOS battery.

As we discussed back in Chapter 5, the CMOS battery powers the storage for a number of values—including the time—while the system is completely off. Refer back to the procedure in the "Losing CMOS RTC Settings" section in Chapter 5 for more details on how to replace the CMOS battery.

Chapter Review

Questions

1. Which utility is useful in identifying a program that is hogging the processor?

   A. Task Manager

   B. Device Manager

   C. System Monitor

   D. System Information

2. Which Windows utility uses points in time that allow you to return your system to a previous date and state?

   A. System Configuration utility

   B. Snapshot Manager

   C. System Restore

   D. Restart Services

3. Andre's Windows 10 computer is taking longer to boot up than it did when he first got it. Which of the following options is the easiest way to speed up his sluggish boot time?

   A. Disable unnecessary startup programs

   B. Rebuild the master boot record

   C. Do a system restore

   D. Upgrade the fans

4. What is the name of the Windows utility that displays a graph with several categories including Application failures, Windows failures, Misc. failures, and Warnings and a timeline of when they occurred?

   A. System File Checker

   B. POST

   C. Reliability Monitor

   D. Time Drift

5. Errors in the BIOS configuration, a faulty hard drive, or a damaged master boot record can cause which type of error?

   A. Operating system not found

   B. Low memory

   C. System instability

   D. Verify requirements

6. Which of the following WinRE options is the least disruptive method to repair a damaged master boot record in a Windows PC?

   A. System Restore

   B. Startup Repair

   C. Reset this PC

   D. System Image Recovery

7. Which of the following can cause a computer to lock up or unexpectedly shut down? (Select two.)

   A. Bad RAM

   B. Poorly written application

   C. Windows Installer

   D. Windows remote shutdown

8. Which of the following can cause a user profile to load slowly? (Select two.)

   A. A corrupt profile

   B. Large amounts of data saved to the desktop

   C. Too many user accounts created on one system

   D. A desktop background image that is too large

9. When applications are released too early and are poorly written with error-prone code or buggy programs, you are likely to experience _____.

   A. Burning smells

   B. Boot problems

   C. Applications crashing

   D. Capacitor swelling

10. Melissa is using too many items inserted into her computer's USB ports and has received a USB controller resource warning message on her screen to let her know. Why is this happening?

   A. Her USBs are not compatible with her computer.

   B. There is a virus on one of her USBs.

   C. USB controllers have a set number of endpoints.

   D. USB controllers have a set number of resources.

Answers

1. **A.** The Task Manager utility is useful in identifying a program that is hogging the processor.

2. **C.** The System Restore utility uses points in time that allow you to return your system to a previous date and state.

3. **A.** Andre's best option would be to disable unnecessary startup programs. A system restore might help speed up his boot times, but it'll be much slower and more disruptive than disabling startup programs.

4. **C.** The Reliability Monitor utility displays a graph with several categories including Application failures, Windows failures, Misc. failures, and Warnings and a timeline of when they occurred.

5. **A.** Errors in the BIOS configuration, a faulty hard drive, or a damaged MBR can cause the error message "Operating system not found."

6. **B.** Startup Repair attempts to repair any damage to the MBR along with other boot-related fixes. Unlike the other options, it only attempts to fix boot problems.

7. **A, B.** Bad RAM and poorly written applications can cause a computer to lock up or unexpectedly shut down.

8. **A, B.** A corrupt profile and large data files saved to the desktop can slow down the user profile loading process.

9. **C.** When applications are released too early and are poorly written with error-prone code or buggy programs, you are likely to experience applications crashing.

10. **C.** She is receiving the USB controller resource warning message on her screen because she is using too many of her USB ports. USB controllers have a set number of endpoints.

Answers

Display Technologies

In this chapter, you will learn how to
- Summarize different display technologies
- Understand how computers display and capture video
- Install and configure video
- Troubleshoot basic video problems

The term *video* encompasses a complex interaction among numerous parts of personal computing devices, all designed to put a picture on the screen. The monitor or video display shows you what's going on with your programs and operating system. It's the primary output device for most devices. The *display adapter* handles communication between the CPU and the monitor or display (see Figure 17-1). The operating system needs to know how to handle communication between the CPU and the display adapter, which requires installing drivers specific to each card.

All of these components fall into the category of *display technologies*. This chapter explores monitors, video displays, and display adapters, discusses how to troubleshoot a variety of display issues, and closes with a look at some topics you won't find on the exam—including a review of the display qualities and features you should know in order to understand and compare product listings.

Figure 17-1
Typical monitor and video card

1101

Video Displays

Video displays for computing devices come in three varieties: flat-panel displays, projectors, and virtual reality headsets. Almost every modern personal computer uses a flat-panel display, and there's a pair of similar display panels mounted inside serious virtual reality headsets. You'll find projectors in boardrooms and classrooms, splashing a picture onto a screen. This section explores the technology variations in video displays and describes the connection options.

Flat-Panel Displays

Almost every computing device today uses some sort of flat-panel display as the primary visual output component. Because standalone monitors don't have to be replaced along with the rest of the computer, it's good to keep in mind that there are always some pretty old displays still in service.

The industry is *always* hard at work to create displays that are thinner, faster, prettier, and more efficient, but the biggest leaps usually come after an innovative new display technology is finally good enough or cheap enough to dominate the market. Once we hit that tipping point, things can change quickly! This also means we can see exciting headlines about new display technologies for years—decades, even—without them ever becoming common in desktop monitors.

When the first desktop computers stole our hearts, they did it despite bulky, heavy monitors with tiny (by modern standards) *cathode-ray tube (CRT)* displays—the same technology used in TVs at the time. CRTs ruled our desktops for decades—from the 1970s up through the early 2000s—when flat-panel displays dethroned them (a little over a decade after the first models appeared).

The early flat-panel displays incorporated a *liquid crystal display (LCD)* panel—and LCD monitors still hold the crown despite a healthy challenge from *organic light-emitting diode (OLED)* panels. Let's take a closer look at both of these panel technologies.

NOTE See the "MicroLED" discussion in Beyond A+ for a look at a potential competitor to LCD and OLED. We'll also revisit OLED in Chapter 24 in the context of mobile devices.

LCD Panels

A color LCD screen is composed of tiny liquid crystal molecules (called *sub-pixels*) arranged in rows and columns between polarizing filters. When electric current is applied to the liquid crystal molecules, they act as a shutter to enable light to pass through. A translucent sheet above the sub-pixels is colored red, green, or blue. Each tiny distinct group of three sub-pixels—one red, one green, and one blue—forms a physical *pixel*, as shown in Figure 17-2.

Figure 17-2
LCD pixels

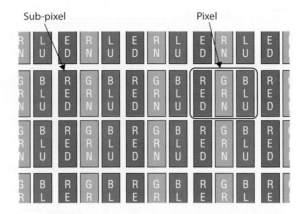

Current LCD monitors use some form of *thin film transistor (TFT)* or *active matrix* technology (see Figure 17-3) with one or more tiny transistors to control each color dot, providing faster picture display, crisp definition, and much tighter color control than the earliest LCD panels could provide.

Figure 17-3
Active matrix
display

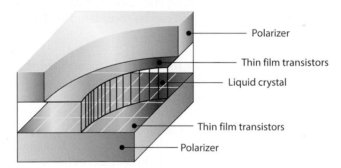

The typical LCD monitor is composed of two main components: an *LCD panel* to create the image, and a *backlight* to illuminate the image so you can see it. Some older models need *inverters* to send power to backlights that require alternating current (AC) electricity. Figure 17-4 shows a typical layout for the internal components of an older LCD monitor.

LCD Panel Technologies   LCD panel manufacturers use a lot of variation in things like the orientation of the liquid crystal molecules within the glass substrates and the underlying electronics to try to create displays that respond quickly to user demands and show accurate color and details. The three most common panel types today are *twisted nematic (TN)*, *in-plane switching (IPS)*, and *vertical alignment (VA)*.

Technically, TN panels are the fastest but offer adequate color; IPS panels display beautiful color at slower speeds; and VA panels fall somewhere in between the two in terms of responsiveness and color accuracy. In reality, the steady march of technological improvement has left us with IPS displays that are fast *enough* for most purposes.

Figure 17-4
LCD components

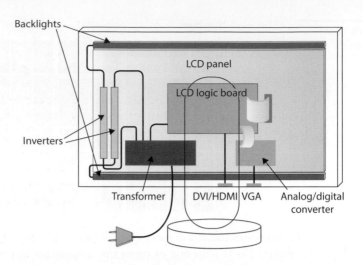

NOTE Samsung offers a proprietary version of IPS called *Plane to Line Switching (PLS)*. Samsung claims PLS is better, naturally, though it functions very similarly to IPS and can be considered an IPS variation.

Backlights   Backlights light up the panel, as mentioned, but vary according to the technology used and the implementation of the lighting. Current LCDs use *light-emitting diode (LED)* technology for backlights; early generations used cold cathode fluorescent lamp (CCFL). These modern monitors are marketed as *LED displays* to differentiate them from the older CCFL panels. LEDs took over from CCFLs because LEDs use DC electricity (just like the logic boards and panels in LCDs), consume much less electricity, and give off little heat. LEDs enable super thin screens like you see on almost every computing device today, from smartphones to tablets to desktop monitors. Figure 17-5 shows an illustration of a typical modern LCD (note the inverters missing from the previous figure).

Figure 17-5
Modern LCD
internals

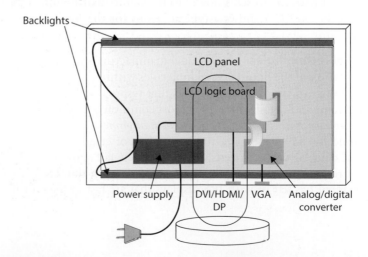

The LCD illustrated in Figure 17-5 has two backlights: one at the top and one at the bottom. That's a typical implementation for backlights, called *edge LED backlighting*. The drawback is that you can sometimes see that the edges are a little brighter than the center.

Direct LED backlighting puts a bank of LEDs behind the panel, providing better uniformity of image. This is more expensive and uses more electricity than edge backlighting, but it's becoming more common on higher-end LCD televisions and filtering into computer monitors as well.

NOTE You'll find a variety of improvements to direct LED backlighting technologies in real displays (none of which are included in the exam objectives). Mini LED, for example, uses smaller LEDs to better control how the display is lit. Quantum dots (QD) are also sometimes used to improve the overall color accuracy and brightness of the display.

OLED Panels

OLED screens use organic compounds between the glass layers that light up when given an electrical charge. Since they emit their own light, they don't require backlight—and this makes them perfect for ultra-thin, energy-efficient displays. OLED pixels can turn off completely, enabling pure black and thus phenomenal contrast compared with LCD panels.

OLED is generally more expensive than LCD, so much of its success has been limited to a small number of niches. Since OLED first started appearing in teeny-tiny displays in the early 2000s, it has built up three niches where it is most competitive: high-end televisions, viewfinders for mirrorless interchangeable lens cameras, and small mobile/wearable devices (including smart watches, smartphones, and virtual reality headsets).

After a few false starts, OLED panels finally started turning up in a growing number of laptops and desktop monitors in the late 2010s and early 2020s. There's a decent chance you'll need to support users with OLED displays, but the continued evolution of LCD technology makes me skeptical that OLED will ever wear the crown.

NOTE OLED displays have created an exciting learning opportunity for early adopters (and those using massive OLED TVs as monitors) who missed tough lessons we learned with older CRT and plasma displays. Much like these earlier technologies, OLED panels have image retention problems that are exacerbated by using them as computer monitors. We'll take a closer look at these image retention issues in the "Troubleshooting Monitors" section.

Projectors

Projectors generate an image in one device and then use light to throw (or project) it onto a screen or some other object. You'll mostly encounter *front-view* projectors, which shoot an image out the front and count on you to place a screen in front at the proper distance.

Front-view projectors connected to PCs running Microsoft PowerPoint have been the cornerstone of every meeting almost everywhere since the 1990s (see Figure 17-6). This section deals exclusively with front-view projectors that connect to PCs.

Figure 17-6
Front-view
projector
(photo courtesy
of Dell Inc.)

Much like monitors, projector technologies evolve over time. Their two main needs are also similar: generating an image, and generating enough light to project the image onto distant objects. I'll give you a quick overview of the most-common image technologies, and then we'll focus a little more closely on three things you should understand about the process of generating and projecting tons of light: lumens, throw, and light sources.

Image Technologies

It may sound like the exciting part of the process, but most modern projectors generate the image in one of two ways, and you're already pretty familiar with one of them by now! Given that light shines through an LCD panel, LCD projectors (see Figure 17-7) are a natural fit for front projection. Just like their monitor equivalent, LCD projectors have a specific native resolution.

Figure 17-7
LCD projector
(photo courtesy
of ViewSonic)

The other main option, proprietary *Digital Light Processing (DLP)* technology from Texas Instruments, uses an array of tiny mirrors to project a front-view image. The technology differs substantially from LCD. DLP projectors produce better color and a softer image than LCD. DLP projectors also tend to weigh less than LCD projectors.

Lumens

The brightness of a projector is expressed in *lumens*, a measure of the amount of visible light given off by a light source. A higher number of lumens means a brighter projector, but the "right" lumen rating depends on the size of the room and how dark it will be when the projector is in use. There's no single answer, but use this as a rough guide:

If you use a projector in a small, dark room, 1000 to 1500 lumens will work well. If you use a projector in a mid-sized room with typical lighting, you'll need at least 2000 lumens. Projectors for large rooms have ratings over 10,000 lumens and are very expensive.

Throw

A projector's *throw* indicates the size of the image at a certain distance from the screen. All projectors have a recommended minimum and maximum throw distance that you need to take into consideration. Throw is expressed in terms of the distance between a video projector lens and the screen on which it shines. For example, for an 80-inch diagonal screen, a standard-throw projector needs to be 132–144 inches feet away from the projection surface. A short-throw projector needs just 48 inches, and an ultra-short-throw projector needs a mere 15 inches away (although such a lens is expensive). Figure 17-8 illustrates the different throw distances.

Figure 17-8
Projector throw
variations

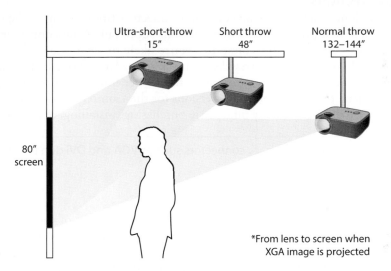

Light Sources

Most projectors use one of three light sources: powerful light bulbs, LEDs, or lasers.

Lamps—light bulbs that produce a lot of lumens in a small form factor—have been the standard for a long time. They're also the bane of traditional projectors. They produce tons of heat, have to warm up before you can use them, need a noisy fan to cool them off both while the projector runs and after you turn it off, and only last about 3000 hours. Replacement lamps are also expensive, usually in the range of a few hundred dollars (U.S.).

LED-based projectors don't generate as much heat, so their fans are smaller and quieter. LED projectors used to cost more than lamp-based ones, but that price difference has narrowed. They haven't historically offered nearly as many lumens (they typically require a much darker room), but they have also narrowed this gap over the years. LED light sources also have long lifespans of 30,000+ hours.

Laser-based projectors produce vibrant, high-contrast images. Laser-based projectors are currently more expensive than competing technologies, but the price is coming down, and laser light source can last 20,000+ hours.

TIP You may also see LED and laser-based light sources referred to as *light engines*, light modules, or similar. Since they don't need a long warm-up time, projectors with these light sources are ready to work more or less instantly. The light source may or may not be replaceable.

Common Display Features

All standalone video displays share characteristics that you need to know for purchase, installation, maintenance, and troubleshooting. They vary in connection types, on-screen controls for adjustments, mounting brackets, and additional features such as built-in USB hubs, webcams, speakers, and microphones.

Connections

Standalone displays have one or more connectors (most often on the back) for connecting them to a video source. I want to zoom out to talk about connector *versions*, and then I'll show you each of the connectors you're likely to see in the wild.

Much like USB, modern video connector standards (HDMI, DisplayPort, and Thunderbolt) are occasionally updated with new versions as the technology improves. You don't need to know about these versions for the CompTIA A+ exams, but you will need to have them in mind any time you're purchasing, installing, or troubleshooting displays.

NOTE Legacy connectors such as VGA and DVI don't have versions to keep track of.

To take full advantage of the bandwidth and features of the latest version of a standard, your display, cable, and video source must all support at least that version. You should also pay careful attention to the bandwidth and features supported by the different connectors on both the video source and display. For example, a given video source or monitor might have three different connectors, but only one may support the device's highest refresh rate and resolution—and only if the video source, cable, and display *all* support this refresh rate and resolution.

VGA *Video Graphics Array (VGA)* is as old as the hills by this point, but you'll still find a 15-pin, three-row, D-type connector (see Figure 17-9) on quite a few monitors. This legacy connector has a *lot* of names, including *D-shell* and *D-subminiature*, but most people simply call it the *VGA connector*. VGA is the oldest and least-capable monitor connection type.

DVI The *Digital Visual Interface (DVI)* standard helped build a bridge between the world of old analog displays and modern digital ones (and even served as the foundation of HDMI, which we'll discuss next). DVI is actually three different connectors that look very much alike: DVI-D (digital), DVI-A (analog), and DVI-A/D or DVI-I (interchangeable—it accepts either a DVI-D or DVI-A).

Figure 17-9
A VGA connector

As a legacy standard, DVI appears on fewer and fewer new devices—but DVI-D and DVI-I connectors (which may be single-link or dual-link) can still power low-end displays. *Single-link DVI* can drive a display with a resolution of 1920 × 1080 at a refresh rate of 60 Hz, and *dual-link DVI* (see Figure 17-10) can drive a 2048 × 1536 display at 60 Hz. (We'll take a closer look at resolution and refresh rate later in the chapter.)

Figure 17-10
Dual-link DVI-I
connector

HDMI   Many monitors, projectors, and VR headsets connect to a computer via the *High-Definition Multimedia Interface (HDMI)* connector, which carries both video and audio signals (see Figure 17-11). The latest version of HDMI can handle just about any resolution, but keep in mind that an older version may not.

Figure 17-11
HDMI port on a
monitor

NOTE   The CompTIA A+ exam objectives don't touch on them, but HDMI technically has more than one type of connector. They aren't common, but don't be shocked if you see an HDMI logo next to an unfamiliar mini or micro port on a compact device such as a digital camera.

DisplayPort, Thunderbolt, and USB Type-C   *Using DisplayPort (DP), Thunderbolt,* and *USB Type-C* connections are an increasingly common way to supply video and audio to displays.

 EXAM TIP   On the CompTIA 1102 Exam, *USB Type-C* is referred to as *USB-C*. They are both used interchangeably and are both trademarks of USB Implementers Forum. To remain consistent with our previous CompTIA A+ publications, we will continue to use the *USB Type-C* designation wherever mentioned in this chapter.

Each of these is technically its own standard with different capabilities, but I'm lumping them together here for a reason. Full-sized DP connections are common these days, like with my Dell monitors (see Figure 17-12). These connect to full-sized DP ports on display adapters, as you would expect.

Figure 17-12
DisplayPort
connection on
monitor

Thunderbolt 1 and Thunderbolt 2 adopted the same connector type that's used for the small version of DisplayPort, called Mini DisplayPort (mDP). Thunderbolt 3 and 4, however, use the USB Type-C connector. USB 3 and 4 also both support using the Type-C connector to drive a display without Thunderbolt.

If that isn't confusing enough, buckle up: you'll find monitors that connect mDP-to-mDP without using Thunderbolt 1 or 2, and many USB Type-C connectors and cables lack Thunderbolt 3 or 4 support. If you're lucky, you'll find a little Thunderbolt symbol next to the ports (see Figure 17-13) to distinguish them—but it isn't always present. Your best bet is to consult the manufacturer's documentation!

Figure 17-13   Logos for plain mDP (left), Thunderbolt 2 mDP (center), Thunderbolt 3/4 USB
Type-C (right)

HDBaseT   Some projectors use a connection technology called *HDBaseT* (see
Figure 17-14) that enables long-range connectivity for uncompressed HD video
and audio over Cat 5a or Cat 6 network cables (we'll talk about network cabling in
Chapter 18). This enables you to connect a projector in a conference room via runs
of up to 100 meters. HDBaseT isn't on the CompTIA A+ 1101 exam, but you might
encounter it in the real world.

Figure 17-14
HDBaseT port on
a projector

Adapters   You will most likely find yourself in a situation where you need to connect a
display and video source that don't have a connector in common. In such a case, you can
use a small *adapter* device, like the *DVI-to-VGA adapter* in Figure 17-15. There are tons
of these things out there.

Figure 17-15
DVI-to-VGA
adapter

Using an adapter is a good solution if you already have a cable for connecting the devices, but if you don't, getting a cable with different end connectors may be more convenient. Figure 17-16 shows a typical DVI-to-HDMI cable.

Figure 17-16
DVI-to-HDMI
cable

Adjustments

It's almost always possible to fiddle with a range of display properties to adjust a display's color balance, brightness, contrast, and so on—but the process differs from display to display. All monitors have an On/Off button; additional buttons may enable you to select among multiple inputs, directly control features like brightness, contrast, and volume, or bring up and navigate the *onscreen display (OSD)* menu (see Figure 17-17).

Every monitor maker provides a different way to access its OSD menu, but each provides at least two functions: physical screen adjustment (bigger, smaller, move to the left, right, up, down, and others) and image adjustments like brightness, contrast, and color. Make sure the user understands how to adjust these settings.

VESA Mounts

Almost every monitor these days has a standardized bracket option for mounting the monitor on the wall or on a special stand called a VESA mount. Figure 17-18 shows the bracket option on a monitor. Figure 17-19 shows a stand for mounting two monitors side-by-side. VESA mounts vary with size—big televisions need a larger mounting bracket than 24-inch computer monitors.

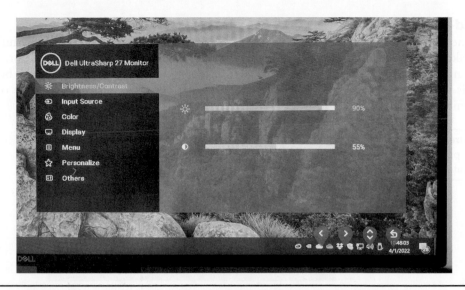

Figure 17-17   Typical OSD menu controls

Figure 17-18
VESA mounting
option on
monitor

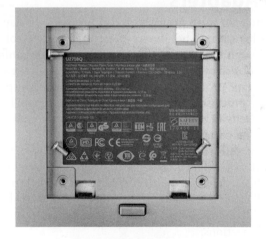

Figure 17-19
Dual-monitor
stand that uses
VESA mounts

Add-on Features

Some monitor manufacturers add extra features to their products, such as USB hubs, speakers, webcams, and microphones. These are supported by an *upstream* USB port on the monitor that you connect to a USB port on the computer. On newer devices, both ends usually use Type-C connectors. Figure 17-20 shows USB ports on the side of a monitor—it's a very handy feature!

Figure 17-20
USB ports on monitor

Display Adapters

The video source for most monitors is a computer's display adapter (also called a graphics card or video card). This device handles a number of video-related chores for the computer—though the most fundamental is processing information from the CPU and sending it to the display. The display adapter is a complex set of devices. A graphics processor of some type processes data from the CPU and outputs commands to the display. Like any other processor, the graphics processor needs RAM. The graphics processor needs fast connectivity between it, the CPU, and system RAM. The display adapter must have a connection compatible with the monitor.

Traditionally, and still quite commonly in Windows PCs, the display adapter was an expansion card that plugged into the motherboard (see Figure 17-21). Although many new systems have the display adapter circuitry built into the CPU and motherboard, most techs still call it the video card, so we'll start there. This section looks at five aspects that define a video card: motherboard slot, graphics processor, video memory, integrated GPUs, and connections.

Motherboard Slot

Every current discrete video card plugs into the PCIe slot on a motherboard. As mentioned, many CPUs/motherboards have the display adapter built-in. I'll discuss integrated graphics after talking about graphics processors and memory types, at which point the topic will make more sense. For now, let's look at PCIe.

Figure 17-21
Typical video
card

PCIe

The *PCI Express (PCIe)* interface was developed to replace the older *Peripheral Component Interconnect (PCI)* and *Accelerated Graphics Port (AGP)* interfaces. PCIe was a natural fit for video because it is incredibly fast. All PCIe video cards use the PCIe ×16 connector (see Figure 17-22). PCIe replaced AGP as the primary video interface almost overnight.

Figure 17-22
PCIe video card
connected in
PCIe slot

Graphics Processor

The graphics processor handles the heavy lifting of taking commands from the CPU and translating them into coordinates and color information that the monitor understands and displays. Most techs today refer to the device that processes video as a *graphics processing unit (GPU)*.

Video card discussion, at least among techs, almost always revolves around the graphics processor the video card uses and the amount of RAM onboard. A typical video card might be called an MSI Ventus GeForce GTX 3080 Ti 12-GB 384-bit GDDR6X PCI Express 4.0, so let's break that down. (Product listings vary—you won't always see the elements in exactly the same order.) MSI is the manufacturer of the video card; Ventus is one of a few different MSI product lines; GeForce GTX 3080 Ti is the graphics processor; 12-GB 384-bit GDDR6X describes the dedicated video RAM and the connection between the video RAM and the graphics processor; and PCI Express 4.0 describes the motherboard expansion slot the card requires.

NOTE Many video cards come with a digital anti-theft technology called *High-bandwidth Digital Content Protection (HDCP)*. HDCP stops audio and video copying between high-speed connections, such as HDMI, DisplayPort, and DVI. The technology also stops playback of HDCP-encrypted content (like Netflix) on devices designed to circumvent the system.

Many companies make the hundreds of different video cards on the market, but only three companies produce the vast majority of graphics processors found on video cards: NVIDIA, AMD, and Intel. NVIDIA and AMD make and sell graphics processors to third-party manufacturers who then design, build, and sell video cards under their own branding. Intel has long focused on building integrated GPUs into its processors, but it returned to the dedicated GPU market in 2021. Figure 17-23 shows an NVIDIA GeForce RTX 3080 Ti on a board made by EVGA.

Figure 17-23
NVIDIA GeForce
RTX 3080 Ti

Low-end graphics processors usually work fine for the run-of-the-mill user who wants to write letters or run a Web browser. High-end graphics processors are designed for demanding tasks such as powering high-end displays and rendering beautiful 3-D graphics (whether that's for professionals such as graphic designers, animators, architects, and engineers—or for, you know…games!).

Video Memory

When you're working with demanding graphics applications (such as rendering special effects for a movie or playing a game with high-quality assets), video memory can prove to be a serious bottleneck in three ways: data throughput speed, access speed, and simple capacity. Manufacturers address these bottlenecks by upping the width of the bus between the video RAM and video processor, adding more and more total RAM, and developing special-purpose RAM.

Specialized types of video RAM (VRAM)—namely Graphics DDR (GDDR) and High Bandwidth Memory (HBM)—exist to meet these high speed and bandwidth demands. You'll generally find a recent generation of special-purpose video RAM—such as GDDR6X or HBM3—in the latest high-end graphics cards, but keep in mind that you may run into low-budget graphics cards that use a recent generation of generic DDR RAM.

 NOTE HBM has some big performance and efficiency advantages over GDDR, but it's also a newer, more expensive technology. It has appeared on a few consumer graphics cards, but has had better success in GPUs designed for use in data centers. We'll probably still be buying GDDR-based cards for years, but this could change in a hurry if the price of HBM drops.

Integrated GPUs

Some motherboards support CPUs with integrated GPUs and provide HDMI and/or Display ports along with the usual mix of USB, Ethernet, and other I/O connectors. When a system uses the CPU's internal GPU, we often say it has integrated graphics.

Traditionally, integrated GPUs aren't very powerful—but they are still fairly common in laptops because integrating them saves a lot of space and power. That said, gradual innovation driven by the popularity of mobile devices and laptops is starting to overturn this old assumption.

AMD and NVIDIA both make integrated GPU chips, Intel has long integrated the Intel Graphics Media Accelerator (GMA) into its chipsets, and Apple has recently made a splash with its M1 processor family, which combines a powerful CPU and GPU on the same chip.

The *best* of these now rival any CPU/discrete graphics card combination that you'd find in a comparable portable computer and are good enough for casual gaming. Even Intel's integrated graphics, which have long been a bit of a joke for anything beyond basic desktop productivity, have made big strides in recent years. NVIDIA's Tegra line is focused on gaming (Nintendo Switch) and automotive entertainment systems.

NOTE There's a *lot* going on under the hood of a combined CPU/GPU. A single Apple M1 chip, for example, integrates 8 to 20 CPU cores, 7 to 64 GPU cores, 16 to 32 neural cores, 8 to 128 GB of low-power DDR4 memory, and cache memory. Wow!

Connector Types and Associated Cables

Display adapters have one or more connectors you can use to connect them to a video display—make sure you're familiar with each of the connectors we looked at earlier in the chapter:

- VGA
- DVI
- HDMI
- DisplayPort
- Thunderbolt (including mDP Thunderbolt 1 and 2 ports, and USB Type-C Thunderbolt 3 and 4 ports)
- USB Type-C

You can also find video cards (especially older ones) with a number of connector types for interfacing with other media devices such as cameras, projectors, television sets, and so on. The video card shown in Figure 17-24 has three connectors: VGA, DVI-I, and a once-common S-video connector. In the days before HDMI, an S-video connector like this was a *decent* way to connect your computer to a standard definition TV.

Figure 17-24
Video card connectors: VGA, S-video, and DVI-I

EXAM TIP A graphics card isn't the only place you'll find a bunch of video connectors. *Capture cards* sport one or more video connectors to enable us to record, stream, or watch video from another video source. They may also have an output connector so that you can also pass the signal back to a normal display for simultaneous viewing.

The video card in Figure 17-25, in contrast, offers four connectors: HDMI, DP (×3). And yes, in case you were wondering, the card can drive four 4K monitors simultaneously!

Figure 17-25
Video card
connectors:
HDMI and
DisplayPort

Installing and Configuring Video

As long as you have the right connection to your video card or integrated graphics, installing a monitor is straightforward. Installing the video card itself *can* be trickier.

 NOTE The installation steps in this section apply to Windows PCs and Linux computers. None of Apple's current macOS systems (except the super expensive Mac Pro) enable you to upgrade the internal display adapter, but you can still configure it or attach an external GPU. (See the Beyond A+ section "eGPUs" for more details.)

During the physical installation of a video card, watch out for three possible issues: long cards, the proximity of the nearest expansion card, and the presence of power connectors. Some high-end video cards simply won't fit in certain cases or will block access to needed motherboard connectors such as the SATA sockets. Unless your case includes a special mounting bracket for mounting the card in a different orientation, there's no clean fix for such a problem—you simply have to change at least one of the components (video card, motherboard, or case).

Because high-end video cards run very hot, you don't want them sitting right next to another card; make sure the fan on the video card has plenty of ventilation space. I leave the slot next to the video card empty to allow better airflow (see Figure 17-26).

Figure 17-26
Installing a video
card

More powerful video cards have massive heat sinks and large cooling fans, so you don't have any choice but to take up double or triple the space. Midrange to high-end video cards typically require at least one (or two) additional PCIe power connectors because they use more power than the PCIe slot can provide. Make sure that your power supply can provide adequate power and has the correct type (6- or 8-pin) of PCIe power connectors.

Try This!

Install a Video Card

You know how to install an expansion card from your reading in earlier chapters. Installing a video card is pretty much the same, so try this!

1. Refer to Chapter 6 for the steps on installing a new card and refer to Chapter 7 for a visual on video power connectors.

2. Plug the monitor cable into the video card port on the back of the PC and power up the system. If your PC seems dead after you install a video card, or if the screen is blank but you hear fans whirring and the internal speaker sounding off long-short-short-short, your video card likely did not get properly seated. Unplug the PC and try again.

Once you've properly installed the video card and connected it to the monitor, you've fought half the battle for making the video process work properly. You're ready to tackle the drivers and tweak the operating system, so let's go!

Software

Configuring your video software is usually a two-step process. First you need to load drivers for the video card. Then you need to open Display Settings and Personalization Settings. Let's explore how to make the video card and monitor work in Windows, then look briefly at display options in macOS and Linux.

Drivers

Just like any other piece of hardware, a video card needs drivers to function. Display adapter drivers install pretty much the same way as all the other drivers we've discussed thus far: Windows has the driver already; insert the installation media that came with the card; or download the latest driver from the Internet.

Video card makers are constantly updating their drivers. Odds are good that any video card more than a few months old has at least one driver update. If possible, check the manufacturer's Web site and use the driver located there if there is one. If the Web site doesn't offer a driver, it's usually best to use the installation media. Always avoid using the built-in Windows driver as it tends to be the most dated.

We'll explore driver issues in more detail after we discuss the Display Settings and the Personalization Settings. Like so many things about video, you can't fully understand one topic without understanding at least one other!

1102

Using Display and Personalization

With the driver installed, you're ready to configure your display settings. The Display Settings or Personalization Settings provide convenient, central locations for all of your display settings, including resolution, refresh rate, driver information, and color depth.

Display Settings   The *Display Settings* in Windows enable adjusting most display options. Open Display Settings by clicking Start | Settings | System. Figure 17-27 shows the default initial Display Settings screen (on a dual-monitor system). Each monitor attached to the system gets a number, and you can drag and drop them to change the location. Figure 17-28 shows a different system with two monitors stacked vertically.

NOTE   There are small differences between how these elements look and work in Windows 10 and Windows 11, so I'm going to jump back and forth between them for these screenshots. They both have the same functionality, and it's important as a tech to get used to things moving around between different OS versions.

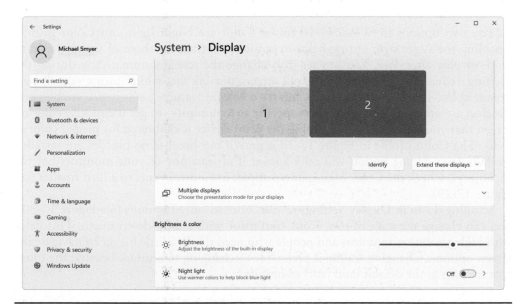

Figure 17-27   Display Settings in Windows 11

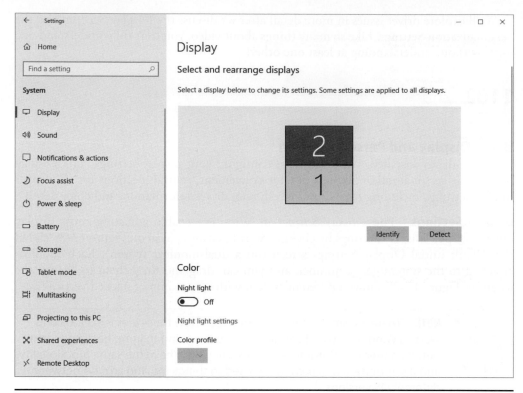

Figure 17-28   Vertically stacked monitors in Windows 10 Display Settings

The two options in Windows 10 under Color are Night light and Color profile. Enabling the *Night light* setting helps to reduce eye strain for those of us who tend to work or play after dark. You can set it to change the screen automatically during the evening, reducing the blue in the default screen, turning the "white" into a vaguely pale orange color. This isn't on the exam, but it's a helpful feature. *Color profile* enables you to select a *profile*—a set of parameters specific to a monitor—to get the precise color on screen that you'll see in print (assuming the print device is calibrated for proper color as well). The Color profile in Figure 17-28 is grayed out because no profiles are installed (in Windows 11 the option will only appear if at least one of your monitors has the capability). Check the Color Management applet in Control Panel to adjust further (see Figure 17-29).

Scrolling down in Display Settings reveals more advanced options (see Figure 17-30). You can change the scale of text, icons, and more with a drop-down menu. This helps with high-resolution monitors and people who need things a little bigger to navigate the screen options. Changing scaling is preferable to changing resolution, because the interface remains at the default (and best) resolution.

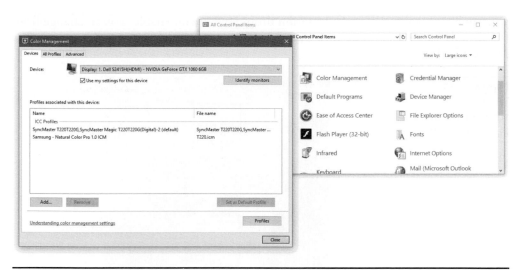

Figure 17-29   Windows 10 Color Management applet in Control Panel

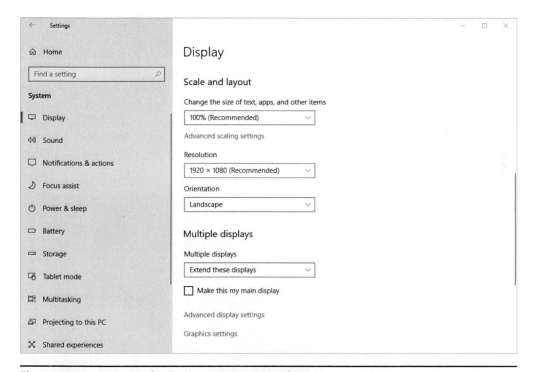

Figure 17-30   More Display Settings options in Windows 10

In some scenarios, you'll need to adjust the resolution or orientation of the monitor. The Resolution drop-down menu enables you to change the resolution (to match a projector, for example, so the presentation you see on the monitor looks the same as your audience will see). The Orientation drop-down menu enables you to change from the default Landscape mode to Portrait mode if you have a monitor that swivels (see Figure 17-31).

Figure 17-31
Windows 10
showing monitor
in portrait mode

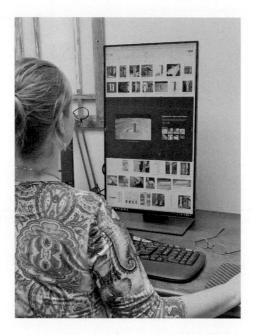

The Multiple displays option gives you control over what shows on the second (or more) screen. The default is *Extend these displays*, which gives you more desktop space for workflow. Figure 17-32 shows my editor working with extended displays configured. You can also duplicate the main display, so the same image shows on all connected monitors, or blank one or the other monitor.

Figure 17-32
My editor hard
at work with two
monitors

NOTE You can readily add additional displays to a system. In years past, you would add a second video card to the system and plug the second monitor into it, then go to the Display Settings to extend the displays. Almost all video cards you can buy today have more than one port, often of different types. Get a cable that matches and plug in for better computing.

Click the *Advanced display* option for specific information about the monitor(s) connected. Figure 17-33 shows the settings for Display 2, an AORUS gaming monitor. Note the screen shows the resolution, refresh rate, and bit depth of the panel (as well as color format and color space, which we'll discuss in Beyond A+).

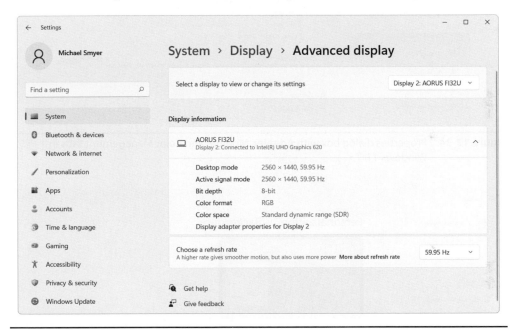

Figure 17-33 Windows 11 Advanced display

This screen also enables you to open the general Properties for the display adapter and monitor by clicking *Display adapter properties* (see Figure 17-34). The Adapter tab shows information about the adapter, such as GPU and RAM. Clicking the Properties button will open a dialog box to update or roll back the driver. See "Working with Drivers" a bit later in this chapter for more information.

Personalization Settings Personalization-branded tools handle user preferences, such as background picture, colors of various interface elements, and that sort of thing. Figure 17-35 shows the *Personalization Settings* background screen. The changes you can make are pretty obvious: make your background a solid color or pick a picture; you can use one of the images that come with Windows or choose your own.

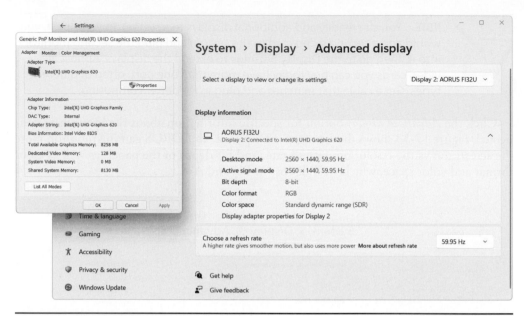

Figure 17-34 Properties dialog box with Adapter, Monitor, and Color Management tabs in Windows 11

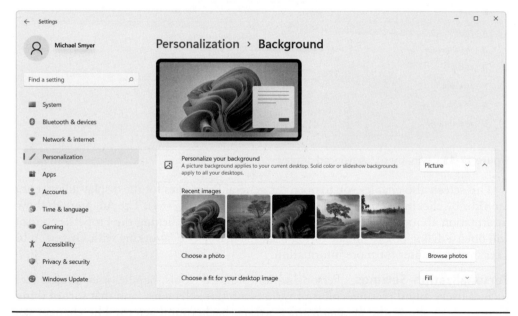

Figure 17-35 Windows 11 Personalization background settings

The list on the left gives you many more options for tweaking the look and feel of Windows, such as customizing a theme (the overall look and feel), changing the default font, and adjusting the Start menu and Taskbar. The Related Settings at the bottom can help people who have trouble with the default interface, with *High contrast settings*. The *Sync your settings* (Windows 10) or *Windows backup* (Windows 11) option under Accounts enables you to synchronize multiple Windows machines that you log on to with your Microsoft account (see Figure 17-36).

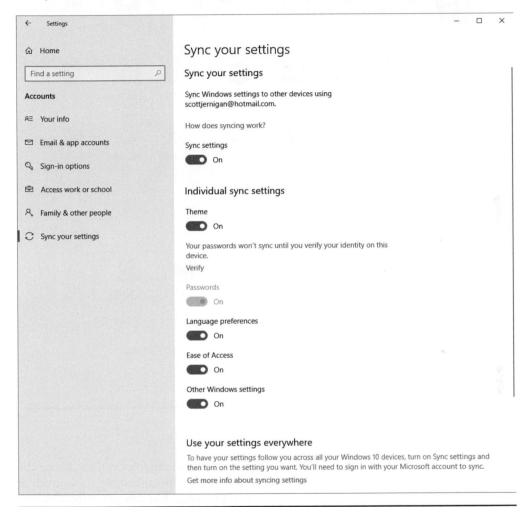

Figure 17-36   Windows 10 Sync your settings options

Display Options in macOS and Linux

macOS and most modern Linux distros offer clear options for changing display settings. To no one's surprise, you'll find the options in macOS in System Preferences (see Figure 17-37). The General settings enable you to change color schemes. You can change the Desktop background in Desktop & Screen Saver.

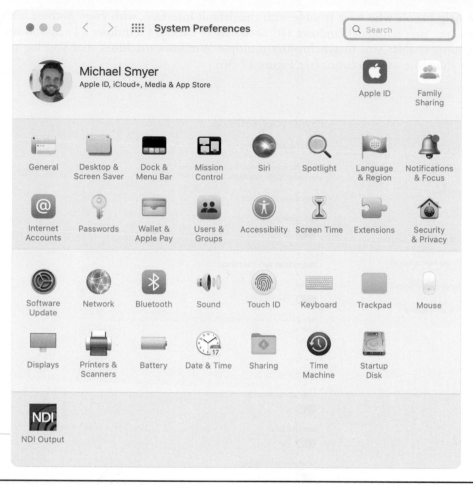

Figure 17-37   System Preferences in macOS

Click the Dock & Menu Bar option to access a screen that enables you to change the user experience a lot (see Figure 17-38). The Dock resides by default along the bottom of the screen. You can make the icons tiny and less distracting. You can move the Dock to the right or left. You can change the default animation behavior for mouseovers.

Different Linux distros put the display options in various places, but you'll commonly find one or more utilities in the System Settings. Figure 17-39 shows the Settings app in Ubuntu, for example, where you can alter most of your system settings, including the background, theme, and Launcher icon size.

All the things you can modify in Windows, you can modify in Linux. You just might have to do a little hunting.

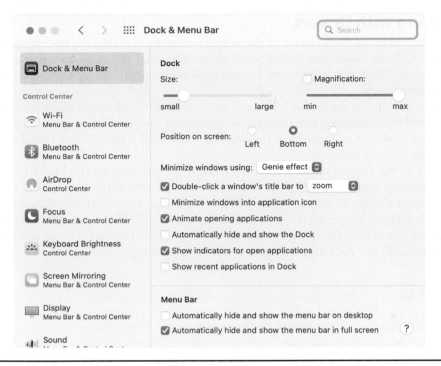

Figure 17-38   Dock & Menu Bar options

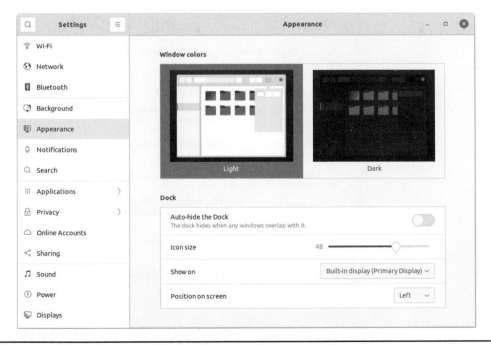

Figure 17-39   Changing the system appearance in Ubuntu's Settings app

Working with Drivers

Now that you know the locations of the primary video tools within the operating system, it's time to learn about fine-tuning your video. You need to know how to work with video drivers from within Settings, including how to update them, roll back updates, and uninstall them.

When you update the drivers for a card, you have a choice of uninstalling the outdated drivers and then installing new drivers—which makes the process the same as for installing a new card—or you can let Windows flex some digital muscle and install the new ones right over the older drivers.

To get to the adapter settings, as you'll recall from earlier, open the Display Settings, click *Advanced display*, and click the *Display adapter properties* link to open the Monitor and Adapter Properties dialog box. Click the Properties button on the Adapter tab to open the Adapter Properties dialog box (see Figure 17-40). (Note that the "Adapter" in the dialog box will be the specific video card.) The General tab gives some information about the card, but the Driver tab gets to the heart of things.

Figure 17-40
Adapter
Properties dialog
box with Driver
tab selected

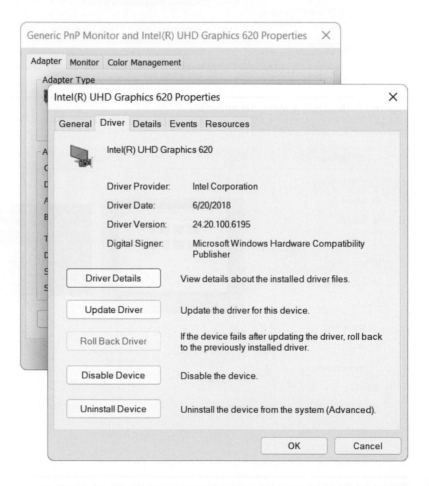

To update drivers, click the Update Driver button. Windows will give you the option of searching for updated drivers on both your computer and the Internet or just on your computer (see Figure 17-41). The former option these days is pretty magical, as long as the computer is connected to the Internet, of course.

Figure 17-41
Windows
looking for
driver updates

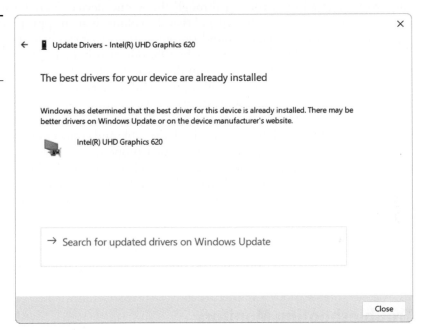

SIM   Check out the excellent "DxDiag" Show! and Click! simulations over in the Chapter 17 section of the hub: https://www.totalsem.com/110X. These will get you prepared for any performance-based questions CompTIA might throw at you.

1101

Troubleshooting Video

Users might temporarily ignore a bad printer or other device, but will holler like crazy when the screen doesn't look the way they expect. Some video problems always point to a specific component, but others have more than one potential cause. To fix the latter kind of video problems quickly, a good place to start is by isolating where, between the computer and the display, the problem lies.

When you run into common problems that could easily be caused by settings built into a monitor, give them a quick check first. If a display turns on but doesn't show anything (or shows the incorrect data/video source), flip through video sources (you might need to do this through an on-screen menu, a physical button, or a remote). If the image is a little bright, dark, washed-out, or has *incorrect color display* issues such as a consistent tint, double-check the image adjustment settings.

The process is similar when *audio issues* are the only problem—usually that the audio isn't working at all or is coming through the wrong device. Start by making sure the expected output device isn't muted and that the volume is at an appropriate level. If that's fine, check the device's audio/sound output settings to make sure the correct output device is selected. The location differs by OS, but each has an option to test a specific output device by playing a tone. If you don't see the correct output, ensure the devices are cabled correctly and that they all support audio. Keep in mind that VGA and DVI cables won't carry sound, and some displays have no speakers.

For rare, obvious visual problems such as a *flashing screen*, streaking, smearing, missing colors, and strange visual distortions, check the cable and connections for *physical cabling issues* first. Confirm the connectors are seated properly. Try another cable. If another cable works, replace the bad cable. If another cable doesn't work, double-check the ports on both ends for any debris or damage. If the cable is particularly long, it's also worth trying a shorter cable just in case you're getting bit by signal loss.

Connect the display to another system. If the cable isn't the culprit and the display works fine on another system, suspect the video card (see the upcoming "Troubleshooting Video Cards and Drivers" section). If the display's problem persists on another system, see the "Troubleshooting Monitors" section (and also the "Troubleshooting Projectors" section, if appropriate).

Troubleshooting Monitors

This section assumes you'll leave display repair to trained professionals and concentrates instead on giving a support person the information necessary to fix basic problems and decide whether a trouble ticket is warranted.

Common Display Problems

I don't recommend opening a monitor to work on it unless you've been trained how to do it safely, but you can still fix many display problems yourself. The following list describes the most common monitor problems and tells you what to do—even when that means sending it to someone else.

- As displays age, they lose brightness. If the brightness control is turned all the way up and the picture seems dim, you'll have to replace the backlight, display, or the entire device. This is a good argument for using the power switch or OS power-management options to turn off displays whenever your systems are idle.

- A display panel may have bad pixels. A bad pixel is any single pixel that does not react the way it should. A pixel that never lights up is a *dead pixel*, a pixel that is stuck on pure white is a *lit pixel*, and a pixel that is always some other specific color is a *stuck pixel*. If you discover bad pixels on a monitor under warranty, the best course of action is to contact the manufacturer. (Fair warning: The warranty of every panel manufacture requires a certain number of bad pixels to be present for the warranty to cover replacement even on a brand-new monitor! You need to check the warranty for your monitor and see how many bad pixels must be present before you may return it.) If the monitor isn't under warranty, you can try to revive the pixel using techniques discussed online, learn to live with the bad pixels, or replace the monitor.

- If a display panel cracks, it is not repairable and must be replaced.

- A flickering image usually points to a problem with the backlight or internal circuits. The exact fix will depend on the technologies in use—but you'll probably have to replace the backlight, display panel, or the whole monitor.

- A *dim image*, especially on only the top or bottom half of the screen, points to a dead or dying backlight.

- If the LCD goes dark but you can still barely see the image under bright lights, you lost either the backlight or the inverter. In many cases, especially with super-thin panels, you'll replace the entire panel and backlight as a unit.

- If an older LCD with a CCFL backlight makes a distinct hissing noise, an inverter is about to fail. You can replace the inverter, but at this point I recommend replacing the display.

- If an image displayed for a long time (common with interface elements in operating systems and games) leaves a shadow or impression, you're seeing image *persistence*. Most persistence problems these days are temporary and should go away if you turn the display off for at least as long as it was on. If not, it may be permanent *display burn-in*. Early generations of each new display technology tend to struggle with burn-in, so it's a good idea to protect them with time-tested solutions: configure the OS to turn off idle displays or protect them with an animated screen saver. Monitors particularly prone to burn-in (such as OLEDs) may also have menu options that help minimize the likelihood or appearance of burn-in. If the burn-in doesn't go away and you can't live with it, you'll have to replace the display.

Bottom line on fixing displays? You can find companies that sell replacement parts, but repairing displays is difficult, and there are folks who will do it for you faster and cheaper than you can. Search for a specialty display repair company. Hundreds of these companies exist all over the world.

Dealing with High-Resolution Monitors

High-resolution monitors offer beautiful visuals, but can make screen elements—buttons, menus, stuff for navigating operating systems and applications—too small for some viewers. If you recall from earlier in the chapter, display panels have a default resolution; the picture will degrade (and may look a little *fuzzy*) if you set the resolution lower than the default. But that's what a lot of people do, because it makes the screen elements bigger and thus useable. That's not the solution!

The best way to deal with the scenario of tiny screen elements is through the Display Settings. Every version of Windows enables you to change the size of screen elements directly, making the screen elements appear larger (or smaller). The resolution doesn't change; only the size of the screen elements change. Figure 17-42 shows the drop-down menu options in Windows 11. Note that changing the size of text, apps, and other items from 100 percent to 125 or 150 percent is a simple selection.

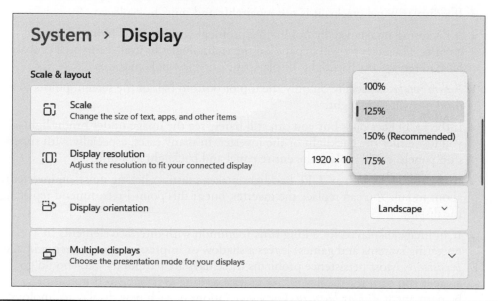

Figure 17-42   Changing the size of text, apps, and other items in Windows 11

Try This!

Scaling the UI

Most of you have access to a Windows computer, so try this! Open Display Settings and experiment with the element size settings. This is something you absolutely need to understand to help users with high-resolution monitors.

Cleaning Monitors

Cleaning monitors isn't like scrubbing a sink or even cleaning a window—you can't just pick whatever cleaning solution and rag are lying around and go to town. Even when a display is protected by a layer of glass, it's still likely to have delicate coatings that reduce glare and resist grime.

Before you dive in, consult your display's manual or other documentation for any special precautions, recommendations, or equipment. Here's what I recommend—as long as your display's documentation doesn't disagree!

- Do not directly spray any liquid onto the screen. If it runs and leaks into any electronics, you could hurt yourself and fry the display.

- Don't use any cleaners or solvents. Multiple display manufacturers explicitly caution against all of them—even common electronics cleaners such as alcohol.

- Don't use prepackaged disposable wipes marketed for cleaning things like lenses or electronics. Some of the ones made specifically for cleaning monitors might be fine, but it isn't always easy to figure out what's in them—and many of them contain alcohol.

- Start with a clean, dry microfiber cloth and gently wipe dirt and grime off the display. Don't push hard, scrape, or scrub—remember the delicate coatings!

- If the screen still has grime on it, apply just enough water to dampen part of the microfiber cloth and continue to gently wipe the screen. This can be frustrating, but it's better to be patient and persistent than to damage an expensive display with force! Promptly dry the screen with the dry portion of your cloth.

Privacy with Multiple Monitors

Adding a second or third monitor to your setup can have a couple of downsides. The added viewing area can increase the potential for glare or reflection from other objects, making optimal monitor placement difficult. The extra visual real estate and viewing angles also make it easy for even casual passersby to see what you're viewing.

Monitor peripheral vendors address these problems with privacy screens. The screens fit over and slightly around the display. They stop wide-angle viewing of the screen and also drop the glare caused by external object reflection.

Multiple Monitor Mishaps

Video cards can handle multiple monitors that differ from one another in size or resolution, but this can create problems. Connecting an older 4:3 aspect ratio projector to a widescreen laptop for a presentation when you're mirroring the displays, for example, can create a pretty bizarre misalignment in layout. Using monitors with different orientation—landscape and portrait—can also produce undesirable effects. Try variations before your presentations!

Also, Windows enables you to designate which monitor is right or left or top or bottom. Making an alignment error here can cause problems when extending a display. You might drag the cursor to the right side of the left monitor, for example, and hit a wall because the "right" monitor is supposed to be on the left. These kinds of issues require a trip to the Display Settings.

Troubleshooting Projectors

Many of the concepts for troubleshooting traditional monitors also apply when you need to troubleshoot a projector, but there are also a few special points to keep in mind.

- Projector lamps can produce a lot of heat. If your projector has a lamp, let it cool off before you work on it. After you turn it off, the fan will run for a while to cool the lamp. If that isn't an option, be very careful where you touch to avoid burning yourself.

- Projector lamps have a relatively short life (usually a few thousand hours) compared to most other display components. They're expensive, but otherwise simple to replace. Keep a spare lamp on hand; not only will you be ready to save the day when one burns out before a big executive meeting, but a spare lamp will help you rule out lamp issues when troubleshooting a projector. You might (depending on the device) be able to do the same with LED or laser light engines (though you won't need to replace them nearly as often).

- Speaking of replacement parts, keep some spare batteries around for the remote. Most projectors are mounted in a hard-to-reach location. If the projector won't respond, try swapping out the remote's batteries before you break out a ladder to reach the projector's physical buttons.

- Projectors have a fan to cool off the lamp. If the fan goes out or the filter gets clogged, the lamp could overheat. The screen may suddenly go black if it goes into an overheat shutdown. If users haven't figured out that this is heat-related, they might describe random, occasional, or *intermittent projector shutdowns*. Trying to turn the projector immediately back on to troubleshoot the issue may not work at all. If it does, it certainly won't help the main problem. Clean dust out of the fans, filters, and vents—and confirm that the fan is working.

- Like any display that goes unused for long enough, a projector might go into sleep mode. It'll usually wake up if you use the computer or press the right button on the remote. If the projector is clearly running but there's no image on the screen, you may have to reboot it.

- If you notice *incorrect color display* issues such as a strong tint that aren't fixed by color adjustments or replacing the cables, an LCD or DLP component has failed and the projector will need service or replacement.

- If the projector throws a *fuzzy image*, the lens might be dirty or out of focus (if its focus is adjustable), or the projector may not be at the intended distance from the screen. Check for dust and dirt, try adjusting the focus, and consult the documentation to ensure it's at the right distance from the screen.

Above all else, don't get *too* focused on the fact that you're dealing with a projector when you have to troubleshoot one. It's easy to jump straight to projector-specific solutions and miss simple problems like a poorly connected cable, or a laptop that isn't configured to extend or mirror its display to the projector.

Troubleshooting Video Cards and Drivers

Video cards rarely go bad, so the majority of video card and driver problems are bad or incompatible drivers or incorrect settings. Always make sure you have the correct driver installed. If you're using an incompatible driver, you might get a Blue Screen of Death (BSoD) as soon as Windows starts to load. A system with a suddenly corrupted driver usually doesn't act up until the next reboot. If you reboot a system with a corrupted driver, Windows will do one of the following: default into a lower resolution, blank the monitor, lock up, or display a garbled screen with weird patterns, incorrect color patterns, or a distorted image.

Whatever the output, reboot into Safe mode and roll back or delete the driver. The drivers may manifest as installed programs under Apps and Features, so check there first before you try deleting a driver via Device Manager. Download the latest driver and reinstall.

Video cards are pretty durable, but they have two components that do go bad: the fan and the RAM. Lucky for you, if either of these goes out, it tends to show the same error—bizarre screen outputs followed shortly by a screen lockup. Usually Windows keeps running; you may see your mouse pointer moving around and windows refreshing, but the screen turns into a huge mess (see Figure 17-43).

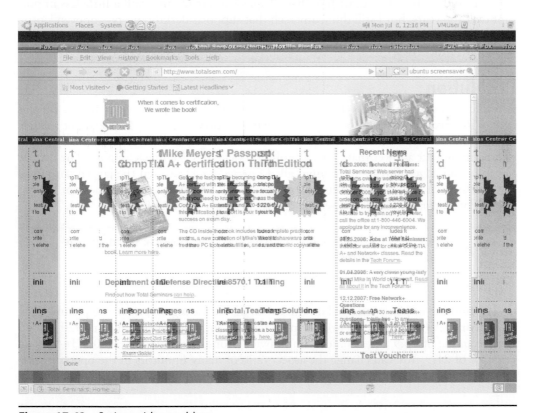

Figure 17-43   Serious video problem

Bad drivers sometimes also make this error, so always first try going into Safe mode to see if the problem suddenly clears up. If it does, you do not have a problem with the video card!

Excessive heat inside the case, even with the video card fan running at full blast, can create some interesting effects. The computer could simply shut down due to overheating. You'll recognize this possible cause because the computer will come back up in a minute or two, but then shut down again as you push it hard enough to heat it up again. Sometimes the screen will show bizarre artifacts or start distorting. Check your case fans and make sure nothing is too close to the video card. You might need to take the whole system outside to blow dust out of its filters, vents, fans, and heatsinks.

Beyond A+

Evaluating Monitors

The CompTIA A+ exam no longer addresses the technical properties that you'll need to know to help your customers find the right monitor for their needs. The popularity of portable and mobile devices with built-in displays has made this skill a little less important over the years, but I still think any tech that supports desktop users—or even laptop users that need a second or third screen—need to know this stuff! Let's look at the most important properties.

Resolution

A resolution, such as 2560 × 1440, describes the number of pixels on a display (in this case, 2560 pixels across and 1440 pixels down). Displays are designed to run at a single *native resolution*. You can't run a display at a resolution higher than the native resolution, and running it at a lower than native resolution degrades the image quality. The display has to use an edge-blurring technique called *interpolation* to soften the jagged corners of the pixels when running at lower than native resolution, which simply does not look as good. The bottom line? Always set the display at native resolution!

 NOTE Two display panels that have the same physical size may have different native resolutions.

The number of pixels arranged on the screen define the *aspect ratio* of the picture, such as 16:9 or 21:9 (see Figure 17-44). A typical widescreen monitor running at 1920 × 1080 is an example of 16:9 aspect ratio. An ultrawide monitor running at 3440 × 1440 is an example of 21:9. You can change the aspect ratio of many monitors in the operating system tools, such as Display in Windows, but the quality of picture will degrade.

Figure 17-44
Various aspect
ratios compared

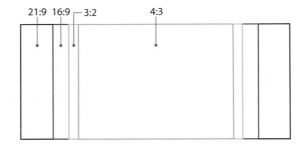

Modern computing devices use different aspect ratios. Many smartphones stick to 16:9, but a lot of newer Android and iPhone models have gone wider with aspect ratios like 18:9 and 19.5:9. Most Apple iPads, in contrast, have a 4:3 aspect ratio screen; the Microsoft Surface laptop uses a 3:2 screen.

Monitor marketing has always been a mess, but display manufacturers usually mention at least the physical size of the display. They often go on to indicate the panel technology, resolution, aspect ratio, and maybe one or two of its most important features.

Once upon a time, a display's native resolution was usually indicated by the name (technically an *initialism*) of the corresponding *video mode*—such as the ancient *VGA* (640 × 480) and *SVGA* (800 × 600) formats. These days, displays are usually marketed with some combination of shorthand borrowed from TV (such as HD, 1080p, FHD, UHD) or film (2K, 4K, 8K, and so on). These formats are easier to remember (mostly because there aren't as many), but it's good to know that these designations (especially the film-style ones) are applied to multiple similar resolutions.

Memorizing every possible resolution isn't a good use of your time (there are a *ton* of resolutions out there), but it is a good idea to be able to recognize the patterns in case you see them in the real world. Table 17-1 shows a mix of these terms and corresponding properties.

Table 17-1
Display
Resolution
Shorthand

Terms	Resolution	Aspect Ratio	Typical Device
VGA	640 × 480	4:3	Ancient monitors
SVGA	800 × 600	4:3	Ancient monitors
HD, 720p	1280 × 720	16:9	Lowest resolution that can be called HD
FHD, 1080p	1920 × 1080	16:9	Full HD resolution
WUXGA	1920 × 1200	16:10	Older widescreen monitors
2K, WQHD	2560 × 1440	16:9	Widescreen displays
4K, Ultra HD, UHD	3840 × 2160	16:9	Televisions, monitors
5K	5120 × 2880	16:9	Monitors (mostly by Apple)
8K, Ultra HD, UHD	7680 × 4320	16:9	Televisions

PPI

The combination of the resolution and physical size of a display determines the *pixels per inch (PPI)* of a panel. The higher the PPI, the finer the picture a monitor can produce. That means, in practical terms, that a smaller high-resolution monitor will look substantially better than a much larger monitor running at the same resolution. A 24-inch 1080p monitor, for example, looks good at just under 100 PPI. A 32-inch 1080p monitor looks kind of grainy, because its PPI is sub-70. This PPI number is part of what makes a MacBook Pro laptop so crisp. The 15.4-inch screen has a resolution of 2880 × 1800, which puts it at 220 pixels per inch. That's sweet! Modern smartphones have outrageous PPI levels, which again is why they look so much better than a typical desktop monitor.

Brightness

The strength of any display's light-emitting components (the backlight, for an LCD, or the LEDs themselves in an OLED display) determine the brightness of the monitor. The brightness is measured in *nits*. Display panels vary from 100 nits on the low end to over 1000 nits or more on the high end. Average displays are around 300 nits, which most monitor authorities consider excellent brightness. Higher brightness levels also make it easier to view displays in bright rooms.

 NOTE One nit equals one candela/m². One candela is roughly equal to the amount of light created by a candle.

Viewing Angle

Flat-panel displays have a limited *viewing angle*, meaning the screen fades out when viewed from the side (or any angle not dead center). Note the viewing angle when shopping for a monitor. Wider is better for typical users. Narrow isn't necessarily bad—especially when you want to limit what anyone but the user can see on the monitor.

Try This!

Test the Viewing Angle

Take a trip to your local computer store to look at displays. Don't get distracted looking at all the latest graphics cards, CPUs, motherboards, and RAM—well, actually, it's okay to look at those things. Just don't forget to look at monitors!

Stand about two feet in front of a display. Look directly at the image on the screen and consider the image quality, screen brightness, and color. Take a small step to your right. Compare the image you see now to the image you saw previously.

Continue taking small steps to the right until you are no longer able to discern the image on the display. You've reached the edge of the viewing angle for that panel.

Do this test with a few different monitors. Do smaller panels, such as 20-inch displays, have smaller viewing angles? Do larger displays have better viewing angles? You might also want to test the vertical viewing angles of some monitors. Try to find a monitor that is on your eye level; then look at it from above or below—does it have a large viewing range vertically? There's also a curved monitor variant not discussed in this chapter, but worth looking at. What kind of viewing angle do they have?

Response Rate

A display's *response rate* is the amount of time it takes for all of the sub-pixels on the panel to change from one state to another. Manufacturers measure these response rates in milliseconds (ms), with lower being better. There are a few ways manufacturers measure this change. One is *black-to-white (BtW)*: how long it takes the pixels to go from pure black to pure white and back again. The most common is *gray-to-gray (GtG)*: how long it takes the pixels to go from one gray state to another.

NOTE Manufacturers of gaming-oriented displays may also use *moving-picture response time (MPRT)*: the minimum time a pixel stays lit once activated. If you're looking for a gaming monitor, look for an MPRT closer to 1 ms. If you *aren't* going to use the display for gaming, treat MPRTs as a sign you may be about to overpay for features you won't be using.

The GtG time will always be faster than the BtW time. A typical modern display has an *advertised* response rate of less than 5 ms. The manufacturer will almost always advertise the GtG response time, though some publish more than one measure. You might find older displays in use with response times over 20 ms—slow enough that you might notice image smearing if you try to watch a movie or play a fast-paced game.

Refresh Rate

The *refresh rate* for a display refers to how often a screen can change or update completely. Think of the refresh rate as a metronome or timer and you'll be close to how it works in a display. For most computing purposes, 60 Hz is fine and that's been the standard for the industry. Higher refresh rates smooth out movement and reduce lag, which is most important in fast-moving games. Common higher-end monitors today, though, go well beyond, offering refresh rates like 144 Hz, 165 Hz, 240 Hz, and so on.

NOTE Higher-end video cards can push well beyond the limits of even the best monitor refresh rates. See the "Adaptive Sync" section later in this Beyond A+ material for the scoop.

Contrast Ratio

A good *contrast ratio*—the difference between the darkest and lightest spots that the monitor can display—is 450:1, although a quick trip to a computer store will reveal displays with lower levels (250:1) and higher levels (1000:1).

Display manufacturers market a *dynamic contrast ratio* number for their monitors, which measures the difference between a full-on, all-white screen, and a full-off, all-black screen. This yields a much higher number than the standard contrast ratio. My Samsung panels have a 1000:1 contrast ratio, for example, but a 20,000:1 dynamic contrast ratio. Sounds awesome, right? In general, the dynamic contrast ratio doesn't affect viewing on computer monitors. Focus on the standard contrast ratio when picking displays.

Color Depth

The typical human eye can see an astonishing variety of colors, luminance (aka brightness), and contrast. Scientists interested in what people see have defined this visual variety into graphs known technically as *chromaticity diagrams* or, more commonly, *color spaces* (see Figure 17-45).

Figure 17-45
Example of a
chromaticity
diagram

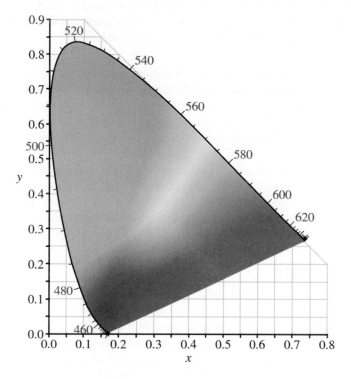

Computers only display a fraction of what people can see and thus use more limited color spaces. Matching color spaces among devices provides some consistency in color output. Several standards define the color space for the IT industry, though *sRGB* has long been the standard for displays. The *color depth* of a display panel indicates how precisely it can replicate colors within the color space it can display.

Very old TN monitors, for example, used a 6-bit panel. That meant that each color channel—red, green, and blue—had 64 (2^6) color variations. Most monitors today use an 8-bit panel, with 256 (2^8) colors per channel. This translates in marketing as 24-bit color, meaning the monitor can display 16.7 million color variations. At the higher end, manufacturers have 10-bit panels that display 1024 (2^{10}) color variations per channel, providing over 1 billion color variations. High levels of precision are especially important if you do a lot of photo editing or video color grading.

Panel Technology

At this point, the vast majority of users will go with an IPS panel with an edge-lit backlight. You'll have amazing color and viewing angle. Size and resolution will be determined by your budget and space considerations.

Once you move beyond the average user, though, things get tricky. Because the exact panel technologies in a given display can have a big impact on its resolution, brightness, contrast, color fidelity, and price, you'll have to spend some time understanding the user's needs and squaring them with the budget. If your budget isn't tight, a full LED backlight or Mini LED backlight can improve the color quality, brightness, and contrast.

 NOTE If you're an excited early adopter, it's worth considering an OLED display (and microLED, if they're available)—but I don't like recommending new computer display technologies until early adopters have beaten them up for a few years and we understand the tradeoffs.

High Dynamic Range

Have you watched the sun rise or set, with the phenomenal difference in brightness between the vibrant sunlit clouds and deep shadows around the trees? That vista encompasses—from its darkest points to its brightest—a very broad *dynamic range*. The world around us has a very broad (or *high* dynamic) range, but photographers and filmmakers have to take special steps to capture enough visual information to get anywhere close.

The standard 8-bit panel uses *standard dynamic range (SDR)*, and that's good enough for almost every computing need, from movies to games to productivity applications. To accurately render *high dynamic range (HDR)* content, displays need to be very bright—at least 400 nits for OLEDs and 600 nits for LCDs—plus support special HDR image formats. The rich details and sparkling highlights make HDR photographs and videos more lifelike—almost like looking out a window!

NOTE I'd love to show you a comparison between SDR and HDR, but it's impossible in print. Go to your local computer store and ask for a demo.

Adaptive Sync

When a graphics card is working hard, the number of frames it can generate in any given second fluctuates wildly. When the display and graphics card are out of sync, different parts of the screen may show different frames. This jarring effect is called *tearing*, and the people who make graphics cards and displays have been working on this problem for years.

An early approach to this problem, vertical sync (V-sync), avoids tearing by using a fixed refresh cycle—at the expense of higher latency. *Adaptive sync* addressed this tradeoff by enabling a display to synchronize its refresh rate with the graphics card's refresh rate. NVIDIA developed proprietary adaptive sync technology it calls *G-Sync*, and in response, AMD developed a royalty-free adaptive sync technology called *FreeSync*. Both technologies are entering their second generations with HDR support: FreeSync Premium Pro and G-Sync Ultimate.

NOTE Dynamic refresh rates have other applications as well. Some portable devices, for example, may lower the refresh rate to save power when there isn't much animation to render.

These technologies are a big improvement for gaming, but there's a downside: minimal cross-compatibility. To take advantage of adaptive sync, your graphics card and monitor either both need to support FreeSync or both need to support G-Sync (although NVIDIA has very recently announced support for a handful of FreeSync monitors via their G-Sync Compatible program). If you want adaptive sync, research the compatibility of your components carefully!

Additional Display Topics

Display technologies play such a huge role in modern computing that it's hard to believe people used computers for years without anything like a modern display. The rapid growth and development of computing technology is nowhere more visible than in the ever-growing selection of super-thin, curved, astonishingly clear, ultra-wide, blazing-fast, efficient, jaw-droppingly huge displays.

The pace of change in display technologies is so fast that it's hard to keep up, but some of these new bells and whistles cost an arm and a leg. A good tech needs to keep up with these developments in order to pick out displays with features that are meaningful to their users, and avoid blowing the budget on features they could live without. With that in mind, let's look at a few additional display topics that you won't find on this edition of the exam, but you're bound to run into in the real world: microLED displays and external GPUs.

MicroLED

Starting in the early 2010s, *microLED (μLED)* displays, which form pixels using groups of microscopic LEDs, have been looming on the horizon. This display technology threatens to outperform both LCD and OLED panels on key qualities like energy efficiency, brightness, contrast, response time, and durability. There's no definite timeline, but several companies have hundreds of engineers working on microLED technology, including heavyweights such as Sony, Samsung, and Apple. It's already mature enough to show up in niche real-world uses such as (projector-less!) movie theater screens and large video walls—but not yet in mass-produced display panels.

eGPUs

Manufacturers have taken advantage of the blistering throughput of the latest USB and Thunderbolt busses to create *external graphics processing units (eGPUs)*, standalone boxes with video cards for video processing and gaming. eGPUs enable you to edit 4K on the go and then play graphics-intensive games on portable computers, such as ultrabooks and MacBook Pros. The portables stay thin and light, unlike dedicated gaming portables. Plus, if you want to edit or game but need an ultra-portable computer, you don't need to shell out for a dedicated video production or gaming machine in addition.

You'll find two main types of eGPUs: those that include a GPU, and empty *enclosures* you can install your own GPU in. Recent versions of the Gigabyte AORUS Gaming Box wrap a high-end Gigabyte-branded NVIDIA gaming card in an enclosure that includes a power supply, water cooling, and several ports for video and peripherals. It has HDMI and DP ports for video, USB ports for key peripherals like a mouse and keyboard, an Ethernet port for wired network access, and a Thunderbolt port for connecting to your computer. This lone Thunderbolt port is powerful enough to supply all of these to a laptop—and even charge it!

Empty enclosures have a similar set of features, but you'll have to do a little research to ensure that your card(s) and enclosure are compatible.

Chapter Review

Questions

1. What do we call the time it takes for all of the sub-pixels on the panel to change from one state to another?

   A. Refresh rate

   B. Redraw rate

   C. Response rate

   D. Transfer rate

2. What provides the illumination for LCD monitors?

    A. Backlights

    B. Inverter

    C. Lamp

    D. LCD panel

3. While he's at his desk, Dudley wants to connect his MacBook Air (which has a pair of Thunderbolt 3 ports) to a flat-panel monitor, USB mouse, and USB keyboard. Which of the following could meet his need?

    A. A monitor with at least two built-in USB ports and a USB Type-C upstream port

    B. Three Thunderbolt-to-USB adapters

    C. A keyboard-video-mouse (KVM) switch

    D. One Thunderbolt-to-DisplayPort adapter and two Thunderbolt-to-USB adapters

4. How do you measure brightness of a projector?

    A. Lumens

    B. Pixels

    C. LEDs

    D. CCFLs

5. Which of these aspect ratios is associated with ultrawide monitors?

    A. 16:9

    B. 21:9

    C. 4:3

    D. 3:2

6. Which type of memory are you most likely to find in a recent high-end dedicated graphics card for a desktop computer?

    A. HBM

    B. DDR

    C. GDDR

    D. LP-DDR

7. Depending on version, Thunderbolt ports manifest as one of which two connector formats?

    A. DisplayPort and Mini DisplayPort

    B. DisplayPort and Mini HDMI

    C. Mini DisplayPort and USB Type-C

    D. Mini HDMI and USB Type-C

8. Which of these is not a light-emitting technology?

   A. CCFL

   B. LED

   C. OLED

   D. LCD

9. A company executive calls complaining that the projector mounted on the ceiling of the conference room suddenly cut off in the middle of her presentation to the board. You go to check it out while the room is not in use, but it seems to work fine. Which of the following is most likely?

   A. The power cord wiggled loose.

   B. The lamp went out.

   C. The projector went to sleep because she forgot to configure her OS to extend the desktop to the projector.

   D. The projector overheated and shut down because the fan stopped working or its filter is clogged.

10. Projectors with which of the following kinds of light source take longer to start up and shut down?

   A. CCFL

   B. Lamp

   C. Laser

   D. LED

Answers

   1. C. The amount of time it takes for all of the sub-pixels on the panel to go from pure black to pure white and back again is called the response rate.

   2. A. The backlights provide the illumination for the LCD panel.

   3. A. If Dudley gets a monitor with at least two USB ports and a USB Type-C upstream port, he can connect the display, mouse, and keyboard all to a single Thunderbolt port on his MacBook Air.

   4. A. The brightness of a projector is measured in lumens.

   5. B. The widest aspect ratio among this group, 21:9, is associated with ultrawide monitors.

   6. B. DDR is the type of memory you will likely find in a high-end graphics card for a desktop computer.

   7. C. Thunderbolt 1 and 2 both use the Mini DisplayPort connector, while Thunderbolt 3 and 4 use the USB Type-C connector.

8. **D.** Because it doesn't emit its own light, liquid crystal display (LCD) technology requires a backlight.

9. **D.** Since the projector worked when you tried it, the lamp didn't go out. It is possible the power cord wiggled loose, but the fact that it's mounted on the ceiling reduces the likelihood that anything could have wiggled the cord. The projector probably didn't go to sleep if she was actively presenting. If the projector overheats due to a dead fan or clogged filter, it will shut down to protect itself.

10. **B.** Projector lamps need time to heat up before the projector is ready and time to cool down after use.

CHAPTER

CHAPTER 18

Essentials of Networking

In this chapter, you will learn how to

- Describe the basic roles of various networked computers
- Discuss network technologies and Ethernet
- Describe a typical Ethernet implementation

It's hard to find a computer that's not connected to a network. Whether you're talking about a workstation that's part of a large enterprise network or discussing that smartphone in your pocket, every computer has some form of network connection. CompTIA includes a lot of networking coverage in the CompTIA A+ exams.

This chapter dives into networks in detail, especially the underlying hardware and technologies that make up the bulk of networks in today's homes and businesses. The discussion starts by examining the roles computers play in networking, helping you associate specific names with devices and services you've undoubtedly used many times already. The second portion, and the heart of the chapter, focuses on the now-standard network technology used in most networks, regardless of operating system. The final section examines how this network technology looks in a normal workplace.

1101

Roles Hosts Play in Networks

Take a moment to think about what you do on a network. Most of us, when asked, would say, "surf the Internet," or "watch YouTube videos," or maybe "print to the printer downstairs." These are all good reasons to use a network, but what ties them together? In each of these situations, you use your computer (the *local host*) to access "stuff" stored on a *remote host* (not your local computer). A *host* is any computing device connected to a network. So what do remote computers have that you might want (see Figure 18-1)?

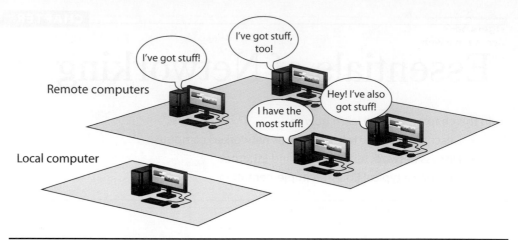

Figure 18-1 Accessing remote computers

NOTE Terminology shifts as soon as computing devices network together. Because a computing device can take many forms, not just a PC or workstation, we need a term to define networked devices. A *host* is any computing device connected to a network. A *local host*, therefore, refers to what's in front of you, like your macOS workstation. A *remote host* refers to some other computing device on the network or reachable beyond the network (more on those later).

Each networked host fulfills a certain *role*. A remote computer called a *Web server* stores the files that make up a Web site. The Web server uses server programs to store and share the data. So the role of the Web server is to provide access to Web sites. Two popular Web server programs are Apache HTTP Server and Microsoft Internet Information Services (IIS). When you access a Web site, your *Web browser* (likely Mozilla Firefox, Google Chrome, Safari, or Microsoft Edge) asks the Web server to share the Web page files and then displays them (see Figure 18-2). Because your computer asks for the Web page, we call it the *client*. That's the role of the local host in this example. The remote computer that serves the Web site is a *server*.

NOTE Any computer that's running a sharing program is by definition a server.

But what about YouTube? YouTube also uses Web servers, but these Web servers connect to massive video databases. Like a normal Web server, these remote computers share the videos with your client device, but they use special software capable of sending video fast enough that you can watch it without waiting (see Figure 18-3).

Figure 18-2
Accessing a Web
page

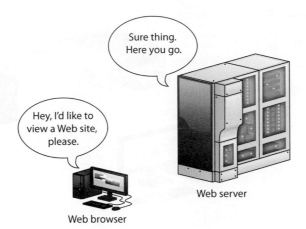

But we don't need the Internet to share stuff. Figure 18-4 shows a small home network with each computer running Windows. One of the computers on the network has a printer connected via a USB port. This computer has enabled a printer-sharing program built into Windows so that the other computers on the network can use the printer. That computer, therefore, takes on the role of a *print server*.

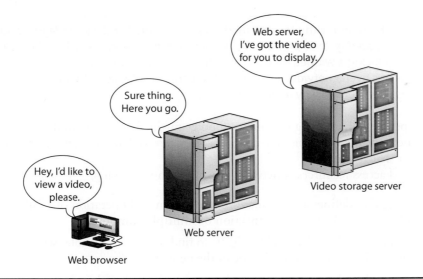

Figure 18-3   Accessing a YouTube page

Figure 18-4
Sharing a printer
in Windows

No matter how big the network, we use networks to share and access stuff. This stuff might be Web pages, videos, printers, folders, e-mail messages, music . . . what you can share and access is limited only by your ability to find a server program capable of sharing it and a client program that can access it.

Each type of server gets a label that defines its role. A networked host that enables you to access a bunch of files and folders is called a file server, or fileshare. The networked host you use to access e-mail messages? It's called a *mail server*. Truth in advertising!

NOTE Along with common modern servers, you'll find a lot of *legacy* and *embedded systems* performing very specific, non-modern tasks. A factory producing a widget, for example, might use a proprietary controller that works over a network. Even though technically obsolete, that network unit isn't broken, so why replace it?

Network people call anything that one computer might share with another a *resource*. The goal of networking, therefore, is to connect computers so that they can share resources or access other shared resources.

To share and access resources, a network must have the following:

1. Something that defines and standardizes the design and operation of cabling, network cards, and the interconnection of multiple computers

2. An addressing method that enables clients to find servers and enables servers to send data to clients, no matter the size of the network

3. Some method of sharing resources and accessing those shared resources

Let's look now at the first of these network needs and discuss current industry standards.

Networking Technologies

When the first network designers sat down at a café to figure out how to get two or more computers to share data and peripherals, they had to write a lot of notes on little white napkins to answer even the most basic questions. The first question was: *How*? It's easy to say, "Well, just run a wire between them!" But that doesn't tell us how the wire works or how the computers connect to the wire. Here are some more big-picture questions:

- How will each computer be identified?
- If two or more computers want to talk at the same time, how do you ensure that all conversations are understood?
- What kind of wire? What gauge? How many wires in the cable? Which wires do what? How long can the cable be? What type of connectors?

Clearly, making a modern network entails a lot more than just stringing up some cable! As you saw a bit earlier, most networks have one or more client machines, devices that request information or services, and a server, the machine that hosts and shares the data. Both clients and servers need *network interface controllers (NICs)* that define or label the machine on the network. A NIC also breaks files into smaller data units to send across the network and reassembles the units it receives into whole files. You also need some medium for delivering the data units between two or more devices—most often this is a wire that can carry electrical pulses; sometimes it's radio waves or other wireless methods. Finally, a computer's operating system has to be able to communicate with its own networking hardware and with other machines on the network. Figure 18-5 shows a typical network layout.

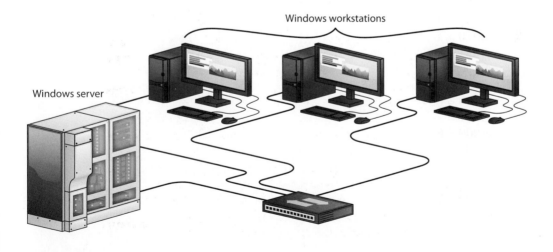

Figure 18-5 A typical network

EXAM TIP Not too many years ago, every NIC came on an expansion card that you added to a motherboard. Most techs called that card a *network interface card* or *NIC*. Now that every motherboard has the networking feature built in, the acronym has shifted to network interface *controller*. You're likely to only see the term *NIC* on the exams, although the objectives this go-around call them *network interface cards*.

Frames and NICs

Data is moved from one device to another in discrete chunks called *frames*. NICs create and process frames.

NOTE You'll sometimes hear the word packet used instead of frames—this is incorrect. Packets are included within a frame. You'll find more information about packets in Chapter 19.

Every NIC in the world has a built-in identifier, an address unique to that network card, called a *media access control (MAC) address*. A MAC address is a *binary number*, meaning it's a string of ones and zeros. Each one or zero is called a *bit*.

The MAC address is 48 bits long, providing more than 281 *trillion* MAC addresses, so there are plenty of MAC addresses to go around. Because people have trouble keeping track of that many ones and zeros, we need another way to display the addresses. *Hexadecimal* is shorthand for representing strings of ones and zeros. One hex character is used to represent four binary characters. Here's the key:

$$0000 = 0$$
$$0001 = 1$$
$$0010 = 2$$
$$0011 = 3$$
$$0100 = 4$$
$$0101 = 5$$
$$0110 = 6$$
$$0111 = 7$$
$$1000 = 8$$
$$1001 = 9$$
$$1010 = A$$
$$1011 = B$$
$$1100 = C$$

1101 = D
1110 = E
1111 = F

So, MAC addresses may be binary, but we represent them by using 12 hexadecimal characters. These MAC addresses are burned into every NIC, and some NIC makers print the MAC address on the card. Figure 18-6 shows the System Information utility description of a NIC, with the MAC address highlighted.

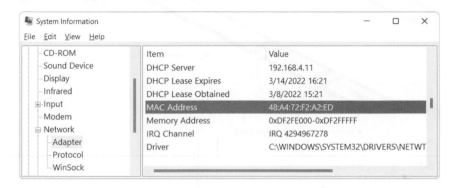

Figure 18-6 MAC address

 NOTE Even though MAC addresses are embedded into the NIC, some NICs allow you to change the MAC address on the NIC.

Hey! I thought we were talking about frames! Well, we are, but you need to understand MAC addresses to understand frames.

The many varieties of frames share common features (see Figure 18-7). First, frames contain the MAC address of the network card to which the data is being sent. Second, they have the MAC address of the network card that sent the data. Third is the data itself (at this point, we have no idea what the data is—certain software handles that question), which can vary in size depending on the type of frame. Finally, the frame must contain some type of data check to verify that the data was received in good order. Most frames use a clever mathematical algorithm called a cyclic redundancy check (CRC).

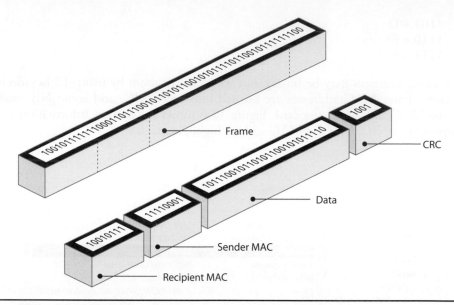

Figure 18-7   Generic frame

Try This!

MAC Address Search

Every personal computing device has a MAC address assigned to each network connection type it offers. Any number of troubleshooting scenarios will have you scrambling to find a device's MAC address, so try this!

You have many ways to discover the MAC address(es) in Windows, macOS, and Linux. The simplest is through the command-line interface. Here's a method in Windows. At the prompt, type **ipconfig /all** and press ENTER. You'll find the MAC address listed as the "Physical Address" under the Ethernet adapter Local Area Connection category.

Which command do you think would work at the Terminal in macOS and Linux? How do you figure out which switch to use? (Refresh your memory of commands in Chapter 15.)

This discussion of frames raises a question: How big is a frame? Or more specifically, how much data do you put into each frame? How do you ensure that the receiving system understands the *way* the data was broken down by the sending machine and can thus put the pieces back together? The hard part of answering these questions is that they encompass so many items. When the first networks were created, *everything* from the frames to the connectors to the type of cable had to be invented from scratch.

To make a successful network, you need the sending and receiving devices to use the same network technology. Over the years, many hardware protocols came and went, but today only one hardware protocol dominates the modern computing landscape: *Ethernet*. Ethernet was developed for wired networking, but even wireless networks use Ethernet as the basis for their signals. If you want to understanding networking, you need to understand Ethernet.

Ethernet

A consortium of companies, including Digital Equipment Corporation, Intel, and Xerox, invented the first network in the mid-1970s. More than just create a network, they wrote a series of standards that defined everything necessary to get data from one computer to another. This series of standards was called *Ethernet*. Over the years, Ethernet has gone through hundreds of distinct improvements in areas such as speed, signaling, and cabling. We call these improvements *Ethernet flavors*.

Through all the improvements in Ethernet, the Ethernet frame hasn't changed in over 25 years. This is very important: you can have any combination of hardware devices and cabling using different Ethernet flavors on a single Ethernet network and, in most cases, the hosts will be able to communicate just fine.

Most modern Ethernet networks employ one of two speeds, *1000BASE-T* or *10GBASE-T*, which were preceded by *10BASE-T* and *100BASE-TX*. As the numbers in the names suggest, 10BASE-T networks run at 10 Mbps, 100BASE-TX networks (called Fast Ethernet) run at 100 Mbps, 1000BASE-T networks (called Gigabit Ethernet) run at 1000 Mbps, or 1 Gbps, and 10GBASE-T runs at speeds of up to 10 Gbps. All four technologies—collectively referred to as just plain Ethernet—use a star bus topology (discussed in the next section) and connect via a type of cable called unshielded twisted pair (UTP).

 NOTE Ethernet developers continue to refine the technology. *Fast Ethernet* (100BASE-TX) is still out there on many older devices. *Gigabit Ethernet* (1000BASE-T) might be the most common desktop standard now, but 2.5-, 5-, and 10-Gigabit Ethernet (10GBASE-T) are becoming more common for desktop power users. 50/100-Gigabit Ethernet is out in datacenter environments as well.

The Ethernet Star Bus

With all Ethernet networks, every individual host connects to a central box. You attach each system to this box via cables to special ports. The box takes care of all the tedious details required by the network to get frames sent to the correct systems. This layout, which looks something like a star, is called a *star bus* topology (see Figure 18-8). (The *bus* refers to the internal wiring in the box. The *star* refers to the wires leading from the box to the hosts.)

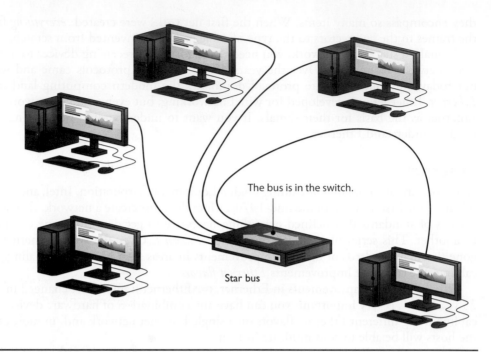

The bus is in the switch.

Star bus

Figure 18-8 Ethernet star bus

 NOTE The term *topology* refers to the physical or logical layout of the network connections—that is, how everything connects. A star bus topology combines two traditional ways to make a network and thus gets another name: a *hybrid topology*.

The central box—the *switch*—provides a common point of connection for network devices. Switches can have a wide variety of ports. Most consumer-level switches have 4 or 8 ports, but business-level switches can have 32 or more ports.

Early Ethernet networks used a *hub*. A switch is a far superior version of a hub and replaced hubs in the 2000s. (Why CompTIA continues to include hubs in the CompTIA A+ objectives is a mystery.) Figure 18-9 shows a typical consumer-level switch.

Figure 18-9
A switch

Hubs and switches look pretty much identical and they perform the same basic job: taking the signal from one host and then repeating the signal out to other hosts. Even though they look the same and do functionally the same job, they do the job differently. Basically, hubs were stupid *repeaters*: anything sent in one port automatically went out all the other connected ports. Switches are smart repeaters: they memorize the MAC addresses of all the connected devices and only send out repeated signals to the correct host. This makes switched networks much faster than hubbed networks.

A simple example demonstrates the difference between hubs and switches. Let's say you have a network of 24 machines, all using 100-Mbps NICs attached to a 100-Mbps hub or switch. We would say the network's *bandwidth* is 100 Mbps. If you put the 24 systems on a 24-port 100-Mbps hub, you would have 24 computers *sharing* the 100 Mbps of bandwidth. A switch addresses this problem by making each port its own separate network. Each system gets to use the full bandwidth. The bottom line? Once switches became affordable, hubs went away.

The connection between a computer and a switch is called a *segment*. With most cable types, Ethernet segments are limited to 100 meters or less. You cannot use a splitter to split a single segment into two or more connections with an Ethernet network that uses this star bus topology. Doing so prevents the switch from recognizing which host is sending or receiving a signal, and no hosts connected to a split segment will be able to communicate. Splitters negatively *affect signal quality*.

Cheap and centralized, Ethernet's star bus topology does not go down if a single cable breaks. True, the network would go down if the switch failed, but that is rare.

Unshielded Twisted Pair

Unshielded twisted pair (UTP) cabling is the specified cabling for 100/1000BASE-T as well as 10GBASE-T and is the predominant cabling system used today. Many types of twisted pair cabling are available, and which type should be used depends on the needs of the network. Twisted pair cabling consists of AWG 22–26 gauge copper wire twisted together into color-coded pairs. Each wire is individually insulated and encased as a group in a common jacket.

 EXAM TIP Know the distinctions between copper and fiber optic cables when making decisions for an organization's infrastructure.

UTP cables come in categories that define the maximum speed at which data can be transferred (also called *bandwidth*). The major categories (Cats) are outlined in Table 18-1.

The Cat level should be clearly marked on the cable, as Figure 18-10 shows.

The *Telecommunication Industry Association (TIA)* establishes the UTP categories, which fall under the ANSI/TIA 568 specification. The *American National Standards Institute (ANSI)* accredits TIA (and many other) standards so that they assure things work across industry and, equally importantly, along with international standards. Currently, most installers use Cat 5e, Cat 6, or Cat 6a cable.

Cat 1	Standard telephone line.
Cat 3	Designed for 10-Mbps networks; a variant that used all four pairs of wires supported 100-Mbps speeds.
Cat 5	Designed for 100-Mbps networks.
Cat 5e	Enhanced to handle 1-Gbps and 2.5-Gbps networks at 100-meter segments.
Cat 6	Supports 1-Gbps, 2.5-Gbps, and 5-Gbps networks at 100-meter segments; 10-Gbps networks up to 55-meter segments.
Cat 6a	Supports 10-Gbps networks at 100-meter segments.
Cat 6e	A nonstandard term used by a few manufacturers for Cat 6 or Cat 6a.
Cat 7	Supports 10-Gbps networks at 100-meter segments; shielding for individual wire pairs reduces crosstalk and noise problems. Cat 7 is not an ANSI/TIA standard.

Table 18-1 Cat Levels

Figure 18-10
Cable markings
for Cat level

Shielded Twisted Pair

Shielded twisted pair (STP), as its name implies, consists of twisted pairs of wires surrounded by shielding to protect them from electromagnetic interference (EMI). STP is pretty rare for 1000BASE-T networks, primarily because there's so little need for STP's shielding; it only really matters in locations with excessive electronic noise, such as a shop floor area with lots of lights, electric motors, or other machinery that could cause problems for other cables. Some STP cables are rated for *direct burial.* A cable rated for direct burial will have a thicker jacket, and some variety of waterproofing to make it suitable for outdoor open-air use or . . . direct burial underground.

Ethernet with Twisted Pair

The 10BASE-T and 100BASE-TX standards required two pairs of wires: a pair for sending and a pair for receiving. 10BASE-T ran on an ancient Cat version called Cat 3, but typically used at least Cat 5 cable. 100BASE-TX required at least Cat 5 to run. 1000BASE-T needs all four pairs of wires in Cat 5e and higher cables, and 10GBASE-T requires all four pairs, but in Cat 6 or higher. These cables use a connector called an *RJ45* connector. The *RJ (registered jack)* designation was invented by Ma Bell (the phone company, for you youngsters) years ago and is still used today.

NOTE There are Cat levels for connectors as well as cables. Don't even try to use a Cat 5e RJ45 connector with a Cat 6 cable.

Currently only two types of RJ connectors are used for networking: RJ11 and RJ45 (see Figure 18-11). *RJ11* connects a traditional telephone to the telephone jack in the wall of your house. It supports up to two pairs of wires, though most phone lines use only one pair. The other pair is used to support a second phone line. RJ11 connectors are primarily used for telephone-based Internet connections (see Chapter 21). RJ45 is the standard for UTP connectors. RJ45 has connections for up to four pairs and is visibly much wider than RJ11. Figure 18-12 shows the position of the #1 and #8 pins on an RJ45 jack.

Figure 18-11
RJ11 (top) and
RJ45 (bottom)

Figure 18-12
RJ45 pin
numbers

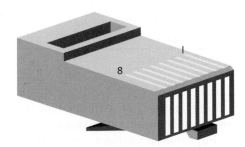

Plenum Versus PVC Cabling

Most workplace installations of network cable go up above the ceiling and then drop down through the walls to present a nice port in the wall. The space in the ceiling, under the floors, and in the walls through which cable runs is called the plenum space. The potential problem with this cabling running through the plenum space is that the protective sheathing for networking cables, called the jacket, is made from plastic, and if you get any plastic hot enough, it creates smoke and noxious fumes.

(continued)

Standard network cables usually use *PVC (polyvinyl chloride)* for the jacket, but PVC produces noxious fumes when burned. Fumes from cables burning in the plenum space can quickly spread throughout the building, so you want to use a more fire-retardant cable in the plenum space. Plenum-grade cable is simply network cabling with a fire-retardant jacket and is required for cables that go in the plenum space. Plenum-grade cable costs about three to five times more than PVC, but you should use it whenever you install cable in a plenum space.

ANSI/TIA has two standards for connecting the RJ45 connector to the UTP cable: *T568A* and *T568B*. Both are acceptable. You do not have to follow any standard as long as you use the same pairings on each end of the cable; however, you will make your life simpler if you choose a standard. Make sure that all of your cabling uses the same standard and you will save a great deal of work in the end. Most importantly, *keep records*!

Like all wires, the wires in UTP are numbered. A number does not appear on each wire, but rather each wire has a standardized color. Table 18-2 shows the official ANSI/TIA Standard Color Chart for UTP.

Pin	T568A	T568B	Pin	T568A	T568B
1	White/Green	White/Orange	5	White/Blue	White/Blue
2	Green	Orange	6	Orange	Green
3	White/Orange	White/Green	7	White/Brown	White/Brown
4	Blue	Blue	8	Brown	Brown

Table 18-2 UTP Cabling Color Chart

 SIM Check out the "568B Wiring" Challenge! sim for Chapter 18. It'll help you memorize the wiring standard for the CompTIA A+ 1101 exam. You find it here: https://www.totalsem.com/110X.

Ethernet with Alternative Connections

UTP is very popular, but Ethernet, as well as other types of networks, can use alternative cabling that you need to be able to identify. Every CompTIA A+ certified tech needs to know about fiber optic cable and coaxial cable, so let's start there.

Fiber Optic

Fiber optic cable is a very attractive way to transmit Ethernet network frames. First, because it uses light instead of electricity, fiber optic cable is immune to electrical problems such as lightning, short circuits, and static. Second, fiber optic signals travel much farther, 2000 meters or more (compared with 100 meters on UTP). Many fiber Ethernet networks use *62.5/125 multimode* fiber optic cable. All fiber Ethernet networks that use this type of cabling require two strands of fiber (one for sending and one for receiving). Figure 18-13 shows three of the more common connectors used in fiber optic networks. The round connector on the left is called a Straight tip, or *ST* connector. The square-shaped middle connecter is called a Subscriber connector, or *SC* connector, and on the far right is a Lucent connector, or *LC* connector.

Figure 18-13
Typical fiber optic cables with ST, SC, and LC connectors

Fiber optics are half-duplex, meaning data flows only one way—hence the need for two cables in a fiber installation. With the older ST and SC connectors, you needed two connectors on every fiber connection. Newer connectors like LC are designed to support two fiber cables in one connector, a real space saver.

Light can be sent down a fiber optic cable as regular light or as laser light. Each type of light requires totally different fiber optic cables. Fiber network technologies based on light-emitting diodes (LEDs) generate light signals that use multimode fiber optic cabling. Light entering a multimode fiber enters from many different angles and these different light rays bounce around the core of the cable. The multiple reflection angles tend to disperse over long distances, so multimode fiber optic cables are used for relatively short connections.

Network technologies that use laser light use single-mode fiber optic cabling. Using laser means that the light rays are aligned, reducing the dispersion over the length of the cable and allowing for phenomenally high transfer rates over long distances. That's why single-mode fiber optic cabling forms the backbone of the Internet!

There are close to 100 different Ethernet fiber optic cabling standards, with names like 10GBASE-SR and 100GBASE-LR1. The major difference is the speed of the network (there are also some important differences in the way systems interconnect, and so on). If you want to use fiber optic cabling, you need a fiber optic switch and fiber optic network cards.

Fiber networks follow the speed and distance limitations of their networking standard, so it's hard to pin down precise numbers on true limitations. Multimode overall is slower and has a shorter range than single-mode. A typical multimode network runs at 10 Gbps, though some can go to 100+ Gbps. Distances for multimode runs generally top out at ~600 meters. With single-mode, speed and distance—depending on the standard—can blow multimode away. The record transmission speed in 2021, for example, was 319 *terabits* per second, and that was over 1800 *miles*!

NOTE There are a number of Ethernet standards that use fiber optic cable instead of UTP.

Coaxial

Early versions of Ethernet ran on *coaxial cable* instead of UTP. While the Ethernet standards using coax are long gone, coax lives on, primarily for cable modems and satellite connections. Coax cable consists of a center cable (core) surrounded by insulation. This in turn is covered with a *shield* of braided cable (see Figure 18-14). The center core actually carries the signal. The shield effectively eliminates outside interference. The entire cable is then surrounded by a protective insulating cover.

Figure 18-14
Typical coax

Coax cables are rated using an RG name. There are hundreds of RG ratings for coax, but the only two you need to know for the CompTIA A+ exam are *RG-59* and *RG-6*. Both standards are rated by impedance, which is measured in ohms. (*Impedance* is the effective resistance to the flow of an alternating current electrical signal through a cable.) Both RG-6 and RG-59 have a 75-ohm impedance. Both of these coax cables are used by your cable television, but RG-59 is thinner and doesn't carry data quite as far as RG-6. The RG rating is clearly marked on the cable.

 NOTE Expect to see more use of the next step up from RG-6, called RG6QS (quad shield) coaxial cable, over the next few years. The extra shielding reduces interference and enables stronger internal signals, useful for pushing more data through the cable. (Think multiple 4K television signals and you'll be on the money about what's driving the upgrade.)

Coax uses a connector known as an *F-type connector*. You might already recognize this connector from the back of your cable modem or TV (see Figure 18-15). There is another type of connector called a BNC connector, but it is largely obsolete and you won't see it on the CompTIA A+ exam.

Figure 18-15
F-type connector

NOTE Coaxial cable implementations can offer acceptable speeds, topping 2 Gbps in some cases. Using splitters to connect multiple hosts to a single cable, however, negatively affects signal quality, lowering the overall speed of the network.

Implementing Ethernet

Regardless of the cabling choice—UTP or fiber—Ethernet networks use a star bus topology. The illustration of a star presented earlier in the chapter in Figure 18-8 doesn't quite translate into real life, so let's turn briefly to look at common implementations of Ethernet.

The Typical LAN

A *local area network (LAN)* is a group of computers located physically close to each other—no more than a few hundred meters apart at most. A LAN might be in a single room, on a single floor, or in a single building. But I'm going to add that a LAN is almost always a group of computers that are able to "hear" each other when one of them sends a broadcast. A group of computers connected by one or more switches is a *broadcast domain* (see Figure 18-16), which means that all nodes receive broadcast frames from every other node.

EXAM TIP For the CompTIA A+ exams, remember that a LAN is a group of networked computers that are close to each other. Also, remember that a LAN is almost always a broadcast domain.

You can set up a LAN in a small office/home office (SOHO) environment in several ways. The most common way—using wireless technology called *Wi-Fi*—dispenses with wires altogether. We'll get there in detail in Chapter 20.

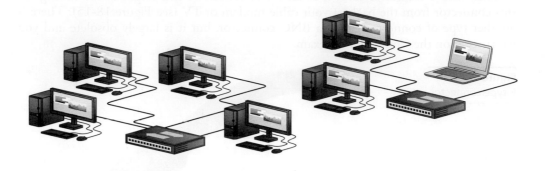

Figure 18-16   Two broadcast domains—two separate LANs

Another option uses the existing electrical network in the building for connectivity. This option, called Ethernet over Power, requires specialized bridges that connect to power outlets. Ethernet over Power has its place in the right situations, and recent innovations have brought speeds up to almost matching Gigabit Ethernet. If you have a computer in a weird place where wireless won't work and traditional cables can't reach, try Ethernet over Power.

Structured Cabling

If you want a functioning, dependable, real-world network, you need a solid understanding of a set of standards collectively called *structured cabling*. These standards, defined by the ANSI/TIA—yes, the same folks who tell you how to crimp an RJ45 onto the end of a UTP cable—give professional cable installers detailed standards on every aspect of a cabled network, from the type of cabling to use to the standards on running cable in walls, even the position of wall outlets.

The CompTIA A+ exams require you to understand the basic concepts involved in installing network cabling and to recognize the components used in a network. The CompTIA A+ exams do not, however, expect you to be as knowledgeable as a professional network designer or cable installer. Your goal should be to understand enough about real-world cabling systems to communicate knowledgeably with cable installers and to perform basic troubleshooting. Granted, by the end of this section, you'll know enough to try running your own cable (I certainly run my own cable), but consider that knowledge extra credit.

The idea of structured cabling is to create a safe, reliable cabling infrastructure for all of the devices that may need interconnection. Certainly this applies to computer networks, but also to telephone, video—anything that might need low-power, distributed cabling.

NOTE   A structured cabling system is useful for more than just computer networks. You'll find structured cabling defining telephone networks and video conferencing setups, for example.

You should understand three issues with structured cabling. We'll start with the basics of how cables connect switches and computers. We'll then look at the components of a network, such as how the cable runs through the walls and where it ends up. This section wraps up with an assessment of connections leading outside your network.

Cable Basics—A Star Is Born

Earlier in this chapter we developed the idea of an Ethernet LAN in its most basic configuration: a switch, some UTP cable, and a few computers—in other words, a typical physical star network (see Figure 18-17).

Figure 18-17   A switch connected by UTP cable to two computers

No law of physics prevents you from placing a switch in the middle of your office and running cables on the floor to all the computers in your network. This setup works, but it falls apart spectacularly when applied to a real-world environment. Three problems present themselves to the network tech. First, the exposed cables running along the floor are just waiting for someone to trip over them, giving that person a wonderful lawsuit opportunity. Simply moving and stepping on the cabling will, over time, cause a cable to fail due to wires breaking or RJ45 connectors ripping off cable ends. Second, the presence of other electrical devices close to the cable can create interference that confuses the signals going through the wire. Third, this type of setup limits your ability to make any changes to the network. Before you can change anything, you have to figure out which cables in the huge rat's nest of cables connected to the switch go to which machines. Imagine *that* troubleshooting nightmare!

"Gosh," you're thinking (okay, I'm thinking it, but you should be, too), "there must be a better way to install a physical network." A better installation would provide safety, protecting the star from vacuum cleaners, clumsy coworkers, and electrical interference. It would have extra hardware to organize and protect the cabling. Finally, the new and improved star network installation would feature a cabling standard with the flexibility to enable the network to grow according to its needs and then to upgrade when the next great network technology comes along. That is the definition of structured cabling.

Structured Cable Network Components

Successful implementation of a basic structured cabling network requires three essential ingredients: a telecommunications room, horizontal cabling, and a work area. Let's zero in on one floor of a typical office. All the cabling runs from individual workstations to a central location, the *telecommunications room*. What equipment goes in there—a switch or a telephone system—is not the important thing. What matters is that all the cables concentrate in this one area.

All cables run horizontally (for the most part) from the telecommunications room to the workstations. This cabling is called, appropriately, *horizontal cabling*. A single piece of installed horizontal cabling is called a *run*. At the opposite end of the horizontal cabling from the telecommunications room is the work area. The *work area* is often simply an office or cubicle that potentially contains a workstation and a telephone. Figure 18-18 shows both the horizontal cabling and work areas.

Figure 18-18
Horizontal
cabling and work
areas

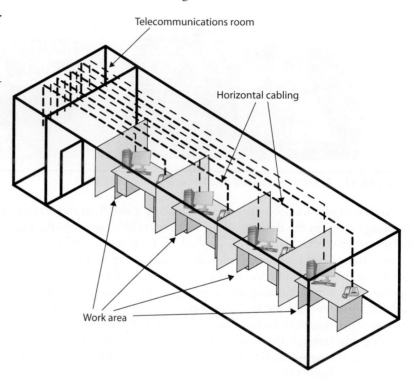

Each of the three parts of a basic star network—the telecommunications room, the horizontal cabling, and the work area(s)—must follow a series of strict standards designed to ensure that the cabling system is reliable and easy to manage. The cabling standards set by ANSI/TIA enable techs to make sensible decisions on equipment installed in the telecommunications room, so let's tackle horizontal cabling first, and then return to the telecommunications room. We'll finish up with the work area.

Horizontal Cabling A horizontal cabling run is the cabling that goes more or less horizontally from a work area to the telecommunications room. In most networks, this cable is a Cat 5e or better UTP, but when you move into structured cabling, the ANSI/TIA standards define a number of other aspects of the cable, such as the type of wires, number of pairs of wires, and fire ratings.

EXAM TIP A single piece of cable that runs from a work area to a telecommunications room is called a *run*. In most networks, this cable is Cat 5e or better UTP.

Solid Core Versus Stranded Core All UTP cables come in one of two types: solid core or stranded core. Each wire in solid core UTP uses a single solid wire. With *stranded core*, each wire is actually a bundle of tiny wire strands. Each of these cable types has its benefits and downsides. Solid core is a better conductor, but it is stiff and will break if handled too often or too roughly. Stranded core is not quite as good a conductor, but it will stand up to substantial handling without breaking. Figure 18-19 shows a close-up of solid and stranded core UTP.

Figure 18-19
Solid and
stranded core
UTP

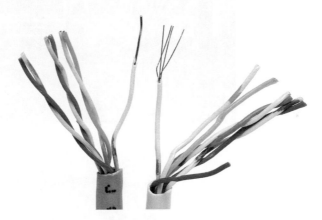

ANSI/TIA specifies that horizontal cabling should always be solid core. Remember, this cabling is going into your walls and ceilings, safe from the harmful effects of shoes and vacuum cleaners. The ceilings and walls enable you to take advantage of the better conductivity of solid core without the risk of cable damage. Stranded cable also has an important function in a structured cabling network, but I need to discuss a few more parts of the network before I talk about where to use stranded UTP cable.

The Telecommunications Room

The telecommunications room is the heart of the basic star. This room is where all the horizontal runs from all the work areas come together. The concentration of all this gear in one place makes the telecommunications room potentially one of the messiest parts of the basic star. Even if you do a nice, neat job of organizing the cables when they are first installed, networks change over time. People move computers, new work areas are added, network topologies are added or improved, and so on. Unless you impose some type of organization, this conglomeration of equipment and cables decays into a nightmarish mess.

Fortunately, the ANSI/TIA structured cabling standards define the use of specialized components in the telecommunications room that make organizing a snap. In fact, it might be fair to say that there are too many options! To keep it simple, we're going to stay with the most common telecommunications room setup and then take a short peek at some other fairly common options.

Equipment Racks   The central component of every telecommunications room is one or more equipment racks. An *equipment rack* provides a safe, stable platform for all the different hardware components. All equipment racks are 19 inches wide, but they vary in height from two- to three-foot-high models that bolt onto a wall (see Figure 18-20) to the more popular floor-to-ceiling models (see Figure 18-21).

Figure 18-20
A short
equipment rack

Figure 18-21
A floor-to-ceiling
rack

 NOTE   Equipment racks evolved out of the railroad signaling racks from the 19th century. The components in a rack today obviously differ a lot from railroad signaling, but the 19-inch width has remained the standard for well over 100 years.

You can mount almost any network hardware component into a rack. All manufacturers make rack-mounted switches that mount into a rack with a few screws. These switches are available with a wide assortment of ports and capabilities. There are even rack-mounted servers, complete with slide-out keyboards, and rack-mounted uninterruptible power supplies (UPSs) to power the equipment (see Figure 18-22).

Figure 18-22
A rack-mounted
UPS

All rack-mounted equipment uses a height measurement known simply as an *RU*. An RU is 1.75 inches. A device that fits in a 1.75-inch space is called a 1RU; a device designed for a 3.5-inch space is a 2RU; and a device that goes into a 7-inch space is called a 4RU. Most rack-mounted devices are 1RU, 2RU, or 4RU.

Patch Panels and Cables   Ideally, once you install horizontal cabling, you should never move it. As you know, UTP horizontal cabling has a solid core, making it pretty stiff. Solid core cables can handle some rearranging, but if you insert a wad of solid core cables directly into your switches, every time you move a cable to a different port on the switch, or move the switch itself, you will jostle the cable. You don't have to move a solid core cable many times before one of the solid copper wires breaks, and there goes a network connection!

Luckily for you, you can easily avoid this problem by using a patch panel. A *patch panel* is simply a box with a row of female connectors (ports) in the front and permanent connections in the back, to which you connect the horizontal cables (see Figure 18-23).

Figure 18-23
Typical patch
panels

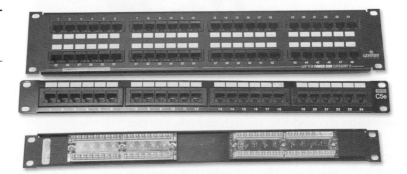

The most common type of patch panel today uses a special type of connector called a *punchdown block,* or sometimes called a *110-punchdown block.* UTP cables connect to a punchdown block using a *punchdown tool.* Figure 18-24 shows a typical punchdown tool, and Figure 18-25 shows the punchdown tool punching down individual strands.

Figure 18-24
Punchdown tool

Figure 18-25
Punching down a punchdown block

The punchdown block has small metal-lined grooves for the individual wires. The punchdown tool has a blunt end that forces the wire into the groove. The metal in the groove slices the cladding enough to make contact.

 EXAM TIP The CompTIA A+ exams expect you to know that a punchdown tool is used for securing UTP connections to a punchdown block. It's not until you go for CompTIA Network+ certification that you'll be expected to know how to use these tools.

Not only do patch panels prevent the horizontal cabling from being moved, but they are also your first line of defense in organizing the cables. All patch panels have space in the front for labels, and these labels are the network tech's best friend! Simply place a tiny label on the patch panel to identify each cable, and you will never have to experience that sinking feeling of standing in the telecommunications room of your nonfunctioning network, wondering which cable is which. If you want to be a purist, there is an official, and rather confusing, ANSI/TIA labeling methodology called ANSI/TIA 606, but many real-world network techs simply use their own internal codes (see Figure 18-26).

Figure 18-26
Typical patch
panels with
labels

Patch panels are available in a wide variety of configurations that include different types of ports and numbers of ports. You can get UTP, STP, or fiber ports, and some manufacturers combine several different types on the same patch panel. Panels are available with 8, 12, 24, 48, or even more ports.

UTP patch panels, like UTP cables, come with Cat ratings, which you should be sure to check. Don't blow a good Cat 6 cable installation by buying a cheap patch panel—get a Cat 6 patch panel! A higher-rated panel supports earlier standards, so you can use a Cat 6 or even Cat 6a rack with Cat 5e cabling. Most manufacturers proudly display the Cat level right on the patch panel (see Figure 18-27).

Figure 18-27
Cat level on
patch panel

Once you have installed the patch panel, you need to connect the ports to the switch through *patch cables*. Patch cables are short (typically two- to five-foot) UTP cables. Patch cables use stranded rather than solid cable, so they can tolerate much more handling. Even though you can make your own patch cables, most people buy premade ones. Buying patch cables enables you to use different-colored cables to facilitate organization (yellow for accounting, blue for sales, or whatever scheme works for you). Most prefabricated patch cables also come with a reinforced (booted) connector specially designed to handle multiple insertions and removals (see Figure 18-28).

Figure 18-28
Typical patch
cable

Rolling Your Own Patch Cables   Although most people prefer simply to purchase premade patch cables, making your own is fairly easy. To make your own, use stranded UTP cable that matches the Cat level of your horizontal cabling. Stranded cable also requires specific crimps, so don't use crimps designed for solid cable. Crimping is simple enough, although getting it right takes some practice.

Figure 18-29 shows the main tool of the crimping trade: an RJ45 *crimper* with both a *wire stripper*, or *cable stripper*, and wire snips built in. Professional cable installers naturally have a wide variety of other tools as well.

 EXAM TIP   The CompTIA A+ exams expect you to know that a cable tech uses a crimper or crimping tool to attach an RJ45 to the end of a UTP cable.

Here are the steps for properly crimping an RJ45 onto a UTP cable. If you have some crimps, cable, and a crimping tool handy, follow along!

1. Cut the cable square using RJ45 crimpers or scissors.

2. Strip off one-half inch of plastic jacket from the end of the cable (see Figure 18-30).

3. Slowly and carefully insert each individual wire into the correct location according to either ANSI/TIA 568A or B (see Figure 18-31). Unravel as little as possible.

4. Insert the crimp into the crimper and press (see Figure 18-32). Don't worry about pressing too hard; the crimper has a stop to prevent you from using too much pressure.

Figure 18-29
Crimper with built-in stripper and snips

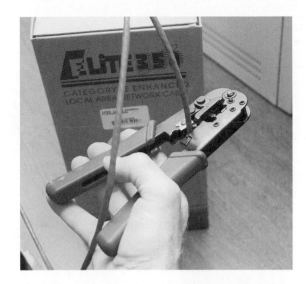

Figure 18-30
Properly stripped cable

Figure 18-31
Inserting the individual strands

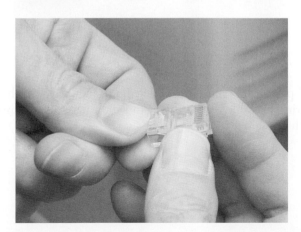

Figure 18-32
Crimping the
cable

Figure 18-33 shows a nicely crimped cable. Note how the plastic jacket goes into the crimp. (The extra strands you can see along with the wires are called *marker threads* or *ripcord*. The Kevlar strands strengthen the cable and enable installers to rip the sheath off easily.)

Figure 18-33
Properly crimped
cable

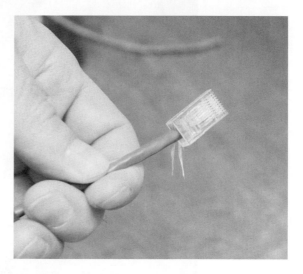

A good patch cable should include a boot. Figure 18-34 shows a boot being slid onto a newly crimped cable. Don't forget to slide each boot onto the patch cable *before* you crimp both ends!

Figure 18-34
Adding a boot

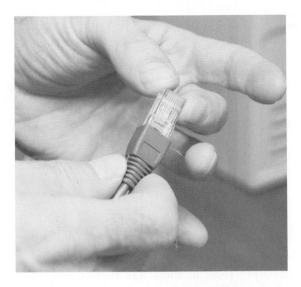

After making a cable, you need to test it to make sure it's properly crimped. I use a handy *cable tester,* available in any good electronics store, to verify all the individual wires are properly connected and in the correct location (see Figure 18-35).

Figure 18-35
Typical tester

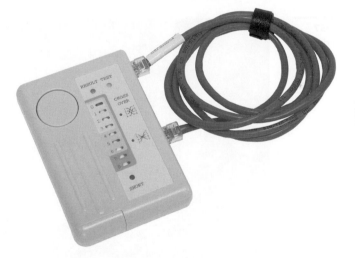

The Work Area

From a cabling standpoint, a work area is nothing more than a wall outlet that serves as the termination point for horizontal network cables: a convenient insertion point for a workstation and a telephone. (In practice, of course, the term "work area" includes the office or cubicle.) A wall outlet itself consists of one or two female jacks to accept the cable, a mounting bracket, and a faceplate. You connect the workstation to the wall outlet with a patch cable (see Figure 18-36).

Figure 18-36
Typical work area outlet

The female RJ45 jacks in these wall outlets also have Cat ratings. You must buy Cat-rated jacks for wall outlets to go along with the Cat rating of the cabling in your network. In fact, many network connector manufacturers use the same connectors, often 110 punchdowns, in the wall outlets that they use on the patch panels (see Figure 18-37). These modular outlets significantly increase the ease of installation.

Figure 18-37
Punching down a modular jack

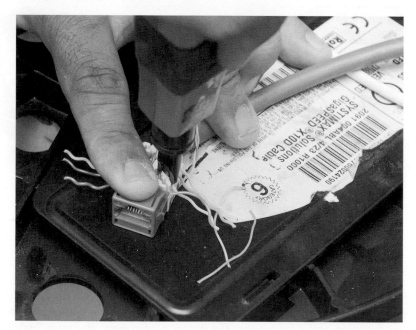

The last step is connecting the workstation to the wall outlet. Here again, most folks use a patch cable. Its stranded cabling stands up to the abuse caused by moving equipment, not to mention the occasional kick.

The work area may be the simplest part of the structured cabling system, but it is also the source of most network failures. When a user can't access the network and you suspect a broken cable, the first place to look is the work area.

Going Wide

A *wide area network (WAN)* is a widespread group of computers connected using long-distance technologies. You connect LANs into a WAN with a magical box called a *router* (see Figure 18-38). The best example of a WAN is the Internet.

Figure 18-38 Two broadcast domains connected by a router—a WAN

You can connect multiple smaller networks into a bigger network, turning a group of LANs into one big WAN, but this raises a couple of issues with network traffic. A computer needs some form of powerful, flexible addressing to address a frame so that it goes to a computer within its own LAN or to a computer on another LAN on the same WAN. Broadcasting is also unacceptable, at least between LANs. If every computer saw every frame, the network traffic would quickly spin out of control! Plus, the addressing scheme needs to work so that routers can sort the frames and send them along to the proper LAN. This process, called *routing*, requires routers and a routing-capable protocol to function correctly.

Routers destroy any incoming broadcast frames, by design. No broadcast frame can ever go through a router. This makes broadcasting still quite common within a single broadcast domain, but never anywhere else.

To go beyond a LAN requires a network protocol—a way machines agree to communicate—that can handle routing. That protocol, for the vast majority of networks, is called TCP/IP, and Chapter 19 begins with the details. For now, review the end-of-chapter material and take some practice exams. See you in Chapter 19!

Chapter Review

Questions

1. How many bits are in a MAC address?
    A. 24
    B. 36
    C. 48
    D. 64

2. What is the minimum Cat level cable required for a 1000BASE-T network?
    A. Cat 1
    B. Cat 5
    C. Cat 5e
    D. Cat 6

3. Which of the following is an example of a hybrid topology?
    A. Bus
    B. Ring
    C. Star
    D. Star bus

4. A typical Cat 6 cable uses which connector?
    A. RJ11
    B. RJ45
    C. Plenum
    D. PVC

5. Why would you use STP over UTP cabling?
    A. Cheaper.
    B. Easier to install.
    C. Better to avoid interference.
    D. They're interchangeable terms.

6. What kind of frame gets received by all NICs in a LAN?
    A. Cat 7
    B. Broadcast
    C. WAN
    D. SC, ST, or LC

7. Safari, Mozilla Firefox, Google Chrome, and Microsoft Edge are all examples of what?

   A. Web servers

   B. Print servers

   C. Web browsers

   D. Proxy servers

8. John's boss asks for a recommendation for connecting the company network to a small satellite building about 1 km from the main campus. The company owns the verdant land in between. Given such a scenario, what network technology implementation should John suggest?

   A. Ethernet over UTP

   B. Ethernet over STP

   C. Ethernet over multimode fiber

   D. Ethernet over single-mode fiber

9. Erin is purchasing cable for the horizontal runs in a new office. What type of UTP cable should Erin order?

   A. Non-plenum/stranded-core

   B. Plenum/solid-core

   C. Plenum/stranded-core

   D. Non-plenum/solid-core

10. Eddard hands Will a cable. Will hands it back and says, meaningfully, "That's a nice F-type connector you've got there." What kind of cable does Eddard have?

   A. Coaxial

   B. Fiber optic

   C. STP

   D. UTP

Answers

1. **C.** MAC addresses are 48-bit.

2. **C.** 1000BASE-T networks need Cat 5 or better UTP.

3. **D.** A star bus topology, like the one used with Ethernet networks, is a hybrid topology.

4. **B.** Cat 6 cables use an RJ45 connector.

5. **C.** Shielded twisted pair cabling handles interference from other electronics much better than unshielded twisted pair.

6. B. All NICs in a LAN will receive broadcast frames.

7. C. All these programs are Web browsers.

8. D. John should suggest the only network technology implementation (listed here) that can cover those distances, Ethernet over single-mode fiber.

9. B. Erin should buy plenum/solid-core cable because it will be used for horizontal runs within the plenum space of the office.

10. A. Eddard has a mighty fine coaxial cable in his hands.

CHAPTER 19

Local Area Networking

In this chapter, you will learn how to
- Explain the basics of interconnecting networks with TCP/IP
- Install and configure wired networks
- Understand network organization and access controls
- Troubleshoot wired networks

Networks dominate the modern computing environment. A vast percentage of businesses have PCs connected in a small local network, and big businesses simply can't survive without connecting their many offices into a single large network.

Because networks are so common today, every good tech needs to know the basics of networking technology, operating systems, implementation, and troubleshooting. Accordingly, this chapter teaches you how to build and troubleshoot a basic network.

The first part of this chapter explores the TCP/IP protocol suite and how Windows uses it in a typical network. Every modern network uses TCP/IP for communicating among devices. You need to know this stuff.

Next, we'll go through the process of setting up a small network from start to finish. This includes details on planning a network, installing and configuring network interface cards (NICs), setting up switches, and configuring TCP/IP.

From there, we'll turn to how we organize modern networks—and control access to all of the resources connected to them.

The chapter closes with troubleshooting a network. Modern operating systems come with plenty of tools to help you when the network stops functioning. I'll show you the tools and combine that with a troubleshooting process that helps you get a network up and running again.

1101/1102

Interconnecting Networks

Ethernet hardware protocol does a fine job of moving data directly from one machine to another inside our network, as you learned in Chapter 18. Up to this point, the only way to distinguish one machine from another is by the MAC address on its network interface card (NIC). But sending a message to any of the billions of networked devices in our world that *aren't* inside our network is a little more complicated. How, for example, would you address a device that doesn't even use Ethernet? (They exist!) How would you send a message to a laptop without knowing whether it's in Alaska or Antarctica?

These questions (and many others) about how to pass messages between networks are answered by another layer of software called the *network protocol*. Over the years there have been many network protocols, most combining multiple simple protocols into groups called *protocol stacks* or *protocol suites*, but *Transmission Control Protocol/Internet Protocol (TCP/IP)* is the primary protocol of most modern networks, including the Internet.

In contrast to physical MAC addresses directly tied to the hardware, IP introduces its own *logical* addressing scheme that isn't coupled to the hardware. IP addressing is hierarchical—devices higher up in each hierarchy know how to direct traffic to addresses within that hierarchy. Each device doesn't need to know exactly how to send a message to every other device—it just needs to know how to send it one step closer to the top of the hierarchy the recipient is under.

Just as switches (which filter and forward by MAC address) interconnect systems on a LAN, we can interconnect LANs themselves into larger *wide area networks (WANs)* with *routers*—devices that filter and forward by *IP address*. A single WAN (see Figure 19-1) might be under the control of a single organization—or it might interconnect multiple organizations, as the Internet does.

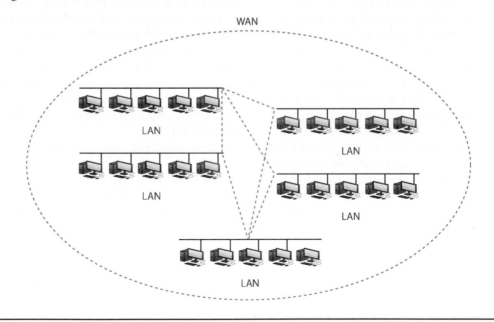

Figure 19-1   WAN concept

Every LAN that connects to the Internet must have a router to interconnect it with an Internet service provider (ISP). A typical SOHO router, like the one shown in Figure 19-2, will have two connections to enable it to connect to two different LANs, but large enterprise routers (like the ones at an ISP) may interconnect dozens of LANs.

Figure 19-2
Typical SOHO
router

One port on the router connects to your LAN's switch and receives an IP address that's part of your network. The other port on the router connects to the next network, usually to your ISP, which in turn connects to millions of other routers and billions of other computers (see Figure 19-3). The IP address of the "LAN" side of your router (the port connected to your LAN) is the address your computer uses to send data to anything outside your network. This is called the *default gateway*.

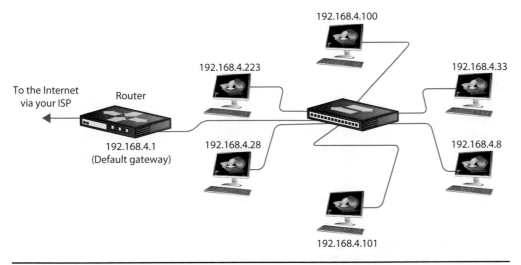

Figure 19-3 Default gateway

In this section, we'll investigate a number of topics related to interconnecting networks, including the two IP network-addressing schemes (IPv4 and IPv6), the role DNS plays, the two main transmission protocols in the TCP/IP suite, and the settings and tools you should understand to actually work with TCP/IP.

Network Addressing with IPv4

Any network address must provide two pieces of information: it must uniquely identify the machine and it must locate that machine within the larger network. In a TCP/IP network, the *IP address* identifies the node and the network on which it resides. If you look at an IP address, it's not apparent which part of the address identifies the network and which part is the unique identifier of the computer.

IP Addresses

The IP address is the unique identification number for your system on the network. Many systems today still rely on the *Internet Protocol version 4 (IPv4)* addressing scheme. IPv4 addresses consist of four sets of eight binary numbers (octets), each set separated by a period. This is called *dotted-decimal notation.* So, instead of a computer being called SERVER1, it gets an address like so:

202.34.16.11

Written in binary form, the address would look like this:

11001010.00100010.00010000.00001011

To make the addresses more comprehensible to users, the TCP/IP folks decided to write the decimal equivalents:

00000000 = 0
00000001 = 1
00000010 = 2
. . .
11111111 = 255

Subnet Mask

Part of every IP address identifies the network (the *network ID*), and another part identifies the local computer (the *host ID,* or host) on the network. A NIC uses a value called the *subnet mask* to distinguish which part of the IP address identifies the network ID and which part of the address identifies the host. The subnet mask blocks out (or masks) the network portion of an IP address.

Let's look at a typical subnet mask: 255.255.255.0. When you compare the subnet mask to the IP address, any part that's all 255s is the network ID. Any part that's all zeros is the host ID. Look at the following example:

IP address: 192.168.4.33
Subnet mask: 255.255.255.0

Because the first three octets are 255, the network ID is 192.168.4 and the host ID is 33.

Every computer on a single LAN must have the same network ID and a unique host ID. That means every computer on the preceding network must have an IP address that starts with 192.168.4. Every computer on the network must have a unique IP address.

If two computers have the same IP address, they won't be able to talk to each other, and other computers won't know where to send data. This is called an *IP conflict*.

You can never have an IP address that ends with a 0 or a 255, so for the preceding example, the LAN can have addresses starting at 192.168.4.1 and ending at 192.168.4.254: a total of 254 addresses.

Originally, subnets fell into "classes," such as A, B, or C, determined by the corresponding octet in the subnet mask. A Class C address, like the one just discussed, had a subnet mask of 255.255.255.0. A Class B address, in contrast, had a subnet mask of 255.255.0.0. The latter class left two full octets (16 bits) just for host numbers. That meant a single Class B network ID could have $2^{16} - 2$ unique host IDs = 65,534 addresses. For completeness, note that a Class A address subnet mask was 255.0.0.0.

 EXAM TIP The addresses that start with "192.168." here are examples of *private addresses*. The architects of IP addressing sliced off three blocks of addresses for use in private networks—one apiece of Class A, Class B, and Class C. If you see an address that starts with "10.", it's a private address from that Class A block. An address that starts with "172.16–31" is from the Class B block, while an address starting with "192.168" is from the Class C block. All other IPv4 addresses are *public addresses*.

Although it's still common to see subnet masks as one to three groups of "255," the class system is long gone. Because the subnet mask numbers are binary, you can make a subnet with any number of ones in the subnet mask.

The current system is called *Classless Inter-Domain Routing (CIDR)* and it works easily in binary, but a little less prettily when you show the numbers in the octets. A quick example should suffice to illustrate this point.

A subnet mask of 255.255.255.0 translates into binary as such:

    11111111.11111111.11111111.00000000

With CIDR, network techs refer to the subnet mask by the number of ones it contains. The preceding subnet mask, for example, has 24 ones. Jill the tech would call this subnet a /24 (*whack twenty-four*). As you've seen already, a /24 network ID offers up to 254 host IDs.

If you want a network ID that enables more host IDs, buy one that has a subnet mask with fewer ones, like this one:

    11111111.11111111.11110000.00000000

Count the ones. (There are 20.) The ones mask the network ID. That leaves 12 digits for the host IDs. Do the binary math: $2^{12} - 2 = 4094$ unique addresses in a single /20 network ID.

When you change the binary number—11110000—to an octet, you get the following:

    255.255.240.0

It might look a little odd to a new tech, but that's a perfectly acceptable subnet mask. The binary behind the octets works.

From a practical standpoint, all you must know as a tech is how to set up a computer to accept an IP address and subnet mask combination that your network administrator tells you to use.

Network Addressing with IPv6

When the early developers of the Internet set out to create an addressing or naming scheme for devices on the Internet, they faced several issues. Of course, they needed to determine how the numbers or names worked, and for that they developed the Internet Protocol and IP addresses. But beyond that, they had to determine how many computers might exist in the future, and then make the IP address space even bigger to give Internet naming longevity. But how many computers would exist in the future?

The 32-bit IPv4 standard offers only 4 billion addresses. That was plenty in the beginning, but seemed insufficient once the Internet went global.

The Internet Engineering Task Force (IETF) developed an IP addressing scheme called *Internet Protocol version 6 (IPv6)* that is slowly replacing IPv4. IPv6 extends the 32-bit IP address space to 128 bits, allowing up to 2^{128} addresses—that should hold us for the foreseeable future!

NOTE If you really want to know how many IP addresses IPv6 provides, here's your number: 340,282,366,920,938,463,463,374,607,431,768,211,456. Say that three times fast!

Although they achieve the same function—enabling computers on IP networks to send packets to each other—IPv6 and IPv4 differ a lot when it comes to implementation. This section provides you with a quick overview to get you up to speed with IPv6 and show you how it differs from IPv4.

EXAM TIP IPv4 addresses use 32 bits and IPv6 addresses use 128 bits. Be sure you can identify their address length differences and address conventions.

IPv6 Address Notation

The notation for a familiar 32-bit IPv4 address—such as 197.169.94.82—contains four octets separated by a period. The 128-bit IPv6 addresses are written like this:

2001:0000:0000:3210:0800:200c:00cf:1234

IPv6 uses a colon as a separator, instead of the period used in IPv4's dotted-decimal format. Each group is a hexadecimal number between 0000 and ffff called, unofficially, a *field* or *hextet*.

NOTE For those who don't play with hex regularly, one hexadecimal character (for example, F/f) represents 4 bits, so four hexadecimal characters make a 16-bit group. For some reason, the IPv6 developers didn't provide a name for the "group of four hexadecimal characters," so many techs and writers have taken to calling them fields or "hextets" to distinguish them from IPv4 "octets."

A complete IPv6 address always has eight groups of four hexadecimal characters. If this sounds like you're going to type in really long IP addresses, don't worry, IPv6 offers a number of ways to shorten the address in written form.

First, leading zeros can be dropped from any group, so 00cf becomes cf and 0000 becomes 0. Let's rewrite the previous IPv6 address using this shortening method:

2001:0:0:3210:800:200c:cf:1234

Second, you can remove one or more consecutive groups of all zeros, leaving the two colons together. For example, using the :: rule, you can write the previous IPv6 address as

2001::3210:800:200c:cf:1234

You can remove any number of consecutive groups of zeros to leave a double colon, but you can only use this trick *once* in an IPv6 address.

Take a look at this IPv6 address:

fe80:0000:0000:0000:00cf:0000:ba98:1234

Using the double-colon rule, you can reduce four groups of zeros; three of them follow the fe80 and the fourth comes after 00cf. Because of the "only use once" stipulation, the best and shortest option is to convert the address to this:

fe80::cf:0:ba98:1234

You may not use a second :: to represent the fourth groups of zeros—only one :: is allowed per address! This rule exists for a good reason. If more than one :: was used, how could you tell how many groups of zeros were in each group? Answer: you couldn't.

Here's an example of a very special IPv6 address that takes full advantage of the double-colon rule, the IPv6 loopback address:

::1

Without using the double-colon nomenclature, this IPv6 address would look like this:

0000:0000:0000:0000:0000:0000:0000:0001

 NOTE The unspecified address (all zeros) can never be used, and neither can an address that contains all ones (in binary) or all *f*s (in hex notation).

IPv6 uses the "*/x*" *prefix length* naming convention, similar to the CIDR naming convention in IPv4. Here's how to write an IP address and prefix length for a typical IPv6 host:

fe80::cf:0:ba98:1234/64

Where Do IPv6 Addresses Come From?

With IPv4, IP addresses come from one of two places: either you type in the IP address yourself (*static IP addressing*) or you use DHCP (also called *dynamic IP addressing*). With IPv6, addressing works very differently. Instead of one IP address, you will have multiple IPv6 addresses on a single network card.

 SIM Check out the excellent "IPv6 Address" Type! simulation in the Chapter 19 section of https://www.totalsem.com/110x. It's good for reinforcing your knowledge of IPv6 and getting practice with performance-based questions.

When a computer running IPv6 first boots up, it gives itself a *link-local address*, IPv6's equivalent to IPv4's APIPA/zeroconf address (we'll explore APIPA/zeroconf later in this chapter). Although an APIPA/zeroconf address can indicate a loss of network connectivity or a problem with the DHCP server, computers running IPv6 always have a link-local address. The first 64 bits of a link-local address are always fe80::, which means every address always begins with fe80:0000:0000:0000. If your operating system supports IPv6 and IPv6 is enabled, you can see this address. Figure 19-4 shows the link-local address for a typical system running the ipconfig utility.

The second 64 bits of a link-local address, the *interface ID*, are generated in two ways. Every current operating system generates a 64-bit random number. Very old operating systems, such as Windows XP and Windows Server 2003, used the device's MAC address to create a 64-bit number called an *Extended Unique Identifier, 64-bit (EUI-64)*.

The link-local address does all the hard work in IPv6, and, as long as you don't need an Internet connection, it's all you need. The old concepts of static and DHCP addressing don't really make much sense in IPv6 unless you have dedicated servers (even in IPv6, servers generally still have static IP addresses). Link-local addressing takes care of all your local network needs.

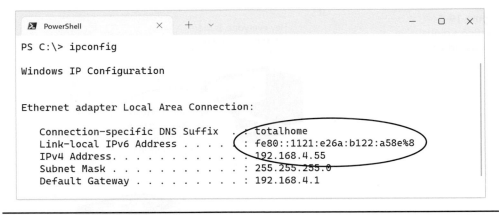

Figure 19-4 Link-local address in ipconfig

IPv6 Prefix Lengths

Systems use IPv6 *prefix lengths* to determine whether to send packets to a local MAC address or to the default gateway to send the packets out to the Internet. But you need to focus on two rules:

- The last 64 bits of an IPv6 address are generated by the NIC, leaving a maximum of 64 bits for the prefix. Therefore, no prefix is ever longer than /64.

- The five Regional Internet Registries (RIRs) pass out /48 prefixes to big ISPs and end users who need large allotments. ISPs and others will borrow another 16 bits for subnetting and then pass out /64 interface IDs to end users. Link-local addressing uses a prefix length of /64. Other types of IPv6 addresses get the subnet information automatically from their routers.

Global Unicast Addresses

To get on the Internet, a system needs a second IPv6 address called a *global unicast address*, often referred to as a "global address." The most common way to get a global address is to request it from the default gateway router, which must be configured to pass out global IPv6 addresses. When you plug a computer into a network, it sends out a very special packet called a *router solicitation (RS)* message, looking for a router (see Figure 19-5). The router hears this message and responds with a *router advertisement (RA)*. This RA tells the computer its network ID and subnet (together called the *prefix*) and DNS server (if configured—more on DNS in a moment).

NOTE   A router solicitation message uses the address ff02::2. This address is read only by other computers running IPv6 in the network. This type of address is different from a broadcast address and is called a *multicast address*. In IPv6, there is no broadcast, only multicast!

Figure 19-5
Getting a global
unicast address

Once the computer gets a prefix, it generates the rest of the address just like with the link-local address. The computer ends up with a legitimate, 128-bit public IPv6 address as well as a link-local address. Figure 19-6 shows the IPv6 information in macOS.

Figure 19-6   macOS system with a global IPv6 address

A global address is a true Internet address. If another computer is running IPv6 and also has a global address, it can access your system unless you have some form of firewall.

 EXAM TIP Computers using IPv6 need a global unicast address to access the Internet.

The addition of IPv6 makes programs such as ipconfig complex. Figure 19-7 shows ipconfig information from a Windows 10 computer.

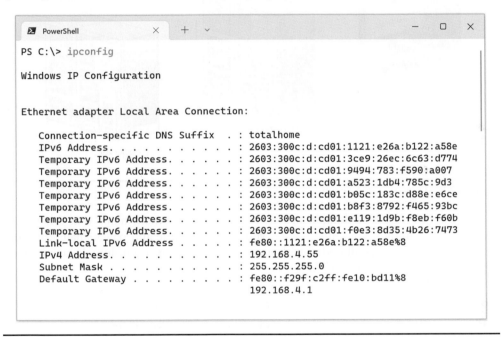

```
PS C:\> ipconfig

Windows IP Configuration


Ethernet adapter Local Area Connection:

   Connection-specific DNS Suffix  . : totalhome
   IPv6 Address. . . . . . . . . . . : 2603:300c:d:cd01:1121:e26a:b122:a58e
   Temporary IPv6 Address. . . . . . : 2603:300c:d:cd01:3ce9:26ec:6c63:d774
   Temporary IPv6 Address. . . . . . : 2603:300c:d:cd01:9494:783:f590:a007
   Temporary IPv6 Address. . . . . . : 2603:300c:d:cd01:a523:1db4:785c:9d3
   Temporary IPv6 Address. . . . . . : 2603:300c:d:cd01:b05c:183c:d88e:e6ce
   Temporary IPv6 Address. . . . . . : 2603:300c:d:cd01:b8f3:8792:f465:93bc
   Temporary IPv6 Address. . . . . . : 2603:300c:d:cd01:e119:1d9b:f8eb:f60b
   Temporary IPv6 Address. . . . . . : 2603:300c:d:cd01:f0e3:8d35:4b26:7473
   Link-local IPv6 Address . . . . . : fe80::1121:e26a:b122:a58e%8
   IPv4 Address. . . . . . . . . . . : 192.168.4.55
   Subnet Mask . . . . . . . . . . . : 255.255.255.0
   Default Gateway . . . . . . . . . : fe80::f29f:c2ff:fe10:bd11%8
                                       192.168.4.1
```

Figure 19-7 The ipconfig command with IPv6 and IPv4

Domain Name System

Knowing that users could not remember lots of IP addresses, early Internet pioneers came up with a way to correlate those numbers with more human-friendly designations. The system they came up with is called the *Domain Name System (DNS)*. Special computers, called *DNS servers,* keep databases that associate IP addresses with names (and store other related information—more on this in a moment).

For example, let's say a machine with the IP address 34.200.194.131 hosts a Web site and we want it to be known as www.totalsem.com. When we set up the Web site, we would pay for a DNS server to register the DNS name www.totalsem.com to the IP address 34.200.194.131. So instead of typing "https://34.200.194.131" to access the Web page, you could type "www.totalsem.com" and press ENTER. Your system would then query the DNS server to get www.totalsem.com's IP address and use that to find the right machine. Unless you want to type in IP addresses all the time, you'll need to use DNS servers (see Figure 19-8).

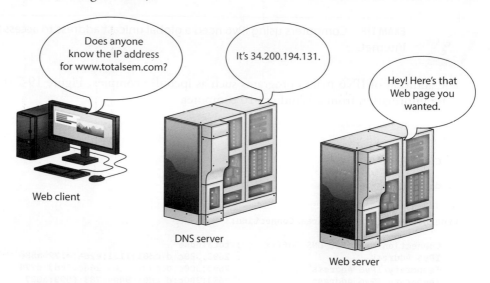

Figure 19-8 Domain name system

The Internet regulates domain names. If you want a domain name that others may access on the Internet, you must register your domain name and pay a small yearly fee. Originally, DNS names all ended with one of the following seven domain name qualifiers, called *top-level domains (TLDs)*:

.com	General business	**.org**	Nonprofit organizations
.edu	Educational organizations	**.gov**	Government organizations
.mil	Military organizations	**.net**	Internet organizations
.int	International		

NOTE Today, Web servers often host multiple Web sites using the same IP address. Don't be surprised if trying to access a site via IP address rather than name doesn't work like you expect.

As more and more countries joined the Internet, a new level of domains was added to the original seven to indicate a DNS name from a country, such as .uk for the United Kingdom. It's common to see DNS names such as www.bbc.co.uk or www.louvre.fr. The *Internet Corporation for Assigned Names and Numbers (ICANN)* has added tons more generic domains such as .name, .app, and .blog.

A lot of the power of DNS comes from the fact that the database stores a little bit more than *just* an IP address and the associated name. DNS has several different types of record, and it can store more than one of each for a given name. The CompTIA A+ 1101 objectives only want you to know about address records (A and AAAA) and two types that play a big role in e-mail: MX and TXT records.

Address Records

Address records are how the DNS database keeps track of the names of individual systems on a network. Each individual *A record* associates one name with an IPv4 address, and each *AAAA record* associates one name with an IPv6 address. If you need to associate a human-friendly name like "accounting" with the accounting department's file server, you'll create an A or AAAA record.

MX Records

MX records enable the servers that handle outgoing e-mail to figure out where e-mail for each domain should go. I let Microsoft 365 handle my e-mail, so the MX record for totalsem.com points to the domain that Microsoft 365 uses for incoming mail. If you shoot me an e-mail at mike@totalsem.com, your outgoing mail server will look up the MX record and know to send the mail on to Microsoft's server.

MX officially stands for *mail exchange*, though the CompTIA A+ 1101 objectives use the term *mail exchanger*.

TXT Records

Text (TXT) records are the junk drawer of the DNS database. People use these free-form records to hold all kinds of things—but the CompTIA A+ 1101 objectives only want you to know the role they play in *spam management*. For decades e-mail administrators waged a battle with scammers who send mountains of unwanted e-mail—*spam*—24 hours a day. To that end, TXT records have three anti-spam purposes:

- **DomainKeys Identified Mail (DKIM) records** Enable receiving servers to verify that the messages they receive were signed by the sending server and have not been altered by intermediate servers.

- **Sender Policy Framework (SPF) records** List the IP or DNS addresses allowed to send e-mail for a domain, enabling receiving servers to discard or flag messages sent by illegitimate servers.

- **Domain-based Message Authentication, Reporting, and Conformance (DMARC) records** Enable domain owners to indicate what receiving servers should do with e-mail that fails the DKIM or SPF checks. They also enable domain owners to receive reports from large e-mail providers about the origin of the mail they received from the domain.

 EXAM TIP These spam management records help others deal with spam claiming to come from your domain. Many servers ignore your mail if you don't set them up. Organizations that manage their own e-mail may run an anti-spam gateway server to dust out spam sent to their users. If so, this anti-spam gateway appliance will also check and enforce the DKIM, SPF, and DMARC records of domains that send it mail.

Entering Client IP Information

When you're configuring a computer to connect to a network, the operating system must provide you an interface to enter the IP address, the subnet mask, the default gateway, and at least one DNS server. Let's review:

- **IP address** Your computer's unique address on the network
- **Subnet mask** Identifies your network ID
- **Default gateway** IP address on the LAN side of your router
- **DNS server** Tracks easy-to-remember DNS names for IP addresses

There are two ways to enter IP information on the operating system: statically or dynamically. Figure 19-9 shows the IP settings dialog box. Here you can enter the information statically.

Figure 19-9
IP settings on a Windows 10 system

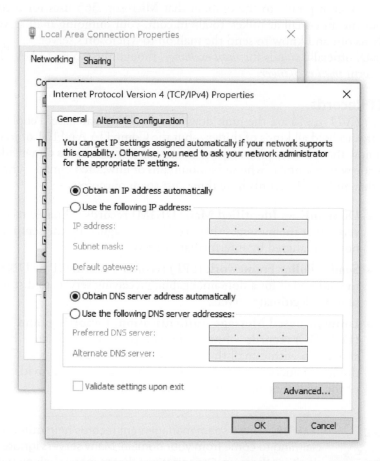

As you look at Figure 19-9, note the radio button for Obtain an IP address automatically. This is a common setting for which you don't need to enter any information. You can use this setting if your network uses *Dynamic Host Control Protocol (DHCP)*.

If you have DHCP (most networks do) and your computer is configured to obtain an IP address automatically, your computer boots up and will broadcast a DHCP request.

A *DHCP server* manages a range of IP addresses (also called its *pool* or *scope*). It provides your computer with an address from this pool in the form of a *lease* containing all the IP information it needs to get on the network (see Figure 19-10) along with the expiration time (after which the computer will need to ask the DHCP server to renew the lease).

NOTE Lease duration is up to the administrator of the DHCP server. Most home and office servers default to leases that last about a week. But for busy networks that have lots of computers coming and going, like a school's student Wi-Fi network, lease times can be as short as an hour.

Figure 19-10
A DHCP server
handing out an
IP address

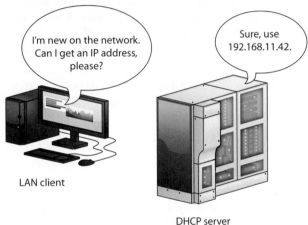

As previously mentioned (and shown in Figure 19-9), you can also manually input an IP address, creating a *static IP address*. Static means it doesn't change until you or some other tech changes it manually. You can also set up the DHCP server to always give a specific IP address to a certain device, such as a server or printer, based on its MAC address. This is called a *DHCP reservation*. Typically, servers have a reserved IP address if they have not been manually configured.

TCP vs. UDP

When moving data from one system to another, the TCP/IP protocol suite needs to know if the communication is connection-oriented or connectionless. When you want to be positive that the data moving between two systems gets there in good order, use a *connection-oriented* application. If it's not a big deal for data to miss a bit or two, then *connectionless* is the way to go. The connection-oriented protocol used with TCP/IP is called the *Transmission Control Protocol (TCP)*. The connectionless one is called the *User Datagram Protocol (UDP)*. Let me be clear: *you* don't choose TCP or UDP. The people who developed the applications decide which protocol to use.

EXAM TIP Expect a question on the CompTIA A+ 1101 exam about TCP vs. UDP. Think connection-oriented vs. connectionless and you'll get the right answer. The objectives also mention DHCP and TFTP as examples of connectionless protocols, and HTTPS and SSH as connection-oriented. Look for more details on TFTP, HTTPS, and SSH in Chapter 21.

Most TCP/IP applications use TCP. TCP gets an application's data from one machine to another reliably and completely without the application developer having to think about how to deal with missing packets. As a result, TCP comes with communication rules that require both the sending and receiving machines to acknowledge the other's presence and readiness to send and receive data.

UDP is the "fire and forget" missile of the TCP/IP protocol suite. UDP doesn't possess any of the extras you see in TCP to make sure the data is received intact. UDP works best when you have a lot of data to send that doesn't need to be perfect or when the application has other ways to deal with any missing packets. A few dropped packets on a Voice over IP (VoIP) call, for example, won't make much difference in the communication between two people. So there's a good reason to use UDP: it's smoking fast compared to TCP.

 NOTE The CompTIA A+ exams expect you to know about other TCP/IP protocols for communicating over the Internet. They're all covered in Chapter 21.

TCP/IP Settings

TCP/IP has a number of unique settings that you must configure correctly to ensure proper network functionality. Unfortunately, these settings can be quite confusing, and there are several of them. Not all settings are used for every type of TCP/IP network, and it's not always obvious where you go to set them.

In Windows 10, you can configure network settings from the Settings app or appropriate Control Panel applet. Go to Start | Settings | Network & Internet | Status. Click *Change adapter options* under the *Advanced network settings* field on the right to get to installed NICs. The Windows 11 Settings app moves things around a little, but from Network & Internet click *Advanced network settings* and then select the NIC you want to configure.

The CompTIA A+ certification exams assume that someone else, such as a tech support person or some network guru, will tell you the correct TCP/IP settings for the network. You need to understand roughly what those settings do and to know where to enter them so the system works.

TCP/IP Tools

All modern operating systems come with handy tools to test and configure TCP/IP. Those you're most likely to use in the field are ping, ipconfig, ifconfig, ip, nslookup, dig, tracert, and traceroute. All of these programs are command-line utilities. Open a command prompt to run them.

ping

The *ping* command provides a really great way to see if you can talk to another system. Here's how it works. Get to a command prompt or terminal and run **ping** followed by an IP address or by a DNS name, such as **ping google.com**. Press the ENTER key and away it goes! Figure 19-11 shows the common syntax for ping.

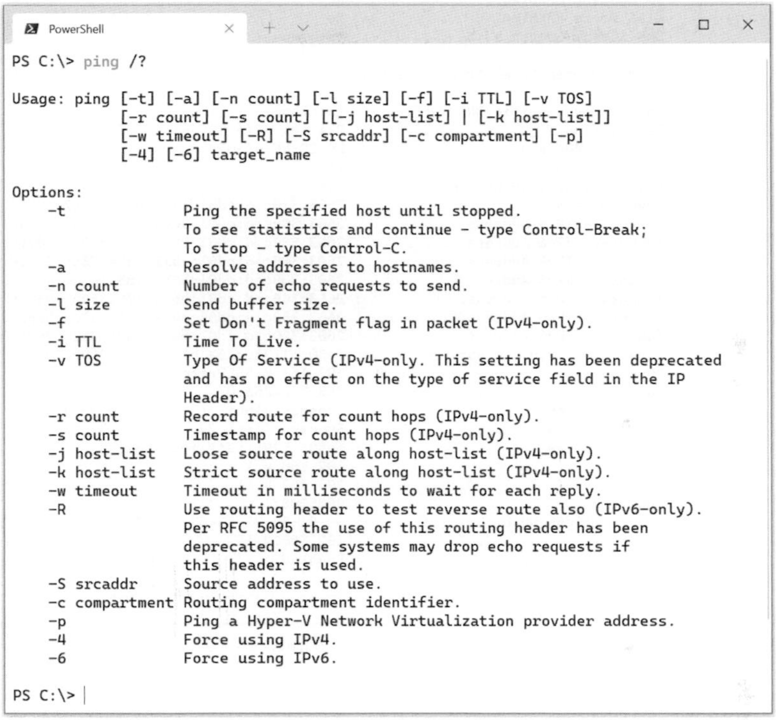

Figure 19-11

The ping command's syntax on Windows

```
PowerShell                    ×    +  ∨              —    □    ×

PS C:\> ping /?

Usage: ping [-t] [-a] [-n count] [-l size] [-f] [-i TTL] [-v TOS]
            [-r count] [-s count] [[-j host-list] | [-k host-list]]
            [-w timeout] [-R] [-S srcaddr] [-c compartment] [-p]
            [-4] [-6] target_name

Options:
    -t              Ping the specified host until stopped.
                    To see statistics and continue - type Control-Break;
                    To stop - type Control-C.
    -a              Resolve addresses to hostnames.
    -n count        Number of echo requests to send.
    -l size         Send buffer size.
    -f              Set Don't Fragment flag in packet (IPv4-only).
    -i TTL          Time To Live.
    -v TOS          Type Of Service (IPv4-only. This setting has been deprecated
                    and has no effect on the type of service field in the IP
                    Header).
    -r count        Record route for count hops (IPv4-only).
    -s count        Timestamp for count hops (IPv4-only).
    -j host-list    Loose source route along host-list (IPv4-only).
    -k host-list    Strict source route along host-list (IPv4-only).
    -w timeout      Timeout in milliseconds to wait for each reply.
    -R              Use routing header to test reverse route also (IPv6-only).
                    Per RFC 5095 the use of this routing header has been
                    deprecated. Some systems may drop echo requests if
                    this header is used.
    -S srcaddr      Source address to use.
    -c compartment  Routing compartment identifier.
    -p              Ping a Hyper-V Network Virtualization provider address.
    -4              Force using IPv4.
    -6              Force using IPv6.

PS C:\> |
```

The ping command has a few useful options beyond the basics. The first option to try in Windows is the -t switch. If you use the -t switch, ping continuously sends ping packets until you stop it with the break command (CTRL-C). That's the default behavior for ping in macOS and Linux; you press CTRL-C again to make it stop. The second option in Windows is the -l switch, which enables you to specify how big a ping packet to send. This helps in diagnosing specific problems with the routers between your computer and the computer you ping.

ipconfig/ifconfig/ip

Windows offers the command-line tool *ipconfig* for a quick glance at your network settings. From a command prompt, run **ipconfig/ all** to see all of your TCP/IP settings (see Figure 19-12). The *ifconfig* command in macOS and other Unixes provides the same level of detail with no switches applied. Much of the Linux world has moved on to the Linux-specific ip command, which is stuffed to the gills with cool features. You can run **ip address** to get the equivalent information.

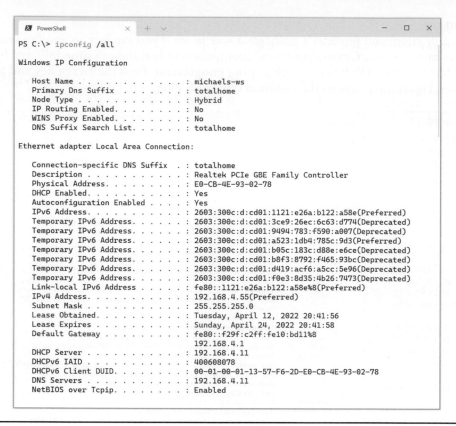

Figure 19-12 An ipconfig /all command in Windows 10

When you have a static IP address, ipconfig does little beyond reporting your current IP settings, including your IP address, subnet mask, default gateway, DNS servers, and WINS servers. When using DHCP, however, ipconfig is also the primary tool for releasing and renewing your IP address. Just run **ipconfig /renew** to get a new IP address or **ipconfig /release** to give up the IP address you currently have.

nslookup/dig

The nslookup command is a powerful command-line program that enables you to determine exactly what information the DNS server is giving you about a specific host name. Every modern OS makes nslookup available when you install TCP/IP, though on Unixes I recommend the *dig* command, which provides more verbose—and more technical—output by default. Figure 19-13 compares what you'll see if you run **nslookup totalsem.com** and **dig totalsem.com**.

```
● ● ●            Terminal — -zsh --no_rcs — 80×30
[michaels-mba-ws% nslookup totalsem.com                              ]
Server:         192.168.4.11
Address:        192.168.4.11#53

Non-authoritative answer:
Name:   totalsem.com
Address: 34.200.194.131

[michaels-mba-ws% dig totalsem.com                                  ]

; <<>> DiG 9.10.6 <<>> totalsem.com
;; global options: +cmd
;; Got answer:
;; ->>HEADER<<- opcode: QUERY, status: NOERROR, id: 59578
;; flags: qr rd ra; QUERY: 1, ANSWER: 1, AUTHORITY: 0, ADDITIONAL: 1

;; OPT PSEUDOSECTION:
; EDNS: version: 0, flags:; udp: 4000
;; QUESTION SECTION:
;totalsem.com.                   IN      A

;; ANSWER SECTION:
totalsem.com.           1367    IN      A       34.200.194.131

;; Query time: 169 msec
;; SERVER: 192.168.4.11#53(192.168.4.11)
;; WHEN: Mon Apr 18 14:04:37 CDT 2022
;; MSG SIZE  rcvd: 57

michaels-mba-ws% ▌
```

Figure 19-13   Running nslookup and dig in macOS

NOTE   If you run **nslookup** by itself, you'll note that the prompt changes. That's because you're running the application interactively. You can run additional nslookup commands without the "nslookup" prefix. Run **exit** to return to the command prompt.

tracert/traceroute

The *tracert* (Windows) and *traceroute* (macOS, Linux) utilities show the route that a packet takes to get to its destination. From a command line, type **tracert** or **traceroute** followed by a space and an IP address or URL. The output describes the route from your machine to the destination machine, including all devices the packet passes through and how long each hop between devices takes (see Figure 19-14).

EXAM TIP   On Windows you can also use the *pathping* command to see similar information to tracert—but with a better statistical summary of the multiple connection attempts it makes.

These commands can help troubleshoot bottlenecks. You can run them to see if a TCP/IP problem is on a machine or connection you control or if you need to contact another network's administrators. The path can differ each time when the destination or networks along the way use a load balancer to spread traffic out over several routes or servers. You might even notice that an intermittent problem only rears its head when packets take a specific route or reach a particular destination server!

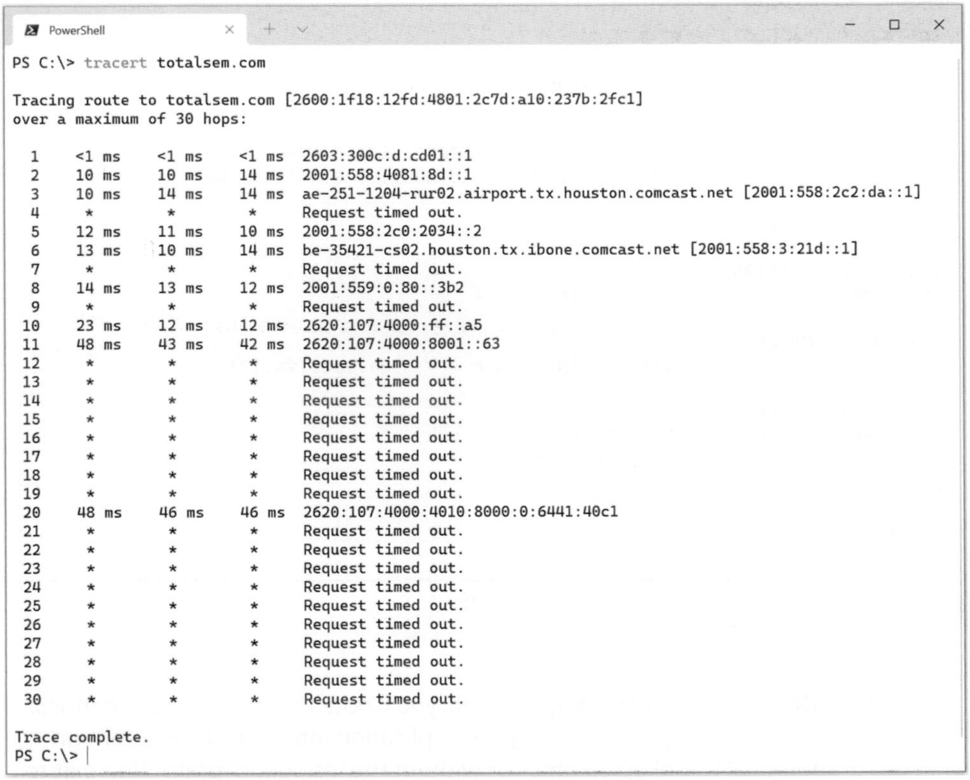

```
PowerShell                                    ×    +   ∨                     —   □   ×

PS C:\> tracert totalsem.com

Tracing route to totalsem.com [2600:1f18:12fd:4801:2c7d:a10:237b:2fc1]
over a maximum of 30 hops:

  1    <1 ms    <1 ms    <1 ms  2603:300c:d:cd01::1
  2    10 ms    10 ms    14 ms  2001:558:4081:8d::1
  3    10 ms    14 ms    14 ms  ae-251-1204-rur02.airport.tx.houston.comcast.net [2001:558:2c2:da::1]
  4     *        *        *     Request timed out.
  5    12 ms    11 ms    10 ms  2001:558:2c0:2034::2
  6    13 ms    10 ms    14 ms  be-35421-cs02.houston.tx.ibone.comcast.net [2001:558:3:21d::1]
  7     *        *        *     Request timed out.
  8    14 ms    13 ms    12 ms  2001:559:0:80::3b2
  9     *        *        *     Request timed out.
 10    23 ms    12 ms    12 ms  2620:107:4000:ff::a5
 11    48 ms    43 ms    42 ms  2620:107:4000:8001::63
 12     *        *        *     Request timed out.
 13     *        *        *     Request timed out.
 14     *        *        *     Request timed out.
 15     *        *        *     Request timed out.
 16     *        *        *     Request timed out.
 17     *        *        *     Request timed out.
 18     *        *        *     Request timed out.
 19     *        *        *     Request timed out.
 20    48 ms    46 ms    46 ms  2620:107:4000:4010:8000:0:6441:40c1
 21     *        *        *     Request timed out.
 22     *        *        *     Request timed out.
 23     *        *        *     Request timed out.
 24     *        *        *     Request timed out.
 25     *        *        *     Request timed out.
 26     *        *        *     Request timed out.
 27     *        *        *     Request timed out.
 28     *        *        *     Request timed out.
 29     *        *        *     Request timed out.
 30     *        *        *     Request timed out.

Trace complete.
PS C:\> |
```

Figure 19-14   The tracert command in action

Try This!

Running tracert/traceroute

Ever wonder why your e-mail takes *years* to get to some people but arrives instantly for others? Or why some Web sites are slower to load than others? Part of the blame could lie with how many hops away your connection is from the target server. You can use tracert/traceroute to run a quick check of how many hops it takes to get to somewhere on a network, so try this!

1. Run **tracert** or **traceroute** on some known source, such as www.microsoft
   .com or www.totalsem.com. How many hops did it take? Did your tracert/
   traceroute time out or make it all the way to the server?

2. Try a tracert/traceroute to a local address. If you're in a university town,
   run a tracert or traceroute on the campus Web site, such as www.rice.edu
   for folks in Houston, or www.ucla.edu for those of you in Los Angeles.
   Did you get fewer hops with a local site?

Configuring TCP/IP

By default, TCP/IP is configured to receive an IP address automatically from a DHCP
server on the network (and automatically assign a corresponding subnet mask). As far as
the CompTIA A+ certification exams are concerned, Network+ techs and administrators give you the client network configuration settings—the IP address, subnet mask,
and default gateway information—and you plug them into the PC. Here's how to do
it manually:

1. In Windows 10/11, open the Settings app and click Network and Internet. From
   here, you can click the Properties button of an already connected network. If the
   adaptor you want to configure is not connected, select the adaptor type from the
   sidebar (Ethernet for instance), then click the name of the adaptor.

2. In the properties screen, click the Edit button under the IP setting header and then
   select Manual from the drop-down menu if currently in Automatic (DHCP) mode.

3. In manual mode, click the toggle switch under IPv4 to reveal the address fields
   (see Figure 19-15)

4. Enter the IP address in the appropriate field.

5. Press the TAB key to skip down to the Subnet prefix length field (Subnet mask in
   Windows 11). Note that in Windows 10 you need to enter the subnet in CIDR
   form (Windows 11 switched back to subnet mask format). As a quick refresher,
   255.255.255.0 is 24 in CIDR format.

6. Optionally, enter the IP address for a default gateway.

7. Optionally, enter the IP addresses of a Preferred DNS server and an Alternate
   DNS server (such as those run by Google or Cloudflare).

8. Click the Save button to close the Properties dialog box.

EXAM TIP Before Microsoft moved these settings into the Settings app, we
used the Network and Sharing Center applet in the Control Panel to do it.
Even though you can use the Settings app to configure these in Windows
10/11, the CompTIA A+ 1102 objectives expect you to know that you can
use the Network and Sharing Center for the same scenarios in Windows 10!

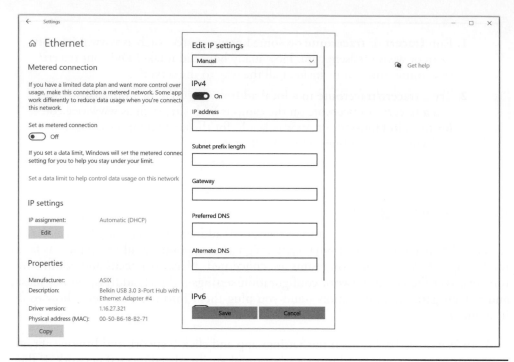

Figure 19-15 Configuring a static IP in Windows 10

Automatic Private IP Addressing

Modern operating systems support a feature called *Automatic Private IP Addressing (APIPA)* in Windows or *zeroconf* in other operating systems that automatically assigns an IP address to the system when the client cannot obtain an IP address automatically. The Internet Assigned Numbers Authority (IANA), the nonprofit corporation responsible for assigning IP addresses and managing root servers, has set aside the range of addresses from 169.254.0.1 to 169.254.255.254 for this purpose.

If the computer system cannot contact a DHCP server, the computer randomly chooses an address in the form of 169.254.*x.y* (where *x.y* is the computer's identifier) and a 16-bit subnet mask (255.255.0.0) and broadcasts it on the network segment (subnet). If no other computer responds to the address, the system assigns this address to itself. When using APIPA/zeroconf, the system can communicate only with other computers on the same subnet that also use the 169.254.*x.y* range with a 16-bit mask. APIPA/zeroconf is enabled by default if your system is configured to obtain an IP address automatically.

NOTE A computer system on a network with an active DHCP server that has an IP address in this range usually indicates a problem connecting to the DHCP server.

Installing and Configuring a Wired Network

To have network connectivity, you need to have three things in place:

- **Connected NIC**   The physical hardware that connects the computer system to the network media.
- **Properly configured IP addressing**   Your device needs correct IP addressing for your network, either via DHCP or static.
- **Switch**   Everything connects to a switch in a wired network.

If you want to share resources on your PC with other network users, you also need to enable Microsoft's File and Printer Sharing. When you install a NIC, by default Windows installs upon setup the TCP/IP protocol, the Client for Microsoft Networks, and File and Printer Sharing for Microsoft Networks. macOS computers come fully set up for networking. Different Linux distros offer setup options similar to the Windows options.

Installing a NIC

The NIC is your computer system's link to the network, and installing one is the first step required to connect to a network. This used to be a big deal and might show up as such in a CompTIA A+ scenario question, but every modern desktop computer has a built-in Gigabit NIC. Windows will automatically install a driver for the NIC at installation.

Full-Duplex and Half-Duplex

All modern NICs run in *full-duplex* mode, meaning they can send and receive data at the same time. The vast majority of NICs and switches use a feature called *autosensing* to accommodate very old devices that might attach to the network and need to run in half-duplex mode. *Half-duplex* means that the device can send and receive, but not at the same time. If you need to adjust the duplex or the *speed* of the NIC manually, you can do so in the NIC's Properties dialog box. Open the Network and Sharing Center in Control Panel and select *Change adapter settings*. In the Network Connections window, right-click the NIC you want to change and select Properties. Click Configure to get to the NIC settings. Click the Advanced tab and scroll down in the Property section until you find Speed & Duplex. Adjust the Value on the right to match whatever ancient device is giving you problems (see Figure 19-16).

Link Lights

Network interfaces have some type of light-emitting diode (LED) *status indicator* that gives information about the state of the NIC's link to whatever is on the other end of the connection. Even though you know the lights are actually LEDs, get used to calling them *link lights*, because that's the term all network techs use. NICs can have between one and four different link lights, and the LEDs can be any color. These lights give you clues about what's happening with the link and are one of the first items to check whenever you think a system is disconnected from the network (see Figure 19-17).

Figure 19-16
Adjusting the Speed & Duplex settings of a NIC in Windows

Figure 19-17
Mmmm, pretty lights!

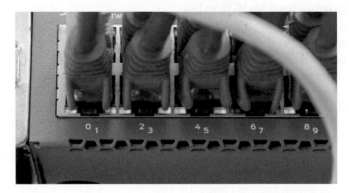

Switches also have link lights, enabling you to check the connectivity at both ends of the cable. If a PC can't access a network, always check the link lights first. Multispeed devices usually have a link light that tells you the speed of the connection. In Figure 19-18, the left link light for port 2 is lit, but the right link light is not, signifying that the other end of the cable is plugged into a 100BASE-T NIC. Port 1, on the other hand, has both link lights lit. It's clearly Gigabit.

Figure 19-18
Multispeed lights

A properly functioning link light is steady on when the NIC is connected to another device. No flickering, no on and off, just on. A link light that is off or flickering shows a connection problem.

Another light is the *activity light*. This little guy turns on when the card detects network traffic, so it makes an intermittent flickering when operating properly. The activity light is a lifesaver for detecting problems, because in the real world, the connection light sometimes lies to you. If the connection light says the connection is good, the next step is to try to copy a file or do something else to create network traffic. If the activity light does not flicker, you have a problem.

On many NICs, a properly functioning link light is on and steady when the NIC is connected to another device—no flickering indicates a good connection. Some NICs use a single LED to display both the link and activity status, in which case the single LED will flicker with activity. That's how the NIC shown in Figure 19-17 works. Read the online documentation from the NIC manufacturer's Web site to determine the meaning of the lights and their steadiness or flickering.

 EXAM TIP   Though no real standard exists for NIC LEDs, you should know that a solid green light means connectivity, a flashing green light means intermittent connectivity, no green light means no connectivity, and a flashing amber light means there are collisions on the network (which is sometimes okay). Also, know that the first things you should check when having connectivity issues are the NIC's LEDs.

Wake-on-LAN

A popular feature of most NICs is the ability to turn on or wake up a powered-down or sleeping PC. You'll learn more about power management in Chapter 23, but for now, know that *Wake-on-LAN* is handy when you want to wake up one or multiple computers that you aren't physically near. To wake up a PC with Wake-on-LAN, you'll need to use a second PC to send either a special pattern or a *magic packet* (a broadcast packet that essentially repeats the destination MAC address many times).

A powered-down or sleeping PC knows to look for this special pattern or packet, at least after configured to do so. Go to the Control Panel and open Network and Sharing Center. Click *Manage network connections* or *Change adapter settings* on the left. For all versions of Windows, right-click the adapter and select Properties. Click the Configure button in the Properties dialog box and then select the Power Management tab (see Figure 19-19). To enable Wake-on-LAN, make sure the checkbox next to *Allow this device to wake the computer* is checked. Optionally, you can select *Only allow a magic packet to wake the computer*, which will instruct the NIC to ignore everything but magic packets.

Figure 19-19
Wake-on-LAN
settings on
the Power
Management tab

Wake-on-LAN is very convenient, but it has one nasty downside. As noted in the Properties dialog box, Wake-on-LAN can wake up or turn on laptops using wireless connections, even when they aren't plugged in or are inside a carrying case. Don't let your laptop overheat or drain its battery—unless you know that you'll need it, turn off Wake-on-LAN on your laptop.

QoS

Quality of service (QoS) enables busy networks to prioritize traffic. While we'll look at QoS from the router's perspective in Chapter 21, individual systems play an important role in the QoS process by tagging their frames, enabling networking hardware to treat them according to rules defined by network administrators. Support for QoS tagging (or priority) should be enabled by default on most network adapters—but if you need to modify this setting, you can find the VLAN option on the Advanced tab of your NIC's Properties dialog box (see Figure 19-20).

Figure 19-20
Network adapter
VLAN setting

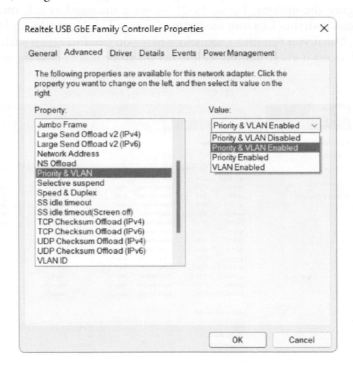

Realtek USB GbE Family Controller Properties

General | Advanced | Driver | Details | Events | Power Management

The following properties are available for this network adapter. Click the property you want to change on the left, and then select its value on the right.

Property:

Jumbo Frame
Large Send Offload v2 (IPv4)
Large Send Offload v2 (IPv6)
Network Address
NS Offload
Priority & VLAN
Selective suspend
Speed & Duplex
SS idle timeout
SS idle timeout(Screen off)
TCP Checksum Offload (IPv4)
TCP Checksum Offload (IPv6)
UDP Checksum Offload (IPv4)
UDP Checksum Offload (IPv6)
VLAN ID

Value:

Priority & VLAN Enabled

Priority & VLAN Disabled
Priority & VLAN Enabled
Priority Enabled
VLAN Enabled

OK   Cancel

NOTE Your BIOS might also have settings for controlling Wake-on-LAN functions. Check your CMOS System Configuration tool to find out.

Configuring IP Addressing

This one's easy. All operating systems by default will be set for DHCP and acquire IP addressing settings automatically. This is true for both IPv4 and IPv6 configuration options. On the off-chance scenario where you need to configure a client to use a static IP address, you can readily do so.

Connecting to a Switch

Every wired computer connects to a switch, enabling communication with other computers on the network. Networks feature two types of switches, unmanaged and managed. An *unmanaged switch* is an automatic device. Plug devices into it and they will communicate via MAC addresses with no configuration needed by techs. An unmanaged switch doesn't do much more than connecting devices.

A *managed switch* offers a lot of extra features that modern networks use to provide added security and efficiency. Managed switches have an IP address that you can use to configure the options. Figure 19-21 shows a managed switch interface. Dealing with managed switches falls into the realm of CompTIA Network+ and CompTIA Security+ techs, but if you run into a scenario where you need to access such a switch, know that you'll access it via IP address with either a web browser or via the command line.

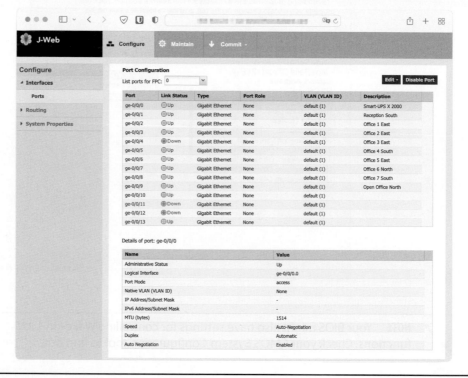

Figure 19-21 Managed switch interface

 EXAM TIP I'm glossing over the complexity involved with managed switches. Some switches have a simple interface like the one pictured in Figure 19-21. Switches (or other devices) that take advantage of *software-defined networking (SDN)* are automatically managed by a separate controller elsewhere on the network.

Let me give you one great example of the power of managed switches: VLANs. You can use special managed switches to break up or *segment* a single physical network into two or more distinct networks. Each *virtual local area network (VLAN)* you create can talk with other computers within the same VLAN, but not to computers on another VLAN.

Here's the cool part. You can have a single switch with, say, 24 computers connected. Normally, all 24 would be on the same network, right? But with a VLAN-capable switch, you can access the management console and assign physical ports to different VLANs. You could assign ports 1 through 12 to VLAN100 and ports 13 through 24 to VLAN200. Computers connected to ports 12 and 13 wouldn't even know the other computer was there. I'll save the big discussion of VLANs and cool things you can do with managed switches for the CompTIA Network+ book in your near future.

Network Organization and Access Control

Windows systems can share all kinds of *resources* across your network: files, folders, entire drives, printers, faxes, Internet connections, and much more. To make it easy to find the right resources and control who should be able to access them, networks (including all of their systems and users) need to be organized in some way to make human sense of all of the wires and addresses. This section looks at how resources (such as files and printers) are shared on a network and explores the two main approaches to organizing modern Windows networks: workgroups and domains.

Shared Resources

When you share resources over a network, every OS uses specific network sharing permissions to allow access, restrict access, or deny access to shared resources. These permissions do not have anything to do with file- or folder-level permissions like the NTFS permissions you saw in Chapter 13 (though file- and folder-level permissions do affect the share permissions). They're also less sophisticated—they don't, for example, support NTFS features such as inheritance.

 EXAM TIP Windows file and print sharing is powered by the Server Message Block (SMB) protocol, which uses TCP port 445 and UDP ports 137–139. Unixes used to use their own Network File System (NFS) protocol, but they have generally settled on SMB as well. Make sure you're prepared to recognize both Common Internet File System (CIFS) and Samba as forms of SMB. CIFS is a deprecated Microsoft dialect of SMB, while Samba is the name of the Linux implementation.

On a non-NTFS volume like an optical media disc or a flash-media USB drive, you have three levels of permission when using the default Sharing Wizard: Read, Read/Write, and Owner, which are discussed later in this chapter. With Advanced Sharing (discussed in the upcoming "Sharing Folders with Advanced Sharing" section), the three permission levels are called Read, Change, and Full Control.

If you share a folder on an NTFS drive, as you normally do these days, you must set *both* the network permissions and the NTFS permissions to let others access your shared resources. You use the network share to share the resource but use NTFS to say what folks can do with that resource. Some good news: This is no big deal! Just set the network permissions to give everyone Full Control, and then use the NTFS permissions to exercise more precise control over *who* accesses the shared resources and *how* they access them. Open the Security tab to set the NTFS permissions. We'll get into the details a little more in the "Organizing with Workgroups" section, next.

EXAM TIP Accessing files over a general-purpose network is convenient for humans, but the performance isn't great—many servers constantly reading and writing huge files can bring a humble SOHO network to its knees! Operations (such as data centers) that need high-performance networked storage often use a separate high-speed *storage area network (SAN)*.

Instead of having internal hard drives, each server has access to block storage devices that live in a massive storage array. They're more or less like local storage devices to the server—it even speaks to them using iSCSI, a network protocol based on the small computer system interface (SCSI) that you encountered back in Chapter 8.

Organizing with Workgroups

Once a network is created, users need to be able to share resources in some organized fashion. Operating systems need a way to determine which users can access resources such as folders and printers and how those resources can be used. Windows networks are organized using workgroups or domains. (These are the Microsoft terms, but the concepts have been adopted by the entire computer industry and apply to macOS and other operating systems.)

Workgroups are an older, simpler approach to the network organizations—so they're a great place to start. They are also the default for almost every fresh installation of Windows.

By default, all computers on the network are assigned to a workgroup called WORK-GROUP. You can see your workgroup name by opening the System applet in Control Panel, as shown in Figure 19-22.

There's nothing special about the name WORKGROUP, except that every computer on the network needs the same workgroup name to be able to share resources. If you want to change your workgroup name, you need to use the System applet. In the *Computer name, domain, and workgroup settings* section on the right, click the Change settings link to open the System Properties dialog box. Then click the Change button to change your workgroup name (see Figure 19-23).

NOTE If you change the workgroup name for one system, you need to change it for all other devices you want connected to that workgroup.

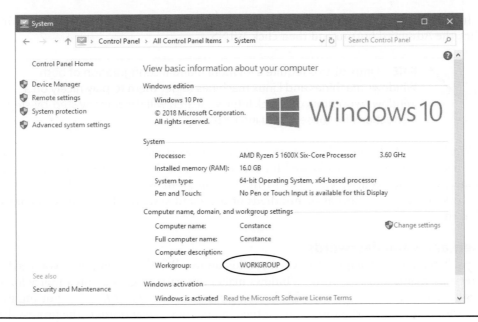

Figure 19-22   Default workgroup

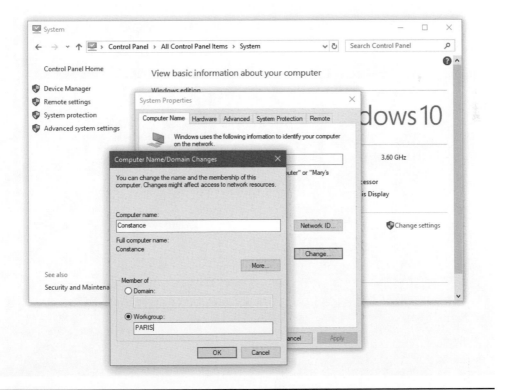

Figure 19-23   Changing the workgroup name in advanced settings

In macOS, you can change the workgroup name in System Preferences | Network. Click the Advanced button and then click WINS.

 NOTE Linux distros require a lot more manual configuration of both Windows machines and Linux machines to get them to play nicely on a Windows workgroup. A quick Internet search will show many step-by-step instructions for those of you interested.

Workgroups lack centralized control over the network; all systems connected to the network are equals. This works well for smaller networks because there are fewer users, connections, and security concerns to think about. But what do you do when your network encompasses dozens or hundreds of users and systems? How can you control all of that?

Usernames and Passwords

As you'll recall from Chapter 13, when you log on to a Windows computer, you need to enter a username and password. Windows makes this easy by giving you a pretty logon interface, as shown in Figure 19-24. Entering a username is *identification*; putting in a password that matches that username in the OS provides *authentication*, the process that enables a system to give a user access to system resources.

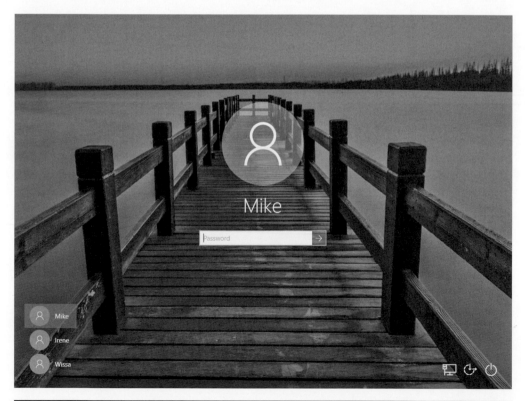

Figure 19-24 Windows logon screen

NOTE The distinction between identification and authentication is not important for the CompTIA A+ exams, though it becomes important for Network+ and Security+. Good to learn it now!

The usernames and their passwords are stored in an encrypted format on your computer. Usernames have a number of jobs on your computer, but at this point the job most interesting to us is to give a user access to the computer. Usernames work well when you access your own computer, but these same usernames and passwords are used to access shared resources on other computers in the network—and that's where we run into trouble. Let's watch a typical folder share take place on a network of Windows systems.

Sharing Folders with the Sharing Wizard

All personal computers can share folders and printers out of the box. Sharing a folder in Windows is easy, for example, because the Sharing Wizard is enabled by default. Just right-click the folder and select Give access to | Specific people to get to the *Choose people to share with* dialog box (see Figure 19-25).

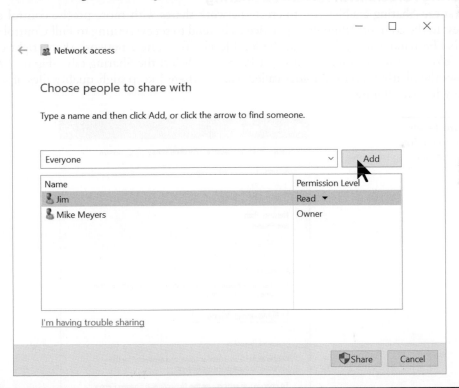

Figure 19-25   Folder sharing in Windows 10

By default, you'll see every user account that's currently on this system. You may give an account Read or Read/Write permission, while the person who created the folder is assigned as Owner. The following list describes these permissions:

- **Read** You can see what's in the folder. You may open files in the folder, but you can't save anything back into the folder.
- **Read/Write** Same as Read but you can save files into the folder.
- **Owner** Same as Read/Write plus you can set the permissions for other users on the folder.

NOTE You'll recall from Chapter 13 that all versions of Windows come with a far more powerful and much more complex form of permissions based on NTFS.

Sharing Folders with Advanced Sharing

Advanced Sharing enables you to create network shares with more precise control over access to the contents (though in practice techs tend to set everything to Full Control and let NTFS handle authorization at the local level). To create a network share, right-click the folder you want to share and select Properties. Select the Sharing tab—Figure 19-26 shows the Sharing tab for a folder called Music, where I keep high-quality files of some of my favorite albums.

Figure 19-26
Sharing tab for
Music folder

Click Advanced Sharing to open the Advanced Sharing dialog box. Then click Share this folder to make it active (see Figure 19-27). Here you can set the share name—by default it's the same as the folder name, but it can be unique. You can also limit simultaneous users and add comments, among other things. Click Permissions to get to the last step (see Figure 19-28).

By default, the Everyone group is set to Read permissions, but you have options here. You can add or remove groups or usernames. Click Add to open the Select Users or Groups dialog box where you can search for users/groups currently on the local computer. (That's important to note, as you'll see in the next section, "Accessing Shared Folders with Workgroups.") Also note the other options here.

You have three permission levels—Read, Change, and Full Control—and you can set those permissions to Allow or Deny. Just like you saw with NTFS permissions, Deny always trumps Allow. Advanced Sharing gives you control over what specific user accounts and groups can do with a network share. You could grant Full Control to a user group, for example, but then add a specific user—Bob in Accounting—and Deny Full Control to that user account. That would effectively give everyone in the group (except for Bob) access to the Music share, to add, rename, delete, and so on.

Figure 19-27
Advanced
Sharing dialog
box, ready for
sharing

Figure 19-28
Permissions for
the about-to-be-
created network
share

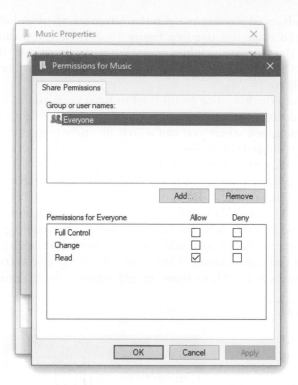

 EXAM TIP Expect a question or two on the CompTIA A+ 1102 exam that requires you to compare *NTFS vs. share permissions*. NTFS applies superior local control over all resources on a computer. Share permissions only apply to network shares (whether created using the Sharing Wizard or Advanced Sharing). *Allow vs. Deny* works similarly in both types of sharing, with Deny trumping Allow.

Accessing Shared Folders with Workgroups

So all this sharing seems to work quite nicely, except for one issue: When you log on to a computer, you access a username and database on that computer. The account you access is stored on the local computer; how do you give someone from another computer access to that shared folder? You have to give that other person a valid username and password. We use the nomenclature <computer name>\<username> to track logons. If you log on to Computer A as Mike, we say you are logged on to ComputerA\ Mike. This nomenclature comes in very handy when networked computers become part of the process.

Figure 19-29 shows Computers A and B. Assume there is a shared folder called Timmy on Computer A and the Mike account has Read/Write permission.

Figure 19-29
Computers A
and B

Computer A\Mike

Computer B\Fred

A person fires up Computer B, logging on as Fred. He opens his Network menu option and sees Computer A, but when he clicks on it he sees a network password prompt (see Figure 19-30).

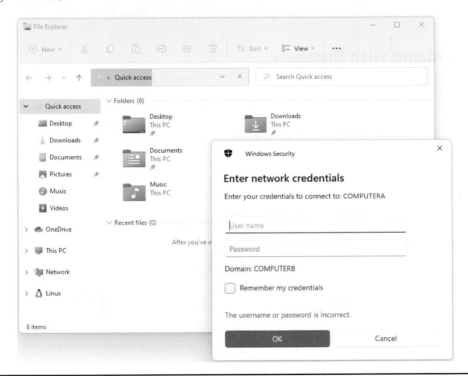

Figure 19-30   Prompt for entering username and password

The reason is that the person is logged on as ComputerB\Fred and he needs to be logged on as ComputerA\Mike to successfully access this folder. So the user needs to know the password for ComputerA\Mike. This isn't a very pretty way to protect user-names and passwords. So what can you do? You have three choices:

1. You can make people log on to shares as just shown.

2. You can create the same accounts (same username and same password) on all the computers and give sharing permissions to all the users for all the shares.

3. You can use one account on all computers. Everyone logs on with the same account, and then all shares are by default assigned to the same account.

 EXAM TIP Moving and copying folders and files within network shares and between network shares and local computers doesn't affect the file attributes. If you copy a read-only file from a network share to your desktop, for example, it'll still be read-only. You can easily change this sort of file attribute by right-clicking the file and selecting Properties.

Organizing with Domains

Workgroups work well in smaller networks (<30 computers), but for larger networks, or if you desire a network with more control and security, it's far better to use a Windows *domain*—a network organization that centralizes user accounts, passwords, and access to resources. Look at Figures 19-31 and 19-32. In a Windows workgroup, each computer has its own set of local user accounts. In a Windows domain, a computer running Windows Server is configured as a *domain controller*. A domain controller stores a set of *domain accounts*. A user logging on to any computer on the domain may use their one domain account to log on to the entire network.

Figure 19-31
Workgroup

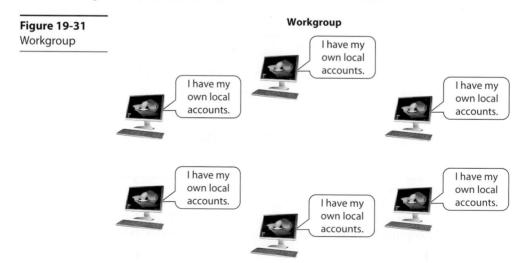

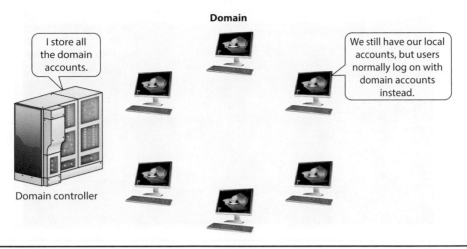

Figure 19-32 Domain

NOTE Even though a computer is on a domain, you can still log on using a local user account, though this is rarely needed. You'll only see this happen with troubleshooting scenarios, like when we rebuilt corrupted profiles in Chapter 16. Otherwise, once you're a member of a domain, you'll log in with your domain account.

A Windows domain (which is not the same as a domain in DNS) makes it easy for anyone with a domain account to log on to any computer in the domain with a single account, a process called *single sign-on (SSO)*. Each user does not need a separate local account stored on every computer. User authentication through the single domain account enables access to all machines on the domain, thus the term single sign-on.

If you have a single computer storing all the domain usernames and passwords, why not take it one step higher and store information about the domain, including printer information, computer names, location information—anything you might need to define the entire network. Modern versions of Windows use an *Active Directory* domain to accomplish these tasks.

EXAM TIP Active Directory is powered by the Lightweight Directory Access Protocol (LDAP), which uses TCP port 389. LDAP generally stays out of sight—but it does important work to keep AD networks running smoothly. It also powers open-source Active Directory alternatives such as OpenLDAP.

To use a domain on a network of Windows machines, for example, you must have a computer running a version of Windows Server (see Figure 19-33) or Linux running Samba. Windows Server is a completely different, much more powerful, and much more expensive version of Windows. You then need to promote the server to a domain controller. This creates the Active Directory.

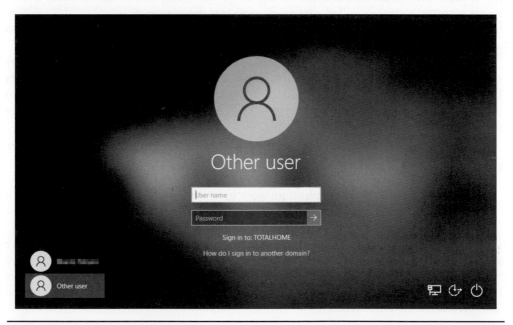

Figure 19-33   Windows Server running in command line only core mode

 EXAM TIP   Look for a comparison question on the CompTIA A+ 1102 exam on *workgroup vs. domain* network setup. The former takes no effort; the latter requires joining an Active Directory domain.

Once a server is set up as a domain controller, creating the Active Directory, each PC on the network needs to join the domain (which kicks you off the workgroup). When you log on to a computer that's a member of a domain, Windows will prompt you for a username instead of showing you icons for all the users on the network (see Figure 19-34).

Figure 19-34   Domain logon screen

When using Active Directory, you don't log on to your computer. Instead, you log on directly to the domain. All user accounts are stored on the domain controller, as shown in Figure 19-35. A lot of domains have names that look like Web addresses, like home. totalsem.com or totalhome.local. Using the previous nomenclature, you can log on to a domain using <domain>\<domain username>. If the domain totalhome.local has a user account called Mike, for example, you would use totalhome.local\Mike to log on.

Figure 19-35
Active Directory
network

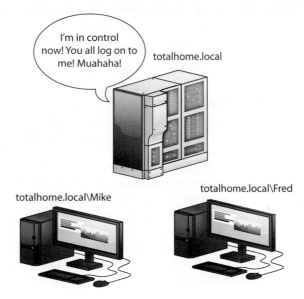

Domain Organization

Active Directory stores everything about a network. One way to see the Active Directory is to log on directly to the domain controller and run the Active Directory Users and Computers utility—the tool that provides basic Active Directory functions (see Figure 19-36). Note the name of the domain (in this case totalhome.local) on the left side. The folders underneath the domain name show the domain's organization.

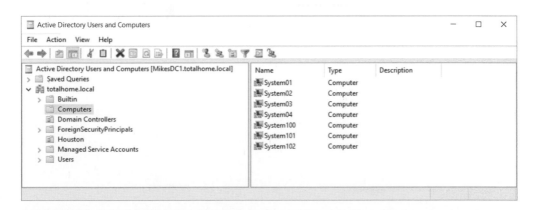

Figure 19-36   Active Directory Users and Computers

Those really aren't folders. They're called organizational units (even though they look like folders), but we'll save that definition for a moment. Here are a few of the more noteworthy folders.

- **Builtin**   This is where all the built-in domain groups are stored, such as Domain Administrators and Users.

- **Computers**   Every system, from servers to workstations, is listed in this folder.

- **Domain Controllers**   It's always a good idea to have more than one domain controller in case one goes down. This folder lists all of them.

- **Users**   This area stores all the non-built-in users for the domain.

Domain Administration

Just as individual systems have an administrator account, the domain also has domain administrators. The accounts are extremely powerful and enable you to join a computer to a domain. Certain domain jobs require domain admin rights. Here's how to deal with adding and removing computers and users from a domain.

To have a computer join a domain, on the Start screen type **Control Panel** and then press ENTER. Then proceed to *System and Security* and click *System*. Under *Computer name, domain, and workgroup settings*, click *Change settings*. To change the *Computer name*, click *Change*. Under *Member of*, click *Domain*, and then type the name of the domain that you want the computer to join, and then press OK. At this point, you will need to restart the computer (see Figure 19-37). Make sure you have access to a Domain account that can join the domain!

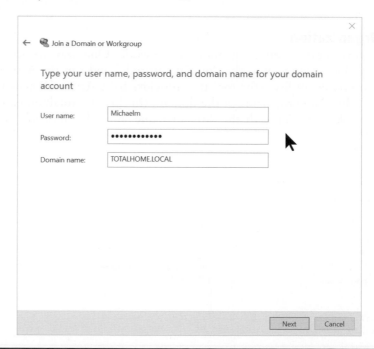

Figure 19-37   Joining a domain

Removing a system from a domain just means accessing the domain controller, going into Active Directory Users and Computers, and right-clicking the computer in question and choosing Properties. Select the Member Of tab, select the unwanted computer, and click the Remove button to remove the computer (see Figure 19-38).

Figure 19-38
Removing a
computer from
the domain

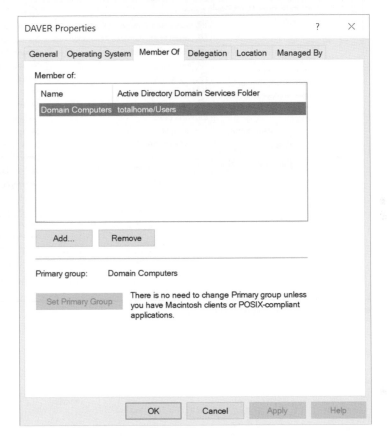

There's no way to promote a local user or group to a domain user or group. A domain admin must create a fresh new domain account on the domain controller using Active Directory Users and Computers. Right-click Users and select New | User (see Figure 19-39) to open the New Object - User dialog box. Figure 19-40 show the dialog box with user account information filled in.

EXAM TIP Groups (or, more accurately, *security groups*) in Active Directory are more or less the same concept as the user groups you encountered in Chapter 13—though Active Directory centralizes them (and can do *much* more with them).

Domain administrators use the Active Directory Users and Computers utility to clean up account issues. To reset a password, right-click a user account and select Reset

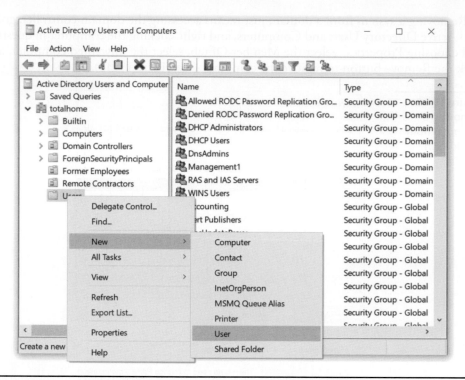

Figure 19-39 Users context menu options

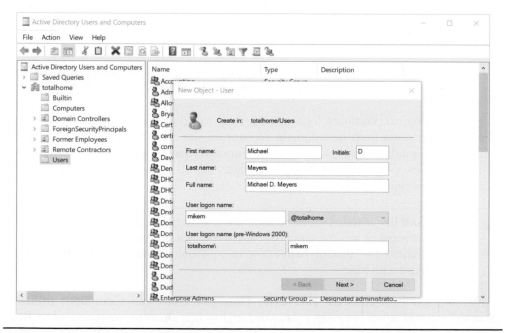

Figure 19-40 Adding a new domain account

Password . . . to open the Reset Password dialog box (see Figure 19-41). Type in a new password, confirm it, and click OK. From the same dialog box, you can select the checkbox to *Unlock the user's account* if needed, such as in the case of accidental, multiple mistyped logon attempts. Finally, you can enable or disable a user account from the context menu by selecting—you guessed it—Enable Account or Disable Account.

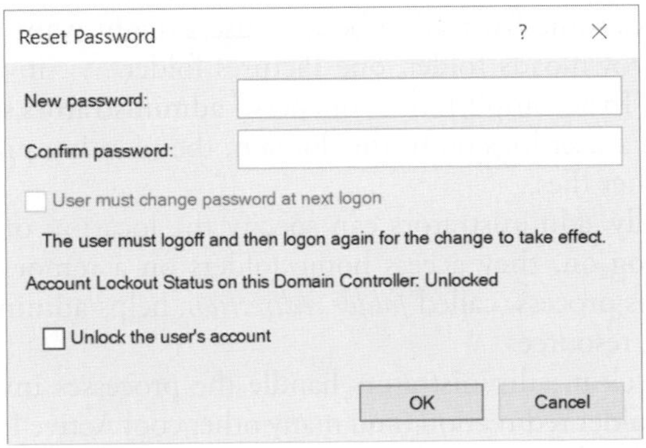

Figure 19-41
Reset Password
dialog box

There's a lot of power in a domain account, allowing features you rarely see in a local account. For example, you can add a *logon script* that runs every time the user logs in that can map network drives, place an information box on the screen, run applications (like anti-malware)—pretty much anything you wish to do. Just add the path and name of the script file under the Profile tab (see Figure 19-42). (Note that CompTIA calls a logon script a *login* script. It's the same thing.)

Figure 19-42
Adding a logon
script to a
domain account

Another great feature built into Active Directory is the ability to pick where you want to store users' *home folders* (such as Pictures, Downloads, Documents, etc.). This requires the use of roaming profiles rather than local profiles. Let me explain. Every time you log on to a computer that's new to your user account, Windows will set up a new home folder for your domain account on that local machine. It won't be populated with any of your stuff, though, because it's a new home folder.

This creates some frustration because users might want to have only one Documents folder, one Downloads folder, one Pictures folder . . . in other words, a single unified home folder. To accomplish this "oneness," administrators set up roaming profiles on the server. When a user logs on to the domain, the roaming profile applies and the user can access his or her files.

Additionally, administrators can specify the location of users' home folders, so that when users log on, they access home folders on a remote server rather than the local machine. This process, called *folder redirection*, helps administrators keep tighter control over network resources.

Just to be clear, administrators handle the processes involved in setting up roaming profiles and folder redirection (and many other cool Active Directory features). CompTIA A+ techs need to know that these features exist so they're not surprised in the field.

Active Directory enables extremely flexible organization of Active Directory users and computers via the use of *organizational units (OUs)* that enable you to organize users and computers by function, location, permission . . . Whatever makes sense for your organization, you can use OUs to manage those assets.

Figure 19-43 shows an example of a heavily modified Active Directory for the totalhome .local domain. Note the OUs for different locations, inactive accounts, and even printers.

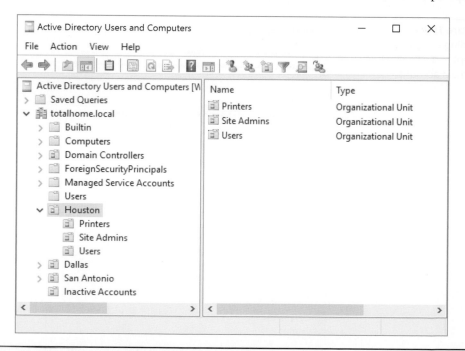

Figure 19-43 totalhome.local domain

EXAM TIP The domain controller authenticates a user when that user logs on to a domain computer. The domain controller is therefore also called an *authentication server*.

File Servers and Drive Mapping

Sharing individual files and folders that are located on user systems may be all users need to collaborate occasionally, but dedicated *file servers* are the way to go when many users need round-the-clock access to a single authoritative copy of important files. When users only need access occasionally, they can just directly access the file server (likely after authenticating), but it's often easier for Windows users that need to interact with a file server constantly to *map* an unused drive letter to a folder on the file server.

Here's how to manually configure a *mapped drive* in Windows. In Windows 11, open File Explorer, click the See More menu, and choose *Map network drive*. In Windows 10, open File Explorer, click This PC on the left-hand side of the screen, and click *Map network drive*. In the Map Network Drive dialog box, select the drive letter you want from the drop-down menu, then click Browse and navigate to the folder you'd like to map (as shown in Figure 19-44). You can also choose in the Map Network Drive dialog box whether the drive will be mapped on sign-in and whether it requires different credentials.

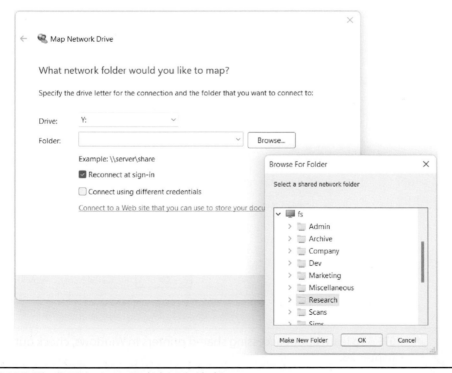

Figure 19-44 Setting up a mapped network drive

NOTE In an Active Directory domain, network shares may be automatically mapped by Group Policy or login scripts. In that case, you'd need to ensure the user is a member of the right group or attach a login script to the user's account. You can learn more about Group Policy in Chapter 27.

Sharing Printers

Sharing printers in Windows follows the same process as sharing files and folders. Assuming that the system has printer sharing services loaded, go to the Devices and Printers settings in the Control Panel and right-click the name of the printer you wish to share. Select Printer properties (not Printers), and then select the Sharing tab (see Figure 19-45). Click *Share this printer*, add a share name, click OK or Apply, and you're done.

Figure 19-45
Giving a name to
a shared printer
on Windows 10

NOTE To learn about accessing shared printers in Windows, check out Chapter 26.

One of the most pleasant aspects of configuring a system for networking under all versions of Microsoft Windows is the amazing amount of the process that is automated. For example, if Windows detects a NIC in a system, it automatically installs the NIC driver, a network protocol (TCP/IP), and Client for Microsoft Networks. So if you want to share a resource, everything you need is automatically installed. Note that although File and Printer Sharing is also automatically installed, you still must activate it by checking the appropriate checkbox in the Local Area Connection Properties dialog box.

Troubleshooting Networks

Once you go beyond a single PC and enter the realm of networked computers, your troubleshooting skills need to take a giant leap up in quality. The secret to finding the right answer to networking problems on the CompTIA A+ exams is to remember that the exams only ask about the skills to get a single computer back on the network. Focus your network troubleshooting answers to scenario questions on getting a single system up and running.

NOTE The troubleshooting issues discussed here apply only to a LAN, and do not cover issues related to troubleshooting Internet access. We'll cover Internet troubleshooting in Chapter 21, using the knowledge you've gained in this chapter and adding even more tools.

CompTIA likes to ask scenario questions that deal with "no connectivity" or "intermittent connectivity." Let's consider two types of connectivity problem: when a computer loses physical connectivity, and when a computer is on the network but can't access a specific resource.

Repairing Physical Cabling

"The network's down!" is one of the most terrifying phrases a network tech will ever hear. Networks fail for many reasons, and the first thing to know is that good-quality, professionally installed cabling rarely goes bad, but you need to know what to do when it does. Let's take a moment now to discuss what to do when you think you've got a problem with your physical network.

Symptoms

Physical connectivity interruptions stand out in Windows. Windows displays a circle-backslash symbol over a globe icon in the notification area to show you're not connected (see Figure 19-46).

Figure 19-46
Windows
no Internet
notification icon

If you encounter this problem, first check the obvious. Run **ipconfig** from the command line. Do you see an APIPA/zeroconf address, like 169.254.15.22? That's a clear sign of a disconnect between the system and the DHCP server. Is the cable unplugged at the system? At the wall outlet? Then go for the less obvious: Is the NIC disabled in Device Manager? If these checks don't solve the problem, take a peek on the other side of the cable. If you're not connected to a running switch, you're going to get the disconnect errors.

EXAM TIP   If you're in macOS or Linux, you can run the **ifconfig** command or **ip** command to get the same information that ipconfig gives you in Windows.

Intermittent connectivity is often the same issue but typically is harder to figure out. Either way, read the next section to see how to get serious about testing for these pesky connectivity problems.

Diagnosing Physical Problems

Look for errors that point to physical disconnection. A key clue that the computer may have a physical problem is that a user gets a "No server is found" error, or tries to use the operating system's network explorer utility (like Network in Windows) and doesn't see any systems besides his or her own.

Multiple systems failing to access the network often points to hardware problems. This is where knowledge of your network cabling helps. If all the systems connected to one switch suddenly no longer see the network, but all the other systems in your network still function, you not only have a probable hardware problem, but also have a suspect—the switch.

Check the Lights

If you suspect a hardware problem, first check the link lights on the NIC and switch. If they're not lit, you know the cable isn't connected somewhere. If you're not physically at the system in question (if you're on a tech call, for example), you can have the user check his or her connection status through the link lights or through software.

EXAM TIP   The CompTIA A+ 1101 objectives mention a problem where the link lights might mislead you. The lights may go off and come back on if you're dealing with *port flapping*—when a connection on a switch or NIC port repeatedly goes up or down—but you may still need to replace the cable, NIC, or switch (or avoid the bad port). It's easier to spot port flapping in the logs on your network devices, but if you start to suspect flapping or notice the link lights cycle off, check for physical problems with the cable, NIC, and switch.

If the problem system clearly cannot connect, eliminate the possibility of a failed switch or other larger problem by checking to make sure other people can access the network, and that other systems can access the shared resource (server) that the problem system can't see. Inspect the cable running from the back of the computer to the outlet. Finally, if you can, plug the system into a known-good outlet and see if it works. A veteran network tech keeps a long patch cable for just this purpose. If you get connectivity with the second outlet, you should begin to suspect the structured cable running from the first outlet to the switch. Assuming the cable is installed properly and has been working correctly before this event, a simple continuity test will confirm your suspicion in most cases.

Check the NIC

Be warned that a bad NIC can also generate a "can't see the network" problem. Use the utility provided by the OS to verify that the NIC works. If you've got a NIC with diagnostic software, run it—this software will check the NIC's circuitry. The NIC's female connector is a common failure point, so NICs that come with diagnostic software often include a special test called a loopback test. A loopback test sends data out of the NIC and checks to see if it comes back. Some NICs perform only an internal loopback, which tests the circuitry that sends and receives, but not the actual connecting pins. A true external loopback requires a *loopback plug* inserted into the NIC's port (see Figure 19-47). If a NIC is bad, replace it.

Figure 19-47
Loopback plug

 NOTE Onboard NICs on laptops are especially notorious for breaking due to frequent plugging and unplugging. On some laptops, the NICs are easy to replace; others require a motherboard replacement. Or you can always use a USB-to-Ethernet adapter.

Cable Testing

The vast majority of network disconnection problems occur at the work area. If you've tested those connections, though, and the work area seems fine, it's time to consider deeper issues.

With the right equipment, diagnosing a bad horizontal cabling run is easy. Anyone running a professional network should own a midrange time-domain reflectometer (TDR) tester such as the Fluke MicroScanner. A TDR sends a signal down the cable, and any sudden change in impedance will cause some of that signal to reflect back. The TDR can then time this reflection and calculate how far down the cable a break is or the total length of a working cable. With a little practice, you can easily determine not only whether a cable is disconnected but also where the disconnection takes place. Sometimes patience is required, especially if the cable runs lack labels, but you will find the problem.

When you're testing a cable run, always include the patch cables as you test. This means unplugging the patch cable from the PC, attaching a tester, and then going to the telecommunications room. Here you'll want to unplug the patch cable from the switch and plug the tester into that patch cable, making a complete test, as shown in Figure 19-48.

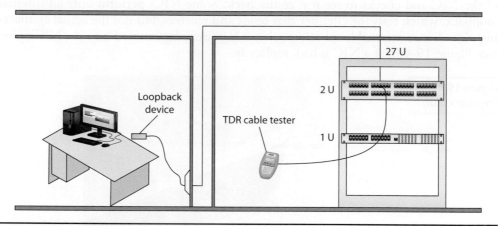

Figure 19-48   Cable tester in action

Testing in this manner gives you a complete test from the switch to the system. In general, a broken cable must be replaced. A bad patch cable is an easy fix, but what happens if the horizontal cable is to blame? In these cases, I get on the phone and call my local installer. If a cable is bad in one spot, the risk of it being bad in another is simply too great to try anything other than total replacement.

Toners

It would be nice to say that all cable installations are perfect and that over the years they won't tend to grow into horrific piles of spaghetti-like, unlabeled cables. In the real world, though, you might eventually find yourself having to locate or *trace* cables. Even in the best-planned networks, labels fall off ports and outlets, mystery cables appear behind walls, new cable runs are added, and mistakes are made counting rows and columns on patch panels. Sooner or later, most network techs will have to be able to pick out one particular cable or port from a stack.

When the time comes to trace cables, network techs turn to a device called a toner for help. Toner is the generic term for two separate devices that are used together: a tone generator and a tone probe. The *tone generator* connects to the cable using alligator clips, tiny hooks, or a network jack, and it sends an electrical signal along the wire at a certain frequency. The *tone probe* emits a sound when it is placed near a cable connected to the tone generator. These two devices are sometimes referred to by the brand name Fox and Hound, a model of toner made by the Triplett Corporation (see Figure 19-49).

Figure 19-49
Well used Fox
and Hound

 EXAM TIP You'll see a tone probe referred to on the CompTIA A+ exam as a *toner probe*.

To trace a cable, connect the tone generator to the known end of the cable in question, and then position the tone probe next to the other end of each of the cables that might be the right one. The tone probe makes a sound when it's placed next to the right cable. Some toners have one tone probe that works with multiple tone generators. Each generator emits a separate frequency, and the probe sounds a different tone for each one. Even good toners are relatively inexpensive ($100 or so); although inexpensive toners can cost less than $25, they don't tend to work well, so spending a little more is worthwhile. Just keep in mind that if you have to support a network, you'd do best to own a decent toner.

Fixing Common Problems

Let's go back and look at the second possible meaning for a loss in connectivity. It's very common to try to connect to a shared resource and either fail or find that a shared resource you've used time and again has suddenly disappeared. This applies (in this chapter, at least) to local resources—shares on the LAN, shared printers, e-mail server, and so on. Troubleshooting access to unavailable resources is part of a tech's bread-and-butter job.

Failing to Connect to a New Resource

When you can't connect to a resource on the first try, it often points to a configuration issue. In most cases, a quick double-check of the sharing system will reveal one of the following problems (and call for the associated solution):

- You don't have the right share name? Go check at the serving system.
- You don't have the required username/password? Ask someone who might have this knowledge, or double-check that your account has access.
- You don't have permission to use/access/connect to the shared resource? Make sure you have the correct permissions.
- You may need a forced Group Policy update if you're in an Active Directory domain. Group Policy updates may take a little while to propagate. The gpresult and gpupdate commands we took a look at in Chapter 15 can help you view the active policy settings and force an update if necessary.
- The folder or printer isn't shared? Share it!
- The folder or printer doesn't exist? Make sure the serving system still hosts the folder you want. Install the network printer if you haven't yet.

Failing to Connect to a Previously Used Resource

If you suddenly can't connect to a resource that you've used many times before, go with the easy answers first:

- Check that you can see the resource using Network.
- Check that the serving system is on.
- Check that the computer is physically connected to the serving system.

The net Command

Windows enables you to view a network quickly from the command line through the *net command*. This works great when you plug into a network for the first time and, naturally, don't know the names of the other computers on that network. To see the many options that net offers, type **net** at a command prompt and press ENTER. The view and use options offer excellent network tools.

You can think of net view as the command-line version of Network. When run, net view returns a list of Windows computers on the network:

```
C:\Users\Mike>net view
Server Name           Remark
-------------------------------------------------
\\SABERTOOTH
\\UBERBOX
\\SERVER1
The command completed successfully.
C:\Users\Mike>
```

 EXAM TIP   \\SABERTOOTH and the other server names here are examples of *network paths*—more technically called Universal Naming Convention (UNC) paths. The CompTIA A+ 1102 objectives want you to know that you can use File Explorer to work with these network paths in Windows. It works both ways. If you navigate the network with File Explorer, you can use it to copy out a network path. If you already have a network path and need to see if it's accessible, type or paste it in File Explorer's address bar!

Once you know the names of the computers, you type **net view** followed by the computer name. The net view command will show any shares on that machine and whether they are mapped drives:

```
C:\>net view server1
Shared resources at SERVER1
Share name  Type  Used as  Comment
-------------------------------------------------------------
FREDC       Disk
Research    Disk  W:
The command completed successfully.
```

The net use command is a command-line method for mapping network shares. For example, if you wanted to map the Research share shown in the previous example to the X: drive, you simply run

```
C:\>net use x: \\server1\research
```

This will map drive X: to the Research share on the SERVER1 computer. *Mapping a drive* means the drive will show up in File Explorer as a selectable resource, just like a local drive.

 NOTE   The net command can give a quick snapshot of the Windows network settings, such as computer name, OS version, workgroup or domain name, and more. Run

    `net config workstation`

It's quick and easy!

The nbtstat Command

The nbtstat command is an old command-line utility that predates Windows. It stands for NetBIOS over TCP/IP Statistics. Many versions ago, Windows used NetBIOS for many aspects of LAN file sharing, and even though NetBIOS is long gone, bits of NetBIOS hang on as a way for Windows to resolve host names on the network when a DNS server is not available.

While not covered on the CompTIA A+ Exam, nbtstat can still provide insight when troubleshooting naming issues in small workgroups. Here are a couple of usage examples; to see what your computer's NetBIOS name is, use the nbtstat -n command:

```
C:\Users\mmeyers>nbtstat -n

Local Area Connection:
Node IpAddress: [192.168.4.43] Scope Id: []

            NetBIOS Local Name Table

      Name               Type         Status
   ---------------------------------------------
      mmeyers-ws    <00>  UNIQUE      Registered
      WORKGROUP     <00>  GROUP       Registered
      mmeyers-ws    <20>  UNIQUE      Registered

C:\Users\mmeyers>
```

You can also query a remote machine by IP to find out its NetBIOS name with nbtstat -A (note the uppercase "A"; use a lowercase "a" if you know the machine's NetBIOS name already):

```
C:\Users\mmeyers>nbtstat -A 192.168.4.52

Local Area Connection:
Node IpAddress: [192.168.4.43] Scope Id: []

          NetBIOS Remote Machine Name Table

      Name               Type         Status
   ---------------------------------------------
      UNITEDKINGDOM  <00>  UNIQUE      Registered
      UNITEDKINGDOM  <03>  UNIQUE      Registered
      UNITEDKINGDOM  <20>  UNIQUE      Registered
      .._MSBROWSE__.<01>  GROUP       Registered
      TOTALHOME      <00>  GROUP       Registered
      TOTALHOME      <1D>  UNIQUE      Registered
      TOTALHOME      <1E>  GROUP       Registered

      MAC Address = 00-00-00-00-00-00
```

Finally, you can see all the names that NetBIOS has in its local cache with nbtstat -c:

```
C:\Users\mmeyers>nbtstat -c

Local Area Connection:
Node IpAddress: [192.168.4.43] Scope Id: []
```

```
            NetBIOS Remote Cache Name Table

     Name              Type      Host Address    Life [sec]
   -------------------------------------------------------------
   CLASS-SERVER    <00>  UNIQUE        192.168.4.50        447
   CLASS-SERVER    <20>  UNIQUE        192.168.4.50        447
   TOTALHOME       <1B>  UNIQUE        192.168.4.12        450
   UNITEDKINGDOM   <20>  UNIQUE        192.168.4.52        417
   UNITEDKINGDOM   <00>  UNIQUE        192.168.4.52        417
   WIN7-64         <20>  UNIQUE        192.168.4.220       450
```

Because the cache is temporary, you may find that it is empty if you haven't browsed your LAN or interacted with another machine recently.

Chapter Review

Questions

1. Steven's Windows system can't connect to the Internet, and he comes to you, his PC tech, for help. You figure out that it's a DHCP problem. What program should you run to troubleshoot his DHCP problem from the client side?

    A. ipconfig

    B. ifconfig

    C. config

    D. dhcp /review

2. What command would you use to view the path taken by an Ethernet packet?

    A. ping

    B. ipconfig

    C. tracert

    D. nslookup

3. Which of the following is the correct net syntax for discovering which network shares on a particular server are mapped on your computer?

    A. net view \\fileserver

    B. net \\fileserver

    C. net map \\fileserver

    D. net share \\fileserver

4. What small device enables you to test a NIC's circuitry?

    A. Loopback plug

    B. Port tester

    C. Multimeter

    D. Integrated network and logic probe

5. Which command can be used to display the cached NetBIOS names for a Windows system?

   A. nslookup

   B. dig --cache

   C. nbtstat -c

   D. nbtstat -A

6. You are down under your desk organizing some wires when you notice that the activity light on your NIC is blinking erratically. Is there a problem?

   A. Yes, the activity light should be on steadily when the computer is running.

   B. Yes, the activity light should be blinking steadily, not randomly.

   C. No, the light blinks when there is network traffic.

   D. No, the light blinks to show bus activity.

7. What is a common symptom of a bad network cable?

   A. Rapidly blinking link lights

   B. No link lights

   C. Solid on link lights

   D. Steady blinking link lights

8. What command-line utility would you run to show a list of network computers?

   A. net send

   B. show net_servers

   C. net use

   D. net view

9. What benefit does full-duplex offer?

   A. It enables NICs to send and receive signals at the same time.

   B. It enables NICs to send data twice as fast.

   C. It enables NICs to receive data twice as fast.

   D. It enables a switch to connect to both coaxial and fiber optic cables.

10. Which is a brand name of toner or tone generator?

    A. TDR

    B. UTP

    C. UDP

    D. Fox and Hound

Answers

1. **A.** You should run ipconfig, or more specifically ipconfig /release and then ipconfig /renew to get a new IP address if a DHCP server is available for Steven's Windows system. This typically resolves most DHCP client-side problems. ifconfig is the program used by macOS and Linux systems for this task. Neither config nor dhcp is valid.

2. **C.** The tracert command in Windows traces the path a data packet takes to get to its destination. macOS and Linux use the traceroute utility for similar purposes.

3. **A.** To see the network shares mapped on your computer, use net view \\fileserver.

4. **A.** A loopback plug will test the NIC's Ethernet port and circuitry.

5. **C.** nslookup and dig only work with DNS, not NetBIOS. nbtstat -A is for querying a remote system's name, but nbtstat -c displays the cached names.

6. **C.** The lights should be blinking to show activity—this is normal.

7. **B.** If there are no link lights, you probably have a bad network cable.

8. **D.** Use the net view command to show a list of computers on the network.

9. **A.** Full-duplex technology enables NICs to send and receive signals at the same time.

10. **D.** Most techs refer to a toner or tone generator as a Fox and Hound, the name of a popular brand of tone generator.

20

Wireless Networking

In this chapter, you will learn how to
- Describe wireless networking components
- Analyze and explain wireless networking standards
- Install and configure wireless networks
- Troubleshoot wireless networks

Wireless networks have been popular for many years now, but unlike wired networks, so much of how wireless works continues to elude people. Part of the problem might be that a simple wireless network is so inexpensive and easy to configure that most users and techs never really get into the *hows* of wireless. The chance to get away from all the cables and mess and just *connect* has a phenomenal appeal. The lack of understanding, though, hurts techs when it comes time to troubleshoot wireless networks. Let's change all that and dive deeply into wireless networking.

Historical/Conceptual

Wireless Networking Components

Instead of a physical set of wires running between network nodes, wireless networks use radio waves to communicate. Various kinds of wireless networking solutions have come and gone in the past (including some that used light instead of radio waves), but most of the wireless networks you'll find yourself supporting these days are *wireless LANs (WLANs)* based on the *IEEE 802.11* wireless Ethernet standard—marketed as Wi-Fi—and on Bluetooth technology.

 EXAM TIP One big difference between LANs and WLANs is security. In a LAN, you can disable ports and limit access to make it hard to sniff your traffic. In a WLAN, all of your packets are zooming through the air and require completely different security mechanisms. Another is that WLANs are a *shared* medium just like old hub-based LANs—the process of communicating over a WLAN is a complex dance with rules to keep devices from talking over each other.

Wireless networking capabilities of one form or another are built into many modern computing devices. Wi-Fi and Bluetooth capabilities are now common as integrated components, and you can easily add them when they aren't. Figure 20-1 shows a PCIe Wi-Fi adapter. You can also add wireless network capabilities by using external USB wireless network adapters or *wireless NICs*, as shown in Figure 20-2.

Figure 20-1
Wireless PCIe
add-on card

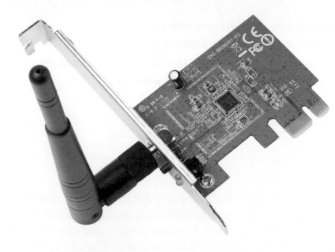

Figure 20-2
External USB
wireless NIC

Wireless networking is not limited to PCs. Most smartphones and tablets have wireless capabilities built in or available as add-on options. Figure 20-3 shows a smartphone accessing the Internet over a Wi-Fi connection.

Figure 20-3
Smartphone
with wireless
capability

NOTE See Chapter 24 for the scoop on mobile devices like smartphones
and tablets.

1101

To extend the capabilities of a wireless Ethernet network, such as connecting to a wired
network or sharing a high-speed Internet connection, you need a *wireless access point
(WAP)*. A WAP centrally connects wireless network devices in the same way that a hub
connects wired Ethernet devices. Many WAPs also act as switches and Internet routers,
such as the ASUS device shown in Figure 20-4.

Like any other electronic devices, most WAPs draw their power from a wall outlet.
More advanced WAPs, especially those used in corporate settings, can also use a feature
called *Power over Ethernet (PoE)*. Using PoE, you only need to plug a single Ethernet
cable into the WAP to provide it with both power and a network connection. The power
and network connection are both supplied by a *PoE-capable switch*.

Figure 20-4
ASUS device
that acts as
wireless access
point, switch,
and router

 EXAM TIP The CompTIA A+ 1101 exam objectives mention *PoE standards*. These include IEEE 802.3af, IEEE 802.3at, and IEEE 802.3bt (which are often marketed respectively as PoE, PoE+, and PoE++). Make sure you recognize them! PoE can power more than just WAPs—and it's especially helpful for devices that are rarely located near power outlets. A *Power over Ethernet injector*, for example, can extend a PoE connection up to 100 meters to connect Ethernet devices such as security cameras.

Wireless communication via Bluetooth comes as a built-in option on newer computers and peripheral devices, or you can add it to an older PC via an external USB Bluetooth adapter. All macOS devices—desktop and portable—have Bluetooth. Most commonly these days, you'll see Bluetooth used to connect a portable speaker to a smartphone, for music on the go, and to connect keyboards to tablets. Figure 20-5 shows a Bluetooth keyboard paired with a Bluetooth-enabled Apple iPad.

 NOTE Wireless access points are commonly known as WAPs, APs, or access points.

Wireless Networking Software

Wireless devices use the same networking protocols and client that their wired counterparts use, and they operate by using the *carrier sense multiple access/collision avoidance (CSMA/CA)* networking scheme. The *collision avoidance* aspect differs slightly from the *collision detection* standard used in wired Ethernet. A wireless device listens in on the wireless medium to see if another is currently broadcasting data. If so, it waits a random amount of time before retrying. So far, this method is exactly the same as the method used by wired Ethernet networks. Because wireless devices have a more difficult time detecting data collisions, however, they offer the option of using the *Request to Send/Clear*

Figure 20-5
Bluetooth
keyboard and
tablet

to Send (RTS/CTS) protocol. With this protocol enabled, a transmitting device sends an RTS frame to the receiving device after it determines the wireless medium is clear to use. The receiver responds with a CTS frame, telling the sender that it's okay to transmit. Then, once the data is sent, the transmitting device waits for an acknowledgment (ACK) from the receiving device before sending the next data packet. This option is very elegant, but keep in mind that using RTS/CTS introduces significant overhead to the process and can impede performance.

In terms of configuring wireless networking software, you need to do very little. Wireless network adapters are plug and play, so any modern version of Windows or macOS immediately recognizes one when it is installed, prompting you to load any needed hardware drivers. You will, however, need a utility to set parameters such as the network name. Modern operating systems include built-in tools for configuring these settings (see Figure 20-6).

Wireless Infrastructure

Wireless networks use one or more WAPs to connect the wireless network devices to a wired network segment, as shown in Figure 20-7. A single WAP servicing a given area is called a *Basic Service Set (BSS)*. This service area can be extended by adding more WAPs.

Larger homes, office buildings, and campuses are a whole different beast. They may have more than one WAP wired up to provide good signal coverage throughout the organization. This is called, appropriately, an *Extended Basic Service Set (EBSS)*. They may also lean on devices known as *wireless repeaters/extenders* that rebroadcast signals

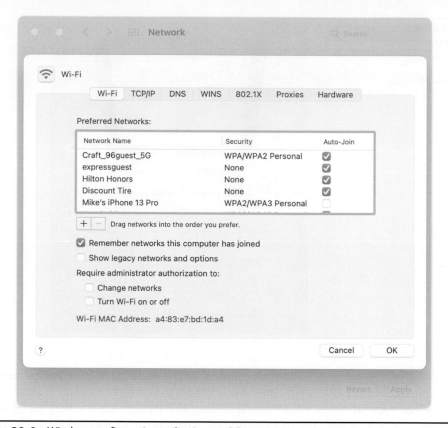

Figure 20-6   Wireless configuration utility in macOS

Figure 20-7
Wireless network
with a single WAP

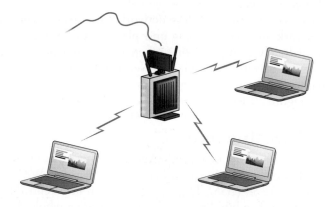

from clients and WAPs to help cover dead zones. Organizations can also "wirelessly wire" buildings up to several miles away. *Long-range fixed wireless*, which uses directional antennas, is a great way to interconnect remote buildings when it's hard or impractical to physically run cable to them.

Many manufacturers also produce sets of Wi-Fi components (each is a bit like a WAP and a bit like an extender) that collaborate to form a *mesh* network—with one of these devices serving as the gateway. The key characteristic of a *wireless mesh network (WMN)* is that the mesh devices act like routers, forwarding traffic for each other. These little mesh networks can improve signal coverage in a house or business that a single router or WAP has trouble covering—with less hassle than if you added more WAPs or extenders.

1102

Wireless Networking Security

One of the classic complaints against wireless networking is that it offers weak security. After all, data packets are floating through the air instead of safely wrapped up inside network cabling—what's to stop an unscrupulous person with the right equipment from grabbing those packets out of the air and reading that data? We have come a long way since the early days of Wi-Fi. In the past, you could access a wireless network by walking into a WAP's coverage area, turning on a wireless device, and connecting. These days, it has grown hard to find accidentally open networks, as hardware makers have trended toward using some type of security by default. Still, issues with these well-intentioned defaults are common, so it's still important to review the settings on new equipment.

Wireless networks use three methods to secure access to the network itself and secure the data being transferred: MAC address filtering, authentication, and data encryption. But before anyone encounters the on-network security, there are some measures we can take to reduce the likelihood our network will be targeted in the first place. Let's take a look at these practices first, followed by the methods for securing the network itself.

SSID

The *service set identifier (SSID)* parameter—also called the *network name*—defines the wireless network. Wireless devices *want* to be heard, and WAPs are usually configured to announce their presence by broadcasting the SSID to their maximum range. This is very handy when you have several wireless networks in the same area, but a default SSID also gives away important clues about the manufacturer (and maybe even model) of an access point.

Always change the default SSID to something unique and change the password right away. Configuring a unique SSID name and password is the very least that you should do to secure a wireless network. Older default SSID names and passwords are well known and widely available online. While newer models may come with unique SSIDs and passwords, the SSID may still leak information about your hardware—and the generated password may use rules that make it easy to break.

These defaults are intended to make setting up a wireless network as easy as possible but can cause problems in places with a lot of overlapping wireless networks. Keep in mind that each wireless access point in a network needs to be configured with the same unique SSID name. This SSID name is then included in the header of every data packet broadcast in the wireless network's coverage area. Data packets that lack the correct SSID name in the header are rejected. When it comes to picking a new unique SSID, it's still good to think about whether the name will make your network a more interesting target or give away details that could help an attacker gain physical or remote access.

Another trick often seen in wireless networks is to tell the WAP not to broadcast the SSID. In theory, people not authorized to access the network will have a harder time knowing it's there, as it won't show up in the list of nearby networks on most devices.

In practice, even simple wireless scanning programs can discover the name of an "unknown" wireless network. Disabling the SSID broadcast just makes it harder for legitimate clients to connect. It doesn't stop bad actors at all—except on a CompTIA A+ exam question.

 EXAM TIP Two of the wireless-specific "security settings" called out in the CompTIA A+ 1102 objectives leave me scratching my head: disabling SSID broadcast and changing channels. Disabling SSID broadcast just makes it harder for legitimate users to find your network; even a simple wireless scanner will still see your network—and no serious attacker will be fooled. Channel selection has nothing to do with security—though it can impact performance. Modern WAPs will generally auto-select channels based on interference, but if not you should do the same manually. Neither of these practices will secure your network—but don't be shocked if they turn up as the right answer on the exam.

Access Point Placement and Radio Power

When setting up a wireless network, keep the space in mind; you can limit risk by hiding the network from outsiders. When using an omni-directional antenna that sends and receives signals in all directions, for example, keep it near the center of the home or office. The closer you place it to a wall, the further away someone outside the home or office can be and still detect the wireless network.

Many wireless access points enable you to adjust the radio power levels of the antenna. Decrease the radio power until you can get reception at the furthest point *inside* the target network space, but not outside. This will take some trial and error.

 EXAM TIP Don't forget to make sure the WAP is also in a *physically* secure location. Most WAPs have physical Ethernet ports in addition to their wireless capabilities. These ports are not password-protected or encrypted. Keep the WAP in a location where unscrupulous folks can't get to it.

Guest Networks

Some WAPs include a guest access feature that makes it easier to set up a network for untrusted users. The CompTIA A+ 1102 objectives mention *disabling guest access* as a wireless-specific security measure—so be prepared to recognize it as a security measure on the exam. In the real world, be conservative: disable guest access unless you need it.

The specifics of this mode can differ, so look into how your device handles guest access if you know you'll need it—and consider an upgrade if you don't like what you discover.

Some devices (especially those designed with businesses like bars, cafes, and coffee shops in mind) have a pretty secure guest mode where guests have access to their own SSID—protected with a different password—and you can prevent them from communicating with each other and the rest of your network. Once again, be conservative: if you need guest networks, enable these protections unless you have a specific reason to let guests interact with each other or the rest of your network.

MAC Address Filtering

Most WAPs support *MAC address filtering*, a method that enables you to limit access to your wireless network based on the physical, hard-wired address of the units' wireless NIC. MAC address filtering is a handy way of creating a type of "accepted users" list to limit access to your wireless network, but it works best when you have a small number of users. A table stored in the WAP lists the MAC addresses that are permitted to participate in the wireless network. Any data packets that don't contain a MAC address listed in the table are rejected.

NOTE MAC filtering might sound airtight, but it isn't. An attacker can use software to listen for the MAC addresses of nearby clients and spoof the address of an accepted client.

Wireless Security Protocols and Authentication Methods

Wireless security protocols provide authentication and encryption to lock down wireless networks. Wireless networks offer awesome connectivity options, but equally provide tempting targets. Wireless developers have worked very hard to provide techs the tools for protecting wireless clients and communication. Wireless authentication accomplishes the same thing wired authentication does, enabling the system to check a user's credentials and give or deny him or her access to the network. Encryption scrambles the signals on radio waves and makes communication among users secure.

This section looks at the most recent generations of wireless security protocols, WPA2 and WPA3, as well as typical authentication methods. (See "Wi-Fi Configuration" later in this chapter for the scoop on enterprise authentication installations.)

EXAM TIP Wireless networks have already been with us for a long time—and the early attempts to secure them were a little...haphazard. These days, Wired Equivalent Privacy (WEP) and the original Wi-Fi Protected Access (WPA) are both deprecated. If you see them on the exam, they're probably wrong answers. If you encounter WEP or WPA on real-world devices where they are the best security available—it's time to go shopping! Wi-Fi Protected Setup (WPS) is also deprecated—but you may still see it on newer devices since it enables less-technical users to add devices to their network by first pressing a button on their WAP.

WPA2   *Wi-Fi Protected Access 2 (WPA2)* uses the *Advanced Encryption Standard (AES)* to provide a secure wireless environment. All current WAPs and wireless clients support WPA2. You may encounter older routers with a "backward compatible" mode for first-generation WPA—but at this point I recommend upgrading or replacing WPA-only devices if at all possible.

EXAM TIP   WPA2 is also compatible with the *Temporal Key Integrity Protocol (TKIP)*, an older encryption method that was introduced with the original WPA. You may see it as an option (both on the exam and in WPA2 devices), but—as an option for backward compatibility with even older devices—enabling it will make a modern network less secure (and potentially slow it down).

WPA3   The successor to WPA2 was announced in early 2018. *Wi-Fi Protected Access 3 (WPA3)* addresses some security and usability issues, including encryption to protect the data of users on open (public) networks.

NOTE   WPA2 was the best option we had for well over a decade. The transition to WPA3 is under way, but WAPs tend to have a pretty long life—expect WPA2 to be the best option on many older devices. Implement WPA3 networks when practical, and eventually disable WPA2 once all of the devices you need to support are WPA3-compatible.

1101

Wireless Networking Standards and Regulations

Most wireless networks use *radio frequency (RF)* technologies, in particular the 802.11 (Wi-Fi) standards. (Other standards such as Bluetooth hold a much smaller place in today's market.) These technologies use parts of the RF signal spectrum that were already in use for other purposes, so they are tightly regulated to minimize their impact on those users. To help you gain a better understanding of wireless network technologies, this section provides a brief look at the standards they use and some aspects of how regulations come into play.

NOTE   Radio frequency is the part of the electromagnetic spectrum used for radio communication.

IEEE 802.11-Based Wireless Networking

The IEEE 802.11 wireless Ethernet standard, more commonly known as *Wi-Fi*, defines methods devices may use to communicate via *spread-spectrum* radio waves. Spread-spectrum broadcasts data in small, discrete chunks over the frequencies available within a certain frequency range.

NOTE Wi-Fi and other wireless communication technologies use radio frequencies that fall in *industrial, scientific, and medical (ISM) radio bands*. This can lead to interference with other devices such as microwave ovens and baby monitors.

The 802.11-based wireless technologies broadcast and receive on one of three radio bands: 2.4 GHz, 5 GHz, and 6 GHz. A band is a contiguous range of frequencies that is usually divided up into discrete slices called *channels*. Over the years, the original 802.11 standard has been extended to 802.11a, 802.11b, 802.11g, 802.11n, 802.11ac, and 802.11ax variations used in Wi-Fi wireless networks. Each of these versions of 802.11 uses one of the two bands, with the exception of 802.11n, which uses one but may use both. Don't worry; I'll break this down for you in a moment.

Newer wireless devices typically provide backward compatibility with older wireless devices. If you are using an 802.11n WAP, all of your 802.11g devices can use it. An 802.11ac WAP is backward compatible with 802.11b, g, and n. The exception to this is 802.11a, which requires a 5-GHz radio, meaning only 802.11ac and dual-band 802.11n WAPs are backward compatible with 802.11a devices. The following paragraphs describe the important specifications of each of the popular 802.11-based wireless networking standards. Let's take a look at Wi-Fi Channels first.

Understanding Wi-Fi Channels

Here's the simple part: each Wi-Fi channel is a little 20-MHz slice of its broader radio band. Unfortunately, you still need to know a good bit more about what channels are, and how they operate to configure and manage modern Wi-Fi networks. One of the big reasons for this is that channels are a little bit different between the 2.4-GHz, 5-GHz, and 6-GHz bands—and different countries regulate them differently.

2.4 GHz   In the 2.4-GHz band, most countries allow for either 11 or 13 channels, with a *big* catch—they overlap! Overlapping channels are not so great for performance, so in the United States we're left with three nonoverlapping channels: 1, 6, and 11. We're also at the mercy of other nearby networks. If your weird neighbor chooses a weird channel—maybe their favorite number is 8—they can make it harder for everyone else. Be a good neighbor—pick 1, 6, or 11!

5 GHz   Thankfully, channels in the 5-GHz band are *nonoverlapping*. The big catch here, though, is that the number of available channels *and* the exact ones that are available can differ from country to country. In the United States, we have 25 channels to choose from. You can also (depending on the Wi-Fi standard) "bond" two or four channels into a *wide* (40 MHz) or *ultra-wide* (80 MHz) channel, increasing throughput at the expense of making your network more vulnerable to interference. At least for now, 5 GHz is the preferred band—use it if you can!

NOTE   Technically, you can use 40-MHz channels in the 2.4-GHz band, but they may hurt your performance. I don't recommend it.

6 GHz   As of this writing, the 6-GHz band is already available for Wi-Fi 6E devices in some countries (including the United States) and is working its way through the regulatory process in others. Its main promise is, of course, less congestion. The new band significantly increases the space available for Wi-Fi networks, giving us many more nonoverlapping channels to spread out over. It's so much more room, in fact, that it can support bonding eight channels into one *super-wide* (160 MHz) channel.

NOTE   The 6-GHz band has its own catches. For example, some people already have licenses for parts of the 6-GHz spectrum, and Wi-Fi devices aren't allowed to interfere with them. For now, this means it's easiest to use the 6-GHz band indoors on devices that have limited power and nonremovable antennas. WAPs designed for use outdoors must support Automated Frequency Coordination (AFC), a technology with which the WAP sends its location, antenna height, and other details to a central database, which then tells the WAP what channels it can use and at what power level.

802.11a

Despite the "a" designation for this extension to the 802.11 standard, *802.11a* was actually on the market after 802.11b. The 802.11a standard differs from the other 802.11-based standards in significant ways. Foremost is that it's the first Wi-Fi standard to operate in the 5-GHz frequency range. This means devices using this standard are less prone to interference from other devices that use the same frequency range. 802.11a also offers considerably greater throughput than 802.11 and 802.11b, at speeds up to 54 Mbps, though its actual throughput is no more than 25 Mbps in normal traffic conditions. Although its theoretical range tops out at about 150 feet, its maximum range will be lower in a typical office environment.

802.11b

802.11b was the first standard to take off and become ubiquitous in wireless networking. The 802.11b standard supports data throughput of up to 11 Mbps (with actual throughput averaging 4 to 6 Mbps)—on par with older wired 10BASE-T networks—and a maximum range of 300 feet under ideal conditions. In a typical office environment, its maximum range is lower. The main downside to using 802.11b is that it uses a very popular frequency. The 2.4-GHz ISM band is already crowded with baby monitors, garage door openers, microwaves, and wireless phones, so you're likely to run into interference from other wireless devices.

802.11g

802.11g came out in 2003, taking the best of 802.11a and b and rolling them into a single standard. 802.11g offers data transfer speeds equivalent to 802.11a, up to 54 Mbps, with the wider 300-foot range of 802.11b. More important, 802.11g runs in the 2.4-GHz ISM band, so it is backward compatible with 802.11b, meaning that the same 802.11g WAP can service both 802.11b and 802.11g wireless clients.

802.11n

The *802.11n* standard (now also known as *Wi-Fi 4*) brought several improvements to Wi-Fi networking, including faster speeds and new antenna technology implementations.

The 802.11n specification requires all but hand-held devices to use multiple antennas to implement a feature called *multiple in/multiple out (MIMO)*, which enables the devices to make multiple simultaneous connections. With up to four antennas, 802.11n devices can achieve amazing speeds. The official standard supports throughput of up to 600 Mbps, although practical implementation drops that down substantially (to 100+ Mbps at 300+ feet).

NOTE Because cellular telephones typically support both cellular networks and 802.11x Wi-Fi networks, many can be used to bridge the gap. Using internal utilities or apps, you can set up your phone as a Wi-Fi WAP that can pass signals to and from the Internet via its cellular connection. Turning your phone into a WAP is known as creating a *hotspot*; using it to bridge to the cellular network is called *tethering*. Check out Chapters 21 and 24 for the scoop on these techniques.

Many 802.11n WAPs employ *transmit beamforming*, a multiple-antenna technology that helps get rid of dead spots—or at least make them not so bad. The antennas adjust the signal once the WAP discovers a client to optimize the radio signal.

Like 802.11g, 802.11n WAPs can run in the 2.4-GHz ISM band, supporting earlier, slower 802.11b/g devices. 802.11n also supports the more powerful so-called *dual-band* operation. To use dual-band, you need a more advanced (and more expensive) WAP that runs at both 5 GHz and 2.4 GHz simultaneously; some support 802.11a devices as well as 802.11b/g devices.

802.11ac

802.11ac, now also known as *Wi-Fi 5*, is a natural expansion of the 802.11n standard, incorporating even more streams, wider bandwidth, and higher speed. To avoid device density issues in the 2.4-GHz band, 802.11ac only uses the 5-GHz band. The latest versions of 802.11ac include a new version of MIMO called *Multiuser MIMO (MU-MIMO)*. MU-MIMO gives a WAP the ability to broadcast to multiple users simultaneously. Like 802.11n, 802.11ac supports dual-band operation. Some WAPs even support tri-band operation, adding a second 5-GHz signal to support a lot more 5-GHz connections simultaneously at optimal speeds.

802.11ax

802.11ax—which is also known as *high efficiency wireless (HEW)*, brings a number of improvements that should help optimize congested networks and reduce power use on client devices. 802.11ax is marketed as *both Wi-Fi 6* and *Wi-Fi 6E* (for *extended*), and the latter marks a really exciting development in wireless networking—even if the designations are a little slippery. The initial 802.11ax devices, marketed under the Wi-Fi 6 designation, can use both the 2.4-GHz and 5-GHz bands. Newer Wi-Fi

6E devices (technically 802.11ax-2021) use the 2.4-GHz, 5-GHz, *and* 6-GHz bands. The 6-GHz band can support more nonoverlapping Wi-Fi channels, is not as saturated with existing Wi-Fi networks, and doesn't suffer as much interference from other devices.

EXAM TIP Back in October 2018, the Wi-Fi Alliance announced new branding for 802.11n (Wi-Fi 4), 802.11ac (Wi-Fi 5), and 802.11ax (Wi-Fi 6). Many people also extend this style of naming back to older standards (they refer to 802.11g as Wi-Fi 3, and so on), but don't get too distracted by these newfangled names! The CompTIA A+ 1101 objectives *only* use this style of designation for Wi-Fi 5 and Wi-Fi 6, so you'll still need to have a good grasp of the 802.11*x* standards. I'm not quite sure if CompTIA will ask about Wi-Fi 6E. Prepare for it, but don't be surprised if you see questions that assume Wi-Fi 6 is still the latest-and-greatest thing in the world of Wi-Fi.

Table 20-1 compares the important differences among modern versions of 802.11*x*.

	802.11n	802.11ac	802.11ax
Max. throughput	100+ Mbps	1+ Gbps	9+ Gbps
Max. range	300+ feet	300+ feet	300+ feet
Frequency	2.4 and 5 GHz	5 GHz	2.4 GHz, 5 GHz, 6 GHz
Security	SSID, MAC filtering, industry-standard WEP, WPA, WPA2	SSID, MAC filtering, industry-standard WEP, WPA, WPA2	SSID, MAC filtering, industry-standard WPA2, WPA3
Compatibility	802.11b, 802.11g, 802.11n, (802.11a in some cases)	802.11a, 802.11b, 802.11g, 802.11n	802.11a, 802.11b, 802.11g, 802.11n, 802.11ac
Description	Same as 802.11g but adds the 5-GHz band that 802.11a uses. 802.11n can also make use of multiple antennas (MIMO) to increase its range and speed.	Expands on 802.11n by adding streams, bandwidth, and higher speed in the 5-GHz band. Uses MU-MIMO and beamforming antenna technology to optimize wireless connections.	Optimizes power use on client devices and reduces network congestion. Has features to support more WAPs and clients in a given area. The 802.11ax-2021 update allows for use of the 6-GHz band, which allows for more uncongested channels.

Table 20-1 Comparison of Modern 802.11 Standards

SIM Check out the "Wireless Technologies" Challenge! sim in the Chapter 20 section of https://www.totalsem.com/110X to reinforce the differences among 802.11a, 802.11b, 802.11g, 802.11n, 802.11ac, and 802.11ax. This will help you with any performance-based questions CompTIA might throw your way.

Try This!

802.11ax Products

802.11ax is the standard for any new Wi-Fi rollout. You need to understand variations, so try this! Head out to a big box electronics retail store, like Microcenter or Best Buy (or go online to Newegg). What variations of 802.11ax products do you see? Note the letters and numbers associated with the products. The base models—the least expensive—might list a speed rating like AX1800. Products listed as AX3000 might cost 30 to 50 percent more, and AX6000 might cost a few times more.

Some Wi-Fi 6E devices are starting to turn up—how many models can you find with AXE speed ratings?

Optimizing Wi-Fi Coverage

Good Wi-Fi provides enough data throughput for your devices to do what you need—and covers every spot you need to connect from. Wireless networking data throughput speeds and coverage depend on *many* factors, but the most important are the wireless standards in use, the distances involved, the amount of interference present, and the kind of antennas in use.

NOTE As mentioned earlier, there are simple ways to cover large buildings or campuses. You can install multiple WAPs to permit "roaming" between one WAP's coverage area and another's—an EBSS, described earlier in this chapter. Or you can install a replacement WAP with greater signal strength and range. If that is still not enough, wireless repeaters/extenders or a mesh networking kit may do what you need. Networks of any size may need further optimization.

Depending on the standard used, wireless throughput speeds range from a measly 2 Mbps to a snappy 9+ Gbps. One factor affecting speed is the distance between wireless clients and their access points. Wireless devices dynamically negotiate the top speed at which they can communicate without dropping too many data packets. Speed decreases as distance increases, so the maximum throughput speed is achieved only at extremely close range (less than 25 feet or so). At the outer reaches of a device's effective range, speed may decrease to around 1 Mbps before it drops out altogether.

Interference caused by solid objects and other wireless devices operating in the same frequency range—such as microwaves, cordless phones, baby monitors, radar systems, and so on—can reduce both speed and range. So-called *dead spots* occur when something capable of blocking the radio signal comes between the wireless network clients. Large electrical appliances such as refrigerators block wireless network signals *very* effectively. Other culprits include electrical fuse boxes, metal plumbing, air conditioning units, and similar objects.

NOTE You can check the speed and signal strength on your wireless network by looking at the wireless NIC's status. In Windows, open the Network and Sharing Center, select Change adapter settings, then double-click your wireless NIC to view the status dialog box.

Because of these factors, wireless networking range is difficult to define. This is why you'll see most descriptions use qualifiers like "*around* 150 feet" and "*about* 300 feet." In Table 20-1 you'll see the maximum ranges listed as those presented by wireless manufacturers as the theoretical maximum ranges. In the real world, you'll experience these ranges only under the most ideal circumstances. True effective range is probably about half what you see listed.

EXAM TIP Look for basic troubleshooting questions on the CompTIA A+ certification exams dealing with factors that affect wireless connectivity, range, and speed.

Antennas and Transmission Power

These range figures generally assume you'll set up a WAP with an omni-directional antenna in the center of the area (see Figure 20-8) you want to cover. With an omni-directional antenna, the radio wave flows outward from the WAP. This has the advantage of ease of use—anything within the signal radius can potentially access the network. Most wireless networks, especially in the consumer space, use standard straight-wire *dipole antennas* to provide omni-directional coverage. Dipole antennas look like a stick, but inside they have two antenna arms or poles aligned on the antenna's axis; hence the term "dipole."

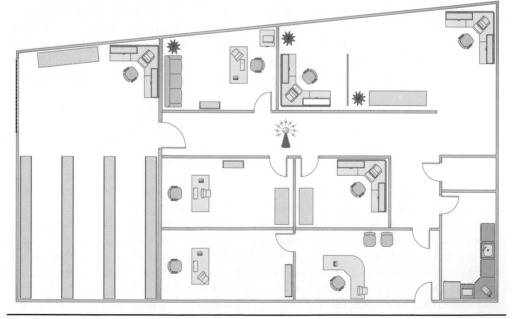

Figure 20-8 Room layout with WAP in the center

Many WAPs have removable antennas that you can replace. To increase the signal in an omni-directional and centered setup, simply replace the factory antennas with one or more bigger antennas (see Figure 20-9). They come in several common flavors. Increasing the size of a dipole will increase its *gain* evenly in all directions. Directional antennas—such as parabolic dish-type antennas—increase gain (and thus range) in a specific direction and reduce gain in all the other directions. The configuration software on some devices will also allow you to tune the transmission power (regardless of which antenna is in use).

NOTE Gain in an antenna strengthens and focuses the radio frequency output from a WAP. The ratio of increase—what's called *gain*—is measured in decibels (dB). The gain from a typical WAP is 2 dB, enough to cover a reasonable area but not a very large room.

In both cases, you should be cautious. A better antenna or higher transmission power may fix your problem, but both are closely regulated. Some antennas may not be legal in your area—or you may not be allowed to use a device with replaceable antennas at all. It may even be possible to increase transmission power to illegal levels and cause trouble for you or your organization.

Figure 20-9
WAP with
replacement
antenna

EXAM TIP If you want to know whether your local café, bookstore, airport, or other public place has a Wi-Fi access point (a hotspot), you can use a *Wi-Fi* or *wireless locator*. Dedicated Wi-Fi locators, also called *Wi-Fi analyzers*, can also be very expensive—but for basic analysis you can just use your smartphone with a free locator/analyzer app.

Long-Range Fixed Wireless

Long-range fixed wireless, which uses directional antennas, is a great way to interconnect remote buildings when it's hard or impractical to physically run cable to them. Using the right antenna and power level can do more than just extend a network's range a few hundred feet. Powerful directional antennas enable organizations to provide a remote building or structure with network access (up to several miles away) without having to run cable to it. There isn't really a specific set of standards for these *point-to-point* connections, but there are regulatory requirements.

- Some organizations use specific equipment, jump through Federal Communications Commission (FCC) regulatory hoops, and pay for a license to use a specific frequency. These may use proprietary or existing wireless protocols.

- Some organizations use normal Wi-Fi standards (and the corresponding unlicensed spectrum) with special equipment.

- Still others may start with a normal Wi-Fi standard (with unlicensed spectrum) but end up tweaking the software or hardware (deviating from the standard) to solve unique problems that they face.

Just like with regular Wi-Fi networks, the level of transmission power plays a big role in the distance you can communicate over. Signals with a higher transmit power can travel farther and penetrate more obstacles. You want to be like Goldilocks here—use enough power for the receiver to hear you loud and clear, but not so much that you waste tons of electricity or interfere with other users. These point-to-point links also have regulatory requirements that cap the maximum transmission power they can use. Adjusting transmit power will be covered later in the chapter.

Bluetooth

Bluetooth wireless technology (named for tenth-century Danish king Harald Bluetooth) is designed to create small wireless networks preconfigured to do very specific jobs. Some great examples are wearable technology, audio devices such as headsets or automotive entertainment systems that connect to your smartphone, *personal area networks (PANs)* that link two computers for a quick-and-dirty wireless network, and input devices such as keyboards and mice. Bluetooth is *not* designed to be a full-function networking solution, nor is it meant to compete with Wi-Fi.

EXAM TIP PANs are the smallest "area network" type included in the CompTIA A+ 1101 objectives. Their scope is exactly what it says on the tin—devices that belong to and are near or on a single person.

Bluetooth, like any technology, has been upgraded over the years to make it faster and more secure. The first generation (versions 1.1 and 1.2) supports speeds around 1 Mbps. The second generation (2.0 and 2.1) is backward compatible with its first-generation cousins and adds support for more speed by introducing Enhanced Data Rate (EDR), which pushes top speeds to around 3 Mbps. The third generation (3.0 + HS) tops out at 24 Mbps, but this is accomplished over an 802.11 connection after Bluetooth negotiation. The High Speed (+ HS) feature is optional. Instead of continuing to increase top speed, the fourth generation (4.0, 4.1, and 4.2), also called Bluetooth Smart, is largely focused on improving Bluetooth's suitability for use in networked "smart" devices/appliances by reducing cost and power consumption, improving speed and security, and introducing IP connectivity. The fifth generation (just *Bluetooth 5*) adds options to increase speed at the expense of range or by changing packet size. Bluetooth 5 adds better support for Internet of Things (IoT) devices, like smart speakers, lights, and so on.

NOTE Chapter 21 details the Internet of Things. We'll get there!

The IEEE organization has made first-generation Bluetooth the basis for its 802.15 standard for wireless PANs. Bluetooth uses a broadcasting method that switches between any of the 79 frequencies available in the 2.45-GHz range. Bluetooth hops frequencies some 1600 times per second, making it highly resistant to interference.

Generally, the faster and further a device sends data, the more power it needs to do so, and the Bluetooth designers understood a long time ago that some devices (such as a Bluetooth headset) could save power by not sending data as quickly or as far as other Bluetooth devices may need. To address this, all Bluetooth devices are configured for one of three classes that define maximum power usage in milliwatts (mW) and maximum distance:

Class	Max. Power Usage	Max. Range
Class 1	100 mW	100 meters
Class 2	2.5 mW	10 meters
Class 3	1 mW	1 meter

Bluetooth personal networks are made to replace the snake's nest of cables that currently connects most PCs to their various peripheral devices—keyboard, mouse, printer, speakers, scanner, and the like—but you probably won't be swapping out your 802.11-based networking devices with Bluetooth-based replacements anytime soon. Despite this, Bluetooth's recent introduction of IP connectivity may bring more and more Bluetooth-related traffic to 802.11 devices in the future.

Having said that, Bluetooth-enabled wireless networking is comparable to other wireless technologies in a few ways:

- Bluetooth is acceptable for quick file transfers where a wired connection (or a faster wireless connection) is unavailable.

- Bluetooth's speed and range make it a good match for wireless print server solutions.

As mentioned earlier in the chapter, Bluetooth hardware comes either built into newer portable electronic gadgets such as smartphones or as an adapter added to an internal or external expansion bus. Bluetooth networking is enabled through device-to-device connections or (rarely) through Bluetooth access points. Bluetooth access points are very similar to 802.11-based access points, bridging wireless Bluetooth segments to wired LAN segments.

1102

Installing and Configuring Wireless Networking

The mechanics of setting up a wireless network don't differ much from a wired network. Physically installing a wireless network adapter is the same as installing a wired NIC, whether it's an internal card, a laptop add-on wireless card, or an external USB device. Simply install the device and let plug and play handle the rest. Install the device's supplied driver when prompted and you're practically finished.

The trick is in configuring the wireless network so that only specific wireless clients are able to use it and securing the data that's being sent through the air.

Wi-Fi Configuration

Typical wireless networks employ one or more WAPs connected to a wired network segment, such as a corporate intranet, the Internet, or both. These networks require that the same SSID be configured on all clients and WAPs.

Most consumer WAPs have an integrated Web server and are configured through a browser-based setup utility. Typically, you open a Web browser on a networked computer and enter the WAP's default IP address, such as 192.168.1.1, to bring up the configuration page. You need to supply an administrative password, included with your

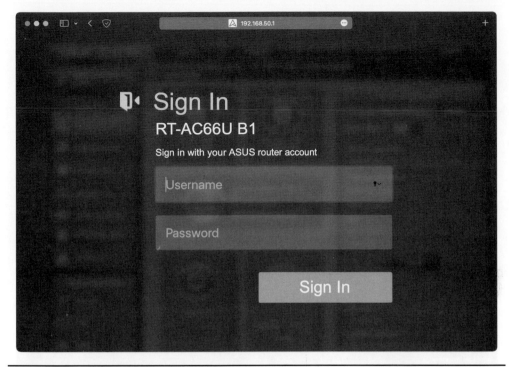

Figure 20-10   Security login for ASUS WAP

WAP's documentation, to log in (see Figure 20-10). Most newer WAPs ask you to create an administrative password at installation. Setup screens vary from vendor to vendor and from model to model. Figure 20-11 shows the initial setup screen for an ASUS WAP/router.

To make life easier, current WAPs come with a Web-based utility that autodetects the WAP and guides the user through setting up all of its features.

When you purchase a new WAP, there is a pretty good chance the vendor already has updated firmware for it. The chance is even greater if you've had your WAP for a while. Before configuring your WAP for your users to access it, you should check for updates. Refer to the section "Software Troubleshooting," later in the chapter, for more on updating WAP firmware.

Configure the SSID option where indicated. Remember that it's better to configure a unique SSID than it is to accept the well-known default one. The default may help an attacker identify your hardware and focus on any vulnerabilities it is known to have. Avoid names that include an address, name, number, or other description that would help an attacker locate the physical device.

Figure 20-11   ASUS WAP home screen

Channel selection is usually automatic, but you can reconfigure this option if you have particular needs in your organization (for example, if you have multiple wireless networks operating in the same area). Use a wireless analyzer to find the "quietest" channel where you intend to install the WAP and select that channel in the appropriate WAP setup/configuration screen. This provides the lowest chance of interference from other WAPs. Clients automatically search through all frequencies and channels when searching for broadcasted SSIDs.

To increase security even more, use MAC filtering. Figure 20-12 shows the MAC filtering configuration screen for an ASUS WAP. Simply click the Add MAC Address button and enter the MAC address of a wireless device that you wish to allow (or deny) access to your wireless network. Set up encryption by setting the security mode on the WAP and then generating a unique security key or password. Then configure all connected wireless devices on the network with the same credentials. Figure 20-13 shows a security settings WAP properties panel configured for WPA2-Personal wireless security.

Figure 20-12   MAC filtering configuration screen for an ASUS WAP

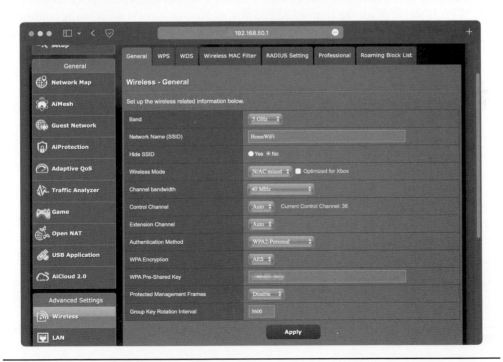

Figure 20-13   Security settings screen for an ASUS WAP

NOTE As noted earlier in the chapter, the WEP protocol is deprecated. It does provide a little security, but it's easily cracked. Use it only as an absolute last resort if there's some reason you can't just upgrade the equipment. WPA3, WPA2, or even WPA are all better choices.

If you're dealing with ancient equipment and find yourself performing the unseemly task of setting up WEP, you should have the option of automatically generating a set of encryption keys or doing it manually; save yourself a headache and use the automatic method. Select an encryption level—the usual choices are either 64-bit or 128-bit—and then enter a unique *passphrase* and click the Generate button (or whatever the equivalent button is called on your WAP). Then select a default key and save the settings. The encryption level, key, and passphrase must match on the wireless client or communication will fail. Many WAPs have the capability to export the WEP encryption key data onto a media storage device so you can easily import it on a client workstation, or you can manually configure encryption by using the Windows wireless configuration utility.

WPA encryption (including the preferred WPA3 or WPA2) is configured in much the same way. While it may seem that there are many configuration options, there are effectively two ways to set up WPA/WPA2/WPA3: Personal/Pre-shared Key (PSK) or Enterprise. Personal is the most common for small and home networks (see Figure 20-14). Enterprise is much more complex, requires extra equipment, and is only used in the most serious and secure wireless networks. After selecting the Personal option, there may be "subselections" such as Mixed mode, which allows a WPA3-encrypted WAP to also support WPA2. You may see the term PSK, Pre-Shared Key, or just Personal in the configuration options. If you have the option, choose WPA3 encryption for the WAP as well as the NICs in your network.

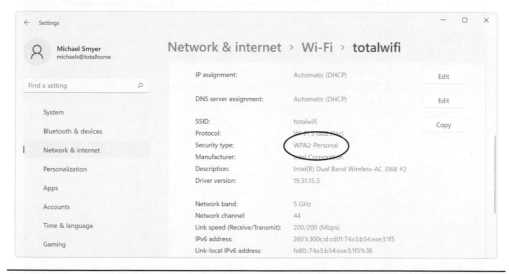

Figure 20-14 Encryption screen on client wireless network adapter configuration utility

Settings such as WPA3 for the Enterprise assume you'll enable authentication by using something called a RADIUS server (see Figure 20-15). Larger businesses tend to need more security than a single network-wide password can offer. Their networks often require individual users to log in with their own credentials. Security-conscious organizations may even require their users to log in with more than just a username and password. You'll learn more about this practice, better known as *multifactor authentication (MFA)*, in Chapter 27.

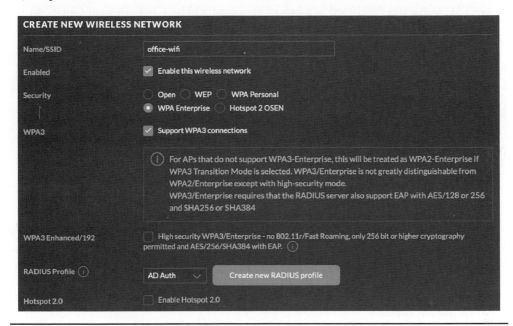

Figure 20-15 Encryption screen with RADIUS option

 EXAM TIP The CompTIA A+ 1101 objectives want you to know about a server role called *authentication, authorization, and accounting (AAA)*—a server that authenticates users, authorizes what resources they may access, and logs all these actions for accountability. Real-world AAA is complex and often entails multiple servers—but RADIUS and TACACS+ are the main protocols that power AAA whether it involves one server or several.

To power AAA, the network uses authentication protocols like RADIUS and TACACS+ to authenticate each user with an authentication server. *Remote Authentication Dial-In User Service (RADIUS)* and *Terminal Access Controller Access-Control System Plus (TACACS+)* are protocols for authenticating network users and managing what resources they may access.

It can be a little tricky to keep TACACS+ and RADIUS straight. I recommend learning more facts than you'll probably need to know about them:

- RADIUS is a completely open standard developed by the Internet Engineering Task Force (IETF) in a whole boatload of RFCs. RADIUS is partially encrypted and usually uses UDP ports 1812 and 1813. It's more likely to be interoperable between different device manufacturers.

- TACACS+ was developed as a proprietary protocol by Cisco, though Cisco has released an "open" description of it so that other companies can also implement it. TACACS+ is fully encrypted and uses TCP port 49. It won't be as well supported on non-Cisco hardware.

EXAM TIP Good network authentication and authorization doesn't stop at the gate! Well-designed networks also validate authentication and authorization when clients access network resources. The *Kerberos* authentication protocol enables a central authorization server to pass out keys that individual clients can present to access resources as needed. You may never deal *directly* with Kerberos, but it's extremely common—it's even hard at work under the hood of Microsoft Active Directory.

Businesses can allow only people with the proper credentials to connect to their Wi-Fi networks. For home use, select the Personal version of WPA3/WPA2/WPA. Use the best encryption you can. If you have WPA3 or WPA2, use it. If not, use WPA. WEP is configured in much the same way, but it is a terrible choice for a general network. If you can't upgrade or replace any WEP-only devices, consider setting up a separate WEP network just for them.

NOTE Always try WPA3-Personal or WPA2-Personal first, depending on what your WAP can handle. If you then have wireless computers that can't connect to your WAP, fall back to WPA2-Personal or WPA-Personal. Use Mixed mode so the newer clients can still take advantage of the extra security provided by WPA3 or WPA2 while older clients can use WPA-Personal.

With most home networks, you can simply leave the channel and frequency of the WAP at the factory defaults, but in an environment with overlapping Wi-Fi signals, you'll want to adjust one or both features. To adjust the channel, find the option in the WAP configuration screens and simply change it. Figure 20-16 shows the channel option in an ASUS WAP.

With multi-band 802.11n, 802.11ac, and 802.11ax WAPs, you can choose whether or not to use the 2.4-GHz, 5-GHz, and 6-GHz bands. In an area with overlapping signals, most of the traffic (at least as of this writing) will be on the 5-GHz frequency.

Figure 20-16
Changing the channel

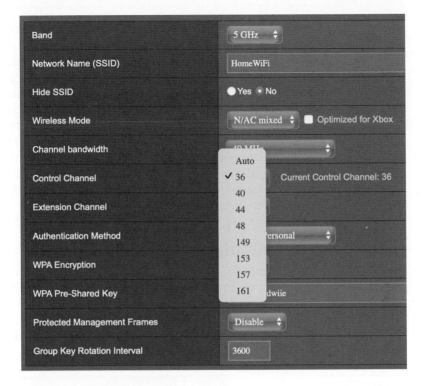

But legacy devices will still be on 2.4 GHz along with other wireless devices such as baby monitors; microwaves also use the 2.4-GHz frequency and can cause a great deal of interference. You can avoid any kind of conflict with your 802.11ac and 802.11ax devices by using the 5-GHz frequency exclusively. Figure 20-17 shows the 2.4-GHz radio being disabled on an 802.11ac WAP.

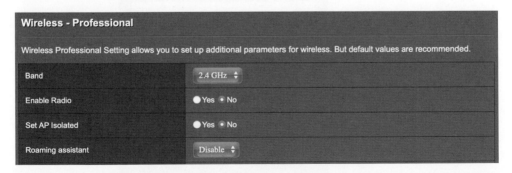

Figure 20-17   Disabling the 2.4-GHz radio

NOTE This chapter (and much of the CompTIA A+ 1102 exam) focuses on SOHO wireless deployment. Techs handle the WAP configuration at each WAP, using the built-in firmware, and that's fine for networks with no more than a few access points. Scaling up to cover an entire campus or enterprise building, on the other hand, makes that configuration impossibly time consuming.

Years ago, manufacturers developed wireless LAN controllers to centralize configuration of many dumb WAPs. An organization might have a thousand WAPs but a single software interface for configuring all of them. These days, that configuration interface can be hosted on a local computer or, increasingly, via a cloud-based infrastructure. The latter uses *cloud-based network controllers*—that's the CompTIA term. You're also likely to see such networks referred to as *cloud-managed WLANs*.

Bluetooth Configuration and Troubleshooting

As with other wireless networking solutions, Bluetooth devices are completely plug and play. Just connect the adapter and follow the prompts to install the appropriate drivers if your OS needs them. Once installed, you'll need to start the *pairing* process to enable the devices to create a secure connection—you wouldn't want every Bluetooth client in range to automatically connect with your smartphone! Figure 20-18 shows a Google Nexus phone receiving a pairing request from an iMac called "mediamac."

Figure 20-18
Goggle Nexus
receiving a
pairing request

Pairing takes a few steps. The first step, of course, is to enable Bluetooth. Some devices, such as Bluetooth headsets, always have Bluetooth enabled because it's their sole communication method. Others, like a Bluetooth adapter in your computer, may be enabled or disabled in the Network and Sharing Center.

Once enabled, the two devices must be placed into pairing mode. Some devices, like the stereo in my car, continuously listen for a pairing request, while others must be set to pairing (or discovery) mode. The devices in pairing mode will discover each other and agree on a compatible Bluetooth version, speed, and set of features.

The final step of the pairing process, the security component, requires you to confirm your intent to pair the devices. Depending on Bluetooth version and device capabilities, there are a number of different ways this could go; these range from the devices confirming the connection without user input to requiring the user to input a short code on one or both devices. If used, these codes are most often four or six digits, but older devices may differ. Refer to your device's documentation for specific details on its pairing process.

Done, right? Well, almost. There remains the final step: make sure everything works. Are you getting sound into your Bluetooth headset or speakers? Does the Bluetooth microphone work when making phone calls or recording notes on your smartphone app? Can you stream music from your smartphone to your car stereo? You get the idea. If something isn't working, it's time to check for two common problems: unsuccessful/incomplete pairing, and configuration issues.

The pairing process is quick and easy to repeat. You may have to delete the pairing from one of the devices first. After re-pairing, test again. If the pairing process never gets started, you have no Bluetooth connectivity. Make sure both devices are on, have Bluetooth enabled, and are in pairing mode. Check battery power in wireless devices and check configuration settings.

If the pairing appears successful but the connection test is not, look for configuration issues. Check microphone input settings and audio output settings. Use any vendor-provided testing and troubleshooting utilities. Keep at it until it works or until you confirm that one or both devices are bad or incompatible.

You'll need to do a little more than just pair devices to connect to a Bluetooth PAN. This connection is handled by your OS in most cases. Figure 20-19 shows the macOS network configuration for a Bluetooth PAN connected through a Nexus phone.

NOTE   Wi-Fi and cellular have made Bluetooth Internet connections a rare sight out in the real world.

Figure 20-19   macOS Bluetooth PAN connected

Troubleshooting Wi-Fi

Wireless networks are a real boon when they work right, but they can also be one of the most vexing things to troubleshoot when they don't. Let's turn to some practical advice on how to detect and correct wireless hardware, software, and configuration problems.

As with any troubleshooting scenario, your first step in troubleshooting a wireless network is to break down your tasks into logical steps. First, of course, identify the problem, then figure out the scope of the problem. Ask yourself *who*, *what*, and *when*:

- Who is affected by the problem?
- What is the nature of their network problem?
- When did the problem start?

In the formal process of troubleshooting, answering these questions is paramount. The answers to these questions dictate at least the initial direction of your troubleshooting.

So, who's affected? If all machines on your network—wired and wireless—have lost connectivity, you have bigger problems than a few wireless machines that cannot access the network. Troubleshoot this situation the way you'd troubleshoot any network failure. Once you determine which wireless devices are affected, it's easier to pinpoint whether the problem lies in one or more wireless clients or in one or more access points.

After you narrow down the number of affected machines, your next task is to figure out specifically what type of error the users are experiencing. If they can access some, but not all, network services, it's unlikely that the problem is limited to their wireless equipment. For example, if they can browse the Internet but can't access any shared resources on a server, they're probably experiencing a permissions-related issue rather than a wireless one.

The last bit of gathering information for this issue is to determine when the problem started. What has changed that might explain your loss of connectivity? Did you or somebody else change the wireless network configuration? For example, if the network worked fine two minutes ago, and then you changed the encryption key or level on the access point, and now nobody can see the network, you have your solution—or at least your culprit! Did your office experience a power outage, power sag, or power surge? Any of these might cause a WAP to fail. And that leads us to the next step of the formal troubleshooting process, establishing a theory of probable cause, which was discussed back in Chapter 1. For now, let's focus on the specifics of troubleshooting Wi-Fi issues.

Once you figure out the who, what, and when, you can start troubleshooting in earnest. Typically, your problem is going to center on your hardware, software, connectivity, or configuration.

Hardware Troubleshooting

Wireless networking hardware components are subject to the same kind of abuse and faulty installation as any other hardware component. Troubleshooting a suspected hardware problem should bring out the technician in you.

Open Windows Device Manager and look for an error or conflict with the wireless adapter. If you see a big exclamation point next to the device, you have a driver error. A downward-facing arrow next to the device indicates that it has been disabled. Enable it if possible or reinstall the device driver as needed.

If you don't see the device listed at all, perhaps it is not seated properly or plugged in all the way. These problems are easy to fix. Just remove and reinstall the device.

 NOTE As with all things computing, don't forget to do the standard PC troubleshooting thing and reboot the computer before you make any configuration or hardware changes!

Software Troubleshooting

Because you've already checked to confirm your hardware is using the correct drivers, what kind of software-related problems are left? Two things come immediately to mind: the wireless adapter configuration utility and the WAP's firmware version.

As I mentioned earlier, some wireless devices won't work correctly unless you install the vendor-provided drivers and configuration utility before plugging in the device. This is particularly true of wireless USB devices. If you didn't do this already, go into Device Manager and uninstall the device, then start again from scratch.

By the time you unpack your new WAP, there's a good chance its firmware is already out of date. Out-of-date firmware could manifest in many ways. Your WAP may enable clients to connect, but only at such slow speeds that they experience frequent timeout errors; you may find that, after a week, your clients can connect but have no Internet access until you reboot the WAP; Apple devices may have trouble connecting or running at advertised speeds. The important thing here is to be on the lookout for strange or erratic behavior.

Manufacturers regularly release firmware updates to fix issues just like these—and many more—so it's good to update the access point's firmware. For older WAPs, go to the manufacturer's Web site and follow the support links until you find the latest firmware version. You'll need your device's exact model number and hardware version, as well as the current firmware version—this is important, because installing the wrong firmware version on your device is a guaranteed way to render it useless! Modern WAPs have built-in administration pages to upload the newly downloaded firmware. Some can even check for firmware updates and install them. Because there are too many WAP variations to cover here, always look up the manufacturer's instructions for updating the firmware and follow them to the letter.

 NOTE When updating the firmware of any device, including your WAP, there's always a chance something could go wrong and render it unusable—and you may hear techs say such a device has been "bricked." Why? It's no more useful than a brick!

Connectivity Troubleshooting

Properly configured wireless clients should automatically and quickly connect to the desired SSID, assuming both the client and WAP support the correct bands. If this isn't taking place, it's time for some troubleshooting. Most wireless connectivity problems come down to either an incorrect configuration (such as an incorrect password) or low signal strength. Without a strong signal, even a properly configured wireless client isn't going to work. Wireless clients use a multi-bar graph (usually five bars) to give an idea of signal strength: zero bars indicate no wireless connectivity and five bars indicates maximum signal. Weak signals or a very busy network (especially with older, closer clients) can both result in *slow network speeds, high latency*, and *intermittent wireless connectivity*.

Whether configuration or signal strength, the process to diagnose and repair is similar to what you'd do for a wired network. Since very few wireless NICs have link lights, you can almost always jump right to checking the Wi-Fi configuration utility. Figure 20-20 shows Windows 10 displaying the link state and signal strength.

Figure 20-20
Windows
10's wireless
configuration
utility

The link state defines the wireless NIC's connection status to a wireless network: connected or disconnected. If your link state indicates that your computer is currently disconnected, you may have a problem with your WAP. If your signal is too weak to receive, you may be out of range of your access point or there may be a device causing interference.

You can fix these problems in a number of ways. Because Wi-Fi signals bounce off of objects, you can try small adjustments to your antennas or WAP placement to see if the signal improves. If your WAP has removable antennas, you can swap out the standard antenna for ones with more transmit power. You can relocate the PC or access point, or locate and move the device causing interference.

You can also run into trouble if there are just too many devices on your network. This can be especially troublesome if you also have some devices that are using old Wi-Fi standards that tie up your WAPs for longer to satisfy the same request than a device using a newer standard would. If you know the network is busy, it might be worth seeing if the problem disappears during off-hours—or even try limiting the number of clients.

If you know you've got old Wi-Fi devices around, replacing them or moving them off onto a separate WAP (that uses a different channel) can increase network performance for everyone.

Other wireless devices that operate in the same frequency range as your Wi-Fi can cause *external interference* as well. Look for wireless telephones, intercoms, and so on as possible culprits. One fix for interference caused by other Wi-Fi devices is to change the channel your network uses. Another is to change the channel the offending device uses, if possible. If you can't change channels, try moving the interfering device to another area or replacing it with a different device.

Configuration Troubleshooting

With all due respect to the fine network techs in the field, the most common type of wireless networking problem is misconfigured hardware or software. That's right—the dreaded *user error*! Given the complexities of wireless networking, this isn't so surprising. All it takes is one slip of the typing finger to throw off your configuration completely. The things you're most likely to get wrong are the SSID and security configuration, though dual-band routers have introduced some additional complexity.

Verify SSID configuration (for any bands in use) on your access point first, and then check on the affected wireless devices. With most wireless devices, you can use any characters in the SSID, including blank spaces. Be careful not to add blank characters where they don't belong, such as trailing blank spaces behind any other characters typed into the name field.

In some situations, clients that have always connected to a WAP with a particular SSID may no longer be able to connect. The client may or may not give an error message indicating "SSID not found." There are a couple possible explanations for this and they are easy to troubleshoot and fix. The simplest culprit is that the WAP is down—easy to find and easy to fix. On the opposite end of the spectrum is a change to the WAP. Changing the SSID of a WAP will prevent the client from connecting. The fix can be as simple as changing the SSID back or updating the client configuration. A client may not connect to a new WAP, even if it has the same SSID and connection configuration as the previous one. Simply delete the old connection profile from the client and create a new one.

If you're using MAC address filtering, make sure the MAC address of the client that's attempting to access the wireless network is on the list of accepted users. This is particularly important if you swap out NICs on a PC, or if you introduce a new device to your wireless network.

Check the security configuration to make sure that all wireless clients and access points match. Mistyping an encryption key prevents the affected client from talking to the wireless network, even if your signal strength is 100 percent! Remember that many access points have the capability to export encryption keys onto a thumb drive or other removable media. It's then a simple matter to import the encryption key onto the PC by using the wireless NIC's configuration utility. Remember that the encryption level must match on access points and clients. If your WAP is configured for WPA2, all clients must also use WPA2.

Chapter Review

Questions

1. Which of the following 802.11 standards functions only on the 5-GHz band?

   A. 802.11g

   B. 802.11n

   C. 802.11ac

   D. 802.11i

2. Which encryption protocol is deprecated?

   A. WAP

   B. WEP

   C. WPA2

   D. WPA3

3. Which device creates a wireless network?

   A. Wireless access point

   B. Wireless extender

   C. Wireless locator

   D. Wireless repeater

4. Which type of wireless network hardware automatically works with its peers to forward traffic?

   A. Access point

   B. Wireless repeater

   C. Wireless extender

   D. Mesh

5. What determines the name of a wireless network?

   A. EAP

   B. MAC address

   C. SSID

   D. WAP

6. What technology enables 802.11n networks to make several simultaneous connections and thus improves speed over previous Wi-Fi standards?

   A. Use of the 2.4-GHz frequency

   B. Use of the 5-GHz frequency

   C. WAP

   D. WPA2

7. What's the top speed for data transfers using 802.11ac technology?

   A. 1+ Mbps

   B. 1+ Gbps

   C. 11+ Mbps

   D. 11+ Gbps

8. Bluetooth technology is most often used to link computers into what sort of network?

   A. Bluetooth area network (BAN)

   B. Personal area network (PAN)

   C. Local area network (LAN)

   D. Wide area network (WAN)

9. What is the name for the common omni-directional antennas found on wireless access points?

   A. Bipole antennas

   B. Dipole antennas

   C. Omni antennas

   D. RF antennas

10. Ralph has installed a wireless network in his house, placing the wireless access point in the kitchen, a centralized location. The Wi-Fi works fine in the living room and dining room but goes out almost completely in the bedroom. What's most likely the problem?

   A. Interference with some metal object

   B. Improper antenna setup

   C. Use of the default SSID

   D. The SSID overlapping with a neighbor's SSID

Answers

1. **C.** The 802.11ac standard functions exclusively on the 5-GHz band, while 802.11g functions on 2.4 GHz, 802.11n functions on both, and 802.11i is a security standard called WPA2.

2. **B.** WEP is a deprecated wireless encryption technology.

3. **A.** A wireless access point (WAP) enables clients to join a wireless network.

4. **D.** In wireless mesh networks, each network device can forward traffic for the others (while one of the devices serves as the gateway).

5. **C.** The SSID determines the name of a wireless network.

6. **C.** The multiple in/multiple out (MIMO) technology implementing multiple antennas enables 802.11n networks to run at much faster speeds than previous Wi-Fi networks.

7. **B.** Data transfers using 802.11ac top out around 1+ Gbps.

8. **B.** Bluetooth most often creates personal area networks.

9. **B.** Standard omni-directional antennas are called dipole antennas.

10. **A.** Watch out for microwave ovens, refrigerators, and pipes in the walls. They can interfere with a Wi-Fi signal and create dead spots.

CHAPTER 21

The Internet

In this chapter, you will learn how to

- Explain how the Internet works
- Connect to the Internet
- Use Internet application protocols
- Troubleshoot an Internet connection

The Internet was once the domain of academics and technologists, but over the past few decades it has mushroomed into a dense fabric that interconnects literally billions of devices—including devices used mainly by people and devices that just *do their own thing*. The Internet was once a place we went intentionally. I'd come home from a long day at work and sit down to be *transported* into the fantasy universe of a game that I could play with millions of other gamers around the world. I still enjoy escaping into a good game—but these days the Internet itself is the nervous system of modern society!

This chapter covers the skills you need as a tech to help connect devices to the Internet. It starts with a brief section on how the Internet works, along with the concepts of connectivity, and then it goes into the specifics of the protocols and software that you use to make the Internet work for you (or for your client). Finally, you'll learn how to troubleshoot a bad Internet connection. Let's get started!

Historical/Conceptual

How the Internet Works

Thanks to the Internet, people can communicate with one another over vast distances, often in the blink of an eye. As a tech, you need to know how computers communicate with the larger world for two reasons. First, knowing the process and pieces involved in the communication enables you to troubleshoot effectively when that communication goes away. Second, you need to be able to communicate knowledgeably with a network technician who comes in to solve a more complex issue.

You probably know that the Internet joins gajillions of devices together to form the largest network on earth, but not many folks know much about how these computers are organized. Most importantly, the Internet is a *network of networks*. Some of these networks are large, and others are tiny. Some of these networks belong to families or small shops, while others belong to hospitals, local governments, Internet service providers (ISPs), and of course technology giants like Amazon, Apple, Google, Microsoft, and so on.

Deep inside the infrastructure that makes up the Internet, the largest of these networks are stitched together into a globe-spanning fabric by a piece of equipment called a backbone router. *Backbone routers* sit along long-distance high-speed fiber optic networks called *backbones* and connect to more than one other backbone router, creating a framework for transferring massive amounts of data. Figure 21-1 illustrates the decentralized and interwoven nature of the Internet.

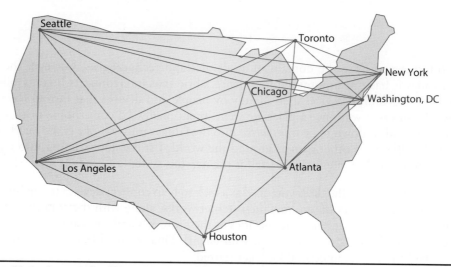

Figure 21-1   Internet backbone connections between cities

The key reason for interweaving the backbones of the Internet was to provide alternative pathways for data if one or more of the routers went down. If Jane in Houston sends a message to her friend Polly in New York City, for example, the shortest path between Jane and Polly in this hypothetical situation might be: Jane's message originates at Rice University in Houston, bounces to Emory University in Atlanta, flits through Georgetown University in Washington, DC, and then zips into SUNY in New York City (see Figure 21-2). Polly happily reads the message and life is great. The Internet functions as planned.

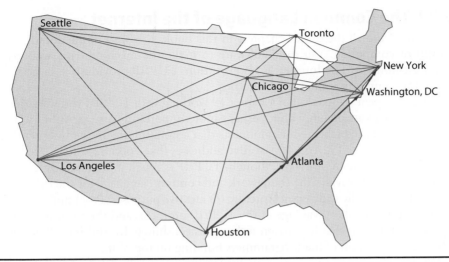

Figure 21-2   Message traveling from Houston to NYC

But what would happen if the entire southeastern United States were to experience a huge power outage and Internet backbones in every state from Maryland to Florida were to go down? Jane's message would fail to go through, so the Rice computers would resend Jane's message. Meanwhile, the routers would update their list of good routes and then attempt to reroute the message to functioning nodes—say, Rice to University of Chicago, to University of Toronto, and then to SUNY (see Figure 21-3). It's all in a day's work for the highly redundant and adaptable Internet. At this point in the game, the Internet simply cannot go down fully—barring, of course, a catastrophe of Biblical proportions.

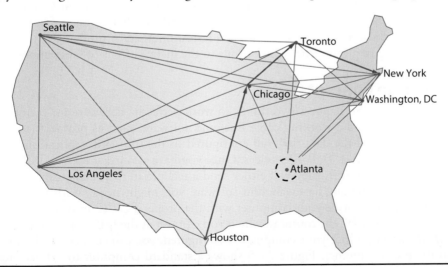

Figure 21-3   Rerouted message from Houston to NYC

TCP/IP: The Common Language of the Internet

As you know from all the earlier chapters in this book, hardware alone doesn't cut it in the world of computing. You need software to make the machines run and create an interface for humans. The Internet is no exception. TCP/IP provides the basic software structure for communication on the Internet.

Because you spent a good deal of Chapter 19 working with TCP/IP, you should have an appreciation for its adaptability and, perhaps more importantly, its extensibility. TCP/IP provides the addressing scheme for computers that communicate on the Internet through IPv4 addresses (such as 192.168.4.1) or IPv6 addresses (like 2603:b23c:d:a421:edcd:9c82 :41a4:7a5b). As a suite of protocols, though, TCP/IP is much more than just an addressing system. TCP/IP provides the framework and common language for the Internet. And it offers a phenomenally wide-open structure for creative purposes. Programmers can write applications built to take advantage of the TCP/IP protocols and their features. The cool thing about TCP/IP is that it's proven to be an astonishingly fruitful foundation limited only by the imagination of the programmers building on top of it.

At this point, you have an enormous functioning network. All the backbone routers connect redundant, high-speed backbone lines, and TCP/IP enables communication and services for building applications that enable humans and machines to interface across vast distances. What's left? Oh, of course: How do you tap into this great network and partake of its goodness?

Internet Service Providers

Most of us connect to the Internet by renting access through a company called an *Internet service provider (ISP)*. ISPs come in all sizes. Comcast, the cable television provider, has multiple huge-capacity connections into the Internet, enabling its millions of customers to connect from their local machines and access the Internet. Contrast Comcast with Electric Power Board (EPB) of Chattanooga, an ISP in Chattanooga, Tennessee (see Figure 21-4), which bills itself as "the world's fastest internet." Unfortunately, EPB only offers its blazing 10 gigabit fiber connections to the lucky citizens of Chattanooga.

Connection Concepts

Connecting to an ISP requires two things to work perfectly: hardware for connectivity, such as a modem and a working cable line; and software, such as protocols to govern the connections and the data flow (all configured in the OS) and applications to take advantage of the various TCP/IP services. Once you have a contract with an ISP to grant you access to the Internet, they will either send a technician to your house or mail you a package containing any hardware and software you might need. With most ISPs, a DHCP server will provide your computer with the proper TCP/IP information. As you know from Chapter 19, the router to which you connect at the ISP is often referred to as the *default gateway*. Once your computer is configured, you can connect to the ISP and get to the greater Internet. Figure 21-5 shows a standard computer-to-ISP-to-Internet connection. Note that various protocols and other software manage the connectivity between your computer and the default gateway.

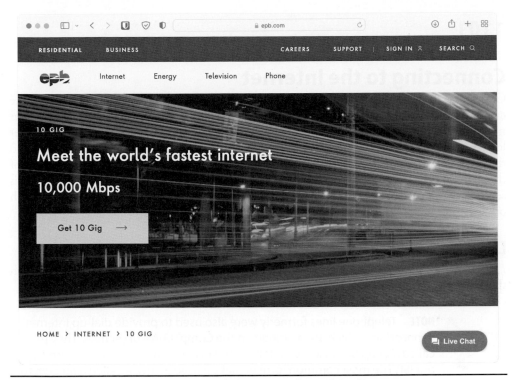

Figure 21-4 Electric Power Board (EPB) of Chattanooga home-based Internet page

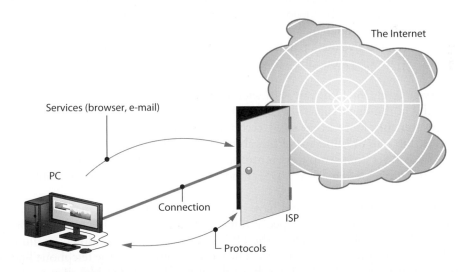

Figure 21-5 Simplified Internet connectivity

1101

Connecting to the Internet

Computers commonly connect to an ISP through their wired or wireless router. If the customer purchased the router, it will have an Ethernet connection to a box (often—but not always—called a modem) that interconnects it with the ISP's network. If the customer leased a router from their ISP, it will often have a built-in modem. The connection to the ISP could use one of many wired or wireless technologies—the modem takes care of the details. Let's take a look at all these various connection options, and then finish this section by discussing basic router configuration and sharing an Internet connection with other computers.

DSL

Digital subscriber line (DSL) connections to ISPs use a standard telephone line with special equipment on each end to create always-on Internet connections.

 NOTE Telephone lines formerly were also used to provide dial-up Internet connections, which are no longer in the CompTIA A+ objectives. They're called *dial-up* because we literally typed in a telephone number owned by our ISP. The most common form of dial-up used a device called a *modem* to literally convert digital data to and from analog sound. Integrated Services Digital Network (ISDN) connected a lot faster than analog dial-up and had more bandwidth. Both were very slow by modern standards, and the proliferation of faster connection technologies has made it hard to find an active dial-up or ISDN connection in the wild—but there are still a few kicking around!

Service levels for DSL can vary widely. At the low end of the spectrum, speeds are generally in the single digits—less than 1 Mbps upload and around 3 Mbps download. Where available, more recent *x*DSL technologies can offer competitive broadband speeds measured in tens or hundreds of megabits per second.

DSL requires little setup from a user standpoint. A tech comes to the house to install the DSL receiver, often called a DSL modem (see Figure 21-6), and possibly hook up a wireless router.

Even if you skip the tech and have the installation equipment mailed to you, all you have to do is plug a couple of special filters in and call your ISP. These *DSL microfilters* remove the high-pitch screech of the DSL signal, enabling traditional landline phones and fax machines to operate correctly. The receiver connects to the telephone line and the computer (see Figure 21-7). The tech (or the user, if knowledgeable) then configures the DSL modem and router (if there is one) with the settings provided by the ISP, and that's about it! Within moments, you're surfing the Web. You don't need a second telephone line. You don't need to wear a special propeller hat or anything. The only kicker is that your house has to be within a fairly short distance from a main phone service switching center (central office). This distance can depend on the DSL variant and can range from several hundred feet to around 18,000 feet.

Figure 21-6
A DSL receiver

Figure 21-7
DSL connection

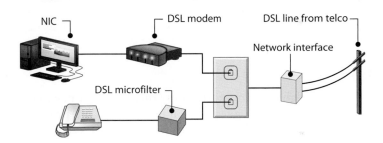

NOTE The two most common forms of DSL you'll find are *asymmetric (ADSL)* and *symmetric (SDSL)*. ADSL lines differ between slow upload speed (such as 384 Kbps, 768 Kbps, and 1 Mbps) and faster download speed (usually 3–15 Mbps). SDSL has the same upload and download speeds, but telecom companies charge a lot more for the privilege. DSL encompasses many such variations, so you'll often see it referred to as *x*DSL. (If you see it marketed at all—DSL appears to be going the way of dial-up. Some DSL providers have stopped accepting new customers or ended service altogether.)

Cable

Cable offers a different approach to high-speed Internet access, using regular cable TV cables to serve up lightning-fast speeds. It offers faster service than most DSL connections, with upload speeds from 5 to 35+ Mbps and download speeds ranging anywhere from 15 to 2000+ Mbps. *Cable Internet* connections are theoretically available anywhere you can get cable TV.

NOTE The term *modem* has been warped and changed beyond recognition in modern networking. Both DSL and cable—fully digital Internet connections—use the term *modem* to describe the box that takes the incoming signal from the Internet and translates it into something the computer can understand.

Cable Internet connections start with an RG-6 or RG-59 cable coming into your house. The cable connects to a *cable modem* that then connects to a small home router (you will often see the modem and router combined into a single box today) or your network interface card (NIC) via Ethernet. Figure 21-8 shows a typical cable setup using a router.

Figure 21-8
Cable connection

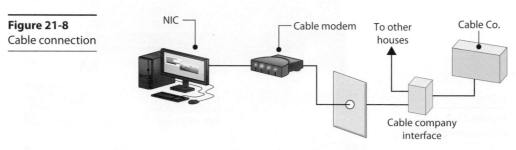

Fiber

In the past, high costs meant that only those with money to burn could enjoy the super-fast speeds of a fiber connection. Subsequently, DSL providers developed very popular fiber-to-the-node (FTTN) and fiber-to-the-premises (FTTP) services that provide Internet (and often Internet and telephone services over the same connection), making them head-to-head competitors with the cable companies. Entrants like Google Fiber and local municipalities have added momentum to the fiber rollout.

With FTTN, the fiber connection runs from the provider to a box somewhere in your neighborhood. This box connects to your home or office using normal coaxial or Ethernet cabling. FTTP runs from the provider straight to a box in your home or office, using fiber the whole way. You might expect this box (which does convert data to and from light) to be called a *fiber modem*—but it has a better name: an *optical network terminal (ONT)*. The ONT has an input for the fiber connection, and an Ethernet or coax connection for a router which then provides wireless (or Ethernet) to connect your computers to the Internet.

One popular fiber-based service is AT&T Internet (formerly called U-verse), which generally offers download speeds from 10 to 100 Mbps and upload speeds from 1 to 20 Mbps for their FTTN service. AT&T Fiber is their FTTP service that gives you 300 Mbps to 5 Gbps for download and upload (see Figure 21-9). Verizon's Fios service is the most popular and widely available FTTP service in the United States, providing upload and download speeds ranging from 300 Mbps to 1 Gbps. Google Fiber, for its part, offers a 1- and 2-Gbps upload/download service.

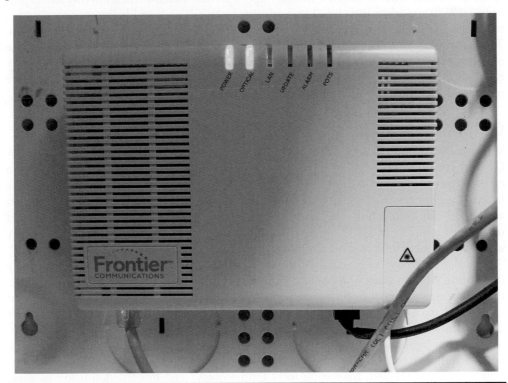

Figure 21-9 A Frontier FiOS FTTP ONT in my closet

Wi-Fi

Wi-Fi (or 802.11 wireless) is so prevalent that it's the way many of us get to the Internet. Wireless access points (WAPs) designed to serve the public abound in coffee shops, airports, fast-food chains, and bars. Even some cities provide partial to full Wi-Fi coverage.

 EXAM TIP An 802.11 network that covers a single city is an excellent example of a *metropolitan area network (MAN)*.

We covered 802.11 in detail in Chapter 20, so there's no reason to repeat the process of connecting to a access point. Do remember that most open networks do not provide any level of encryption, meaning it's easy for a bad guy to monitor your connection and read everything you send or receive.

WISP

Another form of wireless Internet service—appropriately called *wireless Internet service provider (WISP)*—works a little bit like a traditional wired broadband Internet service with a twist: the last segment or two uses a point-to-point long-range fixed wireless connection. The customer just needs to install an antenna provided by the WISP—usually on the outside of their house—and they are online. Since WISPs don't have to run cable to every home they cover, they can often provide cheaper service—or provide service in areas where other broadband providers aren't.

Cellular

Who needs computers when you can get online with any number of mobile devices? Okay, there are plenty of things a phone or tablet can't do, but with the latest advances in cellular data services, your mobile Internet experience will feel a lot more like your home Internet experience than it ever has before. The most common way to access the Internet with a cellular connection—which the CompTIA A+ 1101 exam objectives also refer to as *wireless WAN (WWAN)*—is directly through a mobile device. It's far from the only way, though! Let's look at the technology first, and then consider how to put it to use.

Cellular data services have gone through a number of names over the years, so many that trying to keep track of them and place them in any order is extremely challenging. In an attempt to make organization somewhat clearer, the cellular industry developed a string of marketing terms using the idea of generations: first-generation devices are called 1G, second-generation are 2G, followed by 3G, 4G, and 5G. On top of that, many technologies use G-names such as 2.5G to show they're not 2G but not quite 3G. You'll see these terms on your phones, primarily if you're not getting the best speed possible (see Figure 21-10). Marketing folks tend to bend and flex the definition of these terms in advertisements, so you should always read more about the device and not just its generation.

Figure 21-10
iPhone
connecting
over 5G

The first generation (1G) of cell phone data services was analog and not at all designed to carry packetized data. It wasn't until the early 1990s that two fully digital technologies called the Global System for Mobile Communications (GSM) and code division multiple access (CDMA) came into wide acceptance. GSM evolved into GPRS and EDGE, while CDMA introduced EV-DO. GPRS and EDGE were 2.5G technologies, while EV-DO was true 3G. Standards, with names like UTMS, HSPA+, and HSDPA, have brought GSM-based networks into the world of 3G and 3.5G. These mobile data services provide modest real-world download speeds of a few (generally under 10) Mbps.

We're now at the tail end of the fourth generation. Devices and networks using *Long Term Evolution (LTE)* technology rolled out worldwide in the early 2010s and now dominate wireless services. As early as 2013, for example, LTE already had ~20 percent market share in the United States, and even higher in parts of Asia. The numbers have only grown since then. Marketed as and now generally accepted as a true *4G* technology, LTE networks feature theoretical speeds of up to 1 Gbps download and 100 Mbps upload (see Figure 21-11).

Figure 21-11
Real-world LTE
speed test

The fifth-generation cellular networks—appropriately called *5G*—saw a big development push in 2018, and rollout started in 2019. The IMT-2020 specifications call for speeds up to *20 Gbps*—blazingly fast—but real-world speeds are often a far cry from this (and may vary a lot depending on the carrier and location).

Both 4G and 5G can readily replace wired network technology anywhere there's sufficient cellular data coverage. Most of the big cellular carriers offer home service—a stand-alone cellular modem you can plug into the wall and connect to your router. You can also use a *mobile hotspot*—a device that connects via cellular and shares its Internet access—when you're away from home.

EXAM TIP While any Internet connection type might be *metered* (i.e., you pay based on how much data you use), it is more common with cellular providers. In Windows, the settings for each network have a toggle you can use to indicate that the connection is metered. Marking a connection as metered will cause well-behaved apps to minimize their data use. The exact change will depend on the app. Common changes in data usage you might see are delaying large downloads until you're on a non-metered connection, not auto-playing media, downloading lower-quality media assets, and so on. For its part, Windows will avoid downloading updates on a metered connection!

Hotspots can be dedicated devices or simply a feature of a modern smartphone. (See Chapter 24 for a deep dive into smartphone technologies.) Using a hotspot to connect to the Internet is often called *tethering*. Figure 21-12 shows an iPhone in hotspot mode with tethering instructions for Wi-Fi, Bluetooth, and USB.

Figure 21-12
Tethering in iOS

Satellite

Satellite connections to the Internet get the data beamed to a satellite dish on your house or office. Traditionally, providers such as HughesNet and Viasat have used a small number of satellites in very high-altitude geostationary orbits to cover absolutely massive sections of the globe with about 25 Mbps download and 3 Mbps upload speeds. It also means you need to make sure the satellite dish points toward the satellite (generally toward the south if you live in the northern hemisphere)—so you'll usually want it professionally installed with line-of-sight to the satellite. A coax cable runs from the dish to your satellite modem. The satellite modem has an RJ-45 connection, which you may then connect directly to your computer or to a router.

As both satellites and the costs to develop and launch them have shrunk, there's been a surge of interest in satellite Internet services that use a very large number of satellites in low Earth orbit. This kind of service depends on having enough satellites passing over a given area to provide continuous service, but Starlink (one of the most visible providers) is already delivering several times more download and upload bandwidth where it offers service.

Getting your Internet from the stars has some downsides. The first significant issue is the upfront cost of the dish and installation. The signal can also degrade or drop entirely in foul weather such as rain and snow. Many providers also have usage limits, to ensure a small number of users don't degrade the service for everyone on the same satellite. Finally, there's the distance the signal must travel to the satellite. Although low-orbit constellations can provide a level of *latency*—how long it takes the signal to make the round-trip—that's just a little worse than wired broadband, traditional high-orbit service comes with several hundred milliseconds of latency. This is usually unnoticeable for general Web use, but can make any real-time activity such as gaming or voice/video chat difficult in the best of circumstances.

Connection to the Internet

So you went out and signed up for an Internet connection. Now it's time to get connected. You basically have two choices:

1. Connect a single computer to your Internet connection
2. Connect a network of computers to your Internet connection

Connecting a single computer to the Internet is easy. If you're using wireless, you connect to the WAP using the provided information, although a good tech will always go through the proper steps described in Chapter 20 to protect the wireless network. If you choose to go wired, you run a cable from whatever type of box is provided to the computer.

If you want to connect multiple computers using wired connections, make sure your router has a built-in switch with enough ports. Several manufacturers offer robust, easy-to-configure routers that are a nice upgrade from the routers provided by the ISP. These boxes require very little configuration and provide firewall protection between the primary computer and the Internet, which you'll learn more about in Chapter 27. All it takes to install one of these routers is simply to plug your computer into any of the LAN ports on the back, and then to plug the cable from your Internet connection into the port labeled Internet or WAN.

There are hundreds of perfectly fine choices for SOHO (small office/home office) routers (see Figure 21-13 for an example). Most have four Ethernet switch ports for wired connections, and one or more Wi-Fi radios for any wireless computers you may have. All SOHO routers use a technology called *Network Address Translation (NAT)* to perform a little network subterfuge: It presents an entire LAN of computers to the Internet as a single machine. It effectively hides all of your computers and makes them appear invisible to other computers on the Internet. All anyone on the Internet sees is your *public* IP address. This is the address your ISP gives you, while all the computers in your LAN use private addresses that are invisible to the world. NAT therefore acts as a firewall, protecting your internal network from probing or malicious users on the outside.

Figure 21-13
Common SOHO
router with Wi-Fi

 EXAM TIP   Many computers can share a smaller pool of routable IP addresses with dynamic NAT (DNAT). A NAT might have 10 routable IP addresses, for example, to serve 40 computers on the LAN. LAN traffic uses the internal, private IP addresses. When a computer requests information beyond the network, the NAT doles out a routable IP address from its pool for that communication. Dynamic NAT is also called Pooled NAT.

This works well enough—unless you're the unlucky 11th person to try to access the Internet from behind the company NAT—but has the obvious limitation of still needing many true, expensive, routable IP addresses.

Basic Router Configuration

SOHO routers require very little in the way of configuration and in many cases will work perfectly (if unsafely) right out of the box. In some cases, though, you may have to deal with a more complex network that requires changing the router's settings. The vast majority of these routers have built-in configuration Web pages that you access by typing the router's IP address into a browser. The address varies by manufacturer, so check the router's documentation. If you typed in the correct address, you should then receive a prompt for a username and password, as in Figure 21-14. As with the IP address, the default username and password vary depending on the model/manufacturer. Once you enter the correct credentials, you will be greeted by the router's configuration pages (see Figure 21-15). From these pages, you can change any of the router's settings.

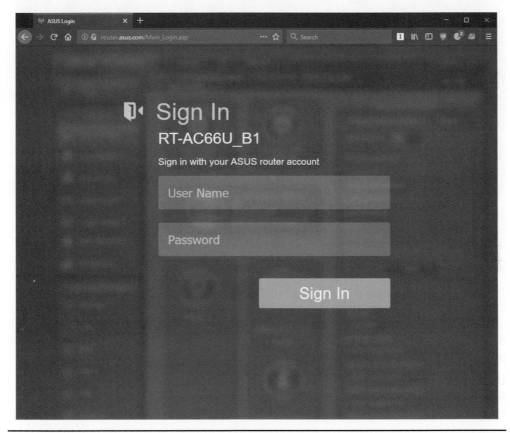

Figure 21-14   Router asking for username and password

Figure 21-15   Configuration home page

Now we'll look at a few of the basic settings that CompTIA wants you to know. (We'll discuss more advanced settings in Chapter 27 that help keep your network and the computers on it secure while they use services available over the Internet.)

UPnP   A lot of networking devices designed for the residential space use a feature called *universal plug and play (UPnP)* to find and connect to other UPnP devices. Common UPnP devices include things like media servers and printers. Since this feature enables seamless interconnectivity at the cost of somewhat lowered security, leave it disabled (as shown in Figure 21-16) if you don't need it.

Figure 21-16 Disabled UPnP option

Changing Default Credentials Since all routers have a default username and default password combination that gives you access to the configuration screen, anyone who has access to your LAN or WLAN can easily gain access to the router and change its settings. One of the first things you should do is change these default login credentials as shown in Figure 21-17.

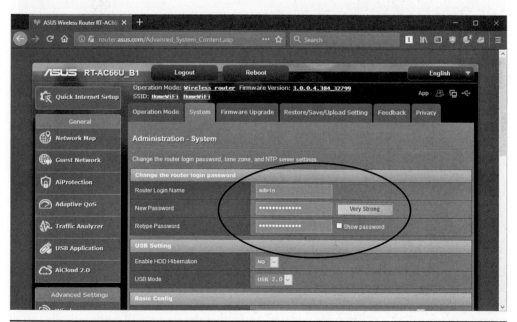

Figure 21-17 Changing the password

Setting Static IP Addresses   In most cases, when you plug in the router's Internet connection, it receives an IP address (from your ISP) using DHCP just like any other computer. Of course, this means that your Internet IP address can change from time to time. This isn't a problem for most people, but some home users and businesses may want a stable IP address to host their own sites and services. Most ISPs enable you to order a static IP address (for an extra monthly charge) and then either supply you with a preconfigured router or give you IP settings to manually enter into your router. My router has an Internet Setup configuration section where I enter the settings that my ISP has provided (see Figure 21-18). Remember to change your connection type from Automatic/DHCP to Static IP to enter the new addresses.

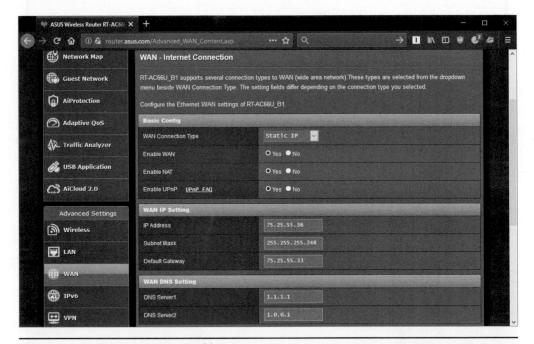

Figure 21-18   Entering a static IP address

 EXAM TIP   The CompTIA A+ 1102 exam objectives call this a *static wide-area network (WAN) IP*. If you get a question about a static IP address, make sure to figure out whether it's a static LAN or WAN IP before you jump to the answers!

Updating Firmware

Routers are just like any other computer in that they run software—and software has bugs, vulnerabilities, and other issues that sometimes require updating. The router manufacturers call these "firmware updates" and either the router will automatically install them or the manufacturer will make them available for manual install either through the router's administration interface or on the manufacturer's Web site for easy download.

NOTE While these methods are generally true of routers available commercially, routers provided by your ISP will update automatically.

If the firmware update is available directly through your router's administration interface, a firmware update may be a few clicks away. If not, download the latest firmware from the manufacturer's Web site to your computer. Then enter the router's configuration Web page and find the firmware update screen. On my router, it looks like Figure 21-19. From here, just follow the directions and click Upgrade (or your router's equivalent). A quick word of caution: Unlike a Windows update, a firmware update gone bad can *brick* your router. In other words, it can render the hardware inoperable and make it as useful as a brick sitting on your desk. This rarely happens, but you should keep it in mind when doing a firmware update.

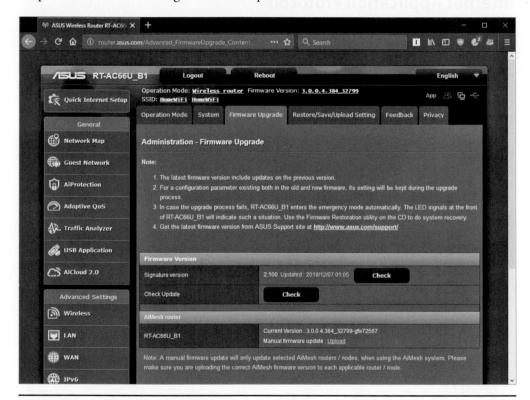

Figure 21-19 Firmware update page

Using the Internet

The Internet is constantly teeming with activity, but it doesn't actually do a whole lot all by itself. Once you've established a connection to the Internet, you need applications to get anything done. If you want to surf the Web, you need an application called a

Web browser, such as Mozilla Firefox, Google Chrome, Microsoft Edge, or Apple Safari. If you want to communicate with people, you might need an e-mail client or one of the many real-time communication applications like Discord, Skype, Slack, Telegram, Teams, Zoom—and tons more. If you want to watch streaming video, you'll need Netflix or one from its always-growing list of competitors.

Underneath the hood, these applications all use one or more application protocols to communicate with the servers that power them. The CompTIA A+ exams expect you to know about a few of the many thousands of applications and application protocols that you might encounter on the Internet—or in your own networks—so this section starts with an overview of the application protocols you may see on the exam, and then looks at how those protocols manifest in different kinds of applications. That's a lot of ground to cover, so buckle up!

Internet Application Protocols

It's *possible* for application developers to invent their own proprietary protocol for their application and servers to communicate with—but creating a good, *secure* protocol is a lot of work. Most application developers turn to well-known application protocols that anyone can use. Web browsers use the *Hypertext Transfer Protocol (HTTP)* to transfer Web pages and related resources. E-mail clients use Post Office Protocol 3 (POP3) or Internet Message Access Protocol (IMAP) to receive e-mail and Simple Mail Transfer Protocol (SMTP) to send e-mail.

Each protocol has its own rules and its own port numbers. Here's an example: most sensitive information sent over the Web (things like credit card information and phone numbers) are sent using an encrypted version of HTTP called *Hypertext Transfer Protocol Secure (HTTPS)*. Although HTTPS looks a lot like HTTP from the point of view of a Web browser, HTTPS uses its own port: 443. It's easy to tell if a Web site is using HTTPS because the Web address starts with the protocol—note the *https* shown in Figure 21-20, instead of just *http*.

Though there are tens of thousands of application protocols in existence, lucky for you, CompTIA only wants you to understand the following commonly used application protocols (except SFTP and SIP, which CompTIA doesn't list in the objectives but I've added for completeness):

- World Wide Web (HTTP and HTTPS)
- E-mail (POP3, IMAP, and SMTP)
- Telnet
- SSH
- FTP/SFTP
- Remote Desktop Protocol (RDP)
- VoIP (SIP)

Figure 21-20 A secure Web page

In addition to the application protocols we see and use daily, there are hundreds, maybe thousands, of application protocols that run behind the scenes, taking care of important jobs to ensure that the application protocols we do see run well. You've encountered a number of these hidden application protocols back in Chapter 19. Take DNS. Without DNS, you couldn't type www.google.com in your Web browser and end up at the right address. DHCP is another great example. You don't see DHCP do its job, but without it, any computers relying on DHCP won't receive IP addresses.

In order to differentiate the application protocols you see from the application protocols you don't see, I'm going to coin the term "utility protocol" to define any of the hidden application protocols. So, using your author's definition, HTTP is an application protocol and DNS is a utility protocol. All TCP/IP protocols use defined ports, require an application to run, and have special settings unique to that application. You'll look at several of these services and learn how to configure them. As a quick reference,

Table 21-1 lists the names, functions, and port numbers of the application protocols CompTIA would like you to know (except, again, SFTP and SIP). Table 21-2 does the same for utility protocols.

Application Protocol	Function	Port Number
HTTP	Web pages	80
HTTPS	Secure Web pages	443
FTP	File transfer	20, 21
SFTP	Secure file transfer	22
IMAP	Incoming e-mail	143
POP3	Incoming e-mail	110
SMTP	Outgoing e-mail	25
Telnet	Terminal emulation	23
SSH	Encrypted terminal emulation	22
RDP	Remote Desktop	3389
SIP	Voice over IP	5060

Table 21-1 Application Protocol Port Numbers

Utility Protocol	Function	Protocol	Port Number
DNS	Allows the use of DNS naming	UDP	53
DHCP	Automatic IP addressing	UDP	67, 68
LDAP	Querying directories	TCP	389
SNMP	Remote management of network devices	UDP	161, 162
SMB/CIFS	Windows folder/file sharing	TCP	445
		UDP	137, 138, 139
NetBIOS/NetBT	NetBIOS over TCP/IP	TCP	137, 139
		UDP	137, 138

Table 21-2 Utility Protocol Port Numbers

You've already encountered a few of these protocols in earlier chapters. The rest of this section will explore many of the different ways to use the Internet, and how the rest of these protocols enable those uses.

EXAM TIP It's important to know what protocols and ports an application uses. Refer to Chapter 19 if you need a refresher on the TCP and UDP protocols. The CompTIA A+ 1101 exam objectives also expect you to know all of the protocols and ports listed in Tables 21-1 and 21-2 (except SFTP and SIP).

1102

Browsing the Web

If some shadowy character in a trench coat stepped out of an alley, handed you a USB drive, and told you to run the program it holds, I *hope* you'd be too cautious to just plug it into the same computer you use for work, online shopping, or banking. It may be a surprise if you've never looked under the hood of a Web browser, but what they do isn't that much different!

A Web browser downloads code, images, and other resources from servers more or less anywhere in the world and then runs that code on your own computer in order to render the Web site. To download these resources, the browser interacts with these *Web servers* using the HTTPS protocol on port 443 and HTTP on port 80. Figure 21-21 shows the home page of my company's Web site, https://www.totalsem.com, in Mozilla Firefox. Where is the server located? Does it matter? It could be in a closet in my office or in a huge data center in Northern Virginia.

Figure 21-21   Mozilla Firefox showing a Web page

NOTE The most common browsers are Apple Safari, Google Chrome, Microsoft Edge, and Mozilla Firefox—and I recommend you keep at least two of these installed. This gives you a quick fix if you run into a site that has a problem or if a nasty security vulnerability is discovered in your usual browser. These common browsers aren't the only ones, either—there are many other browsers focused on providing some feature or supporting a workflow that the mainstream browsers don't support. If you want to nerd out, there are even browsers you can use from the command line—take Lynx and Browsh for a spin!

Because people use browsers for lots of really important things—like banking and shopping—it's really important to make sure they're secure. Let's take a closer look at what browsers are, where to get them, and a few ways to use them to stay safe.

Installing Browsers

These days, almost all operating systems come with a browser or a simple way to install one. Because we need to be able to trust browsers, it's super important to be cautious about where you get them from. An illegitimate copy of Google Chrome could look and smell just like the real thing—but be subtly compromised to give attackers access to your data or system. Make sure you only install browsers from *trusted sources* such as your operating system provider's official app store or package manager, or the browser vendor's own Web site.

Your operating system's app store or package manager should automatically help ensure (but not guarantee) that the software you install is legitimate. If you download the installer on your own, it's a good idea to take some additional steps to verify the installer before you run it. The specifics differ, but whether it's done by an app store, package manager, or by hand, this process always involves one or more cryptographic techniques such as *hashing* and/or *code signing*.

EXAM TIP Some operating systems (like Linux) make it very easy to install software from untrusted sources. Others (especially smartphone operating systems) make it much harder. Don't install browsers (or, heck, *any* software) from *untrusted sources*! Make sure to verify the hashes or code signatures— and don't ignore verification errors from your OS.

Many (but not all) software developers will publish their own checksums for all of the software they release. A *checksum* is created by running that file through a *cryptographic hash function*, which outputs a digital fingerprint for a file. We can repeat this same hashing process after we download the files to confirm that the fingerprints match.

Code signing takes this idea one step further. The developer registers their own digital certificate with whoever develops the OS, app store, or package manager—and uses the certificate to sign the software they release. Your OS, app store, or package manager can then verify these signatures to ensure that the software was released by the registered developer (and not, say, someone who guessed their password). You can check these signatures yourself in Windows by right-clicking the file, selecting Properties, and switching to the Digital Signatures tab (see Figure 21-22).

Figure 21-22
Digital signatures
(signed by
Google, LLC) for
a Google Chrome
installer

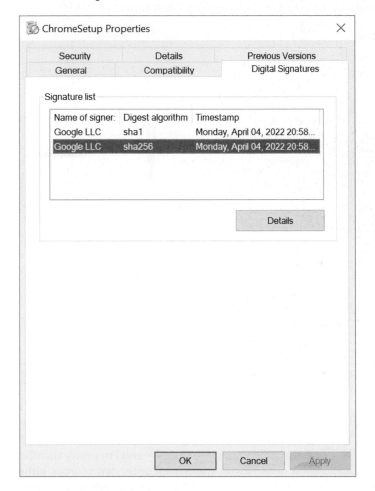

NOTE   Digital certificates are also powered by cryptography. We'll take a closer look at them a little later in this section, and then again in Chapter 27.

Browser Extensions and Plug-ins

Most modern browsers support additional *extensions* or *plug-ins* that modify or extend how they work. There are all kinds of extensions out there, but some common examples are extensions that restyle Web pages, save articles for reading later, block ads, translate pages, and so on. Each browser generally has one trusted source for extensions—either an extension store just for the browser or the operating system's app store. Figure 21-23 shows the *Gesturefy* extension for Firefox, which enables me to quickly navigate the Web by holding down a key and wiggling my mouse!

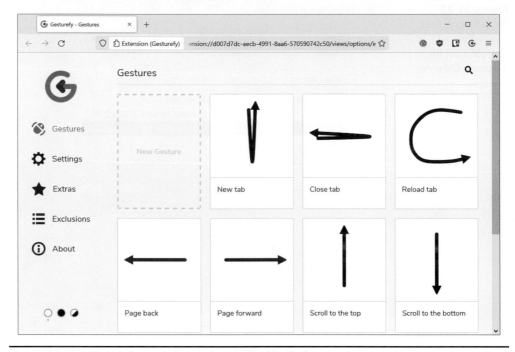

Figure 21-23   Gesturefy extension settings in Mozilla Firefox

 EXAM TIP   Browser extensions have a lot of power: they can usually read, track, and modify every Web site you visit. It's every bit as important to be careful which ones you install—and I'm pretty sure CompTIA expects you to know not to install them from untrusted sources, either. The real world is a little more complicated than this, though. If your organization has its own private browser extension, for example, it probably won't come from the trusted extension store.

Password Managers

Back in *ye olde days* we just had to remember or write down the passwords to all of the different online accounts we needed to log on to. That didn't work very well—it made things *very* easy for hackers. These days, it's a good idea to use a *password manager*, which helps you out by storing your passwords and the accounts or Web sites they're associated with. You can find standalone password managers, password manager extensions for browsers (shown in Figure 21-24), and even password managers directly built into modern browsers.

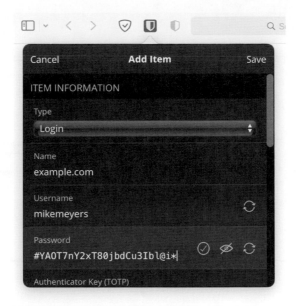

Figure 21-24
Adding a password to the Bitwarden password manager extension in Safari

Password managers aren't perfect. Using one can increase the chances that someone with physical or remote access to one of your devices can log on to any of your accounts, for example. But using a password manager also makes it easier to use a different very strong password for every account. A good password manager also helps you identify passwords that are weak, used for more than one service, or have been found in databases of stolen credentials. A good password manager will also make it easy for you to generate strong passwords.

Secure Connections and Sites

Any time you browse the Web—but *especially* when you're doing sensitive things like logging in to accounts, transferring funds, or making purchases—it's best to make sure you have a secure connection with every site.

Secure connections are supported by an intricate dance that enables the server you're corresponding with to demonstrate that it is registered with a trusted third party known as a *certificate authority (CA)*. Your browser will check to ensure it's a valid certificate, and then negotiate an encrypted connection between your browser and the server. When there's a problem with one of the steps in this dance, your browser will give you some visual indication that the connection may be compromised (as shown in Figure 21-25).

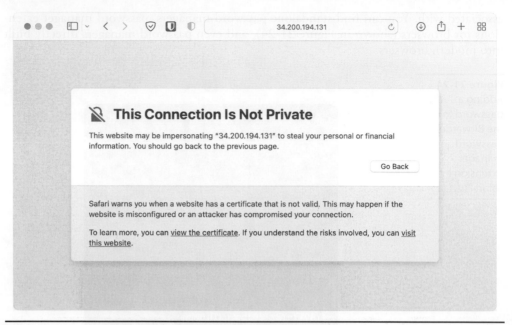

Figure 21-25   Certificate error in Safari

NOTE   Depending on how severe this issue is, your browser may or may not give you the option to ignore the error. Don't get in the habit of clicking through these warnings without thinking. They may be the only thing standing between you and an attacker!

Pop-up and Ad Blockers

Since the earliest days of the Web, users and browsers have been in a back-and-forth war with scammers and advertisers. Two of the main tools at our disposal are the ability to block *pop-ups* (new windows that open when you visit a site, generally with ads in them) and advertisements. The ability to block these is built directly into some browsers, but pop-up and ad blockers are also some of the most frequently used browser extensions. Figure 21-26 shows my favorite ad-blocking extension hard at work!

EXAM TIP   Pop-ups are not necessarily *bad*—it's just very disruptive when a scammer exploits them to open new windows faster than you can close them. It's common, for example, for online stores or browser-based games to make use of pop-ups. Since pop-up blockers keep these from working correctly, any pop-up blocker worth using will have a way to temporarily allow pop-ups and settings you can use to permanently enable them on a given site.

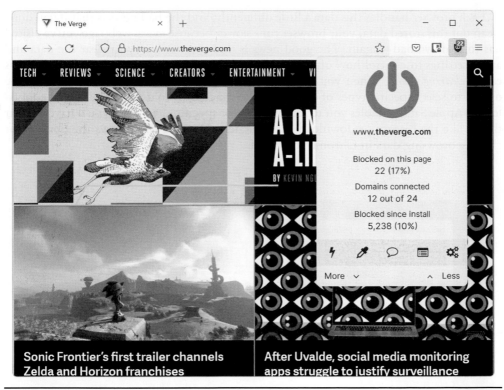

Figure 21-26 uBlock Origin obliterating ads in Firefox!

Browsing Data

Because we use browsers to do weird things like collect rare Beanie Babies, spend so much time bingeing old soap operas that Netflix has to ask if we're okay, and ask a search engine about this strange spot on the back of our hands, a lot of people are concerned about the privacy and security implications of the data trail that browsers create.

The CompTIA A+ 1102 exam objectives touch on four different ways to work with browsing data, but before we consider those I want to zoom out and just think about the main kinds of data our browsers accumulate:

- A running list (called the history) of each page we visit (and potentially which pages are currently open or were open the last time you closed the browser)
- Scripts running on sites we visit (i.e., *cookies* and *local storage*)
- Site-specific settings and passwords we configure
- Form data (such as our postal address) that we enable the browser to auto-fill
- *Cached* copies of recently downloaded resources
- A list of recently downloaded files

Each browser handles this data a little differently, and the bad news is that if you don't clean out this stored data, your browser runs slower because every webpage you've visited has to re-download—again. The good news is that there is a way to clear the data and apply settings to control how often you would like for your cache to be cleared. This is called *clearing cache*. When you go to clear browsing data in Chrome, you'll have the option to select specific types of data, and how much of it to delete. The closest equivalent in Apple Safari enables you to remove data for specific sites—but you'll have to clear things like the history or download list separately. Figure 21-27 shows the options for clearing browsing data in Chrome and Safari.

Figure 21-27 Clearing browsing data in Google Chrome (left) and Apple Safari (right)

Privacy concerns aren't the only reason to clear your browser's cache and or site data. From time to time, your browser or the site you're visiting will make a mistake and you'll end up with some incomplete, incorrect, or simply outdated data in your browser. Clearing the cache, cookies, local storage, and any other browser data for a site can be an important troubleshooting step whenever a Web site or an application you access through your browser is misbehaving.

All of the big browsers also support some kind of *private-browsing mode* that will disable some forms of data collection and discard most other types of data as soon as you close the private window. These browser modes aren't perfect—some sites will still be tracking you on their end—but it can be a quick way to avoid leaving a bunch of your data behind when you use a shared computer.

Some browsers also support something like the opposite of this—the ability to *sign in* (either to the browser itself, or your OS provider's cloud account) and have your browser data synchronized among multiple devices. If you use your browser's built-in password manager, it can be particularly useful to have browser data in sync across all the devices you use. You probably shouldn't, however, sign in and set up synchronization on a shared device.

Configuring Web Browsers

Most of the big Web browsers have a built-in settings menu that you'll find inside the main application menu, which usually has a button in the top-right corner. In Google Chrome and Microsoft Edge, you can click the three-dot icon in the upper-right corner of the browser and select Settings. In Mozilla Firefox, the icon is in the same place but looks like a stack of horizontal lines—click it and select Options. (Safari is the outlier, here. In it, you open the Safari menu on the menu bar and select Preferences.)

These menus are very similar but differ from browser to browser (and they change over time). Figure 21-28 shows what the Settings menu in Google Chrome looks like. Take some time to download all the big browsers that you have access to, use each one a bit, and explore their settings. Knowledge of one browser will help you set up the others.

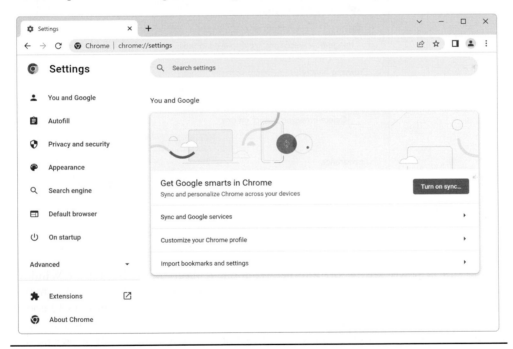

Figure 21-28   Google Chrome Settings

Internet Options

Back in the 1990s, Microsoft made a mistake that we're all *still* paying for: it deeply integrated its Web browser at the time, *Internet Explorer (IE)*, with Windows. Instead of configuring IE directly in the application, Microsoft gave this job to a Control Panel applet named *Internet Options*. Nearly 30 years later, Internet Options (see Figure 21-29) contains a grab-bag of settings that affect Internet Explorer, Microsoft Edge, and potentially any other program that uses the Internet.

Figure 21-29
Internet Options
applet

The sun is slowly setting on Internet Explorer. It hasn't been the default Windows browser since 2015, and as of June 2022 it's no longer supported in the most common version of Windows 10. The CompTIA A+ 1102 exam objectives for Windows 11 appear to be leaving Internet Options behind—but the objectives for Windows 10 still expect you to recognize scenarios that make use of the old Internet Options applet. It's hard to know exactly what CompTIA has in mind, so I'll give you a quick outline of the options.

EXAM TIP I *think* CompTIA is most likely to give you scenarios involving legacy intranet applications or proxy servers. The most obvious reason to use Internet Options is to configure IE—but most people don't need to do this anymore. The big exception is organizations that built or bought applications for internal use that depend on old IE features that modern browsers have removed for security reasons. The next most likely case is that you need to configure the system to use a *proxy server*.

The Internet Options applet has seven tabs:

- The General tab has settings to control the most basic features of Internet Explorer: the home page, tab management, your browsing history, searching, and other appearance controls. It's where you'd delete or change how Internet Explorer stores the Web sites you've visited.

- The Security tab enables you to adjust security settings for a particular zone, such as the Internet, your local intranet, trusted sites, and restricted sites. You can configure which Web sites fall into which zones. This is where you'd relax security rules for an intranet site.

- The Privacy tab works a lot like the Security tab, except it controls privacy matters (like cookies, location tracking, pop-ups, and whether browser extensions run in private browsing mode). There is a slider that enables you to control what is blocked—everything is blocked on the highest setting; nothing is blocked on the lowest.

- The Content tab controls what your browser will and will not display. This is where you'd gate access to insecure or objectionable sites and tweak the AutoComplete feature that pre-fills some forms.

- The Connections tab enables you to set up a connection to the Internet via broadband or dial-up; connect to a VPN; or adjust some LAN settings, which you probably won't need to deal with except perhaps to configure a proxy server connection.

- Finally, there are the Programs and Advanced tabs. These two are not used much today, but here you can find settings to control add-ons for Internet Explorer, what editor to use for editing HTML, and a list of settings to control how IE works at a granular level. In addition, many of these controls you will find here have been moved to the Settings app or other applets and the buttons in Internet Options are just links to that setting's new location.

 EXAM TIP Some organizations use a proxy server to filter employee Internet access for unsafe content. A *proxy server* enables multiple connections to the Internet to go through one protected computer. Applications send requests to the proxy server instead of trying to access the Internet directly, which both protects the client computers and enables the network administrator to monitor and restrict Internet access. Normally, you'll just configure the proxy server's address through the Settings app by searching for proxy settings or selecting Network & Internet and clicking Proxy.

Communicating with Others

If you're like me, one of the most important things you do on the Internet these days is communicate with your friends, family, and coworkers. It wasn't all that long ago, really, that you either talked in person, talked on the phone, or wrote a letter, but now there are dozens of ways to keep in touch with people you know—and even strangers! The CompTIA A+ 1102 exams only focus on the two of the oldest and most business-oriented: e-mail and VoIP.

E-mail

To set up and access e-mail, you have a lot of choices today. You can use the traditional ISP method that requires a dedicated e-mail application. Today, though, people use e-mail clients built into whatever device they use. Finally, you can use a Web-based e-mail client accessible from any device. The difficulty with this section is that all of this is blending somewhat with the advent of account-based access to devices, such as using your Microsoft account to log on to your Windows PC.

All e-mail addresses come in the *accountname@Internet domain* format. To add a new account, provide your name, e-mail address, and password. Assuming the corporate or organization server is set up correctly, that's all you have to do today.

In the not so distant past, however, and still referenced on the CompTIA A+ exams, setting up an e-mail client had challenges. Not only did you have to have a valid e-mail address acquired from the provider and a password, you had to configure both the incoming and outgoing mail server information. You would add the names of the *Post Office Protocol version 3 (POP3)* or *Internet Message Access Protocol version 4 (IMAP4)* server and the *Simple Mail Transfer Protocol (SMTP)* server. The POP3 or IMAP server is the computer that handles incoming (to you) e-mail. Most mail happens through the latest version of IMAP, IMAP4. The SMTP server handles your outgoing e-mail.

 EXAM TIP Make sure you know your port numbers for these e-mail protocols! POP3 uses port 110, IMAP uses port 143, and SMTP uses port 25. Also, you will almost certainly get one or two questions on which protocol handles incoming mail (POP3 or IMAP) and outgoing mail (SMTP).

Integrated Solutions All mobile devices have an integrated e-mail client, fully configured to work within the mobile ecosystem. Apple devices, such as the iPad, enable you to create and use an *iCloud* account that syncs across all your Apple devices. The iCloud e-mail setup process assumes you'll use iCloud for all that sending and receiving stuff and thus you have no other configuration to do. All the settings for IMAP, POP, SMTP, and so on happen behind the scenes. CompTIA calls this sort of lack of configuration *integrated commercial provider email configuration*. That's pretty accurate, if a little bland. You will see more of this in Chapter 24.

Web Mail Most people use Web-based e-mail, such as Yahoo! Mail, Gmail from Google, or Exchange Online from Microsoft, to handle all of their e-mail needs (see Figure 21-30). Web-based mail offers the convenience of having access to your e-mail from any Internet-connected computer, smartphone, tablet, or other Internet-connected device. While desktop clients may offer more control over your messages and their content, Web-based e-mail has caught up in most respects. For example, Web services can provide superior spam-filtering experience by relying on feedback from a large user base to detect unwanted or dangerous messages.

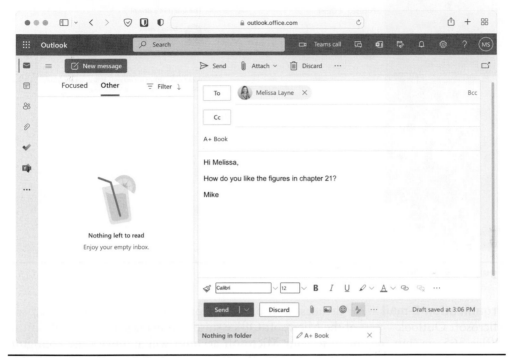

Figure 21-30   Web-based e-mail

 EXAM TIP   One of the big benefits of using somebody else's e-mail service is that *they* do most of the work to deal with spam. If you use your own domain for e-mail, you'll have to set up some DNS records that you saw back in Chapter 19. In addition to the MX records that other e-mail providers use to decide where to route e-mail for your domain, you'll also have to set up a number of *spam management* records (DKIM, SPF, and DMARC) to have much hope of your own outgoing mail being delivered.

Unified Internet Accounts   When I log on to my Windows desktop computer, I use my Microsoft account, a fully functional e-mail account hosted by Outlook. Doing so defines the default e-mail experience on that machine. When I access the Mail client, for example, it immediately accesses my Hotmail account (see Figure 21-31). There's no configuration from a user's or tech's perspective. The same is true when you log on to any Apple device, whether it's a mobile device or smartphone, or a macOS desktop machine. Microsoft calls this feature *Live sign in*.

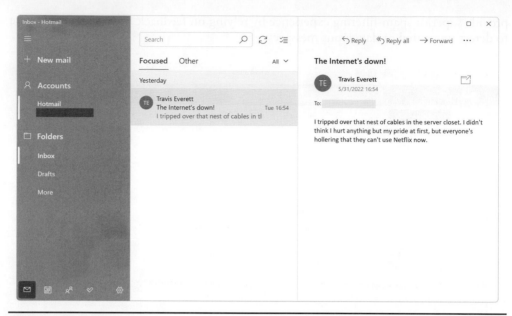

Figure 21-31   Windows Mail

Organization E-mail   For decades now, businesspeople around the world have used Microsoft Outlook—part of the Microsoft Office suite—to manage their e-mail. In the Office 365 era, just logging in to your Microsoft account will automatically configure Outlook to use the correct *Exchange* server. If your organization runs its own Exchange server, you may need to set it up manually. The main times you'll need to intervene are when there isn't a domain network to lean on, when something's changing (like when a company rebrands itself), or when the existing Outlook profile gets broken (see Figure 21-32).

Figure 21-32
Mail applet in
Windows 10

EXAM TIP   You can usually reconfigure Outlook directly, but the CompTIA A+ 1102 exam objectives for Windows 10 also want you to know that you can also do this with the Mail applet in Control Panel. Scenarios where you might find the Mail applet helpful include setting up new users or accounts for an organization-operated Exchange server; the Outlook profile is broken (since this can make it impossible to open Outlook); or you need to update the profile while making sure you don't see the user's mail!

Voice over IP

You can use *Voice over IP (VoIP)* to make *voice calls* over your computer network. Why have two sets of wires, one for voice and one for data, going to every desk? Why not just use the extra capacity on the data network for your phone calls? That's exactly what VoIP does for you. VoIP works with every type of high-speed Internet connection, from DSL to cable to satellite.

VoIP doesn't refer to a single protocol but rather to a collection of protocols that make phone calls over the data network possible. The most common VoIP application protocol is Session Initiation Protocol (SIP), but some popular VoIP applications such as Skype are completely proprietary.

Vendors such as Skype, Cisco, Vonage, Arris, and Comcast offer popular VoIP solutions, and many corporations use VoIP for their internal phone networks. VoIP isn't confined to your computer, either. It can completely replace old copper phone lines. Two popular ways to set up a VoIP system are to either use dedicated *VoIP phones*, like the ones that Cisco makes, or use a dedicated VoIP box (see Figure 21-33) that can interface with your existing analog phones.

Figure 21-33
Arris VoIP
telephony
modem

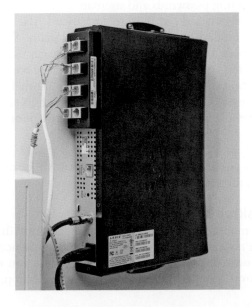

True VoIP phones have RJ-45 connections that plug directly into the network and offer advanced features such as HD-quality audio and video calling. Unfortunately, these phones require a complex and expensive network to function, which puts them out of reach of most home users.

For home users, it's much more common to use a VoIP phone adapter to connect your old-school analog phones. These little boxes are very simple to set up: just connect it to your network, plug in a phone, and then check for a dial tone. With the VoIP service provided by cable companies, the adapter is often built right into the cable modem itself, making setup a breeze.

Remote Access

One of the big advantages of a ginormous, always-on network of networks is that many people can do some or all of their work remotely—whether that means from another city, or just without walking from workstation to workstation. You can take advantage of remote access technologies to manage servers and workstations and use them to train users or troubleshoot their problems. Likewise, you'll almost certainly need to configure some resource to ensure it's available remotely.

The CompTIA A+ 1102 exam objectives want you to know about quite a few remote access technologies, so let's dive in!

Telnet and SSH

Telnet is a terminal emulation program for TCP/IP networks that uses port 23 and enables you to connect to a server or fancy router and run commands on that machine as if you were sitting in front of it. This way, you can remotely administer a server and communicate with other servers on your network. Unfortunately, Telnet shares FTP's bad habit of sending passwords and usernames as clear text, so you should generally use it only as a last resort, and only within your own LAN.

The secure, modern alternative to Telnet, *Secure Shell (SSH)*, has replaced Telnet almost everywhere Telnet used to be popular. As a user, SSH works just like Telnet. Behind the scenes, SSH uses port 22, and the entire connection is encrypted to prevent eavesdroppers from reading your data. SSH has another trick up its sleeve: it can move files or any type of TCP/IP network traffic through its secure connection. This practice, called *tunneling*, plays a role in other secure networking technologies that we'll discuss later in the chapter such as SFTP and VPN.

SSH is encrypted, but its security is only as strong as your password. If you have a machine with a publicly accessible SSH server, it will be under constant attack by hackers trying to guess the password!

Remote Desktop

The kind of remote command-line access you can get with SSH is great for a lot of geeky administrative tasks, but it isn't so good at general productivity—like accessing an application that is only installed on one machine. When you need remote access to the full graphical desktop, you need a remote desktop application.

NOTE Because "remote desktop" is a generic term, you may find some programs with confusingly similar names. Microsoft and Apple both at one point made a program called *Remote Desktop* (the latter is a paid offering), though Microsoft's version is called *Remote Desktop Connection* in current versions of Windows. Then there's Microsoft's *Remote Desktop Connection for Mac*, which is just for enabling macOS machines to connect to a Windows remote desktop.

While some operating systems include a remote desktop client, many third-party remote desktop applications are also available. Most of these make use of either the *Remote Desktop Protocol (RDP)* or *Virtual Network Computing (VNC)*. TightVNC, for example, is totally cross-platform, enabling you to run and control a Windows system remotely from your Mac or vice versa, for example. Figure 21-34 shows TightVNC in action. The Screen Sharing app built into macOS also uses VNC; it's modest, but it's good enough for basic remote access, collaboration, and light remote troubleshooting.

Figure 21-34 TightVNC in action

Windows offers an alternative to VNC: Remote Desktop Connection. *Remote Desktop Connection* provides control over a remote server with a fully graphical interface. Your desktop *becomes* the server desktop (see Figure 21-35).

Figure 21-35
Windows
Remote Desktop
Connection
dialog box

Wouldn't it be cool if, when a client called about a technical support issue and says that something doesn't work, you could transfer yourself from your desk to your client's desk to see precisely what the client sees? This would dramatically cut down on the miscommunication that can make a tech's life so tedious. Microsoft Remote Assistance (MSRA) does just that (though there are also other third-party applications that offer the same capability). *Remote Assistance* enables you to give anyone control of your desktop or take control of anyone else's desktop. If a user has a problem, that user can request support (see Figure 21-36) directly from you. Upon receiving the support-request e-mail, you can then log on to the user's system and, with permission, take the driver's seat.

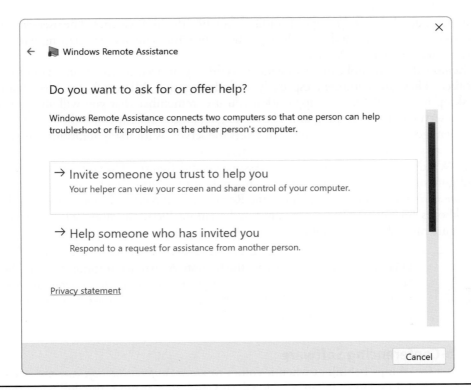

Figure 21-36   Remote Assistance wizard

   EXAM TIP   These remote desktop programs generally require direct network access to the system you want to use. There are also Internet-based *screen sharing* or remote desktop services that enable access from anywhere you have an Internet connection. This may sound great, but be careful! These services basically punch a hole in your network that anyone who compromises the user's credentials with the service can walk through.

With Remote Assistance, you can do anything you would do from the actual computer. You can troubleshoot some hardware configuration or driver problem. You can install drivers, roll back drivers, download new ones, and so forth. You're in command of the remote machine as long as the client allows you to be. The client sees everything you do, by the way, and can stop you cold if you get out of line or do something that makes the client nervous! Remote Assistance can help you teach someone how to use a particular application. You can log on to a user's computer and fire up Outlook, for example, and then walk through the steps to configure it while the user watches. The user can then take over the machine and walk through the steps while you watch, chatting with one another the whole time. Sweet!

Remote desktop applications provide everything you need to access one system from another. They are common, especially considering that Microsoft provides Remote Desktop for free. Whichever application you use, remember that you will always need both a server and a client program. The server goes on the system you want to access and the client goes on the system you use to access the server. With many solutions, the server and client software are integrated into a single product.

In Windows, you can turn Remote Assistance and Remote Desktop on and off and configure other settings. Go to the System applet in Control Panel and then select the *Remote settings* link on the left. Under the Remote tab in System Properties you will see checkboxes for both Remote Assistance and Remote Desktop, along with buttons to configure more detailed settings.

 EXAM TIP   You can also access the Remote Assistance settings through the Settings app. Open the System settings, select About, click *Advanced system settings*, and select the Remote tab. This is the exact same interface you'd reach via the Control Panel!

Video-Conferencing Software

The first few things I think of when it comes to *video-conferencing software* are a screen with a grid of little faces and an occasional cat wandering around, the dull background roar from that guy who called in from his car on the highway, and people trying to talk over each other. But there are some interesting surprises lurking in the presentation-focused features of programs like Microsoft Teams and Zoom.

These programs not only make it easy for someone to share windows or even their entire desktop with whoever else is on the call—but they enable you to give someone else on the call control of your desktop. As a tech, you can use this feature to help a user troubleshoot a problem just like you would in Remote Assistance.

Virtual Private Networks

It's been possible to connect to a remote network for a long time, but back before the Internet existed the main connection options were a telephone line or an outrageously expensive private connection. The introduction of the Internet gave people a way to stop using dial-up and expensive private connections and use the Internet instead, but they wanted to do it securely.

A popular way to secure connections like this entails setting up an encrypted tunnel between the two points—over the open Internet (see Figure 21-37)—creating what we call a *virtual private network (VPN)*.

Figure 21-37
VPN connecting
computers across
the United States

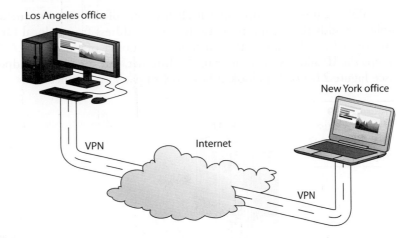

An encrypted tunnel requires endpoints—the ends of the tunnel where the data is encrypted and decrypted. In the SSH tunnel you've seen thus far, the client for the application sits on one end and the server sits on the other. VPNs do the same thing. Either some software running on a computer or, in some cases, a dedicated Internet appliance such as an *endpoint management server* must act as an endpoint for a VPN (see Figure 21-38).

Figure 21-38
Typical tunnel

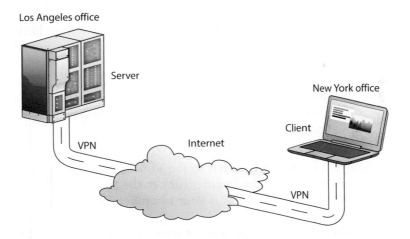

 NOTE An *Internet appliance* is a dedicated box that accomplishes a specific function or functions. You'll see these in many other uses in Chapter 27.

VPNs require a protocol that itself uses one of the many tunneling protocols available and adds the capability to ask for an IP address from a local DHCP server to give the tunnel an IP address that matches the subnet of the local LAN. The connection keeps the IP address to connect to the Internet, but the tunnel endpoints act like NICs (see Figure 21-39). Let's look at how to set up a VPN connection.

Figure 21-39
Endpoints must have their own IP addresses.

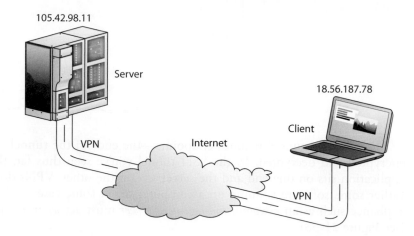

In Windows, type **VPN** in Start | Search and select *VPN settings*. Clicking *Add a VPN connection* presents you with a screen where you can enter all your VPN server information (see Figure 21-40). Your network administrator will most likely provide this information to you. The result is a virtual network card that, like any other NIC, gets an IP address from the DHCP server back at the office.

NOTE A system connected to a VPN looks as though it's on the local network but often performs much slower than if the system were connected directly back at the office.

When your computer connects to the VPN server on the private network, it creates a secure tunnel through the Internet back to the private LAN. Your client takes on an IP address for that network, as if your computer were plugged into the LAN back at the office.

Depending on the configuration of your VPN connection, your Internet traffic may go through your office first. This can help secure the rest of your Internet traffic—but it can also slow it down (and large downloads can bottleneck the organization network if it doesn't have enough bandwidth). VPN connections are convenient, but they can give an attacker an easy way to get into your network—especially if they steal a user's credentials or a user device configured to automatically log in.

Figure 21-40
Adding a VPN
connection in
Windows

Add a VPN connection

VPN provider

Connection name

Server name or address

Type of sign-in info

User name and password

User name (optional)

Password (optional)

☑ Remember my sign-in info

Save   Cancel

File Transfer Software

Sometimes users don't even need direct access to organization's network or workstations
to get their work done remotely—they just need access to the right files! There's a whole
ecosystem of services that enable you to share, synchronize, and transfer files among
different users or among a single user's devices. Some of the best-known examples are
Dropbox, Apple iCloud, Google Drive, and Microsoft OneDrive—but there are plenty
more. In general, software like this comes with an application that you'll install on every
device you want to synchronize files across, and then use the application to specify
exactly what gets synchronized.

These services can be an obvious alternative to opening up your entire network to
attack if someone's credentials are swiped—but they also make it a lot easier for users to
intentionally or accidentally leak files with sensitive information. Each organization will
have to make its own call on these trade-offs.

EXAM TIP The CompTIA A+ 1102 exam objectives include *file transfer software* as a kind of remote access technology, so that's how I'm approaching it here. There's also an emerging *managed file transfer* industry that focuses on providing enterprise-grade file transfer services that make it easy for big organizations to audit who has access to which files and track who has actually downloaded them. These services focus on helping large organizations do things like better secure their files, meet regulatory requirements, or transfer massive files between organizations.

Desktop Management Software

The remote access technologies you've seen so far are fairly limited. They give you a specific kind of access, but otherwise leave the rest up to you. *Desktop management software*, however, gives you a full suite of management tools you can use to configure devices, update or install software, open a remote desktop session to interactively fix issues, enforce security policies, manage user accounts, turn off idle systems—and much more. You may also hear people call this software *endpoint management* software (especially when the software also manages mobile devices).

Remote Monitoring and Management (RMM)

Remote monitoring and management (RMM) software builds on the capabilities of desktop or endpoint management software by also layering in robust monitoring and management of your network—including network devices and servers. Organizations that use an RMM solution have one place to go to understand and manage the health of their wired and wireless network infrastructure, ensure the servers running in their network have the latest security updates, and monitor workstations for unauthorized software!

EXAM TIP *Simple Network Management Protocol (SNMP)* enables remote monitoring and configuration of just about anything on a network. Assuming all your computers, switches, routers, and so on are SNMP-capable, you can use programs to query the network for an unimaginable amount of data. SNMP is a popular protocol to check on your network, but it's the sort of thing you probably won't need to use unless you're a Network+ tech. You'll also find SNMP (along with other protocols) hard at work under the hood of RMM software.

Sharing and Transferring Files

Once upon a time, someone had to physically move their body to share files with someone else or move files between systems. You'd put them on some kind of disk, and then walk the disk over (or throw it like a frisbee) to whoever needed it. At the dawn of the computing era, it was even common for people to "install" software by hand-typing from a paper copy of the program's source code!

All of this extra work is a big part of why early networks were really exciting even long before they were connected to the Internet. Sharing and transferring files is every bit as important in the Internet era—so much so that the way we transfer files has been reinvented a few times over. Let's look at a few of the most common ways it's been done.

File Transfer Protocol

File Transfer Protocol (FTP) emerged in the early 1970s (though it's been updated several times since then) as a great way to transfer files between client systems and an FTP server. It was also *the* way to download software or update your Web site on the early Internet. FTP server software exists for most operating systems, so you can use FTP to transfer data between any two systems regardless of the OS. FTP uses ports 20 and 21.

To access an FTP site, you must use an FTP client such as *FileZilla* or *Cyberduck* (shown in Figure 21-41). For much of the Internet's life, it was possible to access FTP servers through a Web browser—but the sun set on this era in 2021, when both Mozilla Firefox and Google Chrome removed support.

FTP servers require you to log on, though many public download-only servers (and clients) will use "anonymous" as the default. Most FTP clients can store username and password settings to make it easy to reconnect to servers you use regularly. Beware that FTP was developed during a more trusting time—your username and password will be sent over the network in easily intercepted clear text. Don't use the same password for an FTP server that you use for your domain logon at the office!

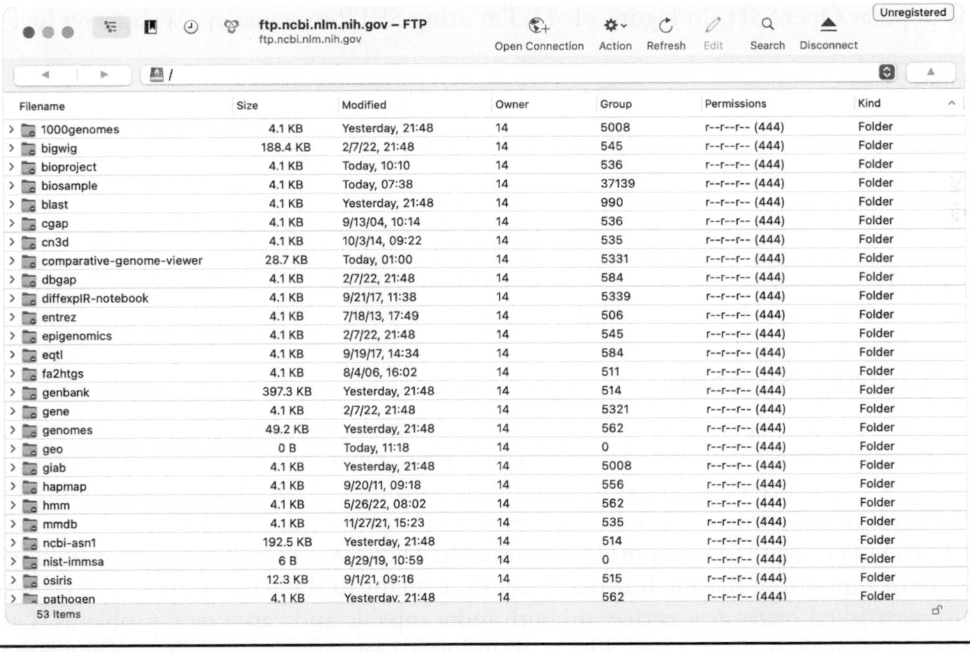

Figure 21-41   The Cyberduck FTP program running on macOS

TFTP

Trivial FTP (TFTP) is an old, bare-bones file transfer protocol that lacks many of the features—like authentication and listing files—that FTP includes. It isn't very popular, but its simplicity gives it a leg up in some narrow cases such as downloading system images to boot a device from the network. If you recall that a big difference between UDP and TCP is that TCP can detect and recover from errors, you might be surprised to know TFTP uses UDP port 69. File transfer does need to avoid errors, and TFTP has its own built-in mechanisms for doing so.

 EXAM TIP The CompTIA A+ 1101 objectives list TFTP and DHCP as examples of *connectionless* (UDP) protocols, and HTTPS and SSH as examples of *connection-oriented* (TCP) protocols. I am not sure exactly why CompTIA wants you to know these four specific protocols—but it's worth memorizing them just in case you see a question that asks you to pick connectionless or connection-oriented protocols out of a lineup!

SFTP

Secure FTP is a network protocol for transferring files over an encrypted SSH connection. You can (and should!) use SFTP for the same things you'd use FTP for—but it is technically its own distinct protocol. The SFTP protocol was written as an extension of SSH, so you can find SFTP client and server support built into SSH software, such as the popular OpenSSH. In Figure 21-42, I'm using SFTP to transfer a Web server log.

Figure 21-42
OpenSSH

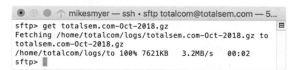

1101

Embedded Systems

One easy-to-miss aspect of the computing landscape is that there are tons and tons of computers out there that don't look like computers. These computers, known as *embedded systems*, have been built into all kinds of stuff—things like appliances, game consoles, cars, medical equipment, missiles, equipment in factories—for decades now.

For a long time, these computers were modest. They played small roles in controlling a device or supporting specific features. Over time, many of these computers have evolved into networked *smart devices* that are both more capable and cause new problems. Let's consider what these devices look like in an industrial setting first, and then see how they manifest in day-to-day life.

Industrial Control Systems

Once upon a time, factories were just a place where a bunch of people came together and used human-powered tools to build things. Waves of new technologies slowly transformed them. For much of the 19th and 20th centuries, factories were places where humans directly controlled or worked in tandem with powerful machines driven by steam or electricity. In the 21st century, our most-advanced factories are becoming fully automated, palace-sized machines maintained by a small number of people.

This latest transformation is being driven by increasingly sophisticated *industrial control systems (ICSs)* that monitor and control (or, at least, help humans monitor and control) many if not all parts of the equipment, materials, and processes they oversee.

Some key industrial technologies (like railroads, power grids, networks of water pumps, pipelines, and so on) that tend to be distributed over wide areas often use a specialized type of ICS. *Supervisory control and data acquisition (SCADA)* systems are designed to manage processes that are spread out over a wide area—and to help with the problem of operating the system safely when something temporarily disrupts connectivity between parts of the system.

Organizations that operate these control systems must carefully balance two needs that can come into conflict. Since these systems might be monitoring and controlling dangerous high-energy processes such as a hydroelectric dam, nuclear power plant, or a process for melting and pouring molten metal, keeping them secure can be a matter of life and death. The other side of this coin is that remote access can make it much easier to manage these systems efficiently and safely.

The Internet of Things

Some embedded systems go a step beyond just being able to use the Internet for remote monitoring and management. These devices, which *actively* use the Internet all on their own during their regular operation, are said to be part of the *Internet of Things (IoT)*. Some of the IoT devices you're most likely to encounter in day-to-day life include things like refrigerators, thermostats, light switches, security cameras, door locks, and smart speakers/digital assistants—but the IoT also includes less-obvious things like parking meters, vending machines, and environment sensors.

 EXAM TIP   Network-accessible embedded systems and IoT devices—and especially *legacy* embedded systems such as SCADA—can be a security risk. These devices tend to live a long life, may not be designed with network security in mind, and may not receive software updates like other networked devices, and it can be hard to notice that they're compromised. It's a good idea to be cautious about letting them on the network at all. If you must, use VLANs (which we discussed in Chapter 19) to isolate these devices on their own network segments. This protects the devices themselves—and helps protect the rest of the network if they're compromised.

We can access, configure, and command these devices over the Internet, but more importantly, the devices themselves regularly use the Internet to report conditions, initiate credit card transactions, download software updates, and so on. I can't show you how every device works, but let's take a look at one of the most iconic: the Nest smart thermostat (see Figure 21-43).

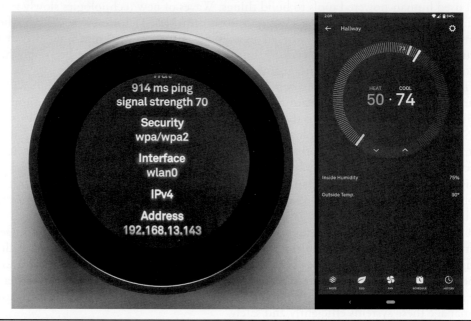

Figure 21-43   Wi-Fi details on a Nest thermostat (left) and Nest smartphone app (right)

You can control a smart thermostat from any device connected to the Internet, such as your computer at the office or your smartphone on the commute. But the Nest thermostat can also use the Internet all on its own—for example, to report when it ran the heater or air conditioner or to automatically adjust its usage to the real-time price of electricity in your area.

 NOTE   IoT devices use a number of protocols that are carefully designed for embedded devices (including Thread, Z-Wave, Zigbee, and more), and the ecosystem is evolving rapidly. Some common themes are lowering power use and leveraging mesh networks to route messages through other IoT devices.

Internet Troubleshooting

There isn't a person who's spent more than a few hours on a computer connected to the Internet who hasn't run into some form of connectivity problem. I love it when I get a call from someone saying, "The Internet is down!" as I always respond the same way: "No, the Internet is fine. It's the way you're trying to get to it that's down." Okay, so I don't make a lot of friends with that remark, but it's actually a really good reminder of why we run into problems on the Internet. Let's review the common symptoms CompTIA lists on their objectives for the CompTIA A+ 220-1101 exam and see what we can do to fix these all-too-common problems.

The dominant Internet setup for a SOHO environment consists of some box from your ISP such as a cable/DSL modem, fiber ONT, etc. that connects via Ethernet cable to a home router. This router is usually 802.11 capable and includes four Ethernet ports. Some computers in the network connect through a wire and some connect wirelessly (see Figure 21-44). It's a pretty safe assumption that CompTIA has a setup like this in mind when talking about Internet troubleshooting, and we'll refer to this setup here as well.

Figure 21-44
Typical SOHO
setup

One quick note before we dive in: Most Internet connection problems are network connection problems. In other words, everything you learned in Chapter 19 applies here. We're not going to rehash those repair problems in this chapter. The following issues are Internet-only problems, so don't let a bad cable fool you into thinking a bigger problem is taking place.

No Connectivity

As you'll remember from Chapter 19, "no connectivity" has two meanings: a disconnected NIC or an inability to connect to a resource. Since Chapter 19 already covers wired connectivity issues and Chapter 20 covers wireless issues, let's look at lack of connectivity from a "you're on the Internet but you can't get to a Web site" point of view:

1. Can you get to other Web sites? If not, go back and triple-check your local connectivity.

2. Can you ping the site? Go to a command prompt and try pinging the URL as follows:

```
C:\>ping www.cheetos1.com
Ping request could not find host www.cheetos1.com.
Please check the name and try again.
C:\>
```

The ping is a failure, but we learn a lot from it. The ping shows that your computer can't get an IP address for that Web site. This points to a DNS failure, a very common problem. To fix a failure to access a DNS server, try these options:

- In Windows, go to a command prompt and type **ipconfig /flushdns**:

```
C:\>ipconfig /flushdns
Windows IP Configuration
Successfully flushed the DNS Resolver Cache.
C:\>
```

NOTE   While the commands are similar, ifconfig and iwconfig aren't suitable for flushing the DNS cache, if it exists, in macOS or Linux.

- In Windows 10, go to Network & Internet in the Settings app and click *Network troubleshooter* (see Figure 21-45). (This option still exists in Windows 11, but you may have to use *Find a setting* to search for it.)

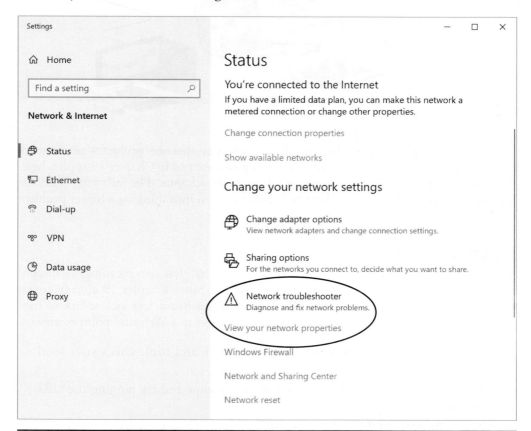

Figure 21-45   Diagnosing a network problem in Windows 10

- Try using another DNS server. There are lots of DNS servers out there that are open to the public. Try Google's famous 8.8.8.8 and 8.8.4.4 or Cloudflare's 1.1.1.1 and 1.0.0.1.

If DNS is OK, make sure you're using the right URL. This is especially true when you're entering DNS names into applications such as e-mail clients.

Limited Connectivity

Limited connectivity points to a DHCP problem, assuming you're connected to a DHCP server. Run **ipconfig** and see if you have an APIPA address:

```
C:\>ipconfig
Windows IP Configuration
Ethernet adapter Local Area Connection:
        Connection-specific DNS Suffix  . :
        IP Address. . . . . . . . . . . . : 169.254.0.16
        Subnet Mask . . . . . . . . . . . : 255.255.0.0
        Default Gateway . . . . . . . . . :
C:\>
```

Uh-oh! No DHCP server! If your router is your DHCP server, try restarting the router. If you know the Network ID for your network and the IP address for your default gateway (something you should know—it's your network!), try setting up your NIC statically.

Local Connectivity

Local connectivity means you can access network resources but not the Internet. First, this is a classic symptom of a downed DHCP server since all the systems in the local network will have APIPA/link local addresses. However, you might also have a problem with your router. You need to ping the default gateway; if that's successful, ping the other port (the WAN port) on your router. The only way to determine the IP address of the other port on your router is to access the router's configuration Web page and find it (see Figure 21-46). Every router is different—good luck!

You can learn a lot by looking at your WAN IP address. Take a look at Figure 21-47. At first glance, it looks the same as Figure 21-46, but notice that there is no IP address. Most ISPs don't provide static IP addresses—they simply give you the physical connection, and your router's WAN network card uses DHCP, just like most internal networks. If you're lucky, you can renew your DHCP address using some button on the router's configuration. If not, try resetting the cable/fiber/DSL modem. If that doesn't work, it's time to call your ISP.

Slow Network Speeds

No matter how fast the connection is, we all want our Internet to go faster. People tolerate a certain amount of waiting for a large program to download or an HD video to buffer, but your connection can sometimes slow down to unacceptable speeds.

Figure 21-46 Router's WAN IP address

Remember that your Internet connection has a maximum speed at which it can transfer. If you divide that connection between multiple programs trying to use the Internet, all of your programs will connect very slowly. To see what's happening on your network, open a command prompt and type **netstat**, which shows all the connections between your computer and any other computer. Here's a very simplified example of netstat output:

```
C:\>netstat
Active Connections
  Proto  Local Address          Foreign Address        State
  TCP    10.12.14.47:57788      totalfs3:microsoft-ds  ESTABLISHED
  TCP    192.168.15.102:139     Sabertooth:20508       ESTABLISHED
  TCP    192.168.15.102:50283   Theater:netbios-ssn    ESTABLISHED
  TCP    192.168.15.102:60222   dts1.google.com:https  ESTABLISHED
  TCP    192.168.15.102:60456   www.serve2.le.com:http ESTABLISHED
  TCP    192.168.15.102:60482   64.145.92.65:http      ESTABLISHED
  TCP    192.168.15.102:60483   12.162.15.1:57080      TIME_WAIT
C:\>
```

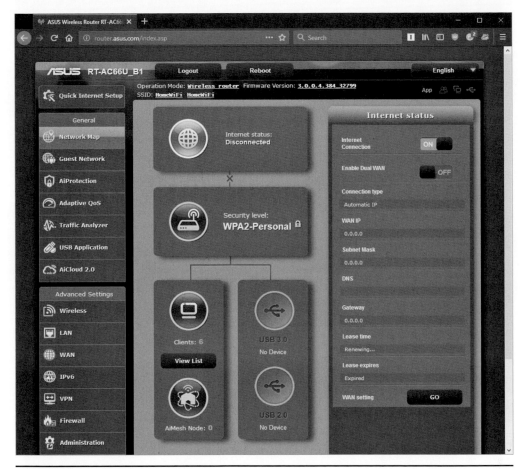

Figure 21-47   No WAN connection

If you look at the Foreign Address column, you'll see that most of the connections are Web pages (HTTP and HTTPS) or shared folders (microsoft-ds, netbios-ssn), but what is the connection to 12.162.15.1:57080? Not knowing every connection by heart, I looked it up on Google and found out that there was a background torrent program running on my machine. I found the program and shut it down.

When everyone on the network is getting slow Internet connectivity, it's time to check out the router. In all probability, you have too many people who need too much bandwidth—go buy more bandwidth!

When additional bandwidth isn't an acceptable solution, you'll need to make the most of what you have. Your router can use a feature called *Quality of Service (QoS)* to prioritize access to network resources. QoS enables you to ensure certain users, applications, or services are prioritized when there isn't enough bandwidth to go around by limiting the bandwidth for certain types of data based on application protocol, the IP address of a computer, and all sorts of other features. Figure 21-48 is a typical router's QoS page.

Figure 21-48 QoS

Latency and Jitter

Any real-time application—things like VoIP, teleconferencing, streaming video, and video games—can prove unworkable if you have miserable high latency. In all of these cases, but especially with VoIP, a key to troubleshooting is that low network latency is more important than high network speed (as long as your connection meets the minimum bandwidth that the application needs). The higher the latency, the more problems, such as noticeable delays during your VoIP call.

Another kind of latency problem, *jitter*, is caused by rapid latency fluctuations, which can in turn make packets arrive in bursts or out of order. While true high latency generally just causes long delays, jitter can garble audio and video signals or break the connection altogether. In all cases, you can assess the latency (and how consistent it is) with tools such as ping, tracert/traceroute, and pathping.

Try This!

Checking Latency with ping

Latency is the bane of any VoIP call because of all the problems it causes if it is too high. A quick way to check your current latency is to use the ever-handy ping, so try this!

1. Run ping on some known source, such as www.microsoft.com or www.totalsem.com.

2. When the ping finishes, take note of the average round-trip time at the bottom of the screen. This is your current latency to that site.

Poor VoIP Call Quality

When the main symptom users are reporting is *poor VoIP quality*, you may need to draw on your knowledge of multiple problems to find a fix. Many VoIP providers have a dashboard where you can log in and see call statistics. The dashboard may not answer your exact question, but most dashboards usually have some kind of call-quality metric (as shown in Figure 21-49) that you can quickly check for signs of obvious trouble.

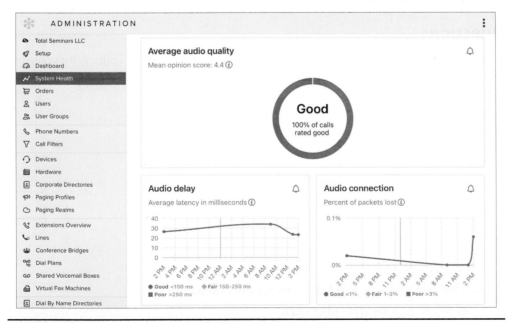

Figure 21-49   Call quality metric in GoTo Administration Panel

Here are a few things to keep in mind if you need to dig deeper:

- Most VoIP problems could be on the other end of the call. Before you jump into diagnosing your own network, see if calls to other locations and networks have the same problem.
- If your organization uses standalone VoIP phones, it's a good idea to see if swapping the phone out for another fixes the issue.
- If the conversation has long delays that are making it hard to communicate, check for high latency.
- If the audio is choppy or distorted, check for jitter. (Some VoIP providers track this for you.)
- If the audio quality is really low, look into whether the network is congested or just doesn't have enough bandwidth.
- Networks often need to use QoS to avoid VoIP call-quality issues—especially when the network is busy—so each of these call-quality problems might indicate that QoS isn't enabled or working correctly. Ensure your router supports QoS and that it's enabled on your router and/or VoIP router. If it's enabled, you may need to tune the settings to prioritize VoIP traffic.

Chapter Review

Questions

1. Of the following four Internet connection options, which typically is most likely to have the *highest* latency?

   A. Cable

   B. Fiber optic

   C. DSL

   D. Satellite

2. What port does POP3 use?

   A. 22

   B. 110

   C. 42

   D. 256

3. What advantage does WISP have over fiber optic?

   A. WISP is faster than fiber optic.

   B. WISP is cheaper to deploy, so it's more likely to be available in smaller communities.

   C. Fiber optic is more likely to be disrupted during rainstorms.

   D. None. WISP has no advantages over fiber optic.

4. Which protocol can you use to send e-mail?

   A. IMAP

   B. POP3

   C. PPP

   D. SMTP

5. Which protocols can you use to receive e-mail? (Select two.)

   A. IMAP

   B. POP3

   C. PPP

   D. SMTP

6. What advantage does satellite have over cable for connecting to the Internet?

   A. Satellite is faster than cable.

   B. Cable degrades in stormy weather; satellite does not.

   C. Cable requires you to be within 18,000 feet of a central switch.

   D. Cable is limited to areas with cable installed; satellite is not.

7. Which of the following represent invalid port to protocol matchups? (Select two.)

   A. 137, 138, 139, 445 = SMB

   B. 3398 = RDP

   C. 80 = HTTPS

   D. 22 = SSH

8. What option often enables you to diagnose TCP/IP errors such as connection problems?

   A. FTP

   B. ping

   C. QoS

   D. APIPA

9. Which of the following cellular data technologies is often considered 4G?

   A. EDGE

   B. UMTS

   C. LTE

   D. CDMA

10. Which of the following remote access technologies should be avoided due to security issues?

   A. SSH

   B. Virtual network computing

   C. RDP

   D. Telnet

Answers

1. **D.** Though newer low-orbit satellite access can be similar to other broadband methods, satellites in a geosynchronous orbit have much higher latency.

2. **B.** Post Office Protocol 3 (POP3) uses port 110.

3. **B.** Because WISP services don't need to run cable to every home or business, it can be easier and cheaper to deploy in less populous areas.

4. **D.** You can use Simple Mail Transfer Protocol (SMTP) to send e-mail messages.

5. **A, B.** You can use either Internet Message Access Protocol (IMAP) or POP3 to receive e-mail messages.

6. **D.** Clearly, satellite cuts you loose from the wires!

7. **B, C.** Remote Desktop Protocol (RDP) uses port 3389. Hypertext Transfer Protocol Secure (HTTPS) uses port 443; HTTP uses port 80.

8. **B.** You can often use the ping command to diagnose TCP/IP problems.

9. **C.** Long Term Evolution (LTE) is usually considered a 4G cellular data technology.

10. **D.** Telnet provides absolutely no security. Use SSH instead!

22

Virtualization

In this chapter, you will learn how to
- Explain why virtualization is so highly adopted
- Describe the service layers and architectures, and characteristics of cloud computing

The subject of this chapter, virtualization, can be a little slippery and hard to understand. A big reason is that virtualization isn't one concrete thing you can grab with your hands. There are many kinds of virtualization, and the thread tying them together isn't very obvious—it's just an idea.

The important idea at the heart of every kind of *virtualization* is to take an existing component (anything in or attached to the system) and make it more flexible by replacing it with a layer of software that (as far as anything interacting with the component can tell) behaves the same. This idea is so fundamental to modern computing that, way back in Chapter 4, we looked at a well-known application of it: virtual memory.

Once upon a time, computer programs had *direct* access to the system's RAM. Programs in modern systems actually access virtual memory—a layer of software that, as far as the program can tell, is RAM. Operating systems use the extra flexibility this layer of software provides to store the memory contents of active programs in RAM but swap the memory contents of idle programs out to a storage drive.

To *virtualize* something is to replace it with this more flexible layer of software. Why do we virtualize things? The answer is almost always because the extra flexibility enables us to do something new, makes things easier to manage, or both.

This chapter delves into virtualization in detail, starting with the reasons why virtualization is important today, and then looking at a collection of technologies that use virtualization extensively: cloud computing. Let's get started.

1101

Hardware Virtualization

One of the most important kinds of virtualization, *hardware virtualization*, takes the entire computer that an OS expects to interact with and virtualizes it. The physical *host* computer uses software known as a *hypervisor* to create environments (each saved in a separate file) that have virtual versions of all the "hardware" devices you need to install and run an OS. The hypervisor allocates fractions of the host's real hardware resources to power these virtual devices.

 EXAM TIP For clarity, I will specify what kind of virtualization I mean and only use the term "virtualization" by itself to refer to the broader idea. If you see "virtualization" by itself on the exam, however, it will almost certainly mean hardware virtualization!

These environments are called *virtual machines (VMs)* or *guests*. Figure 22-1 shows one such example: a Windows host system using a hypervisor called Hyper-V to run two guest virtual machines, one running Ubuntu Linux and another running Windows 10.

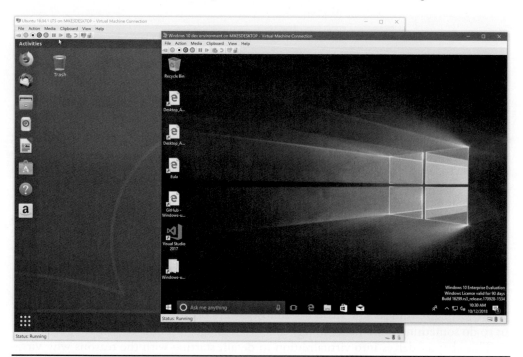

Figure 22-1 Hyper-V running Linux and Windows 10

The CompTIA A+ 1101 objectives expect you to be able to *summarize the purpose of virtual machines*. We'll build up to the list of purposes CompTIA has in mind by the end of this section, but first I want to get philosophical so that we don't lose sight of something.

Just as a hammer is a tool for the purpose of hitting things, a computer is a tool for the purpose of computing things. Virtualizing a computer doesn't change this—the purpose of a virtual machine is still to run computations! The benefits of hardware virtualization are to make virtual machines more convenient than physical computers in some situations, but they are just another tool we can use to meet a need or solve a problem.

Let's take a closer look how we can use hardware virtualization on our own local systems, and then address the elephant in the room—what are the benefits of *virtual* computers and what on Earth can you do with them? Then, I'll walk you through the process of setting up a VM of your own to experiment with, and finish the section with a look at how hardware virtualization tends to manifest on a server.

Client-side Virtualization

A normal operating system installed directly on the hardware uses programming called a *supervisor* (better known as the *kernel*) to handle very low-level interaction among hardware and software, such as task scheduling, allotment of time and resources, and so on. Figure 22-2 shows how the supervisor works between the OS and the hardware.

Figure 22-2
Supervisor on a
generic single
system

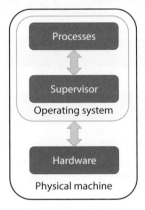

Hardware virtualization enables one machine—the host—to run multiple guest operating systems simultaneously. The CompTIA A+ 1101 objectives focus mostly on what CompTIA calls *client-side virtualization*—when the VM host also serves as someone's day-to-day workstation.

EXAM TIP   If you see the words "client-side" and "virtualization" in the same question on the exam, keep an open mind! As a term, "client-side virtualization" is vague. It refers to where the work is done—usually in contrast to *server-side virtualization*—and omits what kind of virtualization it is. I think CompTIA means client-side hardware virtualization, but CompTIA might mean client-side desktop virtualization. We'll discuss desktop virtualization later in the chapter.

In hardware virtualization, the hypervisor takes on the role of the supervisor—plus the added chore of dividing up the hardware resources among active virtual machines. Figure 22-3 shows a single hypervisor hosting three different guest virtual machines.

Figure 22-3
Hypervisor on a generic single system hosting three virtual machines

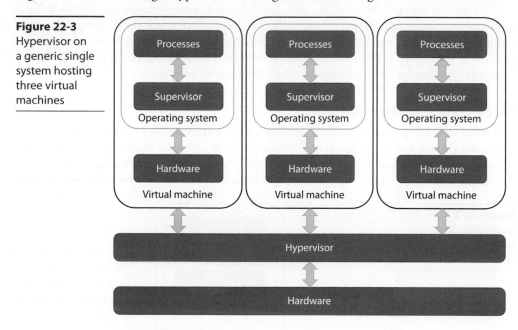

There are a fair number of hypervisors to choose from. Microsoft's Hyper-V (shown earlier in Figure 22-1) is included in Windows Server and Windows Pro. Another very popular hypervisor is Oracle VM VirtualBox (see Figure 22-4), which runs on Windows, macOS, and Linux.

This is in no way a complete list. Many Linux users swear by KVM, for example, and VMware has long made a number of popular commercial hypervisors.

Benefits of Virtualization

One of the tricks to getting your mind around any given kind of virtualization is understanding why anyone bothers—what benefits are they getting from the extra flexibility? Hardware virtualization unlocks a lot of little benefits, so I'll focus on two big categories: saving resources and making systems easier to manage.

Saving Resources

A dirty little secret of modern life is that most people have things they almost never use—and big organizations are no different! When it comes to resource use, most computers and cars have a lot in common: they spend most of the time just sitting there, a little time partly occupied, and are only rarely used to their full capacity.

Before hardware virtualization, each OS needed a physical system. With a hypervisor, though, you can place multiple virtual servers or clients on a single physical system. Rather than one machine running a Windows file server, another Windows system

Figure 22-4   Oracle VM VirtualBox

acting as a DNS server, and a third machine running Linux for a DHCP server, why not use one physical computer to handle all three servers simultaneously as virtual machines?

The flexibility of virtual machines makes it possible to consolidate multiple systems down into a single box. Every physical computer requires a minimum amount of hardware, and a lot of that hardware—like its fans, power supply, and motherboard—require a minimum amount of electricity just to turn on. When organizations reduce the number of physical systems they need to do the same amount of work, they benefit from ongoing energy savings (see Figure 22-5).

Figure 22-5
Hardware
virtualization
saves power.

300 watts

600 watts

Lowering your energy bill is great, but it's just where the benefits start. Hardware consolidation reduces the time and money an organization spends maintaining hardware and enables it to entirely avoid purchasing expensive hardware that rarely if ever runs at full capacity during its useful lifetime.

These benefits are biggest for servers, but they also apply to desktop computers. A Windows user who needs regular access to Linux doesn't need two computers or a complex multi-boot setup—they just need a Windows hypervisor and a Linux VM. Likewise, support techs who need occasional access to every OS version they support can have a single system with a VM for each.

Complex desktop PCs can also be replaced with simple but durable *thin clients* that offload most of their work on servers. Each thin client still needs a keyboard, mouse, and monitor—but they may not need hard drives or fans. They can usually get away with simpler motherboards and less-powerful CPUs, GPUs (which can be built into the CPUs), and RAM.

Simplifying System Management and Security

The most popular reason for virtualizing is probably the benefits we reap from easy-to-manage systems. We can take advantage of the fact that VMs are simply files: like any other files, they are easy to copy around. It's easy to set up new employees with a department-specific virtual machine that has all of the software they need already installed.

These management advantages turn out to be a nice security advantage, too. Let's say you have set up a new employee with a traditional physical system. If that system goes down—due to hacking, malware, or so on—you need to restore the system from a backup (which may or may not be easily at hand) or break out the OS installation media. With hardware virtualization, the host machine, hypervisor, and any other VMs it runs are generally unaffected and uninfected; you merely need to shut down the virtual machine and reload an alternate (clean) copy of it. And because VMs are just files, these are easy to keep around.

 TIP VMs on a network face the same risks—and pose the same risks to other networked devices—as any other networked computer. Networked VMs have *security requirements* similar to a physical system and should usually get whatever security treatment you'd give physical systems. VMs need regular OS and software updates, firewalls, anti-malware software, accounts with strong passwords, backups, and good general security hygiene.

Most virtual machines also let us make a *snapshot* or *checkpoint*, which saves the virtual machine's state at that moment, allowing us to quickly return to this state later. Snapshots are great for doing risky (or even not-so-risky) maintenance with a safety net. They also give you the freedom to install updates without worrying they'll render the OS unusable, making it easier to keep systems secure. These aren't, however, a long-term backup strategy—each snapshot may reduce performance and should be removed as soon as the danger has passed. Figure 22-6 shows VMware ESXi saving a snapshot.

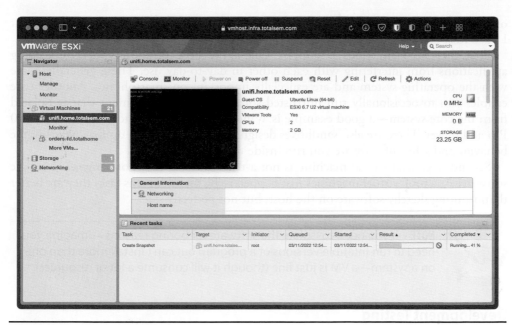

Figure 22-6 Saving a snapshot

 TIP Virtualized operating systems use the same security features as real operating systems. For each virtual machine user account, you'll need to keep track of user names, passwords, permissions, and so on, just like on a normal PC.

Purpose of Virtual Machines

As I said earlier: like physical computers, virtual machines are just another tool for computing things. This means you can find people using virtual machines to do almost anything they can do with physical computers. It also means you'll find people using physical computers for things virtual machines do well.

Above all else, it means that—just like with physical computers—people are constantly finding new ways to use virtual machines. Let's review the list of purposes you should know for the CompTIA A+ 1101 exam—but keep in mind that the best problem you ever solve with a VM may not be on this list!

Sandboxing

We'll take a closer look at security topics in Chapter 27, so for now I just want to touch lightly on a fundamental idea. If you need to run software that you don't trust, the safest way to do it is to run it on a separate computer where it can't interact with real data and programs.

Isolating untrusted software this well is rarely practical, so the next-best thing is to run the software inside a tightly restricted execution environment—a *sandbox*—which limits how the software can interact with the host system and any files and other programs on it. CompTIA wants you to know that virtual machines can serve as a sandbox—but I need to split a few hairs.

First, there are many kinds of sandbox. One of the most common types is for keeping applications from interfering with each other in day-to-day use. These generally come with the operating system and are especially important on smartphones. Another type enables you to occasionally run untrusted software in an environment that is isolated from the core system—a good example is Windows Sandbox, included in Windows 10 Pro and newer. There are also sandboxes designed from the ground up for analyzing the behavior and safety of software you run inside them.

Second, a general virtual machine is not a true sandbox. It is not *designed* to isolate software! As a tool, virtual machines just happen to be useful for this task; they are better than running sketchy software on the host, but not perfectly safe.

NOTE   If you need to isolate the software for boring reasons—imagine you need to run multiple versions of a program but can't install more than one on a system—a VM is just fine (though it will consume a lot of resources).

Development Testing

When it comes to programming, there's always a chance that differences between systems will cause the software that developers are working on to run differently—or not at all! For this reason, developers often test the software they are writing in a *development environment* that matches the intended environment (i.e., where the software should run) as closely as possible. Virtual machines are a popular choice for these environments.

EXAM TIP   The CompTIA A+ 1101 objectives call this purpose *test development*. I think CompTIA means "test" as a verb—to test development work. But there's a chance CompTIA means "development" as the verb—to develop tests. Know that VMs are a popular way to test development work and look for "VM" in the answers if you see a question about creating or developing tests.

It isn't enough to just use *any* VM, though. Surprisingly small differences between systems can cause trouble. Not only are two systems set up by hand likely to differ, but differences accumulate on every system as users install different software in them, run updates at different times, create different files, and so on. Developers may regularly run special software to prepare a fresh VM—to *provision* it with the exact operating system, files, and software specified in configuration files shared among everyone working on the project.

Application Virtualization

The final purpose of VMs that CompTIA focuses on is application virtualization. *Application virtualization* entails virtualizing the OS capabilities that an application would normally use to install and do its work. The flexibility this creates enables some neat tricks, such as being able to run an application without installing it, run applications that only work in a different version of your OS, run applications that would normally interfere with each other, and even run applications that were written for another OS entirely.

 EXAM TIP The CompTIA A+ 1101 objectives call out two of these tricks: running applications for a different OS version (identified as *legacy software/ OS*), and running applications written for another OS (identified as *cross- platform virtualization*). Look for "application virtualization" or "virtual machines" as an answer to questions about running applications for a different or older OS.

I need to be clear about two things here. First, there are different approaches to application virtualization out there and they don't all use virtual machines. Second, you can manually use virtual machines to accomplish these same tricks, but application virtualization means more than just running an application in a VM. The point is to have your cake and eat it, too.

Here's an example of application virtualization. Having to run a full Windows 7 VM to access a legacy app on macOS is clunky. Users must jump through hoops to move files around between the host system and the VM, and they'll almost certainly catch themselves trying to use macOS keyboard shortcuts inside the Windows VM or Windows keyboard shortcuts outside of it.

In contrast, some forms of application virtualization are so seamless that users will launch it just like any other native desktop app and not even know they are interacting with old software written for Windows 7.

Creating a Virtual Machine

Before we go any further, let's take the basic pieces you've learned about hardware virtualization and put them together in one of its simplest forms: a virtual machine on your local system.

The basic process for creating virtual machines is as follows:

1. Set up your system's hardware to support virtual machines and verify it can meet the resource requirements for running them.

2. Install a hypervisor on your system.

3. Create a new virtual machine that has the proper virtualized hardware requirements for the guest OS.

4. Start the new virtual machine and install the new guest OS exactly as you'd install it on a new physical machine.

Hardware Support and Resource Requirements

While any computer running Linux, Windows, or macOS will support a hypervisor, there are a few hardware requirements we need to address.

Every Intel-based CPU since the late 1980s is designed to support a supervisor for multitasking, but it's hard work for that same CPU to support multiple supervisors on multiple VMs. Both AMD and Intel added extra features to their CPUs just to support hypervisors: Intel's *VT-x* and AMD's *AMD-V*. This is *hardware virtualization support*, and VMs will run better with it enabled.

If your CPU and BIOS support hardware virtualization, you can turn it on or off inside the system setup utility (it may or may not be enabled by default). Figure 22-7 shows the virtualization setting in a typical system setup utility. Note that AMD's AMD-V virtualization is often referred to as SVM mode, as shown in Figure 22-7.

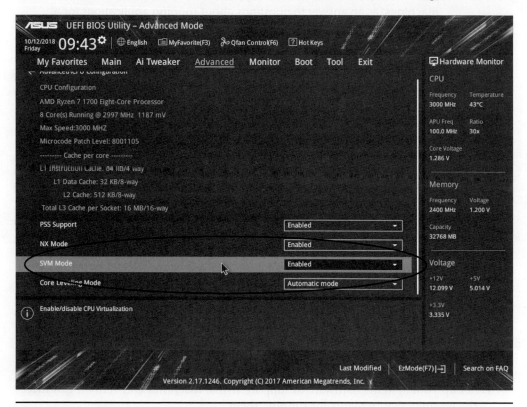

Figure 22-7   BIOS setting for CPU hardware virtualization support on an AMD-based system

RAM   The most important concern is RAM. Each virtual machine needs just as much RAM as a physical one, so it's common practice to stuff your host machine with large amounts of RAM. The more virtual machines you run, the more RAM you need. Generally, you need to leave enough RAM (4 GB recommended) for the hypervisor and every VM you intend to run simultaneously.

 NOTE   As we discussed way back in Chapter 4, different motherboards can support different quantities of RAM. If you plan to build a PC to run virtual machines, it pays to do your research. You don't want to get stuck with a board that maxes out at 16 GB of RAM.

VM Storage   VM files can be huge because they include everything installed on the VM. Depending on the OS and how the VM is used, the VM file could range from megabytes to hundreds of gigabytes. On top of that, every snapshot or checkpoint you make requires space. Figure 22-8 shows a newly minted Windows 10 VM taking about 10 GB of storage space.

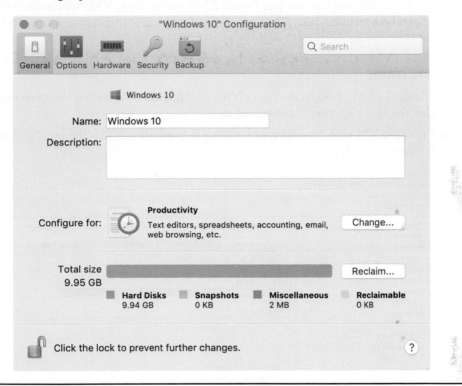

Figure 22-8   Single VM file taking about 10 GB

The particulars of VM storage depend on your circumstances, but here are a few basic recommendations:

- Make sure you have plenty of storage space for all of the VMs you plan to have, and room to grow.
- Your VM files are precious. Plan ahead to protect them with good RAID arrays and regular backups to make sure they are available when you need them.
- If performance is critical for your VMs, plan to store them on an SSD.

Virtual Networks
Probably one of the coolest features of VMs is that you can "virtually" network them in many different ways. Don't just limit yourself to thinking, "Oh, can I get a VM to connect to the Internet?" Well, sure you can, but hypervisors do so much more.

Every hypervisor has the capability to connect each of its virtual machines to a network in a number of different ways. All of these options depend on virtual switches, but the way this looks will vary a lot from hypervisor to hypervisor.

Some common ways to network VMs include the following:

- Create an *internal network* (see Figure 22-9) for multiple VMs within the same hypervisor, enabling them to communicate with each other (and optionally the outside world).

- Place a VM on a virtual network that only enables it to communicate with the host system.

- "Bridge" a VM's NIC to the host's NIC, enabling the VM to join the same network that the host computer is connected to.

- Provide a VM with no network, isolating it from other VMs, the host, and the broader network.

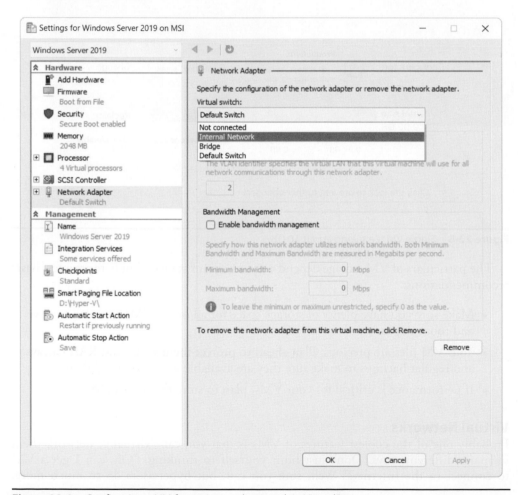

Figure 22-9   Configuring a VM for an internal network in VirtualBox

Installing a Virtual Machine

The actual process of installing a hypervisor is usually no more complicated than installing any other type of software. Let's use Hyper-V as an example. If you have a Windows 10 or 11 Professional system, you can enable Microsoft's Hyper-V by going to the Programs and Features Control Panel applet and selecting *Turn Windows features on or off*, which opens the Windows Features dialog box, as shown in Figure 22-10.

Figure 22-10
Installing
Hyper-V in
Windows

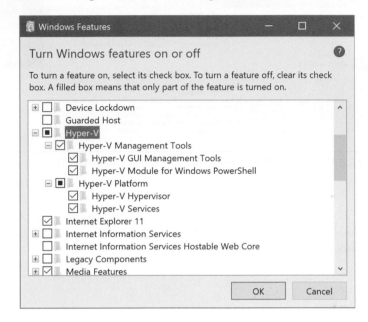

Once you've installed the hypervisor of choice, you'll have a *virtual machine manager (VMM)* that acts as the primary place to create, start, stop, save, and delete guest virtual machines. Figure 22-11 shows the manager for VirtualBox.

NOTE   If you are using Windows 10/11 Home, Hyper-V is not available from this menu. Use a third-party virtualization tool.

How to Build a Virtual Machine

Now that you've got a hypervisor, you can set up a virtual machine. On pretty much any virtual machine manager, this is simply a matter of selecting New | Virtual Machine, which starts a wizard to ensure you're creating the right virtual machine for your guest OS. Most hypervisors have presets for crucial settings (such as virtual RAM, storage space, and so on) to ensure your guest OS has the virtual hardware it needs to run.

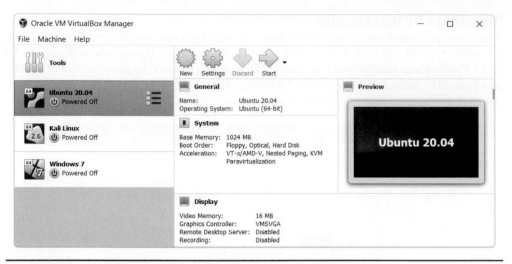

Figure 22-11 Oracle VM VirtualBox Manager (three VMs installed)

Figure 22-12 shows the VirtualBox wizard asking what OS you intend to install in the Machine Folder field. You also need to give the virtual machine a name. For this overview I'm going with Fedora Workstation.

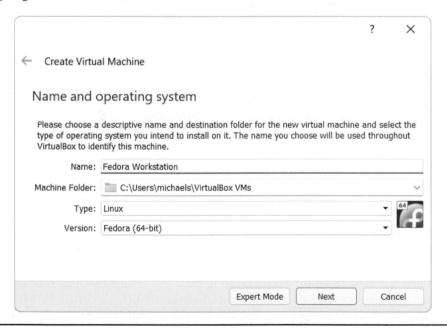

Figure 22-12 Creating a new VM in Oracle VirtualBox

NOTE Use descriptive names for virtual machines. This will spare you a lot of confusion when you have multiple VMs on a single host.

Click Next, and you get to pick how much memory you want for your VM (see Figure 22-13). VirtualBox recommends at least 1 GB for Fedora, but I'm going with 2 GB.

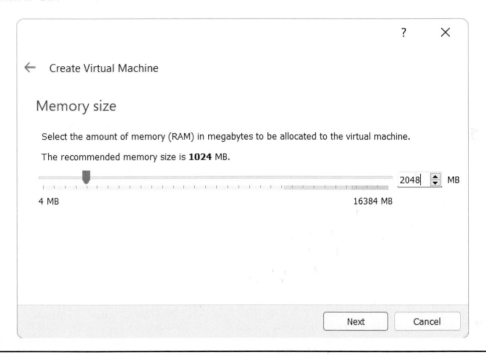

Figure 22-13 Selecting the amount of memory for the VM

After clicking Next, you get to create the virtual hard drive. Clicking Create opens the Create Virtual Hard Disk wizard, which asks several technical questions about hard disk file type and how it should allocate the space. I'm just going with the defaults, but it can be useful to change them in certain situations. Finally, on the last screen, you get to set how big the virtual disk will be, the default being 8 GB. That's a bit small for me, so I've gone with 25 GB, as shown in Figure 22-14. With that, you've created a new virtual machine.

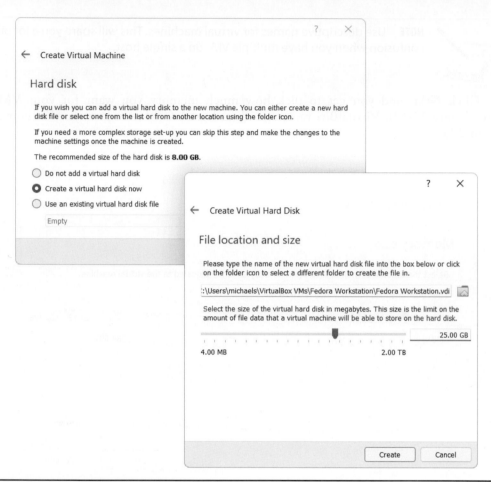

Figure 22-14   Setting the virtual drive size

Installing the Operating System

Once you've created the new guest VM, it's time to install a guest operating system. Would you like to use Microsoft Windows in your virtual machine? No problem, but every Windows virtual machine requires a separate, legal copy of Windows; this also goes for any licensed software installed in the VM.

All good virtual machine managers enable you to load installation media from removable media on the host, but the easy way is to tell the new virtual machine to treat an ISO file as its own optical drive. In Figure 22-15, I'm installing Fedora Workstation on a VirtualBox virtual machine. I downloaded an ISO image from the Fedora Web site (https://getfedora.org) and selected it as the installation media. From here I click Start and install Fedora like any other installation.

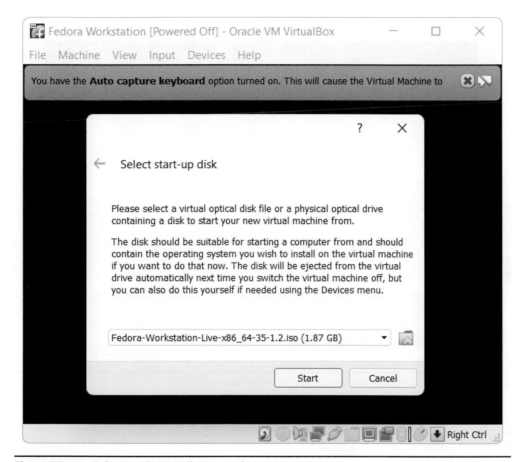

Figure 22-15 Selecting the installation media

After you've gone through all the configuration and OS installation screens, you can start using your virtual machine. Figure 22-16 shows VirtualBox running the newly installed Fedora Workstation.

Like with a real system, you can add or remove hardware—but adding hardware won't take a trip to the electronics store or a box from Newegg. With a good hypervisor, you can easily add and remove virtual hard drives, virtual network cards, virtual RAM, and so on, helping you adapt your VM to meet changing needs. Figure 22-17 shows the Settings System screen from VirtualBox.

 SIM Check out the excellent Chapter 22 Show! and Click! sims on "Virtual Hardware" over at https://www.totalsem.com/110X. These help reinforce terminology and typical steps for setting up a virtual machine.

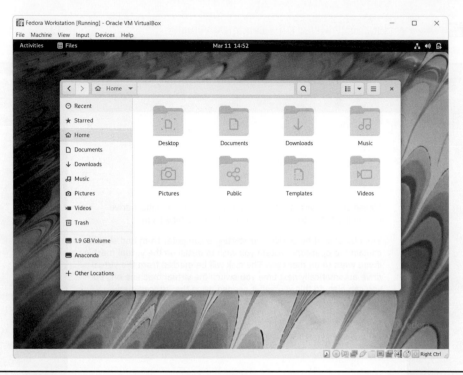

Figure 22-16   Fedora Workstation running in VirtualBox

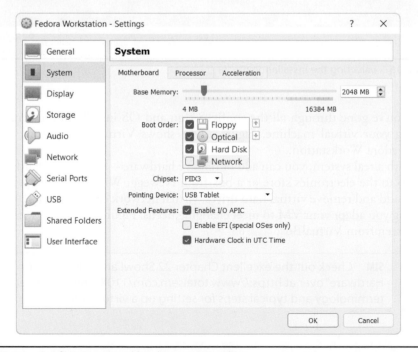

Figure 22-17   Configuring virtual hardware in VirtualBox

Server-side Virtualization

When it comes to servers, hardware virtualization has pretty much taken over everywhere. Many of the servers we access, such as those that power Web sites and video streaming services, are virtualized. These severs usually aren't running in a desktop hypervisor such as VirtualBox because that type of hypervisor requires the host to have a full operating system.

This full host OS not only ties up at least enough resources to run a full VM—it also adds a little overhead to every operation. For this reason (and others), most server VMs run on a powerful hypervisor/OS combination called a *bare-metal* hypervisor. We call it bare metal because there's no other software between it and the hardware—just bare metal. The industry also refers to this class of hypervisors as *Type-1*, and applications such as VirtualBox as *Type-2* (see Figure 22-18).

Figure 22-18
Type-1 versus
Type-2
hypervisors

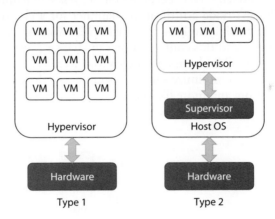

I hope by this point that you have a sense of what hardware virtualization is—but don't worry if you're still a bit confused about why it's a big deal. One hurdle to understanding how and why virtualization is continually revolutionizing IT is that the flexibility it creates is often most helpful at very large scales (like data centers with tens of thousands of servers) that aren't familiar to most people. In the next section, we'll see how this flexibility plays out on a massive scale.

To the Cloud

Before we look at what "the cloud" is, I want to take a step back and talk about something that will sound unrelated: money. One of the really great things money does is give us common, easily divisible units we can exchange for the goods and services we need. When we don't have money, we have to trade goods and services to get it, and before money was invented, humans had to trade goods and services for other goods and services.

Let's say I'm starving and all I have is a hammer, and you just so happen to have a chicken. I offer to build you something with my hammer, but all you really want is a hammer of your own. This might sound like a match made in heaven, but what if my hammer is actually worth at least five chickens, and you just have one? I can't give you a fifth of a hammer, and once I trade the hammer for your chicken, I can't use it to build anything else. I have to choose between going without food and wasting most of my hammer's value. If only my hammer was money!

In the same vein, a top-of-the-line physical server can be a bit like a really expensive hammer. It has the resources to do *a lot* of work, but it is often underused because you would have to find tasks in which to take advantage of its various resources. Installing a hypervisor on this server sets us on the path to using it in a new, more productive way.

In this new model, servers become (a little) less like hammers and (a little) more like money. I still can't trade a fifth of my hammer for a chicken, but a powerful physical server has the flexibility to host one huge VM, two large VMs, or one large VM and a dozen tiny ones—and this configuration can change constantly!

As the number of VM hosts and guest VMs increases, so do the options for distributing VMs across hosts to minimize unused resources (see Figure 22-19). At larger scales, the hosts become more and more like a pool of common, easily divisible units we can use to solve problems—more and more like money.

Figure 22-19
No vacancy on these hosts

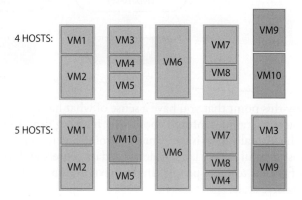

Many organizations use this flexibility to make their own data centers more efficient, but its most impressive use is in the services offered by massive cloud computing providers. These companies cobble together massive pools of computing resources from data centers all around the world.

When we talk about *the cloud*, we're talking not just about friendly file-storage services like Dropbox or Google Drive, but about all of the services that enable us to dip into the vast pools of computing resources sold by Amazon (see Figure 22-20), Microsoft, and many other companies over the open Internet. The technology at the heart of these innovative services is virtualization (and they apply it to far more than just virtual servers).

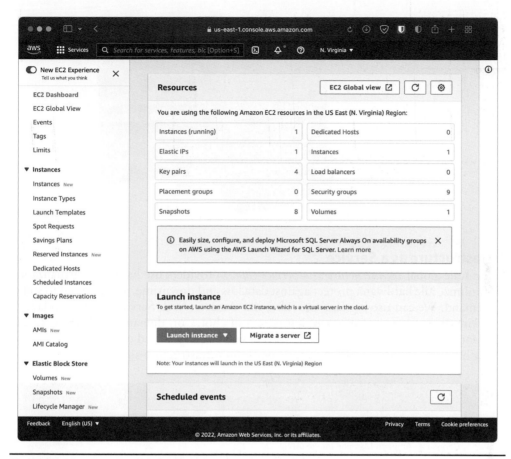

Figure 22-20   Amazon Web Services Management Console

The Service-Layer Cake

Service is the key to understanding the cloud. At the hardware level, we'd have trouble telling the difference between the cloud and the servers and networks that comprise the Internet as a whole. We use the servers and networks of the cloud through layers of software that add great value to the underlying hardware by making it simple to perform complex tasks or manage powerful hardware. As end users we generally interact with just the sweet software icing of the service-layer cake—Web applications like Dropbox, Gmail, and Facebook, which have been built atop it. The rest of the cake exists largely to support Web applications like these and their developers. Let's slice it open (see Figure 22-21) and start at the bottom.

Figure 22-21
A tasty three-
layer cake

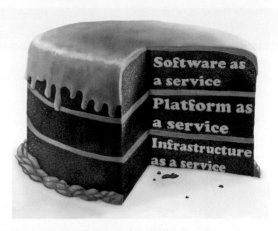

Infrastructure as a Service

Large-scale global *Infrastructure as a Service (IaaS)* providers use hardware virtualization to minimize idle hardware, protect against data loss and downtime, and respond to spikes in demand. We can use big IaaS providers like Amazon Web Services (AWS) to launch new virtual servers using an operating system of choice on demand (see Figure 22-22) for pennies an hour. The beauty of IaaS is that you no longer need to purchase expensive, heavy hardware. You are using Amazon's powerful infrastructure as a service.

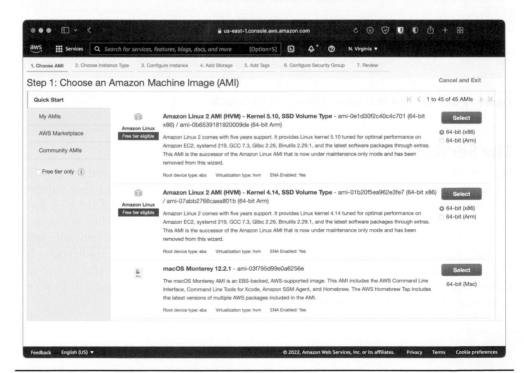

Figure 22-22   Creating an instance on AWS

A huge number of Web sites are really more easily understood if you use the term *Web applications.* If you want to access Mike Meyers' videos, you go to https://hub.totalsem .com. This Web site is really an application that you use to watch videos, practice simulation questions, and so forth. This Web application is a great tool, but as more people access the application, we often need to add more capacity so you won't yell at us for a slow server. Luckily, our application is designed to run distributed across multiple servers. If we need more servers, we just add as many more virtual servers as we need. But even this is just scratching the surface. AWS provides many of the services needed to drive popular, complex Web applications—unlimited data storage (see Figure 22-23), database servers, caching, media hosting, and more—all billed by usage.

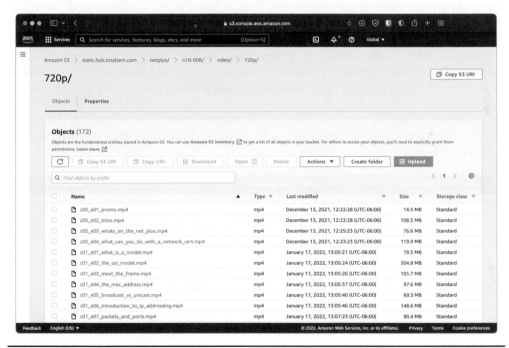

Figure 22-23   Amazon Simple Storage Service (S3)

The hitch is that, while we're no longer responsible for the hardware, we are still responsible for configuring and maintaining the operating system and software of any virtual machines we create. This can mean we have a lot of flexibility to tune it for our needs, but it also requires knowledge of the underlying OS and time to manage it. If you want someone to handle the infrastructure, the operating system, and everything else (except your application), you need to move up to Platform as a Service (PaaS).

Platform as a Service

Web applications are built by programmers. Programmers do one thing really well: they program. The problem for programmers is that a Web application needs a lot more than just a programmer. Developing a Web application requires people to manage the infrastructure: system administrators, database administrators, general network support, and so on. A Web application also needs more than just hardware and an operating system.

It needs development tools, monitoring tools, database tools, and potentially hundreds of other tools and services. Getting a Web application up and running is a big job.

A *Platform as a Service (PaaS)* provider gives programmers all the tools they need to deploy, administer, and maintain a Web application. The PaaS provider starts with some form of infrastructure, which could be provided by an IaaS, and on top of that infrastructure the provider builds a platform: a complete deployment and management system to handle every aspect of a Web application.

The important point of PaaS is that the infrastructure underneath the PaaS is largely invisible to the developer. The PaaS provider is aware of their infrastructure, but the developer cannot control it directly, and doesn't need to think about its complexity. As far as the programmer is concerned, the PaaS is just a place to deploy and run his or her application.

Heroku, one of the earliest PaaS providers, creates a simple interface on top of the IaaS offerings of AWS, further reducing the complexity of developing and scaling Web applications. Heroku's management console (see Figure 22-24) enables developers to increase or decrease the capacity of an application with a single slider, or easily set up add-ons that add a database, monitor logs, track performance, and more. It could take days for a tech or developer unfamiliar with the software and services to install, configure, and integrate a set of these services with a running application; PaaS providers help cut this down to minutes or hours.

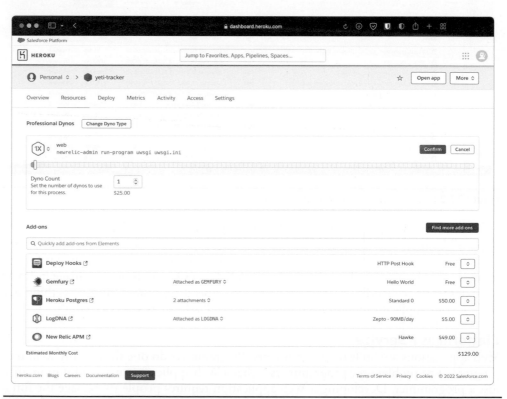

Figure 22-24   Heroku's management console

Software as a Service

Software as a Service (SaaS) sits at the top layer of the cake. SaaS shows up in a number of ways, but the best examples are the Web applications we just discussed. Some Web applications, such as Total Seminars Training Hub, charge for access. Other Web applications, like Google Maps, are offered for free. Users of these Web applications don't own this software; you don't get an installation DVD, nor is it something you can download once and keep using. If you want to use a Web application, you must get on the Internet and access the site. While this may seem like a disadvantage at first, the SaaS model provides access to necessary applications wherever you have an Internet connection, often without having to carry data with you or regularly update software. At the enterprise level, the subscription model of many SaaS providers makes it easier to budget and keep hundreds or thousands of computers up to date (see Figure 22-25).

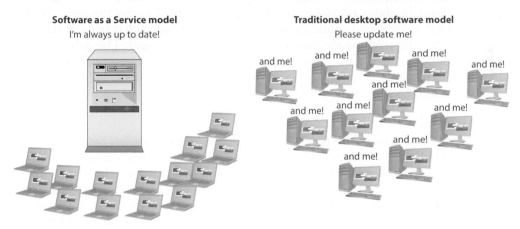

Figure 22-25   SaaS versus updating every desktop

The challenge to defining SaaS perfectly is an argument that almost anything you access on the Internet could be called SaaS. A decade ago we would've called the Google search engine a Web site, but it provides a service (search) that you do not own and that you must access on the Internet. If you're on the Internet, you're arguably always using SaaS.

It isn't all icing, though. In exchange for the flexibility of using public, third-party SaaS, you often have to trade strict control of your data. Security might not be crucial when someone uses Google Drive to draft a blog post, but many companies are concerned about sensitive intellectual property or business secrets traveling through untrusted networks and being stored on servers they don't control.

 EXAM TIP   Know the differences between basic cloud concepts such as SaaS, IaaS, and PaaS.

Ownership and Access

Security concerns like those just discussed don't mean organizations have to forfeit all of the advantages of cloud computing, but they do make their management think hard about the trade-offs between cost, control, customization, and privacy. Some organizations also have unique capacity, performance, or other needs no existing cloud provider can meet. Each organization makes its own decisions about these trade-offs, but the result is usually a cloud network that can be described as public, private, community, or hybrid.

Public Cloud

Most folks usually just interact with a *public cloud,* a term used to describe software, platforms, and infrastructure delivered through networks that the general public can use. When we talk about *the* cloud, this is what we mean. Out on the open, public Internet, cloud services and applications can collaborate in ways that make it easier to think of them collectively as *the cloud* than as many public clouds. The public doesn't *own* this cloud—the hardware is often owned by companies like Amazon, Google, and Microsoft—but there's nothing to stop a company like Netflix from building its Web application atop the IaaS offerings of all three of these companies at once.

Private Cloud

If a business wants some of the flexibility of the cloud, needs complete ownership of its data, and can afford both, it can build an internal cloud the business actually owns—a *private cloud.* A security-minded company with enough resources could build an internal IaaS network in an onsite data center. Departments within the company could create and destroy virtual machines as needed and develop SaaS to meet collaboration, planning, or task and time management needs all without sending the data over the open Internet. A company with these needs but without the space or knowledge to build and maintain a private cloud can also contract a third party to maintain or host it.

Community Cloud

While a community center is usually a public gathering place for those in the community it serves, a *community cloud* is more like a private cloud paid for and used by more than one organization. Community clouds aren't run by a city or state for citizens' use; the community in this case is a group of organizations with similar goals or needs. If you're a military contractor working on classified projects, wouldn't it be nice to share the burden of defending your cloud against sophisticated attackers sponsored by foreign states with other military and intelligence contractors?

Hybrid Cloud

Sometimes we *can* have our cake and eat it too. Not all data is crucial, and not every document is a secret. Needs that an organization can only meet in-house might be less important than keeping an application running when demand exceeds what it can handle onsite. We can build a *hybrid cloud* by connecting some combination of public, private, and community clouds, allowing communication between them. Using a hybrid cloud model can mean not having to maintain a private cloud powerful enough to meet peak demand—an application can grow into a public cloud instead of grind to a halt, a technique called *cloud bursting*.

But a hybrid cloud isn't just about letting one Web application span two types of cloud—it's also about integrating services across them. Let's take a look at how Jimmy could use a hybrid cloud to expand his business.

 EXAM TIP   Know the differences between public, private, community, and hybrid cloud models.

Jimmy runs a national chain of sandwich shops and is looking into drone-delivered lunch. He'll need a new application in his private cloud to calculate routes and track drones, and that application will have to integrate with the existing order-tracking application in his private cloud. But then he'll also need to integrate it with a third-party weather application in the public cloud to avoid sending drones out in a blizzard, and a flight-plan application running in a community cloud to avoid other drones, helicopters, and aircraft (and vice versa). The sum of these integrated services and applications *is* the hybrid cloud that will power Jimmy's drone-delivered lunch.

Cloud Characteristics

When it comes to whether and how to make use of cloud computing, every organization has to weigh the positives and negatives of the cloud against a more traditional approach. Different organizations will care about different things, but let's take a moment to discuss five cloud characteristics that CompTIA wants you to know for the exam.

Shared Resources

Cloud computing focuses less on individual physical systems and more on the underlying resources. Instead of renting out each physical unit separately, cloud providers aggregate them into a pool of *shared resources* that they make available on-demand. The provider's customers draw from this pool as they need additional resources and release them back into the pool when they are done.

This flexibility is one of the cloud's big strengths. For example, this makes it practical to spin up tons of resources to render special-effects animations for an upcoming movie and release the resources once the job's done. Unfortunately, this also means jobs for other users are likely running on the same hardware—and that's not always acceptable.

Most cloud neighbors are fine, but you never know! There's always a chance that a cloud neighbor could be intentionally exploiting a weakness in the host system to spy on their neighbors, could get hacked or infected with malware, or could overuse shared resources in a way that hinders performance for everyone else.

Rapid Elasticity

Let's say you start a new Web application. If you use an IaaS provider such as Amazon, you can start with a single server and get your new Web application out there. But what happens if your application gets really, really popular? No problem! Using AWS features, you can easily expand the number of servers, even spread them out geographically, with just a click of the switch. This capability is known as *rapid elasticity*.

Metered Utilization

Ah, the biggest downside to using someone else's cloud: you have to write a check to whoever is doing the work for you—and boy can these cloud providers get creative about how to charge you! In many cases they charge a precise *metered utilization* rate based on factors such as the traffic that goes in and out of your Web application and how much data you store. In other cases you pay for the exact amount of time that every single one of your virtualized servers is running.

Regardless of how costs are measured, this differs from more traditional hosting with a fixed monthly or yearly fee. You pay for what resources you use, rather than a more general fee for all the hardware of a system.

High Availability

For every small organization with a single physical server doing some critical job 24 hours a day, there's a tech who doesn't sleep well at night. All kinds of problems can knock a single system out of commission for hours or days, and many organizations can't justify the cost of hiring someone to keep an eye on the server closet all night just in case.

Large cloud providers, however, have an army of automated systems and technicians perpetually watching over their global network of data centers. This already reduces the odds of an extended outage, enabling many cloud providers to promise that most of their services will be available 99.9 percent of the time or more.

Cloud computing enables organizations to get as close to 100 percent uptime as they can afford. Sometimes this is as simple as paying the cloud provider extra for a service to guarantee greater uptime. Organizations can also design their cloud deployments for *high availability*—for example, they can set up redundant servers all around the world and automatically reroute traffic whenever a server is down.

 NOTE High availability isn't limited to the cloud—it is a huge topic in its own right! If you continue on to take the CompTIA Network+ exam, you'll learn more about how important high availability is in networking and data centers.

File Synchronization

Cloud file storage services, like Dropbox and Box, were early smash successes in getting people to move to the cloud for some of their storage needs. Most of these services provide file *synchronization* apps that propagate file changes to the storage provider on to any other connected devices. Synchronization apps make it easy to access the same set of files across multiple devices.

These days, file synchronization is often bundled with productivity suites (i.e., collections of apps that enable you to edit documents, spreadsheets, presentations, and so on) such as Microsoft 365 and Google Workspaces. Regardless of how your organization approaches it, file synchronization makes it easier for users to collaborate or work on the same files from multiple devices without having to shuffle files around.

Unfortunately, cloud-based file synchronization also means giving up a lot of control over the organization's files to the provider. It also makes it easier for disgruntled users to pass documents on to people who shouldn't have access to them.

Desktop Virtualization

Desktop virtualization tries to apply the flexibility associated with both hardware virtualization and cloud computing to user workstations. The most common forms of *desktop virtualization* entail using a client program on one device to connect to a *virtual desktop*, providing access to a user's files and applications.

If each human user still needs a system to access their virtual desktop, why would an organization be eager to also set aside server resources for them? Some of the big reasons are control, security, and management. Every user walking around with a laptop stuffed to the gills with sensitive organization data and applications is a huge risk! Desktop virtualization enables users to access the apps and files they need without storing them on local devices that could get lost or stolen at any time.

Some folks do desktop virtualization with just a remote desktop client and a user account on a multiuser OS such as Windows Server. The CompTIA A+ 1101 objectives focus on a form called *virtual desktop infrastructure (VDI)*, in which each user's client program connects to an automatically managed virtual machine running on a central server. In many organizations these VDI servers will be on premises, but it's also possible to set up VDI servers in the cloud.

 NOTE CompTIA didn't include cloud-based Desktop as a Service (DaaS) in the 1101 objectives, but any organization considering cloud-based VDI will likely consider using DaaS as well. They both accomplish roughly the same goal, but differ when it comes to cost, licensing, control, flexibility, and management.

Chapter Review

Questions

1. Upgrading which component of a host machine would most likely enable you to run more virtual machines simultaneously?

    A. CPU

    B. Hard drive

    C. RAM

    D. Windows

2. Which of the following could an organization use to enable its users to access their files and applications from multiple devices?

   A. Virtual desktop

   B. Client-side virtual machine

   C. File-synchronization service

   D. Virtual memory

3. What feature lets you save a VM's state so you can quickly restore to that point? (Choose two.)

   A. Checkpoint

   B. Save

   C. Snapshot

   D. Zip

4. What do you need to install a legal copy of Windows 10 into a virtual machine using VirtualBox?

   A. A valid Windows 10 license

   B. Valid Windows 10 installation media

   C. A valid ESXi key

   D. A second NIC

5. Which of the following is an advantage of a virtual machine over a physical machine?

   A. Increased performance

   B. Hardware consolidation

   C. No backups needed

   D. Operating systems included

6. Janelle wants to start a new photo-sharing service for real pictures of Bigfoot, but doesn't own any servers. How can she quickly create a new server to run her service?

   A. Public cloud

   B. Private cloud

   C. Community cloud

   D. Hybrid cloud

7. After the unforeseen failure of her Bigfoot-picture-sharing service, bgFootr— which got hacked when she failed to stay on top of her security updates—Janelle has a great new idea for a new service to report Loch Ness Monster sightings. What service would help keep her from having to play system administrator?

   A. Software as a Service

   B. Infrastructure as a Service

   C. Platform as a Service

   D. Network as a Service

8. Which kind of hypervisor is installed and run from within a full operating system?

   A. Bare-metal

   B. Virtual-metal

   C. Type-1

   D. Type-2

9. When a virtual machine is not running, how is it stored?

   A. Firmware

   B. RAM drive

   C. Optical disc

   D. Files

10. BigTracks is a successful Bigfoot-tracking company using an internal service to manage all of its automated Bigfoot monitoring stations. A Bigfoot migration has caused a massive increase in the amount of audio and video sent back from their stations. In order to add short-term capacity, they can create new servers in the public cloud. What model of cloud computing does this describe?

    A. Public cloud

    B. Private cloud

    C. Community cloud

    D. Hybrid cloud

Answers

1. **C.** Adding more RAM will enable you to run more simultaneous VMs. Upgrading a hard drive could help, but it's not the best answer here.

2. **A.** Users can access a virtual desktop, which may include their files and applications, from different devices.

3. **A, C.** The saved state of a VM is called a snapshot or checkpoint. Not to be confused with a true backup.

4. **A.** You need a valid Windows 10 license to run Windows legally.

5. **B.** A big benefit of hardware virtualization is hardware consolidation.

6. **A.** Using the public cloud will enable Janelle to quickly create the servers she needs.

7. **C.** By switching to a PaaS, Janelle can concentrate on creating her service and leave the lower-level administration up to the PaaS provider.

8. **D.** A Type-2 hypervisor runs inside a full operating system.

9. **D.** VMs are just files, usually stored on a hard drive.

10. **D.** BigTracks is creating a hybrid cloud by connecting its internal private cloud to a public cloud to quickly expand capacity.

8. Which kind of hypervisor is installed and run from within a full operating system?

   A. Bare-metal

   B. Virtualized

   C. Type 1

   D. Type 2

9. When a virtual machine is not running, how is it stored?

   A. In RAM

   B. RAM drive

   C. Optical disc

   D. Files

10. BizTrack is a successful flight-tracking company using an internal service to manage all of its automated flight monitoring stations. A big fleet migration has caused a massive increase in the amount of audio and video sent back from their stations. In order to add short-term capacity they can create new servers in the public cloud. What model of cloud computing does this describe?

   A. Public cloud

   B. Private cloud

   C. Community cloud

   D. Hybrid cloud

Answers

1. C. Adding more RAM will enable you to run more simultaneously. VMs. Upgrading a hard drive could help but it's not the best answer here.

2. C. It lets you access a virtual desktop, which may include data, files, and applications from different devices.

3. A, C. The saved state of a VM is called a snapshot, or the pause. Not to be confused with a stored state.

4. A. You need a 64-bit Windows 10 license to run 8 Windows 10 apps.

5. B. A type 1 hypervisor is hardware virtualization. It is not a container domain.

6. A. Leaving the public cloud will enable the family to quickly create the apps in its model.

7. C. By switching to a PaaS, familie can concentrate on the learning, bear service and leave the lower-level administration up to the PaaS provider.

8. D. A Type 2 hypervisor runs inside a full operating system.

9. D. A VM at rest is usually stored on a hard drive.

10. D. BizTrack is creating a hybrid cloud because they retain their internal private cloud to a public cloud to quickly expand capacity.

CHAPTER 23

Portable Computing

In this chapter, you will learn how to

- Describe the many types of portable computing devices available
- Explain ways to expand portable computers
- Manage and maintain portable computers
- Upgrade and repair portable computers
- Troubleshoot portable computers

There are times when the walls close in, when you need a change of scenery to get that elusive spark that inspires greatness...or sometimes you just need to get away from your coworkers for a few hours because they're driving you nuts! For many occupations, that's difficult to do. You need access to your documents and spreadsheets; you can't function without e-mail or the Internet. In short, you need a computer to get your job done.

Portable computing devices combine mobility with accessibility to bring you the best of both worlds; portables enable you to take some or even all of your computing capabilities with you when you go. Featuring all the bells and whistles of a desktop system, many portables offer a seamless transition from desk to café table.

This chapter looks at the classic portable computer, essentially a desktop transformed into a mobile format. Classic portables usually run the same operating systems as their desktop counterparts—Windows, macOS, or Linux. However there are some operating systems—like Chrome OS, based on Linux—that are unique to portable computers.

Historical/Conceptual

Portable Computing Devices

All portable devices share certain features. For output, they use LCD screens, although these vary from 20-inch behemoths to diminutive 10-inch displays. Portable computing devices employ sound of varying quality, from bland mono playback to fairly nice faux-surround reproductions. All of them run on DC electricity stored in batteries when not plugged into an AC outlet.

When asked about portable computing devices, most folks describe the traditional clamshell *notebook* computer, such as the one shown in Figure 23-1, with built-in LCD monitor, keyboard, and input device (a trackpad, in this case). The notebook is also called a portable or a laptop. All the terms are synonymous. A typical laptop functions as a fully standalone computer, but there are always trade-offs that come with portability. Common trade-offs are price, weight, size, battery life, computing power, input devices, ports, drives, support for hardware upgrades, storage capacity, durability, and the quality of any warranty/support programs. Finding the *right* portable is easier if you can figure out what it will be used for and narrow your search to only devices with essential features and exclude those with unacceptable trade-offs.

Figure 23-1
An older notebook computer

Taxonomy

The companies making mobile and portable devices experiment a lot, so the terms we use to describe these devices are always in flux. New device categories and their related marketing terms may flood the market and blur the lines between existing categories one year, only to fall out of use within a few years.

The CompTIA A+ objectives don't focus on these terms and categories, but it's still a good idea to keep up with them. Knowing how to categorize portable and mobile devices makes it easier to identify devices that are a good fit for specific uses. It also helps you apply the best troubleshooting procedures for a given device. These categories can be slippery, so don't think of them as mutually exclusive. Sometimes more than one of these terms apply to a single device.

Portable vs. Mobile

Over the years, the lines between portable computing devices such as laptops and mobile devices such as smartphones have blurred. Smartphones have become more powerful, laptops have incorporated touch screens and smaller form factors, and many tablets allow the use of external keyboards and mice. Despite these blurred lines, portable computing devices and mobile devices are separate concepts, with unique use cases and applications. A good rule of thumb is to look at the operating system that the device uses. If it uses the same operating system as its desktop counterparts, it is a portable device. If it uses a dedicated mobile operating system like Android, iOS, or iPadOS, it is a mobile device.

Types of Laptops

There are many terms that address the size or purpose of traditional clamshell laptops/ notebooks, but over time, a lot of these distinctions have become less important. As the technology has been developed, use cases for many laptops have started to overlap. Terms like ultrabook, thin and light, and business laptop are mostly for marketing at this point, because apart from the examples I'm about to mention, laptops in general are a lot thinner, lighter, and more powerful than they were when many of these terms were coined (see Figure 23-2).

Figure 23-2
Older full-size laptop (left) versus the thin-slice aesthetic of the MacBook Air (right)

- *Gaming laptops*, which tend to have flashy designs, typically come loaded with the latest top-end processors, graphics cards, RAM, SSDs, and large, high-quality displays. They also tend to come with thoughtful touches like RGB lighting.

- A *Chromebook* is a portable computer running Google's Linux-based Chrome OS. Chrome OS is a proprietary Linux-based operating system developed by Google. Thanks to Chrome OS, Chromebooks offer an experience focused on Web applications by making use of virtually unlimited data storage in the cloud and Software as a Service (SaaS) applications available over the Web. Using primarily cloud-based applications and storage allows users to get by with less powerful hardware, and as a result saves on cost. Because they offload so much work, Chromebooks have a reputation for being cheap and light, but premium Chromebooks are increasingly common.

- *2-in-1s* are touch-screen computers somewhere along the spectrum from laptop-and-tablet to tablet-and-laptop. We'll take a closer look at pure mobile tablets (such as the Apple iPad and various Android tablets) in Chapter 24. Some 2-in-1s have removable screens that separate from the rest of the laptop to function as a tablet (see Figure 23-3). Others have special hinges that enable you to fold the entire device up and use it in tablet form. 2-in-1s are also sometimes referred to as *convertibles* or *hybrids*.

Figure 23-3
Microsoft Surface
Pro 6 with its
keyboard cover
(Used with
permission from
Microsoft)

 NOTE Innovative portable form factors like those in the 2-in-1 category
are often designed to be handled, rotated, flipped, and passed around. As
a result, Windows now supports the automatic screen-rotation tricks we've
seen on smartphones and tablets for years. Anyone who has used a device
like this for long knows that occasionally you'll run into problems with the
automatic screen-orientation sensor; see the "Troubleshooting Portable
Computers" section later in the chapter for fixes.

1101

Input Devices

Portable computers come with a variety of input devices. Most have a fully functional keyboard and a device to control the mouse pointer.

Keyboard Quirks

Laptop keyboards differ somewhat from those of desktop computers, primarily because manufacturers have to cram all the keys onto a smaller form factor. They use the QWERTY format, but manufacturers make choices with key size and placement of the non-alphabet characters.

Almost every portable keyboard uses a Function (FN) key to enable some keys to perform an extra duty. You'll either hold the FN key to access the extra function, or you'll hold it to access the traditional function (the latter is more common with extra functions on the F1–F12 keys). On some systems, you can also configure this behavior. Figure 23-4 compares a laptop keyboard with a standard desktop keyboard. Note that the former has no separate number pad on the right and is a more compact layout.

Figure 23-4   Keyboard comparison

Pointing Devices

Portables need a way to control your mouse pointer, but their smaller size requires manu-facturers to come up with clever solutions. Beyond the built-in solutions, portables usu-ally have USB ports and can use every type of pointing device you'd see on a desktop. Early portables used *trackballs*, often plugged in like a mouse and clipped to the side of the case. Other models with trackballs placed them in front of the keyboard at the edge of the case nearest the user, or behind the keyboard at the edge nearest the screen.

 NOTE   The FN key also enables you to toggle other features specific to a portable, such as GPS tracking or the keyboard backlight, to save battery life.

The next wave to hit the laptop market was IBM's TrackPoint device, a joystick the size of a pencil eraser, situated in the center of the keyboard (see Figure 23-5). With the TrackPoint, you can move the pointer around without taking your fingers away from the "home" typing position. You use a forefinger to push the joystick around, and then click or right-click, using two buttons below the spacebar. This type of pointing device has since been licensed for use by other manufacturers, and while it continues to appear on some business-focused laptops today, it has primarily been replaced by our next link in the pointing device chain.

Figure 23-5
IBM TrackPoint

By far the most common laptop pointing device found today is the *trackpad* (see Figure 23-6)—a flat, touch-sensitive pad just in front of the keyboard. To operate a track-pad, you simply glide your finger across its surface to move the pointer and tap or press the surface once or twice to single- or double-click. You can also click by using buttons just below the pad on some older devices. Most people get the hang of this technique after just a few minutes of practice. The main advantage of the trackpad over previous laptop pointing devices is that it uses few moving parts—a fact that can really extend the life of a hard-working laptop.

Figure 23-6
Trackpad on
a laptop

 EXAM TIP Use the Settings | Devices | Mouse dialog box or the Mouse applet in Control Panel for *trackpad configuration*. You can change sensitivity and much more in either tool.

Many manufacturers today include a multitouch trackpad that enables you to perform gestures, or actions with multiple fingers, such as scrolling up and down or swiping to another screen or desktop. The *Multi-Touch trackpad* on Apple's laptops pioneered such great improvements to the laptop-pointing-device experience that the lack of a mouse is no longer a handicap on many laptops.

 TIP In the past it was common to accidentally "use" a trackpad with your palm while typing, so you may find some devices with a hardware switch or FN key combination for disabling the trackpad. More recent trackpads are usually capable of detecting and ignoring accidental input like this on their own.

Continuing the trend of mobile's influence on more traditional portables, a number of laptops come equipped with a *touch screen* like you would find on a smartphone or tablet, again relying heavily on gestures to enable users to fluidly perform complex actions. In some cases these are otherwise very traditional laptops that happen to include a touch screen, but in other cases they are devices that are intended to be used as both a tablet *and* a laptop. Many of these touch screens are designed to take advantage of dedicated touch pens, also known as a stylus. These pens enable users to be more precise with their touch-screen interactions, hand write notes, draw, and keep the screen free of fingerprints. We'll take a closer look at touch screens when we discuss mobile devices in Chapter 24.

Webcams and Microphones

The ability to communicate with others through real-time video is such a common expectation of mobile and portable devices these days that most of these devices (including laptops) come equipped with some sort of front-facing video camera—a *webcam* in the case of laptops—and one or more built-in microphones. A single *microphone* may be suitable for picking up the user's voice, and additional microphones can help noise-cancellation routines improve the audio quality.

Even though most of us may just use the microphone in conjunction with the webcam, a growing number of programs support voice commands. Microsoft, for example, promotes its *Cortana* functionality built into Windows 10 (and optionally added to Windows 11). Any Windows 10 or 11 user on a system with a microphone, as long as they can live with letting Windows listen in on them, can perform voice searches and other actions from anywhere within earshot (mic-shot?) of their device.

The downside of these input devices becoming ubiquitous is the security risk they pose. It might be bad enough if a nefarious hacker or government agency (from any country) managed to get malware into my computer to see everything I click or type, but the risks are amplified if they can also hear and see anything going on near the device. It's common enough for webcams to include a light that indicates when they're recording, but built-in microphones don't do the same. In some cases, vulnerabilities allow the recording indicator to be disabled anyway.

Display Types

Laptops come in a variety of sizes and at varying costs. One major contributor to the overall cost of a laptop is the size of the LCD screen. Most laptops offer a range between 10.1-inch to 17.3-inch screens (measured diagonally), while a few offer just over 20-inch screens.

In the past, 4:3 aspect ratio screens were common, but these days it's hard to find one on anything but special-purpose or ruggedized laptops; almost all regular laptops come in one of two widescreen format ratios. *Aspect ratio* is the comparison of the screen width to the screen height, as you'll recall from Chapter 17. While widescreens can have varying aspect ratios, *almost* all of the screens you find in present-day laptops will be 16:9 or 16:10.

 EXAM TIP Laptop LCDs are the same in almost every way as desktop LCDs with a TFT screen and a LED backlight (add an inverter and swap in a CCFL backlight for older laptops). You know all about these screens from Chapter 17. Expect questions about laptop displays but know that they're pretty much the same as desktop displays. The only major difference is that the LCD frame contains an antenna, and may contain a camera and microphone, but we'll discuss this later in the chapter.

Laptop screens typically come with one of two types of finish: matte or high-gloss. The matte finish was the industry standard for many years and offered a good trade-off between color richness and glare reduction. The better screens have a wide viewing angle and decent response time. The major drawback for matte-finished laptop screens is that they wash out a lot in bright light. Using such a laptop at an outdoor café, for example, can be very difficult without a bright enough display.

Manufacturers released high-gloss laptop screens more than a decade ago, and they rapidly took over many store shelves. The high-gloss finish offers sharper contrast, richer colors, and wider viewing angles when compared to the matte screens. The drawback to the high-gloss screens is that, contrary to what the manufacturers claim, they pick up lots of reflection from nearby objects, including the user! So, although they're usable outside during the day, you'll need to contend with increased reflection as well. Higher-end laptops include various anti-reflective solutions to mitigate this issue, with varying degrees of success.

With the advent of LED backlighting for LCD panels, many manufacturers have switched back to an anti-glare screen, though they're not quite the matte screens of old. When the LED brightness is up high, these are lovely screens. (See the "Troubleshooting Portable Computers" section, later in this chapter, for issues specific to LED-backlit portables.)

As with other LCD technologies that you'll recall from Chapter 17, most LCD/LED screens initially used *twisted nematic (TN)* technology. Most modern laptop screens use *in-plane switching (IPS)* panels for the greater viewing angle and better color quality. You'll mostly find TN panels on older portables.

 EXAM TIP You may recall from Chapter 17 that there is another LCD panel type, *vertical alignment (VA)*. While you're very unlikely to encounter a VA panel on a laptop, it is possible and CompTIA may ask about one on the A+ 1101 exam. Just be aware that while they are uncommon for laptops, it isn't impossible.

Organic light-emitting diode (OLED) displays are becoming more common on laptops (originally, due to their cost, they were limited primarily to large desktop monitors and TVs). OLED screens sip energy when compared to LCDs, and while less expensive and more common than they used to be, you'll mostly find them on smartphones and tablets today. Chapter 24 discusses OLED screen technology.

 EXAM TIP The CompTIA A+ 1101 exam objectives may refer to OLED displays for laptops. Manufacturers were slow to incorporate OLED display technology in laptops, but OLED displays have gradually seen more adoption in recent years, particularly on higher-end devices. You may not see many in the wild yet, but know they exist for the exam!

Extending Portable Computers

In the dark ages of mobile computing, you had to shell out top dollar for any device that would operate unplugged, and what you purchased was what you got. Upgrade a laptop? Connect to external devices? You had few if any options, so you simply paid for a device that would be way behind the technology curve within a year and functionally obsolete within two.

Portable computers today offer a few ways to enhance their capabilities. Most feature external ports that enable you to add completely new functions, such as attaching a scanner, mobile printer, or both. You can take advantage of the latest wireless technology breakthrough simply by slipping a card into the appropriate slot on the laptop.

I'll first describe single-function ports, and then turn to networking options. Next, I'll cover card slots, and then finish with a discussion of general-purpose ports.

Single-Function Ports

All portable computers come with one or more single-function ports. You'd have a hard time finding a portable computing device that doesn't have an audio jack, for example. Laptops often provide a video port for hooking up an external monitor, though wireless screen sharing and screencasting are gaining popularity as an alternative.

 NOTE Some laptop manufacturers, in a quest to make increasingly thinner and lighter devices, have moved away from including single-function ports like HDMI. Not only have they done away with most single-function ports, but they have also removed some common general-purpose ports like USB-A, in favor of a smaller number of USB-C or Thunderbolt ports. This port deficiency is often compensated for with a USB-C dongle, replacing on-board ports with optional expansion instead.

Ports work the same way on portable computers as they do on desktop models. You plug in a device to a particular port and, as long as the operating system has the proper drivers, you will have a functioning device when you boot.

Audio

Most portable computers have a 3.5-mm audio jack that is used for audio-out. This jack is quite often a combined *headset jack* that also supports microphone-in on the same three-ring plug. Older laptops might have a similarly sized microphone-in jack (see Figure 23-7), though built-in microphones are most common. You can plug in headphones, regular PC speakers, or even a nice surround sound setup to enable the laptop to play music just as well as a desktop computer can.

You can control the sound (both out and in) through the appropriate Settings app area or Control Panel applet in Windows, System Preferences in macOS, or some kind of switches on the laptop. The portable shown in Figure 23-8, for example, enables you to mute the speakers by pressing a special mute button above the keyboard. Other portables

Figure 23-7
3.5-mm audio
jacks

use a combination of the FN key and another key to toggle mute on and off, as well as to play, pause, fast-forward, and rewind audio (or any other media options). Most portables have volume up/down controls in the same location.

As Bluetooth wireless headphones have increased in popularity, some laptop manufacturers have excluded a dedicated 3.5-mm audio jack altogether. This isn't a common or particularly popular move, but if you encounter a portable device with no dedicated audio jacks, don't be surprised, because you heard about it here first.

Figure 23-8
The mute button
on a laptop

Display

Most laptops support a second monitor via a digital port of some sort. There are many of these—you may find HDMI (including Mini-HDMI and Micro-HDMI) or Display-Port (including USB Type-C and Thunderbolt); on ancient or special-purpose portables, there's even a chance you may still find a VGA or DVI port. With a second monitor attached, you can duplicate your screen to the new monitor, or extend your desktop across both displays, letting you move windows between them. Not all portables can do all variations, but they're more common than not.

Most portables use the FN key plus another key on the keyboard to cycle through display options. To engage the second monitor or to cycle through the modes, hold the FN key and press F8 (see Figure 23-9).

Figure 23-9
Laptop keyboard
showing
Function (FN)
key that enables
you to access
additional key
options, as on
the F8 key

NOTE Although many laptops use the Function key method to cycle the monitor selections, that's not always the case. You might have to pop into Settings to do so. Just be assured that if the laptop has a video output port, you can cycle through monitor choices!

You can control what the external monitor shows by adjusting your operating system's display settings. In Windows 10/11, this is all contained in the Display area of the Settings app. Open the Settings app and navigate to System | Display; from there scroll down till you find the Multiple displays section (see Figure 23-10). You'll see a drop-down menu with several options. *Extend these displays* makes your desktop encompass both the laptop and the external monitor. *Duplicate these displays* places the same thing on both displays. You'd duplicate these displays for a presentation, for example, rather than for a workspace.

Near-Field Scanner

It isn't really a port, but you'll find some portable computers—especially ones designed for and marketed to business users—with a very thin slot the width of a credit card on one side or the other. No, it isn't an expansion or memory card slot—it's a *smart card reader*. If you've seen a credit or debit card with a little metallic chip (see Figure 23-11), you've seen a smart card. Smart card readers make use of a *near-field scanner*. While smart cards have tons of uses, what matters here is that you can log in to a portable device (if it has a built-in or USB smart card reader) using *your* smart card and a PIN number. We'll go into a little more detail on the use of smart cards for authentication in Chapter 27.

Networking Options

Rarely will you find a portable computer without at least one network connection option. Today's portables come with some combination of 802.11, Bluetooth, and wired Ethernet connections. Generally they work exactly as you've seen in previous chapters, but you may stumble into a few issues that are unique to portables. (Mobile devices—tablets, smartphones—have even more options, as you'll see in Chapter 24.)

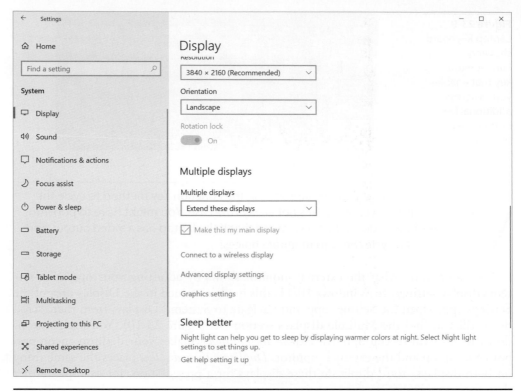

Figure 23-10 Multiple-display options menu in Windows 10

Figure 23-11
Smart card

802.11 Wireless

Most portables today have Wi-Fi built directly into the chipset for connecting the device to a wireless access point (WAP) and from there to a bigger network, such as the Internet. The 802.11n standard is common on older laptops; newer portable computers use 802.11ac (Wi-Fi 5) or 802.11ax (Wi-Fi 6).

NOTE While the newest portables are shipping with 802.11ax, which is backward compatible with older standards, be aware that, especially as portables are getting powerful enough to live longer useful lives, you may see a few previous standards built into devices in the wild.

Bluetooth

802.11 isn't the only wireless technology commonly found in portable devices. Nearly all modern portables use Bluetooth as well. Bluetooth is really handy on a laptop because, as you may recall from Chapter 20, it enables you to add wireless peripherals such as mice, keyboards, and headsets, as well as communicate with smartphones, speakers, and other Bluetooth devices.

Hardware Switches

Portable computers that come with wireless technologies such as 802.11, mobile broadband, GPS, or Bluetooth have some form of on/off switch to toggle the antenna off or on so that you may use the laptop in areas where emissions aren't allowed (like a commercial aircraft, hence the term "airplane mode"). The switch may be hardwired on older devices, like the one shown in Figure 23-12, or if you're using a more modern machine, will be a toggle of the FN key plus another key on the keyboard. Also, if you're not using Wi-Fi or Bluetooth, turn them off to save some electricity and lengthen the portable's battery life.

Figure 23-12
Wireless switch

EXAM TIP Hardware switches or special Function key toggles enable you to switch features on and off, such as wireless networking, cellular networking, and Bluetooth. Toggle them off when in a scenario where battery life takes priority over networking.

Wired Ethernet

Some *full-size* laptops have an RJ45 wired Ethernet connection like the one shown in Figure 23-13. These work exactly like any other Ethernet jack—they have link lights and connect via UTP cable. Be aware, however, that wired Ethernet is one of the things many smaller contemporary laptops leave out.

Figure 23-13
Ethernet port
on laptop

There are two issues with RJ45s on laptops. First, they do not have an on/off switch like the 802.11 and Bluetooth connections. You can turn them off just like you would turn off the NIC on a desktop: disable the NIC in Device Manager or turn the NIC off in BIOS. The other issue is the relative weakness of the physical connection. If you ever plug a laptop into a wired network and the OS doesn't see a connection, check the RJ45 port.

Portable-Specific Expansion Slots

The makers of portable computers have developed methods for you to add features to a portable via specialized connections known generically as *expansion slots*. For many years, the *Personal Computer Memory Card International Association (PCMCIA)* established standards involving portable computers, especially when it came to expansion cards and slots. Once a common feature on laptops, these specialized expansion slots are almost impossible to find due to the dominance of USB. The last standard was called ExpressCard.

Storage Card Slots

Many portable computers offer one or more flash memory card slots to enable you to add storage to the portable. Particularly popular with photographers and videographers, these slots also enable the fast transfer of data from the card to the portable, and vice versa. They come in the standard varieties that you already know from Chapter 10, such as SD or microSD.

General-Purpose Ports

Portable computers rarely come with all of the hardware you want. Today's laptops usually include at least USB-A or USB-C ports to give you the option to add more hardware. A few special-purpose laptops may still provide legacy general-purpose expansion ports (PS/2, RS-232 serial ports, eSATA, FireWire, and so on) for installing peripheral hardware, but these are increasingly less common. Most portables focus on more modern ports like USB-C or Thunderbolt. If you're lucky, you will have a docking station or port replicator so you don't have to plug in all of your peripheral devices one at a time.

USB and Thunderbolt

Universal serial bus (USB) and Thunderbolt enable users to connect a device while the computer is running—you won't have to reboot the system to install a new peripheral. With USB and Thunderbolt, just plug in the device and go! Because portables don't have a desktop's multiple internal expansion capabilities, USB and Thunderbolt are some of the more popular methods for attaching peripherals to laptops and other portables (see Figure 23-14). Keeping with the trend toward fewer and more standardized general-purpose ports, many modern laptop manufacturers design their devices to charge using USB-C rather than the older AC adapters or more proprietary solutions.

Figure 23-14
Devices attached to USB on a portable PC

Docking Stations

Docking stations offer legacy and modern single- and multifunction ports (see Figure 23-15). The traditional docking station uses a proprietary connection, though the high speeds of USB 3.*x* and Thunderbolt 3 and 4 have made universal docks more common. A docking station makes an excellent companion to small portables with fewer ports.

Figure 23-15
Docking station

Port Replicators

A *port replicator* supplies one of the most critical aspects of docking stations, but in a smaller, more portable format: support for connectors that the laptop lacks. A modern USB Type-C port replicator, for example, will plug into a laptop's USB-C port and offer an array of other port types, such as VGA, HDMI, USB Type-A (2, 3, 3.1), RJ45, and more. Port replicators work great with ultra-light, ultra-thin laptops to enhance the capabilities of the machine.

Smaller port replicators are also often referred to as dongles or USB-C dongles. Modern port replicators support something called pass-through charging, enabling the user to connect their charger to the port replicator. Be careful, because sometimes a port replicator won't allow enough power through to the laptop, which can lead to slow charging, or even losing charge while plugged in.

 EXAM TIP Over time, the lines between docking station, port replicator, and dongle have blurred, and you'll hear the terms used interchangeably in the IT world. Nonetheless, there are distinctions between docking stations and port replicators. A docking station is an external device that attaches to a mobile computer or other device, has a power connection, and allows connections to peripherals such as a keyboard and a mouse. It usually also includes slots for memory cards, optical disc drives, and other devices. Docking stations are perfect for professionals who need their work desk while traveling. A port replicator is an external device that provides connections to peripherals through ports. They are also perfect for travelers who just need to access email and communicate with others. Keep these differences in mind when you're taking the CompTIA A+ exam.

USB Adapters

When you don't need access to a number of ports at once, you can often find a USB adapter for whatever you need to connect. When it comes to drives or connectors that you need only occasionally, these adapters can enable you to use a much more portable device.

Two great examples of this are wired Ethernet and optical drives. I don't know about you, but I haven't spun up an optical disc in months, nor am I sure when I last opened my laptop within a few feet of a wired Ethernet connection. A USB to Ethernet (RJ45) dongle and a USB optical drive can provide these features when and where I need them, leaving me a much smaller laptop to carry the rest of the time.

Another good use for USB adapters is updating connectivity support for older devices. A USB to Wi-Fi dongle or a USB Bluetooth adapter can let me update an old laptop to 802.11ax, or add Bluetooth to a laptop that didn't come with it built in.

 EXAM TIP The CompTIA A+ 1101 exam expects you to be familiar with USB to Ethernet adapters.

Managing and Maintaining Portable Computers

Most portables come from the factory fully assembled and configured. From a tech's standpoint, your most common work on managing and maintaining portables involves taking care of the batteries and extending the battery life through proper power management, keeping the machine clean, and avoiding excessive heat.

Everything you normally do to maintain a computer applies to portable computers. You need to keep current on OS updates and use stable, recent drivers. Use appropriate tools to monitor the health of your storage drives and clean up unwanted files. That said, let's look at issues specifically involving portables, with one caveat: because more compact or hybrid portables are often built like mobile devices, you may need to approach those devices by combining steps mentioned here with troubleshooting ideas from Chapter 25.

Batteries

Manufacturers over the years have used a few types of batteries for portable computers: Nickel-Cadmium (Ni-Cd), Nickel-Metal Hydride (Ni-MH), and *Lithium-Ion (Li-Ion)*. Today, only Li-Ion is used because that battery chemistry provides the highest energy density for the weight and has few problems with external factors.

The Care and Feeding of Batteries

In general, keep in mind the following basics. First, always store batteries in a cool place. Although a freezer might seem like an excellent storage place, the moisture, extreme freezing cold, metal racks, and food make it a bad idea. Second, keep the battery charged, at least to 70–80 percent. Many modern laptops include *optimized charging* features that can prevent your battery from charging over a certain percentage while it's plugged in, and in some cases, like with modern MacBooks, even learn your charging routine and adjust itself accordingly. Third, never drain a battery all the way down unless required to do so as part of a *battery calibration* (where you, in essence, reset the battery according to steps provided by the manufacturer). Rechargeable batteries have only a limited number of charge-discharge cycles before overall battery performance is reduced. Fourth, *never* handle a battery that has ruptured or broken; battery chemicals are very dangerous and flammable (check YouTube for videos of what happens when you puncture a Li-Ion battery). Finally, always recycle old batteries.

Try This!

Recycling Old Portable Device Batteries

Got an old portable device battery lying around? Well, you need to get rid of it, and there are some pretty toxic chemicals in that battery, so you can't just throw it in the trash. Sooner or later, you'll probably need to deal with such a battery, so try this!

1. Do an online search to find the battery recycling center nearest to you. Electronics retailers are getting much better about accepting a wide array of e-waste, including batteries, though they may place quantity limits.

2. Sometimes, you can take old laptop batteries to an auto parts store that disposes of old car batteries—I know it sounds odd, but it's true! See if you can find one in your area that will do this.

3. Many cities offer a hazardous materials disposal or recycling service. Check to see if and how your local government will help you dispose of your old batteries.

Power Management

Many different parts are included in the typical laptop, and each part uses power. The problem with early laptops was that every one of these parts used power continuously, whether or not the system needed the device at that time. For example, the hard drive continued to spin even when it was not being accessed, the CPU ran at full speed even when the system was doing light work, and the LCD panel continued to display even when the user walked away from the machine.

Over the years, a lot of work has gone into improving the battery life of portable devices. Beyond engineering better batteries and ever-more-efficient components, the system firmware and OS of most modern portables collaborate with the firmware of individual components to manage their power use. To reduce power use, the computer can power off unused components until they are needed, enter a low-power mode when the device isn't in use, and throttle the performance of power-hungry components like the CPU to fit the current workload. This process of cooperation among the hardware, BIOS, and OS to reduce power use is known generically as power management.

Low-Power Modes

If you don't know what's going on under the hood, computers usually appear to be clearly off or on. In reality, most computers (both desktops and portables!) that appear to be off are using at least a little power, and may be in one of a few low-power modes. The CompTIA A+ 220-1102 exam focuses on configuring basic power options in the Windows Control Panel, but it's good to have a handle on low-power modes in general.

 NOTE Low-power mode names can differ from OS to OS (and even from version to version), but the basic concepts are the same.

When the computer is off, turning it on will boot the OS from scratch. You can think of there being two kinds of true off mode:

- **Mechanical off mode** The system and all components, with the exception of the real-time clock (RTC), are off.

- **Soft power-off mode** The system is mostly off except for components necessary for the keyboard, LAN, or USB devices to wake the system.

Computers that appear to be off may actually be in a *sleep* (also called *standby* or *suspend*) mode: waking them will resume any programs, processes, and windows that were open when they entered the low-power mode. There are a number of fine-grained sleep modes, but the highlights are:

- A device can wake quickly from normal sleep mode (sometimes called suspend to RAM) because it doesn't power down the RAM, enabling the system to save its place. If the device loses power unexpectedly, it can lose whatever was in RAM.

- Devices wake more slowly from a deeper sleep mode called *hibernate* (or suspend to disk) because they save everything in RAM to a hard drive or SSD (and restoring it all takes a moment) before powering down. On the up side, hibernation saves more power and won't lose its place if the device loses power.

Configuring Power Options

You configure power options via the system setup utility or through the operating system. OS settings override CMOS settings. Implementations differ, but certain settings apply generally, like the ability to enable or disable power management; configure which devices can wake the system; configure what the power button does; and configure what the system should do when power is restored after an outage.

Operating systems tend to use friendly terms like *Energy Options* or *Power Options*, but you might run into some more technical terms in a system configuration utility. Many CMOS versions present settings to determine wake-up events, such as directing the system to monitor a modem or a NIC. You'll see this feature as *Wake on LAN*, or something similar.

In Windows, power options can be found in the Settings | System | Power & sleep | in Windows 10/11 and the Control Panel applet Power Options. Windows offers *power plans* that enable better control over power use by customizing a Balanced, Power saver, or High performance power plan (see Figure 23-16).

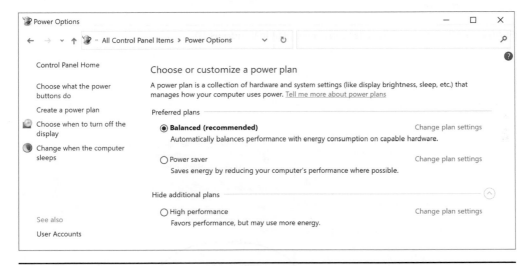

Figure 23-16 Windows 10 Balanced, Power saver, and High performance power plan options

NOTE While you can customize most laptops' power plans to your heart's content, on some models, such as Microsoft's Surface Pro line, you are restricted to just the default Balanced plan.

You can customize a power plan for your laptop, for example, and configure it to turn off the display at a certain time interval while on battery versus plugged in or configure it to put the computer to sleep (see Figure 23-17). To see the specific power plans, click

Additional power settings or go directly to the Control Panel Power Options applet. There you can tweak a lot more, including choices like hibernation (see Figure 23-18).

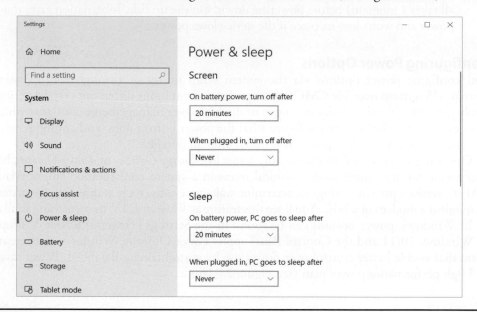

Figure 23-17   Customizing a laptop power plan in Windows 10

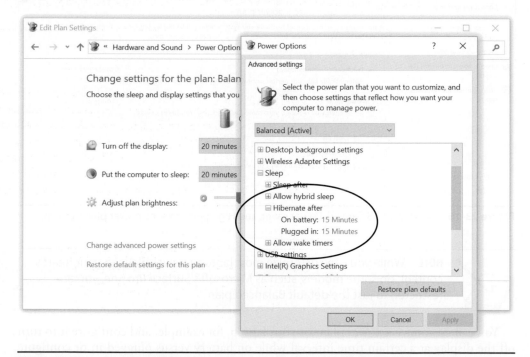

Figure 23-18   Windows 10 hibernation settings in the Power Options applet

Manual Control over Power Use

Most portables give you several manual options for reducing battery use in certain circumstances. We've already discussed using the on/off switch or keyboard combinations for disabling the Wi-Fi antenna or shutting off Bluetooth, but many modern portables borrow a feature from smartphones and tablets for disabling most or all of their wireless components at once: *airplane mode*. Beyond its intended use, airplane mode is also a great way to disable power-sucking components quickly. On the flipside, some newer gaming laptops include something known as a MUX switch, which enables a user to disable the computer's integrated graphics in favor of the dedicated graphics card, which increases performance, but decreases battery life significantly.

Try This!

Adjusting Your System's Power Management

Go into the Power Options applet on a Windows computer and look at the various settings. What is the current power plan for the computer? Check to see if it is running a Balanced or High performance power plan. If it is, change the power plan to Power saver and click *Change plan settings*. Familiarize yourself with some of the advanced power settings (click the *Change advanced power settings* link).

Try changing the individual settings for each power scheme. For instance, set a new value for the *Turn off the display* setting—try making your display turn off after five minutes. Don't worry; you aren't going to hurt anything if you fiddle with these settings.

Note that Microsoft changed power settings for laptops in Windows 10 to be Balanced. You can still adjust advanced power settings and tweak everything.

Laptops with backlit keyboards or RGB lighting will have some way you can disable this feature when it's not needed, usually with a keyboard combination. You can also reduce the output of the LCD backlight using a combination of FN and another key to eke out a few more precious minutes of computing time before you have to shut down. Figure 23-19 shows a close-up of the FN-activated keys for adjusting screen brightness.

Figure 23-19
Keys for adjusting
screen brightness

One of the best ways to conserve battery is to plan ahead for times when you'll be unplugged. This can mean a lot of different things in practice, but they all boil down to thinking of ways to minimize the number of programs and hardware devices/radios you'll need to use while your laptop is running on battery power. When I travel, for example, and know that I'm going to need a certain set of files stored on my file server at the office, I put those files on my laptop before I leave, while it's still plugged into the AC. It's tempting to throw the files on a thumb drive so I don't have to break out my laptop at the office, or to let Dropbox do my syncing for me when I get to a Wi-Fi hotspot, but both USB and Wi-Fi use electricity.

Better than that, Windows enables me to designate the files and folders I need as *offline files*, storing a local, duplicate copy of the files and folders on my hard drive. When I connect my laptop to my office network, those offline files are automatically synced with the files and folders on the file server. Anything I changed on the laptop gets written to the server. Anything anyone changed in those folders on the server gets written to my laptop. If changes were made on both sides, a sync conflict pops up automatically, enabling me to resolve problems without fear of overwriting anything important.

To designate a folder and its contents as offline files, right-click the folder you want and select *Always available offline* from the context menu. The sync will occur and you're done. When you want to open the files offline, go to the Control Panel and open the Sync Center applet (see Figure 23-20). Click the *Manage offline files* link to open the Offline Files dialog box (see Figure 23-21). Click the *View your offline files* button and you're in.

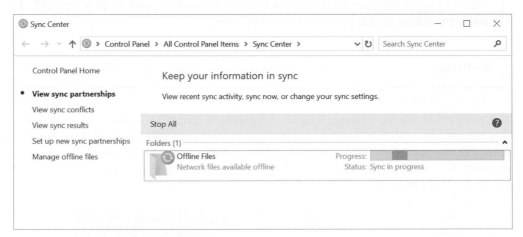

Figure 23-20   Sync Center applet

 EXAM TIP   Another option for extending battery life is to bring a spare battery. While most modern laptops don't have easily swappable batteries, larger power banks enable you to charge your laptop on the go, much like you'd do with your smartphone.

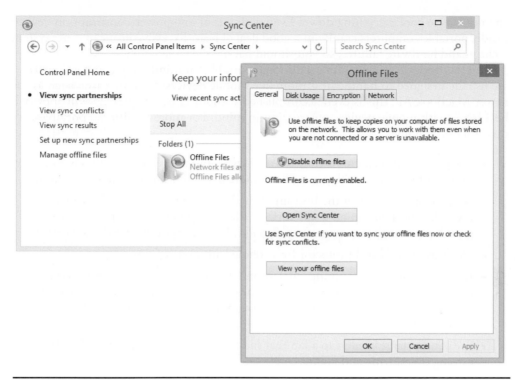

Figure 23-21   Offline Files dialog box

Cleaning

Most portable computers take substantially more abuse than a corresponding desktop model. Constant handling, travel, airport food on the run, and so on can radically shorten the life of a portable if you don't take action. One of the most important things you should do is clean the device regularly. Use an appropriate screen cleaner (not a glass cleaner!) to remove fingerprints and dust from the fragile LCD panel. (Refer to Chapter 17 for specifics.) Using a dedicated screen cleaner is important, otherwise you run the risk of doing permanent damage to the display.

We'll go into greater detail on environmental threats in Chapter 27, but if you've had the portable in a smoky or dusty environment where air quality alone can cause problems, try cleaning it with compressed air. Compressed air works great for blowing out dust and crumbs from the keyboard and for keeping any ports, slots, and sockets clear. Don't use water on your keyboard! Even a little moisture inside the portable can toast a component.

Heat

To manage and maintain a healthy portable computer, you need to deal with heat issues. Every portable has a stack of electronic components crammed into a very small space. Unlike their desktop brethren, portables don't have lots of freely moving air space that enables fans to cool everything down. Even with lots of low-power-consumption devices inside, portable computers crank out a good deal of heat. Excessive heat can cause system lockups and hardware failures, so you should handle the issue wisely.

The following steps have more traditional portables in mind; very compact portables are usually designed to handle heat more like mobile devices; in some cases, such as the newer MacBook Air, this is even accomplished without fans. Chapter 25 will approach heat issues with mobile device construction in mind. For more traditional portables, try this as a starter guide:

- Use power management, even if you're plugged into the AC outlet. This is especially important if you're working in a warm (more than 80 degrees Fahrenheit) room.

- Keep air space between the bottom of the laptop and the surface on which it rests. Putting a laptop on a soft surface, such as a pillow on your lap, creates a great heat-retention system—not a good thing! Always use a hard, flat surface.

- Don't use a keyboard protector for extended amounts of time.

- Listen to your fan, assuming the laptop has one. If it's often running very fast—you can tell by the whirring sound—examine your power management settings, environment, and running programs so you can change whatever is causing heat retention.

- Speaking of fans, be alert to a fan that suddenly goes silent. Fans do fail on laptops, causing overheating and failure.

Protecting the Machine

Even midrange laptops can be pricey, and replacing them before you're ready is always a pain. To protect your investment, you'll want to adhere to certain best practices. You've already read tips in this chapter to deal with cleaning and heat, so let's look at the "portable" part of portable computers.

Tripping

Pay attention to where you run the power cord when you plug in a laptop. One of the primary causes of laptop destruction is people tripping over the power cord and knocking the laptop off of a desk. This is especially true if you plug in at a public place such as a café or airport. Remember, the life you save could be your portable's!

Storage

If you aren't going to use your portable for a while, storing it safely will go a long way toward keeping it operable when you do power it up again. A quality case is worth the extra few dollars—preferably one with ample padding. Not only will this protect your system on a daily basis when transporting it from home to office, but it will keep dust and pet hair away as well. Also, protect from battery leakage, at least on devices with removable batteries, by removing the battery if you plan to store the device for an extended time. Regardless of whether the battery is removable or built in, it's a good idea to store the battery partially charged and top it up occasionally to keep it from fully discharging.

Travel

If you travel with a laptop, guard against theft. If possible, use a case that doesn't look like a computer case. A well-padded backpack makes a great travel bag for a laptop and appears less tempting to would-be thieves, though some brands and styles of these are still quite obvious. Smaller portables can often hide in less obvious bags. Don't forget to pack any accessories you might need, like modular devices, power banks, and AC adapters. Most importantly—back up any important data before you leave!

Make sure to have at least a little battery power available. Heightened security at airports means you might have to power on your system to prove it's really a computer and not a transport case for questionable materials. And never let your laptop out of your sight. If going through an x-ray machine, request a manual search. The x-ray won't harm your computer like a metal detector would, but if the laptop gets through the line at security before you do, someone else might walk away with it. If flying, stow your laptop under the seat in front of you where you can keep an eye on it.

If you travel to a foreign country, be very careful about the electricity. North America uses ~115-V power outlets, but most of the world uses ~230-V outlets. Most portable computers have *auto-switching power supplies*, meaning they detect the voltage at the outlet and adjust accordingly (but most people just call it a *charger*). An auto-switching power supply will have an input voltage range printed on it somewhere (see Figure 23-22).

Figure 23-22
Input and output
voltages on
laptop power
brick

Double-check the charger to make sure its supported range covers voltages used in any country you plan to visit. If it doesn't, you may need a full-blown electricity-converting device, either a step-down or step-up *transformer*. You should be able to find converters and transformers at electronics retailers, travel stores, and, of course, online.

Shipping

Much of the storage and travel advice can be applied to shipping. If possible, remove batteries and optical discs from their drives. Pack the portable well and disguise the container as best you can. Back up any data and verify the warranty coverage. Ship with a reputable carrier and always request a tracking number and, if possible, delivery signature. It's also worth the extra couple of bucks to pay for the shipping insurance. And when the clerk asks what's in the box, it's safer to say "electronics" rather than "a new 17-inch laptop computer."

Security

The fact is, if someone really wants to steal your laptop, they'll find a way. While we cover securing devices against physical theft in Chapter 27, there are some things you can do to make yourself, and your portable devices, less desirable targets. As you've already learned, disguise is a good idea.

Another physical deterrent is a laptop lock. Not all laptops are able to use one, but they can be helpful if the option is available for your device. Similar to a steel bicycle cable, there is a loop on one end and a lock on the other. The idea is to loop the cable around a solid object, such as a bed frame, and secure the lock to the small security hole on the side of the laptop (see Figure 23-23). Again, if someone really wants to steal your computer, they'll find a way. They'll dismantle the bed frame if they're desperate. The best protection is to be vigilant and not let the computer out of your sight.

Figure 23-23
Cable lock

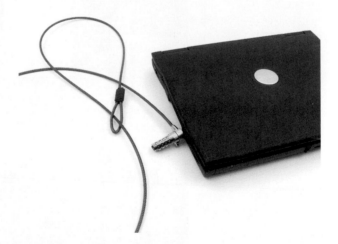

An alternative to securing a laptop with a physical lock is to use a software tracking system that makes use of GPS. It won't keep your device from being taken, but tracking software can use the many sensors and networking capabilities of modern devices to help recover them. While functionality differs by application, common features include seeing the location of the stolen computer, capturing images or audio with its sensors, and wiping sensitive files from the device. Because this functionality is more common in mobile devices, we'll save the details for Chapter 25.

Theft isn't the only security risk that laptop owners face; modern laptops account for the need to protect user privacy and data as well. Screen locks have been around for a long time, requiring a user to enter a PIN or password before being able to actually use the device. In recent years, these features have been enhanced using *biometrics*. Biometrics are measurements of physical characteristics that are documented and verified through the use of scanners. Biometrics can be used to match a physical characteristic of a user with a valid user account in order to authenticate the user. Common biometric security features found on laptops include fingerprint scanners located on the keyboard or facial recognition software that uses the device's webcam. These are popular because they allow a user to quickly access their device without needing to enter a complex password every time they open the lid or come back from a lunch break.

Upgrading and Repairing Laptop Computers

A competent tech can upgrade and repair portable computers to a degree, though true laptop techs are specialists. Over the years, laptops have become more and more based on proprietary parts, to a point where some laptops can only really be repaired by the manufacturer or authorized third parties, and in some cases, upgrades are off the table altogether. Upgrading the basics usually means breaking out the trusty screwdriver and avoiding electrostatic discharge (ESD). *Repairing* portables successfully, on the other hand, requires research, patience, organization, special tools, and documentation. Plus, you need a ridiculously steady hand. This section provides an overview of the upgrade and repair process. Keep in mind that the growing number of form factors and the shrinking size of portable devices mean there are many exceptions, especially for very compact portables; these devices may be trickier to take apart, and components may be soldered on or use less-common interfaces.

Disassembly Process

Disassembling a portable PC is usually pretty easy, if it was designed to be upgraded or serviced by casual users. Putting it back together in working condition is the hard part! You need to follow a four-step process to succeed in disassembly/reassembly.

 NOTE Many modern laptops are designed with portability in mind over repairability and, as a result, are not easily repairable without access to proprietary tools or parts. In laptops like this, even components like RAM or an SSD may be soldered onto the motherboard. Nonetheless, knowing your way around the inside of a laptop is a great skill as a tech.

First, *document and label every cable and screw location*. Laptops don't use standard connectors or screws. Often you'll run into many tiny screws of varying threads. If you try to put a screw into the wrong hole, you could end up stripping the screw, stripping the hole, or getting the screw wedged into the wrong place.

Second, *organize any parts you extract from the laptop.* Seriously, put a big white piece of construction paper on your work surface, lay each extracted piece out in logical fashion, and clearly mark where each component connects and what it connects to as well. You may even want to use a smartphone camera to take pictures or a webcam to record your workspace in case something goes missing.

Third, *refer to the manufacturer's resources.* I can't stress this point enough. Unlike desktops, portables have no standardization of internal structure. Everything in the portable is designed according to the manufacturer's best engineering efforts. Two portables from the same manufacturer might have a similar layout inside, but it's far more likely that every model differs a lot.

Finally, you need to *use the appropriate hand tools.* A portable, especially on the inside, will have a remarkable variety of tiny screws that you can't remove/reinsert without tiny-headed Phillips or Torx drivers. You'll need tiny pry bars—metal and plastic—to open components. Figure 23-24 shows an entry-level toolkit for a laptop tech that you can order from iFixit (https://www.ifixit.com; more on this site in a moment). Their professional toolkit version has 70 tools, plus there's an expansion kit! Like I said at the beginning of this section, portable techs are specialists.

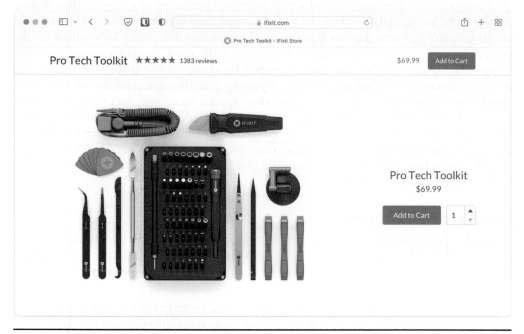

Figure 23-24   Bare-minimum laptop repair tools

Now that you have the official line on the disassembly process, let's get one thing clear: a lot of manufacturers don't provide access to their resources to just any tech, but only to authorized repair centers. So what do you do when faced with an unfamiliar laptop that a client brought in for repair?

You have essentially two options. First, you can find a dedicated laptop tech and refer your client to that person. If the problem is exceptionally complicated and the portable in question is mission critical, that's often the best option. If you want to tackle the problem or it looks like something you should be able to do, then you go to third-party sources: YouTube and iFixit.

Every portable computer has a specific make and model. Open up a Web browser and go to YouTube. Type in precisely what you want to do, such as "Dell XPS 13 keyboard replacement," and see what pops up (see Figure 23-25). You'll most likely get results back, especially if the laptop in question is a couple of years old. People all over the world have to deal with broken devices, so you're not alone.

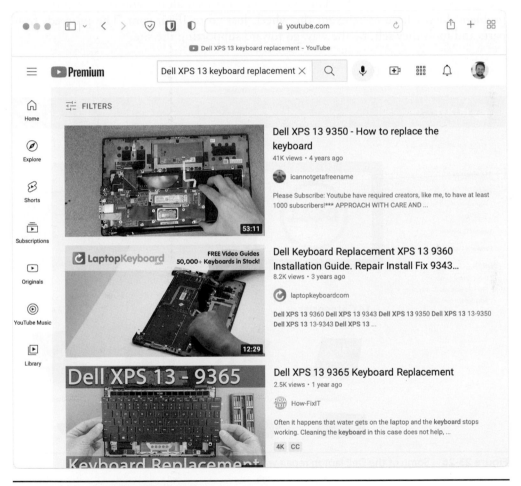

Figure 23-25 YouTube search result

Once you've found the appropriate video or something that's close enough to enable the repair attempt, watch it. If it's too difficult for your skill level or requires a set of expensive tools, then fall back to step one and go find a dedicated tech. Otherwise, figure out what tools and parts you need. Parts specific to a laptop (as in that Dell keyboard in the preceding example) will need to be purchased from the manufacturer. More generic parts, like hard drives, CPUs, and so on can be purchased from Newegg (my favorite tech store) or some other online retailer.

For general tools, parts, and a lot of very detailed step-by-step instructions, I highly recommend iFixit. Billed as "Repair guides for everything, written by everyone," iFixit is built by techs like you and me who conquer a problem, document the steps, and post the details (see Figure 23-26). This means the next tech along who runs into the same problem doesn't have to reinvent the wheel. Just go to iFixit.com. The proceeds from parts and tools they sell, by the way, go toward supporting the site.

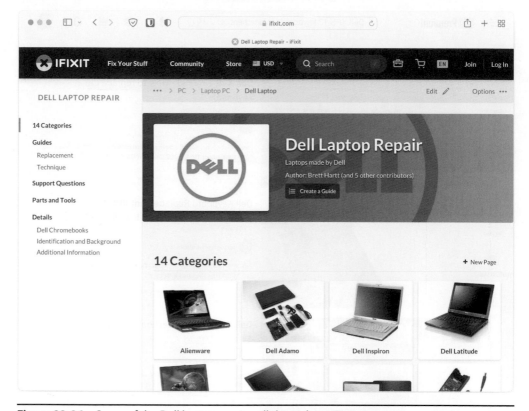

Figure 23-26 Some of the Dell laptop repair walkthroughs at iFixit.com

Standard Upgrades

Every CompTIA A+ tech should know how to perform the two standard upgrades to portable computers: adding RAM and replacing a hard drive. Let's go through the steps.

Upgrading RAM

Not every modern laptop has the option to upgrade RAM, but there are still plenty that do. As a result, one of the more common laptop upgrades you'll be called on to do is to add more RAM. A quick Google search of the make and model that you're working on will tell you whether or not the RAM is soldered or replaceable. If it's replaceable, you'll need to make sure you know what kind you need.

EXAM TIP Expect a question or two on the CompTIA A+ 1101 exam about scenarios where you should install (and configure) laptop memory—as in random access memory (i.e., RAM). Adding RAM or replacing existing sticks with more RAM can dramatically improve performance.

How to Add or Replace RAM Upgrading the RAM in a laptop requires a couple of steps. Once you've determined that the specific device you're working on can be upgraded, you need to get the correct RAM. Refer to the manufacturer's Web site or to the manual (if any) that came with the laptop for the specific RAM needed. Once you know the type, you need to make sure you know the configuration of any existing RAM in the system. If you are planning to upgrade from 8 GB to 16 GB, you need to know if your portable already has one module at 8 GB or two modules at 4 GB.

Second, every portable offers a unique challenge to the tech who wants to upgrade the RAM, because there's no standard location for RAM placement in portables. The RAM slots may not even be in the same spot. More often than not, you need to unscrew or pop open a panel on the underside of the portable or remove the entire back plate (see Figure 23-27). Then you press out on the restraining clips and the RAM stick pops up (see Figure 23-28). Gently remove the old stick of RAM and insert the new one by reversing the steps.

Figure 23-27
Removing the
back plate

Figure 23-28   Releasing the RAM

Always remove all electrical power from the laptop before removing or inserting memory. Disconnect the AC cord from the wall outlet. Take out any removable batteries! Failure to disconnect from power can result in a fried laptop. In the case of systems with built-in batteries, consult the manufacturer's resources to evaluate the safety of working on the system and any additional steps or precautions you should take.

Upgrading Mass Storage

You can replace a hard disk drive (HDD) or solid-state drive (SSD) in some laptops fairly easily, while others (like MacBooks) cannot be upgraded at all. Contemporary laptops with upgradeable storage make use of the small M.2 form factor in order to save space, although a fair number of systems, particularly older ones, will also use 2.5-inch SATA drives. Using smaller form-factor drives enables manufacturers to include a second slot for easy mass storage expansion.

mSATA and M.2   If you have a newer portable, chances are the computer uses one of the smaller SSD formats—mSATA or M.2. You read about them in detail back in Chapter 8, but glance back to refresh your memory if necessary.

Most manufacturers make it fairly easy to replace or upgrade an mSATA or M.2 drive. Remove the bottom plate or dedicated drive bay covering from the computer. Remove the tiny retaining screw and pop the old drive out. Put the new drive in its place, insert the retaining screw, and reattach the covering. You're good to go, at least from the hardware side of things.

One of the best upgrades you can make on a laptop is to migrate from an HDD to an SSD. You may get less storage capacity for the money, but the trade-offs are worth it. Beyond improved reliability, the SSD will use a lot less electricity than an HDD, thus extending battery life. Additionally, any SSD is rip-roaringly faster than an HDD and performance across the board will be boosted. An upgrade from an HDD to an SSD can breathe new life into an otherwise sluggish older system.

The process of replacing a hard drive mirrors that of replacing RAM. You find the hard drive hatch—either along one edge or in a compartment on the underside of the computer—and release the screws. If the device doesn't have a hatch, you may need to remove the bottom of the chassis (as previously shown in Figure 23-27). Remove the old drive and then slide the new drive into its place (see Figure 23-29). Reattach the hatch or cover and boot the computer. If you're replacing your boot drive, grab a bootable USB flash drive and prepare to reinstall.

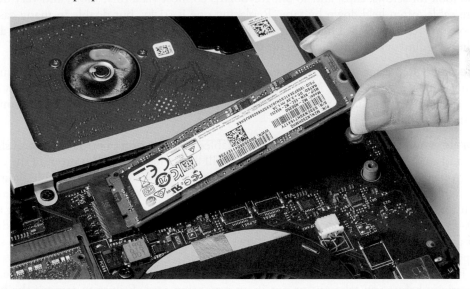

Figure 23-29 Inserting a replacement drive

Hardware/Device Replacement

Once you get beyond upgrading RAM and replacing a hard drive on a portable, you take the plunge into the laptop-repair specialty. You can replace some components by lifting them out, detaching a ribbon cable, and then reversing the steps with the replacement part. Other parts require a full teardown of the laptop to the bare bones, which presents a much greater magnitude of difficulty. Because every portable differs, this section provides guidance, but not concrete steps, for replacement. Be aware, as mentioned earlier, that many systems are trending toward more integrated parts; make sure the part you're replacing is actually replaceable in the specific system you're working on.

Components

Replaceable components require more work than the RAM or drive upgrades, but replacing them generally falls into the category of "doable." What I call *components* are the battery, keyboard, internal speaker(s), and expansion cards.

Battery   If a battery's performance falls below an acceptable level, you can replace it with a battery from the manufacturer or from an aftermarket vendor. Although this should be a simple swap replacement (and usually is, at least if the battery isn't built in), you might encounter a situation where the real problem wasn't the battery per se, but an inadequate or malfunctioning charging system. The new battery might not give you any better performance than the old one. Try it.

Keyboard   Getting a keyboard off a laptop computer often requires little pry bars, but also look for screws, clips, and so on. Keyboards connect via a tiny, short, and very delicate cable, often held down by tape. Replacing one is tricky, but doable in many cases. Look up steps for detaching and reattaching keys on a specific device if possible, and otherwise find generic instructions for the clip type before proceeding.

Speaker   Replacing the internal speaker or speakers on a laptop will most likely require you to open up the device. Most laptop speakers are inside the chassis, so if you want to replace them, you need to dismantle the portable to get to them. (See the upcoming "Integral Parts" section.)

Wireless and Expansion Cards   Many portables have one or more true expansion slots for add-on cards. The more modular varieties will have a hatch on the bottom of the case that opens like the hatch that gives you access to the RAM slot(s). This enables you to change out an older wireless cards (alternative names Wi-Fi card and WLAN card), for example, with one that support current Wi-Fi card standards, thus greatly enhancing the Wi-Fi experience on this device. Similarly, you could change out a Bluetooth module for an upgraded version. Figure 23-30 shows a wide-open laptop with the expansion slot exposed for the insertion of a WLAN card.

Just like when installing RAM in a portable, you must avoid ESD and remove all electricity before you take out or put in an expansion card. Failure to remove the battery and the AC adapter (or follow any extra steps and precautions in the manufacturer's resources if the battery is built in) can and probably will result in a shorted-out laptop motherboard, and that just makes for a bad day.

 NOTE   Check with the portable manufacturer to get a Wi-Fi card that's compatible with the portable. Just because a card will fit in the slot does not, in this case, mean it will work.

The only other consideration with expansion cards applies specifically to wireless. Not only will you need to connect the card to the slot properly, but you must reattach the antenna connection and often a separate power cable. Pay attention when you remove the card as to the placement of these vital connections.

Figure 23-30
M.2 expansion
slot on laptop
with WLAN card

You'll find one of two types of expansion slots in a portable: Mini-PCIe and M.2. The older ones (think 2013 and earlier) use Mini-PCIe and are uncommon to see today, while newer devices use M.2.

Display and Its Components   A laptop screen presents unique challenges when faced with a replacement scenario. The display has the typical parts you'd expect in an LCD, such as the panel, backlight(s), and inverter (on older portables); plus, the display typically has other components along for the ride, such as the Wi-Fi antenna, a webcam, and a microphone. Finally, a touch-screen display offers even more of a challenge.

NOTE   For a deeper dive on the type of display technologies that exist, refer back to Chapter 17. Laptops typically make use of the same technologies that desktop monitors use, just in smaller sizes.

The process for replacing the screen (flat, touch screen, digitizer), inverter, Wi-Fi antenna, webcam, or microphone follows the same steps. You pry the plastic frame off the display, most commonly using a spudger or other tool from your toolkit, then remove any exposed screws. The screen will lift out, and you'll need to detach the internal parts.

I can't give you precise details, because every model differs, but the parts are usually secured with tiny screws or compression, or mild adhesive. Plus, you'll need to gently disconnect data cables for each component. If you're just replacing a defective webcam or microphone, you won't need to disconnect other parts (most likely), but if you need to replace the screen or inverter, you'll have to remove everything.

Take pictures with your phone. Keep track of which connectors go where. Don't rush the process when dealing with so many tiny connectors and parts. Document the locations and types of screws. The extra work you do to record each step or layer will pay off with a properly repaired laptop. Trust me!

 EXAM TIP Expect a question or two on the CompTIA A+ 1101 exam on a typical scenario where replacement of the screen or components within the display needs to happen. These are obvious—cracked screen, failure of the digitizer/touch screen, Wi-Fi antenna malfunction, and so on. (Note that the specific objective language on the antenna is *WiFi antenna connector/placement*, which refers to the wireless antenna wires—yes, that's an oxymoron—that run along the top and sides of the display and connect with a tiny ribbon cable.) While you don't need to know the steps of the repair process for the exam, you need to at least be able to understand the differences between display components and troubleshoot issues that they may have.

Integral Parts

Some hardware replacements require you to get serious with the laptop, opening it fully to the outside, removing many delicate parts, and even stripping it down to the bare chassis. I leave these repairs to the professional laptop repair folks, simply because they have the specific tools and expertise to do the job efficiently. To understand the process, I've outlined it here. This pertains to three components: DC jack, trackpad, and system board.

 NOTE While a few laptops used to have removable/replaceable video cards, these were few and far between and you are very unlikely to encounter them in the wild. Modern devices have the GPU as part of the system board.

Portables generally open in two different ways, depending on the manufacturer. You either peel away layers from the top down, through the keyboard, or from the bottom up, through the base. Either direction requires careful attention to detail, part connectivity, and locations. You'll need a system to keep track of the dozens of tiny screws.

Every one of the replacements here requires you to detach the screen from the main chassis of the portable. Aside from finding the connection points and removing the proper screws, you need to pay attention to the connection points for the data stream to the monitor and the antenna that's in the frame of the display, as mentioned earlier.

Once you have the portable stripped down, you replace whichever component you're in there to replace and then begin the process of building it back up into a coherent unit. Pay incredibly careful attention to getting data cables connected properly as you rebuild. I can't imagine a worse tech experience than replacing a trackpad and rebuilding a laptop only to have missed a connection and having to do it all over again.

 EXAM TIP The DC jack requires extra-special love when you need to replace one. The part is soldered to the main board, so replacing it means you'll need to not only strip the laptop to the bare metal, but also unsolder the old part and solder the new part. Then you'll rebuild the laptop and hope you got everything right. CompTIA cannot expect a CompTIA A+ technician to know how to do this stuff. Expect a question that explores whether it *can* be done. Rest assured, specialized techs can replace *any* component on a laptop, even the DC jack.

Troubleshooting Portable Computers

Many of the troubleshooting techniques you learned about for desktop systems can be applied to laptops. For example, take the proper precautions before and during disassembly. Use the proper hand tools, and document, label, and organize each plastic part and screw location for reassembly. Additionally, here are some laptop-specific procedures to try.

Power and Performance

Some of the most common portable device issues relate to how well they do (or don't!) run—so let's take a look at a few issues related to power, performance, and heat.

Laptop Won't Power On

- If a laptop won't power up—a *no power* scenario—verify AC power by plugging another electronic device into the wall outlet. If the other device receives power, the outlet is good.

- If the outlet is good, connect the laptop to the wall outlet and try to power on. If no LEDs light up, you may have a bad AC adapter. Swap it out with a known-good power adapter.

- A faulty peripheral device might keep the laptop from powering up. Remove any peripherals such as USB or Thunderbolt devices.

Poor Performance

- The most common reason for slow performance is that a running application or process is consuming high resources. All operating systems have a utility to check this—such as the Task Manager in Windows or Activity Monitor in macOS—and look into any problems it finds. The application or process may need to be closed or stopped, you may need to reboot, or the application may need an update.

- Extreme performance issues may lead to a frozen system. If they don't resolve on their own and you can't interact with the device, you may need to perform a hard reboot (which may result in the loss of any unsaved work). Usually, holding down the power button for 10 seconds is sufficient, though you may need to check the manufacturer's resources for the proper procedure. If the battery is removable, you may be able to reboot the device by pulling the battery out and replacing it.

 NOTE Be aware, that you might find official or third-party resources discussing hard and soft resets. These are *not* the same as hard and soft reboots, so you should pay careful attention to the instructions and make sure you're performing the correct procedure. See Chapter 25 for more on hard and soft resets.

Battery Issues

- A *swollen battery* will probably go unnoticed at first, and the symptoms it creates may be hard to identify if you aren't aware it can happen. The cause is usually over-charging, perhaps due to a failure in the circuits that should prevent it, but the early symptoms might be a laptop that doesn't quite sit right on flat surfaces, a screen that doesn't fit flush when closed, problems with input devices like the trackpad or keyboard, and trouble removing or inserting a removable battery. Eventually, the device's case may be obviously deformed. While battery packs are designed to handle a little swelling, it increases the risk they'll puncture—and a punctured battery can be dangerous. Don't ignore these symptoms; open the case carefully to check the battery, and very carefully deliver it to an e-waste recycling or disposal site.

- If you have a laptop with a battery that won't charge up—a *poor battery health* problem—it could be one of three things: The device has a setting that limits how much charge the battery can hold to preserve its lifespan, the battery might be cooked, or the AC adapter isn't doing its job, also known as *improper charging*. To troubleshoot, first go to the devices battery settings and look to see if there is a charge limiting setting. If there isn't, you can try removing the battery and run the laptop on AC power only. If it works, you know the AC adapter is good. If it doesn't work, you probably need to replace the adapter. Another option is to replace the battery with a known-good battery. If the new battery works, you've found the problem. Just replace the battery.

- The reasons for very short battery life in a battery that charges properly are fairly benign. The battery has usually outlived its useful life and needs to be replaced, or some programs or hardware are drawing much more power than usual. Check wireless devices you usually keep disabled to make sure they aren't on. Follow recommendations in the preceding "Poor Performance" section to address problem programs.

Overheating

- Because overheating can be both a symptom and a cause of a variety of issues, you should be alert to any device that is running hotter than usual. Note which parts of the device are hot—this can give you important clues. If the device feels dangerously hot, err on the side of protecting the device from heat damage instead of trying to diagnose the cause. Power the device down and remove the battery if possible. Set it on a cool, hard surface, out of direct sunlight, with the hottest part of the device exposed to air if possible.

- Likewise, look for possible signs a device is overheating—like inconsistent reboots, graphical glitches, system beeps—and rule out heat issues.

- Listen for fans. While some portables don't have any, complete silence may indicate a failed fan, and unusual noise may signal one on its way out. Before you open the device to check the fans, make sure that the device isn't set to some type of silent mode. Many modern laptops include software that allows you to run the laptop quietly or silently when not doing resource-intensive tasks. If this setting is active, it may be the reason for the lack of fan noise.

- Dust build-up in the laptop can lead to major overheating issues over time. If a computer is having overheating issues, it's very possible that there is dust, pet hair, or residue from smoke gumming up the works. To fix this, you should first check the fan vents for obstructions, grab your ESD wrist strap, then open the laptop and disconnect the battery. Once this is done, use a can of compressed air to blow the dust out of the chassis using short bursts from different angles. Be careful, laptop fans can be fragile, so don't be too aggressive when you clean them.

- Know when to expect a hot device. Busy or charging devices can create a lot of heat; follow the steps mentioned in the preceding "Poor Performance" and "Battery Issues" sections for identifying components that shouldn't be on, especially if they are hot to the touch, and finding runaway programs. If the device is charging, unplug it and see if the device cools. If you find nothing unexpected and the device is unusually hot, it may have an airflow problem.

- If the entire device is hot, it may have simply been left in direct sunlight or a hot environment. Cool the device down and see if the trouble goes away.

Components

Various hardware components can encounter issues, including the display, wireless networking, audio, and input devices.

Display Problems

- If the laptop is booting (you hear the beeps and the drives) but the screen doesn't come on properly—a *no display* problem—first, make sure the display is turned on. Press the FN key and the key to activate the screen a few times until the laptop display comes on. If the device is a 2-in-1 with a removable screen, make sure it is properly attached and that it is receiving power.

- If the laptop display is very dim—a *dim display* problem—it may be as simple as adjusting the brightness settings. Most laptops allow you to do this by using the FN key and the key to adjust the brightness. If this doesn't work, it may also be due to some power saving setting. Check the power saving settings to see if the screen brightness is being limited there. If those options don't fix the problem, you may be dealing with a failing backlight. This can be caused by failed inverters on older laptops.

- If the screen won't come on or is cracked, most laptops have a port for plugging in an external monitor, which you can use to log in to your laptop.

- If you plug a laptop into an external monitor and that monitor does not display, remember that you have both a hardware and an OS component to making dual displays successful. There's usually a combination of FN and another key to toggle among only portable, only external, and both displays. Plus, you have the Display area of Settings or the Display in the Control Panel to mirror or extend the desktop to a second monitor.

- If you have a *flickering display*, you should check for software issues before you try to open the laptop chassis. Laptop displays can flicker because of bad device drivers or application issues just like desktop displays. Unlike desktop displays, laptops are more likely to be dropped or accidentally knocked off a table. This can loosen connectors inside the display and lead to flickering as well. If software isn't the problem, loose connections just might be.

- If the screen orientation on a Windows portable doesn't change when the device is rotated, auto-rotation may be disabled. Likewise, if the orientation changes at the wrong time, you can lock rotation in Settings, or via the Display in the Control Panel. If the rotation needs to remain locked, you can still change the orientation via Settings/Display, or possibly with FN key combinations.

Wireless Devices (Bluetooth, Wi-Fi, NFC, or GPS) Don't Work or Work Intermittently

- If the wireless doesn't work at all, check along the front, rear, or side edges of the laptop for a physical switch that toggles the internal wireless adapter, Bluetooth adapter, or airplane mode on and off. Also check your notification area for an airplane icon.

 EXAM TIP Expect a couple of questions on the CompTIA A+ 1101 exam that explore poor/no connectivity scenarios where a client experiences issues with wireless connectivity or Bluetooth connectivity issues.

- If a tech has recently replaced a component that required removal of the laptop display, dead wireless could mean simply a disconnected antenna. Most portables have the antenna built into the display panel, so check that connection.

- Try the special key combination for your laptop to toggle the wireless or Bluetooth adapter, or one for toggling airplane mode. You usually press the FN key in combination with another key.

- You might simply be out of range or, if the wireless works intermittently, right at the edge of the range. Physically walk the laptop over to the wireless router or access point to ensure there are no out-of-range issues. You might also be experiencing congestion, too many wireless devices operating in the same frequency range.

- With Bluetooth specifically, remember that the pairing process takes action or configuration on both devices to succeed. Turn on the Bluetooth device, actively seek it, and try again.

- If only the GPS is not functioning, privacy options may be preventing applications from accessing your GPS location information. Check the Control Panel or the Privacy section of the Settings app to see whether the GPS device is enabled, and if location services are enabled both system-wide and for the appropriate applications. Check System Preferences in macOS or a similar location in Linux for the same options.

- While we won't discuss Near Field Communication (NFC) in depth until Chapter 24, some portable computers may have NFC support; if NFC isn't functioning, you may need to enable a setting to enable communication with nearby devices. In Windows, open the Proximity applet in the Control Panel (only present if you have NFC hardware) and make sure Proximity support is enabled.

Audio Problems

- If audio isn't working when it should be, check for a hardware mute or volume button or switch and verify through the notification area Volume icon that the audio output isn't muted. Verify proper output device configuration through the operating system, and verify the application is using the right output device.

- If no sound is coming from the device speakers, try plugging in a pair of headphones or some external speakers. If these work fine, there's a chance the built-in speakers have been damaged. Depending on their location, it can be easy to get them wet.

- If the device has had repairs or upgrades lately, make sure the speakers are properly connected.

- If headphones work fine with the device, the speakers may need replacing. First, make sure the device has been rebooted, double-check the audio output device settings, try changing and resetting the default output device, and try disabling and re-enabling the appropriate device.

Input Problems

- Before assuming an input problem is hardware related, confirm that the system is otherwise running smoothly. Input devices may appear not to work or work erratically if the system is freezing up. Refer to the earlier "Power and Performance" section for troubleshooting a frozen system.

- If none of the keys work on your laptop, there's a good chance you've unseated the keypad connector. These connectors are quite fragile and are prone to unseating from any physical stress on the laptop. Check the manufacturer's disassembly procedures to locate and reseat the keypad.

- If you're getting numbers when you're expecting to get letters, the number lock (NUM LOCK) function key is turned on. Turn it off. Pay attention to the NUM LOCK indicator lights, if any, on a portable if you experience these sorts of problems.

- Laptop keyboards take far more abuse than the typical desktop keyboard, because of all those lunch meetings and café brainstorm sessions. Eating and drinking while over or around a keyboard just begs for problems. If you have a portable with sticking keys, look for the obvious debris in the keys. Use compressed air to clean them out. If you have serious goo and need to use a cleaning solution, disconnect the keyboard from the portable first. Make sure it's fully dried out before you reconnect it or you'll short it out.

- A laptop keyboard key that doesn't register presses or feels sticky may also have had its switch knocked out of place, especially if the key appears slightly raised or tilted. These switches can be delicate, so be careful if you want to avoid ordering replacements. Research what kind of switch your device's keyboard uses, and be aware that a single keyboard may use a few different kinds. Look up steps for detaching and reattaching keys on that specific device if possible, and otherwise find generic instructions for the clip type before proceeding.

- If the trackpad is having problems, a shot of compressed air does wonders for cleaning pet hair out of the trackpad sensors. You might get a cleaner shot if you remove the keyboard before using the compressed air. Remember to be gentle when lifting off the keyboard and make sure to follow the manufacturer's instructions.

- The trackpad driver might need to be reconfigured. Try the various options in the Control Panel | Mouse applet, or the equivalent location in System Preferences.

- If the touch screen is unresponsive or erratic, a good first step is to check the screen for dirt, grease, or liquids, which can make the sensors go haywire; wipe it down with a dry microfiber cloth.

- Some touch screens may appear to work improperly if they are registering an unintentional touch. Depending on the design of the device, it may be tempting to hold it in a way that leaves some part of your hand or arm too close to the edge of the screen; some devices will register this as a touch.

- Your device may have touch-screen diagnostics available through hardware troubleshooting menus accessible through the BIOS. Refer to the manufacturer's resources for how to access these diagnostics. If available, they are a quick way to identify whether you're looking at a hardware or software/configuration issue. The Mouse applet in the Control Panel or Settings enables you to calibrate or reset your touch support. macOS has a Trackpad applet in System Preferences. Attempt to reset and recalibrate the display.

EXAM TIP The troubleshooting issue known as a *cursor* drift can mean one of two things. First, the display shows a trail of ghost cursors behind your real cursor as you move it. This might point to an aging display or an improperly configured refresh rate. Second, the cursor moves erratically or drifts slowly in a steady direction (also known as *touch calibration*), whether you are touching the trackpad or not. If a reboot doesn't fix the pointer drift, the trackpad has probably been damaged in some way and needs to be replaced.

Chapter Review

Questions

1. Which of the following are good ideas when it comes to batteries? (Select two.)
   A. Keep the contacts clean by using alcohol and a soft cloth.
   B. Store them in the freezer if they will not be used for a long period of time.
   C. Toss them in the garbage when they wear out.
   D. Store them in a cool, dry place.

2. To replace a wireless antenna in a laptop, what must you do?
   A. Remove the keyboard.
   B. Remove the screen.
   C. Remove the expansion slot cover on the bottom of the laptop.
   D. This cannot be done.

3. Which of the following SSD form factors are commonly used in laptops? (Select two.)
   A. 2.5 inch
   B. M.2
   C. 3.5 inch
   D. 1.8 inch

4. Clara just finished a long road trip on a hot day in a car with a broken air conditioner. When she arrives at her destination, she immediately opens her laptop, which was working before she left, to check her e-mails. For some reason, every time she tries to power up the computer, it shuts down again within a few seconds. What is the most likely problem?
   A. The laptop's hard drive died and needs to be replaced.
   B. The laptop display is faulty and needs to be replaced.
   C. The laptop fans are very dusty and need to be cleaned.
   D. The laptop is already hot from sitting in the car and needs time to cool off.

5. What is a type of sensing device that detects the locations and duration of contact across its face, usually by a finger or stylus?

   A. Trackpad

   B. Touchscreen

   C. Touchpad

   D. Laptop

6. Which of the following display types will you commonly find on a laptop today?

   A. CRT

   B. LCD

   C. CCFL

   D. Plasma

7. Steve complains that his aging Windows laptop still isn't snappy enough after upgrading the RAM. What might improve system performance?

   A. Add more RAM.

   B. Replace the power supply.

   C. Replace the battery.

   D. Replace the HDD with an SSD.

8. Jim likes his laptop but complains that his wireless seems slow compared to all the new laptops. On further inspection, you determine his laptop runs 802.11n. What can be done to improve his network connection speed?

   A. Add more RAM.

   B. Replace the display with one with a better antenna.

   C. Replace the 802.11n card with an 802.11ac card.

   D. Get a new laptop, because this one can't be upgraded.

9. Edgar successfully replaced the display on a laptop (a toddler had taken a ballpoint pen to it), but the customer called back almost immediately complaining that his wireless didn't work. What could the problem be?

   A. The problems are unrelated, so it could be anything.

   B. Edgar inadvertently disconnected the antenna from the 802.11 card.

   C. Edgar replaced the display with one without an internal antenna.

   D. Edgar failed to reconnect the antenna in the new display.

10. Rafael gets a tech call from a user with a brand new laptop complaining that his display is flickering. What is the most likely issue?

   A. The laptop uses a plasma display.

   B. The laptop uses a CRT display.

   C. The laptop display drivers are outdated.

   D. The laptop display is faulty and needs to be replaced.

Answers

1. **A, D.** Keeping a battery in the freezer is a good idea in theory, but not in practice. All batteries contain toxic chemicals and should *never* be treated like regular trash.

2. **B.** The antenna for laptop Wi-Fi connections is located in the screen portion of the laptop. To access the antenna, remove the screen (or at least the plastic frame parts).

3. **A, B.** 2.5-inch and M.2 solid-state drives are commonly used in laptops.

4. **D.** Because Clara just had a long road trip in a hot car, the laptop is most likely already hot and needs time to cool off.

5. **B.** A touchscreen is a type of sensing device that detects the locations and duration of contact across its face, usually by a finger or stylus.

6. **B.** You'll only see LCD displays on portables today (though they may be marketed as LED displays).

7. **D.** Replacing the HDD with an SSD will speed up the system.

8. **C.** Replacing the 802.11n wireless card with an 802.11ac NIC should improve his network connection speed.

9. **D.** A disconnected antenna makes Wi-Fi unhappy.

10. **C.** Flicker is most commonly caused by software issues like outdated or corrupted drivers.

24

Mobile Devices

In this chapter, you will learn how to
- Explain the features and capabilities of mobile devices
- Describe the major mobile operating systems
- Describe how to configure mobile devices

It's hard to imagine that most of the mobile devices we use today (in particular the popular iPhone, iPad, and Android devices) at one time sounded like science fiction rather than reality. Mobile devices have revolutionized the way we work and play. Devices such as smartphones and tablets enable people to access unique tools and features from just about anywhere and accomplish essential tasks on the go.

As amazing as mobile devices are, it's not easy to find a definition of *mobile device* that everyone agrees on. If you ask folks who are comfortable with these devices, you'll get lots of descriptions of functions and capabilities as opposed to what they are. In essence, the following aspects make a device mobile (and even these will sometimes create debate):

- Lightweight, usually less than two pounds
- Small, designed to move with you (in your hand or pocket)
- Touch or stylus interface; no keyboard or mice
- Sealed unit lacking any user-replaceable parts
- Non-desktop OS; mobile devices use special mobile operating systems

The last one is important—as discussed in Chapter 23, a device's OS is the easiest way to differentiate between something like a 2-in-1 laptop in a tablet form factor and a plain tablet mobile device. Your typical portable computer runs a desktop OS such as Windows, macOS, or some Linux distribution such as Ubuntu. A true mobile device will typically run Apple iOS, iPadOS, or some form of Google's Android.

 EXAM TIP CompTIA A+ 1102 objective 1.8 lists iPadOS, iOS, and Android under cell phone/tablet OSs. The same objective lists Windows, Linux, macOS, and Chrome OS under workstation OSs. Be aware that while there are some tablets that run versions of Windows, for exam purposes, Windows is treated as a desktop operating system rather than a mobile one.

This chapter explores mobile devices in detail. We'll first look at the hardware features and capabilities of devices common in the mobile market. Next, we'll examine mobile operating system software. The chapter finishes with the details of configuring the devices for personal use. We'll save mobile device troubleshooting and security for Chapter 25. The CompTIA A+ certification exams are serious about mobile devices and we have a lot of ground to cover, so let's get started.

1101

Mobile Computing Devices

The specialized hardware of mobile devices defines to a large degree the capabilities of those devices. This first section examines smartphones and tablets and then looks at specific hardware common to many of these devices.

Device Variants

Most modern mobile devices fall into one of a few categories, including smartphones, tablets, and wearable technology, which all have similar features and capabilities. There are a few other mobile device types, and they are best understood as devices purpose-built to be better at some task than a general-purpose device such as a smartphone or tablet; an e-reader is a good example. The CompTIA A+ 1101 exam objectives focus on smartphones and tablets, but be aware that these other types of mobile devices exist.

Smartphones

One of the earliest types of mobile device was the personal digital assistant (PDA), such as the Compaq iPaq from the late 1990s. PDAs had the basic features of today's mobile devices but lacked cellular connectivity, so you couldn't make a phone call. Many people, your author included, spent close to ten years carrying a mobile phone and a PDA, wondering when somebody would combine these two things. Starting around 2003–2005, companies began marketing PDAs that included cellular telephones (although cool features like using the PDA to access Internet data weren't well developed). Figure 24-1 shows an early PDA-with-a-phone, the once very popular RIM BlackBerry.

While these tools were powerful for their time, it wasn't until Apple introduced the iPhone (see Figure 24-2) in 2007 that we saw the elements that define a modern *smartphone*:

- A multi-touch interface as the primary input method for using the smartphone
- A well-standardized application programming interface (API) enabling developers to create new apps for the system
- Tight consolidation of cellular data to the device, enabling any application (Web browsers, e-mail clients, games, and so on) to exchange data over the Internet
- Synchronization and distribution tools that enable users to install new apps and synchronize or back up data

Figure 24-1
RIM BlackBerry
(courtesy of the
TotalSem Tech
Museum)

Figure 24-2
Early Apple
iPhone

Since then, smartphones have developed many more features and uses. They have come to play a big role in the trend toward ever-present connectivity and seamless data access across all of our devices. Because smartphones do so much more than simply make and receive phone calls—we surf the Web with them, stream music and video, send and receive e-mail, and even do work with them—the infrastructure and technologies that connect smartphones with a mesh of networked data and services must be fast, robust, and secure.

Most smartphones run one of the big two operating systems: Google Android or Apple iOS (see Figure 24-3). iOS runs exclusively on Apple hardware, such as the iPhone. Phones running Android come from a multitude of manufacturers. Smartphones typically have no user-replaceable or field-replaceable components, and have to be brought into specialized (and in some cases, authorized) service centers for repair.

Figure 24-3
Examples of
the big two
smartphone OSs:
Android (left),
iOS (right)

Tablets

Tablets are very similar to smartphones; they run the same (or at least similar in the case of Apple's tablets) OSs and apps, and use the same multi-touch screens. From a tech's perspective, they are like large smartphones (without the phone). While a typical smartphone screen is around 5 to 6 inches, tablets run around 7 to 12.9 inches (see Figure 24-4).

Unlike smartphones, tablets generally lack a cellular data connection (unless you buy a model specifically designed for it), instead counting on 802.11 Wi-Fi to provide Internet connectivity. Tablets are available at many price points, from more budget-friendly options that sacrifice performance and build quality in favor of affordability, all the way to high-end devices that use cutting-edge hardware, premium materials, and the most advanced available features. Tablets have come a long way since they debuted, and are now fairly ubiquitous not only for individual users but also in business settings.

Figure 24-4
Typical tablet

Mobile Hardware Features

Much of the usefulness of mobile devices is driven by the many hardware features they include. This section explores the basics: screen technologies, cameras, microphones, digitizers, and GPS connectivity.

Screen Technologies

Mobile devices use a variety of screen types. Most tablets use some type of LCD panel, just like portable devices and desktop monitors. The less expensive ones use twisted nematic (TN); the better ones, like the Apple iPad, use an in-plane switching (IPS) panel for richer colors and better viewing angles. Refer back to Chapter 17 if you need to review the difference between these panel types. We'll take a look at the technology that turns these screens into touch interfaces in the upcoming "Digitizers" section.

Some smaller devices, like the better smartphones, use a related technology—*organic light-emitting diode (OLED)*—that lights the screen with an organic compound. Applying an electric current causes the organic layer to glow in the precise spots desired. Displaying a checkerboard pattern of black and white, in other words, only lights up the white squares. OLEDs and AMOLEDs don't use backlights at all, which means they *can* display true black, they're lighter, and they use less electricity than LCDs.

 EXAM TIP OLED screens use an organic compound exposed to electrical current for lighting; they don't have a traditional backlight.

 NOTE Some devices use *active matrix OLED (AMOLED)*, which adds a TFT layer for more control over the screen. AMOLED is more expensive than OLED, but provides a better picture that uses less electricity.

Cameras

Many mobile devices have distinct front-facing and rear-facing cameras. These cameras enable chatting with Grandma over Facetime, tearful YouTube confessionals, and Instagram selfies! Devices with a camera can transmit video over cellular and IP-based networks (such as the Internet) just like dedicated or built-in webcams on full-fat desktops and laptops.

Smartphone cameras have come a long way since the grainy, low-resolution images of yesteryear. Many of them now rival all but the high-end dedicated point-and-shoot cameras used by advanced hobbyists and professional photographers (see Figure 24-5).

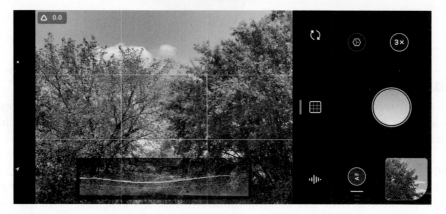

Figure 24-5 Author's camera app on his iPhone

Modern smartphone camera features include high dynamic range (HDR), light compensation, and other functions that enable the user to finely tune a photo or video. Manufacturers have even incorporated advances in artificial intelligence to their image-processing software to enhance the end results. Higher-end and even midrange devices often have more than one camera lens built in, allowing for more versatile photography. Additionally, these cameras offer a variety of options when taking photos and video; some cameras enable you to take "bursts" of shots (like ten in a single second) to make sure you capture faster-moving objects and action shots, as well as slow-motion video. When coupled with the multitude of apps available for mobile devices, you can edit photos and videos on-the-fly, adding light-filter effects, cleaning up shots, and even adding special effects.

Microphones

Almost all mobile devices incorporate at least one microphone. Smartphones certainly wouldn't be of much value without a microphone, and you wouldn't be very effective at communicating over Skype or FaceTime without them. Additionally, many people use mobile devices to dictate speech or record other sounds, so microphones serve many purposes on mobile devices.

As with the portable devices discussed in the previous chapter, mobile devices commonly have more than one microphone to enable noise-cancelling routines to work their magic. In contrast to those more traditional portables, you may need to take more care to avoid blocking any of the microphones on a mobile device.

Digitizers

When electrical engineers talk about a digitizer, they refer to a component that transforms analog signals into digital ones; that is to say, it digitizes them. That's not what we techs talk about when discussing digitizers on mobile devices. A *digitizer* refers to the component that provides the "touch" part of a touch screen. When your finger contacts a touch screen, the digitizer's fine grid of sensors under the glass detects your finger and signals the OS its location on the grid. As with modern trackpads, you can use one or more fingers to interact with most touch screens.

 EXAM TIP The CompTIA A+ 1101 exam objectives mention touch-screen configuration as something you do on a laptop or mobile device. While this used to only really apply to touch-screen laptops, some configuration options for touch screens have made their way to tablets and smartphones as well.

Location Services

One major feature of mobile devices is the ability to track the device's location through *global positioning system (GPS) services,* cellular, or Wi-Fi connections. Users rely on *cellular location services* to conveniently find things near them, such as stores and restaurants, or to determine when their Uber driver will show up. This section discusses some of what a mobile device such as a smartphone can do with GPS capability, followed by a look at privacy concerns associated with location tracking.

A great example of how smartphones can use GPS is the traffic and navigation app *Waze* (see Figure 24-6). Waze not only navigates, but its crowd-sourced data collection provides you with amazing real-time knowledge of the road ahead.

Figure 24-6
Waze in action

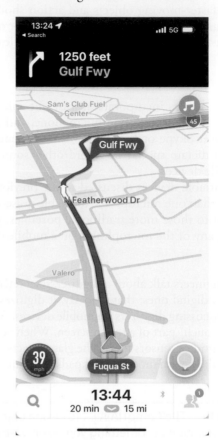

Another cool use of GPS is finding your phone when it's missing. The iPhone offers the Find My iPhone app (see Figure 24-7), for example. This feature is part of the iCloud service that comes free with any iOS device.

Figure 24-7
Find My iPhone
app

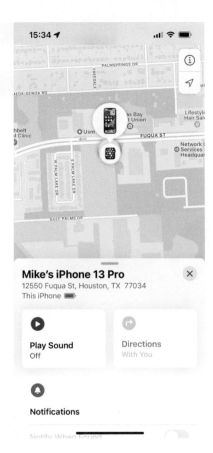

Location Tracking and Privacy Tracking your location is generally a good thing…
when you want to be tracked. By default, mobile OSs track and in many cases record
your location for an extended amount of time. This is called *geotracking*, and not everyone
likes it. If you don't like this feature, turn it off. Figure 24-8 shows turning off Location
on an Android phone.

EXAM TIP Because mobile devices tap into the Internet or cellular phone
networks, the devices have identifying numbers such as a MAC address.
The cell phone companies and government agencies can use the ID or MAC
address to pinpoint where you are at any given time. *Geotracking* has a lot of
room for abuse of power.

Figure 24-8
Turning off
Location

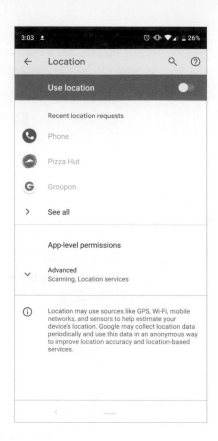

1102

Mobile Operating Systems

Most mobile devices run either Apple iOS or Google Android. This section discusses their development and implementation models, as well as some of their major features, including how their app stores work.

Development Models

Before we look at each mobile operating system in detail, let's step back to consider the big picture. The different underlying philosophies inspiring these operating systems—and guiding the companies that make them—help us understand why they do something one way instead of another. We'll start with a look at closed source and open source as development models. You may have heard these terms regarding how software is released and licensed (if not, Chapter 28 will discuss how these terms apply to licensing), but they also provide an interesting framework for looking at how products are developed and released. Then we'll discuss how these models apply to operating systems.

Closed Source

When it comes to development models, it may help to think of *closed source* as another way to refer to the traditional practice of making and selling a product without telling anyone how you made it. The traditional model makes intuitive sense, at least in our culture; how your product is made is a trade secret—something that gives you a competitive edge—and sharing it could inspire competitors to use your design, or potential customers to make it themselves.

Vendor-Specific and Proprietary   We sometimes apply the terms *vendor-specific* or *proprietary* to a closed-source product or technology, most often when we're trying to highlight something that doesn't use common, open standards. The terms are related to closed source, but don't confuse them; they aren't interchangeable. These labels often imply that the product may not play nice (or be interoperable) with other products, may have connectors and cables that are hard to find or expensive, may not be friendly to users who want to tinker with or modify it, may be harder to repair, and may pose a host of other problems.

The concept behind and use of these terms is sometimes slippery. As you'll see later in the chapter, a device maker may use a common standard such as USB 3.0, but design its own connector. Even though the device maker is technically using part of the open USB 3.0 standard, we'll still call the device's ports and cables proprietary.

Open Source

In this broader sense, you can think of a product as *open source* if its maker releases the instructions for making it—it doesn't have to be software (though that's usually the context). When a company commits to open sourcing one or more products, it has to operate differently than companies using a closed-source model. Secrecy, for example, is necessarily a smaller part of its business; knowing that anyone could make its products, the company has to focus on other factors (such as price, service, support, convenience, quality, innovation, etc.) to stay competitive.

Just because a company releases these instructions to the public doesn't mean anyone else gets to own them. Much as artists and authors set terms that specify whether the rest of us can legally copy or modify their work, the owners or authors of the instructions for making a product will specify terms for how others are allowed to use them. Sometimes the owners or authors may just say they're releasing the instructions for personal use or educational purposes—you can study what they've done and make your own product, but you can't start selling copies. When it comes to open-source software, these terms commonly dictate whether companies who modify the software are obliged to publish their changes, and whether they're allowed to profit from how they use it.

Development Models and the Mobile OS

The development model is one of many choices that reflect underlying company philosophy and goals. A company that makes an open-source mobile operating system like Google Android has little control over how the OS will be used and who can modify it. A company that makes a closed-source operating system like Microsoft Windows but licenses the OS to device makers has more control—the company knows the OS won't be modified and can be picky about which devices to license it for. A company making a closed-source OS like Apple iOS for its own devices can tailor-fit the software to the hardware it will run on. A company that builds an OS others can use and modify as they see fit and a company that builds an OS handcrafted exclusively for its own hardware obviously have very different underlying philosophies and goals.

The big thing to keep in mind with an open-source operating system like Android is that companies building devices that use the OS don't have to share the OS developer's underlying philosophy—they can have wildly varying goals and development models of their own. If the operating system's license allows it, each of the device makers could modify the OS before installing it on their own device—and never release those modifications. The modifications might just enable special hardware to work, but they could also install apps you don't want and can't remove, cause third-party apps coded without knowledge of the modifications to malfunction, or collect information about how you use the device.

To bring this all together, the point is that a manufacturer can put an open-source operating system on an otherwise closed-source device—don't assume a device is itself open source just because the mobile OS it uses is. In fact, vanishingly few of the devices with an open-source OS are best seen as open-source products.

Think back to the earlier discussion of an open-source development process and apply it to a smartphone. The most extreme interpretation of an open-source smartphone is that the maker has released all of the instructions and code someone else would need to manufacture an identical smartphone and all of the components inside it. A more likely (but still exceptional) scenario is that all of the software on the device when it leaves the factory is open sourced, including the operating system, drivers, and the firmware powering its components.

Apple iOS and iPadOS

Apple's closed-source mobile operating system, *iOS* (see Figure 24-9), runs on the iPhone. (The Apple iWatch runs a different OS, called watchOS. It is also closed source.) The Apple model of development is very involved: Apple tightly controls the development of the hardware, OS, developer tools, and app deployment platform. Apple's disciplined development model is visible in its strict development policies and controls for third-party developers, and this control contributes to the high level of security in iOS.

iOS apps are almost exclusively purchased, installed, and updated through Apple's *App Store*. An exception is providers of line-of-business apps specific to a particular organization. These internal development groups reside within an organization and can develop iOS apps, but deploy them only to devices that are under the organization's control, skipping the public App Store. They still have to undergo a type of Apple partnering and enterprise licensing approval process.

Apple's famous iPad tablet used to run iOS, but over time, the needs of tablet users evolved, and it now runs *iPadOS* (see Figure 24-10) The differences between iOS and iPadOS are slight, and the experience of using an iPad is very similar to that of using an iPhone. The average user may not notice the differences, but there are some important distinctions between the two that a good tech should aware of.

Figure 24-9
iOS 15

Figure 24-10
iPadOS in action

One key difference is in *touch pen* compatibility. Touch pens are, in general, an advanced version of the traditional stylus, which usually is just a plastic pointer with some kind of rubber point. Apple's touch pen is called the Apple Pencil and only works with iPadOS-equipped devices. Beyond keeping the screen clear of fingerprints, a touch pen can be used to effectively handwrite notes and draw precise and often professional-caliber artwork. Tablet users have gravitated toward using tablets as laptop substitutes in some cases, so iPadOS accommodates this by incorporating some of the features more commonly associated with macOS, such as multitasking functionality, mouse and key-board support, and the ability to connect external storage via USB-C. On the flipside, there are things that iOS does that iPadOS doesn't. Most notably, iOS allows direct pair-ing with Apple's smartwatch, while iPadOS does not.

Google Android

For simplicity, think of Android and iOS as opposites. *Android* (see Figure 24-11) is an open-source platform, based on yet another open platform, Linux, and is owned by Google. Because Android is open source, device manufacturers can (and do!) alter or customize it as they see fit; there are differences among the implementations from vari-ous vendors. Google writes the core Android code and occasionally releases new versions (naming each major update after a dessert or candy of some sort), at which point vendors customize it to add unique hardware features or provide a branded look and feel.

Figure 24-11
Android 12
(Snow Cone)

Android apps are available to purchase and download through various app stores, such as *Google Play* and the Amazon Appstore. Android app stores tend to be fairly open in contrast to the high standards and tight control Apple applies to its third-party app developers, and Android makes it easier to install arbitrary applications downloaded from a Web site.

 NOTE Android-based devices may be more open than iOS ones on average, but it isn't a given. How open or closed an individual Android device is will depend greatly on how its manufacturer has modified the OS.

Mobile OS Features

Mobile operating systems come in a variety of flavors and sometimes have different features as well as different interfaces. But they also have a great deal in common, because consumers expect them to perform most of the tasks they are used to seeing in other mobile devices, regardless of operating system. Whether you are using an iPhone, an Android phone, or a smart watch, you still expect to be able to send texts, check your e-mail, and make video calls. Because of this, mobile OS differences boil down to hardware and app support, look and feel, and philosophical differences that manifest in how the OS goes about a common task. We'll take a quick look at some of the features common to all mobile operating systems and point out differences along the way.

User Interfaces

All mobile OSs have a *graphical user interface (GUI)*, meaning you interact with them by accessing icons on the screen. Current models do not offer a command-line interface. Each OS usually has either a major button or a row of icons that enables the user to navigate to the most prominent features of the device. They also all support touch *gestures*, such as *swiping* to navigate between screens or *pinching* to zoom in or out. Most mobile OSs have some type of menu system that enables the user to find different apps and data.

iOS offers some customization of the user interface. You can group apps together into folders, for example, and reposition most apps for your convenience. The iOS look and feel, however, will remain consistent.

Android offers a very different GUI experience by employing programs called *launchers* that enable users to customize their Android device extensively. Many companies make launchers, and different manufacturers ship devices preloaded with launchers they make or prefer. Samsung devices use the TouchWiz launcher, for example. I use the Nova launcher on my Android phone. The launcher enables you to change nearly every aspect of the GUI, including icon size, animations, gestures, and more.

Most mobile devices include an *accelerometer* and a *gyroscope*, one to measure movement in space and the other to maintain proper orientation of up and down. These extend the user interface to include how you move the device itself; a common use is changing the *screen orientation* when you rotate a device from vertical to horizontal, for example, to enhance watching videos on YouTube.

Wi-Fi Calling

While every mobile device that calls itself a phone must have support for cellular wireless, another feature that many mobile devices include is *Wi-Fi calling*, the capability to make regular phone calls over Wi-Fi networks. Wi-Fi calling is very useful if you often find yourself in a place with poor cellular coverage but good Wi-Fi. To use Wi-Fi calling, first both your phone and carrier need to support it, then you need to enable it in your phone settings (see Figure 24-12). Once Wi-Fi calling is enabled, the phone will use any Wi-Fi network it's connected to (assuming the performance is acceptable) for all phone calls.

Figure 24-12
Option to enable
Wi-Fi calling on
an iPhone 13 Pro

Virtual Assistants

> "Hey, Siri!"
> "Yes, Mike?"
> "What's the weather like today?"
> "Always sunny where you are, Mike."

Okay, maybe they're not quite that cool, but the *virtual assistants* on smartphones and tablets enable quick, vocal interaction to accomplish common goals. For example, one only has to ask Siri (Apple's virtual assistant) how to find the nearest restaurant or tourist attraction, and she (Siri's voice is female by default) will respond with the information sought.

Virtual assistants can also be useful in performing Internet searches and, in some cases, even activating and using certain apps on the mobile device. This helps people who may have certain disabilities that may prevent them from tapping or typing on the device, by enabling them to use voice commands.

A virtual assistant is also useful if you must use your smartphone while driving (although *anything* that diverts your attention from the road is discouraged for safety reasons). You can speak to the smartphone's virtual assistant to place a call or get directions while driving, especially if the smartphone is paired with the car's Bluetooth system. The Windows 10/11 equivalent to Siri is called Cortana, and essentially serves the same functions and provides the same services and features. Google's virtual assistant, Google Assistant, is also available for iOS and any of Google's many platforms like Google Home and Android TV. In addition to the big three's virtual assistants, there are also apps you can download that provide other virtual assistant services, depending upon your platform.

Software Development Kits

Most mobile operating systems come with some sort of software development kit (SDK) or application development kit that you can use to create custom apps or add features to existing apps on the device. Figure 24-13 shows the development (programming) environment for the iOS SDK, *Xcode*, with the code for an iOS app open in the background window, and the same app code running in an iPhone simulator on top.

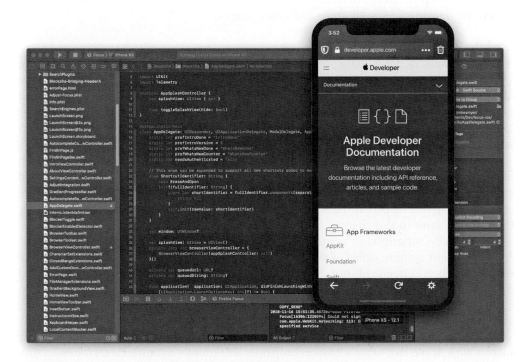

Figure 24-13   Xcode running an app written with the iOS SDK

Each mobile OS poses its own challenge to app developers. Apple's rigid development model makes it such that your app must pass a rigorous testing program before it is allowed into the App Store. Microsoft's development model, while not typically as rigid, is similar in nature. Google, on the other hand, allows anyone to create Android apps and distribute them to the masses without much interference.

Emergency Capabilities

One feature almost all currently marketed smartphones have built in is the emergency notification feature that enables them to receive broadcasts from national emergency broadcast systems, such as the Emergency Alert System (EAS) in the United States. This can be a very useful feature during severe weather, enabling you to receive warning text messages. In the event someone reports a child missing in your immediate area, it enables you to get AMBER Alerts. Many of these emergency broadcast system alerts also force your phone to emit a very loud sound or vibrate incessantly in order to get your attention.

While modern smartphones can place 911 calls effectively, the old 911 system relied on the Public Switched Telephone Network (PSTN) to trace a call and determine its location, in order to dispatch emergency responders to the correct address quickly. This was problematic with mobile devices, so legislation was passed (the Wireless Communications and Public Safety Act of 1999) requiring carriers to be able to pinpoint the location of a mobile device, such as a smartphone. The *Enhanced 911 (E911)* system uses GPS and cellular networks to triangulate the location of a phone by its distance from cell towers, its transmission delay time, and other factors.

Mobile Payment Service

As smartphones and other mobile devices have become so much more commonplace in our daily lives, we've become very reliant on them to store our personal and sensitive information such as passwords, credit card numbers, financial documents, receipts, and more. Over time, smartphone manufacturers, as well as merchants, realized that the next logical step was to enable you to pay for goods and services simply by scanning your smartphone or using an app.

The app connects to your bank information and automatically transfers the funds from your bank to the merchant. This feature is called *mobile payment service*. Near field communication (NFC) applications refine the process further: simply place your device on or near the special pad at the register in order to authorize payment to the merchant. (See "NFC," later in this chapter, for the scoop on these tiny networks.)

Additionally, smartphone manufacturers produce their own payment systems. The Apple payment system, called *Apple Pay*, was first implemented with the iPhone 6, and support has been integrated into the Apple Watch. Apple Pay supports major credit card payment terminals and point-of-sale systems, including those fielded by Visa, MasterCard, and American Express. Apple Pay can use contactless payment terminals with NFC and supports in-app payments for online purchases.

Mobile payment systems have become a lot more popular over time. Since Apple saw success with Apple Pay, other software companies and mobile manufacturers followed suit. Samsung, one of the most prominent manufacturers of Android smartphones, released Samsung Pay in 2015. Google released their version in 2018, and predictably named it

Google Pay. These apps have expanded their functionality to serve as full-blown digital wallets, allowing you to do more than just pay for things. One of the coolest features is that users can now store and transfer digital tickets for concerts and sporting events, making forgotten or lost tickets largely a thing of the past.

Airplane Mode

Airplane mode is simply a switch (either an actual hardware switch located on the mobile device or a software switch that can be located in the device's configuration settings) that turns off all cellular and wireless services, except Bluetooth (see Figure 24-14). The aptly named mode disables these communications so passengers can comply with restrictions protecting aircraft instruments from interference, though you can also use it as a shortcut for turning off communication functions.

Figure 24-14
Airplane mode
enabled on iOS 15

VPN

As you'll recall from earlier chapters, VPNs establish secure connections between a remote client and the corporate infrastructure, or between two different sites, such as a branch office and the corporate office. VPNs are typically implemented using tunneling methods through an unsecure network, such as the Internet. In a client VPN setup, the host has client VPN software specially configured to match the corporate VPN server or concentrator configuration. This configuration includes encryption method and strength, as well as authentication methods.

A site-to-site VPN scenario uses VPN devices on both ends of the connection, configured to communicate only with each other, while the hosts on both ends use their respective VPN concentrators as a gateway. This arrangement is usually transparent to the users at both sites; hosts at the other site appear as if they are directly connected to the user's network.

VPNs can use a variety of technologies and protocols. The most popular ways to create a VPN are to use either a combination of the Layer 2 Tunneling Protocol (L2TP) and IPsec (see Figure 24-15), or Secure Sockets Layer (SSL)/Transport Layer Security (TLS). When using the L2TP/IPsec method, UDP port 1701 is used and must be opened on packet-filtering devices. In this form of VPN, users connect to the corporate network and can use all of their typical applications, such as their e-mail client, and can map shares and drives as they would if they were actually connected onsite to the corporate infrastructure.

Figure 24-15
Configuring
a VPN

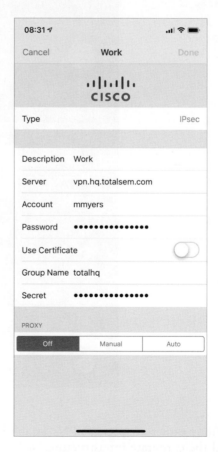

An SSL/TLS-based VPN, on the other hand, uses the standard SSL/TLS port, TCP 443, and is typically used through a client's Web browser. SSL/TLS-based VPNs don't normally require any special software or configuration on the client itself, but they don't give the client the same direct access to resources on the corporate network. Therefore, users may have to access these network resources through the client browser via an access portal.

NOTE SSL has been entirely replaced by TLS, but you'll often still see things referred to as SSL/TLS or SSL. VPNs are one example where this is the case.

1101

Configuring a Mobile Device

Mobile devices require some setup and configuration to function seamlessly in your life, though the industry is constantly refining and simplifying this process. Mobile devices typically come preconfigured with everything but your user account and network credentials. Just because you don't have to do much to get up and running anymore doesn't mean you're out of the woods, though. You may well need to configure corporate e-mail accounts, device add-ons, apps, synchronization settings, and other advanced features.

You can add capabilities by enhancing hardware and installing productivity apps. You also need to set up network connectivity, add Bluetooth devices, configure e-mail account(s), and enable the devices to synchronize with a computer. Plus you have a lot of add-on options; let's take a look.

Enhancing Hardware

A mobile device is a computer, just like your desktop or laptop, with the same basic components doing the same basic things. The construction centers on a primary circuit board, the motherboard, onto which every other component is attached. The biggest of these components is often the *system on a chip (SoC)*, a wonder of miniaturization combining a CPU, GPU, and sundry other support logic onto a single silicon die, saving a lot of space and power in the process. An interesting aside about the CPUs used in these devices is that they are rarely Intel x86 based; instead, you are much more likely to run across an ARM architecture chip when perusing the spec sheets of your new tablet or smartphone. The iPad uses Apple-designed ARM A-series or M-series chips, for example, while Samsung's smartphones and tablets generally use ARM chips from Qualcomm's Snapdragon line-up.

Mobile devices use storage, though you'll never see one using a traditional magnetic *hard disk drive (HDD)* with spinning platters. Mobile devices use flash media such as a *solid-state drive (SSD)* or microSD card because they are smaller, use less power, and are much, much faster than spinning HDDs. Plus they're cooler, just like you.

Mobile devices differ from their larger brethren in two very significant areas of importance to techs. First, none of them offer any user-replaceable parts. If something breaks, you send the device back to the manufacturer, visit a local manufacturer-supported retail outlet such as the Apple Store, or take it to a specialized repair shop. Second, you can't upgrade mobile devices at all. Even a laptop enables you to upgrade RAM or a mass storage drive, for example, but the mobile device you buy is exactly what you get. You want something better? Buy a new one.

That said, every mobile device enables you to attach some kind of peripheral or external storage device. But every device offers different expansion capabilities, so it's hard to generalize about them. The closest you can get is the audio jack, but many smartphones no longer include them, in favor of Bluetooth connectivity. That being said, audio jacks are still around on some devices (see Figure 24-16).

Figure 24-16
Earbuds
plugged into a
smartphone

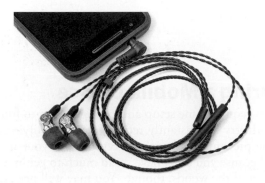

Note this is quickly changing as Apple dropped the jack as of the iPhone 7, and many Android devices have started leaving the port off as well, as Bluetooth wireless earbuds and speakers continue to become more popular, reliable, and affordable. Current iPhones and most iPads use the Lightning jack or USB-C, respectively, for physical external connections.

Apple Expansion Options

Apple devices offer the least expansion capability of all mobile devices, so even though they dominate the U.S. marketplace, there's not much to say about them. Most of the expansion on Apple devices is limited to proprietary cables and devices. The iPhone and iPad have historically used a single proprietary *Lightning port* for charging the device and connecting to the few external devices available. Figure 24-17 shows the typical use for the port: connecting to a USB AC adapter to charge.

Figure 24-17
USB charger
connected to
proprietary
Lightning port

While the vast majority of Apple's iOS devices stick with the proprietary Lightning connector, Apple has switched to USB Type-C with most iPad variants. Who knows what this means for the iPhone line, but it is nice to see Apple expanding its use of the industry standard. We'll return to USB Type-C, along with a number of other connectors, later in the chapter.

iPhones and iPads enable you to mirror the screen to a multimedia device such as a projector or a smart TV. This enables seamless presentations, for example, through the excellent Apple Keynote program (see Figure 24-18). The multimedia connection originally required another adapter (see Figure 24-19), but if you're using your device with a smart TV or another Apple device like an iMac, you can achieve this wirelessly with a feature called AirPlay.

Figure 24-18
Apple Keynote on an iPad and a projector

Figure 24-19
Apple Digital AV Adapter

Android Expansion Options

Devices that use Google Android come with a variety of connections and expansion capabilities. Some offer microSD slots for adding storage in the form of these tiny flash memory cards (see Figure 24-20), but this is becoming less common.

Figure 24-20
microSD card
and slot

Android devices used to have a more diverse range of connectors available, both for charging and connecting peripherals. Older devices sometimes used miniUSB, or proprietary power connectors, and some Android smartphones even had a tiny Micro-HDMI port. This has largely gone the way of the dinosaurs though, and most Android devices you'll see today make use of USB-C or occasionally still use microUSB.

Finally, some tablets (but rarely smartphones) sport a connector for attaching the device to an external monitor, such as a big screen or projector. Figure 24-21 shows a Micro-HDMI port and connector.

Figure 24-21
Micro-HDMI port
and connector

Bluetooth

The last way that mobile devices expand their physical capabilities is wirelessly, most often using the Bluetooth standard (if you need a refresher on Bluetooth, refer back to Chapter 20). Traditionally, extending a mobile device with Bluetooth has meant adding a headset, mouse (though not with Apple iOS products), keyboard, or speaker. Figure 24-22 shows a diminutive Apple keyboard for the iPad and the iPad resting in a stand to make typing a little easier than using the virtual keyboard.

With Bluetooth-enabled wearable devices growing in popularity, it can be tricky to decide how self-sufficient one of these must be before it stops counting as a mobile enhancement and enters the realm of full-fledged mobile device.

Figure 24-22
Keyboard
associated
with iPad

 NOTE   See the "Bluetooth" section toward the end of this chapter for the steps to set up a mobile device with a Bluetooth speaker.

Installing and Configuring Apps

Mobile devices come from the manufacturer with a certain number of vital apps installed for accessing e-mail, surfing the Web, taking notes, making entries in a calendar, and so on. Almost all mobile devices offer multimedia apps to enable you to listen to music, take pictures, watch YouTube videos, and view photos. You'll find instant messaging tools and, in the case of smartphones, telephone capabilities.

Beyond these essentials, you'll install most other apps through an app store. As you read about the app ecosystem for each mobile OS, consider how well the details of each ecosystem mesh with the development models discussed earlier in the chapter. Even though the rules of each app ecosystem usually reflect this development model, don't assume the apps on offer will follow suit—you'll find plenty of closed-source apps available on Android and open-source apps available for iOS.

iOS/iPadOS Apps

Apple iPhone and the iPad use the iOS and iPadOS operating systems, respectively. Apple exerts more control over the user experience than any other manufacturer by insisting all app developers follow strict guidelines.

Apple maintains strict control over what apps can be installed onto iOS/iPadOS devices, meaning that if you want to get an app for your iPhone or iPad, you can only get it from the Apple App Store (see Figure 24-23). Apple must approve any app before it goes into the App Store, and Apple reserves the right to refuse to distribute any app that fails to measure up.

Figure 24-23
App Store

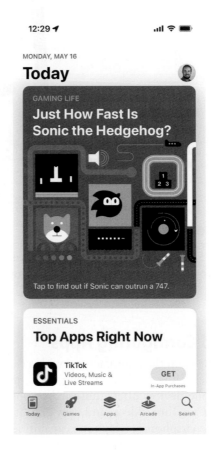

To add an app, select the App Store icon from the home screen. You can explore featured apps in the Today tab or peruse by category. You can check out the popular games, or simply search for what you want (see Figure 24-24).

Figure 24-24
Searching for
Monument
Valley 2

The first time you try to purchase an app through the App Store, you'll be prompted to set up an account. You can use an account that you created previously through the Apple iTunes music and video store or create a new Apple ID account. You can create a new Apple ID account with a few quick steps (see Figure 24-25) and a valid credit card.

Another iCloud feature, the iCloud Keychain, builds on the Keychain feature in macOS to synchronize user information, passwords, payment information, and other credentials with all of your Apple devices. (See "Synchronization," a little later in the chapter.) Keychain can seamlessly store many non-Apple credentials as well, such as logins for Facebook, Amazon, and other providers, and use them to auto-complete repetitive forms in both device apps and on Web sites. The real benefit is that you can authorize Apple to save this sensitive information, instead of authorizing each individual app or site to keep a copy.

Figure 24-25
Creating an
Apple ID for
iCloud and App
Store purchases

Android Apps

Google Android powers many smartphones and a solid portion of tablets. Unlike Apple iOS, Google gives core Android away, enabling manufacturers to differentiate their Android devices from those of other manufacturers. A Samsung tablet, in other words, uses a version of Android that differs somewhat from the Android an ASUS tablet uses. Likewise, OnePlus developed a custom interface called OxygenOS to change the look and feel of Android on its devices.

Because of these modifications, few Android users ever use "stock" or unmodified Android. Despite the shared core OS, Android users familiar with devices from one manufacturer may get tripped up by the different interface on Android devices from a different maker. These differences make it important to combine knowledge of the Android version a smartphone or tablet runs with knowledge about the manufacturer and its modifications to Android. The manufacturer will typically assign a version number to each release of its modifications.

Android devices can usually get apps from more than one source. The most common is Android's default app store, Google Play (which offers well over 2 million apps)—but some manufacturers (such as Amazon, for its line of Fire devices) modify Android to change this.

Many manufacturers offer a store with apps developed or customized to work with their devices. These *vendor-specific* stores enable you to get apps that should work well with your Android smartphone or tablet.

You can also go to a third-party app store or market for apps developed "for Android" that probably will work with your device, but there's no guarantee that they'll work on all Android devices. This Wild West approach to apps makes the Android smartphone or tablet experience vastly different from the experience on iOS.

Network Connectivity

Mobile devices connect to the outside world through the cellular networks or through various 802.11 Wi-Fi standards. You learned specifics about the standards in Chapter 20, so I won't rehash them here. This section looks at standard configuration issues from the perspective of a mobile device.

When you want to connect to a Wi-Fi network, you need to enable Wi-Fi on your device and then actively connect to a network. If the network is properly configured with WPA2, or WPA3 encryption, then you also need to have the logon information to access the network. The most common way to connect is through the Settings app (see Figure 24-26).

Figure 24-26
Selecting the
Settings icon

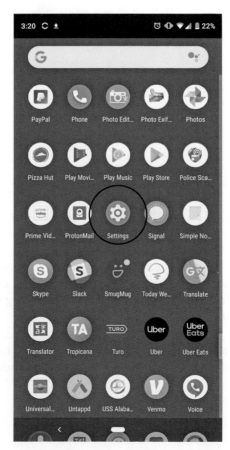

The Settings app enables you to do the vast majority of configuration necessary to a mobile device. To join a network, for example, tap the Wi-Fi (or Networks) option to see available networks (see Figure 24-27). Simply select the network you want to join and type in the passphrase or passcode. Give the mobile device a moment to get IP and DNS information from the DHCP server, and you're on the network.

Figure 24-27
Browsing
available
networks

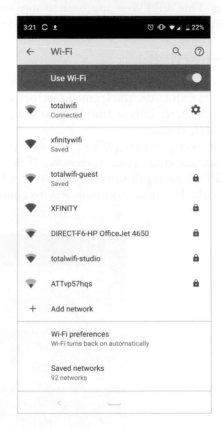

After you connect to a network successfully, all mobile devices store that network access information automatically, creating a *profile* for the network based on its SSID. This works just like with any other device that connects to a Wi-Fi network. If the SSID of a network changes after you've connected to that network, your mobile device will fail to connect to the rechristened network. You need to delete the profile and reconnect. Delete the profile through the Settings app by choosing the Wi-Fi network and selecting *Forget this network*.

 EXAM TIP You can use the Settings app to turn off Wi-Fi or to go into airplane mode to stop the device from sending any signals out.

Cellular Data Networks

Anyone with a smartphone these days can enjoy the convenience of using wireless cellular technology. Who doesn't love firing up an Android phone or an iPhone and cruising the Internet from anywhere? As cell-phone technology converges with Internet access technologies, competent techs need to understand what's happening behind the scenes. That means tackling an alphabet soup of standards. Regardless of the standard, the voice and data used on smartphones and some tablets (unless you have 802.11 wireless turned on) moves through a cellular wireless network with towers that cover the world. Back in Chapter 21, we discussed the technologies that make up cellular networking, so now we're going to talk about how it can be enabled and disabled on most mobile devices.

As discussed earlier in this chapter in the context of mobile operating systems, Android and iOS have a lot in common and that includes similar ways to enable and disable your cellular network. The way to accomplish it is fairly simple: swipe down from the top of the screen to check for a quick option, labeled with something like Data or Cellular. Alternatively, you can use the Settings app (introduced in the previous section). Once you've found it, look for the menu option that says Data or Cellular, and toggle it on or off.

Radio Firmware

Mobile devices use a wide variety of radio technologies to access the Internet, e-mail, and corporate infrastructures. Generally, mobile devices have two types of radios: 802.11 and Bluetooth. If the device can make calls, it also has some form of cellular radio.

PRL, PRI, and Baseband Updates   As mobile devices travel, they frequently have to pass through areas that don't have strong signals, or into areas that the carrier does not service. When a mobile device connects to different carriers' networks, we say it is *roaming*; roaming may result in additional service charges, depending upon the carriers involved.

Your phone's firmware will receive occasional automatic updates to its *Preferred Roaming List (PRL)* from the carrier; the PRL is a priority-ordered list of the other carrier networks and frequencies it should search for when it can't locate its home carrier's network. Updates to this list are sent via your phone's cellular connection (called baseband updates, or over-the-air updates) or, in some cases, through firmware updates during normal operating system and firmware upgrades via synchronization.

CDMA devices may also receive *product release instruction (PRI)* updates, which modify a host of complex device settings. Don't worry about specifics, here—these settings can pertain to the intricacies of many functions such as GPS, cellular connectivity, and messaging—but instead focus on the fact that carriers use these product release instructions to ready the device for deployment on their networks, enable the network to route calls or messages to the device, and more. As such, PRI updates may be needed if the network is evolving during the lifetime of a device, the device needs to be moved to a new network, or the device has a new owner.

   EXAM TIP   PRL updates are handled automatically during firmware/OS updates. They are only for CDMA networks. No one but the nerdiest of nerds will ever see these updates.

IMEI, ICCID, and IMSI   There are three particular identifiers you will need to understand in order to effectively manage mobile devices. The *International Mobile Equipment Identity (IMEI)* number is a 15-digit number used to uniquely identify a mobile device. IMEI numbers are unique to devices using the *Global System for Mobile Communications (GSM)* family of technologies, including its present-day descendants: 4G LTE and 5G. You can typically find this number printed inside the battery compartment of the mobile device, but you may not need to take the device apart: some operating systems enable you to view it inside the device configuration settings (see Figure 24-28).

Figure 24-28
IMEI settings
on an Android
phone

The IMEI number can be used to identify a specific device and even to block that device from accessing the carrier's network. If the device is lost or stolen, the user can notify her carrier, and the carrier can make sure the device can't be used on the network.

 NOTE   Always write down your IMEI number when you get a new phone, as it can prove you are the actual owner if the phone is stolen or lost.

The ICCID number, which stands for Integrated Circuit Card Identifier, uniquely identifies a subscriber identity module (SIM). The SIM contains information unique to the subscriber (the owner of the phone), and is used to authenticate the subscriber to the network. SIMs can be moved from phone to phone, usually with no problems.

The third number is the *International Mobile Subscriber Identity (IMSI)* number. It is also included on the SIM, but represents the actual user associated with the SIM. This number is not normally accessible from the phone, but is usually available from the carrier, to ensure that stolen phones are not misused. The IMSI number can also be used to unlock a phone.

You might want to record these numbers for each managed device in the enterprise, whether for inventory purposes or so that you have them handy when you work with your *mobile device management (MDM)* software (look for a more in-depth explanation about MDM software in Chapter 25). The MDM software typically collects these identifiers along with other device information (such as the telephone number or MAC address) during the provisioning process and stores them in the mobile device inventory for you. Figure 24-29 shows how IMEI and ICCID numbers are listed for a newer Android device in the device settings.

Figure 24-29
IMEI and ICCID numbers

Data

Many mobile devices can use the cellular data services discussed in Chapter 20 to access the Internet. This way you can use your smartphone, tablet, or other mobile devices to get e-mail or browse the Web pretty much anywhere.

By default, mobile devices that use cellular networks for Internet connectivity use *data roaming*, meaning they'll jump from cell tower to cell tower and from your provider to another provider without obvious notice. This is no big deal when you travel within your own country where competing providers have inexpensive roaming agreements.

Watch out for data roaming outside your country! If you travel to another country, your mobile device will happily and seamlessly connect via another cell provider if one is available. This can lead to some shockingly huge bills from your cell phone company when you get back from that cruise or international trip. If you're going outside your cell provider's coverage area, get a plan that specifies that you're traveling. It'll still be more expensive than your regular plan, but not nearly as crazy as an accidental roaming charge.

If you don't need to connect when out of country, turn data roaming off. You'll find the feature in the Settings app, as you might expect. You can also turn off cellular data entirely or only turn off cellular services selectively if your device can do more than one type. You would want to turn off cellular data, for example, if you don't have an unlimited data plan and are getting near your limits. There are also some security reasons to disable cellular connections while traveling, which we'll explore further in Chapter 25.

E-mail

Every mobile device uses an e-mail service set up specifically from the mobile OS developer. Plus, you can configure devices to send and receive standard e-mail as well. Let's look at the integrated options first.

All mobile devices offer e-mail services from the manufacturer or the OS developer. iOS and iPadOS devices integrate perfectly with iCloud, Apple's one-stop shop for e-mail, messaging, and online storage. Android devices assume a Gmail account, so they feature a Gmail option front and center.

Aside from the integrated e-mail options, mobile devices enable you to set up standard corporate and ISP e-mail configurations as well. The process is similar to that of setting up e-mail accounts that you learned about in Chapter 21. Apple devices go through the Settings app, tap Mail, then tap the Accounts option (see Figure 24-30). Tap the Add Account option to bring up the default e-mail options (see Figure 24-31). If you want to connect to a Microsoft Exchange Server–based e-mail account, tap the appropriate option here and type in your e-mail address, domain, username, password, and description.

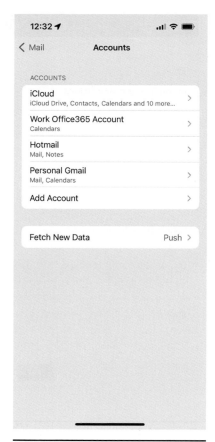

Figure 24-30   Accounts screen on iPhone

Figure 24-31   Default e-mail types on iPhone

Neither POP3 nor IMAP4 is one of Apple's suggested options, so if you want to set up an account of either type, you'll need to tap the Other option on the initial Add Account screen. Eventually you'll get prompted to choose POP3 or IMAP and type in addresses for the sending (SMTP) and receiving servers.

Android-based devices assume you'll have a Gmail account as your primary account, so you'll find Gmail's distinctive app icon on the home screen (see Figure 24-32). Gmail also can talk to other, non-Gmail e-mail services for setting up Exchange, POP3, or IMAP4 accounts; you configure it the same way as you would a desktop e-mail application, including putting in the port number and security type, in this case, TLS, if the server lacks autoconfigure (see Figure 24-33).

Figure 24-32 Gmail app

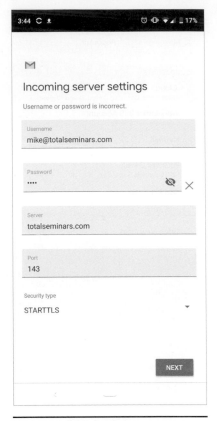

Figure 24-33 Setting up a secure IMAP account

EXAM TIP The latest versions of Android simply query the e-mail server to configure port numbers and security types automatically, just like modern desktop-based e-mail clients. Even though current devices automate this process, the CompTIA A+ 1101 objectives include port numbers, so you need to know them.

The CompTIA A+ 1101 exam will hit you pretty hard on e-mail settings, specifically on TCP port numbers for the various e-mail protocols. We've covered these in earlier chapters, but here's a quick cheat sheet and a few alternative numbers for real-world applications:

- POP3 uses TCP port 110.
- IMAP4 uses TCP port 143.
- SMTP uses TCP port 25.

Many servers block these default ports; plus, when you move to more secure versions of the protocols, you need to use other port numbers. I have no clue whether CompTIA will quiz on the secure ports for POP3, IMAP4, and SMTP, but here they are:

- Secure POP3 uses TCP port 995.
- Secure IMAP4 uses TCP port 993.
- Secure SMTP uses TCP port 465 or 587.

Finally, you may also have to configure other settings, such as *Secure/Multipurpose Internet Mail Extensions (S/MIME)* standard, used to configure digital signature settings for e-mail, and contacts from the corporate address book, depending on how the corporate e-mail server is set up.

 EXAM TIP Be familiar with corporate e-mail configuration settings for Gmail, Yahoo, Outlook, and iCloud (You'll get a closer look at them in Chapter 25). Know the corporate and ISP e-mail configuration settings for POP3, IMAP4, port and security settings, and Exchange.

Synchronization

From the first day mobile devices came into existence there was a problem: synchronizing data. People don't want their contacts on their mobile devices to be different than the contacts on their desktop—or online contacts. People don't want to edit e-mail on their mobile device and then have to go online to make the same changes. People only want one calendar. If you have a mobile device, you're going to want a method for all these different sets of data to synchronize so you only have one set of contacts, one e-mail inbox, one calendar, and so forth.

To keep files and data up to date, smartphones and tablets can *synchronize*, or *sync*, with cloud-based servers over the Internet or with local machines. These files and data include personal documents, Internet bookmarks, calendar appointments, social media data, e-books, and even location data. Older devices, such as BlackBerry and Palm Pilot, had a specialized sync program you installed on your computer to sync contacts, calendars, and so on. Today's devices sync through the cloud or optionally use a dedicated program.

Various mobile devices sync differently, depending upon the device vendor and software required. iOS/iPadOS devices use Apple iCloud to sync iPhones, iPads, and Macs via the cloud. Android devices can use Google's many services to sync certain configuration settings, apps, photos, texts, and so on. In some cases individual apps will synchronize directly; for example, a podcast app might synchronize data such as subscribed shows. Older versions of iOS needed to sync to a laptop or desktop computer via Apple's iTunes application. While this is still fully supported, most users will just let iCloud handle everything in the background.

EXAM TIP Synchronization enables mobile devices to keep up to date with a lot of essential information. You should know the types of data typically synced, including contacts, e-mail, photos, and calendar information for the exam, and other types of data to be a great tech. It's a lot. You can do this!

Synchronize to the Automobile

Automobile makers know you will talk on the phone while driving. While inherently dangerous—a good conversation can distract you from surroundings, including other 3000-pound death machines—everyone does it. Modern automobiles come equipped with voice communication systems, hands-free calling that uses your smartphone via Bluetooth (see Figure 24-34). *Synchronizing to the automobile* enables voice-activated contact calling, among other things, and often hooks up with a car's navigation system to help you get from point A to point B.

Figure 24-34
Calling via an iPhone using a car's built-in entertainment system

Exchange ActiveSync

Exchange ActiveSync (EAS) is a Microsoft protocol used to synchronize Microsoft Exchange e-mail, contacts, and calendars that has become widely used across a range of mobile OS platforms and hardware vendors, including Apple and Android devices. It was originally developed as a synchronization protocol for Microsoft Exchange corporate users, but has evolved over time to include more device control and management features. EAS not only has the capability to set up and configure network connectivity and secure e-mail options for clients that connect to Microsoft Exchange corporate servers, but also has the capability to control a much wider range of functions. Some of these functions include the ability to set password policies, remotely wipe or lock a mobile device, and control some device settings.

Synchronization Methods

In the old days, mobile devices were synchronized to a desktop (uphill, both ways, in the snow!), using a specific type of synchronization software provided with the device. Also, the type of data was typically limited to contact information, but we liked it because it was all we had. Now, there are newfangled ways you can sync device contacts, media files, and even apps. You can also get updates and patches from the device manufacturer by syncing your device.

With faster cellular and Wi-Fi networking technologies, you can skip the desktop and sync even large amounts of data to the cloud. Each phone vendor has its own cloud technology that can tie to your user account and store personal data from your mobile device. Apple has iCloud, Microsoft has OneDrive, and Google has Google Drive, as do some of the individual manufacturers that make Android devices.

There are also independent cloud providers that enable you to store your personal data, and even share it with others. Dropbox is a prime example of this type of provider, although there are many others. Most cloud storage services require you to set up security measures to protect your data, such as requiring a username and password for authentication. Some cloud providers also allow you to encrypt data stored in their cloud.

Synchronizing your data to a personal computer (or laptop) has both advantages and disadvantages. Some advantages of syncing to a personal computer are that you can be in full control of storing and protecting your own data, encrypted any way you choose, and can also move it to portable storage in case you need a backup of it later. A disadvantage is that you must be able to connect to your computer—a small problem if you can't bring it with you.

Syncing to the cloud also has its advantages and disadvantages. If you have a good cellular or wireless signal, you can sync from anywhere. You do have to be careful of syncing over insecure public wireless networks, however, since there is a possibility that your data could be intercepted and read over these insecure networks. Another disadvantage of syncing to the cloud is that once your data is in the cloud, you no longer fully control it. You are at the mercy of the security mechanisms and privacy policies of your provider. You have to accept whatever security mechanisms they use, such as encryption strength (or lack thereof), and you have to abide by their privacy policies, which may allow them to turn your data over to other companies for marketing, or even to law enforcement. Additionally, some cloud providers may limit the type and amount of data you are allowed to store in their cloud. These restrictions are typically in place to prevent software, movie, and music piracy.

These are all considerations you'll have to think carefully about when choosing whether to sync to the desktop, the cloud, or both.

 EXAM TIP The CompTIA A+ 1102 objectives cover synchronization extensively, and this overlaps with an 1102 objective, single sign-on (SSO). Be aware that a properly coded application on a modern mobile device can enable you to log in with one of the other accounts you're probably already logged into, such as Google, Apple ID, Facebook, Twitter, etc. The process for using your active authenticated session with one of these common services to sign you into other services is called *single sign-on (SSO)*. This may come up on the 1101 exam in the context of mobile device synchronization or on the 1102 exam in the context of single sign-on.

Synchronization Issues

The most common synchronization issue is a connectivity, device, or remote infrastructure problem that leaves data partially synced. A partial sync could result in incompletely downloaded e-mail or even duplicate messages as the device tries over and over to successfully sync, repeatedly downloading the same e-mail messages. A device may attempt to sync to download an OS patch or update and may fail. The most likely culprit is connectivity issues with Wi-Fi or cellular connections, and the problem can usually be resolved by moving the device to an area with a stronger signal. This doesn't prevent upstream connectivity issues, which may also have to be examined.

There are other problems that prevent synchronization, including authentication issues, OS version issues, or incorrect configuration settings. If a device won't sync even after getting it to a stronger, more stable connection, these are some of the things you should examine. Another problem may be the remote end of the connection. This may be the enterprise e-mail server, or even the entry point into the enterprise network. Failure to properly authenticate or meet the requirements of the entry device may prevent a device from synchronizing.

Another issue you may want to examine when you have synchronization trouble is that multiple sources may be trying to sync the same data. A device can synchronize from an enterprise app store, for example, as well as the vendor app store; personal e-mail services, such as Gmail and Yahoo Mail; and even from third-party providers of "whatever-as-a-service" and cloud storage. This could be as simple as a configuration change you had to make for one service preventing another from working—or the sources might be independently trying to sync different data to the same location. In the enterprise environment, it's the mobile device management team's job to put together a management and technical strategy that will ensure minimal conflict between different synchronization sources.

Account Setup and Management

If you or someone you know uses mobile devices for work, you've most likely done or at least seen some form of account setup or management. Most productivity apps, like *Microsoft 365, Google Workspace*, and Apple's suite of apps that use *iCloud*, are designed to be synchronized across multiple devices. This means that the document you were reviewing or the e-mail you were carefully writing on your laptop before you had to leave for an appointment can be paused, synchronized, and resumed on another computer or, you guessed it, a mobile device. This sort of cross-platform synchronization has become essential to businesses and it's going to be something you'll encounter on the CompTIA A+ exam, as well as on the job in IT.

The big question you probably have now is about how to synchronize these accounts. In this regard, mobile devices work mostly in the same way as a desktop or a laptop. The mobile versions of productivity apps generally mimic most of the functionality of their desktop counterparts, with optimized user interfaces to account for things like the smaller display, touchscreen, screen rotation, and other mobile device characteristics. They're also optimized to make it as easy as possible to synchronize. In many cases, it's as simple as installing the mobile version of an app like Microsoft 365, entering the e-mail and password associated with the account, and waiting a few seconds until your Teams chat or Outlook e-mails are available to you on the go.

Most of these apps give users or administrators the ability to make adjustments, including to synchronization settings. Some device synchronization settings may, for example, cause your device to save things you're working on in local storage. If this happens, you may be happy about it, or you may wonder why your smartphone suddenly started displaying a notification that your storage is full. You may also notice that your accounts aren't synchronizing. In this case, one of the first places you should look is your account settings; the fix may be as simple as turning on synchronization in your mobile app.

Mobile Device Communication and Ports

Mobile devices wouldn't be nearly as useful if they didn't have ways to interconnect with the outside world. This section looks at the many technologies and connections mobile devices use to get data flowing to the Internet and other devices.

MicroUSB/MiniUSB

If you have an Android device made before 2017, it's very likely it has either a micro- or mini-USB port to charge, connect to laptops or desktops, and sync between those devices. *MicroUSB* or *miniUSB* connectors were standard on most Android devices. That's not to say that you won't be able to find devices using proprietary connectors; Google makes the OS available to multiple device manufacturers, and some manufacturers do maintain a proprietary connector.

Lightning Connector

With the iPhone 5, Apple introduced its most recent proprietary connector, known as the *Lightning* connector. It replaced the older 30-pin dock connector that Apple used on previous iPhones and iPads. The Lightning connector is an 8-pin connector (see Figure 24-35) that can be inserted without regard to proper orientation; in other words, it's not "keyed" to insert a specific way (such as right-side up or upside down, as traditional USB connectors are) into the device.

 NOTE   Earlier-model iPads made use of the Lightning connector, but in 2018, Apple released the first USB-C iPad Pro. Since then, Apple has gradually transitioned its various other iPad models, like the Air and Mini, to USB-C. You'll only find Lightning connectors in use on older models, or the basic iPad still sold by Apple at the time of writing.

Figure 24-35
Lightning
connector

The proprietary nature of the Lightning cable means it's more expensive than a normal USB cable. It is licensed to other manufacturers through the *Made for iPhone (MFi)* program, but to prevent widespread production of fake Lightning connectors by unlicensed manufacturers, it contains a small chip that identifies it as a true Lightning connector, and cables without that chip typically won't work or will only have limited use.

NOTE The Apple Lightning standard is the epitome of *proprietary vendor-specific ports and connectors*. Only iOS devices use Lightning for communication and power. Android devices typically use industry-standard, vendor-neutral ports and connectors.

USB Type-C

USB Type-C (see Figure 24-36), the newest iteration of USB connectors, is quickly becoming the de facto standard port on Android devices today, which is awesome because you can use one charger for your laptop and phone. As we touched on earlier, Apple has gradually adopted USB-C for its iPad lineups since 2018 due to its compatibility with a huge number of peripherals and its higher power handling that provides faster charging.

Figure 24-36
USB Type-C
connector

Like the Lightning connector, the USB Type-C connector is not keyed, allowing it to be inserted right-side up or upside down. It can (but doesn't have to) support USB 3.1 technology with very fast data transfer rates of up to 10 Gbps. Don't assume Type-C is synonymous with a specific version of USB—some devices using a Type-C connector are using it with USB 2.0.

EXAM TIP You will likely see micro- and mini-USB, USB-C, and Lightning mobile device connection types on the exams. Know their characteristics and differences.

Bluetooth

While we discussed Bluetooth at some length, including configuring and pairing, in Chapter 20, let's review an outline of how the process will work on a mobile device. You can pair a Bluetooth device with a mobile device using a simple process that begins with enabling Bluetooth on the mobile device (if it isn't already enabled). Steps vary, but you can accomplish this in the quick settings menu or the full device settings menu. Next, power on the other Bluetooth device (or ensure Bluetooth is enabled if the device is already on). Return to the mobile device to discover and select the Bluetooth device for pairing, and then enter the appropriate personal identification number (PIN) code (see Figure 24-37). To add *Bluetooth speakers*, for example, the smartphone or tablet will display a set of characters for you to type on the keyboard. Once you type in the PIN code, the devices connect.

Figure 24-37
Prompting
for PIN

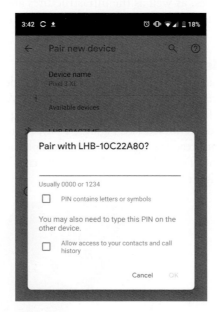

EXAM TIP Not all Bluetooth pairings require a PIN code, but there's always some kind of pairing action to perform on both devices.

Always remember to test the connectivity between a mobile device and a newly added Bluetooth accessory. If you've added a speaker, open up your favorite music app or podcast and tap play to make sure it works.

 EXAM TIP Most mobile devices have Bluetooth discovery disabled by default to conserve battery life. An active search for devices to pair with uses electricity, as does completed pairing, so use Bluetooth only when you need to use it and be prepared for the battery hit.

NFC

Near Field Communication (NFC) uses chips embedded in mobile devices that create electromagnetic fields when these devices are close to each other. The typical range for NFC communications is anywhere from a very few centimeters to only a few inches. The devices must be very close to or touching each other, and can be used to exchange contact information, small files, and even payment transactions through stored credit cards using systems like Apple Pay and Google Pay. This technology is seeing widespread adoption in newer mobile devices, as well as the infrastructures and applications that support them. *Tap pay devices* are increasingly common, using NFC and your phone so your credit cards stay in your wallet or purse.

Magnetic Readers and Chip Readers

Merchants can attach a magnetic reader or a chip reader to a smartphone to enable very quick credit card transactions via the cellular network. Vendors appreciate the portability of *credit card readers*, for example, which take credit card payments from a mobile device for goods and/or services rendered (see Figure 24-38). It's not unusual to see a food truck use a portable credit card reader plugged into the headphone port on an iPad, or being used at the Texas Renaissance Festival to take the Totalsem crew's money when they dressed up and went to play (see Figure 24-39). Cheers!

Figure 24-38
Magnetic credit card reader attached to smartphone

Figure 24-39
Totalsem crew
at the Texas
Renaissance
Festival

Infrared

Now largely replaced by other, faster technologies, such as Bluetooth and 802.11 wireless, infrared (IR) was previously used to transfer data between mobile devices, such as laptops and some older PDAs. Infrared was used to create the first real personal area networks (PANs). Infrared uses the wireless Infrared Data Association (IrDA) standard, and at one time was widely used to connect devices such as wireless remotes, printers, wireless mice, digitizers, and other serial devices. IrDA requires *line of sight*, meaning that devices have to be directly facing each other, requires very short distances (sometimes inches) between devices, and has very slow data rates.

 EXAM TIP You may have noticed that CompTIA included *serial interfaces* on the A+ 1101 objectives. A serial interface is a connection that sends data one bit at a time. The venerable RS232 port found on legacy devices is one example, but infrared is also a type of serial interface. You can also get adapters to convert another port into a serial port, and these exist for many different types of devices. Keep all of these possible types of serial interfaces in mind because you may see them on the exam.

Hotspots and Tethering

A *mobile hotspot* is a small device that shares access to cellular technologies such as 4G, 4G LTE via Wi-Fi, and 5G. Most of these devices can be purchased from wireless providers such as Verizon, Sprint, AT&T, T-Mobile, or other carriers, and are usually specific to their type of broadband network. A mobile hotspot is basically a wireless router that routes traffic between Wi-Fi devices and broadband technologies, providing wireless access for up to five to ten devices at a time.

Depending upon the carrier, many cellular phones, as well as tablets, can act as portable hotspots. You'll recall this from Chapter 21. When used in this manner, it's called *tethering* to the cell phone. While some devices configured as hotspots can use your existing data plan with your carrier, some carriers separate out and limit the amount of data that can be used for tethering.

To configure a device as a hotspot, you typically enable its cellular data connection and turn on an additional hotspot setting that causes the device to broadcast a Wi-Fi network. Now the mobile device serves as a router between the cellular network and the traditional Wi-Fi network it is broadcasting. Then any devices that you wish to tether to the hotspot simply see the device as a wireless router. You can also configure a password so that not just anyone can connect to the hotspot. Figure 24-40 shows a screenshot of an Android phone serving as a portable hotspot.

Figure 24-40
An Android
phone acting as a
portable hotspot

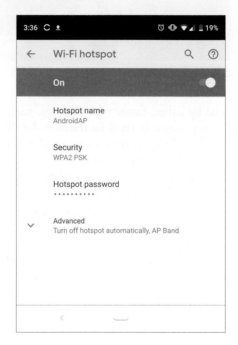

Accessories

Mobile device accessories come in a wide variety of types, packing a huge range of features. Some of the most common accessories that people want for their mobile device, particularly smartphones and tablets, include devices that wirelessly connect to them, typically using Bluetooth technologies. It's not unusual to find Bluetooth *headsets* and high-quality *external speakers* for users to listen to music and chat with friends.

Game controllers, including gamepads and other accessories that plug into tablets via a USB port or connect via Bluetooth, are also common, effectively turning tablets into full-scale gaming platforms. Additionally, cloud gaming has started to materialize as a viable option, and people are now able to use some mobile devices to stream their console and PC games and play on the go.

One feature that some Android mobile devices offer is the ability to use removable external storage, such as *miniSD* or *microSD memory cards*, effectively upgrading the storage capacity of the device. This is something Apple hasn't embraced with its devices, and in fact has become less common with Android devices as well.

There are also accessories no mobile device user should be without, including an *external power bank* or a phone or device charger. To recharge mobile devices, *device chargers* either plug into a wall outlet and the mobile device, or plug into a computer and the mobile device, while *power banks* are just portable batteries that you can charge up and plug your phone or tablet into to get some extra juice when you don't have the ability to plug into the wall.

Some chargers don't require connection to the device at all; they simply require you to lay the device on top of a special pad that recharges the battery wirelessly. Specifics differ a little depending on whether the device was designed for wireless charging or the capability is being added with an aftermarket kit—but in either case the pad creates an electromagnetic field for transmitting power to an antenna in the device. Despite being a wireless technology, the range is measured in centimeters and charging works best when the mobile device is on the pad.

The marketplace has settled on the Qi (pronounced "chee") standard from the Wireless Power Consortium (WPC) as the wireless charging standard of choice. Apple's 2017 decision to adopt the Qi standard and become a member of that consortium sealed the fate of early rival standards. Apple has even expanded wireless charging functionality to include power banks for some iPhone models.

Some devices also have specialized accessories, including *docking stations* (much like the docks discussed for portables in Chapter 23). Although these docking stations are typically used for tablets, they are also used for credit card readers.

Another important accessory is a case for the device. These include an almost unimaginable variety of designer cases, as well as hardened cases designed to withstand falls and other impacts. There also screen protectors—*protective covers*—that range from flimsy plastic all the way to hardened glass that can protect a mobile device screen from scratches and impact. You can find cases made of plastic, leather, rubber, wood, metal, and unicorn horn. Some of these cases are even waterproof, allowing the more adventurous folks to take their phones with them while they are diving in oceans or river-rafting.

We've covered only a few of the hundreds of accessories that are available for mobile devices. Many accessories also come with apps to help control or get the most out of the accessory.

Chapter Review

Questions

1. Which of the following is used in mobile devices to convert analog video and sound to digital video and sound?

   A. Calibrator

   B. SDK

   C. Virtual assistant

   D. Digitizer

2. John has a high-resolution image on his iPad of his two-year-old son and the family dog. The image initially displays smaller than the screen, so he wants to zoom in to get the details of his son's expression. What gesture can he use to accomplish this task?

   A. Click the mouse in the middle of the picture to select it, then use the scroll wheel on the mouse to zoom in.

   B. Tap the picture with his index finger on his son's face.

   C. Long-press on the image and select zoom from the pop-up menu.

   D. Touch his son's face on the screen with his thumb and finger, then pinch outward to scroll in.

3. Which mobile device screen technology uses no backlight?

   A. BYOD

   B. LCD

   C. LED

   D. OLED

4. What can a government use to determine your location at a specific time as long as you're using your mobile device?

   A. Multifactor authentication

   B. Geotracking

   C. Google Earth

   D. Authenticator applications

5. What are the steps involved in pairing a Bluetooth speaker with a tablet?

   A. Enable Bluetooth on the tablet; turn on the Bluetooth speaker; find the device with the tablet; enter a PIN code or other pairing sequence.

   B. Turn on the Bluetooth speaker; find the device with the tablet; enter a PIN code or other pairing sequence.

    C. Search for the Bluetooth speaker from the tablet; select **pair** from the options to enable the speaker.

    D. Enable Bluetooth on the tablet; turn on the Bluetooth speaker; find the device with the tablet; select **pair** from the options to enable the speaker.

6. Which of the following connectors is unique to Apple devices?

    A. Lightning

    B. USB-C

    C. Molex

    D. USB-A

7. John returned from a cruise to the Bahamas and got a bill from his cell phone company (Sprint) that was over $1000. What could have happened?

    A. John connected to the Internet with his smartphone using the cruise ship company's Wi-Fi.

    B. John's smartphone connected to the Internet in the Bahamas via a cell provider that wasn't Sprint.

    C. John used his smartphone to do Internet gambling, and Sprint frowns on that activity.

    D. Bills after international trips are always reported in the currency of the country visited. When translated from Bahamian dollars to U.S. dollars, the amount is the same he normally pays.

8. Leonard just purchased a very expensive comic book and paid for it using the stored credit card information on his smartphone. What technology did he use to make the transaction?

    A. Swipe lock

    B. Wi-Fi calling

    C. NFC

    D. BitLocker To Go

9. What information do you need to connect an Android-based tablet to an IMAP account?

    A. POP3 server DNS name

    B. Username and password

    C. Username, password, sending and receiving server addresses

    D. Exchange server name, username, and password

10. Which mobile OS enables device manufacturers to customize it to better suit their specific devices?

   A. Android

   B. Blackberry

   C. iOS

   D. iPadOS

Answers

1. D. Digitizers are used in mobile devices to convert analog video and sound to digital video and sound, or to interpret analog signals associated with touch movement on a screen into digital equivalents.

2. D. John should touch his son's face on the screen with his thumb and finger, then pinch outward to zoom in.

3. D. OLED technology does not use a backlight.

4. B. Geotracking can locate you and your GPS-equipped mobile device.

5. A. To pair a Bluetooth speaker with a tablet, enable Bluetooth on the tablet, turn on the Bluetooth device, find the Bluetooth device in the tablet's settings screen, then enter a PIN code or finalize the pairing.

6. A. Lightning connectors are an Apple proprietary connector type developed to be used with Apple's mobile devices.

7. B. John's smartphone connected to the Internet in the Bahamas via a cell provider that wasn't Sprint, causing him to incur high data roaming charges.

8. C. Leonard likely purchased his comic book using Near Field Communication (NFC) technology, which can be used for payment transactions through stored credit card information in mobile applications.

9. C. To connect an Android-based tablet to an IMAP account, you need a username and password and the sending and receiving server addresses.

10. A. Google Android is open source, enabling manufacturers to make modifications to better suit their specific devices.

CHAPTER 25

Maintaining and Securing Mobile Devices

In this chapter, you will learn how to

- Troubleshoot common mobile device and application issues
- Explain basic mobile device security
- Describe typical mobile OS and application security issues

Mobile devices are packed with tightly integrated hardware, aren't designed to be upgraded by their users, and come with mobile-oriented operating systems. Because of these major differences, the troubleshooting and security practices for mobile devices differ a lot from those for desktop computers, and somewhat from those for other portable devices. This chapter explores general troubleshooting of mobile devices and their apps first, then covers security features and capabilities of devices common in the mobile market. The chapter finishes by jumping into preventing, detecting, and addressing security issues with mobile operating systems and applications. CompTIA loves those performance-based scenario questions, so get ready for some real-world issues when it comes to security and application troubleshooting.

1101/1102

Troubleshooting Mobile Device Issues

The CompTIA A+ exam objectives divide mobile device problems into two groups: general issues with mobile device hardware and software (1101 exam), and security issues (1102 exam) with the mobile OS and apps. In this section we're going to cover tools for troubleshooting general hardware, OS, and app issues, and apply these tools to common problems. These common problems happen across all varieties, types, and manufacturers of mobile devices. This chapter includes references to Apple's iOS and iPadOS, as well as Google Android. We talked about the differences between iOS and iPadOS in Chapter 24, and while they are very similar, there are some areas where troubleshooting may differ, so keep both their similarities and differences in mind.

NOTE Few mobile devices have components you can service in the field. In the event of a hardware problem, send the device to a service center for repair. Companies like iFixit (https://www.ifixit.com) are making some components field-replaceable, but usually only for skilled techs.

Troubleshooting Tools

Because mobile device hardware typically can't be repaired or replaced by a user or field tech, mobile device troubleshooting focuses on ruling out software issues. The few things you can try are common to almost all mobile devices, and it's best to start with ones that inconvenience the user least. Sometimes these tools will fix the problem, but other times they'll just restore normal functionality until the problem recurs, or help you rule out causes.

Just because you'll troubleshoot a mobile device a little differently doesn't mean you should throw out what you already know. Reflect on the troubleshooting methodology covered in Chapter 1, and use the troubleshooting tools you learn about here to help you work through that process. If the troubleshooting process doesn't fix the problem or identify a cause you can resolve in-house, the next step is to take or send the device to an authorized service center.

Keep in mind that the steps you'll need to take to perform any of these operations will depend on the specific device, its operating system, and the OS version. Be prepared to consult manufacturer and OS resources for exact steps. Let's dive in.

NOTE Most of these tools either are guaranteed to erase data and customizations or have some risk of doing so under the right circumstances. Remember to communicate with the device's user what steps you'll be taking, including what kinds of data loss it can entail, and give the user a chance to back up his or her data.

Try This!

Practice on the Real Deal

If you have access to a smartphone or tablet, practice getting to the tools used for troubleshooting mobile devices. You're going to read about a bunch of places to adjust things such as screen brightness, close or uninstall apps, and much more. Access the device's Settings and explore. Just don't do anything specifically to any device without proper permissions.

Check and Adjust Configuration/Settings

Modern mobile operating systems have tons of configurable settings, as do many of the apps users install on them. Always be on the lookout for "problems" that sound a lot like a simple configuration issue and investigate these early if they seem likely. It won't cost you much (except time) to check relevant settings, but it might save you from having to perform later steps that require backing up and restoring user data.

If the issue isn't likely related to configuration, save your time and revisit configuration after you've tried rebooting the device, which we'll discuss in the upcoming "Soft Reset" section; you don't want to waste tons of time toggling settings if a reboot could fix the problem. If you find a setting that doesn't seem right and want to see if a change resolves the issue, make sure to keep track of what you changed and what the previous setting was!

Close Running Apps

All of the mobile operating systems provide at least one way to close running applications—the most common is to swipe the app in a particular direction from the device's list of *recent apps*. If you come at this with a traditional mindset shaped by how desktop operating systems work, there's a chance you'll misunderstand when and why we close mobile apps, so let's consider a much-simplified version of what goes on under the hood.

On a traditional computer, you open an application when you need it, and it will run until it completes its work, crashes, or you close it. Because mobile devices have more limited computing resources and battery power, you don't want open apps eating up big chunks of resources and burning power while they aren't in focus or the device isn't even being used. To address this problem, modern mobile OS versions manage running apps to optimize performance and battery life.

The catch is that the way they manage apps makes the term "running" a little slippery. While your current app may be running in the traditional sense, the various processes that power your recent out-of-focus apps may keep running if they have work to do, be cached until you return to the app, or get killed if the OS needs its resources for other apps. For the most part the OS will do a good job of managing well-designed apps, but you may still need to close an app if it has frozen, begins to malfunction, or you suspect it is causing the device to misbehave.

 NOTE When closing an app, keep in mind that the user may lose unsaved data when you close it, and (depending on the app) that their device may lose certain functionality they expect it to have until the app is restarted.

Some apps may (intentionally or accidentally) leave background processes running even after the GUI has closed. In Android, the Application Manager will let you *force stop* an app, also killing its background processes (Figure 25-1). In iOS and iPadOS, a swipe will generally do the job.

Figure 25-1
Force stop in
Android

Soft Reset

To maintain mobile devices, it's important to understand the terminology surrounding resets, especially if you're coming at this from a desktop-oriented mindset. On a desktop, you typically initiate a soft reboot from within the operating system or trigger it by pressing a button dedicated to restarting the system; the hallmark of a soft reboot is that the machine never powers all the way down. In contrast, you can perform a hard reboot by holding down the system's power button for several seconds until it turns completely off; you don't want to reboot this way if you can avoid it, but you'll need to if the system is frozen.

On mobile devices, the term *soft reset* describes restarting the device, whether you do it from within the OS or with hardware buttons on the device. If the device still won't restart, confirm the soft reset procedure in the manufacturer resources; if you know you're performing it correctly, and the device allows for it, you can force a device with a removable battery to power down by removing the back cover and the battery.

Much like a reboot on a traditional computer, you can fix all kinds of strange behavior on a mobile device with a soft reset. I'm listening to Spotify on my Android device as I write this section, for example, and when I got started this morning the playback was stopping every few songs; I performed a soft reset and now it's working fine. The soft reset is the easy reset, but there's another reset you need to know; we'll continue this discussion in the "Reset to Factory Default" section coming up in a moment.

Uninstall/Reinstall Apps

Uninstalling and reinstalling apps can be an important troubleshooting process. You can uninstall apps through either the app store they were installed with or the device's *application manager*; you can also, of course, reinstall them via the app store. If the user started having trouble shortly after installing a new app, uninstalling it to see if the problem goes away is an obvious way to rule out a potential cause. If they've been successfully using the app, make sure to jot down important settings and back up their data if possible before you uninstall it.

The problems you can fix or troubleshoot by uninstalling and reinstalling aren't always as obvious as this. If a user has had an app for a long time and it only recently started acting up, it's possible the app's developers released a bad update; after a bad update, the app might not work at all, or it might work fine if you uninstall and reinstall it. Sometimes this can be a no-win situation for a tech—what if the only fix to a user's problem is removing an app they use daily until its developers fix a problem?

Reset to Factory Default

This other reset—known by many names such as *hard reset*, *factory reset*, or *reset to factory default*—will clear all user data and setting changes, returning the device (well, its software) to the state it was in when it left the factory. Take extra care not to confuse a hard reset with a hard reboot; if you're reading documentation or a how-to page that uses the terms reboot and reset interchangeably, pay close attention to what the author intends you to do—and consider finding a less-ambiguous resource.

Because the hard reset removes all of a user's data and settings changes, it's the most disruptive option here—typically one you won't perform until after backing up the user's data (which we'll discuss later in the chapter). The big exception is when you're intentionally performing a factory reset in order to clear user data off a device before it is sold, recycled, or assigned to a new user.

Despite the inconvenience, resetting a device to factory defaults is an important troubleshooting step on the way to determining whether it should be sent to a service center. If a factory reset fixes the device's issues but they return some time after restoring a backup of user data and programs, return to earlier steps for tracking down the troublemaking app.

Touchscreen and Display Issues

Modern mobile devices are almost all screen, and some provide little beyond a touchscreen and a power button for interacting with the device. While display issues tend to be urgent for most devices, the touchscreen's integral role in controlling a modern mobile device makes it all the more so. We already touched on some important steps for troubleshooting a touchscreen in the "Input Problems" section at the end of Chapter 23, so be prepared to integrate those steps with the more mobile-centric issues discussed here.

Dim Display

Mobile devices have a *brightness control* that can be set to auto mode or controlled manually. These settings don't always work perfectly, and sometimes apps that need special control over brightness settings can cause the device's display to be too dark or bright for the user's comfort.

A dim display might be a sign that there's a problem with the panel, but first you need to check the display settings. Turn off any auto-adjustment setting and manually change the display brightness from the dimmest to brightest setting and observe whether it covers an appropriate range of output. If it doesn't, there may be a problem with the display panel; if it does, there may be something keeping the auto-adjustment from working right.

The auto-adjustment is affected by how much light a sensor or camera on the front of the device can detect. Make sure the sensor isn't covered with dirt or some other obstruction. If the display is too bright in a dim room, check the surroundings for bright light that isn't close enough to illuminate the area, but that the sensor might pick up if pointed in the right direction.

Be on the lookout for apps that tinker with the display's brightness. These apps may use distinct brightness settings, or they may modify system-wide brightness. Reading apps, like Amazon Kindle, are one example. See if a soft reset returns the display to normal operation, and then investigate whether using these apps causes the brightness issue to return. Every once in a while, Kindle on my Android tablet will interfere with the system's *auto-brightness,* causing all sorts of strange brightness changes until I restart the tablet by performing a soft reset. The solution in this case may be as simple as teaching the user to reset their device when an app like this has caused a problem.

Autorotation Problems

Much like brightness controls, mobile devices also have automatic and manual controls for rotating the screen. The autorotate mode uses the device's accelerometer to change the screen between portrait and landscape orientations when the user rotates the device. When the *screen does not autorotate*, usually either autorotation is off (the screen orientation is locked) or the app currently being used does not support both portrait and landscape orientations, which is necessary for autorotation to work.

You might also run into an autorotation problem caused by OS, resource, or hardware problems on the device. If autorotation doesn't work after a soft reset, you may need to wait for an OS update or take the device in for service.

Touchscreen Responsiveness

When a user tries to interact with a mobile device but finds the touchscreen nonresponsive or gets an inaccurate touchscreen response, there are a few simple things to rule out first: dirt, accidental touches, and performance issues. Any of these can cause *digitizer issues* (we talked about what a digitizer is in more detail in Chapter 24), some of which can be resolved quickly, others require specialist diagnostic and repair. With those out of the way, we'll turn to more catastrophic causes.

Accidental Touch The simplest issue to resolve is an accidental touch. Sometimes a user will hold a device in such a way that its touchscreen detects some part of their arm or hand as an intentional touch, and it may not react at all when they try to manipulate it intentionally. Oversensitive sensors or bad design might exacerbate this, but the fix is always the same: show the user how the sensors pick up an accidental touch and teach them how to hold the device to avoid them.

Dirty Screen Another simple issue to resolve is a dirty screen. Sometimes simply wiping the touchscreen down with a dry microfiber cloth to get rid of fingerprints, dust, dirt, grease, and other foreign objects will fix a responsiveness problem (see Figure 25-2).

Figure 25-2
Cleaning a
smartphone

Performance Problems Much like a mouse cursor may slow, freeze, or move erratically when a traditional computer is having performance issues, a touchscreen may appear not to work at all or have severe accuracy and response problems if the mobile device is performing poorly. Be patient with the device and look for signs it is struggling to keep up. Is it displaying the right time? If it has an animated lock screen or wallpaper, are the animations playing smoothly?

If the device appears to have network connectivity, are weather or stock widgets on the lock screen updating? Is it slow to respond when you press unrelated hardware buttons? If the device can receive them, see if it responds normally when you call or text it. If the problem seems to be performance related, perform a soft reset and see if the touchscreen starts working.

A lot of users add a screen protector to their mobile devices to give a little extra help in case of a drop. A poorly installed screen protector can cause touchscreens not to work properly. Check the guidelines from the manufacturer and remove and replace a subpar screen protector.

Calibration and Diagnostics If a soft reset doesn't get the touchscreen working, look online for information about whether the device has a hidden *diagnostics menu* or *service menu*. You might reach this menu by inputting a series of digits into the device's dialer, or by holding specific buttons while the device is booting up during a soft reset. If the device has a touchscreen diagnostic here, it should help you decide whether the touchscreen itself is in good working order. Some Android devices may also have a setting in either the primary OS settings menu or a hidden device menu for calibrating the touchscreen.

Physical Damage While we covered the previous issues when we discussed portable devices in Chapter 23, smaller mobile and wearable devices have a greater risk of some problems that are rarer with larger portables. Everyone knows a quick dip in a toilet, margarita glass, or swimming pool can kill a mobile device, but sometimes getting one wet or dropping it on a hard surface can cause trouble short of complete death. A smartphone in your pocket when you get caught in the rain, or on a table when you spill a drink, could end up with liquid in all sorts of nooks and crannies.

Although some mobile devices can handle a little bit of moisture, most can't handle immersion at all. Dropping a smartphone in a toilet makes for a very bad day. Without removable batteries, there's not much you can do to save a liquid-soaked mobile device, and as a result, this level of *liquid damage* is often a death sentence for mobile devices.

If you rule out the simplest explanations and fixes in this section and the touchscreen is still not responding properly, it's time to inspect the device for evidence it has been dropped or gotten wet. There's always the old-fashioned way—ask the user. Just be aware that it may be hard to get someone to admit their touchscreen stopped working after they sprayed milk through their nose because they tried to read XKCD while eating breakfast.

NOTE For a good dose of tech-oriented humor, check out the comics at https://xkcd.org. Geeky fun at its finest!

A *broken screen* doesn't require the glass itself to be cracked; drops or impacts can break internal connections, rendering the device difficult or impossible to use. Moisture can cause internal shorts, and lingering liquid could cause sensors to behave in really strange ways. Most mobile devices will contain a few *liquid contact indicator (LCI)* stickers that change color when exposed to water, as shown in Figure 25-3. While these are really so the carrier or manufacturer can refuse to cover water damage under warranty, look up their locations online and then check them on the device. There's often one on the battery or in the battery compartment, if it's accessible; it'll usually be white if it hasn't gotten wet.

Figure 25-3
Pristine LCI sticker (top) and LCI sticker absorbing a drop of water (bottom)

Apps Not Launching

A mobile device app may fail to launch or install correctly for a few reasons. First, the app may not be compatible with some combination of the mobile device's hardware, operating system version, or vendor/carrier customizations to the OS. With Android devices, for example, different manufacturers can tweak the OS to suit their own needs, which may cause compatibility issues with other vendors' apps.

 NOTE This section details reasons an app may always fail to launch or install correctly. Remember, an app may fail to install or launch correctly before you perform a soft reset, but do so fine afterward. Perform a soft reset and then try reinstalling and launching the app.

Another reason an app may not launch is that the device doesn't meet the app's hardware requirements. These might be more traditional requirements such as amount of available RAM, storage space, and processor type, but the app might also require a sensor or radio your device lacks or requires capabilities that your device's camera doesn't support. It's always a good idea to review an app's requirements before installing it (or when you run into trouble).

Both Apple and Android devices track errors with applications. You'll need third-party tools to access *app log errors*—or what I assume are *logs of app errors* (thanks, CompTIA!). Something to keep in mind if a senior tech or app programmer (in the case of custom apps for an organization) needs help with troubleshooting.

Overheating

Just as with the portable devices discussed in Chapter 23, overheating can cause permanent damage to a mobile device; most of the recommendations given there still apply. That said, our relationship with mobile devices is a little different. They are usually on, spend more time in our hands and pockets, and we take them places we wouldn't dream of taking a larger portable. A mobile device is more likely to get left on the car seat on a hot summer day or be nestled close to our body in well-insulated winter clothing.

Focus on overheating as a combination of the heat a mobile device produces itself, heat added to it by external sources like the sun or a lamp, and how well its environment dissipates or retains heat. Since we handle these devices more often, we have a lot of chances to notice what's normal and what isn't; when a device is hot, combine these three factors and see how well they explain the device's temperature. The process of looking for a good explanation can help you catch performance problems before they drain the battery, prevent heat damage to components, or identify problems with the battery or power systems before they become dangerous.

Charging, large data transfers, frozen apps, recording HD video, and other intensive tasks can all make a mobile device much hotter than normal; avoid letting the device do intense work in hot or well-insulated spaces. If you can avoid it, don't bring mobile devices into very hot environments; if you can't, minimize risk by turning the device off altogether. If the device is hot to the touch in a cool environment, you can put it into airplane mode, close all running programs, and see if it cools down. If it doesn't, turn it off until it cools and then try again.

Your biggest concerns are a device that overheats for no obvious reason or gets hot enough that it could burn someone. These problems are usually caused by some sort of hardware issue, possibly a defective battery or other power circuit within the device. There's really not much you can do; turn it off to protect the device from further damage and take it to a service center.

The dangers of not addressing an overheating mobile device—even one that is overheating for otherwise benign reasons—are, at best, an eventual device failure and requisite data loss. At worst, a severely overheating device can become a safety risk with the potential to burn or shock a user and, especially if the battery ruptures, cause a fire or explosion.

Update Failures

Ideas like app stores and regular automatic updates are now common on computer operating systems, but these things cut their teeth in the world of iPhone, Android, and even the failed Windows Phone. Ease of use rules this world, so installing software and updates on a mobile device is dead simple. But don't think it's too simple to fail! If you manage enough mobile devices, you'll see a case where the *OS fails to update* or an *application fails to update*.

Usually, the reason an update fails is that the device doesn't have enough free space to install the update. It might auto-purge some files to make room, but you'll have to jump in to remove some apps or files (back them up first) if it fails. Corrupt downloads won't install; check your device's documentation on how to delete the bad update and retry with a strong connection. Running out of battery mid-update can cause big trouble; it's best to plug in the device before updating the OS.

Slow Response

Mobile devices can be *slow to respond* like regular desktop computers and laptops, and often for the same reasons. Response issues can be caused by storage space being almost filled up on a mobile device, making it unable to save data or install apps efficiently. Mobile devices can also be slow to respond when there are too many apps running at the same time, eating up RAM.

Usually, the mobile device's OS has configuration settings that enable you to stop apps or view their resource usage, including memory and storage space. If storage space is an issue, you may have to uninstall some apps, or reinstall them so that they are stored on removable storage devices, such as microSD or miniSD memory cards.

A device with response issues will often be running hot, and this heat can be a big clue. Use the recommendations in the previous section to evaluate whether the device or the environment is the source of this heat. A hot, sluggish device could be using *thermal throttling* to protect the device's CPU from heat damage by reducing its power; in this case, performance should pick up as it cools.

One of the first troubleshooting steps you can take in resolving response issues is to perform a soft reset of the device; this clears running apps—perhaps even ones that are frozen or malfunctioning—from RAM. As far as troubleshooting tools go, you can use the device settings or third-party apps to measure the device's performance.

Sometimes those apps can help point the way to what's causing the performance problems. If you ultimately determine that a hardware issue is causing performance problems, you should take the device to an authorized repair facility.

Battery Life

Just like the portable devices discussed in Chapter 23, modern mobile devices use Lithium-Ion (Li-Ion) batteries. It's usually not too hard to make use of a more traditional portable computer while it's charging, but the ergonomics of mobile devices can make it miserable to use one while it's charging—so it's even more important to make sure your device has power when you need it. Our purpose here is to look at how you can manage any battery to get the most out of it, but first we need to talk about the cornerstone of good battery management.

Meeting User Power Needs

Mobile devices are rated in terms of how long their battery should power a device during "normal" use, how long the device can go between battery charges, and the levels of power that both the battery provides and requires in order to charge. Make sure you and your users have mobile devices that have a chance to last long enough to perform normal activities for an adequate amount of time.

The battery life numbers advertised by a device's maker are a good start, but be suspicious of these figures. Mobile device review sites will benchmark the performance of more popular mobile devices and tell you how long they survived while performing some battery-sucking tasks like playing HD video. Know how long a given user's device will need to last on a charge, and try to make sure they get a device that can last at least 20 percent longer to account for how the battery's capacity will dwindle over its lifetime, known as its *battery life*.

If there's no existing device that can meet the user's needs most of the time, make sure they either have a device with a removable battery and a spare or have a portable external battery recharger. You can plug a mobile device into a *portable battery recharger* (sometimes called *external battery*, *power pack*, or *portable charger*) to recharge when there's no available outlet.

Managing Battery Life

There are two ways to think about battery life: how long it will last on each charge, and how long the battery can meet your needs before you have to replace it. Luckily, you can optimize both of these at the same time. When you waste battery life on device features you aren't using, not only will your device need to recharge sooner than necessary, but the extra recharge cycles will also shorten the useful life of your battery, also known as your *battery health*. Let's take a look at the biggest battery drains while keeping in mind that these are generalizations: check your device's battery usage monitor to see what is consuming most of its power.

Display While it depends somewhat on how big your device's screen is and what kind of display it uses, the fastest way to drain most modern mobile devices is leaving the screen on. Keep the display off when you can, and use the lowest acceptable brightness setting.

Because the screens look so much more vibrant at full brightness, there's a good chance this will be their default setting. The battery savings from using the lowest setting may be enticing, but the best compromise is usually to configure the device to control brightness automatically. Figure 25-4 displays the battery usage for an iPhone 13 Pro. Notice how much of the battery is being drained by the screen alone!

Figure 25-4
Battery usage for a smartphone

There are more options for optimizing how much power your display uses, though some of these differ by device or manufacturer. You can usually adjust how long the screen will stay on without input, and whether it will turn on when you receive a notification. Some devices have *power-saving modes* and may even be able to save power by displaying grayscale instead of full color. OLED displays use less power to display darker colors; if your device uses an OLED panel, you can also reduce power consumption by using black wallpapers and configuring apps to use a dark theme if the option is available.

Wireless Communication   To paint with a very broad brush, another big battery drain is the process of communicating without wires. It's good to keep in mind that every form of wireless communication your mobile device is capable of (such as cellular voice, cellular data, Wi-Fi, Bluetooth, Near-Field Communication [NFC], etc.) corresponds to a radio inside the device. In order to use that type of communication, the radio needs to be on and drawing power. If you aren't actively using that mode of communication but the radio is on, you're wasting power. Each communication technology draws varying amounts of energy under different circumstances, but here are two helpful guidelines: searching for signals is power intensive, and your device's apps will do more work in the background when connections are available.

Especially when traveling outside of populated areas, a mobile device can use lots of power talking with distant towers and base stations; this constant search can significantly drain battery power. You may be able to control this power drain through configuration changes that limit device roaming or searching for new wireless networks, but another approach is disabling these communications technologies until you need them or are back in an area with good coverage. You don't want to get stuck in the snow on a rural highway only to discover that your phone has almost completely drained its battery searching for cellular signals.

Even when the device maintains a strong connection, it constantly uses power to transmit and receive data. Having the connection available is often worth this slow drain, but beware that some of your apps will lightly sip power while disconnected and burn through much more doing background work when a connection is present. The easy way to rein this in is to disable communication, but the operating system (and sometimes the app itself) will have settings for controlling when an app can send and receive data in the background, and what connections it can use.

Location   While you can apply the same guidelines for managing GPS or location services, some small differences make it worth discussing separately. When location services are on, the device's apps can query the location of the device. Depending on how you've configured the device, it may approximate your location using low-power (less-accurate) methods like nearby cellular and Wi-Fi networks, higher-accuracy (higher-power) methods like GPS, or combine both of these. This could be for apps that require location data in the background, or for active apps, such as mapping software, that use the GPS receiver. The power drain here can vary widely between an app occasionally checking approximate location in the background, and one constantly requesting high-quality updates.

The simplest solution is to keep location services off when they aren't required, but you may be able to find a happy medium by setting per-app restrictions. When an app requires location data (common examples are apps for navigating, mapping, geocaching, or finding nearby users, restaurants, garage sales, or movie theaters) but location is disabled, the device will usually prompt you to turn it on.

Because apps for which location data is less critical may happily use a stale location, the best combination of trade-offs will ultimately depend on how you use your device and what apps you have running. If you regularly use the device to take location-tagged pictures cataloging graffiti or potholes, you may want the highest quality location data available at all times, regardless of the battery drain. Another tip is to review configuration settings for apps that use location services and disable the ones that don't need to have immediate location data.

EXAM TIP Be familiar with the factors that can reduce battery power and battery life.

Charging Issues

Charging a mobile device is one of the most regular interactions a user will have with it. As a result, charging issues can arise, leading to inconvenience and frustration. There are a range of possible causes for *improper charging*, from something as simple as having too many apps running in the background, all the way to broken hardware in the device. Depending on the source of the problem, the device may charge slowly or not at all. Let's have a look at some of the main causes, how to identify them, and most importantly, how to fix them.

If your device is charging more slowly than usual, there are a few possibilities. The first thing to check is whether anything is using an unusually high amount of battery. Sometimes, resolving the issue is as simple as closing out of some background apps.

Slow charging can also be caused by issues with your charger or cable. If the charger you're using wasn't designed with the device in mind, or you're just using a cable you grabbed out of a drawer, it may not be able to provide enough power. You'll know fairly quickly if the phone is charging slowly; most devices display the estimated charging time somewhere, either on the home screen or in the battery menu in Settings. If you encounter slow charging and you've ruled out background apps, grab a different charger, preferably one that you know works with the device. If it charges normally, the issue was almost certainly with the charger or cable. If it doesn't, you may have bigger problems and should look to the device hardware.

NOTE In Chapter 24 we talked about different types of ports you'll find on smartphones and tablets. Issues related to charging cables are especially common, particularly for smartphones, because people often use their devices while they are plugged in. The result is that the cables can end up fraying, or the connector can become damaged. If a charging cable that worked well suddenly starts charging slowly, it's very possible that it just didn't hold up to the higher amount of wear and tear mobile devices experience. If the cable is micro-USB, the odds of this being the problem are especially high.

If you've already ruled out issues with background battery usage, chargers, and cables, it's time to explore the possibility that the charging port itself has a problem. For example, you may have a *physically damaged port*. This is the worst-case scenario, because, as we discussed when we addressed field repair, mobile device hardware repair is very difficult without access to specialized tools and parts. If you closed out the extraneous apps, restarted the device, tested a few different charging cables, and the device still won't charge, there's really one more thing that you can test before its time to take it to a specialist. It may sound silly but try plugging the charger into a different outlet. I've plugged in my charger to one outlet, felt the creeping despair that comes with potential hardware issues, moved it to another outlet, and had the device charge normally. Sometimes the issue isn't with the device at all. If none of these steps work though, the device may require some form of specialized diagnostic or repair.

Swollen Battery

As we discussed in Chapter 23, one of the more insidious problems you'll see in mobile devices is a swollen battery. The main cause is overcharging, usually when the circuits designed to prevent overcharging fail. Non-OEM chargers or batteries, especially if they aren't rated for the correct voltage and wattage, represent an additional risk, as does overheating. Sometimes the battery is just bad. Overcharging has become less common as mobile device manufacturers continue to improve their hardware and implement software that helps to prevent it, but swollen batteries can still be a serious problem.

Prevention may be the best cure. Don't let batteries overheat, especially while charging. Prefer OEM chargers and batteries. Check the manufacturer's documentation for specific actions to take or avoid. Regardless, prevention can't always work, and swollen batteries may rupture, leak, and catch fire. It's important to be aware it can happen, vigilant for signs it is occurring, and careful when disposing swollen batteries.

Look for subtle clues, like changes in how the device's frame and screen come together, how it sits on a flat surface, how the back cover sits on the device, weird creaking or popping, inexplicable heat, and so forth. If the device has a removable cover, it's pretty simple to check the battery. If it doesn't, you may need to find a service center or a mobile technician who is comfortable taking the device apart to check.

When you encounter a swollen battery, dispose of it according to the recommendations in the "Try This! Recycling Old Portable Device Batteries" section of Chapter 23 and replace it with a known-good battery, preferably from the original device vendor.

 CAUTION You should never try to repair a battery under any circumstances, let alone when it's swollen, as it can cause bodily harm and damage to equipment.

Random Reboots and Freezes

A mobile device can *randomly reboot* or freeze up just like a desktop system (and for the same reasons). The main difference is that there aren't as many ways to successfully deal with a frozen mobile device. In that case, the immediate goal is getting the device back to a usable state. If the device isn't responding, you'll need to perform a soft reset, and without access to the OS you'll have to follow the manufacturer's steps for performing a soft reset—probably either by holding the power button for a few seconds or removing the battery.

 NOTE When a device seems to be frozen, there's also a chance the touchscreen just isn't responding. Check if the device responds normally to hardware button presses or enabled voice and gesture commands before assuming it is frozen.

If the device is still at least partially responsive, you can try to close an offending process from your list of recent apps. Even if you get the app to close, you may find the device unstable again as soon as you reopen the app. It's often best to save yourself wasted time: close the offending app, save any work in other open apps, and perform a soft reset.

When the device is usable again, there may be more steps to take. If you know the device rebooted or froze when you opened a newly installed or updated app, you may need to uninstall it and consider waiting for an update or looking for a replacement. Sometimes operating system issues can cause reboots and freezes, especially right after a device update, so look for follow-up OS patches correcting these types of issues. If the device randomly (and with increased frequency) reboots or freezes up, whenever using apps performing similar tasks (any app that uses the GPS or camera, for example), then your device likely has a hardware issue and needs service.

There's also a chance you'll find that the device is still unusable after the soft reset, in which case you'll need to look for the manufacturer's documentation on how to boot the device into any special modes that enable you to either remove an offending app, repair the OS installation, or reset the device to factory default. If this process also fails to render the device stable, you'll need to send it to a service center.

Cannot Broadcast to an External Monitor

Back in Chapter 24 we saw that some mobile devices have video output that enables you to broadcast the display onto an external monitor or projector. When done correctly, this is usually an almost automatic process: plug some adapter into your mobile device, plug that adapter into your external monitor's VGA, DVI, DP, or HDMI port, and it all just works.

Well, that's the theory. In reality, broadcasting your mobile device's screen to an external monitor is fraught with problems. While these vary by type of device, here are a few tried-and-true things to check when your device cannot broadcast to an external monitor:

- Is your source correct on the external monitor? All monitors, TVs, and projectors have lots of inputs. Is the external monitor pointing at the right source?

- Do you have the right adapter for your device? Apple alone has come out with five different types of video adapters in the last few years—and don't even get me started on the many adapters for Android! Make sure you have an adapter that is known to work for your device.

- Does your adapter need its own power source?

- For HDMI: Did the HDMI recognize your device and your external monitor? Depending on the make and model, you may need to reset one or both devices to give the HDMI time to see connections and set itself up.

No Sound from Speakers

Sound issues are also common on mobile devices. The most obvious (and probably most common) is that the volume was turned down or muted through software configuration or an app. This is easy to fix, but sometimes you have to go through many configuration settings for both the device and apps to figure out which one is controlling the volume at the moment or which one may actually be muting the speakers. A device may have separate settings for media, call volume, notifications, and more—and sometimes it's easy to change the wrong one.

The versatile nature of mobile devices means that we are often switching from one use to another. This can sometimes lead to people forgetting that their device was paired with some peripheral. One of the most common peripherals you'll see with mobile devices are wireless Bluetooth headphones. If you aren't getting any sound from the speakers, it may be a good idea to double-check for paired audio devices—the sound may just be coming from somewhere you didn't expect.

Some mobile devices also have hardware volume controls on them, so check them. If that doesn't work, then start going into the configuration settings for the device and apps. If none of these steps works, then you may have a hardware issue: the speakers have been damaged or come disconnected inside the device. As with all other hardware issues, you'll likely have to take the device to a service center for repair.

Connectivity and Data Usage Issues

General network connectivity issues—the kind that can affect all devices—have been covered elsewhere within the book. For mobile devices in particular, you should be aware of some additional network connectivity issues that you will likely encounter at some point. We'll discuss these in respect to cellular signals, but the first issue applies to *Wi-Fi* and *Bluetooth* network connections as well. For the most part you can't directly fix these connection issues, but you'll inevitably find a connection issue is responsible for some problem, or at least need to rule it out on the way to the ultimate cause.

One of the most prominent connection issues plaguing mobile devices is weak signal. The signal might be weak because you're deep inside a building, nestled between skyscrapers, crossing the no-man's-land between cell towers in sparsely populated areas, or any of a wide array of similar situations. The primary symptoms of a weak signal are dropped connections, delays, slow transmission speeds, battery drain, and frequent indications that the device is searching for a signal.

There isn't much you can do to troubleshoot a weak signal except monitor it. There are cellular signal boosters you can purchase, but these are of dubious value in some situations. These are most effective when the user is stationary in a location far from the cell tower, and usually aren't useful while the user is on the move.

 NOTE In addition to signal issues, performance problems on the device itself can cause the symptoms of slow data connectivity. We've covered these already, but they include high utilization of resources such as CPU, RAM, and network bandwidth, and a device's struggle to maintain a solid network connection.

Even if your signal is good, you may still run into connectivity problems—and they may be tricky to spot if you aren't aware of them. The first of these is an *overloaded network*, which is common during large public gatherings (such as a sporting event) or a widespread emergency that causes a surge in network use. Your device might have full bars but be unable to place calls, send texts, or transfer data. Another explanation for connectivity problems despite a strong signal are restrictions and limits the carrier enforces. You may experience slow data speeds while roaming just because the carrier of the network you are roaming on limits data rates for nonsubscribers. Exceeding the *data usage limits* that your carrier sets can also lead to slow data speeds.

The carrier will usually notify the user by e-mail or text message, but the user might not notice. What happens next is up to the carrier and the terms of the user's plan. Some carriers stop cellular data use beyond the preset limits, bill the user for additional data, or throttle the speed of the connection. Each causes complications, but you can minimize them by *recognizing data caps*. Configure data hogs like cloud storage apps to synchronize only on Wi-Fi, monitor data use and disable cellular data usage in the configuration settings of the device (see Figure 25-5) as needed, or pay to raise the data cap.

Figure 25-5
Option to disable
cellular data
in iOS

While the abstract side of data usage limits is important, the essential part is that you think about how these various scenarios could manifest on real devices. If you have a corporate plan, knowing the data limits and what happens when they're exceeded will give you a big leg up. What should you suspect when a user turns up at the end of the month with a device that suddenly has terrible call quality in Skype while using cellular data but works fine over Wi-Fi? Or a traveling employee says she keeps getting calls from colleagues asking why she hasn't weighed in on an important e-mail discussion that hasn't turned up on her device, despite a good connection? A quick check to see whether the user is over the plan limit could spare both of you hours of troubleshooting.

GPS and Location Services Problems

Sometimes the location services on mobile devices will be better at finding where you aren't than where you are. Some inaccuracy can be explained by the hardware a device has available; a Wi-Fi-only tablet with no GPS can get only a general location.

Symptoms of location issues can vary depending on what apps are trying to use location services. Photos might end up tagged with the wrong location, or the coffee shop you picked because it was closest might actually be further away than your device suggests. A navigation app might have trouble identifying your location at all, or it might be sure it knows where you are even when you know you're blocks away. Other symptoms can include prompts and error or informational messages from the OS or apps that rely on location data (see Figure 25-6).

Figure 25-6
GPS prompt

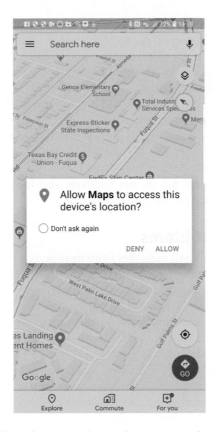

Troubleshooting location problems begins with simple actions such as making sure that your GPS, cellular data, and Wi-Fi are turned on and functioning properly, as sometimes these services can be inadvertently turned off by the user or by an app, and have to be periodically reactivated. Typically, a warning message will indicate that GPS or data services are turned off, so this is easy to identify and fix. Specific apps may have trouble if they are configured not to access or use location services. This is usually a matter of going into the app configuration or location settings and allowing the app to make use of those services.

EXAM TIP   If you run into GPS error questions on the exam, remember that all apps will tell you if GPS is turned off and usually ask you if want to turn on GPS. Otherwise, before digging deeper, first consider simple issues such as whether you are in a place where you can get a good GPS signal.

Once you've checked the obvious software reasons for location trouble, it's a good idea to think about the physical environment before you go on a wild-goose chase. GPS won't work underground, will probably be spotty indoors unless you're near a window, and can really struggle in dense urban areas with tall buildings. Don't be spooked into a long search for subtle GPS problems if your device occasionally has trouble deciding which downtown street you're strolling along.

When you're sure there are frequent location problems unexplained by the environment, it's time to dig deeper. Along with the OS issues discussed previously, incorrect OS configuration settings for GPS, cellular, and Wi-Fi services may prevent location services from functioning properly. These configuration items should be checked when multiple apps are having location issues.

If the issues persist, there's a good chance the problem is in the actual GPS or network hardware inside the device, or the OS code that interfaces with it. Look online to see if other device owners report similar trouble on the same device software versions. If you don't see other reports of trouble, the device likely needs a trip to the service center. Although mobile devices may have removable network or GPS modules in them, most of these components are not user serviceable and have to be replaced or repaired by authorized service technicians.

Encryption Problems

Methods to secure e-mail messages from anyone but the intended recipient generally fall well outside the accepted parameters of the CompTIA A+ certification, but it's useful to know how to troubleshoot mobile device encryption issues. To understand the issue, we'd need to dive into a number of topics you won't see until you take the CompTIA Security+ exam. Instead, let's focus on the basics.

For an e-mail message to be secure, it must be *encrypted*—scrambled according to some kind of standard, such as *Pretty Good Privacy (PGP)* or *Secure/Multipurpose Internet Mail Extensions (S/MIME)*. For the recipient to read the e-mail message, he or she needs to have software that can unscramble or *decrypt* the message. To ensure the sender and recipient alone can access the contents of the e-mail message, both people need specific keys that enable encryption and decryption. A *key* is a string of bits used by a computer program to encrypt or decrypt data.

In practice, there are a few reasons a mobile device won't be able to decrypt an e-mail. The simplest of these is that the e-mail client or application doesn't support the encryption standard used to encrypt the message; the fix may be a plug-in or an entirely new client. Once you confirm that the e-mail client or app supports this encryption method, follow any steps for configuring the client to use it. Finally, the e-mail client will need access to keys for decrypting the message. With some standards, keys may always be exchanged manually; someone will need to contact the sender to exchange keys. In other cases, keys may be exchanged automatically in at least some circumstances (if you're part of the same organization, for example).

Securing Mobile Devices

Just like any computer we use to input or access sensitive data and network resources, we need to secure our mobile devices. Whether the device is company owned or personal, we still need to protect ourselves from the needless inconvenience of easily prevented damage, theft, or malware infections, as well as from the chance of important data being lost completely or falling into the wrong hands.

BYOD Versus Corporate-Owned Devices

The *bring your own device (BYOD)* war was briefly fought and lost by organizations hoping to continue the long-held tradition that IT assets belonged to (and were strictly controlled by) the company, not the individual. As mobile devices proliferated, however, IT folks realized the genie was out of the bottle; they couldn't control these new technologies completely. Some companies enforce a policy prohibiting the use of personal devices to access corporate data and resources, particularly in high-security environments. Companies at the other end of the spectrum allow (and even encourage) the use of personal devices to save corporate IT dollars and keep employees happy.

Most organizations fall in the middle of the spectrum and have a mixed environment with both corporate-owned and employee-owned mobile devices. Some organizations institute a cost-sharing program, subsidizing an employee's personally owned device with a monthly phone stipend or discount agreement with mobile device and telecommunications vendors. Regardless of how comfortable an organization is with BYOD, there are important questions to answer.

One question is how much control the corporation has versus the individual. If corporate data is processed or stored on the device, the organization should have some degree of control over it. On the other hand, if the device also belongs to the employee, then the employee should have some control. Another question is who pays for the device and its use. If the organization allows the user to use her own device for company work, does the organization help pay for the monthly bill or compensate the user for its use? Again, this issue is best solved via formal policy and procedures. Yet another important question in a BYOD environment is how to handle employee privacy. If policy allows the organization some degree of control over the device, what degree of privacy does the user maintain on her own device? Can the organization see private data, or have the ability to remotely access a user's personal device and control its use?

The proliferation of mobile devices in the workplace has led to the development of *mobile device management (MDM) policies* that often combine a specialized app on the devices and specialized infrastructure to deal with those devices. These policies also inform *corporate versus end-user device configuration options*; in other words, who should make configuration decisions on things such as e-mail, wireless access, and so forth. As you might imagine, MDM policies are a big deal at the big organization level (the enterprise) because of the scale and complexity of the issues. A CompTIA A+ technician comes in to facilitate the installation of the MDM app, for example, or to help fix key infrastructure problems (like an overloaded WAP because all 25 members of a department bought Apple Watches at the same time). Mobile device management isn't always necessary. Sometimes, the organization is concerned just with a specific app or group of apps. In this case, you'll find the use of *mobile application management (MAM)*.

 EXAM TIP Both mobile device management and mobile application management are included in the CompTIA A+ exam objectives for a reason. They sound similar but serve different purposes. MDM is for entire devices, while MAM is for specific applications used by the organization. Keep this in mind so that you don't get them mixed up on the exams.

Profile Security Requirements

A *profile* is a collection of configuration and security settings that an administrator has created in order to apply those settings to particular categories of users or devices. A profile can be created in several different ways, including through the MDM software, or in a program such as the Apple Configurator, for example. Profiles are typically text-based files, usually in an eXtensible Markup Language (XML) format, and are pushed out to the different devices that require them. Profiles should be developed based on the needs of the organization. You can develop a profile specific to certain platforms, operating systems, or devices, so that a particular type of device will get certain settings.

You can also develop profiles that are specific to different user categories or management groupings (such as mobile sales representatives, middle managers, senior managers, and executives). Your senior organizational executives might have a specific profile applied to their devices granting them additional permissions and access to special apps or connections.

You might also apply group-specific profiles to external users, such as consultants or business partners. These users may require limited access to organizational resources using their own mobile device, their organization's mobile devices, or even mobile devices temporarily issued by your organization. A group-specific profile applied to these external users may give them particular network configuration and security settings so that they can access a business extranet, for example, or use specific VPN settings. They may also require access to particular enterprise or business-to-business (B2B) apps hosted on your organization's servers. In any case, both device- and user-specific profiles can be very helpful in managing larger groups of users, delivering uniform security and configuration settings to their devices based on different mission or business requirements.

Depending on your organizational needs, you could conceivably apply several different profiles to a device at once, based on platform, user group, and so forth. When multiple profiles are applied, there's a chance some settings will conflict. For example, some restrictive settings for a device profile may not be consistent with some less-restrictive ones in a group or user profile. When both are applied to the device, the different configuration settings may conflict and overwrite each other. The solution is to pay special attention to profile precedence and configure the MDM server to resolve conflicts using criteria such as user group membership or security requirements.

You should also develop profiles that apply to corporate-owned versus employee-owned devices. A profile applied to a device in a BYOD environment may be considerably different than one applied to a company-owned device. This would be based on policy settings affecting privacy, acceptable use of the device, and so on. Figure 25-7 shows how you can conceptually apply different profiles to different device and user groups.

Preventing Physical Damage

For something shaped a lot like a bar of soap and sometimes almost as slippery, mobile phones can cost a lot of money. That means you need to take steps to prevent damage. The first step you should take to protect your slippery investment is a case, protective

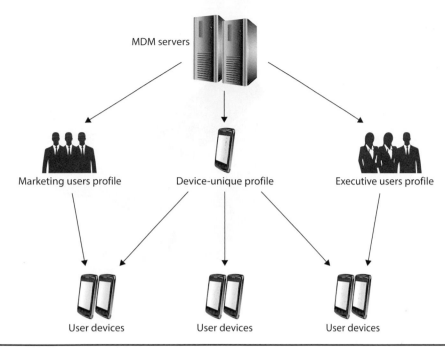

MDM servers

Marketing users profile   Device-unique profile   Executive users profile

User devices   User devices   User devices

Figure 25-7   Applying profiles to different device and user groups

cover, or sleeve for the mobile device. It doesn't help the HD camcorder in your new iPad if you get a scratch across the lens! You'll get a scratched, blurry movie even though the camcorder is capable of much, much more. Apple makes very nice covers for iPhones and iPads, plus you can get many third-party covers and sleeves (see Figure 25-8).

Depending on the amount of money you're willing to spend, you can get a cover that helps protect your screen from scratches, impacts, and small amounts of water. Like to scuba with your Android device? Get a specialty waterproof case and go post your deep thoughts to Facebook from 40 feet underwater.

Do the obvious to protect your devices. Don't get them anywhere near liquids. Don't run your smartphone through the wash in your trousers. Don't even think about placing heavy objects on that ~$600 tablet! Use common sense.

Combating Malware

Malware on mobile devices is an interesting issue. Tight controls on the OS and apps make traditional malware infections almost impossible on iOS and Android devices. When malware strikes, the OS maker supplies periodic OS updates, automatic updates and operating system patches. Android's more open nature means there are third-party *antivirus* and *anti-malware* single-user (user-level) and enterprise-level solutions available if you have corporate regulations that require such software. Figure 25-9 shows an example of user-level antivirus software for an Android device.

Figure 25-8
Putting an Apple
Smart cover on
an iPad

Figure 25-9
Antivirus app for
Android

NOTE We discuss operating system updates and their importance to security in detail in Chapter 27. Be aware that OS updates are just as important for mobile device security as they are for desktops and laptops.

In an ideal world, your mobile anti-malware software will cover all threats and work on all the devices used in your corporate network. In a heterogeneous real-world infrastructure, because there may be a variety of mobile devices from different vendors using different operating systems, a one-size-fits-all anti-malware solution probably won't work. Multiple solutions may be necessary for the different devices present on a network, or different modules covering specific types of devices may be available from the vendor to integrate with an enterprise-level anti-malware solution.

In any case, the most important part of an enterprise-level anti-malware solution is delivering timely updates to the devices on a routine basis. Network access control (NAC) solutions can ensure a device is checked for the latest anti-malware signatures and updated as necessary when it attempts to connect to the network. In the case of user-managed devices, you may need policy, NAC, and other technical solutions to ensure users are updating their own devices in a timely manner.

NOTE Chapter 27 goes into much depth on malware, including the types of malware as well as the most common sources and symptoms of malware infections.

Dealing with Loss

The best way to make sure you're ready to survive losing a mobile device is to assume it's inevitable. Say it to yourself: every mobile device will get lost at least once. I hope most of your users will prove you wrong, but the odds are good we'll all misplace every device we own at least once. Most of us will be lucky and find it right where we left it, but it could just as easily go the other way.

When you start with the assumption that your device will end up at the mercy, kindness, or ignorance of strangers at least once, it's obvious: you should protect your data from access by putting a good *screen lock* on the device. Most mobile devices enable you to set a screen lock through Settings (see Figure 25-10). Do it right now! There are many types of these locks; the most common require you to input a password, *PIN code*, pattern, fingerprint, or successful *facial recognition* to unlock the mobile device so you can use it. Modern iOS and Android use *device encryption* to protect the built-in storage, so even a "finder" who dismantles the device to access the drive will not get your documents.

As we discussed in the "System Lockout" section earlier, mobile devices may also have *failed login attempt restrictions* which restrict the number of login attempts that can fail before system lockout occurs. This system lockout slows down someone trying to guess the passcode of a found mobile device while you use *locator applications* or services to recover or remotely wipe it.

Figure 25-10
Passcode (screen
lock) option in
Settings

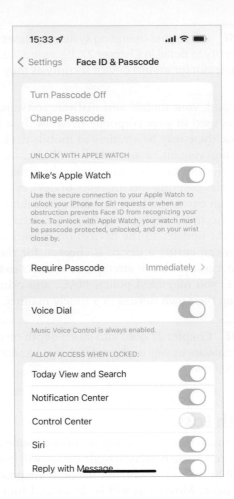

15:33 ✈

< Settings   Face ID & Passcode

Turn Passcode Off

Change Passcode

UNLOCK WITH APPLE WATCH

Mike's Apple Watch

Use the secure connection to your Apple Watch to
unlock your iPhone for Siri requests or when an
obstruction prevents Face ID from recognizing your
face. To unlock with Apple Watch, your watch must
be passcode protected, unlocked, and on your wrist
close by.

Require Passcode   Immediately >

Voice Dial

Music Voice Control is always enabled.

ALLOW ACCESS WHEN LOCKED:

Today View and Search

Notification Center

Control Center

Siri

Reply with Message

EXAM TIP For the purposes of the CompTIA A+ 1102 exam, know that *fingerprint lock, facial recognition, pattern lock, swipe lock,* and *PIN code* are screen lock methods used to secure mobile devices.

Apple and Google offer locator services for discovering the whereabouts of a misplaced mobile device. Using Apple's iCloud as an example, log in to your iCloud account and click the Find My iPhone button (despite the name, it also works for iPads). As soon as the device in question accesses the Internet (and thus receives an IP address and posts its MAC address), iCloud will pinpoint the location within a few yards (see Figure 25-11). Very slick!

Recovering from Theft

If your mobile device gets stolen and contains sensitive information, then you have a couple of options for dealing with it. Locator applications and services help, but if you have credit card information or other risky data on your mobile device, you need to act quickly.

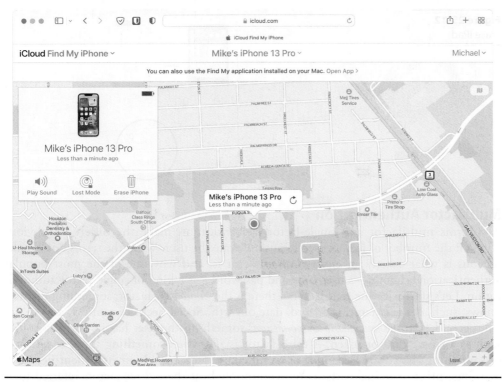

Figure 25-11   Locating a phone in iCloud

First, make sure you keep your data backed up. You should have everything synced to a local machine and, if possible, backed up to one of the *remote backup applications*—like Microsoft's OneDrive cloud service—to put your data beyond the reach of even a disaster that takes out your house. With Apple devices, for example, you back up and restore with one of several services, such as iCloud or iTunes, or use the Apple Configurator to handle a fleet of iOS devices. Android devices use the Google Sync feature to back up and restore.

Second, you can *remotely wipe* your mobile device. Apple, for example, makes it supremely easy through your Apple account. Log in, locate, and nuke your device (see Figure 25-12). You may never get the device back, but at least the bad guys won't have your data. It's equally simple with Android devices. Log in and follow the same process— locate and nuke.

Securing Your Data

Every security scenario we've discussed so far (remote wipe excepted) was designed to secure the device itself. Let's turn to how we can protect our actual data.

Figure 25-12
Erase iPad

Mike's iPad

1 minute ago

Play Sound   Lost Mode   Erase iPad

Multifactor Authentication

The terms multifactor and single-factor authentication make the difference obvious enough: the number of factors used to authenticate the user. What the terms don't make obvious is what exactly an *authentication* factor is, and why one of the most popular authentication schemes—a username and password—is a kind of single-factor authentication. Let's start with the factors. First, there is the *knowledge* factor: something the user knows, such as a username, password, date of birth, Social Security number, and so on. The second factor is *ownership* or *possession*: something the user has in her possession, such as a smart card or token. A third factor is *inherence*: something the user either is or something they do. An example of an inherence factor is a biometric identifier, such as a fingerprint or retinal pattern. You commonly hear these three factors referred to as something the user knows, something the user has, and something the user is.

Other authentication factors exist but are not as commonly considered in security authentication. For example, there's the *location* factor: somewhere you are. This can be used if the individual's location can be pinpointed via GPS or some other method. The individual may be required to be at a certain location in order to log in to the system, for example. Yet another is the *temporal* factor. As the name implies, schemes using the temporal factor may require logon at a certain time of day, or even within so many seconds or minutes of another event. Token methods of authentication also use time factors, as the PIN displayed on a token is only good for a finite amount of time.

Armed with the factors, let's consider authenticating with a single factor. The most common schemes require a username and password; both are something you know, so the scheme uses a single factor. You can also think of a traditional door lock as *single-factor authentication*; the key it requires is something the user has—a possession factor.

During the initial push to move beyond single-factor authentication, the term *two-factor authentication* grew common—and you'll still hear people use this term. Over the years, however, authentication methods using more than two factors have grown increasingly common, so it has become more correct to say multifactor authentication. *Multifactor authentication (MFA)* can use a variety of methods, as long as it uses more than one.

Just because the term sounds fancy and might make us think of complex systems at secret government installations, don't assume multifactor authentication hasn't played a role in everyday life for decades. For example, when you use a bank's ATM, you're using MFA: something you possess (the ATM card) and something you know (the correct PIN).

EXAM TIP Don't confuse the username and password combination with multifactor authentication. Only one factor is being used here, the knowledge factor, making this a form of single-factor authentication.

Biometric Authentication

Combined with other authentication factors, biometric elements can provide a very secure multifactor authentication mechanism. An example of *biometric authentication* is presenting a smartcard to a proximity badge reader and then placing your finger on a fingerprint reader to access a secure area.

NOTE Not every type of biometric authentication is a good fit for mobile devices. You'll get a closer look at the different types and other uses for them in Chapter 27.

Mobile devices use biometrics, too. Laptops have included fingerprint readers for several years already, and they are common in other mobile devices such as smartphones. A prime example is Apple's Touch ID; starting with the iPhone 5s, the iPhone can unlock with a fingerprint. Current iOS devices use facial recognition to identify and authenticate users. Check out Figure 25-13.

Authenticator Applications

Access to third-party or corporate networks often requires strong authentication methods. Access to a corporate VPN, for example, may require a specific app, approved and published by the organization, configured with the correct security settings. Generic apps have the ability to use multiple sets of credentials to access different Web sites, networks, or network-based services (for example, corporate e-mail, VPN access, and so forth). There are also apps that can act as tokens or issue temporary session PINs for multifactor authentication. The key to these apps is configuration; settings vary per app, but might include network configuration, authentication or encryption settings, and properly registering a given service with the authenticator app. You'll get a further look at authenticator applications in Chapter 27 as well.

Trusted Sources Versus Untrusted Sources

For the most part, getting software from *trusted sources*—legitimate app stores run by the major vendors, such as Apple, Google, Microsoft, and Amazon—is both easy and secure. Different vendors have their own requirements (including security) that developers must meet in order to get an app into the vendor's store. Most differences stem from the development and support model used by the vendor.

Apple strictly controls all aspects of the device and the apps available in the App Store (though organizations have some freedom to distribute apps developed in-house to their own devices). For example, Apple has exact requirements for how developers must create an app sold via the App Store. Android, on the other hand, has much less central control. One way Android's relaxed controls manifest is the ability to install apps from *untrusted sources*.

Figure 25-13
Face ID options

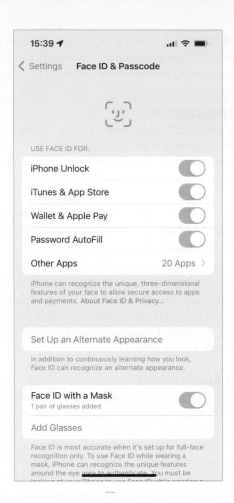

The operating system flavors developed by different Android device makers can change which sources are and aren't trusted. What may run on devices sold by one vendor isn't necessarily guaranteed to run on another vendor's device, even though they all use variations of the Android operating system. A prime example is Amazon's line of Fire devices (including products like Fire TV and Fire Tablet), which can only get apps from the Amazon Appstore. Additionally, even apps from the Google Play store aren't subject to guidelines as strict as the ones Apple uses. That doesn't mean they are necessarily less secure, but it does make security issues more likely.

The security weakness third-party app stores create is essentially apps from *unapproved* or *unofficial* sources. There are definitely legitimate app sources outside of Google Play, such as device manufacturers, communications carriers, and in-house corporate development sources. Some sources are not so legitimate, and are usually unapproved by the vendors, manufacturers, and corporate customers. You may also need to modify your mobile OS to run some apps you obtain through unofficial channels. These third-party apps may be perfectly fine, or they may be malicious and pose a security risk to your device or orga-nization. See "Unauthorized Root Access, Developer Mode, and Sideloading," later in the chapter, for more details.

When getting apps from questionable sources, risks include apps that contain malware or steal personal data and transmit it to a third party. Additionally, some apps require replacing the operating system with one that's not approved by the vendor; this not only invalidates the warranty on most devices, but could cause the device to be unstable and not operate properly.

Firewalls

While we'll discuss them in greater depth in Chapter 27, for now it's enough to know that software *firewalls* on individual hosts protect them from network-based threats. It isn't completely clear what CompTIA expects you to know about firewalling mobile devices. Generally, mobile devices don't use a firewall, because they don't have lots of services listening on open ports (like a traditional computer would). But, because they aren't listening, you can think of them as having a de facto firewall. The cellular and Wi-Fi networks mobile devices use also employ firewalls to protect all networked devices.

Depending on the OS, you may be able to find and install more traditional soft-ware firewall packages. One example of a software firewall for Android is shown in Figure 25-14. Android software firewall packages include basic rule elements for con-structing rules to filter specific traffic coming into the host. Many of these packages also include solutions for anti-malware and basic intrusion detection.

Figure 25-14
An Android
firewall app

Some of these software firewall solutions are standalone and must be configured and managed by the user, whereas some are enterprise-level solutions and can be centrally configured, updated, and managed by the systems administrator. Keep in mind that software firewall packages work at a very basic level and can't possibly contain every single network threat. Still, they serve as a second line of defense for the host, and are part of any good, layered, defense-in-depth security design.

Mobile OS and Application Security Issues

Security is a complicated, ever-evolving topic. We've already discussed aspects of mobile device security at various points in the chapter, but there are some additional security issues the user and organization need to be aware of and take steps to prevent. We'll begin with a discussion of tools you can use to troubleshoot mobile OS and application security issues broadly, and then turn to some of the common risks, symptoms, and clues related to mobile security issues.

Troubleshooting Tools

While the foundation of good security is staying informed of new threats and being vigilant about the patches, configuration updates, policy changes, anti-malware updates, and user re-education required to address these new threats, this foundation boils down to not giving attackers an easy win. Beyond this, we have to cope with security issues that require constant vigilance: novel threats, avoiding insecure applications, and irresolvable vulnerabilities.

Though your greatest assets are your own curiosity, instincts, and persistence, you can augment these with a variety of technical tools for troubleshooting mobile security issues. Let's look at some of these tools, grouped in terms of the issues they are most useful in addressing: network attacks and app security.

Network Attacks

Device makers originally designed mobile devices to be gregarious by nature—they are more useful this way—but network attacks can exploit such openness. We'll consider specific issues a little later in the "Unintended Connections" section and focus now on tools for identifying and mitigating risks: device security settings, user training, Wi-Fi analyzers, and cell tower analyzers.

Device Security Settings   Because network attacks generally prey on devices that are overeager to connect, the first step to mitigating these threats is to make sure your devices won't automatically connect to any open Wi-Fi network or nearby Bluetooth device. You can apply these settings manually on each device, but you can also use MDM software or similar software made for managing more than one device, such as Apple Configurator.

User Training   It won't help (much) to configure your devices to avoid automatic connections if your users still select any open Wi-Fi network or agree to any pairing request without considering the consequences. Similarly, your network will be at risk if your users don't recognize any of the warning signs that their connection to your organization's secure Wi-Fi network has been intercepted by an evil-twin wireless access point (WAP). Teach them what is normal, and train them to stop and report anything that seems out of place.

Wi-Fi Analyzer   In addition to using a *Wi-Fi analyzer* for tasks such as figuring out what channel a network should use, optimizing WAP placement, or finding dead spots, you can use one to map out nearby networks (see Figure 25-15). Most of these are probably genuine networks in neighboring buildings or offices, but there's always a chance someone will set up a WAP for the wrong reasons.

Figure 25-15
A Wi-Fi analyzer
app on Android
showing several
SSIDs in the area

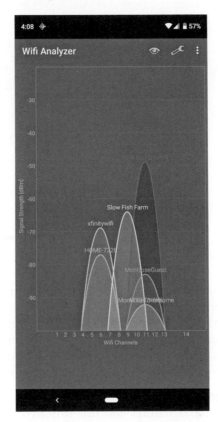

Cell Tower Analyzer   Like a Wi-Fi analyzer, a *cell tower analyzer* helps identify nearby cellular signals, estimate their distance and direction (see Figure 25-16), measure their signal strength, and collect other information such as the technologies they are using, network names, and more. A simple use might be to confirm signal quality for a user having trouble connecting, or to map out access in the building. There's also a chance you'll spot an illegitimate tower operating nearby—and your organization might be the target.

Figure 25-16
My Android-
based cell
tower analyzer
estimating the
location of a cell
tower

App Security

One of the important things to understand about malware is that the "best" malware accomplishes its objective without anyone detecting it. Almost anyone could figure out that malware is to blame for a device that runs like it's full of molasses and constantly redirects your searches or Web requests to sites that announce that you've won a round-trip to Mars. Because the most dangerous malware is subtle, you need to use tools to help you catch the easy stuff, freeing your attention to see subtle signs something is amiss.

Anti-Malware and App Scanners   Mobile anti-malware apps, much like their desktop counterparts, use signatures and lists to scan a device in order to identify, block, remove, or warn about known malware. An *app scanner*, by contrast, looks through the permissions requested by your installed apps to assess the risk they pose to security and privacy. You may find some separate apps for performing each of these tasks, or combined apps that can do both. You won't find these apps available for iOS, but many of the same features are available through the Settings app.

App scanners typically run before an app is installed or updated and can give you information such as what network connectivity the app requires, what permissions it needs, and what access the app has to certain hardware and functions on your device. App scanners can also tell you what type of data access the app has to your personal information, such as contacts and media files (see Figure 25-17).

Figure 25-17
Combined anti-malware and app scanner

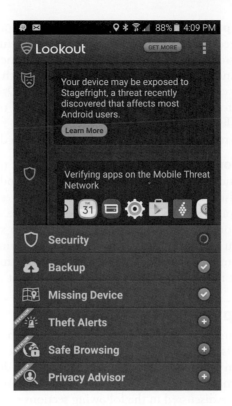

The usefulness of app scanners as a security tool becomes more apparent if you think of every installed app as posing a few different risks. First, there's the direct risk that the app is designed to spy on you or steal your data. Next, there's the risk that the app maker will lose control of your personal information once it leaves your device. Finally, there's the risk that a vulnerability in the app will allow an attacker to use it against you.

Some users are savvy enough to avoid directly installing malware. But how many of those users know enough to assess the risk that an attacker in the future will be able to exploit a vulnerability in an app they're installing today? And what about malware that doesn't require the user to do anything at all for it to find its way onto their device?

NOTE Malware is always evolving, and always being developed. Sometimes, the software isn't necessarily intended to be used maliciously. A high-profile example of this was software known as Pegasus. Originally designed to be used by law enforcement agencies to address terrorism and organized crime, it also ended up being used to spy on journalists, activists, and even world leaders. The scariest part was that it didn't require the user to click or install anything in order to get to a mobile device and start spying. This is an example both of how insidious malware can be and how important it is to stay vigilant in securing and monitoring devices.

Remote Backup Applications   Maintaining a current backup of your device is one measure you need to take in case all else fails. Different tools used to perform remote backups and restore data include MDM software, iTunes, and the various synchronization tools for Android; another option is to back up the data to the manufacturer's or third-party user cloud storage, such as Microsoft OneDrive or Apple iCloud.

Some malware can put down deep roots and be hard to expunge. A recent full backup predating the infestation can give you the confidence to focus on making sure you get rid of the malware, rather than focusing on being sure you don't lose important data.

App Troubleshooting Tools   We've already looked at tools for troubleshooting general mobile device and app issues: force stop, uninstalling and reinstalling apps, and a factory reset. You can also use these tools to pinpoint and address app security issues.

Whenever you see clues or symptoms of malware or another app security issue, remember that one way you can isolate the cause is to stop apps until you identify the cause. When you know what is causing the symptoms, uninstall it. If the app is reputable and the symptoms could be non-malicious, reinstall it to see if this fixes the problem. If these steps don't resolve the behavior, use a factory reset to cleanse the device.

Risks, Symptoms, and Clues

The value of your curiosity, intuition, and persistence begins to show in a big way when we look at the risks, symptoms, and clues that malware or some other security problem is present. When you read about a potential risk here, don't assume you'll only see it by itself. Because malware and other attacks can be creative, complex, and multifaceted, view the scenarios discussed in the following sections as risks to understand and manage, symptoms of malware or an attack, or merely clues of an attack underway.

Much like you shouldn't assume you'll see these things as isolated incidents, you shouldn't assume when you encounter one or more of them that malware or an attack is necessarily present. In fact, we've already discussed many of the issues in this section as they relate to other kinds of mobile device problems.

Unexpected Resource Use

If you think about it, malware is just software or a program that uses your device for work or tasks you don't want it to do. Like any program working hard, malware can cause resource issues. Because resource issues can also be relatively benign problems fixed by a soft reset, it's easy to shrug them off. Be suspicious, especially if you see patterns and can't find an obvious explanation; the first clues of an ongoing attempt to spy on your company may well be an uptick in data outbound from affected cellular devices.

Sluggish Response Time   A hot phone, high resource use, and excessive *power drain* can be common signs that an app is frozen or malfunctioning, but they might also be symptoms that your device is doing precisely what a malware developer intends. The device might be hot, have *sluggish response time*, or be low on battery because it's a live recording device uploading everything it records in real time, or because it's copying files available on the network to a remote location.

High Network Traffic   Likewise, high network traffic can cause network issues, signal-quality problems, frozen apps, regular syncing of large files—or a sign the device is busy uploading or downloading something without your knowledge. High network traffic may also clue you in to one or more devices that are attempting to use an illegitimate WAP or cell tower that has a lower capacity than its official counterpart.

Data-Usage Limit Notification   As discussed earlier, a data transmission limit is a line in the sand that indicates when a device has used more data than its plan or carrier allots for it. Perhaps the user drove across the country while listening to Spotify, or perhaps the device is uploading stolen data from the device and other networked locations. If you see an inexplicable *data-usage limit notification*, it may be time to start checking the mobile device for malware.

Unexpected Behaviors

Security threats don't only cause unexpected resource usage, they can also cause unexpected device and application behavior. Much like their desktop counterparts, mobile devices can start to behave strangely when they are infected with malware. A *high number of ads*, *fake security warnings*, and *unexpected application behavior* from individual apps can all be indicators of a security issue, whether it's malware or breached credentials. These issues will be explored in greater detail in Chapter 27, but be aware when you take the CompTIA A+ exams that these issues can also indicate that your mobile device is compromised. As with other computing devices, if you start to see any of these signs, consider scanning for malware as part of your troubleshooting efforts.

Unintended Connections

A major security issue is unintended network connections (such as cellular, Wi-Fi, and Bluetooth). Unintended cellular network connections aren't common since these are preprogrammed into the phone by the carrier and periodically updated, but there is a technique called *tower spoofing* that involves setting up equipment to spoof a carrier's tower and infrastructure and cause a cellular device to use it instead of the normal tower equipment. It requires overpowering the nearest legitimate cell signal, causing the cellular device to lock onto it instead. Equipment used in tower spoofing can also eavesdrop on any conversation, even if it is encrypted. In some cases, the equipment can fool the device into turning off encryption completely—and sophisticated attacks can even install malware on the device.

Just as hackers have been using this technique for a few years, law enforcement officials have been reportedly using it as well. Since 2010, there have been numerous court cases highlighted in the media questioning the admissibility of evidence obtained from cell signal interception. Media reports say various federal, state, and local law enforcement agencies use a device called a "Stingray" to intercept a suspect's cell traffic using tower spoofing equipment and techniques. There's even an aircraft-mounted version, known as a "Dirtbox."

 NOTE   Though much of the news coverage on tower spoofing focuses on U.S. law enforcement agencies using the Stingray, you could just as easily encounter malicious cellular or Wi-Fi networks run (for a variety of reasons) by individuals, businesses, organized crime, and governments anywhere in the world.

Unintended Wi-Fi connections and *unintended Bluetooth pairings* can enable malicious people to access, steal, or modify data. Configure your mobile device not to connect to unknown Wi-Fi networks or automatically pair with other Bluetooth devices. This will require you to manually connect to known and trusted Wi-Fi networks, and manually pair with Bluetooth devices—but it's worth it. If the device is centrally managed, MDM software can enforce these protections via profile settings.

Connectivity Issues

Earlier, we looked at dropped and weak signals in terms of their impact on battery life, power management, and running apps. Sometimes these signal issues go unnoticed or are only a minor inconvenience. When it comes to cellular signals, they can also be one of the few clues you'll get that your device is interacting with a spoofed cell tower.

If you or your users are in an area where the signal quality should be (and usually is) excellent, be curious—especially if you have multiple reports of difficulty. Check with the relevant cellular providers to see if they have any known tower issues in the area. Fire up a cell tower analyzer and compare nearby signals with what you've seen in the past, or with third-party resources online.

If users are suddenly reporting that Wi-Fi quality is low in an area where it was high, or you notice your device sees a network with a strong signal and the correct SSID in what used to be a dead spot, check it out. There may be a rogue WAP on the loose. *Limited* or *no Internet connectivity* can be a tricky problem to troubleshoot. As you've seen both earlier in the book and here in this chapter, there are many potential causes, but if you've ruled out hardware problems and provider issues and are still having limited or no connectivity, it may be time to investigate a security issue as the potential culprit.

Unauthorized Data Access

Securing data stored on a mobile device is hard. The building's security guards might stop a courier from walking out with a desktop under his arm, but they probably won't notice an extra phone in his pocket. Even if they do, he might just confidently claim he has to carry an extra phone for work and go on his way. If I accidentally leave my phone behind at lunch, there's a chance I won't notice until I head to my car that evening. Device locks and remote wipe can usually prevent unauthorized users from accessing data on a mobile device—as long as you wipe the device before it is compromised.

Data can leak out other ways, though, such as removable memory storage cards, and data sharing settings in the device's OS or applications. Removable memory cards should be encrypted if they contain sensitive data, so an unauthorized person can't access data if they are removed from the device. Security and privacy settings on the device can help protect personal data, and the same settings can be configured in different apps that need to access personal data.

One of the more obvious risks to every networked app with access to data is the possibility that it will leak some of that data (whether intentionally or not). In some cases, it can be hard to figure out where the leak is. If an attacker used tax returns you stuck in

Dropbox to obtain a loan in your name, where and when did the data go? You had local copies on your phone, laptop, and desktop, plus what was available if your Dropbox credentials were compromised, and any copies that transited over the network. Perhaps the attacker stole them directly from the company that did your taxes.

The point is that leaked files are a risk, a potential symptom of an ongoing security issue, and a possible clue to what that issue might be. A full audit of the many ways an important file could've leaked out of a networked environment is beyond what can be expected of a CompTIA A+ tech, but he or she may well get the first chance to escalate the issue or write it off as a compromised login and make the user change passwords.

EXAM TIP Portable and mobile devices present amazing opportunities for your personal information to become much less personal and a lot more public. The CompTIA A+ 1102 exam calls this "leaked personal files/data," but it could just as easily be translated as "your phone password wasn't strong and you left the phone in a kiosk at the ski resort." (Not that this has ever happened to me.)

Unauthorized Account Access

Unauthorized account access is a big deal not only for the mobile device itself, but also for all organizational networks it can connect to. If someone steals the account credentials or is able to access a mobile device configured to remember the credentials, then they have an entry point into an organizational network. As discussed earlier, you should plan based on the assumption every device will be lost.

To keep VPN and e-mail connections secure, the device should not store usernames and passwords for connecting automatically. This way, lost or stolen devices can't be used to access these services (at least not without also stealing credentials) because they still require authentication. Unauthorized account access can lead to a malicious person stealing or accessing data not only on the device, but also on the larger network.

When a device is lost, act with an abundance of caution. Treat the previously described precaution as something to protect you until the device is reported missing. Once you know it is missing, change the user's credentials. Keep in mind that compromised account credentials could also be a clue that one of the user's devices itself has been compromised and may be an ongoing threat to the organization.

Unauthorized Root Access, Developer Mode, and Sideloading

To help secure the device, mobile operating systems all restrict the actions (such as installing apps or changing settings) that a user can normally perform. There are ways around these restrictions, though the name of each method differs by OS, depending on how the OS restricts what the user can do. To fully remove these restrictions, a user may have to *jailbreak* (iOS) or *root* (Android) the device. Android also has two less intrusive options: developer mode and sideloading. Let's take a look at each.

EXAM TIP Know jailbreak, root access, and the OS associated with each, but keep in mind that it's common to see both of these terms used in relation to removing access restrictions from any given device.

Jailbreaking means the user installs a program on the iOS device that changes settings Apple didn't intend for users to change. Jailbreaking allows a user to install blocked software, such as apps that don't come from the App Store or apps that don't meet Apple's legal and quality requirements. Jailbreaking also enables a user to unlock functionality on the device.

Rooting an Android device is a similar procedure to grant the user full administrative access to the lower-level functionality of the device. As in the case of jailbreaking, this is also done to install software or enable functions that could not otherwise be used on the device. Although none of the popular Android device vendors condone rooting, they have little recourse beyond voiding the warranty if the user owns the device.

Developer mode is another Android-specific mode, but unlike rooting, it doesn't present the same level of catastrophic risk that rooting can. You don't void your warranty, you don't leave your phone unusable if you make a mistake, and you don't introduce major security risks. However, a user who isn't familiar with developer mode options may end up changing settings that make using the device more difficult. Developer mode gives users access to features like USB debugging, more advanced resource monitoring, and the ability to go a step farther by rooting the device. As a result, developer mode doesn't present its own security risks, but it does give Android users access to functionality that might.

In the same vein, another unique aspect of Android when compared to Apple's mobile OSs is the ability to sideload applications without using a dedicated app store. *Sideloading* allows an Android user to use a file called an *Android package (APK) to* install an app that they got from a Web site or source other than the Google Play store onto their device. Sideloading can have some advantages like allowing a user to bypass geographic limitations or install software that was previously available on the app store and removed for whatever reason.

Sideloading also comes with security risks. Some APKs can be *bootleg applications*, which can pose legal issues. Other APKs may be *malicious applications*, designed to act similarly to a Trojan horse (explained in more detail in Chapter 27). *Application spoofing* can be a very dangerous attack method when used against mobile devices, as many people wrongly assume that mobile devices aren't vulnerable the same way desktop and laptop computers are. As with any other class of devices, a false sense of security can lead to real-world security problems.

The important thing to keep in mind with jailbreaking, rooting, and sideloading is that they give the user more power at the expense of disabling protections that limit the damage malicious apps can do to the device. There are some things you just can't use a device for without removing these restrictions, but the benefit should always be weighed against the risk, especially when it comes to deciding whether to allow jailbroken/rooted devices on your network.

NOTE Organizational networks may use MDM software to detect and block devices that have used one of these methods to remove restrictions.

The manufacturer or service provider may prevent a device from connecting to their services if they detect the change. There are also immediate risks: a failed attempt could brick the device, or perhaps just render it unusable until you restore it completely from a backup (removing the jailbreaking/rooting software in the process).

Unauthorized Location Tracking

We discussed the benefits of GPS and location tracking earlier, but there are also risks involved. Configuration settings in the OS and apps may allow a user's location to be sent to third parties, sometimes without explicit consent or knowledge. The best way to prevent this is to turn off the GPS function or location services unless they are needed. Another way is to configure the device and apps that use geotracking to prevent unauthorized tracking, if the device allows it. Some apps—or specific features—simply won't work until geotracking is enabled (see Figure 25-18).

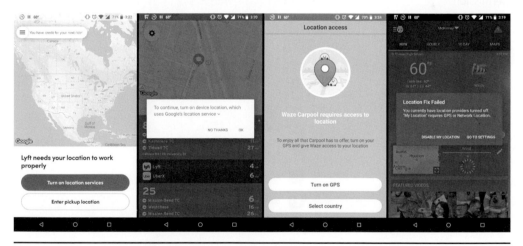

Figure 25-18 Four Android apps prompting the user to enable location services

Keep in mind that the GPS functionality in a mobile device is not the only way to track its location; cellular networks and Wi-Fi are also used to track device location, although not as precisely as GPS. Some of the network attacks in the "Unintended Connections" section can also be used to locate or track a device.

Unauthorized Camera and Microphone Activation

App features, malware, and unauthorized network connections can potentially be used to activate (or disable!) some features on a mobile device. Any built-in cameras and microphones are of particular concern, because they enable an attacker to move beyond sensitive data on the device and effectively spy on anyone near it.

NOTE Some of the most sophisticated attacks using methods discussed in the earlier "Unintended Connections" section can reportedly cause a device to appear to power down while still leaving its microphone active. Attacks of this quality may be unavoidable until carriers and device makers secure their networks and devices against them, but you can still be on the lookout for strange behavior.

The ways to prevent these exploits are by restricting camera and microphone permissions in apps or operating systems (when they allow it), taking steps previously described to prevent unauthorized network connections, and using anti-malware solutions on the device. Even when you're looking at a popular app by a trustworthy developer, such as the iOS apps with camera permissions in Figure 25-19, keep in mind that any vulnerabilities in a networked app with camera and microphone permissions could allow an attacker to listen in.

Figure 25-19
Apps with permission to access my iPhone's camera

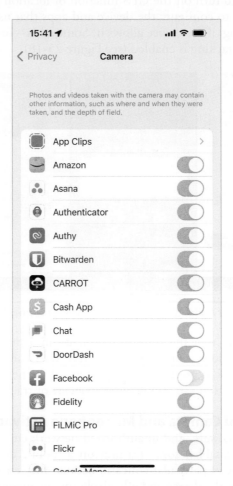

Chapter Review

Questions

1. After five minutes of struggling with a painfully sluggish device, you finally manage to close the offending application. What's the best next step?

   A. Reopen the application and hope it doesn't freeze again.

   B. Uninstall the application and look for a replacement.

   C. Perform a soft reset and see if the app runs smoothly afterward.

   D. Close all open applications and attempt to reopen the application to see if it freezes again.

2. Which of the following would be a legitimate reason a mobile device is running slowly?

   A. Incorrect calibration

   B. RAM too slow

   C. Lack of storage space

   D. Incorrect version of application

3. Joyce notices her GPS map app gives the error "GPS coordinates not available." What should she try first?

   A. Run another GPS app.

   B. Stop and start GPS on the mobile device.

   C. Move to a place where she can get a good GPS signal.

   D. Update the mobile device's firmware.

4. You've lost your iPhone. What would you use to try to find it?

   A. iTunes

   B. iFind

   C. Location Services

   D. iCloud

5. Fred wants to play *World of Warcraft* on his desktop system. He logs in and then the game asks for a code that is generated by an authenticator app on his Android phone. This is an example of _____.

   A. Multifactor authentication

   B. Factor authorization

   C. Multifactor authorization

   D. Factor authentication

6. Jailbreaking an iPhone gives access to _____.

   A. The administrator account

   B. The root account

   C. The /bin folder

   D. The system BIOS

7. A great way to protect data on a removable media card is to _____.

   A. Encrypt it

   B. Lock it

   C. Remove it when unneeded

   D. Format it

8. What type of file would you use to sideload an app onto an Android device?

   A. APK

   B. ZIP

   C. GIF

   D. EXE

9. Users bringing personally owned mobile devices into an enterprise environment is called _____.

   A. Importing

   B. CYMK

   C. Providing

   D. BYOD

10. What do app scanners do?

   A. Scan QR codes and barcodes for hidden codes

   B. Analyze the traffic into and out of an application for suspicious behavior

   C. Analyze the permissions used by installed applications to highlight security risks

   D. Analyze Wi-Fi signals to identify evil-twin WAPs

Answers

1. **C.** After five minutes of struggling with a painfully sluggish device, definitely perform a soft reset and see if the app runs smoothly afterward.

2. **C.** Lack of storage space would be a legitimate reason a mobile device is running slowly.

3. **C.** Joyce needs to move to a place where she can get a good GPS signal.

4. **D.** Apple's iPhone uses the Find My iPhone feature of iCloud.

5. **A.** Using both a password and a security code is an example of multifactor authentication.

6. **B.** Jailbreaking is unique to iOS to provide access to the root account.

7. **A.** A great way to protect data on a removable media card is to encrypt it.

8. **A.** An Android Package (APK) is the file type that is used to sideload applications onto Android devices.

9. **D.** Users bringing personally owned mobile device into an enterprise environment is known as bring your own device (BYOD).

10. **C.** App scanners analyze the permissions used by installed applications to highlight security risks.

5. A. Using both a password and a security code is an example of multifactor authentication.

6. B. Jailbreaking is unique to iOS to provide access to the root account.

7. A. A great way to protect data on a removable media card is to encrypt it.

8. A. An Android Package (APK) is the file type that is used to sideload applications onto Android devices.

9. D. Users bringing personally owned mobile device into an enterprise environment is known as bring your own device (BYOD).

10. C. App scanners analyze the permissions used by installed applications to highlight security risks.

Printers and Multifunction Devices

In this chapter, you will learn how to

- Describe current printer and multifunction device consumables
- Explain the laser printing process
- Install and configure a printer or multifunction device consumable
- Recognize and fix basic printer and multifunction device problems

Despite all the talk about the "paperless office," paper documents continue to be a vital part of the typical office. Some computers are used exclusively for the purpose of producing paper documents. Many people simply still prefer dealing with a hard copy, even as portable devices have proliferated. Developers cater to this preference by using metaphors such as *page*, *workbook*, and *binder* in their applications.

In the past, your average office had an array of electronic and mechanical devices dedicated to performing a single task with paper documents. Think printers, copiers, scanners, and fax machines. Back in the 1990s, the *multifunction device (MFD)*, also known as a *multifunction printer (MFP)*, tried to consolidate multiple functions (often printing and scanning) into a single device. At first these devices weren't terribly great at any of their functions, but today's mature multifunction devices get their many jobs done well.

The CompTIA A+ certification strongly stresses the area of printing and expects a high degree of technical knowledge of the function, components, maintenance, and repair of all types of printers and multifunction devices.

This chapter examines the common varieties of printers and scanners, then looks at specifics of how a laser printer works. The chapter continues with the steps for installing a multifunction device in a typical personal computer and concludes with troubleshooting issues.

Printer and Multifunction Device Consumables

The multifunction devices commonly used in SOHO environments typically sit on a desk, shelf, or countertop, and they tend to be fairly similar in appearance. Because of this, when most of us think about MFDs, we picture small desktop *all-in-one* devices (which can usually be used as a printer, scanner, copier, and fax machine) connected to a nearby computer (see Figure 26-1 for an example).

Figure 26-1
All-in-one
printer/scanner/
fax machine/
copier/iPhone
dock

The reality is that these desktop devices, descendants of the desktop printer and scanner, are just the low end of the market. As you head upmarket, multifunction printers look more like the descendants of copy machines and even small printing presses. Despite how different from SOHO MFDs these high-end devices may look, they still share a core set of components—a printer and scanner of some sort—with the all-in-ones you're probably familiar with. As you go upmarket, the greatest improvements tend to be in speed/capacity, durability, and document handling/finishing features such as sorting, stapling, binding, and so on.

Because MFDs are so varied, we'll look at some of the individual components and technologies you may find inside them separately—be prepared to encounter these components as both standalone devices and included with other components in an MFD. I've added 3-D printers to this section; you won't find these as anything but standalone devices, not MFDs.

Printers

No other piece of your computer system is available in a wider range of styles, configurations, and feature sets than a printer, or at such a wide price variation. What a printer can and can't do is largely determined by the type of printer technology it uses—that is, how it gets the image onto the paper. Modern printers can be categorized into several types: impact, inkjet, thermal, laser, 3-D, and virtual.

Impact Printers

Printers that create an image on paper by physically striking an ink ribbon against the paper's surface are known as *impact printers*. Although *daisy-wheel* printers (essentially an electric typewriter attached to the computer instead of directly to a keyboard) have largely disappeared, their cousins, *dot-matrix printers*, still soldier on in many offices. Although dot-matrix printers don't deliver what most home users want—high quality and flexibility at a low cost—they're still widely found in businesses for two reasons: dot-matrix printers have a large installed base in businesses, and they can be used for multipart forms because they actually strike the paper. Impact printers tend to be relatively slow and noisy, but when speed, flexibility, and print quality are not critical, they provide acceptable results. Computers that print multipart forms, such as *point of sale (POS)* machines, use special *impact paper* that can print receipts in duplicate, triplicate, or more. These POS machines represent the major market for new impact printers, although some older dot-matrix printers remain in use.

Dot-matrix printers use a grid, or matrix, of tiny pins, also known as printwires, to strike an inked printer *ribbon* and produce images on paper (see Figure 26-2). The case that holds the printwires is called a *printhead*. Using either 9 or 24 pins, dot-matrix printers treat each page as a picture broken up into a dot-based raster image. The 9-pin dot-matrix printers are generically called *draft quality*, while the 24-pin printers are known as *letter quality* or near-letter quality (NLQ). The BIOS for the printer (either built into the printer or a printer driver) interprets the raster image in the same way a monitor does, "painting" the image as individual dots. Naturally, the more pins, the higher the resolution. Figure 26-3 illustrates the components common to dot-matrix printers. Some dot-matrix printers use continuous-feed paper with holes on its sides that are engaged by metal sprockets to pull the paper through—this is known as *tractor-feed paper* because the sprockets are reminiscent of the wheels on a tractor.

Figure 26-2
An Epson FX-880+ dot-matrix printer (photo courtesy of Epson America, Inc.)

Inkjet Printers

Inkjet printers (also called *ink-dispersion printers*) like the one shown in Figure 26-4 are relatively simple devices. An inkjet printer uses a *printhead* connected to a *carriage* that contains the ink. A *carriage belt* and motor move the carriage back and forth so the ink can cover the whole page. A *roller* grabs paper from a paper tray (usually under or inside the printer) or *feeder* (usually on the back of the printer) and advances it through the printer (see Figure 26-5).

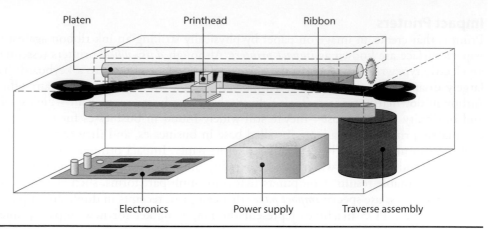

Figure 26-3   Inside a dot-matrix printer

Figure 26-4
Typical inkjet
printer

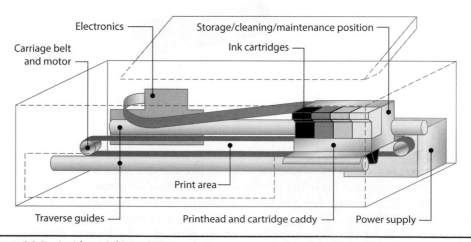

Figure 26-5   Inside an inkjet printer

The ink is ejected through tiny tubes. Most inkjet printers use heat to move the ink, while a few use a mechanical method. The heat-method printers use tiny resistors or electroconductive plates at the end of each tube that literally boil the ink; this creates a tiny air bubble that ejects a droplet of ink onto the paper, thus creating a portion of the image (see Figure 26-6).

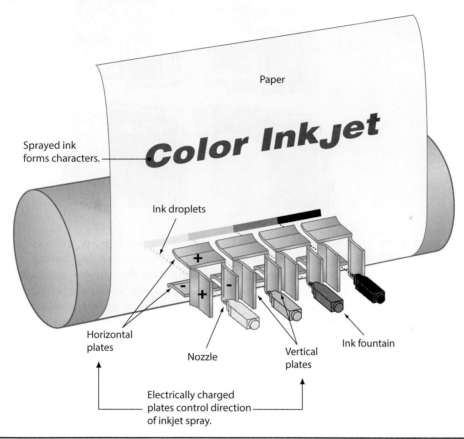

Figure 26-6 Detail of the inkjet printhead

The ink is stored in special small containers called *ink cartridges*. Older inkjet printers had two cartridges: one for black ink and another for colored ink. The color cartridge had separate compartments for cyan (blue), magenta (red), and yellow ink, to print colors by using a method known as CMYK (you'll read more about CMYK later in this chapter). If your color cartridge ran out of one of the colors, you had to purchase a whole new color cartridge or deal with a messy refill kit.

Printer manufacturers began to separate the ink colors into three separate cartridges so that printers came with four cartridges: one for each color and a fourth for black (see Figure 26-7). This not only was more cost-effective for the user, but it also resulted in higher-quality printouts. Today you can find color inkjet printers with six, eight, or more color cartridges. In addition to the basic CMYK inks, the additional cartridges provide for green, blue, gray, light cyan, dark cyan, and more. Typically, printers using more ink cartridges produce higher-quality printed images—and cost more.

Figure 26-7
Inkjet ink
cartridges

In recent years, manufacturers such as Epson and Canon have introduced ink-jet printers with refillable ink tanks, radically changing the economics of printing. Rather than selling printers inexpensively and raking in money on throw-away ink cartridges, consumers and businesses can print in glorious color without the hassle (or guilt). The printers, such as the Epson EcoTank line, cost a lot more than previous models (think $300–$700 rather than $60–$120), but come with a couple of years' worth of ink fresh out of the box. Let the color flow.

The two key features of an inkjet printer are the print resolution—how densely the printer lays down ink on the page—and the print speed. Resolution is measured in horizontal and vertical *dots per inch (dpi)*, such as 2400 × 2400 dpi. Higher numbers mean that the ink dots on the page are closer together, so your printed documents will look better. Resolution is most important when you're printing complex images such as full-color photos, or when you're printing for duplication and you care that your printouts look good. Print speed is measured in *pages per minute (ppm)*, and this specification is normally indicated right on the printer's box. Most printers have one (faster) speed for monochrome printing—that is, using only black ink—and another for full-color printing.

Another feature of inkjet printers is that they can support a staggering array of print media. Using an inkjet printer, you can print on a variety of matte or glossy photo papers, iron-on transfers, and other specialty media; some printers can print directly onto specially coated optical discs, or even fabric. Imagine running a T-shirt through your printer with your own custom slogan (how about "I'm CompTIA A+ Certified!"). The inks have improved over the years, too, now delivering better quality and longevity than ever. Where older inks would smudge if the paper got wet or start to fade after a short time, modern inks are smudge-proof and of archival quality—for example, some inks by Epson are projected to last up to 200 years.

For best results with all this variety of media available, you need to make sure the print settings match the paper/media type. In Windows 10, for example, go to Settings | Devices | Printers & scanners. Select the printer installed, click Manage, and go to Printer preferences. There you can change the media type to match.

NOTE Print resolution is measured in dots per inch (dpi) and print speed is measured in pages per minute (ppm).

Try This!

Pages per Minute Versus Price

Printer speed is a key determinant of a printer's price, and this is an easy assertion to prove, so try this!

1. Open a browser and head over to the Web site for HP (https://www .hp.com), Canon (https://www.canon.com), Epson (https://www.epson .com), Brother (https://www.brother.com), or Samsung (https://www .samsung.com). These five companies make most of the printers on the market today.

2. Pick a printer technology and check the price, from the cheapest to the most expensive. Then look for printers that have the same resolution but different ppm rates.

3. Check the prices and see how the ppm rate affects the price of two otherwise identical printers.

Thermal Printers

Thermal printers use a heated printhead to create a high-quality image on special or plain paper. You'll see two kinds of thermal printers in use. The first is the *direct thermal* printer, and the other is the *thermal wax transfer* printer. Direct thermal printers use a *heating element* to burn dots into the surface of special *heat-sensitive thermal paper*. If you remember the first generation of fax machines, you're already familiar with this type of printer. Many retail businesses still use it as a receipt printer, using large rolls of thermal paper housed in a *feed assembly* that automatically draws the paper past the heating element; some receipt printers can even cut the paper off the roll for you.

Laser Printers

Using a process called *electro-photographic imaging*, *laser printers* produce high-quality and high-speed output of both text and graphics. Figure 26-8 shows a typical laser printer. Laser printers rely on the photoconductive properties of certain organic compounds.

Photoconductive means that particles of these compounds, when exposed to light (that's the "photo" part), will *conduct* electricity. Laser printers usually use lasers as a light source because of their precision. Some lower-cost printers use LED arrays instead.

Figure 26-8
Typical laser
printer

The first laser printers created only monochrome images; you can also buy a color laser printer, but most laser printers produced today are still monochrome. Although a color laser printer can produce complex full-color images such as photographs, they really shine for printing what's known as *spot color*—for example, eye-catching headings, lines, charts, or other graphical elements that dress up an otherwise plain printed presentation.

NOTE Some printers use *consumables*—such as ink—at a faster rate than others, prompting the industry to rank printers in terms of their cost per page. Using an inexpensive printer (laser or inkjet) costs around 4 cents per page, while an expensive printer can cost more than 20 cents per page—a huge difference if you do any volume printing. This hidden cost is particularly pernicious in the sub-$100 inkjet printers on the market. Their low prices often entice buyers, who then discover that the cost of consumables is outrageous—these days, a single set of color and black inkjet cartridges can cost as much as the printer itself, if not more!

The CompTIA A+ certification exams take a keen interest in the particulars of the laser printing process—or specifically, the *imaging process*—so it pays to know your way around a laser printer (see Figure 26-9). Let's take a look at the many components of laser printers and their functions. The imaging process is described in detail later in the chapter in the section "The Laser Printing Process."

Toner Cartridge The *toner cartridge* in a laser printer is so named because of its most obvious activity: supplying the toner that creates the image on the page (see Figure 26-10). To reduce maintenance costs, however, many other laser printer parts, especially those that suffer the most wear and tear, have been incorporated into the toner cartridge. Although this makes replacement of individual parts nearly impossible, it greatly reduces the need for replacement; those parts that are most likely to break are replaced every time you replace the toner cartridge.

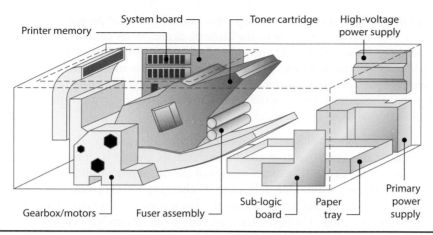

Figure 26-9 Components inside a laser printer

Figure 26-10
Laser printer's
toner cartridge

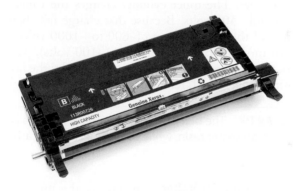

NOTE Color laser printers have four toner cartridges: black, cyan, magenta, and yellow.

Imaging Drum The *imaging drum* (also called the photosensitive drum) is an aluminum cylinder coated with particles of photosensitive compounds. The drum itself is grounded to the power supply, but the coating is not. When light hits these particles, whatever electrical charge they may have "drains" out through the grounded cylinder.

Erase Lamp The *erase lamp* exposes the entire surface of the imaging drum to light, making the photosensitive coating conductive. Any electrical charge present in the particles bleeds away into the grounded drum, leaving the surface particles electrically neutral.

Primary Corona/Charge Roller   The *primary corona* wire (or *primary charge roller*, in newer laser printers), located close to the imaging drum, never touches the drum. When the primary corona or primary charge roller is charged with an extremely high voltage, an electric field (or corona) forms, enabling voltage to pass to the drum and charge the photosensitive particles on its surface. The primary grid regulates the transfer of voltage, ensuring that the surface of the drum receives a uniform negative voltage of between ~600 and ~1000 volts.

Laser   The *laser* acts as the writing mechanism of the printer. Any particle on the drum struck by the laser becomes conductive and its charge is drained away into the grounded core of the drum. The entire surface of the drum has a uniform negative charge of between ~600 and ~1000 volts following its charging by the primary corona wire or charge roller. When particles are struck by the laser, they are discharged and left with a ~100-volt negative charge. Using the laser, we can "write" an image onto the drum. Note that the laser writes a positive image to the drum.

Toner   The *toner* in a laser printer is a fine powder made up of plastic particles bonded to pigment particles. The toner cylinder charges the toner with a negative charge of between ~200 and ~500 volts. Because that charge falls between the original uniform negative charge of the imaging drum (~600 to ~1000 volts) and the charge of the particles on the drum's surface hit by the laser (~100 volts), particles of toner are attracted to the areas of the imaging drum that have been hit by the laser (that is, areas that have a relatively positive charge with reference to the toner particles).

 EXAM TIP   The black toner used in laser printers is typically carbon mixed into polyester resin, while color toner trades carbon for other pigments.

Transfer Corona/Transfer Roller   To transfer the image from the imaging drum to the paper, the paper must be given a charge that will attract the toner particles off of the drum and onto the paper. In older printers, the *transfer corona*, a thin wire, applied a positive charge to the paper, drawing the negatively charged toner particles to the paper. Newer printers accomplish the same feat using a *transfer roller* that draws the toner onto the paper. The paper, with its positive charge, is also attracted to the negatively charged drum. To prevent the paper from wrapping around the drum, a *static charge eliminator* removes the charge from the paper.

In most laser printers, the transfer corona/roller is outside the toner cartridge, especially in large, commercial-grade machines. The transfer corona/roller is prone to a build-up of dirt, toner, and debris through electrostatic attraction, and it must be cleaned. It is also quite fragile—usually finer than a human hair. Most printers with an exposed transfer corona/roller provide a special tool to clean it, but you can also—very delicately—use a cotton swab soaked in denatured alcohol (don't use rubbing alcohol because it contains emollients). As always, never service any printer without first turning it off and unplugging it from its power source.

Fuser Assembly   The *fuser assembly* is almost always separate from the toner cartridge. It is usually quite easy to locate, as it is close to the bottom of the toner cartridge and usually has two rollers to fuse the toner. Sometimes the fuser is somewhat enclosed and difficult to recognize because the rollers are hidden from view. To help you determine the location of the fuser, think about the path of the paper and the fact that fusing is the final step of printing.

The toner is merely resting on top of the paper after the static charge eliminator has removed the paper's static charge. The toner must be melted to the paper to make the image permanent. Two rollers, a pressure roller and a heated roller, are used to fuse the toner to the paper. The pressure roller presses against the bottom of the page, and the heated roller presses down on the top of the page, melting the toner into the paper. The heated roller has a nonstick coating such as Teflon to prevent the toner from sticking to it.

Power Supplies   All of the devices described in this chapter have power supplies, but when dealing with laser printers, techs should take extra caution. The corona in a laser printer requires extremely high voltage from the power supply, making a laser printer power supply one of the most dangerous devices in computing! Turn off and unplug the printer as a safety precaution before performing any maintenance.

Turning Gears   A laser printer has many mechanical functions. First, the paper must be grabbed by the *pickup roller* and passed over the *separation pad*, which is a small piece of cork or rubber that separates the sheets as they are pulled from the paper feed tray. A separation pad uses friction to separate a single sheet from any others that were picked up. Next, the photosensitive roller must be turned and the laser, or a mirror, must be moved back and forth. The toner must be evenly distributed, and the fuser assembly must squish the toner into the paper. Finally, the paper must be kicked out of the printer and the assembly must be cleaned to prepare for the next page.

 EXAM TIP   Be sure you are familiar with laser printer components, particularly the imaging drum, fuser assembly, transfer belt, transfer roller, pickup rollers, separation pads, and duplexing assembly.

More sophisticated laser printers enable duplex printing, meaning they can print on both sides of the paper. This is another mechanical function with a dedicated *duplexing assembly* for reversing the paper.

All of these functions are served by complex gear systems. In most laser printers, these gear systems are packed together in discrete units generically called *gear packs* or *gearboxes*. Most laser printers have two or three gearboxes that you can remove relatively easily in the rare case one of them fails. Most gearboxes also have their own motor or solenoid to move the gears.

All of these mechanical features can wear out or break and require service or replacement. See the "Troubleshooting Printers" section, later in this chapter, for more details.

System Board   Every laser printer contains at least one electronic board. On this board is the main processor, the printer's ROM, and the RAM used to store the image before it is printed. Many printers divide these functions among two or three boards dispersed around the printer (also known as sub-logic boards, as shown back in Figure 26-10). An older printer may also have an extra ROM chip and/or a special slot where you can install an extra ROM chip, usually for special functions such as PostScript.

On some printer models, you can upgrade the contents of these ROM chips (the *firmware*) by performing a process called *flashing* the ROM. Flashing is a lot like upgrading the system BIOS, which you learned about in Chapter 5. Upgrading the firmware can help fix bugs, add new features, or update the fonts in the printer.

Of particular importance is the printer's RAM. When the printer doesn't have enough RAM to store the image before it prints, you get a memory overflow problem. Also, some printers store other information in the RAM, including fonts or special commands. Adding RAM is usually a simple job—just snapping in a SIMM or DIMM stick or two—but getting the *right* RAM is important. Call or check the printer manufacturer's Web site to see what type of RAM you need. Although most printer companies will happily sell you their expensive RAM, most printers can use generic DRAM like the kind you use in a computer.

Ozone Filter   The coronas inside laser printers generate ozone (O_3). Although not harmful to humans in small amounts, even tiny concentrations of ozone will cause damage to printer components. To counter this problem, most laser printers have a special ozone filter that needs to be vacuumed or replaced periodically.

Sensors and Switches   Every laser printer has a large number of sensors and switches spread throughout the machine. The sensors are used to detect a broad range of conditions such as paper jams, empty paper trays, or low toner levels. Many of these sensors are really tiny switches that detect open doors and so on. Most of the time these sensors/switches work reliably, yet occasionally they become dirty or broken, sending a false signal to the printer. Simple inspection is usually sufficient to determine if a problem is real or just the result of a faulty sensor/switch.

3-D Printers

3-D printers (see Figure 26-11) use melted material to create prints of three-dimensional objects. The flat surface from which the 3-D printer deposits this melted material to build an object is called the *print bed*. The most common 3-D printers use *plastic filament* or *resin* on spools (see Figure 26-12). Some 3-D printers enable you to print with multiple colors.

A typical 3-D printer is made of many distinct parts. Take a look at Figure 26-13 for a breakdown of some of the more important components.

3-D printers take a 3-D illustration and build it in tiny layers or slices, one by one. 3-D filament printers work by melting the plastic and allowing it to cool as the 3-D image builds. 3-D resin printers work by placing liquid resin down and curing it with UV light. Simple printers can create relatively simple shapes, such as blocks, pyramids, and so on.

Figure 26-11
3-D printer

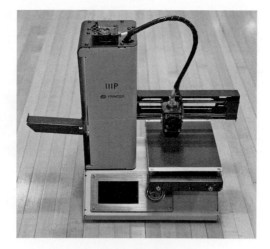

Figure 26-12
3-D printer
plastic filament

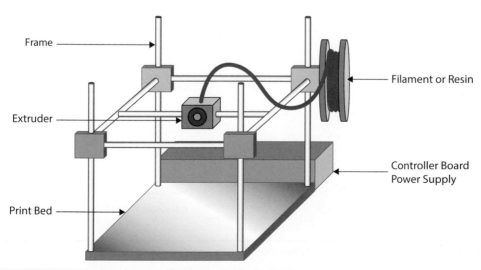

Frame

Extruder

Print Bed

Filament or Resin

Controller Board
Power Supply

Figure 26-13   3-D printer

Better printers can create more exciting shapes, such as the stylized replacement game pieces for the popular board game Settlers of Catan pictured in Figure 26-14. Even better 3-D printers can make elaborate structures, with lots of holes and gaps within the layers.

Figure 26-14
3-D-printed
game pieces
(photo courtesy
of Donny Jansen)

Installation of 3-D printers requires more than the typical printer installation. The connections (USB) and drivers are typical, but 3-D printers also need manual connection of the plastic filament(s) to the print device. You'll also need specialized software designed to print in 3-D. Most manufacturers' 3-D printing software enables you to use standard 3-D drawings, such as STL, OBJ, and CAD files. Figure 26-15 shows the Ultimaker Cura software pushing a print job to a 3-D printer. Sweet!

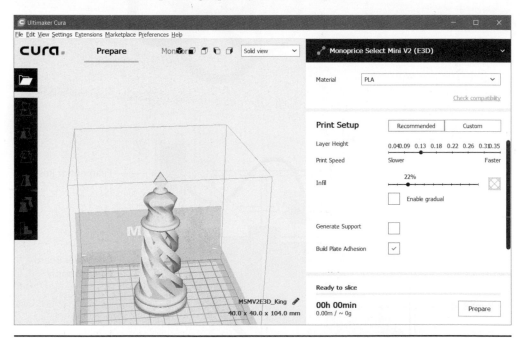

Figure 26-15   Managing a new 3-D print job

Virtual Printers

The most quizzical printer of all, the *virtual printer*, doesn't look like much, but it's actually still pretty similar to physical or "real" printing. When you print to a virtual printer, your system goes through all the steps to prepare a document for printing and sends it off to a virtual printer—a program that converts the output from your computer into a specific format and saves the result to a portable file that looks like the printed page would have. You can print this file later if you like, or maybe send it to someone else to print, but you can also just keep it in digital format. Virtual printers provide a nice way to save anything you can print, and they're particularly good for saving reference copies of information found on the Web.

Print to PDF   One of the most popular virtual printing options is the ability to *print to PDF*, a feature every operating system supports out of the box these days. Windows didn't join the party until Windows 10, however, so be aware that you'll need to install a virtual PDF printer on older versions of Windows. You can get these through official Adobe software, but there are also some third-party options.

Cloud and Remote Printing   Blurring the line between traditional and virtual printing, a variety of cloud services, such as Google Cloud Print, will install a virtual printer on your system that wraps up your document and sends it out over the Internet or other network to a cloud server, which eventually ends up routing it to a real printer for printing—all without needing to have a driver installed for it.

Printer Languages

Now that you've learned about the different types of print devices and techniques, it's time to take a look at how they communicate with the computer. How do you tell a printer to make a letter *A* or to print a picture of your pet iguana? Printers are designed to accept predefined printer languages that handle both characters and graphics. Your software must use the proper language when communicating with your printer, in order to output paper documents. Following are the more common printer languages.

EXAM TIP   One thing to remember for the exam is the importance of choosing the appropriate driver for the OS. A common printing mistake, for example, is that you may be printing to a PostScript printer with a PCL driver.

NOTE   You might think of the American Standard Code for Information Interchange (ASCII) language as nothing more than a standard set of characters. ASCII actually contains a variety of control codes for transferring data, some of which can be used to control printers. For example, ASCII code 10 (or 0A in hex) means "Line Feed," and ASCII code 12 (0C) means "Form Feed." These commands have been standard since before the creation of IBM computers, and all printers respond to them. If they did not, the PRT SCR (print screen) key would not work with every printer. Being highly standardized has advantages, but the control codes are extremely limited. Printing high-end graphics and a wide variety of fonts requires more advanced languages.

PostScript   Adobe Systems developed the *PostScript* page description language in the early 1980s as a device-independent printer language capable of high-resolution graphics and scalable fonts. PostScript interpreters are embedded in the printing device. Because PostScript is understood by printers at a hardware level, the majority of the image processing is done by the printer and not the computer's CPU, so PostScript printers print faster. PostScript defines the page as a single raster image; this makes PostScript files extremely portable—they can be created on one machine or platform and reliably printed out on another machine or platform (including, for example, high-end typesetters).

HP Printer Command Language   HP developed its *Printer Command Language (PCL)* as a more advanced printer language to supersede simple ASCII codes. PCL features a set of printer commands greatly expanded from ASCII. HP designed PCL with text-based output in mind; it does not support advanced graphical functions. The most recent version of PCL, PCL6, features scalable fonts and additional line-drawing commands. Unlike PostScript, however, PCL is not a true page description language; it uses a series of commands to define the characters on the page. Those commands must be supported by each individual printer model, making PCL files less portable than PostScript files.

 EXAM TIP   The CompTIA A+ Acronym list identifies PCL as *Printer Control Language*. *Control* or *Command* is rather irrelevant at this point in time. HP refers to PCL as simply PCL in all its documentation.

Windows GDI and XPS   Windows uses the *graphical device interface (GDI)* component of the operating system to handle print functions. Although you can use an external printer language such as PostScript, most users simply install printer drivers and let Windows do all the work. The GDI uses the CPU rather than the printer to process a print job and then sends the completed job to the printer. When you print a letter with a TrueType font in Windows, for example, the GDI processes the print job and then sends bitmapped images of each page to the printer. The printer sees a page of TrueType text, therefore, as a picture, not as text. As long as the printer has a capable enough raster image processor (explained later in this chapter) and plenty of RAM, you don't need to worry about the printer language in most situations. We'll revisit printing in Windows in more detail later in this chapter.

Windows Vista also introduced a new printing subsystem called the XML Paper Specification (XPS) print path in 2006. In 2009, the ECMA-388 standard formally named XPS the Open XML Paper Specification (OpenXPS), although Microsoft and others continue to use only *XPS* in documentation and screen elements. XPS provides several improvements over GDI, including enhanced color management (which works with Windows Color System, introduced in the "Optimizing Print Performance" section later in the chapter) and better print layout fidelity. The XPS print path requires a driver that supports XPS. Additionally, some printers natively support XPS, eliminating the requirement that the output be converted to a device-specific printer control language before printing.

EXAM TIP Laser and inkjet printers can also use *duplexing assemblies*, which enable the printer to automatically print on both sides of the paper. Some printers include this built-in feature, while others require a piece of additional hardware that flips the paper for the printer.

Scanners

You can use a scanner to make digital copies of existing paper photos, documents, drawings, and more. Better scanners give you the option of copying directly from a photographic negative or slide, providing images of stunning visual quality—assuming the original photo was halfway decent, of course! In this section, you'll look at how scanners work and then turn to what you need to know to select the correct scanner for you or your clients.

How Scanners Work

All *flatbed scanners*, the most common variety of scanner, work the same way. You place a photo or other object face down on the glass (called the platen), close the lid, and then use software to initiate the scan. The scanner runs a bright light along the length of the platen once or more to capture the image. Figure 26-16 shows an open scanner.

Figure 26-16
Scanner open
with photograph
face down

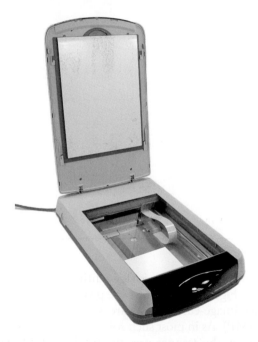

 NOTE Many serious flatbed scanners and multifunction devices will have an automatic document feeder (ADF) to remove most of the manual labor from this process. Check out the upcoming "Automatic Document Feeder" section for more details.

The scanning software that controls the hardware can manifest in a variety of ways. Nearly every manufacturer has some combination of drivers and other software to create an interface between your computer and the scanner. When you push the front button on the Epson Perfection scanner, for example, the Epson software loads, ready to start scanning (see Figure 26-17).

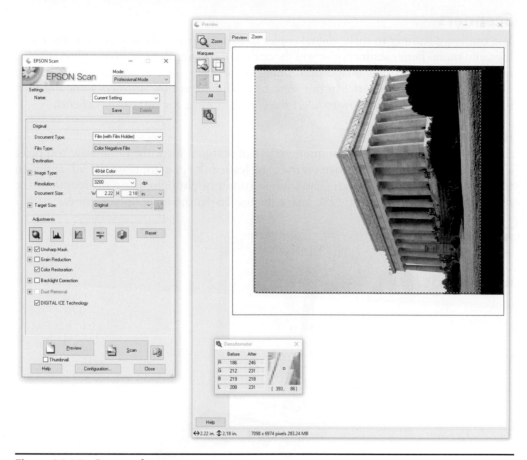

Figure 26-17   Epson software

You can also open your favorite image-editing software first and choose to acquire a file from a scanner. Figure 26-18 shows the process of acquiring an image from a scanner in the popular free image-editing software, GNU Image Manipulation Program (otherwise known as GIMP). As in most such software, you choose File | Create and then select Scanner. In this case, the scanner uses the traditional TWAIN drivers. *TWAIN* stands for *Technology Without an Interesting Name*—I'm not making this up!—and has been the default driver type for scanners for a long time.

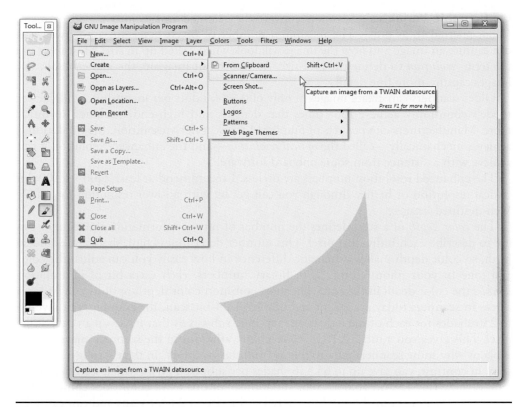

Figure 26-18 Acquiring an image in GNU Image Manipulation Program (GIMP)

At this point, the drivers and other software controlling the scanner pop up, providing an interface with the scanner (as shown in Figure 26-17). Here you can set the resolution of the image as well as many other options.

NOTE In addition to loading pictures into your computer, many scanners offer a feature called *optical character recognition (OCR)*, a way to scan a document and have the computer turn the picture into text that you can manipulate by using a word processing program.

How to Choose a Scanner

You must consider four primary variables when choosing a scanner: resolution, color depth, grayscale depth, and scan speed. You can and will adjust the first three during the scanning process, although probably only down from their maximum. The scan speed relates to all four of the other variables, and the maximum speed is hard-coded into the scanner.

Configurable Variables   Scanners convert the scanned image into a grid of pixels (often referred to as dots). The maximum number of pixels determines how well you can capture an image and how the image will look when scaled up in size. Most folks use the term *resolution* to define the grid size. As you might imagine, the higher-resolution images capture more fine detail.

Older scanners can create images of only 600 × 600 dots per inch (dpi), while newer models commonly achieve four times that density, and high-end machines do much more. Manufacturers cite *two* sets of numbers for a scanner's resolution: the resolution it achieves mechanically—called the *optical resolution*—and the enhanced resolution it can achieve with assistance from some onboard software.

The enhanced resolution numbers are useless. I recommend at least 2400 × 2400 dpi optical resolution or better, although you can get by with a lower resolution for purely Web-destined images.

The *color depth* of a scan defines the number of bits of information the scanner can use to describe each individual pixel. This number determines color, shade, hue, and so forth, so color depth makes a dramatic difference in how easily you can adjust the color and tone in your photo editor. With binary numbers, each extra bit of information *doubles* the color detail in the scan. The most common color depth options you will run across in scanners today are 24-bit and 48-bit. A 24-bit scan, for example, can save up to 256 shades for each of the red, green, and blue sub-pixels that make up an individual pixel. This gives you a total of 16,777,216 color variations in the scanned image, which explains why some scanners refer to this as "millions of colors" in their settings. A 48-bit scan, in contrast, can save up to 65,536 shades per subpixel, giving you a scan that holds a massive 281,474,976,710,656 color variations. All this extra color does come with a downside: images scanned at 48 bits are twice the size of 24-bit scans and can easily be hundreds of megabytes per file!

These days, 48-bit scanners are common enough that you shouldn't have to settle for less, even on a budget. Figures 26-19, 26-20, and 26-21 show pretty clearly the difference resolution makes when scanning.

Figure 26-19   Earring scanned at 72 dpi and 24-bit color

Figure 26-20   Same earring, scanned at 300 dpi and 24-bit color

Figure 26-21   Same earring, scanned at 1200 dpi and 24-bit color

Scanners differ a lot in *grayscale depth*, a number that defines how many shades of gray the scanner can save per pixel. This matters if you work with black-and-white images in any significant way, because grayscale depth may be advertised with a much lower number than color depth. Current consumer-level scanners come in 8-bit, 12-bit, and 16-bit grayscale varieties. You might recognize these three numbers from the previous color depth discussion, because grayscale images only need a third the information it takes to represent the red, green, and blue values that make up a color image. I recommend 16-bit.

Scanning Speed   Scanners have a maximum scanning speed defined by the manufacturer. The time required to complete a scan is also affected by the parameters you set; the time increases as you increase the amount of detail captured. A typical low-end scanner, for example, takes upward of 30 seconds to scan a 4 × 6 photo at 300 dpi. A faster scanner, in contrast, can crank out the same scan in 10 seconds.

Raise the resolution of the scan to 600 dpi at 48-bit resolution, and that faster scanner can take a full minute to complete the scan. Adjust your scanning settings to optimize for your project. Don't always go for the highest quality scan if you don't need the resolution and color depth.

Network Scan Services

If you've ever had to fill out a paper document and upload it, you've used a scanner, but you may not be aware of how many ways networking can make scanning easier. You can use cloud services like we talked about for printers earlier in the chapter, but that's not all. Remember the SMB protocol from Chapter 19? It's not just for print sharing.

You can also use *SMB* for scan sharing, enabling the scanning of a lot of data directly to a networked folder that other people on the network can access. It can save a few steps by removing the need to scan locally and then manually move the scanned files to the file share; but be careful, using SMB can introduce security vulnerabilities (you'll learn all about security and vulnerabilities in the next chapter). Many multifunction devices are older, and as a result, may only support older versions of the protocol. If the device only supports SMB 1.0, then you'll probably want to find an alternative way to get your scanned documents onto a network share.

Scanning can even make use of the humble email. Many multifunction devices include a scan to *e-mail* feature, which lets you scan a document and have it automatically e-mailed from you to someone else. This is useful when you want to send a scanned document to an individual or small group rather than to a dedicated network share.

Scanning Tips

As a general rule, you should obtain the highest quality scan you can manage, and then play with the size and image quality when it's time to print it or share it over the Web. The amount of RAM in your system—and to a lesser extent, the processor speed—dictates how big a file you can handle.

 NOTE   If you're set to do some heavy scanning—like archiving all those old family photos—check out Wayne Fulton's Web site, https://www.scantips .com. The site has a simple, direct interface, and a treasure trove of excellent information on scanners and scanning. I've used his knowledge for years now and recommend it highly.

If you travel a lot, you'll want to make sure to use the locking mechanism for the scanner light assembly. Just be sure to unlock before you try to use it or you'll get a light that's stuck in one position. That won't make for very good scans!

Copy and Fax Components

The scanning and printing capabilities of a multifunction device enable manufacturers to add copy-machine features easily. To copy a document or photo, you essentially scan a document or photo and then print it, but all with a single press of the Copy button.

Faxing generally requires separate functions in the machine, such as a document feed and a connection to a traditional, analog phone line. Assuming you have those and an account with the local telecom company, the process of faxing is pretty simple. You put a document in the feeder, plug in the fax number, and press the Send button (or whatever the manufacturer labels it).

Automatic Document Feeders

An MFD uses an *automatic document feeder (ADF)* to grab pages to copy, scan, or fax. An ADF is typically on top of the MFD and you place a stack of pages in the tray (see Figure 26-22). Different machines require documents face up or face down; they'll typically have some marking to show which way to feed the pages (see Figure 26-23).

Figure 26-22
Typical automatic document feed loaded with pages to copy

Figure 26-23
Wonderfully descriptive markings on MFD telling user to load pages face up in ADF

Connectivity

Most printers, scanners, and multifunction devices connect to a computer via a USB port, but Wi-Fi or Ethernet network connections are also very popular. You'll need to know how to support network connections as well as the plug-and-play USB ones.

USB Connections

New printers and multifunction devices use USB connections that you can plug into any USB port on your computer. USB printers may not come with a USB cable, so you need to purchase one when you purchase a printer. (It's quite a disappointment to come home with your new printer only to find you can't connect it because it didn't come with a USB cable.) Most printers use the standard USB type A connector on one end and the smaller USB type B connector on the other end, although some use two type A connectors. Whichever configuration your USB printer has, just plug in the USB cable—it's that easy!

Network Connections

Connecting a printer or multifunction device to a network isn't just for offices anymore. More and more homes and home offices are enjoying the benefits of network printing. It used to be that you would physically connect the printer to a single computer and then share the printer on the network. The downside to this was that the computer connected to the printer had to be left on for others to use the printer.

Today, the typical *network printer* comes with its own built-in 802.11 (a, b, g, n, ac, ax) Wi-Fi adapter to enable wireless printing over infrastructure, though you should avoid ad hoc connections for security reasons when possible (see Chapter 20 for more on setting up an ad hoc wireless network).

Other printers include an onboard network adapter that uses a standard RJ-45 *Ethernet* cable to connect the printer directly to the network by way of a router. The printer can typically be assigned a static IP address, or it can acquire one dynamically from a DHCP server. (Don't know what a router, IP address, or DHCP server is? Take a look back at Chapter 18 and Chapter 19.) Once connected to the network, the printer acts independently of any single computer. Alternatively, some printers offer a Bluetooth interface for networking.

 NOTE   Since printers tend to have longer lives than most other computing devices, be aware that printers with a built-in wireless print connection may be using older Wi-Fi or Bluetooth standards than you're used to encountering.

Even if a printer does not come with built-in Ethernet, Wi-Fi, or Bluetooth, you can purchase a standalone network device known as a *print server* to connect your printer to the network—but beware that you may not be able to use all features of an MFD connected to a print server. These print servers, which can be Ethernet or Wi-Fi, enable one or several printers to attach via USB cable (or even parallel port, if you still have a printer that old). You may not need to go to the store to find a print server, though—check your router, first, to see if it has an *integrated print server*. If it does, you may be able to plug your printer into a USB port on the router. So take that ancient Image-Writer dot-matrix printer and network it—I dare you!

EXAM TIP As discussed in Chapter 18 in the context of the roles of networked hosts, print servers aren't necessarily physical devices. You'll find print servers outside network devices. In fact, your Windows system is capable of operating as a print server. Anytime you plug a printer into a computer and share the printer (printer share) over the network, the sharing system can be referred to as a print server.

Physical Installation

Ooh! Few things are more exciting than installing a new printer, scanner, or MDF in your office! While fun (and always a crowd pleaser), you should consider several factors before you pull out the box cutters!

Location

So where do you put this thing? Not only does your new device need to be in a location that is convenient for everyone who needs to use it, but that location should also provide good power and ventilation. Equally, the device ought to be in a place that's not in anyone's way, like a hallway or a person's office, so that no one is constantly interrupted by people grabbing print jobs.

Unboxing

Unboxing a printer or MFD, especially a large office printer or MDF, is a tricky business and one that should be considered with great care. In particular, read the instructions included with the device before you start unboxing it. The instructions should provide very specific steps in which to unbox the various components of the device.

NOTE All printers and scanners come with internal packaging that must be removed before use. Again, read the documentation to make sure you don't overlook removing from the device a piece of Styrofoam or cardboard.

The Laser Printing Process

The *imaging process* with a laser printer breaks down into seven steps, and the CompTIA A+ 1101 exam expects you to know them all. As a tech, you should be familiar with these phases, as this can help you troubleshoot printing problems. If an odd line is printed down the middle of every page, for example, you know there's a problem with the imaging drum or cleaning mechanism and the toner cartridge needs to be replaced.

The seven steps to the laser printing process may be performed in a different order, depending on the printer, but it usually goes like this:

1. Processing

2. Charging

3. Exposing

4. Developing

5. Transferring

6. Fusing

7. Cleaning

Processing

When you click the Print button in an application, several things happen. First, the CPU processes your request and sends a print job to an area of memory called the print spooler. The *print spooler* enables you to queue up multiple print jobs that the printer will handle sequentially. Next, Windows sends the first print job to the printer. That's your first potential bottleneck—if it's a big job, the OS has to dole out a piece at a time and you'll see the little printer icon in the notification area at the bottom right of your screen. Once the printer icon goes away, you know the print queue is empty—all jobs have gone to the printer.

Once the printer receives some or all of a print job, the hardware of the printer takes over and processes the image. That's your second potential bottleneck, and it has multiple components.

Raster Images

Impact printers transfer data to the printer one character or one line at a time, whereas laser printers transfer entire pages at a time to the printer. A laser printer generates a *raster image* (a pattern of dots) of the page, representing what the final product should look like. It uses a device (the laser imaging unit) to "paint" a raster image on the imaging drum. Because a laser printer has to paint the entire surface of the imaging drum before it can begin to transfer the image to paper, it processes the image one page at a time.

A laser printer uses a chip called the *raster image processor (RIP)* to translate the raster image into commands to the laser. The RIP takes the digital information about fonts and graphics and converts it to a rasterized image made up of dots that can then be printed. An inkjet printer also has a RIP, but it's part of the software driver instead of onboard hardware circuitry. The RIP needs memory (RAM) to store the data that it must process.

A laser printer must have enough memory to process an entire page. Some pages printed at high resolution and containing very complex designs (lots of fonts, complex formatting, high-resolution graphics, and so on) require more memory. Insufficient memory will usually be indicated by a memory overflow ("MEM OVERFLOW") error. If you get a memory overflow or *low memory error*, try reducing the resolution, printing smaller graphics, reducing the complexity, or turning off RET (see the following section for the last option). Of course, the best solution to a memory overflow error is simply to add more RAM to the laser printer.

Do not assume that every error with the word *memory* in it can be fixed simply by adding more RAM to the printer. Just as adding more RAM chips will not solve every conventional computer memory problem, adding more RAM will not solve every laser printer memory problem. The message "21 ERROR" on an HP LaserJet, for example, indicates that "the printer is unable to process very complex data fast enough for the print engine." This means that the data is simply too complex for the RIP to handle. Adding more memory would *not* solve this problem; it would only make your wallet lighter. The only answer in this case is to reduce the complexity of the page image.

Resolution

Laser printers can print at different resolutions, just as monitors can display different resolutions. The maximum resolution a laser printer can handle is determined by its physical characteristics. Laser printer resolution is expressed in dots per inch (dpi), such as 2400 × 600 dpi or 1200 × 1200 dpi. The first number, the horizontal resolution, is determined by how fine a focus can be achieved by the laser. The second number is determined by the smallest increment by which the drum can be turned.

Higher resolutions produce higher-quality output, but keep in mind that higher resolutions also require more memory. In some instances, complex images can be printed only at lower resolutions because of their high memory demands. Even printing at 300 × 300 dpi, laser printers produce far better quality than dot-matrix printers because of *resolution enhancement technology (RET)*.

RET enables the printer to insert smaller dots among the characters, smoothing out the jagged curves that are typical of printers that do not use RET (see Figure 26-24). Using RET enables laser printers to output high-quality print jobs, but it also requires a portion of the printer's RAM. If you get a MEM OVERFLOW error, disabling RET will sometimes free up enough memory to complete the print job.

Figure 26-24
RET fills in gaps with smaller dots to smooth out jagged characters.

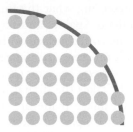 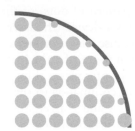

Charging

Now we turn to the physical side of the printing process. To make the drum receptive to new images, it must be charged (see Figure 26-25). Using the primary corona wire or primary charge roller, a uniform negative charge is applied to the entire surface of the drum (usually between ~600 and ~1000 volts).

Figure 26-25
Charging the
drum with a
uniform negative
charge

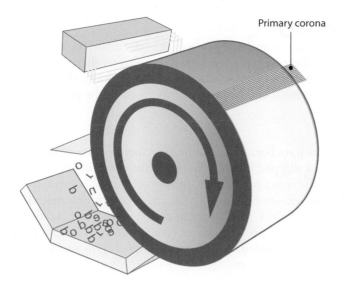

Exposing

A laser is used to create a positive image on the surface of the drum. Every particle on the drum hit by the laser releases most of its negative charge into the drum.

Developing

Those particles with a lesser negative charge are positively charged relative to the toner particles and attract them, creating a developed image (see Figure 26-26).

Figure 26-26
Writing the
image and
applying the
toner

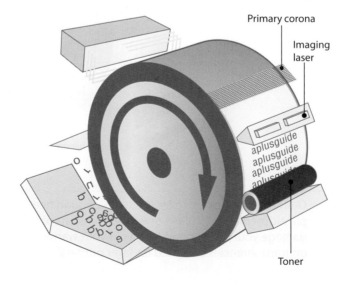

Transferring

The printer must transfer the image from the drum onto the paper. The transfer corona or transfer roller gives the paper a positive charge; then the negatively charged toner particles leap from the drum to the paper. At this point, the particles are merely resting on the paper and must still be permanently fused to the paper.

Fusing

The particles have been attracted to the paper because of the paper's positive charge, but if the process stopped here, the toner particles would fall off the page as soon as you lift it. Because the toner particles are mostly composed of plastic, they can be melted to the page. Two rollers—a heated roller coated in a nonstick material and a pressure roller—melt the toner to the paper, permanently affixing it. Finally, a static charge eliminator removes the paper's positive charge (see Figure 26-27). Once the page is complete, the printer ejects the printed copy and the process begins again with the physical and electrical cleaning of the printer.

Figure 26-27
Transferring the image to the paper and fusing the final image

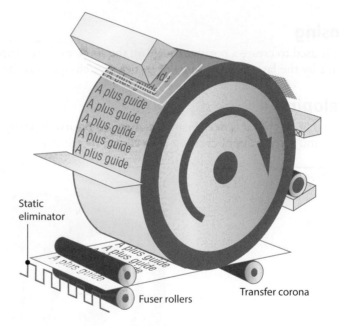

Static eliminator

Fuser rollers

Transfer corona

 CAUTION The heated roller produces enough heat to melt some types of plastic media, particularly overhead transparency materials. This could damage your laser printer (and void your warranty), so make sure you print on transparencies designed for laser printers!

Cleaning

The printing process ends with the physical and electrical cleaning of the imaging drum (see Figure 26-28). Before printing another new page, the drum must be returned to a clean, fresh condition. All residual toner left over from printing the previous page must be removed, usually by scraping the surface of the drum with a rubber cleaning blade. If residual particles remain on the drum, they will appear as random black spots and streaks on the next page. The physical cleaning mechanism either deposits the residual toner in a debris cavity or recycles it by returning it to the toner supply in the toner cartridge. The physical cleaning must be done carefully—a damaged drum will cause a mark to be printed on every page until it is replaced.

Figure 26-28
Cleaning and
erasing the drum

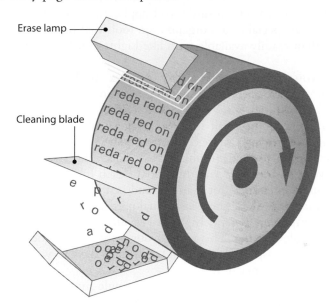

The printer must also be electrically cleaned. One or more erase lamps bombard the surface of the drum with the appropriate wavelengths of light, causing the surface particles to discharge into the grounded drum. After the cleaning process, the drum should be completely free of toner and have a neutral charge.

 NOTE Color laser printers use four different colors of toner (cyan, magenta, yellow, and black) to create their printouts. Most models send each page through four different passes, adding one color at each pass to create the needed results, while others place all the colors onto a special *transfer belt* and then transfer them to the page in one pass. In some cases, the printer uses four separate toner cartridges and four lasers for the four toner colors, and in others the printer simply lays down one color after the other on the same drum, cleaning after each of four passes per page.

Installing a Multifunction Device

Installing a multifunction device differs a lot from installing single-function devices. In the consumer space, the process is messy because of the complexity of the devices. Here's the scoop.

First, most multifunction devices today connect via USB and wirelessly, so you need to consider connectivity. Second, you need to install drivers for each of the various functions of the MFD. Initially, that seems fine, because you can use the driver disc/download that came with the MFD and can install everything for the OS you choose.

That default process can rapidly turn into a mess, though, because of several factors. The drivers are often outdated. Updating specific drivers takes time and clicking. Worse, manufacturers often add absurdly bad applications to "support" specific functions of MFDs, such as special photo organization tools that bog down the system and function far worse than readily available tools like Lightroom from Adobe (not free, but reasonably priced).

Third, you're dealing with a very complex machine that can break in interesting ways. Maintenance and troubleshooting take on new dimensions by the sheer number of options to consider, from ink levels to scanner mechanics to dogged-out phone lines. Although none of these fall into the category of installation, you can minimize the problems by practicing a more compartmentalized installation.

Rather than focus on the multifunction aspect of MFDs, you will often fare better for you and your customers if you think about each function as a separate action. Pull the machine apart in essence, for example, and install a printer, a scanner, a copy machine, and a fax machine. Share these individual parts as needed on a network. Update drivers for each component separately. Conceptualize each function as a separate device to simplify troubleshooting. This way, if your print output goes south, for example, think about the printer aspects of the MFD. You don't have to worry about the scanner, copy, or fax aspects of the machine.

The next sections cover installation of single-function devices, though the bulk of information is on printers. That's both what the CompTIA A+ exams cover and what you'll have to deal with as a tech for the most part.

 EXAM TIP   The CompTIA A+ exams test you on installing and troubleshooting printers, so read these sections carefully!

Setting Up Printers in Windows

You need to take a moment to understand how Windows handles printing, and then you'll see how to install, configure, and troubleshoot printers.

To Windows, a printer is not a physical device; it is a *program* that controls one or more physical printers. The *physical* printer is called a print device by Windows (although I continue to use the term "printer" for most purposes, just like almost every tech on the planet). Printer drivers and a spooler are still present, but in Windows, they are integrated into the printer itself (see Figure 26-29). This arrangement gives Windows amazing flexibility. For example, one printer can support multiple print devices, enabling a system to act as a print server. If one print device goes down, the printer automatically redirects the output to a working print device.

Figure 26-29
Printer driver
and spooler in
Windows

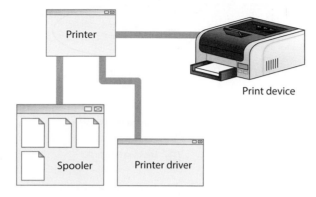

Print device

Spooler

Printer driver

Printer

The general installation, configuration, and troubleshooting issues are basically identical in all modern versions of Windows. Here's a review of a typical Windows printer installation. Setting up a printer is quite easy. Most printers are plug and play, so installing a printer is reduced to simply plugging it in and loading the driver if needed. With USB printers, Windows won't even wait for you to do anything; Windows immediately detects and installs a printer once you connect it.

If Windows does not immediately detect the printer, you can use the classic Devices and Printers applet in the Control Panel (introduced in the "Sharing Printers" section of Chapter 19), but most users will opt for the simpler Settings | Devices | Printers & scanners interface for setting up a printer (see Figure 26-30). Click the *Add a printer or scanner* option to find a connectable printer.

Standard Users and Printers

A standard user—that is, not an administrator—can install a printer just fine in Windows. The user can also use one of the built-in printer drivers and print fine.

Windows will balk with an "Unable to install printer. Operation could not be completed" error message and accompanying code when the user tries to install software and drivers from an optical disc or downloaded from the Internet. For those options, you need administrative rights.

If you're stuck in that position, such as rolling out corporate laptops to company employees who will want to install printers at home, you can work around the problem. Microsoft suggests changing the Group Policy Driver Installation policy to allow non-administrators to install drivers for printers.

You should be able to find detailed instructions on this if need be at https://docs .microsoft.com. We'll discuss Group Policy editing in Chapter 27.

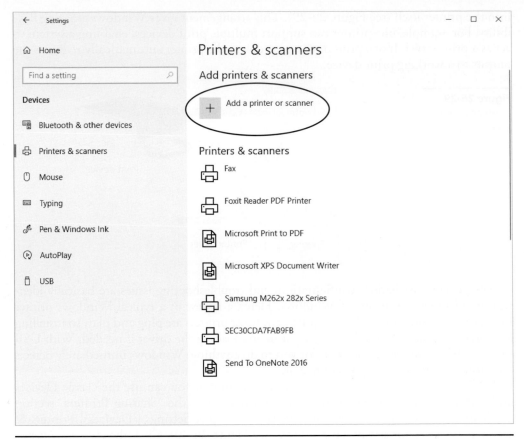

Figure 26-30   Printers & scanners in Settings

The Add Printer Wizard and the Settings app both let you install a local printer or a network printer. This distinction is actually a little misleading. Windows divides printer installation into two scenarios: a printer connected directly to a computer (your local system or another one on a network), or a standalone printer directly connected to a switch or router. While you might expect the local and network installation options to divide these scenarios nicely, they don't. Let's take a quick look at both local and network installations so you know when to use each.

Installing a Local Printer

At first glance, you might think the local printer installation option is used to install your standard USB printer, but don't forget that Windows will automatically detect and install USB printers (or any other plug-and-play printer). So what do you use it for? This option is most commonly used to install standalone network printers using an IP address. Using current versions of Windows and a modern printer, you shouldn't need the IP address to install a standalone network printer, but it can be a helpful alternative if Windows refuses to detect it any other way.

If you need to install a standalone network printer, use its hostname or IP address. In Windows, click *Add a printer or scanner* (shown in Figure 26-30). If Windows doesn't automatically detect your new printer, click *The printer that I want isn't listed* and select *Add a printer using TCP/IP address or hostname*. In Windows 10 and 11, both the Settings app and the Control Panel app give you the same choices.

Whether you use a USB port or a TCP/IP port, you'll need to select the proper driver manually (see Figure 26-31). Windows includes a lot of printer drivers, but you can also use the handy Have Disk option to use the disc that came with the printer. If you use the driver included on the disc, Windows will require administrator privileges to proceed; otherwise, you won't be able to finish the installation. The Windows Update button enables you to grab the latest printer drivers via the Internet.

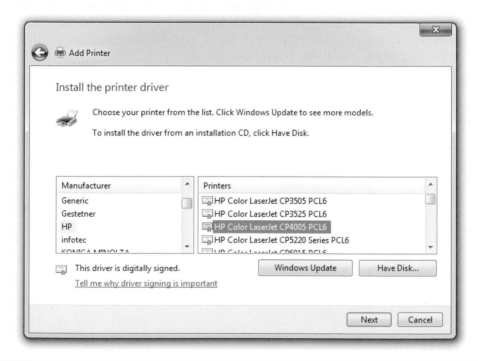

Figure 26-31   Selecting drivers

After clicking the Next button, you'll be asked if the new local printer should be the default printer and whether you want to share it with other computers on the network. And before you ask, yes, you can share a standalone network printer connected to your computer via a TCP/IP port using the *File and printer sharing* option located at Control Panel | Network and Sharing Center | Change advanced sharing settings, though the printer would be disabled for other users any time you turned off your computer. You'll be asked to print a test page to make sure everything works. Then you're done!

NOTE Windows-based printer sharing isn't the only game in town. Apple's *AirPrint* functionality can be used in conjunction with its *Bonjour Print Service* (installed separately, or along with iTunes) to share a printer connected to a Windows system with AirPrint-compatible macOS and Apple iOS devices.

Installing a Network Printer

Setting up network printers in a typical SOHO LAN doesn't require much more effort than setting up local printers. When you try to install a network printer, the Settings app or Add Printer Wizard will scan for any available printers on your local network. More often than not, the printer you are looking for will pop up in a list (see Figure 26-32). When you select that printer and click Add device or Next, Windows will search for drivers. If you need to, you can pick from a list of available drivers or use the disc that came with the printer. Either way, you're already done.

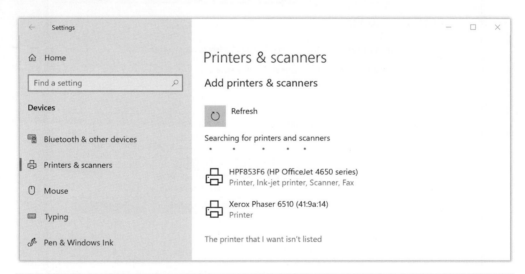

Figure 26-32 List of available shared printers on a network

If Windows fails to find your printer, you'll need to configure the network printer manually. Every version of Windows includes multiple methods of doing this. These methods change depending on whether you are connected to a domain or a workgroup.

 NOTE Remember printer sharing from Chapter 19? Here's the other side of the operation. Keep in mind that after you install a shared printer onto your computer, you can actually share it with others. Windows considers it *your* printer, so you can do what you want with it, including sharing it again.

If you are on a workgroup, you can browse for a printer on your network, connect to a specific printer (using its name or URL), or use a TCP/IP address or hostname, as you see

in Figure 26-33. In a domain, most of these options remain the same, except that instead of browsing the workgroup, you can search and browse the domain using several search parameters, including printer features, printer location, and more. Once you've found your printer, you might be prompted for drivers. Provide them using the usual methods described earlier and then you are finished!

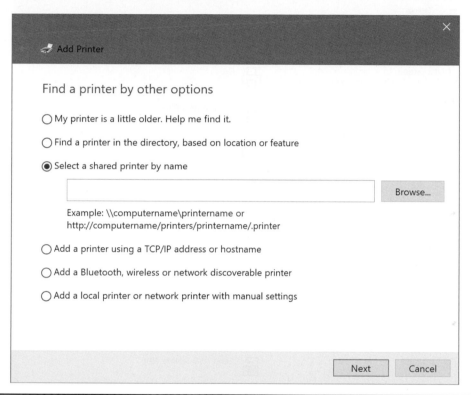

Figure 26-33   Options for finding network printers

Remember that Windows doesn't always see your network's printers exactly how they are physically arranged. Imagine you have a network with three computers. Andy's computer has a printer connected via USB, whereas Beth's computer and Carol's computer have no printers. There is, however, a second printer connected directly to their router via Ethernet. Beth has configured her system to connect directly to the network printer using an IP address. As a result, she can actually share that printer with the rest of her network, even though it's not attached to her computer—Windows doesn't care where it is. The process for sharing a local printer and a network printer is identical because Windows considers both printers to be installed on your computer and under your control. So now Andy and Beth both share printers. When Carol goes looking for shared printers to use, the network printer attached to the router will look like Beth's printer, as if it were directly connected to Beth's machine.

Figure 26-34 shows the Printers & scanners screen on a system with multiple printers installed. Note the text *Default* below the printer's name; this shows that the device is the default printer. If you have multiple printers, you can change the default printer by right-clicking the printer's icon and selecting Set as default printer.

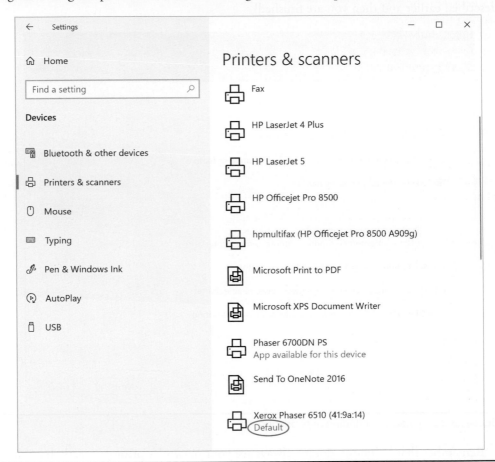

Figure 26-34   Installed default printer in Printers & scanners in Settings

In addition to the regular driver installation outlined previously, some installations use printer emulation. *Printer emulation* simply means using a substitute printer driver for a printer, as opposed to using one made exclusively for that printer. You'll run into printer emulation in two circumstances. First, some new printers do not come with their own drivers. They instead emulate a well-known printer (such as an HP LaserJet) and run perfectly well on that printer driver. Second, you may see emulation in the "I don't have the right driver!" scenario. I keep about three different HP LaserJet and Epson inkjet printers installed on my computer because I know that with these printer drivers, I can print to almost any printer. Some printers may require you to set them into an *emulation mode* to handle a driver other than their native one.

1102

As you might imagine, setting up printers and MFDs in an enterprise environment differs from the process in a SOHO environment. Here's a scenario. Bayland Widgets Corporation has 30 users who share access to two high-end color laser printers, two very fast black-and-white laser printers, one MFD (mainly used for scanning and copying purposes, but it also prints), and a trio of very nice inkjet printers. The printers and MFD are located in various places for convenience and managed by a single print server.

To make things a lot simpler than going to each client machine and installing these networked printers, Tony the Admin deploys the printers and MFD using Windows group policy to map the correct printers for all 30 workstations (plus several laptops as well). As users log in each morning, the group policy maps the MFD and the closest color laser printer to all of the workstations and laptops. It only maps the high-quality inkjet printers to the marketing department workstations, however, and the fast black-and-white laser printers to accounting. This all happens automatically with the correct drivers loaded as necessary.

NOTE Sharing a printer or MFD in a SOHO LAN is pretty easy. It's also easy to install a shared network printer. Once you scale up, though, management of many workstations and printers/MFDs becomes a pain unless you map via a group policy that applies to a lot of computers or users. You can also automate printer mapping via an Active Directory domain *logon script*, as discussed back in Chapter 19.

We'll hit group policy in Chapter 27. But deploying or mapping printers and multifunction devices in this way enables much faster rollout, updates, replacements, and so on.

NOTE In addition to the Devices and Printers applet, Windows also includes the Print Management console. This tool enables you to view and modify the printers and drivers on your system, connected to your network, or manage any Windows print servers connected to the network. Many of Print Management's advanced features go beyond the scope of the CompTIA A+ exams, but know that it centralizes (and in a few cases, enhances) the standard printer controls in Windows. You can find Print Management in Control Panel | Administrative Tools | Print Management. However, note that Windows 10 Home doesn't offer Print Management.

Configuring Print Settings

Once your printer is installed, a good first stop is the Printing preferences menu, accessible by right-clicking the desired printer in the Devices and Printers applet in the Control Panel. This is where you'll be able to control how your printer will print your documents. Be aware that these settings can vary depending on features available on your printer or multifunction device, but let's take a look at some of the ones you're most likely to find.

Layout

The settings you're most likely to change from time to time are probably the layout settings, which control how the printer determines what to print where.

- The *duplex* setting lets you specify whether and how to use each side of a printed page. Simple duplexing will just use the front and back of each sheet sequentially, but you may find more advanced options for laying out booklets.

- The *orientation* setting lets you specify whether to print in *landscape* or *portrait* mode.

- The *multiple page* setting will let you print multiple document pages on each physical page.

- The *scaling* setting, not to be confused with the multiple page setting, is usually for fitting a large document to a single page or scaling a small document up to the size of a full page.

- *Reverse* or *invert* options let you print the mirror image of your document, which is useful for printing on transfer paper and other special-use cases.

Paper

Many of the settings you'll find are for telling your printer what kind of paper it will be using, and (especially if the printer has multiple paper trays) where to find it.

- Set the *paper size* to one of several common paper sizes or define a custom one.

- Specify the *paper type*, which may involve setting thickness, coating, and special formats such as envelopes and labels.

- A *paper source* setting will let you select any available paper settings, and possibly *manual feed*, in which case the printer will wait for you to feed it each sheet individually. This is useful if you need to feed in one-off items or paper that won't fit in the tray.

- *Tray settings* allow you to select the printer tray to input the paper (if there are multiple trays). Many printers have the option to choose "automatically select" which also tells the printer to pull the paper from the main tray. When the main tray is out of paper, the printer will automatically choose another tray that has existing paper.

Quality

There are usually a number of different settings that have bearing on quality, but you should be aware that the name or description of some settings that affect quality may discuss ink or toner use (and may as such be located with other ink/toner-related settings).

- The most obvious of these, *resolution*, specifies what dpi the document should be printed at.

- Some printers may let you choose some mode or quality presets that optimize printing for graphics or text or choose to manually configure your own advanced settings.

- Some printers may have settings that reduce ink or toner used, for economic and environmental reasons.

Other Common Settings

Some print devices offer options useful in specific, but limited, occasions.

- The *apply a watermark* setting will let you choose from presets or define your own. A watermark is a lightly printed mark across every page. Use a watermark to designate a draft copy of a document, for example, rather than a final copy.

- *Header/footer* settings can be used to add information about when a document was printed and who printed it.

- A *collate* option lets you specify the order in which multiple copies of a multi-page document are printed. If the option is unchecked and you print ten copies, each page will be printed ten times before the printer moves on. If the option is checked, the printer will print the full document before starting over.

Optimizing Print Performance

Although a quality printer is the first step toward quality output, your output relies on factors other than the printer itself. If you've ever tweaked a photograph until it looked perfect on your screen only to discover the final printout was darker than you hoped, you made an important discovery. What you see on the screen may not match what comes out of the printer unless both devices are properly calibrated.

Color calibration uses hardware to generate an International Color Consortium (ICC) color profile, a file that defines the color characteristics of a hardware device. The operating system then uses this profile to correct any color shifts in your monitor. With a calibrated monitor, you know any color shifts in your photograph are really in the photo, not an artifact of your monitor.

 EXAM TIP *Calibration* is a general term for a manual or automatic process that corrects differences between how a device or component currently works and how it *should* work. All kinds of devices need calibration, but the CompTIA A+ 1101 objectives focus on calibrating inkjet and laser printers. This section describes one kind of calibration—but keep an eye out for additional calibration steps in the "Inkjet Printer Maintenance" and "Laser Printer Maintenance" sections later in this chapter.

Where these ICC color profiles really start to get interesting is that they can be created for printers as well. Just like with a monitor, they let the computer know the unique color quirks of a specific printer on a specific paper. When your printer and monitor have been properly calibrated and the profiles installed, your prints and monitor display should match. Color profiles are sometimes included on the installation media with a printer, but you can create or purchase custom profiles as well. Windows includes *Windows Color System (WCS)* to help build color profiles for use across devices. WCS is based on a newer component Microsoft calls the *color infrastructure and translation engine (CITE)*.

 NOTE Two of the best monitor calibration hardware manufacturers are Datacolor Spyder—that's the one I use most—and X-Rite ColorMunki Display. Get one. You'll be much happier with your print outcome! Here are the main URLs: https://www.datacolor.com and https://www.xrite.com.

Managing Public/Shared/Networked Devices

While we've looked at a few of the ways you can share a printer or multifunction device over a network, there's more to know about sharing these devices than just how to set them up. A few big issues are network security and data privacy.

Network Print Security

The ease of access that makes wired or wireless network printers and multifunction devices so useful is also a big risk; networked printers are subject to unique security issues. Luckily for us, the CompTIA A+ exams concentrate on just a few basic but important security issues with printer and multifunction devices, so let's look at these.

User Authentication   Allowing only the right people to use a device is an old issue and one that's been covered in one way through user permissions in Windows, but there's more to user authentication. For example, what if you have an expensive color laser printer? Many color laser printers use user authentication to determine, for example, if a user can print color or only black and white. These types of user authentications are based in the printer or printer server but happily work with Windows domains. In Windows 10, printer authentication can be configured in Printers and scanners.

Badging   Who hasn't seen the classic episode of *The Office* where Dwight requires everyone to use a badge to access the photocopier? While individual codes are rare, user badges that enable you to scan or photocopy are still quite common. These badges use every kind of technology, although NFT is the most common.

Audit Logs   Printers and scanners have audit logs just like any other device. These logs commonly reside in the printer itself, although other solutions work with Windows Event Viewer or Linux Syslog. The bottom line is that if you want to know what happened to a printer, check the logs!

Secured Prints   Ever find yourself printing something you don't want others to see? Do you ever find yourself running to the printer to grab it before anyone can see? That's what secure printing is all about.

Secure printing works by first requiring the user to enter a password or PIN code before a print job starts. After the job is sent to the printer (or print server), the job doesn't automatically print. To make the job print, the user must enter the passcode again at the printer, therefore making sure no one but that user can see the confidential print job.

If you think about it, a lot of sensitive information can pass through a printer or MFD in most organizations, especially in places like schools and hospitals where privacy is strictly regulated. When all of this information passes through the printer or MFD, it's important to make sure it isn't leaking out. Unfortunately, it's common for modern devices to contain a hard drive or other storage media used to cache copies of documents the device prints, scans, copies, or faxes. Depending on the device, you may be able to disable this feature, schedule regular deletion of the cache, or manually clear the cache regularly to limit the amount of damage a compromise could cause. It's also important to clear this information before disposing of the device.

Disabling features like this wouldn't be much good if anyone who could use the device could also change the settings, so enterprise models often allow for *user authentication* on the device. This can address a number of the risks these devices present by limiting use to authenticated users and restricting the features each user can access to only what they need.

Just because the data on your device is secure doesn't mean documents rolling off of it are free from prying eyes. User authentication can also help out by letting users send documents to the printer but waiting to print them until the user authenticates at the device. It can also minimize some of the risk to unsupervised documents by restricting the ability of less-trusted users to scan/copy/e-mail a document from the device, limiting the ease with which they could steal a copy of an unattended document and leave the original.

 NOTE Every printer is different. Read the documentation included with your printer to learn how you can perform the tasks listed in this section.

1101

Maintaining and Troubleshooting Printers

Once set up, printers tend to run with few issues, assuming that you install the proper drivers and keep the printer well maintained. But printer errors do occasionally develop. This section provides an overview of troubleshooting the most common print problems, as well as problems that crop up with specific printer types.

Maintaining and Troubleshooting General Issues

Printers of all stripes share some common problems, such as print jobs that don't print, strangely sized prints, and misalignment. Other issues include disposing of consumables, sharing multiple printers, and crashing on power-up. Let's take a look at these general troubleshooting issues, but start with a recap of the tools of the trade.

NOTE Don't forget to check the obvious. Many printers include tiny displays that can clue you in to what's wrong. Most brands use a series of *error codes* that indicate the problem. Use the manual or the manufacturer's Web site to translate the error code into meaningful information.

Tools of the Trade

Before you jump in and start to work on a printer that's giving you fits, you'll need some tools. You can use the standard computer tech tools in your toolkit, plus a couple of printer-specific devices. Here are some that will come in handy:

- A multimeter for troubleshooting electrical problems such as faulty wall outlets
- Various cleaning solutions, such as denatured alcohol
- An extension magnet for grabbing loose screws in tight spaces and cleaning up iron-based toner
- An optical disc or USB thumb drive with test patterns for checking print quality
- Your trusty screwdrivers—both a Phillips-head and flat-head, because if you bring just one kind, it's a sure bet that you'll need the other

Print Job Never Prints

If you click Print but the printer will not print, first check all the obvious explanations. Is the printer on? Is it connected? Is it online? Is there an error message on its display? Does it have paper? Is your computer online?

If the printer is on, the display might have a useful message. It'll usually let you know if the printer is out of paper, has a paper jam that needs to be resolved, or has had a *memory full/low memory error*. If so, refill the paper, resolve the jam, or try reprinting the job at a lower quality, accordingly.

If you can't connect to the printer, check all cables, ports, and power involved. If everything is plugged in and ready to go, check the printer's display for any indication that it has *no connectivity* (you may need to navigate its menu system to view its connectivity status). If the printer was previously connected, turn it off for a moment, and then turn it back on and see if it successfully connects. If it doesn't, the menu system will typically have an option to manually configure network settings. Try resetting or manually configuring them.

If the printer does have connectivity, double-check the appropriate printer applet for your version of Windows. If you don't see the printer you are looking for, you'll need to reinstall it.

If you attempt to use a printer shared by another computer but Windows pops up with an "Access Denied" error, you might not have permission to use the printer. Go to the host system and check the Security tab of the Printer Properties dialog box. Make sure your user account is allowed to use the printer.

Assuming the printer is in good order, it's time to look at the spooler. You can see the spooler status either by double-clicking the printer's icon in the appropriate printer Control Panel applet or by double-clicking the tiny printer icon in the notification area if it's present. If you're having a problem, the printer icon will almost always be there. Figure 26-35 shows the print spooler status window open.

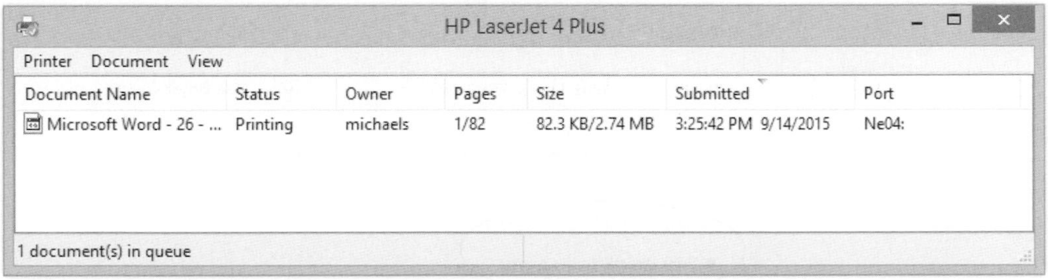

Document Name	Status	Owner	Pages	Size	Submitted	Port
Microsoft Word - 26 - ...	Printing	michaels	1/82	82.3 KB/2.74 MB	3:25:42 PM 9/14/2015	Ne04:

HP LaserJet 4 Plus — Printer Document View — 1 document(s) in queue

Figure 26-35   Print spooler status

Multiple prints pending in a queue can easily overflow or become corrupt due to a lack of disk space, too many print jobs, or one of a thousand other factors. The status window shows all of the pending print jobs and enables you to delete, start, or pause jobs. I usually just delete the affected print job(s) and try again.

Print spoolers are handy. If the printer goes down, you can just leave the print jobs in the spooler until the printer comes back online. If you have a printer that isn't coming on anytime soon, you can simply delete the print job in the spooler window and try another printer.

If you have problems with the print spooler, you can get around them by changing your print spool settings. Go into the Printers/Devices and Printers applet, right-click the icon of the printer in question, and choose Printer properties. In the resulting Properties dialog box (see Figure 26-36), choose the *Print directly to the printer* radio button on the Advanced tab and click OK; then try sending your print job again. Note that this window also offers you the choice of printing immediately—that is, starting to print pages as soon as the spooler has enough information to feed to the printer—or holding off on printing until the entire job is spooled.

If that isn't enough, try restarting the print spooler service. Right-click the Start button and select Computer Management. In the column on the left, double-click Services and Applications, and then click Services. The Services console should appear in the center of the Computer Management window. Scroll down and find the service named Print Spooler. Right-click the service and simply click Restart, if available; otherwise, click Stop, wait for it to stop, right-click the service again, and select Start. You should be able to print using the print spooler again.

Another possible cause for a stalled print job is *incorrect paper size*—the printer is simply waiting for the correct paper! Laser printers in particular have settings that tell them what size paper is in their standard paper tray or trays. If the application sending a

Figure 26-36
Print spool
settings

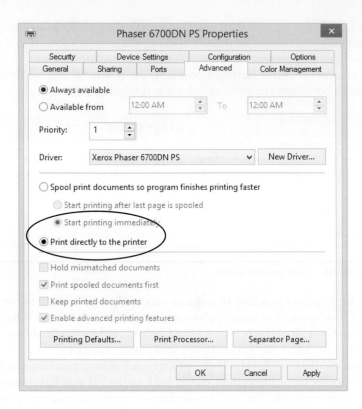

print job specifies a different paper size—for example, it wants to print a standard No. 10 envelope, or perhaps a legal sheet, but the standard paper tray holds only 8.5 × 11 letter paper—the printer usually pauses and holds up the queue until someone switches out the tray or manually feeds the type of paper that this print job requires. You can usually override this pause, even without having the specified paper, by pressing the OK or GO button on the printer.

The printer's default paper tray and paper size options will differ greatly depending on the printer type and model. To find these settings, go into the printer's Properties dialog box from the Printers/Devices and Printers applet, and then select the Device Settings tab. This list of settings includes Form to Tray Assignment, where you can specify which tray (in the case of a printer with multiple paper trays) holds which size paper.

Strange Sizes

A print job that comes out an unexpected size usually points to a user mistake in setting up the print job. All applications have a Print command and a Page Setup interface. The Page Setup interface enables you to define a number of print options, which vary from application to application. Figure 26-37 shows the Page Setup options for Microsoft Word. Make sure the page is set up properly before you blame the printer for a problem.

Figure 26-37
Page Setup
options for
Microsoft Word

If you know the page is set up correctly, recheck the printer drivers. If necessary, uninstall and reinstall the printer drivers. If the problem persists, you may have a serious problem with the printer's print engine, but that comes up as a likely answer only when you continually get the same strangely sized printouts using a variety of applications.

Grinding Noises

The only noise you want to hear from your printer is the printing of a document. Sometimes, however, we may try to either stuff too much paper in the tray, or the paper feeder is misaligned and you hear awful *grinding noises*. All you have to do is realign the paper in the paper feeder. You may also want to take a look at the rollers to see if they need some cleaning.

Finishing Issues/Staple Jams and Hole Punches

Some of the more high-end printers have built-in staplers and capabilities to place hole punches into documents—which is fantastic. However, what is not so great is when you experience a *staple jam* or *hole punch* error on your control panel. Fixing a staple jam in a printer is much like fixing a staple jam in a stapler. You open up the stapling mailbox, remove the stapler cartridge and any jammed staples, insert the cartridge back into the stapling mailbox and your stapler jam is fixed. With a *hole punch* print option there may be compatibility issues when you combine printing options (stapling and hole punch). Also, feeding the paper in horizontally (rather than vertically) sometimes creates some issues.

Incorrect Page Orientation

Have you ever tried to print a document that you intended to output as portrait, but instead came out as a landscape orientation? *Incorrect page orientation* settings can be easily fixed by going to your Printer settings | Printing preferences | Orientation and selecting which page orientation you would prefer *before* you print.

Misaligned or Garbage Prints

Misaligned or garbage printouts (CompTIA calls this *garbled print*) often point to a corrupted or incorrect driver, but it's worth trying to reboot the printer before jumping to conclusions. If that doesn't help, make sure you're using the right driver (it's hard to mess this up, but not impossible) and then uninstall and reinstall the printer driver. If the problem persists, you may be asking the printer to do something it cannot do. For example, you may be printing to a PostScript printer with a PCL driver. Check the printer type to verify that you haven't installed the wrong type of driver for that printer!

If none of these solutions help, it's also worth making sure there isn't a data cable or power issue. Swap out the data cable for one you know is good. Move the printer to another outlet (with no power strip or surge protector). If the printer supports more than one type of connection, try a different one.

Dealing with Consumables

All printers tend to generate a lot of trash in the form of consumables. Impact printers use paper and ribbons, inkjet printers use paper and ink cartridges, and laser printers use paper and toner cartridges. In today's environmentally sensitive world, many laws regulate the proper disposal of most printer components. Be sure to check with the local sanitation department or disposal services company before throwing away any component. Of course, you should never throw away toner cartridges—certain companies will pay for used cartridges!

Both laser printers and computers require more power during their initial power-up (the POST on a computer and the warm-up on a laser printer) than once they are running. HP recommends a reverse power-up. Turn on the laser printer first and allow it to finish its warm-up before turning on the computer. This avoids having two devices drawing their peak loads simultaneously.

> **NOTE** When in doubt about how to dispose of any computer component, check a *material safety data sheet (MSDS)*. These standardized forms provide detailed information about potential environmental hazards associated with different components but also proper disposal methods. For example, surf to https://epson.com/support/sds to find the latest MSDS for all Epson products. This isn't just a printer issue—you can find an MSDS for most computer components.

> **EXAM TIP** MSDSs contain important information regarding hazardous materials such as safe use procedures and emergency response instructions. An MSDS is typically posted anywhere a hazardous chemical is used.

> **NOTE** Used toner cartridges are toxic to the environment, so you need to dispose of them properly. There are some different ways to do this and do your part in saving our earth and water. You can take them to a supply store like Office Depot; place them in a plastic bag and deposit into a green recycle bin; or send them back to the manufacturer.

Incorrect Chroma Display

If you print in color, sooner or later something is going to come out in the *wrong* color. A good first step is printing out the appropriate diagnostic/test page—this should help separate problems with the printer from problems with what or how you're printing.

Some pretty simple things can cause an *incorrect chroma display*, so let's check those first. If you print a document with color and it comes out in black and white, double-check both the app you used to print and your print settings to make sure they aren't configured to use grayscale. Double-check the color ink/toner levels.

If something you expected to come out black comes out an odd tone, your printer may be low on black ink/toner. Colors that *appear* black may be a *rich black* with other colors mixed in—if there isn't enough black in the mix, you might end up with something unexpected.

If your printer's color registration is out of whack, you might see a sliver of unexpected color (usually cyan, magenta, or yellow) to either side of larger elements. This can be less obvious with text—it may just look blurry, discolored, or appear to have an unexpected shadow. If so, run your printer's registration or alignment routine.

Check the print settings on your system and the printer itself to see if it's configured to adjust any colors. If so, it may be misconfigured. If your printer has a color calibration routine, run it to see if the issue improves. It's also possible your system is using the wrong color profile for either the printer or the monitor. In the first case, your printer might be *right* and your *monitor* might be wrong. Make sure your system isn't using an incorrect color profile for either device. If the profiles are correct and you have the right tools to color calibrate either device, go ahead and do so.

Some reasons for color problems are a lot less fun. If your printer has separate cartridges or tanks for different colors, it's possible someone installed the wrong color in one of the slots/tanks. If it's an inkjet, *someone* will need to spend a good bit of time cleaning the incorrect ink out of the tubing and printheads. If the right colors are in the right slots, a gunked-up printhead may be keeping the printer from laying down the right amount of a color—but the solution will still be cleaning.

No Image on Printer Display

The small menu display screens included on many modern printers and multifunction devices can, like any other display screen, have a number of issues. The display might freeze or get stuck on a specific screen; it might not come on at all; it might light up but never show an image; it might only display a single color, have artifacts such as lines showing on the display, or even just slowly fade from decades of steady use. Unfortunately, there's not a lot you can do about these problems. Turning the device off and back on is a good start, and some manufacturers recommend completely unplugging it for a few minutes. If the screen is still misbehaving but the device is otherwise functional and the problem didn't appear immediately after a firmware update, it's time to take the device to a service center.

Maintaining and Troubleshooting Impact Printers

Maintaining an impact printer is a lot like scheduling regular maintenance on your car. When you treat your car with care and love, it will return the love by not having as many problems and visits to the mechanic. Although maintaining an impact printer may seem overwhelming, this regular maintenance is offset by the few problems you'll encounter with them.

Impact Printer Maintenance

Impact printers require regular maintenance but will run forever as long as you're diligent. Keep the platen (the roller or plate on which the pins impact) and the printhead clean with denatured alcohol. Be sure to lubricate gears and pulleys according to the manufacturer's specifications. Never lubricate the printhead, however, because the lubricant will smear and stain the paper. Don't forget to replace the ink ribbon every so often.

Most impact printers use paper continuously fed from a roll or ream, so changing or *replacing the paper* is a little more involved than adding sheets to the tray. First you'll need to swap out the rolls or move the new ream into position, and then you'll need to feed the new paper. If there is already paper in the printer, you'll need to finish feeding it out first. Like with other printers, paper quality, debris, and improperly fed paper can all lead to jams, which you'll typically clear by feeding the paper one way or the other.

For all of these processes, look up the printer's documentation; if you don't follow the instructions, there's a chance you'll damage the printer. There's often a manual feeding wheel or roller, or you may just need to pull the paper firmly from one side of the printer; both of these can break the feeding system if performed improperly.

Impact Printer Problems

The primary issues to troubleshoot are bad-looking text and bad-looking pages. White bars going through the text point to a dirty or damaged printhead. Try cleaning the printhead with a little denatured alcohol. If the problem persists, replace the printhead. Printheads for most printers are readily available from the manufacturer or from companies that rebuild them. If the characters look chopped off at the top or bottom, the printhead probably needs to be adjusted. Refer to the manufacturer's instructions for proper adjustment. If the characters have simply degraded or grown faint over time and your printer is used frequently, the printhead may be wearing out; replace it.

Bad-Looking Page

If the page is covered with dots and small smudges—the "pepper look"—the platen is dirty. Clean the platen with denatured alcohol. If the print is faded, and you know the ribbon is good, try adjusting the printhead closer to the platen. If the print is okay on one side of the paper but fades as you move to the other, the platen is out of adjustment. Platens are generally difficult to adjust, so your best plan is to take it to the manufacturer's local warranty/repair center.

Maintaining and Troubleshooting Thermal Printers

Compared to other printer styles, thermal printers are simple to troubleshoot and maintain. With direct thermal printers, you only need to worry about three things: the heating element, the rollers, and the paper. With thermal wax printers, you also need to care for the wax ribbon.

Thermal Printer Maintenance

To *clean the heating element*, turn off the thermal printer and open it according to the manufacturer's instructions. Use denatured alcohol and a lint-free cloth to wipe off the heating element. You might need to use a little pressure to get it completely clean. Clean the rollers with a cloth or compressed air. Make sure to *remove debris* so they can properly grip the paper. *Replacing the paper* is as easy as sliding off the old roll and replacing it with a new one. Remember to feed the paper through the heating element, because otherwise you won't print anything. Replacing the ribbon is similar to replacing the roll of paper; make sure to feed it past the heating element, or the printer won't work properly. Your printer's manufacturer should include any special instructions for installing a new ribbon.

Maintaining and Troubleshooting Inkjet Printers

Maintenance on inkjet printers is interesting. One would think that using a printer on a regular basis would make it prone to more issues, right? Not the inkjet printer. They rely on regular use (but not abuse) to minimize printing issues, therefore minimizing the need to troubleshoot.

Inkjet Printer Maintenance

Inkjet printers are reliable devices that require little maintenance as long as they are used within their design parameters (high-use machines will require more intensive maintenance). Because of the low price of these printers, manufacturers know that people don't want to spend a lot of money maintaining them.

If you perform even the most basic maintenance tasks on inkjet printers, they will soldier on for years without a whimper. Inkjets generally have built-in maintenance programs that you should run from time to time to keep them in good operating order. Inkjet printers don't get nearly as dirty as laser printers, and most manufacturers do not recommend periodic cleaning. Unless your manufacturer explicitly tells you to do so, don't vacuum an inkjet. Inkjets generally do not have maintenance kits, but most inkjet printers come with extensive maintenance software (see Figure 26-38). Usually, the hardest part of using this software is finding it in the first place. Look for an option in Printing Preferences, a selection on the Start menu, or an option on the printer's management Web page. Don't worry—it's there!

When you first set up an inkjet printer, it normally instructs you to perform a routine to align, or to *calibrate* the printheads properly. Specifics differ, but the printer will usually print at least one *test page* and either ask you to place it in the scanner (if it has one) or use the menu to indicate which sets of numbered lines align best. If this isn't done, the print quality will show poor color *registration*—a fancy way of saying the different color layers that make up your print aren't aligned properly. The good news is that you can perform this procedure at any time. If a printer is moved or dropped or it's just been working away untended for a while, it's often worth running the alignment/registration routine. Some printers will even do this automatically from time to time.

Replacing cartridges in inkjet printers usually is easy, but the exact process can vary widely from printer to printer. Refer to the documentation, but typically you'll open a compartment on the printer and see one or more cartridges attached to the printhead. If the printhead isn't accessible, don't try to force it out; printheads often move to the center of the printer for easy access, in which case you'll need the printer to be on before you replace cartridges.

Cartridges may simply slide into place, but the printer may also have clips to lock them in. Check the clips or slots on the printhead for an indicator of which cartridge goes where. Follow the manufacturer's instructions for removing the cartridge you need

Figure 26-38 Inkjet printer maintenance screen

to change, then remove the new cartridge from its packaging. Look for a piece of tape or other protective covering over its nozzles or contacts; you'll need to remove that before inserting it. Make sure you follow the insertion process carefully, as an improperly seated cartridge may catch on other components when the printhead moves. Once you insert the new cartridges and close the compartment, the printhead should move back into place.

Did I say that you never should clean an inkjet? Well, that may be true for the printer itself, but there is one part of your printer that will benefit from an occasional cleaning: the inkjet's printer head nozzles. The nozzles are the tiny pipes that squirt the ink onto the paper.

 NOTE All inkjet inks are water-based, and water works better than denatured alcohol to clean them up. Every inkjet printer has a different procedure for cleaning the printhead nozzles. On older inkjets, you usually have to press buttons on the printer to start a maintenance program. On more modern inkjets, you can access the head-cleaning maintenance program from Windows.

CAUTION Cleaning the heads on an inkjet printer is sometimes necessary, but I don't recommend that you do it on a regular basis as preventive maintenance. The head-cleaning process uses up a lot of that very expensive inkjet ink—so do this only when a printing problem seems to indicate clogged or dirty printheads!

Definitely use inkjet printers regularly—that's good maintenance. Keeping the ink flowing through the printheads prevents them from drying up and clogging. If you don't have anything "real" to print for a week, run a test page.

Inkjet Printer Problems

A common problem with inkjet printers is the tendency for the ink inside the nozzles to dry out when not used even for a relatively short time, blocking any ink from exiting. If your printer is telling Windows that it's printing and feeding paper through, but either nothing is coming out (usually the case if you're just printing black text) or only certain colors are printing, the culprit is almost certainly dried ink clogging the nozzles.

Another problem that sometimes arises is the dreaded *multipage misfeed.* This is often not actually your printer's fault—humidity can cause sheets of paper to cling to each other—but sometimes the culprit is an overheated printer, so if you've been cranking out a lot of documents without stopping, try giving the printer a bit of a coffee break. Also, fan the sheets of the paper stack before inserting it into the paper tray.

Finally, check to see if excess ink overflow is a problem. In the area where the printheads park, look for a small tank or tray that catches excess ink from the cleaning process. If the printer has one, check to see how full it is. If this tray overflows onto the main board or even the power supply, it will kill your printer. If you discover that the tray is about to overflow, you can remove excess ink by inserting a twisted paper towel into the tank to soak up some of the ink. It is advisable to wear latex or vinyl gloves while doing this. Clean up any spilled ink with a paper towel dampened with distilled water.

Maintaining and Troubleshooting Laser Printers

Quite a few problems can arise with laser printers, but before getting into those details, you need to review some recommended procedures for *avoiding* those problems.

CAUTION Before you service a laser printer, always, *always* turn it off and unplug it! Don't expose yourself to the very dangerous high voltages found inside these machines.

Laser Printer Maintenance

Unlike computer maintenance, laser printer maintenance follows a fairly well-established procedure. Of course, you'll need to *replace toner* every so often, but keeping your laser printer healthy requires following these maintenance steps.

Keep It Clean   Laser printers are quite robust as a rule. A good cleaning every time you replace the toner cartridge will help that printer last for many years. I know of many examples of original HP LaserJet I printers continuing to run perfectly after a dozen or more years of operation. The secret is that they were kept immaculately clean.

Your laser printer gets dirty in two ways: Excess toner, over time, will slowly coat the entire printer. Paper dust, sometimes called *paper dander*, tends to build up where the paper is bent around rollers or where pickup rollers grab paper. Unlike (black) toner, paper dust is easy to see and is usually a good indicator that a printer needs to be cleaned. Usually, a thorough cleaning using a can of compressed air to blow out the printer is the best cleaning you can do. It's best to do this outdoors, or you may end up looking like one of those chimney sweeps from *Mary Poppins*! If you must clean a printer indoors, use a special low-static vacuum—often called a toner vac—designed especially for electronic components, like some of the great products from Metro Vacuum (https://metrovac.com).

Every laser printer has its own unique cleaning method, but the cleaning instructions tend to skip one little area. Every laser printer has a number of rubber guide rollers through which the paper is run during the print process. These little rollers tend to pick up dirt and paper dust over time, making them slip and jam paper. They are easily cleaned with a small amount of 90 percent or better denatured alcohol on a fibrous cleaning towel. The alcohol will remove the debris and any dead rubber. If the paper won't feed, you can give the rollers and separator pads a textured surface that will restore their feeding properties by rubbing them with a little denatured alcohol on a nonmetallic scouring pad.

CAUTION   The imaging drum, usually (but not always) contained in the toner cartridge, can be wiped clean if it becomes dirty, but be very careful if you do so! If the drum becomes scratched, the scratch will appear on every page printed from that point on. The only repair in the event of a scratch is to replace the toner cartridge or imaging drum.

If you're ready to get specific, get the printer's service manual. They are a key source for information on how to keep a printer clean and running. Sadly, not all printer manufacturers provide these, but most do. While you're at it, see if the manufacturer has a Quick Reference Guide; these can be very handy for most printer problems!

Periodic Maintenance   Although keeping the printer clean is critical to its health and well-being, every laser printer has certain components that you need to replace periodically. Your ultimate source for determining the parts that need to be replaced (and when to replace them) is the printer manufacturer. Following the manufacturer's maintenance guidelines will help to ensure years of trouble-free, dependable printing from your laser printer.

Many manufacturers provide kits that contain components that you should replace on a regular schedule. These maintenance kits include sets of replacement parts, such as a fuser, as well as one or more rollers or pads. Typically, you need to reset the page counter after installing a maintenance kit so the printer can remind you to perform maintenance again after a certain number of pages have been printed.

Some ozone filters can be cleaned with a vacuum and some can only be replaced—follow the manufacturer's recommendation. You can clean the fuser assembly with 90 percent or better denatured alcohol. Check the heat roller (the Teflon-coated one with the light bulb inside) for pits and scratches. If you see surface damage on the rollers, replace the fuser unit.

Most printers will give you an error code when the fuser is damaged or overheating and needs to be replaced; others will produce the error code at a preset copy count as a preventive maintenance measure. Again, follow the manufacturer's recommendations.

NOTE Failure of the thermal fuse (used to keep the fuser from overheating) can necessitate replacing the fuser assembly. Some machines contain more than one thermal fuse. As always, follow the manufacturer's recommendations. Many manufacturers have kits that alert you with an alarm code to replace the fuser unit and key rollers and guides at predetermined page counts.

The transfer corona can be cleaned with a 90 percent denatured alcohol solution on a cotton swab. If the wire is broken, you can replace it; many just snap in or are held in by a couple of screws. Paper guides can also be cleaned with alcohol on a fibrous towel.

As with inkjet printers, some laser printers also have calibration routines to ensure the quality of color prints. *Registration* routines ensure that each color prints in the correct location, and *color calibration* ensures that the printer lays down the right amount of each color. Some devices will perform these automatically from time to time. If not, the printer's manual or menu panel should recommend when to run these routines and should walk you through the process.

CAUTION The fuser assembly operates at 200 to 300 degrees Fahrenheit, so always allow time for this component to cool down before you attempt to clean it.

Laser Printer Problems

Laser printer problems usually result in poor output. One of the most important tests you can do on any printer, not just a laser printer, is called a *diagnostic print page* or an *engine test page*. You do this by either holding down the On Line button as the printer is started or using the printer's maintenance software. If the print quality is poor, check for a calibration routine on your device, and see if this resolves the issue.

Faded Prints or Blank Pages   If a laser printer is spitting out *faded prints* or even *printing blank pages*, that usually means the printer is running out of toner. If the printer does have toner and nothing prints, print a diagnostic/test page. If that is also blank, remove the toner cartridge and look at the imaging drum inside. If the image is still there, you know the transfer corona or the high-voltage power supply has failed. Check the printer's maintenance guide to see how to focus on the bad part and replace it.

Dirty or Smudged Printouts   If the fusing mechanism in a laser printer gets dirty, it will leave a light dusting of toner all over the paper, particularly on the back of the page. When you see toner *speckling on printed pages*, you should get the printer cleaned.

If the printout looks smudged or readily rubs off on your fingers, the fuser isn't properly fusing the toner to the paper (CompTIA calls it *toner not fusing to paper*). Depending on the paper used, the fuser needs to reach a certain temperature to fuse the toner. If the toner won't fuse to the paper, try using a lighter-weight paper. You might also need to replace the fuser.

Double/Echo Images   Echo images sometimes appear at regular intervals on the printed page. This happens when the imaging drum has not fully discharged and is picking up toner from a previous image or when a previous image has used up so much toner that either the supply of charged toner is insufficient or the toner has not been adequately charged. Sometimes it can also be caused by a worn-out cleaning blade that isn't removing the toner from the drum.

Light Echo Images Versus Dark Echo Images   A variety of problems can cause both light and dark echo images, but the most common source of light echo images is "developer starvation." If you ask a laser printer to print an extremely dark or complex image, it can use up so much toner that the toner cartridge will not be able to charge enough toner to print the next image. The proper solution is to use less toner. You can fix echo image problems in the following ways:

- Lower the resolution of the page (print at 300 dpi instead of 600 dpi).
- Use a different pattern.
- Avoid 50 percent grayscale and "dot-on/dot-off patterns."
- Change the layout so that grayscale patterns do not follow black areas.
- Make dark patterns lighter and light patterns darker.
- Print in landscape orientation.
- Adjust print density and RET settings.
- Print a completely blank page immediately prior to the page with the echo image, as part of the same print job.

In addition to these possibilities, low temperature and low humidity can aggravate echo image problems. Check your user's manual for environmental recommendations. Dark echo images can sometimes be caused by a damaged drum. It may be fixed by replacing the toner cartridge. Light echo images would *not* be solved in this way. Switching other components will not usually affect echo image problems because they are a side effect of the entire printing process.

Lines Down the Printed Page   *Lines down the printed page* usually occur when the toner is clogged, preventing the proper dispersion of toner on the drum. Try shaking the toner cartridge to dislodge the clog. If that doesn't work, replace the toner cartridge.

Blotchy Print   Blotches are commonly a result of uneven dispersion of toner, especially if the toner is low. Shake the toner from side to side and then try to print. Also be sure that the printer is sitting level. Finally, make sure the paper is not wet in spots. If the blotches are in a regular order, check the fusing rollers and the imaging drum for any foreign objects.

Spotty Print   If spots appear at regular intervals, the drum may be damaged or some toner may be stuck to the fuser rollers. Try wiping off the fuser rollers. Check the imaging drum for damage. If the drum is damaged, get a new toner cartridge.

Embossed Effect   If your prints are getting an embossed effect (like putting a penny under a piece of paper and rubbing it with a lead pencil), there is almost certainly a foreign object on a roller. Use 90 percent denatured alcohol or regular water with a soft cloth to try to remove it. If the foreign object is on the imaging drum, you're going to have to use a new toner cartridge. An embossed effect can also be caused by the contrast control being set too high. The contrast control is actually a knob on the inside of the unit (sometimes accessible from the outside, on older models). Check your manual for the specific location.

Incomplete Characters   You can sometimes correct incompletely printed characters on laser-printed transparencies by adjusting the print density. Be extremely careful to use only materials approved for use in laser printers.

Creased Paper   Laser printers have up to four rollers. In addition to the heat and pressure rollers of the fuser assembly, other rollers move the paper from the source tray to the output tray. These rollers crease the paper to avoid curling that would cause paper jams in the printer. If the creases are noticeable, try using a different paper type. Cotton bond paper is usually more susceptible to noticeable creasing than other bonds. You might also try sending the output to the faceup tray, which avoids one roller. There is no hardware solution to this problem; it is simply a side effect of the process.

Paper Jams   Every printer jams now and then. To *clear jams*, always refer first to the manufacturer's jam removal procedure. It is simply too easy to damage a printer by pulling on the jammed paper! If the printer reports a jam but there's no paper inside, you almost certainly have a problem with one of the many jam sensors or paper feed sensors inside the printer, and you'll need to take it to a repair center.

Multipage Misfeed   If the printer grabs multiple sheets at a time, this is called a *multipage misfeed*. To fix this issue first try opening a new ream of paper and loading that in the printer. If that works, you have a humidity problem. If the new paper angle doesn't work, check the separation pad on the printer. The separation pad is a small piece of cork or rubber that separates the sheets as they are pulled from the paper feed tray. A worn separation pad looks shiny and, well, worn! Most separation pads are easy to replace.

Paper Not Feeding   If your printer has paper in the tray but you try to print and notice *paper not feeding*, you might need to clean (or even replace) your printer's pick-up rollers. First, rule out some simple alternatives. Make sure the printer is configured to use the same tray you're expecting it to use. Check the paper: make sure the tray isn't overfilled and confirm the paper there is well aligned, positioned correctly in the tray, and not ripped or bent. See if the weight or coating are different than what you normally use and whether the print settings specify the correct kind of paper. If the paper is different than what you normally use, test whether it'll pick up the normal paper just fine. If the tray has adjustable guides, make sure they aren't holding the paper too tightly.

Warped, Overprinted, or Poorly Formed Characters   Poorly formed characters can indicate either a problem with the paper (or other media) or a problem with the hardware.

Incorrect media cause a number of these types of problems. Avoid paper that is too rough or too smooth. Paper that is too rough interferes with the fusing of characters and their initial definition. If the paper is too smooth (like some coated papers, for example), it may feed improperly, causing distorted or overwritten characters. Even though you can purchase laser printer–specific paper, all laser printers print acceptably on standard photocopy paper. Try to keep the paper from becoming too wet. Don't open a ream of paper until it is time to load it into the printer. Always fan the paper before loading it into the printer, especially if the paper has been left out of the package for more than just a few days.

The durability of a well-maintained laser printer makes hardware a much rarer source of character printing problems, but you should be aware of the possibility. Fortunately, it is fairly easy to check the hardware. Most laser printers have a self-test function—often combined with a diagnostic printout, but sometimes as a separate process. This self-test shows whether the laser printer can properly develop an image without actually having to send print commands from the computer. The self-test is quite handy to verify the question "Is it the printer or is it the computer?" Run the self-test to check for connectivity and configuration problems.

Possible solutions include replacing the toner cartridge, especially if you hear popping noises; checking the cabling; and replacing the data cable, especially if it has bends or crimps or if objects are resting on the cable. If you have a front menu panel, turn off advanced functions and high-speed settings to determine whether the advanced functions are either not working properly or not supported by your current software configuration (check your manuals for configuration information). If these solutions do not work, the problem may not be user serviceable. Contact an authorized service center.

Troubleshooting 3-D Printers

Creating objects by melting and reforming plastic has a lot of potential for a big mess. Common issues include unwanted strings connecting open spaces (called *stringing* or *oozing*), overheating to melt part of the final product, and *layers shifting* so that they don't align properly. All filaments differ in quality, just to make an already complex process more problematic. Using poor-quality filament might save money up front but lead to *clogged extruders* in short order.

 NOTE   CompTIA doesn't specify any maintenance steps for 3-D printers.

Although 3-D printers have been around for a decade or so, the technology still has growing pains. Troubleshooting 3-D printers is way outside the scope of the CompTIA A+ exams, primarily because the processes and such vary tremendously among the many models of printers. For the most part, check the manufacturer's Web site for help. Try one of the many excellent enthusiast sites out there for help guides, such as https://www.fabbaloo.com. Good luck!

Chapter Review

Questions

1. What mechanism is used by most inkjet printers to push ink onto the paper?
   A. Electrostatic discharge
   B. Gravity
   C. Air pressure
   D. Electroconductive plates

2. With a laser printer, what creates the image on the imaging drum?
   A. Primary corona
   B. Laser imaging unit
   C. Transfer corona
   D. Toner

3. What is the proper order of the laser printing process?
   A. Process, clean, charge, expose, develop, transfer, and fuse
   B. Process, charge, expose, develop, transfer, fuse, and clean
   C. Clean, expose, develop, transfer, process, fuse, and charge
   D. Clean, charge, expose, process, develop, fuse, and transfer

4. On a dot-matrix printer, what physically strikes the ribbon to form an image?
   A. Electromagnets
   B. Printwires
   C. Character wheel
   D. Print hammers

5. Which of these items are considered to be dot-matrix printer consumables? (Select all that apply.)
   A. Drive motor
   B. Paper
   C. Flywheel
   D. Ribbon

6. What part of a laser printer must be vacuumed or replaced periodically to prevent damage caused by the action of the corona?

   A. The rubber rollers

   B. The ozone filter

   C. The transfer filter

   D. The cleaning blade

7. Which one of the following port types do most printers support?

   A. PS/2

   B. USB

   C. Infrared

   D. RS-232

8. A standalone printer prints a test page just fine, but it makes gobbledygook out of your term paper. What's probably wrong?

   A. Out of toner

   B. Fuser error

   C. Printer interface

   D. Faulty software configuration

9. Which printing process ends with the physical and electrical cleaning of the imaging drum?

   A. Thermal

   B. Inkjet

   C. Impact

   D. Laser

10. Which tool would help you determine why a print job didn't print?

    A. Printer driver

    B. Printer setup

    C. Print spooler

    D. System setup

Answers

1. **D.** Most inkjet printers use electroconductive plates to push the ink onto the paper.

2. **B.** The laser imaging unit creates an image on the imaging drum.

3. **B.** Process, charge, expose, develop, transfer, fuse, and clean is the proper process.

4. **B.** Printwires physically strike the ribbon in dot-matrix printers.

5. B, D. Both paper and ribbons are considered dot-matrix printer consumables.

6. B. The ozone filter of a laser printer should be periodically vacuumed or changed.

7. B. You'll find almost all non-networked printers hooked up to USB ports.

8. D. The application (software) that is trying to print is probably configured incorrectly.

9. D. The laser printing process ends with the physical and electrical cleaning of the imaging drum.

10. C. The print spooler can help you determine why a print job didn't print.

Securing Computers

In this chapter, you will learn how to
- Explain the threats to your computers and data
- Describe key security concepts and technologies
- Explain how to protect computers from network threats

Your PC is under siege. Through your PC, malicious people can gain valuable information about you and your habits. They can steal your files. They can run programs that log your keystrokes and thus gain account names and passwords, credit card information, and more. They can run software that takes over much of your computer processing time and use it to send spam or steal from others. The threat is real and immediate. Worse, they're doing these things to your clients as I write these words. You need to secure your computer and your users' computers from these attacks.

But what does computer security mean? Is it an anti-malware program? Is it big, complex passwords? Sure, it's both of these things, but what about the fact that your laptop can be stolen easily or that improper ventilation can cause hard drives and other components to die?

To secure computers, you need both a sound strategy and proper tactics. For strategic reasons, you need to understand the threat from unauthorized access to local machines as well as the big threats posed to networked computers. Part of the big picture is knowing what policies, software, and hardware to put in place to stop those threats. From a tactical in-the-trenches perspective, you need to master the details to know how to implement and maintain the proper tools. Not only do you need to install anti-malware programs in your users' computers, for example, but you also need to update those programs regularly to keep up with the constant barrage of new malware.

1102

Analyzing Threats and Vulnerabilities

Threats to your data and PC come from two directions: accidents and malicious people. All sorts of things can go wrong with your computer, from users getting access to folders they shouldn't see to a virus striking and deleting folders. Files can be deleted, renamed, or simply lost (what Nancy Drew might call "The Case of the Disappearing Files"). Hard drives can die, and optical discs get scratched and rendered unreadable. Accidents happen, and even well-meaning people can make mistakes.

Threats need some way to access a network or facility, whether they are accidental or malicious, internal or external, and that's where vulnerabilities come in. A *vulnerability* is a weak spot in your defenses that enables a threat to cause harm. Vulnerabilities can exist in an organization's physical security or in its networks. Understanding different types of vulnerabilities and the threats that will try to exploit them is vital to protecting your organization's data, reputation, and safety. We'll look at threats first, followed by vulnerabilities that threats exploit to do their harm.

Threats

Unfortunately, a lot of people out there intend to do you harm. Combine that intent with a talent for computers, and you have a dangerous combination. Let's look at the following issues:

- Malicious actors
- Unauthorized access
- Social engineering
- Insider threats
- Data destruction, whether accidental or deliberate
- Administrative access
- System crash/hardware failure
- Physical theft
- Malware
- Spam

Malicious Actors

In some cases, the threat in question is an individual, also known as a *threat actor*. Whether they're an external malicious actor like a hacker or an internal malicious actor like a disgruntled employee, threat actors need some way to use vulnerabilities to their advantage. This is known as an *attack*, or an *exploit*. The general order of operations goes something like this: a threat actor identifies one or more vulnerabilities in a network or physical security system, uses some combination of attacks to exploit the vulnerability or vulnerabilities, and proceeds to carry out their nefarious plans. You'll notice that I didn't say that a threat actor will use only one attack or exploit only one vulnerability. There's good reason for this. Very rarely will a malicious actor make use of only one method. For example, a malicious actor attacking from outside the organization may employ a phishing scam to gain user login credentials, use those credentials to gain initial access to a network, then deploy a zero-day attack to take over the network administrator's account.

If some of these terms sound unfamiliar now, don't worry. You're about to get a crash course in some of the many threats and attacks you'll encounter in the world of IT.

 EXAM TIP Be aware that while many of these terms are considered types of attacks, CompTIA's A+ 1102 exam objectives classify them all as *social engineering* or *threats*. For the purpose of the 1102 exam, threats and attacks are one and the same, but in most other contexts, threats and attacks are separate concepts.

Zero-Day Attack A *zero-day attack* is an attack on a vulnerability that wasn't already known to the software developers. It gets the name because the developer of the flawed software has had zero days to fix the vulnerability. Microsoft, Apple, and other software developers regularly post patches to fix flaws as they're discovered.

Spoofing *Spoofing* is the process of pretending to be someone or something you are not by placing false information into your packets. Any data sent on a network can be spoofed. Here are a few quick examples of commonly spoofed data:

- Source MAC address and IP address, to make you think a packet came from somewhere else
- E-mail address, to make you think an e-mail came from somewhere else
- Web address, to make you think you are on a Web page you are not on
- Username, to make you think a certain user is contacting you when in reality it's someone completely different

Generally, spoofing isn't so much a threat as it is a tool to make threats. If you spoof my e-mail address, for example, that by itself isn't a threat. If you use my e-mail address to pretend to be me, however, and to ask my employees to send in their usernames and passwords for network login? That's clearly a threat. (And also a waste of time; my employees would *never* trust me with their usernames and passwords.)

On-Path Attack In an *on-path attack*, an attacker taps into communications between two systems, covertly intercepting traffic thought to be only between those systems, reading or in some cases even changing the data and then sending the data on. A classic on-path attack would be a person using special software on a wireless network to make all the clients think his laptop is a wireless access point. He could then listen in on that wireless network, gathering up all the conversations and gaining access to passwords, shared keys, or other sensitive information.

 EXAM TIP While CompTIA prefers and uses the term *on-path attack*, you'll more commonly hear it referred to by its original name, *man-in-the-middle*, out in the world. Just be aware that the two terms are interchangeable, and that on-path attack is how it will be referred to on the exam.

Session Hijacking Somewhat similarly to on-path attacks, *session hijacking* tries to intercept a valid computer session to get authentication information. Unlike on-path attacks, session hijacking only tries to grab authentication information, not necessarily listening in like an on-path attack.

Brute-Force Attack CompTIA describes brute force as a threat, but it's more of a method that threat agents use. Brute force is a method where a threat agent guesses many or all possible values for some data. Most of the time the term *brute force* refers to an attempt to crack a password, but the concept also applies to other attacks. You can brute force a search for open ports, network IDs, usernames, and so on. Pretty much any attempt to guess the contents of some kind of data field that isn't obvious (or is hidden) is considered a *brute-force attack*.

There are two other tools attackers use to brute force passwords: dictionaries and rainbow tables. A *dictionary attack* is a form of brute-force attack that essentially guesses every word in a dictionary. Don't just think of Webster's dictionary—a *dictionary* used to attack passwords might contain every password ever leaked online.

Before we can talk about rainbow tables, we need to look closer at password leaks. One (terrible!) way to authenticate users is to save a copy of their password in a database and check it every time they log in. Hackers *love* to steal these databases because they can go try the username and password on popular services, and use the passwords to improve the dictionaries they use to guess passwords.

In response to this threat, authentication systems only save a special value (called a *hash*) computed from the password; each time the user logs in, the system re-computes this special value and compares it with the saved copy. If an attacker steals one of these databases, they only get a bunch of usernames and hashes. Hashes are special because the computation that creates them is irreversible; the only way to figure out what password produced a given hash is to guess a password, perform the same computation, and see if the hashes match.

Attackers fought back by pre-computing large lookup tables—known as *hash tables*—of passwords and the corresponding hash. When they find a large database of hashed passwords, they can just look up the corresponding password in their hash table. Hash tables for passwords more than a few characters long eat tons of storage space, so they're turned into *rainbow tables* to save space (at the expense of a little speed and accuracy.) *Rainbow tables* use complicated math to condense dictionary tables with hashed entries dramatically. They're binary files, not text files, and can store amazing amounts of information in a relatively small size. Rainbow tables generally fall into the realm of CompTIA Security+ or even higher-level certifications, but the phrase has become common enough that CompTIA A+ techs need to know what it means.

Denial of Service A *denial of service (DoS)* attack uses various methods to overwhelm a system, such as a Web server, to make it essentially nonfunctional. DoS attacks were relatively common in the early days of the Web. These days you'll see *distributed denial of service (DDoS)* attacks that use many machines simultaneously to assault a system. A DDoS attack is generally executed using a botnet. A botnet consists of any number (usually a large one) of systems infected with malware designed to allow them to be controlled by an attacker and used to send disruptive traffic designed to bring down a resource. You'll get a closer look at botnets and how they work later on in the chapter when we discuss malware.

Cross-Site Scripting   Most companies have Web sites, and Web sites can sometimes be very vulnerable to attacks by the bad guys. One such attack that can pose a threat to your Web applications is known as cross-site scripting. *Cross-site scripting (XSS)* is an attack in which the attacker injects malicious code into the Web app in order to trick it into sending things it shouldn't to other users of the Web site. Generally, this occurs due to errors in the application's code, which the attacker finds and exploits. XSS can lead to account takeovers, stolen data, or even a full takeover of the Web site or app. The nitty-gritty details of XSS, specific variants of the attack, and how to prevent them are things you'll learn more about in CompTIA Security+, but for the CompTIA A+ 1102 exam, be aware that cross-site scripting can pose a major threat to an organization's Web site(s).

SQL Injection   You've most likely deduced by now that accessing, stealing, and destroying data are common goals of malicious actors, so let's take a look at one of the favorite methods hackers use to achieve them. Before I can tell you about the dreaded SQL injection, I'm going to have to tell you what SQL is. SQL is an acronym for *Structured Query Language*. SQL is a language that enables a program to interact with a database using various commands and queries. If you've started thinking that attacking a database sounds like a dangerous threat, you're right. An *SQL injection* occurs when an attacker enters SQL commands into an input field like you'd see in a Web app, in order to gain access to data in a database that they shouldn't be able to see. You won't need to know the ins and outs of how SQL injection is performed, but know that preventing it is done at the programming level, with something known as *input validation*.

Unauthorized Access

Unauthorized access occurs when a person accesses resources without permission. "Resources" in this case means data, applications, and hardware. A user can alter or delete data; access sensitive information, such as financial data, personnel files, or e-mail messages; or use a computer for purposes the owner did not intend.

Not all unauthorized access is malicious—often this problem arises when users who are poking around in a computer out of curiosity or boredom discover they can access resources in a fashion the primary user did not have in mind. Unauthorized access becomes malicious when people knowingly and intentionally take advantage of weaknesses in your security to gain information, use resources, or destroy data!

One way to gain unauthorized access is intrusion. You might imagine someone kicking in a door and hacking into a computer, but more often than not it's someone sitting at a home computer, trying various passwords over the Internet. Not quite as glamorous, but it'll do. Another insidious method is manipulating people into giving privileged information or access that would be otherwise unavailable to a would-be attacker. This takes us into a discussion of one of the most common and dangerous categories of threats.

Social Engineering

Although you're more likely to lose data through accidents, the acts of malicious users get the headlines. Most of these attacks come under the heading of *social engineering*—the process of using or manipulating people inside the organization to gain access to its network or facilities—which covers the many ways humans can use other humans to gain unauthorized information. This information may be a network login, a credit card number, company customer data—almost anything you might imagine that one person or organization may not want outsiders to access.

 NOTE Social engineering attacks are often used together, so if you discover one of them being used against your organization, it's a good idea to look for others.

Social engineering attacks aren't hacking—at least in the classic sense of the word—but the goals are the same and the attacks will often be used by hackers in conjunction with other methods. Let's look at a few of the more classic types of social engineering attacks.

Infiltration Hackers can use *impersonation* to enter your building physically disguised as cleaning personnel, repair technicians, messengers, and so on. They then snoop around desks, looking for whatever they can find. They might talk with people inside the organization, gathering names, office numbers, department names—little things in and of themselves but powerful tools when combined later with other social engineering attacks.

Dressing the part of a legitimate user—with fake badge and everything—enables malicious people to gain access to locations and thus potentially your data. Following someone through the door, for example, as if you belong, is called *tailgating*. Tailgating is a common form of infiltration.

To combat tailgating, facilities often install a*n access control vestibule* at the entrance to sensitive areas, or sometimes at the entrance to the whole building. Traditionally called a *mantrap*, an access control vestibule is a small room with a set of two doors, one to the outside, unsecured area and one to the inner, secure area. When walking through the access control vestibule, the outer door must be closed before the inner door can be opened. In addition to the double doors, the user must present some form of authentication. For additional security, an access control vestibule is often controlled by a *security guard* who keeps an *entry control roster*. This document keeps a record of all comings and goings from the building.

Information Gathering You're probably familiar with the old saying that "knowledge is power." The good news is that when it comes to securing systems and facilities, the saying is true. The bad news is that it's also true when someone is trying to compromise those systems and facilities. Social engineering is often used by threat actors to gather information that makes it easier for them to successfully gain access. Here are some common ways that they get ahold of information that they aren't supposed to have.

Dumpster diving is the generic term for searching garbage for information. This is also a form of intrusion. The amount of sensitive information that makes it into any organization's trash bin boggles the mind! Years ago, I worked with an IT security guru who gave me and a few other IT people a tour of our office's trash. In one 20-minute tour of the personal wastebaskets of one office area, we had enough information to access the network easily, as well as to seriously embarrass more than a few people. When it comes to getting information, the trash is the place to look!

Shoulder surfing is another technique for gathering information and gaining unauthorized access. Shoulder surfing is simply observing someone's screen or keyboard to get information, often passwords. As the name implies, it usually requires the bad guy looking over your shoulder to see what you are doing.

Vishing   *Vishing* is one of the most common social engineering attacks. In this case, the attacker makes a phone call to someone in the organization to scam them into revealing information gain information. The attacker attempts to come across as someone inside the organization and uses this to get the desired information. Probably the most famous of these scams is the "I forgot my username and password" scam. In this gambit, the attacker first learns the account name of a legitimate person in the organization, usually using the infiltration method. The attacker then calls someone in the organization, usually the help desk, in an attempt to gather information, in this case a password.

> **Hacker:** "Hi, this is John Anderson in accounting. I forgot my password. Can you reset it, please?"
> **Help Desk:** "Sure, what's your username?"
> **Hacker:** "j_w_anderson."
> **Help Desk:** "OK, I reset it to e34rd3."

Vishing certainly isn't limited to attempts to get network access. There are documented vishing attacks against organizations aimed at getting cash, blackmail material, or other valuables.

Phishing   *Phishing* is the act of trying to get people to give their usernames, passwords, or other security information by pretending to be someone else electronically. A classic example is when a bad guy sends you an e-mail that's supposed to be from your local credit card company asking you to send them your username and password. Phishing is by far the most common form of social engineering done today.

Phishing refers to a fairly random act of badness. The attacker targets anyone silly enough to take the bait. *Spear phishing* is the term used for targeted attacks, like when a bad guy goes after a specific celebrity. The dangerous thing about spear phishing is that the bait can be carefully tailored using details from the target's life. A particularly dangerous form of phishing specifically targets people who are high up in an organization, such as executives or administrators. This is known as *whaling*.

Evil Twin   One of the reasons infiltrations can be so dangerous is that a malicious actor may be able to plant devices inside an organization's network. A particularly dangerous example of this is known as an *evil twin*. An evil twin is a fake wireless access point configured to mimic the traits of a legitimate device and network, in order to lure unsuspecting users to connect to the attacker's device. By doing this, the attacker can snoop on Internet traffic, steal user credentials, and use this information to do additional damage.

Insider Threats

Threats to your network or facility don't only come from the outside. Sometimes, the threat exists within the organization itself. This is known as an *insider threat*. An insider threat is any security risk that originates from a person inside an organization. Sometimes, the insider in question is malicious, out to steal funds or information. They may also be a disgruntled current or former employee looking to get back at the company.

Don't make the mistake of thinking that all insider threats are malicious though—sometimes accidents happen, and the insider threat is a well-meaning person just trying to make their or someone else's job easier. The real threat here is the access to systems and facilities that they have and what they can do with it. There are several ways to mitigate the risks of insider threats, most which center on access control. Only giving users access to what they need to do their jobs and deleting relevant user and administrator accounts when someone leaves the company are both examples of insider threat mitigation. Some methods to mitigate the risk of insider threats will be discussed in greater detail later in the chapter in the "Logical Security" section.

Data Destruction

Often an extension of unauthorized access, data destruction means more than just intentionally or accidentally erasing or corrupting data. It's easy to imagine some evil hacker accessing your network and deleting all your important files, but authorized users may also access certain data and then use that data beyond what they are authorized to do. A good example is the person who legitimately accesses a Microsoft Access product database to modify the product descriptions, only to discover that she can change the prices of the products, too.

This type of threat is particularly dangerous when users are not clearly informed about the extent to which they are authorized to make changes. A fellow tech once told me about a user who managed to mangle an important database when someone gave him incorrect access. When confronted, the user said: "If I wasn't allowed to change it, the system wouldn't let me do it!" Many users believe that systems are configured in a paternalistic way that wouldn't allow them to do anything inappropriate. As a result, users often assume they're authorized to make any changes they believe are necessary when working on a piece of data they know they're authorized to access.

Administrative Access

Every operating system enables you to create user accounts and grant those accounts a certain level of access to files and folders in that computer. As an administrator, supervisor, or root user, you have full control over just about every aspect of the computer. This increased control means these accounts can do vastly more damage when compromised, amplifying the danger of several other threats. The idea is to minimize both the number of accounts with full control and the time they spend logged in.

Even if a user absolutely needs this access, uses strong passwords, and practices good physical security, malware installed by a convincing spear phishing attack could leverage that control to access files, install software, and change settings a typical account couldn't touch.

System Crash/Hardware Failure

As with any technology, computers can and will fail—usually when you can least afford for it to happen. Hard drives crash, the power fails...it's all part of the joy of working in the computing business. You need to create redundancy in areas prone to failure (such as installing backup power in case of electrical failure) and perform those all-important data backups. A security-specific example would be having redundant firewalls to protect the network in the event that one of them fails. Chapter 14 goes into detail about using backups and other issues involved in creating a stable and reliable system.

Physical Theft

A fellow network geek once challenged me to try to bring down his newly installed network. He had just installed a powerful and expensive firewall router and was convinced that I couldn't get to a test server he added to his network just for me to try to access. After a few attempts to hack in over the Internet, I saw that I wasn't going to get anywhere that way.

So, I jumped in my car and drove to his office, having first outfitted myself in a techy-looking jumpsuit and an ancient ID badge I just happened to have in my sock drawer. I smiled sweetly at the receptionist and walked right by my friend's office (I noticed he was smugly monitoring incoming IP traffic by using some neato packet-sniffing program) to his new server.

I quickly pulled the wires out of the back of his precious server, picked it up, and walked out the door. The receptionist was too busy trying to figure out why her e-mail wasn't working to notice me as I whisked by her carrying the 65-pound server box. I stopped in the hall and called him from my cell phone.

> **Me (cheerily):** "Dude, I got all your data!"
> **Him (not cheerily):** "You rebooted my server! How did you do it?"
> **Me (smiling):** "I didn't reboot it—go over and look at it!"
> **Him (really mad now):** "YOU <EXPLETIVE> THIEF! YOU STOLE MY SERVER!"
> **Me (cordially):** "Why, yes. Yes, I did. Give me two days to hack your password in the comfort of my home, and I'll see everything! Bye!"

I immediately walked back in and handed him the test server. It was fun. The moral here is simple: Never forget that the best network software security measures can be rendered useless if you fail to protect your systems physically!

Protecting Laptops Physical security for your systems extends beyond the confines of the office as well. The very thing that makes laptops portable also makes them tempting targets for thieves. One of the simplest ways to protect your laptop is to use a basic *cable lock*. The idea is to loop the cable around a solid object, such as a bed frame, and secure the lock to the small security hole on the side of the laptop.

Malware

Networks are without a doubt the fastest and most efficient vehicles for transferring computer viruses among systems. News reports focus attention on the many malicious software attacks from the Internet, but a huge number of such attacks still come from users who bring in programs on optical discs and USB drives. The "Network Security" section of this chapter describes the various methods of virus infection and other malware and what you need to do to prevent such attacks from damaging your networked systems.

Spam

If you have an e-mail address, there's a 100 percent chance that you've seen spam at some point in your life. *Spam* is the digital equivalent of junk mail; it's bulk e-mail sent out to as many people as possible in the hopes that at least some of them engage with it. Sometimes spam is just an annoyance, but it can also be a threat to your network. Phishing attempts, malicious links, and attachments that contain malware are just some of the dangers that spam can present. *Spam management* methods and tools were covered in detail back in Chapter 19.

Vulnerabilities

Threats to your computers and facilities can be scary, but they need some way to gain access before they can cause trouble. Threats compromise a system by exploiting vulnerabilities in a computer, network, company policy, or physical security to gain access. Once a vulnerability is exploited, whether by an outside hacker, a disgruntled employee, or even inadvertently by a well-meaning person just trying to make their job easier, chaos can ensue. Data deletion, data theft, extortion, and all sorts of other nasty things can happen if vulnerabilities aren't identified and addressed. As a CompTIA A+ technician, you likely won't be expected to know the nitty-gritty details of how to fix all vulnerabilities, but you should understand the fundamentals of different types of vulnerability, and how they can threaten an organization. Here are a few common vulnerabilities that you may run across while working as a technician.

Have you ever been working on your computer, playing a game, or having a Zoom meeting, and suddenly your operating system nags you to install updates that require a reboot? I know I have, and as disruptive as that can be, the disruptions that could result from ignoring those messages are even worse. That's because these warnings are telling you to patch your operating system, and oftentimes, those patches are intended to address a security risk. *Unpatched systems* are vulnerable to an ever-growing list of vulnerabilities that attackers know about and are actively exploiting. Leaving a system unpatched is like leaving a second-story window open while you go on vacation. Sure, you may get home and see that everything is fine, but you may also have been robbed blind. Patching systems is key and will be discussed in more detail later in this chapter when we address malware prevention.

If leaving your systems unpatched is like leaving a second-story window open when you go on vacation, an unprotected system is like leaving your front door open with a sign on the lawn inviting people to break in. An *unprotected system* lacks key security tools like anti-malware software and firewalls. Without these in place, there is nothing stopping a hacker from doing whatever they want in your network. They can send malware, try to connect directly to your internal network, and try to steal or destroy your sensitive information, and do all of this with a relatively low chance of being detected. An unprotected system is a serious vulnerability, whether it's at home, in a small business, or in a major corporation. If you must have unprotected systems, make sure to isolate and monitor them!

Operating systems also have lifespans. Over time, as new and sometimes improved operating systems launch, older ones are phased out. Once an old OS is phased out completely, it stops receiving security updates as new vulnerabilities are discovered. These operating systems are known as *end-of-life (EOL) operating systems* and can present a major vulnerability to a network if even one device is still using an EOL OS. It's a fairly common problem, because operating system upgrades can be expensive and disruptive to a business's operations. Regardless, making sure that operating systems are well supported and still receiving regular security updates is an important way to mitigate vulnerabilities.

While the concept of *bring your own device (BYOD)* was discussed in the context of securing mobile devices back in Chapter 25, the potential security risks extend past mobile devices to personal laptops as well. While BYOD may be popular with employees and more friendly to an organization's budget, BYOD can also be a security vulnerability. An external threat can use the fact that personal devices may not all be maintained with standard security features to gain access from the outside. Additionally, insider threats, whether malicious or accidental, can use personal devices to introduce malware, or remove privileged data from the security of the company's internal network.

In the best of all possible worlds, your organization will use a mix of policies, systems, and elbow grease to ensure the devices in your networks never have vulnerabilities like these. But in reality, a system may need to defer updates for weeks while it's busy rendering special effects. Users may need time to comply or need network access to do it. The accounting department might require software that only works on an EOL OS. A computer that serves as the interface to an old ICS system may not even have a software firewall (we'll look at these later in the chapter). Unless you check compliance continually, new violations will appear between checks. In short, compliance is an aspiration, and you'll often have to manage the vulnerabilities and risks that *non-compliant systems* represent (often by isolating them and monitoring them well).

Security Concepts and Technologies

Once you've assessed the threats to your computers and networks, you need to take steps to protect those valuable resources. Depending on the complexity of your organization, this can be a small job encompassing some basic security concepts and procedures, or it can be exceedingly complex. The security needs for a three-person desktop publishing firm, for example, would differ wildly from those of a defense contractor supplying top-secret toys to the Pentagon.

From a CompTIA A+ certified technician's perspective, you need to understand the big picture (that's the strategic side), knowing the concepts and available technologies for security. At the implementation level (that's the tactical side), you're expected to know where to find such things as security policies in Windows. A CompTIA Network+ or CompTIA Security+ tech will give you the specific options to implement. (The exception to this level of knowledge comes in dealing with malicious software such as viruses, but we'll tackle that subject in the second half of the chapter.)

Controlling access is the key. If you can control access to the data, programs, and other computing resources, you've secured your systems. *Access control* is composed of interlinked areas of physical and logical security that a good security-minded tech should think about: physical security, authentication, users and groups, and security policies. Much of this you know from previous chapters, but this section should help tie it all together as a security topic. The first step is understanding physical security, which includes methods of preventing physical access to facilities, systems, and information, and the second is understanding logical security to learn how to protect your network, authenticate users, and employ effective security policies.

Physical Security

For most people, when they hear the word security, the first thing they think of are things like guards, fences, security cameras, and the like. That's because they're thinking about physical security. Physical security is often the first line of defense for an organization. It includes the fences and gates that keep people off the property, the locks that keep people from entering a building or area they aren't supposed to, and the guards who use surveillance tools and alerts to keep an eye on things. *Physical security* is all about defending facilities and systems from—you guessed it—physical threats, both internal and external. There are layers to physical security that can and often do overlap with logical security tools to provide effective security coverage. Let's start our investigation by looking at some specific goals and methods of physical security.

Securing Facilities

The first order of security is limiting access to your physical hardware. The security market is huge, but the options basically boil down to fences, doors, locks, alarms, and keeping a close eye on things. The first step is understanding that all of these pieces can (and will) fail or be beaten; great security involves arranging and layering many pieces so that they can enhance each other's strengths and compensate for each other's weaknesses.

Think back to the access control vestibule introduced earlier in the chapter. A low-tech solution like a traditional door lock is just a speed-bump to someone with a lock-pick and a moment alone with the lock. Access control vestibules are great because they combine simple measures like doors, *door locks*, *security guards*, and an entry control roster in a way that is much harder to beat than one or two locked doors. Some facilities may enhance their entrance security further by adding a *magnetometer*, better known as a metal detector. As pointed out earlier in the chapter when we talked about different types of threats, some threats originate from inside the organization as well as outside. A metal detector is a good way to help prevent people from bringing in dangerous items that they could use to cause harm, and to prevent them from walking out with something that doesn't belong to them.

Sometimes access control needs to be extended past the door itself, out to the property. Many facilities have more than one entrance, or multiple buildings. As a result, organizations may add an additional line of defense to keep unauthorized people off company property altogether. *Fences* are often used to stop people from snooping around where they aren't supposed to. *Bollards*, those short concrete or metal posts that you'll sometimes see in areas with heavy foot traffic, can be used to prevent vehicles from getting too close for comfort (see Figure 27-1).

Figure 27-1
Example of
a bollard

Security guards are great, but they can't be everywhere at once. They need some way to keep an eye on things. That's where the following tools come into play:

- Video surveillance can be used by security personnel to monitor the facility from a centralized location.

- Good *lighting* makes it harder for a would-be bad guy to avoid detection, with the added benefit of decreasing the likelihood of workplace accidents for staff.

- *Motion sensors* can be used to let them know if someone or something is detected so they can take a closer look.

- *Alarm systems* can serve a variety of functions, from warning the IT department of an attempted network breach, to informing staff of a security issue, to alerting security staff or law enforcement if a break-in happens after hours.

Any combination of these tools makes a great addition to a robust security plan, but it's also important to make sure that people inside the organization don't have access to things they aren't supposed to. This brings us to the next set of access control options.

Traditional door locks aren't terrible, but keys are easy to copy and the cost of frequently re-keying locks adds up fast. An organization ready to move beyond the basics can step up to a keyless lock system driven by employee *ID badges*—especially ones with authentication tools such as *radio frequency identification (RFID)* or smart cards (see "Authentication," later in this chapter)—to control building and room access. Figure 27-2 shows a typical badge.

Figure 27-2
Typical employee
badge/smart
card

Lock Down Systems

Once an attacker has physical access to the building, protecting your hardware gets a lot harder. There are some options here, but don't plan on them doing much more than slow someone down by a few minutes and make it obvious to anyone watching that they're up to no good:

- Lock the doors to your workspaces. A fast, reliable keyless lock system can make it painless to lock them even when the user steps out for a moment.
- *Equipment locks* can keep someone from quickly walking off with the hardware.
- *USB locks* make it harder to plug in a USB drive to load malware for stealing data.
- *RJ45 locks* limit an intruder's ability to gain access to the wired network.
- *Server locks* limit access to a server's ports and drives. There are also locking rack doors to limit access to the front or back of an entire server rack.

These devices are meaningless if an intruder can walk in like they belong, sit down at an unattended, logged-in computer, and get to work. Don't leave a logged-in PC unattended, even if it's just a Standard or Guest user. May the gods help you if you walk away from a server still logged in as an administrator. You're tempting fate.

If you must step away for a moment, manually lock the computer (or screen) with a hotkey or the primary OS menu. On a Windows system, just press WINDOWS-L on the keyboard to lock it. It's also a good idea to set up a screensaver with a short wait time and configure it to show the logon screen on resume.

EXAM TIP If you're in charge of multiple-user security best practices, using screensaver locks—configured to show the logon screen on resume—can help a lot with users who might forget to lock their systems when taking a break or going to lunch. Both Windows and macOS enable you to take this a step further and set automatic *timeout* and a *screen lock*, where the screen goes blank after a few minutes and a password is required for logon.

Protect Sensitive Information

Locking unattended systems is a great habit, but it won't help much if the intruder manages to watch the user enter their password or is able to read it off a sticky note on the monitor. Don't write down passwords and leave them in plain sight. Teach users to follow the strong password guidelines set forth in Chapter 13. Be aware of the risk of shoulder surfing. Ideally, the office layout should make it impossible for someone to watch the user without their knowledge.

If users need to work with sensitive information anywhere someone unauthorized could see the screen, they may need a privacy filter (also called a privacy screen)—a framed sheet or film that you apply to the front of your monitor. Privacy filters reduce the viewing angle, making it impossible to see the screen unless you're directly in front of it (see Figure 27-3). Lock up paper copies of critical, personal, or sensitive documents out of sight and shred any you don't need immediately.

Figure 27-3 Privacy filter

Logical Security

While physical security is focused on preventing unauthorized access to facilities and equipment, *logical security* is primarily focused on denying access to computers and data. Logical and physical security features are generally combined for maximum effectiveness. In some cases, like with biometrics, the security tool can be used for both logical and physical security applications. Let's dig deeper into some of the more commonly implemented logical security controls.

MAC Address Filtering

It's far from bulletproof, but if an attacker does gain physical access to your site, you may be able to throw up another hurdle to limit their ability to access your network with any of their own devices. Both wired and wireless networks can use *MAC filtering* to enable you to *blacklist* or *whitelist* devices based on their MAC address.

Use a *blacklist* to block specific computers, adding their MAC addresses to the ranks of the undesired. You can use a *whitelist* to pre-specify the only MAC addresses allowed access. I say this isn't bulletproof because a savvy attacker *can* spoof an address (they'll have a much easier time sniffing a valid Wi-Fi MAC address than a wired one, though) from another device accessing the network.

Keeping devices you don't control out of your network is a big win! If the attacker can't gain access to your network with one of their own devices (which they have probably preloaded with tools for attacking your systems or network), they'll have to resort to breaking into one of your devices to do the heavy lifting.

MAC addresses aren't the only way to filter traffic to and from your network. IP addresses can also be used to help keep unwanted traffic from entering or leaving your network. Like MAC filtering, IP filtering is a tool often available with routers and firewalls. *IP filtering* enables an administrator to set rules about whether packets should be sent or received based on the source or destination IP address. IP filtering isn't a surefire solution to security issues, but it can be an extra hurdle in the same way MAC filtering is.

Authentication

Security requires properly implemented *authentication*, which means in essence how the computer determines who can or should access it and, once accessed, what that user can do. A computer can authenticate users through software or hardware, or a combination of both.

You can categorize ways to authenticate into three broad areas: knowledge factors, ownership factors, and inherence factors. You read about *multifactor authentication* in detail in Chapter 25 in the context of mobile device security. It works the same way when securing a desktop computer, a laptop, a server, or a building. There's no reason to rehash it here. The only thing to add is that many organizations use *two-factor authentication*. An example is a key fob that generates a numeric key. A user authenticates by entering his or her username and password (something the user knows) and enters the key (something the user has) when prompted. Another popular method of authentication is to use an authenticator application. An *authenticator application* adds an additional layer of security similar to many multifactor authentication methods, by generating some form of key or password to be entered in conjunction with standard login credentials.

EXAM TIP The CompTIA A+ 1102 exam will quiz you on multifactor and two-factor authentication. This applies to all computing devices.

Software Authentication: Proper Passwords It's still rather shocking to me to power up a friend's computer and go straight to his or her desktop, or with my married-with-kids friends, to click one of the parents' user account icons and not be prompted for a password. This is just wrong! I'm always tempted to assign passwords right then and there—and not tell them the passwords, of course—so they'll see the error of their ways when they try to log on next. I don't do it but always try to explain gently the importance of good passwords.

You know about passwords from Chapter 13, so I won't belabor the point here. Suffice it to say that you must require that your users have proper passwords. Don't let them write passwords down or tape them to the underside of their mouse pads either!

It's not just access to Windows that you need to think about. There's always the temptation for people to do other mean things, such as change CMOS settings, open up the case, and even steal hard drives. Any of these actions renders the computer inoperable to the casual user until a tech can undo the damage or replace components. All modern CMOS setup utilities come with a number of tools to protect your computer, such as drive lock, intrusion detection, and of course system access BIOS/UEFI passwords such as the one shown in Figure 27-4. Refer to Chapter 5 to refresh yourself on what you can do at a BIOS level to protect your computer.

Figure 27-4
BIOS/UEFI
access password
request

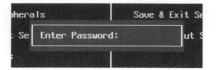

Hardware Authentication Gates, doors, and computers can make use of *badge readers*, *smart card readers*, and *biometric scanners* to authenticate users with more authority than mere passwords. *Smart cards* are credit card–sized cards with circuitry that can identify the bearer of the card. Smart cards are relatively common for tasks such as authenticating users for mass transit systems but are fairly uncommon in computers. Figure 27-5 shows a smart card and keyboard combination.

Figure 27-5
Keyboard-
mounted smart
card reader
being used for
a commercial
application
(photo courtesy
of Cherry Corp.)

Security tokens are devices that store some unique information that the user carries on their person. They may be digital certificates, passwords, or biometric data. They may also store an RSA token. *RSA tokens* are random-number generators that are used with usernames and passwords to ensure extra security. Most security *hard tokens* come in the form of *key fobs*, as shown in Figure 27-6.

Figure 27-6
RSA key fob
(photo courtesy
of EMC Corp.)

Apps and services that use security codes usually prompt you to enter the code after you supply your username and password. Some offer to send you a code via e-mail, text message (via short message service [SMS]), or voice call. Figure 27-7 shows PayPal prompting me for a code from my authenticator app (left) and my bank offering to send me a security code (right).

Figure 27-7 Prompt for a security code (left) and offer to send a security code (right)

An authenticator application is a software security token (a soft token) that turns a mobile device into a security token. As shown in Figure 27-8, these apps can generate a security code like the one on the RSA key fob shown previously in Figure 27-6. Hardware tokens are more secure than soft tokens and send-a-code options.

Figure 27-8
Getting a security code from my authenticator app

People can guess or discover passwords, but it's a lot harder to forge someone's fingerprints. The Apple keyboard shown in Figure 27-9 authenticates users on a local machine by using a *fingerprint scanner*. Other devices that will do the trick are key fobs, retina scanners, and palmprint scanners. Devices that require some sort of physical, flesh-and-blood authentication are called *biometric scanners* or *biometric locks*. In some rare cases, an organization may decide that fingerprints just aren't enough authentication. In these cases, you may find the much newer *palmprint reader*. Palmprint is a bit of a misnomer, as what the scanner is actually doing is using infrared light to map the unique structure of veins in your palm. Advantages of a palmprint reader include being much more difficult, if not impossible, to fake, and the fact that it requires a person to have blood flow, which is a built-in guarantee that the person being authenticated is alive.

Figure 27-9
Apple TouchID
fingerprint
reader on a
MacBook Air

The main disadvantage is cost, with palmprint readers often costing significantly more than their fingerprint scanning counterparts.

Clever manufacturers have developed key fobs and smart cards that use RFID to transmit authentication information so users don't have to insert something into a computer or card reader. The Privaris plusID combines, for example, a biometric fingerprint fob with an RFID tag that makes security as easy as opening a garage door remotely!

Retina scanners loom large in media as a form of biometric security, where you place your eye up to a scanning device. While retina scanners do exist, I have been in hundreds of high-security facilities and have only seen one retina scanner in operation in almost 30 years as a tech. Figure 27-10 shows about the only image of a retina scanner in operation you'll ever encounter.

Figure 27-10
Retina scanner in
Half-Life 2

Current smartphones and tablets use full facial recognition for identification and authentication, although they also use passcodes for when the recognition fails.

Figure 27-11 shows a user logging in to an Apple iPhone via facial recognition. (Note the open lock. Hard to show the process in action because it happens so fast!)

Figure 27-11
Unlocking an
iPhone via facial
recognition

Users and Groups

Windows uses user accounts and groups as the bedrock of access control. A user account is assigned to a group, such as Users, Power Users, or Administrators, and by association gets certain permissions on the computer. Using NTFS enables the highest level of control over data resources.

Assigning users to groups is a great first step in controlling a local machine, but this feature really shines in a networked environment. Let's take a look.

NOTE The file system on a hard drive matters a lot when it comes to security. On modern systems, the file system on the boot drive has support for an *access control list (ACL)*, a rich form of user and groups permissions. But this security only extends to drives/cards formatted with modern file systems such as NTFS, APFS, HFS+, and ext3/4. If you copy a file to a drive/card formatted with exFAT or the older FAT32, such as many cameras and USB flash drives use, the OS will strip all permissions and the file will be available for anyone to read!

Access to user accounts should be restricted to the assigned individuals, and those who configure the permissions to those accounts must follow the *principle of least privilege*: accounts should have permission to access only the resources they need and no more. Tight control of user accounts is critical to preventing unauthorized access. Disabling unused accounts is an important part of this strategy, but good user account management goes far deeper than that.

Groups are a great way to achieve increased complexity without increasing the administrative burden on network administrators, because all operating systems combine permissions. When a user is a member of more than one group, which permissions does that user have with respect to any particular resource? In all operating systems, the permissions of the groups are *combined*, and the result is what you call the *effective permissions* the user has to access a resource. As an example, if Rita is a member of the Sales group, which has List Folder Contents permission to a folder, and she is also a member of the Managers group, which has Read and Execute permissions to the same folder, Rita will have both List Folder Contents *and* Read and Execute permissions to that folder.

Watch out for *default user accounts and groups*—they can become secret backdoors to your network! All network operating systems have a default Everyone group that can be used to sneak into shared resources easily. This Everyone group, as its name implies, literally includes anyone who connects to that resource. Windows gives full control to the Everyone group by default, for example, so make sure you know to lock this down! The other scary one is the Guest account. The Guest account is the only way to access a system without a username and password. Unless you have a compelling reason to provide guest access, you should always make sure the Guest account is disabled.

All of the default groups—Everyone, Guest, Users—define broad groups of users. Never use them unless you intend to permit all of those folks access to a resource. If you use one of the default groups, remember to configure it with the proper permissions to prevent users from doing things you don't want them to do with a shared resource!

 NOTE You can use directory permissions to limit access to sensitive information on a shared file server, protect user-specific files from snooping by other users on a multiuser system, and protect the system's own software from being compromised by any scripts or programs the user runs. The job doesn't end here, though! Anyone with physical access to a drive can ignore your controls. Use full-disk *data-at-rest encryption* to protect data (data in storage, not in use or moving around the network).

Security Policies

We've already discussed policies in Chapters 13 and 19, but let's do a quick review and then see how we put it all together to help secure a network. Although permissions control how users access shared resources, there are other functions you should control that are outside the scope of resources. For example, do you want users to be able to access a command prompt on their Windows system? Do you want users to be able to install software? Would you like to control what systems a user can log on to or at what time of day a user can log on? All network operating systems provide you with some capability to control these and literally hundreds of other security parameters, under what Windows calls *policies*. I like to think of policies as permissions for activities, as opposed to true permissions, which control access to resources.

A policy is usually applied to a user account, a computer, or a group. Let's use the example of a network composed of Windows systems with a Windows Server. Every Windows client has its own local policies program, which enables policies to be placed on that system only. Figure 27-12 shows the tool you use to set local policies on an individual system, called *Local Security Policy*, being used to deny the Guest account the capability to log on locally.

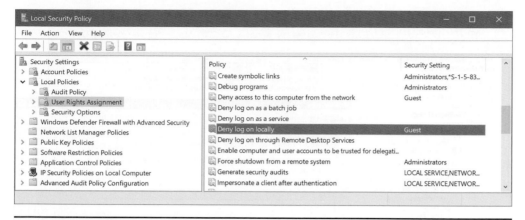

Figure 27-12   Local Security Policy

Local policies work great for individual systems, but they can be a pain to configure if you want to apply the same settings to more than one PC on your network. If you want to apply policy settings en masse, you need to step up to features of domain-based Windows Active Directory. You can use *organizational units (OUs)* that organize users and devices logically into a folder-like hierarchy; then exercise deity-like (Microsoft prefers the term granular) control to apply a different *group policy* to the network clients in each unit.

One important thing to keep in mind about Active Directory group policies is that they supersede local policies. For example, if you have a local policy in place that allows a specific user to install third-party software, then set a group policy for the domain that prevents all users from doing so, the user won't be able to install the software. If you run into a situation like this, you'll find that the gpupdate and gpresult commands we discussed back in Chapter 15 are helpful. They're a quick way to double-check which group policies are applied to which users and make changes if there's a conflict. Now let me explain group policy a little more and show you some examples of what it can do.

 EXAM TIP   Group policy changes may not immediately apply to all systems. Windows will fetch the group policy when the system boots or someone logs in. It will also refresh the policy from time to time while running, though some policy changes won't apply without a reboot anyways. You can run gpupdate/force from the command line to update group policy for a specific computer immediately.

Want to set the default wallpaper for every PC in your domain? Group policy can do that. Want to make certain tools inaccessible to everyone but authorized users? Group policy can do that, too. Want to control access to the Internet, redirect home folders, run scripts, deploy software, or just remind folks that unauthorized access to the network will get them nowhere fast? Group policy is the answer. Figure 27-13 shows group policy; I'm about to change the default title on every instance of Internet Explorer on every computer in my domain!

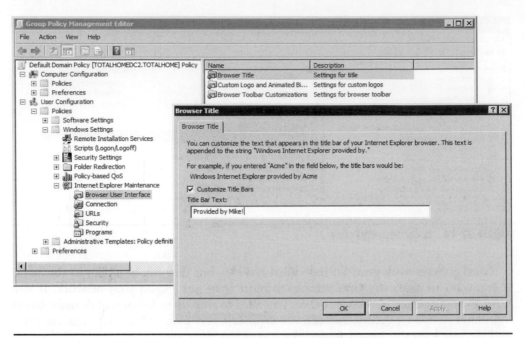

Figure 27-13 Using group policy to make IE title say "Provided by Mike!"

That's just one simple example of the settings you can configure by using group policy. You can apply literally hundreds of tweaks through group policy, from the great to the small, but don't worry too much about familiarizing yourself with each and every one. Group policy settings are a big topic on most of the Microsoft certification tracks, but for the purposes of the CompTIA A+ exams, you simply have to be comfortable with the concept behind group policy.

Although I could never list every possible policy you can enable on a Windows system, here's a list of some commonly used ones:

- **Prevent Registry Edits** If you try to edit the Registry, you get a failure message.

- **Prevent Access to the Command Prompt** Keeps users from getting to the command prompt by turning off the Run command and the Command Prompt shortcut.

- **Log On Locally** Defines who may log on to the system locally.

- **Shut Down System** Defines who may shut down the system.

- **Minimum Password Length** Forces a minimum password length.

- **Account Lockout Threshold** Sets the maximum number of logon attempts a person can make before being locked out of the account.

- **Disable Windows Installer** Prevents users from installing software.

- **Printer Browsing** Enables users to browse for printers on the network, as opposed to using only assigned printers.

Although the CompTIA A+ exams don't expect you to know how to implement policies on any type of network, you are expected to understand that policies exist, especially on Windows networks, and that they can do amazing things to control what users can do on their systems. If you ever try to get to a command prompt on a Windows system only to discover the Run command is dimmed, blame it on a policy, not the computer!

 EXAM TIP Account management security policy best practices dictate that you should implement restrictive user permissions, login time restrictions, account lockout based on failed attempts, disable guest accounts, and disable the operating system's built-in AutoRun or AutoPlay features. Finally, you should always change default system usernames and passwords where possible.

Network Security

Networks are under threat from the outside as well, so this section looks at issues involving Internet-borne attacks, firewalls, and wireless networking. This content is the security bread and butter for a CompTIA A+ technician, so you need to understand the concepts and procedures and be able to implement them properly.

Malicious Software

The beauty of the Internet is the ease of accessing resources just about anywhere on the globe, all from the comfort of your favorite chair. This connection, however, runs both ways, and people from all over the world can potentially access your computer from the comfort of their evil lairs. The Internet is awash with malicious software that is, even at this moment, trying to infect your systems.

The term *malware* defines any program or code that's designed to do something on a system or network that you don't want done. Malware comes in quite a variety of guises, such as viruses, worms, ransomware, spyware, Trojan horses, keyloggers, cryptojacking, and rootkits. Let's examine all these forms of malware, look at what they do to infected systems, and then examine how these nasties get onto your machines in the first place.

Forms of Malware

Malware has been pestering PC users since the 1980s and has evolved into many forms over the years. From the classic boot sector viruses of the '90s to the more recent threats of ransomware and attacks on critical infrastructure, malware is an ever-changing threat to your users and data. To better understand these threats, you need to understand the different forms that malware can take.

Virus A *virus* is a program that has two jobs: to replicate and to activate. *Replication* means it makes copies of itself, by injecting itself as extra code added to the end of executable programs, or by hiding out in a drive's boot sector. *Boot sector viruses* can be particularly nasty because they live inside your system's boot partition and activate their malicious code before the security software is able to start up and prevent it. *Activation* is when a virus does something like corrupting data or stealing private information.

A virus only replicates to other drives, such as thumb drives or optical media. It does not self-replicate across networks. A virus needs human action to spread.

Worm   A *worm* functions similarly to a virus, except it does not need to attach itself to other programs to replicate. It can replicate on its own through networks, or even hardware like Thunderbolt accessories. If the infected computer is on a network, a worm will start scanning the network for other vulnerable systems to infect.

Trojan   A *Trojan* (named for the Trojan Horse) is a piece of malware that appears or pretends to do one thing while, at the same time, it does something evil. A Trojan horse may be a game, like poker, or ironically, a fake security program. The sky is the limit. Once installed, a Trojan horse can have a hold on the system as tenacious as any virus or worm; a key difference is that installed Trojan horses do not replicate.

Keylogger   *Keylogger* malware does pretty much what you might imagine, recording the user's keystrokes and making that information available to the programmer. You'll find keylogging functions as part of other malware as well. Keyloggers are not solely evil; a lot of parental control tools use keyloggers.

Rootkit   For malware to succeed, it often needs to come up with some method to hide itself. As awareness of malware has grown, anti-malware programs make it harder to find new locations on a computer to hide malware. A *rootkit* is a program that takes advantage of very low-level operating system functions to hide itself from all but the most aggressive of anti-malware tools. Worse, a rootkit, by definition, gains privileged access to the computer. Rootkits can strike operating systems, hypervisors, and even firmware (including hard drives and accessories . . . yikes!).

The most infamous rootkit appeared a while back as an antipiracy attempt by Sony on its music CDs. Unfortunately for the media giant, the rootkit software installed when you played a music CD and opened a backdoor that could be used maliciously.

Cryptominers   Malicious actors are often motivated by financial gain, so sometimes, they try to kill two birds with one stone by installing malware that can mine cryptocurrency. These *cryptominers* take control of a computer's hardware resources and use them to mine cryptocurrency, which is then deposited into a crypto wallet belonging to the attacker. A telltale sign a system is infected with this kind of malware may be inexplicably high GPU or CPU utilization. There are other problems that can lead to excessive hardware utilization, but if you see it, it might be a good idea to check for cryptominer malware.

Behavior

Knowing what form the malware takes is all well and good, but what really matters is how "mal" the malware will be when it's running rampant on a system. To get things started, let's dive into an old favorite: spyware.

Spyware   *Spyware*—malicious software, generally installed without your knowledge—can use your computer's resources to run distributed computing applications, capture keystrokes to steal passwords, or worse. Classic spyware often sneaks onto systems by being bundled with legitimate software—software that functions correctly and provides some form of benefit to the user. What kind of benefit? Way back in 2005, Movieland (otherwise known as Movieland.com and Popcorn.net) released a "handy" movie download service. They didn't tell users, of course, that everyone who installed the software was "automatically enrolled" in a three-day trial. If you didn't cancel the "trial," a pop-up window filled your screen demanding you pay them for the service that you never signed up for. The worst part, however, was that you couldn't uninstall the application completely. The uninstaller redirected users to a Web page demanding money again. (Movieland was shut down in 2007.)

For another classic example, look at Figure 27-14: the dialog box asks the user if she trusts the Gator Corporation (a well-known spyware producer from ages ago). Because everyone eventually knew not to trust Gator, they would click No, and the company faded away.

Figure 27-14
Classic Gator
Corporation's
acknowledgment
warning

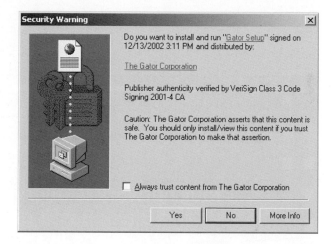

If Movieland was a problem back in 2005, what are the big spyware applications today? Unfortunately, I can't tell you—not because it's a secret, but because we don't know about them yet. You'll probably only run into spyware these days on the CompTIA A+ 1102 exam.

Ransomware   As bad as spyware can be, at least you still have access to your data. *Ransomware*, on the other hand, encrypts all the data it can gain access to on a system. To top it off, many versions of ransomware can even encrypt data on mapped network drives!

EXAM TIP   Know the various types of malware, including viruses, worms, Trojan horses, keyloggers, rootkits, cryptominers, spyware, and ransomware.

Once it has locked up all your data, the ransomware application pops up a message asking for money (often bitcoins) to decrypt your data (see Figure 27-15). Also, to encourage a faster payment, this ransom is presented with a timer that, when it reaches 0, triggers deletion of the encryption keys, leaving you with a drive full of scrambled data. In some particularly dastardly cases, the ransomware doesn't actually have the ability to decrypt built in, and will just leave your drives encrypted or wipe the data altogether when that clock hits 0.

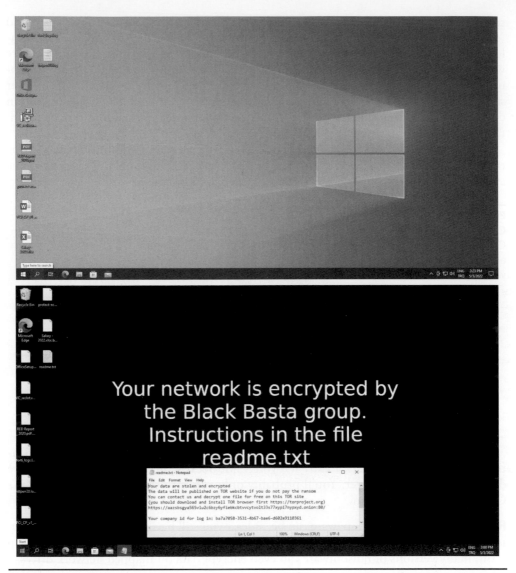

Figure 27-15 Clean computer (top) and same computer (bottom) encrypted by Black Basta group malware (Courtesy of National Cyber Labs)

A Bot on the Net Full of Zombies   Another type of malware I want to talk about is the botnet ("bot" as in robot, get it!). As we touched on when we discussed Denial of Service attacks, a *botnet*, as "net" in its name implies, isn't a single type of malware, but rather, a network of infected computers (*zombies*) under the control of a single person or group. Botnets can be massive, easily growing into the millions of zombies for the largest networks.

With that many machines under their control, botnet operators have command of massive computing and network resources. Some of the most common uses of botnets are sending spam or launching distributed denial of service attacks. If you've ever wondered how spammers and hackers pay for all that bandwidth, they don't! They use the bandwidth of millions of zombie machines spread all around the world, from grandma's e-mail machine to hacked Web servers.

Spam is but one use of a botnet. The criminals who run these networks also use all that collective power to launch a DDoS attack against companies and governments and demand a ransom to call off the attack.

Malware Signs and Symptoms

If your PC has been infected by malware, you'll bump into some strange things before you can even run an anti-malware scan. Like a medical condition, malware causes unusual symptoms that should stand out from your everyday computer use. You need to become a PC physician and understand what each of these symptoms means.

Malware's biggest strength is its flexibility: it can look like anything. In fact, a lot of malware attacks can feel like normal PC "wonkiness"—momentary slowdowns, random one-time crashes, and so on. Knowing when a weird application crash is actually a malware attack is half the battle.

Slow performance in a PC can mean you're running too many applications at once, or that you've been hit with malware. Applications can crash at random, even if you don't have too many loaded. How do you tell the difference? In this case, it's the frequency. If it's happening a lot, even when all of your applications are closed, you've got a problem. This goes for frequent lockups, too—whether it seems to be *PC-* or *OS-based lockups*. If Windows starts misbehaving (more than usual), run your anti-malware application right away.

Malware, however, doesn't always jump out at you with big system crashes. Some malware tries to rename system files, change file permissions, or hide files completely. You might start getting e-mail messages from colleagues or friends questioning a message "you" sent to them that seemed spammy. You might get *automated replies from unknown sent e-mail* that you know you didn't send. An increase in *desktop alerts* that don't seem to have a legitimate cause, or *unwanted notifications within the OS* may also be signs that it's time to check for malware. You may even get *false alerts regarding your computer's antivirus protection*. Most of these issues are easily caught by a regular anti-malware scan, so as long as you remain vigilant, you'll be okay.

 NOTE While it's not necessarily a malware attack, watch out for **hijacked e-mail** accounts belonging either to you or to someone you know. Hackers can hit both e-mail clients and Webmail users. If you start receiving some fishy (or phishy) e-mail messages, change your Webmail username and password and scan your PC for malware.

Some malware even fights back, defending itself from your many attempts to remove it. If your Windows Update feature stops working, preventing you from patching your PC, you've got malware. (CompTIA speak: *OS update failures*.) If other tools and utilities throw up an "Access Denied" road block, you've got malware. If you lose all Internet connectivity, either the malware is stopping you or the process of removing the malware broke your connection. (CompTIA refers to this as being *unable to access the network*, which seems very polite.) In this case, you might need to reconfigure your Internet connection: reinstall your NIC and its drivers, reboot your router, and so on.

Even your browser and anti-malware applications can turn against you. If you type in one Web address and end up at a different site than you anticipated, this is known as a *browser redirection* and it means that a malware infection might have overwritten your *hosts* file. The hosts file overrules any DNS settings and can redirect your browser to whatever site the malware adds to the file. Most browser redirections point you to phishing scams or Web sites full of free downloads (that are, of course, covered in even more malware). In fact, some free anti-malware applications are actually malware—what techs call *rogue anti-malware* programs. You can avoid these rogue applications by sticking to the recommended lists of anti-malware software found online at reputable tech sites, like Ars Technica, Tom's Hardware, Anandtech, and others. *Random/frequent pop-ups* can be another annoying sign that your system is infected with some form of malware. *Pop-up* blocking has become fairly effective over the years, so if you've already ruled out the possibility that the browser isn't up to date or that the pop-up blocker is off, it may be time to start looking for malware.

Watch for security alerts in Windows, either from Windows' built-in security tools or from your third-party anti-malware program. Windows built-in tools alert you via the Action Center or the Windows Defender Security Center (Windows 10/11). The notification in Figure 27-16 is prompting us to activate Defender Antivirus.

Figure 27-16
Notification
to activate
Defender
Antivirus in
Windows 11

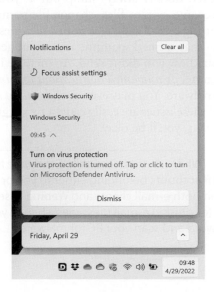

You don't configure much here; it just tells you whether or not you are protected. The Action Center or Security Center will pop up a notification in the notification area whenever Windows detects a problem.

Malware Prevention and Recovery

The only way to permanently protect your PC from malware is to disconnect it from the Internet and never permit any potentially infected software to touch your precious computer. Because neither scenario is likely these days, you need to use specialized anti-malware programs to help stave off the inevitable assaults. Even with the best anti-malware tools, there are times when malware still manages to strike your computer. When you discover infected systems, you need to know how to stop the spread of the malware to other computers, how to fix infected computers, and how to remediate (restore) the system as close to its original state as possible.

Dealing with Malware

You can deal with malware in several ways: anti-malware programs, training and awareness, patch/update management, and remediation.

At the very least, every computer should run an anti-malware program. If possible, add an appliance that runs anti-malware programs against incoming data from your network. Also remember that an anti-malware program is only as good as its updates—keep everyone's definition file (explained a bit later) up to date with, literally, nightly updates! Users must be trained to look for suspicious ads, programs, and pop-ups, and understand that they must not click these things. The more you teach users about malware, the more aware they'll be of potential threats. Your organization should have policies and procedures in place so everyone knows what to do if they encounter malware. Finally, a good tech maintains proper incident response records to see if any pattern to attacks emerges. He or she can then adjust policies and procedures to mitigate these attacks.

 NOTE One of the most important malware mitigation procedures is to keep systems under your control patched and up to date through proper *patch management*. Microsoft, Apple, and the Linux maintainers do a very good job of putting out bug fixes and patches as soon as problems occur. If your systems aren't set up to update automatically, then perform manual updates regularly.

Anti-Malware Programs

An *anti-malware program* such as a classic *antivirus program* protects your PC in two ways. It can be both sword and shield, working in an active seek-and-destroy mode and in a passive sentry mode. When ordered to seek and destroy, the program scans the computer's boot sector and files for viruses and, if it finds any, presents you with the available options for removing or disabling them. Antivirus programs can also operate as *virus shields* that passively monitor a computer's activity, checking for viruses only when certain events occur, such as a program execution or file download.

NOTE The term *antivirus* (and antispyware, or anti-anything) is becoming obsolete. Viruses are only a small component of the many types of malware. Many people continue to use the term as a synonym for anti-malware.

Antivirus programs use different techniques to combat different types of viruses. They detect boot sector viruses simply by comparing the drive's boot sector to a standard boot sector. This works because most boot sectors are basically the same. Some antivirus programs make a backup copy of the boot sector. If they detect a virus, the programs use that backup copy to replace the infected boot sector. Executable viruses are a little more difficult to find because they can be on any file in the drive. To detect executable viruses, the antivirus program uses a library of signatures. A *signature* is the code pattern of a known virus. The antivirus program compares an executable file to its library of signatures. There have been instances where a perfectly clean program coincidentally held a virus signature. Usually, the antivirus program's creator provides a patch to prevent further alarms.

Windows comes with Windows Defender (simply called Virus & threat protection in Windows 10/11, as shown in Figure 27-17), a fine tool for catching most malware, but it's not perfect. You can also supplement Windows Defender with a second malware removal program. My personal favorite is Malwarebytes.

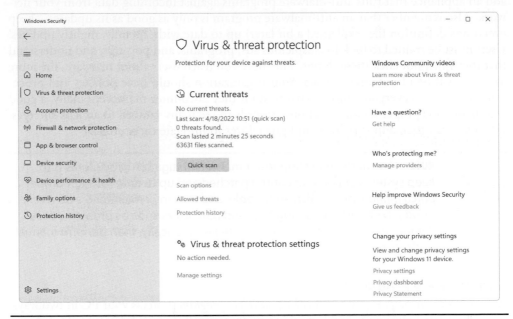

Figure 27-17   Windows 11 Virus & threat protection

These applications work exactly as advertised. They detect and delete malware of all sorts—hidden files and folders, cookies, Registry keys and values, you name it. Malwarebytes is free for personal use. Figure 27-18 shows Malwarebytes in action.

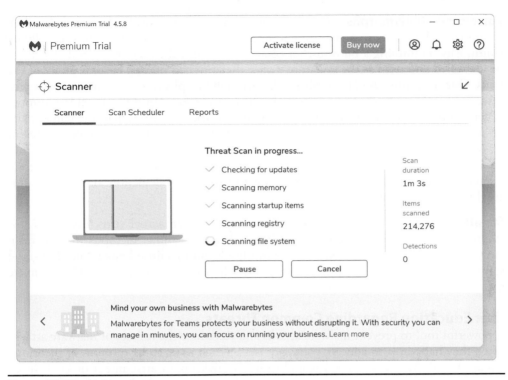

Figure 27-18 Malwarebytes

Try This!

Malwarebytes

If you haven't done this already, do it now. Go to https://www.malwarebytes.com and download the latest copy of Malwarebytes. Install it on your computer and run it. Did it find any malware that slipped in past your defenses?

Now that you understand the types of viruses and how antivirus programs try to protect against them, let's review a few terms that are often used to describe virus traits.

SIM Check out the excellent Challenge! sim, "Fixing Viruses," in the Chapter 27 sims over at https://www.totalsem.com/110X.

Polymorphic/Polymorphs   A *polymorphic virus*, often shortened to a *polymorph*, attempts to change its signature to prevent detection by antivirus programs, usually by continually scrambling a bit of useless code. Fortunately, the scrambling code itself can be identified and used as the signature—once the antivirus makers become aware of the virus. One technique used to combat unknown polymorphs is to have the antivirus program create a checksum on every file in the drive. A *checksum* in this context is a number generated by the software based on the contents of the file rather than the name, date, or size of that file. The algorithms for creating these checksums vary among different antivirus programs (they are also usually kept secret to help prevent virus makers from coming up with ways to beat them). Every time a program is run, the antivirus program calculates a new checksum and compares it with the earlier calculation. If the checksums are different, it is a sure sign of a virus.

Stealth   The term "stealth" is more of a concept than an actual virus function. Most *stealth virus* programs are boot sector viruses that use various methods to hide from antivirus software. The AntiEXE stealth virus hooks on to a little-known but often-used software interrupt, for example, running only when that interrupt runs. Others make copies of innocent-looking files.

User Education Regarding Common Threats

A powerful tool to prevent malware attacks and to reduce the impact of malware attacks when they happen is to educate your end users. Teach users to be cautious of incoming e-mail they don't clearly recognize and to never click on an attachment or URL in an e-mail unless they are 100 percent certain of the source. With the rise in ransomware attacks over time, good anti-phishing training has become an absolutely essential tool in the IT security toolbox. *Anti-phishing training* involves teaching users how to recognize and critically examine incoming e-mails to better avoid falling prey to phishing attempts. Anti-phishing training has benefits that extend beyond the confines of the organization, as phishing attacks happen in SOHO environments as well. Regardless of where or why a person is using their device, this is some very useful education.

Explain the dangers of going to questionable Web sites to your users and teach them how to react when they see questionable actions take place. All Web browsers have built-in attack site warnings like the one shown in Figure 27-19.

Nobody wants their systems infected with malware. Users are motivated and happy when you give them the skills necessary to protect themselves. The bottom line is that educated and aware users will make your life a lot easier.

Malware Prevention Tips

The secret to preventing damage from a malicious software attack is to keep from getting malware on your system in the first place. One way to do this is with a variation on traditional DNS—secure DNS. Secure DNS can describe software or a remote DNS provider that implements some additional filtering to block your devices from visiting all kinds of malicious Web sites.

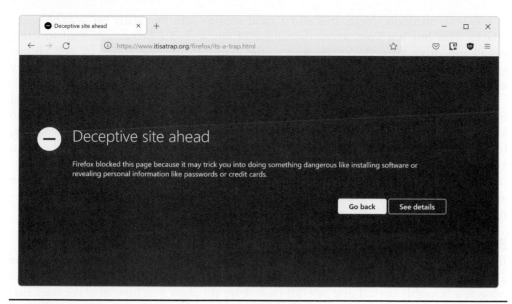

Figure 27-19   Attack site warning

If you can't keep the malware from reaching your system, a good next step is catching it on the way in the door. All good antivirus/anti-malware programs (like the built-in Windows Defender Antivirus) include a virus shield that scans e-mail, downloads, running programs, and so on automatically (see Figure 27-20).

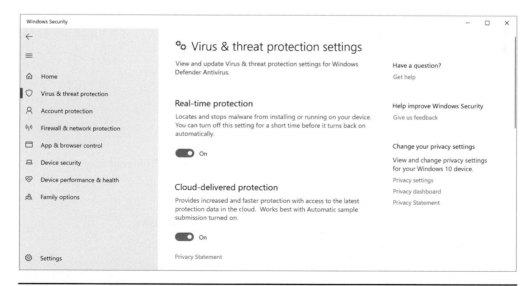

Figure 27-20   A Windows 10 virus shield (Defender Antivirus) in action

Use your antivirus shield. It is also a good idea to scan PCs daily for possible virus attacks. Last but not least, know the source of any software before you load it. Only install apps from trusted sources, such as the manufacturer's Web site, or well-known app stores like Valve's Steam service. Avoid untrusted software sources, like free registry cleaners from some support domain, at all costs.

Keep your antivirus and anti-malware programs (including Defender Antivirus) updated. New viruses and other malware appear daily, and your programs need to know about them. The list of virus signatures your antivirus program can recognize, for example, is called the *definition file*, and *updated definitions* play a critical role in keeping the latest malware out of your system. Fortunately, most antivirus programs update themselves automatically. Further, you should periodically update the core anti-malware software programming—called the *engine*—to employ the latest refinements the developers have included.

Boot Media Anti-Malware Tools

If you run anti-malware software and your computer still gets infected, especially after a reboot, you need a more serious anti-malware tool. Many anti-malware companies provide a bootable optical disc or USB flash drive (or show you how to make one) that enables you to boot from a known-clean OS and run the same anti-malware software, but this time not corrupted by the malware on your system.

Malware Recovery Tips

When the inevitable happens and either your computer or one of your user's computers gets infected by malware such as a computer virus, you need to follow certain steps to stop the problem from spreading and get the computer back up safely into service. The CompTIA A+ 1102 exam outlines the following multistep process as the *best practice procedures for malware removal*:

1. Investigate and verify malware symptoms.

2. Quarantine infected systems.

3. Disable System Restore in Windows.

4. Remediate infected systems.

   A. Update anti-malware software.

   B. Scanning and removal techniques (e.g., Safe Mode, Preinstallation Environment).

5. Schedule scans and run updates.

6. Enable System Restore and create a restore point in Windows.

7. Educate the end user.

EXAM TIP In addition to this malware removal process, the CompTIA A+ 1102 objectives also mention *OS reinstallation* as another way to make sure your system is malware-free—just restore a full system backup (in Windows, you can take or restore one with the Backup and Restore utility). There are hurdles to using this approach.

You must have space to store one or more full backups, plan far enough ahead to have one or more recent backup available, know at least one is malware-free, and be prepared to either back up user files/data separately or lose any created/modified since the last backup. You won't always have this option, but a good way to get started is to back up user files and data *separately* and take a full backup of the system itself once you have all of the software you need installed and configured. If you attempt to reinstall your OS from a backup and you find that your system is still infected, it may be time to try what is known as a *clean install*, which means just starting from a fresh copy of Windows and treating it like a new device. This has disadvantages as well, since it means starting from scratch with your system's apps and data. In some cases, this may be your only choice, but it isn't always ideal.

Recognize and Quarantine   The first step is to identify and recognize that a potential malware outbreak has occurred. If you're monitoring network traffic and one computer starts spewing e-mail, that's a good indicator of malware. Or users might complain that a computer that was running snappily the day before seems very sluggish.

Many networks employ software such as the open source PacketFence that automatically monitors network traffic and can cut a machine off the network if that machine starts sending suspicious packets. You can also quarantine a computer manually by disconnecting the network cable. Once you're sure the machine isn't capable of infecting others, you're ready to find the virus or other malware and get rid of it.

At this point, you should disable System Restore. If you make any changes going forward, you don't want the virus to be included in any saved restore points. To turn off System Restore in Windows, open the Control Panel and then the System applet. Click the System protection link to open the System Properties window with the System Protection tab displayed. In the Protection Settings section, select a drive and click Configure. In the System Protection dialog box that opens, select Turn off system protection. Repeat the procedure for each hard drive on the system.

Search and Destroy   Once you've isolated the infected computer (or computers), you need to get to a safe boot environment and run anti-malware software. You can try the Windows Recovery Environment in Windows 10/11, because it doesn't require anything but a reboot. If that doesn't work, or you suspect a boot sector virus, you need to turn to an external bootable source, such as a bootable optical disc or USB flash drive.

Get into the habit of keeping around a bootable anti-malware flash drive or optical media. If you suspect a virus or other malware, use the boot media, even if your anti-malware program claims to have eliminated the problem. Turn off the PC and reboot it from the anti-malware disc or flash drive (you might have to change CMOS settings to boot to optical or USB media). This will put you in a clean boot environment that you know is free from any boot sector viruses. If you only support fairly recent computers, you will likely be booting to a USB flash drive, so you can put a boot environment on a thumb drive for even faster start-up speeds.

You have several options for creating the bootable optical disc or flash drive. First, some antivirus software comes in a bootable version. Second, you can download a copy of Linux that offers a live USB or DVD option such as Ubuntu. With a live bootable device, you boot to the device and install a complete working copy of the operating system into RAM, never touching or accessing the hard drive, to give you full Internet-ready access so you can reach the many online anti-malware sites you'll need for access to anti-malware tools.

Finally, you can download and burn a copy of the Ultimate Boot CD. Don't worry, you can use it with a USB drive. It comes stocked with several antivirus and anti-malware programs, so you won't need any other tool. Find it at https://www.ultimatebootcd.com. The only downside is that the anti-malware engines will quickly be out of date, as will their malware libraries.

Once you get to a boot environment, update your anti-malware software and then run its most comprehensive scan. Then check all removable media that were exposed to the system, and any other machine that might have received data from the system or that is networked to the cleaned machine. A virus or other malicious program can often lie dormant for months before anyone knows of its presence.

E-mail is still a common source of viruses, and opening infected e-mails is a common way to get infected. Viewing an e-mail in a preview window opens the e-mail message and exposes your computer to some viruses. Download files only from sites you know to be safe and avoid the less reputable corners of the Internet, the most likely places to pick up computer infections.

 EXAM TIP CompTIA considers the process of removing a virus part of the remediation step. Since you can't remediate a PC until after a virus is gone, I've laid out the steps as you see here.

Remediate Malware infections can do a lot of damage to a system, especially to sensitive files needed to load Windows, so you might need to remediate formerly infected systems after cleaning off the drive or drives. *Remediation* simply means that you fix things the virus or other malware harmed. This can mean replacing corrupted Windows Registry files or even startup files.

If you can't start Windows after the malware scan is finished, you need to boot to the Windows Preinstallation Environment and use the Windows Recovery Environment/System Recovery Options.

With the Windows Recovery Environment (covered in detail in Chapter 16), you have access to more repair tools, such as Startup Repair, System Restore, System Image Recovery, Refresh, and Command Prompt (see Figure 27-21). Run the appropriate option for the situation and you should have the machine properly remediated in a jiffy.

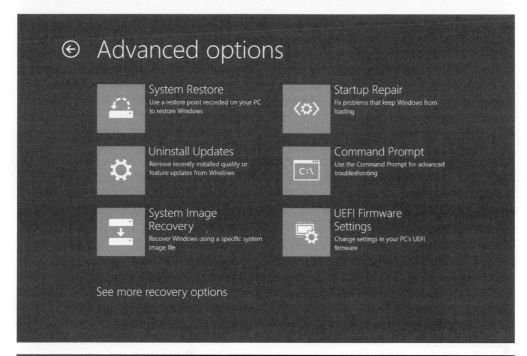

Figure 27-21   System Recovery Options

 EXAM TIP   Remember to re-enable System Restore and create a new restore point once the system has been repaired. Be aware that you may see recovery environment referred to as *recovery mode* on the exam, so don't let that throw you off.

Educate End Users   The best way to keep from having to deal with malware is education. It's your job as the IT person to talk to your users, especially the ones whose systems you've just spent an hour ridding of nasties, about how to avoid these programs. Show them samples of dangerous e-mails they should not open, Web sites to avoid, and the types of programs they should not install and use on the network. Any user who understands the risks of questionable actions on their computers will usually do the right thing and stay away from malware.

Finally, have your users run antivirus and antispyware programs regularly. Schedule them while interfacing with the user so you know it will happen.

1101

Firewalls

Much as anti-malware programs are essential tools in the fight against malicious programs on the Internet, *firewalls* are devices or software that protect an internal network from unauthorized access to and from the Internet at large. Firewalls use a number of methods to protect networks, such as hiding IP addresses and blocking TCP/IP ports.

A typical network uses one of two types of firewalls: *hardware firewalls*, often built into routers, and *software firewalls* that run on your computers. Both types of firewall protect your computer and your network. You also run them at the same time. Let's look at both a typical SOHO router's firewall features and your computer's software firewall to see how they protect your network and your computers.

Hardware Firewall Settings

Most SOHO networks use a hardware firewall, often as a feature built into a router like the ASUS model shown in Figure 27-22. A hardware firewall protects a LAN from outside threats by filtering the packets before they reach your internal machines, which you learned about back in Chapter 21. Routers, however, have a few other tricks up their sleeves. From the router's browser-based settings screen (see Figure 27-23), you can configure a hardware firewall. Let's walk through a few of the available settings.

Figure 27-22
ASUS router as a
firewall

Figure 27-23   Default Web interface

A hardware firewall watches for and stops many common threats—all you have to do is turn it on (see Figure 27-24). Hardware firewalls use *Stateful Packet Inspection (SPI)* to inspect each incoming packet individually. SPI also blocks any incoming traffic that isn't in response to your outgoing traffic. You can even disable unused ports entirely, blocking all traffic in or out. But what if you want to allow outside users access to a Web server on the LAN? Because Network Address Translation (NAT) hides the true IP address of that system (as described in Chapter 21), you'll need a way to allow incoming traffic past the router/firewall and a way to redirect that traffic to the right PC.

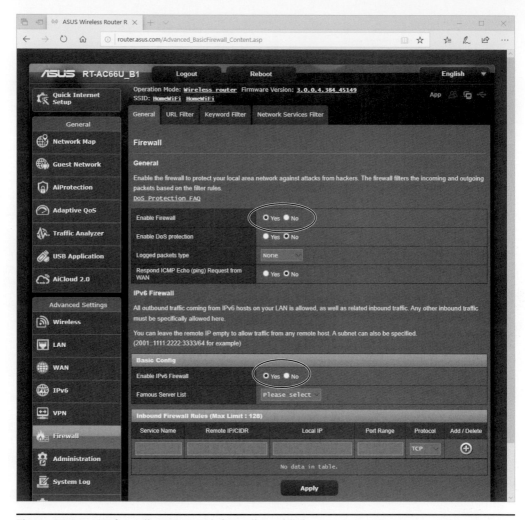

Figure 27-24 SPI firewall settings with firewalls enabled

Port forwarding/mapping enables you to open a port in the firewall and direct incoming traffic on that port to a specific IP address on your LAN. In the case of the Web server referenced in the previous paragraph, you would open port 80 (for HTTP packets) and instruct the router to send all incoming traffic to the server machine. Figure 27-25 shows port forwarding configured to send all HTTP packets to an internal Web server.

Port forwarding isn't the only way to open ports on a firewall. *Port triggering* enables you to open an incoming connection to one computer automatically based on a

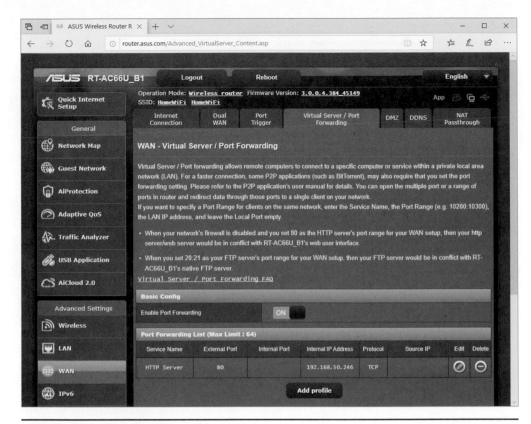

Figure 27-25   Port forwarding

specific outgoing connection. The *trigger port* defines the outgoing connection, and the *destination port* defines the incoming connection. If you set the trigger port to 3434 and the destination port to 1234, for example, any outgoing traffic on port 3434 will trigger the router to open port 1234 and send any received data back to the system that sent the original outgoing traffic. Figure 27-26 shows a router set up with port triggering for an Internet Relay Chat (IRC) server.

If you want to go beyond port forwarding and port triggering and open every port on a machine, you need a screened subnet. A *screened subnet* puts systems with the specified IP addresses outside the protection of the firewall, opening all ports and enabling all incoming traffic (see Figure 27-27). If you think this sounds incredibly dangerous, you are right! Any PC inside the screened subnet will be completely exposed to outside attacks. Don't use it!

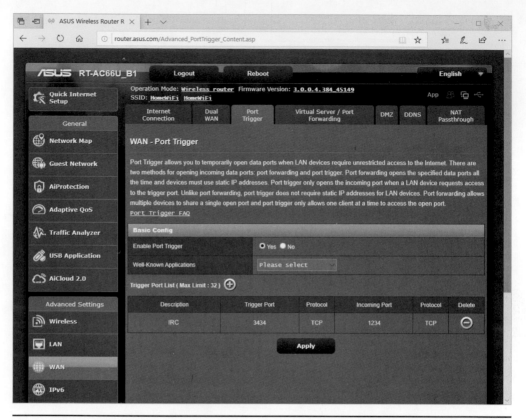

Figure 27-26 Port triggering

EXAM TIP CompTIA uses the term *screened subnet* in the A+ 1102 exam objectives, so be ready in case you see it on the exam, but on the job, you'll more likely encounter the term *demilitarized zone* or *DMZ* (as shown in Figure 27-27).

Software Firewalls

While a hardware firewall does a lot to protect you from outside intruders, you should also use a software firewall, such as the firewalls built into each version of Windows, called (appropriately) Windows Defender Firewall or Windows Defender Firewall with Advanced Security. (Earlier versions of Windows just called the tool(s) *Windows Firewall*.) Windows Defender Firewall (see Figure 27-28) handles the heavy lifting of port blocking, security logging, and more.

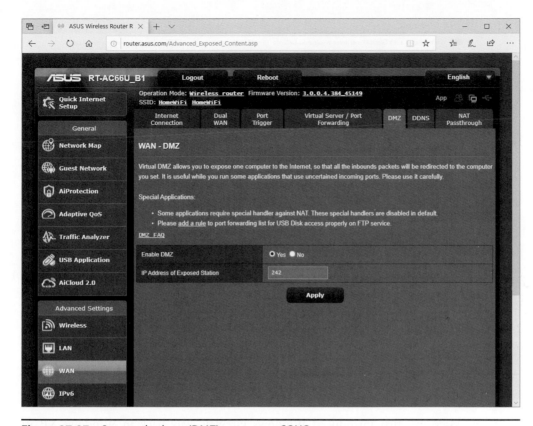

Figure 27-27   Screened subnet (DMZ) set up on a SOHO router

You can configure Windows Defender Firewall via the Windows Defender Firewall applet in Control Panel. Here you can fine-tune *port security* by setting up *exceptions* to open individual ports, or adjust *application security* by adding exceptions to let specific programs and services pass through the firewall. If you wanted to run a *Minecraft* server (a game that requires an Internet connection), for example, it would need to be on the list of exceptions for your firewall. Most programs you install add themselves to this list automatically, otherwise Windows Defender Firewall prompts you the first time you run it and asks if you want to add the program as an exception.

EXAM TIP   You can also manage Windows Defender Firewall through the Windows Security app. To activate or deactivate the firewall, visit the Firewall & network protection section. To activate, click the Turn on button under each network type you use. To deactivate, click the network name and then toggle Defender Firewall off.

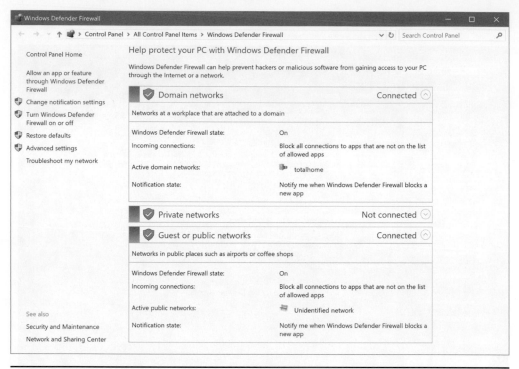

Figure 27-28 Windows 10 Firewall settings

When Microsoft first introduced Windows Firewall, way back in Windows XP, its biggest shortcoming was that it failed to consider that a single PC, especially a portable, might connect to multiple networks. You don't necessarily want the same firewall settings used for both public and private networks. Microsoft developed a way for you to separate trustworthy networks (like the one in your house or at the office) from non-trustworthy networks (like a public Wi-Fi Internet connection at the airport) by including three network types: Domain, Private, and Guest or Public.

- A *Domain* network is a Windows network controlled by a Windows domain controller that runs Active Directory Domain Services. In this case, the domain controller itself tells your machine what it can and cannot share. You don't need to do anything when your computer joins a domain.

- A *Private* network enables you to share resources, discover other devices, and allow other devices to discover your computer safely.

- A *Guest or Public* network prevents your computer from sharing and disables all discovery protocols.

When your computer connects to a network for the first time, Windows will prompt you to choose the network type. Windows 10/11 asks if you want to allow other devices on the network to discover your PC (see Figure 27-29). It will mark the network Private if you answer yes; Public if you answer no. In either case, Windows uses your answer to decide whether to share files and resources or lock them down tight.

Figure 27-29
Windows 10
network options,
public or private?

When your computer joins a domain, Windows automatically sets your network location to Domain (unless your domain controller chooses something different, which is unlikely).

When running on a Private (Home or Work) network, Windows enables Network Discovery and File and Printer Sharing as exceptions. When running on a Guest or Public network, Windows disables these exceptions.

 EXAM TIP The Network Discovery setting dictates whether a computer can find other computers or devices on a network, and vice versa. Even with Network Discovery activated, several firewall settings can overrule certain connections.

That's the end of the story if your Windows machine never changes networks, but what about machines (mainly laptops) that hop from one network to another (see Figure 27-30)? In that case, you need different firewall settings for each network the system might encounter.

Figure 27-30
Many machines need more than one network setting.

One firewall setting is enough for me.

I need different firewall settings depending on where I am.

EXAM TIP Expect a scenario question on home vs. work vs. public network options on the CompTIA A+ 1102 exam. Just remember that you trust home and work networks, but don't trust public ones.

Once you've picked a network type, you might want to customize the firewall settings further. If you click the Advanced settings option in the Windows Defender Firewall applet, you'll discover a much deeper level of firewall configuration. In fact, it's an entirely different tool called *Windows Defender Firewall with Advanced Security* (see Figure 27-31). You can also access it directly through the Administrative Tools in Control Panel.

From the Windows Defender Firewall with Advanced Security snap-in, you have much more control over how Windows treats exceptions. In the standard Windows Defender Firewall applet, you can only choose a program and make it an exception, giving it permission to pass through the firewall. But programs both send and receive network data, and the basic applet doesn't give you much control over the "inbound" and "outbound" aspect of firewalls. The Windows Defender Firewall with Advanced Security snap-in takes the exceptions concept and expands it to include custom rules for both inbound and outbound data. Figure 27-32 shows the outbound rules for a typical Windows system.

A rule always includes at least the following:

- The name of the program
- Group: an organizational group that helps sort all the rules
- The associated profile (All, Domain, Public, Private)

- Enabled/disabled status
- Remote and local address
- Remote and local port number

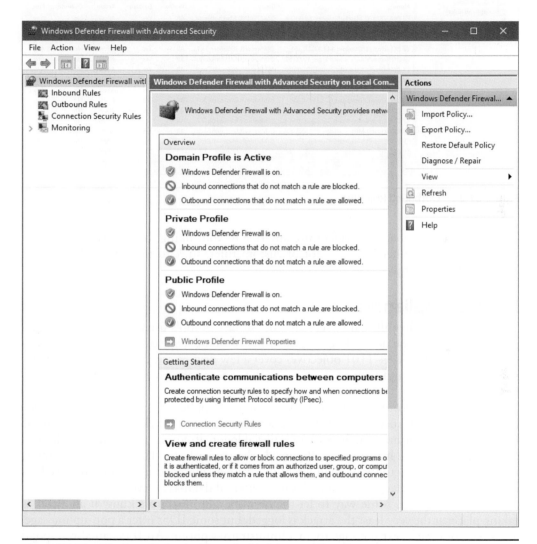

Figure 27-31   Windows Defender Firewall with Advanced Security

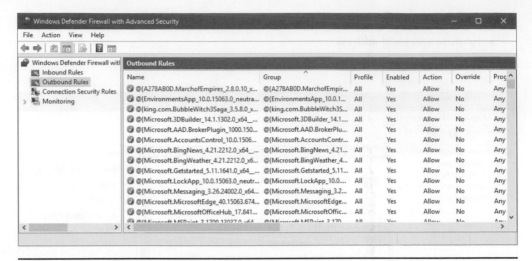

Figure 27-32 Outbound Rules list

You can add, remove, and customize any rule to your liking. It quickly gets complicated, so unless you need to set a lot of custom rules, stick to the standard Windows Defender Firewall applet.

Internet Appliances

The discussion of firewalls barely scratches the surface of tools used to secure a large network. While enterprise networking is generally beyond the scope of a CompTIA A+ tech's duties, the CompTIA A+ 1101 objectives cover a few devices critical to modern network security—IDS, IPS, and network taps—plus the concept of unified threat management. Let's take a look.

An *intrusion detection system (IDS)* is an Internet application that inspects packets, looking for active intrusions. An IDS functions inside the network, watching for threats that a firewall might miss, such as viruses, illegal logon attempts, and other well-known attacks. Plus, because it inspects traffic inside the network, the IDS can discover internal threats, like the activity of a vulnerability scanner smuggled in on a flash drive by a disgruntled worker planning an attack on an internal database server.

An IDS always has some way to let the network administrators know if an attack is taking place: at the very least the attack is logged, but some IDSs offer a pop-up message, an e-mail, or even a text message to an administrator's phone. An IDS can also respond to detected intrusions with action. The IDS can't stop the attack directly, but can request assistance from other devices—like a firewall—that can.

An *intrusion prevention system (IPS)* is very similar to an IDS, but an IPS sits directly in the flow of network traffic. This active monitoring has a trio of consequences. First, an IPS can stop an attack while it is happening. There's no need to request help from any other devices. Second, the network bandwidth and latency take a hit. Third, if the IPS goes down, the network link might go down too. Depending on the IPS, it can block incoming packets on-the-fly based on IP address, port number, or application type. An IPS might go even further, literally fixing certain packets on-the-fly.

A *network tap* is a piece of network monitoring hardware (although there are also smaller-scale software options) that sits between devices on the network and copies the traffic between them for later analysis. This comes in handy because, rather than directly interacting with the traffic and potentially interfering with it, a network tap allows the traffic to flow normally. The copied network traffic can then be inspected without the risk of network disruptions. Network taps can also be part of a virtual network, with a lot of additional flexibility in how they are used. Figure 27-33 shows an example of how a network tap might be used.

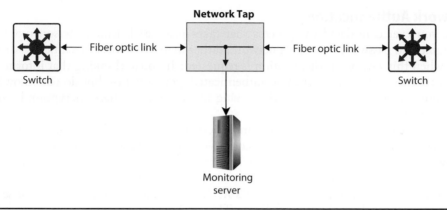

Figure 27-33 One potential configuration of a network tap

All these network Internet appliances, no matter how advanced and aware they become, are still singular tools in the box used to protect networks. That is why modern dedicated firewall/Internet appliances are built around providing *unified threat management (UTM)*. UTM takes the traditional firewall and packages it with many other security services such as IPS, VPN, load balancing, antivirus, and many other features depending on the make and model. The UTM approach to building network gear helps build robust security deep into the network, protecting what really matters: our data.

1102

Authentication and Encryption

You know that the first step in securing data is authentication, through a username and password. But when you throw in networking, you're suddenly not just a single user sitting in front of a computer and typing. You're accessing a remote resource and sending login information over the Internet. What's to stop someone from intercepting your username and password?

Firewalls do a great job of controlling traffic coming into a network from the Internet and going out of a network to the Internet, but they do nothing to stop interceptor hackers who monitor traffic on the public Internet looking for vulnerabilities.

Worse, once a packet is on the Internet itself, anyone with the right equipment can intercept and inspect it. Inspected packets are a cornucopia of passwords, account names, and other tidbits that hackers can use to intrude into your network. Because we can't stop hackers from inspecting these packets, we must turn to *encryption* to make them unreadable.

Network encryption occurs at many levels and is in no way limited to Internet-based activities. Not only are there many levels of network encryption, but each encryption level also provides multiple standards and options, making encryption one of the most complicated of all networking issues. You need to understand where encryption comes into play, what options are available, and what you can use to protect your network.

Network Authentication

Have you ever considered the process that takes place each time a person types in a username and password to access a network, rather than just a local machine? What happens when this *network* authentication is requested? If you're thinking that information is sent to a server of some sort to be authenticated, you're right—but do you know how the username and password get to the serving system? That's where encryption becomes important in authentication.

In a local network, authentication and encryption are usually handled by the OS. In today's increasingly interconnected and diverse networking environment, there is a motivation to enable different operating systems to authenticate any client system from any other OS. Modern operating systems such as Windows and macOS use standard authentication encryptions such as MIT's *Kerberos*, enabling multiple brands of servers to authenticate multiple brands of clients. These LAN authentication methods are usually transparent and work quite nicely, even in mixed networks.

Data Encryption

Encryption methods don't stop at the authentication level. There are a number of ways to encrypt network *data* as well. The encryption method is dictated to a large degree by what method the communicating systems will connect with. Many networks consist of multiple networks linked together by some sort of private connection, usually some kind of WAN connection such as old T1s or Metro Ethernet. Microsoft's encryption method of choice for this type of network is called *IPsec* (derived from *IP security*). IPsec provides transparent encryption between the server and the client.

A virtual private network (VPN) can also use IPsec, but VPNs typically use other encryption methods. Speaking of VPNs, if you're on an untrusted network, you can also protect your network traffic by tunneling it all through a VPN connection. Security-conscious organizations may even require all of their portable devices access the Internet through a VPN connection to one of their home offices.

Application Encryption

When it comes to encryption, even TCP/IP applications can get into the swing of things. The most famous of all application encryptions is the *Secure Sockets Layer (SSL)* security protocol, which was used to secure Web sites. Everyone uses *Transport Layer*

Security (TLS) in *HTTPS* (HTTP over TLS) protocol these days. (SSL has been replaced by TLS, in other words.) These protocols make it possible to secure the Web sites people use to make purchases over the Internet. You can identify HTTPS Web sites by the *https://* (rather than http://) included in the URL (see Figure 27-34).

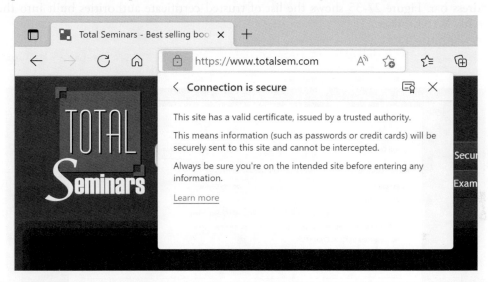

Figure 27-34   A secure Web site

 NOTE   HTTPS originally meant HTTP over SSL, so the "S" in HTTPS made sense. Most Web sites use the more robust TLS to encrypt connections. The Internet people just quietly switched TLS for SSL, but didn't make a new acronym such as "HTTPT." CompTIA refers to the "S" as standing for "secure," which is a great way to remember the main difference between HTTP and HTTPS.

To make a secure connection, your Web browser and the Web server must encrypt their data. That means there must be a way for both the Web server and your browser to encrypt and decrypt each other's data. To do this, the server sends a public key to your Web browser so the browser knows how to decrypt the incoming data. These public keys are sent in the form of a *digital certificate*. This certificate is signed by a trusted *certificate authority (CA)* that guarantees that the public key you are about to get is actually from the Web server and not from some evil person trying to pretend to be the Web server. A number of companies issue digital certificates, such as Verisign, Comodo, and many others.

Your Web browser has a built-in list of trusted certificate authorities, referred to as *trusted root CAs*. If a certificate comes in from a Web site that uses one of these highly respected companies, you won't see anything happen in your browser; you'll just go to the secure Web page, where a small lock icon will appear in the browser status bar or address bar. Figure 27-35 shows the list of trusted certificate authorities built into the Firefox Web browser.

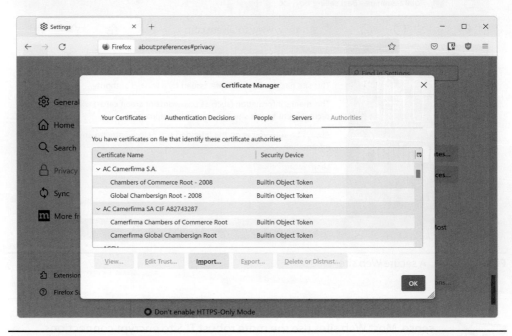

Figure 27-35 Trusted certificate authorities

If you receive a certificate that your browser thinks is fishy, such as one that is expired or one for which the browser does not have a trusted root CA, the browser will warn you and usually give you some way to make an exception for the certificate, as shown in Figure 27-36.

We all have to make our own decisions here, but you should usually heed the browser's warning and advice. Most *certificate warnings* are invalid for boring reasons, like the site owner forgetting to update the certificate on time. But the certificate warnings could just as easily indicate that the site or your connection to it is compromised! Only add an exception if you *know* it's safe. You might, for example, need to add an exception to access a site on your organization's intranet.

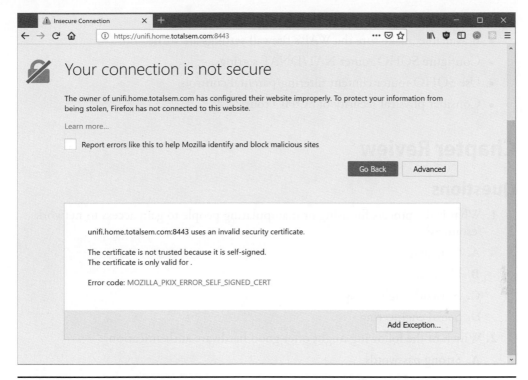

Figure 27-36 Incoming certificate

Wireless Issues

Wireless networks add a whole level of additional security headaches for techs to face, as you know from Chapter 20. Here are a few points to consider:

- Set up wireless encryption, at least WPA2 but preferably the more secure WPA3 if your device supports it, and configure clients to use it.
- Disable DHCP and require your wireless clients to use a static IP address.
- If you need to use DHCP, only allot enough DHCP addresses to meet the needs of your network, to avoid unused wireless connections.
- Change the WAP's SSID from the default.
- Filter by MAC or IP address to help limit network access to known clients only.
- Change the default username and password. Even if the defaults are generated and look secure, knowledge of how they were generated might make them easier to guess.

- Update the firmware as needed.
- If available, make sure the WAP's firewall settings are turned on.
- Configure SOHO router NAT/DNAT settings.
- Use SOHO router content filtering/parental controls.
- Consider physical security of SOHO router.

Chapter Review

Questions

1. What is the process for using or manipulating people to gain access to network resources?

   A. Cracking

   B. Hacking

   C. Network engineering

   D. Social engineering

2. Which of the following might offer good hardware authentication?

   A. Strong passwords

   B. Encrypted passwords

   C. NTFS

   D. Smart cards

3. Which of the following is used for biometric authentication?

   A. Motion sensor

   B. RSA token

   C. Palmprint scanner

   D. Kerberos

4. Which hardware firewall feature enables incoming traffic on a specific port to reach an IP address on the LAN?

   A. Port forwarding

   B. NAT

   C. Screened subnet

   D. Multifactor authentication

5. Zander downloaded a game off the Internet and installed it, but as soon as he started to play, he got a Blue Screen of Death. Upon rebooting, he discovered that his Documents folder had been erased. What happened?

   A. He installed spyware.

   B. He installed a Trojan.

   C. He broke the Group Policy.

   D. He broke the Local Security Policy.

6. Which of these choices would provide better security for Mary's Wi-Fi router?

   A. Secure DNS

   B. WEP

   C. WPA2

   D. WPA3

7. Malware that encrypts a hard drive and demands payment in exchange for decryption is known as what?

   A. Trojan

   B. Cryptominer

   C. Ransomware

   D. Keylogger

8. John dressed up in a fake security guard uniform matching the ones used by a company and then walked into the company's headquarters with some legitimate employees in an attempt to gain access to company resources. What kind of attack is this?

   A. Administrative access

   B. Data destruction

   C. Spoofing

   D. Tailgating

9. Andre, CEO of a midsized company, received an e-mail that appeared to be from a colleague that wanted to close a major deal. Suspicious because the deal in question didn't exist, he called in his IT security team who determined that it came from a spoofed IP address. Which of the following best describes this attempted attack?

   A. Phishing

   B. Whaling

   C. Zero-day

   D. Tailgating

10. Edna wants to put a policy in place at her company to prevent or at least limit viruses. What policies would offer the best solution?

    A. Install antivirus software on every computer. Teach users how to run it.

    B. Install antivirus software on every computer. Set up the software to scan regularly.

    C. Install antivirus software on every computer. Set up the software to update the definitions and engine automatically. Set up the software to scan regularly.

    D. Install antivirus software on every computer. Set up the software to update the definitions and engine automatically. Set up the software to scan regularly. Educate the users about sites and downloads to avoid.

Answers

1. **D.** Social engineering is the process of using or manipulating people to gain access to network resources.

2. **D.** Smart cards are an example of hardware authentication devices.

3. **C.** Palmprint scanners are a method of biometric authentication.

4. **A.** To open a port on your hardware firewall and send incoming traffic to a specific PC, use port forwarding.

5. **B.** Zander clearly installed a Trojan, a virus masquerading as a game.

6. **D.** Mary should set up WPA3 on her Wi-Fi router.

7. **C.** Malware that demands money in exchange for hard drive decryption is called ransomware.

8. **D.** John just practiced tailgating on the unsuspecting company.

9. **B.** Andre was the target of a whaling attempt.

10. **D.** The best policy includes updating the software engine and definitions, scanning PCs regularly, and educating users.

28

Operational Procedures

In this chapter, you will learn how to

- Implement best practices associated with documentation and support systems information management
- Explain basic change-management best practices
- Summarize environmental impacts and local environmental controls
- Explain the importance of prohibited content/activity and privacy, licensing, and policy concepts

The term *operational procedures* encompasses a lot for any organization, from best practices for safety (Chapter 1) to dealing with security risks (Chapter 27); from organizational polices for limiting access to sensitive data (also Chapter 27) to proper communication techniques and professionalism all techs should employ (again, Chapter 1). The CompTIA A+ 1102 exam even throws in basics of scripting (Chapter 15) and remote access technologies (Chapter 21) as operational procedures (though labeling them as such feels like a reach to me).

This chapter explores another aspect of operational procedures—namely, business practices that enable *continuity*, a fancy way of saying that an organization should keep working more or less the same in the face of both mundane day-to-day change and sudden disasters. We'll focus here on four categories of business continuity and operational procedures: documentation and support systems management, basic change management, environmental impacts and controls, and prohibited content/activity, privacy, licensing, and policies.

1102

Implementing Best Practices Associated with Documentation and Support Systems Information Management

Organizations need documentation to provide continuity and structure. Documentation can take many forms, but the four categories of concern to a new tech are asset management, custom installation of software packages, ticketing systems, and knowledge base/articles.

Asset Management

Techs help organizations institute *asset management* practices to protect organizational assets. These include inventory lists, database systems, and barcodes, among other things.

 EXAM TIP Although the term "barcode" is not likely to appear on the CompTIA A+ 1102 exam, organizations still use this technology to track assets.

Inventory Lists

Have you ever worked for a company that issued you a piece of equipment that had a company-specific tag on it? This could be anything from a number engraved onto the handle of a shovel to an RFID tag attached to a computer. Regardless of the form, every organization has to track the physical and virtual assets that it has in its inventory at any given time. For a tech company, the inventory might include, for example, 32 Dell laptops, 32 USB-C power adapters, 32 copies of Microsoft Office, and so forth. Regardless of the form, *inventory lists* are found in every organization and document the assets that the organization has deployed and holds in reserve. Keeping track of these assets is an essential function. Inventory lists document the *who, what,* and *where* of each asset so that an organization can track all its assets.

Database System

For now, let's keep this really simple. In the context of asset management, *database systems* are used to track things like *who* has the asset (e.g., Melissa Layne), *what* type of asset this person has (e.g., a laptop), and *where* this asset is located (e.g., the research and innovation department). Sometimes database systems document *why* the person is using the asset (e.g., to analyze quantitative and qualitative data for her department). Asset management database systems can also be used for things like

- Recording an asset's description: make, model, serial numbers, asset barcode, asset category, etc.
- Recording an asset's acquisition and disposal information
- Linking purchase receipts, manuals, and other digital documents to asset records
- Tracking an asset's status and location
- Obtaining a report listing assets assigned to a department or employee
- Recording asset maintenance and repair histories (date, details, costs, etc.)

Some of the listed items will be discussed further in the "New User Set-Up Checklist" and "End-User Termination Checklist" sections later in the chapter. As you progress through more advanced topics and courses, there will be much more to learn about database systems.

NOTE The difference between an inventory list and a database system is that an inventory list keeps track of the assets that the organization has given out to people and that it has as "extras." A database system tracks more detailed information about the assets.

Barcodes

Many inventory items have simple stickers or printed labels with *barcodes*—unique symbols/numbers that track specific items. Figure 28-1 shows a typical barcode. A barcode acts as a fingerprint for an item, binary code that can be readily scanned. One drawback to barcodes is that they're read-only. You can't add data or information to them at all.

Figure 28-1
Barcode on an
SSD encoding its
serial number

Asset Tags and IDs

Asset tags can use the *radio frequency identification (RFID)* wireless networking protocol to also keep track of inventory (see Figure 28-2). The asset tag includes an RFID tag (consisting of a microchip and antenna), which an RFID scanner or reader can electronically read and identify even without line of sight to the item. Most RFID tags are passive, meaning that the tag receives all the power it needs from the scanner's signal! An active RFID tag, on the other hand, uses a battery or external power source to send out and receive signals. Both types of RFID tags enable asset management. Unlike barcodes, the information stored in an RFID tag can be updated with new details.

Figure 28-2
RFID tag

Procurement Life Cycle

This is one of those topics that is a pain to talk about because every organization has its own process. For small companies, the procurement life cycle can be as simple as picking up the phone, making a few calls, and getting what they need. For highly bureaucratic organizations, the procurement life cycle can be a years-long process involving thousands of pages of rules. At its core, the *procurement life cycle* is the process involved in buying assets that your project needs. However, we are going to try to keep this simple and break down the procurement life cycle into six simple phases.

Identify Needs   Develop an understanding of what you need and why you need it. This can involve simple statements of work or complex documents detailing very specific objectives. This phase will vary from organization to organization and across use cases.

Evaluate Suppliers   Once you know what you need and why you need it, you need to scope out who provides the product or service you require. Sometimes this can be completed with a simple Web search. Other times it may require you to conduct a lengthy series of interviews. Typically, the cost of an implementation is directly proportional to the amount of time you spend evaluating the best supplier.

Negotiate Terms and Finalize the Purchase Order   When you have decided on the best supplier, you need to contact that supplier and enter into a negotiation of terms. Think of this as buying a car, but at a much larger scale. Everyone is willing to make concessions. In the world of business, it is how many concessions you can get, while maintaining quality, that matters in the end.

So, now you have bargained your way down to the very best terms that you can extract from the supplier. This is known as their best and final offer. You agree that this works for your organization, which then sends to the supplier a purchase order (PO) with relevant payment information. The supplier in turn sends an invoice to your organization to initiate the billing process.

Receive Invoice and Process Payment   Your organization receives an invoice, aligned with the purchase order, and sends the supplier the funds to facilitate payment. Are you finished? Not just yet.

Delivery and Audit   After the supplier has been paid, they deliver the service or product as promised. Upon implementation, you begin to monitor how effective the new service or product is compared to your previous state. This is called the audit.

Maintain Records for Future Audits   Everything is up and running. You are happy. The supplier is happy. Now you must continue to track effectiveness versus the return on investment (ROI), to assess periodically whether this solution is still effective or, if you need a new approach.

Warranty and Licensing

In the role of an asset manager, you will also need to keep track of *warranty* and *licensing* documentation. Although this may seem like an overwhelming task, as long as you have established solid security measures and adhere to licensing compliance requirements, you will be able to easily manage and update this important documentation. This in no way means that this job is easy. It's not. In terms of licensing compliance, the stakes are high. If, for example, a company has 50 unlicensed copies of a software application running on 400 of its computers, the company could face fines as high as $500,000!

Unlicensed assets are also linked to potential data loss. Data loss leads to privacy violations, and the snowball continues to get bigger and bigger. There are, however, software applications that can make the tracking job easier, such as various Software as a Service (SaaS) products that make maintaining compliance a little easier.

Assigned Users

Your organization may receive a set number of licenses for a particular product, such as software. This represents how many people in your organization can use the product. Sometimes suppliers are flexible, and they will say, "As long as you don't have more than ten people accessing our product, then everything is fine." Other times, suppliers want to know specifically who is using their product, and if this changes they will want to know who the replacement is. In this case the users are known as *assigned users*.

Individual organizations may also have their own rules about assigning user roles to individuals, even if the supplier does not require the organization to provide identities for individual users. When this is the case, it is often related to audits that determine if the right people are receiving access to the right products or services to ensure optimal performance of the organization as a whole.

Documentation for Policies, Procedures, Industry Standards, and Compliance

Organizations of every size should have a library of documents that cover the organization's policies and procedures and any industry standards and compliance regulations that apply to the organization. New employees should be given a package of these documents the first week on the job and instructed to review them. The onus, however, is on the employer to have these documents ready for new employees and to instill the need to apply the core principles contained within them to the organizational culture. Doing so will prevent issues, avoid inefficiencies, and create a sense of ownership.

Standard Operating Procedures

From a technician's point of view, the most common operating issue revolves around software, such as what sort of software users are allowed to install on their computers or, conversely, why you have to tell a user that he can't install the latest application that may help him do his job more effectively because that software isn't on the approved list. This can lead to some uncomfortable confrontations, but it's part of a tech's job.

EXAM TIP The CompTIA A+ 1102 exam objectives call out *procedures for custom installations of software packages*. If your organization has rules about what software you can and can't install, it probably also has processes that lay out what to do when users request job-related software that isn't on the approved list. For example, folks who work out at NASA's Johnson Space Center here in Houston have to open a support ticket with the IT department if they need a program that isn't on the approved list. From there, the process governs how to decide if the software's license is acceptable, whether it will cause security or compatibility problems, and so on.

The concepts behind standard operating procedures (SOPs) are not meant to make a tech's life difficult and mundane. They are meant, for example, to stop users with insufficient technical skill or knowledge from installing malicious programs or applications that will destabilize their systems, thus keeping technical support calls down, which in turn enables techs to focus on more serious problems.

Organizations largely develop standard operating procedures for employees for two reasons: to enhance the success of the organization, and to meet government-related compliance requirements. *Organizational policies* include regulatory compliance policies, acceptable use polices, and password policies, among others. Because security is growing to include SOPs associated with regulatory compliance, risk management, end-user training, and so forth, those who have service desk responsibilities will likely have to eventually incorporate these SOPs to keep the organization secure.

Acceptable Use (AUP)

An *acceptable use policy (AUP)* describes what employees can and cannot do with the organization's property. An example of a common AUP provision is that a company laptop can be used only for company business. Another common AUP provision bars employees from accessing illegal Web sites from the organization's computers. AUPs are often very detailed and specific documents that employees must read, agree to, and sign as a step in the employment process.

Network Topology Diagrams

Network documentation provides a road map for current and future techs who need to make changes or repairs over time. For the most part, CompTIA Network+ techs and system administrators handle the oversight of the network, but CompTIA A+ techs do a lot of the implementation of fixes. A *network topology diagram* provides a map for how everything connects in an organization's network. These diagrams include switches, routers, WAPs, servers, and workstations (see Figure 28-3). More complex diagrams identify connection types and speeds, and the technologies in use (listing a WAP as an 802.11ax or Wi-Fi 6, for example). Many organizations rely on the Cisco icon set as a universal visual aid for creating these diagrams (see Figure 28-4).

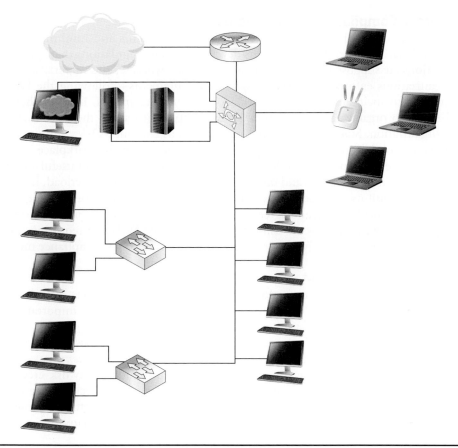

Figure 28-3　Typical network topology diagram

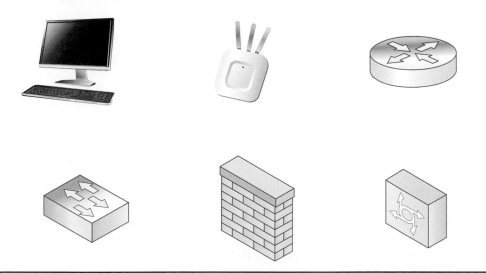

Figure 28-4　A sampling of Cisco network diagram icons

Regulatory Compliance Requirements

Part of a government's job is to ensure safe work environments and minimize exploitation of workers. To this end, governments develop rules and regulations that specify how organizations are supposed to manage their workplaces, workers, and materials. Properly run organizations enforce *regulatory compliance* requirements—following the laws and regulations—to maintain a healthy workforce. *Compliance* means, in a nutshell, that members of an organization must abide by or comply with all of the rules that apply to the organization. Statutes with funny names such as Sarbanes-Oxley impose certain behaviors or prohibitions on what people can and cannot do in the workplace.

It has become commonplace for Web sites and applications to collect useful and informative data about their visitors and users. In this age of information overload, it's equally important that visitors and users understand that their usage data is being collected. To ensure there is understanding and agreement from both parties, many organizations have integrated a *splash screen* prior to using the application or Web site requiring users to agree to things such as data privacy, terms and conditions, or other compliance measures.

New-User Setup Checklist

To make the first day of work easier for new employees, most employers have developed documentation to make sure that they are not overwhelmed and, more importantly, that they have everything they need to start working.

One of these documents is a *new-user setup checklist*, which is a best practice associated with the documentation and *support systems information management* that techs use to ensure that a new user is set up with the proper equipment, network credentials, company policies and procedures, and so forth. New-user setup checklists are flexible, meaning that predefined items can be listed in a set order (1, 2, 3, etc.). Although the items may vary based on the employee's position and role in the company, here are some common items you might need to provide to a new employee:

- Technology: PC, laptop, mouse/mouse pad, keyboard, phone, webcam, external storage
- Software: product/project development, analytical, statistical, etc.
- E-mail/messaging setup (e.g., Microsoft Outlook, Teams, Zoom, Teams, etc.)
- Password security
- Documentation for hardware or software for further reference on functionality provided
- Documentation on data privacy policies for new employee to read and sign
- Contact information provided if new employees have questions, issues, concerns, etc.

Good onboarding gets users to the point where they have everything they need to perform their job functions, they understand how to use it, and they understand and agree to any related security policies that could have a significant negative impact on them and the organization should they not practice them.

End-User Termination Checklist

For any number of reasons, voluntary or involuntary, an employee may leave an organization. Regardless of the reason, the IT department should complete an *end-user termination checklist* to ensure that the departing employee returns all equipment issued by the organization, that their network access has been removed, and, where applicable, that knowledge transfer is facilitated, such as requesting documents the user has created that could help their successor. If you are given this responsibility in your organization, you need to follow your organization's checklist carefully to make sure that the former employee cannot engage in malicious behavior.

Ticketing Systems

Ticketing systems help handle requests for technical assistance. Many companies use ticketing software internally to provide employees with technical support. Some companies also offer consumer ticketing services. For example, if a user encounters a problem with software, the system might allow them to submit a ticket to the software vendor to resolve the problem.

A ticketing system for internal use usually involves requests to an IT department. It streamlines the process for submitting problems and getting them resolved. Ticketing software for consumers might be assigned to a support person who is familiar with typical technical issues. According to CompTIA, some of the information needed to resolve an issue using a ticketing system might include:

- User information (name, location, job position, etc.)
- Date
- Device information (type of device, model, serial, etc.)
- Categories
- Severity
- Escalation levels
- Problem description (clarity here is very important)
- Progress notes
- Problem resolution (never forget this, always document your findings)

Clear, concise writing is critical when it comes to the problem description, notes, and resolution. You probably won't be the only tech responding to every ticket, so it's important that your coworkers can understand what the problem is and how it is being addressed. Figure 28-5 shows how this information might be presented on a trouble ticket.

Here is an example of how a ticketing system process might play out. Jamie's company computer is not starting. She contacts the IT department by submitting a helpdesk "ticket" in which she provides necessary information (name, date, device information, description of problem, etc.) that helps the responding tech, Jamal, get an initial idea of what the issue is and how to help resolve the issue.

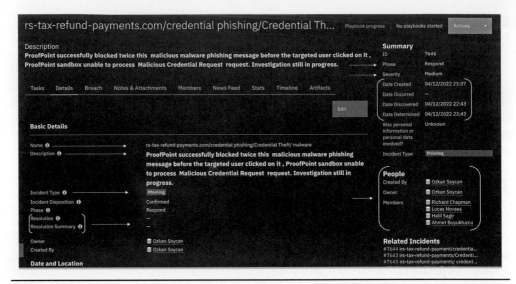

Figure 28-5 A typical interface for a ticketing system

Next, depending on the type of ticketing system, Jamal the tech contacts user Jamie and asks her to explain in further detail what is wrong with the computer. Jamal starts troubleshooting by asking questions such as "Is the computer plugged in?" and "Is the power source completely plugged into the PC?" He also takes notes, documenting his questions and her responses, and any information about their interaction regarding the issue. Jamie responds to Jamal's questions until they have pinpointed the issue with the computer. Depending on the severity of the issue, the issue either will be resolved and the ticket will be closed or, if the issue cannot be resolved, the ticket will be escalated to another tech who might have more in-depth experience and guidance to help solve Jamie's PC issue.

Knowledge Base/Articles

Organizations use documentation to enable cooperation among employees and coordination among departments. From a tech's perspective, documentation helps in troubleshooting various issues. Creating and maintaining a company *knowledge base*—a set of documents that tell the tale of equipment used, problems encountered, and solutions to those problems—provides an essential tool for current and future techs. The articles could be, for example, articles from third-party tech sources that apply to the organization's equipment, such as Cisco articles about the routers the organization uses.

Change-Management Best Practices

CompTIA A+ techs are well positioned to offer valuable *change management* insights. You see what works, what doesn't, and what needs to change. The old laser printers in the accounting department, for example, can't keep up with user needs and you're spending way too much time each week keeping them running. And you're tired of users complaining to you. Change is needed.

Change isn't only grass-roots driven, but often comes from the top. Every organization has formal and informal change-management processes and a designated individual to oversee these processes. You can't just buy a new laser printer, for example, without considering the cost and impact. You can't upgrade the operating systems for 100 users without thorough testing and analysis of the OS. Let's take a closer look at change-management best practices, which include documented business processes and the change-management process.

Documented Business Processes

Every step of a change needs *documented business processes*. Documented business processes include a plan to return an infrastructure to its pre-change environment, the steps to create an operational environment for development and/or testing, as well as appointing an individual who is responsible for these types of processes. Let's take a look at these three documented business processes, which the CompTIA A+ 1102 objectives identify, respectively, as *rollback plan*, *sandbox testing*, and *responsible staff member*.

Rollback Plan

What if an executed change is a failure? This happens more than you think. Therefore, before a change occurs, a *rollback plan* must be in place that defines the steps needed to return the infrastructure to its pre-change environment. OS rollbacks, uninstallation, or return to old equipment are all possible parts of a good rollback plan.

For example, Jamie at Bayland Widgets Corp. (BWC) wants to upgrade 16 systems in the design lab from Windows 7 to Windows 11. She obtains approval from management and subsequently implements the upgrade. After a few days, several users have complained that an important CAD application BWC uses is having issues, such as software freezes.

Jamie looks at the rollback plan documentation that lays out the steps for undoing the upgrades. She follows through with the undo process, making notes about the steps, then awaits further instructions for how to get the design lab computers upgraded without failures.

Sandbox Testing

Simply put, a *sandbox* is a place where you can experiment without messing up the primary system. A sandbox usually is a virtualized environment (refer to Chapter 22) that isolates the test machine from the host machine to avoid causing additional problems. The ability to restore a VM or container from a snapshot makes each of them an ideal choice for *sandbox testing*, which entails checking out new and updated applications without putting the systems and data you depend on at risk.

Responsible Staff Member

Activities like rollback plans and sandbox testing (and change management, discussed in the next section) are typically led by a *responsible staff member (RSM)*. This individual leads projects like these by following policies, processes, and procedures that have been developed (and likely refined over time) toward facilitating, coordinating, and implementing projects.

For example, Janice, the director of the accounting department, needs 20 of her employees' computers upgraded to Windows 11. Who does she contact to initiate this change? The responsible staff member, of course! This person is appointed by IT department leadership and will assist Janice from the beginning of the upgrade all the way to the end. Depending on the size of your organization, the RSM may be the person who addresses the problem themselves or a manager who coordinates with others to get it fixed.

Change-Management Process

A change-management process enables organizations to implement changes to IT infrastructure in a safe and cost-effective manner. Any organization with a change-management process should have documents that lay out the steps, who performs them, and how they go about it.

One of your first jobs as a tech is to consult these documents so that—when change comes your way (either from you or from on high)—you'll already understand the process. When it's time for a change, start by reviewing this process to avoid being embarrassed about (and possibly disciplined for) missing some important step.

There's no single guide to change management, though most organizations follow common-sense guidelines. This section provides an outline of the change-management best practices CompTIA recommends. A package created by a CompTIA A+ tech should include all the documentation just discussed, plus receipts, overtime records, an inventory of changed systems, lists of new users created, signed end-user acceptance forms, and so on.

Request Forms

A *request form* kicks off the change-management process. At some point, someone (maybe you or maybe the CIO of the company you work for) identifies a problem that needs to be fixed and submits a basic request form to IT. Depending on your organization, this form may range from a simple one-pager to an extremely complex set of documents. However, regardless of the level of complexity, all request forms have three things in common. They state the problem, what needs to be fixed, and what the desired outcome is.

Beyond these essentials, other information may be needed, such as why this change is important, who it will benefit, how soon it needs to be implemented, and a host of other factors. Again, these requirements all vary depending on the organization you work for and the procedures and requirements it has put in place. The key thing to remember here is that if you submit a change request form, you should be ready to explain why the change is needed. If you can do that, the rest is all a matter of following processes, which you will pick up quickly.

Determine the Purpose of the Change

No organization is ever going to give you new equipment or allow you to make upgrades without knowing why they are needed. To propose a change, you'll almost certainly need to document the *purpose of the change*. Returning to the scenario from the earlier "Rollback Plan" section in which Jamie at BWC wanted to upgrade 16 systems in the design lab from Windows 7 to Windows 11, users have demanded the latest OS from Microsoft to better serve customers who have (all) jumped to Windows 11. The purpose of the change, therefore, is improved performance and support for clients.

Determine the Scope of the Change

Usually included as part of the purpose of the change, the *scope of the change* defines who and what this change will affect. This includes an inventory of all systems involved, the number of people involved in making the change, how long the change will take, and often the estimated cost of the change.

In our design lab scenario, Jamie estimates that in order to upgrade 16 comput-ing devices to Windows 11, she will need approximately three people to help with the upgrade, and it should be completed in three days. With this information, in addition to a determination of which edition of Windows 11 will be installed, Jamie now has a pretty good idea of what her overall budget will be.

Document the Date and Time of the Change

Knowing when changes will be deployed is essential. Depending on the application and your organization, anywhere from a few people to literally thousands of people may be impacted. Thus, a clearcut date and time needs to be established for when any system changes will occur. You don't want to be "that guy" who pushes the big red button and sends their company into complete chaos. Imagine that your alarm clock has been set to play heavy metal music at maximum volume and you have no idea what time it will go off. If the music starts to blare before you want to get up, you would very likely wake up extremely grumpy and the day that followed would be far from optimal. This is exactly what your colleagues will be like if you don't adequately document the date and time associated with system changes.

Determine Impact

This phase of change management can be a little tricky, depending on the existing level of documentation related to your systems. Your goal here is to identify which systems the change will impact (both the system the change is made to and its interconnected sys-tems) and to what extent they will be impacted (e.g., unavailable to users for two hours). In a perfect world, every organization should have a complete architectural mapping of all systems and the interrelationships that exist between components. When this is the case, you can reference the documentation and trace where connections exist and deduce where the change will likely impact other systems. This enables you to give everyone a heads-up as to what to expect, when it will happen, and what steps they might need to take. However, you aren't always going to be in a situation where you have access to a complete overview of how systems are connected.

There is an old joke in the IT world that goes like this, "There is only one guy who knows how this all works and he died three years ago." Yea, it's rather gallows humor, but unfortunately it is frequently applicable in a general sense. As organizations grow, they have the tendency to stack systems upon systems, with little or no documentation explaining what happened, when it happened, or why it happened. If this describes your organization, you are in the unenviable spot of basically flying with one eye covered.

However, by acquainting yourself with the systems that you will be working with, you will quickly learn how things are connected, and when asked to perform this type of assessment, you can make assumptions as to where interrelationships exist. The key here is to remember the old adage "Better safe than sorry." So, if anything, be overly cautious and prepare others for the worst-case scenario.

Analyze the Level of Risk

All changes to infrastructure come with risk. A proper change-management request will certainly require a *risk analysis*, a detailed assessment of possible problems that could result from the change to determine the *risk level* of the change. Determining the risk level will include the development of a non-exhaustive list of questions covering as many possible things that could go wrong during the change. What if the upgrade fails? Has the new application been tested on a sample system? Will the new computers have adequate firewalls? Don't panic (well, not too much), as any risk analysis will almost certainly be passed off to a security person in your organization—but that person might have great interest in your opinions and concerns!

Change Board Approvals

So, Jamie has all this documentation to back up her request to upgrade 16 design lab computers to Windows 11. She has documented the purpose and scope of the change, the proposed date and time of the change, the affected systems and corresponding impact, and the level of risk the changes poses. Now she needs to submit this documentation to the *change board* to obtain their approval. The change board consists of techs and representatives from management, IT security, and administration who meet on a regular basis (quarterly is common). They review the change documentation and either approve or deny the change, but more often than not they first ask for more information or details, making a "proposal–rejection–fix–back to change board" cycle that repeats itself until everyone is satisfied.

Plan for the Change

If you receive approval from the change board, you'll need to plan for the change. What needs to be done before the change starts? What needs to be purchased? Where will new, uninstalled equipment be stored? On which days will you implement this change? During what time period? Who will cover your other duties while you're otherwise engaged? Anything that needs to be ready before you start is covered in the plan for the change.

End-User Acceptance

Part of successful change management is educating the end users in both the need for the change and how to adapt to changed systems. *End-user acceptance* is vital for successful change. More than anything else this means training. Do the users know how to use the new features on your super printer? What new features in this OS upgrade do end users need to learn? Are the end users versed in the new application (and know not to use the old one)?

Now let's shift gears and discuss how you and end users need to be aware of environmental impacts and how to control them so that your organization's existing technology is protected, as well as technology you may have proposed to implement in a potential change-management plan.

Environmental Impacts and Local Environmental Controls

Computers are surrounded by a host of dangers all just waiting to wreak havoc. In addition to power surges, brownouts, and blackouts, discussed in Chapter 7, there are other factors that could negatively affect your computer. Environmental factors such as chemicals stored near your computer, dust, heat, cold, wet…it's a jungle out there!

Managing environmental controls requires a person who can multitask. They must make sure the equipment is working properly and is maintained and monitored, and they must also be ready for any unexpected variables to pop up in the interim. A person in this type of position undoubtedly needs clear processes and procedures in place to make sure that a certain level of protection has been met.

 EXAM TIP   Expect questions on environmental threats, impacts, and how to control them on the CompTIA A+ 220-1102 exam.

Temperature, Humidity, and Ventilation

Proper local environmental controls help secure servers and workstations from the environmental impact of excessive heat, dust, and humidity. Such environmental controls include air conditioning, proper ventilation, air filtration, and monitors for temperature and humidity. A CompTIA A+ technician maintains an awareness of temperature, humidity level, and ventilation, so that he or she can tell very quickly when levels or settings are out of whack.

A computer works best in an environment where the air is clean, dry, and room temperature. CompTIA doesn't expect you to become an environmental engineer, but it does expect you to explain and deal with how dirty or humid or hot air can affect a computer. We've covered all of these topics to some extent throughout the book, so let's just do a quick overview with security in mind.

Ventilation Patrol

Most computers are designed to operate at room temperature, which is somewhere in the area of 22°C (72°F) with the relative humidity in the 30–40 percent range. Colder and dryer is better for computers (but not for people), so the real challenge is when the temperature and the humidity go higher.

A modern office will usually have a good heating, ventilation, and air conditioning (HVAC) system, so your job as a tech is to make sure that nothing interferes with the proper functioning of your HVAC system. That means you're pretty much always on ventilation patrol. Watch for the following to make sure air is flowing:

- Make sure ducts are always clear of obstructions.
- Make sure duct dampers are adjusted for proper airflow (not too hot or too cold).
- Make sure equipment is located in an area with proper ventilation.

Dirty Air

Dust and debris aren't good for any electronic components. Your typical office air conditioning does a pretty good job of eliminating the worst offenders, but not all computers are in nice offices. No matter where the computers reside, you need to monitor your systems for dirt. The best way to do this is observation as part of your regular work. Dust and debris will show up all over the systems, but the best place to look are the fans. Fans will collect dust and dirt quickly (see Figure 28-6).

Figure 28-6
Dirty fan

Dust Cleanup   All electronic components get dirty over time. To clean them, you need to use either compressed air or a nonstatic vacuum. So which one do you use? The rule is simple: If you don't mind dust blowing all over the place, use compressed air. If you don't want dust blowing all over the place, use a vacuum.

Airborne Particle Protection   Computers and the individuals operating them are typically in enclosed, indoor environments. Just as you would in your own home, changing the air filters on a regular basis reduces the amount of airborne particles coming through the filters. Dedicate a certain date to change all of the filters and make sure to always keep an inventory of the correct size filters ready for the next filter change. Another option to protect against airborne particles is to wear a mask such as the N95 masks sold in many home improvement and hardware stores.

Location/Equipment Placement   Equipment closets filled with racks of servers need proper airflow to keep things cool and to control dusty air. Make sure that the room is ventilated and air-conditioned (see Figure 28-7) and that the air filters are changed regularly.

Figure 28-7
Air-conditioning vent in a small server closet

If things are really bad, you can enclose a system in a dust shield. Dust shields come complete with their own filters to keep a computer clean and happy even in the worst of environments.

   EXAM TIP   Always use proper ventilation, air filters, and enclosures. To protect against airborne particles, consider wearing a protective mask.

Hazardous Materials

Offices are filled with chemicals and substances that pose health risks. Some of these risks are immediate—hazardous materials can burst into flames or damage your skin, lungs, and eyes. Others may cause cancer or other health conditions through regular exposure over many years. The CompTIA A+ 1102 objectives want you to know about compliance to government regulations that apply to working with these substances.

Regulations may sound intimidating, but the goal here is simple: people who work with or around dangerous substances deserve to know what the risks are, what precautions they should take, and what to do if there's an accident. You'll need to consult and comply with local regulations, but you should at least be familiar with the *material safety data sheet (MSDS)*—a document that details the risks, precautions, and clean-up/disposal procedures—for any substances you work with regularly and know how to find the MSDS if something you aren't familiar with spills. For specific information on proper battery and toner disposal, and other device and asset disposal, take a look at Chapters 11 and 26.

Recycling E-Waste

Most U.S. cities have one or more environmental services centers that you can use to recycle electronic components. For your city, try a Google (or other search engine) search on the term "environmental services" and you'll almost certainly find a convenient place for e-waste disposal.

Prohibited Content/Activity and Privacy, Licensing, and Policies

Organizations need policies and procedures in place to deal with negative events that affect their networks and systems—an *incidence response*. The larger the organization, the more detailed the incidence response, ranging from the team involved to the planning and steps in every contingency. This is a gigantic topic that is covered in more advanced certifications, such as CompTIA Security+. From a CompTIA A+ tech's standpoint, you need to understand your role and what you should (and definitely should not) do when responding to an incident involving prohibited content or activity. This section explains how prohibited content, computer-related activity, and licensing can trigger negative events and also outlines the important steps to take in the unfortunate instance that such a negative event happens.

Try to stay away from any personal information on a PC. If you find something private (that isn't illegal), ignore it and forget about it. If you find something illegal, you must follow the proper procedures. If a device you work on becomes evidence in legal proceedings, isolate the system and document everything that happens going forward. Pay special attention to the chain of custody or whoever is currently in control of the machine.

Data Classification

Larger organizations, such as government entities, benefit greatly from organizing their data according to its sensitivity—what's called *data classification*—and making certain that computer hardware and software stay as uniform as possible. In addition, many government and internal regulations apply fairly rigorously to these organizations.

Data classification systems vary by the organization, but a common scheme classifies documents as public, internal use only, highly confidential, top secret, and so on.

Using a classification scheme enables employees such as techs to know very quickly what to do with documents, the drives containing documents, and more. Your strategy for recycling a computer system left from a migrated user, for example, will differ a lot if the data on the drive was classified as internal use only or top secret.

Data classification goes hand in hand with *data retention requirements*, which dictate how long data needs to be kept by an organization, and is often related to how it has been classified. Customer data, security logs, and employee data, all can be covered under a company's data retention requirements. After the pre-determined period of retention, data can be disposed of, but until then, it needs to be kept just as safely as data that is currently still in use.

Regulated Data

Regulated data is data that requires specific privacy and security safeguards as mandated by federal, state, or local laws or regulations or by industry standards or regulations. An organization's technology policies must clearly address these privacy and security safeguards. There are four types of regulated data that IT departments must protect. Let's look at each.

Credit Card Transactions

The *Payment Card Industry Data Security Standard (PCI DSS)* is a rigorous set of rules for securing systems that accept, transmit, process, or store credit/debit card payments.

Personally Identifiable Information

Personally identifiable information (PII) is a big umbrella term for any data that can lead back to a specific individual. Regulating and protecting PII will continue to be an issue for industries and government organizations for a long, long time. The *General Data Protection Regulation (GDPR)* is a fairly new law that defines a broad set of rights and protections for the personal information of citizens living in countries in the European Union. Consult your superiors about your organization's policies for working with regulated data.

Laws protecting data have been developed so that organizations can create their own PII documentation for their employees to follow. The main premise behind these laws is that some information collected from individuals contains sensitive information that could easily identify who they are. Also, these regulatory laws specify that any PII data should be permanently deleted if there is no use for it. Never, in any circumstance, should PII be shared with anyone.

A sub-category of PII is personal government-issued information. *Personal government-issued information* consists of things like social security numbers, driver's license or passport numbers, a birth certificate, all of which, unsurprisingly, are issued by the government. These documents and the information they contain are sensitive and can leave someone vulnerable to serious identity theft if they fall into the wrong hands, and special care must be taken to protect them.

Protected Healthcare Data

Protected health information (PHI), or simply *healthcare data*, is basically any data that involves a person's health status, medical records, and healthcare services they have received. Like PII, PHI should never be shared unless given permission by the owner of that information.

Compliance

Compliance means that members of an organization must abide by or comply with all of the rules that apply to the organization. As we discussed earlier when we talked about standard operating procedures, the most common compliance issue revolves around software, such as what sort of software users are allowed to install on their computers. Compliance keeps technical support calls down and enables techs to focus on more serious problems—like an incident response.

Licensing, End-User License Agreement, and Digital Rights Management

Software licensing has many twists that can easily lead a user or a tech out of compliance. Like other creative acts, programmers are granted copyright to the software they create. The copyright owner then decides how he or she or it (the corporation) will license that software for others to use. Licenses can be for personal use or corporate use. They can also be valid licenses or non-expired licenses. Licenses can be closed source or open source. Each of these options has variations as well, so this gets complex. Let's start at the top and work through the variations.

Personal Use License Versus Corporate Use License

For moral or philosophical reasons, some developers want their software to be free for some or all purposes. When Linus Torvalds created the Linux operating system, for example, he made it freely available for everyone. GIMP image-editing software likewise is available to download and use for free.

Personal use licenses have variations. Many personal use programs are "free" only for personal use. If you want to use the excellent TeamViewer remote access program at your office, for example, you need to buy a corporate license. But if you want to log in to your home machine from your personal laptop, you can use TeamViewer for free. When software is released under a *corporate use license*, you have a legal obligation to pay money for access to it—but a lot of variations apply. Traditionally, you bought a copy of a program and could use it forever, sell it to someone else, or give it away. You bought copies for each user with a personal use license, or multiple users with an enterprise license.

Today, the picture is muddier. You can buy the use of Microsoft Office, for example, as long as you pay a monthly or yearly fee. The personal use license enables you to share the software with several other people or accounts and use it on several of your personal machines.

License Validity and Expiration

Many software licenses come with strings attached, and as techs we must pay careful attention to them. For example, a license might say how many systems you can install it on, how many human users it can have, how many CPUs you can run it on, whether you're allowed to use it for commercial purposes, whether someone who owns a valid license can transfer it to anyone else, which version(s) of the software the license is valid for, or even how long the license will remain valid.

A license is *valid* when your organization complies completely with these stipulations. Some programs that demand a license key may straight-up tell you if the license key itself is no longer valid—but confirmation that the license key is valid doesn't mean you're off the hook when it comes to complying with every last clause in the license. Some licenses stipulate that you can *only* use the software with a *non-expired license*. Other licenses permit you to keep using the installed version after the license has expired but cut off your access to updates and security patches until you renew the license.

 EXAM TIP At first glance, valid licenses and non-expired licenses seem to mean the same thing; however, it's important to know the distinctions between the two for the 1102 exam, objective 4.6.

Open Source Licenses

Another huge variation in software use and licensing is what you can do with the source code of an application. *Open source licenses* generally allow you to take the original code and modify it. Some open source licenses require you to make the modified code available for free download; others don't require that at all. *Closed source licenses* stipulate that you can't modify the source code or make it part of some other software suite.

End-User License Agreements

The *end-user license agreement (EULA)* that you must accept to be able to proceed when opening or installing new software obligates you to abide by the use and sharing guidelines stipulated by the software copyright holder. When you agree to the EULA, in other words, you're agreeing not to do things like make illegal copies of the software or attempt to reverse-engineer how it works. The EULA may also give the copyright holder permission to collect data on you and how you use the software and limit whether (or for how much) you can sue the copyright holder if it mangles your files or causes other problems.

Digital Rights Management

Software and media companies use various forms of *digital rights management (DRM)* technology to try to enforce their policies regarding when, where, and how we can use the software or access media such as video, music, and books. In short, DRM is one way the industry has tried to fight software and media piracy over the years. Many programs require activation over the Internet, for example, or a special account with the copyright holder. Some media files can only be opened by the provider's official app.

NOTE The key for a tech is to know the specific licenses paid for by the tech's organization and ensure that the organization abides by those licenses. Using pirated software, exceeding the use limits set by a EULA, and using programs that aren't licensed for commercial use in a corporate setting all expose your organization to lawsuits.

Incident Response

Organizations have *incident response* policies and procedures to deal with negative events. CompTIA A+ techs might be members of the incident response team. As such they need to understand first response actions, identification and reporting of incidents, and chain of custody. Let's start by looking at first response actions.

First Response

First response means securing the area, determining the scope of the incident, and analyzing the impact the incident might have on the organization. If you're part of the incident response team, your first response duties will be spelled out in detail in the incident response plan. Most likely, your team's first action when something bad happens is to secure the area. Securing the area can mean physical lockdown—no one in or out—or other lockdown—no network traffic in or out of the affected section.

Incident Reporting

An *incident report* means telling your supervisor about the data you've gathered regarding a computer or network incident. This provides a record of what you've done and accomplished. It also provides information that, when combined with other information you may or may not know, could reveal a pattern or bigger problem to someone higher up the chain.

This can be accomplished with a *documentation of incident.* Many companies have pre-made forms that you simply fill out and submit. Other places are less formal. Regardless, you need to do this!

Tracking specific problems through incident reports documentation helps current and future techs deal with problematic hardware and individuals. If you have five identical color laser printers in five departments, for example, and one starts jamming regularly after 10,000 pages, documenting the problem—the incident—and the solution will point very clearly to the potential problems with the other four printers when they reach that same usage level.

Once you've gathered data about a particular system or dealt with a computer or network problem, what's next?

Inform Management/Law Enforcement as Necessary

So, you have documented all of the necessary information needed about the incident. Now it's time for you to make a decision. Is the incident at a low risk level and can be resolved at your level? Or, is it something that has escalated to a higher risk level where you need to inform your supervisor? Determine the scope of the incident (single system, whole group of users, and so on) and explore its seriousness and potential impact on the organization. Determining the scope of the incident can be accomplished by questioning users, reviewing log files, and so on. Your network and security people will handle possible impact scenarios and determine if the impact is serious enough to include law enforcement in the investigation.

Chain of Custody

When responding to an incident involving prohibited content or activity, there must be an end-to-end process for identifying who owns what, where it is, and who is liable for it. It asks and answers, "Whose responsibility is this?" when assets, digital or physical, transfer hands in an organization. For example, *who* is in charge and liable for *data integrity* (ensuring that the data is in its original and uncorrupted form) and *data preservation* (ensuring that the data is backed up and kept available)? *Where* is the data stored (i.e., drive, server)? This process, called the *chain of custody*, begins when the evidence is initially seized or collected and establishes a continuous accounting of where the evidence is at all times, who has possessed it, what activities were performed on it, and the details of its storage, use, and transfer. This process helps to ensure the integrity of evidence and minimizes the possibility that it has been altered or tampered with. Chain of custody contributes to the admissibility and value of evidence in court.

Beyond A+

Whew! You've just finished a book that covers everything you need to know to take and pass the CompTIA A+ 1101/1102 exams. Congratulations! What's next?

First, go back to the Introduction and review the study chart and guidelines. Review, review, review! Take the practice exams and look for exam sources online to get even more scoop on the types of questions you'll see.

Second, schedule your exams if you haven't already done so (pressure and diamonds and all that). Having that endpoint in sight helps focus.

Go back to my original question once you've taken and passed both CompTIA A+ exams: What's next? The two logical steps are to start studying for CompTIA Network+ and CompTIA Security+. These complete CompTIA's Core curriculum and round out tech skills needed for today's interconnected and security-heightened world. There are a lot of great writers and videographers out there who have excellent materials on CompTIA Network+ and Security+ (including me), so you won't find it hard to get study materials.

Good luck, my friend, and keep in touch!

Chapter Review

Questions

1. Henry gets a help desk call from Arthur in accounting who reports that his keyboard is not working. This seems like a familiar problem, one that another tech mentioned a short time back. Where should Henry look to find information on the problem?

    A. Change documentation

    B. Incident reports

    C. Asset management documentation

    D. Risk management documentation

2. Annie wants to mark several Mac laptops issued to salespeople so that she can set up a scanner at the office door to track each time the laptops enter and leave the building. What will help her accomplish this goal?

    A. Add a barcode sticker to each laptop.

    B. Add an RFID tag to each laptop.

    C. Submit a change document to the change board.

    D. It can't be done, because the laptops run macOS.

3. Joan has proposed upgrading the inkjet printers in the marketing department with color laser printers. The purpose of the change is to reduce the cost per page printed, because toner is less expensive than ink and the duty cycle of laser printers is longer than that of inkjet printers. The marketing department currently has three inkjet printers. What's her logical next step?

    A. She should complete the scope of change part of the change document to factor in the price of the printers.

    B. She should perform a risk analysis to determine any potentially negative consequences.

    C. She should download the documentation on the new printers and begin the education process for the marketing department on how to use them.

    D. She should contact the change board with her initial proposal.

4. Once the change board has reviewed and approved Joan's plan for the new printers, what's her next step?

    A. Create a rollback plan in case the quality of print with the laser printers isn't sufficient for the marketing materials.

    B. Test the rollback plan.

    C. Finalize the change documentation.

    D. Implement the change plan.

5. What broad term describes the process of creating a road map for current and future techs to make changes or repairs over time for an organization?

    A. Change documentation

    B. Change management

    C. Management documentation

    D. Network documentation

6. What broad term describes the process of enabling organizations to implement changes to IT infrastructure in a safe and cost-effective manner?

    A. Change documentation

    B. Change management

    C. Management documentation

    D. Network documentation

7. As part of the change-management process, educating users on new systems is an important component in which of the following?

    A. Rollback plan

    B. Accessibility training

    C. End-user acceptance

    D. Risk analysis

8. Which of the following is an example of an environmental control?

    A. HVAC system

    B. Temperature and humidity

    C. Surge protector

    D. Fire extinguisher

9. Which of the following is a detailed assessment of possible problems that could result from change?

    A. Acceptable use policy

    B. New-user setup checklist

    C. Regulatory requirements

    D. Risk analysis

10. What does an IT department use for a departing employee to ensure that all equipment has been returned, access has been removed, and, where possible, knowledge transfer has been facilitated?

    A. End-user termination checklist

    B. New-user setup checklist

    C. Network topology diagram

    D. Acceptable use policy

Answers

1. **B.** Henry should check the incident reports to see if there's a history of problems with the computer at that workstation.

2. **B.** Annie should add a radio frequency identification (RFID) tag to each laptop and install a scanner at the door to track when the laptops are taken out of the office and returned.

3. **A.** Joan hasn't finished the scope of change yet, so she should include the price of the printers.

4. **A.** Once the change board has approved the change plan, Joan should make sure to have a good rollback plan in place in case something unforeseen and negative happens.

5. **D.** The term network documentation describes the road map for current and future techs to make changes or repairs over time for the organization.

6. **B.** The term change management describes the process organizations use to implement changes to IT infrastructure in a safe and cost-effective manner.

7. **C.** Training users in new or updated systems leads to end-user acceptance of the changes.

8. **A.** An HVAC system is an example of an environmental control.

9. **D.** A risk analysis is a detailed assessment of possible problems that could result from change.

10. **A.** When an employee parts ways with an organization, the IT department uses an end-user termination checklist to ensure that the employee has returned all equipment, that their access has been removed, and, where possible, knowledge transfer has been facilitated.

Mapping to the CompTIA A+ Objectives

220-1101 Exam Objectives

Exam 220-1101 Objectives	Chapter(s)
3.4 Given a scenario, install and configure motherboards, central processing units (CPUs), and add-on cards.	
Motherboard form factor	6
Advanced Technology eXtended (ATX)	6
Information Technology eXtended (ITX)	6
Motherboard connector types	6, 7, 8
Peripheral Component Interconnect (PCI)	6
PCI Express (PCIe)	6
Power connectors	7
SATA	8
eSATA	8
Headers	6
M.2	8
Motherboard compatibility	3
CPU sockets	3
Advanced Micro Devices, Inc. (AMD)	3
Intel	3
Server	3
Multisocket	6
Desktop	3
Mobile	3
Basic Input/Output System (BIOS)/Unified Extensible Firmware Interface (UEFI) settings	5
Boot options	5
USB permissions	5
Trusted Platform Module (TPM) security features	5
Fan considerations	5
Secure Boot	5
Boot password	5
Encryption	5
TPM	5
Hardware security module (HSM)	5
CPU architecture	3
x64/x86	3
Advanced RISC Machine (ARM)	3
Single-core	3
Multicore	3
Multithreading	3
Virtualization support	3

220-1102 Exam Objectives

Exam 220-1102 Objectives	Chapter(s)
4. Remediate infected systems	27
a. Update anti-malware software	27
b. Scanning and removal techniques (e.g., safe mode, preinstallation environment)	27
5. Schedule scans and run updates	27
6. Enable System Restore and create a restore point in Windows	27
7. Educate the end user	27
3.4 Given a scenario, troubleshoot common mobile OS and application issues.	
Common symptoms	24, 25
Application fails to launch	25
Application fails to close/crashes	25
Application fails to update	25
Slow to respond	25
OS fails to update	24
Battery life issues	25
Randomly reboots	25
Connectivity issues	16, 23, 25
Bluetooth	23
WiFi	23
Near-field communication (NFC)	25
AirDrop	16
Screen does not autorotate	25
3.5 Given a scenario, troubleshoot common mobile OS and application security issues.	
Security concerns	25
Android package (APK) source	25
Developer mode	25
Root access/jailbreak	25
Bootleg/malicious application	25
Application spoofing	25
Common symptoms	25
High network traffic	25
Sluggish response time	25
Data-usage limit notification	25
Limited Internet connectivity	25
No Internet connectivity	25
High number of ads	25
Fake security warnings	25
Unexpected application behavior	25
Leaked personal files/data	25

Exam 220-1102 Objectives	Chapter(s)
Change management	28
Request forms	28
Purpose of the change	28
Scope of the change	28
Date and time of the change	28
Affected systems/impact	28
Risk analysis	28
Risk level	28
Change board approvals	28
End-user acceptance	28
4.3 Given a scenario, implement workstation backup and recovery methods.	
Backup and recovery	14
Full	14
Incremental	14
Differential	14
Synthetic	14
Backup testing	14
Frequency	14
Backup rotation schemes	14
On site vs. off site	14
Grandfather-father-son (GFS)	14
3-2-1 backup rule	14
4.4 Given a scenario, use common safety procedures.	
Electrostatic discharge (ESD) straps	1
ESD mats	1
Equipment grounding	1
Proper power handling	1
Proper component handling and storage	1
Antistatic bags	1
Compliance with government regulations	1
Personal safety	1
Disconnect power before repairing PC	1
Lifting techniques	1
Electrical fire safety	1
Safety goggles	1
Air filtration mask	1

About the Online Content

This book comes complete with

- A video from Mike Meyers introducing the CompTIA A+ certification exams
- TotalTester Online practice exam software with practice exam questions for both exam 220-1101 and 220-1102, as well as pre-assessment tests for each exam to get you started.
- More than an hour of sample video training episodes from Mike Meyers' CompTIA A+ Certification video series
- More than 20 sample simulations from Total Seminars' TotalSims for CompTIA A+
- Links to a collection of Mike Meyers' favorite tools and utilities for PC troubleshooting

System Requirements

The current and previous major versions of the following desktop browsers are recommended and supported: Chrome, Microsoft Edge, Firefox, and Safari. These browsers update frequently, and sometimes an update may cause compatibility issues with the TotalTester Online or other content hosted on the Training Hub. If you run into a problem using one of these browsers, please try using another until the problem is resolved.

Your Total Seminars Training Hub Account

To get access to the online content you will need to create an account on the Total Seminars Training Hub. Registration is free, and you will be able to track all your online content using your account. You may also opt in if you wish to receive marketing information from McGraw Hill or Total Seminars, but this is not required for you to gain access to the online content.

Privacy Notice

McGraw Hill values your privacy. Please be sure to read the Privacy Notice available during registration to see how the information you have provided will be used. You may view our Corporate Customer Privacy Policy by visiting the McGraw Hill Privacy Center. Visit the **mheducation.com** site and click **Privacy** at the bottom of the page.

Single User License Terms and Conditions

Online access to the digital content included with this book is governed by the McGraw Hill License Agreement outlined next. By using this digital content you agree to the terms of that license.

Access   To register and activate your Total Seminars Training Hub account, simply follow these easy steps.

1. Go to this URL: **hub.totalsem.com/mheclaim**

2. To register and create a new Training Hub account, enter your e-mail address, name, and password on the **Register** tab. No further personal information (such as credit card number) is required to create an account.

    If you already have a Total Seminars Training Hub account, enter your e-mail address and password on the **Log in** tab.

3. Enter your Product Key: `c34m-cnm7-nk9w`

4. Click to accept the user license terms.

5. For new users, click the **Register and Claim** button to create your account. For existing users, click the **Log in and Claim** button.

    You will be taken to the Training Hub and have access to the content for this book.

Duration of License   Access to your online content through the Total Seminars Training Hub will expire one year from the date the publisher declares the book out of print.

Your purchase of this McGraw Hill product, including its access code, through a retail store is subject to the refund policy of that store.

The Content is a copyrighted work of McGraw Hill, and McGraw Hill reserves all rights in and to the Content. The Work is © 2023 by McGraw Hill.

Restrictions on Transfer   The user is receiving only a limited right to use the Content for the user's own internal and personal use, dependent on purchase and continued ownership of this book. The user may not reproduce, forward, modify, create derivative works based upon, transmit, distribute, disseminate, sell, publish, or sublicense the Content or in any way commingle the Content with other third-party content without McGraw Hill's consent.

Limited Warranty   The McGraw Hill Content is provided on an "as is" basis. Neither McGraw Hill nor its licensors make any guarantees or warranties of any kind, either express or implied, including, but not limited to, implied warranties of merchantability or fitness for a particular purpose or use as to any McGraw Hill Content or the information therein or any warranties as to the accuracy, completeness, correctness, or results to be obtained from, accessing or using the McGraw Hill Content, or any material referenced in such Content or any information entered into licensee's product by users or other persons and/or any material available on or that can be accessed through the licensee's product (including via any hyperlink or otherwise) or as to non-infringement of third-party rights. Any warranties of any kind, whether express or implied, are disclaimed. Any material or data obtained through use of the McGraw Hill Content is at your own discretion and risk and user understands that it will be solely responsible for any resulting damage to its computer system or loss of data.

Neither McGraw Hill nor its licensors shall be liable to any subscriber or to any user or anyone else for any inaccuracy, delay, interruption in service, error or omission, regardless of cause, or for any damage resulting therefrom.

In no event will McGraw Hill or its licensors be liable for any indirect, special or consequential damages, including but not limited to, lost time, lost money, lost profits or good will, whether in contract, tort, strict liability or otherwise, and whether or not such damages are foreseen or unforeseen with respect to any use of the McGraw Hill Content.

TotalTester Online

TotalTester Online provides you with a simulation of the CompTIA A+ exams. Exams can be taken in Practice Mode or Exam Mode. Practice Mode provides an assistance window with hints, references to the book, explanations of the correct and incorrect answers, and the option to check your answer as you take the test. Exam Mode provides a simulation of the actual exam. The number of questions, the types of questions, and the time allowed are intended to be an accurate representation of the exam environment. The option to customize your quiz allows you to create custom exams from selected domains or chapters, and you can further customize the number of questions and time allowed.

To take a test, follow the instructions provided in the previous section to register and activate your Total Seminars Training Hub account. When you register, you will be taken to the Total Seminars Training Hub. From the Training Hub Home page, select your certification from the list of Your Topics on the Home page, and then click the TotalTester link to launch the TotalTester. Once you've launched your TotalTester, you can select the option to customize your quiz and begin testing yourself in Practice Mode or Exam Mode. All exams provide an overall grade and a grade broken down by domain.

Pre-Assessment

In addition to the sample exam questions, the TotalTester also includes a CompTIA A+ Pre-Assessment test for each of the CompTIA Core 1 (1101) and Core 2 (1102) exams. The pre-assessment exams are designed to help you assess your understanding of the topics before reading the book. To launch the pre-assessment tests, click **Pre-Assessment Test** for the exam you want to take. The A+ Pre-Assessment tests are 50 questions each and run in Exam Mode. When you complete the test, you can review the questions with answers and detailed explanation by clicking **See Detailed Results**.

Playing the CompTIA A+ Introduction Video

You can watch the video introduction to the CompTIA A+ exams online. Select **CompTIA A+ All-in-One 11e (1101 & 1102) Resources** from the list of "Your Topics" on the Home page. Click the Book Resources tab, and then select the **A+ Intro** from the list of resources on the right.

Mike's CompTIA A+ Video Training Sample

Over an hour of training videos, starring Mike Meyers, are available for free. Select **CompTIA A+ All-in-One 11e (1101 & 1102) Resources** from the list of "Your Topics" on the Home page. Click the TotalVideos tab. The videos are organized by chapter, and there are over an hour of free videos available for study. You can purchase Mike's complete video training series from the Total Seminars website www.totalsem.com.

TotalSims Sample for CompTIA A+

 From your Total Seminars Training Hub account, select **CompTIA A+ All-in-One 11e (1101 & 1102) Resources** from the list of "Your Topics" on the Home page. Click the TotalSims tab. The simulations are organized by chapter, and there are over 20 free simulations available for reviewing topics referenced in the book. You can purchase access to the full TotalSims for A+ with over 200 simulations from the Total Seminars website, www.totalsem.com.

Mike's Cool Tools

Mike loves freeware/open-source PC troubleshooting and networking tools! Access the utilities mentioned in the text by selecting **CompTIA A+ All-in-One 11e (1101 & 1102) Resources** from the list of "Your Topics" on the Home page. Click the Book Resources tab, and then select **Mike's Cool Tools**.

Technical Support

For questions regarding the TotalTester or operation of the Training Hub, visit **www.totalsem.com** or e-mail **support@totalsem.com**.

For questions regarding book content, visit **www.mheducation.com/customerservice**.

100BASE-T   Ethernet cabling system designed to run at 100 Mbps on twisted pair cabling. Also called Fast Ethernet.

1000BASE-T   Ethernet cabling system designed to run at 1000 Mbps on twisted pair cabling. Also called Gigabit Ethernet.

1000BASE-TX   Similar to 1000BASE-T but uses two pairs of wires rather than four. Not as commonly used as 1000BASE-T.

10GBASE-T   Ethernet standard that supports speeds of up to 10 Gbps and is common on server-to-server connections. Requires Cat 6 or better twisted pair or fiber optic cabling.

2-in-1   Portable devices that serve as both a laptop and a tablet.

3G   Third-generation cellular data technologies (such as EV-DO, UTMS, HSPA+, and HSDPA) with real-world speeds under 10 Mbps.

4G   Fourth-generation cellular data technologies. Most popularly implemented as Long Term Evolution (LTE), a wireless data standard with theoretical download speeds of 1 Gbps and upload speeds of 100 Mbps.

5G   Fifth-generation cellular data technologies, launched in 2019. Their specifications call for up to 20 Gbps, but real-world speeds are often less and can vary depending on the carrier and location.

64-bit processing   A type of processing that can run a compatible 64-bit operating system, such as Windows 10 and 11, and 64-bit applications. 64-bit PCs have a 64-bit-wide address bus, enabling them to use more than 4 GB of RAM.

802.11a   Wireless networking standard that operates in the 5-GHz band with a theoretical maximum throughput of 54 Mbps.

802.11ac   Wireless networking standard that operates in the 5-GHz band and uses multiple in/multiple out (MIMO) and multi-user MIMO (MU-MIMO) to achieve a theoretical maximum throughput of 1+ Gbps.

802.11ax   Wireless networking standard that operates in the 2.4-, 5-, and 6-GHz bands. Also known as high-efficiency wireless, it introduces improvements that optimize congested networks and reduce power use on client devices. The main improvement is the introduction of the 6-GHz band, which supports more channels, is less saturated, and suffers less interference. Also known as *Wi-Fi 6* or *Wi-Fi 6E* (if it supports the 6-GHz band).

802.11b   Wireless networking standard that operates in the 2.4-GHz band with a theoretical maximum throughput of 11 Mbps.

802.11g   Wireless networking standard that operates in the 2.4-GHz band with a theoretical maximum throughput of 54 Mbps and is backward compatible with 802.11b.

802.11n   Wireless networking standard that can operate in both the 2.4-GHz and (optionally) 5-GHz bands and uses multiple in/multiple out (MIMO) to achieve a theoretical maximum throughput of 100+ Mbps.

AC (alternating current)   Type of electricity in which the flow of electrons alternates direction, back and forth, in a circuit.

acceptable use policy (AUP)   Defines what actions employees may or may not perform on company equipment, including computers, phones, printers, and even the network itself. This policy defines the handling of passwords, e-mail, and many other issues.

access control list (ACL)   A clearly defined list of permissions that specifies what actions an authenticated user may perform on a shared resource.

access control vestibule   Small room with a set of doors—one to the unsecured area and one to a secured area. Only one door can open at a time, and individuals must authenticate to continue through the door to the secured area. Combats tailgating. Also commonly known as a mantrap.

access point   *See* WAP.

Accounts (Windows Settings)   Windows Settings category that includes e-mail and account options.

activation (software)   Process of confirming that an installed copy of a Microsoft product (most commonly Windows or a Microsoft Office application) is legitimate. Usually done at the end of software installation.

active partition   On a hard drive, the primary partition that contains an operating system.

actively listen   Part of respectful communication involving listening and taking notes without interrupting.

activity light   An LED on a NIC, hub, or switch that blinks rapidly to show data transfers over the network.

Address Resolution Protocol (ARP)   Protocol in the TCP/IP suite used with the command-line utility of the same name (arp) to determine the MAC address that corresponds to a particular IP address

administrative shares   Administrator tool to give local admins access to hard drives and system root folders.

Administrative Tools   Group of Control Panel applets, including Computer Management, Event Viewer, Performance Monitor, and Task Scheduler.

administrator account   User account, created when the OS is first installed, that is allowed complete, unfettered access to the system without restriction.

administrator password   Credentials for the system administrator account.

Administrators group   List of members with complete administrator privileges.

ADSL (asymmetric digital subscriber line)   Fully digital, dedicated connection to the telephone system that provides average download speeds of 3–15 Mbps and upload speeds of 384 Kbps to 1.5 Mbps. *Asymmetric* identifies that upload and download speeds are different, with download usually being significantly faster than upload.

Advanced Encryption Standard (AES)   A block cipher created in the late 1990s that uses a 128-bit block size and a 128-, 192-, or 256-bit key size. Practically uncrackable.

Advanced Micro Devices (AMD)   *See* AMD.

AirDrop   Apple feature for its various operating systems that enables easy wireless sharing of files between Apple devices.

algorithm   Set of rules for solving a problem in a given number of steps.

AMD (Advanced Micro Devices)   CPU and chipset manufacturer that competes with Intel. Produces FX, A-Series, Ryzen, and Opteron CPUs and APUs. Also produces video card processors (GPUs) under its Radeon brand.

amperage   *See* current.

amperes (amps or A)   Unit of measure for amperage, or electrical current.

analog   Device that uses a physical quantity, such as length or voltage, to represent the value of a number. By contrast, digital storage relies on a coding system of numeric units.

Android application package (APK)   Installation software for Android apps.

ANSI/TIA   A major telecommunication standards agency. The Telecommunication Industry Association (TIA) establishes the UTP categories under the ANSI/TIA 568 specification. The American National Standards Institute (ANSI) accredits TIA standards to ensure compatibility of industry and international standards. *See also* UTP.

anti-malware program   Software designed to identify and block or remove malware. Typically powered by frequently updated definition files containing the signatures of known malware.

antistatic bag   Bag made of antistatic plastic into which electronics are placed for temporary or long-term storage. Used to protect components from electrostatic discharge.

antistatic mat   Special surface on which to lay electronics to prevent electrostatic discharge. Includes a grounding connection designed to equalize electrical potential between a workbench and one or more electronic devices.

antistatic wrist strap   Special device worn around the wrist to prevent electrostatic discharge. Includes a grounding connection designed to equalize electrical potential between a technician and an electronic device.

antivirus program   Software designed to combat viruses by either seeking out and destroying them or passively guarding against them. Typically, it is frequently updated with new definition files to enable up-to-date protection from newly discovered viruses.

API (application programming interface)   Enables computer programs to "talk" to each other. Unlike a user interface, an API is not visible to the user. Documented APIs enable one vendor to create software that can communicate with another vendor's software.

APIPA (Automatic Private IP Addressing)   Feature of Windows that automatically assigns an IP address to the system when the client cannot obtain an IP address automatically. *See also* zeroconf.

App Store   Apple's mobile software storefront, where you can purchase apps for your smartphone, tablet, and other Apple products.

Apple File System (APFS)   Apple's proprietary file system, introduced to replace the older HFS+.

applet   Generic term for a program in the Windows Control Panel.

application manager   Mobile device interface for removing and managing apps running on the device.

application programming interface   *See* API.

application spoofing   The act of disguising a malicious mobile app as a legitimate one for the purpose of infecting a target device with malware or stealing credentials like passwords.

application virtualization   Process that virtualizes OS capabilities that an application would normally use to install and do its work. Enables the use of an application without actually installing it, running an application that only works on an older OS version, or even running an application that only works on a different OS.

Applications   Tab in Task Manager that lists running applications.

Apps (Windows Settings)   Windows settings category that enables you to list, view, manage autostart, and uninstall apps.

Apps & features   Area of the Windows 10 Settings Apps category that enables users to add and remove programs and Windows features.

apt-get   Linux command for installing or updating a program using the advanced packaging tool.

ARM (Advanced RISC Machine)   Energy-efficient processor design frequently used in mobile devices and also used by the latest macOS computers using the M1 and M2 processors.

ARP   *See* Address Resolution Protocol.

aspect ratio   Ratio of width to height of a display. Wide-screen displays such as modern TVs, desktop computer monitors, portable computer displays, and even smartphones commonly use 16:9 or 16:10, although you can find devices with many other aspect ratios.

assertive communication   Means of communication that is not pushy or bossy but is also not soft. Useful in dealing with upset customers as it both defuses their anger and gives them confidence that you know what you're doing.

asset tag   Inventory tracking tags (which may be simple barcodes or use wireless networking protocols such as RFID) that help an organization track items such as equipment.

attack vector   The route or methods used by a given attack (including malware).

attributes   Values in a file that determine the hidden, read-only, system, and archive status of the file.

ATX (Advanced Technology Extended)   Popular motherboard form factor that generally replaced the AT form factor.

audio jack   Very popular connector used to transmit two audio signals; perfect for stereo sound. Confusingly, you can find the diameter described as both 1/8 inch and 3.5 mm.

AUP   *See* acceptable use policy.

authentication   The process of identifying and granting access to some user trying to access a system.

authorization   The process that defines which resources an authenticated user may access and what the user may do with those resources.

AutoPlay   A Windows feature that opens a dialog box when removable media is inserted into the computer, providing options based on what Windows finds on the drive, including starting the Autorun application.

Autorun   A feature that enables Windows to look for and read a file called autorun.inf immediately after a removable media device (optical disc or thumb drive) is inserted and automatically run whatever program the file lists.

Backup and Restore   Windows 7's backup utility. It offers two options: create a backup or restore from a backup. Windows 10 still supports making and restoring these backups, which it calls Backup and Restore (Windows 7). *See also* File History.

backup testing   The process of ensuring that file or system backups have produced backups from which you can restore usable systems and files.

badge reader   *See* smart card reader.

bandwidth   The capacity of a network to transmit a given amount of data during a given period.

bash   Default command shell on macOS and most Linux distributions. *See* shell.

basic disk   Hard drive partitioned in the "classic" way with a master boot record (MBR) and partition table. *See also* dynamic disks.

battery health   The amount of charge a battery can hold. Decreases over time as the battery is charged and discharged.

battery life   The length of time a battery can be used before needing to be recharged.

binary numbers   Number system with a base of 2, unlike the number systems most of us use that have bases of 10 (decimal numbers), 12 (measurement in feet and inches), and 60 (time). Binary numbers are preferred for computers for precision and economy. An electronic circuit that can detect the difference between two states (on–off, 0–1) is easier and more inexpensive to build than one that could detect the differences among ten states (0–9).

biometric authentication   Authentication process using biometric data such as voice, fingerprints, or retinal scans.

biometric scanner   Hardware device used to support authentication; works by scanning and remembering a unique aspect of a user's body part (e.g., retina, iris, face, or fingerprint) by using some form of sensing device such as a retinal scanner.

BIOS (basic input/output services) (basic input/output system)   Classically, software routines burned onto the system ROM of a PC. More commonly seen as firmware that directly controls a particular piece of hardware. This firmware handles startup operations and low-level control of hardware such as disk drives, the keyboard, and monitor.

bit   Single binary digit. Also, any device that can be in an on or off state.

BitLocker Drive Encryption   Drive encryption software offered in high-end versions of Windows. BitLocker requires a special chip to validate hardware status and to ensure that the computer hasn't been hacked.

Bluetooth   Wireless technology designed to create small wireless networks preconfigured to do specific jobs, but not meant to replace full-function networks or Wi-Fi.

Blue Screen of Death (BSoD)   Infamous error screen that appears when Windows encounters an unrecoverable error. This is an example of a proprietary crash screen.

bollard   Short post made of metal, concrete, or another solid material used to prevent vehicles from entering or driving onto an area. Often used to protect pedestrian areas or deny vehicles from getting too close to a secure area.

boot To initiate an automatic routine that clears the memory, loads the operating system, and prepares the computer for use. Term is derived from "pull yourself up by your bootstraps." Necessary because RAM doesn't retain program instructions when power is turned off.

boot method Media a computer uses to initiate the booting process. Includes optical media, removable drives, or a networked location. For the related CMOS setting, *see* boot sequence.

boot options Settings in the system setup program that define which devices the system will attempt to boot from (and in what order).

boot sector First sector on a storage drive. The boot-up software in ROM tells the computer to load whatever program is found there. If a system disk is read, the program in the boot record directs the computer to the root directory to load the operating system.

bootable disk Any storage device with a self-starting operating system.

bootleg application Fake application designed to trick users into installing it. *See also* application spoofing.

bootmgr Windows Boot Manager. Manages the boot process using information from the Boot Configuration Data (BCD) file.

bootrec A Windows Recovery Environment troubleshooting and repair tool that repairs the master boot record, boot sector, or BCD store.

botnet Network of computers infected with malware that can be controlled to do the bidding of the malware developers, or anyone who pays them. A common use is carrying out distributed denial of service (DDoS) attacks.

broadband Commonly understood as a reference to high-speed, always-on communication links that can move large files much more quickly than a regular phone line.

broadcast A network transmission addressed for every node on the network.

broadcast domain Group of computers connected by one or more switches—that is, a group of computers that receive broadcast frames from each other.

browser Program specifically designed to retrieve, interpret, and display Web pages.

brute-force attack Simple attack that attempts to guess credentials or identify vulnerabilities by trying many possibilities.

BSoD *See* Blue Screen of Death.

bug Programming error that causes a program or a computer system to perform erratically, produce incorrect results, or crash. The term was coined when a real bug was found in one of the circuits of one of the first ENIAC computers.

bus   Series of wires connecting two or more separate electronic devices, enabling those devices to communicate. Also, a network topology where computers all connect to a main line called a bus cable.

BYOD (bring your own device)   An organizational policy that permits employees to use their own phones or other mobile devices instead of company-issued ones.

byte   Unit of 8 bits; fundamental data unit of personal computers. Storing the equivalent of one character, the byte is also the basic unit of measurement for computer storage.

cable Internet   Fast Internet connection from a cable TV provider via RG-6 or RG-59 cable and a cable modem.

cable lock   Simple anti-theft device for securing a laptop to a nearby object.

cable modem   Device that enables Internet connection over existing coaxial cable television infrastructure by translating signals into a form that networked devices can understand.

cable tester   Device for verifying that the connectors and wires in a cable (such as UTP) are in good order.

cache (disk)   Special area of RAM that stores the data most frequently accessed from the hard drive. Cache memory can optimize the use of your systems.

cache (L1, L2, L3, etc.)   Special section of fast memory, usually built into the CPU, used by the onboard logic to store information most frequently accessed by the CPU.

calibration   Process of matching the print output of a printer to the visual output of a monitor.

card reader   Device with which you can read data from one of several types of flash memory.

Cat 5   Category 5 wire; an ANSI/TIA standard for UTP wiring that can operate at up to 100 Mbps.

Cat 5e   Category 5e wire; ANSI/TIA standard for UTP wiring that can operate at up to 1 Gbps.

Cat 6   Category 6 wire; ANSI/TIA standard for UTP wiring that can operate at up to 10 Gbps.

Cat 6a   Category 6a wire; augmented Cat 6 UTP wiring that supports 10-Gbps networks at the full 100-meter distance between a node and a switch.

Cat 7   Supports 10-Gbps networks at 100-meter segments; shielding for individual wire pairs reduces crosstalk and noise problems. Cat 7 is not an ANSI/TIA standard.

catastrophic failure   A failure in which a component or whole system will not boot; usually related to a manufacturing defect of a component. Could also be caused by overheating and physical damage to computer components.

cd Command-line utility for changing the focus of the command prompt from one directory to another. Shorthand for "change directory."

cellular location services Mobile device feature that can detect the device's location, enabling apps to request and use this information to provide location-aware services, such as finding nearby restaurants.

certificate authority (CA) Trusted entity that signs digital certificates to guarantee that the certificate was signed by the Web site in question (and not forged).

chain of custody A documented history of who has been in possession of a system or component.

change board A group of representatives from around the organization who review and approve change proposals.

change documentation Collected documentation for all aspects of a change process, including plans leading up to the change as well as receipts, overtime documents, an inventory of changed systems, a list of created users, and signed end-user acceptance forms.

change management A well-defined process composed of many planning and execution steps that enables organizations to change their IT infrastructure in a safe, cost-effective manner.

checksum Value generated from some data, like a file, and saved for comparing to other checksums later. Can be used to identify identical data, such as files on a user's system that match known viruses. Checksums can also be used to monitor whether a program is changing itself over time, which is a strong warning sign that it may be malware that evolves to avoid detection.

chipset Electronic chips, specially designed to work together, that handle all of the low-level functions of a PC. In the original PC, the chipset consisted of close to 30 different chips. For most of the 1990s and 2000s, chipsets usually consisted of one, two, or three separate chips embedded into a motherboard. Today's CPUs have controllers built in, such as the memory and display controllers. Almost all chipsets are now a single chip.

chkdsk (checkdisk) Hard drive error detection and, to a certain extent, correction utility in Windows, launched from the command-line interface. Originally a DOS command (chkdsk.exe); also the executable for the graphical Error checking tool.

chmod Linux command used to change user and group permissions for a file.

chown Linux command used to change ownership over a directory or file.

Chrome OS Google's Linux-based operating system designed to connect users via the Internet into Google applications, such as Gmail, Google Docs, and more. Chrome OS comes preinstalled on purpose-built hardware such as the Chromebook portable computers.

Chromebook   Strictly, any portable computer running Google's Chrome OS. Chromebooks offer an experience focused on Web applications by making use of virtually unlimited data storage in the cloud and Software as a Service (SaaS) applications available over the Web. Because they offload so much work, Chromebooks have a reputation for being cheap and light, but premium Chromebooks are increasingly common.

Classless Inter-Domain Routing (CIDR)   Current system for creating and notating IPv4 subnets; replaced the older, less flexible three-class system.

clean installation   Installing an operating system on a fresh drive, following a reformat of that drive. Often it's the only way to correct a problem with a system when many of the crucial operating system files have become corrupted.

clearing cache   The process of clearing stored app or browser settings in order to resolve performance issues. Commonly used to resolve issues with Web browsers or to free up resources on mobile devices.

client   Computer program that uses the services of another computer program. Also, software that extracts information from a server; a Web browser is a client, and the Web site that it accesses is the server. Also, a machine that accesses shared resources on a server.

client/server   Relationship in which client software obtains services from a server on behalf of a person.

client-side virtualization   Using a hypervisor installed on a client machine to run a virtual machine. The VM may be created and stored on the client machine or accessed over the network.

clock cycle   Single charge to the clock wire (CLK) of a CPU, informing the CPU that another piece of information is waiting to be processed.

clock speed   The maximum number of clock cycles that a CPU can handle in a given period of time, measured in MHz or GHz. In modern CPUs, the internal speed is a multiple of the external speed. *See also* clock-multiplying CPU.

clock-multiplying CPU   CPU that takes the incoming clock signal and multiples it inside the CPU to let the internal circuitry of the CPU run faster.

cloud computing   A model for enabling and accessing computing storage and other shared (or not shared) resources on demand. The "cloud" is based on servicing models that include, among others, Infrastructure as a Service (IaaS), Platform as a Service (PaaS), and Software as a Service (SaaS), as well as hybrid mixtures of these services.

CMOS (complementary metal-oxide semiconductor)   Defunct technology used in earlier computer systems that hooked up a small amount of RAM to a small battery to hold system settings for the BIOS firmware even with the computer off. This has long since been incorporated into the chipset. CMOS is often informally used to refer to the CMOS setup program or system setup utility.

CMOS battery   A coin cell lithium-ion battery that maintains power to the CMOS memory chip when the computer is otherwise unpowered. The usual battery size is CR2032.

CMOS clear   A jumper setting or button on the motherboard that, when set, will revert CMOS settings to the factory defaults. Sometimes labeled CLRTC on the motherboard.

CMOS setup program   Program enabling you to access and update CMOS data. Also referred to as the system setup utility, BIOS setup utility, UEFI/BIOS setup, and similar names.

coaxial cable   Cabling in which an internal conductor is surrounded by another, outer conductor, thus sharing the same axis.

code   Set of symbols representing characters (e.g., ASCII code) or instructions in a computer program (a programmer writes source code, which must be translated into executable or machine code for the computer to use).

code-division multiple access (CDMA)   Wireless data standard for mobile devices.

color depth (display)   The number of bits (the bit depth) necessary to represent the number of colors in a graphics mode. Common color bit depths are 16-bit and 32-bit, representing 65,536 colors and 16.7 million colors (plus an 8-bit alpha channel for transparency levels), respectively.

command   A request, typed from a terminal or embedded in a file, to perform an operation or to execute a particular program.

command prompt   Text prompt for entering commands.

command-line interface (CLI)   Text user interface. Users input text commands and receive text output. CLI commands, which are more flexible and often faster (or use fewer resources) than a graphical equivalent, are also easy to compose into scripts for performing frequent tasks.

community cloud   Cloud network that serves a community or group with shared needs and interests, such as hospitals or defense contractors.

compatibility modes   Feature of Windows to enable software written for previous versions of Windows to operate in newer versions.

compliance   Concept that members of an organization must abide by the rules created by and applying to that organization (including government regulations). For a technician, compliance often defines what software can or cannot be installed on an organization's computers.

component failure   Occurs when a system device fails due to a manufacturing defect or some other type of defect.

compression   Process of squeezing data to eliminate redundancies, allowing files to use less space when stored or transmitted.

Computer Management Applet in Windows' Administrative Tools that contains several useful snap-ins, such as Device Manager and Disk Management.

connector Small receptacle used to attach a cable to a device or system. Common types of connectors include USB, PS/2, RJ-45, VGA, HDMI, DVI, HD15, DisplayPort, and Thunderbolt.

consumables Materials used up by printers, including paper, ink, ribbons, 3-D printer filament, and toner cartridges.

container file A file that contains multiple data streams, such as a ZIP archive file or an MP4 movie file. Also called a *wrapper*.

context menu Small menu brought up by right-clicking on objects in Windows.

contrast ratio Difference in intensity between the lightest and the darkest spot that a device can display (in the case of a monitor) or capture (in the case of a camera or scanner).

Control Panel Collection of Windows applets, or small programs, that can be used to configure various pieces of hardware and software in a system.

controller card Card adapter that connects devices, such as a drive, to the main computer bus/motherboard.

copy command Command-line tool used to make a copy of a file and paste it in another location.

counter Used to track data about a particular object when using Performance Monitor.

cp Copy command in Linux.

CPU (central processing unit) "Brain" of the computer. Microprocessor that handles primary calculations for the computer. CPUs are known by names such as Core i7 and Ryzen.

CRC *See* cyclic redundancy check.

credit card reader Device that can be attached to mobile phones and tablets to take credit card payments.

crimper A specialized tool for connecting network cables to a connector, such as twisted pair wires to an RJ-45 connector or coaxial cable to an RG-6 connector. Also called a *crimping tool*.

cross-site scripting (XSS) An attack in which the attacker injects malicious code into a Web app in order to trick it into sending things that it shouldn't to other users of the Web app.

cryptominer A form of malware that enlists the hardware of the target system to mine cryptocurrency without the knowledge of the system's owner.

CSMA/CA (carrier sense multiple access/collision avoidance)   Networking scheme used by wireless devices to transmit data while avoiding data collisions, which wireless nodes have difficulty detecting.

CSMA/CD (carrier sense multiple access/collision detection)   Networking scheme used by Ethernet devices to transmit data and resend data after detection of data collisions.

current   Amount of electrons moving past a certain point on a wire, measured in units called amperes. Also called amperage.

cyclic redundancy check (CRC)   Very accurate mathematical method used to check for errors in long streams of transmitted data. Before data is sent, the main computer uses the data to calculate a CRC value from the data's contents. If the receiver calculates from the received data a different CRC value, the data was corrupted during transmission and is re-sent. Ethernet packets use the CRC algorithm in the FCS portion of the frame.

DAC   *See* discretionary access control.

data classification   System of organizing data according to its sensitivity. Common classifications include public, highly confidential, and top secret.

Data Collector Sets   Windows log repository that accepts log entries from other Windows computers.

data roaming   A feature of cellular data systems that enables the signal to jump from cell tower to cell tower and from your provider to another provider without obvious notice.

data storage   Saving a permanent copy of your work so that you can come back to it later.

data usage cap   Restrictions on how much data a user may consume. Once the user exceeds the limit, data may be blocked entirely or bandwidth may be throttled.

database system   A representation of the relationship between two or more objects. Often used in asset management to keep track of who has possession of various assets and why they have them.

DB-9   A two-row DB connector (male) used to connect the computer's serial port to a serial-communication device such as a modem or a console port on a managed switch.

DC (direct current)   Type of electricity in which the flow of electrons is in a complete circle in one direction.

DDoS (distributed denial of service)   An attack on a computer or network device in which multiple computers send data and requests to the device in an attempt to overwhelm it so that it cannot perform normal operations.

DDR3 SDRAM   Type of SDRAM that sends 8 bits of data in every clock cycle.

DDR4 SDRAM   Type of SDRAM that offers higher density and lower voltages than DDR3 and can handle faster data transfer rates. Maximum theoretical capacity of DDR4 DIMMs is up to 512 GB.

DDR5 SDRAM   The successor to DDR4, offering doubled bandwidth, decreased power consumption, quadrupled DIMM capacity, and up to 7200 MT/s at the time of writing.

DE (desktop environment)   Name for the various user interfaces found in Linux distributions.

debug   To detect, trace, and eliminate errors in computer programs.

decrypt   To pass decryption keys and encrypted data through the appropriate decryption algorithm in order to retrieve the original unencrypted data. *See* encryption.

dedicated server   Machine that is not used for any client functions, only server functions.

default gateway   In a TCP/IP network, the nearest router to a particular host. This router's IP address is part of the necessary TCP/IP configuration for communicating with multiple networks using IP.

default user accounts/groups   Users or groups that are enabled by default. Some, such as the guest account, represent a security risk.

definition file   List of malware signatures that enables anti-malware programs to identify malware on your system and clean them. This file should be updated often. Also called a *signature file*.

defragmentation (defrag)   Procedure in which all the files on a hard disk drive are rewritten on disk so that all parts of each file reside in contiguous clusters. The result is an improvement in disk speed during retrieval operations.

degaussing   Data destruction procedure used to reduce or remove the electromagnetic fields that store data on magnetic hard drives.

del (erase)   Command-line tool used to delete/erase files.

denial of service   *See* DoS.

Desktop   User's primary interface to the Windows operating system.

desktop virtualization   A traditional desktop operating system installed in a VM. *See also* virtual machine.

device charger   Plugs into a power source and charges a device through one of its ports, such as USB or Lightning. Convenient for charging while the device stays on.

device driver   Program used by the operating system to control communications between the computer and peripherals.

device encryption   Enhances mobile device security by encrypting the device's internal storage.

Device Manager   Utility that enables techs to examine and configure all the hardware and drivers in a Windows PC. It is both an MMC snap-in and a Windows 10 Control Panel utility.

Devices (Windows Settings)   Windows Settings category that enables users to make changes to attached devices such as printers, scanners, keyboard, and mouse.

DFS (distributed file system)   A storage environment where shared files are accessed from storage devices within multiple servers, clients, and peer hosts.

DHCP   *See* Dynamic Host Configuration Protocol.

diagnostics menu   Hidden mobile device menu that contains tests and diagnostics for verifying the functionality of various device hardware.

dictionary attack   Type of brute-force attack using a dictionary to guess things like usernames and passwords. Don't think *Webster's*—these dictionaries may be full of usernames and passwords that have leaked or been used as defaults over the years.

dig   Linux command that queries DNS to enable troubleshooting and monitoring.

digital certificate   Form in which a public key is sent from a Web server to a Web browser so that the browser can decrypt the data sent by the server.

digital rights management (DRM)   Code schemes for enforcing what users can and can't do with commercial software or digital media files.

digitizer   The touchscreen overlay technology that converts finger and stylus contact into input data for the device to use.

dilithium crystal   Controlling agent in a faster-than-light warp drive.

DIMM (dual inline memory module)   32- or 64-bit type of DRAM packaging with the distinction that each side of each tab inserted into the system performs a separate function. DIMMs come in a variety of sizes, with 184-, 240-, and 288-pin being the most common on desktop computers.

dipole antenna   Standard straight-wire antenna that provides the most omnidirectional function.

dir   Command-line tool used to display the entire contents of the current working directory.

direct burial   Rating applied to shielded twisted pair (STP) cabling that indicates a thicker jacket and some form of waterproofing for use outdoors or underground.

direct LED backlighting   Matrix of LEDs that illuminates a display from directly behind the display panel.

directory   Another name for a folder.

discretionary access control (DAC)   Authorization method based on the idea that there is an owner of a resource who may at his or her discretion assign access to that resource. DAC is considered much more flexible than mandatory access control (MAC).

Disk Cleanup (cleanmgre.exe)   Utility built into Windows that can help users clean up their hard drives by removing temporary Internet files, deleting unused program files, and more.

Disk Defragmenter (dfrgui.exe)   A program that maintains performance by rearranging chunks of data on a storage device to ensure chunks that comprise a file are stored contiguously. Filename is dfrgui.exe. Renamed to Optimize Drives in Windows 8 and up.

disk duplexing   Type of disk mirroring using two separate controllers rather than one; marginally faster than traditional mirroring because one controller does not write each piece of data twice.

disk initialization   A process that places special information on every hard drive installed in a Windows system.

Disk Management (dismgmt.msc)   Snap-in available with the Microsoft Management Console that enables techs to configure the various disks installed in a system; available in Computer Management | Administrative Tools.

disk mirroring   Process by which data is written simultaneously to two or more disk drives. Read and write speed is decreased, but redundancy in case of catastrophe is increased.

disk quota   Application allowing network administrators to limit hard drive space usage.

disk striping   Process by which data is spread among multiple (at least two) drives. Increases speed for both reads and writes of data. Considered RAID level 0 because it does not provide fault tolerance.

disk striping with parity   Method for providing fault tolerance by writing data across multiple drives and then including an additional drive, called a parity drive, that stores information to rebuild the data contained on the other drives. Requires at least three physical disks: two for the data and a third for the parity drive. This provides data redundancy at RAID levels 5, 10, and 0+1 with different options.

disk thrashing   Hard drive that is constantly being accessed due to lack of available system memory. When system memory runs low, a Windows system will utilize hard disk space as "virtual" memory, thus causing an unusual amount of hard drive access.

Disk Utility   macOS tool that checks for hard drive errors.

display adapter   Handles all the communication between the CPU and the monitor. Also known as a *video card* or *graphics card*.

Display Settings   Windows utility that enables a user to change color schemes, font sizes, and other aspects of what appears on the computer monitor.

DisplayPort   Digital video connector used by some Apple Mac desktop models and some PCs, notably from Dell. Designed by VESA as a royalty-free connector to replace VGA and DVI.

distended capacitors   Failed capacitors on a motherboard, which tend to bulge out at the top. This was especially a problem during the mid-2000s, when capacitor manufacturers released huge batches of bad capacitors.

distributed denial of service   *See* DDoS.

distribution (distro)   A specific variant of Linux.

DLP (Data Loss Prevention)   System or set of rules designed to stop leakage of sensitive information. Usually applied to Internet appliances to monitor outgoing network traffic.

DMZ   *See* screened subnet.

DNS (Domain Name Service)   TCP/IP name resolution system that translates a host name into an IP address. Uses UDP port 53.

DNS domain   Specific branch of the DNS name space. Top-level domains (TLDs) include .com, .gov, and .edu.

docking station   Device that provides a portable computer extra features such as an optical drive, in addition to legacy and modern ports. Similar to a port replicator. Also, a charging station for mobile devices.

document the findings, actions, and outcomes   Recording each troubleshooting job: what the problem was, how it was fixed, and other helpful information. (Step 6 of 6 in the CompTIA troubleshooting methodology.)

domain   Groupings of users, computers, or networks. In Microsoft networking, a domain is a group of computers and users that share a common account database and a common security policy. On the Internet, a domain is a group of computers that share a common element in their hierarchical name. Other types of domains exist—e.g., broadcast domain, etc.

domain controller   A computer running Windows Server that stores a set of domain accounts.

domain-based network   Network that eliminates the need for logging on to multiple servers by using domain controllers to hold the security database for all systems.

DoS (denial of service)   An attack on a computer resource that prevents it from performing its normal operations, usually by overwhelming it with large numbers of requests in an effort to monopolize its resources.

DRAM (dynamic random access memory or dynamic RAM)   Memory used to store data in most personal computers. DRAM stores each bit in a "cell" composed of a transistor and a capacitor. Because the capacitor in a DRAM cell can only hold a charge for a few milliseconds, DRAM must be continually refreshed, or rewritten, to retain its data.

drive cloning   Taking a PC and making a duplicate of the hard drive, including all data, software, and configuration files, and transferring it to another PC. *See also* image deployment.

drive letter   A letter designating a specific drive or partition.

driver signing   Digital signature for drivers used by Windows to protect against potentially bad drivers.

DSL (digital subscriber line)   High-speed Internet connection technology that uses a regular telephone line for connectivity. DSL comes in several varieties, including asymmetric (ADSL) and symmetric (SDSL), and many speeds. Typical home-user DSL connections are ADSL, with faster download speeds than upload speeds.

dual boot   Refers to a computer with two operating systems installed, enabling users to choose which operating system to load on boot. Can also refer to kicking a device a second time just in case the first time didn't work.

dual-channel architecture   Using two sticks of RAM to increase throughput. *See also* triple-channel architecture *and* quad-channel architecture.

dual-channel memory   Form of memory access used by many motherboards that requires paired identical sticks of RAM.

dumpster diving   To go through someone's trash in search of information.

duplexing   Similar to mirroring in that data is written to and read from two physical drives, for fault tolerance. Separate controllers are used for each drive, both for additional fault tolerance and for additional speed. Considered RAID level 1. Also called *disk duplexing* or *drive duplexing*.

duplexing assembly   Mechanical feature of some printers that can automatically flip the paper to print on both sides.

DVI (digital visual interface)   Special video connector designed for digital-to-digital connections; most commonly seen on PC video cards and LCD monitors. Some versions also support analog signals with a special adapter.

dynamic disks   Special feature of Windows that enables users to span a single volume across two or more drives. Dynamic disks do not have partitions; they have volumes. Dynamic disks can be striped, mirrored, and striped or mirrored with parity.

Dynamic Host Configuration Protocol (DHCP)   Protocol that enables client hosts to request and receive TCP/IP settings automatically from an appropriately configured server. Uses UDP ports 67 and 68.

ECC (error correction code) Special software, embedded on hard drives, that constantly scans the drives for bad blocks.

ECC RAM/DRAM (error correction code RAM/DRAM) RAM that uses special chips to detect and fix memory errors. Commonly used in high-end servers where data integrity is crucial.

effective permissions User's combined permissions granted by multiple groups.

EFS (encrypting file system) Storage organization and management service, such as NTFS, that has the capability of applying a cipher process to the stored data. The professional editions of Windows offer a feature called the Encrypting File System (EFS), an encryption scheme that any user can use to encrypt individual files or folders on a computer.

electromagnetic interference (EMI) Electrical interference from one device to another, resulting in poor performance of the device being interfered with. Examples: static on your TV while running a blow dryer, or placing two monitors too close together and getting a "shaky" screen.

electromagnetic pulse (EMP) Potentially damaging burst of electromagnetic energy caused by events such as electrostatic discharge (ESD), lightning, nuclear detonations, and so on.

electrostatic discharge (ESD) Uncontrolled rush of electrons from one object to another. A real menace to PCs, as it can cause permanent damage to semiconductors.

eliciting answers Communication strategy designed to help techs understand a user's problems better. Works by listening to a user's description of a problem and then asking cogent questions.

embedded system A computer that is dedicated to a specific task and often is included as part of a larger and more complex system. Embedded systems are found in everything from medical devices to power plants to toys to railway control systems.

emergency notification Feature built into smartphones enabling them to receive messages from emergency broadcast systems, such as the Emergency Alert System (EAS) in the United States.

encrypted Data that has been passed through an encryption algorithm, rendering it unreadable without the decryption keys. *See* encryption.

encryption Making data unreadable by those who do not possess a key or password.

end process Option in Task Manager to halt a program or background process. Other supporting processes continue to run after ending a process they support.

end process tree Option in Task Manager to halt a program or background process and all of its supporting processes.

end task   Process of forcibly exiting a program or application, initiated using Task Manager in Windows or Activity Monitor in macOS.

end-user acceptance   Change management step that entails educating and training users about what has changed and how to use any new systems, devices, or features.

end-user license agreement   *See* EULA.

Enhanced 911 (E911)   Improves 911 service for cellular phones by using GPS and cellular network triangulation to locate the device and dispatch emergency responders.

entry control roster   Document for recording who enters and leaves a building.

environment variables   System data such as the date and time, currently logged-in users, running operating system version, and more. Scripts and programs on a system often use these variables to tailor their behavior to the system's capabilities and configuration.

environmental control   Practice of protecting computing equipment from environmental damage by taking measures such as air conditioning, proper ventilation, air filtration, temperature monitoring, and humidity monitoring.

equipment rack   A metal structure used in equipment rooms to secure network hardware devices and patch panels. Most racks are 19 inches wide. Devices designed to fit in such a rack use a height measurement called *units*, or simply *U*.

erase lamp   Component inside laser printers that uses light to make the coating of the photosensitive drum conductive.

Error checking   Windows graphical tool that scans and fixes hard drive problems. Often referred to by the name of the executable, chkdsk, or Check Disk. The macOS equivalent is the Disk Utility, and Linux offers a command-line tool called fsck.

error correction code   *See* ECC.

eSATA   Serial ATA-based connector for external hard drives and optical drives.

escalate   Process used when person assigned to repair a problem is not able to get the job done, such as sending the problem to someone with more expertise.

ESD mat   *See* antistatic mat.

ESD strap   *See* antistatic wrist strap.

establish a plan of action to resolve the problem and implement the solution   After establishing and testing a theory about a particular problem, techs solve the problem. (Step 4 of 6 in the CompTIA troubleshooting methodology.)

establish a theory of probable cause (question the obvious)   After identifying a problem, techs question the obvious to determine what might be the source of the problem. (Step 2 of 6 in the CompTIA troubleshooting methodology.)

Ethernet   Name coined by Xerox for the first standard of network cabling and protocols that define everything necessary to get data from one computer to another. Since its inception, Ethernet as a hardware protocol has gone through hundreds of improvements and even forms the basis of wireless networking signals.

Ethernet over Power (EoP)   Uses a building's existing electrical network for Ethernet. Requires specialized bridges between the Ethernet network and power outlets.

Ethic of Reciprocity   Golden Rule: Do unto others as you would have them do unto you.

EULA (end-user license agreement)   Agreement that accompanies a piece of software, to which the user must agree before using the software. Outlines the terms of use for the software and also lists any actions on the part of the user that violate the agreement.

Event Viewer (eventvwr.msc)   Utility made available in Windows as an MMC snap-in that enables users to monitor and audit various system events, including network bandwidth usage and CPU utilization.

evil twin   Substitute wireless access point configured to look the same as the real one in order to gather information from users who accidentally connect to it.

exFAT   A Microsoft-proprietary file system that breaks the 4-GB file-size barrier, supporting files up to 16 exabytes (EB) and a theoretical partition limit of 64 zettabytes (ZB). Envisioned for use with flash media devices with a capacity exceeding 2 TB.

expansion slots   Connectors on a motherboard that enable users to add optional components to a system. *See also* PCIe.

ext4 (Fourth Extended File System)   File system used by most Linux distributions.

extended partition   Type of nonbootable hard disk partition. May only have one extended partition per disk. Purpose is to divide a large disk into smaller partitions, each with a separate drive letter.

external enclosure   Casing that encloses an external hard drive.

external speaker   Portable device that can substantially improve on the audio output of a mobile device or portable computer. Typically connects via Bluetooth or a regular headphone jack.

facial recognition   Technology that enables use of facial features to unlock a mobile device or personal computer.

factory recovery partition   *See* recovery partition.

factory reset   Returns a device's software to how it left the factory by removing all user-installed data, programs, and customizations.

FAT (file allocation table)   Hidden table that records how files on a hard disk are stored in distinct clusters. The address of the first cluster of a file is stored in the directory file. The FAT entry for the first cluster is the address of the second cluster used to store that file. In the entry for the second cluster for that file is the address for the third cluster, and so on until the final cluster, which gets a special end-of-file marker. There are two FATs, mirror images of each other, in case one is destroyed or damaged. Also refers to the 16-bit file allocation table when used by Windows 2000 and later NT-based operating systems.

FAT32   File allocation table that uses 32 bits to address and index clusters. Commonly used with USB flash-media drives and versions of Windows prior to XP.

fiber optic cable   High-speed cable for transmitting data, made of high-purity glass sealed within an opaque tube. Much faster than conventional copper wire such as coaxial cable. Most common connectors include ST, SC, and LC.

file   A named collection of any form of data that is stored beyond the time of execution of a single job. A file may contain program instructions or data, which may be numerical, textual, or graphical information.

File Explorer   A tool in Windows that enables users to browse files and folders.

file extension   Two, three, four, five, or more letters that follow a filename and identify the type of file (file format). Common file extensions are .zip, .exe, .doc, .java, and .xhtml.

file format   How information is encoded in a file. Two primary types are binary (pictures) and ASCII (text), but within those are many formats, such as BMP and GIF for pictures. Commonly represented by a suffix (the file extension) at the end of the filename; for example, .txt for a text file or .exe for an executable.

File History   Control Panel applet introduced in Windows 8 for backing up personal files and folders.

file permission   Specifies what degree of access the system should grant a user or group to a particular file.

file server   Computer designated to store software, courseware, administrative tools, and other data on a LAN or WAN. It "serves" this information to other computers via the network when users enter their personal access codes.

file system   Scheme that directs how an OS stores and retrieves data on and off a drive; FAT32 and NTFS are both file systems. Used interchangeably with the term "data structure."

File Transfer Protocol   *See* FTP.

file-level backup   Manually or automatically copying individual files or folders to one or more backup locations.

filename   Name assigned to a file when the file is first written on a disk. Every file on a disk within the same folder must have a unique name. Filenames can contain any character (including spaces), except the following: \ / : * ? " < > |

fileshare   A server set up to share documents and other files with other users on a network.

find   Linux command used to locate files in the filesystem.

Finder   macOS's file and folder browser.

fingerprint lock   Type of biometric device that enables a user to unlock a mobile device using a fingerprint.

fingerprint scanner   Scanner that reads the unique pattern of a person's fingerprint to authenticate them. Used primarily to unlock devices like smartphones and some laptops.

firewall   Device that restricts traffic between a local network and the Internet.

firmware   Embedded programs or code stored on a ROM chip. Generally OS-independent, thus allowing devices to operate in a wide variety of circumstances without direct OS support. The system BIOS is firmware.

firmware update   Process by which the BIOS of a motherboard can be updated to reflect patched bugs and added features. Performed, usually, through CMOS, though some motherboard manufacturers provide a Windows program for performing a firmware update.

flash ROM   ROM technology that can be electrically reprogrammed while still in the PC. Overwhelmingly the most common storage medium of BIOS in computers today, as it can be upgraded without a need to open the computer on most systems.

flux capacitor   A rectangular-shaped compartment with three flashing Geissler-style tubes arranged in a "Y" configuration that makes time travel possible.

folder permission   Specifies what degree of access the system should grant a user or group to a particular folder.

force stop   Terminate an Android app and all associated background processes. More extreme than simply closing the app, which may leave background processes running.

form factor   Standard for the physical organization of motherboard components and motherboard size. Most common form factors are ATX, microATX, and Mini-ITX.

format   Command-line tool used to format a storage device.

formatting   The process of preparing a partition to store files by creating a file system to organize the blocks and creating a root directory.

fragmentation   Occurs when files and directories get jumbled on a fixed disk and are no longer contiguous. Can significantly slow down hard drive access times and can be repaired in windows by using Optimize Drives. *See also* defragmentation.

frame   A data unit transferred across a network. Frames consist of several parts, such as the sending and receiving MAC addresses, the data being sent, and the frame check sequence.

freeware   Software that is distributed for free, with no license fee.

FRU (field replaceable unit)   Any part of a PC that is considered to be replaceable "in the field," i.e., a customer location. There is no official list of FRUs—it is usually a matter of policy by the repair center.

FTP (File Transfer Protocol)   Rules that enable two computers to talk to one another during a file transfer. Protocol used when you transfer a file from one computer to another across the Internet. FTP uses port numbers 20 and 21.

F-type connector   Common coax connector secured with a screw connector.

full device encryption   Enhances mobile device security by encrypting the device's internal storage.

full format   Format process that tests every sector to mark out the unusable ones in the file allocation table (FAT). *See* formatting.

full-duplex   Any device that can send and receive data simultaneously.

Full-Speed USB   USB standard that runs at 12 Mbps. Also known as *USB 1.1*.

fully qualified domain name (FQDN)   A complete, bottom-to-top label of a DNS host going from the specific host to the top-level domain that holds it and all of the intervening domain layers, each layer being separated by a dot. FQDNs are entered into browser bars and other utilities in formats like *mail.totalseminars.com*.

Function (FN) key   Special key on many laptops that enables some keys to perform a third duty.

Gaming (Windows Settings)   Windows Settings category that contains options to optimize and modify gaming experiences.

GDDR5   Fifth generation of graphical DDR RAM found on high-performance video cards.

General Data Protection Regulation (GDPR)   European Union law that defines a broad set of rights and protections of personal information for citizens of the EU.

general protection fault (GPF)   Error code usually seen when separate active programs conflict on resources or data. Can cause an application to crash.

geofencing   Using mobile device features to detect when the device enters or exits a defined area.

geotracking   Feature in cellular phones that enables cell phone companies and government agencies to use the ID or MAC address to pinpoint where a phone is at any given time.

gestures Specific motions the user performs on a touchscreen, such as pinching or swiping, that have a special meaning to the app being used.

giga Prefix for the quantity 1,073,741,824 (2^{30}) or for 1 billion. One gigabyte would be 1,073,741,824 bytes, except with hard drive labeling, where it means 1 billion bytes. One gigahertz is 1 billion hertz.

Global Positioning System (GPS) Technology that enables a mobile device to determine where you are on a map.

global user account Login information and associated settings maintained at a location accessible by any computer, irrespective of location or local account configuration.

globally unique identifier (GUID) partition table (GPT) Partitioning scheme that enables you to create more than four primary partitions without needing to use dynamic disks.

Google Play Google's app and media store for Android devices.

Google Workspace Google's suite of productivity tools and applications. Can be synchronized across multiple devices to enable more efficient workflow.

gpresult Windows command for listing group policies applied to a user.

GPS *See* Global Positioning System.

GPU (graphics processing unit) Specialized processor that helps the CPU by taking over all of the 3-D rendering duties.

gpupdate Windows command for making immediate group policy changes in an individual system.

graphical user interface (GUI) *See* GUI.

grep Linux command to search through text files or command outputs to find specific information or to filter out unneeded information.

group Collection of user accounts that share the same access capabilities.

group policy Means of easily controlling the settings of multiple network clients with policies such as setting minimum password length or preventing Registry edits.

Group Policy Editor (gpedit.msc) MMC snap-in used to change or modify group policy in Windows.

GSM (Global System for Mobile Communications) Wireless data standard for mobile devices.

guest An operating system running inside a virtual machine.

guest account Very limited built-in account type for Windows; a member of the Guests group.

Guests group   User group that enables someone without an account to use a system. *See* group.

GUI (graphical user interface)   Interface that enables user to interact with computer graphically, by using a mouse or other pointing device to manipulate icons that represent programs or documents, instead of using only text as in early interfaces. Pronounced "gooey."

half-duplex   Transmission mode where a device can either send or receive, but not do both at once.

hang   Occurs when a computer or program stops responding to keyboard commands or other input; a computer or program in such a state is said to be "hung."

hang time   Number of seconds a too-often-hung computer is airborne after you have thrown it out a second-story window.

hard drive   *See* HDD.

hard reset   For mobile devices, another term for a factory reset. Don't confuse this with a hard reboot. *See* factory reset.

hard token   Dedicated device that contains information used as an authentication factor when logging on to a secure site.

hardware   Physical computer equipment such as electrical, electronic, magnetic, and mechanical devices. Anything in the computer world that you can hold in your hand. A hard drive is hardware; Microsoft Word is not.

hardware firewall   Firewall implemented within networking hardware such as a router. *See* firewall.

hardware protocol   Defines many aspects of a network, from the packet type to the cabling and connectors used. Ethernet is an example of a hardware protocol.

hardware virtualization   Processor features that speed up and simplify virtualization. Required for some hypervisors to function. *See also* hypervisor.

hardware-assisted virtualization   Virtualization that makes use of the host machine's hardware to enable the virtualized software to function.

hash   A special value computed from some other value using an irreversible computation. Has many uses in computing, and plays a key role in modern authentication systems. Instead of saving user passwords directly in a database (which would make them a huge target for attackers), well-designed authentication systems compute and save only a (salted) hash of each password. When the user attempts to log in, the system hashes the provided password to see if it matches the saved hash. *See also* salted hash.

HDD (hard disk drive)   Data-recording system using solid disks of magnetic material turning at high speeds to store and retrieve programs and data in a computer.

HDMI (High-Definition Multimedia Interface) Single multimedia connection that includes both high-definition video and audio. Used to connect a computer to LCDs, projectors, and VR headsets.

heat dope *See* thermal paste.

heat sink A specially designed hunk of metal such as aluminum or copper that conducts heat away from a CPU or other heat-producing component and out into fins that transfer the heat to circulating air. When used to cool a CPU, a heat sink is typically paired with a fan assembly to improve its performance.

hex (hexadecimal) Base-16 numbering system using ten digits (0 through 9) and six letters (A through F). In the computer world, shorthand way to write binary numbers by substituting one hex digit for a four-digit binary number (e.g., hex 9 = binary 1001).

hibernate Power management setting in which all data from RAM is written to the hard drive before the system goes into sleep mode. Upon waking up, all information is retrieved from the hard drive and returned to RAM. Also called *suspend to disk*.

hidden attribute File attribute that, when used, does not allow the dir command to show a file.

hierarchical directory tree Method by which Windows organizes files into a series of folders, called directories, under the root directory. *See also* root directory.

high availability A trait of systems that indicates an emphasis on reliable operations with minimal or no downtime.

High Dynamic Range (HDR) Video technology that increases the bandwidth of display colors and light intensity above standard dynamic range.

high-level formatting Format that sets up a file system on a drive.

Hi-Speed USB USB standard that runs at 480 Mbps. Also referred to as USB 2.0.

horizontal cabling Cabling that connects the equipment room to the work areas.

host (networking) On a TCP/IP network, a single device that has an IP address—any device (usually a computer) that can be the source or destination of a data packet. Also, in virtualization, a computer running one or more virtual operating systems.

host (virtualization) The system running (or hosting) a virtual machine.

host ID The address of a TCP/IP device such as a computer, printer, camera, or other device.

hostname Windows command for displaying the name of a computer.

hotspot A mobile device that broadcasts a small Wi-Fi network to share its mobile data network connection with nearby Wi-Fi devices. Often a standalone device, though many cellular phones and data-connected tablets can be set up to act as hotspots.

hot-swappable   Any hardware that may be attached to or removed from a PC without interrupting the PC's normal processing.

hot-swapping   Replacing a bad drive in a RAID array without needing to reboot or power down.

HTML (Hypertext Markup Language)   ASCII-based, script-like language for creating hypertext documents such as those on the World Wide Web.

HTTP (Hypertext Transfer Protocol)   Extremely fast protocol used for network file transfers in the WWW environment. Uses port 80.

HTTPS (HTTP over Secure Sockets Layer)   Secure form of HTTP used commonly for Internet business transactions or any time when a secure connection is required. Uses port 443.

hub   Electronic device that sits at the center of a star bus topology network, providing a common point for the connection of network devices. Hubs repeat all information out to all ports and have been replaced by switches, although the term "hub" is still commonly used. A USB hub shares a single USB connection and its bandwidth among connected devices.

hybrid   A network topology that combines features from multiple other topologies, such as the star bus topology.

hybrid cloud   A combination of cloud resources from more than one of the three cloud types (community, private, and public).

Hyper-Threading   Intel CPU feature (generically called *simultaneous multithreading*) that enables a CPU to run more than one thread at once.

hypervisor   Software that enables a single computer to run multiple operating systems simultaneously.

I/O (input/output)   General term for reading and writing data to a computer. "Input" includes data entered from a keyboard, identified by a pointing device (such as a mouse), or loaded from a disk. "Output" includes writing information to a disk, viewing it on a monitor, or printing it to a printer.

IaaS   *See* Infrastructure as a Service.

iCloud   Apple cloud-based storage. iCloud enables a user to back up all iPhone or iPad data, and makes that data accessible from anywhere. This includes any media purchased through iTunes as well as calendars, contacts, reminders, and so forth.

ID badge   Small card or document for confirming the identity of its holder and what access they should be granted. May use built-in authentication tools such as RFID or smart card to function as a "something you have" authentication factor.

IDE (Integrated Drive Electronics)   PC specification for small- to medium-sized hard drives in which the controlling electronics for the drive are part of the drive itself, speeding up transfer rates and requiring only a simple adapter (or "paddle") connection on a motherboard. IDE only supported two drives per system of no more than 504 MB each, and has been completely supplanted by Enhanced IDE. EIDE supports four drives of over 8 GB each and more than doubles the transfer rate. The more common name for PATA drives.

identify the problem   To question the user and find out what has been changed recently or is no longer working properly. (Step 1 of 6 in the CompTIA troubleshooting methodology.)

IEC-320 connector   Connects the cable supplying AC power from a wall outlet into the power supply.

IEEE (Institute of Electronic and Electrical Engineers)   Leading standards-setting group in the United States.

IEEE 802.11   Wireless Ethernet standard more commonly known as Wi-Fi.

image deployment   Operating system installation that uses a complete image of a hard drive as an installation media. Helpful when installing an operating system on a large number of identical PCs.

image file   Bit-by-bit image of data to be burned on optical media or flash drive—from one file to an entire disk—stored as a single file on a hard drive. Particularly handy when copying from CD to CD or DVD to DVD.

image-level backup   Backing up a complete volume, including any OS, boot files, applications, and data it contains.

IMAP4 (Internet Message Access Protocol version 4)   An alternative to POP3 that retrieves e-mail from an e-mail server; IMAP uses TCP port 143.

IMEI (International Mobile Equipment Identity)   A 15-digit number used to uniquely identify a mobile device, typically a smartphone or other device that connects to a cellular network.

impedance   Amount of resistance to an electrical signal on a wire. Relative measure of the amount of data a cable can handle.

impersonation   A social engineering attack in which a person pretends to be someone else in order to gain access to confidential data or to launch attacks against a computer network.

incident report   Record of the details of an accident, including what happened and where it happened.

incident reporting   Process of reporting gathered data about a system or problem to supervisors. Creates a record of work accomplished and may help identify patterns. Often documented on an incident report form.

Infrastructure as a Service (IaaS)   Cloud-hosted provider of virtualized servers and networks.

inheritance   NTFS feature that passes on the same permissions in any subfolders/files resident in the original folder.

in-place upgrade   *See* upgrade installation.

insider threat   Threat to an organization that originates from within. An insider threat can be malicious or accidental, but either way, it introduces some type of risk to safety, data, and the business.

installation media (drivers)   Optical media or drive (such as a USB flash drive) that holds all the necessary device driver files for a specific device such as a printer, scanner, or motherboard.

installation media (operating systems)   Optical media or drive (such as a USB flash drive) that holds all the necessary files for installing an operating system or an application (program).

integrated GPU   GPU integrated with the motherboard or processor, in contrast to GPUs on separate graphics cards. This typically lowers power consumption, saves space, reduces heat, and may speed up communication with the GPU.

Intel   One of the two major CPU manufacturers and the original creator of the x86 CPU architecture. Competes directly with AMD in desktop, laptop, and server processors.

interface   Means by which a user interacts with a piece of software.

Internet of Things (IoT)   Everyday home objects that incorporate computing and networked features to enable enhanced functionality. Smart home devices, home security systems, and even refrigerators can be part of the Internet of Things.

Internet service provider (ISP)   Company that provides access to the Internet, usually for money.

interrupt/interruption   Suspension of a process, such as the execution of a computer program, caused by an event external to the computer and performed in such a way that the process can be resumed. Events of this kind include sensors monitoring laboratory equipment or a user pressing an interrupt key.

intrusion detection system (IDS)   Application that inspects packets, looking for active intrusions. Functions inside the network, looking for threats a firewall might miss, such as viruses, illegal logon attempts, and other well-known attacks. May also discover threats from inside the network, such as a vulnerability scanner run by a rogue employee.

intrusion prevention system (IPS) Application similar to an intrusion detection system (IDS), except that it sits directly in the flow of network traffic. This enables it to stop ongoing attacks itself, but may also slow down the network and be a single point of failure.

inventory management A process for protecting devices and equipment by tagging them with barcodes or asset tags and keeping track of these tagged devices.

inverter Device used to convert DC current into AC. Commonly used in older laptops and flatbed scanners with CCFLs.

iOS The operating system of Apple iPhones.

IoT *See* Internet of Things.

ip Command-line utility for Linux servers and workstations that displays the current TCP/IP configuration of the machine. Similar to ipconfig in Windows.

IP address Numeric address of a computer connected to the Internet. An IPv4 address is made up of four octets of 8-bit binary numbers (32 bits total) translated into their shorthand numeric values. An IPv6 address is 128 bits long. The IP address can be broken down into a network ID and a host ID. Also called *Internet address*.

iPadOS The operating system of Apple's iPad tablets.

ipconfig Command-line utility for Windows servers and workstations that displays the current TCP/IP configuration of the machine. Similar to ip in Linux.

IPS (in-plane switching) Display technology that replaces the older twisted nematic (TN) panels for more accurate colors and a wider viewing angle.

IPsec (Internet Protocol security) Microsoft's encryption method of choice for networks consisting of multiple networks linked by a private connection, providing transparent encryption between the server and the client.

IPv4 (Internet Protocol version 4) Internet standard protocol that provides a common layer over dissimilar networks; used to move packets among host computers and through gateways if necessary. Part of the TCP/IP protocol suite. Uses the dotted-decimal format—*x.x.x.x*. Each *x* represents an 8-bit binary number, or 0–255. Here's an example: 192.168.4.1.

IPv6 (Internet Protocol version 6) Protocol in which addresses consist of eight sets of four hexadecimal numbers, each number being a value between 0000 and ffff, using a colon to separate the numbers. Here's an example: fedc:ba98:7654:3210:0800:200c:00cf:1234.

ISO file Complete copy (or image) of a storage media device, typically used for optical discs. ISO image files typically have a file extension of .iso.

ISP *See* Internet service provider.

ITX (Information Technology eXtended)   A family of motherboard form factors. Mini-ITX is the largest and the most popular of the ITX form factors but is still quite small.

jack (physical connection)   Part of a connector into which a plug is inserted. Also referred to as a *port*.

jailbreaking   Process for circumventing the security restrictions present on an iOS device.

jitter   Network issue in which packets are delayed by variable lengths of time, leading to poor performance.

joule   Unit of energy describing (in this book) how much energy a surge suppressor can handle before it fails.

jumper   Pair of small pins that can be shorted with a shunt to configure many aspects of PCs. Often used in configurations that are rarely changed.

Keep my files   Windows Recovery Environment option in Windows 10 that rebuilds the OS but preserves user files, settings, and Microsoft Store applications (while deleting all other applications on the system).

Kerberos   Authentication encryption developed by MIT to enable multiple brands of servers to authenticate multiple brands of clients.

kernel   Core portion of program that resides in memory and performs the most essential operating system tasks.

kernel panic   The Linux/macOS equivalent of the Windows BSoD. An error from which the OS can't recover without a reboot. *See also* Blue Screen of Death.

key fob   Generically, just about anything attached to a key ring that isn't a key. Some security tools, such as hardware security tokens and RFID authentication devices, are commonly designed as key fobs.

Keychain   A macOS password management and storage service that saves passwords for computer and non-computer environments. Also, the *iCloud Keychain* adds synchronization among any macOS and iOS devices connected to the Internet for a user account.

keylogger   Software, usually malware, that copies, saves, and sometimes uploads all keystrokes and other inputs on a computer. Keyloggers are used to gather information such as passwords, Web sites visited, and other activities performed on a computer.

kill   Command in UNIX shells (such as Bash) and in PowerShell that terminates an indicated process.

KVM (keyboard, video, mouse) switch   Hardware device that enables multiple computers to be viewed and controlled by a single mouse, keyboard, and screen.

LAN (local area network)   Group of computers connected via cabling, radio, or infrared that uses this connectivity to share resources such as printers and mass storage.

laser   Single-wavelength, in-phase light source that is sometimes strapped to the head of sharks by bad guys. Note to henchmen: Lasers should never be used with sea bass, no matter how ill-tempered they might be. They should, however, be used in optical disc technology, laser-based projectors, single-mode fiber optic cables, and/or laser printers.

latency   Amount of delay before a device may respond to a request; most commonly used in reference to RAM.

launcher   An Android app that serves as the device's desktop, often with more extensive customization features than launchers provided by Google or the device maker.

LBA (logical block addressing)   *See* logical block addressing.

LC   *See* Lucent connector.

LCD (liquid crystal display)   Type of display commonly used on portable computers. LCDs have also replaced CRTs as the display of choice for desktop computer users. LCDs use liquid crystals and electricity to produce images on the screen.

lease   A temporary IP address assignment to a device on the network from a pool of available addresses.

LED (light-emitting diode)   Solid-state device that vibrates at luminous frequencies when current is applied.

Level 1 (L1) cache   First RAM cache accessed by the CPU, which stores only the absolute most accessed programming and data used by currently running threads. Always the smallest and fastest cache on the CPU.

Level 2 (L2) cache   Second RAM cache accessed by the CPU. Much larger and often slower than the L1 cache, and accessed only if the requested program/data is not in the L1 cache.

Level 3 (L3) cache   Third RAM cache accessed by the CPU. Much larger and slower than the L1 and L2 caches, and accessed only if the requested program/data is not in the L2 cache.

LGA (land grid array)   Arrangement of a large number of pins extending from the CPU socket to corresponding contact points on the bottom of the CPU.

Libraries   Feature in Windows that aggregates folders from multiple locations and places them in a single, easy-to-find spot in File Explorer. Default libraries in Windows include Documents, Music, Pictures, and Videos.

Lightning   An 8-pin connector, proprietary to Apple, that can be inserted without regard to orientation. Used to connect mobile devices to a power or data source.

Lightweight Directory Access Protocol (LDAP)   Protocol used for obtaining directory information over a network. Uses port 389.

Li-Ion (Lithium-Ion)   Battery commonly used in portable computing devices. Li-Ion batteries don't suffer from the memory effects of Nickel-Cadmium (Ni-Cd) batteries and provide much more power for a greater length of time.

link light   An LED on NICs, hubs, and switches that lights up to show good connection between the devices.

link-local address   IPv6 address a computer gives itself when it first boots. IPv6's equivalent to IPv4's APIPA address.

Linux   Open-source UNIX-clone operating system.

liquid cooling   A method of cooling a PC that works by running some liquid—usually water—through a metal block that sits on top of the CPU, absorbing heat. The liquid gets heated by the block, runs out of the block and into something that cools the liquid, and is then pumped through the block again.

load balancer   A device that spreads network traffic across multiple servers in order to improve availability of resources.

local area network   *See* LAN.

Local Security Policy   Windows tool used to set local security policies on an individual system.

local share   File sharing server that only shares with local devices on a LAN.

local user account   List of usernames and their associated passwords with access to a system, contained in an encrypted database.

local username   Username that is stored on the device, rather than on an Active Directory domain controller.

Local Users and Groups (lusrmgr.msc)   Tool enabling creation and changing of group memberships and accounts for users.

location data   Information provided by a mobile device's GPS; used for mapping functions as well as for location-aware services, such as finding nearby restaurants or receiving coupons for nearby shops.

locator application   Application designed to enable the user of a mobile device or laptop to locate the device in the event that it was lost or stolen.

log files   Files created in Windows to track the progress of certain processes.

logical block addressing (LBA)   Addressing scheme that presents storage chunks on a storage device to the OS as a sequence of blocks beginning with LBA0. This saves the OS from having to deal directly with the details of how storage space is arranged on a hard drive or SSD.

logical drives   Sections of an extended partition on a hard drive that are formatted and (usually) assigned a drive letter, each of which is presented to the user as if it were a separate drive.

logical security   Security measures focused on denying access to networks, systems, and data.

logon screen   First screen of the Windows interface, used to log on to the computer system.

Long Term Evolution (LTE)   Fourth-generation cellular network technology supporting theoretical download speeds up to 1 Gbps and upload speeds up to 100 Mbps. Marketed as and now generally accepted as a true 4G technology.

long-range fixed wireless   Method of wirelessly connecting networks when it isn't feasible to run cables. Uses directional antennas and can connect buildings up to several miles away.

loop   Control construct used in a script or program to repeat a sequence of instructions when certain conditions are met. For example, a script could use a loop to a set of instructions for resizing an image once for every image file in a directory.

loopback plug   Device used during loopback tests to check the female connector on a NIC.

loopback test   Special test to confirm a NIC can send and receive data. A full external loopback test requires a loopback plug inserted into the NIC's port.

ls   UNIX equivalent of the dir command, which displays the contents of a directory.

LTE   *See* Long Term Evolution.

Lucent connector (LC)   Type of fiber optic connector. *See* fiber optic cable.

M.2   Type of space-efficient expansion slot common in recent portable computers. Also found on some desktop motherboards. M.2 is available in different configurations to support Wi-Fi cards and SSDs.

Mac   Also *Macintosh*. Common name for Apple Computers' flagship operating system, as well as their desktop and laptop computers; Apple calls the current operating system *macOS*.

MAC (mandatory access control)   Authorization method in which the system grants access to resources based on security labels and clearance levels. Less flexible than discretionary access control (DAC), which lets users assign access levels to resources they own. MAC may be used in organizations with very high security needs.

MAC (media access control) address   Unique 48-bit address assigned to each network card. IEEE assigns blocks of possible addresses to various NIC manufacturers to help ensure that the address is always unique. The Data Link layer of the OSI model uses MAC addresses to locate machines.

MAC address filtering   Method of limiting wireless network access based on the physical, hard-wired address of the wireless NIC of a computing device.

machine language   Binary instruction code that is understood by the CPU.

macOS   Operating system from Apple that powers its desktop and portable computers. Based on UNIX; most versions of macOS run on Intel/IBM-based hardware, just like Microsoft Windows. The latest versions of macOS also support Apple's new M1 and M2 ARM-based processors. Before 2016, it was known as OS X. *See also* Mac.

magnetic hard drives   Storage devices that read and write data encoded magnetically onto spinning aluminum platters.

magnetometer   A fancy way of saying *metal detector*.

mail server   Networked host or server that provides e-mail service.

maintenance kit   Set of commonly replaced printer components provided by many manufacturers.

malware   Broadly, software designed to use your computer or device against your wishes. Includes adware, spyware, viruses, ransomware, etc. May be part of seemingly legitimate software or installed by exploiting a vulnerability in the device.

MAM   *See* mobile application management.

man   Linux command short for manual. Brings up user manual for a wide variety of other Linux commands and utilities.

MAN (metropolitan area network)   802.11 network that covers a single city.

mandatory access control   *See* MAC (mandatory access control).

man-in-the-middle attack   *See* on-path attack.

mass storage   Hard drives, optical discs, removable media drives, etc.

master boot record (MBR)   Tiny bit of code that takes control of the boot process from the system BIOS.

Material Safety Data Sheet (MSDS)   Standardized form that provides detailed information about potential environmental hazards and proper disposal methods associated with various computing components.

md (mkdir)   Command-line tool used to create directories.

MDM   *See* mobile device management.

media access control   *See* MAC (media access control) address.

mega-   Prefix that stands for the binary quantity 1,048,576 (2^{20}) or the decimal quantity of 1,000,000. One megabyte is 1,048,576 bytes. Sometimes shortened to *Meg*, as in "my video card has 8 Megs of video RAM." One megahertz, however, is a million hertz.

memory   Device or medium for temporary storage of programs and data during program execution. Synonymous with storage, although it most frequently refers to the internal storage of a computer that can be directly addressed by operating instructions. A computer's temporary storage capacity is measured in kilobytes (KB), megabytes (MB), or gigabytes (GB) of RAM (random-access memory). Long-term data storage on hard drives and solid-state drives is also measured in megabytes, gigabytes, and terabytes.

mesh topology   Network topology where each computer has a dedicated line to every other computer, most often used in wireless networks.

metered utilization   Fee charged by cloud service providers on the basis of how much of a resource was used. Fees may be based on things like access time, bandwidth used, bytes uploaded or downloaded, CPU usage, and other resource usage metrics.

metropolitan area network   *See* MAN.

MFA   *See* multifactor authentication.

MFD   *See* multifunction device.

MFT (master file table)   Enhanced file allocation table used by NTFS. *See also* FAT.

micro Secure Digital (microSD)   The smallest form factor of the SD flash memory standard. Often used in mobile devices.

microATX (μATX)   Variation of the ATX form factor, which uses the ATX power supply. MicroATX motherboards are generally smaller than their ATX counterparts but retain all the same functionality.

microprocessor   "Brain" of a computer. Primary computer chip that determines relative speed and capabilities of the computer. Also called the central processing unit (CPU).

Microsoft 365   Microsoft's subscription suite of productivity apps; includes Word, Teams, Outlook, SharePoint, PowerPoint, and numerous other applications used in homes and businesses around the world.

Microsoft Management Console (MMC)   A shell program in Windows that holds individual utilities called snap-ins, designed for administration and troubleshooting. The MMC enables an administrator to customize management tools by picking and choosing from a list of snap-ins. Available snap-ins include Device Manager, Event Viewer, Local Users and Groups, and Computer Management.

Microsoft Remote Assistance (MSRA)   Feature of Windows that enables users to give anyone control of his or her desktop over the Internet.

microUSB   USB connector commonly found on a variety of devices including Android phones. Slowly being replaced by USB Type-C connectors (especially in Android phones).

migration   Moving users from one operating system or hard drive to another. Particularly common when upgrading operating systems or migrating from a mechanical hard drive (HDD) to a solid-state drive (SSD).

MIMO (multiple in/multiple out)   Feature of 802.11n devices that enables the simultaneous connection of up to four antennas, greatly increasing throughput. 802.11ac also uses Multiuser MIMO (MU-MIMO), which gives a WAP the capability to broadcast to multiple users simultaneously.

mini connector   One type of power connector from a PC power supply unit. Supplies 5 and 12 volts to peripherals.

Mini-ITX   The largest and the most popular of the three ITX form factors. At a miniscule 6.7 by 6.7 inches, Mini-ITX competes with microATX and proprietary small form factor (SFF) motherboards.

miniUSB   Smaller USB connector often found on digital cameras.

mirror set   A type of mirrored volume created with RAID 1. *See also* mirroring.

mirror space   Storage Space that mirrors files across two or more drives, like RAID 1 or RAID 10. *See* Storage Spaces.

mirrored volume   Volume that is mirrored on another volume. *See also* mirroring.

mirroring   Reading and writing data at the same time to two drives for fault tolerance purposes. Considered RAID level 1. Also called *drive mirroring*.

Mission Control   A feature of macOS that enables switching between open applications, windows, and more.

mkdir   *See* md.

MMC   *See* Microsoft Management Console.

mobile application management (MAM)   Enables IT to make and enforce policies regarding appropriate and safe application use on business devices and premises as well as allowing them to push updates and make changes to specific applications.

mobile device   Small, highly portable computing device with tightly integrated components designed to be worn or carried by the user. Includes smartphones, tablets, and wearable devices.

mobile device management (MDM)   A formalized structure that enables an organization to account for all the different types of devices used to process, store, transmit, and receive organizational data.

mobile device management (MDM) policies   Technical controls that govern how mobile devices are used as tools in the workplace.

mobile hotspot   *See* hotspot.

Molex connector   Computer power connector used by optical drives, hard drives, and case fans. Keyed to prevent it from being inserted into a power port improperly.

monitor   Screen that displays data from a PC. Typically a flat-panel display, such as an LCD.

motherboard   Flat piece of circuit board that resides inside your computer case and has a number of connectors on it. Every device in a PC connects directly or indirectly to the motherboard, including CPU, RAM, hard drives, optical drives, keyboard, mouse, and video cards.

motherboard book   Valuable resource when installing a new motherboard. Normally lists all the specifications about a motherboard, including the type of memory and type of CPU usable with the motherboard.

move   Command-line tool used to move a file from one location to another.

mSATA   Standardized smaller SATA form factor for use in portable devices.

MSDS   *See* Material Safety Data Sheet.

msinfo32 (System Information)   Provides information about hardware resources, components, and the software environment.

multiboot installation   OS installation in which multiple operating systems are installed on a single machine.

multicore processing   Using two or more execution cores on one CPU die to divide up work independently of the OS.

multifactor authentication (MFA)   Authentication schema requiring more than one unique authentication factor. The factors are knowledge, possession, inherence, location, and temporal. For example, a password (knowledge factor) and a fingerprint (inherence factor) is a basic form of multifactor authentication.

multifunction device (MFD)   Single device that consolidates functions from more than one document-handling device, such as a printer, copier, scanner, or fax machine.

multimeter   Device used to measure voltage, amperage, and resistance.

multimode   Type of fiber optic cabling capable of transmitting multiple light signals at the same time using different reflection angles within the cable core. Signals tend to degrade over distance, limiting multimode cable to short distances. *See* fiber optic cable.

multiple Desktops   A GUI feature that enables a computer to have more than one Desktop, each with its own icons and background. macOS supports multiple Desktops with Spaces. Most Linux distros use multiple Desktops, often called workspaces. Microsoft introduced the feature with Windows 10.

multitasking   Process of running multiple programs or tasks on the same computer at the same time.

multitouch   Input method on many smartphones and tablets that enables you to perform gestures (actions with multiple fingers) to do all sorts of fun things, such as using two fingers to scroll or swipe to another screen or desktop.

Multiuser MIMO (MU-MIMO) New version of MIMO included in 802.11ac that enables a WAP to broadcast to multiple users simultaneously.

mv The move command in Linux and macOS.

NAT (Network Address Translation) A means of translating a system's IP address into another IP address before sending it out to a larger network. NAT manifests itself by a NAT program that runs on a system or a router. A network using NAT provides the systems on the network with private IP addresses. The system running the NAT software has two interfaces: one connected to the network and the other connected to the larger network. The NAT program takes packets from the client systems bound for the larger network and translates their internal private IP addresses to its own public IP address, enabling many systems to share a single IP address.

native resolution Resolution on an LCD monitor that matches the physical pixels on the screen.

Near-Field Communication *See* NFC.

near-field scanner Enables mobile devices to use near-field communication to read things like barcodes and bank cards.

net Command-line utility in Windows that enables users to view and change a whole host of network settings and information.

net use Subcommand of the Windows net command that enables a user to connect, disconnect, and view information about existing connections to network resources.

net user Subcommand of the Windows net command that enables a user to create, delete, and change user accounts.

NetBIOS (Network Basic Input/Output System) Protocol that operates at the Session layer of the OSI seven-layer model. This protocol creates and manages connections based on the names of the computers involved. Uses TCP ports 137 and 139, and UDP ports 137 and 138.

netstat Command-line tool in Windows and Linux to identify inbound and outbound TCP/IP connections with the host.

network Collection of two or more computers interconnected by telephone lines, coaxial cables, satellite links, radio, and/or some other communication technique that communicate with one another for a common purpose.

Network Interface in File Explorer that displays networked computers and other devices, such as network printers.

Network & Internet (Windows Settings) Windows Settings category that contains options and settings relating to networks and Internet connectivity, including checking connection status, network sharing, and VPN settings.

network attached storage (NAS)   A device that attaches to a network for the sole purpose of storing and sharing files.

network connection   A method for connecting two or more computers together. *See also* network.

network documentation   A road map to an organization's network configuration and topology to guide techs who need to change or repair the network.

network ID   Logical number that identifies the network on which a device or machine exists. This number exists in TCP/IP and other network protocol suites.

network interface card (or controller)   *See* NIC.

network protocol   Software that takes the incoming data received by the network card, keeps it organized, sends it to the application that needs it, and then takes outgoing data from the application and hands it to the NIC to be sent out over the network.

network topology diagram   A map of how everything in an organization's network (including switches, routers, WAPs, services, and workstations) connects. May indicate connection types, speed, technologies, and so on.

NFC (Near Field Communication)   Mobile technology that enables short-range wireless communication between mobile devices. Now used for mobile payment technology such as Apple Pay and Google Pay.

NIC (network interface card or controller)   Expansion card or motherboard interface that enables a PC to connect to a network via a network cable. A *wireless NIC* enables connection via radio waves rather than a physical cable. Also commonly called a wireless card or Wi-Fi card.

nit   Value used to measure the brightness of an LCD display. A typical LCD display has a brightness of between 100 and 400 nits.

nonvolatile   Describes storage that retains data even if power is removed; typically refers to a ROM or flash ROM chip, but also could be applied to hard drives, optical media, and other storage devices.

notification area   Windows GUI feature that contains icons representing background processes, the system clock, and volume control. Located by default at the right edge of the Windows taskbar. Many users call this area the system tray.

nslookup   Command-line program in Windows used to determine exactly what information the DNS server is providing about a specific host name.

NTFS (New Technology File System)   Robust and secure file system introduced by Microsoft with Windows NT. NTFS provides an amazing array of configuration options for user access and security. Users can be granted access to data on a file-by-file basis. NTFS enables object-level security, long filename support, compression, and encryption.

NTFS permissions   Restrictions that determine the amount of access given to a particular user on a system using NTFS.

NVIDIA Corporation   One of the foremost manufacturers of graphics cards and chipsets.

NVMe (Non-Volatile Memory Express)   SSD technology that supports a communication connection between the operating system and the SSD directly through a PCIe bus lane, reducing latency and taking full advantage of the speeds of high-end SSDs. NVMe SSDs come in a few formats, such as an add-on expansion card, though most commonly in M.2 format. NVMe drives are a lot more expensive currently than other SSDs, but offer much higher speeds. NVMe drives use SATAe.

object   System component that is given a set of characteristics and can be managed by the operating system as a single entity.

ohm(s)   A unit of measurement of electronic resistance; used to measure cable's impedance.

OLED (organic light-emitting diode)   Display technology where an organic compound provides the light for the screen, thus eliminating the need for a backlight or inverter. Used in high-end TVs and small devices such as smart watches, smartphones, and VR headsets.

on-path attack   Attacker serves as an intermediary between two systems, enabling the attacker to observe, redirect, or even alter messages passing in either direction. Also commonly known as a *man-in-the-middle (MITM) attack.*

operating system (OS)   Series of programs and code that creates an interface so users can interact with a system's hardware; for example, Windows, macOS, and Linux.

optical disc/media   Types of data discs (such as DVDs, CDs, BDs, etc.) that are read by a laser.

optical drive   Drive used to read/write to optical discs, such as CDs or DVDs.

optical network terminal (ONT)   Works like a modem, but for fiber optic networks. Enables your networked devices to communicate with an Internet service provider.

optimization   Changes made to a system to improve its performance.

OS   *See* operating system.

overclocking   To run a CPU or video processor faster than its rated speed.

overloaded network   A mobile network that, often due to a large public event, emergency, or network equipment failure, is unable to keep up with user demand. Users may have good signal quality but be unable to access data, text, or voice services.

owner   In both NTFS and UNIX permissions, usually the user that created a given file or folder, although both systems support changing ownership to another user.

Ownership permission   Special NTFS permissions granted to the account that owns a file or folder. Owners can do anything they want to the files and folders they own, including changing their permissions.

PaaS   *See* Platform as a Service.

packet   Basic component of communication over a network. Group of bits of fixed maximum size and well-defined format that is switched and transmitted as a single entity through a network. Contains source and destination addresses, data, and control information. Packets are included within (and are not the same thing as) a frame.

page file   *See* virtual memory.

PAN (personal area network)   Small wireless network created with Bluetooth technology and intended to link computers and other peripheral devices.

parallel execution   When a multicore CPU processes more than one thread.

parity RAM   Earliest form of error-detecting RAM; stored an extra bit (called the parity bit) to verify the data.

parity space   Storage Space that adds resiliency similar to RAID 5 or RAID 6. *See* Storage Spaces.

partition   Section of the storage area of a hard disk. Created during initial preparation of the hard disk, before the disk is formatted. Also called a *volume*.

partition boot sector   Sector of a partition that stores information important to its partition, such as the location of the OS boot files. Responsible for loading the OS on a partition.

partition table   Table located in the boot sector of a hard drive that lists every partition on the disk that contains a valid operating system.

partitioning   Electronically subdividing a physical drive into one or more units called partitions (or volumes).

passcode lock   Mobile device security feature that requires you enter a series of letters, numbers, or motion patterns to unlock the mobile device each time you press the power button.

password   Key used to verify a user's identity on a secure computer or network.

password manager   Software that uses strong encryption to protect stored passwords, removing the need to remember all the various and complex passwords a person uses for their various online accounts.

patch   Small piece of software released by a software manufacturer to correct a flaw or problem with a particular piece of software. Also called an *update*.

patch cables   Short (typically two- to five-foot) UTP cables that connect patch panels to a switch or router.

patch management   Process of keeping software updated in a safe, timely fashion.

patch panel   A panel containing a row of female connectors (ports) that terminate the horizontal cabling in the equipment room. Patch panels facilitate cabling organization and provide protection to horizontal cabling.

path   Route the operating system must follow to find an executable program stored in a subfolder.

pattern lock   Mobile device screen lock that requires the user to swipe a certain pattern in order to be authenticated and unlock the device.

PCI (Peripheral Component Interconnect)   Design architecture for the expansion bus on the computer motherboard that enabled system components to be added to the computer. Used parallel communication, and was replaced by PCIe.

PCI DSS (Payment Card Industry Data Security Standard)   A standard that sets common rules for systems that accept, process, transmit, or store credit/debit card payments. Often referred to as just *PCI*.

PCIe (PCI Express)   Serialized successor to PCI and AGP that uses the concept of individual data paths called lanes. May use any number of lanes, although a single lane (×1) and 16 lanes (×16) are the most common on motherboards.

PCIe 6/8-pin power connector   Connector on some power supplies for powering a dedicated graphics card.

peer-to-peer network   Network in which each machine can act as both a client and a server.

Performance   Tab in Task Manager that tracks PC performance, including CPU usage, available physical memory, size of the disk cache, and other details about memory and processes.

Performance Monitor (perfmon.msc)   Windows tool for tracking system resources over time.

Performance Options   Tool that enables users to configure CPU, RAM, and virtual memory settings.

peripheral   Any device that connects to the system unit.

permission propagation   Describes what happens to permissions on an object, such as a file or folder, when you move or copy it.

personal area network   *See* PAN.

Personalization (Windows Settings)   Windows Settings category that enables users to configure preferences such as the background picture for both the desktop and lock screen, colors of interface elements, themes, which elements show on the Start screen, and so on.

personally identifiable information (PII)   Any data that can lead back to a specific individual.

PGA (pin grid array)   Arrangement of a large number of pins extending from the bottom of the CPU package into corresponding holes in the CPU socket.

Phillips-head screwdriver   Most important part of a PC tech's toolkit.

phishing   A social engineering attack intended to get people to give their usernames, passwords, or other security information by pretending to be someone else electronically.

physical security   Security measures intended to protect facilities and systems from physical threats like unauthorized entry, burglary, or other threats.

ping   Command-line utility used to send a "ping" message to another computer, which can be used to verify another system is on the network, spot potential DNS issues, identify latency problems, and so on.

Pinwheel of Death   *See* Spinning Pinwheel of Death.

pipe   Command-line operator that uses the | symbol to "pipe" output from one command to another, instead of printing it to the screen.

pipeline   Processing methodology where multiple calculations take place simultaneously by being broken into a series of steps. Often used in CPUs and video processors.

pixel (picture element)   In computer graphics, smallest element of a display space that can be independently assigned color or intensity.

pixels per inch (PPI)   Density of pixels on a display or a light sensor; the higher the density, the greater the resolution.

PKI (public key infrastructure)   Authentication schema where public keys are exchanged between all parties using digital certificates, enabling secure communication over public networks.

Platform as a Service (PaaS)   Cloud-based virtual server(s) combined with a platform that gives programmers the tools needed to deploy, administer, and maintain a Web application.

plenum   Space in the ceiling, walls, and floor where special plenum-grade (fire-retardant) network cables can be run out of sight.

plug and play (PnP)   Combination of smart PCs, smart devices, and smart operating systems that automatically configure all necessary system resources and ports when you install a new peripheral device.

policies   Control permission to perform a given action, such as accessing a command prompt, installing software, or logging on at a certain time of day. Contrast with true permissions, which control access to specific resources.

POP3 (Post Office Protocol 3)   One of the two protocols that receive e-mail from SMTP servers. POP3 uses TCP port 110. While historically most e-mail clients used this protocol, the IMAP4 e-mail protocol is now more common.

port (networking)   In networking, the number used to identify the requested service (such as SMTP or FTP) when connecting to a TCP/IP host. Examples include application protocol ports such as 80 (HTTP), 443, (HTTPS), 21 (FTP), 23 (Telnet), 25 (SMTP), 110 (POP3), 143 (IMAP), and 3389 (RDP).

port (physical connection)   Part of a connector into which a plug is inserted. Physical ports are also referred to as jacks.

port forwarding   Router configuration that enables outside traffic to reach a particular node on a secured network, such as a server. Port forwarding translates the IP address and port number used to reach the network by a remote client into the IP address and port number used by a particular node on the network.

port replicator   Device that plugs into a USB port or Thunderbolt port and offers common PC ports, such as VGA, HDMI, USB, network, and so on. Plugging a laptop into a port replicator can instantly connect the computer to nonportable components such as a printer, scanner, monitor, or full-sized keyboard. Port replicators are typically used at home or in the office with the nonportable equipment already connected.

portable battery recharger   Device containing a rechargeable battery that can be used to charge other devices, typically over USB, when no outlets are available.

POST (power-on self-test)   Basic diagnostic routine completed by a system at the beginning of the boot process to make sure a display adapter and the system's memory are installed. In the event that there is some problem with the hardware, you'll generally hear some combination of beeps indicating where the problem is; consult the motherboard book. It then searches for an operating system. If it finds one, it hands over control of the machine to the OS.

POST card   Device installed into a motherboard expansion slot that assists in troubleshooting boot problems by providing a two-digit code indicating the stop of the boot process where the problem is occurring.

potential   The amount of electrical energy stored in an object.

power conditioning   Ensuring and adjusting incoming AC wall power to as close to standard as possible. Most UPS devices provide power conditioning.

power management   Cooperation between hardware, BIOS, and OS to reduce power consumption.

Power Options   Windows Control Panel applet that enables better control over power use by customizing a Balanced, Power saver, or High-performance power plan.

Power over Ethernet (PoE)   Technology that provides power and data transmission through a single network cable.

power plan   Preconfigured profiles (such as Balanced, High performance, and Power saver) in the Power Options applet that modify a Windows system's behavior to adjust power consumption.

power supply unit (PSU)   Provides the electrical power for a PC. Converts standard AC power into various voltages of DC electricity in a PC.

Power Users group   After Administrator/Administrators, the second most powerful account and group type in Windows. Power users have differing capabilities in different versions of Windows.

power-saving modes   Special power modes that limit or modify device functionality in order to prolong battery life. May take steps such as disabling communications, reducing processor speed, limiting programs, and dimming the screen.

PowerShell   *See* Windows PowerShell.

preboot execution environment (PXE)   Technology that enables a PC to boot without any local storage by retrieving an OS from a server over a network.

primary partition   Partition on a Windows hard drive that can store a bootable operating system.

principle of least privilege   Accounts should have permission to access only the resources they need and no more.

print server   Server, computer, or standalone network device that shares access to a printer over a network.

printed circuit board (PCB)   Copper etched onto a nonconductive material and then coated with some sort of epoxy for strength.

Privacy (Windows Settings)   Windows Settings category that contains options related to privacy.

private cloud   Cloud network built and maintained by or explicitly for a specific company or organization. Often onsite, but may be provided by a third party. While a public cloud network often requires more expertise and costs more, especially up front, it also enables greater customization and security.

PRL (Preferred Roaming List)   A list that is occasionally and automatically updated to a phone's firmware by the carrier so that the phone will be configured with a particular carrier's networks and frequencies, in a priority order, that it should search for when it can't locate its home carrier network.

Processes Tab in Task Manager that lists all running processes on a system. Frequently a handy tool for ending buggy or unresponsive processes.

product key Code used during installation to verify legitimacy of the software.

profile (MDM) A collection of mobile device management (MDM) configuration and security settings that an administrator has created in order to apply those settings to particular categories of users or devices.

profile (network) Collection of information necessary to automatically connect to a network, stored by the network's SSID. Enables mobile and portable devices to easily use many networks.

profile (user) Describes a Windows user account's customized environment, including Desktop preferences, color schemes, shortcuts, and so on.

program/programming Series of binary electronic commands sent to a CPU to get work done.

Programs and Features Windows Control Panel applet; enables uninstalling or changing program options and altering Windows features.

projector Device for projecting video images from PCs or other video sources, usually for audience presentations.

prompt A character or message provided by an operating system or program to indicate that it is ready to accept input.

proprietary Technology unique to a particular vendor.

proprietary crash screen A screen, differing between operating systems, that indicates an NMI. *See also* BSoD *and* Spinning Pinwheel of Death.

protected health information (PHI) Personally identifiable information that relates to a person's health status, medical records, and healthcare services they have received.

protocol Agreement that governs the procedures used to exchange information between cooperating entities. Usually includes how much information is to be sent, how often it is to be sent, how to recover from transmission errors, and who is to receive the information.

proxy server Software that enables multiple connections to the Internet to go through one protected computer. Common security feature in the corporate world. Applications that want to access Internet resources send requests to the proxy server instead of trying to access the Internet directly, which both protects the client computers and enables the network administrator to monitor and restrict Internet access.

ps Linux command for listing all processes running on the computer.

public cloud Cloud network built and maintained by a large company for use by any individual or company who wants to create an account and start paying for services.

Public folder   Folder that all users can access and share with all other users on the system or network.

public key infrastructure   *See* PKI.

punchdown block   Connector used to connect UTP cable to a patch panel. Wires are attached to the block using a punchdown tool.

punchdown tool   A specialized tool for connecting UTP wires to a punchdown block.

PVC (polyvinyl chloride)   Material used to make the plastic protective sheathing around many basic network cables. Produces noxious fumes when burned.

pwd   Linux command that displays the user's current path.

QR scanner   An application or device capable of scanning and interpreting QR codes.

quad-channel architecture   Feature similar to dual-channel RAM, but making use of four sticks of RAM instead of two.

Quality of Service (QoS)   Router feature used to prioritize access to network resources. Ensures certain users, applications, or services are prioritized when there isn't enough bandwidth to go around by limiting the bandwidth for certain types of data based on application protocol, the IP address of a computer, and all sorts of other features.

quick format   High-level formatting that creates just the file allocation table and a blank root directory. *See also* formatting.

radio frequency (RF)   The part of the electromagnetic spectrum used for radio communication.

radio frequency identification (RFID)   Wireless technology that uses small tags containing small amounts of digital information, and readers capable of accessing it. Passive RFID tags operate by harvesting some of the power a scanner or reader emits, enabling a vast array of applications. Common uses such as tracking inventory, identifying lost pets, contactless payments, authentication, and wireless door locks are just scratching the surface. *See also* asset tag, ID badge, key fob, *and* smart card.

RAID (redundant array of independent [or inexpensive] disks)   Method for creating a fault-tolerant storage system. RAID uses multiple hard drives in various configurations to offer differing levels of speed/data redundancy.

RAID 0   Uses byte-level striping and provides no fault tolerance.

RAID 0+1   A RAID 0 configuration created by combining two RAID 1 arrays. Provides both speed and redundancy, but requires at least four disks.

RAID 1   Uses mirroring or duplexing for increased data redundancy.

RAID 5   Uses block-level and parity data striping. Requires three or more drives.

RAID 5 volume (dynamic disks)   A software-based RAID 5 volume made up of three or more dynamic disks with equal-sized unallocated space. Created with Windows Disk Management.

RAID 6   Disk striping with extra parity. Like RAID 5, but with more parity data. Requires four or more drives, but you can lose up to two drives at once and your data is still protected.

RAID 10   The opposite of RAID 0+1, two mirrored RAID 0 configurations. Provides both speed and redundancy, and also requires four disks.

RAM (random access memory)   Memory that can be accessed at random—that is, memory that you can write to or read from without touching the preceding address. This term is often used to mean a computer's main memory.

ransomware   A nasty form of malware that encrypts data or drives on the infected system and demands payment, often within a limited timeframe, in exchange for the keys to decrypt the data.

rapid elasticity   Characteristic of cloud computing that enables cloud consumers to add or remove capacity quickly. Because cloud servers are powered by virtual machines, customers can start or shut down new instances of VMs or move the VMs to more powerful hardware.

rd (rmdir)   Command-line tool used to remove directories.

read-only attribute   File attribute that does not allow a file to be altered or modified. Helpful when protecting system files that should not be edited.

real-time clock (RTC)   Device within the CMOS memory chip that provides date and time information to the computer and operating system.

recent apps   Interface for viewing a list of recently used apps on a mobile device.

reciprocity   *See* Ethic of Reciprocity.

recovery partition   Small hidden partition on a system's primary hard drive with a factory-fresh OS image to recover and reinstall from.

Recycle Bin   Location to which files are moved when they are deleted from a modern Windows system. To permanently remove files from a system, they must be emptied from the Recycle Bin.

refresh rate   Time required for a monitor to redraw the whole screen.

regedit.exe   Program used to edit the Windows Registry.

registration (printing)   Describes how accurately the printer lays down each color layer that makes up a page or image. Poor registration can result in muddled colors or a fringe of pure color around a shape or image. Printers usually have a routine (which may mention calibration, alignment, or registration) for detecting and fixing alignment issues.

registration (product)   Usually optional process that identifies the legal owner/user of the product to the supplier.

Registry   Complex binary file used to store configuration data about a particular Windows system. To edit the Registry, users can use the Registry Editor or use regedit.

Registry Editor (regedit.exe)   Program used to edit the Windows Registry.

remediation   Repairing damage caused by a virus.

remnant   Potentially recoverable data on a hard drive that remains despite formatting or deleting.

Remote Assistance   *See* Microsoft Remote Assistance.

remote desktop   Generically, the process of using one system to access the desktop or graphical user interface (GUI) of a remote system.

Remote Desktop Connection   Windows tool used to form a remote desktop connection and graphically access the GUI of a remote system.

Remote Desktop Protocol (RDP)   Protocol used for Microsoft's Remote Desktop tool. Uses port 3389.

remote network installation   A common method of OS installation where the source files are placed in a shared directory on a network server. Then, a tech who needs to install a new OS can boot the computer, connect to the source location on the network, and start the installation from there.

remotely wipe   The ability to remotely delete user data from a mobile device that has been lost or stolen.

removable media   Any storage on a computer that can be easily removed. For example, optical discs, flash drives, or memory cards.

Remove everything   Windows Recovery Environment option in Windows 10 that deletes all apps, programs, user files, and user settings, resulting in a fresh installation of Windows. Use as a last resort when troubleshooting (and back up data first).

replication   When a virus makes copies of itself, often by injecting itself into other executables. *See* malware *and* virus.

reset to factory default   Another term for a factory reset.

resistance   Difficulty in making electricity flow through a material, measured in ohms.

resistor   Any material or device that impedes the flow of electrons. Antistatic wrist straps and mats use tiny resistors to prevent a static charge from racing through the device.

resolution   Measurement for monitors and printers expressed in horizontal and vertical dots or pixels. Higher resolutions provide sharper details and thus display better-looking images.

Resource Monitor (resmon.exe)   Windows utility that displays detailed performance information about a computer's CPU, memory, disk, and network activity.

resources   Data and services such as files, folders, drives, printers, connections, and so on.

response rate   The amount of time it takes for all the sub-pixels on an LCD panel to change from one state to another. This change is measured in one of two ways: black-to-white (BtW) measures how long it takes the pixels to go from pure black to pure white and back again, and gray-to-gray (GtG) measures how long it takes the pixels to go from one gray state to another.

restore point   A snapshot of a computer's configuration at a specific point in time, created by the System Restore utility and used to restore a malfunctioning system. *See also* System Restore.

retina scanner   Biometric security device that authenticates an individual by comparing retinal scans. Rarer in the real world than in media such as movies or video games.

RFI (radio frequency interference)   Another form of electrical interference caused by radio wave–emitting devices, such as cell phones, wireless network cards, and microwave ovens.

RG-6   Coaxial cabling used for cable television. It has a 75-ohm impedance and uses an F-type connector.

RG-59   Coaxial cable used for cable television, cable modems, and broadcast TV; thinner than RG-6, which makes it suitable for shorter patch cables.

riser card   Special adapter card, usually inserted into a special slot on a motherboard, that changes the orientation of expansion cards relative to the motherboard. Riser cards are used extensively in slimline computers to keep total depth and height of the system to a minimum. Sometimes called a daughter board.

risk analysis   A detailed assessment of any problems that could result from a change.

RJ (registered jack) connector   UTP cable connector, used for both telephone and network connections. RJ-11 is a connector for four-wire UTP; usually found in telephone connections. RJ-45 is a connector for eight-wire UTP; usually found in network connections.

RJ-11   *See* RJ (registered jack) connector.

RJ-45   *See* RJ (registered jack) connector.

rm   Linux command for deleting files.

rmdir   *See* rd (rmdir).

roaming   When a mobile device connects to a network not owned by its home carrier.

robocopy   Powerful command-line utility for copying files and directories, even over a network.

rogue anti-malware   Free application that claims to be anti-malware but is actually malware.

ROM (read-only memory)   Generic term for nonvolatile memory that can be read from but not written to. This means that code and data stored in ROM cannot be corrupted by accidental erasure. Additionally, ROM retains its data when power is removed, which makes it the perfect medium for storing BIOS data or information such as scientific constants.

root directory   Directory that contains all other directories. Also known as *root folder*.

root keys   Five main categories in the Windows Registry:

- HKEY_CLASSES_ROOT
- HKEY_CURRENT_USER
- HKEY_LOCAL_MACHINE
- HKEY_USERS
- HKEY_CURRENT_CONFIG

rooting   Process for circumventing the security restrictions and gaining access to the root user account on an Android device.

rootkit   Program that takes advantage of very low-level functionality to gain privileged system access and hide itself from all but the most aggressive anti-malware tools. Can strike operating systems, hypervisors, and even device firmware.

router   Device connecting separate networks; forwards a packet from one network to another based on the network address for the protocol being used. For example, an IP router looks only at the IP network number. Routers operate at Layer 3 (Network) of the OSI seven-layer model.

RSA token   Random-number generator used along with a username and password to enhance security.

RU (rack mounted unit)   Height measurement used for rack-mounted equipment. An RU is 1.75 inches. A device that fits in a 1.75-inch space is called a 1RU; a device designed for a 3.5-inch space is a 2RU; and a device that goes into a 7-inch space is called a 4RU.

run (networking)   A single piece of installed horizontal cabling.

Run as administrator   Method of running a Windows program with elevated privileges, disabling protections that normally limit a program's ability to damage the system.

SaaS   *See* Software as a Service.

Safe Mode   Important diagnostic boot mode for Windows that runs only very basic drivers and turns off virtual memory.

safety goggles   Protective glasses that keep stuff out of your eyes.

salted hash   *See* salting.

salting   The process of protecting password hashes from being easily reversed with a rainbow table by adding additional values to each password before hashing and storing it.

SAN   *See* storage area network.

sandbox   Virtualized computer used as a restricted environment to safely run untrusted applications or test new applications without posing risk to an actual system or network.

SAS (Serial Attached SCSI)   Fast, robust storage interface based on the SCSI command set. Also supports SATA drives. Used mainly in servers and storage arrays.

SATA (serial ATA)   Serialized version of the ATA standard that offers many advantages over PATA (parallel ATA) technology, including thinner cabling, keyed connectors, and lower power requirements.

SATA 3.2   Another term for SATAe. *See* SATA Express.

SATA Express (SATAe)   Version of SATA that ties capable drives directly into the PCI Express bus on motherboards. Each lane of PCIe 3.0 is capable of handling up to 8 Gbps of data throughput. A SATAe drive grabbing two lanes, therefore, could move a whopping 16 Gbps through the bus.

SATA power connector   15-pin, L-shaped connector used by SATA devices that support the hot-swappable feature.

SC   *See* subscriber connector.

SCADA   *See* supervisory control and data acquisition.

scope of the change   Defines who and what the change will affect. May include an inventory of systems to change, people involved, time required, and estimated cost.

screen lock   Mobile device and Windows feature that locks the screen until some form of authentication challenge is passed.

screen orientation   Describes whether a mobile device screen is in portrait or landscape mode, and the device settings that govern when the orientation may change. When the screen orientation setting is in automatic mode, the user interface (UI) will switch between portrait and landscape modes based on the device's orientation in physical space.

screened subnet   A lightly protected or unprotected subnet network positioned between an outer firewall and an organization's highly protected internal network. Screened subnets are used mainly to host public address servers (such as Web servers). Also commonly known as a *demilitarized zone (DMZ)*.

script Set of text instructions that tells a computer a series of commands to execute in a repeatable fashion.

scripting language Set of commands, syntax, variables, and format for scripts to be used in a specific computer environment. For example, *bash* is a scripting language often used in the Bash shell, which is common on UNIX environments.

SCSI (small computer system interface) Long-lived storage drive technology once common in the server market. Has been through many iterations. Today, the SCSI command set lives on in Serial Attached SCSI (SAS) hard drives. *See also* SAS.

SDRAM (synchronous DRAM) Dynamic RAM that is synchronous, or tied to the system clock. This type of RAM is used in all modern systems.

Search (box or field) Location on the Windows 10 taskbar next to the Start button where users can input text and see relevant suggestions (for settings, programs, files, and popular Web searches).

sector Magnetically preset storage areas on traditional magnetic hard drives. On older hard drives, a sector held 512 bytes of data; modern drives use 4096-byte Advanced Format (AF) sectors.

Secure Boot UEFI feature that secures the boot process by requiring properly signed software. This includes boot software and software that supports specific, essential components.

Secure Shell (SSH) Terminal emulation program similar to Telnet, except that the entire connection is encrypted. Uses port 22.

Secure Sockets Layer (SSL) Security protocol used by a browser to connect to secure Web sites. Replaced by Transport Layer Security (TLS).

security token Device that stores some unique information that a user carries with them. May contain digital certificates, passwords, biometric data, or RSA tokens.

segment The connection between a computer and a switch.

self-grounding A less-than-ideal method for ridding yourself of static electricity by touching a metal object such as a computer case.

Serial Attached SCSI *See* SAS.

serial presence detect (SPD) Information stored on a RAM chip that describes the speed, capacity, and other aspects of the RAM chip.

server Computer that shares its resources, such as printers and files, with other computers on a network. Example: network file system server that shares its disk space with a workstation that does not have a disk drive of its own.

Server Message Block (SMB) Windows' network file and print sharing protocol, though every major OS now supports it. Protocol of choice for LAN file servers. Uses TCP port 445 and UDP ports 137, 138, and 139.

service   A process that runs in the background of a PC but displays no icons anywhere. You can view a list of services in the Windows Task Manager. Also, a program stored in a ROM chip.

service menu   Hidden device menu containing tools for technicians servicing the device. May contain diagnostics, reports, or interfaces for changing otherwise inaccessible settings.

service pack   Collection of software patches released at one time by a software manufacturer.

Services   Tab in Windows Task Manager that lists all running services on a system. *See also* service.

Settings app   Windows app that combines a huge number of otherwise disparate utilities, apps, and tools traditionally spread out all over your computer into one fairly unified, handy interface.

sfc (System File Checker)   Command-prompt program (sfc.exe) that scans, detects, and restores Windows system files, folders, and paths.

SFTP (Secure FTP)   Secure version of the File Transfer Protocol (FTP) that uses port 22. *See also* FTP.

shared resources   Consolidating resources from many systems into a smaller number of more powerful systems, reducing power, maintenance, and hardware costs.

shell   Tool that interprets command-line input, also known as the command-line interpreter.

shielded twisted pair   *See* STP.

shoulder surfing   Social engineering attack where a malicious actor obtains credentials or other sensitive information by watching someone use a computer or device, often over their shoulder.

shunt   Tiny connector of metal enclosed in plastic that creates an electrical connection between two posts of a jumper. Also known as a *jumper block*.

shutdown   Windows and Linux command-line tool for shutting down the computer.

SID (security identifier)   Unique identifier for every PC that most techs change when cloning.

side-by-side apps   Windows feature for quickly pinning an app to the left or right half of a screen.

signature (malware)   Code pattern of a known virus or malware that antivirus/anti-malware software uses to detect malware.

signature file   *See* definition file.

signed driver   A driver designed specifically to work with Windows that has been tested and certified by Microsoft to work stably with Windows.

Simple Mail Transport Protocol   *See* SMTP.

Simple Network Management Protocol   *See* SNMP.

simple space   Storage Space that just pools storage space, like just a bunch of disks (JBOD). *See* Storage Spaces.

simple volume   Volume created when setting up dynamic disks. Acts like a primary partition on a dynamic disk.

single sign-on (SSO)   Process that uses an account or credentials for a popular service (such as a Google Account) to sign on or authenticate with other services.

single-factor authentication   A less-secure authentication process using only one of the authentication factors. *See also* multifactor authentication.

single-mode fiber optic cabling   Type of fiber optic cabling that uses laser light to transmit at very high rates over long distances. Still fairly rare. *See also* fiber optic cable.

single-sided RAM   Has chips on only one side, as opposed to double-sided RAM.

sleep mode   Power management setting in which all data from RAM is preserved by powering down much of the computer but maintaining power to RAM, or by writing the contents of RAM to the mass storage drive before the system goes into a reduced-power mode. Upon waking up, the information is retrieved from the HDD or SSD and returned to RAM if necessary; the system continues where it left off.

slot covers   Metal plates that cover up unused expansion slots on the back of a PC. Useful in maintaining proper airflow through a computer case.

S.M.A.R.T. (Self-Monitoring, Analysis, and Reporting Technology)   Monitoring system built into hard drives that tracks errors and error conditions within the drive.

smart card   Hardware authentication involving a credit card–sized card with circuitry that can be used to identify the bearer of that card.

smart card reader   Device that scans the smart card chip, such as those in ID badges. Common applications include enhancing the security of doors or laptops.

smartphone   A cell phone enhanced to do things formerly reserved for desktop and laptop computers, such as Web browsing, document viewing, and media consumption.

SMTP (Simple Mail Transport Protocol)   Main protocol used to send electronic mail on the Internet. Uses port 25.

snap-ins   Utilities that can be used with the Microsoft Management Console.

snapshot   Virtualization feature that enables you to save an extra copy of the virtual machine as it is exactly at the moment the snapshot is taken.

SNMP (Simple Network Management Protocol)   A set of standards for communication with devices connected to a TCP/IP network. Examples of these devices include routers, hubs, and switches. Uses ports 161 and 162.

social engineering   Using or manipulating people inside the networking environment to gain access to that network from the outside.

SO-DIMM (small-outline DIMM)   Memory used in portable PCs because of its small size.

soft power   Characteristic of ATX motherboards, which can use software to turn the PC on and off. The physical manifestation of soft power is the power switch. Instead of the thick power cord used in AT systems, an ATX power switch is little more than a pair of small wires leading to the motherboard.

soft reset   The equivalent of a reboot or restart for a mobile device. An important troubleshooting step because it clears running programs from memory and restarts the operating system. Some portable devices that closely resemble mobile devices may also use soft resets.

soft token   Programming (usually running on a general computing device such as a smartphone or portable computer) that enables the device to serve as an authentication factor when logging on to a secure resource.

software   Single group of programs designed to do a particular job; always stored on mass storage devices.

Software as a Service (SaaS)   Cloud-based service to store, distribute, and update programs and applications. The SaaS model provides access to necessary applications wherever you have an Internet connection, often without having to carry data with you or regularly update software. At the enterprise level, the subscription model of many SaaS providers makes it easier to budget and keep hundreds or thousands of computers up to date.

software firewall   Firewall implemented in software running on servers or workstations. *See* firewall.

software-defined networking (SDN)   Networking method that uses software tools to control network administration and traffic. SDN allows for the programming of the network to improve efficiency.

solid core   A cable that uses a single solid (not hollow or stranded) wire to transmit signals.

solid-state drive   *See* SSD.

spam   Unsolicited e-mails from both legitimate businesses and scammers that account for a huge percentage of traffic on the Internet.

spam gateway   Software used to filter incoming e-mail to prevent spam.

spanned volume   Volume that uses space on multiple dynamic disks.

SPD   *See* serial presence detect.

speaker   Device that outputs sound by using a magnetically driven diaphragm.

spear phishing   Dangerous targeted phishing attack on a group or individual that carefully uses details from the target's life to increase the odds they'll take the bait.

spindle speed   Fixed speed in revolutions per minute (RPM) at which a given HDD's platters spin. The two most common speeds are 5400 and 7200 RPM; higher-performance drives (far less common) run at 10,000 and 15,000 RPM. Also called *rotational speed*.

Spinning Pinwheel of Death (SPoD)   A spinning rainbow wheel (sometimes referred to as a "beach ball") that serves as the macOS indicator that an application isn't responding and may be busy or frozen.

spoofing   Pretending to be someone or something else by placing false information into packets. Commonly spoofed data include a source MAC address or IP address, e-mail address, Web address, or username. Generally a useful tool for enhancing or advancing other attacks, such as social engineering or spear phishing.

spyware   Software that runs in the background of a user's PC, sending information about browsing habits back to the company that installed it onto the system.

SQL attack   *See* Structured Query Language (SQL) attack.

SRAM (static RAM)   Very high-speed RAM built into CPUs that reduces wait states by preloading as many instructions as possible and keeping copies of already run instructions and data in case the CPU needs to work on them again.

SSD (solid-state drive)   Data storage device that uses flash memory to store data.

SSH   *See* Secure Shell.

SSID (service set identifier)   Parameter used to define a wireless network; otherwise known as the network name.

SSL   *See* Secure Sockets Layer.

ST   *See* straight tip.

standard user account   User account in Windows that has limited access to a system. Part of the Users group. Accounts of this type cannot alter system files, cannot install new programs, and cannot edit some settings by using the Control Panel without supplying an administrator password.

standby   *See* sleep mode.

standoffs Small mechanical separators that screw into a computer case. A motherboard is then placed on top of the standoffs, and small screws are used to secure it to the standoffs.

star bus topology A hybrid network topology where the computers all connect to a central bus—a switch—and have a layout resembling a star.

Start button Clickable element on the Windows taskbar that enables access to the Start menu.

Start menu Menu that can be accessed by clicking the Start button on the Windows taskbar. Enables you to see all programs loaded on the system and to start them.

Start screen Windows 10 version of the Start menu, which functions as a combination of the traditional Start menu and Windows 8/8.1 Modern UI.

Startup Repair A one-stop, do-it-all troubleshooting option that performs a number of boot repairs automatically.

Stateful Packet Inspection (SPI) Used by hardware firewalls to inspect each incoming packet individually for purposes such as blocking traffic that isn't in response to outgoing requests.

static IP address Manually set IP address that will not change.

storage area network (SAN) Storage setup in which, rather than using internal drives, a device accesses a separate block of hard drives on a network separate from the normal network, reading them logically as one drive.

storage pool One or more physical drives grouped into a single Storage Space.

Storage Spaces In Windows, a software RAID solution that enables users to group multiple drives into a single storage pool.

STP (shielded twisted pair) Cabling for networks, composed of pairs of wires twisted around each other at specific intervals. Twists serve to reduce interference (also called crosstalk)—the more twists, the less interference. Cable has metallic shielding to protect the wires from external interference.

straight tip (ST) Type of fiber optic connector. *See* fiber optic cable.

stranded core A cable that uses a bundle of tiny wire filaments to transmit signals. Stranded core is not quite as good a conductor as solid core, but it will stand up to substantial handling without breaking.

streaming media Broadcast of data that is played on your computer and immediately discarded.

string In programming and scripting, a non-numeric sequence of alphanumeric data.

stripe set Two or more drives in a group that are used for a striped volume.

striped volume   RAID 0 volumes. Data is spread across two drives for increased speed.

strong password   Password containing at least eight characters, including letters, numbers, and punctuation symbols.

structured cabling   ANSI/TIA standards that define methods of organizing the cables in a network for ease of repair and replacement.

Structured Query Language (SQL)   A language that enables a program to interact with a database using various commands and queries.

Structured Query Language (SQL) attack   An attack that occurs when an attacker enters SQL commands into an input field on a Web app in order to gain access to data or an entire database that the attacker isn't supposed to see.

su   Older Linux command for gaining root access.

subfolder   A folder located inside another folder.

subnet mask   Value used in TCP/IP settings to divide the IP address of a host into its component parts: network ID and host ID.

sub-pixels   Tiny liquid crystal molecules arranged in rows and columns between polarizing filters used in LCDs. A pixel is composed of a red, a green, and a blue sub-pixel.

subscriber connector (SC)   Type of fiber optic connector. *See* fiber optic cable.

su/sudo   Linux command for gaining root access.

SuperSpeed USB   A fast form of USB, with speeds up to 5 Gbps. Also called USB 3.0, USB 3.1 Gen 1, or USB 3.2 Gen 1.

SuperSpeed USB 10 Gbps   Updated form of SuperSpeed USB providing speeds up to 10 Gbps. Also called USB 3.1 or USB 3.2 Gen 2.

supervisory control and data acquisition (SCADA)   Hardware and software combination used to monitor and control the operational technology used in industrial settings such as public transit systems, power plants, and refineries.

surge suppressor   Inexpensive device that protects your computer from voltage spikes.

suspend   *See* sleep mode.

swap file   *See* virtual memory.

swap partition   Special partition found on Linux and UNIX systems that behaves like RAM when your system needs more RAM than is installed.

swipe lock   Mobile device feature that uses a swipe gesture to unlock the mobile device.

switch   Device that filters and forwards traffic based on some criteria. A bridge and a router are both examples of switches. In the command-line interface, a switch is a function that modifies the behavior of a command.

swollen battery   A Li-Ion battery that has begun to swell as it fails, often due to manufacturing defects, heat, or overcharging. May also deform the device containing it. It is an explosion and fire risk if it ruptures, so dispose of it quickly and safely.

sync   The process of keeping files on mobile devices up to date with the versions on desktop computers or over the Internet via cloud-based services.

Sync Center   Windows Control Panel applet where network files marked as *Always available offline* may be viewed.

synchronize   *See* sync.

syntax (command)   The proper way to write a command-line command so that it functions and does what it's supposed to do.

System (Windows Settings)   The proverbial "junk drawer" category of Windows Settings categories. System contains everything from display options, to sound settings, to notifications settings.

system BIOS   Primary set of BIOS stored on a flash ROM chip on the motherboard. Defines the BIOS for all the assumed hardware on the motherboard, such as keyboard controller, basic video, and RAM.

system bus speed   Speed at which the CPU and the rest of the PC operates; set by the system crystal.

System Configuration (msconfig.exe)   Windows tool to edit and troubleshoot operating system and program startup processes and services.

system crystal   Crystal that provides the speed signals for the CPU and the rest of the system.

system fan   Any fan controlled by the motherboard but not directly attached to the CPU.

System File Checker   *See* sfc.

System Information tool   *See* msinfo32.

system lockout   Protects against attempts to brute-force a lock screen or login system by locking the user out until they perform some more thorough authentication process. Occurs when too many consecutive login attempts fail.

system on a chip (SoC)   Single silicon die containing a CPU, GPU, and other important support logic.

System Preferences   macOS tool containing many administrative functions.

System Protection   Tab in Windows System Properties dialog box that enables you to configure how and when the system will create restore points and provides easy access to existing restore points via System Restore.

system resources In classic terms, the I/O addresses, IRQs, DMA channels, and memory addresses. Also refers to other computer essentials such as hard drive space, system RAM, and processor speed.

System Restore Utility in Windows that enables you to return your PC to a recent working configuration when something goes wrong. System Restore enables you to select a restore point and then returns the computer's system settings to the way they were at that restore point—all without affecting your personal files or e-mail.

system ROM Flash ROM chip that stores the system BIOS.

system setup utility *See* CMOS setup program.

system tray *See* notification area.

system unit Main component of the desktop PC, in which the CPU, RAM, optical drive, hard drive, and power supply reside. All other devices—the keyboard, mouse, and monitor—connect to the system unit.

system/application log errors May indicate the presence of a malware infestation and the scope of its effects.

%SystemRoot% The path where the operating system is installed.

T568A Wiring standard for Ethernet cable.

T568B Wiring standard for Ethernet cable.

tablet A mobile device consisting of a large touchscreen, enabling the user to browse the Web, view media, and even play games.

tailgating Form of infiltration and social engineering that involves following someone else through a door as if you belong in the building.

Take Ownership Special permission allowing users to seize control of a file or folder and potentially prevent others from accessing the file/folder.

Task Manager Windows utility that shows all running programs, including hidden ones, and is accessed by pressing CTRL-SHIFT-ESC. You can use the Task Manager to shut down an unresponsive application that refuses to close normally.

Task Scheduler (taskschd.msc) Windows utility enabling users to set tasks to run automatically at certain times.

taskbar Contains the Start button, Search box, pinned apps, running apps, and the notification area. Located by default at the bottom of the desktop.

taskkill Windows command-line tool for killing running processes.

tasklist Windows command-line tool for listing and managing processes.

TCP *See* Transmission Control Protocol.

TCP/IP (Transmission Control Protocol/Internet Protocol)   Communication protocols developed by the U.S. Department of Defense to enable dissimilar computers to share information over a network. TCP/IP is the primary protocol of most modern networks, including the Internet.

TCP/IP services   Services such as HTTP or SSH that run atop TCP/IP.

TDR (time-domain reflectometer)   Device for testing network cabling by measuring impedance (which is similar to resistance); any impedance means a bad cable.

tech toolkit   Tools a PC tech should never be without, including a Phillips-head screwdriver, a pair of plastic tweezers, a flat-head screwdriver, a hemostat, a star-headed Torx wrench, a parts retriever, and a nut driver or two.

telecommunications room   Area where all the cabling from individual computers in a network converges.

Telnet   Terminal emulation program for TCP/IP networks that allows one machine to control another as if the user were sitting in front of it. Uses port 23.

tera-   Prefix that usually stands for the binary number 1,099,511,627,776 (2^{40}). When used for mass storage, it's often shorthand for 1 trillion bytes.

terminal   Dumb device connected to a mainframe or computer network that acts as a point for entry or retrieval of information.

Terminal   A command-line tool available in macOS and various Linux distros.

terminal emulation   Software that enables a computer to communicate with another computer or network as if the computer were a specific type of hardware terminal.

test the theory to determine the cause   Attempt to resolve the issue by either confirming the theory and learning what needs to be done to fix the problem, or by not confirming the theory and forming a new one or escalating. (Step 3 of 6 in the CompTIA troubleshooting methodology.)

tethering   The act of using a cellular network–connected mobile device as a mobile hotspot.

theory of probable cause   One possible reason why something is not working; a guess or hypothesis.

thermal compound   *See* thermal paste.

thermal pad   Heat-transferring pad that can be used as an alternative to thermal paste. Typically preapplied to OEM heat sinks supplied with processors and covers for M.2 drives.

thermal paste   Paste-like material with very high heat-transfer properties. Applied between the CPU and the cooling device, it ensures the best possible dispersal of heat from the CPU. Also called *heat dope* or *thermal compound*.

thermal printer Printer that uses heated printheads to create high-quality images on special or plain paper. Common in retail receipt printers, which use large rolls of thermal paper housed in a feed assembly that automatically draws the thermal receipt paper over the heating element.

thin provisioning Creating a Storage Space that reports a size greater than the actual capacity installed in the computer, with the ability to later add more physical capacity up to the reported size. *See also* Storage Spaces.

This PC Commonly used interface for Windows Explorer that displays hard drives and devices with removable storage.

thread Smallest logical division of a single program.

throttling Power reduction/thermal control capability allowing CPUs to slow down during low activity or high heat build-up situations.

throw Size of the image a projector displays at a certain distance from the screen.

Thunderbolt An open standards connector interface that is primarily used to connect peripherals to devices, including mobile devices, if they have a corresponding port.

Time & Language (Windows Settings) Windows Settings category that allows you to change the date, time, and language on a Windows system.

Time Machine macOS backup tool that enables you to create full system backups, called *local snapshots*, and to recover some or all files in the event of a crash; it also enables you to restore deleted files and recover previous versions of files.

TLS *See* Transport Layer Security.

TN (twisted nematic) Older technology for LCD monitors. TN monitors produce a decent display for a modest price, but they have limited viewing angles and can't accurately reproduce all the color information sent by the video card.

tone generator *See* toner.

tone probe *See* toner.

toner Generic term for two devices used together—a tone generator and a tone probe (locator)—to trace cables by sending an electrical signal along a wire at a particular frequency. The tone probe then emits a sound when it distinguishes that frequency.

topology The way computers connect to each other in a network.

touch interface The primary user interface on modern mobile devices where keys are replaced with tactile interaction.

touch pen Device designed to be used in conjunction with touchscreens to create a drawing or writing experience. Touch pens can be as simple as a plastic stylus, all the way to the advanced Apple Pencil, which uses sensors and a Bluetooth connection to the device to enhance its effectiveness.

touchscreen   Monitor with a type of sensing device (a digitizer) across its face that detects the location and duration of contact, usually by a finger or stylus.

traceroute   macOS and Linux command-line utility for following the path a packet takes between hosts. The Windows version is named tracert.

tracert   Windows command-line utility used to follow the path a packet takes between two hosts. The utility is traceroute in macOS and Linux.

traces   Small electrical connections embedded in a circuit board.

trackpad   Flat, touch-sensitive pad that serves as a pointing device for most laptops.

transfer rate   Rate of data transferred between two devices, especially over the expansion bus.

Transmission Control Protocol (TCP)   Connection-oriented protocol used with TCP/IP. *See also* User Datagram Protocol *and* TCP/IP.

transmit beamforming   Multiple-antenna technology that adjusts the signal when clients are discovered, to optimize quality and minimize dead spots. Employed in many 802.11n WAPs and standard in 802.11ac and 802.11ax WAPs.

Transport Layer Security (TLS)   Encryption protocol used to securely connect between servers and clients, such as when your Web browser securely connects to Amazon's servers to make a purchase. Replaces SSL.

triple-channel architecture   A chipset feature similar to dual-channel RAM, but making use of three matched sticks of RAM instead of two.

Trojan   Program that does something other than what the user who runs the program thinks it will do. Used to disguise malicious code, also known as a *Trojan horse*.

troubleshooting methodology   Steps a technician uses to solve a problem. CompTIA A+ defines six steps: identify the problem; establish a theory of probable cause (question the obvious); test the theory to determine the cause; establish a plan of action to resolve the problem and implement a solution; verify full system functionality and, if applicable, implement preventive measures; and document findings, actions, and outcomes.

Trusted Platform Module (TPM)   A hardware platform for the acceleration of cryptographic functions and the secure storage of associated information. BitLocker, for example, requires a TPM chip on the motherboard or equivalent to validate on boot that the computer has not changed. Recent Intel and AMD processors include TPM functions.

trusted root CA   A highly respected certificate authority (CA) that has been placed on the lists of trusted authorities built into Web browsers.

trusted source   Legitimate app stores run by the major OS vendors such as Apple, Google, Microsoft, and Amazon.

tunneling Creating an encrypted link between two programs on two separate computers.

two-factor authentication Authentication process that provides additional security by requiring two different authentication factors. *See also* multifactor authentication.

UAC (User Account Control) Windows feature implemented to stop unauthorized changes to Windows. UAC enables standard accounts to do common tasks and provides a permissions dialog box when standard and administrator accounts do certain things that could potentially harm the computer (such as attempt to install a program).

UDP *See* User Data Protocol.

UEFI (Unified Extensible Firmware Interface) Modern 32- or 64-bit firmware programming interface. Replaced the original 16-bit PC BIOS. UEFI supports large-capacity storage drives, additional features, and a more direct booting process.

unattended installation A type of OS installation where special scripts perform all the OS setup duties without human intervention.

unauthorized access Anytime a person accesses resources in an unauthorized way. This access may or may not be malicious.

UNC (Universal Naming Convention) Describes any shared resource in a network using the convention \\<*server name*>\<*name of shared resource*>.

unified threat management (UTM) Providing robust network security by integrating traditional firewalls with many other security services such as IPS, VPN, load balancing, anti-malware, and more.

unpatched system Provides robust network security by integrating traditional firewalls with many other security services such as IPS, VPN, load balancing, anti-malware, and more.

unshielded twisted pair *See* UTP.

untrusted source Stores or sites where apps can be obtained outside of the legitimate trusted sources run by major vendors. *See* trusted source.

UPC (Universal Product Code) Barcode used to track inventory.

update *See* patch.

Update & Security (Windows Settings) Windows Settings category that includes options related to Windows updates and security features, including Windows Defender.

upgrade installation Installation of Windows on top of an earlier installed version, thus inheriting all previous hardware and software settings.

UPS (uninterruptible power supply)   Device that supplies continuous clean power to a computer system the whole time the computer is on. Protects against power outages and sags (and corresponding data loss).

URL (uniform resource locator)   An address that defines the location of a resource on the Internet. URLs are used most often in conjunction with HTML and the World Wide Web.

USB (universal serial bus)   General-purpose serial interconnect for keyboards, printers, joysticks, drives, scanners, and many other devices. Enables hot-swapping of devices.

USB host controller   Integrated circuit normally built into the chipset that acts as the interface between the system and every USB device that connects to it.

USB hub   Device that extends a single USB connection to two or more USB ports, almost always directly from one of the USB ports connected to the root hub.

USB root hub   Part of the host controller that makes the physical connection to the USB ports.

USB thumb drive   Flash memory device that has a standard USB connector.

USB Type-C (connector)   Reversible USB-type cable that supports up to USB 3.2 with a top speed of 10 Gbps. Quickly becoming the de facto standard port on Android devices. Thunderbolt-enabled USB Type-C ports can reach top speeds of 40 Gbps. *See also* Thunderbolt.

user account   Container that identifies a user to an application, operating system, or network. Includes name, password, username, groups to which the user belongs, and other information based on the user and the OS being used. Usually defines the rights and roles a user plays on a system.

User Accounts   Applet in Control Panel that enables you to make changes to local user accounts, and gives you access to the Settings app when you opt to add a new account.

User Datagram Protocol (UDP)   Connectionless protocol used with TCP/IP. *See also* Transmission Control Protocol *and* TCP/IP.

user interface   Visual representation of the computer on the monitor that makes sense to the people using the computer, through which the user can interact with the computer. This can be a graphical user interface (GUI) like Windows 10 or a command-line interface (CLI) like Windows PowerShell.

user password   Credentials assigned to a login account that does not have administrative capabilities.

user profile   Settings that correspond to a specific user account and may follow the user regardless of the computers where they log on. These settings enable the user to have customized environment and security settings.

Users   Tab in Task Manager that shows other logged-in users and enables you to log off other users if you have the proper permissions. Also includes information on resources consumed by programs the user is running.

Users folder   Windows default location for content specific to each user account on a computer. It is divided into several folders such as Documents, Pictures, Music, and Videos.

Users group   List of local users not allowed to edit the Registry or access critical system files, among other things. They can create groups, but can only manage the groups they create.

USMT (User State Migration Tool)   Advanced application for file and settings transfer of many users.

Utilities   macOS folder that contains tools for performing services on a Mac beyond what's included in System Preferences, including Activity Monitor and Terminal.

UTP (unshielded twisted pair)   Popular type of cabling for telephone and networks, composed of pairs of wires twisted around each other at specific intervals. The twists serve to reduce interference (also called crosstalk). The more twists, the less interference. Unlike shielded twisted pair (STP), UTP cable has no metallic shielding to protect the wires from external interference. 1000BASE-T uses UTP, as do many other networking technologies. UTP is available in a variety of grades, called categories, as follows:

- **Cat 1 UTP**   Regular analog phone lines—not used for data communications.
- **Cat 2 UTP**   Supports speeds up to 4 Mbps.
- **Cat 3 UTP**   Supports speeds up to 16 Mbps.
- **Cat 4 UTP**   Supports speeds up to 20 Mbps.
- **Cat 5 UTP**   Supports speeds up to 100 Mbps.
- **Cat 5e UTP**   Supports speeds up to 1000 Mbps.
- **Cat 6 UTP**   Supports speeds up to 10 Gbps.
- **Cat 6a UTP**   Supports speeds up to 10 Gbps.
- **Cat 7 UTP**   Supports 10-Gbps networks at 100-meter segments; shielding for individual wire pairs reduces crosstalk and noise problems. Cat 7 is not an ANSI/TIA standard.

variables   In scripting and programming, named labels for some portion of in-memory data. The actions taken by the script or program may change or replace the data in the variable.

verify full system functionality and, if applicable, implement preventive measures   Making sure that a problem has been resolved and will not return. (Step 5 of 6 in the CompTIA troubleshooting methodology.)

vertical alignment (VA)　Display technology used in mid-range LCD panels. VA refers to how the liquid crystal matrix is arranged within the panel.

VESA mount　A screen or display bracket that follows the industry standard—established by the Video Electronics Standards Association (VESA)—which specifies size, location, and type of mounting points.

VGA connector　A 15-pin, three-row, D-type VGA monitor connector. Goes by many other names, such as D-shell, D-subminiature connector, DB-15, DE15, and HD15. The oldest and least-capable monitor connection type.

vi　Linux and macOS command-line tool for editing text files.

video capture　Computer jargon for the recording of video information, such as TV shows or movies.

video card　Expansion card that works with the CPU to produce the images displayed on your computer's display.

video display　*See* monitor.

viewing angle　Width (measured from the center to the side of a display) range within which the image can be fully seen.

virtual assistant　Voice-activated technology that responds to user requests for information. Virtual assistants can be used to search the Internet, make reminders, do calculations, and launch apps.

virtual desktop infrastructure (VDI)　Hosting desktops (Windows, Linux, or macOS) on a server so they can be used in VMs on remote devices. Not to be confused with VDI virtual machine disk images.

virtual machine (VM)　A complete environment for a guest operating system to function as though that operating system were installed on its own computer.

virtual memory　Portion of the hard drive set aside by an OS to act like RAM when the system needs more RAM than is installed. A file containing this data is typically called a *page file* in Windows and a *swap file* in UNIX platforms like Linux and macOS.

Virtual Network Computing (VNC)　Protocol enabling remote desktop connections. *See also* remote desktop.

virus　A program that has two jobs: to replicate and to activate. *Replication* means it copies itself. *Activation* is when a virus damages a system or data. A virus can't self-replicate across networks; it needs human action to spread to other drives. *See also* definition file.

virus shield　Passive monitoring of a computer's activity, checking for viruses only when certain events occur, such as a program execution or file download.

vishing   A social engineering attack in which the attacker uses the phone to scam an unsuspecting user out of information that can be used to cause further harm.

VoIP (Voice over Internet Protocol)   Collection of protocols that makes voice calls over a data network possible.

VoIP phone   Device that looks like a regular landline phone but uses VoIP to communicate over a computer network.

volatile   Memory that must have constant electricity to retain data.

volts (V)   Measurement of the pressure of the electrons passing through a wire, or voltage.

volume   *See* partition.

VPN (virtual private network)   Encrypted connection over the Internet between a computer or remote network and a private network.

vulnerability   Weakness in a system, network, or organization that an attacker will exploit to gain access, steal information, and cause other harm.

WAN (wide area network)   A widespread group of computers connected using long-distance technologies.

WAP (wireless access point)   Device that centrally connects wireless network nodes.

wattage (watts or W)   Measurement of the amps and volts needed for a particular device to function.

Web browser   Program designed to retrieve, interpret, and display Web pages.

Web server   A computer that stores and shares the files that make up Web sites.

whaling   A phishing attack in which the attacker specifically targets someone high up in an organization, like the CEO.

wide area network   *See* WAN.

Wi-Fi   Common name for the IEEE 802.11 wireless Ethernet standard.

Wi-Fi 6   *See* 802.11ax.

Wi-Fi 6E   *See* 802.11ax.

Wi-Fi calling   Mobile device feature that enables users to make voice calls over a Wi-Fi network, rather than a cellular network.

wildcard   Character—usually an asterisk (*) or question mark (?)—used during a search to represent search criteria. For instance, searching for *.**docx** will return a list of all files with a .docx extension, regardless of the filename. The * is the wildcard in that search. Wildcards can be used in command-line commands to act on more than one file at a time.

Windows 10   Operating system developed by Microsoft that powers most desktop and portable computers in use today.

Windows 10 Enterprise   Windows edition that includes all the power and features of Windows 10 Pro for Workstations but also includes a feature called Long-Term Servicing Branch. LTSB turns off automatic updates, removes the Microsoft Store, and disables the automatic installation of Microsoft's Edge browser. Windows 10 Enterprise is not available in stores; it has to be purchased through a Microsoft sales representative.

Windows 10 Home   The most basic edition of Windows. Designed for home users, it has the fewest features. Supports up to 128 GB of RAM.

Windows 10 Pro   A more robust edition of Windows, which supports up to 2 TB of RAM. Windows 10 Pro is the most basic edition that supports joining an Active Directory domain. It also allows the use of Remote Desktop Protocol and BitLocker encryption.

Windows 10 Pro for Workstations   A beefier edition of Windows Pro that supports up to 6 TB of RAM and is intended for the most high-end and resource-heavy systems. Along with the features of Windows 10 Pro. Windows 10 Pro for Workstations is intended for the most high-end and resource-heavy systems.

Windows 11   Operating system developed by Microsoft and released in 2021, intended to replace Windows 10 and become the default desktop and laptop operating system.

Windows Hardware Compatibility Program   Microsoft's rigorous testing program for hardware manufacturers, which hardware devices must pass before their drivers can be digitally signed.

Windows key   Key on a keyboard bearing the Windows logo that traditionally brings up the Start menu, but is also used in some keyboard shortcuts.

Windows Memory Diagnostic   Windows tool that can automatically scan up to 4 GB of a computer's RAM when a problem is encountered.

Windows PowerShell   Command-line tool included with Windows. Offers a number of powerful scripting tools for automating changes both on local machines and over networks.

Windows Preinstallation Environment (WinPE)   The installation program for Windows.

Windows Recovery Environment   *See* WinRE (Windows Recovery Environment).

Windows Update   Microsoft application used to keep Windows operating systems up to date with the latest patches or enhancements.

WinRE (Windows Recovery Environment)   A special set of tools in the Windows setup that enables you to access troubleshooting and system recovery options.

winver   Command that displays a system's current Windows version.

wireless access point   *See* WAP.

wireless Internet service provider (WISP)   An Internet service provider for which the last segment or two uses a point-to-point long-range fixed wireless connection.

wireless mesh network (WMN)   A hybrid wireless topology in which most nodes connect in a mesh network while also including some wired machines. Nodes act like routers; they forward traffic for other nodes, but without wires.

wireless repeater/extender   Device that receives and rebroadcasts a Wi-Fi signal to increase coverage.

work area   In a basic structured cabling network, often simply an office or cubicle that potentially contains a PC attached to the network.

workgroup   A simple, decentralized network that Windows PCs are configured to use by default.

working directory   The current directory used by command-line commands unless they explicitly specify a target file or directory. The prompt usually indicates the working directory.

World Wide Web (WWW)   System of Internet servers that supports documents formatted in HTML and related protocols. Can be accessed by applications that use HTTP and HTTPS, such as Web browsers.

worm   Similar to a virus, except it does not need to attach itself to other programs to replicate. It can replicate on its own through networks, or even hardware like Thunderbolt accessories.

WPA2 (Wi-Fi Protected Access 2)   Wireless security protocol, also known as IEEE 802.11i. Uses the Advanced Encryption Standard (AES) and replaces WPA.

WPA3 (Wi-Fi Protected Access 3)   The successor to WPA2, addresses usability and security issues that affected its predecessor by including encryption to protect data of users on open (public) networks.

wrapper   *See* container file.

WWW   *See* World Wide Web.

x86   Describes 32-bit operating systems and software.

x86-64   Describes 64-bit operating systems and software. Sometimes known as x64.

zeroconf (zero-configuration networking)   Operating system feature that provides a random Class B IP address to a system set for DHCP when a DHCP server cannot be found. Enables networking without static IP addressing in such an environment. *See also* APIPA.

zero-day attack   Attack targeting a previously unknown bug or vulnerability that software or hardware developers have had zero days to fix.

ZIF (zero insertion force) socket   Socket for CPUs that enables insertion of a chip without the need to apply pressure. Intel promoted this socket with its Overdrive upgrades, but ZIF is currently used by both Intel and AMD. The chip drops effortlessly into the socket's pin grid array holes or land grid array, and a small lever locks it in.

zsh   Command-line shell used by macOS. Short for Z Shell.

zombie   Computer infected with malware that has turned it into a botnet member.

INDEX

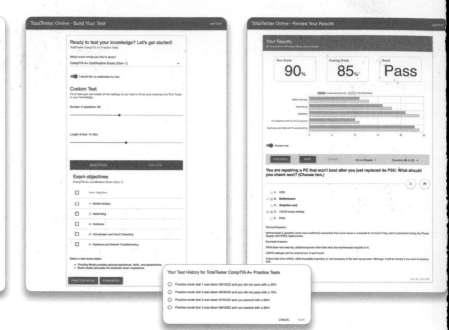